Handbook of Reading Research, Vol

The *Handbook of Reading Research* is *the* research handbook for the field. Each volume has come to define the field for the period of time it covers. *Volume IV* follows in this tradition. To identify the dominant themes, topics, and developments in the field, the editors surveyed reading research studies and reading policy trends since the year 2000, when *Volume III* was published. As in previous volumes, the focus is on reading research, rather than a range of literate practices. When taken as a set, the four volumes provide a definitive history of reading research. *Volume IV* brings the field authoritatively and comprehensively up-to-date.

Michael L. Kamil is Professor Emeritus of Education at Stanford University. He is a member of the Psychological Studies in Education Committee and on the faculty of the Learning, Design, and Technology Program.

P. David Pearson is a faculty member in the Language and Literacy program and the Cognition and Development program at the Graduate School of Education at the University of California, Berkeley, where he served as Dean from 2001–2010.

Elizabeth Birr Moje is an Arthur F. Thurnau Professor of Literacy, Language, and Culture in Educational Studies, a Faculty Affiliate in Latina/o Studies, and Faculty Associate in the University's Institute for Social Research—Research Center for Group Dynamics at the University of Michigan, Ann Arbor, MI.

Peter P. Afflerbach is a Professor of Curriculum and Instruction and Director of the Reading Center at the University of Maryland at College Park.

Handbook of Reading Research

Volume IV

Editors

Michael L. Kamil
P. David Pearson
Elizabeth Birr Moje
Peter P. Afflerbach

Routledge
Taylor & Francis Group

NEW YORK AND LONDON

First published 2011
by Routledge
711 Third Avenue, New York, NY 10017

Simultaneously published in the UK
by Routledge
2 Park Square, Milton Park, Abingdon, Oxon OX14 4RN

Routledge is an imprint of the Taylor & Francis Group, an informa business

Typeset in Minion by EvS Communication Networx, Inc.

Library of Congress Cataloging in Publication Data
Handbook of reading research / [edited by] Michael L. Kamil [et al.].
p. cm.
Includes bibliographical references and index.
1. Reading. 2. Reading—Research—Methodology. I. Kamil, Michael, L.
LB1050.H278 2000
428.4'072—dc20
96-10470

ISBN 13: 978-0-8058-5342 -1 (hbk)
ISBN 13: 978-0-8058-5343 -8 (pbk)
ISBN 13: 978-0-203-84041-2 (ebk)

Contents

Dedication

Volume IV is dedicated to Rebecca Barr and Peter Mosenthal
Their memory, their legacy, their families

In 1981, four soon to be editors of the first *Handbook* assembled, at the invitation of David, in Michael's apartment in Chicago. After that first meeting, at least twice and often three or more times a year, from 1981 through 2002, we had the privilege of meeting with Becky and Peter to plan for, work on, or celebrate the (then) forthcoming volume of the *Handbook of Reading Research*. These meetings were held during annual conferences or in Chicago because of its convenience, and they were usually accompanied with good food—and even better wine!

These meetings served three purposes for us. One was work, pure and simple—planning, and revising (and revising again…) the themes, outlines, authorial teams, and draft chapters for the next *Handbook*. And, yes, nagging each other about our authors' laggardly chapters. A second was mutual professional learning—each informing or challenging the others to think and rethink our individual and collective views on reading theory, research, and practice. We may have gotten our start on research in the various graduate schools we attended, but we honed our craft in these regular meetings. We learned from each other, debated issues, argued about data and theory, reconciled differences, and gained great insights into reading research, practice, policy, publishing and the idiosyncrasies of many of the leading reading researchers. Those interactions enriched our professional work beyond measure. The third was sheer friendship and collegiality. Over the years, we developed both, and one could never have asked for better colleagues and friends than Becky and Peter. The work never seemed like work because it was wrapped in the sheer pleasure of being with the best friends and colleagues we could have imagined. Becky was always one to keep all of us on task; Peter kept us organized and up to date with his complete analyses of the research literature, long before it was fashionable to do such tracking of research.

When we (Peter, Becky, Michael, and David) agreed to work together back in 1981, we made a commitment that we would each assume the role of lead editor for one volume—and then we would turn over the reins to the next generation of scholars to continue the tradition. So when we started the planning for *Volume IV*, we knew it was Peter's turn to be lead editor: his turn to deal with the arrangements with the publisher, his turn to suffer the queries and complaints from all the authors wondering how things were coming and why this or that change was necessary. That never happened. Peter was taken from us before the cycle could be completed. So the dedication of the *HRR4* goes double for Peter. He has been the lead editor in spirit and principle if not in person.

We are blessed to have known them for as long as we did. We are doubly blessed to have worked with them as closely as we did. We are triply blessed for the examples they, and by association we, set for leading the field in this once a decade effort to take stock of what we know about reading research.

Michael and David

Transitions
Looking Back and Looking Ahead

Looking Back. As the two of us look back on the nearly 30 years in which we have been involved in the *Handbook*, the first agenda is a very large thank you:

- To the three editors who have labored with us to bring each of the four volumes into reality:
  - Lane Akers, then at Longman's, who took the initial risk (and plunge) with *HRR1* on somewhat less than a lick and a promise.
  - Ray O'Connell, who, still at Longman's, was willing to expand the total volume of words of *HRR2* by 65%. May he rest in peace.
  - Naomi Silverman, who has been our guide, conscience, and cheerleader through *HRR3* and *HRR4*.
- To the authors of the 131 chapters who have graced the pages of one or more of the four volumes with their scholarly insights and compelling prose.
- To all of the persons who worked on production of the four volumes, editorial assistants and copy editors.
- To all who tolerated, encouraged, and helped us while we worked on the volumes—spouses, friends, and other colleagues.

Looking Ahead. Perhaps the last decision the original four of us made as a team was that for *HRR4*, we would bring on two scholars as associate editors from the next generation of literacy scholars. We planned to have them work in apprentice roles while we did *HRR4* and then cede to them the reins to future *Handbooks*. We wanted scholars who, while academically younger than we, had established their scholarly credentials—research excellence, international prominence, and professional generosity. It would take all three of those attributes, we thought, to carry on the tradition of the *Handbook*. After literally hours of deliberation among the four of us, not to mention more than one bottle of a good Rhone, we settled on Elizabeth Moje and Peter Afflerbach. And we could not have been wiser in our choices, for Elizabeth and Peter have been exemplary in taking on the work of creating *HRR4*. Of course, when we planned the transition, we planned on four incumbents to mentor two successors. We did not know that the team of mentors would be reduced by half. So Peter and Elizabeth were thrust into positions that we (and they) had not imagined when we made the decision in 2002. They took on that role with a sense of commitment, enthusiasm, diligence, and professionalism that has been remarkable. We leave our editorial roles knowing that the *Handbook* is in good hands!

As the two of us prepare to step out of this remarkably privileged position, we look back on a history filled with wonderful memories of great results, hard work and amazing collegiality. We look forward to a portfolio of future volumes destined to continue and enhance a tradition that has been a part of our lives and our souls for nearly 3 decades. We leave knowing that we are experiencing exciting times for literacy that will be well-represented in the future *Handbooks*. Good reading and good researching!

David and Michael

Preface

Reading Research in a Changing Era

An Introduction to the *Handbook of Reading Research, Volume IV*

Michael L. Kamil, Peter P. Afflerbach,
P. David Pearson, and Elizabeth Birr Moje

The challenge for this, the fourth volume of the *Handbook* has been to capture the range of reading research done in a rapidly changing world. Both our work and the settings in which we carry it out are wider in scope and deeper in nuance than at any other time in our history. The purposes of reading research over the last 15 years have varied from finding ways in which instruction and learning can become more effective to examining the cognitive processes that underpin acts of reading to unpacking the social and cultural practices that motivate and mediate literate practice and learning. The authors of the chapters in this volume have spent a great deal of time and effort trying to determine the most effective ways of representing this diversity. Volume IV of the *Handbook of Reading Research* (hereafter *HRR4*) is an attempt to help resolve our current understandings of the sources, purposes, methods, findings, and consequences of reading research. As with earlier volumes, we view the new volume not as a replacement for, but rather as a complement to, earlier volumes of the *Handbook*.

READING RESEARCH: A BIT OF HISTORY

A century ago, Huey (1908) provided to the field what can arguably be regarded as the first review of research on reading and reading instruction. *The Psychology and Pedagogy of Reading* represents the first in a long line of efforts to synthesize what it is that we know for certain about the conditions and practices under which we read and learn to read. The path from Huey's work to *HRR4* is neither direct nor smooth, although it is clearly traceable. The current emphasis on synthesizing research can easily be singled out as one part of the path upon which Huey set forth. Moreover, Huey recognized that the volume of reading research was too vast to be synthesized or represented in a single volume (although his effort came very close). At best, only a sample of the broad range of studies, even in the early 1900s, could be represented in any given review.

Although Huey felt that there was an overwhelming body of research, he could not have imagined the explosion in reading research that would be ushered in by shifts in the dominant paradigms of psychological research and federal funding in the late 1960s and early 1970s. Most significantly, cognitive psychology paved the way for a renaissance in reading research by licensing scholars to discuss what happened inside the black box we call the mind, an activity that had been discouraged if not forbidden for the half decade preceding that paradigm shift. This accelerated interest in bringing research to bear on the problems of reading produced exponentially larger volumes of research. The establishment of the Center for the Study of Reading at the University of Illinois in 1975 with its focus on the mental models (schema) that drove comprehension and Durkin's (1978–79) work on the lack of comprehension instruction intensified the interest in doing reading research, particularly on the problems of text understanding.

Becoming a Nation of Readers called attention to the need for higher quality reading instruction and, consequently, for research to uncover the ways in which such a goal could be achieved.

The first volume *(HRR1)* of the *Handbook of Reading Research* (1984) was an attempt to bring together as much of that the newly conducted and published research as possible. The promissory notes issued by researchers in areas like metacognition, comprehension instruction, materials, and technology were partially redeemed. Federal support for research increased steadily over the next three decades, and with that support came a concomitant increase in the heft and sophistication of the research produced. Debates about the proper kind of research methods, problems, analyses occurred along the way. By the time the second *Handbook of Reading Research* was published in 1991, reading research was a thriving enterprise with its attendant "Reading or paradigm wars" (see, for example, Adams, 1990; Adams & Bruck, 1995; Stanovich, 1990; Kamil, 1995; McKenna, Robinson, & Miller, 1990a, 1990b; Edelsky, 1990).

By 1997 a Congressional mandate charged the "Director of the National Institute of Child Health and Human Development (NICHD), in consultation with the Secretary of Education, to convene a national panel to assess the status of research-based knowledge, including the effectiveness of various approaches to teaching children to read" (NICHD, 2000, 1-1). This effort, dubbed the National Reading Panel (NRP for short) was intended to do for reading something similar to what Huey had intended to do in 1908, but with an additional standard—that we as a field employ a specific set of research protocols to determine what research was ready for use to guide instruction. Those protocols emphasized internal validity (privileged causal over correlational designs) as well as external validity (generalizability to as many settings and populations as possible). The National Reading Panel (NRP) reported that there were over 100,000 research studies produced between 1966 and 2000, with some 16,000 prior to that time. These numbers illustrate the exponential growth in the research base stimulated by both research funding and urgent concern for improving reading instruction.

When *HRR2* was published in 1991, reading research had begun to incorporate the social and contextual variables that had only been hinted at in *HRR1*. Reviews describing research on society and literacy constituted an entire section of *HRR1*. The "reading wars" were in full swing as was the somewhat related (and sometimes confounded) debate about research methodology—focusing mainly on the relative validity of quantitative versus qualitative approaches. Despite the intensity of those debates, the *Handbook* was never able to secure a review of research related to the whole language movement and other constructivist pedagogies, the important chapter on response to literature notwithstanding.

A review of research on linguistically diverse readers was included for the first time. *HRR2* also included reviews of research on text more finely divided by genres than previously acknowledged. *HRR2* included an attempt to model progress in reading research. Renewed emphasis on teacher variables was apparent in reviews in *HRR2*, presaging the current interests in teacher quality. All of these suggest the highly varied, often disparate, and sometimes complementary nature of reading research. It was clear that the reading research, while growing in volume was also growing in perspective, epistemology, methodology, and substance.

When *HRR3* was published in 2000, a very different context for reading research existed. *HRR3* used the concept of verges to describe the new frontiers of research that were represented in the extant body of reading research. This was not the only significant change that had occurred. Federal involvement in education policy and funding was on the rise. Efforts at conducting systematic syntheses of reading research, as well as more rigorous methods of analyzing research, were growing.

Perhaps the two most important developments represented in *HRR3* were globalization and methodology. A series of reviews based on research around the globe was included to reflect the growing nature of reading and reading instructions from perspectives other than those of the United States or western Europe. The expansion and varied nature of methodologies prompted us to include a series of reviews on the uses of methodologies. These chapters were eventually reprinted as a stand-alone volume; the success of that volume indexed the importance of these issues. In terms of content, a chapter on neurological research in reading represented a clear "new" direction. There were two reviews of technology and two of second language learners, also suggesting the increasing diversity of reading research.

Stretching back to the early 1980s, *HRR1* was stimulated by the increased funding for reading research, but other forces—such as the paradigm shift in psychology—played an important role. By contrast, *HRR3* reflected a point in time during which reading research was becoming a lever for policy decisions. For the very first time, a briefing was held for Members of Congress and aides and assistants on the content of *HRR3* and its relevance for policy, marking at least some recognition of the importance of research in the formulation of policy decisions. *HRR3* also included a separate chapter on reading policy, the very first ever in the *Handbook*.

Some of the issues that seemed important in *HRR1* and *HRR2* did not "make the cut" in subsequent volumes. The strong interest in schema theory and metacognition had morphed into new developments, most notably the emphasis on mental models and a whole generation of research on comprehension instruction. Other important research foci that took hold in *HRR3* included work in linguistics, discourse processes, media literacy, and knowledge-comprehension relations.

WHAT HAS CHANGED SINCE THE PUBLICATION OF *HRR3*?

Despite earlier concerns raised by many about the quality of educational research (e.g., Kaestle, 1993; Labaree, 2003, 2004, 2008), reading research has occupied a central role in the past decade. Perhaps the most obvious sign is that federal educational policy has, for the first time in our history, been driven quite directly by reading research; more specifically what is deemed *scientifically based* reading research is codified into law in No Child Left Behind (NCLB). While the attempts are not without controversy, there is no denying the explicit emphasis on synthesizing reading research literature to determine (a) what practices are ready for adoption in schools, (b) what is missing in the research literature, and (c) even what to do to improve the quality of reading research. Coupled with these efforts to determine what the research can offer as guidance has been targeted research funding for those areas of greatest importance to fill extant gaps in the research literature.

Research Methodologies

In *HRR3*, there were 10 reviews of the uses of different methodologies that had been used in reading research. These approaches differed from the two chapters on experiments and ethnography in *HRR1* and the absence of any explicit discussion of methodologies in *HRR2*. The beginnings of the emphasis on scientific-based practice in reading research were reflected, albeit imperfectly, by the emphasis on high quality research as the foundation for practice. Policy eventually limited the types of research that were used in policy decisions, but the emphasis on research has provided even more stimulation of the amount and quality of research conducted. *HRR3* was prepared while *Preventing Reading Difficulties* was being written and before the emergence of *The NRP Report, Reading First, NCLB,* and other documents and policies that have assumed great importance in the past decade. One of the chapters in *HRR3* was on research synthesis, a methodology that has assumed high prominence in current policy considerations. Some of the national-level efforts to conduct syntheses have included the National Reading Panel, the National Literacy Panel for Language Minority and Youth, the National Early Literacy Panel. While these Panels have been specifically focused on limited areas, the What Works Clearinghouse (WWC) has assumed a broader role. The WWC conducts reviews of instructional research in reading and mathematics, provides syntheses of the research, and makes the results available (http://ies.ed.gov/ncee/wwc/).

A different effort is Doing What Works (DWW), a web site (http://dww.ed.gov/) that offers research, instructional methods, and other resources for teaching in a number of areas. Related to the efforts in What Works Clearinghouse is a new series of Practice Guides from the Institute for Education Sciences. These Guides look across research with the intent of making recommendations for instructional practice. The recommendations are differentially rated as a function of the soundness of the evidence supporting them. A secondary purpose of the Practice Guides is to help create a culture of research-awareness among school-based practitioners.

Government Education Policy

Over the past half decade, important shifts in government education policies can be seen in the move from an almost exclusive focus on elementary reading instruction under Goals 2000, Reading Excellence, Reading First and Early Reading First to a focus on middle and high school literacy concerns. The programs for Striving Readers and Struggling Readers have received dramatically increased funding while the funding for Reading First has been curtailed, despite strong state level evidence about its efficacy. There remains, however, at least a promise of continued, and even increased, emphasis on early childhood language and literacy.

Assessment assumed an importance in the last decade never before granted to it. Indeed, it became first among equals among policy levers. First, the role of the National Assessment of Educational Progress (NAEP) expanded with the influence of NCLB and the emphasis on accountability; NAEP was to be benchmark, the gold standard, against which all state assessments would be validated. Second, changes in federal research funding through the Institute of Education Sciences elevated the role of validated externally developed assessments as the standard for judging the efficacy of interventions. Third, NCLB, with its provision for validated systems of assessment (outcome measures to evaluate programs, frequently administered curriculum-based assessments to monitor progress, and diagnostic assessments to prescribe instruction), increased the prominence of assessment at every level within the education system—classroom, school, district, and state. As *HRR4* was sent to the printers, there was a call for national funding to permit states to develop more challenging tests to monitor school performance.

Standards have emerged once again as an important focus for policy, although to date there has been little direct research or evidence on the effects of standards. With the national movement (National Governors Association & Council of Chief State School Officers, 2009) to establish a common set of standards, it can be expected that there will be a great deal of attention on standards in the near future. The effort is a joint project by the National Governors Association, Council of Chief State School Officers, ACT, and Achieve, Inc. While the standards themselves promise to be research-based, conducting research on the effects on reading instruction and achievement of adopting such standards may be extremely difficult. Because most states have already committed to this project, there may be few, if any opportunities for comparison conditions, at least in the most rigorous, "gold standard" methods that have become so important in national policy. The study of the common standards work may be exactly the kind of study that calls for observational and qualitative analyses to ascertain how, why, and when the common standards are taken up and put into practice. Such observational work could reveal whether what is commonly prescribed is always commonly enacted; given the nature of the common core standards work, which seeks to offer a broad range of possibilities, the opportunity for comparative studies of reading instruction and achievement seems to have great potential. Equally important, much of the common core work is accompanied by work on logical text progressions across the grade levels and concomitant progression of comprehension skill across the grades, suggesting multiple opportunities for focused study of the effects of offering these progressions to teachers as guides for reading instruction across the grades and subject areas. The effort is also attendant with the development with new forms of assessments to allow for determinations of whether or not students meet the standards.

Research Policy

For researchers, the past decade has seen a great infusion of resources for research in reading and literacy, as well as other areas. Research funding has come from both traditional and non-traditional sources. NICHD was influential in the growth of research funding for both basic and applied research in reading and literacy. The establishment of the Institute for Education Sciences (IES) has also had an important effect on federal research policy, by upping the ante for more emphasis on experimental designs and developing a "theory" of how research should progress across its goals of exploration, development, efficacy, and scale-up.

Stimulated by the Report of the RAND Reading Study Group (2002), *Reading for Understanding,* reading research has, at least in part, been driven by similar programmatic efforts to examine basic processes, program development, scaling up existing programs, and the development of assessments. Unquestionably, the research funding has largely focused on experimental trials, but other methodologies are encouraged, particularly for the exploration and development goals. This program has looked at basic processes, development of programs, scaling up existing programs, and the development of assessments. Although the research funding has largely focused on experimental trials, other methodologies are encouraged, particularly for the exploration and development goals.

A different sort of development has been the use of large-scale national evaluations to judge effectiveness of programs. These evaluations have employed randomized control trials of programs that have been previously developed and used, either on experimental or commercial bases. In general, the results of these evaluations have not shown dramatic effects in favor of these programs (e.g., Dynarski et al., 2007; James-Burdumy et al., 2009; Kemple et al., 2008), the public claims of efficacy notwithstanding. One problem with this body of research is that many of these reports are based on relatively short-term applications, typically two years, of large-scale, complex, whole-school reform efforts. While short-term evaluations can do both the programs and the public a disservice, they do emphasize the need for extended evaluations as well. We know that (a) these efforts may require extended time in application for effects to be measured reliably, and (b) sometimes initial effects fade over time. The recognition that large-scale reform takes time has important implications for how reading interventions at such a scale should be studied, including questions about the length of time required for robust findings to emerge, to questions about the size of effects that can be expected in at various stages in the life of an intervention, to deciding how big an effect is required for educators to take it seriously as a path to reform. Given that the findings have generally shown effect sizes of less than 0.2, the body of evaluations is at least cautionary for the hope that there are quick or singular fixes for the problems of struggling readers.

THE CHANGING FOCI OF READING RESEARCH

The quarter century that has passed since the publication of *HRR1* has witnessed a decided shift in the topics and content of reading research. The shift in the past decade, since the publication of *HRR3*, has been almost as dramatic. The most obvious change has been the shift from emphasis on elementary reading to focus on adolescent reading, defined, generally, as anything above Grade 3. (This has largely been the result of prior focus on grades 1–3 as a result of Reading First funding and policy.) One result of the changes in policy and funding is likely to be increased attention to research on and for older students.

Although the focus of federally funded work has largely been on experimental work, the field has seen an important shift in research models to mixed methods, which combine statistical and qualitative data to obtain more complete pictures of the both the nature of the phenomena under study and the contexts in which research takes place. Nowhere is this more important than in the evaluation studies of large-scale interventions, where an emphasis on *what* works needs to be accompanied by an analysis of *why* and *how* various practices or curricula work for which students. The mantra of *what works for whom, and when* is increasingly taken up by those interested in student learning.

Similarly, the field has witnessed an increased realization that cognitive variables interact with social and cultural variables in complex ways, necessitating the use of more complex methods of data collection. One of the signs of the shift in methodologies is indicated by the suggestions made by Shavelson and Towne (2002) that research designs should be dictated by the questions being asked, rather than attempting to fit questions into methodologies.

Research funding also privileges programmatic research more than ever before, with more funding opportunities for complex, multi-year projects. Many recent funding opportunities also mandate a broader-based research team that includes scholars from many disciplines and practitioners as well as researchers. The increase in the number of opportunities for research and the amount of resources available threatens to overwhelm the reading research. As a consequence, multiple organizations—from private foundations (e.g., the Spencer Foundation) and academies (e.g., the National Academy of Education), to reading research associations (e.g., the International Reading Association and the Literacy Research Association (formerly the National Reading Conference)—have promoted the continuing and advanced education of education researchers in a number of ways. Targeted doctoral fellowships have been offered in targeted areas by both federal agencies and private funders. While these are not immediate fixes, they do presage improvement over the long term.

The increase in the number of private companies engaged in sponsored research is another sign of the stress in the research infrastructure. Contract research organizations such as American Institutes for Research, SRI International, ABT Associates, RMC Research Corporation, and many more have filled the need to supervise and coordinate large-scale research projects and evaluations. Many of these functions have also been assumed by the Regional Educational Laboratories, such as Education Northwest, PREL, Serve, WestEd or Learning Point Associates, albeit with more constrained directions for research and projects based on regional issues and contexts.

In regard to the substance of reading research, some trends in research foci appeared extremely promising when *HRR3* was published. For example, research in neurological/neuropsychological variables in the development of reading and learning to read was viewed as the cutting edge of reading research because it provided what some thought to be a more scientific view of the impact of reading interventions due to the ability to examine neurological, rather than only behavioral outcomes, which are thought to be subject to observer bias. The challenge to neurological research, however, is that in addition to extremely high costs, clear results of the impact of an intervention on reading extended prose are difficult to obtain, due to the research mechanisms necessary. Thus, although neurological studies remain an active research area, the results do not yet seem to have had a substantial impact on research about either the theoretical or practical aspects of reading.

Another research area that continues to demand attention is the area of computer (and other) technologies related to reading. *HRR3* offered two reviews of research on reading and technology, without a great deal of overlap. The promise of computer application and multimedia technologies for reading and reading instruction seemed to be looming on the horizon as an important tool in classrooms and other education settings. The National Evaluation of Educational Technology (Dynarski et al., 2007), however, showed that the applications involved did not produce dramatic results over conventional teaching. These findings are borne out in the second year of the evaluation (Capuano et al., 2009). Nevertheless, the penetration of computer technology in schools is extensive. The Internet has become a primary source of information and research in higher education and in many economically enfranchised school districts. There is every reason to believe that computers and Internet access will have continued effects on reading and reading instruction.

Professional development appears to have been the greatest growth area since the publication of *HRR3*. The concern for teacher quality has been coupled with professional development and appears as a concern in a great deal of funded projects. The National Reading Panel Report showed that a small body of literature demonstrated the direct effects of professional development on student achievement. That body of literature has not grown by a great deal over the last decade, but the concerns shifted, thanks largely to generous funding of coaches in the Reading First initiative within NCLB, from more conventional professional development to coaching and other sustained and intensive delivery models. Although little research exists currently to support the efficacy of coaching, there is a growing body of research that illustrates how and when coaching can be effective. Whether this becomes an area of further growth in research depends upon whether policies to sustain the use of coaches are retained in the post-NCLB journey on which we are about to embark as *HRR4* is sent to the printer.

THE CURRENT VOLUME: AN OVERVIEW

The *Handbook of Reading Research, Volume IV* (*HRR4*), offers what we hope is a comprehensive sample of research being done in the first decade of the 21st century. As noted in the previous sections, *HRR4* is situated in relation to an era of great challenge and promise for research. As a field, we are navigating competing ideas about the nature and role of reading research, the best means to foster reading development, the nature of reading processes, the role of context in reading, and even about the value of reading itself. Different schools of thought, some aligned, some seemingly opposed, represent varied traditions of inquiry and related knowledge. Debates about how to define, study, teach, and assess reading, its components, and the best means of helping students learn to read are waged not only within, but also across fields. The accumulation of knowledge from diverse and affiliate fields (or from fields not typically associated with reading) makes more complex the questions and answers of reading research. The complexity of reading research is increased by the demand to analyze acts of reading as situated in diverse contexts and practiced by diverse groups of people. Most challenging, perhaps, is the fact that reading researchers need to wade through the complexity to develop consensus understandings of the nature of reading, standards for reading achievement, how reading may be effectively taught, engagingly learned, and enthusiastically used.

HRR2 cited two themes, "Broadening the definition of reading," and "Broadening the reading research agenda." Breadth emerges again for *HRR4*. Indeed, the last decade of reading research is notable for the emergence of inquiry that employs multiple methods/mixed methods in an attempt to examine more fully the complex contexts, varied texts, and diverse experiences of readers and teachers that converge in the act of reading. Reading research benefits from the situated characterization, moving beyond "cold cognition" to skill and strategy that are always embedded in social milieu, used by readers who are both individuals and cultural beings with specific goals, experiences and levels of achievement. As readers are situated, so too is reading research.

HRR3 carried a theme of "verges" to characterize the state of reading research in 2000, a "place of encounter between something and something else" (Boorstin, 1987, p. xv). In *HRR4* the verges have expanded in both number and complexity. Increased sources of information, in the form of research results, policy briefs, and popular reports, inform reading instruction and policy, and there is an increased awareness of the forces that act, in manner subtle or stark, to influence both acts of reading and research on reading. Our view is that reading research continues to be broad in conceptualization and scope, but as research is situated in political and social contexts, the breadth of inquiry may be challenged by privilege—the likelihood that particular kinds of reading research may gain more traction in the public policy sphere. One result of differential privilege for particular research practices is that individual studies or entire classes of research may or may not reach the threshold required to inform theory and practice. The long-term effect might be decrease the relative influence that reading research, in toto, has. We are at a crossroads at which reading researchers have access to diverse methodologies, traditions of inquiry, foci, interpretations, and uses of research. At the same time, influences on research, from dedicated funding streams (contrast the IES with the NICHD with Spencer Foundation, for example) to differential preferences within professional organizations (contrast, for example, the focus of reading research at the Literacy Research Association (formerly NRC), the International Reading Association, the Society for Scientific Studies of Reading, and the American Educational Research Association) render a portrait of diversity or division, depending on one's perspective.

Thus, as we planned *HRR4*, we drafted questions intended to limn the borders and the scope of reading research which, in turn, provides a frame for contents of *HRR4*. These questions revolved around what we know about the nature, conduct, and validity of reading research; the onset and development of skilled reading; the nature of reading processes; the teaching and learning of reading; and the contexts that shape when, how, and why reading occurs.

ON READING RESEARCH—ITS NATURE, CONDUCT, AND VALIDITY

The previous three volumes of the *Handbook of Reading Research* share a clear focus on the cognitive components of reading, their development, and instruction that fosters students' reading growth. This research emanates from traditions in cognitive psychology and educational psychology. Also present, but less pronounced, is research from affiliated fields, including sociology, anthropology, critical theory and discourse analysis. A consistent subtext in some chapters relates to economic and political influences on reading research. Addressing each of these questions begs the question of just who does reading research.

Who Is the Reading Researcher?

Is the reading researcher the academic, politician, teacher, or policy maker? The last decade, with emphases on effect size, meta-analyses, and large budget studies, favors a particular kind of academician, the researcher interested in testing or evaluating interventions. But the study of reading is a complex endeavor, with contributions to knowledge (i.e., basic research) continuing to be critical in a period of increasing information exchange through new forms of communication, increased diversity of background and experience represented by both students and teachers, and changing social practices around forms of communication. What's more, design research is increasingly valuable as it examines applications of basic research in practice before attempting to generalize laboratory research to living populations of people who must engage in teaching and learning in real contexts. As a consequence, we have included research reviews from a range of different types of researchers, including those whose work focused on developing statistical models to be tested in large-scale programmatic interventions to those who study the literate practices of families, single classrooms, or young people engaged in reading and producing popular cultural texts.

What Can Reading Research Do? What Should It Do?

A primary purpose of reading research is to inform theory, from which we may derive educational policy and practice. In simple form, a significant research finding is all that is needed to amend theory, and to inform instructional approach. A more nuanced form is guided by the understanding that situated nature of what is researched (and research itself) matters, and that the complexities of human learning, classroom and school communities, and society influence actions based on research results, in predictable or unanticipated manner. The more we learn, the more we need to know. To this end, we invited authors who represent varied communities of research that should inform theory and practice. The research ranges from basic research in the cognitive processes of reading to how teachers and students are situated in classrooms, nested in schools, all situated within the greater context of an information-laden 21st century.

The chapters in *HRR4* represent traditions of inquiry that are well-established and well-accepted, and those who are newcomers to reading research. In some cases some of these new research traditions may be met with skepticism, especially in an era wherein intervention or evaluation research may be considered the most valuable form of research for a field such as reading.

What Research Methods Matter for HRR4?

Since the publication of *HRR3* (Kamil, Mosenthal, Pearson, & Barr, 2000), the idea of "gold standards" of instructional programs and practices has gained a great deal of strength. We note that this phenomenon has had varied effects. The question of, "What works?" might be preceded by "what is allowed to matter?" or "What is selected to determine if it works?" That said, our decisions about the kinds of chapters to include in *HRR4* reflect the current policy emphasis on evaluating what works.[1] For example, Hoffman, Maloch, and Sailors contributed a chapter on the use of direct observation tools that allow for the measurement of reading instruction in classrooms. In other words, although naturalistic observations are valued as a part of such work, it seems essential in an evaluation-focused policy environment that reading researchers to find ways to *measure* instructional practice in ways that can be tied to learners' reading achievement. Similarly, Graesser, McNamara, and Louwerse offer an intricate system for measuring the multiple dimensions of text complexity via a system known as *Coh-Metrix*. This system acknowledges the multiple ways that texts can scaffold or constrain comprehension. The power of the tool Graesser et al. describe is its speed and efficiency in providing information to teachers, curriculum developers, and researchers about what instructional approach may be necessary with a given text being read by a given group of students. Schatschneider and Petscher's chapter on statistical modeling also speaks to an evaluation model by illustrating how and why statistical models can be useful in reading research that seeks to test theories about the most appropriate forms of reading instruction. And Deshler, Hock, Ihle, and Mark take up that model in describing the necessary conditions and methods for conducting rigorous and sound analyses of programmatic interventions.

In each chapter, the methodological emphasis seems to be on advancing tools and procedures that document, measure, and evaluate reading instruction, texts, or acts of reading within a prescribed range of practices and outcomes. And yet, in each of the chapters—whether studies of programmatic interventions, statistical models, computer-based text analysis tools, or classroom measurement protocols—the authors not only acknowledge the complexity of the reading acts and practices they seek to study, but also call for close and contextually bound studies of these very practices. That is, not one of the methodological chapter authors—focused as they are on *measurement* of practices and outcomes—assumes that those measurements tell the complete story of what it means to engage with, learn from, or teach with a range of texts in a range of classrooms. We concur with this argument about the importance of additional sources of information, *especially* in evaluation studies, and thus, the section concludes with Rueda's review of research methods that work from cultural perspectives. Rueda reviews studies that have examined culture and literacy learning, and emphasizes the need for studies that examine how acts and practices reading, reading instruction, and even reading research are embedded in social, cultural, and political spheres of influence.

On Reading Development and Reading Processes

A good portion of *HRR4* is dedicated to addressing research on the component processes of reading—a dimension which has been covered in previous *Handbooks*—as well as to examining research on the *development* of skilled reading. We made this distinction between processes and development to exploit the recent recognition that learning to read does not end with the development of phonemic awareness or fluent reading ability, but is a process that occurs throughout life as one enters new domains and encounters new types of texts. This is a new dimension of *HRR4*, as development across the lifespan has not been explicitly attended to in past volumes.

HRR4 thus includes four chapters on development of skilled reading. Although we do not intend to suggest that reading development is a neatly linear, staged process, the chapters proceed, not surprisingly from the critical periods of emergent literacy and primary grades reading development (see Paratore, Cassano, & Schickedanz, as well as Foorman & Connor chapters) to reviews of adolescent (Alexander & Fox) and adult (Brooks) reading development. The inclusion of reviews on adolescent and adult development reflects increased emphasis on adolescent and adult literacy skill development in school reform movements and in the popular presses. Much of this emphasis is shaped by what appears to be diminishing reading performance as children age (as measured by test scores), but is also prompted by changing workplace demands and increased access to information rendered in print, image, and sound.

Across more than a century, records of reading research reveal evolving notions of the reader. Reading, from a research perspective, has been described as a response to print, a processing of information, and a set of strategies and skills that yield meaning. Reading also involves motivations, self-concept, and prior experiences that can reinforce of diminish the reading experience. Reading is situated, an endlessly varied phenomenon involving individual readers of unique experience, involving texts and tasks that vary in terms of goals, difficulty, and time. Each of these points suggests questions for the development and processes of skilled reading. For example, what is the shifting role of print, image, and sound in developing reading skill as people move across the lifespan and how do these forms of representation change in relation to one another? How do people's motivations to read and purposes for reading change as they age and move through different life contexts? These, and a number of other questions about lifespan development of skilled and flexible reading processes, are taken up throughout many of the chapters of *HRR4*, with the chapters explicitly focused on development dovetailing nicely with the chapters on reading processes, our next dimension of the new volume.

The chapters on reading processes examine reading in its finer aspects, with a focus on questions about what reading is, what counts as reading comprehension, and what are the key components of skilled reading. The chapters cover the range of what we considered to be central aspects of reading processes, from orthographic processing (Cunningham) to oral discourse and reading (Lawrence and Snow) to word recognition processes (Shefelbine) and the development of fluent reading (Rasinski, Reutzel, Chard, & Linan-Thompson). The section concludes with Duke and Carlisle's comprehensive treatment of the development of comprehension processes in the earlier years of schooling.

Teaching and Learning

The chapters dealing with the teaching and learning of reading continue a long tradition in the *Handbook*. Every volume has devoted considerable emphasis to this area. The question of purpose is taken up in the chapters explicitly dedicated to teaching and learning, but is also addressed implicitly in chapters that examine the contexts that shape acts and practices of reading.

Much of the research literature assumes a fairly narrow band of purpose for acts and practices of reading, most prominently the learning of text content. Increasingly, reading purpose includes the idea that readers act with the meanings they bring to and construct from reading. Reading can serve the purpose of helping individuals create their personae, and claim social group membership. The purpose of reading can be to extract information, to learn new words, concepts, or practices; to use the ideas to carry out a task; to emancipate or enable participation in social and political processes; or to maintain the status quo (e.g., Freebody & Freiberg; Hiebert & Nagy; Li; Kucan & Palincsar; Wilkinson & Son).

Who is the Reader? A necessary question in addressing the teaching and learning of reading skill is the question of who is a reader? Is the reader an information processor, a strategist, a situated thinker, a digital native? Is s/he the texter, the twitterer, and the Internet junkie? Is the reader engaged, dispassionate, curious, or resigned? Is the reader the "A" student who lacks motivation but perseveres, the "failing" student who excels in reading non-traditional text, the individual who identifies as a reader, or the individual who feels reading as an imposition? Is the reader part of a family, seeking to get work done or meet familiar and or cultural demands? These possibilities and more are explored in chapters in this section and beyond, including chapters by Afflerbach and Cho; Alexander and Fox; Alvermann; Brooks; Foorman and Connor; Goldenberg; Li; Rodriguez-Brown; Rueda; and Wilkinson and Son.

What is a Text? Just as the question, *Who is the reader?* must be addressed in the study of teaching people to read, so too must the question, *What is a text?* Across each section of *HRR4*, chapters address aspects of text by examining research methods for studying text (Graesser, McNamara, & Louwerse), how digital texts are read and taught (Afflerbach & Cho; Alvermann), the role of texts in disciplinary learning (Moje, Stockdill, Kim, & Kim), the impact of popular cultural texts (Alvermann), and how texts are read critically (Freebody & Freiberg). Across these chapters questions about the similarities and differences between reading in traditional and "new" forms, are addressed. In each case, authors acknowledge the importance of traditional print texts in school learning, but point to the role that Internet and hypertexts, multimedia, and texts that readers and writers themselves create might shape one's identity as a reader, world knowledge, and school-based, subject-matter learning (Alexander & Fox; Brooks; Foorman & Connor; Goldenberg; Moje et al.; Rueda).

The chapters as a set cover the range of teaching and learning practices that need to be considered in any discussion of teaching people how to read. Thus, we have included chapters on teaching and learning at the word level (a chapter by Tunmer and Nicholson, on teaching and learning of word recognition, in concert with Hiebert & Nagy, on vocabulary teaching and learning), together with chapters on comprehension and disciplinary literacy teaching (see Wilkinson & Son and Moje, Stockdill, Kim, & Kim, respectively). We did not stop, however, at what might be considered the basic dimensions of teaching people how to read, but also included chapters on the development of critical (Freebody & Freiberg) and cultural literacy skills (Li on the role of culture in teaching and learning literacy). Finally, this section includes reviews of research on teaching for remediation of reading difficulties (Kucan & Palincsar), and on assessments for literacy teaching and learning (Afflerbach & Cho).

What, and When, is a Context for Reading?

HRR4 departs from previous volumes by devoting a section to immediate and broad contexts that shape reading skill development, the cognitive processes of reading, and teaching and learning practices. Reading context, as a dimension of reading, and thus, reading research, was largely absent from *HRR1*, except insofar as particular methods of research took up contextual issues (e.g., L. Guthrie & Hall's "Ethnographic Approaches to Reading Research") and research on basic processes that acknowledged something "social" in the reading process (e.g., Bloom & Green's "Directions in the Sociolinguistic Study of Reading" and Wigfield & Asher's, "Social and Motivational Influences on Reading").

HRR2 presented a strong contrast to *HRR1*, devoting an entire section to *Society and Literacy,* with chapters examining historical and cross-cultural aspect of literacy, linguistic diversity, the role of the publishing industry and textbooks in developing literacy learning, and the impact of politics and policy on reading research. *HRR2* expanded notions of context with attention to reading research in different regions of the world and also revisited the role of social context in methods by again examining ethnographic approaches and adding a focus on discourse and sociocultural perspectives, while also treating contexts in terms of policies that influence how reading is taught and learned.

In *HRR4*, we have focused on the various contexts for reading, separating out research on social, policy, school, and out of-school contexts, with a range of different chapters each addressing these dimensions of context. As part of an examination of social contexts, Alvermann takes on the question of how popular cultures shape literacy practices in and out of school. Coburn and colleagues, by contrast, introduce policy contexts on a broad scale, and Taylor and her colleagues examine reading and school reform initiatives prompted by reading policies, whereas Dillon, O'Brien, Sato, and Kelly examine professional development and teacher education as yet another policy context that shapes how reading is taught and learned. In regard to school contexts, Goldenberg offers a review of research on one of the most pressing aspects of school-based literacy instruction: the effects of various reading and writing instructional programs on and for English language learners in the United States. Turning to out-of-school contexts, Kirkland and Hull analyze the research on community-based and after-school programs for literacy development, and Rodriguez-Brown investigates family contexts as sites for literacy learning. In each case, the reviews emphasize the power of context for shaping everything from how an individual reads, how a teacher teaches a group of students, how common standards are developed, how funding streams are articulated and awarded, and to how and why reading researchers do their work. Ultimately, this section of *HRR4* is a reminder that despite a current emphasis in research and policy on attempting to determine *what works,* contexts matter. The fact that contextual influences are multiple and complex makes the work of reading researchers more difficult, and pushes the field to remember that the focus need be on *what works, for whom, when, why, and how.* Such work requires meaningful research questions, rigorous methods, deep and broad knowledge, and generative collaborations across disciplinary and methodological perspectives.

SUMMING UP AND MOVING FORWARD: READING RESEARCH FOR A NEW ERA

Attention to these multiple, diverse, and increasingly powerful contexts reminds the reader that acts of reading—and therefore, acts of reading instruction and reading research—do not occur in a vacuum. Reading researchers face numerous challenges to the way they do their work, from debates over what counts as reading to challenges in how to assess what skilled reading is. As we consider the challenges facing reading research, we are reminded of the following quote from Rosenblatt, which captures our perspective that incorporating ways of knowing and seeing and doing from outside the mainstream can be particularly useful in producing new knowledge and, at times, new ways of doing:

> The special meaning, and more particularly, the submerged associations that [these] words and images have for the individual reader will largely determine what the work communicates... The reader brings to the work personality traits, memories of past events, present needs and preoccupations, a particular mood of the moment, and a particular physical condition. These and many other elements in a never-to-be-duplicated combination determine ... response to the peculiar contribution of the text. (Rosenblatt, 1938, p. 30)

That this description of reading was written more than 70 years ago reminds us that findings about the act of reading or the practice of teaching a person to read can come from many perspectives and offer unique insights, even when the means by which authors collect data and offer theories may not meet someone else's standards for research and hypothesizing.

In conclusion, we return to the idea that research, carefully conceptualized, conducted, analyzed, and considered, must be the main informant of reading theory and practice. The chapters assembled in *HRR4* remind the reader that there are different paths to constructing an understanding of reading, as well as different applications of the knowledge gained from research. This is a sign of health for reading research, and should encourage us all to remember that comprehensive theories of reading, learning to read, and of teaching reading are the beneficiaries of rigor, triangulation, and attention to the situated and social nature of the construct we seek to understand.

NOTE

1. One other motive guided our selection of methods chapters: Where we felt that the content and perspective provided by a methods chapter in *HRR3* was still timely and relevant, we decided not to provide an update. This, of course, is consistent with our tradition of designating each new *Handbook* a volume rather than an edition. The idea is that chapters in the older volumes speak to important issues even 25 years after their publication.

REFERENCES

Adams, M. (1990). *Beginning to read: Thinking and learning about print*. Cambridge, MA: MIT Press.

Adams, M. J., & Bruck , M. (1995). Resolving the great debate. *American Educator, 19*(7), 10–20.

Barr, R., Kamil, M., Mosenthal, P., & Pearson, P. D. (Eds.). (1991). *Handbook of reading research, Volume II*. New York: Longman.

Boorstin, D. J. (1987). *The landmark history of the American people*. New York: Random House.

Capuano, L., Dynarski, M., Agodini, R., & Rall, K. (2009). *Effectiveness of reading and mathematics software products: Findings from two student cohorts* (NCEE 2009-4041). Washington, DC: National Center for Education Evaluation and Regional Assistance, Institute of Education Sciences, U.S. Department of Education.

Durkin, D. (1978–79). What classroom observations reveal about reading comprehension instruction. *Reading Research Quarterly, 14*(4), 481–533.

Dynarski, M., Agodini, R., Heaviside, S., Novak, T., Carey, N., Campuzano, L., et al. (2007). *Effectiveness* of reading and mathematics software products: Findings from the first student cohort. Washington, DC: U.S. Department of Education, Institute of Education Sciences.

Edelsky, C. (1990). Whose agenda is this anyway? A response to McKenna, Robinson, and Miller. *Educational Researcher, 19*, 7–11.

Huey, E. B. (1908). *The psychology and pedagogy of reading, with a review of the history of reading and writing and of methods, texts, and hygiene in reading.* New York: Macmillan.

James-Burdumy, S., Mansfield, W., Deke, J., Carey, N., Lugo-Gil, J., Hershey, A., et al. (2009). *Effectiveness of selected supplemental reading comprehension interventions: Impacts on a first cohort of fifth-grade students* (NCEE 2009-4032). Washington, DC: National Center for Education Evaluation and Regional Assistance, Institute of Education Sciences, U.S. Department of Education.

Kaestle, C. (1993). The awful reputation of educational research. *Educational Researcher, 22*(1), 23–31.

Kamil, M. L. (1995). Some alternatives to paradigm wars. *Journal of Reading Behavior, 27*, 243–261.

Kamil, M., Mosenthal, P., Pearson, P. D., & Barr, R., (Eds.). (2000). *Methods of literacy research: The methodology chapters from the handbook of reading research volume III.* Mahwah, NJ: Erlbaum.

Kemple, J., Corrin, W., Nelson, E., Salinger, T., Herrmann, S., & Drummond, K. (2008). *The enhanced reading opportunities study: Early impact and implementation findings (NCEE 2008-4015).* Washington, DC: National Center for Education Evaluation and Regional Assistance, Institute of Education Sciences, U.S. Department of Education.

Labaree, D. F. (2003, May). The peculiar problems of preparing and becoming educational researchers. *Educational Researcher, 3*(4), 13–22.

Labaree, D. F. (2004). *The trouble with ed schools.* New Haven, CT: Yale University Press.

Labaree, D. F. (2008, October). The dysfunctional pursuit of relevance in educational research. *Educational Researcher, 37*(7), 421–423.

McKenna, M., Robinson, R., & Miller, J. (1990a). Whole language: A research agenda for the nineties. *Educational Researcher, 19*, 3–6.

McKenna, M., Robinson, R., & Miller, J. (1990b). Whole language and the need for open inquiry: A rejoinder to Edelsky. *Educational Researcher, 19*, 12–13.

National Academy of Education Commission on Reading & Anderson, R. C. (1985). *Becoming a nation of readers: The report of the Commission on Reading.* Washington, DC: National Academy of Education, National Institute of Education, Center for the Study of Reading.

National Governors Association & Council of Chief State School Officers. (2009, November 10). *Common core state standards k-12 work and feedback groups announced* (Press release). Retrieved January, 2010, from http://www.nga.org/portal/site/nga/menuitem.6c9a8a9ebc6ae07eee28aca9501010a0/?vgnextoid=709db26363bd4210VgnVCM1000005e00100aRCRD&vgnextchannel=6d4c8aaa2ebbff00VgnVCM10 00001a01010aRCRD

National Institute of Child Health and Human Development. (2000). *Report of the National Reading Panel. Teaching children to read: an evidence-based assessment of the scientific research literature on reading and its implications for reading instruction: reports of the subgroups* (NIH Publication No. 00-4769). Washington, DC: U.S. Government Printing Office.

Pearson, P. D., Mosenthal, P., Kamil, M., & Barr, R. (Eds.). (1984). *Handbook of reading research.* New York: Longman.

RAND Reading Study Group. (2002). *Reading for understanding: Toward an R&D program in reading comprehension.* Santa Monica, CA: RAND Science and Technology Policy Institute.

Rosenblatt, L. (1938). *Literature as exploration.* New York: Appleton-Century.

Shavelson, R. J., & Towne, L. (Eds.). (2002). *Scientific research in education.* Washington, DC: National Research Council, National Academy Press.

Stanovich, K. (1990). A call for an end to the paradigm wars in reading research. *Journal of Reading Behavior, 22*(3), 221–231.

Part 1

Conduct of Reading Research

1 Researching the Teaching of Reading through Direct Observation

Tools, Methodologies, and Guidelines for the Future

James V. Hoffman, Beth Maloch
The University of Texas at Austin

Misty Sailors
The University of Texas at San Antonio

When all was quiet, one of the pupils called out: "I ain't got no ruler." In answer to this the teacher, without correcting or even paying the slightest attention to the incorrect language that had been used by the child, said to him: "You don't need a ruler. Do it the way you done it yesterday." Then the words of the oft-repeated (spelling) list were slowly dictated by the teacher. When the word "steal" was reached, she remarked: "Spell the 'steal' you spelled this morning, not the 'steel' you spelled yesterday." When the word "their" was reached, the teacher asked, "How do you spell 'their'?" "T-h-e-i-r – their," sang the children. What kind of a 't' do you use in their?" "Capital 't'" one of the pupils answered. "That's right," said the teacher ... Here the teacher said to me, "They don't use capital letters regularly in this class; I only let them use capitals when they write proper names and proper things."

(Joseph Mayer Rice, 1893, p. 72)

Joseph Mayer Rice has been variously credited as the "inventor of the comparative test" (Engelhart & Thomas, 1966); a "founder of the progressive movement" (Graham, 1966); and even as the "father of research in teaching" (Berliner, 2007). Whether these titles exaggerate Rice's contributions to education or not, it is widely agreed that Rice, a medical physician, was one of the very first to venture into classrooms to study teaching. Rice was fundamentally concerned with the quality of schooling in America. He had studied education in Europe and was impressed with the "scientific" approach being taken there. Over a period of 5 months, beginning in January of 1892 and finishing in 1893, he visited classrooms in 36 cities to "witness" as much teaching as possible (p. 2). He relied only on "personal observation of teaching" (p 5). In every school district he observed in at least 30 to 35 classrooms, claiming to have observed over "twelve hundred" teachers. It is not entirely clear the method Rice used to record his observations nor is there detail on his process of analysis. The book is filled with some transcripts of classroom interactions suggesting that his noting taking could have been quite detailed. Rice recorded his observations and reported his findings over a series of years using both periodical writing (chiefly in *The Forum*) and in book form (Rice, 1893). Rice was highly critical of the schools he visited and the teaching he observed identifying only four of the systems he visited as deserving of positive attention and decrying most of the others as being "unscientific" and "mechanical."

Rice believed strongly in the connection between "scientific" practices and student achievement. He returned to the four systems he identified as having outstanding teaching and gathered additional student data on spelling, arithmetic, reading, and writing. He argued that these data (all positive in terms of student performance) supported his claim for the close relationship between teaching and learning. In 1897 Rice presented his claims supported by classroom research to an annual meeting of school superintendents in New Jersey (Berliner, 2007). Leonard P. Ayers (1912) reported on the event:

> The presentation of these data threw that assemblage into consternation, dismay, and indignant protest. But the resulting storm of vigorously voiced opposition was directed, not against the methods and results of the investigation, but against the investigator who had pretended to measure the results of teaching spelling by testing the ability of the children to spell. In terms of scathing denunciation the educators there present, and the pedagogical experts who reported the deliberations of the meeting to the educational press, characterized as silly, dangerous, and from every viewpoint reprehensible the attempt to test the efficiency of the teacher by finding out what the pupils could do. With striking unanimity they voiced the conviction that any attempt to evaluate the teaching of spelling in terms of the ability of the pupils to spell was essentially impossible and based on a profound misconception of the function of education. (p. 300)

Rice was not deterred from his purpose by this response and continued making his appeals directly to the public. Rice was convinced that the flaws in public education were the result of poor organization and leadership in schools as well as poor teacher preparation.

> I asked one of the primary grade teachers whether she believed in the professional training of teachers. "I do not," she answered emphatically. "I speak from experience. A graduate of the Maryland Normal School once taught under me, and she wasn't as good a teacher as those who come from the High School." One of the primary teachers said to me: "I formerly taught in the higher grades, but I had an attack of nervous prostration some time ago, and the doctor recommended rest. So I now teach in the primary, because teaching primary does not tax the mind." (Rice, 1893, p. 58)

Rice attempted, in his writing, to walk the fine line between "blaming" teachers and "blaming" the system that created them. He hoped that his inspection of teaching could lead to the reform of teaching from the mechanical to the scientific.

By today's standards for educational research, we would likely judge Rice's efforts as short on methodological rigor (e.g., descriptions of the tools used in the observations) and just slightly over the top on subjectivity, politics, and passion. The most disappointing aspect of Rice's work, however, comes in the fact that while he may have transformed educational measurement and the emphasis for linking teaching to testing, he failed to inspire educational researchers to move into classrooms to conduct more rigorous examinations of teaching. One must fast-forward at least 75 years from the turn of the century to begin to find significant research in the teaching of reading that was conducted in the context of classrooms (Dunkin & Biddle, 1974). This is particularly the case, as we will document in this chapter, with respect to research in the teaching of reading.

Our focus for this chapter will be on describing the tools and methodologies used to observe the teaching of reading in classrooms. Our path takes us from the conceptual, to the historical, to the present, and then to the future.

TOOLS AND MEDIATION IN OBSERVATIONAL RESEARCH

All observational research studies, regardless of methodology, rely on tools. These tools include the means for the recording of data (e.g., the pencil, the computer, the video camera), the formatting or organization of these data (e.g., a checklist, a blank page), and the mental operations or frames of the observer that filter what is recorded (e.g., purposes, expectations, attention, experience). While there is a strong tradition in physical and social science research to use the term "instrumentation" to describe methods, we favor the use of "tools". Instrumentation has strong technical and deep behavioral roots in research. In contrast, the term tool recognizes the social mediation involved in all human activity and knowledge construction. The tools of research always mediate the processes of data gathering and the interpretation of the data.

The dual concepts of "tool" and "mediation" are central to the socio-cultural theory of Vygotsky and his colleagues (see Cole, 1996). The structure and development of human psychological processes are co-constituted by the interaction with tools. The tools are physical and psychological (including language) and mediate learning. In Cole's terms, the mediational triangle includes the inquirer, the object of the inquiry and, indirectly, the tool(s) of inquiry (Cole, 1996). This means, according to Cole, that humans are part of their world and unable to step outside and view the world from the "outside." Pertinent to research, Cole (1996) points out: "traditional dichotomies of subject and object, person and environment, and so on, cannot be analytically separated and temporally ordered into independent and dependent variables" (p. 103). Cole (1996, p. 203) describes Wartofsky's (1973) framework for artifacts (including tools and language) as represented in three levels. Artifacts, according to Wartofsky, can be viewed as primary, secondary, and tertiary. Primary artifacts are associated with tools of production (e.g., a pencil). Secondary artifacts grow out of the application of primary artifacts (e.g., a list of practices). Tertiary artifacts are far removed from practice and are essentially conceptual or imaginative (e.g., Rice's publication and presentation of his findings to leverage for change in practice). Tool use in research can be seen in terms of primary artifacts (associated with production) as in the use of a computer to record data; secondary artifacts (as in the data as represented in various forms through stages of analysis); and tertiary artifacts (as in the ways in which communities interpret these data into larger cultural meanings).

Just as our experiences with the world are shaped by and shape our thinking, the tools and technology used in observations also have a similar effect. This is seen in the evolution of tools for research in the natural sciences (e.g., the study of planets and the cosmos). We align ourselves with Mitcham (1994), who claims that (we) "think through technology" as well as Ihde (1991) who argues that instruments used in research do not merely "mirror reality" but mutually constitute the investigated reality. Ihde maintains that perception is co-determined by the tools or technology of inquiry. Certain aspects are placed in the foreground (and others in the background) by the technology used and can make certain aspects of the observed visible that might otherwise be invisible. According to Ihde, neglecting the role of instruments (i.e., technological artifacts) in science leads to naïve realism. In considering the tools of observation in research it is important to emphasize a "particular" use of a tool in a time and place does not generalize to all other contexts. The social situatedness of tool use and its local meaning must always be recognized.

Given the important role of tools in the conduct of observational research, we focus attention in our review on the qualities and descriptions of the tools used to observe. Our intention is to inspect the ways in which tools come to embody a way of thinking (i.e., a culture of inquiry) that is passed on from one generation (of researchers) to the next—sometimes without a critical analysis of the historical roots and meanings embodied in the tools used.

We believe that the tools of scientific research must meet the highest standards for rigor. We believe that, as these tools are refined, the field of reading research will be better positioned to increase understandings of teaching, of the relationships between teaching and learning, and of the relationship of teaching to teacher knowledge.

GOALS

Through this research review we will attempt to:

1. Characterize the range of tools and methodologies used to gather observational data on teachers;
2. Identify trends in the uses of the tools and methodologies;
3. Discuss concerns or cautions over the tools and methodologies;
4. Describe emerging and promising tools and methodologies; and
5. Propose a set of guidelines for observational research in reading.

We have organized this chapter into four parts. We set the stage for the movement into observational studies of teaching reading in part 1 through a look at the foundational reading research in the 1960s and 1970s as well as a broader look at the research in teaching literature. We describe the procedures we have followed in the identification of tools and methodologies that have been used to study the teaching of reading in part 2. Next, we describe our findings related to the use of tools and strategies that reflect a "quantitative" research perspective (part 3) and the use of tools and strategies that reflect a "qualitative" research perspective (part 4). Finally, we use the findings from our review to articulate a set of guidelines that we hope can help guide the future of observational research in reading in positive directions.

PART 1. BACKGROUND: FOUNDATIONAL RESEARCH

Jeanne Chall's (1967) classic and enormously popular book *Learning to Read: The Great Debate* can be used to characterize the dominant research paradigm for reading research through the first half of the twentieth century. Chall believed that scientific research could be used to resolve questions related to what works and what is best. The science of teaching, as envisioned within the emerging field of psychology, would be informed by experimental research that relied on valid and reliable measures of student learning according to Chall. Chall's review of research surrounding success in learning to read led her to claim that a code-emphasis approach to beginning reading produced better results than a meaning emphasis approach when student achievement was used as the criterion for success. Chall was not the first in this era to make this claim. There were Flesch (1955), Terman and Walcutt (1959), and Walcutt (1961) who all claimed to have the answer to the question: "What is the best way to teaching reading?" All claimed that the status quo for methods, as represented in the popular "Look-Say" basals, did not follow research. Interestingly, none of the studies cited in Chall's review drew on data from the observation of teaching in classrooms. Far from resolving the debate (see Rutherford, 1968), Chall's arguments only served to fuel the fire and turn up the heat on an already heated debate.

In the mid-1960s, the federal government funded the "Cooperative Research Program in First-Grade Reading Instruction." A total of 27 individual research studies from across the country were included in this study. While the project had many dimensions, the focus on determining the best method of reading instruction using student learning outcomes as the determining factor received the most attention. Data were pooled across the studies with respect to the effectiveness questions. The findings from the study disappointed many. There was no clear "winner" among the various methods (Bond & Dykstra, 1967). Frequently, the treatments did not yield the same results across different projects (p. 122). There were numerous project-by-treatment interactions. There were standard "measures" of teachers applied across the methods comparison studies (e.g., experience). However, there were no standard measures of teaching practices applied nor were there any required observations of teachers that would attest to implementation of the treatment.

Only 3 of the 27 first-grade studies included significant observations of teachers. Ironically, Chall and Feldman's (1966) study of teacher beliefs in relation to the implementation of commercial programs was one of the three. The Chall and Feldman study, though not included as one of the methods comparison studies, found little relationship between what teachers reported they were doing and what they did. She did find strong relationships, however, between what they did and what their students' learned.

Wolf, King, and Huck (1968) also used significant observations of teaching within the first-grade studies. Teachers in this study were observed interacting with children in classroom instruction using a categorization scheme developed by the authors and based on Bloom's (1965) taxonomy of the cognitive domain and Guilford's (1967) work on the structure of the intellect. The authors concluded that interpreting, analyzing, and evaluating questions produced more critical responses from children than other types of teachers' questions. The third study from the first-grade studies deserves particular attention in terms of methodology. Harris and Serwer (1966) directed one of the methods comparison studies in which they contrasted the effects of skills-based methods with language experience methods. Harris and Serwer were also interested in the issue of "time" spent in reading activities as a causal (i.e., a rival hypothesis or confounding variable to the "method" used) explanation for student achievement growth. Teachers maintained time logs on activities in reading. The findings from these logs yielded significant correlations to student gain. Teachers in this study were also observed using OScAR-R (Observational Scaling and Rating Reading) developed by Donald Medley for use in this study. The "static" side of this instrument focused on the description of the range of materials used. The "dynamic" section focused on teacher behavior and yielded a coded recording for each teacher statement and interchanges between teachers and students.

The post-first-grade study period in reading research was largely silent with respect to research in reading that focused on teaching in classrooms. Outside of the Wolf et al. (1968) and the Harris and Serwer (1966) studies reported earlier, no study that used significant and systematic observation of teaching was published in the *Reading Research Quarterly* in the decade that followed the publication of the first-grade studies (1967–1977). In contrast, the field of research in teaching (Dunkin & Biddle, 1974; Travers, 1973) blossomed during this same period. Rosenshine and Furst (1973) described the use of direct observation of teaching with a focus on methods. Close to 100 classroom observation systems were developed during this time (Simon & Boyer, 1974) with a large number of these drawing on the observational scheme developed by Ned Flanders (1970). Flanders was interested in the "talk" in classrooms as it might reflect a "democratic" or "authoritative" classroom structure. The Flanders observation system, known as FIAC, was focused on the characterization of teacher and pupil talk in classroom along the dimensions of direct and indirect. Direct teacher talk, for example, included content questions directed at students or reprimands in the behavioral area. Student talk, for example, included coding of student responses to questions or student initiated questions. The coding of talk through the Flanders system was then used to study the relationship between patterns of talk and student outcomes—ranging from achievement to attitudes toward school and learning. The system was designed to record the sequence of behavioral events. The behaviors were divided between teacher talk (Indirect Influence: accepts feelings, praises or encourages, accepts or uses ideas of student, asks questions; Direct Influence: lecturing, giving ideas, criticizing or justifying authority) and Student talk (student talk—response, student talk—initiation, silence or confusion). The observer using the FIAC recorded behaviors every 3 seconds. The most basic form of analysis is to compute frequency analysis for the categories and more complex analyses focus on contingencies and co-occurrence.

Most of the observation systems developed during this period within the research in teaching community were focused solely on observable behaviors. Some of the systems emphasized "high-inference" coding while other systems relied more heavily on "low-inference" systems. Rosenshine and Furst (1973) define a low-inference measure as a rating system that classifies specific, denotable, relatively objective classroom behavior and is recorded as frequency accounts by the observer. They describe high-inference measures as a rating system that requires an observer to make an inference from a series of classroom events using specific constructs, such as satisfaction, enthusiasm, and clarity. Many of these systems included both types of information. Research on teaching flourished as it relied on tools to observe teaching behaviors (termed "process" variables) and correlated them with student outcome measures (termed "product" variables). Rosenshine and Fursts' call for studies that would progress following a "descriptive-correlation-experimental feedback loop" (p. 131) set the standard for the next decade of research in teaching.

Three large programs of research during the early and mid-1970s helped to frame the "process product" research literature. These research programs focused on reading, relied on tools and strategies from the research in teaching literature to conduct classroom observations, and were pursued "outside" of the traditional reading research community. Further, the federal government supported each of these studies, like the first-grade studies, by large-scale funding.

The Follow-Through Studies

In February 1967, President Johnson requested that Congress establish a program to "follow through" on Head Start. These studies were to document the impact of an early education intervention and to identify the features of the intervention that had the greatest impact on student achievement growth. The evaluation model was described as planned variation. Seven different models of early childhood education were compared in research (Stallings, 1975). Classroom observations were conducted across all of the different models and were designed to document activities, materials used, grouping patterns, and interactions. Data were gathered in 35 first-grade and 36 third-grade classrooms. The COI (Classroom Observation Instrument) was developed for data collection. The COI included 602 categories describing behaviors of teachers and students. Interactions were scored in five-minute sequences. Observers completed an average of four observation sequences each hour during a 5-hour observation day. The behaviors included attention to such areas as focus (e.g., academic, social) and discourse patterns (e.g., question, statement). In addition to the interaction data, the observer would gather data on grouping and organization in the classroom as well as the availability of materials. Observers using this system went through rigorous training to achieve high levels of reliability. Monitoring of the observers was also systematic. Stallings' research indicated strong positive relationships between the use of behaviors associated with direct instruction models and student achievement gains. These findings were consistent across measures of reading and mathematics.

The Texas Teacher Effectiveness Studies

These studies were designed to explore the relationship between teacher expectations and student achievement. They focused, in part, on the documentation of classroom teaching behaviors associated with levels of expectation. Additionally the studies examined the relationship between teacher behaviors and student achievement. Brophy (1973) first studied a group of elementary teachers to determine the "stability" of their effects on student achievement. Brophy continued to study a sub-group of these teachers who were stable in terms of their impact on student achievement. This follow-up study relied on a combination of low-inference and high-inference observation systems to measure classroom processes including the *Brophy & Good, Dyadic Interaction Coding System* (Brophy & Good, 1970). Thousands of correlations were computed between scores on process measures and student gain. The findings from these studies suggested a large number of process variables related to both academic (e.g., the use of sustaining feedback to incorrect or incomplete responses) and managerial aspects of teaching (e.g., seating patterns in the classroom). In several areas, differences between the effects of certain teacher behaviors were noted in relation to work in high-SES versus low-SES classrooms. Reading achievement was one of the major student outcome variables studied.

The BTES (Beginning Teacher Evaluation Studies, Phase II)

The goal of this study was to relate classroom observations of teaching to student achievement growth in reading and mathematics. The study was framed around John Carroll's (1963) theoretical work on learning as it relates to aptitude and the opportunity to engage with the content to be learned. Within this study, the variables related to "time" (i.e., engaged/on-task time, allocated time) were found to be highly associated with student achievement. In addition, the researchers found support in the observational data for a model of direct instruction that featured specific elements of effective lessons (see Rosenshine, 1983, for a description of the direct instruction lesson model that emerged out of this research effort). Differences in effective practices were noted across grade levels and different content areas (Berliner, 1990; Fisher et al., 1978; McDonald & Elias, 1976).

Summary

Up through the mid-1970s, research into the teaching of reading that relied on direct observations was sparse. Instructional research in reading during this era was focused primarily on comparison studies directed toward the identification of "the best" methods. In contrast, the field of research in teaching was aggressively moving into classrooms to study teaching effectiveness and often the focus settled on reading instruction and reading achievement. The focus in the research in teaching literature was on the identification of the "best" teaching practices. The bulk of this research, as within the reading research community, was quantitative in nature and rooted in the post-positivist search for cause and effect relationships—specifically in revealing the relationship between specific teaching processes and student learning. These contrasting paradigms for research and the tools and strategies for conducting research operated in a kind of "parallel universe"—largely ignoring each other, as Duffy noted in his 1981 research address to the National Reading Conference (Duffy 1991). However, changes in the late 1970s and early 1980s brought some changes. These changes gained momentum during the decade of the 1990s.

PART 2. TOOLS AND STRATEGIES FOR THE STUDY OF TEACHING READING: EXAMINING THE RESEARCH LITERATURE

Our task was to inspect the research literature focused on reading that relied on the direct observation of teaching and to report on the range of methods and strategies used. We developed an initial set of criteria to focus our search. We limited our focus to research reports that:

- were published in scholarly, refereed research journals;
- reported on the gathering of new data or on a new analysis of existing data;
- focused on teachers and teaching in the area of reading:
- described some authentic act(s) of teaching;
- reported on the methods used to observe teaching; and
- were conducted in classrooms and/or clinic settings (EC through High School).

Even with these criteria we were challenged at times in deciding as to whether a study should or should not be included in our review. To guide us in these decisions, we operated under the rule of "cast the net widely" first (i.e., include even the doubtful cases) and then consider each of the borderline cases using a consensus process within our team. In reporting our findings we will expand on our rationale for including studies that may have been outside of our original criteria.

We made a decision to limit our search to the 30-year period of 1977–2006. Several factors contributed to our decision to set 1977 as the formal starting period. First, our historical review of the earlier period suggested that there was limited research in reading that focused on the direct observation of teaching. These earlier studies were described in the previous section. Second, this was a time when two new research centers were beginning to formulate research agendas that recognized and emphasized the importance of reading and teaching (the Center for the Study of Reading (CSR) at the University of Illinois and the Institute for Research in Teaching (IRT) at Michigan State University). And third, our initial searches of the literature turned up little, beyond the research described in the background section, prior to the 1977 period.

We searched the research literature using a combination of hand searches and electronic search methods. The hand search was completed by one member of the research team and included all articles from 1977 to the present appearing in the *American Educational Research Journal*; the *Journal of Reading Behavior* (later the *Journal of Literacy Research*); the *Yearbook of the National Reading Conference*; the *Journal of Scientific Studies in Reading* (starting in 1997); *Research in the Teaching of English; Teaching and Teacher Education*; the *Elementary School Journal*; the *Journal of Educational Psychology*; and the *Reading Research Quarterly*. In addition, we searched the Web of Science using the following descriptors: with the number of "hits" indicated (TS=(reading AND (teaching OR instruction) AND research AND (primary OR elementary OR secondary OR middle) AND ((participant OR participants) OR (subject OR subjects) OR (student OR students) OR (pupil OR Pupils))) (139 hits). We searched ERIC using the following descriptors: Reading instruction (thesaurus descriptor) AND Classroom research (thesaurus descriptor) AND Elementary (34 hits) and Secondary (9 hits). All of the studies that met the criteria were included in the database for analysis. Each of the articles identified through the electronic and hand search methods was read and considered against the criteria we had established.

During this process, we excluded a study if there was no clear act of an observation of teaching involved. For example, Fukkink (2005) conducted a sequential analysis of think-aloud protocols for looking at the process of deriving word meaning from a written context with primary students—there was no study of an act of teaching in this study. We also excluded studies that did not focus on preservice or inservice classroom teachers or if it was unclear who the teacher was. For example, Mansett-Williamson and Nelson (2005) used paid tutors in their study, but it was unclear if the tutors were preservice or inservice teachers, and Hitchcock, Prater, and Dowrick (2004) studied the effects of tutoring with parents as implementers. Studies like these were not accepted into our database. We also excluded studies if they were not focused on reading such as the science study conducted by Mastropieri and colleagues (2006) who investigated class wide peer tutoring versus teacher-directed instruction for students with mild disabilities in an eighth grade. Other studies used observational methods, but were focused on writing rather than reading, such as McIntyre's (1995) and McCarthey's (1992) studies. Each of the studies was reviewed by at least two or more members of the research team until a consensus decision for inclusion or exclusion was reached.

We have organized our review of the literature as well as the reporting of findings around the frames of qualitative and quantitative research methods. We relied primarily on the theoretical writing of Erickson (1986), Linn and Erickson (1990), and Mertens (2005) to guide us in our categorization processes. The qualitative studies tended to be "interpretive" in nature, and while these studies may have included some quantification of data (e.g., the frequency of certain kinds of teacher actions and percentages that related to a developing theme), they did not rely on inferential statistics. Quantitative studies tended to be "post-positivist" in nature and were focused on describing or exploring the associative or causal relationships among predetermined variables. Not all quantitative studies relied heavily on statistics. Some descriptive studies, in particular those relying on pre-existing variable descriptions, were classified as quantitative (post-positivist) in nature. Studies that drew on both quantitative and qualitative methods were included in both data pools. For purposes of our analysis and reporting, the data collection strategies of the research methods in these mixed-methods studies are considered within the respective categories of quantitative and qualitative research.

In the review process, all studies were examined by at least two of the members of the authoring team. A consensus was required for a study to move into the review. A total of 296 studies met the criteria we established for this review. In Figure 1.1 we present the distribution of studies over time by methodologies (i.e., Quantitative, Qualitative and Mixed). We present the distribution of studies by research journal across methodologies in Table 1.1. Note that the studies in Figure 1.1 are grouped in 2-year pairs. In the next two parts of this report, we offer our analysis of these studies focused on the tools and strategies for observation under the broad methodologies of qualitative and quantitative. We used a constant-comparative methodology (Strauss & Corbin, 1990) within the quantitative and qualitative sections to identify significant themes and patterns (e.g., purposes for use of the instrument). For both the quantitative and qualitative sections, we reviewed each article, entering relevant methodological information (e.g., participants, research questions or purpose, observation methods or techniques, procedures of analysis) into a table. After the two tables were complete, we read and reread the information in these extensive tables noting patterns in techniques and researchers' decisions related to classroom observation. Repeated reading and reviewing of these articles suggested that the variations in observational tools and methods were in some ways related to the differing purposes of the studies. The table was then cut apart, by individual study, and sorted according to observational purpose.

PART 3: USE OF QUANTITATIVE METHODS IN OBSERVATIONAL STUDIES

In this section, we report on our inspection of studies that used quantitative methods of data collection and analysis for the observation of teaching. We identified 108 studies that used quantitative methods only and 14 that used mixed methods (see Table 1.1). Our analysis revealed

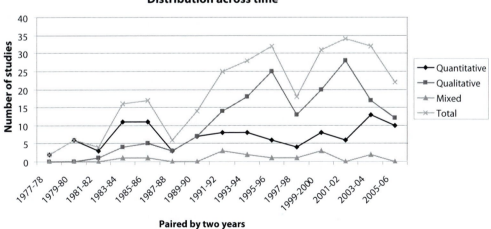

Figure 1.1 Distribution of studies across time.

Table 1.1   Journals Publishing Observational Studies

Journal	Total	Quan	Qual	Mixed
American Educational Research Journal	11	8	2	1
British Journal of Educational Psychology	2	2	0	0
Canadian Modern Language Review	1	0	1	0
Cognition and Instruction	1	0	1	0
Early Childhood Review Quarterly	1	1	0	0
Elementary School Journal	32	19	12	1
Journal for Research in Mathematics Education	1	0	1	0
Journal of Deaf Studies and Deaf Education	1	1	0	0
Journal of Educational Psychology	13	10	3	0
Journal of Learning Disabilities	2	2	0	0
Journal of Literacy Research/Journal of Reading Behavior	37	7	30	0
Journal of Research in Science Teaching	1	0	1	0
Learning Disabilities Quarterly	1	1	0	0
National Reading Conference Yearbook	101	26	71	4
Remedial and Special Education	2	2	0	0
Research in the Teaching of English	22	4	18	0
Reading Research and Instruction	2	0	2	0
Reading Research Quarterly	45	23	17	5
School Effectiveness and School Improvement	1	1	0	0
Scientific Studies of Reading	3	0	3	0
Teaching and Teacher Education	9	1	5	3
Totals	289	108	167	14

several interesting patterns. First, our analysis revealed trends across time and within journals. Second, observational studies were focused on particular aspects of reading instruction and that focus expanded over time. Third, not only the use of the tools varied widely, but the quality of the description of the tools did, as well. Finally, our analysis revealed that one topic in particular, seemed to evolve as the instruments used to examine it evolved. We report on each of these findings in this section.

Trends across Time and Journals

The majority of observational studies that used quantitative methods have been published in the *National Reading Conference Yearbook* (29), *Reading Research Quarterly* (29), the *Elementary School Journal* (20), the *Journal of Educational Psychology* (10), the *American Educational Research Journal* (9), and the *Journal of Reading Behaviors/Journal of Literacy Research* (7) (see Table 1.1). Five observational studies using quantitative methods were published in the 1970s with a surge of them following in the 1980s (33), 1990s (37), and 2000s (26) (see Figure 1.1). This trend would seem to indicate an increased appreciation for and attention to the use of this methodology in reading research across time. This increased attention is true for *Elementary School Journal, Journal of Educational Psychology, Journal of Reading Behavior/Journal of Literacy Research*, and *American Educational Research Journal*, but not for the *Yearbook of the*

National Reading Conference (YBNRC) and *Reading Research Quarterly (RRQ)*, where there is a significant drop in the number of observational studies that used quantitative research from the 1980s to the 2000s (*RRQ* dropped from 9 in the 1980s to 3 in the 2000s; *NRCYB* dropped from 13 in the 1980s to 1 in the 2000s).

Trends across Topics

Observational studies that used quantitative methods focused on a variety of topics. These foci were particular to decades and their representation in the literature reflected the growing attention to areas of reading and reading instruction in the larger area of reading research. For example, in the 1980s, the majority of the studies in our database investigated some aspect of instruction with students, namely, instructional interactions between teachers and students in classrooms. Some of the interactions examined involved questioning strategies and patterns of teachers (e.g., Fagan, Hassler, & Szabo, 1981), while others looked at the feedback teachers gave to miscues (Hoffman & Clements, 1984). Other studies explored the comprehension instruction such as the work of Duffy and his colleagues (Duffy et al., 1986, 1987). Still other studies explored teachers' expectations (Brophy, Rohrkemper, Rashid, & Goldberger, 1983); theoretical orientations (DeFord, 1985); and instruction in special education classrooms (Allington & McGill-Franzen, 1989).

In the 1990s, observational studies expanded to include the description (and importance) of the print environment in literacy instruction (see, for example, Morrow, 1991) and struggling readers as part of special populations (e.g., Lindsey, 1990). The field of educational psychology contributed to the understanding of reading as a process during this decade as evident through the work of Pressley and his colleagues (Brown, Pressley, Van Meter, & Schuder, 1996). Finally, this decade of "what works" (as called for in *A Nation at Risk*) brought with it descriptions and comparisons of models, programs, and approaches to reading instruction. Some of the studies compared broad approaches to literacy instruction with a broad instructional approach (see, for example, Fisher & Hiebert, 1990), while others compared specific models of reading instruction, such as shared reading to traditional models of reading (Reutzel, Hollingsworth, & Eldredge, 1994). Still others studied the effects of specific programs, such as Success for All (Ross & Smith, 1994) and Peer-Assistance Learning Strategies (Fuchs, Fuchs, & Kazden, 1999), on reading instruction and student achievement.

In the 2000s, research that used observational methods continued to examine these same foci; however, the researchers used observational methods to expand what was studied, including the role of schools and effective teachers (Taylor, Pearson, Clark, & Walpole, 2000) and the role of teacher education (Hoffman et al., 2005) in literacy learning. Similarly, studies of special populations (especially English language learners) expanded during this time (see, for example, Vaughn et al., 2006).

Patterns in the Use of Instruments

In addition to the expanding notion of what could be observed in classrooms, our examination also revealed a variety of tools used across these studies. A small number of the studies in this database used a validated observational instrument as a tool to collect data; the remainder varied greatly in their description of the tool used. Of the studies that did not use (or modify) an existing instrument, some used a checklist, some used a categorical coding scheme and some used a rating scheme to collect or mark data.

In addition to the ways observational data were collected, tools were used for different purposes, including (a) as windows into instruction; (b) to establish fidelity of implementation of an innovation; (c) to characterize classroom/context; and (d) as instrument development. We explored each of these focusing on the tools used in each.

Windows into Instruction.   Almost half of the studies in our database used observational data as a means of directly answering their research question(s). A handful of studies (5) used a low-inference frequency count. For example, Gambrell (1984) measured time-on-task to help describe the time structure of teacher-directed reading instruction and help determine how much time children in grades 1–3 spent engaged in contextual reading experiences. Another handful of studies (8) used a rating system to capture more theoretical data, such as the data Duffy and his colleagues (Duffy, Roehler, & Rackliffe, 1986) collected when they tested the effects of explicit teacher explanations on the use of reading strategies in low reading groups. A more recent study involved data collection through the use of a laptop computer, which may be a wave of the next decade. Through the use of the CLASS 3 program, data collectors in middle school classrooms captured and rated class discussions and related activities, focusing on the types of questions that teachers and students asked, materials used, and interactions with each other (Applebee, Langer, Nystrand, & Gamoran, 2003).

The majority of the other studies in this group (26) used a low-inference categorical system for capturing and/or marking data, although many of the systems were quite complex. For example, in examining the characteristics of basal reading programs and their influence on instruction, Barr and Sadow (1989) coded "running records" of exchanges between teachers and students to determine time spent on reading and non-reading activities. They further coded their data to determine the nature and duration of each activity and what type of activities teachers and students were engaged (activities were classified as word id/word meaning/general comprehension activities). Almasi (1995) also used a categorical system, one that she marked qualitatively (through constant-comparison), exploring the nature of episodes of sociocognitive conflict among fourth-grade readers in peer-led and teacher-led discussions of narrative text. She also employed a statistical analysis of students' ability to recognize and resolve episodes of sociocognitive conflict as well as the discourse associated with sociocognitive conflict.

Establishment of Fidelity of Implementation of Innovation.   While many of the studies in our database used observation instruments to document, assess, and describe classroom instruction, other studies used observational instruments to establish the fidelity of implementation of the innovation under study. Fidelity of implementation in research confirms that the independent variable was correctly manipulated, determines how adequately appropriate model was implemented, or assesses the conformity to prescribed elements (Mowbray, Holter, Teague, & Bybee, 2003). The quality of the measures used across this category varied widely. In some studies, fidelity of implementation was documented only in passing. For example, in van Keer's (2004) quasi-experimental study in which he examined the effects of explicit reading strategies instruction followed by practice in (a) teacher-led, whole class activities; (b) reciprocal same age activities; or (c) cross age peer tutoring activities, fidelity was conducted through "regular observations" (p. 44). In other studies, fidelity was determined through prepared forms used to record notes regarding teaching methods, fidelity of practices to procedures, classroom behavior, and engaged time (see, for example, Ross & Smith, 1994). Still other studies described a more elaborate description of the instrument and a rating system for determining the degree of implementation. For example, in the comparison study of the innovative CORI model to more traditional models of comprehension instruction, Guthrie and his colleagues (2004) measured the fidelity of implementation through a rating scale (4 = thorough implementation; 3 = partial implementation; 2 = limited implementation; 1 = no visible implementation) and used the ratings as a covariates in their analysis.

Characterization of Classroom/Context.   In a very small number of studies, researchers used observational means to characterize the classroom as one sort of instruction or another or to confirm the differences in the instruction. The quality of those instruments varied widely. For example, Fisher and Hiebert (1990) used a categorical system to classify instructional approaches of the teachers in their study. These researchers examined the learning opportunities available to students in classrooms with different approaches to literacy. Using a task perspective, the researchers first identified the tasks and subtasks and then categorized the tasks and subtasks based on their duration, general and specific subject matter, and cognitive complexity. The activities were categorized by product type, product specification by students, format, and activity duration. These observations "made it clear that literacy experiences for the two instructional approaches were qualitatively different" (Fisher & Hiebert, 1990, p. 5). In other studies, the examination of the context was not as systematic, as in a study of the effects of teacher-directed print concept instruction in a print rich environment on print concept development of kindergarteners (Reutzel, Oda, & Moore, 1989). In this study, the researchers determined there were "no observable differences in the quantity or quality of instruction" between the groups of teachers at the onset of the study (p. 202) through the use of a pre-existing, school-based instrument that was not focused on literacy.

Development of an Observation Instrument.   Finally, in 11 studies in our database, researchers used observational means as a mechanism for creating and/or validating observational instruments. The majority of these studies were conducted in the most recent decade. The quality of these instruments (including the descriptions and reporting of each) was very different from our three previous categories. Some of the instruments were developed to answer the research question. In many cases, data was being collected for which no instrument existed. For example, in their research, Taylor, Pearson, Peterson, and Rodriguez (2003) investigated the effects of teaching on students' reading achievement in "beating the odds" schools. The researchers created and used the CIERA School Change Observation Scheme to describe the ways that teachers maximized students' cognitive engagement in literacy activities and to evaluate the efficacy of a school-wide framework aimed at cognitive engagement. This instrument combined field-notes with a quantitative coding process—the narrative data from the field-notes were coded on task behavior; who was providing the instruction; grouping patterns; major literacy activities; salient literacy events; materials; teacher interactive style; and expected responses of the students. The instrument was validated within the study and used to describe the role of effective schools and teachers in the literacy development of children from low-income and minority backgrounds across the country.

Other studies in this category were focused on the validation of an instrument as the purpose of the study. For example, Hoffman, Sailors, Duffy, and Beretvas (2004) and Wolfersberger, Reutzel, Sudweeks, and Fawson (2004) focused on the creation and validation of instruments that captured and measured the print environment of classrooms as a way of describing literacy instruction. More recent studies have used observations to validate contemporary ways of documenting instruction. For example, Camburn and Barnes (2004) have used triangulation to assess teacher logs (a 4-page self-administered questionnaire in which teachers report the instructional experiences of a target student for an entire day) as a viable mechanism for describing language arts instruction. In their study, observers collected full day observations in math and language arts instruction, filled out a log and then compared their logs to logs the observed teachers filled out. They found a high correlation between what the observers saw (and marked on the log) and what the teachers marked on their logs. Through their work, Camburn and Barnes are expanding the notion of what counts as classroom observations.

The Evolution of a Topic through the Evolution of "Tool"

Our analysis of patterns across topics revealed that there was one topic in particular (print-rich environments and their role in literacy development) that seemed to evolve as the observational instruments used to document it evolved. Within the 11 studies that centered on the topic of print-rich environments, 3 used the instrument in their study to measure the implementation of the innovation and/or the instrument was not described well enough for us to analyze its use. Therefore, we only analyzed eight studies; we discuss these eight studies in this section. We first present a brief summary of those studies, followed by the themes that emerged across these eight studies, focusing on the prominent role that the instrument played in the study.

The eight studies in our database represent a continuously expanded focus on what "counts" (and with whom it "counts") in print environment research. For example, in the earliest study in our database, Taylor, Blum, and Logsdon (1986) studied kindergarten teachers' implementation of a theory-based pre-reading curriculum, the observable factors which characterized implementing classrooms, and the effects of implementation on the reading achievement of children. In order to answer the research question, the team observed all six classrooms, identifying and documenting features and incidences of print through written descriptions as well as slides and videotapes. Incidences were compared across classrooms and distinguishing properties and aspects of print were described four categories were built. Included in these categories were: (a) type of language used in display; (b) location of print in room; (c) availability of print to children; and (d) time frame of activities with displays. A checklist was then created by operationally defining their curriculum; the checklist was used as a rating scale to determine implementation. This rating scale measured the implementation of the curriculum by describing the print environment of these kindergarten classrooms as implemented (a) very effectively, (b) effectively, (c) to a limited degree, or (d) not at all. Participating classrooms were then classified as "implementing" or "not implementing" and children's reading achievement was compared across groups. The tool in this study was constructed using the theory behind the intervention.

Morrow (1991) also collected data on the physical print environment of classrooms, but expanded this notion to include a documentation of the ways in which teachers and children used literacy during the observational periods. Morrow set out to determine the factors that motivated literacy behavior in play. Her study looked at the relationships of (a) the frequency of literacy behaviors by children at play, (b) specific materials and physical design elements in kindergarten play areas, and (c) teacher guided experiences related to literacy and play. She collected observational data in 35 kindergarten classrooms including information on the print found in the environment. To do so, she modified the Survey of Displayed Literacy Stimuli and also creating a "questionnaire" that documented the number of participants (including children and teachers) engaged in literacy activities and the perceived motivations behind the behaviors. She collected data across four different days during four different weeks while children were at play. Morrow used the observational data in her analysis and reported on the ways participating teachers modeled, discussed, or suggested the use of literacy in the presence of children. Morrow's modified instrument expanded the notion of what counts within the print-rich environment research.

During this same time, Ross, Smith, Lohr, and McNelis (1994) developed and validated the Elementary Classroom Observation Measure (ECOM) for their study in which they examined how classroom conditions, resources, and teaching methods compared across 40 remedial and regular tracked first-grade classrooms. While the instrument developed for this study did not focus (in its entirety) on the print environment, it did include it as one significant aspect. The ECOM considered the classroom ecology and resources (print); makeup and physical environment; interval coding (including grouping configurations and teacher and student behaviors); a rating of teacher behaviors that positively support learning; teaching methods; and open comments. The instrument contained interval coding (based on a low inference system), holistic ratings and descriptions that "reflected more global, subjective impressions of the events observed" (p. 108). Interestingly, the researchers found no significant differences in the resources offered to children in these two types of classrooms. This study is evidence that an expanding community of researchers was coming to understand of the importance of a print-rich environment.

In her seminal formative experiment, Neuman (1999) connected theory to practice in her examination of the impact of flooding 330 child-care centers with high quality children's books and providing training to child-care staff. Neuman collected pre-post intervention data on the physical environments of classrooms, including the arrangement of books in library corners and shelves (through the use of photography). Neuman also used momentary time samples to collect data on the literacy related interactions between teachers and children (in sample classrooms). Her instrument began as field-notes that were codified as either a literacy interaction initiated by or directed at the focus child of the observation. She also collected data on the storybook reading activities in both groups. The photos of the physical environments were analyzed to establish categories of change in environment and frequency counts of interactions were reported in percentages. Neuman's work capitalized on the use of technology to capture data and to help the field "see" those differences in classrooms due to the intervention. That is, Neuman used clear lines between the data she collected, analyzed, and reported.

Duke (2000) connected theory to practice in her study of the exposure to and the types of experiences with informational text offered to students in 10 low-SES and 10 high-SES first grade classrooms. In her work, Duke recorded print on the walls (referred to as displayed print) and in the classroom library (books and magazines) and activities in which children were engaged with print. She coded activities by genre, what was done with the text in the activity, and the length (in time) of the activity. She piloted her instrument prior to this study. Coding over 6,000 pieces of displayed print for this study, Duke carefully reported her descriptions of how she identified and coded texts that appeared in her database, especially those texts that appeared between her visits to these classrooms. Duke tallied each of the focus areas of the study (displayed print, classroom libraries, and activities) and employed MANOVA comparisons of low- and high-SES classrooms. Although her findings were quite alarming (there was an overall scarcity of informational texts in these first grade classrooms), her work continued to move research centered on print-rich environments forward through her use of an observational tool and its clear path between the theory that drove her work and the collection and coding of data and analysis.

The final set of studies in this section demonstrated this careful mapping between theory, data collection and data analysis as well as the role of the instrument in that mapping. All were centered on the validation of an observational instrument. For example, Wolfersberger and colleagues (2004) designed and described the development and validation of the Classroom Literacy Environment Profile (CLEP), an assessment tool for measuring "print richness" of elementary classrooms. The CLEP contained 33 items; each item was rated on a scale from 1 (lowest level of implementation) to 7 (highest level of implementation). In their report, the authors demonstrated the move from the theoretical to the practical as the instrument went through three phases. In phase I, the research team used naturalistic methods to develop the items that would appear in the instrument. In phase II, the team used test theory to refine the content (constructing, reviewing, and rating the items). In phase III, the team validated the instrument in 21 classrooms (K–6). An analysis of variance was conducted on each item and subscale, demonstrating the discrimination reliability of the CLEP.

The next instrument in our database was published in the same journal as the CLEP, just one volume later. In this study, Hoffman and his colleagues (2004) reported on the development and validation of an instrument that centered on a strong theoretical framework for thinking about print rich classrooms. Through their work, the team documented the connection between print rich classrooms and student reading achievement. The research team followed a protocol similar to the Wolfersberger team—first conducting a literature review and developing tentative categories of text types and rubrics for each. Feedback from classroom teachers was solicited on all three components. The team then field-tested the instrument and revisions were made. The instrument contained three components. The first measured the physical print environment of classrooms (grades K–6). The second documented the uses of texts by students and teachers. The third documented the understandings of the texts (forms, functions, and uses) by students and teachers. These three components were rated individually. Each component was highly correlated with student achievement in reading (as measured on the GRADE) in 33 classrooms (grades K–6) across six states. The work of Hoffman and his colleagues provided an additional component to consider in the observational documentation of the print-rich environment—the understandings of the purposes, functions, and uses of the print in the environment by students and teachers (drawn from the social practice perspective) and the connection of the print environment to student reading achievement.

In the final study in our database, Baker and his colleagues (Baker, Gersten, Haager, & Dingle, 2006) also validated a classroom observation measure to use with English language learners in Grade 1, the English Language Learner Classroom Observation Instrument (ELLCO). While the formal development of the instrument is discussed in other publications, the authors did report on the reliability of the instrument and the correlation between subscales. The ELLCO contains six subscales with individual items in each. Subscales include (a) explicit teaching, (b) quality of instruction, (c) sheltered English instruction, (d) interactive teaching, (e) vocabulary development, and (f) phonemic awareness and decoding. Ratings within the subscales (except for phonemic awareness and decoding instruction) were correlated to reading achievement (as measured through a composite reading score consisting of posttest performance on oral reading fluency and the reading comprehension measure) in the 14 classrooms in which the team worked in California. The subscales were used to measure the reliability. Because they considered their work to be exploratory, the team offered suggestions for future work on the instrument in refining the subscales. The work of Baker and his colleagues followed the same clear path as the other studies in this analysis while continuing to expand the notion of "what counts" and "for whom" in the literature on print-rich environments.

Our examination of these eight studies illustrated the ways in which the evolution of the tools used to capture and describe print-rich environments informed the understanding of its role in literacy development. First, the purpose of all of the print-rich studies, regardless of the role of the instrument, was to demonstrate the existence and importance of the topic. Second, there was a careful refining of the instruments used to study classroom teaching and literacy learning. While there were some that simply mentioned it (Duke, 2000) others described it in detail (see, for example, Taylor et al., 1986). Third, the approach to the collection of data through the use of these instruments varied greatly. For example, some instruments were open-ended field-notes that were examined (Morrow, 1992) while others contained a more systematic and quantitative documentation of data. Regardless, the pattern across studies was that they all offered a careful description of how data was collected and coded. And finally, there was a very close connection between the theoretical frame of the study and the data collected and codified. This expanding notion of "what counts," "for whom," "under what conditions," and "for what purposes and intentions" is a direct and parallel path to the evolution of the instruments developed and used. That is, perhaps without the refinement and development of instruments, the field might be thinking only in terms of books in classrooms with the very youngest of children without a particular look at why and how.

Summary

In summary, our analysis of studies that used quantitative methods for data collection and analysis varied widely, as did the use of the instruments, and demonstrated a growing recognition of the importance of observational methods. The use of instruments in this database focused on a variety of topics, reflecting the growing understanding of reading instruction. The variety of ways in which the tools were used reflected the flexible ways tools were used to examine teaching through observational research methods. For example, tools in our database were classificatory, categorical, frequency counts, and rating systems, depending on the purpose and intention of the use of the tool. And, our analysis revealed that at least one topic developed parallel with the instrumentation used to understand it. This all reflects a growing advancement of both the method of quantitative means for observational research.

However, there are a few caveats to consider. While the field of reading research has seen a surge of observational studies, it would appear that only a few journals are continuing to publish this type of methodology. While the *National Reading Conference Yearbook* and *Reading Research Quarterly* were some of the first journals to widely recognize observational studies, the contributions of observational studies using quantitative methods to these journals have decreased significantly. We are unclear as to why this trend is taking place. Perhaps with the expansion of acceptance and recognition of observational studies (using quantitative means) as a viable mechanism for understanding literacy instruction, authors have more choices in outlets for their work. Or perhaps, authors find their work appreciated in the journals that focus more generally on teaching and teacher education.

Our analysis also indicated that the quality of descriptions of the instruments used varied widely, with some studies meticulously noting the instrumentation used and others just mentioning the instrument in passing. Again, we were unclear as to this pattern. Perhaps it is because authors choose not engage in careful documentation, publishers do not require it, or there is simply not enough space in journals to report this information. Regardless, this was a growing concern as we analyzed this database.

PART 4: STUDIES USING QUALITATIVE OBSERVATIONAL TECHNIQUES

Between the years 1977 and 2006, we identified 181 studies that used qualitative methods in classroom observations. The qualitative observational techniques reviewed in this section constitute a departure from the observational tools and protocols discussed in the quantitative section. Most of the studies reviewed in this section documented teaching through participant observation, recording the data through written field-notes and, in many cases, audio or video records. There is a strong tradition in qualitative work, and in the work we review for this section, of documenting observations through field-notes with an open-ended format rather than an observational protocol to which the researcher attends. Lincoln and Guba (1985), along with other qualitative researchers (Bogdan & Biklen, 2007; Glaser & Strauss, 1967), argues that the researcher is the "instrument of choice" and highlights the need to consider the subjectivity of the researcher. In this tradition, the use of more open-ended formatting for observational documentation is necessarily accompanied by increased attention to the biases, beliefs, and experiences of the researcher, as well as considerations of how researchers might guard against these biases in their note-taking. That is, while recognizing the influence of the researcher's values, assumptions, beliefs, and biases, researchers—as evidenced in our review here—have sought to address these concerns in a variety of ways. Thus, the variation in observational technique in these studies was related less to the format of the observational protocol—in most cases there was no protocol—and more to the frequency, focus, and length of observations.

In this section, we discuss trends across the 30 years under review, explain our review procedures, and describe the range of observational methods used in the studies.

Trends

Across the 30 years we considered in our review, the number of qualitative studies involving the observation of teaching increased dramatically. We found no studies using qualitative observational methods until 1981. In the 1980s, we identified only nineteen studies, including those using qualitative methods solely (17) or in a mixed methods design (2). The first, Sanders' study (1981) of the interactional language that occurred in literacy learning lessons in a first grade classroom, was published in the *National Reading Conference Yearbook*. Of the 19 studies published during the 1980s, 14 were published in the *NRC Yearbook*, a number indicating that the *Yearbook* may have provided an outlet for early observational research related to literacy—particularly those that used qualitative methods. Only five were published in major research journals—one in *Reading Research Quarterly* (Alvermann & Hayes, 1989), one in *Research in the Teaching of English* (Eeds & Wells, 1989), one in *Elementary School Journal* (Duffy, Roehler, & Rackliffe, 1986), and two in *Teaching and Teacher Education* (Alpert, 1987; Magliaro & Borko, 1986).

In the 1990s, 89 studies were published. As discussed below, during this time, literacy researchers spent extended time in classrooms, particularly engaging in in-depth study of single or small numbers of classrooms. The *NRC Yearbook* continued to feature studies utilizing qualitative observational techniques, publishing almost half (40) of the studies included in our qualitative database. However, qualitative observational studies also began to make more regular appearances in prominent research journals such as *Reading Research Quarterly, Journal of Literacy Research, Research in the Teaching of English*, and *Elementary School Journal*. That trend continued into the current decade. From 2000 to 2006, over 70 reports of research have been published that met our criteria. With this trend, it is possible that by the end of the 2000s, we will see upwards of 100 research articles reporting qualitative observational techniques. These articles are appearing in both the *NRC Yearbook* and across a variety of research journals (see Table 1.1).

Across the studies reviewed, observational duration (from 3 days to 4 years), observational frequency (from 3 total lessons, to daily observations), and number of participants (from 1 teacher to 44) varied. Our review and analysis (described above) of these 181 studies suggested that they fell into four broad groups, categorized according to the purpose of the observations. Observations were employed to accomplish one of four somewhat broadly construed purposes:

- For the purpose of exploring existing classroom practices (79 studies)
- For the purpose of understanding interventions or innovations (51 studies)
- For the purpose of inspecting a particular aspect or event of a classroom or clinic (26 studies)
- For the purpose of supporting, contrasting, or corroborating another data source (25 studies)

We explain and discuss each of these four categories of studies in the following sections. In each section, we describe the purposes of these studies, how these purposes related to the researchers' techniques for collecting observational data, and representative examples of each category.

Exploring Existing Classroom Practices

In the first, and largest, group of studies (totaling 79), observations were used for the purpose of investigating research questions as contextualized within classrooms or teaching situations as wholes. In these studies, researchers were participant observers in classrooms for extended periods of time (usually at least a semester) and sought to make sense of the teaching within the context of the classroom and its participants. Although observations were used as the primary data source, researchers also used other sources to make sense of teaching in the context of the classroom. Although one particular time of the day or event was the focus (e.g., literature circles), attempts were made to document the whole of the classroom so that findings were con-textualized. While there were a few studies of this type in the early 80s (e.g., Bloome, 1983, 1984), they became more prominent through the years, reaching their prime in the mid-1990s.

Sixty-four of the 79 studies (81%) in this group focused on one or two teachers and were more ethnographic in nature. In these studies, the researchers spent considerable time in one or two classrooms in order to examine literacy instruction as situated within particular classroom contexts. For example, Moje (1996) observed a high school content area teacher over a period of 2 years as she and her students engaged in literacy activities. Engaging in "intensive, long term, participant observation" (p. 179), Moje documented the teacher's instruction via daily field-notes for a period of 3 months the first year, and throughout the second year. These notes, like many of the studies in this category, were analyzed using the constant-comparative method (Glaser & Strauss, 1967). Within the studies focusing on one or two teachers, the length of the data collection period varied from 12 weeks to 3 years. While not all were as extensive as Moje's study, all set out to understand teaching as situated in a particular classroom.

Because researchers used open-ended field-notes as a data collection tool or method, they often (but not always) described the focus or procedures of this documentation. For example, Knapp (2002) described her note-taking carefully, saying, she "wrote a running longhand nar-rative of what happened in class, containing time notations, descriptions of activities, and notes on the teacher's and students' discourse, actions, and interactions" (p. 66). To give the reader a sense of how much observational data was collected, researchers tended to report the frequency of the observations (e.g., weekly; 3–4 mornings per week; twice weekly), the number of pages of field-notes, the total number of hours spent observing (e.g., researchers logged a total of 300 hours of observations) and/or video recordings (e.g., 60 hours of videotaped data).

Teacher research studies, in which at least one of the researchers was the teacher under study, comprised a small subset of these studies (five). Baumann and Ivey (1997), for example, report on Baumann's year long sabbatical as a second grade teacher. His teaching was documented through a combination of his reflective journal, audio/videotapes, and Ivey's field-notes that she took as a participant observer in his classroom.

Fifteen of the 79 studies (19%) documented the teaching of more than two teachers. While focused on understanding literacy instruction as a whole, the amount of observational data col-lected varied, depending on how many teachers were observed. For example, in a study focused on the experiences of five diverse students, McCarthey (1997) sought to understand how home and school were connected. In order to explore how these experiences varied across students, she selected five students and conducted 1–3 hour observations three times each week for a year, documenting those observations through field-notes and audiotape records. The length and frequency of these observations afforded opportunities to observe each of these five students carefully over the course of a year. On the other hand, in a study of 30 teachers, Pressley and his colleagues (Pressley, Wharton-McDonald, Mistretta-Hampston, & Echevarria, 1998; Pressley et al., 2001; Wharton-McDonald, Pressley, & Mistretta-Hampston, 1998) sought to identify and describe effective first-grade literacy instruction by observing multiple classrooms. The pur-pose of this research was to determine cross-classroom features, not to examine the contex-tual nuances of each classroom, and as a result, researchers observed more classrooms but each teacher was observed only twice monthly during their language arts block.

A methodological component of research characterized by both multiple participants and multiple researchers was the need to align observational practices across researchers, and report how these were aligned. In those studies in which multiple researchers collected observational data, more attention was paid to describing the observation procedures and how procedures were aligned. For example, Wharton-McDonald et al. (1998) wrote of their field notes,

Two complete sets of field notes were maintained, and the two primary observers frequently reviewed each other's notes and discussed similarities and differences in their observations of the same classrooms. In order to maximize the accuracy of the notes and facilitate later analyses, the three language principles recommended by Spradley (1980) were followed in taking field notes. For each entry, the language used—whether it was the observer's or the teacher's—was noted (the language identification principle). Whenever possible, the language of the teachers and students was recorded verbatim (the verbatim principle). Interactions or events were recorded using concrete language; the observers tried not to use abstract jargon in field notes (the concrete principle). (p. 106)

Here, like other authors in the same situation, they attempted to lay out, as clearly as possible, their procedures for field-notes, borrowing from Spradley's work on participant observation. This kind of description, although not always as detailed, was present in many of the research articles in our database.

Understanding Innovation or Intervention

In the second group of studies (totaling 51), observations were used for the purpose of investigating interventions or innovations in classrooms or clinics (e.g., Alvermann & Hayes, 1989; Worthy & Beck, 1997). In these studies, research questions related to interventions or innovations offered by researcher/university or district, and the studies were typically intended to document the teacher's implementation of these innovations or interventions. Many of these articles emerged from larger studies and were attempts to better understand the process teachers went through as they attempted to implement a program in which they were "trained." For example, Roehler, Duffy, and Meloth (1984) conducted a post-hoc analysis of the teachers involved in an "explicit explanation" study to determine how these explanations might be characterized. Similarly, El-Dinary, Pressley, and Schuder (1992) followed up a larger study of transactional strategies instruction with an examination of the "process of becoming a SAIL [Students' Achieving Independent Learning] teacher." In this study, the researchers followed three of the larger set of teachers, analyzing 24–27 observations per teacher documented through audiotapes and fieldnotes. Observations over the course of a year, across these three teachers, afforded an opportunity to understand this process of change for SAIL teachers. From the same larger study, Brown and Coy-Ogan (1993) followed one teacher across 3 years, documenting her reading/teaching of the same story over 3 years, with three different sets of second graders. This analysis afforded more in-depth insights about how one teacher traversed the transition across more than 1 year and with different classrooms of students. These analyses that emerged from the larger quantitative or mixed methods studies were attempts to more qualitatively characterize and understand the "inside" of these interventions and how they played out in teachers' classrooms.

Studies investigating interventions, particularly those studies conducted by multiple researchers, often employed more focused observational techniques. For example, Paterson, Henry, O'Quin, Ceprano, and Blue (2003) engaged in a mixed methods study of sixteen classrooms to determine the effectiveness of the Waterford Early Reading Program. Researchers first conducted a qualitative analysis of observations. These observations—four per teacher—were documented using an observational protocol in which "observers noted the starting and ending times of an event or activity, then described that activity as fully as possible, noting teacher's actions and strategies, the children's actions, and the children's activities in the Waterford centers" (p. 187). Qualities of these classrooms identified through the qualitative analysis of this observational data were then entered into a multi-variate analysis to discover "how factors other than the Waterford Program might affect literacy learning" (p. 195).

In addition, several studies were designed to document the ways a teacher (or more often, teachers) took up a particular innovation (e.g., whole language, literature-based instruction, use of response logs) after learning about it in professional development. For example, Borasi, Siegel, Fonzi, and Smith (1998) examined the implementation of transactional reading strategies in four secondary mathematics classes. After participating in a semester long seminar to learn the strategies, teachers joined researchers in collaboratively planning five "instructional experiences" (p. 282) and implementing these lessons in their classrooms. To understand and track how the teachers implemented these strategies in the classroom, the researchers documented each of these experiences (lasting anywhere from 2 to 18 weeks) in their entirety through extensive field-notes and audio/videotaping. Researchers and teachers worked together through the implementation process.

Similarly, a few researchers studied and documented teachers' existing practices, and offered ongoing feedback and consultation as teachers made efforts to revise or grow these practices. For example, Alvermann and Hayes (1989) worked with teachers to modify discussions to reflect higher-order thinking and critical reading. After documenting existing discussion patterns, Alvermann and Hayes observed/videotaped classroom discussion, then met with the teacher to discuss and offer feedback on future discussions. This videotaping/debriefing cycle was repeated with teachers several times over the course of 6 months, and the entire process was documented.

Inspecting a Particular Aspect or Event of a Classroom or Clinic

A third set of studies employed observations primarily for the purpose of investigating a particular aspect or event of a classroom or clinic. In these studies, observations focused on a particular event (e.g., read aloud; content area reading discussions) or aspect (e.g., story-book reading style, textbook use), with the duration of the study often tied to this focus (e.g., length of unit, duration of a set of activities). Across these 26 studies, observations ranged from three lessons for one teacher (Sweetland, Abel-Carrick, & Kinzer, 1987) to 192 lessons observed across nine teachers (Armbruster et al., 1991). In all but one instance, researchers documented teaching either through recordings (with transcription following) or through what most would call "general" field-notes.

The vast majority of these studies made use of audio or videotapes to record instruction or activities. Interestingly, over half of the studies used transcriptions of these recordings as the primary or sole documentation of the teaching. That is, field-notes were not used to document teaching while in the classroom (at least not as it was reported in writing); audio/videotapes were transcribed and used as the sole observational data source for analysis. Use of transcription as the primary observational data source occurred in those studies with fewer observations, most hovering around three to four total observations per teacher.

For example, Martinez and Teale (1993) examined the storybook reading styles of six kindergarten teachers reading the same four storybooks. To do so, they transcribed the audiotaped read alouds of these four books. At least one researcher was present for each reading to note nonverbal behaviors in an attempt to make the transcript more complete. These transcripts became the primary data source for the analysis. For studies in which there were a small number of observations per teacher (e.g., Alvermann, 1990; Martinez & Teale, 1993; Sipe & Brightman, 2006), the recording and transcribing of these observations allowed for a more thorough and complete (and archivable) documentation, in some ways a "thicker" record of the few instances of recorded teaching. As well, many of these studies focused on interactions around text (e.g., role of the teacher in nonfiction discussions; content area reading discussions; storybook reading). This research focus may have led to the researchers' decisions to sample fewer instances of teaching and to document that teaching through transcribed recordings.

For the remaining studies in this category, researchers documented more instances of teaching, and they were likely to document this teaching through the combination of field-notes, audio/video recordings, and some transcription. For example, Sosniak and Stodolsky (1993) examined the roles textbooks played in classrooms by observing four teachers, 10 times each, and documenting these observations through field-notes. Whether documenting through audio/videotape recordings (with subsequent transcription) or through open-ended field-notes, all studies within this category used observations as a way of understanding a particular aspect or event in a classroom.

Providing a Secondary Data Source

In the final category (totaling 25), we grouped studies in which observations were used for the purpose of offering support or contrast with another data source (usually interviews) or as a secondary source for verification/contextualization (e.g., Konopak et al., 1990; Garcia et al., 2006). Often concerned with more "internal" states such as thoughts, decision-making, or beliefs, interviews in these studies frequently served as a primary data source while observations were employed to supplement, make sense of, or corroborate what the researchers were finding through the interviews. Research questions such as, "How do secondary, content-area teachers think about reading when they plan?" (Hinchman, 1985), "Is there consistency between Chapter 1 teachers' beliefs and their instructional planning?" (Mitchell, Konopak, & Readence, 1991), and "How did our former students' beliefs about literacy teaching evolve and change as they went from methods course, to student teaching, to their first year of teaching?" (Pierce & Pomerantz, 2006) were typical of these studies.

This category of studies, not as common as the first three discussed, includes several that examined the consistency between beliefs and practices. Observations, in these cases, were used as a way of comparing teachers' beliefs to what they actually did in the classroom. For example, Konopak et al. (1990) investigated how teacher beliefs about reading for content learning (i.e., Science) were realized during instruction. Five days of observation were preceded and followed by one-on-one interviews. Then, these data sources were analyzed together to assess the consistency and variances of the teachers' beliefs and practices.

Across this set of studies, there were several consistencies in the recording or documentation of teaching. First, most of these studies used some form of note-taking to record the observation. Second, 12 of the 25 studies also audio or video recorded these observations, although only four actually transcribed them. Third, little description was included as to the form of the field-notes or note-taking. Occasionally, note-taking was not even mentioned in the data collection section, even though the findings section suggested that researchers did indeed document the teaching through some form of narrative written record. All of these consistencies were related to the purpose of the observations—to supplement or confirm findings from other data sources. Because observations were not the primary or central data sources in these studies, less attention and description was devoted to them in the reports.

Summary

Despite limitations mentioned in the above section, as we look across all of the studies using qualitative methods, we were encouraged by the range and complexity of ways researchers are capturing and documenting literacy instruction in qualitative ways. It is clear that researchers were working creatively and thoughtfully to understand literacy instruction. Whereas quantitative observational studies vary in the types and formats of observational protocols used and focused on particular aspects of practice, the studies reviewed in this section ranged in how and how often observations were accomplished, how these observations were documented and recorded, and how researchers chose to "sample" the observational data available to them during both data collection and data analysis phases of their research.

Researchers "sampled" instruction in different ways. Their decisions concerning when and how often they might observe teaching related to their overall purposes or focus of the research. In the case of innovation and intervention, for example, researchers were interested in how teaching developed or progressed over time so many of these researchers decided to sample teaching in such a way to tap into this temporal aspect of development. For example, Kong and Pearson (2003), hoping to capture "any changes that might have occurred during the school year," concentrated their observational data collection within three time periods: (a) 6 weeks at the beginning of the year, (b) 2 weeks in February, and (c) 2 weeks in May. Between these periods, the researchers visited the classroom every other week. Rex (2001) documented the first 31 days in their entirety through audio/videotapes and field-notes, in order to examine the ways in which students were inducted into a particular class community. Kantor, Miller, and Fernie (1992) documented the first 2 weeks of each quarter through video recordings (with six camera locations around the room), as well as daily field-notes written by four participant observers. All of these researchers sampled teaching through their observations in ways appropriate to their focus and research questions. Their decisions to do so, as do all decisions researchers make about sampling, impacted the data they collected.

Finally, in consideration of our emphasis on observational tools and methods, it is important to consider the theoretical and practical notion of the researcher as instrument. In the studies reviewed in this section, the researchers, in most cases, did not use particular observational protocols or checklists but instead noted their observations through open-ended field-notes. As the primary observational instrument, the researcher's beliefs, perspectives, and focus influenced decisions about what to observe and what to record. While we note that this is always true of observational research (both quantitatively and qualitatively oriented), qualitative researchers have perhaps more responsibility to lay these perspectives and foci out because they are not made apparent in the categories of a protocol. The best of the studies reviewed here described well their decisions, their foci, and their perspectives, although across the database, there were variations in these descriptions. A number of studies failed to provide sufficient detail as to how and when observations were conducted, how these observations were conducted, and how they were used in analysis. In some of the earliest studies, detail was limited to "we observed in classrooms" or something similar. As we moved into the 1990s, more literacy researchers began entering classrooms as ethnographers. Partly as a function of the paradigm within which they wrote and partly in an effort to address criticism, methodological description became thicker and more detailed. However, while a good many researchers continue to provide appropriate and detailed description of methods, we came across a number of studies published recently in which description was insufficient or lacking. We see this as an area for concern and urge researchers and editors to push themselves towards detailed description of observational procedures.

DISCUSSION

Jaap Tuinman began his Presidential address to the National Reading Conference in 1977 with the statement "My major contention today is that reading researchers do not spend enough time in the schools and classrooms when reading is taught and learned" (1979, p. 9). Later, in the same talk, he posed the question: "Do we as reading researchers stay away from the classroom for fear of not being able to cope with the complexity of the phenomena?" (p. 16). Tuinman sounded the alarm—although for all apparent signs—the challenge fell on deaf ears and his question regarding "why" was left hanging. In the 10 years following his presidential address (1977 to 1987) not one research article examining the teaching of reading in classrooms was published in the National Reading Conference's major research journal (*The Journal of Reading Behavior*). The data gathered through our review suggest that the situation is changing. More and more researchers have ventured into classrooms and accepted the challenge to study the teaching of reading in all its complexity.

Our inspection and analysis across these observational studies leave us in a state of worried hope/hopeful worry. The increased attention to field-based, observational studies in the research literature from a sheer quantitative perspective is cause to celebrate—a little. We worry that the number of observational studies is still pitifully few in relation to the number of studies conducted annually and painfully small in relation to the formulation of policies that shape practice. Quantity is not the only issue. The attention to rigor is sometimes lacking. Whether the absence of rigor is a failure on the part of the researcher (and the editors who let these studies move into publication) or the failure of the editors who do not allow space for researchers to provide a detailed description of methods in research reports we cannot determine. But the problem is real. We take issue in particular with studies that do not offer critical attention to the tools used to observe teaching.

We continue to worry, as well, with the favoring of quantitative over qualitative research studies at several levels in the policy context. The disparityof funding for quantitative vs. qualitative research (e.g., through the IES) and the requirements for the use of experimental studies to justify the selection of programs, materials, or particular instructional practices (e.g., through NCLB and Reading First) are at best shortsighted, if not anti-scientific. The rigor within the qualitative research studies we encountered in this review is at least equal to if not surpassing the rigor with the quantitative studies. The findings from both sides offer important insights and evidence to guide policy and practice.

On the hopeful side, there are a substantial and growing number of high-quality, observational studies in both quantitative and qualitative traditions. In our analysis, we have attempted to feature these studies. We have seen at least four areas of promise that deserve special mention. First, there has been an increase in the quantity, quality and valuing of qualitative research. It is important that observational research that reveals teaching in all its complexity continues to grow. Second, there has been an emergence of a small but substantial number of mixed-methods studies that offer combined and complimentary use of qualitative and quantitative methods to observe teaching. We would point, in particular, to the work of Paterson et. al. (2003) and Almasi (1995). A third area of hope is to be found in the work of individuals who offer a program of work that relies on multiple methods and clearly builds on previous work. Duffy's, as referenced in both the quantitative and qualitative sections, has demonstrated these qualities. A fourth area of hope relates to the introduction of new methodologies and related tools of inquiry. We note the promising use of design and formative experiments (e.g., Reinking & Watkins, 2000) following Brown (1992) and Collins (1992) as just one example of this trend. Formative and design experiments position the researcher close to practice (see Reinking & Bradley, 2007). Since the teaching of reading is an endeavor "practiced" by professionals this makes good sense as a lead to follow for the future. Knowledge of practice (and we purposefully avoid using the term "effective" practice) and practical knowledge emerge in the context of solving old and facing new challenges. Observational research in this context offers the promise of capturing the construction of new knowledge (situated learning) that can become the basis for initial and continuing professional development.

Based on our analyses of these observational studies of teaching reading, we propose five guidelines for future observational research in reading. Here we focus on those aspects of research that are particularly important to the methodology surrounding observational research and not to educational research or reading research more generally considered. These five guidelines can be applied across quantitative, qualitative, and mixed methods studies.

Five Guidelines for Observational Research in Reading:

1. TOOL SELECTION: Researchers must be clear in describing the selection or development process and the criteria used for the tools used to observe teaching. There should be a particular attention to the tool qualities and the purposes and contexts for the study. For example, Paterson et al. (2003), a mixed methods study of the effectiveness of the Waterford Early Reading Program, offered detailed information regarding their focused, qualitative observational protocol. Designed to inquire into the characteristic classroom practices of Waterford and non-Waterford classrooms (variables that later figured into a multi-variate analysis), researchers documented observations using uniform worksheets, following the work of Durkin (1978–1979). In this article, the researchers explained the parameters of the protocol (described earlier in this chapter) and provided an excerpt of a sample of the protocol. Importantly, they also made clear why a focused protocol of this kind, instead of more open-ended field-notes, fit within both the purpose of their study—to contrast Waterford and non-Waterford classrooms according to variables of instruction—and the logistical issues related to employing consistent observational practices across multiple observers.

2. TOOL DESCRIPTION: Researchers must offer detailed documentation on the history/past experiences with the tools being used as well as the features of the tools and procedures required with particular attention to any modifications made for the study. For example, Duffy and his colleagues (Duffy et al., 1987) provided the rationale behind the use of his modified instrument used to measure the explicitness of treatment and treated-control teachers' explanations of reading strategies. Similar to one used in earlier studies (Duffy et al., 1986), the instrument used in the 1987 study was modified to reflect descriptive findings about explanations that came as a result of the 1986 study. The research team presented the instrument in the appendix of the study.

3. TOOL USE: Researchers must provide specific detail on the use of the tool including the sampling of observations, the schedule for observations, and the intensity/duration of the observations. Additional required information relates to any special training of data collectors and moderation of the use of the instruments or procedures. Wharton-McDonald et al. (1998), for example, clearly delineated observational procedures for their study of nine first grade classrooms. These researchers noted the frequency of their observations—twice monthly for 7 months, the time of day they sampled during their observations—"scheduled language arts period. . . typically last[ing] from one and two hours" (p. 105), and how the observers aligned observational practices (e.g., maintaining two observers per classroom who frequently consulted with one another and clearly communicating goals and procedures for observations).

4. TOOL PRODUCTS (or "secondary artifacts"). Researchers must describe the path from the raw data collected using the observational tools and the subsequent stages of analysis leading to the presentation of the data interpreted in a report. For example, Duke (2000) quite succinctly described her theoretical frame for the data she collected (informational texts and genre development), the means by which she collected that data (predetermined coding system based on print in classrooms and library and the activities that surrounded that print), and her stages of analysis (three databases, one for each coding system and tallies of each) in her study of the print environments offered in different SES settings.

5. TOOL EVALUATION: Researchers must describe their evaluation of the tools that they used in the research to capture the critical elements of teaching, including any adaptations or innovations that might be useful for future research efforts. For example, in their seminal work, Camburn and Barnes (2004) validated the use of teacher self-reports (through the use of language arts logs) as a research instrument. They used triangulation strategies— multiple methods, data sources, and researchers in an attempt to develop an alternative way of describing classroom practices. In their concluding remarks, the research team suggested that the validation of self-reports of teachers is extremely complex. So complex in fact that

there may not be a shared understanding of terms between researchers and teachers and that observers may not be able to provide judgments that are interchangeable with those made by teachers. Finally, the research team believed that the strategy of triangulation was useful as a means of checking the validity of self-reports of teachers as well as a measurement and analysis strategy in its own right. We know this group continues to develop the use of logs as a means of describing classroom instruction.

We believe that the adoption of these guidelines within the reading research community could be useful in promoting quality research. We believe that these guidelines can be of great use to researchers designing studies, editorial advisors reviewing manuscripts, journal editors forming guidelines and making decisions on manuscripts, and to faculty mentoring the next generation of reading researchers.

CONCLUSION

There are many factors that discourage literacy researchers from conducting quality studies that require the observation of teachers and teaching. The costs for this kind of research, in terms of time and resources, are enormous. The work is labor intensive and demands deep understanding of research methods. The complexity of teaching in classrooms is multidimensional and therefore daunting—just as Tuinman had warned. However, the benefits far outweigh the costs of not doing this kind of research. At the policy level, we cannot leave classroom literacy research vulnerable to those who, like Joseph Rice, are motivated to gather data useful in criticizing schools and teachers in order to advance their own agenda for reform. Nor can we afford to leave teachers vulnerable to policy mandates that draw on research 'findings' from contrived experimental studies conducted far from the complexity of classroom life. The development of strong theoretical perspectives around the teaching and learning of reading also demands observational studies. As long as the questions that drive our inquiry into literacy are directed toward classroom practices we have no choice but to do observational research. The choices we face are centered on how to do it well. Hopefully, the examples we have identified and discussed and the guidelines we have drawn will offer some important direction to future researchers.

REFERENCES

Allington, R., & McGill-Franzen, A. (1989). School response to reading failure: Chapter 1 and special education. *The Elementary School Journal, 89*, 529–542.

Almasi, J. F. (1995). The nature of fourth graders' sociocognitive conflicts in peer-led and teacher led-discussions of literature. *Reading Research Quarterly, 30*, 314–351.

Alpert, B. R. (1987). Active, silent and controlled discussions: Explaining variations in classroom conversation. *Teaching and Teacher Education, 3*, 29–40.

Alvermann, D., & Hayes, D. (1989). Classroom discussion of content area reading assignments: An intervention study. *Reading Research Quarterly, 24*, 305–355.

Alvermann, D. E. (1990). Discussion versus recitation in the secondary classroom. In J. Zutell & S. McCormick (Eds.), *39th yearbook of the National Reading Conference* (pp. 113–119). Chicago: NRC.

Applebee, A. N., Langer, J. A., Nystrand, M., & Gamoran, A. (2003). Discussion-based approaches to developing understanding: Classroom instruction and student performance in middle and high school English. *American Educational Research Journal, 40*, 685–730.

Armbruster, B. B., Anderson, T. H., Armstrong, J. O., Wise, M. A., Janisch, C., & Meyer, L. A. (1991). Reading and questioning in content area lessons. *Journal of Reading Behavior, 23*, 35–59.

Ayers, L. (1912). Measuring educational processes through educational results. *School Review, XX,* 300–309.

Baker, S. K., Gersten, R., Haager, D., & Dingle, M. (2006). Teaching practice and the reading growth of first-grade English learners: Validation of an observation instrument. *Elementary School Journal, 107,* 199–221.

Barr, R., & Sadow, M. W. (1989). Influence of basal programs on fourth-grade reading instruction. *Reading Research Quarterly, 24,* 44–71.

Baumann, J. F., & Ivey, G. (1997). Delicate balances: Striving for curricular and instructional equilibrium in a second-grade, literature/strategy-based classroom. *Reading Research Quarterly, 32,* 244-275.

Berliner, D. (1990). The nature of time in schools: Theoretical concepts, practitioner perceptions. In C. Denham & A. Lieberman (Eds.), *Time to learn* (pp. 33–63). Washington, DC: National Institute of Education.

Berliner, D. (2007). Educational psychology: Searching for essence throughout a century of influence. In P. Alexander & P. Winne (Eds.), *Handbook of educational psychology* (pp. 3–28). Mahwah, NJ: Erlbaum.

Bloom, B. S. (1965). *Taxonomy of educational objectives: The classification of educational goals.* New York: David McKay Company.

Bloome, D. (1983). Classroom reading instruction: A socio-communicative analysis of time on task. In J. A. Niles & L.A. Harris (Eds.), *32nd yearbook of the National Reading Conference* (pp. 275–281). Rochester, NY: NRC.

Bloome, D. (1984). A socio-communicative perspective of formal and informal classroom reading events. In J. A. Niles & L. A. Harris (Eds.), *33rd yearbook of the National Reading Conference* (pp. 117–123). Rochester, NY: NRC.

Bogdan, R., & Biklen, S. (2007). *Qualitative research for education: An introduction to theories and methods.* Boston: Pearson.

Bond, G., & Dykstra, R. (1967). The Cooperative research program in first-grade reading instruction. *Reading Research Quarterly, 2,* 1–142.

Borasi, R., Siegel, M., Fonzi, J., & Smith, C. F. (1998). Using transactional reading strategies to support sense-making and discussion in mathematics classrooms: An exploratory study. *Journal for Research in Mathematics Education, 29,* 275–305.

Brophy, J. E. (1973). Stability of teacher effectiveness. *American Educational Research Journal, 10*(3), 245–252.

Brophy, J. E., & Good, T. (1970). Teacher-Child Dyadic Interactions: A New Method of Classroom Observation. *Journal of School Psychology, 8*(2), 131–137.

Brophy, J., Rohrkemper, M., Rashid, H., & Goldberger, M. (1983). Relationships between teachers' presentations of classroom tasks and students' engagement in those tasks. *Journal of Educational Psychology, 75,* 544–552.

Brown, A. L. (1992). Design experiments: Theoretical and methodological challenges in creating complex interventions in classroom settings. *Journal of the Learning Sciences, 2*(2), 141–178.

Brown, R., & Coy-Ogan, L. (1993). The evolution of transactional strategies instruction in one teacher's classroom. *Elementary School Journal, 94,* 221–233.

Brown, R., Pressley, M., Van Meter, P., & Schuder, T. (1996). A quasi-experimental validation of transactional strategies instruction with low-achieving second-grade readers. *Journal of Educational Psychology, 88,* 18–37.

Camburn, E. & Barnes, C. A. (2004). Assessing the validity of a language arts instruction log through triangulation. *Elementary School Journal, 105,* 49–74.

Carroll, J. S. (1963). A model of school learning. *Teachers College Record, 64,* 723–733.

Chall, J. S. (1967). *Learning to read: The great debate.* New York: McGraw-Hill.

Chall, J. S., & Feldman, S. (1966). First-grade reading: An analysis of the interactions of professed methods, teacher implementation, and child background. *The Reading Teacher, 19,* 569–575.

Cole, R. (1996). *Culture in mind.* Cambridge, MA: Harvard University Press.

Collins, A. (1992). Toward a design science of education. In E. Scanlon & T. O'Shea (Eds.), *New directions in educational technology* (pp. 15–22). New York: Springer.

DeFord, D. (1985). Validating the Construct of Theoretical Orientation in Reading Instruction. *Reading Research Quarterly, 20,* 351–367.

Duffy, G. (1991). What counts in teacher education? Dilemmas in educating empowered teachers. In J. Zutell & S. McCormick (Eds.), *Learner factors/teacher factors: Issues in literacy research and instruction* (pp. 1–18). Chicago: National Reading Conference.

Duffy, G. G., Roehler, L. R., Meloth, M. S., Vavrus, L. G., Book, C., Putnam, J., et al. (1986). The relationship between explicit verbal explanations during reading skills instruction and student awareness and achievement: A study of reading teacher effects. *Reading Research Quarterly, 21,* 237–252.

Duffy, G. G., Roehler, L. R., & Rackliffe, G. (1986). How teachers' instructional talk influences students' understanding of lesson content. *The Elementary School Journal, 87,* 3–16.

Duffy, G. G., Roehler, L. R., Sivan, E., Rackliffe, G., Book, C., Meloth, M. S., et al. (1987). Effects of explaining the reasoning associated with using reading strategies. *Reading Research Quarterly, 22,* 347–368.

Duke, N. K. (2000). 3.6 Minutes per day: The scarcity of informational texts in first grade. *Reading Research Quarterly, 35,* 202–224.

Dunkin, M., & Biddle, B. (1974). *The study of teaching.* New York: Holt, Rinehart and Winston.

Durkin, D. (1978–1979). What classroom observations reveal about reading comprehension instruction. *Reading Research Quarterly, 14*(4), 481–533.

Eeds, M., & Wells, D. (1989). Grand conversations: An exploration of meaning construction in literature study groups. *Research in the Teaching of English, 23,* 4–29.

El-Dinary, P. B., Pressley, M., & Schuder, T. (1992). Teachers learning transactional strategies instruction. In C. K. Kinzer & D. J. Leu (Eds.), *41st yearbook of the National Reading Conference* (pp. 453–462). Chicago: NRC.

Engelhart, M. D., & Thomas, M. (1966, Summer). Rice as the inventor of the comparative test. *Journal of Educational Measurement, 3*(2), 141–145.

Erickson, F. (1986). Qualitative methods in research in teaching. In M. C. Wittrock (Ed.), *Handbook of research in teaching* (3rd ed., pp. 119–161). New York: Macmillan.

Fagan, E. R., Hassler, D. M., & Szabo, M. (1981). Evaluation of questioning strategies in language arts instruction. *Research in the Teaching of English, 15,* 67–73.

Fisher, C. W., & Hiebert, E. H. (1990). Characteristics of tasks in two approaches to literacy instruction. *Elementary School Journal, 91,* 3–18.

Fisher, C., Filby, N., Marliave, R., Cahen, L., Dishaw, M., Moore, J., et al. (1978). *Teaching behaviors: Academic learning time and student achievement: Final report of phase III-B, beginning teacher evaluation study.* San Francisco: Far West Laboratory for Educational Research and Development.

Flanders, N. A. (1970). *Analyzing teaching behavior.* Reading, MA: Addison-Wesley Publishing.

Flesch, R. (1955). *Why Johnny can't read.* New York: Harper and Row.

Fuchs, L. S., Fuchs, D., & Kazden, S. (1999). Effects of peer-assisted learning strategies on high school students with serious reading problems. *Remedial and Special Education, 20,* 309–318.

Fukkink, R. G. (2005). Deriving word meaning from written context: A process analysis. *Learning and Instruction, 15,* 23–43.

Gambrell, L. (1984). How much time do children spend reading during teacher-directed reading instruction? In J. A. Niles & L. A. Harris (Eds.), *National Reading Conference yearbook, 33* (pp. 193–198). Rochester, NY: NRC.

Garcia, G. E., Bray, T.M., Mora, R.A., Ricklefs, M.A., Primeaux, J., Engel, L. C., et al. (2006). Working with teachers to change the literacy instruction of Latino students in urban schools. In J. V. Hoffman, D. L. Schallert, C. M. Fairbanks, J. Worthy, & B. Maloch (Eds.), *55th yearbook of the National Reading Conference* (pp. 155–170). Oak Creek, WI: NRC.

Glaser, B. G., & Strauss, A. L. (1967). *The discovery of grounded theory: Strategies for qualitative research.* New York: Aldine.

Graham, P. A. (1966). Joseph Mayer Rice as a founder of the progressive education movement. *Journal of Educational Measurement, 3*(2), 129–133.

Guilford, J. (1967). *The nature of human intelligence.* New York: McGraw-Hill.

Guthrie, J. T., Wigfield, A., Barbosa, P., Perencevich, K. C., Taboada, A., Davis, et al. (2004). Increasing reading comprehension and engagement through Concept-Oriented Reading Instruction. *Journal of Educational Psychology, 96,* 403–423

Harris, A., & Serwer, B. (1966). The CRAFT project: instructional time in reading research. *Reading Research Quarterly, 2,* 27–57.

Haynes, M. C., & Jenkins, J. R. (1986). Reading instruction in special education resource rooms. *American Educational Research Journal, 23*, 161–190.

Hinchman, K. (1985). Reading and the plans of secondary teachers: A qualitative study. In J. V. Hoffman, D. L. Schallert, C. M. Fairbanks, J. Worthy, & B. Maloch (Eds.), *55th yearbook of the National Reading Conference* (pp. 251–256). Oak Creek, WI: NRC.

Hitchcock, C. H., Prater, M. A., & Dowrick, P. W. (2004). Reading comprehension and fluency: Examining the effects of tutoring and video self-modeling on first-grade students with reading difficulties. *Learning Disability Quarterly, 27*, 89–103.

Hoffman, J. V., & Clements, R. (1984). Reading miscues and teacher verbal feedback. The *Elementary School Journal, 84*, 423–439.

Hoffman, J. V., Roller, C. M., Maloch, B., Sailors, M., Duffy, G. G., Beretvas, S. N., & The National Commission on Excellence in Elementary Teacher Preparation for Reading. (2005). Teachers' preparation to teach reading and their experiences and practices in the first three years of teaching. *Elementary School Journal, 105*(3), 267–289.

Hoffman, J. V., Sailors, M., Duffy, G. G., & Beretvas, S. N. (2004). The effective elementary classroom literacy environment: Examining the validity of the TEX-IN3 Observation System. *Journal of Literacy Research, 36*, 303–334.

Ihde, D. (1991). *Instrumental realism: The interface between philosophy of science and philosophy of technology.* Bloomington: Indiana University Press.

Kantor, R., Miller, S. M., & Fernie, D. (1992). Diverse paths to literacy in a preschool classroom: A sociocultural perspective. *Reading Research Quarterly, 27*, 184–201.

Knapp, N. F. (2002). Tom and Joshua: Perceptions, conceptions and progress in meaning-based reading instruction. *Journal of Literacy Research, 34*, 59–98.

Kong, A., & Pearson, P. D. (2003). The road to participation: The construction of a literacy practice in a learning community of linguistically diverse learners. *Research in the Teaching of English, 38*, 85–123.

Konopak, B., Cothern N., Jampole, E., Mitchell, M., Dean, R., Holomon, L., et al. (1990). Reading instruction in science at the transitional grades: Beliefs versus practice. In J. Zutell & S. McCormick (Eds.), *39th yearbook of the National Reading Conference* (pp. 129–136). Chicago: NRC.

Lincoln, Y., & Guba, E. (1985). *Naturalistic inquiry.* New York: Sage.

Lindsey, M. (1990). The curricular experiences of at-risk first graders in programs designed to promote success. In J. Zutell & S. McCormick (Eds.), *NRC yearbook, 39* (pp. 79–86). Chicago: NRC.

Linn, R. L., & Erickson, F. (1990). *Qualitative methods.* London: Collier Macmillan.

Magliaro, S., & Borko, H. (1986). The reading instruction of student teachers and experienced teachers: A social organizational perspective. In J.A. Niles & R.V. Lalik (Eds.), *35th yearbook of the National Reading Conference* (pp. 272–279). Rochester, NY: NRC.

Mansett-Williamson, G., & Nelson, J. M. (2005). Balanced, strategic reading instruction for upper-elementary and middle school students with reading disabilities: A comparative study of two approaches. *Learning Disability Quarterly, 28*, 59–74.

Martinez, M.G., & Teale, W.H. (1993). Teacher storybook reading style: A comparison of six teachers. *Research in the Teaching of English, 27*, 175–99.

Mastropieri, M. A., Scruggs, T. E., Norland. J. J., Berkeley, S., McDuffle, K., Tornquist, E. H., et al. (2006). Differentiated curriculum enhancement in inclusive middle school science: Effects on classroom and high-stakes tests. *Journal of Special Education, 40*, 130–137.

McCarthey, S. J. (1992). The influence of classroom discourse on student texts: The case of Ella. *Yearbook of the National Reading Conference.* Chicago: NRC.

McCarthey, S. J. (1997). Connecting home and school literacy practices in classrooms with diverse populations. *Journal of Literacy Research, 29*, 145–182.

McDonald, F. J., & Elias, P. (1976). A report on the results of phase I I of the beginning teacher evaluation study: An overview. *Journal of Teacher Education, 27*, 315–316.

McIntyre, E. (1995, June). Teaching and learning writing skills in a low-SES, urban primary classroom. *Journal of Reading Behavior, 27*(2), 213–242.

Mertens, D. (2005). *Research and evaluation in education and psychology* (2nd ed.). Thousand Oaks, CA: Sage.

Mitcham, C. (1994). *Thinking through technology: The path between engineering and philosophy.* Chicago: The University of Chicago Press.

Mitchell, M. M., Konopak, B. C., & Readence, J. E. (1991). The consistency between chapter I teachers' beliefs about reading and their instructional decision-making and interactions. In J. Zutell & S. McCormick (Eds.), *40th yearbook of the National Reading Conference* (pp. 377–384). Chicago: NRC.

Moje, E. B. (1996). "I teach students, not subjects": Teacher-student relationships as contexts for secondary literacy. *Reading Research Quarterly, 31,* 172–195.

Morrow, L. M. (1991). Relationships among physical design of play centers, teachers' emphasis on literacy in play, and children's literacy behaviors during play. In J. Zutell & S. McCormick (Eds.), *Fortieth yearbook of the National Reading Conference: Learner factors/teacher factors: Issues in literacy research and instruction* (pp. 127–140). Chicago: NRC.

Morrow, L. M. (1992). The impact of a literature-based program on literacy achievement, use of literature, and attitudes of children from minority backgrounds. *Reading Research Quarterly, 27,* 250–275.

Mowbray, C. T., Holter, M. C., Teague, G. B., & Bybee, D. (2003). Fidelity criteria: Development, measurement, and validation. *American Journal of Evaluation, 24,* 315–340.

Neuman, S. B. (1999). Books make a difference: A study of access to literacy. *Reading Research Quarterly, 34,* 286–311.

Paterson, W. A., Henry, J. J., O'Quinn, K., Ceprano, M. A., & Blue, E. A. (2003). Investigating the effectiveness of an integrated learning system on early emergent readers. *Reading Research Quarterly, 38,* 172–207.

Pierce, M., & Pomerantz, F. (2006). From pre-service to in-service: The evolution of literacy teaching practices and beliefs in novice teachers. In J. V. Hoffman, D. L. Schallert, C. M. Fairbanks, J. Worthy, & B. Maloch (Eds.), *55th yearbook of the National Reading Conference* (pp. 235–248). Oak Creek, WI: NRC.

Pressley, M., Wharton-McDonald, R., Allington, R., Block, C. C., Morrow, L., Tracey, D., et al (2001). A study of effective first-grade literacy instruction. *Scientific Studies of Reading, 5,* 35–58.

Pressley, M., Wharton-McDonald, R., Mistretta-Hampston, J., & Echevarria, M. (1998). Literacy instruction in 10 fourth- and fifth-grade classrooms in upstate New York. *Scientific Studies of Reading, 2,* 159–194.

Reinking, D., & Bradley, B. (2007). *On formative and design experiments.* New York: Teachers College Press.

Reinking, D., & Watkins, J. (2000). A formative experiment Investigating the use of multimedia book reviews to increase elementary students' independent reading. *Reading Research Quarterly, 35,* 384–419.

Reutzel, D. R., Hollingsworth, P. M., & Eldredge, J. L. (1994). Oral reading instruction: The impact on student reading development. *Reading Research Quarterly, 29,* 41–62.

Reutzel, D. R., Oda, L. K., & Moore, B. H. (1989). Developing print awareness: The effect of three instructional approaches on kindergarteners' print awareness, reading readiness, and word reading. *Journal of Reading Behavior, 21*(3), 197–217.

Rex, L. A. (2001). The remaking of a high school reader. *Reading Research Quarterly, 36,* 288–314.

Rice, J. (1893). *Public-school system of the United States.* New York: Century Press.

Roehler, L. R., Duffy, G. G., & Meloth, M. S. (1984). The effects and some distinguishing characteristics of explicit teacher explanation during reading instruction. In J. A. Niles & L. A. Harris (Eds.), *33rd yearbook of the National Reading Conference* (pp. 223–239). Rochester, NY: NRC.

Rosenshine, B. (1983). Teaching functions in instructional programs. *The Elementary School Journal, 83*(4), 335–351.

Rosenshine, B., & Furst, N. (1973). The use of direct observation to study teaching. In R. Travers (Ed.), *Second handbook of research on teaching* (pp. 122–183). Chicago: Rand McNally.

Ross, S. M., & Smith, L. J. (1994). Effects of the success for all model on kindergarten through second-grade reading achievement, teacher's adjustment, and classroom-school climate at an inner-city school. *Elementary School Journal, 95,* 121–138.

Ross, S. M., Smith, L. J., Lohr, L., & McNelis, M. (1994). Math and reading instruction in tracked first-grade classes. *Elementary School Journal, 95,* 105–119.

Rutherford, W. (1968). Learning to read: A critique. *Elementary School Journal, 69*(2), 72–83.

Sanders, T. S. (1981). Three first graders' concept of word and concepts about the language of literacy instruction. In M. K. Kamil (Ed.), *30th yearbook of the National Reading Conference* (pp. 266–272). Washington, DC: NRC.

Simon, A. E., & Boyer, G. (1974). *Mirrors for behavior III: An anthology of observation instruments.* Philadelphia: Communications Materials Center.

Sipe, L. R., & Brightman, A. (2006). Teacher scaffolding of first-graders' literary understanding during read alouds of fairytale variants. In J. V. Hoffman, D. L. Schallert, C. M. Fairbanks, J. Worthy, & B. Maloch (Eds.), *55th yearbook of the National Reading Conference* (pp. 276–292). Oak Creek, WI: NRC.

Sosniak. L. A., & Stodolsky, S. S. (1993). Teachers and textbooks: Materials use in four fourth-grade classrooms. *Elementary School Journal, 93,* 249–275.

Spradley, J. (1980). *Participant observation.* New York: Harcourt Brace Jovanovich.

Stallings, J. (1975). Implementation and child effects of teaching practices in Follow Through classrooms. *Monographs of the Society for Research in Child Development, 40,* nos. 7 and 8 (Serial No. 163).

Strauss, A., & Corbin, J. (1990). *Basics of qualitative research: Grounded theory procedures and techniques.* New York: Sage.

Sweetland, J. J., Abel-Carrick, D., & Kinzer, C. K. (1987). An analysis of ambiguous oral discourse during reading instruction. In J. E. Readence & R. S. Baldwin (Eds.), *36th yearbook of the National Reading Conference* (pp. 187–193). Chicago: NRC.

Taylor, B. M., Pearson, P. D., Clark, K., & Walpole, S. (2000). Effective schools and accomplished teachers. *Elementary School Journal, 101,* 121–165.

Taylor, B. M., Pearson, P. D., Peterson, D. S., & Rodriguez, M. C. (2003). Reading growth in high-poverty classrooms: The influence of teacher practices that encourage cognitive engagement in literacy learning. *Elementary School Journal, 104,* 3–28.

Taylor, N. E., Blum, I. H., & Logsdon, D. M. (1986). The development of written language awareness: Environmental aspects and program characteristics. *Reading Research Quarterly, 21,* 132–149.

Terman, S. W., & Walcutt, C. (1959). *Reading: Chaos and cure.* New York: McGraw-Hill.

Travers, R. (Ed.). (1973). *Second handbook of research on teaching.* Chicago: Rand McNally.

Tuinman, J. (1979). An instructional perspective on basic research in reading. In M. Kamil & A. Moe (Eds.), *28th yearbook of the National Reading Conference* (pp. 9–18). Clemson, SC: Clemson University.

Van Keer, H. (2004). Fostering reading comprehension in fifth grade by explicit instruction in reading strategies and peer tutoring. *British Journal of Educational Psychology, 74,* 37–70.

Vaughn, S., Cirino, P. T., Linan-Thompson, S., Mathes, P. G., Carlson, C. D., Hagan, E. C., et al. (2006). Effectiveness of a Spanish intervention and an English intervention for English-language learners at risk for reading problems. *American Educational Research Journal, 43,* 449–487.

Walcutt, C. (1961). *Tomorrow's illiterates.* Boston, MA: Little, Brown.

Wartofsky, M. (1973). Perception, representation, and the forms of action: Towards an historical epistemology. In M. Wartofsky (Ed.), *Models: Representation and the scientific understanding* (pp. 188–210). London: Reidel.

Wharton-McDonald, R., Pressley, M., & Mistretta-Hampston, J. M. (1998). Literacy instruction in nine first-grade classrooms: Teacher characteristics and student achievement. *Elementary School Journal, 99,* 121–128.

Wolf, W., King, M. L., & Huck, C. S. (1968). Teaching critical reading to elementary school children. *Reading Research Quarterly, 3*(4), 435–498.

Wolfersberger, M. E., Reutzel, D. R., Sudweeks, R., & Fawson, P. C. (2004). Developing and validating the Classroom Literacy Environmental Profile (CLEP): A tool for examining the "print richness" of early childhood and elementary classrooms. *Journal of Literacy Research, 36,* 211–272.

Worthy, J., & Beck, I. (1997). On the road from recitation to discussion in large-group dialogue about literature. In C. K. Kinzer, K. A. Hinchman, & D. J. Leu (Eds.), *46th yearbook of the National Reading Conference* (pp. 312–324). Chicago: NRC.

2   Methods of Automated Text Analysis

*Arthur C. Graesser, Danielle S. McNamara,
and Max M. Louwerse*
University of Memphis

This chapter describes methods of analyzing the structures, functions, and representations of text. The lens is on the text, but we will selectively identify salient implications for cognitive processes and educational practice. The primary emphasis is also on automated methods of text analysis. That is, a computer system receives the text, performs processes that implement computational algorithms, and produces a text analysis on various levels of language and discourse structure. However, sometimes there are theoretical components of text that cannot be handled by computers so it is necessary to have human experts annotate or structure the text systematically. Human annotation schemes are identified in cases when it is beyond the scope of computer technologies to perform such text processing mechanisms.

A systematic analysis of the text is no doubt important to any comprehensive theory of reading and any application designed to improve reading in school systems. Reports on reading comprehension research acknowledged that there is a complex interaction among characteristics of the reader, the tasks that the reader is to perform, the socio-cultural context, and the properties text itself (National Reading Panel, 2000; McNamara, 2007; Snow, 2002). Investigations of such interactions are facilitated by precise measures of the properties of the text at various levels of analysis: words, sentences, paragraphs, entire texts. Readers may excel at some levels, but have deficits at others, so it is necessary to measure and record the various levels. Interventions to improve reading are expected to be precise on what characteristics of the text are being targeted in the intervention. From the standpoint of assessment, developers of high stakes tests need to be specific on the characteristics of the text in addition to the cognitive processes that are being measured and aligned to reading standards.

This is a unique point in history because there is widespread access to computer tools that analyze texts at many levels of language and discourse. This increased use of automated text analysis tools can be attributed to landmark advances in such fields as computational linguistics (Jurafsky & Martin, 2008), discourse processes (Pickering & Garrod, 2004; Graesser, Gernsbacher, & Goldman, 2003), cognitive science (Lenat, 1995; Landauer, McNamara, Dennis, & Kintsch, 2007), and corpus linguistics (Biber, Conrad, & Reppen, 1998). Thousands of texts can be quickly accessed and analyzed on thousands of measures in a short amount of time.

The chapter is into divided four sections. The first section provides a brief historical background on theoretical approaches to analyzing texts between 1970 and 2000. The second section covers some current theoretical and methodological trends, most of which are interdisciplinary in scope. The third section describes how the text analysis systems are scored in assessments of accuracy and reliability. The fourth section identifies text analysis tools that assist researchers and practitioners. These tools span a large range of text units (words, clauses, propositions, sentences, paragraphs, lengthy documents) and levels of representation and structure (syntax, semantics, mental models, text cohesion, genre). Throughout the chapter we will point out some of the ways that automated text analyses have been put into practice, as in the case of intelligent tutoring systems that coach reading skills, feedback on student writing, and the selection of texts to match reader profiles.

HISTORICAL BACKGROUND FROM 1970 TO 2000

Reading researchers have always explored methods of analyzing the structures, functions, and representations of text (Ausubel, 1968; Gibson & Levin, 1975; Goldman & Rakestraw, 2000; Williams, 2007), but there were some dramatic breakthroughs in the 1970s when the field of reading became more interdisciplinary. The fields of text linguistics, artificial intelligence, psychology, education, and sociology were particularly influential. Below are some of the landmark contributions that launched the 1970s.

1. ***Text linguistics.*** Structural grammars that had originally been applied to phonology and sentence syntax were applied to meaning units in text and connected discourse (Van Dijk, 1972). In some analyses, texts were decomposed into basic units of meaning called *propositions,* which refer to events, actions, goals, and states that are organized in a hierarchical structure. Each proposition contains a *predicate* (e.g., main verb, adjective, connective) and one or more *arguments* (e.g., nouns, embedded propositions) that play a thematic role, such as agent, patient, object, time, or location. Below is an example sentence and its propositional meaning representation.

> When the board met on Friday, they discovered they were bankrupt.
> PROP 1: meet (AGENT = board, TIME = Friday)
> PROP 2: discover (PATIENT = board, PROP 3)
> PROP 3: bankrupt (OBJECT: corporation)
> PROP 4: when (EVENT = PROP 1, EVENT = PROP 2)

The arguments are placed within the parentheses and have role labels, whereas the predicates are outside of the parentheses. The propositions, clauses, or other similar conceptual units are connected by principles of cohesion, many of which were identified by Halliday and Hasan (1976). Referential cohesion occurs when a noun, pronoun, or noun-phrase refers to another constituent in the text. For example, if the above example sentence were followed by "The meeting lasted several hours," the noun-phase *the meeting* refers to PROP-1. Cohesion between propositions or clauses is often signaled by various forms of discourse markers, such as connectives (e.g., *because, in order to, so that*), adverbs (*therefore, afterwards*), and transitional phrases (*on the other hand*).

At a higher level of rhetorical structure, the propositions or other analogous conceptual units are organized into rhetorical structures that are affiliated with particular text genres. The rhetorical structure specifies the global organization of discourse, such as setting+plot+moral, problem+solution, compare-contrast, claim+evidence, question+answer, and argue+counter-argue (Meyer, 1975). Formal text grammars specify the elements and composition of these rhetorical patterns explicitly and precisely. For example, story grammars (Rumelhart, 1975; van Dijk, 1972) decompose simple stories in the oral tradition into structures that are captured by rewrite rules, such as:

> Story → Setting+Plot+Moral
> Setting → Location+Time+Characters
> Plot → Complication+Resolution
> Complication → Episode*

The specific goals of these compositional analyses in text linguistics were to segment texts into units, to assign the units to theoretical categories, and to organize the units into structures (typically hierarchical structures). Such a detailed decomposition was viewed as essential to any rigorous analysis of meaning, content, and discourse. Human experts were needed to segment, annotate, and structure these text representations because the theoretical distinctions were too complex or subtle for naïve coders to understand. However, it is hardly the case that the experts agreed on these structured representations when social scientists collected inter-judge agreement in the experts' judgments of segmentations, annotation, and structure. Inter-judge agreement was typically found to be significantly above chance, but modest, unless the experts had substantial training and feedback on their analyses to the point that they had similar analytical mindsets. Given that experts yielded imperfect agreement, automated computer analyses were similarly limited. At present, there are no computer programs that can translate texts into these structured text representations automatically, although there have been some attempts with modest success to automate propositional analyses (see section on text analysis tools).

2. *Artificial intelligence (AI).* Computer models in the 1970s attempted to interpret texts (Woods, 1977), generate inferences (Rieger, 1978; Schank, 1972), and comprehend simple, scripted narratives (Schank & Abelson, 1977). Most AI researchers were convinced that syntactic parsers and formal semantics would not go the distance in achieving natural language understanding because it is necessary to have world knowledge about people, objects, situations, and other dimensions of everyday experience. AI researchers identified packages of the generic world knowledge, such as person stereotypes, spatial frames, scripted activities, and schemas (Schank & Abelson, 1977). For example, scripts are generic representations of everyday activities (e.g., eating at a restaurant, washing clothes, playing baseball) that have actors with goals and roles, sequences of actions that are typically enacted to achieve these goals, spatial environments with objects and props, and so on. These scripts and other generic knowledge packages are activated during comprehension through pattern recognition processes and subsequently guide the course of comprehension by monitoring attention, generating inferences, formulating expectations, and interpreting explicit text.

AI researchers quickly learned that it was extremely difficult to program computers to comprehend text even when the systems were fortified with many different classes of world knowledge (Lehnert & Ringle, 1982). Modest successes were achieved when the texts were organized around a central script (Schank & Riesbeck, 1981) or when the computer achieved shallow rather than deep comprehension (Lehnert, 1997). Shallow comprehension is sufficient to answer questions such as *who, what, when,* and *where,* which elicit a single word that is likely to be mentioned in a text. Deep comprehensions requires substantial inferences and answer questions such as *why, how, what if,* and *so what.* AI research in natural language comprehension eventually became transformed into a new field called computational linguistics. This new field systematically evaluated the accuracy of computer programs that processed language or discourse at particular levels.

3. *Psychology and education.* Researchers in psychology and education empirically tested some of the theories in text linguistics and AI, as well as models of their own. They did this by collecting reading times, recall for text units, summarization protocols, answers to questions, ratings on various dimensions, and other data. Some researchers sampled naturalistic texts in their investigations whereas others prepared experimenter-constructed *textoids* that controlled for extraneous variables.

The results of the psychological research were quite illuminating on a number of fronts. For example, the number of propositions in a text predicted reading times (after controlling for the number of words), whereas recall for the text could be predicted by structural composition (Frederiksen, 1975; Haberlandt & Graesser, 1985; Kintsch, 1974). The distinction between given (old) and new information in a text predicted reading times for sentences and activation of inferences (Haviland & Clark, 1974). The structures generated by story grammars predicted recall and summaries of narrative text (Mandler & Johnson, 1977; Rumelhart, 1975). Recall memory for expository text also was systematically influenced by the text's rhetorical organization (Meyer, 1975). Memory for a vague or ambiguous text dramatically improved when there was a world knowledge schema that clarified and organized the sentences in the text (Bransford & Johnson, 1972). Indeed, reading times, memory, inferences, and other psychological processes were all facilitated by the scripts postulated by the AI researchers and the world knowledge schemas postulated by the social scientists (Anderson, Spiro, & Montague, 1977; Bower, Black, & Turner, 1979; Graesser, Gordon, & Sawyer, 1979; Spilich, Vesonder, Chiesi, & Voss, 1979).

The complexity of the psychological models grew as researchers collected more data in these psychological studies. Comprehension came to be viewed as a transaction between an author and a reader through the medium of a text, as opposed to being a bottom-up extraction of language codes and meaning (Rosenblatt, 1978). Interactive models of reading assumed there was a mixture of top-down and bottom-up processes among the multiple levels of language and discourse during the process of comprehension (Rumelhart & Ortony, 1977). These models were very different from the strictly bottom-up models (Gough, 1972).

4. *Sociology, philosophy, and communication*. Researchers in these fields emphasized the social, pragmatic, and communication processes that underlie text and discourse. Speech acts were basic units of conversation that could be assigned to categories such as question, command, assertion, request, promise, and expressive evaluation (Searle, 1969). These same categories were believed to play a functional role in printed text just as they do in oral conversation. Rommetveit (1974), for example, proposed that a printed text is a structured, pragmatic, social interaction between an author and reader. Patterns of turn-taking in conversation were explored by Sacks, Schegloff, and Jefferson (1974), whereas Grice (1975) identified the conversational postulates that underlie smooth conversation, including the cooperation principle and the maxims of quality, quantity, relation, and manner. Some AI researchers attempted to capture the pragmatic foundations of speech acts in discourse in structured symbolic representations (Cohen & Perrault, 1979).

Unfortunately, these pragmatic mechanisms have never been successfully automated on computers, except for very narrow applications (airline reservations, verifying train schedules; Allen, 1995) in which there are few alternative actions, goals, and people.

By the end of the 1970s a new multidisciplinary field of discourse processes was launched on the foundations of the above research traditions. The first publication of the journal *Discourse Processes* appeared in 1978, founded by Roy Freedle, a research scientist at Educational Testing Service in the fields of psychology and education. In 1990, the Society for Text and Discourse (ST&D) was founded as a society dedicated to investigating text and discourse processing through the lenses of the above disciplines. Discourse processing researchers continued to apply systematic methods of text analysis by human experts and computers. They continued to investigate the psychological processes that underlie the comprehension and production of discourse. However, the field changed in some fundamental ways that are addressed in the next section.

CURRENT THEORETICAL AND METHODOLOGICAL TRENDS

The theoretical metaphors in text analysis have shifted in recent years. There has been a shift from deep, detailed, structured representations of a small sample of texts to comparatively shallow, approximate, statistical representations of large text corpora. In the 1970s, text analysts were absorbed in identifying idea nodes in a complex web of knowledge structures. Today's researchers are inspecting high-dimensional semantic spaces that serve as statistical representations of document corpora as large as an encyclopedia or Wikipedia. This is the era when computers can analyze millions of words in thousands of documents in minutes or even seconds. Researchers are exploring computational models that specify how statistical patterns of words in documents map onto theoretical components of form and meaning. This section describes some new trends.

Corpus-Based Statistical Representations

As we discussed in the previous section, researchers in psychology and education concluded that world knowledge has a large impact on reading and comprehension. Among the various classes of world knowledge are scripted activities, spatial frames, stereotypes about people, taxonomic hierarchies of plants and animals, the functioning of devices and artifacts, and so on. A psychological or computational model has to get a handle on how to represent the vast repertoire of world knowledge in the cognitive system. However, world knowledge has traditionally been an insurmountable challenge to text analysts because it is boundlessly large and semantically unruly. Decades of research in the cognitive sciences has converged on the view that the most forms of world knowledge, other than pure mathematics, are open-ended, imprecise, ill-defined, incomplete, and often vague.

Fortunately, however, the new statistical approach to representing world knowledge and the meaning of texts has provided an approximate solution to the problem of world knowledge. Two notable examples of statistical, corpus-based approaches to analyzing text meaning and world knowledge are *Latent Semantic Analysis* (Kintsch, 1998; Landauer & Dumais, 1997; Landauer et al., 2007) and the *Linguistic Inquiry Word Count* (LIWC; Pennebaker, Booth, & Francis, 2007).

Latent Semantic Analysis (LSA) uses a statistical method called "singular value decomposition" (SVD) to reduce a large Word-by-Document co-occurrence matrix to approximately 100–500 functional dimensions. The Word-by-Document co-occurrence matrix is simply a record of the number of times word W_i occurs in document D_j. A document may be defined as a sentence, paragraph, or section of an article. Each word, sentence, paragraph, or entire document ends up being a weighted vector on the K dimensions. One important use of LSA is it provides a match score between any two texts (A and B) on the extent to which the texts are similar in meaning, relevance, or conceptual relatedness. The match score between two texts A and B (where a text can be either a single word, a sentence, or a larger text excerpt) is computed as a geometric cosine between the two vectors, with values ranging from approximately 0 to 1.

LSA-based technology is currently being used in a large number of learning technologies and applications in education (see Landauer et al., 2007). The Intelligent Essay Assessor grades essays as reliably as experts in English composition (Landauer, Laham, & Foltz, 2003); a similar achievement on essay grading in computational linguistics has been achieved by the *E-rater* at Educational Testing Service (Burstein, 2003). LSA is used in *Summary Street* to give feedback on students' summaries of texts that they read (E. Kintsch, Caccamise, Franzke, Johnson, & Dooley, 2007), in *iSTART* to give feedback on students' self-explanations on the text as they read (McNamara, Levinstein, & Boonthum, 2004), in *RSAT* to infer reading strategies from a reader's think aloud protocols (Millis et al., 2004), and in *AutoTutor* to guide tutorial dialogue as students work on problems by holding a conversation in natural language (Graesser, Lu, et al., 2004; VanLehn, Graesser et al., 2007). LSA-based technologies are currently being assimilated in the textbook industry for retrieving documents and for giving students feedback on their writing. Because students get immediate feedback on their writing, they spend substantially more time revising their essays than they normally would if they had to wait days or weeks to receive feedback from their instructor. The accuracy of LSA technologies are often quite impressive and have been steadily improving, but are not perfect (either are humans, of course). The impact of these technologies on reading and writing quality will undoubtedly receive more attention in the future.

Pennebaker's LIWC accesses 70+ dictionaries that search for specific words or word stems in any individual or group of text files (Pennebaker, Booth, & Francis, 2007). Each dictionary in LIWC was constructed with the help of groups of judges who evaluated the degree to which each word is conceptually related to the broader category of which it is part. Most of the categories are psychologically-oriented (e.g., negative or positive emotions, intentions, traits, causality), whereas others are more standard linguistic categories (e.g., first person singular pronouns, prepositions, connectives). LIWC has been used to analyze a vast diversity of texts and has uncovered relations between these text analyses and psychological variables. For example, the narratives written by victims of traumatic events can predict how well they cope with the trauma and the number of times they visit a medical doctor (Pennebaker & Chung, 2007). Analyses of hundreds of thousands of text files reveal that people are remarkably consistent in their function word use across context and over time. For example, most everyone uses far more pronouns in informal settings than formal ones (Pennebaker & King, 1999) and are quite consistent in their writing over the course of their careers (Pennebaker & Stone, 2003). The distribution of function words in a person's writing is diagnostic of different social and personality characteristics, such as leadership, loneliness, deception, and inclinations toward suicide. LIWC has been developed in English, Arabic, Dutch, German, Hungarian, Italian, Korean, Norwegian, and Spanish at the time of this writing.

It is important to acknowledge that LSA and LIWC do not address the order of words in the text so they are hardly perfect representations of meaning. Word order is known to be an important aspect of comprehension. For example, the sequence of words *are you here?* conveys a question, whereas *here you are* is an assertion and *you are here* is possibly a command. *John loves Mary* has a different meaning than *Mary loves John*. Advances in computational linguistics (Allen, 1995; Jurafsky & Martin, 2008) have provided syntactic parsers and semantic modules that are more structured and sensitive to word order. Some of these systems are reported later in the section on text analysis tools. One brut-force approach to word order is an *n-gram* analysis that examines sequences of words of length *n*. For example, an n-gram analysis of length 3 considers word triplets. One very promising automated method of grading is an algorithm that combines LSA and n-gram analysis.

It is quite apparent that computers can glean much from a text by merely inspecting the distribution of words, their co-occurrence with other words in a text, and their ordering. These statistical analyses of the new millennium are an order of magnitude more informative than the computer analyses that measure text difficulty with readability formulae. Most readability formulas rely exclusively on word length and sentence length, with occasional consideration of word frequency in the language. For example, Flesch-Kincaid Grade Level (Klare, 1974–75) considers only the number of words in a sentence and the number of syllables in a word in the readability formula. Sentence length and word length do in fact robustly predict reading time (Haberlandt & Graesser, 1985; Just & Carpenter, 1987; Rayner, 1998), but certainly there is more to text difficulty than word and sentence length. These other measures of text difficulty are addressed later when we discuss the Coh-Metrix system (Graesser, McNamara, Louwerse, & Cai, 2004).

Psychological Models of Text Comprehension

Discourse psychologists have developed and tested a number of models that attempt to capture how humans comprehend text. Among these are the Collaborative Action-based Production System (CAPS) Reader model (Just & Carpenter, 1992), the Construction-Integration model

(Kintsch, 1998), the constructivist model (Graesser, Singer, & Trabasso, 1994), the structure-building framework (Gernsbacher, 1990), the event indexing model (Zwaan & Radvansky, 1998), the landscape model (Van den Broek, Virtue, Everson, Tzeng, & Sung, 2002), and embodiment models (Glenberg, 1997; de Vega, Glenberg, & Graesser, 2008). Many of these are complex processing models that combine symbolic representations and statistical representations that satisfy constraints at multiple levels of language and discourse. This subsection considers the CAPS/Reader and Construction-Integration (CI) model because these are the closest candidates to building a completely automated computer system that comprehends naturalistic text.

Just and Carpenter's (1992) CAPS/Reader model directs comprehension with a large set of production rules. The production rules play a variety of roles in the cognitive system, such as (a) scanning the words in the explicit text, (b) governing the operations of working memory, (c) changing activation values of information in working memory and long-term memory, and (d) performing other cognitive or behavioral actions. The production rules have an "IF <state>, THEN <action>" form and are probabilistic, with activation values and thresholds. For example, if the contents of working memory has some state S that is activated to a degree that meets or exceeds some threshold T, then action A is executed by spreading activation to one or more other information units in working memory, long-term memory, or response output. All of the production rules are evaluated in parallel within in each cycle of the production system, and multiple rules may get activated within each cycle. The researcher can therefore trace the activation of information units (i.e., word or proposition nodes) in the text, working memory, and long-term memory as a function of the cycles of production rules that get activated. Just and Carpenter have reported that these profiles of nodal activation can predict patterns of reading times for individual words, eye tracking behavior, and memory for text constituents. However, one drawback to the CAPS Reader model is that the researcher needs to formulate all of the production rules ahead of time.

Kintsch's (1998) CI model directs comprehension with a connectionist network. As text is read, sentence by sentence (or alternatively, clauses by clause), a set of word concepts and proposition nodes are activated (constructed). Some nodes match constituents in the explicit text whereas others are activated inferentially by world knowledge. The activation of each node fluctuates systematically during the course of comprehension, sentence by sentence. When any given sentence S (or clause) is comprehended, the set of activated nodes include (a) N explicit and inference nodes affiliated with S and (b) M nodes that are held over in working memory from the previous sentence by virtue of meeting some threshold of activation. The resulting N+M nodes are fully connected to each other in a weight space. The set of weights in the resulting (N+M) by (N+M) *connectivity matrix* specifies the extent to which each node activates or inhibits the activation of each of the other N+M nodes. The values of the weights in the connectivity matrix are theoretically motivated by multiple levels of language and discourse. For example, if two word nodes (A and B) are closely related in a syntactic parse, they would have a high positive weight; if two propositions contradict each other, they would have a high negative weight.

The dynamic process of comprehending sentence S has a two stage process, namely construction and integration. During construction, the N+M nodes are activated and then the connectivity matrix operates on these initial node activations in multiple activation cycles until there is a settling of the node activations to a new final stable activation profile. At that point, integration of the nodes has been achieved. Sentences that are more difficult to comprehend would require more cycles to settle. These dynamic processes have testable implications for psychological data. Reading times should be correlated with the number of cycles during integration. Recall of a node should be correlated with the number of cycles of activation. Inferences should be activated to the extent that they are activated and survive the integration phases. Kintsch (1998) summarizes substantial empirical evidence that support these and other predictions from the CI model.

The original CI model was not completely automated because researchers had to supply the world knowledge and the connectivity matrix that captures the language and discourse constraints. However, now that there has been substantial progress in the field of computational linguistics, it is possible to generate the weights in a principled fashion computationally by a computer. There are syntactic parsers (Charniak, 2000; Lin, 1998) that can assign syntactic tree structures to sentences automatically and these can be used to generate the syntactic connectivity matrix. Kintsch (1998) has used LSA to automatically activate concepts (near neighbors) from long-term memory that are associated with explicit words and to generate weights that connect the N+M nodes. One current technical limitation is that there is no reliable mechanism for translating language to propositions, an important functional unit in the CI model. However, there has been progress on this front, as will be discussed in the section on text analysis tools.

Annotation Schemes in Linguistics

The linguistics literature does not have a uniform method for representing text, but propositions are not normally the functional discourse units. Linguists have assumed, for example, that the functional discourse segments are clauses (Givón, 1983), conversational turns (Sacks et al., 1974), sentences (Polanyi, 1988), prosodic units (Grosz & Hirschberg, 1992) or intentional units (Grosz & Sidner, 1986). Such differences in fundamental discourse units end up having an impact on the resulting taxonomies of discourse categories and coherence relations.

Two of the most frequently mentioned annotation schemes for discourse relations were developed by Hobbs (1985) and Mann and Thompson (1988). Hobbs integrates a theory of coherence relations within a larger knowledge-based theory of discourse interpretation. According to Hobbs, readers attempt to establish text coherence as they read. Coherence relations guide the readers' text building strategies but inferences are often needed to establish the coherence. Hobbs identified 9 coherence relations, such as occasion, evaluation, background, explanation, contrast, parallel, and elaboration.

Mann and Thompson's (1988) *Rhetorical Structure Theory* (RST) is similar to Hobbs but there are more relations and parts of it have been computationally implemented (Marcu, 2000). RST specifies the relations among *text spans*, regardless of whether or not they are marked by linguistic devices. RST assumes that relations in the text are between text spans, which are usually but necessarily identical to clauses. The text spans have variable size, ranging from two clauses to multi-sentence segments. RST proposes that a set of rhetorical relations tend to dominate in most texts, but the door is open for additional rhetorical relations that the writer needs. Mann and Thompson (1988) identified 23 rhetorical relations, including circumstance, solutionhood, elaboration, background, purpose, and non-volitional result. Thus, RST analysis starts by dividing the text into functional units that are called text spans. Two text spans form a nucleus and a satellite (Mann & Thompson, 1988); the nucleus is the part that is more essential to the writer's purpose than the satellite. Rhetorical relations are then composed between two non-overlapping text spans and form schemas. These schemas are rearranged into larger schema applications. The result of the analysis is a rhetorical structure tree, which is a hierarchical system of schema applications.

SCORING OF TEXT ANALYSIS SYSTEMS

A systematic scoring method is needed to assess the reliability of humans or computers in analyzing texts. There are two fundamental questions that guide these scoring systems: How similar are the text analyses of two or more humans? How similar are the analyses of humans and computers? Scoring procedures are needed to assess the segmentation of texts into theoretical units (such as propositions, clauses, sections, or text spans), the assignment of text units to theoretical categories (such as speech act categories, cohesion relations, or rhetorical categories), the structural relations between text units (such as relational links, connectives, or superordinate/subordinate relations), and the ratings of texts on quantitative dimensions (such as importance, quality, difficulty, or cohesion). We refer to these four procedures as segmentation, classification, linking, and rating, respectively.

Some of these scoring decisions are categorical (or qualitative) whereas others are continuous (or quantitative). An example categorical classification task would involve assigning sentences to one of several speech act categories (e.g., assertion, command, question, request, etc.). A Cohen's kappa score is normally used to assess the similarity of humans in their classification categories, or the similarity of humans and computers. The kappa scores vary from 0 to 1 and statistically adjust for the base rate likelihood that observations are in the various categories. It should be noted that percent agreement in the decisions of 2 or more parties (humans or computers) is inappropriate because of base rate problems and possibilities of inflating the score via highly skewed frequency distributions. An example quantitative rating task is the grading of essays on quality, with values ranging from 0 to 1. A Cronbach's alpha score is normally used to assess the similarity of ratings of humans or the similarity of humans and computers, although correlation coefficients (Pearson, Spearman) can also serve the sample purpose. These measures of agreement are quite familiar to researchers in education, psychology, and most other fields.

Researchers in computational linguistics use different quantitative methods of scoring agreement between human and computer decisions (Jurafsky & Martin, 2008). Human experts normally serve as the gold standard when measuring the performance of computers in making a decision or in assigning a text unit to category X. Recall and precision scores are routinely reported in the field of computational linguistics, as defined below.

Recall score is the proportion of computer decisions that agree with human decisions: $p(X_{computer} \mid X_{expert})$.

Precision score is the proportion of human decisions that agree with computer decisions: $p(X_{expert} \mid X_{computer})$.

An *F-measure* is a combined overall score (varying from 0 to 1) that takes both recall and precision into account. An alternative to these recall, precision, and F-measure scores is to perform signal detection analyses (Green & Swets, 1966), as defined below.

Hit rate = recall score
Miss rate = (1.0 - hit rate)
False alarm rate = $p(X_{computer} \mid \text{not } X_{expert})$
Correct rejection rate = (1.0 - false alarm rate)

An overall *d'* score is a measure in theoretical standard deviation units of the computer's discriminating the occurrence of X versus not-X, when using the human expert as the gold standard. The *d'* score is highest when the hit rate is 1 and the false alarm rate is 0.

The field of computational linguistics has benefited from some large-scale initiatives, funded by Department of Defense, that have systematically measured the performance of different systems developed by the computational linguists. These systems perform a variety of different useful functions, such as (a) accessing relevant documents from large document corpora (called *information retrieval*) and (b) extracting lexical, syntactic, semantic, or discourse information from text (called *information extraction*, or *automated content extraction*). The performance of information and content extraction systems has been assessed and reported in the Message Understanding Conferences (MUC; DARPA, 1995) and the Document Understanding Conferences (DUC), sponsored by the Association of Computational Linguistics. The National Institute of Standards and Technology (NIST) is a neutral party that selects the benchmark tasks, performance measures, and scheduling of the assessments. This assures that the performance of dozens of different systems can be evaluated and compared with fairness and objectivity. The different systems are compared quantitatively on various capabilities, although it is explicitly emphasized that the goal is to mark progress in the field as a whole rather than to hold competitions.

Comparisons of performance between a computer program and human experts (or between experts) are not expected to be perfect, but the question arises as to what level of performance is considered impressive, modest, or disappointing. How high should we expect the scores to be when examining kappa, alpha, recall, precision, or F-measures? There is no iron-clad, defensible answer to this question, but our labs regard kappa and F-measure scores of .70 or higher to be impressive, .30 to .69 to be modest, and .29 or lower to be disappointing. However, comparisons between computer and humans should be evaluated relative to the scores between two human judges. If two experts have a kappa score of only .40, then a kappa score between computer and expert of .36 would be impressive. We often consider the ratio of [kappa(computer, expert) / kappa (expert1, expert2)] to be the most relevant metric of the performance of the computer system (see Graesser, Cai, Louwerse, & Daniel, 2006), as long as the agreement between experts is modest or higher.

TEXT ANALYSIS TOOLS

This section identifies computer tools that can be used to analyze texts on different levels of language and discourse. We focus here on completely automated text analysis systems, as opposed to the large array of tools in which the human and computer collaboratively annotate the text. We will start with the most conventional simple systems and end with the most complex systems that analyze text at global levels.

Conventional Measures of Text Difficulty

Readability formulae.   Readability formulae (Klare, 1974–75) have had a major influence on the textbook industry because they are routinely used as a standard for the selection of texts in K–12 and college. For example, if the students are in the sixth grade, a textbook at the third-grade level would be considered too easy and a textbook at the ninth-grade level would be considered too difficult for the students. A text that is scaled at the fifth- through seventh-grade level would be considered closer to the sixth graders' zone of proximal development.

Readability formulas have widespread use even though they rely exclusively on word length, sentence length, and sometimes word frequency. For example, the output of the *Flesch Kincaid Reading Grade Level* is specified in formulae 1.

Flesch Reading Grade Level = (.39 x ASL + 11.8 x ASW – 15.59 (1)

ASL refers to the average sentence length in the text whereas ASW is the average number of syllables per word. This simple metric is easy to score but ignores dozens of language and discourse components that are theoretically expected to influence comprehension difficulty, as will be described later. Texts tend to take more time to read when there are longer words and lengthier sentences (Haberlandt & Graesser, 1985; Just & Carpenter, 1987, 1992). Longer words tend to be less frequent in the language, as we know from Zipf's law (1949), and longer sentences tend to place more demands on working memory (Just & Carpenter, 1992). Nevertheless, there are a host of other variables that are also expected to influence reading difficulty.

There is also a potential risk of these readability formulas when they are mechanically applied to alter texts. It would not be wise to superficially shorten words and sentences in a text in order to have it fall under the rubric of an earlier grade level. For example, one could shorten words by substituting pronouns (*it, this, that, he, she, we*) for nouns, noun-phrases, or clauses. But that would functionally increase difficulty whenever the reader incorrectly binds the pronoun to a referent. One could shorten a sentence by chopping it up into shorter sentences. But that would functionally increase text difficulty whenever the reader has trouble conceptually relating the shorter sentences. The textbook industry has on occasion shorted texts in this mechanical way and thereby made texts less coherent rather than easier to read.

Lexile and DRP.   Measures such as Lexile (Stenner, 1996) and Degrees of Reading Power (DRP; B.I. Koslin, Zeno, & S. Koslin, 1987) capitalize on the predictive power of word and sentence length as automated signatures of word familiarity and sentence complexity. The precise formulae that compute reading difficulty of texts are not publically released, but the Lexile and DRP scores for texts are highly correlated with Flesch Kincaid Readability scores ($r > .90$ in our analyses). Moreover, the metrics of text difficulty also take into consideration the students' comprehension performance at different ages. Students' comprehension ability can be measured using cloze tests, for example, in which the student fills in a missing word in a sentence, usually by choosing one of four possibilities. A cloze score of .75 means that the correct word is selected 75% of the time; this .75 benchmark may be adopted as an adequate threshold for comprehension in the Lexile analysis. The Lexile score measures both text difficulty and student ability in terms of the same unit, namely **lexiles**. A student is expected to comprehend 75% of a text, if the text has a Lexile score of 800 lexiles and the student's ability is estimated at 800 lexiles A students' expected comprehension of a text is a function of the difference between the difficulty of the text and the student's comprehension ability. One practical use of these measures is that they match readers to texts by providing automated text difficulty and comprehension ability indices, with the assumption that students can be encouraged to read texts that they understand at a specified level.

Some advantages of these types of reading programs are that they encourage students to read, the students can see their progression from level to level, and the predictive power of these types of formulae is relatively good. However, their predictive power largely stems from their predicting the same shallow level of comprehension as the level of difficulty measured in the text. Once again, we believe it is important to develop automated indices of text difficulty and comprehension that go beyond surface understanding and surface text characteristics by measuring deeper, more conceptual levels of comprehension.

Word-Level Measures

Hundreds of lexicons are available that analyze words on different dimensions of form, syntax, meaning, and psychological attributes. In this section we identify many of the word-based measures. Most of these measures can be accessed through Coh-Metrix (Graesser, McNamara, et al., 2004; McNamara, Lowerse, & Graesser, 2007; http://cohmetrix.memphis.edu/cohmetrixpr/index.html), a facility on the Web that analyzes texts on characteristics of language and discourse.

Word Frequency.   Word frequency estimates the frequency of a word appearing in published documents in the real world, based on a designated corpus of texts with millions of words.

One impressive estimate is *CELEX*, the database from the Dutch Centre for Lexical Information (Baayen, Piepenbrock, & Gulikers, 1995), based on a corpus of 17.9 million words. About 1 million of the word tokens are collected from spoken English (news transcripts and telephone conversations) whereas the remainder come from written corpora (newspapers and books). Some other well-known word frequency norms, all based on smaller corpora, are those of Francis and Kucera (1982) and Brown (1984).

Psychological Dimensions of Words. We have already described Pennebaker's Linguistic Inquiry Word Count (LIWC; Pennebaker & Francis, 1999), which includes psychological indices of words on such dimensions as positive and negative emotions, causality, and personality traits. Researchers had to rate or classify words in the lexicon on each of these psychological indices. Another important lexicon is the MRC Psycholinguistic Database (Coltheart, 1981), a collection of human ratings of 150,837 words along four psychological dimensions: meaningfulness, concreteness, imagability, familiarity, and age of acquiring the word. These ratings are based on work by Paivio, Yuille, and Madigan, (1968), Toglia and Battig (1978), and Gilhooly and Logie (1980).

WordNet. WordNet® (Fellbaum, 1998; Miller, Beckwith, Fellbaum, Gross, & Miller, 1990) is an online lexicon whose design was inspired by cognitive science and psycholinguistics. English nouns, verbs, adjectives and adverbs are organized into semantic fields of underlying lexical concepts. For example, some words are functionally synonymous because they have the same or a very similar meaning. Polysemy is the number of senses of a word; for example, *bank* has one sense that is affiliated with money and another that is affiliated with rivers. A word's hypernym count is defined as the number of levels in a conceptual taxonomic hierarchy that is above (superordinate to) a word; *table* (as a concrete object) has 7 hypernym levels: seat -> furniture -> furnishings -> instrumentality -> artifact -> object -> entity. A word having many hypernym levels tends to be more concrete, whereas few hypernym levels is diagnostic of abstractness.

Parts of Speech. There are over 70 part-of-speech (POS) tags derived from the Penn Treebank (Marcus, Santorini, & Marcinkiewicz, 1993). The tags include content words (e.g., *nouns, verbs, adjectives, adverbs*) and function words (e.g., *prepositions, determiners, pronouns*). Brill (1995) developed a POS tagger that automatically assigns a POS tag to each word. The Brill tagger assigns POS tags even to words that are not stored in its lexicon, based on the syntactic context of the other words in the sentence. Content words are more important than function words when it comes to identifying the background world knowledge for a text. However, the function words are also important for syntactic processing and are affiliated with the psychological profile of the writer (Pennebaker & Stone, 2003). Pronouns are particularly diagnostic of the writers' psychological states according to research by Pennebaker (Pennebaker & Chung, 2007).

Syntax

Computational linguists have developed a large number of syntactic parsers that automatically assign syntactic tree structures to sentences (Jurafsy & Martin, 2008). Two popular contemporary parsers are Apple Pie (Sekine & Grishman, 1995) and the Charniak parser (2000). These parsers capture surface phrase-structure composition rather than deep structures, logical forms, or propositional representations. The Charniak (2000) parser generates a parse tree from an underlying formal grammar which can be induced from a corpus of texts via machine learning algorithms. The root of the tree, or highest level, divides the sentence into intermediate branches that specify nodes that include noun phrase (NP), verb phrase (VB), prepositional phrase (PP), and embedded sentence constituents. The tree terminates at leaf nodes, or words of the sentence that are labeled for their part of speech. Hempelmann, Rus, Graesser, and McNamara (2006) evaluated the accuracy and speed of generating the parse trees for a number of syntactic parsers and concluded that the Charniak parser fared the best.

The syntactic complexity of sentences can be evaluated by two tools on the Web, namely Coh-Metrix (Graesser, Lu, et al., 2004) and QUAID (Question Understanding Aid; Graesser et al., 2006). Syntactic complexity is assumed to increase with the degree to which sentences have embedded phrases, nodes that directly dominate many subnodes, and high working memory loads. One index is noun phrase density, calculated by taking the mean number of modifiers (e.g., *adjectives*) per noun phrase. A second index computes the extent to which there are embedded constituents by calculating the mean number of high-level constituents per word. A third index computes the number of words in the sentence that appear before the main verb of the main clause; as this number increases, the comprehender is expected to hold more words in working memory. Coh-Metrix also provides a metric of the extent to which sentences in the text have different syntactic structures, i.e., a form of syntactic diversity.

Propositions

Researchers in AI and computational linguistics have not been able to develop a computer program that can automatically and reliably translate sentences into a propositional representation or logical form, even in large-scale evaluations that aspire to such a goal (Rus, 2004; Rus, McCarthy, & Graesser, 2006). The assignment of noun-phrases to thematic roles (e.g., agent, recipient, object, location) is also well below 80% correct in the available computer systems (DARPA, 1995). However, progress will hopefully be made in future years through two avenues. First, there is a corpus of annotated propositional representations in PropBank (Palmer, Kingsbury, & Gildea, 2005), so researchers can work on developing and refining their algorithms for automatic proposition extraction. Second, a tool called AutoProp (Briner, McCarthy, & McNamara, 2006) has been designed to "propositionalize" texts that have already been reduced to clauses. This is a promising tool that might eventually achieve adequate performance.

Coreference and Cohesion

Coh-Metrix (Graesser, McNamara, et al., 2004) was explicitly designed to analyze text cohesion and coherence by incorporating recent advances in computational linguistics. McNamara, Louwerse, and Graesser (2007) have reviewed over 40 studies that evaluated the accuracy of Coh-Metrix and also how it was tested in psychological experiments on text comprehension and memory. This subsection covers measures of Coh-Metrix, but it is beyond the scope of this chapter to review the research that has assessed its validity.

Coreference.   Coreference is perhaps the most frequent definition of cohesion among researchers in discourse processing and linguistics (Britton & Gulgoz, 1991; Halliday & Hasan, 1976; Kintsch & van Dijk, 1978; McNamara, Kintsch, Songer, & Kintsch, 1996). As discussed earlier in the chapter, referential cohesion occurs when a noun, pronoun, or noun-phrase refers to another constituent in the text. There is a referential cohesion gap when the words in a sentence do not connect to words in surrounding text or sentences. Coh-Metrix tracks five major types of lexical coreference by computing overlap in nouns, pronouns, arguments, stems, and content words. Noun overlap is the proportion of all sentence pairs that share one or more common nouns, whereas pronoun overlap is the proportion of sentence pairs that share one or more pronoun. Argument overlap is the proportion of sentence pairs that share nouns or pronouns (e.g., *table/table, he/he*). Stem overlap is the proportion of sentence pairs in which a noun (or pronoun) in one sentence has the same semantic morpheme (called a lemma) in common with any word in any grammatical category in the other sentence (e.g., the noun *photograph* and the verb *photographed*). The fifth coreference index, content word overlap, is the proportion of content words that are the same between pairs of sentences. Some of these measures consider only pairs of *adjacent* sentences, whereas others consider *all possible pairs* of sentences in a paragraph.

Connectives. Connectives help increase the cohesion of a text by explicitly linking ideas at the clausal and sentential level (Britton & Gulgoz, 1991; Halliday & Hasan, 1976; Louwerse & Mitchell, 2003; McNamara et al., 1996; Sanders & Noordman, 2000). Most of the connectives in Coh-Metrix are defined according to the subcategories of cohesion identified by Halliday and Hasan (1976) and Louwerse (2001). These include connectives that correspond to additive cohesion (e.g., *also, moreover, however, but*), temporal cohesion (e.g., *after, before, until*), and causal/intentional cohesion (e.g., *because, so, in order to*). Logical operators (e.g., variants of *or, and, not,* and *if–then*) are also cohesive links that influence the analytical complexity of a text. The measures of connectives are computed as a relative frequency score, the number of instances of a category per 1,000 words.

Cohesion of the Situation Model. An important level of text comprehension consists of constructing a situation model (or mental model), which is the referential content or microworld of what a text is about (Graesser et al., 1994; Kintsch, 1998). Text comprehension researchers have investigated five dimensions of the situational model (Zwaan & Radvansky, 1998): causation, intentionality, time, space, and protagonists. A break in cohesion or coherence occurs when there is a discontinuity on one or more of these situation model dimensions. Whenever such discontinuities occur, it is important to have connectives, transitional phrases, adverbs, or other signaling devices that convey to the readers that there is a discontinuity; we refer to these different forms of signaling as particles. Cohesion is facilitated by particles that clarify and stitch together the actions, goals, events, and states conveyed in the text. Coh-Metrix computes the ratio of cohesion particles to the incidence of relevant referential content; given the occurrence of relevant content (such as clauses with events or actions), what is density of particles that stitch together the clauses. In the case of temporality, Coh-Metrix computes a repetition score that tracks the consistency of tense (e.g., *past* and *present*) and aspect (*perfective* and *progressive*) across a passage of text. The repetition scores decrease as shifts in tense and aspect are encountered. A low particle-to-shift ratio is a symptom of problematic temporal cohesion.

Latent Semantic Analysis (LSA). Coh-Metrix assesses conceptual overlap between sentences by LSA (Landauer et al., 2007), the corpus-based statistical representation that considers implicit knowledge. LSA-based cohesion was measured in several ways in Coh-Metrix, such as LSA similarity between adjacent sentences, LSA similarity between all possible pairs of sentences in a paragraph, and LSA similarity between adjacent paragraphs. The Coh-Metrix research team has also developed a tool with an LSA-based measure that automatically computes the relative amount of *given* versus *new* information that each sentence has in a text and then computes the average newness among all sentences in the text (Chafe, 1976; Halliday, 1967; Haviland & Clark, 1974; Prince, 1981). Hempelmann et al. (2005) reported that the span method has a high correlation with the theoretical analyses of give/new developed by Prince (1981), as well as other linguists who have analyzed the given-new distinction in discourse.

Genre

There are many types of discourse, or what some researchers call *genre*, conversational *registers,* or simply discourse categories (the expression we adopt here). There are prototypical discourse categories in the American culture, such as folktales, scientific journal articles, and news editorials. These three examples would funnel into more superordinate classes that might be labeled as narrative, exposition, and argumentation, respectively. Some texts will be hybrids, of course.

Biber (1988) conducted a very ambitious investigation of discourse categories . Biber used 23 spoken and written categories from the Lancaster-Oslo-Bergen (LOB) corpus and the London-Lund corpus, and computed the frequency of 67 linguistic features in these categories. The normalized frequencies of these features in each of the discourse categories were then entered in a factor analysis, from which six factors emerged. These factors can be seen as dimensions on which discourse categories can be placed. Biber's analysis showed that no single dimension comprised a difference between speech and writing, but there were the following relations or features among the texts: (a) Involved versus informational production, (b) narrative versus non-narrative, (c) explicit versus situation dependent reference, (d) overt expression of persuasion, (e) abstract versus non-abstract information, and (f) online informational elaboration. For example, categories such as romantic fiction, mystery fiction, and science fiction were positioned high on the second dimension (narrative). In contrast, categories such as academic prose, official documents, hobbies, and broadcasts scored low (non-narrative).

Biber's (1988) study and the multi-feature multidimensional approach have become a standard in corpus linguistics (McEnery, 2003) and have led to various extensions (Conrad & Biber, 2001), as well as to assessments of the validity, stability, and meaningfulness of the approach (Lee, 2004). An automated version of Biber's system is available in his laboratory whereas the 67 features of language and discourse are automated in Coh-Metrix. Coh-Metrix also has other algorithms that significantly differentiate science, narrative, versus history texts (McCarthy, Myers, Briner, Graesser, & McNamara, in press).

CLOSING COMMENTS

As we close the first decade of the new millennium, we are confident that automated text analyses will continue to progress and lead to useful new applications. Few of our colleagues would have placed their bets 20 years ago on computer systems that would grade student essays as well as experts in composition, that would train students to read at deeper levels, or that would tutor students on science topics in natural language. However, there are now systems that achieve these practical goals, as we have pointed out in this chapter. Moreover, they are now being scaled up to the point of being used in school systems, the textbook industry, and eLearning. Of course, the use of these technologies throughout the world is at the early phase of adoption and it will take awhile before they are fully evaluated with respect to their impact on reading proficiency.

This chapter will close with two examples that should have a profound impact on reading researchers in the future. The first is that the textbook industry will eventually use these tools to improve the quality of textbooks. Existing textbooks in science and other academic topics are frequently not well written because they fail to consider the world knowledge of the reader and they have gaps in text cohesion. As discussed earlier, writers in the textbook industry run the risk of shortening words and sentences in order to minimize the text difficulty scores of the texts that are targeted for grades 1–4. The problem with shortening words by substituting pronouns for long content words is that it is sometimes difficult to ground pronouns in appropriate referents, so comprehension and coherence suffers. The problem with shortening the sentences is that there is a potential penalty in lowering the cohesion among the ideas expressed in sentences. The unfortunate consequence of these mechanical alterations is that students end up with an incoherent reading experience. Writers of textbooks of the future are expected to take a closer look at the automated text analysis tools as they prepare materials for school systems. Moreover, the text analysis systems need to consider the full range of levels of language and discourse—not merely word and sentence length.

The second example addresses the selection of texts for the learner. How can we optimize the assignment of the next text for the student to read? We presumably would not want to assign a text that is too easy or too difficult, but rather to assign a text that is at the reader's zone of proximal development. The computer can play an important role in suggesting the ideal text for the reader at the right time and place. It would be important for the text to be relevant to the immediate curriculum and also to match the reader's profile of world knowledge, comprehension skills, and interests. Technologies are currently available to make such assignments of texts to readers. However, more research and development is needed to refine these technologies and advance the science of reading comprehension mechanisms. Once again, however, the text analysis systems need to consider the full range of levels of language and discourse.

AUTHOR NOTES

The research on was supported by the National Science Foundation (SBR 9720314, SES 9977969, REC 0106965, REC 0126265, ITR 0325428, REESE 0633918), the Institute of Education Sciences (R305G020018, R305H050169, R305B070349, R305A080589), and the Office of Naval Research (N00014-00-1-0917). Any opinions, findings, and conclusions or recommendations expressed in this material are those of the authors and do not necessarily reflect the views of NSF, IES, or ONR.

REFERENCES

Allen, J. (1995). *Natural language understanding.* Redwood City, CA: Benjamin/Cummings.

Anderson, R. C., Spiro, R. J., & Montague, W. E. (Eds.). (1977). *Schooling and the acquisition of knowledge.* Hillsdale, NJ: Erlbaum.

Ausubel, D. (1968). *Educational psychology: A cognitive view.* New York: Holt, Rinehart, and Winston.

Baayen, R. H., Piepenbrock, R., & Gulikers, L. (1995). *The CELEX lexical database* [CD-ROM]. Philadelphia: Linguistic Data Consortium, University of Pennsylvania.

Bransford, J. D., & Johnson, M. K. (1972). Contextual prerequisites for understanding: Some investigations of comprehension and recall. *Journal of Verbal Learning and Verbal Behavior, 11,* 717–726.

Biber, D. (1988). *Variations across speech and writing.* Cambridge, MA: Cambridge University Press.

Biber, D., Conrad, S., & Reppen, R. (1998). *Corpus linguistics: Investigating language structure and use.* Cambridge, UK: Cambridge University Press.

Bower, G. H., Black, J. B., & Turner, T. J. (1979). Scripts in memory for text. *Cognitive Psychology, 11,* 177–220.

Brill, E. (1995). Transformation-based error-driven learning and natural language processing: A case study in part-of-speech tagging. *Computational Linguistics, 21,* 543–566.

Briner, S. W., McCarthy, P. M., & McNamara, D. S. (2006). Automating text propositionalization: An assessment of AutoProp. In R. Sun & N. Miyake (Eds.), *Proceedings of the 28th Annual Conference of the Cognitive Science Society* (pp. 24–49). Austin, TX: Cognitive Science Society.

Britton, B. K., & Gulgoz, S. (1991). Using Kintsch's computational model to improve instructional text: Effects of repairing inference calls on recall and cognitive structures. *Journal of Educational Psychology, 83,* 329–345.

Brown, G. D. A. (1984). A frequency count of 190,000 words in the London-Lund Corpus of English Conversation. *Behavioral Research Methods Instrumentation and Computers, 16,* 502–532

Burstein, J. (2003). The *e-rater* scoring engine: Automated essay scoring with natural language processing. In M. D. Shermis & J. Burstein (Eds.), *Automated essay scoring: A cross-disciplinary perspective* (pp. 113–122). Hillsdale, NJ: Erlbaum.

Chafe, W. (1976). Givenness, contrastiveness, definiteness, subjects, and topics. In C. Li (Ed.), *Subject and topic* (pp. 25–76). New York: Academic Press.

Charniak, E. (2000). A maximum-entropy-inspired parser. *Proceedings of the First Conference on North American Chapter of the Association for Computational Linguistics* (pp. 132–139). San Francisco: Morgan Kaufmann Publishers.

Cohen, P. R., & Perrault, C. R. (1979). Elements of a plan-based theory of speech acts. *Cognitive Science, 3*, 177–212.

Conrad, S., & Biber, D. (2001). *Variation in English: Multi-dimensional studies.* Harlow, UK: Longman.

Coltheart, M. (1981). The MRC Psycholinguistic Database. *Quarterly Journal of Experimental Psychology, 33A*, 497–505.

DARPA. (1995). *Proceedings of the Sixth Message Understanding Conference* (MUC-6). San Francisco: Morgan Kaufman Publishers.

De Vega, M., Glenberg, A. M., & Graesser, A. C. (Eds.). (2008). *Symbols and embodiment: Debates on meaning and cognition.* Oxford, UK: Oxford University Press.

Fellbaum, C. (Ed.). (1998). *WordNet: An electronic lexical database.* Cambridge, MA: MIT Press.

Francis, W. N., & Kucera, N. (1982). *Frequency analysis of English usage.* New York: Houghton-Mifflin.

Frederiksen, C. H. (1975). Representing logical and semantic structure of knowledge acquired from discourse. *Cognitive Psychology, 7*, 371–458.

Gernsbacher, M. A. (1990). *Language comprehension as structure building.* Hillsdale, NJ: Erlbaum.

Gibson, E. J., & Levin, H. (1975). *The psychology of reading.* Cambridge, MA: MIT Press.

Gilhooly, K. J., & Logie, R. H. (1980). Age of acquisition, imagery, familiarity and ambiguity measures for 1944 words. *Behavioral Research Methods and Instrumentation, 12,* 395–427.

Givón, T. (1983). Topic continuity in discourse: An introduction. In T. Givón (Ed.), *Topic continuity in discourse: Quantified cross-linguistic studies* (pp. 347–363). Amsterdam: John Benjamins.

Glenberg, A. M. (1997). What memory is for. *Behavioral and Brain Sciences, 20*, 1–19.

Goldman, S. R., & Rakestraw, J. A. (2000). Structural aspects of constructing meaning from text. In M. L. Kamil, P. B. Mosenthal, P. D. Pearson, & R. Barr (Eds.), *Handbook of reading research* (Vol. III, pp. 311–336). Mahwah, NJ: Erlbaum.

Gough, P. B. (1972). One second of reading. In J. F. Kavanaugh & J. G. Mattingly (Eds.), *Language by ear and by eye* (pp. 331–358). Cambridge, MA: MIT Press.

Graesser, A. C., Cai, Z., Louwerse, M., & Daniel, F. (2006). Question Understanding Aid (QUAID): A web facility that helps survey methodologists improve the comprehensibility of questions. *Public Opinion Quarterly, 70*, 3–22.

Graesser, A. C., Gernsbacher, M. A., & Goldman, S. R. (Eds.). (2003). *Handbook of discourse processes.* Mahwah, NJ: Erlbaum.

Graesser, A. C., Gordon, S. E., & Sawyer, J. D. (1979). Recognition memory for typical and atypical actions in scripted activities: Tests of a script pointer plus tag hypothesis. *Journal of Verbal Learning and Verbal Behavior, 18*, 319–322.

Graesser, A. C., Lu, S., Jackson, G. T., Mitchell, H., Ventura, M., Olney, A., et al. (2004). AutoTutor: A tutor with dialogue in natural language. *Behavioral Research Methods, Instruments, and Computers, 36*, 180–193.

Graesser, A. C., McNamara, D. S., Louwerse, M. M., & Cai, Z. (2004). Coh-Metrix: Analysis of text on cohesion and language. *Behavioral Research Methods, Instruments, and Computers, 36*, 193–202.

Graesser, A. C., Singer, M., & Trabasso, T. (1994). Constructing inferences during narrative text comprehension. *Psychological Review, 101*, 371–395.

Green, D. M., & Swets, J. A. (1966). *Signal detection theory and psychophysics.* New York: Wiley.

Grice, H. P. (1975). Logic and conversation. In P. Coleand & J. L. Morgan (Eds.), *Syntax and semantics* (Vol. 3): *Speech acts* (pp. 41–58). New York: Seminar Press.

Grosz, B., & Hirschberg, J. (1992, October 13–16). Some intonational characteristics of discourse structure. In J. J. Ohala, T. M. Nearey, B. L. Derwing, M. M. Hodge, & G. E. Wiebe (Eds.), *Proceedings of the International Conference on Spoken Language Processing* (pp. 429–432). Banff, Canada. Retrieved from http://www.isca-speech.org/archive/icslp_1992

Grosz, B. J., & Sidner, C. L. (1986). Attention, intentions, and the structure of discourse. *Computational Linguistics, 12*(3), 175–204.

Haberlandt, K. F., & Graesser, A. C. (1985). Component processes in text comprehension and some of their interactions. *Journal of Experimental Psychology: General, 114,* 357–374.

Halliday, M. (1967). *Intonation and grammar in British English.* The Hague: Mouton.

Halliday, M. A. K., & Hasan, R. (1976). *Cohesion in English.* London: Longman.

Haviland, S. E., & Clark, H. H. (1974). What's new? Acquiring new information as a process in comprehension. *Journal of Verbal Learning and Verbal Behavior, 13,* 515–521.

Hempelmann, C. F., Dufty, D., McCarthy, P., Graesser, A. C., Cai, Z., & McNamara, D. S. (2005). Using LSA to automatically identify givenness and newness of noun-phrases in written discourse. In B. Bara (Ed.), *Proceedings of the 27th Annual Meetings of the Cognitive Science Society* (pp. 941–946). Mahwah, NJ: Erlbaum.

Hempelmann, C. F., Rus, V., Graesser, A. C., & McNamara, D. D. (2006). Evaluating the state-of-the-art treebank-style parsers for Coh-Metrix and other learning technology environments. *Natural Language Engineering, 12,* 131–144.

Hobbs, J. R. (1985). *On the coherence and structure of discourse* (Technical Report CSLI-85-37). Center for the Study of Language and Information, Stanford University, Palo Alto, CA.

Jurafsky, D., & Martin, J. H. (2008). *Speech and language processing: An introduction to natural language processing, computational linguistics, and speech recognition.* Upper Saddle River, NJ: Prentice-Hall.

Just, M. A., & Carpenter, P. A. (1987). *The psychology of reading and language comprehension.* Boston: Allyn & Bacon.

Just M. A., & Carpenter, P. A. (1992). A capacity theory of comprehension: Individual differences in working memory. *Psychological Review, 99,* 122–149.

Kintsch, E., Coccamise, D., Franzke, M., Johnson, N., & Dooley, S. (2007). Summary street: Computer-guided summary writing. In T. Landauer, D. S. McNamara, S. Dennis, & W. Kintsch (Eds.), *Handbook of latent semantic analysis* (pp. 263–278). Mahwah, NJ: Erlbaum.

Kintsch, W. (1974). *The representation of meaning in memory.* Hillsdale, NJ: Erlbaum.

Kintsch, W. (1998). *Comprehension: A paradigm for cognition.* Cambridge, UK: Cambridge University Press.

Kintsch, W., & Van Dijk, T.A. (1978). Toward a model of text comprehension and production. *Psychological Review, 85,* 363–394.

Klare, G. R. (1974–1975). Assessing readability. *Reading Research Quarterly, 10,* 62–102.

Koslin, B. I., Zeno, S., & Koslin, S. (1987). *The DRP: An effective measure in reading.* New York: College Entrance Examination Board.

Landauer, T. K., & Dumais, S. T. (1997). A solution to Plato's problem: The latent semantic analysis theory of acquisition, induction, & representation of knowledge. *Psychological Review, 104,* 211–240.

Landauer, T. K., Laham, D., & Foltz, P. W. (2003). Automated essay assessment. *Assessment in education: Principles, Policy, and Practice, 10,* 295–308.

Landauer, T., McNamara, D. S., Dennis, S., Kintsch, W. (Eds.). (2007). *Handbook of latent semantic analysis.* Mahwah, NJ: Erlbaum.

Lee, D. Y. W. (2004). *Modeling variation in spoken and written English.* London: Routledge.

Lehnert, W. (1997). Information extraction: What have we learned? *Discourse Processes, 23,* 441–470.

Lehnert, W. G., & Ringle, M. H. (Eds.). (1982). *Strategies for natural language processing.* Hillsdale, NJ: Erlbaum.

Lenat, D. B. (1995). CYC: A large-scale investment in knowledge infrastructure. *Communications of the ACM, 38,* 33–38.

Lin, D. (1998, May). Dependency-based evaluation of MINIPAR. Paper presented at *Workshop on the Evaluation of Parsing Systems.* Granada, Spain.

Louwerse, M. M. (2001). An analytic and cognitive parameterization of coherence relations. *Cognitive Linguistics, 12,* 291–315.

Louwerse, M. M., & Mitchell, H. H. (2003). Toward a taxonomy of a set of discourse markers in dialog: A theoretical and computational linguistic account. *Discourse Processes, 35,* 199–239.

Mandler, J., & Johnson, N. (1977). Remembrance of things parsed: Story structure and recall. *Cognitive Psychology, 9,* 111–151.

Mann, W. C., & Thompson, S. A. (1988). Rhetorical structure theory: Toward a functional theory of text organization. *Text, 8,* 243–281.

Marcu, D. (2000). *The theory and practice of discourse parsing and summarization.* Cambridge, MA: MIT Press.

Marcus, M., Santorini, B., & Marcinkiewicz, M. A. (1993). Building a large annotated corpus of English: The Penn Treebank. *Computational Linguistics, 19,* 313–330.

McCarthy, P. M., Myers, J. C., Briner, S. W., Graesser, A. C., & McNamara, D. S. (in press). Are three words all we need? A psychological and computational study of genre recognition. *Journal for Computational Linguistics and Language Technology.*

McNamara, D. S. (2007). (Ed.). *Theories of text comprehension: The importance of reading strategies to theoretical foundations of reading comprehension.* Mahwah, NJ: Erlbaum.

McNamara, D. S., Kintsch, E., Songer, N. B., & Kintsch, W. (1996). Are good texts always better? Text coherence, background knowledge, and levels of understanding in learning from text. *Cognition and Instruction, 14,* 1–43.

McNamara, D. S., Levinstein, I. B., & Boonthum, C. (2004). iSTART: Interactive strategy trainer for active reading and thinking. *Behavioral Research Methods, Instruments, and Computers, 36,* 222–233.

McNamara, D. S., Louwerse, M. M., & Graesser, A. C. (2007). *Coh-Metrix: Automated cohesion and coherence scores to predict text readability and facilitate comprehension.* Unpublished final report on Institute of Education Science grant, University of Memphis.

McEnery, T. (2003). Corpus linguistics. In R. Mitkov (Ed.), *The Oxford encyclopedia of computational linguistics* (pp. 448–463). Oxford, UK: Oxford University Press.

Meyer, B. J. F. (1975). *The organization of prose and its effect on memory.* New York: Elsevier.

Miller, G. A., Beckwith, R., Fellbaum, C., Gross, D., & Miller, K. J. (1990). Introduction to wordnet: An on-line lexical database. *Journal of Lexiography, 3,* 235–244.

Millis, K. K., Kim, H. J., Todaro, S. Magliano, J., Wiemer-Hastings, K., & McNamara, D. S. (2004). Identifying reading strategies using latent semantic analysis: Comparing semantic benchmarks. *Behavior Research Methods, Instruments, & Computers, 36,* 213–221.

National Reading Panel. (2000). *Teaching children to read: An evidence-based assessment of the scientific research literature on reading and its implications for reading instruction* (NIH Pub. No. 00-4769). Jessup, MD: National Institute for Literacy.

Paivio, A., Yuille, J. C., & Madigan, S. A. (1968). Concreteness, imagery, and meaningfulness values for 925 nouns. *Journal of Experimental Psychology Monograph Supplement, 76,* 1–25.

Palmer, M., Kingsbury, P., & Gildea, D. (2005). The Proposition Bank: An annotated corpus of semantic roles. *Computational Linguistics, 31,* 71–106.

Pennebaker, J. W., Booth, R. J., & Francis, M. E. (2007). *Linguistic inquiry and word count.* Austin, TX: LIWC.net (www.liwc.net).

Pennebaker, J. W., & Chung, C. K. (2007). Expressive writing, emotional upheavals, and health. In H. S. Friedman & R. C. Silver (Eds.), *Foundations of health psychology* (pp. 263–284). New York: Oxford University Press.

Pennebaker, J. W., & Francis, M. E. (1999). *Linguistic inquiry and word count (LIWC).* Mahwah, NJ: Erlbaum.

Pennebaker, J. W., & King, L. A. (1999). Linguistic styles: Language use as an individual difference. *Journal of Personality and Social Psychology, 77,* 1296–1312.

Pennebaker, J. W., & Stone, L. D. (2003). Words of wisdom: Language use over the life span. *Journal of Personality and Social Psychology, 85,* 291–301.

Pickering, M. J., & Garrod, S. (2004). Toward a mechanistic psychology of dialogue. *Brain and Behavioral Sciences, 27,* 169–190.

Polanyi, L. (1988). A formal model of the structure of discourse. *Journal of Pragmatics, 12,* 601–638.

Prince, E. F. (1981). Toward a taxonomy of given-new information. In P. Cole (Ed.), *Radical pragmatics* (pp. 223–255). New York: Academic Press.

Rayner, K. (1998.) Eye movements in reading and information processing: 20 years of research. *Psychological Bulletin, 124,* 372–422.

Rieger, C. (1978). GRIND-1: First report on the Magic Grinder story comprehension project. *Discourse Processes, 1,* 267–303.

Rommetveit, R. (1974). *On message structure.* New York: Wiley.

Rosenblatt, L.M. (1978). *The reader, the text and the poem: The transactional theory of the literary work.* Carbondale: Southern Illinois University Press.

Rumelhart, D. E. (1975). Notes on a schema for stories. In D. G. Bobrow & A. Collins (Eds.), *Representation and understanding* (pp. 211–236). New York: Academic Press.

Rumelhart, D. E., & Ortony, A. (1977). The representation of knowledge in memory. In R. C. Anderson, R. J. Spiro, & W. E. Montague (Eds.), *Schooling and the acquisition of knowledge* (pp. 99–135). Hillsdale, NJ: Erlbaum.

Rus, V. (2004, July). A first exercise for evaluating logic form identification systems. *Proceedings Third International Workshop on the Evaluation of Systems for the Semantic Analysis of Text (SENSEVAL-3)*, at the Association of Computational Linguistics Annual Meeting. Barcelona, Spain: ACL.

Rus, V., McCarthy, P. M., & Graesser, A.C. (2006). Analysis of a text entailer. In A. Gelbukh (Ed.), *Lecture notes in computer science: Computational linguistics in intelligent text processing: 7th international conference* (pp. 287–298). New York: Springer Verlag.

Sacks, H., Schegloff, E. A., & Jefferson, G. (1974). A simple systematic for the organization of turn taking in conversation. *Language, 50*, 669–735.

Sanders, T. J. M., & Noordman, L. G. M. (2000). The role of coherence relations and their linguistic markers in text processing. *Discourse Processes, 29*, 37–60.

Schank, R. C. (1972). Conceptual dependence: A theory of natural language understanding. *Cognitive Psychology, 3*, 552–631.

Schank, R. C., & Abelson, R. P. (1977). *Scripts, plans, goals, and understanding: An inquiry into human knowledge structures*. Hillsdale, NJ: Erlbaum.

Schank, R., & Riesbeck, C. (1981). *Inside computer understanding*. Hillsdale, NJ: Erlbaum.

Searle, J. R. (1969). *Speech acts*. London: Cambridge University Press.

Sekine, S., & Grishman, R. (1995). A corpus-based probabilistic grammar with only two nonterminals. *Fourth International Workshop on Parsing Technologies* (pp. 260–270). Prague/Karlovy Vary, Czech Republic.

Snow, C. (2002). *Reading for understanding: Toward an R&D program in reading comprehension*. Santa Monica, CA: RAND Corporation.

Spilich, G. J., Vesonder, G. T., Chiesi, H. L., & Voss, J. F. (1979). Text processing of domain related information for individuals with high and low domain knowledge. *Journal of Verbal Learning and Verbal Behavior, 18*, 275–290.

Stenner, A. J. (1996, October). *Measuring reading comprehension with the Lexile framework*. Paper presented at the California Comparability Symposium. Retrieved January 30, 2006, from http://www.lexile.com/DesktopDefault.aspx?view=re

Toglia, M. P., & Battig, W. F. (1978). *Handbook of semantic word norms*. Hillsdale, NJ: Erlbaum.

Van den Broek, P., Virtue, S., Everson, M.G., & Tzeng, Y., & Sung, Y. (2002). Comprehension and memory of science texts: Inferential processes and the construction of a mental representation. In J. Otero, J. Leon, & A. C. Graesser (Eds.), *The psychology of science text comprehension* (pp. 131–154). Mahwah, NJ: Erlbaum.

Van Dijk, T. A. (1972). *Some aspects of text grammars*. The Hague: Mouton.

VanLehn, K., Graesser, A. C., Jackson, G. T., Jordan, P., Olney, A., & Rose, C. P. (2007). When are tutorial dialogues more effective than reading? *Cognitive Science, 31*, 3–62.

Williams, P. J. (2007). Literacy in the curriculum: Integrating text structure and content area instruction. In D. S. McNamara (Ed.), *Reading comprehension strategies: Theories, interventions, and technologies* (pp. 199–219). Mahwah, NJ: Erlbaum.

Woods, W. (1977). Transition network grammars for natural language analysis. *Communications of the Association for Computing Machinery, 13*, 591–606.

Zipf, G. K. (1949). *Human behaviour and the principle of least effort*. Cambridge, MA: Addison-Wesley Press.

Zwaan, R. A., & Radvansky, G. A. (1998). Situation models in language comprehension and memory. *Psychological Bulletin, 123*, 162–185.

3 Statistical Modeling in Literacy Research

Christopher Schatschneider and Yaacov Petscher
Florida State University

> Remember that all models are wrong; the practical question is how wrong do they have to be to not be useful.
>
> (Box & Draper, 1987, p. 74)

Statistical modeling is ubiquitous in scientific research. Across the vast differences in the subject matter studied by biologists, psychologists, anthropologists, physicists, and educational researchers, one of the constants is the widespread use of statistical modeling. This is not to say that there are not other forms of research that do not use statistical models. In fact, if one were to look at the *Handbook of Reading Research: Volume III* (Kamil, Mosenthal, Pearson, & Barr, 2000), one might get the impression that few literacy researchers engage in statistical modeling. Of the 10 chapters on methods of literacy research, only one chapter (Shanahan, 2000) explicitly talks about using statistical modeling as a part of the methodological approach. With the recent broadening of our "methodological tool bag" in literacy research, it would be useful to examine the benefits and limitations of statistical modeling. To that end, this chapter provides a brief conceptual overview of statistical models, including a discussion of what statistical modeling entails as well an exploration into the philosophical underpinnings of statistical modeling. We also provide a brief overview of statistical modeling in literacy research and end with a discussion of limitations inherent in these models.

WHAT ARE STATISTICAL MODELS?

A formal definition of a statistical model is, oddly enough, beyond the scope of this chapter. A useful starting place would be to define a statistical model as an equation or set of equations that attempts to describe a phenomena being studied. Statistical models accomplish this by using mathematical equations that generate predictions about the observed phenomena. These predictions can be compared to the actual observations to assess how well the model performs in replicating the observed phenomena. By using probability distributions, statistical models also provide inferences about the likelihood that a relation being modeled from a set of observations is due to chance. Finally, in the construction of most statistical models there is an attempt to balance two competing goals—fit and parsimony. A simple illustration may be useful, both in terms of understanding the purpose and usefulness of statistical models, and also revealing some of the basic assumptions that often go unexamined. Let's say that a reading researcher has collected 100 measurements of student reading ability. These observations may show that some students are quite skilled at reading, others are not as skilled, and still others struggle with reading. From these observations, we can attempt to fit some simple statistical models. Models can be useful in describing these reading scores by distilling a large amount of quantitative information into a smaller set of numbers that conveys some potentially useful information about the observations. With these 100 observations, we could compute a mean and variance, for example. Computing a mean and variance is one of the most basic of statistical models. This simple act contains much of the same benefits and limitations that apply to almost all statistical modeling procedures. In computing a mean, we are using a mathematical equation in an attempt to describe a particular phenomenon. In computing the variance, we are using the mean as a predictor of each score, in an attempt to see how well the mean adequately describes the set of observations. The variance is a direct measure of how well the model fits the data. A relatively large variance estimate implies that the mean does not provide as good of a description of those observations while a smaller variance estimate implies that the mean is a better representation of those observations.

This simple example can also shed light on the balancing act of adequate fit to the data versus parsimony of explanation. All statistical models strive to adequately describe the observations to which they are fit. But many researchers also value parsimony as a general principle of science (although others view parsimony as an epistemological preference and not a general principle; see Courtney & Courtney, 2008). Parsimony in the scientific sense refers to the idea that "the simplest explanation is usually the best." Statistical parsimony typically refers to the number of components or parameters in a model (in our example of computing variance, the statistical model had one parameter—the mean) in such a way that all else being equal, fewer parameters are regarded as better or more parsimonious. In our previous example, we used the mean of the observations as our parameter in a statistical model to try and predict each observation. This is one of the simplest models that one can fit to a set of observations, but it is rarely adequate in describing a set of observations. That is, this model is parsimonious, but probably does not represent the data well.

The real strength of statistical modeling comes when we develop two or more models and compare them in terms of their parsimony and model fit (Maxwell & Delaney, 2004). Almost any statistical model that one can think of either implicitly or explicitly entails the comparison of two or more models based on the increase in model fit in relation to the increase in model complexity. Statistical models have a structured way in which they can be compared in order to judge whether a more complicated model sufficiently improves the description of the observations to justify the relative loss of parsimony. Models accomplish this with the help of probability distributions. A probability distribution describes the likelihood that a particular value or estimate will occur under a particular set of conditions. Some probability distributions give the likelihood of observing a particular value or estimate when nothing is operating except differences due to random sampling. These are called central distributions. In common statistical analyses, the t distribution for tests of differences between means and the F distribution for analyses of variance represent just such "known" central distributions. If the value of a statistic derived from a model (such as an F-ratio or t-ratio) is found to be large enough that values that large or larger only occur 5% of the time in a distribution where only random sampling is operating, then most researchers will conclude that it is not likely that this particular F – or t – ratio occurred by chance, and this model provides a significant improvement in explaining the data The use of known probability distributions allows researchers to assign a probability value to the difference between two models that provides a basis by which we can select the more complex model over the simpler model.

PHILOSOPHICAL UNDERPINNINGS IN THE USE OF STATISTICAL MODELS

Statistical models serve as useful tools for scientists who are grounded in the philosophy of empiricism and analytic reductionism. Empiricism is the idea that knowledge arises from experience and observation. Empiricism often favors observations derived from experimentation over passive observations, and rejects evidence based on intuition or reasoning alone. Analytic reductionism is the belief that we can gain understanding of a complex system by understanding the parts of the system and how they interact.

A foundational assumption of empiricism is that nature is lawful (Underwood, 1957; Maxwell & Delaney, 2004). The assumption of lawfulness implies that observations made about nature and used by statistical models are not random or chaotic, and that an inspection of observations can reveal general principles. In this sense, statistical models could be used as mathematical formalizations of our ideas about the general principle being observed (but do not necessarily need to). The assumption of lawfulness has a number of corollaries. One is that nature is also consistent or uniform. The assumption of uniformity implies that the regularity seen in a limited amount of observations should generalize universally. For social science research, this assumption is questionable. But in terms of statistical models, it implies that the model developed on a particular set of observations should be applicable to a new set of observations if the observations come from the same population of observations.

Analytic reductionism rests on the idea of finite causation (Maxwell & Delaney, 2004), or that a phenomena being studied have a finite number of causes. The ability to read, for example, is a complex behavior that has many causes and correlates. The reasons why any one person can comprehend texts are numerous (ranging from cognitive, genetic, neuroanatomical to instruction, home environments, and cultural contexts). Some would argue that the potential causes of reading we investigate are not causes at all, but are actually INUS conditions (Shadish, Cook, & Campbell, 2002). INUS stands for an Insufficient but Nonredundant part of an Unnecessary but Sufficient condition. Let's take reading instruction in the classroom as an example of an INUS condition for a student learning to read. Reading instruction in the classroom is insufficient for the student learning how to read because other factors must be present (the child must be able to attend to the instruction, must not have any neurological damage that would prevent reading, etc.), and it is nonredudant in that it can contribute something unique to all the other reasons a child might learn how to read (either on their own or with help from their parents), it is unnecessary in that there are other mechanisms by which the student could learn how to read (perhaps at home), but it is part of sufficient condition in that in combination with other factors, can also lead to students learning to read. But in terms of finite causation, this implies that there are only a limited number of causes (or INUS conditions) that will explain the ability to read. If there are an unlimited number of causes that can produce reading behavior, then generalizations of findings would be impossible.

Most statistical models are a mathematical outgrowth of empiricism and analytic reductionism. Many scientists believe that nature is lawful and consistent, and that knowledge about a phenomenon can be obtained by making observations. Many scientists also believe that it is fruitful to study only parts of a phenomenon as a way of understanding the whole. *Statistical models facilitate this endeavor by using observations as a means for inferring lawful relationships.* Statistical models are mathematical representations of the scientist's ideas about the lawful relations that exist in nature. Given a set of observations, scientists develop mathematical models that they believe will explain this relationship. Statistical models take into account the fallible nature of observations and that they contain errors. They provide a mathematical basis for judging the adequacy with which the proposed lawful relation explains the observations. But it is important to remember that the use of these models typically implies an adherence to a philosophical tradition to which not all literacy researchers subscribe.

One final comment about statistical models in general. As we stated previously, the inputs into a statistical model are the observations made by the researcher. These observations can come from a variety of environments (research designs), and it is these environments that determine what can be concluded from the results of statistical modeling. As Lord (1953, p. 750) stated, the "numbers don't know where they came from." Statistical models don't know where the numbers come from either. The researcher is responsible to knowing how the observations were obtained, and what conclusions can be drawn from the results of the statistical model.

STATISTICAL MODELING IN LITERACY RESEARCH

Statistical modeling has had an enormous impact on literacy research. The uses of statistical modeling in advancing literacy research can be grouped into a few broad areas that we describe next.

Observation and Measurement

The foundation of an empirical approach to science is observation. However, these observations must take on some kind of symbolic form in order to be useful. Whether these observations are turned into hand-written notes, transcribed verbal recordings, or numeric representations, some kind of symbol-system must be used to record observations. Additionally, it is rare that a researcher in the social sciences is studying something that can be continuously observed. Instead, observations must be sampled from the phenomena being studied, with the assumption that a sample of observations will be a good representation of the phenomena under investigation.. Finally, it is often the case that observations of certain behaviors are easier to obtain if they are elicited by the researcher. Literacy researchers will often set up an artificial environment where reading behaviors can be recorded, for example, or they may ask a teacher to deliver a particular activity or lesson that can provide the researcher with just such behaviors.

Recorded observations take on many forms and serve many purposes. But all observations have one thing in common: To a greater or lesser degree, all observations are prone to error. The idea that observations and measurements contain errors has been around for a long time, and the systematic study of errors in observations since the early 19th century (Tabak, 2005). Every measurement has the possibility of being influenced by error. A researcher can miss something that is occurring in the classroom, students may not answer a question correctly because they are not feeling well, or perhaps they didn't understand what was being asked, or conversely, a student may get an answer correct by luck in guessing. A researcher could also simply miscode a particular response or observation. These are just a couple of examples of potential errors that occur in literacy research. Errors in measurement are unavoidable when conducting science. However, statistical models can aid the researcher in a number of ways. First, the effectiveness of statistical models in helping researchers minimize the impact of error of measurement stems from the notion that most errors in measurement are random rather than systematic; that is, there is no systematic way in which errors are influencing the observations. If the influence of errors on observation is random, then, over the long run, they will cancel each other out. Statistical models can estimate the amount of random error that is influencing a set of observations. Classical Test Theory (CTT: Nunnally & Bernstein, 1994) employs a number of statistical models for which the primary purpose is to estimate the errors in measurements. CTT assumes that anything that can be measured has a "true score" component and an "error score" component, and the models developed in CTT are designed to estimate the percentage of each.

These models are useful to the literacy researcher in a number of ways. First, they help to refine measurements and observations. Statistical models can estimate the amount of error in an observation and can point to ways in which these errors can be minimized. Item-total correlations can be estimated to inspect an items utility in representing the domain being sampled, estimates of inter-observer agreements can be calculated to see where two or more people observing the same phenomena agree or disagree on what is being observed and can give an indication as to which behaviors are most troublesome to find agreement. Statistical models produce estimates of error that can be expected for published observation instruments which aids the literacy researcher in selecting a pre-developed observation instrument if the researcher chooses that route.

More recently, advances in Item Response Theory (IRT; Hambleton, Swaminathan, & Rogers, 1991) have proved to be useful to literacy researchers and have been seen as an improvement over classical test theory. IRT rests on a simple idea—the probability that someone will respond in a particular way is directly related to how much of a particular attribute a person possesses. For example, the probability that a student will be able to read a particular word is dependent upon how much "word reading ability" the student has. The statistical models that support IRT are fairly complex. However, these models also provide a number of useful products. IRT provides for a straightforward way to develop alternate assessment forms so students can be assessed over time while minimizing practice effects. IRT also provides a very powerful means to detect item bias (termed differential item function in IRT) so that items that behave differently for different populations can be removed or minimized. IRT also aids other statistical models in that the ability estimates obtained via IRT are on a true interval scale, which is often one of the assumptions of other statistical models.

Many of the norm-referenced and standardized tests of reading and reading related ability used by researchers have been developed using IRT. Tests such as the Wide Range Achievement Test – 4 (Wilkinson & Robertson, 2006), Woodcock Reading Mastery Test – Revised (Woodcock, 1998), and the Peabody Picture Vocabulary Test – Third Edition (Dunn & Dunn, 1997) are examples of assessments that use IRT as the basis for test development and score reporting. Using scores from an IRT based assessment provides the researcher with a number of benefits including an assurance that the scores obtained from the instrument are on the same scale over the entire age range that is covered in the assessment, which is critical for longitudinal research.

Construct Validation

All areas of science are concerned with establishing the viability of potentially important variables and constructs and statistical modeling can be useful in this endeavor. Construct validity is a problem of generalizing the observations made on a given phenomena to the higher order constructs these observations represent (Shadish et al., 2002). Constructs such as "decoding ability" and "vocabulary knowledge," for example, are unobservable constructs, assumed to exist by researchers; however, the existence of these constructs must be inferred by researchers from samples of behaviors. It would scarcely be possible to conduct science without operationally defining our constructs of interest. Nunnally and Bernstein (1994) argue that there are three major aspects to construct validation: (a) Specify the domain of observables thought to be related to the construct, (b) determine whether those observables are measuring the same thing or different things, and (c) conduct research to see which of those constructs (or really the measures created to represent them) behave in ways are consistent with hypotheses made about those constructs. Statistical modeling is the primary tool for the second aspect of construct validation—determining whether the relationships among our observations are being produced by the same construct or different constructs.

One statistical modeling technique that is ideally suited to this task is structural equation modeling (SEM: Bollen, 1989). SEM provides a means by which a researcher fit different statistical models to a set of observations to see if the covariation seen among the observations is best captured by one or more constructs. One influential example of the use of statistical modeling to assess construct validity is the study conducted by Wagner, Torgesen, Laughon, Simmons, and Rashotte (1993). In this particular study, Wagner and colleagues were attempting to operationally define the construct of phonological processing that was originally posed in Wagner and Torgesen (1987). They constructed a number of assessments that were thought to measure different aspects of phonological processing ability. In this study, they first used SEM to investigate the individual factors that they believed comprised phonological processing. The statistical models that were fit to these data were able to provide these researchers with evidence the items that they had developed were either all tapping the same factor or were tapping different factors. Once they were satisfied with their measurement models, they used SEM to test alternate models of phonological processing that would best represent the construct of phonological processing. As stated in the beginning of this chapter, one of the biggest strengths of statistical modeling is to compare different models against each other in terms of fit and parsimony. These researchers started with the simplest model—that all of the observations developed to assess phonological processing measure just one construct. They then proposed more complex models that may also best represent the covariation seen among the observations. The results of these model comparisons revealed two phonological awareness constructs (phonological analysis and synthesis), a phonological memory construct, and two phonological code retrieval efficiency constructs. Further research on phonological awareness found that the two phonological awareness constructs are probably better characterized as one unitary construct (Schatschneider, Francis, Foorman, Fletcher, & Mehta, 1999; Anthony et al., 2002). This study is an excellent example of the use of statistical modeling in literacy research to inform construct validation. Further research has also validated the usefulness of phonological processing as a useful construct when studying how students learn to read.

Identifying Relationships

Studies of individual difference have fruitfully used statistical modeling to identify important relationships between constructs as they relate to reading (Bowey, 2005). A variety of statistical models have been employed to analyze data from these individual differences studies. Simple correlations, multiple regression and SEM are the most common statistical models in an individual difference study. In most individual difference studies of literacy, researchers attempt to find important correlates of word reading and/or comprehension skills. Many of the individual differences studies of cognitive correlates of reading ability are searching for the cognitive subcomponents that are thought to be necessary for efficient word reading or reading comprehension skills. Bowey (2005) reviewed a large body of individual difference studies and identified six constructs that have consistently been found to reliably relate to reading ability in the early grade: (a) verbal ability (Bowey, 1995; Cronin & Carver, 1998), (b) phonological memory (Badian, 2000; Wagner, Torgesen, & Rashotte, 1994); (c) speech perception and production (Scarborough, 1990); (d) phonological awareness (Wagner et al., 1994; Schatschneider, Fletcher, Francis, Carlson, & Foorman, 2004); (e) letter name knowledge (deJong & van der Leij, 1999; Schatschneider et al., 2004); and (f) rapid automatized naming (Wagner et al., 1994; Wolf, Bally, & Morris, 1986; Schatschneider et al., 2004).

Individual differences studies in reading are not restricted to the search for cognitive correlates of reading skill. Many literacy researchers have also looked for environmental and social factors that correlate with reading ability. Broad environmental factors such as socioeconomic status (Arnold & Doctoroff, 2003) and mother's education (Riciutti, 1999) as well as parental expectations of achievement (Hill, 2001), and home literacy environments (Burgess, Hecht, & Lonigan, 2002) have all been shown to be consistently correlated with children's reading ability.

Statistical models such as multiple regression and SEM have helped identify these constructs as important correlates of reading ability. These models have done so by providing the researcher the ability to identify which constructs have a unique relationship with reading, above and beyond other constructs. This is an important tool for researchers to have because these models provide evidence that a particular construct provides non-redundant information in its relation to reading ability. If we view reading ability as something with multiple causes, the use of statistical models in individual differences studies can provide the literacy researcher with clues as to which construct may be an INUS condition for reading ability.

Of course, it is well known that correlations do not prove causation. Many constructs may be correlated with reading because of a shared relationship with another construct. However, correlations do provide a minimally necessary condition for a causal relationship between two constructs. If there is no correlation, there can be no causal relationship. Individual differences studies provide crucial information to literacy researchers in that they point to constructs that, if interventions can be developed to improve, may help children become better readers. Not all of the constructs identified through correlational research will be helpful, and some of them may only be helpful for certain students in certain contexts. However, the statistical models used in individual difference studies can provide us with good leads in the search for identifying possible causes in the individual differences seen in students reading ability. But it remains for experimental research to determine whether interesting correlations represent real causes.

Experiments and Causal Conclusions

Empiricism has its basis in observation, and especially in observations of experiments (Maxwell & Delaney, 2004). The goal of experimentation is to discover the effects of potential causes (Shadish et al., 2002). How can we know if something is a "cause" of something else? Philosopher John Stuart Mill (1843/1987) proposed three conditions for inferring cause: (a) The potential cause must *precede* the effect, (b) the potential cause must be *related* to the effect, and (c) there is no other plausible alternative explanation for the effect. Shadish and colleagues (2002) suggest that experiments are well suited to studying cause and effect relationships because they (a) ensure that a presumed cause is deliberately manipulated and, thereby, precedes the observed effect, (b) incorporate procedures that help determine whether the cause is related to the effect, and (c) incorporate procedures to minimize and/or assess the influence of extraneous factors that could produce the effect presumed to be attributed to the cause.

To be able to infer that a potential cause has had an effect in an experiment, it is crucial that we have some knowledge of what would have happened if the potential cause is absent. Inferring effects by comparing them to what would have happened if the potential cause had been absent is called counterfactual inferencing (Shadish et al., 2002). The essence of counterfactual inferencing is that we can only know if event C caused event E if it were the case that if C had not occurred, E would not have occurred.

In literacy research, it is not possible to know what would have happened if a particular intervention, for example, had not been delivered. This is why hypothetical counterfactuals are developed through the use of random assignment. The control group in a randomized experiment represents our best guess as to what would have happened to the treatment group had they not been given treatment.

Statistical models play a large role in the analysis of observations from experiments in literacy research. Because hypothetical counterfactuals have to be employed based on other groups of students, it is certainly possible that the control group may differ from the treatment group based solely on chance. Statistical models are ideally suited to help the researcher discern chance differences between groups from real effects. Statistical models do so by assigning a probability value to the possibility that the observations made in an experiment are solely due to chance factors. This is accomplished by comparing two models—one where the only actor operating in the experiment is chance differences due to sampling variation and another where both chance differences and treatment group differences explain the results. If the statistical model that includes the treatment group in its equation is a better model than the alternative model that does not include the experimental grouping, then the researchers have evidence to conclude that the experimental manipulation is the cause of the difference. A "better model" in this context is defined as one that provides a significantly better prediction of the subjects observed scores by knowing whether or not they received the treatment, in relation to the loss of parsimony that comes from the addition of this grouping variable into the equation. Whether the model that contains the group membership variable is a significantly better model is determined by comparing the improvement in prediction obtained using this model to a known probability distribution (at distribution, for example), and if the probability that this improvement in prediction occurred by chance is sufficiently low (most commonly set at less than a 5% chance), then we would conclude that this model is a better model. The number of experimental studies in literacy has grown rapidly over the past decade. In the United States, the Institute for Education Science (IES) was created in 2002 as a part of the U.S. Department of Education. Its mission is "to provide rigorous evidence on which to ground education practice and policy. By identifying what works, what doesn't, and why, we intend to improve the outcomes of education for all students, particularly those at risk of failure" (http://ies.ed.gov/director/). To advance that mission, IES provides millions of dollars for randomized controlled research trials to determine whether particular programs and practices have a causal relationship to improved reading outcomes.

However, it bears repeating that in literacy research, we are not typically studying cause and effect relationships, but INUS conditions. In a true causal relationship, when a cause occurs, an effect will occur every time. INUS conditions, however, are a sufficient condition in that only in combination with other factors, do they contribute to reading ability. This has profound implications for drawing conclusions from randomized controlled experiments in literacy research. What this means is that an effect will most likely not occur every time for every student. Because the ability to read has multiple causes, and the experiment being conducted could not possibly intervene on all of them, some students will not respond to a particular intervention, or some may respond more than others. In this sense, our models become "probabilistic prediction models" (Stanovich, 2003) in that an identified "effective" intervention only increases the probability that a student will benefit from the intervention. It is of critical importance that literacy researchers explain what they mean when they say they are running studies that draw "causal conclusions," and discuss the limitations of their findings. Additionally, consumers of science need to be made aware that these studies do not guarantee that an intervention will work for every student, and also that if an intervention does not work for one student, it does not negate the possibility that it would work for another.

USE OF STATISTICAL MODELING IN LITERACY RESEARCH: AN EXEMPLAR

Statistical models serve as valuable tools for conducting empirical research. From assessing the quality of our measurements to determining the effectiveness of our interventions, statistical models provide an objective means by which we can evaluate our research questions. In this chapter, we have touched upon a number of broad uses of statistical models. At this point, we thought it would be illuminating to describe the use of statistical models in the context of a single study. Out of the hundreds of potential studies to describe in more detail, we selected Wagner et al. (1993). We chose Wagner et al. as an exemplar because their work has been influential in our study of early reading skills and they used some relatively sophisticated statistical models to perform construct validation and to identify important relationships.

Wagner et al. (1993) administered a number of assessments that were hypothesized to be related to early reading development to a group of kindergarten and second grade students. Many of the assessments used in the study were developed by Wagner and colleagues and the choice of which assessments to give to the students was grounded in the theoretical work done by Wagner and Torgesen (1987). In their 1987 paper, Wagner and Torgesen hypothesized the existence of three correlated but distinct constructs that they believed to be causally related to early reading development: Phonological awareness, phonological recoding in lexical access, and phonetic recoding in working memory. These three conceptual constructs comprise the superordinate construct of phonological processing. In order to provide evidence for the existence of these constructs, Wagner and colleagues employed or created measures that they believed would tap the skills that were thought to encompass these three constructs and administered them to kindergarten and second grade children in order to obtain estimates of how much these measures covary with each other. These covariances provide the basis by which researchers hypothesize what causes some measures to covary. Measures that covary highly are thought to do so because performance on those measures is determined by the same underlying latent (unobserved) ability. Performances on assessments that do not covary strongly are thought to be driven by different cognitive constructs.

Wagner et al. (1993) then fit a series of structural equation models to the covariance matrix of the measures of phonological processing. Structural equation models create predicted covariance matrices that can be compared to the observed covariance matrix obtained from the data. The comparison of the predicted covariance matrices to the observed covariance matrix determines the model fit, or how well the model explains the original variances and covariances of the observed variables. The difference between the predicted and observed covariance matrix from any structural equation model can be expressed as a chi-square value (which represents the sum of the squared difference between the elements in the predicted and observed covariance matrices weighted by sample size). This chi-square value can then be compared to a chi-square distribution table to determine statistical significance. Because the chi-square is based on the squared differences between observed and predicted covariances, models that fit better will have smaller chi-square values, and nonsignficant probability values associated with a model will typically indicate a good fit.

A stronger use of structural equation models comes when we can compare two predicted models against each other in terms how well each explains the observed covariance matrix. Wagner et al. (1993) employed this model comparison approach when they proposed to test a series of five alternate models of phonological processing abilities. They argued for the potential viability of each of these models including models where all of the covariance observed can be explained by one common latent factor (the most parsimonious solution) and another model where each of the abilities thought to measure phonological processing was its own latent construct (least parsimonious but most likely will provide the best fit to the data).

But as is true with many proposed hypotheses, the models did not directly conform to their pre-conceived ideas. As stated before, the researchers proposed that three abilities were thought to comprise phonological processing: Phonological awareness, phonological recoding in lexical access, and phonetic recoding in working memory. However, when testing their models, they found that their measures of phonological awareness were better modeled as having two latent factors instead of only one. They named the two factors phonological analysis and phonological synthesis. Additionally, the measures thought to tap phonological recoding in lexical access were also best represented by two latent constructs that they subsequently named isolated naming and serial naming. This unexpected finding raised the number of models they wanted to test from five to seventeen. After fitting a series of models, assessing their fit, and comparing them to each other, Wagner et al. (1993) arrived at a four factor solution for kindergarten students and a five factor solution in second grade. These models were found to be the best balance between model fit and parsimony. Once they arrived at these solutions, they then used the best fitting model from second grade and used those factors to predict word recognitions skills. After controlling for general cognitive ability, they found that the phonological processing factors accounted for an additional 20% of the variance observed in word recognition skills above and beyond general cognitive ability.

In Wagner et al. (1993) we see many of the advantages of using statistical modeling. First, by formally testing their measurement models, they uncovered that in their data phonological awareness and phonological recoding in lexical access should be represented by two factors each instead of only one. Without examining this first, the researcher can only argue on conceptual grounds that measures tap the same latent ability. In the case of Wagner et al., measures that tap these constructs may have been aggregated together inappropriately. Second, their use of the model comparison approach gave them an empirical justification for deciding which constructs comprise the domain of phonological processing. Finally, the usefulness of assessing phonological processing was supported by the statistical models that demonstrated the explanatory power of these constructs in predicting word reading skills above and beyond general cognitive processing.

LIMITATIONS OF STATISTICAL MODELING

Statistical modeling is an incredibly powerful tool for literacy researchers. Statistical models aid in the construction of observational tools, the development and identification of constructs, and in understanding the relations of constructs to one another and to reading. They can be used for prediction, and they also assist in the identification of "causal" relationships. It is our belief that every literacy researcher should have statistical modeling in their methodological toolbag as one of the useful means by which questions in literacy can be answered.

To that end, it is also helpful to discuss the limitations of statistical models. There is a tool for every job, and it's important to know the strengths and weaknesses of each tool. First, there is the obvious limitation that all statistical models rest upon certain mathematical assumptions. The consequences of violating these assumptions range from minimal to severe. Much has been written about the assumptions that underlie our models and the consequences of violating those assumptions. Less obvious are the conceptual limitations of statistical modeling. First, statistical models are limited to observations that can be turned into numbers (or at least categories). This limits models to those areas of literacy research where our observations of literacy can be quantified. Statistical models are not designed to directly analyze or synthesize qualitative information. This can often limit the types of questions that can get asked if a literacy researcher only uses statistical models. Just as we recommended that all literacy researchers should be versed in the use of statistical models, we also advocate that literacy researchers need to be able to do more than just employ statistical modeling. As the saying goes, if the only tool one has is a hammer, then one tends to see every problem as a nail.

Another limitation of statistical models is that they are only as good as the observations made by the researcher. The researcher interjects his bias in regards to which observations about a phenomena are made and which are not collected. In studying literacy, it would be almost impossible for a researcher to collect observations on all the biological, cognitive, social, emotional, and environmental influence on reading behavior, even though most literacy researchers would acknowledge the importance of all these areas. Statistical models can only provide information in regards to the observations that are collected, not the information that is ignored.

Another issue arises when two or more statistical models cannot be differentiated from each other. That is, is oftentimes the case that two or more models can provide a reasonable explanation of a set of observations (Breiman, 2001). These models may provide different estimates as to the importance of particular constructs, or perhaps may not even include the same constructs. Statistical models also have a difficult time distinguishing between nonlinear relationships and interactions (Lubinski & Humphreys, 1990), which also has implications for inferring which constructs are more closely related to reading ability than others.

A final limitation is related to the quote that opens this chapter. All models are wrong. But what does this statement mean? It means that all models are imperfect representations of what is occurring in nature. Models by their very nature are reductionistic and will not be able to fully explain the complex relationships we are attempting to understand. Statistical models will never tell us with certainty whether something is an exact cause of something else. Probability is inherent in every statistical model, and probabilities imply the possibility that a model is incorrect. But simply because this is true, it does not imply that models are not useful. Statistical models provide us with an incrementally better understanding of reading ability and development. They aid us in advancing our understanding of the components and correlates of reading, they give us ideas about which correlates may be fruitful to intervene with in order to enable more students to read, and they provide us with the ability to predict if our interventions will work on future students.

REFERENCES

Anthony, J. L., Lonigan, C. J., Burgess, S. R., Driscol, K., Phillips, B. M., & Cantor, B. G., (2002). Structure of preschool phonological sensitivity: Overlapping sensitivity to rhyme, words, syllables, and phonemes. *Journal of Experimental Child Psychology, 82*, 65–92.

Arnold, D. H., & Doctoroff, G. L. (2003). The early education of socioeconomically disadvantaged children. *Annual Review of Psychology, 54*, 517–545.

Badian, N. A. (2000). Do preschool orthographic skills contribute to the prediction of reading? In N. A. Badian (Ed.), *Prediction and prevention of reading failure* (pp. 31–56). Parkton, MD: York.

Bollen, K. A. (1989). *Structural equations with latent variables: Wiley Series in Probability and Mathematical Statistics.* New York: Wiley

Box, G. P., & Draper, N. R. (1987). *Empirical model-building and response surfaces.* New York: Wiley.

Bowey, J. A. (1995). Socioeconomic status differences in preschool phonological sensitivity and first grade reading achievement. *Journal of Educational Psychology, 87*, 476–487.

Bowey, J. A. (2005). Predicting individual differences in learning to read. In M. J. Snowling & C. Hulme (Eds.), *The science of reading: A handbook* (pp. 155–172). Malden, MA: Blackwell.

Breiman, L. (2001). Statistical modeling: The two cultures. *Statistical Science, 16*, 199–231.

Burgess, S. R., Hecht, S. A., & Lonigan, C. J. (2002). Relations of home literacy to the development of reading-related abilities: A one-year longitudinal study. *Reading Research Quarterly, 37*, 408–426.

Courtney, A., & Courtney, M. (2008). Comments regarding "On the nature of science." *Physics in Canada, 64*, 7–8.

Cronin, V., & Carver, P. (1998). Phonological sensitivity, rapid naming, and beginning reading. *Applied Psycholinguistics, 19*, 447–461.

de Jong, P. F., & van der Leij, A. (1999). Specific contributions of phonological abilities to early reading acquisition: Results from a Dutch latent variable longitudinal study. *Journal of Educational Psychology, 91*, 450–476.

Dunn, L. M., & Dunn, L. M. (1997). *Peabody Picture Vocabulary Test–Third Edition.* Circle Pines, MN: American Guidance Service.

Hambleton, R. K., Swaminathan, H., & Rogers, H. J. (1991). *Fundamentals of item response theory.* Newbury Park, CA: Sage.

Hill, N. E. (2001). Parenting and academic socialization as they relate to school readiness: The role of ethnicity and family income. *Journal of Educational Psychology, 93*, 686–697.

Kamil, M. L., Mosenthal, P. B., Pearson, P. D., & Barr, R. (2000). *Handbook of reading research: Volume III.* Mahwah, NJ: Erlbaum.

Lord, F. M. (1953). On the statistical treatment of football numbers. *American Psychologist, 8*, 750–751.

Lubinski, D., & Humphreys, L. G. (1990). Assessing spurious "moderator effects": Illustrated substantively with the hypothesized "synergistic" relation between spatial and mathematical ability. *Psychological Bulletin, 107*, 385–393.

Maxwell, S. E., & Delaney, H. D. (2004). *Designing experiments and analyzing data: A model comparison approach* (2nd ed.). Mahwah, NJ: Erlbaum.

Mill, J. S. (1987). A system of logic. In J. S. Mill, J. Bentham, & R. Ryan (Eds.), *Utilitarianism and other essays* (pp. 113–131). New York: Viking. (Original work published 1843)

Nunnally, J., & Bernstein, I. (1994). *Psychometric theory* (3rd ed.). New York: McGraw Hill.

Riciutti, H. N. (1999). Single parenthood and school readiness in White, Black, and Hispanic 6- and 7-year-olds. *Journal of Family Psychology, 13,* 450–465.

Scarborough, H. S. (1990). Very early language deficits in dyslexic children. *Child Development, 61,* 1728–1743.

Schatschneider, C., Fletcher, J. M., Francis, D. J., Carlson, C., & Foorman, B. R. (2004). Kindergarten prediction of reading skills: A longitudinal comparative analysis. *Journal of Educational Psychology, 96,* 265–282.

Schatschneider, C., Francis, D. J., Foorman, B. F., Fletcher, J. M., & Mehta, P. (1999). The dimensionality of phonological awareness: An application of item response theory. *Journal of Educational Psychology, 91,* 467–478.

Shadish, W. R., Cook, T. D., & Campbell, D. T. (2002). *Experimental and quasi-experimental designs for generalized causal inference.* New York: Houghton Mifflin.

Shanahan, T. (2000). Research syntheses: Making sense of the accumulation of knowledge in reading. In M. L Kamil, P. B. Mosenthal, P. D. Pearson, & R. Barr (Eds.), *Handbook of reading research: Volume III* (pp. 209–226). Mahwah, NJ: Erlbaum.

Stanovich, K. E. (2003). Understanding the styles of science in the study of reading. *Scientific Studies of Reading, 7,* 105–126.

Tabak, J. (2005*). Probability and statistics: The science of uncertainty.* New York: Checkmark Books.

Underwood, B.J . (1957). *Psychological research.* New York: Appleton, Century, and Crofts.

Wagner, R. K., & Torgesen, J. K. (1987). The nature of phonological processing and its causal role in the acquisition of reading skills. *Psychological Bulletin, 101,* 192–212.

Wagner, R. K., Torgesen, J. K., Laughon, P., Simmons, K., & Rashotte, C. A. (1993). Development of young children's phonological processing abilities. *Journal of Educational Psychology, 85,* 83–103.

Wagner, R. K., Torgesen, J. K., & Rashotte, C. A. (1994). Development of reading-related phonological processing abilities: New evidence of bidirectional causality from a latent variable longitudinal study. *Developmental Psychology, 30,* 73–87.

Wilkinson, G. S., & Robertson, G. J. (2006). *Wide Range Achievement Test Fourth Edition.* Lutz, FL: Psychological Assessment Resources.

Wolf, M., Bally, H., & Morris, R. (1986). Automaticity, retrieval processes, and reading: Longitudinal study in average and impaired readers. *Journal of Educational Psychology, 91,* 415–438.

Woodcock, R. W. (1998). *Woodcock Reading Mastery Tests-Revised/Normative Update.* Circle Pines, MN: American Guidance Service.

4 Designing and Conducting Literacy Intervention Research

Donald D. Deshler, Michael F. Hock,
Frances M. Ihle, and Caroline A. Mark
University of Kansas

Increasingly, literacy intervention research is being used by policy makers and school leaders to inform decision-making, as well as by practitioners to influence how instruction is provided to improve student outcomes (Pressley, Graham, & Harris, 2006). As a result, intervention researchers must design interventions and conduct studies that are seen as credible by these various stakeholders. In short, interventions must lead to statistically and socially significant outcomes *and* it must be feasible to implement them within the prevailing constraints and complexities of school settings.

The purpose of this chapter is to (a) provide a synopsis of the Pigott and Barr (2000) chapter in the *Handbook of Reading Research, Volume III* on intervention research; (b) summarize important federal initiatives that have influenced the reading research enterprise; (c) describe defining features and trends in conducting literacy research in school settings; (d) discuss emerging trends in literacy research; and (e) discuss implications for theory, practice, policy, and research.

BUILDING ON PIGOTT AND BARR

Pigott and Barr (2000) established a strong foundation for conceptualizing and understanding the multiple roles and importance of well-designed research in their chapter, *Designing Programmatic Interventions.* Their overall goal was to inform researchers about how to conduct rigorous studies of programmatic interventions so that theory, practice, and policy decisions were, in fact, informed decisions. As such, the authors cautioned researchers to think carefully about how to conduct studies of literacy. They defined programmatic intervention as going beyond typical intervention research in which a single intervention is tested for a relatively short period of time to evaluation of a line of program research. Short-term, smaller studies are often confounded with validity issues (e.g., nested nature of the data, lack of statistical power, issues of dosage) that can be better controlled in a line of programmatic research extended over time.

The authors also described research designs that can be used to demonstrate *effectiveness* (experimental and quasi-experimental), inform our understanding of *how* interventions work (qualitative studies), and enhance the design and development of interventions (design studies). According to the authors, the overarching goal of the research methods they were advocating is to determine if the intervention works, how it works, and for whom (teachers and students) it works. While that language has been modified somewhat to include issues of cultural context, Pigott and Barr's points are as relevant today as they were in 2000. From this strong foundation, we extend the knowledgebase of programmatic research by discussing recent changes in federal policy and emerging trends in research designs, and situate knowledge in the complex world of schools and schooling.

IMPORTANT MILESTONES AFTER 2000

During the first few years of the 21st century, several federal initiatives and federally financed reports have had a significant influence on the funding and conducting of reading research, including the way research findings are viewed and used. After more than two years of intensive work, the National Reading Panel (NRP) submitted its report to Congress in April of 2000. This report contained an extensive review of the reading literature based on experimental and quasi-experimental research studies and a synthesis of findings in several areas of reading instruction. The research findings pointed to an approach to teaching reading that included the following five components: (a) phonemic awareness, (b) phonics, (c) fluency, (d) vocabulary, and (e) text comprehension (National Institute of Child Health and Human Development [NICHD], 2000). The immediate impact of the NRP report was seen when the Reading First initiative, under the auspices of No Child Left Behind (NCLB), integrated the five essential areas of reading into its implementation requirements.

Despite the wide-reaching impact of the NRP report as it exerted its influence on policy and practice in reading instruction, debate about the definition of education research persisted. Some policy makers viewed education research as broken (Sroufe, 2003), and disagreement about how to narrow the achievement gap continued (McDaniel, Sims, & Miskel, 2001). However, Reading First exponentially increased the demand for funding to implement scientifically based reading instruction, yet a centralized information and funding source for rigorous and instructionally relevant research did not exist. The Department of Education's Office of Education Research and Improvement (OERI), though perhaps suited to assume this role in name, did not have the capacity to address states' needs. When the House introduced H.R. 4875 (February, 2001) to reauthorize OERI, the language defining educational research in this bill differed from the definition of educational research in NCLB.

These differing definitions led the U.S. Department of Education's National Educational Research Policy and Priorities Board to charge the National Research Council (NRC) with the responsibility of examining the nature of scientific research in education. The NRC committee concluded that guiding principles, rather than specific methods, should define scientific research in education. Shavelson and Towne's *Scientific Research in Education* (2002) was the culmination of the NRC work. It included six guiding principles:

- Pose significant questions that can be investigated empirically.
- Link research to relevant theory.
- Use methods that permit direct investigation of the question.
- Provide a coherent and explicit chain of reasoning.
- Replicate and generalize across studies.
- Disclose research to encourage professional scrutiny and critique. (p. 52)

A new piece of legislation, which ultimately became the Education Sciences Reform Act of 2002, used these recommendations to broaden the definition of scientific research in education. This law defined scientifically based research in a manner similar to the NRC report by emphasizing the importance of direct investigation, a logical chain of reasoning, and generalizable results. This law also established the Institute of Education Sciences (IES). IES's mission is to provide rigorous evidence upon which to ground education practice and policy (Eisenhart & Towne, 2003; Sroufe, 2003). The impact of the NRP and NRC reports on reading researchers continues to be significant because they brought about changes in how reading research was viewed and led to legislation that contained current standards for "scientific" research in education.

Another significant initiative during this period was the establishment of the Partnership for Reading (authorized by NCLB). This partnership is a collaborative effort by three federal agencies: the National Institute for Literacy, the Eunice Kennedy Shriver National Institute for Child Health and Human Development, and the U.S. Department of Education. Following the NRP, the Partnership for Reading funded panels that reviewed the literature on both early childhood and adult literacy. The newly formed IES likewise funded the efforts of a panel that studied language-minority children and youth (McCardle & Chhabra, 2004). Though few Department of Education dollars have traditionally been designated for the purposes of dissemination, the Partnership's stated purpose is to disseminate information regarding evidenced practices in education.

DEFINING FEATURES AND TRENDS IN LITERACY RESEARCH

Given the difficulty of teaching students to become proficient readers and the complex dynamics that exist in today's schools, designing interventions that are powerful, practical, and robust is a great challenge. These challenges are especially pronounced when working with students who have learning disabilities or who are English learners; moreover, the challenge is magnified when working with these students in secondary school settings (Deshler & Schumaker, 2006).

To overcome these challenges, researchers must use sophisticated research tools and approaches. Additionally, since policy makers increasingly rely on research findings to inform public policy decisions, it is incumbent on researchers to address policy-relevant questions and communicate their findings in easy-to-understand ways.

Pressley and colleagues (2006) analyzed the state of educational intervention research through a literacy lens. A summary of four of the key factors that they described as characterizing intervention research follows.

1. *Diverse theoretical orientations.* The literacy interventions described in the research literature are often grounded in or influenced by a broad array of theories ranging from theories about how phonological processes are foundational in language (Adams, 1990) to how images are represented in the mind (Sadoski & Paivio, 2000) to how schemata are formed and enhance comprehension (Anderson & Pearson, 1984). Instructional methodology (teaching), like the interventions themselves, has also been linked to specific theoretical orientations. Most of them can be conceptualized on a continuum from more mechanistic protocols (e.g., direct explanation and modeling) to more socio-constructivist protocols (e.g., learner adaptation and generalization of initially learned strategies).

2. *Interventions of varying complexity.* Most of the research on literacy interventions has focused on specific interventions that are targeted on a given skill or strategy (e.g., a self-questioning strategy). Such interventions are taught with a prescribed instructional methodology that typically involves modeling, scaffolded practice opportunities, and generalization instruction (e.g., Schumaker & Deshler, 2006). Increasingly, intervention packages consisting of several components have been designed to address the literacy needs of children in a more coordinated, comprehensive manner (e.g., Schoenbach, Greenleaf, Cziko, & Hurwitz, 1999). Intervention packages are often based on an array of smaller, focused interventions that are orchestrated together across classes or grades and may be designed as a school-wide literacy program (e.g., Slavin & Madden, 2006). Designing and conducting evaluations on focused, distinct interventions is generally easier than assessing more complex interventions (Raudenbush, 2005). Alternate research strategies/designs are needed to enable us to better understand the complex dynamics at play in multi-component interventions across multiple settings that involve several implementers (Deshler, 1996).

3. *Diverse research approaches.* Recently, renewed attention has been given to the potential value of randomized control trials (RCTs), sometimes referred to as the "gold standard" of the research enterprise (e.g., Coalition for Evidence-based Policy, 2003). In many instances, however, randomization is not possible or feasible. In such cases, quasi-experimental designs may be used in which students, classrooms, or schools are carefully matched.

Even when randomized field trials are possible, recent thinking about the assumptions underlying RCTs has come under scrutiny. For example, the use of RCTs in and of themselves does not guarantee that threats to internal validity will be controlled (McMillan, 2007). Such threats include random assignment at a level of analysis that ignores the nested nature of the intervention, lack of within-intervention fidelity, differential mortality of participants, weakness in instrumentation, diffusion of the intervention across treatments, subject and experimenter effects, and novelty effects due to change to established procedures. Indeed, according to McMillan, in some cases RCTs pose more threats to internal validity than highly controlled quasi-experiments. In short, despite their advantages, RCTs still require that researchers rigorously address threats to validity.

When experimental or quasi-experimental designs are used, important information may be missed if the primary focus of an experiment is on student outcomes alone. Thus, increased attention is being given to qualitative or naturalistic research strategies that can be used to study the broader context and the broad array of processes and conditions that potentially influence the implementation of the intervention and the behavior of teachers and students as they interact with the intervention (Lincoln & Guba, 1985). Such strategies can help illuminate the dynamics surrounding very complex interventions or programs. Additionally, in conjunction with RCTs or quasi-experimental studies, qualitative methodologies can shed light on some of the unintended consequences induced by the intervention in specific contexts.

Finally, new statistical tools enable researchers to examine differences in effects relative to rates of growth (growth curve analysis) as well as interactions among interventions and school and child variables (nested models such as hierarchical linear modeling). In short, as the complexity of the intervention increases (the number of components, the number of players involved, the breadth of reach of the intervention, etc.), the value of using mixed-methods models that tap both quantitative and qualitative methods becomes increasingly apparent (Chatterji, 2004).

4. *Diverse measures.* Intervention research on literacy increases in value as the number and variety of measures increase. Specifically, it is important to measure *both* the impact of an intervention *and* how it works (i.e., how the student responds to it or how the teacher teaches it). For example, if students are taught a self-questioning strategy, it is important to determine the impact of this instruction on key dependent measures (e.g., increase in reading comprehension scores). It is equally as informative to take measures on how students respond to certain lesson features, as well as how fluently teachers teach various lesson components, and so on.

Data that measure factors other than the expected outcomes can shed important light on interactions between teachers, students, and intervention materials; they may even reveal serendipitous transfer (or, alternatively, unanticipated depressing effects on other features of the curriculum). Use of such data can facilitate adjustments and refinements in various intervention components. This is not a trivial matter, especially in consequential policy contexts. That is, if the primary measures are outcomes on large-scale tests (e.g., state assessments), decision makers may prematurely jettison an intervention program for the wrong reasons or adopt a program that shows superficial gains to the detriment of deep learning.

EMERGING TRENDS IN LITERACY RESEARCH

With Pressley et al.'s (2006) summary of the literacy intervention research literature as a backdrop, we unpack three factors that are (or should be) gaining increased attention by literacy researchers; specifically, (a) expanding the methodological landscape, (b) determining the cost-effectiveness of literacy interventions, and (c) rethinking knowledge creation and utilization strategies. Finally, we offer an example of an integrated intervention research model that embodies many of these elements.

Expanding the Methodological Landscape

As literacy researchers continue to seek ways to more fully understand and meaningfully study literacy instruction within the context of complex educational environments, the need for increasingly sophisticated research tools is more acute (McCardle, Chhabra, & Kapinus, 2008). As mentioned earlier, statistical tools such as hierarchical linear modeling and growth curve analysis have added to the methodological toolbox for researchers traditionally operating primarily from a quantitative perspective (Shavelson & Towne, 2002).

The late 1980s and early 1990s witnessed the emergence of lines of work that represented a different orientation to the educational research enterprise. Specifically, several researchers began to question the ecological validity of the contexts in conventional experiments. Work by Newman (1990, 1992), Brown (1992), and Collins (1992) gave rise to a paradigm that came to be known by several names, including design research, design experiments, design studies, formative experiments, formative evaluation, and engineering research (van den Akker, Gravemeijer, McKenney, & Nieveen, 2007). For our purposes, the term "design research" will be used.

Plomp (2007) defined educational design research as "the systematic study of designing, developing and evaluating educational interventions (i.e., programs, teaching-learning strategies and materials, products and systems) as solutions to such problems … (design research) also aims at advancing our knowledge about the characteristics of these interventions and the processes to design and develop them" (p. 9).

Van den Akker (1999) and the Design-Based Research Collective (2003) argued that traditional educational research is often divorced from the problems and issues of everyday practice and as such provides information of limited value to practitioners. Additionally, they posited that many traditional research approaches (experiments, surveys, and correlational analyses with their emphasis on description) do not sufficiently account for the contextual complexities of the educational process and, therefore, do not provide prescriptions that are useful for the problems practitioners encounter on the front lines.

Despite the general agreement among researcher regarding the utility of design studies, there is some confusion in the field as to what constitutes this methodology. Reinking and Bradley (2008) have attempted to provide some clarity to this issue by identifying seven defining characteristics of design research (they refer to these studies as formative and design experiments). According to the authors, the fewer of these characteristics that are evident, the less likely it is that researchers are operating within the general parameters of this approach:

1. *Intervention-centered in authentic instructional contexts.* The primary function of design research is to study instructional interventions. The intervention can be a new one that is in its formative stages of development or a well-established intervention that is being studied using methodologies that were not used when it was initially designed or validated. The intervention might be a set of activities designed to accomplish a particular instructional goal (e.g., Gersten, 2005). Regardless, the investigation takes place in authentic settings with

all of the inherent variations and complexities that are often controlled by the researcher in more traditional, tightly designed studies.

2. *Theoretical.* As in traditional research paradigms, theory plays a role, but the role is different. Cobb, Confrey, diSessa, Lehrer, and Schauble (2003) noted that the purpose of design research is "to develop a class of theories about both the process of learning and the means that are designed to support learning" (p. 9). They further indicate that the theories that emerge from design research tend to be more modest and local than many overarching explanatory theories. Palincsar (2005) reminded us that while a primary goal of design research is to improve the way in which an instructional protocol operates, it also places a premium on advancing theory or developing theory that applies to specific local conditions.

3. *Goal-oriented.* Since design research is focused on improving student outcomes in authentic educational settings, it follows that researchers' work is driven by explicit goals about the intervention and why the intervention is important. This goal(s) becomes the benchmark against which daily work with the intervention is measured and against which refinements or adjustments are made. In short, the importance of the goal provides the rationale for conducting the study.

   An example would be the research of Fritschmann, Deshler, and Schumaker (2007), who designed interventions to enhance the ability of struggling adolescent learners to draw inferences from written text. Multiple iterations of the intervention were tested in order to develop an instructional design that was powerful enough to enable students to achieve predetermined instructional targets.

4. *Adaptive and iterative.* One of the most salient characteristics of design research is the commitment of researchers to ongoing adaptations in the design of the intervention to increase the responsiveness of the intervention to the needs of students and teachers. Researchers who employ traditional experimental studies are concerned with issues surrounding fidelity of implementation. In order to be satisfied that outcomes observed are due primarily to the effects of the intervention, it is imperative that evidence be collected to verify that it was taught with fidelity in accordance with the specified intervention protocol (e.g., O'Donnell, 2008; Sterling-Turner, Watson, & Moore, 2002).

   Design researchers take a contrary perspective; they fully anticipate that the parameters of their intervention will evolve over time as they learn what changes must be made in certain features of the intervention to better meet the needs of participants within a given setting.

5. *Transformative.* An intervention that is the object of a design study may have the potential to positively transform the environment for teaching and learning. Indeed, Kelly (2007) indicated that design research was best suited for open, or what Rittel and Webber (1973) called wicked, problems. While these kinds of problems are the most vexing, and often the most resistant to intervention, if a solution is found, it is likely to have a transformative effect on teaching and learning. For example, most interventions for struggling adolescent readers have fallen short of closing the large achievement gap that many of these students face (Deshler, Palincsar, Biancarosa, & Nair, 2007; Viadro, 2009). Given the shortage of instructional time available to educators and the escalating dropout rates among failing adolescent learners, any intervention that showed dramatic gains for these students would have the potential of having a transformative effect on instructional programming for these students.

6. *Methodologically inclusive and flexible.* Design researchers generally embrace a mixed-methods philosophy (Nieveen, McKenney, & van den Akker, 2006). Their desire to be responsive to the contextual realities that they encounter in school settings necessitates that they be willing to use a host of methods as they collect and analyze data (e.g., Chatterji, 2004).

7. *Pragmatic.* Design researchers are concerned with issues of whether an intervention is palatable to and doable by classroom teachers; that is, whether classroom teachers will accept it and can implement it in their current teaching context. If an intervention has a large effect size but is cumbersome to use (e.g., difficult to understand, lacks support materials, requires a difficult record-keeping system, and demands an inordinate amount of out-of-class preparation time), its likelihood of adoption and sustained use is minimal (e.g., Deshler & Deshler, 2007).

Relatively few peer-reviewed design research studies exist. One obstacle is that there are no journals devoted specifically to the publication of design studies. Frequently cited examples of literacy-based design studies in the professional literature include Brown (1992); Lenski (2001); Palincsar, Magnusson, Collins, and Cutter (2001) and Reinking and Watkins (2000).

Brown's (1992) foundational work on design experiments was centered on introducing teaching activities that enabled readers to become metacognitive in their approach to text. A second example is a study by Palincsar et al. (2001) studied a process called "Guided Inquiry Supporting Multiple Literacies" (GIsML) designed to promote scientific understanding of texts in upper-elementary students with special needs. In subsequent iterations of the intervention, teachers tended to focus on particular elements of the intervention that matched student needs. Lenski (2001) developed a reading process called directed reading-connecting activity with the goal of increasing the number and variety of elementary students' intertextual references during discussions. Teachers were observed clarifying their beliefs about learners and modified their instruction accordingly. A final example is the work of Reinking and Watkins (2000), who taught a process for using multimedia rather than traditional book reviews. An unintended beneficial consequence was teachers involving parents in the intervention through interactions with their children at home.

While there is a burgeoning literature on design research (e.g., Kelly, Lesh, & Baek, 2008; Plomp & Nieveen, 2007; Reinking & Bradley, 2008), a host of challenges remain to be addressed by its advocates. First, Schoenfeld (2006) stressed that the methodological openness valued by design researchers is not shared by most federal funding agencies in education. Thus, the opportunities for conceptual and operational growth of the design research field will be limited. Second, the lack of agreement among design researchers relative to conceptual clarity of the construct, operational definitions of elements, and standards of rigor complicate communication and growth in the literature (Kelly, 2007). Finally, Clements (2008) argued that "[design researchers] can be swept awash by too much data and too many interacting variables and possibilities, with too little theoretically determined constraints" (p. 221). To this end, Clements and other design researchers are beginning to advance frameworks and bring order to design intervention research.

Determining the Cost-Effectiveness of Literacy Interventions

According to Levin and McEwan (2001), "the purpose of cost-effectiveness analysis is to provide a method for choosing among alternatives in order to select those that are able to accomplish a given result most parsimoniously" (p. 1). Expenditures in the education sector in the United States are second only to expenditures in the health care sector. Interestingly, investments in each of these sectors exceed expenditures by the military sector. In light of the massive investments made in education, it is important that researchers carefully consider *both* effectiveness *and* costs when evaluating an intervention or making recommendations based on their research findings.

In spite of the logic of the need for information on both intervention effects and costs, such data are relatively sparse in the research literature on interventions. One study by Clune (1999) was conducted to determine how cost-effectiveness was treated in the research literature. Using the ERIC database for studies incorporating the term "cost-effectiveness," he found over 9,000 titles. He analyzed the abstracts of the studies to determine exactly how cost-effectiveness was treated in the studies. He used a four-category rubric to analyze the methodological rigor of the studies: (a) *Rhetorical*—cost-effectiveness claims with no data on either costs or effects; (b) *Minimal*—minimal data, such as potential categories of effectiveness or cost feasibility with no evidence of systematic study; (c) *Substantial*—attempts to mount data on cost and effectiveness but with serious flaws; and (d) *Plausible*—ingredients or resource approaches to costs and a strong effectiveness design with comparisons among alternatives.

To make the study manageable, he removed studies that did not focus on outcomes of school-aged students, thus reducing the sample to 541 studies. Results showed that more than 80% of the studies were Rhetorical (56%) or Minimal (27%). Only 1% fell between Substantial and Plausible, with the remaining 15% being Substantial.

Levin (2001) attempted to explain why relatively little attention is given to rigorous cost-effectiveness analyses when evaluating educational interventions. He offered three plausible explanations: (a) Lack of training—He found that very limited attention is given in either evaluation textbooks or university training programs. (b) Lack of effects—Since many rigorous studies seem to yield statistically insignificant results or differences in effect sizes are so small that they lack practical significance (e.g., Viadero, 2009), it is not useful to conduct cost-effectiveness evaluations. (c) Lack of demand by policy makers—Levin and Meister (1987) found that decision-makers may ignore cost-effectiveness data in their decisions to allocate resources because they find such information to be a distraction.

Cost-effectiveness information may be helpful in guiding the decision-making process, but it should not be the sole criterion in evaluating educational options. Intervention researchers can enhance the value of their work by incorporating methods to measure and analyze costs of interventions being studied in addition to our historic emphasis on effects.

Levin and McEwan (2001) outlined the following basic steps to designing and implementing a cost analysis with comparing multiple interventions. First, the resources or ingredients required for each alternative are identified. In short, the task is to identify the resources that accounted for the levels of effectiveness of each of the alternatives. Typical ingredients would be personnel (specifying both qualifications and time commitments), facilities, equipment, and other program inputs. Second, values are placed on each of the ingredients using current market prices. Items not directly purchased for the intervention (e.g., the shared cost of a facility) are proportionately valued. Third, costs of all ingredients are summed to determine total costs. Fourth, once costs of effects and costs have been determined, they are combined in a ratio for each alternative. The ratios can then be ordered to identify the alternatives that provide a given level of effectiveness for the least cost, or the highest effectiveness for a given cost.

Rethinking Knowledge Creation and Utilization Strategies

During the past 75 years, knowledge has been viewed in vastly different ways. For example, prior to the 1970s, knowledge was viewed as a largely stable, objective commodity; however, the report of the 1977 National Dissemination Forum (Bickell, 1977) noted a dramatic shift in this view:

> At the most fundamental level, there seems to be a tension between two vastly different, almost diametrically opposed, conceptions of knowledge acquisition. One extreme seems to be a conception of filling an "empty vessel" with facts or information. Information is "objective," easily communicated, and easily apprehended. Facts speak for themselves. Products and programs can be adopted and implemented. At the other extreme we find images of engaging or supporting "communities of learners," of individual learning as a

complex reconstruction of cognitive frames and meanings/values, or of organizations that must "restructure" and become "learning organizations." Somewhere between these two extremes seems to be much of our current "in-practice" models of knowledge utilization. (p. 121)

To understand the varying perspectives on knowledge and their evolution, Hood (2002) mapped knowledge frameworks along four dimensions: (a) Objective–Constructed; (b) Simple–Complex; (c) Explicit–Tacit; and (d) Individual–Social. He summarized these varying perspectives on knowledge and the evolving landscape:

We have moved from preoccupations with tangible, formal formats and channels to inclusion of less tangible, informal formats and channels. And especially during the last decade, we have contended with the implications of digitalization, hyper-media, the Internet and computer-augmented learning and information processing. Finally, as we have dealt with needs of users in fields beyond the scientific disciplines (e.g., business, industry, health, education, public policy) we have discovered that scientific and technical information alone is rarely sufficient to meet users' needs. Craft knowledge usually must be melded with scientific knowledge. All these changes have had a profound effect on our conceptions of the design and operation of effective information systems, and more fundamentally on our conceptions of knowledge and the processes of knowledge utilization. (p. 5)

The topic of knowledge utilization often highlights the significant differences that sometimes exist between researchers and practitioners relative to their assumptions and beliefs about knowledge claims and warrants; it also brings into focus differences in the knowledge the two groups value and how they want information configured, displayed, and related. In short, researchers and practitioners frequently operate within different communities and make sense of the world through different lenses (Spillane, Reiser, & Reimer, 2002). These differences may help explain the infamous research-practice gap. Indeed, the size and intractability of this gap may be influenced by how firmly rooted researchers and practitioners are in their core assumptions, values, and ideologies.

An alternative literature exists, however, that underscores both strategies for and resultant advantages of researchers and practitioners deliberately seeking to work together. Rynes, McNatt, and Bretz (1999) found that researchers who spent more time at organizational sites interacting with practitioners reported more personal learning than those who did not. Similar findings were reported in the physical sciences by Cohen, Florida, Randazzese, and Walsh (1998) and in the life sciences by Louis, Blumenthal, Gluck, and Stoto (1989). Collectively, these studies indicate that the divide between researchers and practitioners can be closed when researchers spend time in the field working alongside practitioners and use those experiences to influence the research questions they ask, the nature of the interventions they use, and the interpretation they bring to their findings.

A deliberate strategy being used in education to bring practitioners and researchers together is the Strategic Education Research Plan (SERP). The goal of SERP is to promote new, long-term collaborations among the research, practice, and policy communities. SERPs are designed to create large-scale, well-coordinated, cumulative research and development enterprises focused on the problems of educational practice (NRC, 2003).

SERP is conceptualized as an independent, non-profit organization that, in its mature state, is intended to plan and steer a program of work carried out primarily in "field sites" around the country—schools and school districts in which long-term research and development is conducted as a collaborative effort of researchers, practitioners, and developers. Work across field sites, research protocols, and data collection efforts will be coordinated from the beginning and planned in accordance with key SERP principles, so that knowledge can accumulate across projects and over time. In short, SERPs pay particular attention to the notion of building "critical mass" with "requisite variety" (including researchers and practitioners) working in school-based settings over substantial periods of time (Alberts & Donovan, 2009; Donovan, Wigdor, & Snow, 2003).

The National Academy of Education's (NAE) *Recommendations Regarding Research Priorities* (1999) voiced a similar message: "progress toward high achievement for all students has been impeded by the belief that research, students' learning, and teachers' learning can be studied in isolation from important matters of context" (p. 8). In essence, both the SERP framework and the NAE recommendations support research and development that is conducted in "Pasteur's Quadrant" (Stokes, 1997). Stokes argued that scientific research should be conceptualized as falling into four quadrants. One quadrant contains scientists who conduct pure basic research and have little interest in potential use of findings; a second quadrant contains scientists who conduct pure applied research with little interest in the scientific aspects of their work; a third is neither overly theoretical nor applied; the fourth quadrant [Pasteur's] is devoted to "use-inspired basic science" or research that has potential real-world utility but does not lose sight of the need to advance scientific understanding. Stokes argued that the majority of federal funding should be invested in Pasteur's Quadrant.

Research conducted within the use-inspired paradigm directly addresses the need to carefully attend to the salient conditions and contexts within which interventions are applied. In order to centralize the role of context, research must be designed with a long-term perspective in mind, be field-based, be collaborative, be focused on authentic outcomes, and involve close researcher-practitioner partnerships.

In light of the staggering number of students who continue to struggle in basic literacy attainment, literacy researchers have a responsibility not only to produce research of the highest caliber but also to carefully consider what strategies they should (could) use or develop to ensure the effective transfer of the knowledge and its optimal use in practice and policy (Neilson, 2001). Hood (2002) raised a host of questions surrounding the challenges that literacy researchers in the 21st century must ask of themselves, including (a) What characterizes the knowledge that is used in practice? (b) Who is the user—what do I know and assume about the user? (c) What specific outcomes are expected on the front lines? and (d) What do we need to know about the context within which interventions are applied?

Beyond these questions, researchers need to ask themselves the following: (a) What do I see as my role and responsibility in knowledge creation, transfer, and utilization to be? (b) How should I think about the burgeoning number of new mechanisms for sharing information (e.g., Web 2.0, e-journals, partnerships with publishers)? (c) How, if at all, should I leverage these new tools and prevailing mindsets toward accessing knowledge and knowledge utilization?

Clearly, the Internet is shaping not only how information is created and shared but also the expectations that people have about the knowledge creation and utilization process (Fabos, 2009). It is important for literacy researchers to grapple with these questions and to become students of the current and rapidly evolving dynamics surrounding knowledge creation, packaging, dissemination, and utilization. The answer to these and related questions will define, to some degree, the influence of educational researchers (Davenport, 2005).

An Example of an Integrated Intervention Research Model

Since its inception in 1978, the mission of the University of Kansas Center for Research on Learning (CRL) has tried to embody these qualities. We have worked to establish a collaborative network between our research staff and staff at partnering schools as we attempt to fulfill our mission to markedly improve (a) the performance of struggling adolescent learners, (b)

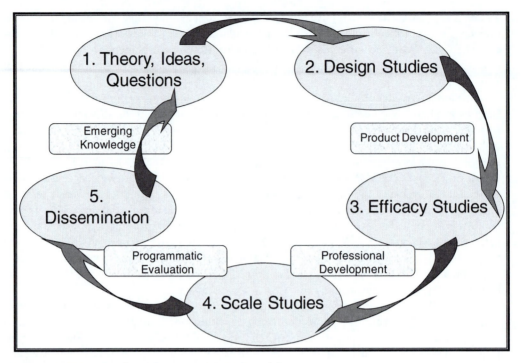

Figure 4.1 CRL comprehensive intervention R&D model.

how teachers instruct academically diverse classes, (c) how secondary schools are structured to improve outcomes, (d) how our validated practices can reach thousands of practitioners in the field, and (e) how public policy initiatives are crafted to support struggling adolescent learners. To assist us in remaining focused on and true to our mission, the R&D work of CRL researchers has been driven by the model depicted in Figure 4.1.

Within our model, work on an idea for a new intervention idea is generally grounded in field observations or conversations with practitioners, who raise questions about a particular need shown by students (e.g., struggling readers having difficulty integrating graphics with written text materials) or teacher need (e.g., teachers having difficulty engaging students in academic goal setting). These needs, problems, or questions (see oval #1 labeled "Theory, Questions, Ideas") become the basis of helping us define or begin to understand the exact nature of the need, the situations under which the problem is observed, the pervasiveness of the problem, and so on. Our conversations are guided by a model of adolescent reading developed by Deshler and Hock (2007) that is grounded in the proposition that a balanced combination of word-level, comprehension, and executive process theories should define the nature of adolescent reading interventions and the process of learning to read in older students. Most generally, the outcome of these deliberations is an initial product (e.g., a skeletal instructional protocol) that is designed to address the identified student need or instructional problem.

This product then becomes the basis of a series of Design Studies (oval #2). These initial studies might take place in one or two classrooms using a single-subject design (Kennedy, 2005; Shadish, Cook, & Campbell, 2002). After each iteration of the intervention, adjustments and refinements are made to the intervention protocol. Subsequent quasi-experimental studies are conducted in other classrooms under different conditions (i.e., different group size, teachers with different professional preparation, etc.). Frequently, focus groups are held with teachers and/or students to solicit their input regarding the intervention. In addition to the refinements of the intervention during this phase of our work, we are developing intervention-specific measures to test factors such as fidelity and palatability of the intervention (Schumaker & Deshler, 2003) for use during the next phase of our R&D model, Efficacy Studies.

Efficacy Studies (oval #3) are conducted with the goal of determining causal effects between intervention and student outcomes. Both quantitative and qualitative designs are used to measure outcomes and features of independent variables and contextual factors that might influence intervention outcomes (e.g., measures of time on task, student attendance, fidelity of implementation, classroom management/student behavior variables). After an acceptable level of effects has been demonstrated (e.g., see Bulgren & Schumaker, 2006; Schumaker & Deshler, 2006), professional development supports (e.g., PowerPoint slides, simulation activities, sample scoring protocols, case studies) are developed and made available to members of the CRL International Professional Development Network (IPDN) (www.kucrl.org). The IPDN consists of nearly 1,500 educators who have been certified to work with teachers and administrators on an ongoing basis to provide high-quality professional development in the use of the targeted intervention developed by CRL researchers. This professional development is grounded in a partnership model of instructional coaching (Knight, 2009; www.instructionalcoach.org).

Interventions validated through efficacy studies are tested on a broad basis in Scale Studies to verify generalizability in a broad array of settings and environments (oval #4). A part of the Scale Study process is the development of "off-the-shelf" materials and supports for classroom teachers and coaches to enable implementation of the intervention independent of the researchers. CRL researchers and staff members have made a significant commitment to the development of instructional materials (e.g., instructional manuals, technology supports) for teachers. Over 80 separate curriculum packages have been developed to support scaled implementation of our interventions (e.g., Fisher, Deshler, & Schumaker, 1999; Hock, Schumaker, & Deshler, 2003; Lancaster, Schumaker, Lancaster, & Deshler, in press).

Program scale studies conducted by external evaluators are done to determine program effects in large-scale random control studies (e.g., Corrin et al., 2008). These studies are designed to measure the robustness of interventions using group reading tests (e.g., the Group Reading Assessment and Diagnostic Evaluation; Williams, 2001). A part of our efficacy and scaling efforts includes taking cost-effectiveness measures consistent with the Levin and McEwan (2001) frameworks (e.g., Knight, Hock, & Skrtic, 2006).

The final component of our model is dissemination (oval #5). This component involves the use of a broad array of tools to communicate information about our interventions and situations within which they have been found to work. These tools include traditional vehicles such as journal articles and conference presentations as well as teacher support web sites, blogs, newsletters, annual conferences for members of the IPDN, webcasts, and so on (see www.kucrl.org). Our most recent dissemination initiative is the establishment of a national learning community known as CRL Learns (see http://crllearns.kucrl.org). The majority of our dissemination mechanisms are designed to be highly interactive between our center researchers and practitioners in the field or members of our IPDN. These interactions surface new knowledge, insights, questions, and ideas that, in turn, inform new research ideas (see oval #1).

Our R&D model has been modified based on input provided to our center by Drs. Elizabeth Moje and Carol Lee. The work of these literacy researchers has been richly informed by their meticulous efforts to study the broader contexts and cultures from which children come and in which they live and learn. Their work has underscored the vital role of situating all literacy events in relationship to people, texts, and broader contextual factors and influences (e.g., Lee, 2007; Moje, 1996; Moje, Dillon, & O'Brien, 2000). How we think about the interventions we design, the measures that we take, and the perspectives that we seek to understand are changing as a result of their scholarship.

In short, this model has been helpful in guiding our work. However, its greatest value has been the way in which it has evolved as our thinking about schooling, learning, contexts, and the research process have changed.

This chapter would be incomplete without pointing to the work of some other centers that have likewise aimed to foster research that is closely informed by practice. For example, the Juniper Garden Children's Project (JGCP), initiated in the mid-1960s, began with the premise that the local community was capable of identifying the developmental and educational needs of its children (Hall, Schiefelbusch, Greenwood, & Hoyt, 2006). This community-university partnership has resulted in significant contributions to the field, including interventions such as class-wide peer tutoring and screening tools like the Individual Growth and Development Indicators for Infants and Toddlers (Carta et al., 2002). The center is frequently recognized for its rigorous and meaningful research, which is generally connected directly to the needs of the community and continues to be an exemplar intervention development site.

Another research and development model is that followed by the Center for Applied Special Technology (CAST). The primary focus of CAST has been to develop technologies that allow for inclusive educational settings. Their interventions have been directed by the needs of "learners who often get pushed aside," but have utility for the majority of students (CAST, 2009). CAST has been central in the effort to increase the use and development of universal designs for learning (Rose & Meyer, 2002) and, in the process, has developed online tools and software such as the UDL *Book Builder* (http://bookbuilder.cast.org/) and *Thinking Reader* (e.g., Dalton & Palincsar, 2006). CAST also offers numerous opportunities for professional development and remains in constant contact with educators, schools, and universities.

IMPLICATIONS FOR THEORY, PRACTICE, POLICY, AND RESEARCH

Education, like many disciplines, has been criticized for suffering from the "silo effect." That is, the various entities within the organization suffer from a lack of communication and common goals. A silo mentality is the opposite of a systems-thinking approach to organizational design; or, a framework based on the premise that the component parts of a system can best be understood in the context of relationships with each other and with other systems, rather than in isolation (Senge, 2007).

Since the beginning of this decade, some notable events and trends have somewhat reduced the seemingly intractable silos that have existed between research and practice. The major precipitating event has been the passage of No Child Left Behind and the accompanying expectation for schools to use evidence-based practices to reach Adequate Yearly Progress (AYP) goals. The evidence-based requirements set forth in NCLB influenced the formation of the Institute of Education Sciences and, in turn, its establishment of the What Works Clearinghouse (http://ies.ed.gov/ncee/wwc/). Through this chain of policy initiatives, researchers and practitioners began to reconsider and, in many cases, redefine their relationships to one another—if not out of choice, out of necessity. Practitioners and publishers needed evidenced-based tools to meet their instructional and publishing needs, and researchers needed partnerships and sites in which to conduct their studies and outlets through which their findings could be disseminated.

A second trend has been the growing influence of computers (Levy & Murnane, 2004) and the Internet on the processes of knowledge creation and knowledge utilization (Rynes, Bartunek, & Daft, 2001). Technology has redefined the landscape relative to the definition of knowledge and how it is produced, who can produce it, and who can share it. Interestingly, the *elements* of the information cycle (i.e., creation, validation, dissemination, re-creation, etc.) have not been substantially changed due to technology. However, the *process* has been significantly altered. Creation is now as simple as a podcast or blog post. Dissemination and peer review occur through "crowd sourcing" methods such as ratings on Amazon or comments on Diigo (a knowledge-sharing online community), online articles, open access journals, blogs, videos, and Second Life builds. Information is now mutable, participatory, democratic, and rapidly recreated. While the implications for researchers and practitioners are not clear and are still emerging, we must seek to understand these new realities and how they will impact our work.

Trends *within* the research community itself have also contributed to a breakdown of firmly entrenched silos. As discussed in this chapter, the rapidly growing interest in design research has brought researchers and practitioners together in partnership roles in which the expertise and perspectives of each are linked, valued, and leveraged in the search for effective interventions. While the importance and value of randomized controlled experiments is recognized and supported, an increased reliance on mixed-methods underscores the recognition by a growing number of educators and policy makers of the importance of understanding contextual variables as much as learner and intervention variables.

Regardless of the research paradigm followed, even under the best of circumstances, conducting high-quality intervention research in school settings is an extremely difficult undertaking (Supovitz, 2008). The list of challenges and obstacles that intervention researchers must overcome can be both daunting and sizable (e.g., condensed timeframes for intervention implementation and insufficient time for site "buy-in;" recruitment, cooperation, and retention of sites in randomized controlled trials; conducting intervention studies in unstable school environments with high staff turn-over or high student absenteeism).

The point in surfacing these problems is to prompt discussion and action among education funding agencies, professional organizations, and research and practitioner communities to collectively generate strategies to address the most vexing of these obstacles to doing intervention research. Bringing researchers, practitioners, funding agencies, and professional associations together to address these issues would make strategic sense so the limited resources available for educational R&D could be more effectively spent addressing the actual research questions. It is hoped, in an environment in which silos are coming down between researchers and practitioners (or at least communication linkages between members of these communities are being built), these kinds of challenges can be taken on and mutually solved.

At best, educational policy makers, practitioners, and researchers are "loosely coupled" communities (Weick, 1985). As such, they are weakly related and fairly independent relative to function, structure, and culture (Sanchez, 1997). However, the level of productivity between loosely coupled organizations or communities is enhanced if all parties recognize the important role of human sense-making in the communication process. Spillane et al. (2002) elaborated on what is involved in sense-making:

> Successful implementation of complex policies necessitates substantial changes in implementing agents' schemas. Most conventional theories of change fail to take into account the complexity of human sense making.... Sense-making is not a simple decoding of the policy message, in general, the process of comprehension is an active process of interpretation that draws on the individual's rich knowledge base of understandings, beliefs, and attitudes. (p. 394)

In short, to the degree that members of these different stakeholder communities work toward understanding the values, beliefs, and attitudes of the other, efforts will be better aligned and coordinated—a fundamental requirement for narrowing the achievement gap.

REFERENCES

Adams, M. J. (1990). *Beginning to read.* Cambridge, MA: Harvard University Press.

Alberts, B., & Donovan, S. (2009). *Collaboration and innovation.* Washington, DC: Strategic Education Partnership.

Anderson, R. C., & Pearson, P. D. (1984). A schema-theoretic view of basic processes in reading. In P. D. Pearson (Ed.), *Handbook of reading research* (pp. 255–291). New York: Longman.

Bickell, H. M. (1977). *National dissemination forum, 1977: Final report.* Washington, DC: Education Resources Information Center.

Brown, A. L. (1992). Design experiments: Theoretical and methodological challenges in creating complex interventions in classroom settings. *The Journal of the Learning Sciences, 2*(2), 141–178.

Bulgren, J., & Schumaker, J. B. (2006). Teaching practices that optimize curriculum access. In D. D. Deshler & J. B. Schumaker (Eds.), *Teaching adolescents with disabilities: Accessing the general education curriculum* (pp. 79–120). New York: Corwin.

Carta, J. J., Greenwood, C. R., Walker, D., Kaminski, R., Good, R., & McConnell, S. (2002). Individual growth and development indicators (IGDIs): Assessment that guides intervention for young children. *Young Exceptional Children Monograph Series, 4*, 15–28.

CAST. (2009). Research and Development in Universal Design for Learning. Retrieved from http://www.cast.org/research/index.html

Chatterji, M. (2004). Evidence on "what works": An argument of extended-term mixed-method (ERMM) evaluation designs. *Educational Researcher, 33*(9), 3–13.

Clements, D. H. (2008). Design experiments and curriculum research. In A. E. Kelly, R. A. Lesh, & J. Y. Baek (Eds.), *Handbook of design research methods in education* (pp. 217–233). New York: Routledge.

Clune, W. H. (1999). *Methodological strength and policy usefulness of published research on cost-effectiveness in education.* Unpublished paper, Center for Policy Research in Education, Madison, WI.

Coalition for Evidence-based Policy. (2003). *Identifying and implementing educational practices supported by rigorous evidence.* Washington, DC: National Institute for Literacy.

Cobb, P., Confrey, J., diSessa, A., Lehrer, R., & Schauble, L. (2003). Design experiments in educational research. *Educational Researcher, 32*(1), 9–13.

Cohen, W., Florida, R., Randazzese, L., & Walsh, J. (1998). Industry and the academy: Uneasy partners in the cause of technological advance. In R. G. Noll (Ed.), *Challenges to research universities* (pp. 171–199). Washington, DC: Brookings Institution Press.

Collins, A. (1992). Towards a design science of education. In E. Scanlon & T. O'Shea (Eds.), *New directions in educational technology* (pp. 15–22). Berlin: Springer.

Corrin, W., Somers, M. A., Kemple, J. J., Nelson, E., Sepanik, J., Salinger, T., et al. (2008). *The enhanced reading opportunities study: Findings from the second year of implementation.* New York: MDRC.

Dalton, B., & Palincsar, A. (2006). *Reading to learn: Investigating general and domain specific supports in a technology-rich environment with diverse readers learning from informational text.* Washington, DC: U.S. Department of Education, Institute of Education Sciences.

Davenport, T. H. (2005). *Thinking for a living: How to get better performance and results from knowledge workers.* Cambridge, MA: Harvard Business School Press.

Deshler, D. D. (1996). Influencing effective practice through IDEA-supported research. *Exceptionality, 6*(2), 69–80.

Deshler, D. D., & Schumaker, J. B. (2006). *Teaching adolescents with disabilities: Accessing the general education curriculum.* New York: Corwin Press.

Deshler, D. D., Palincsar, A. S., Biancarosa, G., & Nair, M. (2007). *Informed choices for struggling adolescent readers: A research-based guide to instructional programs.* Newark, DE: International Reading Association.

Deshler, R. T., & Deshler, D. D. (2007). School and district change to improve adolescent literacy. In D. D Deshler, A. S. Palincsar, G. Biancarosa, & M. Nair (Eds.), *Informed choices for struggling adolescent readers: A research-based guide to instructional programs* (pp. 92–110). Newark, DE: International Reading Association.

Deshler, D. D., & Hock, M. F. (2007). Adolescent literacy: Where we are, where we need to go. In M.

Pressley, A. K. Billman, K. H. Perry, K. E. Reffitt, & J. M. Reynolds (Eds.), *Shaping literacy achievement: Research we have, research we need* (pp. 98–128). New York: Guilford.

Design-Based Research Collective. (2003). Design-based research: An emerging paradigm for educational inquiry. *Educational Researcher, 32*(1), 5–8.

Donovan, M. S., Wigdor, A. K., & Snow, C. E. (2003). *Strategic education research partnership.* Washington, DC: National Academies Press.

Eisenhart, M., & Towne, L. (2003). Contestation and change in national policy on "scientifically based" education research. *Educational Researcher, 32*(7), 31–38.

Fabos, B. (2009). The price of education: critical literacy, education, and today's Internet. In J. Coiro, M. Knobel, C. Lankshear, & D. Leu (Eds.), *Handbook of research on new literacies* (pp. 839–870). New York: Routledge.

Fisher, J. B., Deshler, D. D., & Schumaker, J. B. (1999). The effects of an interactive multimedia program on teachers' understanding and implementation of an inclusive practice. *Learning Disability Quarterly, 22*(2), 127–142.

Fritschmann, N. S., Deshler, D. D., & Schumaker, J. B. (2007). The effects of instruction in an inference strategy on the reading comprehension skills of adolescents with disabilities. *Learning Disability Quarterly, 30*(4), 1–18.

Gersten, R. (2005). Behind the scenes of an intervention research study. *Learning Disabilities Research and Practice, 20*(4), 200–212.

Hall, R. V., Schiefelbusch, R. L., Greenwood, C. R., & Hoyt, R. K. (2006). The Juniper Gardens Children's Project. In R. L. Schiefelbusch & S. R. Schroeder (Eds.), *Doing science and doing good: A history of the Bureau of Child Research and the Schiefelbusch Institute for Life Span Studies at the University of Kansas* (pp. 125–140). Baltimore, MD: Brookes.

Hock, M., Schumaker, J. B., & Deshler, D. D. (2003). *Possible selves: Nurturing student motivation.* Lawrence, KS: Edge Enterprises.

Hood, P. (2002). *Perspectives on knowledge utilization in education.* San Francisco: WestEd.

Kelly, A. E. (2004). Design research in education: Yes, but is it methodological? *The Journal of the Learning Sciences, 13,* 115–128.

Kelly, A. E. (2007). Quality criteria for design research. In J. J. van den Akker, K. Gravemeijer, S. McKenney, & N. Nieveen, N. (Eds.), *Educational design research* (pp. 121–136). New York: Routledge.

Kelly, A. E., Lesh, R. A., & Baek, J. Y. (2008). *Handbook of design research methods in education: Innovations in science, technology, engineering, and mathematics learning and teaching.* New York: Routledge.

Kennedy, C. H. (2005). *Single case designs for educational research.* Boston: Pearson.

Knight, J. (2009). What can we do about teacher resistance? *Phi Delta Kappan,* 508–513.

Lancaster, P. E., Schumaker, J. B., Lancaster, S.J.C., & Deshler, D. D. (in press). Efficacy of computerized instruction in the Test-taking Strategy: A field test with secondary students with high-incidence disabilities. *Learning Disability Quarterly.*

Lee, C. D. (2007). *Culture, literacy, and learning: Taking bloom in the midst of whirlwind.* New York: Teachers College Press.

Lenski, S. D. (2001). Intertexual connections during discussion about literature. *Reading Psychology, 22,* 313–335.

Levin, H. M. (2001). Waiting for Godot: Cost-effectiveness analysis in education. In R. Light, *New directions in evaluation* (pp. 58–68). San Francisco: Jossey-Bass.

Levin, H. M., & McEwan, P. J. (2001). *Cost-effectiveness analysis: Methods and applictions.* Thousand Oaks, CA: Sage.

Levy, F., & Murnane, R. J. (2004). *The new division of labor: How computers are creating the next job market.* New York: Russell Sage Foundation.

Lincoln, Y. S., & Guba, E. G. (1985). *Naturalistic inquiry.* Thousand Oaks, CA: Sage.

Louis, K. S., Blumenthal, D., Gluck, M. E., & Stoto, M. (1989). Entrepreneurs in academe: An exploration of behaviors among life scientists. *Administrative Sciences Quarterly, 34,* 110–131.

McCardle, P., & Chhabra, V. (2004). The accumulation of evidence: A continuing process. In P. McCardle & V. Chhabra (Eds.), *The voice of evidence in reading research* (pp. 463–478). Baltimore: Brookes.

McCardle, P., Chhabra, V., & Kapinus, B. (2008). *Reading research in action: A teacher's guide to student success.* Baltimore: Brookes.

McDaniel, J. E., Sims, C. H., & Miskel, C. G. (2001). The national reading policy arena: Policy actors and perceived influence. *Educational Policy, 15*(1), 92–114.

McMillan, J. H. (2007). Randomized field trials and internal validity: Not so fast my friend. *Practical Assessment Research & Evaluation, 12*(15). Retrieved from http://pareonline.net/getvn.asp?v=12&n=15

Moje, E. B. (1996). "I teach students, not subjects": Teacher-student relationships as contexts for secondary literacy. *Reading Research Quarterly, 31*(2), 172–195.

Moje, E. B., Dillon, D. R., & O'Brien, D. (2000), Reexamining roles of learner, text, and context in secondary literacy. *Journal of Educational Researcher, 93*(3), 165–180.

National Institute of Child Health and Human Development. (2000). *Report of the National Reading Panel. Teaching children to read: An evidence-based assessment of the scientific research literature on reading and its implications for reading instruction* (NIH Publication No. 00-4769). Washington, DC: U.S. Government Printing Office.

National Research Council, Committee on a Strategic Education Research Partnership, Donovan, M. S., Wigdor, A. K., & Snow C. E. (Eds.). (2003). *Strategic education research partnership.* Washington, DC: National Academy Press.

Neilson, S. (2001). *Knowledge utilization and public policy processes: A literature review.* Ottawa, ONT, Canada: International Development Center, Evaluation Unit.

Newman, D. (1990). Opportunities for research on the organizational impact of school computers. *Educational Researcher, 19*, 8–13.

Newman, D. (1992). Formative experiments on the co-evolution of technology and the educational environment. In E. Scanlon & T. O'Shea (Eds.), *New directions in educational technology* (pp. 61–70). New York: Springer-Verlag.

Nieveen, N., McKenney, S., & van den Akker, J. V. D. (2006). Educational design research: The value of diversity. In J. V. D. Akker, K. Gravemeijer, S. McKenney, & N. Nieveen (Eds.), *Educational design research* (pp. 151–158). New York: Routledge.

O'Donnell, C. L. (2008). Defining, conceptualizing, and measuring fidelity of implementation and its relationship to outcomes in K-12 curriculum intervention research. *Review of Educational Research, 78*(1), 33–84.

Palincsar, A. S. (2005). Working theory into and out of design experiments. *Learning Disabilities Research and Practice, 20*(4), 15–32.

Palincsar, A. S., Magnusson, S. J., Collins, K. M., & Cutter, J. (2001). Making science accessible to all: Results of a design experiment in inclusive classrooms. *Learning Disability Quarterly, 24*(1), 15–32.

Pigott, T. D., & Barr, R. (2000). Designing programmatic interventions. In M. L. Kamil, P. B. Mosenthal, P. D. Pearson, & R. Barr (Eds.), *Handbook of reading research* (Vol. III, pp. 545–561). Mahwah, NJ: Erlbaum.

Plomp, T. (2007). Educational design research: An introduction. In T. Plomp & N. Nieveen (Eds.), *An introduction to educational design research* (pp. 9–36). Amsterdam, Netherlands: Netherlands Institute for Curriculum Development.

Plomp, T., & Nieveen, N. (2007). *An introduction to educational design research.* Amsterdam, Netherlands: Netherlands Institute for Curriculum Development.

Pressley, M., Graham, S., & Harris, K. (2006). The state of educational intervention research as viewed through the lens of literacy intervention. *British Journal of Educational Psychology, 76*, 1–19.

Raudenbush, S. (2005). Learning from attempts to improve schooling: The contributions of methodological diversity. *Educational Researcher, 34*(5), 25–31.

Reinking, D., & Bradley, B. A. (2008). *Formative and design experiments: Approaches to language and literacy.* New York: Teachers College Press.

Reinking, D., & Watkins, J. (2000). A formative experiment investigating the use of multimedia book reviews to increase elementary students independent reading. *Reading Research Quarterly, 35*(3), 384–419.

Rittel, H. W. J., & Webber, M. M. (1973). Dilemmas in a general theory of planning. *Policy Science, 4*, 155–169.

Rose, D. H., & Meyer, A. (2002). *Teaching in the digital age: Universal design for learning.* Alexandria, VA: ASCD.

Rynes, S. L., Bartunek, J. M., & Daft, R. L. (2001). Across the great divide: Knowledge creation and transfer between practitioners and academics. *Academy of Management Journal, 44*(2), 340–455.

Rynes, S. L., McNatt, D. B., & Bretz, R. D. (1999). Academic research inside organizations: Inputs, processes, outcomes. *Personnel Psychology, 85*, 314–322.

Sadoski, M., & Paivio, A. (2000). *Imagery and text: A dual coding theory of reading and writing.* Mahwah, NJ: Erlbaum.

Sanchez, R. (1997). Preparing for an uncertain future: Managing organizations for strategic flexibility. *International Studies of Management & Organization, 27*(2), 71–94.

Schoenbach, R., Greenleaf, C., Cziko, C., & Hurwitz, L. (1999). *Reading for understanding.* New York: Corwin.

Schoenfeld, A. H. (2006). Design experiments. In J. L. Green, G. Camilli, P. B. Elmore, A. Skukauskaite, & E. Grace (Eds.), *Handbook of complementary methods in education research* (pp. 193–205). Mahwah, NJ: Erlbaum.

Schumaker, J. B., & Deshler, D. D. (2003). Designs for applied educational research. In H. L. Swanson, K. R. Harris, & S. Graham (Eds.), *Handbook of learning disabilities* (pp. 483–500). New York: Guilford.

Schumaker, J. B., & Deshler, D. D. (2006). Teaching adolescents to be strategic learners. In D. D. Deshler & J. B. Schumaker (Eds.), *Teaching adolescents with disabilities: Accessing the general education curriculum* (pp. 121–156). New York: Corwin.

Senge, P. (2007). Give me a lever long enough... and single-handed I can move the world. *The Jossey-Bass reader on educational leadership* (2nd ed., pp. 3–16). San Francisco: Jossey-Bass.

Shadish, W. R., Cook, T. D., & Campbell, D. T. (2002). *Experimental and quasi-experimental designs for generalized causal inference.* Boston: Houghton Mifflin.

Shavelson, R. J., & Towne, L. (2002). *Scientific research in education.* Washington, DC: National Academy Press.

Slavin, R. E., & Madden, N. A. (2006). *Success for all—Roots & wings: 2006 summary of research on achievement outcomes.* Baltimore: Johns Hopkins University, Center for Research and Reform in Education.

Spillane, J. P., Reiser, B. J., & Reimer, T. (2002). Policy implementation and cognition: Reframing and refocusing implementation research. *Review of Educational Research, 72*(3), 387–431.

Sroufe, G. (2003). Legislative reform of federal education research programs: A political annotation of the education sciences reform act of 2002. *Peabody Journal of Education, 78*(4), 220–229.

Sterling-Turner, H. E., Watson, T. S., & Moore, J. W. (2002). The effects of direct training and treatment outcomes in school consultation. *School Psychology Quarterly, 17*(3), 47–77.

Stokes, D. E. (1997). *Pasteur's quadrant: Basic science and technological innovation.* Washington, DC: Brookings Institution.

Supovitz, J. A. (2008). Implementation as iterative refraction. In J. A. Supovitz & E. H. Weinbaum (Eds.), *The implementation gap: Understanding reform in high schools* (pp. 151–172). New York: Teachers College Press.

van den Akker, J. (1999). Principles and methods of development research. In J. J. van den Akker, N. Nieveen, R. M. Branch, K. L. Gustafson, & T. Plomp (Eds.), *Design approaches and tools in education and training* (pp. 1–14). Dordrecht, The Netherlands: Kluwer.

van den Akker, J., Gravemeijer, K., McKenney, S., & Nieveen, N. (2007). *Educational design research.* New York: Routledge.

Viadero, D. (2009, April 1). 'No effects' studies raising eyebrows. *Education Week, 28*(27), 1, 14–15.

Weick, K. E. (1985). The significance of corporate culture. In P. Frost, L. Moore, M. Louis, C. Lundberg, & J. Martin (Eds.), *Organizational culture* (pp. 381–389). Beverly Hills, CA: Sage.

Williams, K. T. (2001). *Group reading assessment and diagnostic evaluation.* San Antonio, TX: Pearson.

5 Cultural Perspectives in Reading

Theory and Research

Robert Rueda

University of Southern California

Culture is a ubiquitous feature of daily life and is characteristic of human activity, including reading and literacy. In fact, reading and literacy are cultural inventions constructed over the course of history to enable more effective solutions to everyday needs such as recording important events, facilitating commerce, and broadening means of communication (Cole, 1996; Lee & Smagorinsky, 2000). Thus, the connections between literacy and culture are deep. In this chapter, we will explore these connections. This will include a discussion of culture as a construct, an historical overview of culture in reading research, and a review and critique of research related to cultural factors in literacy acquisition and teaching, and a proposal for a research agenda for the field. Finally, the chapter will provide a model for examining cultural factors in literacy research as a means of guiding this agenda.

A NOTE ON LITERACY AND READING

Before exploring the meaning of culture, it is worth noting the distinction between literacy and reading, primarily because of the potential for confusion in both theory and research and the implications for understanding cultural factors. Literacy and reading are often used interchangeably in spite of the fact that various authors may have very different meanings. We draw the distinction here because of the implications for understanding work related to culture. A recent National Research Council report (Snow, Burns, & Griffin, 1998) defined reading as "... the use of the products and principles of the writing system to get at the meaning of a written text" (p. 42). In essence, it focuses on the individual psychological processes involved in decoding and comprehending text. In contrast, while literacy includes reading, it looks more broadly not only at the act of reading but at the beliefs, attitudes, and social practices that literate individuals and social groups follow in a variety of settings and situations (Pearson & Raphael, 2000). For example, literacy involves knowledge of the underlying discourses in a group (Gee, 1992); that is, the values, viewpoints, "funds of knowledge" (Gonzalez, Moll, & Amanti, 2005), and language patterns established by members of that discourse group, patterns internally resistant to criticism.

While the psychological processes involved in reading are most often seen as universal (we will discuss this point in more detail later), literacy is often seen as much more culturally specific, opening the possibility of multiple literacies. For example, the language patterns, types and uses of text, vocabulary, syntax, and shared meanings and values in school-based literacy may be very different than those found in some home and community settings (Bloome, Katz, Solsken, Willett, & Wilson-Keenan, 2000). While the cultural practices in home and community settings are normally *acquired*, the literate cultural practices associated with school are often thought to be *learned* (Gee, 1992). In both cases, the discourses around literacy in different cultural settings have to do with language patterns and internally accepted meanings and ways of behaving.

One characteristic of the reading research field in terms of reading and literacy is that cultural research has often been part of the latter but not the former. Moreover, research in one area is sometimes used to suggest pedagogy and policy in the other, a fact that may help explain some of the disagreements within the field. To avoid additional confusion, the next section begins with an overview of culture as a construct, taking care to differentiate culture specifically from a range of other sociocultural variables. An historical overview follows, examining connections to earlier work in past volumes of the *Handbook of Reading Research*. Finally, we will talk about what changes in the educational context might have implications for this topic, and provide an overview of research in this area, describing the implications for theory, practice, policy, and future research.

Culture as a Construct

While the term "culture" is commonly used in the everyday vernacular and in the social and behavioral literature as well, there is a great deal of variance in meaning. One view sees culture and cultural progress as universal, representing the general inheritance of humankind reflected in such collective achievements such as artistic refinements, science, knowledge, cultural institutions, etc. In this view, societies do not have discrete cultures; rather, they embrace and exhibit greater or lesser degrees of the general culture created by humankind up to the present time. Such a view allows the ranking of various social groups according to their degree of culture and the extent to which they incorporate and/or contribute to the general cultural progress (for a discussion, see Gallego & Cole, 1998, and Erikson, 2004).

The competing view, and the one adopted here, is more relativistic and related to the particular historical circumstances of specific groups (Goodenough, 1994). It refers to the daily patterns of living (cultural practices) that allow individuals to relate to the surrounding social order. That is, "Each culture...is an historically unique configuration of the residue of the collective problem solving activities of a social group in its efforts to survive and prosper within its environment(s)" (Gallego & Cole, 1998, p. 367). In this view, there is not one grand culture, but many different cultures. Furthermore, culture is learned, and develops because of the need to evolve in response to adaptive challenges and tasks faced by a given group (Weisner, 1994). While culture is most often referenced in the literature primarily with respect to students from nonmainstream cultural and linguistic backgrounds, culture is in fact a universal feature of daily life for all humans (Rogoff, 2003). At the most basic level, culture helps determine what is customary and "normal." But it is not static knowledge. Culture and cultural processes are dynamic and are expressed through cultural practices (behavior, artifacts, rules, etc.) that characterize daily life (Gallimore & Goldenberg, 2001). In a given ecological niche, these represent historically evolved and shared ways of perceiving, thinking, and storing possible responses to adaptive challenges and changing conditions (Gallimore & Goldenberg, 2001).

Thus, used here in its most general sense, culture refers to the socially inherited body of past human accomplishments that serves as the resources for the current life of a specific social group (D'Andrade, 1996). Early writing by Kroeber and Kluckholn provided a more specific definition:

> Culture consists of patterns, explicit and implicit, of and for behavior acquired and transmitted by symbols, constituting the distinctive achievements of human groups, including their embodiment in artifacts; the essential core of culture consists of traditional (i.e., historically derived and selected) ideas and especially their attached values; cultural systems may on the one hand be considered as products of action, on the other as conditioning elements of further action. (1963, p. 181)

D'Andrade and Strauss (1992) and others (Gee, 2000; Strauss & Quinn, 1998) suggested that cultural beliefs and practices are organized as *cultural models*, which are situated, social constructions of the world that shapes one's understanding of the world and one's behavior in it. These cultural models are thought to be so familiar that they are often invisible and unnoticed by those who hold them (Gallimore & Goldenberg, 2001). From a research perspective, culture and cultural processes are notoriously difficult to define and operationalize because: (a) much of what we consider cultural knowledge is automated, and therefore not always transparent or easily accessible to the individual or external observers, and (b) they involve values, ideas, beliefs, and practices that are relative.

Although culture has been visible in literacy research for some time, an unfortunate tendency in the past has been to focus on surface differences and treat culture as if it were a homogenous, static, and internally consistent set of rules for behavior that continually shape an individual's everyday activities in predictable ways. Most often, however, these cultural models impact behavior in variable and inconsistent ways (D'Andrade & Strauss, 1992; Gallimore & Goldenberg, 2001; Levine & White, 1986; Strauss, 1992). Summing up these points, Gallimore and Goldenberg noted that:

> Values and practices encoded in cultural models are not necessarily internally consistent or consistently related to behavior. This seeming "irrationality" can be understood as preparation for shifting challenges, for which different cultural models may be required...This variability in model enactment means that culture is not a nominal variable to be attached equally to every individual like a "social" address, in the same way that age, height, or gender might be. Treating culture in this way assumes that everyone who claims membership in or is assigned to a group has common natal experiences and acts on available cultural models in a uniform, unvarying fashion. In many cases they do not. *Assuming homogeneity of experience and behavior of individuals within cultures, without empirical evidence, is unwarranted* [italics in original]. A parallel error is to treat national or ethnic status as equivalent to a common cultural experience for individuals. (pp. xii–xiii)

Rather than assuming that cultural models develop automatically based on things like race, ethnicity, gender, etc., it is important to realize that it is really an individual's specific experiences that influence the cultural models that develop. Thus, as some have argued, it is critical to examine what people actually *do* in terms of cultural practices rather than making unwarranted assumptions about these factors based on unsubstantiated inferences about presumed beliefs and values and how these might mediate behavior (Gutierrez & Rogoff, 2003). As these authors note, cultural influences are variable both across individuals and across settings for the same individual.

RESEARCH AND THEORY ON CULTURAL PERSPECTIVES

Changes in the Educational Context

Before looking at some of the research and theory, it is worth taking note of the larger educational context that has had a bearing on research on culture and the treatment of cultural factors in reading research. These factors include national demographic changes, national educational policy initiatives such as NCLB, and the focus on evidence-based approaches.

Demographic Changes.   Between 1966 and 2006 the U.S. population grew by 100 million. The Hispanic population increased from 8.5 million in 1966–67 to 44.7 million today. Latinos thus accounted for 36% of the 100 million people added to the population in the last four decades, the most of any racial or ethnic group. The White population grew from 167.2 million in 1966–67 to 201.0 million today, which represented 34% of the 100 million added since 1966–67. The Black population increased from 22.3 million to 38.7 million and accounted for about 16% of the population growth. The Asian and Pacific Islander population increased from 1.5 million to about 14.3 million, representing about 13% of the increase (Pew Hispanic Center, 2006). A significant number of these students came from homes where English is not the primary language. For example, between 1979 and 2005, the number of school-age children (ages 5–17) who spoke a language other than English at home increased from 3.8 to 10.6 million (from 9 to 20% of the school-age population). Among school-age children who spoke a non-English language at home, the total number who spoke English with difficulty increased from 1.3 million (3% of all 5- to 17-year-olds) to 2.9 million (6%) between 1979 and 2000 (Livingston, 2007). It is difficult to ignore cultural factors in the classroom setting given these massive changes in the makeup of the school age population.

Accountability.   Passage of No Child Left Behind (NCLB) marked a turning point in the move toward accountability for schools. The result of this legislation and other related initiatives has been increased pressure on schools to see that all children achieve at high levels. As part of NCLB's school accountability measures, schools cannot meet their Annual Yearly Progress goals unless all major subgroups at the school meet achievement targets. Teachers as well as administrators are thus under tremendous pressure to produce demonstrable results. The measure of choice in the quest for accountability has been large scale high stakes tests, sometimes leading to attempts to focus the curriculum on test-related material to the exclusion of other material. In this context, cultural considerations have often been absent from the discussion about curricular and instructional approaches.

Evidence-Based Approaches.   A long history of research has focused on cultural factors in schools, classrooms, and communities (Goldenberg, Rueda, & August, 2006a; Rogoff, 2003). Much of this work has been observational and qualitative in nature, typically focusing on a single or small number of specific cultural contexts (Au, 2000; Wilkinson & Silliman, 2000). Over the past several years, however, a push has been made at the federal level and within some arenas of the research domain to embrace what have come to be known as evidence-based instructional approaches (Mayer, 2001; Feuer, Towne, & Shavelson, 2002; Slavin, 2002; Whitehurst, 2002). Some interpretations of this agenda have focused on a relatively narrow view of acceptable methodological approaches, specifically randomized, control group experiments. This cause-effect emphasis has come to be seen as the hallmark of acceptable research for determining instructional approaches and deciding policy matters. While the matter has been vigorously debated within the education community, given the qualitative nature of much research on cultural factors, this is an important consideration. It has shifted the research agenda in many cases away from questions and methodologies not amenable to quantitative and controlled approaches that emphasize generalization of results.

Taken together, these changes in the educational landscape have undoubtedly (and will continue to) influenced the role that cultural factors play in educational research and practice. They should be kept in mind as the discussion examines the theory and research in this area.

THEORETICAL CONSIDERATIONS

Work on what might be termed sociocultural factors in language and literacy has a long history in the research literature, as noted previously. Some of the earliest such work focused on sociolinguistic studies of classroom language use and communicative patterns (Cazden, John, & Hymes, 1972). Wilkinson and Silliman (2000) noted that beginning in the 1970s, this research developed from a variety of disciplinary perspectives, including psychologists looking at individual differences in language use, linguists examining communicative functions, sociologists studying social organization and communication processes, educators examining the organization of lessons, speech and language researchers looking at language disabilities, and educational anthropologists looking at verbal and nonverbal communication within and between cultural groups.

Ethnographic work, especially that based in educational anthropology, has been especially prominent in studies focusing specifically on culture and on comparative studies between cultures in classrooms and home settings (Florio-Ruane & McVee, 2000). As Florio-Ruane and McVee pointed out, the work in educational anthropology has maintained a particular interest in "...cross cultural comparisons, focusing primarily on differential treatment and access to knowledge within the school of a society characterized by diversity in race, language, ethnicity, and social class." (p. 156). One characteristic of much of this work is that it has relied heavily on a social constructivist perspective (Florio-Ruane & McVee, 2000; Lave, 1988; Wilkinson & Silliman, 2000), in particular that reflecting social historical theory of neo-Vygotskian scholars (Cole, 1996; Lee, 2005a, 2005b; Lee & Smagorisnky, 2000; Gutierrez, Baquedano-Lopez, Alvarez, & Chiu, 1999; Moll, 1990; Moll & Gonzalez, 2004; Scribner & Cole, 1981) and thus slowly began to merge the traditional anthropological focus on cultural groups with the study of individual learning. The social constructivist framework has been especially prominent in bridging the social and the learning-related cognitive concerns (Brown, Collins, & Duguid, 1989; Lave, 1988; Lave & Wenger, 1991, 1998; Rogoff, Turkanis, & Bartlett, 2001; Rogoff, 2003; Tharp & Gallimore, 1988; Wenger, 1999; Wells & Claxton, 2002; Wertsch, 1991).

Social constructivist theorists argue that learning, including reading and literacy, is a function of the activity, context and culture in which it occurs (i.e., it is situated). Social interaction is a critical aspect of situated learning, as learners move from novice to expert in a specific "community of practice" which embodies certain beliefs and behaviors to be acquired, such as those surrounding reading and literacy in school settings. Brown et al. (1989) emphasize the idea of cognitive apprenticeship within this process, in which expertise advances through collaborative social interaction and the social construction of knowledge between a novice learner and a more competent facilitator (Rogoff et al., 2001).

This trend toward an emphasis on student learning and instruction, with a specific focus on the acquisition of literacy for students from culturally diverse backgrounds, was clearly exemplified in the work based on the Kamehameha Early Education Project (KEEP) in Hawaii during the 1980's (Au, 2000) and subsequent work in other cultural settings (Lee, 2007, 2008).

While social constructivist theory has been prominent in the research on cultural and sociocultural factors in reading and literacy research (Gaffney & Anderson, 2000), it is not the only perspective. Gee (2000) provided an overview of the multitude of theoretical and disciplinary perspectives that have guided research on sociocultural factors in reading. These include: (a) ethnomethodology and conversational analysis, (b) interactional sociolinguistics, (c) ethnography of speaking, (d) sociohistorical psychology, (e) situated cognition, (f) cultural models theory, (g) cognitive linguistics, (h) the new science and technology studies, (i) modern composition theory, (j) sociocultural literacy studies, (k) connectionism, (l) modern sociology, and (m) poststructuralist or postmodernist work. Gee contended that there is mounting convergence in these areas along themes that have traditionally formed tensions in the reading research: cognition vs. context, skills vs. meaning, formal language structures vs. communicative functions, and the individual vs. the social.

RESEARCH ON CULTURALLY RESPONSIVE INSTRUCTION AND CULTURAL ACCOMMODATIONS

A long-standing history focuses on the importance of cultural factors in the acquisition of school-based literacy. The earliest work in this area suggested that clear differences in language, discourse, and interactional patterns existed between students from different racial, ethnic, and cultural groups, especially compared to mainstream Anglo American students and teachers (Au, 1980; Hale-Benson, 1986; Heath, 1983; Labov, 1972). A major hypothesis of subsequent work in this area has been that students whose discursive styles are incongruent with school and mainstream cultural norms may encounter more obstacles to school achievement than peers who use styles that approximate such norms (Nieto, 1999; Gay, 2000). The absence of a shared cultural frame of reference is thought to impact students' participation in classroom activities including reading and literacy events (Gay, 2000; Lue, Green, & Smalley, 2002; Wiley, 2005), and, in the worst cases, lead to negative outcomes such as special education placement (Klinger et al., 2005). Thus, as Florio-Ruane & McVee (2000) noted, a major focus for the last two decades has been an effort to provide culturally responsive instruction and cultural accommodations.

Gay (2000) defined culturally responsive teaching as using the cultural knowledge, prior experiences, and performance styles of students to make learning more appropriate and effective for them by teaching to their strengths. She described this form of instruction as embracing the following elements:

1. It acknowledges the legitimacy of the cultural heritages of different ethnic groups, both as legacies that affect students' dispositions, attitudes, and approaches to learning and as worthy content to be taught in the formal curriculum.
2. It builds bridges of meaningfulness between home and school experiences as well as between academic abstractions and lived sociocultural realities.
3. It uses a wide variety of instructional strategies connected to different learning styles.
4. It teaches students to know and praise their own and each other's cultural heritages.
5. It incorporates multicultural information, resources, and materials in all the subjects and skills routinely taught in schools. (p. 29)

Au (2000) discussed the issue of cultural responsiveness in terms of literacy instruction, and noted some evidence (see Au & Kawakami, 1994) for "...positive results when teachers accepted and built on students' home language; structured interaction with students in a manner consistent with their home values; kept expectations high and focused on meaning-making rather than lower level skills; recognized that storytelling and question answering may take different forms in different cultures; and capitalized on students' ability to learn from peers" (p. 839). Drawing on a social constructivist perspective, Au noted that literacy achievement is a function of the interaction of multiple levels, including districts, schools, communities, teachers, students, and families. Interestingly, Au (1998, 2000) raised the possibility that factors in addition to cultural compatibility might be equally important to student outcomes, specifically instructional factors. Au and Mason (1981) noted the following about the research base at the time:

It has been implied that the presence of culturally congruent elements in lessons given to minority children may help to prevent damaging conflicts between teacher and students. This idea has much intuitive appeal, but we have very little evidence to support the notion that the presence of school situations resembling those in the home leads to improved academic achievement by minority children. (p. 150)

The most current comprehensive review of this issue is found in the report of the National Literacy Panel (August & Shanahan, 2006), which conducted a wide-ranging, evidence-based review of the research literature on the development of literacy among language minority children and youth. The Panel report covered a variety of topics related to the literacy acquisition of second language learners, including the development of literacy, cross-linguistic relationships, instructional approaches and professional development, and assessment. Of most concern to the present discussion, the report included a review of sociocultural factors in literacy development (Goldenberg, Rueda, & August, 2006a, 2006b; Rueda, August, & Goldenberg, 2006). Sociocultural factors were defined broadly, and the following questions examined:

1. What is the influence of immigration (generation status and immigration circumstances) on literacy development, defined broadly?
2. What is the influence of differences in discourse and interaction characteristics between children's homes and classrooms?
3. What is the influence of other sociocultural characteristics of students and teachers?
4. What is the influence of parents and families?
5. What is the influence of policies at the district, state, and federal levels?
6. What is the influence of language status or prestige?

One section of the report (Goldenberg et al., 2006b) examined these issues with the stipulation that some student outcome measure was included in the studies examined. This was purposely defined broadly to include any observational indicators, ethnographic descriptions, examples or analyses of student products, motivational measures, participation or engagement measures, self- or teacher reports, and standardized or quantitative measures. A total of 50 studies fit this criterion. A second section of the report focused on the same questions, but with no requirement for reported student outcomes, finding an additional 25 of the most relevant descriptive studies.

The aspect of the report with the most relevance to the present discussion focuses on the second question, specifically the impact of efforts to accommodate classroom instruction to cultural differences. The major conclusions from the report in this domain suggested the following. First, it is clear that there are differences between the interactional and discourse features, norms, and expectations of home/community and school for many culturally and linguistically diverse students. An especially rich descriptive literature paints a picture of how these differences are exhibited in classroom settings in a variety of activities. Second, surprisingly few studies have included student outcomes, and most of the available studies use proximal indicators of achievement (i.e., engagement) rather than direct measures of reading or literacy acquisition. Third, a large number of the existing studies are plagued by methodological issues, which include the following:

1. Insufficient specification about investigator time spent in the research setting.
2. Insufficient specification of data-collection techniques, data-analysis techniques, number of subjects, and number of observations.
3. Data not presented to confirm/disconfirm author's point of view explicitly.
4. No information about how representative examples were selected.
5. No information about the frequency or typicality of reported key occurrences.
6. No information about whether competing interpretations were considered and evaluated.
7. Insufficient triangulation across several data sources.
8. Making inferences and drawing conclusions not warranted by the data reported. (Goldenberg et al., 2006a, p. 260)

The report also indicated that some support exists for the impact of related factors such as culturally familiar text and/or language on reading comprehension. That is, students tend to understand more when it is in the language they know better and when the text they are reading deals with culturally recognizable content.

While the National Literacy Panel report is the most current and comprehensive review of the impact of cultural factors on literacy acquisition, admittedly it focused on second language learners and thus excluded other populations (Gay, 2000; Hollins & Oliver, 1999; Ladson-Billings, 1994, 1995; Lee, 2005b). The general conclusions reached in this report, however, do not change significantly even when other populations are considered. The current research base does not offer good guidance (other than general principles and plausible hypotheses along with descriptions of specific projects or sites where they have been used and accounts of the impact) for school personnel who are trying to consider cultural issues in literacy instruction.

It is important to recognize that lack of extensive evidence is not the same as negative evidence. In fact, many of the hypotheses regarding cultural accommodations and the influences of cultural processes on reading and literacy outcomes are highly plausible and likely. As noted above, it is certainly the case that differences between most classroom settings and the home and community settings are real and able to be documented for many students from diverse backgrounds. It should also be kept in mind that the extensive work in educational anthropology and related areas demonstrate that early views of these differences as deficits are misguided, and in fact the rich cultural and linguistic resources of students can be used advantageously to engage students in high level academic work (Gonzalez et al., 2005).

One reason there is not extensive evidence for the impact of cultural accommodations and culturally responsive instruction is that, as noted earlier, culture is difficult to define, at least in ways that allow for quantitative measurement and observation. By definition, culture is dynamic, contextually variable, and unevenly expressed (Erickson, 2004; Gallego, Cole, & LCHC, 2001). Moreover, because of strong ties to anthropology, a major focus has been on detailed and accurate description of social, cultural, and linguistic processes in specific settings and activities. The research has focused more on the "what is?" question regarding cultural processes and cultural factors rather than the "what are the effects of?" question.

However, there is another possible reason for the lack of research addressing the issue of impact related to cultural factors. This is the lack of theoretical or conceptual models relating social and cultural factors to student learning and other outcomes without trivializing or narrowly and artificially defining and measuring cultural processes. While Gee (2000) noted some convergence around key issues from a multitude of diverse disciplines and theoretical orientations that look at sociocultural factors in reading, there is no framework that can help tie the descriptive work on literacy with the more experimentally-based work on reading. The following section discusses some possibilities in this regard.

What Ties Cultural Factors To Reading and Literacy Outcomes?

As the previous section suggests, there does not appear to be a clear answer to this question, since conceptual models, especially those with clear instructional ties and connections to student learning, are missing. Thus this section offers some possibilities in this regard, in particular in the area of reading comprehension, which may be helpful in stimulating future work.

A Note on Reading Comprehension.   The RAND Reading Study Group (2002) offered the following definition of reading comprehension:

> The process of simultaneously extracting and constructing meaning through interaction and involvement with written language. Comprehension has these elements: the reader,

the text, and the activity, or purpose for reading. These elements define a phenomenon—reading comprehension—that occurs within a larger sociocultural context that shapes and is shaped by the reader and that infuses each of the elements. All are influenced by the broader context. (p. xi)

In discussing the role of the reader, the report goes on to say:

The reader brings to the act of reading his or her cognitive capacities (attention, memory, critical analytic ability, inferencing, and visualization), motivation (a purpose for reading, interest in the content, self efficacy as a reader), knowledge (vocabulary, domain, and topic knowledge, linguistic and discourse knowledge, knowledge of comprehension strategies), and experiences. (p. xi–xii)

Where might comprehension break down for students from diverse language or cultural backgrounds? A preliminary list might include the following:

1. Attention—there may be differences in the cues students attend to in classroom instruction.
2. Encoding—the input from text, the teacher, or peer discussions may not be comprehensible because of language differences or because of differences in genre or vocabulary, or the formal register used in academic contexts or "academic English" (Bailey, 2007) or typical discourse patterns (Cazden, 1988; Mehan, 1979).
3. Strategic processing and self-regulation—because of the complex interplay among race, ethnicity, and socioeconomic status, students from some households may not have been exposed to large numbers of schooled adults who might model strategies useful in processing text.
4. Background knowledge—the knowledge and skills that students have acquired may not map easily onto that in curriculum materials or books or activities.
5. Motivation—students may come to school with different learning goals (Goldenberg, Gallimore, Reese, & Garnier, 2001; Ogbu & Simmons, 1998), poor self-efficacy due to past academic experiences, or low task value because the structure or purpose of instructional activities do not map onto known experiences and abilities and interests.

In addition to these factors, language and cultural differences may influence how significant others such as teachers or peers respond to and interact with individual students, whether these differences are real or perceived. These differences may influence teacher expectations, for example, and result in differential treatment, thus mediating student participation, engagement, and other opportunities to learn. Given these possibilities, it is possible to hypothesize that cultural factors can have both primary intrapersonal effects on reading and literacy and secondary interpersonal effects. The former might be reflected by the impact on individual cognitive processes and motivational and affective states, while the latter might operate in a variety of interpersonal contexts or activity settings serving to facilitate or constrain participation and interaction. We will discuss each below, drawing on Rueda (2006).

Primary Intrapersonal Effects—Cognitive Processes.   While most cognitive psychologists and information processing theorists consider basic human cognitive processes to be universal, there is some evidence that even basic processes may be influenced by cultural factors. Bransford, Brown, and Cocking (1999) suggested, "Prior knowledge also includes the kind of knowledge that learners acquire because of their social roles, such as those connected with race, class, gender, and their culture and ethnic affiliations" (p. 60). As one example, primacy (remembering the first thing heard in a sequence) and recency (remembering the last thing heard) effects, often thought to reflect universal aspects of human memory performance, are influenced by cultural background and the type of schooling children have (Valsiner, 1988). Schooling may influence even basic, seemingly universal, cognitive processes such as visual-perceptual processing, attention, and visual and verbal memory (Cole & Scribner, 1977; Ostrovsky-Solis, Ramirez, & Ardilia, 2004; Rogoff, 1981).

In the domain of reading, recent work on cognitive load theory seems especially relevant in the attempt to link cultural processes with cognitive and academic outcomes. A major focus of this work is the capacity limitations of working memory (Paas, Renkl, & Sweller, 2003; Sweller, 1988; Sweller, van Merriënboer, & Paas, 1998). This work focuses on how constraints in working memory help determine what types of instruction are effective. A basic tenet of cognitive load theory is that learning is mediated by human limitations on working memory capacity, and processing and/or storage not directly relevant for learning makes it less efficient. When this occurs, working memory capacity is taxed (i.e., cognitive load is high) and thus learning is negatively affected. These limitations in working memory can be reduced, in part, by enabling the use of schemas, an organization that incorporates multiple elements of information into a single element with a single function stored in long term memory (LTM), enabling a learner to process information more efficiently.

LTM contains huge amounts of domain-specific knowledge structures (including culturally specific knowledge) that can be described as hierarchically organized schemas allowing one to categorize different problem states and decide the most appropriate solution to a given problem. This might include important issues as what is considered a problem to solve in the first place, how to frame or mentally represent the problem to be solved, or what solutions would be considered appropriate.

Another way in which cognitive load can be reduced is when cognitive processes operate automatically rather than under conscious control. Automatic processing of schemas requires minimal working memory resources and allows problem solving to proceed with minimal effort. In the domain of reading, as an example, difficulties in decoding make the processing of text very difficult for a reader, such that the cognitive load is high. Reading fluency, however, helps reduce the cognitive demand and thus makes text comprehension easier for the reader.

Categories of Cognitive Load.   Cognitive load theory specifies different types of cognitive load with very different and instructionally relevant features. *Intrinsic cognitive load* refers to the demands on working memory capacity intrinsic to the material being learned such as a specific text. Different materials or learning activities differ in their level of intrinsic cognitive load, and modifying instruction cannot change this. Changing a task so that it is a simpler learning task that omits some interacting elements, however, can reduce the cognitive load and thus the efficiency of the learning. A basic finding regarding human cognition is that working memory—where all conscious cognitive processing is thought to occur—can handle no more than two or three novel interacting elements. In contrast, LTM is made up of schemas. Such organization helps lighten the load—bringing the schema from LTM into working memory means only one element must be processed, even though the schema may incorporate many interacting elements. Thus schemas accomplish the same purpose as a factor analysis in a statistical context—simplifying many things into fewer so it is simpler to process and less draining on the available resources.

Extraneous or *ineffective cognitive load* is due to the manner in which information is presented or the nature of the learning activities. Ineffective cognitive load imposes an unnecessary burden on learning. Most instructional design work, where cognitive load theory has been most frequently applied, has focused on trying to reduce extraneous cognitive load because it is amenable to instructional characteristics. Extraneous cognitive load is primarily important when intrinsic cognitive load is high (i.e., reading a difficult or complex text) because the two forms of cognitive load are additive. If intrinsic cognitive load is low (as with simple recreational text), levels of extraneous cognitive load may be less important because the total cognitive load may not exceed working memory capacity.

Germane or *effective cognitive load* refers to demands placed on working memory capacity by mental activities that contribute directly to learning, defined in cognitive load theory as schema acquisition and automation. Germane cognitive load enhances learning and is influenced by instructional design. Also, increases in effort or motivation can increase the cognitive resources devoted to a task. If these additional resources are relevant to schema acquisition and automation, it also constitutes an increase in germane cognitive load.

Applications to Cultural Accommodations and Reading Comprehension Instruction. An important principle in this work is that intrinsic, extraneous, and germane cognitive load are additive, and furthermore, the total load cannot exceed working memory resources available if learning is going to occur. Culture can be thought of (admittedly narrowly, but for purposes of the current discussion) as an automated schema that helps simplify cognitive demands in everyday tasks and activities. If every behavior or thought or sentence were novel, the cognitive demands would be very high. However, familiar schemas lighten this load, and when these are automated, cognitive load is further reduced. Thus, being in a culturally familiar setting is relatively effortless compared with being in a strange cultural setting. A culturally unfamiliar text (because of unfamiliar text structure or unfamiliar concepts or ideas) could impose intrinsic cognitive load even if the text could be decoded. In addition, culturally familiar materials, settings, and activities may help focus attention in ways that might promote learning. In essence, focusing one's attention represents more efficient and task-relevant use of those scarce resources in the limited working memory store.

The applications of this work to conceptualizing cultural accommodations and reading comprehension specifically should be apparent. In essence, culturally unfamiliar reading materials and texts, reading-related activities, and even ways of talking and speaking during reading instruction may represent sources of extraneous cognitive load and thus make learning less efficient and more burdensome. Recall that the different types of cognitive load are additive. Therefore, as the total cognitive load surpasses the capacity of the cognitive system, learning and comprehension will suffer. In essence, cognitive load may serve as a mediator between external cultural and sociocultural factors and environments on the one hand and internal cognitive processes on the other to facilitate or diminish learning. Cultural unfamiliarity with specific tasks, texts, discourse and interactional processes, and other important classroom features may therefore lead to the types of negative outcomes that the descriptive literature reviewed earlier has so long suggested. The reverse situation is likewise possible, whereby the cultural schemas some students bring to classroom learning activities advantage them in ways that reduce cognitive load and thus make learning more efficient. Thus, as many authors have suggested, when culturally responsive instruction is introduced, students can access their relevant schemas or "funds of knowledge" (Moll & Gonzalez, 2004) in such a way that extraneous cognitive load is reduced.

Rueda (2006) termed the processes just described "facilitative encoding". Under ideal circumstances, where students' cultural knowledge helps them access text and classroom activities, extraneous and thus overall cognitive load should be reduced in ways that facilitate learning and comprehension. Thus, while culturally compatible instruction and classroom settings may make students feel better about being there, which is not a trivial consideration, these approaches may also make tasks more comprehensible and amenable to connections with existing prior knowledge. A somewhat related concept from the literature on second language acquisition, comprehensible input, has long been proposed as an important instructional principle for second language learners (Krashen, 1982). If the preceding argument holds true, teachers of students from diverse backgrounds need to be well informed about the cultural knowledge that their students bring to school, and the ways in which reading materials, instructional activities, and other aspects of comprehension instruction can serve to unduly increase cognitive load, leading to impaired learning. Similarly, it also suggests that children's existing schemas can be broadened such that previously unfamiliar material, activities, and settings are well integrated into long term memory.

Primary Intrapersonal Effects—Motivational Processes.   Motivation has often been considered as a trait inherent to students. Contemporary motivational theory, in contrast, has focused on one's context-specific personal beliefs around specific tasks and activities and one's ability to engage in those tasks. Schunk, Pintrich, and Meece (2008) suggest that the central indicators of motivation include active choice, persistence, and mental effort, all of which are assumed to impact achievement. While there is wide agreement on these indices of motivation, motivation theory in general comprises a family of related theories rather than one singular theory. Thus, because the aim of this chapter is heuristic, not all possible motivational variables will be addressed. Rather, we will attempt to illustrate how motivational processes can be linked to cultural processes. One motivation theory that has been particularly influential is known as expectancy x value theory, and because of its relevance to the discussion, it will be the focus here.

A Social-Cognitive Expectancy Value Perspective on Motivation.   Eccles and Wigfield and their colleagues (Eccles, 1983, 1987, 1993; Eccles & Midgley, 1989; Wigfield, 1994; Wigfield & Eccles, 1992, 2000) outlined the motivational framework known as expectancy x value theory, which focuses on two key components of motivation. Expectancy is how well one expects to do on a given task, and value is how much one values a given task or activity. In this framework, greatly simplified here because of space limitations, aspects of the social world (cultural milieu, socializers' behaviors, and past performances) influence motivational beliefs (task value and expectancy) and individuals' cognitive processes (perceptions of the social environment and causal attributions), which in turn produce motivated behavior (active choice, persistence, mental effort) (Schunk et al., 2008). The key aspects of an expectancy x value approach are explained below.

The value component of this theory focuses on beliefs related to how individuals answer the question, "Why should I do this task?" There are four basic aspects of task value, including interest, importance, utility, and cost. Expectancy, on the other hand, refers to beliefs related to the question, "Am I able to do this task?" and the basic aspects include self-efficacy, perceived task difficulty, and causal attribution. The assumption here is that cultural factors (i.e., familiarity or unfamiliarity) can shape one or more of these motivational variables and thus mediate one's choice of activities, effort, and persistence. In cases where students have strong expectations for being successful in a task or activity and have high value and interest, engagement will be increased and vice versa. Thus, in culturally compatible situations, students may believe they are more likely to succeed and the task is less difficult, and attribute errors to lack of effort rather than lack of ability. They may also be more interested and believe the task or materials are more important, that mastering the task has some usefulness in other situations, and that the task will not require an unreasonable amount of effort. Thus cultural factors impact student outcomes and achievement at least in part through their mediation of basic motivational processes. Similar to facilitative encoding, which focuses on cognitive factors, the parallel here in the motivational arena can be termed "facilitative engagement."

In a comprehensive review of current work and issues in motivation, Pintrich (2003) outlined key motivational generalizations based on current research and theory. These include: (a) adaptive self-efficacy and competence beliefs motivate students, (b) adaptive attributions and control beliefs motivate students, (c) higher levels of interest and intrinsic motivation motivate students, (d) higher levels of value motivate students, and (e) goals motivate and direct students (p. 672).

It can be hypothesized that culturally compatible instruction and culturally responsive learning environments and materials can have a significant impact on these key motivational areas and thus mediate student participation in ways that help (or hinder) their reading, comprehension, and ultimately achievement. Consistent with this hypothesis, some of the descriptive research on cultural factors described increased student engagement as a product of culturally compatible teaching (Au, 1980). While engagement is not necessarily the same as achievement, fostering engagement is not a trivial concern. A robust literature, in fact, suggests that mental effort is associated with motivational beliefs such as interest (Salomon, 1984), and that academic engagement and other "achievement-related behaviors" are associated with measured achievement (Fredericks, Blumenfeld, & Paris, 2004) and reading comprehension in particular (Guthrie et al., 2004; Guthrie et al., 2006).

In addition to cognitive and motivational intrapersonal ways in which cultural processes can impact reading and comprehension, a social constructivist perspective would suggest that intrapersonal processes play a role as well. These are discussed next.

Secondary Interpersonal Effects—Social Processes.   These effects can be thought of as influences on individual learning mediated by the processes and organization of the social context. That is, the nature of students' participation in classroom activities has a major impact on learning (Lave & Wenger, 1998; Rogoff, 1991, 1995; Rogoff, Baker-Sennett, Lacasa, & Goldsmith, 1995; Wenger, 1999). These mediating effects might be reflected through social interactions with others in places like classrooms, and may ultimately influence important factors such as opportunity to learn through diminished participation, negative interactions with teachers, etc. (Cazden, 1985). There is evidence that everything a teacher does has a motivational impact on students (Stipek, 1996). Teachers' beliefs about their ability to teach and about their students' learning abilities and cognitive abilities influence their relationships with students (Davis, 2003). This is reflected in areas such as type of feedback given, the use of reward structures, praise and criticism, help, and overall classroom climate (Schunk et al., 2008). One way this may operate in classroom settings is when teachers or school personnel such as psychologists interpret the performance of culturally diverse students as reflective of cognitive or linguistic deficiencies because of nonmainstream discourse and/or interactional patterns (Labov, 1982; Lee, 2005b, 2007).

This section has outlined some possible mechanisms to begin connecting cultural processes and cultural differences, such as those found in many classroom settings, with cognitive and motivational factors which ultimately connect to achievement. As the overview of research in this area suggests, such factors have long been hypothesized to play a role in the lagging performance in reading and literacy of students of color. The work has been primarily qualitative in nature, however, for reasons outlined earlier, and there is no strong causally oriented research base linking such factors to student outcomes. The nature of the construct makes it difficult to manipulate experimentally. Equally important, however, is the lack of a theoretical framework to suggest possible mechanisms that link cultural processes and learning. Given the lack of models that might guide such research, we made suggestions for ways in which cultural factors might impact learning. These included primary intrapersonal effects, including facilitative encoding and facilitative engagement, focusing on cognitive and motivational factors respectively. In addition, we described secondary interpersonal effects, focusing on ways that social and interactional processes can be mediated by cultural factors and thus constrain or facilitate student participation and the nature of day-to-day interactions.

IMPLICATIONS FOR THEORY, PRACTICE, POLICY, AND FUTURE RESEARCH

Research and Theoretical Concerns

One interesting observation related to the treatment of cultural processes in the literature is that cultural factors are often discussed solely with reference to students from diverse cultural and linguistic backgrounds, as opposed to being a pervasive feature of all human activity. In addition, culture is often treated as a function of students primarily, rather than as a feature that permeates social contexts and learning processes in classrooms and schools. Although culture has been a consistent concern of previous volumes of the *Handbook of Reading Research*, there is still a significant amount that we do not know. As noted earlier, previous research focused more on the descriptive "what is" type of questions through careful, contextualized description of specific cultural settings and processes involving reading and literacy. This has been augmented by work that attempted to adjust classroom teaching and classroom settings to make them more culturally responsive to students, most often through various forms of cultural accommodations. In addition, over time, there has been a trend away from negative views of students' cultural practices from home and community toward using these cultural practices as an instructional resource.

The task remaining is to develop a knowledge base that allows instructional practices developed in this fashion to be more strategic, and theoretically and empirically driven. From a research perspective, a significant need in the field is to examine more systematically the impact of cultural factors, to provide better guidance to teachers and schools. Part of the challenge in this regard is reducing or eliminating the cognitive-cultural divide, and building models that will integrate work from different perspectives—including models that speak to how cultural factors should or might impact reading and literacy processes specifically. It also involves connecting work on cultural processes and practices with work on learning. Consideration of a learning framework allows the development of specific testable hypotheses and provides some guidance about relevant constructs to assess and/or manipulate when considering literacy in general and reading comprehension instruction in particular. There are some examples of attempts to address multiple interacting dimensions of determinants of student achievement (e.g., Fredericks et al., 2004).

From a research perspective, questions of interest include:

1. Do culturally responsive teaching practices reduce cognitive load in learning activities? If so, does this result in better achievement?
2. Which types of accommodations are the most effective in mediating cognitive load?
3. Does the systematic use of culturally relevant text produce higher student engagement and/or outcomes (greater interest and task value, thus impacting the choice to read more, to persist at reading tasks, to exert more effort with challenging text, and finally to increased comprehension)?
4. Does culturally accommodated instruction lead to higher self-efficacy, or facilitate connections to prior knowledge, thus decreasing cognitive load?
5. Do features of culturally accommodated instructional routines or activities increase student interest, importance, and utility, thus influencing choice, persistence, or effort?

These and many other related questions have not been extensively explored to date, with a few notable exceptions (Au, 1980, 2000; Lee, 2005a). Instructional and curriculum designers are left to rely on intuition or educated guesses regarding if, when, and how to design and implement these approaches. Systematic work drawing on current understandings of learning and motivation promises to help unravel these questions. As this work on cultural factors becomes more integrated into mainstream reading and literacy research, we need to see that it begins to be reflected in state and federal reading policy as well.

Instructional Considerations

Sociocultural theorists (Lee & Smagorinsky, 2000; Lee & Ball, 2005) remind us that learning and achievement are not solely a function of individual students and intrinsic characteristics, but rather reside in the interaction between the student and the environment. When students come to school with nontraditional backgrounds, those educators who try to facilitate literacy and reading comprehension processes need to systematically consider the learning and motivational implications of the classroom activities and materials they provide. Currently, the research base does not permit offering guidance (other than general principles) for school personnel who are trying to consider cultural issues in literacy instruction. The work of authors such as Gallimore and Goldenberg (2001), Gutierrez and Stone (2000), Lee (2000), and Rogoff (2003) on cultural models suggested that at a minimum the following types of questions would be important to explore in order to form the foundation of culturally responsive pedagogy that many have argued for (Au, 2000; Gay, 2000):

1. What is the range and nature of cultural settings that a learner has had experience with?
2. Who are/were the participants?
3. What is the range and nature of things people do or did in those settings? (This can bring in all of the traditional sociocultural influences, such as ethnicity, race, gender, socio-economic status, etc., without having to make monolithic judgments about individual characteristics based on group labels—the answers to these questions provides a window into how these factors operate a specific individual but not for an entire group).
4. Based on experience in these settings, what types of cultural models have individuals developed?

In terms of classroom settings, parallel concerns might include:

1. What are the typical and characteristic activity settings in this school and classroom? How are they structured?
2. How and when do they occur?
3. Who participates?
4. What are the cultural models that characterize this classroom or school?

Teachers well informed regarding these questions have at a minimum a principled way and an empirical base for modifications in instruction that will maximize the cultural resources of their students.

We should keep in mind that although the focus on cultural factors in reading and literacy is increasingly prominent in the research literature, problematic aspects of how culture has been treated in the past need to be avoided, including the following:

1. Making monolithic judgments about entire groups (often around racial and/or ethnic lines) without considering within-group and individual differences.
2. Focusing on surface features of culture.
3. Focusing on presumed culturally related variables that have failed to show a relationship to learning such as learning styles.
4. Treating culture as a deficit rather than a resource in learning.

5. Equating group labels, especially racial and ethnic group labels, with cultural characteristics.
6. Assuming cultural influences operate rigidly in all settings.
7. Relying on presumed characteristics without considering empirical validation.

Erickson (2004) noted that the presence of cultural differences in society does not necessarily lead to conflict or problems in school or other social and organizational settings. Rather, conflict is dependent on whether cultural differences are treated as a boundary or a border. Boundaries, which are to be expected, are simply a reflection of the presence of cultural differences. Borders, on the other hand, are social constructs, political in origin, involving the arbitrary exercise of power or authority of one group over another. It is when boundaries are treated as borders, when one's cultural knowledge is scrutinized or "stopped and frisked," as Erickson notes, that problems may arise. While there are descriptive accounts of how these processes operate in classroom settings, we know little about how to overcome these effects in educationally advantageous ways.

REFERENCES

Au, K. H. (1980). Participation structures in a reading lesson with Hawaiian children: Analysis of a culturally appropriate instructional event. *Anthropology and Education Quarterly, 11*(2), 91-115.

Au, K. H. (1998). Social constructivism and the school literacy learning of students of diverse backgrounds. *Journal of Literacy Research, 20*, 297–319.

Au, K. H. (2000). A multicultural perspective on policies for improving literacy achievement: Equity and excellence. In M. L. Kamil, P. B. Mosenthal, P. David Pearson, & R. Barr (Eds.), *Handbook of reading research: Vol III* (pp. 835–852). New York: Erlbaum.

Au, K. H., & Kawakami, A. J. (1994). Cultural congruence in instruction. In E. R. Hollins, J. E. King, & W. Hayman (Eds.), *Teaching diverse populations: Formulating a knowledge base* (pp. 5–23). Albany: State University of New York Press.

Au, K. H., & Mason, J. M. (1981). Social organizational factors in learning to read: The balance of rights hypothesis. *Reading Research Quarterly, 17*(1), 115–152.

August, D., & Shanahan, T. (Eds.). (2006). *Developing literacy in second-language learners: Report of the National Literacy Panel on language-minority children and youth.* Mahwah, NJ: Erlbaum.

Bailey, A. L. (2007). *The language demands of school: Putting academic English to the test.* New Haven, CT: Yale University Press.

Bloome, D., Katz, L., Solsken, J., Willett, J., & Wilson-Keenan, J. (2000). Interpellations of family/community and classroom literacy practices. *Journal of Educational Research, 93*(3), 155–163.

Bransford, J. D., Brown, A. L., & Cocking, R. R. (1999). *How people learn: Brain, mind, experience, and school.* Washington, DC: National Academy Press.

Brown, J. S., Collins, A., & Duguid, S. (1989). Situated cognition and the culture of learning. *Educational Researcher, 18*(1), 32–42.

Cazden, C. B. (1985). Social context of learning to read. In H. Singer & R. B. Ruddell (Eds.), *Theoretical models and the processes of reading* (3rd ed., pp. 595–610). Newark, DE: International Reading Association.

Cazden, C. B. (1988). *Classroom discourse.* New York: Heinemann.

Cazden, C. B., John, V., & Hymes, D. (Eds.). (1972). *Functions of language in the classroom.* New York: Teachers College Press.

Cole, M. (1996). *Cultural psychology: A once and future discipline.* Cambridge, MA: Harvard University Press.

Cole, M., & Scribner, S. (1977). Cross-cultural studies of memory and cognition. In R. V. Kail, Jr., & J. W. Hagen (Eds.), *Perspectives on the development of memory and cognition* (pp. 239–271). Hillsdale, NJ: Erlbaum.

D'Andrade, R. (1996). Culture. *Social science encyclopedia* (2nd ed., pp. 161–163). London: Routledge.

D'Andrade, R. G., & Strauss, C. (Eds.). (1992). *Human motives and cultural models*. Cambridge, UK: Cambridge University Press.

Davis, H. A., (2003). Conceptualizing the role and influence of student-teacher relationships on children's social and cognitive development. *Educational Psychologist, 38*, 207–234.

Eccles, J. (1983). Expectancies, values and academic behaviors. In J. T. Spence (Ed.), *Achievement and achievement motives* (pp. 75–146). San Francisco: Freeman.

Eccles, J. (1987). Gender roles and women's achievement-related decisions. *Psychology of Women Quarterly, 11*, 135–172.

Eccles, J. (1993). School and family effects on the ontogeny of childrens' interests, self-perceptions, and activity choice. In J. Jacobs (Ed.), *Nebraska symposium on motivation: Developmental perspectives on motivation* (pp. 145–208). Lincoln: University of Nebraska Press.

Eccles, J. S., & Midgley, C. (1989). Stage-environment fit: Developmentally appropriate classrooms for young adolescents. In C. Ames & R. Ames (Eds.), *Research on motivation in education* (Vol. 3, pp. 139–186). San Diego, CA: Academic Press.

Erickson, F. (2004). Culture in society and in educational practices. In J. A. Banks & C. A. McGee Banks (Eds.), *Handbook of research on multicultural education* (5th ed., pp. 31–60). New York: Wiley.

Feuer, M. J., Towne, L., & Shavelson, R. J. (2002). Scientific culture and educational research. *Educational Researcher, 11*(31), 4–14.

Florio-Ruane, S., & McVee, M. (2000). Ethnographic approaches to literacy research. In M. L. Kamil, P. B. Mosenthal, P. David Pearson, & R. Barr (Eds.), *Handbook of reading research: Vol III* (pp. 153–162). Mahwah, NJ: Erlbaum.

Fredericks, J., Blumenfield, P., & Paris, A. (2004). School engagement: Potential of the concept, state of the evidence. *Review of Educational Research, 74*, 59–109.

Gaffney, J. S., & Anderson, R. C. (2000). Trends in reading research: Changing intellectual currents over three decades. In M. L. Kamil, P. B. Mosenthal, P. David Pearson, & R. Barr (Eds.), *Handbook of reading research: Vol III* (pp. 53–76). Mahwah, NJ: Erlbaum.

Gallego, M. A., Cole, M., & LCHC. (2001). Classroom culture and culture in the classroom. In V. Richardson (Ed.), *The fourth edition of the handbook of research on teaching* (pp. 951–997). Washington, DC: American Educational Research Association.

Gallego, M., & Cole, M. (1998). Classroom cultures and cultures in the classroom. In V. Richardson (Ed.), *Handbook of research on teaching* (4th ed., pp. 355–490). New York: MacMillan.

Gallimore, R., & Goldenberg, C. (2001). Analyzing cultural models and settings to connect minority achievement and school improvement research. *Educational Psychologist, 36*(1), 45–56.

Gay, G. (2000). *Culturally responsive teaching*. New York: Teachers College Press.

Gee, J. P. (1992). Reading. *Journal of Urban and Cultural Studies, 2*, 65–77.

Gee, J. P. (2000). Discourse and sociocultural studies in reading. In M. L. Kamil, P. B. Mosenthal, P. David Pearson, & R. Barr (Eds.), *Handbook of reading research: Vol III* (pp. 195–208). Mahwah, NJ: Erlbaum.

Goldenberg, C., Gallimore, R., Reese, L., & Garnier, H. (2001). Cause or effect? A longitudinal study of immigrant Latino parents' aspirations and expectations and their children's school performance. *American Educational Research Association Journal, 38*, 547–582.

Goldenberg, C., Rueda, R. S., & August, D. (2006a). Synthesis: Sociocultural contexts and literacy development. In D. August & T. Shanahan (Eds.), *Developing literacy in second-language learners: Report of the National Literacy Panel on language-minority children and youth* (pp. 249–268). Mahwah, NJ: Erlbaum.

Goldenberg, C., Rueda, R. S., & August, D. (2006b). Sociocultural influences on the literacy attainment of language-minority children and youth. In D. August & T. Shanahan (Eds.), *Developing literacy in second-language learners: Report of the National Literacy Panel on language-minority children and youth* (pp. 269–318). Mahwah, NJ: Erlbaum.

Gonzalez, N., Moll, L. C., & Amanti, C. (2005). *Funds of knowledge: Theorizing practices in households, communities, and classrooms*. Mahwah, NJ: Erlbaum.

Goodenough, W. H. (1994). Toward a working theory of culture. In R. B. Borotsky (Ed.), *Assessing cultural anthropology* (pp. 262–273). New York: McGraw-Hill.

Guthrie, J. T., Wigfield, A., Barbosa, P., Perencevich, K. C., Taboada, A., Davis, M. H., Scafiddi, N. T., & Tonks, S. (2004). Increasing reading comprehension and engagement through concept-oriented reading instruction. *Journal of Educational Psychology, 96*(3), 403–423.

Guthrie, J. T., Wigfield, A., Humenick, N. M., Perencevich, K. C., Taboada, A., & Barbosa, P. (2006). Influences of stimulating tasks on reading motivation and comprehension. *Journal of Educational Research, 99*(4), 232–245.

Gutierrez, K. D., Baquedano-Lopez, P., Alvarez, H., & Chiu, M. (1999). Building a culture of collaboration through hybrid language practices. *Theory Into Practice, 38*(2), 87–93.

Gutierrez, K. D., & Rogoff, B. (2003). Cultural ways of learning: Individual styles or repertoires of practice. *Educational Researcher, 32*(5), 19–25.

Gutierrez, K. D., & Stone, L. D. (2000). Synchronic and diachronic dimensions of social practice: An emerging methodology for cultural-historical perspectives on literacy learning. In C. D. Lee & P. Smagorinsky (Eds.), *Vygotskian perspectives on literacy research: Constructing meaning through collaborative inquiry* (pp. 150–164). New York: Cambridge University Press.

Hale-Benson, J. E. (1986). *Black children: Their roots, culture, and learning styles.* Baltimore, MD: John Hopkins University Press.

Heath, S. B. (1983). *Ways with words: Language, life, and work in communities and classrooms.* Cambridge, UK: Cambridge University Press.

Hollins, E. R., & Oliver, E. I. (1999). *Pathways to success in school: Culturally responsive teaching.* Mahwah, NJ: Erlbaum.

Klinger, J. K., Artiles, A. J., Kozleski, E., Harry, B., Zion, S., Tate, W., et al. (2005). Addressing the disproportionate representation of culturally and linguistically diverse students in special education through culturally responsive educational systems. *Education Policy Analysis Archives, 13*(38). Retrieved June 15, 2007, from http://epaa.asu.edu/epaa/v1n38

Krashen, S. (1982). *Principles and practice in second language acquisition.* New York: Pergamon Press.

Kroeber, A. L., & Kluckholn, C. (1963). *Culture: A review of concepts and definitions.* New York: Alfred A. Knopf, Inc., and Random House.

Labov, W. (1972). *Language in the inner city.* Philadelphia: University of Pennsylvania Press.

Labov, W. (1982). Objectivity and commitment in linguistic science: The case of the Black English trial in Ann Arbor. *Language in Society, 11*, 165–201.

Ladson-Billings, G. (1994). *The dreamkeepers: Successful teachers for African-American children.* San Francisco: Jossey-Bass.

Ladson-Billings, G. (1995). But that's just good teaching! The case for culturally relevant pedagogy. *Theory Into Practice, 34*(3), 159–165.

Lave, J. (1988). *Cognition in practice: Mind, mathematics, and culture in everyday life.* Cambridge, UK: Cambridge University Press.

Lave, J., & Wenger, E. (1991). *Situated learning: Legitimate peripheral participation.* Cambridge, UK: Cambridge University Press.

Lave, J., & Wenger, E. (1998). *Communities of practice: Learning, meaning, and identity.* Cambridge, UK: Cambridge University Press.

Lee, C. D. (2000). Signifying in the zone of proximal development. In C. D. Lee & P. Smagorinsky (Eds.), *Vygotskian perspectives on literacy research: Constructing meaning through collaborative inquiry* (pp. 191–225). New York: Cambridge University Press.

Lee, C. D. (2005a). Culture and language: Bidialectical issues in literacy. In J. Flood & P. L. Anders (Eds.), *Literacy development of students in urban schools: Research and policy* (pp. 241–274). Newark, DE: International Reading Association.

Lee, C. D. (2005b). Taking culture in to account: Intervention research based on current views of cognition & learning. In J. King (Eds.), *Black education: a transformative research and action agenda for the new century* (pp. 73–114). Mahwah, NJ: Erlbaum.

Lee, C. D. (2007). *Culture, literacy, and learning: Taking bloom in the midst of the whirlwind.* New York: Teachers College Press.

Lee, C. D. (2008). Synthesis of research on the role of culture in learning among African American youth: The contributions of Asa G. Hilliard, III. *Review of Educational Research, 78*(4), 797–827.

Lee, C. D., & Ball, A. (2005). All that glitters ain't gold: CHAT as a design & analytical tool in literacy research. In R. Beach, J. Green, M. Kamil, & T. Shanahan (Eds.), *Multidisciplinary perspectives on literacy research* (2nd ed., pp. 101–132). Cresskill, NJ: Hampton Press.

Lee, C. D., & Smagorinsky, P. (2000). *Vygotskian perspectives on literacy research: Constructing meaning through collaborative inquiry.* New York: Cambridge University Press.

LeVine, R. A., & White, M. U. (1986). *Human conditions: The cultural basis of educational development.* New York: Routledge & Kegan Paul.

Livingston, A. (2007). *The condition of education 2007 in brief* (NCES 2007–066). U.S. Department of Education. Washington, DC: National Center for Education Statistics.

Lue, M. S., Green, C. E., & Smalley, S. Y. (2002). Communication skills of African American learners with disabilities. In F. E. Obiakor & B. A. Ford (Eds.), *Creating successful learning environments for African American learners with exceptionalities* (pp. 107–117). Thousand Oaks, CA: Corwin Press.

Mayer, R. E. (2001). Resisting the assault on science: The case for evidence-based reasoning in educational research. *Educational Researcher, 10*(30), 29–30.

Mehan, H. (1979). *Learning lessons: The social organization of classroom instruction.* Cambridge, MA: Harvard University Press.

Moll, L. C. (1990). *Vygotsky and education.* New York: Cambridge University Press.

Moll, L. C., & Gonzalez, N. (2004). Engaging life: A funds-of-knowledge approach to multicultural education. In J. Banks & C. A. McGee Banks (Eds.), *Handbook of research on multicultural education* (pp. 699–715). San Francisco: Jossey-Bass.

Nieto, S. (1999). Multiculturalism, social justice, and critical teaching. In I. Shor & C. Pari (Eds.), *Education is politics: Critical teaching across differences, K-12* (pp. 1–20). Portsmouth, NH: Heinemann.

Ogbu, J., & Simmons, H. D. (1998). Voluntary and involuntary minorities: A Cultural-ecological theory of school performance with some implications for education. *Anthropology and Education Quarterly, 29*(2), 155–188.

Ostrovsky-Solis, F., Ramirez, M., & Ardilla, A. (2004). Effects of culture and education on neuropsychological testing: A preliminary study with indigenous and nonindigenous population. *Applied Neuropsychology, 11*(4), 186–193.

Paas, F., Renkl, A., & Sweller, J. (2003). Cognitive load theory and instructional design: recent developments [Special issue]. *Educational Psychologist, 38*(1).

Pew Hispanic Center. (2006). *From 200 million to 300 million: The numbers behind population growth.* Retrieved from http://pewhispanic.org/factsheets/factsheet.php?FactsheetID=25 6/27/2007

Pearson, P. D., & Raphael, T. E. (2000). Toward a more complex vew of balance in the literacy curriculum. In W. D. Hammond & T. E. Raphael (Eds.), *Literacy instruction for the new millennium* (pp. 1–21). Grand Rapids, MI: Center for the Improvement of Early Reading Achievement & Michigan Reading.

Pintrich, P. R. (2003). A motivational science perspective on the role of student motivation in learning and teaching contexts. *Journal of Educational Psychology, 95*(4), 667–686.

RAND Reading Study Group. (2002). *Reading for understanding: Toward an R&D program in reading comprehension.* Santa Monica, CA: RAND Education.

Rogoff, B. (1981). Schooling's influence on memory test performance. *Child Development, 52,* 260–267.

Rogoff, B. (1991). *Apprenticeship in thinking: Cognitive in social context.* New York: Oxford University Press.

Rogoff, B. (1995). Observing sociocultural activity on three planes: Participatory appropriation, guided participation, and apprenticeship. In J. V. Wertsch, P. Del Rio, & A. Alvarez (Eds.), *Sociocultural studies of mind* (pp. 139–164). Cambridge, UK: Cambridge University Press.

Rogoff, B. (2003). *The cultural nature of human development.* New York: Oxford University Press.

Rogoff, B., Baker-Sennett, J., Lacasa, P., & Goldsmith, D. (1995). Development through participation in sociocultural activity. In J. Goodnow, P. Miller, & F. Kessel (Eds.), *Cultural practices as contexts for development* (pp. 45–65). San Francisco: Jossey-Bass.

Rogoff, B., Turkanis, C. G., & Bartlett, L. (Eds.). (2001). *Learning together: Children and adults in a school community.* New York: Oxford University Press.

Rueda, R. (2006). Motivational and cognitive aspects of culturally accommodated instruction: The case of reading comprehension. In D. M. McInerney, M. Dowson, & S. Van Etten (Eds.), *Effective schools: Vol. 6: Research on sociocultural influences on motivation and learning* (pp. 135–158). Greenwich, CT: Information Age.

Rueda, R. S., August, D., & Goldenberg, C. (2006). The sociocultural context in which children acquire literacy. In D. August & T. Shanahan (Eds.), *Developing literacy in second-language learners: Report of the National Literacy Panel on language-minority children and youth* (pp. 319–340). Mahwah, NJ: Erlbaum.

Salomon, G. (1984). Television is "easy" and print is "tough": The differential investment of mental effort in learning as a function of perceptions and attributions. *Journal of Educational Psychology, 76,* 774–786.

Schunk, D. M., Pintrich, P. R., & Meece, J. L. (2008). *Motivation in education: Theory, research, and applications.* Upper Saddle River, NJ: Pearson Merrill/Prentice Hall.

Scribner, S., & Cole, M. (1981). *The psychology of literacy.* Cambridge, MA: Harvard University Press.

Slavin, R. E. (2002) Evidence-based education policies: Transforming educational practice and research. *Educational Researcher, 10*(31), 15–21.

Snow, C. E., Burns, M. S., & Griffin, P. (1998). *Preventing reading difficulties in young children.* Washington, DC: National Academy Press.

Stipek, D. (1996). Motivation and instruction. In D. C. Berliner & R. C. Calfee (Eds.), *Handbook of educational psychology* (pp. 85–113). New York: MacMillan.

Strauss, C. (1992). What makes Tony run? Schemas as motives reconsidered. In R. G. Andrade & C. Strauss (Eds.), *Human motives and cultural models* (pp. 197–224). New York: Cambridge University Press.

Strauss, C., & Quinn, N. (1998). *A cognitive theory of cultural meaning.* New York: Oxford University Press.

Sweller, J. (1988). Cognitive load during problem solving: Effects on learning. *Cognitive Science, 12,* 257–285.

Sweller, J., van Merriënboer, J. G., & Paas, F. G. (1998). Cognitive architecture and instructional design. *Educational Psychology Review, 10,* 251–296.

Tharp, R., & Gallimore, R. (1988). *Rousing minds to life: Teaching, learning, and schooling in social context.* Cambridge, UK: Cambridge University Press.

Valsiner, J. (1988). *Developmental psychology in the Soviet Union.* Bloomington: Indiana University Press.

Weisner, T. S. (1994). The crisis for families and children in Africa: Change in shared social support for children. *Health Matrix Journal of Law/Medicine, 4*(1), 1–29.

Wells, G., & Claxton, G. (Eds.). (2002). *Learning for life in the C21st: Sociocultural perspectives on the future of education.* Oxford, UK: Blackwell.

Wenger, E. (1999). *Communities of practice. Learning, meaning and identity.* Cambridge, UK: Cambridge University Press.

Wertsch, J. V. (1991). *Voices of the mind: A sociocultural approach to mediated action.* Cambridge, MA: Harvard University Press.

Whitehurst, G. (2002). *Charting a new course for the U.S. Office of Educational Research and Improvement.* Paper presented at the annual meeting of the American Educational Research Association, New Orleans.

Wigfield, A. (1994). Expectancy-value theory of motivation and achievement: A developmental perspective. *Educational Psychology Review, 6,* 49–78.

Wigfield, A., & Eccles, J. (1992). The development of achievement task values: A theoretical analysis. *Developmental Review, 12,* 265–310.

Wigfield, A., & Eccles, J. (2000). Expectancy-value theory of achievement motivation. *Contemporary Educational Psychology, 25,* 68–81.

Wiley, T. G. (2005). *Literacy and language diversity in the United* States (2nd ed.). Washington, DC: Center for Applied Linguistics.

Wilkinson, L. C., & Silliman, E. R. (2000). Classroom language and literacy learning. In M. L. Kamil, P. B. Mosenthal, P. David Pearson, & R. Barr (Eds.), *Handbook of reading research: Vol III* (pp. 337–360). Mahwah, NJ: Erlbaum.

Part 2

Development of Reading

6 Supporting Early (and Later) Literacy Development at Home and at School

The Long View

Jeanne R. Paratore
Boston University

Christina M. Cassano
Boston University and Salem State College

Judith A. Schickedanz
Boston University

As we began our work on this chapter, we reviewed the relevant chapters in each of the earlier handbooks. We noted that although previous chapters differed in important ways, they were also unified in the significant goal of seeking to understand "children's literacy knowledge and processes as they move from unconventional to conventional literacy" (Yaden, Rowe, & MacGil-livray, 2000). We, too, adopted this goal, but also considered additional purposes. Our discussions and conversations repeatedly led us to a fundamental question about the consequences of actions taken in the early childhood years to move children from unconventional to conventional literacy. Specifically, we questioned how current conceptions of early foundations reach beyond these years. What we call "the long view" is, at least in part, a response to current concerns that although many children learn to read well enough to make sense of the multiple texts for which they are held accountable, too many do not. Moreover, even among those who do, few meet the benchmarks on national and state assessments for the "advanced" category that is reserved for students who can read and understand, and also evaluate, critique, compare, and judge the worthiness of the arguments (Lee, Grigg, & Donahue, 2007). The idea that this "topping off" at relatively low levels of proficiency can be accounted for by the types of experiences children have in the earliest years and the balance in experiences across different literacy domains has been suggested by others (Curtis, 1990; Juel, 2006; Mills & Jackson, 1990; Snow, 1991). Yet, these ideas seem to have had little effect on present policy and practice. In her essay on the "path to competence," Alexander (2005/06) noted that to reach the goal of a fully literate society,

> We must take another look at what it means to read competently. We must consider what it takes to read well not just in the early years, as children struggle to unravel the mysteries and beauty of written and spoken language, but across the lifespan, as the purposes for reading and the character of written language change. In other words, we can do more to realize the goal of a literate society if we better understand the full nature of reading development. (p. 414)

Likewise, Paris (2005) argued that "traditional reading research has ignored fundamental differences in the developmental trajectories of reading skills" (p. 184). Paris claims that "some skills are more constrained than others; they are learned quickly, mastered entirely, and should not be conceptualized as enduring individual difference variables" (p. 184). Yet, he noted, "constrained skills are analyzed with the same research tools and parametric statistical analyses as unconstrained skills…a mistake that can lead to spurious claims about early reading skills" (p. 184).

As we sought to understand the consequences of early literacy development for later achievement, these ideas provided a constant point of reference. We begin with a concise review of how the "theoretical epochs" encompassing the last 100 years shaped various understandings of early literacy development. We next present a brief definition of "skilled reading," in keeping with our focus on "the long view." In subsequent sections, we examine research related to factors and abilities that predict success in early and later reading and studies that inform acquisition sequences and home and school acquisition supports. We conclude with implications of existing evidence for practice and also suggest questions that must be answered as we look to the future and strive to develop "new" knowledge.

EARLY LITERACY: A BIT OF HISTORY

As Mason (1984) noted in her chapter in the first volume of the *Handbook of Reading Research,* specific concerns about the process of early reading largely originated somewhat late in our educational history, in the 20th century. In 1925, the National Committee on Reading, established to respond to reading failure, outlined five periods of reading development, the first covering preschool, kindergarten, and the early part of first grade. The committee's report (*Twenty-Fourth Year Book of the Society for the Study of Education,* 1925) prompted development of a wide variety of programs, many providing tasks thought useful in developing readiness for reading. Such programs had been in place for nearly 25 years when Millie Almy (1949) asked, "How does it happen that some children reach first grade ready to read and seemingly do not need a period of readiness?"

In the years both preceding and following Almy's publication, much research has been directed at understanding the processes and practices that support early reading. Research and theory have led us from a view of learning to read as largely maturational (e.g., Morphett & Washburne, 1931; Witty & Kopel, 1936) to one that is some interactive combination of innate abilities and experiences (e.g., Horowitz, 2000). In recent years, critiques (Hunt, 1961) and several lines of research have been consequential in clarifying and deepening our understanding of the particular processes and experiences that influence development, and thus the sources of various foundations of literacy learning. In 1987, Greenough and colleagues proposed two kinds of brain plasticity. In their model, "experience expectant" plasticity requires environmental input to finish development in parts of the brain, such as the visual cortex. This input is available across widely varying environments, which guarantees access, except in unusual circumstances (e.g., congenital cataracts, which limit light input to the infant brain). "Experience dependent" plasticity, on the other hand, accounts for "the storage of information that is unique to the individual" (Greenough, Black, & Wallace, 1987, p. 540). Brain processes (i.e., new synaptic formation throughout life) allow experiences of this kind to vary in timing, in contrast to the narrow critical periods for "experience expectant" plasticity. Absence of environmental input of the "experience expectant" type at the appropriate or expected times has mostly negative outcomes, while environmental input of the "experience dependent" kind has positive outcomes, overall, except when it collides with socially established schedules for the acquisition of culturally-privileged knowledge and skill.

Another strand of research brought new understanding to central conceptualizations about fundamental early reading abilities, specifically those focused on visual and auditory perception. A detailed discussion of the research on infant perceptual abilities is beyond the scope of this chapter. (See reviews in Jusczyk, 1997 and Kellman & Arterberry, 1998.) In a nutshell, however, infants prefer patterned visual displays (Fantz, 1963), can accommodate visually to objects at adult levels, by 3- to 4-months of age (Haynes, White, & Held, 1965), and have 20/20 acuity by 12 months of age (Banks & Salapatek, 1983). Six-week-old infants notice differences in the orientation of identical line forms (e.g., Y), while 12-week-old infants show "pattern invariance" (i.e., no longer respond to orientation; Cohen & Younger, 1984). Moreover, infants develop visual categories (e.g., dot patterns, spatial relations, and animals) starting at 6 months of age (Bomba & Siqueland, 1983; Eimas & Quinn, 1994).

The infant research provided new explanations for long-held views about visual and auditory discrimination in preschool children. If the infant was competent in visual and auditory perception, conceptualizations of visual and auditory capacities related to early reading were wrong. Typically, developing youngsters do not lack discrimination *capacity* in either domain. Rather, their failure to respond to differences in the orientation of letters, for example, results from noticing *invariance* of form across typically irrelevant differences. In the auditory domain, infant researchers found keen speech perception in infants (Eimas, Sikqueland, Jusczyk, & Vigorito, 1971) and learned that toddlers discriminate "word pairs that are minimally different" and "hear these differences as accurately as adults" (Liberman & Liberman, 1979, p. 111). In learning to read and write, however, children must come to *think* of spoken words as comprising a series of individual sounds which can be manipulated (Liberman, 1997).

Yet another area of study has focused on the types of literacy experiences children have at home. These studies (e.g., Almy, 1949; Baghban, 1984; Durkin, 1966; Schickedanz, 1990) and others focusing on oral language development in different home contexts (Hart & Risley, 1995; Hoff & Naigles, 2002; Huttenlocher, Haight, Bryk, Seltzer, & Lyons, 1991; Huttenlocher, Waterfall, Vasilyeva, & Vevea, 2007; Pan, Rowe, Singer, & Snow, 2005; Rowe, Levine, Fisher, & Goldin-Meadow, 2009) provide evidence about cognitive and linguistic supports provided in the early years and their relationships to skills foundational to literacy and language development. Such studies have continued to loosen the grip of genetic-based explanations for the wide differences in literacy skill found among different groups of children.

At present, perhaps the most widely held theory of development, including literacy and language abilities, is one that has been articulated by Horowitz (2000):

> Various linear and nonlinear combinations and permutations, constitutional, economic, social, and cultural factors provide the set of circumstances or contexts for development. These circumstances may, in aggregate, generally provide normal advantage, poor advantage, or high advantage... at the ends of the continuum of advantage, a confluence of constitutional, social, economic, and cultural circumstances for poor advantage or enriched advantage can coalesce into what I call "swamping conditions." That is, at the extremes a dense concentration of resources made possible, for example, by high socioeconomic advantage can have the effect of swamping development in a positive manner. Conversely, a dense concentration of disadvantage circumstances can swamp development negatively. (p. 6)

Almost 50 years after Hunt's (1961) masterful critique of intelligence as innate capacity created optimism about greater control over the experiences and nurturing provided to young children, we still search for the factors leading to success in reading, still debate the balance in experiences we should provide in the earliest years, and still struggle to bridge differences between home/community and school language and literacy practices and possibilities. Yet, despite the persistent uncertainties and challenges, much is known about how early experiences pave the way for later success. In the sections that follow, we summarize investigations that provide insight into the abilities and skills that are worthy of instructional attention in the earliest years, examine the state of knowledge about the sequence in which typically performing youngsters acquire these important abilities or understandings, and summarize studies that inform understanding of the instructional actions that contribute to children's learning success. As a backdrop, we begin with a definition of skilled reading, to maintain a clear focus on the types of abilities and knowledge that have a persistent effect on literacy learning in both early and later years.

SKILLED READING

Current federal policy (i.e., NCLB) focuses on five literacy domains as essential to successful reading development: phonemic awareness, phonics, vocabulary, fluency, and comprehension. To these we add motivation and engagement.

Although capable readers depend to some extent on context clues to recognize words, successful word reading depends primarily on decoding abilities (Adams, 1990; Ehri & Wilce, 1987; NICHD, 2005). The skills underlying decoding include letter name knowledge and phonological awareness (Lonigan, Burgess & Anthony, 2000; Muter, Hulme, & Snowling, Stevenson, 2004; Ball & Blachman, 1991; Juel, Griffith, & Gough, 1986), the insight that letters represent (roughly) individual sounds in spoken words (i.e., the alphabetic principle; Ehri, Nunes, Stahl, and Willows, 2001; Foorman, Francis, Novy, & Liberman, 1991; Share & Gur, 1999; Treiman, 1994), knowledge of print conventions (e.g., direction in which print is accessed from the page; Clay, 1979) and an understanding that print conveys meaning (Neuman & Roskos, 1997; Purcell-Gates, 1996). (See Foorman & Connor, this volume, for further discussion.)

Children learning to read are, of course, expected also to comprehend their texts. This is a relatively simple task in the initial phases, with both vocabulary and syntax in beginning texts simplified for easy access (Hiebert & Martin, 2002; Hockett & Neeley, 1936). As a consequence, comprehension difficulties often are not evident until third or fourth grade, when words, grammatical structures, and text topics are less familiar and more complex (Biemiller, 2006; Chall, Jacobs, & Baldwin, 1990; Snow, 1991). As texts become increasingly difficult, automatic word recognition allows the reader to focus attention on constructing meaning rather than on decoding words (LaBerge & Samuels, 1974). However, skillful decoding, alone, is insufficient for successful comprehension (e.g., Applegate, Applegate, & Modla, 2009; Buly & Valencia, 2002; Duke, Pressley, & Hilden, 2004; Hoover & Gough, 1990). Deep stores of vocabulary and concept knowledge allow readers to connect information to prior knowledge and experiences (e.g., Anderson & Nagy, 1991; Ouellette, 2006; Pressley & Afflerbach, 1995). Familiarity with various text structures provides expectations for the organization and grammar of a text, and for the types of information they will encounter, which aids comprehension (see Goldman & Rakestraw, 2001, for a review). Awareness of comprehension strategies (e.g., making predictions, distinguishing between important and unimportant information, categorizing ideas, and monitoring understanding and correcting confusion along the way) enhances the reader's reasoning (Cain, Oakhill, & Bryant, 2004; Duke, Pressley, & Hildin, 2004; Paris & Paris, 2007).

Motivation and engagement are also critical to skillful reading (Wigfield & Asher, 1984). A number of factors contribute to the reader's motivation and engagement, including the goals and purposes for reading (Guthrie & Humenick, 2004); knowledge of reading strategies (Baker & Wigfield,1999; Guthrie & Wigfield, 2000); the text's ease of readability (Klare, 1984); interest in the topic (Guthrie & Humenick, 2004; Wigfield & Asher, 1984); and choices about what to read and how to respond to reading (e.g., peer discussion; written response; Guthrie & Humenick, 2004; Guthrie & Wigfield, 2000).

This general framework of skilled reading in elementary school, coupled with increasing recognition that literacy development begins long before formal reading instruction begins, has helped shape current research designed to find early predictors of reading achievement. Although most research on early predictors has taken a short view that encompasses only beginning reading (e.g., preschool or kindergarten through first or second grade; e.g., Almy, 1949;

Lonigan et al., 2000; Muter et al., 2004; Schatschneider, Fletcher, Francis, Carlson, & Foorman, 2004), some studies conducted over the past decade include longitudinal designs that span pre-school or kindergarten through third or fourth grades. These studies allow examination of how various factors acquired in the early years are related to reading in later years. In the next section, we review longitudinal studies that provide information about the relationships between early literacy foundations and both early and later reading success.

PREDICTORS OF BEGINNING AND LATER READING SUCCESS

Several longitudinal studies have identified critical early foundations that predict success in both beginning and later reading achievement (Muter et al., 2004; NICHD, 2005; Roth, Speece & Cooper, 2002; Sénéchal, Ouellette, & Rodney, 2006; Storch & Whitehurst, 2002). Storch and Whitehurst (2002) analyzed the potential of code-related and oral language abilities, acquired by the end of preschool, to predict children's reading achievement in elementary school. Head Start children (626 preschoolers) were assessed in the spring, then again in kindergarten and in first through fourth grades. Preschool and kindergarten code-related assessments included the Developmental Skills Checklist (DSC; CTB, 1990; e.g. alphabet knowledge, phonological awareness, and print concepts), emergent writing (name writing, drawing a person, and message writing), story retelling (BUS; Glasgow & Cowley, 1994), and receptive and expressive vocabulary (PPVT-R; Dunn & Dunn, 1981 and One Word; Gardner, 1990 respectively). Standardized reading accuracy and comprehension measures, used in first through fourth grades, included Reading Comprehension, Word Reading, Word Study Skills, and Reading Vocabulary from the Stanford Achievement Tests (SAT; Psychological Corporation, 1989a), the Reading subscale of the Wide Range Achievement Test-Revised (W-RAT-R; Jastak & Wilkinson, 1984), and the Word Attack subscale of the Woodcock Reading Mastery Test (WMRT-R; Woodcock, 1987).

Code-related skills (i.e., letter name knowledge, phonological awareness, and name writing) predicted decoding skill in beginning readers. Code-related skills and oral language skills were highly related in the preschool years (48% of variance), somewhat related in kindergarten (less than 10% of variance), and unrelated in first and second grade (i.e., reading ability—word recognition accuracy—in grades 1 and 2 was not directly related to language abilities). By grades 3 and 4, however, oral language ability was a significant predictor of reading comprehension (7% of the variance). Additionally, while oral vocabulary did not account for any unique variance in reading levels until third grade, it had an indirect effect on decoding skill in the early grades through its effect on phonological awareness. Storch and Whitehurst (2002) also found that

> Within the oral language domain, approximately 90% of the variance in a child's oral language ability in kindergarten was accounted for by preschool ability, 96% of the variance in Grade 1–2 oral language was accounted for by kindergarten ability, and 88% of the variance in Grades 3–4 oral language skills was accounted for by Grade 1–2 ability. (p. 940)

Code-related skills showed a similar pattern, though a weaker relationship: 38% of variance in kindergarten code-related skill was explained by preschool code-related skill. Stability in code-related skills, beginning late in preschool (Anthony & Lonigan, 2004; Lonigan, Burgess, & Anthony, 2000), has been found by some other researchers (e.g., Wagner, Torgesen, Laughon, Simmons, & Rachotte, 1993; Wagner et al., 1997), though not all. For example, in a study of Finnish students during the first and second year of formal schooling (mean age 7 years, 3 months; SD = .32), Lerkkanen, Rasku-Puttonen, Aunola, and Nurmi (2004) found that students who began school with stronger comprehension abilities maintained their advantages over their peers in this area, while those who began school with weaker word reading skills often developed competency in this area after receiving formal instruction.

Other longitudinal studies are consistent with Storch and Whitehurst's (2002) main findings that code-related skills are the best predictors of success in early reading, while language-related skills add to the prediction of success in later reading, when texts are more challenging (Muter et al., 2004; NICHD, 2005; Roth, Speece, & Cooper, 2002; Sénéchal, Ouellette, & Rodney, 2006).

In Sénéchal and LeFevre's (2002) study, 168 children were followed from kindergarten through third grade to determine the effects of home literacy (e.g., parent storybook reading and instruction of literacy skills) on later reading achievement. Oral language measures included receptive vocabulary (PPVT-R; Dunn & Dunn, 1981) and listening comprehension (SESAT; Psychological Corporation, 1989b). Code-related skills, assessed at the beginning of Grade 1, included phonological awareness (e.g., matching words using onsets or rimes), print concepts, alphabet knowledge, invented spelling, and word reading. Comprehension and word reading ability were assessed at the end of Grade 1 with standardized subtests (e.g., Woodcock-Johnson Psycho-Educational Battery-Revised; Woodcock & Johnson, 1989). Reading at the end of Grade 3 was measured using the vocabulary and comprehension subtests (MacGinitie & MacGinitie, 1992). Skill-based home literacy experiences, emergent literacy abilities, and phonological awareness contributed to success in learning to read, while oral vocabulary contributed only indirectly through its effect on phonological awareness. By third grade, however, oral vocabulary accounted for unique variance in comprehension (17%). Parents' reports of teaching children to read and print words also "accounted for variance in children's emergent literacy and, in time, children's emergent literacy accounted for variance in reading skills at the end of grade 1" (p. 453).

In a later reanalysis of data from both the 2002 study and one conducted in 2004, Sénéchal, Ouellette, & Rodney (2006) examined vocabulary's role in reading and listening comprehension. Kindergarten vocabulary accounted for unique variance in reading comprehension in the third grade (Study 1, 4%) and fourth grade (Study 2, 15%), and was also predictive of listening comprehension in kindergarten (7%), and in grades 1 (8%) and 3 (7 %). Early literacy skills and phoneme awareness also predicted listening comprehension in kindergarten (8%) but not in Grade 1.

The NICHD study (2005), which spanned the ages birth to third grade (n = 1,137), also found that code-related skills were the best predictors of early reading, and that language-based skills accounted for larger amounts of variance by third grade. In addition to this general pattern, however, "...the direct path from 54-month broad language to first-grade decoding (B = .10, p < .01) was statistically significant" (p. 434). This finding indicated that broad language skills, found before kindergarten entry, independently "predict reading skill during the transition to first grade." Importantly, only broad language measures, not vocabulary measures, were related to first-grade word recognition. The researchers concluded that "both vocabulary and more comprehensive language play unique roles in first-grade reading" (p. 434) with broader measures directly affecting word recognition and vocabulary indirectly affecting word recognition through phonological awareness.

This finding can perhaps be explained by the differences in both the samples and the measures of oral language used in this study compared to the study by Storch and Whitehurst (2002). The NICHD sample was more economically diverse and the study used more language measures, some beyond vocabulary assessment. The broader language measures included the Reynell Developmental Language Scale (Reynell & Gruber, 1977), an assessment of expressive language and verbal comprehension at 36 months; and the Preschool Language Scale (PLS-3; Zimmerman, Steiner, & Pond, 1979), an assessment of auditory comprehension and expressive language at 54 months. The NICHD study also measured vocabulary with the Picture Vocabulary subtest of Woodcock-Johnson Psychological Educations Battery-Revised, Woodcock & Mather (1989, 1989–1990).

In a third study (2-year longitudinal), Muter and colleagues (2004) focused on the prediction of word recognition and reading comprehension from phonological skills, letter naming, vocabulary, and grammatical skills (syntax and morphology) in 90 British children, tested in September/October of their reception year (mean age, 4.9 years) and during the same months of first and second grade. Time 1 assessments included rhyme detection and production, phoneme completion and deletion, and letter knowledge subtests of the Phonological Abilities Test (Muter, Hulme, & Snowling, 1997); the British Picture Vocabulary Scale II (BPVS II; Dunn, Dunn, Whetton, & Burley, 1997); and the Hatcher Early Word Recognition Test (42 high frequency words; Hatcher, Hulme, & Ellis, 1994). Time 2 assessments included all but one Time 1 assessments (the BPVS II), plus a syntactic awareness measure (Word Order Correction Test; Tunmer, 1989) a Morphological Generation Task, and the first 20 words of the British Abilities Scales II Word Reading Test (BAS II; Elliot, 1996). Time 3 assessments included the Hatcher Early Reading Test, the first 50 words of the BAS II, and the NARA II (Neale, 1997). The NARA II passages measured the number of words read accurately and reading comprehension (total number of questions correctly answered). Though limited in its longitudinal reach (only through October of second grade), the study's outcomes were fairly consistent with longer longitudinal research, with phonemic sensitivity and letter knowledge the strongest predictors of word reading, and vocabulary knowledge and grammatical skills contributing to the prediction of reading comprehension, even after controlling for earlier word recognition.

To better understand which language variables are the strongest predictors of early reading achievement, and the point in development when they exert their effects, Roth, Speece, and Cooper (2002) studied 66 children (mean age 5 years, 6 months) from kindergarten through first (n = 8) and second grades (n = 39). The comprehensive language measures for kindergarten included receptive vocabulary, definitional level vocabulary, and word retrieval (PPVT-R; Dunn & Dunn, 1981; Oral Vocabulary Subtest of the TOLD-P:2; Newcomer & Hammill, 1988; Boston Naming Test; Goodglass & Kaplan, 1983), as well as measures of syntax and morphology (TALC-R; Carrow-Woolfolk, 1985; formulated sentences subtests of the CELF-R; Semel, Wiig, & Secord, 1987). Measures of metalinguistics (phoneme blending and elision tasks) and meta-semantics (subsets of the TLC-E; Wiig & Secord, 1988) were also administered in kindergarten, as was a measure of narrative discourse ability (Roth, Spekman, & Fye, 1995) and a modification of the Del Rio English Story Comprehension Test (San Felipe-Del Rio Consolidation Independent School District, 1975). Kindergarten reading abilities were measured using the print awareness, letter/word identification (LWID), and word attack (WA; pseudowords) subtests of the Woodcock-Johnson Psychoeducational Battery-Revised (Woodcock & Johnson, 1989). The testing battery was reduced in first and second grades to the LWID, the WA subtests of the WJ-R, the metalinguistics measures, and the measure of narrative discourse. Data on background variables (SES, family literacy and nonverbal intelligence) were also collected.

Oral language contributed directly to second-grade reading achievement, and indirectly to word recognition through an effect on phonological awareness (for a discussion of the relationship between vocabulary and phonological awareness, see the section on phonological awareness). A post hoc analysis found that "oral language and word retrieval, together, accounted for 23% of the variance in second-grade reading comprehension, beyond the influence of kindergarten print awareness skill" (p. 268). The most important semantic skills for the prediction of reading comprehension were oral definitions and word retrieval, a finding consistent with prior research showing that decontextualized language skill is related to reading comprehension (e.g., Dickinson, Tabors, & Roach, 1996).

Finally, a full picture of predictors of later reading achievement must include social skills. Children who enter kindergarten with antisocial behavior, especially aggressiveness, develop fewer friendships and less positive relationships with teachers than do children who have positive social skills. Peer rejection and conflict with the teacher mediate classroom participation, which, in turn, has a direct effect on achievement. Ladd, Birch, and Buhs (1999) found that initial antisocial behavior and subsequent classroom participation accounted for close to 60% of the indirect effects on achievement. They suggest that teacher-child conflict may reduce teacher-child "instructional dialogues" and may also decrease a child's motivation to engage in instructional activities. Poor peer relationships decrease learning opportunities for aggressive children by marginalizing a child's participation during collaborative activities. Stipek and Miles (2008) followed kindergarten or first grade through fifth grade and found a strong indirect effect of teacher-child relationships on achievement. Other studies (e.g., Wentzel, 1997) of older children have also found a strong link between motivation to engage in school tasks and a positive sense of belonging, which includes teacher support and peer acceptance.

In the early years, behavior problems and attention issues often occur together (e.g., see Velting & Whitehurst, 1997). Self-regulation—the allocation of attention to tasks and the selective use of learning strategies (Blair, 2002)—correlates with academic achievement, including reading (Spira, Bracken, & Fischel, 2005). Early childhood teachers often note regulatory behaviors as among the most important for a child's learning (e.g., Rimm-Kaufman, Pianta, & Cox, 2000), with 60% of kindergarten teachers doing so in Lewit and Baker's (1995) study. When asked how many of their kindergarteners did not have the social skills to engage "productively" in classroom activities, close to half of the teachers said that more than half of the children lacked these skills. Landry and Smith's (2006) intervention study with parents of infants established a causal link between a child's self-regulation skill and a parents' skill in helping an infant maintain a focus of attention, and between maintenance of attention and an infant's cooperation and word learning.

In sum, the development of oral language, code-related skills, and social behavior (i.e., behavior style and self-regulation) in the early years has lasting effects on children's long-term academic achievement. Research on the importance of behavior style and self-regulation skills indicates that these have an early and continuing snowballing effect on achievement through their effects on classroom participation. The effects of code-related skills and oral vocabulary knowledge are more complex, with each cluster accounting for different amounts of reading performance at different points in time. Code-related skills predict the largest amount of variance in early grade reading skill, while oral vocabulary contributes to reading comprehension in grades three and four. When language is broadly defined to include more than vocabulary, and when vocabulary's indirect effects are considered for decoding (i.e., through an effect on phoneme awareness), the role of language in early reading skill becomes more evident. Moreover, given the contributions of oral vocabulary and syntax to the "self-teaching" of orthographic representations through phonological recoding (Share, 1999), their importance for the development of early reading becomes clearer, as does the need to use connected text measures, rather than isolated words or pseudowords, to determine the full effect of language knowledge in the early phases of reading. Children who struggle in the early grades typically continue to experience reading failure (Juel, 1988; Spira et al., 2005) and early differences in critical predictors are evident in preschool. Thus, the major task for the preschool years is to determine how to support development in *all* of the areas related to both beginning and later reading development, regardless of the specific timing of the greatest effect of comprehension-related variables, language skills and background knowledge, because it takes considerable time for children to acquire sufficient levels of these skills to support reading comprehension.

Research on the link between social skills at school entry and later achievement, and between parenting skill and social skills development, suggests that interventions in the early years to reduce later achievement gaps must focus not only on language and literacy skills, but also on social skills. Stipek and Miles (2008) suggest that the protective factor of positive social skills is especially important for low-income children who are also at risk due to a lower level of foundational skills in content domains. This suggestion is consistent with Spira et al.'s (2005) finding that behavioral control/attention predicted reading improvement in struggling readers in first grade and with the findings reported by Torgesen (2000) that the inability to control behavior and attend to instruction interferes with instructional interventions for struggling readers.

ACQUISITION SEQUENCES AND SUPPORT

In this section, we discuss specific details of two important categories of predictors of reading success, code knowledge and oral language. Length constraints preclude a detailed treatment of the self-regulation literature, which, as we noted, is positively related to literacy and mediated through early parenting behavior (Landry & Smith, 2006). Readers can consult several sources (e.g., Beckwith & Rodning, 1992; Landry, Swank, & Baldwin, 1996; Olson, Bates, & Bayles, 1984; Tamis-LeMonda, Bornstein, & Baumwell, 2001) about this important area of development. For code related and oral language categories, we discuss typical acquisition sequences, as well as supportive instructional conditions, often for both home and school contexts. As well, we include a brief discussion of acquisition sequence and instructional support of knowledge and its relationship to reasoning, because reasoning and thinking are fundamentally important to eventual success in reading and writing. Research indicates that when children do not have prior knowledge, or do not relate it sensibly to texts to draw inferences, they have comprehension difficulties (see Carlisle & Rice, 2004; Duke et al., 2004) and that experience with *"why"* questions when reading text for which they have prior knowledge facilitates reasoning (Pressley et al., 1992).

Code Knowledge

Three areas of early literacy skills knowledge provide important foundations for the development of code-related skills: print awareness, phonological awareness, and alphabet knowledge.

Print Awareness

Basic print awareness includes the understandings that print is meaningful (i.e., conveys a message), serves many functions, and varies in organization in relation to function (i.e., a restaurant menu differs from a storybook or a letter to a friend; Purcell-Gates, 1996). At earlier levels of awareness, children depend on physical context and social clues to read print (Goodman, 1986). At later, higher levels, children's reading rests on knowledge of letter names, an understanding of the alphabetic principle (i.e., letters—graphemes represent phonemes in spoken words), and knowledge of print conventions (e.g., directionality, space between words, and uppercase versus lowercase letters and punctuation marks; Ehri & Sweet, 1991; Morris, Bloodgood, Lomax, & Perney, 2003; Treiman, Cohen, Mulqueeny, Kessler, & Schechtman, 2007).

Acquisition Sequence. From observations of others' engagement with print across contexts, children learn to interpret print (Purcell-Gates, 1995, 1996). At first, children depend completely on clues from the physical context of familiar print and cannot read print removed from these settings. Researchers have described levels of print awareness, distinguishing between context dependent "reading" and reading words using letter and sound skills. Mason (1980) described three levels: (a) context dependent (i.e., children "recognize" words only in their environmental contexts); (b) visual recognition (i.e., children also read some words isolated from physical context); and (c) letter-sound analysis (i.e., words are read by sounding out) (pp. 216–217). Levels described by McGee and Richgels (1989; novice, experimenting, and conventional) capture similar shifts from physical context to use of print skills. Context dependent or novice readers fail to recognize classmates' names when they are removed from cubbies and presented in isolation (Share & Gur, 1999), because they lack basic code-related skills and print conventions required to read print on its own bare terms. They also do not know which words say McDonald's and Burger King when these are out of context (Masonheimer, Drum, & Ehri, 1984). Context-dependent readers also fail to notice altered spellings of words in the environment (e.g., Pepsi to Xepsi; McDonalds to MxPonalds; Masonheimer et al., 1984; Reutzel, Fawson, Young, Morrison, & Wilcox, 2003), and fail to recognize words when they are printed in all capital letters rather than in their more conventional, familiar form (Treiman et al., 2007).

Three- and four-year olds use global features of print, such as linear arrangement and multiplicity and diversity of units in a display, to make word versus non-word judgments (Ganapole, 1987; Lavine, 1977; Treiman et al., 2007). In contrast, children 5 years of age and older base word judgments on characteristics of the individual units in a display and their sequence. Movement from the use of only global print features (e.g., linear arrangement and letter strings that look like words) to the use of grapheme and sound knowledge (e.g., invented spelling) is also seen in early writing (Clay, 1975; Genishi & Dyson, 1984; Schickedanz, 1990).

Acquisition Support.   Movement from lower to higher levels of print awareness requires letter name knowledge, phoneme awareness, insight of the alphabetic principle, and print conventions (e.g., left to right progression of print, space between words; Ehri & Sweet, 1991; Masonheimer et al., 1984; Reutzel et al., 2003). Designing literacy-rich dramatic play contexts (Morrow & Schickedanz, 2006; Neuman & Roskos, 1993, 1997) and providing classroom library corners (Morrow & Weinstein, 1986) increase children's use of literacy materials and function knowledge (Neuman & Roskos, 1997). While these opportunities build interest in print and allow children to participate in reading and writing on their own early terms, engagement with environmental print in daily life at home (Purcell-Gates, 1996) or in enriched classroom-play contexts (Neuman & Roskos, 1997) does not by itself lead children to higher levels of print knowledge. When children can rely on non-print clues from the environmental context in which print is embedded, they are unlikely to use graphic features of print or sounds clues (Ehri & Sweet, 1991). Children's ability to read print increases when adults' engagement with environmental print focuses on how print works (Purcell-Gates, 1996) and when environmental print is intentionally manipulated (e.g., matched with its logo context, or assembled from jig-saw puzzle pieces; Christie, Enz, Han, Prior, & Gerard, 2007).

Phonological Awareness

Infants detect minimum contrasts in words (i.e., differences of one phoneme) when producing or understanding talk (Eimas et al., 1971). For reading and writing, however, children must have conscious awareness of sounds in words (Liberman, Cooper, Shankweiler, & Studdert-Kennedy, 1967; Liberman, Shankweiler, Fischer, & Carter, 1974). Compared to lower levels of phonological awareness, phoneme-level awareness is a better predictor of later reading achievement. (For reviews see Adams, 1990; Lonigan, 2006; Snow, Burns, & Griffin, 1998.) The relationship among different levels of phonological awareness (i.e., rhyme sensitivity and phonemic awareness) has been of interest, with evidence suggesting that all are part of the same construct (Anthony & Lonigan, 2004; Anthony et al., 2002; Schatschneider et al., 2004; Wagner et al., 1993; Wagner et al., 1997).

Acquisition Sequence.   Phonological awareness progresses from larger to smaller speech units (i.e., from words and syllables to onset-rime segments and phonemes; Anthony, Lonigan, Driscoll, Philips, & Burgess, 2003; Liberman et al., 1974; MacLean, Bryant, & Bradley, 1987), although children do not master one level before awareness of the next begins (i.e., acquisition is not in rigid stages; Anthony et al., 2003). The easier apprehension of larger units, such as words and syllables, is thought the consequence of their discreteness in speech (i.e., articulation gestures; Liberman et al., 1967; Treiman, 1985). Phonemes, in contrast, can become psychologically perceived, though not articulated distinctly as separate entities in words (Gibson & Levin, 1975; Liberman et al., 1967).

Phonological awareness tasks vary in operation demands, with detection less challenging than production (i.e., "Do these two words rhyme?" versus "Can you think of words that rhyme with___?"), deletion easier than manipulation (e.g., deletion *and* addition of phonemes), and blending easier than segmenting (Lonigan, 2006; Stanovich, Cunningham, & Cramer; 1984; Yopp, 1988). The position of the target phoneme also affects detection and segmentation performance (i.e., initial position is easier than medial or final positions; McBride-Chang, 1995). Presentation format (oral or pictorial), response mode (e.g., oral, or physical, such as clapping), and type of word (e.g., pseudo versus actual) also affect performance. Task variations can lead to under- or over-estimations of children's abilities and make comparisons of data across studies challenging (Backman, 1983).

Acquisition Support.   Oral experiences with rhyming texts (e.g., poems, songs, nursery rhymes), as well as experiences with specific detection and segmentation tasks, promote phonological awareness (Bradley & Bryant, 1983, 1985; Byrne & Fielding-Barnsley, 1995; Justice, Chow, Capellinni, Flanigan, & Colton, 2003; Lundberg, Frost, & Petersen, 1988; O'Connor, Jenkins & Slocum, 1995). Researchers (Baker, Fernandez-Fein, Scher, & Williams, 1998; Crain-Thoreson & Dale, 1999; Sénéchal & LeFevre, 2002; Sonnenschein, Brody, & Munsterman, 1996) have found a direct relationship between parents' self-report of children's engagement in various types of formal and informal language and literacy activities (e.g., hand-clap games, singing, interactions with educational books, writing letters and words) and higher levels of phonological awareness.

Significant correlations have also been found between letter-name knowledge and phoneme awareness (Bowey, 1994; Lonigan, Burgess, Anthony, & Barker, 1998; Muter et al., 2004; MacLean, Bryant, & Bradley, 1987), with prediction mostly from the former to the latter (e.g., Lonigan, Burgess, & Anthony, 2000). Juel (2006) offered this explanation: "Letters are the anchors to which articulatory gestures and approximations of phonemes can be attached" (p. 419). Adult segmentation of words into their constituent phonemes, combined with linking these sounds to letter names (as occurs in shared or scaffolded writing), appears to facilitate phoneme-level awareness (Ball & Blachman, 1991; Bradley & Bryant, 1985; Bus & van IJzendoorn, 1999; Craig, 2006; Ehri & Wilce, 1987). Because studies using letters to represent phonological segments have only been conducted at the kindergarten level, effects on preschoolers are not known.

Vocabulary size and other lexicon features (e.g., "neighborhood density"; Metsala & Walley, 1998, p. 101; age of acquisition of different words) are positively correlated with phoneme awareness (Jackson et al., 2007; Spira, Bracken, & Fischel, 2005; Storch & Whitehurst, 2002). This correlation has been explained in terms of a "lexical restructuring" (Metsala, 1999; Walley, 1993; Walley, Metsala, & Garlock, 2003) hypothesis. Words are first entered into memory in a holistic fashion (i.e., only suprasegmental features); as a child's vocabulary increases, clusters of words, very similar in phonological structure (e.g., *big, bit, bid*), form "dense neighborhoods" (Metsala & Walley, 1998, p. 101). This density forces storage at more segmental levels (e.g., onset-rime and phoneme), which makes onset-rime and phoneme level units psychologically available. In this view, phoneme awareness is not the bringing of previously unconscious units to conscious awareness, but a consequence of these units having become part of spoken word recognition (Metsala, 1999; Walley, 1993; Walley et al., 2003). (See also Foorman & Connor and Duke & Carlisle, this volume, for a further discussion of the relationship between vocabulary knowledge and phonological awareness.)

In light of the positive correlation between oral vocabulary and phoneme awareness, instruction that increases vocabulary development would also likely support phoneme-level awareness. As well, given that syntax "bootstraps" vocabulary learning (Hoff, 2006; Hoff & Naigles, 2002) and also comprehension (Duke & Carlisle, this volume), broad language learning—vocabulary and syntax together—are likely to provide the most robust support of phonological awareness.

Alphabetic Knowledge

Alphabet knowledge includes letter-name knowledge (upper and lowercase) and its level of automaticity, letter-sound knowledge (i.e., the specific sound representations assigned to graphemes), as well as the more general alphabetic principle that letters represent sounds in spoken words.

Acquisition Sequence.   Children learn upper-case letters first, then gradually learn lower-case letters. Letters in the child's first name (Justice, Pence, & Bowles 2006; McGee & Richgels, 1989; Treiman & Broderick, 1998), and other meaningful letters from words encountered frequently, are learned before others. Apart from personal influences, which include familiarity, letters with few overlapping features are distinguished before letters with many visually-similar features (e.g., O/E versus E/F), with those differing only by orientation distinguished last (W/M, d/b, p/q; Gibson & Levin, 1975). Middle-class children know about 20 upper-case letters by the end of preschool years (Mason, 1980; Worden & Boettcher, 1990). Three-year-olds, on average, know only 3 to 5 letters, although some know more than 20 (Worden & Boettcher, 1990). Based on data from Early Reading First projects from 2002–2006, a spring performance target of 18 upper-case letters for 4–year-olds was set by the U. S. Department of Education for 2007 projects (http://www.ed.gov/about/reports/annual/2007plan/edlite-g2eseaearlyread.html).

The alphabetic principle—the understanding that letters (i.e., graphemes) represent sounds in spoken words—rests on both letter knowledge and phonemic awareness. It emerges as both letter knowledge and phonological awareness reach adequate levels, and with experience in seeing letters linked to sounds. Letter-name knowledge predicts letter-sound knowledge (McBride-Chang, 1999; Treiman, Broderick, & Tincoff, 1998). Moreover, in cases where phonemes in letter names match the letter's assignment in the orthography, letter-name knowledge supports children's learning of specific letter-sound correspondences (McBride-Chang, 1999; Treiman & Broderick, 1998), especially when the relevant phoneme is first in the letter's name (e.g., B, /b/, /e/ versus L, /e/ /l/; Treiman & Broderick, 1998). Letter-sound correspondences are harder to learn for letters with multiple mappings or with names that do not contain the phonemes they represent (e.g., W and H). Teaching letter-sound associations through rote memorization shows less benefit to word reading or spelling than does linking phoneme segments and the letter names containing the relevant phonemes through teacher-scaffolded writing activities (Ball & Blachman, 1991; Ehri & Wilce, 1985).

Acquisition Support.   Exposure to a wide variety of letters, through alphabet puzzles, magnetic letters, and alphabet books, allows comparison and detection of minor physical differences between and among letters (e.g., F/E, O/Q, K/X; Gibson & Levin, 1975). This helps children learn that highly similar letters are not different exemplars of the same category, but different categories (Schickedanz, 1998). Because younger preschoolers have limited fine-motor skills and relatively weak mental images of letters (Schickedanz & Casbergue, 2004), their earliest written letters rarely capture a letter's conventional features. Although early writing, including scribbled forms, is a critical early literacy activity for preschoolers, it cannot provide adequate visual access to conventional letters. Thus, interesting and playful experiences that allow for comparing a variety of letters in their conventional forms (Gibson, 1979) and in different fonts (e.g., E, E, **E**; Adams, 1990) are important supports for letter-name learning and likely more motivating than isolated letter instruction, such as introducing one letter a week or teaching letters via flash cards.

Oral Language

Oral language knowledge includes both receptive and expressive language. Although there is significant variability in the rate of children's language development, it follows a relatively predictable sequence.

Acquisition Sequence

Children usually say a first word around 12 months of age and experience a vocabulary "spurt" between 18 and 24 months (Bates, Bretherton, Snyder, 1988; Fenson et al., 1994; Goldfield & Reznick, 1990). Preschoolers acquire initial and limited understandings of words from only a few exposures (i.e., "fast mapping"; Carey, 1978; Dollaghan, 1985; Woodward, Markham, & Fitzsimmons, 1994) and these understandings undergo further development over a number of years (Justice, Pence, & Bowles, 2006). Receptive vocabulary always exceeds expressive vocabulary and child explanations (i.e., definitional vocabulary) require a higher level of word knowledge than either receptive or expressive measures (National Institute for Literacy, 2008; Weizman & Snow, 2001).

Estimates of vocabulary size by age differ depending on the methodology used. Smith's (1941) estimate of first graders' vocabulary was 16,500 basic or root words, Templin's (1957) was 7, 800, and Anglin's (1993) was 10,398. There is agreement that vocabulary levels vary widely among children, and that children with the lowest levels enter first grade with several thousand fewer words than children entering with robust vocabularies (Biemiller, 2006).

Biemiller and Slonim (2001) studied the word knowledge of children in three populations (normative and advantaged populations in grades 2–5 and an English as a second language population in grades 5 and 6) and found correlations (all above $r = .90$) in word meanings. In addition, regardless of age or population, there were words known in common. Moreover, words higher in their designated sequence were known by children with larger vocabularies but not by children with smaller vocabularies, which prompted their claim of a "rough sequence" (Biemiller, 2006) of acquisition of word meanings.

Acquisition Support

In this section, related studies are addressed in two sections: adult talk that supports children's vocabulary learning and contexts that provide opportunities for knowledge acquisition.

Types of Adult Talk.   Density of adult talk (i.e., sheer quantity) surrounding a child was a strong predictor of vocabulary size in many studies (Dickinson & Tabors, 2001; Hart & Risley, 1995; Hoff & Naigles, 2002; Huttenlocher et al., 1991; Weizman & Snow, 2001; Wells, 1985). Hart and Risley's findings, based on data from 42 children of low, middle, and upper SES, followed for 2 years (between 1 and 3 years of age), have been especially influential. The amount that parents talked to their children varied from fewer than 500 words to greater than 3,000 in an average hour. In a year, these differences amounted to an estimated 250,000 utterances compared to 4 million. The more words children heard, the faster their vocabularies developed. The amount of talk and the variety in the type of words used were also correlated: "… more talk meant more subtle variations in immediate context, calling for more different words" (p. 131). Beyond the number and type of words spoken, complexity of adult syntax predicts vocabulary growth

(Duke & Carlisle, this volume; Hoff, 2006; Tabors, Beals, & Weizman, 2001) and child syntax level (Hoff-Ginsberg, 1986; Hoff-Ginsberg & Shatz, 1982; Huttenlocher et al., 2002).

Investigators also have studied the effects of various functions of adult talk to which children are exposed in different settings (Beals, 2001; Beals, DeTemple, & Dickinson, 1994; Davidson & Snow, 1995; DeTemple & Beals, 1991; Dickinson & Beals, 1994; Huttenlocher, Vasilyeva, Cymerman, & Levine, 2002; Tabors, Beals, & Weizman, 2001; Weizman & Snow, 2001). In general, the more that adult talk prompts children to elaborate and clarify, to answer cognitively challenging questions, or to think about language and the child's world, the greater its effects on children's vocabulary development and on some aspects of literacy development (i.e., comprehension). Much has been made of children's preparation for school-like talk (Heath, 1983; Purcell-Gates, 1995), and in this light, Beals' (2001) examination of parents' use of narrative and explanatory talk, two types of discourse commonly used in classrooms, is of particular interest. "Mealtime" data from 68 low-income families with 3-, 4-, or 5-year-old children, provided evidence of similar amounts of narrative talk (11 to 17%)—defined as a type of discourse "about an event that has happened in the past or that will happen in the future and that usually takes shape over several turns in a conversation" (p. 83)—and explanatory talk (14 to 16%), defined as "talk that requested and/or made some logical connection between objects, events, concepts, or conclusions" (p. 86), with slight variations with age. There was a wide range in occurrence of each type of talk across families, with narrative talk ranging from 0% to 65% of talk across the three age groups, and explanatory talk ranging from 0% to 52% of talk. Different types of talk were correlated with different language subskills at different ages. More exposure to explanatory talk was associated with higher vocabulary scores (PPVT-R; Dunn & Dunn, 1981) in 5-year-olds. More exposure to narrative talk at age 5 was also correlated with higher vocabulary scores. For 4-year-olds, higher amounts of narrative talk correlated with higher scores on a story comprehension task.

Studies also suggest a relationship between access to knowledge and concepts and vocabulary development, in particular, and literacy learning in general. Prior to the simplification of beginning reading texts in the early 1900s, over concern about the knowledge required to read texts, research on the relationship between knowledge and reading skill was common (Hildreth, 1933). Assessments of knowledge in this research (e.g., Peck & McGlothlin, 1940), which typically included both vocabulary ("What does 'invite' mean?" p. 662) and knowledge items ("Where would you play with a sled?" p. 661), were highly correlated with success in reading (e.g., Hilliard & Troxell, 1937; Peck & McGlothlin, 1940). A focus on knowledge as it relates to reading has been somewhat lost in recent years, as attention has shifted to skills largely related to word recognition (Juel, 2006), although Neuman (2006) has recently highlighted the importance of knowledge and the wide differences among children with different SES. Some research has focused on correlations between knowledge input and child outcomes. For example, Tabors, Roach, and Snow (2001) found that parents' focus on science process talk in conjunction with magnet play with preschool-age children (i.e., the why/how of magnetism) was moderately to strongly related to kindergarten measures of vocabulary (receptive, definitions, and superordinate categories), story comprehension, and narrative production. Wasik, Bond, and Hindman (2006) also attributed vocabulary gains made by Head Start children in part to the quality of the intervention teachers' conversations in theme-based activities that exposed children naturally and repeatedly to key oral vocabulary. Some researchers (Beals, DeTemple, & Dickinson, 1994; Dickinson, McCabe, & Essex, 2006; Dickinson & Tabors, 2001; Tabors, Roach, & Snow, 2001; Weizman & Snow, 2001) have stressed the contributions of cognitively-rich talk, including "academic talk" (i.e., talk including new information/explanations), to vocabulary and other aspects of language, and have noted that cognitively-rich talk in preschool and kindergarten classrooms requires content-rich curricula (Dickinson et al., 2006; Neuman, 2006).

Types of Contexts.   The relationship between conceptually-rich talk and vocabulary development has prompted examination of settings that afford opportunities for children to hear and engage in such talk (e.g., Beals, DeTemple, & Dickinson, 1994; Cote, 2001; Dickinson, 1984; Hoff, 2006; Tabors, Beals, & Weizman, 2001; Snow & Kurland, 1996). In a study of language use of 53 low-income mothers and their 5-year-old children during play (magnet and toy), book reading (story and information), and mealtime, Weizman and Snow (2001) found the most talk during mealtime and information-book conversations, although the highest exposure to sophisticated words occurred when mothers read the book text. Together, play and mealtime settings generated nearly seven times as many maternally-generated sophisticated word tokens as the book-reading sessions alone. Greater maternal use of sophisticated words and higher frequencies of instructive or helpful interactions that supported sophisticated word meanings were related to vocabulary outcomes at age 5. The quantity and lexical sophistication of vocabulary used by parents also predicted a substantial amount (50%) of the variance in children's second-grade vocabulary knowledge.

Numerous studies have focused specifically on parent-child, shared book reading as a language-learning context. Scarborough and Dobrich (1994) conducted a narrative review of nine research samples (median N = 41) that examined oral language as an outcome variable of parent-child reading. They reported an overall median correlation of only .23. In contrast, Bus, van IJzendoorn, and Pellegrini (1995) conducted a quantitative meta-analysis, and they reported an effect size of $d = .67$ (33 samples, including N = 3410 participants) for the association between book reading and language skills (measured by tests such as the Peabody Picture Vocabulary Test and the Illinois Test of Psycholinguistic Abilities). They concluded that "the strength of the correlation between book reading and literacy/language skills is somewhat greater than one of the most powerful predictors of reading problems, the nonword reading deficit" (p. 15). Bus and colleagues attributed differences in their findings and those of Scarborough and Dobrich to the methodological advantages of the quantitative meta-analysis:

> The contrast between our conclusions and those of Scarborough and Dobrich emphasizes the advantages of quantitative meta-analysis that takes the accumulation of trends into account. In the area of book reading, the sample sizes are mostly small and effects have to be substantial to reveal significant statistics. By simply counting the number of significant effects, reviewers may seriously underestimate the overall effect. (p. 15)

Other comparisons on the effects of particular types of storybook sharing techniques indicate that when children take an active role in shared reading and parents or teachers provide feedback through expansions, modeling, corrections and praise, children learn substantially more words. These results hold across groups of children of different SES and with children scoring below average on language measures (Arnold & Whitehurst, 1994; Valdez-Menchaca & Whitehurst, 1992; Whitehurst et al., 1994).

Other studies have examined the effects of various read-aloud conditions on children's language knowledge. These included interactive and non-interactive, and single and repeated reading conditions. Single reading of a storybook increased children's receptive, but not expressive, vocabulary (Sénéchal & Cornell, 1993), while repeated readings and questions were more likely to increase receptive vocabulary than a single-reading (an effect size of 1.06; Sénéchal (1997). Answering questions during repeated readings (three) resulted in greater word learning than a single reading or rereadings without questioning (Sénéchal, 1997).

Effects of conditions of talk surrounding book reading were also found in the previously cited study by Weizman and Snow (2001). Specifically, parent utterances, characterized as instructive or helpful, "explained as much variance in word learning as did the density of sophisticated words" (p. 27). As explained by DeTemple and Snow (2003), "Children can start to establish a lexical item in their memory after one or two exposures—fast-mapping—but full specification of the item's phonology, meaning, and usage may require many exposures" (p. 20). Word understanding is less likely to occur from passive encounters, and word knowledge is likely to increase from opportunities to connect and link new words to other words and concepts (Nagy & Scott, 2000). Questioning and elaboration during repeated readings very likely support increasingly deeper word meaning, helping children go beyond their initial, superficial, "fast mapping" knowledge (Carey, 1978).

The effects of interactional styles during book reading, however, appear to be mediated by children's initial vocabulary knowledge. While some studies (e.g., Haden, Reese, & Fivush, 1996) have found that children whose mothers emphasized understanding the story had higher vocabulary scores than children whose mothers emphasized describing and labeling objects and ideas, other studies (Reese, Cox, Harte, & McAnally, 2003) have found a more complex relationship. Specifically, children with smaller initial vocabularies showed the greatest vocabulary gains when mothers described and labeled objects, while children with larger initial vocabularies benefited most from a style emphasizing overall story comprehension. Thus, for children with larger vocabularies, conversations need not be related to the word itself, but can be more broadly related to the context in which the word appears (DeTemple & Snow, 2003), while children with smaller vocabularies need more direct support in learning new words. (See Foorman and Connor, this volume, for a similar discussion related to primary-grade children.)

Because shared book-reading makes significant contributions to children's vocabulary development, understanding how parents and teachers learn to read effectively is important. Both teachers and parents vary widely in how they share storybooks with children (Dickinson & Keebler, 1989; Dickinson & Smith, 1994; Reese et al., 2003) and both parents and teachers benefit from some form of instructional intervention (Edwards, 1994, 1995; Krol-Sinclair, 1996; McKeown & Beck, 2006; Paratore, 1993; Paratore, Melzi, & Krol-Sinclair, 1999; Phillips, McNaughton, & MacDonald, 2004; Whitehurst et al., 1994; Zevenbergen & Whitehurst, 2006). (See also Duke & Carlisle, this volume.)

Reasoning

Thinking that involves reasoning requires factual knowledge, but goes beyond it. In reasoning, factual knowledge is used to draw inferences. Reasoning is especially important for listening and reading comprehension, and its development begins early. (See Duke & Carlisle, this volume, for further discussion of reasoning in early and later reading development.)

Acquisition Sequence.   Preschool children's difficulties in reasoning have been the focus of considerable research and a major theory (Piaget, 1963, 1954). A thorough review is beyond the scope of this chapter, but we note here that, even at young ages (i.e., 4 years of age), knowledge interacts with thinking (Hirschfeld & Gelman, 1994). Moreover, conceptual knowledge (i.e., non-perceptible information, such as humans, dogs, cats, and whales are mammals) acts as a strong constraint on what Haskell (2001) calls "runaway transfer" (p. 155), the excessive overgeneralization of knowledge. This tendency has been noted by several researchers (e.g., Beck & McKeown, 2001; Neuman, 1990) in children's responses to higher-level questions about stories read aloud to them.

Acquisition Support.   Considerable differences in reasoning are due to different levels of knowledge and strategies for accessing and relating knowledge, not to differences in thinking capacity (e.g., Brown, 1989; Granott & Gardner, 1994; Hirschfeld & Gelman, 1994). Providing theoretical knowledge to young children (e.g., "You don't need to touch the magnet to the paperclip. The magnetic force goes out from the magnet to attract it. Magnetism is not like glue.") is especially effective in reigning in runaway transfer (Haskell, 2001). A focus on substantive knowledge during the early years, in conjunction with thematically related books and expository texts (Duke & Purcell-Gates, 2003) and the use of higher-level versus lower-level questions in discussions of stories (Collins, 2004; Hansen, 1981), not only builds vocabulary and conceptual knowledge (Wasik et al., 2006; Dickinson, McCabe, & Essex, 2006) but also reasoning skills that predict higher-level reading comprehension (Pressley et al., 1992; Woloshyn, Paivio, & Pressley, 1994).

SUMMARY AND IMPLICATIONS

We began this chapter with the purpose of understanding how and when various behaviors (e.g., code knowledge, vocabulary knowledge, reasoning) acquired at an early age exert their influence on children's literacy achievement in both beginning and later phases. We were motivated by evidence that, despite decades of attention to early intervention, low levels of literacy achievement persist. Our synthesis of evidence leads to a conclusion that, at least in part, low levels of literacy achievement may be explained by inadequate attention in the early years to the full array of abilities that are required for success in the later years. This conclusion suggests a need for attention to a number of research findings, including:

1. Particular skills and abilities acquired in the early childhood years influence competency at different points in the literacy learning trajectory. Code knowledge "shows up" in early-grade achievement (K-1-2); oral language knowledge and reasoning abilities (acquired throughout the early years and added to and refined into later years) "show up" in grades 3, 4, and beyond. The need to support the full array of abilities necessary for later reading is underscored in the conclusion drawn by Whitehurst and Lonigan (2002) that "investing resources to improve both code-related and oral language skills" (p. 21) in preschool children may help to prevent difficulties in later reading achievement. Likewise, Biemiller (2006) noted that a vocabulary gap that arises before children become conventional readers and writers is rarely closed in later years. Consequently, curricula intended to guide both parents and teachers in their interactions with young children must be as relentlessly focused on developing vocabulary and language knowledge as they are on developing code knowledge. Further, a large body of research indicates a need for early intervention to support the development of children's social skills. Ladd, Birch, and Buhs (1999) note that "these findings illustrate the need to revise prevailing theories of early school adjustment.... to incorporate interpersonal risk factors that operate within the classroom environment" (p. 1397).

2. The ways parents and teachers use language matter. Lots of talk is important, but density matters most when talk is rich with rare or sophisticated words and focused on topics that build children's conceptual knowledge. Moreover, utterances are most helpful when they support elaboration, clarification, and reasoning. Because some parents and teachers do not use these types of linguistic interactions, effective language learning requires deliberate and sustained interventions with these adults (Biemiller, 2006; Biemiller & Boote, 2006; Dickinson, 1994; Landry & Smith, 2006). The importance of such training for teachers is evident in data that show that excellent preschools help to make up for homes offering little language support (Cassidy et al., 1995; Dickinson, McCabe, & Essex, 2006). For example, a child's enrollment in a preschool rated "high" on the Preschool Environment composite (90th percentile) predicted above average performance on kindergarten language and literacy assessments, even if the home environment was rated "low" (10th percentile) on

home support for language development (Dickinson & Tabors, 2001). Additionally, teacher knowledge and training can significantly and positively affect children's acquisition of both code-related and oral language skills (for a review see Bowman, Donovan, & Burns, 2001). Highly-trained teachers use more rare words and involve children in more cognitively challenging talk throughout the school day. They also score higher on environmental rating scales and involve children in more analytical talk about books (Dickinson & Tabors, 2001).

3. The types of books parents and teachers share with children matter. Texts that introduce children to unfamiliar topics, interesting and complex syntax, and rare or sophisticated words are likely to contribute more to vocabulary and language learning than books low on these characteristics. Parents and teachers also talk more when reading expository than when reading narrative texts (Price, van Kleek, & Huberty, 2009). Thus, reading both genres with children will likely make a difference in children's language outcomes.

4. The ways parents and teachers share books matter. Children are more likely to acquire vocabulary knowledge from shared reading when readings are repeated and discussions are interactive and elaborative and focused on plot, language, and interesting or important words.

5. Opportunities to develop phonological awareness matter. At home and at school, playful experiences with rhyming texts and with games and activities that emphasize attention to sounds in words (e.g., hand-clapping syllables in their names, singing songs and reciting poems with alliteration, thinking of words that begin with the same sound, thinking of words that have the same phonogram, isolating and manipulating onset-rime) support children's development of phonological awareness.

   Interesting and playful opportunities to solve alphabet, letter, and word puzzles, to use magnetic letters, and to read and respond to alphabet books help children learn letter names, and knowledge of letter names correlates with phoneme awareness. Additionally, shared and scaffolded writing activities in which adults help children to segment words into their constituent phonemes and link letter sounds to letter names also facilitate the development of phonemic awareness.

6. Opportunities to learn about how print works matter. At both home and school, adults should engage children in tasks that require them to attend to and use print (e.g., match print with a logo context, manipulate letters to form known and new words, invent spellings and compose messages, point out the actual print in environmental print displays, when reading it, and read and respond to alphabet books).

FUTURE DIRECTIONS

Although much is now known about the roots of beginning literacy, gaps remain in important areas. Three kinds of research are noted here. First is a need for longitudinal studies of promising practices— intervention studies that begin in the earliest years (i.e., ages 2, 3, and 4) and continue through grades 3 or 4. Longitudinal intervention studies could answer questions about the efficacy of various instructional supports for the acquisition of code knowledge or vocabulary and language knowledge that are more or less helpful in these early years. Second is a need for studies that probe the types of language learning afforded by different types of texts. Intuitively, expository texts that introduce youngsters to unfamiliar topics and rare words would seem to support greater language learning, which is the rationale for asking teachers and parents to broaden the range of texts shared with children (Duke & Purcell-Gates, 2003). Little research has been done to study the differential effects of narrative and expository texts. A recent study of parental reading to preschool children found that parents and children talk far more when reading expository texts compared to narrative, but the effects on child language outcomes were not determined (Price, Van Kleeck, & Huberty, 2009). Thus, we know relatively little about the differential effects of narrative and expository text at these early ages. Third, as Biemiller (2006) noted, at present, there is little evidence that school support for vocabulary learning is paying off in substantial learning gains. Some current interventions hold promise (Beck & McKeown, 2001; Biemiller & Boote, 2006; Duke & Purcell-Gates, 2003; Schickedanz, 2001), but instructional practices that contribute to closing the gap for those children who enter school with smaller vocabularies and that teachers can and will incorporate into their daily teaching repertoires need to be better understood and specified. Finally, since we know that many of the variables we have reviewed make an independent contribution to literacy development, we must learn more about the separate and combined effects of these effective practices. In particular, we need to know the circumstances in which each needs its own place in the instructional program or, alternatively, whether some variables (e.g., knowledge acquisition efforts) might pull others (e.g., vocabulary or phonological awareness) along.

REFERENCES

Adams, M. J. (1990). *Beginning to read: Thinking and learning about print.* Urbana: University of Illinois Center for the Study of Reading.

Alexander, P. A. (2005/06). The path to competence: A lifespan developmental perspective on reading. *Journal of Literacy Research, 37*(4), 413–436.

Almy, M. C. (1949). *Children's experiences prior to first grade and success in beginning reading.* New York: Bureau of Publications, Teachers College, Columbia University.

Anderson, R.C., & Nagy, W. (1991). Word meanings. In R. Barr, M. Kamil, P. Mosenthal, & P. D. Pearson (Eds.), *Handbook of reading research* (Vol. II, pp. 690–723). White Plains, NY: Longman.

Anglin, J. N. (1993). Vocabulary development: A morphological analysis. *Monographs of the Society for Research in Child Development, 58*(10) (Serial No. 238).

Anthony, J. L., & Lonigan, C. J. (2004). The nature of phonological awareness: Converging evidence from four studies of preschool and early grade school children. *Journal of Educational Psychology, 96*(1), 43–55.

Anthony, J. L., Lonigan, C. J., Burgess, S. R., Driscoll, K., Philips, B. M., & Cantor, B. G. (2002). Structure of preschool phonological sensitivity: overlapping sensitivity to rhyme, words, syllables, and phonemes. *Journal of Experimental Child Psychology, 82*(1), 65–92.

Anthony, J. L., Lonigan, C. J., Driscoll, K., Philips, B. M., & Burgess, S. R. (2003). Phonological sensitivity: A quasi-parallel progression of word structure units and cognitive operations. *Reading Research Quarterly, 38*(4), 470–487.

Applegate, M. D., Applegate, A. J., & Modla, V. G. (2009). "She's my best reader; she just can't comprehend": Studying the relationship between fluency and comprehension. *Reading Teacher, 62* (6), 512–521.

Arnold, D. S., & Whitehurst, G. J. (1994). Accelerating language development through picture book reading: A summary of dialogic reading and its effects. In D. K. Dickinson (Ed.), *Bridges to literacy: Children, families, and schools* (pp. 103–128). Cambridge, MA: Blackwell.

Backman, J. (1983). The role of psycholinguistic skills in reading acquisition: a look at early readers. *Reading Research Quarterly, 18*, 466–479.

Baghban, M. (1984). *Our daughter learns to read and write: A case study from birth to three.* Newark, DE: The International Reading Association.

Baker, L., Fernandez-Fein, S., Scher, D., & Williams, H. (1998). Home experiences related to the development of word recognition. In J. L. Metsala & L. C. Ehri (Eds.), *Word recognition in beginning literacy* (pp. 263–288). Mahwah, NJ: Erlbaum.

Baker, L., & Wigfield, A. (1999). Dimensions of children's motivation for reading and their relations to reading activity and reading achievement. *Reading Research Quarterly, 34*(4), 452–477.

Ball, E. W., & Blachman, B. A. (1991). Does phoneme awareness training in kindergarten make a difference in early word recognition and spelling? *Reading Research Quarterly, 26*(1), 49–66.

Banks, M. S., & Salapatek, P. (1983). Infant visual perception. In P. Mussen (Ed.), *Handbook of child psychology: Vol. 2. Infant and developmental psychobiology* (4th ed., pp. 435–571). New York: Wiley.

Bates, E., Bretherton, I., & Snyder, L. (1988). *From first words to grammar: Individual differences and dissociable mechanisms.* New York: Cambridge University Press.

Beals, D. E. (2001). Eating and Reading: Links between family conversations with preschoolers and later language and literacy. In D. K. Dickinson & P. O. Tabors (Eds.), *Beginning literacy with language: Young children learning at home and at school* (pp. 75–92). Baltimore, MD: Brookes.

Beals, D. E., DeTemple, J. H., & Dickinson, D. K. (1994). Talking and listening that support early literacy development of children from low-income families. In D. K. Dickinson (Ed.), *Bridges to literacy: Children, families, and schools* (pp. 19–40). Cambridge, MA: Blackwell.

Beck, L., & McKeown, M. G. (2001). Text Talk: Capturing the benefits of read-aloud experiences for young children. *The Reading Teacher, 55,* 10–20.

Beckwith, L., & Rodning, C. (1992). Evaluating effects of intervention with parebnts of preterm infants. In S. Friedman & M. J. Sigman (Eds.), *The psychological development of low-birthweight children: Annual advances in applied developmental psychology* (Vol. 6, pp. 389–410). Norwood, NJ: Ablex.

Biemiller, A. (2006). Vocabulary development and instruction. In D. Dickinson & S. B. Neuman (Eds.), *Handbook of early literacy research* (Vol. 2, pp. 41–51). New York: Guilford.

Biemiller, A., & Boote, C. (2006). An effective method for building meaning vocabulary in primary grades. *Journal of Educational Psychology, 98*(1), 42–62.

Biemiller, A., & Slonim, N. (2001). Estimating root word vocabulary growth in normative and advantaged populations: Evidence for a common sequence of vocabulary acquisition. *Journal of Educational Psychology, 93,* 498–520.

Blair, C. (2002). School readiness: Integrating cognition and emotion in a neurobiological conceptualization of children's functioning at school entry. *American Psychologist, 57*(2), 111–127.

Bomba, P., & Siqueland, E. R. (1983). The nature and structure of infant form categories. *Journal of Experimental Child Psychology, 35,* 294–328.

Bowey, J. (1994). Phonological sensitivity in novice readers and nonreaders. *Journal of Experimental Child Psychology, 58,* 134–159.

Bowman, B. T., Donovan, M. S., & Burns, M. S. (Eds.). (2001). *Eager to learn: Educating our preschoolers.* Washington, DC: National Academy Press.

Bradley, L., & Bryant, P. E. (1983). Categorizing sounds and learning to read: A causal connection. *Nature, 301,* 419–421.

Bradley, L. L., & Bryant, P. E. (1985). *Rhyme and reason in reading and spelling.* Ann Arbor: The University of Michigan Press.

Brown, A. L. (1989). Analogical learning and transfer: What develops? In S. Vosniadou & A. Ortony (Eds.), *Similarity and analogical reasoning* (pp. 369–412). Hillsdale, NJ : Erlbaum.

Buly, M. R., & Valencia, S. W. (2002). Below the bar: Profiles of students who fail state reading assessments. *Educational Evaluation and Policy Analysis, 24,* 219–239.

Bus, A. G., & van Ijzendoorn, M. H. (1999). Phonological awareness and early reading: A meta-analysis of experimental training studies. *Journal of Educational Psychology, 91*(3), 403–414.

Bus, A. G., van Ijzendoorn, M. H., & Pellegrini, A. D. (1995). Joint book reading makes for success in learning to read: A meta-analysis in intergenerational transmission of literacy. *Review of Educational Research, 65,* 1–21.

Byrne, B., & Fielding-Barnsley, R. (1995). Evaluation of a program to teach phonemic awareness to young children: A 2- and 3-year follow-up and a new preschool trial. *Journal of Educational Psychology, 87,* 488–503.

Cain, K., Oakhill, J., & Bryant, P. (2004). Children's reading comprehension ability: Concurrent prediction by working memory, verbal ability, and component skills. *Journal of Educational Psychology, 96*(1), 31–42.

Carey, S. (1978). The child as word learner. In J. Bresnan, G. Miller, & M. Halle (Eds.), *Linguistic theory and psychological reality* (pp. 264–293). Cambridge, MA: MIT Press.

Carlisle, J. F., & Rice, M. S. (2004). Assessment of reading comprehension. In C. A. Stone, E. R. Silliman, B. J. Ehren, & K. Apel (Eds.), *Handbook of language and literacy: Development and disorders* (pp. 521–540). New York: Guilford.

Carrow-Woolfolk, E. (1985). *Test for the auditory comprehension of language-Revised.* Allen, TX: DLM Teaching Resources.

Cassidy, D. J., Buell, M. J., Pugh-Hoese, S., & Russell, S. (1995). The effect of teacher education on child care teachers' beliefs and classroom quality: Year one of the TEACH early childhood associate degree scholarship program. *Early Research Quarterly, 10,* 171–183.

Chall, J. S., Jacobs, V. A., & Baldwin, L. E. (1990). *The reading crisis: Why poor children fall behind.* Cambridge, MA: Harvard University Press.

Christie, J., Enz, B. J., Han, M., Prior, J., & Gerard, M. (2007). Effects of environmental print games and play props on young children's print recognition. In D. Sluss & O. Jarrett (Eds.), *Investigating play in the 21st century* (pp. 220–228). Lanham, MD: University Press of America.

Clay, M. M. (1975). *What did I write: Beginning writing behaviour.* Portsmouth, NH: Heinemann.

Clay, M. M. (1979). *The early detection of reading difficulties* (3rd ed.). Portsmouth, NH: Heinemann.

Cohen, L.B., & Younger, B. A. (1984). Infant perception of angular relations. *Infant Behavior and Development, 7,* 37–47.

Collins, M. F. (2004). *ESL preschoolers' English vocabulary acquisition and story comprehension from storybook reading.* Unpublished doctoral dissertation, Boston University.

Cote, L. R. (2001). Language opportunities during mealtimes in preschool classrooms. In. D. K. Dickinson & P. O. Tabors (Eds.), *Beginning literacy with language: Young children learning at home and at school* (pp. 205–222). Baltimore, MD: Brookes.

Crain-Thoreson, C., & Dale, P. S. (1999). Enhancing linguistic performance: parents and teachers as book reading partners for children with language delays. *Topics in Early Childhood Special Education, 19*(1), 28–39.

Craig, S. A. (2006). The effects of an adapted interactive writing intervention on kindergarten children's phonological awareness, spelling, and early reading development: A contextualized approach to instruction. *Journal of Educational Psychology, 98,* 714–731.

CTB. (1990). *Developmental skills checklist.* Monterey, CA: McGraw-Hill.

Curtis, M. E. (1990). Development of components of reading skills. *Journal of Educational Psychology, 72,* 656–669.

Davidson, R. G., & Snow, C. E. (1995). The linguistic environment of early readers. *Journal of Research in Childhood Education, 10,* 5–21.

DeTemple, J. M., & Beals, D. E. (1991). Family talk: Sources of support for the development of decontextualized skills. *Journal of Research in Childhood Education, 6,* 11–19.

DeTemple, J., & Snow, C. E. (2003). Learning words from books. In A. vanKleeck, S. A. Stahl, & E. B. Bauer (Eds.), *On reading books to children: Parents and teachers* (pp. 16–36). Mahwah, NJ: Erlbaum.

Dickinson, D. K. (1984). First impressions: Children's knowledge of words gained from a single exposure. *Applied Psycholinguistics, 5,* 359–373.

Dickinson, D. K. (Ed.). (1994). *Bridges to literacy: Children, families and schools.* Cambridge, MA: Blackwell.

Dickinson, D. K., & Beals, D. E. (1994). Not by print alone: Oral language supports for early literacy. In D. Lancy (Ed.), *Children's emergent literacy: From Research to Practice* (pp. 29–40). Westport, CT: Praegar.

Dickinson, D. K., & Keebler, R. (1989). Variation in preschool teachers' styles of reading books. *Discourse Processes, 12,* 353–375.

Dickinson, D. K., McCabe, A., & Essex, M. J. (2006). A window of opportunity we must open to all: The case for preschool with high-quality support for language and literacy. In D. K. Dickinson & S. B. Neuman (Eds.), *Handbook of early literacy research* (Vol. 2, pp. 11–28). New York: Guilford.

Dickinson, D. K., & Smith, M. M. (1994). Long-term effects of preschool teachers' book readings on low-income children's vocabulary and story comprehension. *Reading Research Quarterly, 29,* 105–122.

Dickinson, D. K., & Tabors, P. O. (Eds.). (2001). *Beginning literacy with language: Young children learning at home and at school.* Baltimore, MD: Brookes.

Dickinson, D., Tabors, P., & Roach, K. (1996). Predicting children's fourth grade reading comprehension using individual growth trajectories in vocabulary, decoding, and decontextualized language. In A. Spinillo & J. Oakhill (Chairs), *Thinking about texts: Comprehension and metalinguistic awareness.*

Symposium presented at the XIVth Biennial Meetings of the International Society for the Study of Behavioral Development, Quebec City, Quebec.

Dollaghan, C. (1985). Child meets word: Fast mapping in preschool children. *Journal of Speech and Hearing Research, 28*, 449–454.

Duke, N., Pressley, M., & Hilden, K. (2004). Difficulties with reading comprehension. In C. A. Stone, E. R. Silliman, B. J. Ehren, & K. Apel (Eds.), *Handbook of language and literacy: Development and disorders* (pp. 501–520). New York: Guilford.

Duke, N. K., & Purcell-Gates, V. (2003). Genres at home and at school: Bridging the known to the new. *The Reading Teacher, 57*(1), 30–37.

Dunn, L. M., & Dunn, L. M. (1981). *Peabody picture vocabulary test—revised.* Circle Pines, MN: American Guidance Service.

Dunn, L. M., Dunn, L. M., Whetton, C., & Burley, J. (1997). *British picture vocabulary scale II.* Windsor, England: NFER-Nelson.

Durkin, D. (1966). *Children who read early.* New York: Teachers College Press.

Edwards, P. A. (1994). Responses of teachers and African-American mothers to a book-reading intervention program. In D. K. Dickinson (Ed.), *Bridges to literacy: Children, families, and schools* (pp. 175–210). Cambridge, MA: Blackwell.

Edwards, P. A. (1995). Empowering low-income mothers and fathers to share books with young children. *The Reading Teacher, 48*, 558–565.

Ehri, L., Nunes, S., Stahl, S., & Willows, D. (2001). Systematic phonics instruction helps students learn to read: evidence from the National Reading Panel's meta analysis. *Review of Educational Research, 71*(3), 393–447.

Ehri, L. C., & Sweet, J. (1991). Fingerpoint-reading of memorized text: what enables beginners to process the print? *Reading Research Quarterly, 26*(4), 442–462.

Ehri, L. C., & Wilce, L. S. (1985). Movement into reading: is the first stage of printed word learning visual or phonetic? *Reading Research Quarterly, 20*, 163–179.

Ehri, L. C., & Wilce, L. S. (1987). Cipher versus cue reading: an experiment in decoding acquisition. *Journal of Educational Psychology, 79*, 3–13.

Eimas, P.D., & Quinn, P. (1994). Studies on the formation of perceptually based basic level categories in young infants. *Child Development, 65*, 903–917.

Eimas, P.D., Siqueland, D.R., Jusczyk, P., & Vigorito, J. (1971). Speech perception in infants. *Science, 171*, 303–306.

Elliot, C. D. (1996). *British abilities scales II.* Windsor, England: NFER-Nelson.

Fantz, R.L. (1963). Pattern vision in newborn infants. *Science, 140*, 296–297.

Fenson, L., Dale, P. S., Reznick, J. S., Bates, E., Thal, D. J., & Pethick, S. H. J. (1994). Variability in early communicative development. *Monographs of the Society of Research in Child Development, 59*(5) (Serial No. 242).

Foorman, B. R., Francis, D. J., Novy, D. M., & Liberman, D. (1991). How letter-sound instruction mediates progress in first-grade reading and spelling. *Journal of Educational Psychology, 83*(4), 456–469.

Ganapole, S. J. (1987). The development of word consciousness prior to first grade. *Journal of Reading Behavior, 19*, 415–436.

Gardner, M. F. (1990). *Expressive one-word picture vocabulary test—revised.* Novato, CA: Academic Therapy.

Genishi, C., & Dyson, A. H. (1984). *Language assessment in the early years.* Norwood, NJ: Ablex.

Gibson, E. J. (1979). Theory-based research on reading and its implications for instruction. In J. B. Carroll & J. S. Chall (Eds.), *Toward a literate society* (p. 239–281). New York: McGraw-Hill.

Gibson, E. J., & Levin, H. (1975). *The psychology of reading.* Cambridge, MA: MIT Press.

Glasgow, C., & Cowley, J. (1994). *The Renfrew BUS story—American edition.* Centreville, DE: The Centreville School.

Goldfield, B. A., & Reznick, J. S. (1990). Early lexical acquisition: Rate, content, and the vocabulary spurt. *Journal of Child Language, 17*, 171–183.

Goldman, S. R., Rakestraw, J. A. (2001). Structural aspects of constructing meaning from text. In M.Kamil, P. B. Mosenthal, P. D. Pearson, & R. Barr (Eds.), *Handbook of reading research* (Vol. III, pp. 311–336). Mahwah, NJ: Erlbaum.

Goodglass, H., & Kaplan, E. (1983). *The Boston Naming Test.* Philadelphia: Lea and Febriger.

Goodman, Y. (1986). Children coming to know literacy. In W. Teale & E. Sulzby (Eds.), *Emergent literacy: Writing and reading* (pp. 1–14). Norwood, NJ: Ablex.

Granott, N., & Gardner, H. (1994). When minds meet: Interactions, coincidence, and development of domains of ability. In R. J. Sternberg & R. K. Wagner (Eds.), *Mind in context* (pp. 171–201). New York: Cambridge University Press.

Greenough, W., Black, J. E., & Wallace, C. S. (1987). Experience and brain development. *Child Development, 58*, 539–559.

Guthrie, J. T., & Humenick, N. M. (2004). Motivating students to read: Evidence for classroom practices that increase reading motivation. In P. McCardle & V. Chhabra (Eds.), *The voice of evidence in reading research* (pp. 329–354). Baltimore, MD: Brookes.

Guthrie, J. T., & Wigfield, A. (2000). Engagement and motivation in reading. In M. L. Kamil, P. B. Mosenthal, P. D. Pearson, & R. Barr (Eds.), *Handbook of reading research* (Vol. III, pp. 403–424). Mahwah, NJ: Erlbaum.

Haden, C. A., Reese, E., & Fivush, R. (1996). Mother's extratextual comments during storybook reading: Stylistic differences over time and across texts. *Discourse Processes, 21*, 135–169.

Hansen, J. (1981). The effects of inference training and practice on young children's reading comprehension. *Reading Research Quarterly, 3*, 391–417.

Hart, B., & Risley, T. R. (1995). *Meaningful differences.* Baltimore, MD: Brookes.

Haskell, R. E. (2001). *Transfer of learning: Cognition, instruction, and reasoning.* New York: Academic Press.

Hatcher, P. J., Hulme, C., & Ellis, A. W. (1994). Ameliorating early reading failure by integrating the teaching of reading and phonological skills: The phonological linkage hypothesis. *Child Development, 65*, 41–57.

Haynes, H., White, B. L., & Held, R. (1965). Visual accommodation in human infants. *Science, 148*, 528–530.

Heath, S. B. (1983). *Ways with words: Language, life and work in communities and classrooms.* Cambridge, England: Cambridge University Press.

Hiebert, E. H., & Martin, L. A. (2002). The texts of beginning reading instruction. In S. B. Neuman & D. K. Dickinson (Eds.), *Handbook of early literacy research* (pp. 361–376). New York: Guilford.

Hildreth, G. (1933). Information tests of first-grade children. *Childhood Education 9*, 416–420.

Hilliard, G. H., & Troxell, E. (1937). Informational background as a factor in reading readiness and reading progress. *Elementary School Journal, 38*, 255–263.

Hirschfeld, L. A., & Gelman, S. A. (1994). *Mapping the mind: Domain specificity in cognition and culture.* New York: Cambridge University Press.

Hockett, J. A. & Neeley, D. P. (1936). A comparison of the vocabularies of thirty-three primers, *The Elementary School Journal, 37*, 190–202.

Hoff, E. (2006). Environmental supports for language acquisition. In D. K. Dickinson & S. B. Neuman (Eds.), *Handbook of early literacy research* (Vol. 2, pp. 163–172). New York: Guilford.

Hoff, E., & Naigles, L. (2002). How children use input in acquiring a lexicon. *Child Development, 73*, 418–433.

Hoff-Ginsberg, E. (1986). Function and structure in maternal speech: Their relation to the child's development of syntax. *Child Development, 62*, 782–796.

Hoff-Ginsberg, E., & Shatz, M. (1982). Linguistic input and the child's acquisition of language. *Psychological Bulletin, 92*, 3–26.

Hoover, W. A., & Gough, P. B. (1990). The simple view of reading. *Reading and Writing: An Interdisciplinary Journal, 2*, 127–160.

Horowitz, F. D. (2000). Child development and the PITS: Simple questions, complex answers, and developmental theory. *Child Development, 71*, 1–10.

Hunt, J. M. (1961). *Intelligence and experience.* New York: The Ronald Press.

Huttenlocher, J., Haight, W., Bryk, A., Seltzer, M., & Lyons, T. (1991). Early vocabulary growth: Relation to language input and gender. *Developmental Psychology, 27*, 236–248.

Huttenlocher, J., Vasilyeva, M., Cymerman, E., & Levine, S. (2002). Language input and child syntax. *Cognitive Psychology, 45*, 337–375.

Huttenlocher, J., Waterfall, H. R., Vasilyeva, M., & Vevea, J. L. (2007). The varieties of speech to young children. *Developmental Psychology, 43* (5), 1062–1083.

Jackson, R., McCoy, A., Pistorino, C., Wilkinson, A., Burghardt, J., Clark, M., et al. (2007). *National evaluation of early reading first: Final report*. Washington, DC: U.S. Department of Education, Institute of Education Sciences, U.S. Government Printing Office.

Jastak, S., & Wilkinson, G. S. (1984). *Wide Range Achievement Test—Revised*. Wilmington, DE: Jastak Associates.

Juel, C. (1988). Learning to read and write: A longitudinal study of 54 children from first through fourth grades. *Journal of Educational Psychology, 60*, 437–447.

Juel, C. (2006). The impact of early school experiences on initial reading. In D. K. Dickinson & S. B. Neuman (Eds.), *Handbook of early literacy research* (Vol. 2, pp. 410–426). New York: Guilford.

Juel, C., Griffith, P. L., & Gough, P. B. (1986). Acquisition of literacy: A longitudinal study of children in first and second grade. *Journal of Educational Psychology, 78*, 243–255.

Jusczyk, P. W. (1997). *The discovery of spoken language*. Cambridge, MA: MIT Press.

Justice, L. M., Chow, S. M., Capellinni, C., Flanigan, K., & Colton, S. (2003). Emergent literacy intervention for vulnerable preschoolers: Relative effects of two approaches. *American Journal of Speech-Language Pathology, 12*, 320–332.

Justice, L. M., Pence, K., & Bowles, R. B. (2006). An investigation of four hypotheses concerning the order by which 4-year-old children learn the alphabet letters. *Early Childhood Research Quarterly, 21*(3), 374–389.

Kellman, P. J., & Arterberry, M. (1998). *The cradle of knowledge: Development of perception in infancy*. Cambridge, MA: MIT Press.

Klare, G. P. (1984). Readability. In P. D. Pearson, R. Barr, M. L. Kamil, & P. Mosenthal (Eds.), *Handbook of reading research* (Vol. 1, pp. 681–744). White Plains, NY: Longman.

Krol-Sinclair, B. (1996). Connecting home and school literacies: Immigrant parents with limited formal education as classroom storybook readers. In D. J. Leu, C. K. Kinzer, & K. A. Hinchman (Eds.), *Literacies for the 21st Century: Research and practice* (pp. 270–283). Chicago: National Reading Conference.

LaBerge, D., & Samuels, S.J. (1974). Toward a theory of automatic information processing in reading. *Cognitive Psychology, 6*, 293–323.

Ladd, G. W., Birch, S. H., & Buhs, E. S. (1999). Children's social and scholastic lives in Kindergarten: Related spheres of influence? *Child Development, 70*, 1373–1400.

Landry, S. H., & Smith, K. E. (2006). The influence of parenting on emerging literacy skills. In D. K. Dickinson & S. B. Neuman (Eds.), *Handbook of early literacy research* (Vol. 2, pp. 135–148). New York: Guilford.

Landry, S. H., Swank, P. W., & Baldwin, C. D. (1996). Effects of maternal scaffolding during joint toy play with preterm and full-term infants. *Merrill-Palmer Quarterly, 42*, 177–199.

Lavine, L. O. (1977). Differentiation of letterlike forms in prereading children. *Developmental Psychology, 13*, 89–94.

Lee, J., Grigg, W., & Donahue, P. (2007). *The nation's report card: Reading 2007 (NCES 2007-496)*. Washington, DC: National Center for Education Statistics, Institute of Education Sciences, U.S. Department of Education.

Lerkkanen, M., Rasku-Puttonen, H., Aunola, K., & Nurmi, J. (2004). Predicting reading performance during the first and the second year of primary school. *British Educational Research Journal, 30*(1), 67–92.

Lewit, E. M., & Baker, L. S. (1995). School readiness. *The future of children, 5*, 128–139.

Liberman, A. M. (1997). How theories of speech affect research in reading and writing. In B. A. Blachman (Ed.), *Foundations of reading acquisition and dyslexia* (pp. 3–19). Mahwah, NJ: Erlbaum.

Liberman, A. M., Cooper, F. S., Shankweiler, D., & Studdert-Kennedy, D. (1967). Perception of the speech code. *Psychological Review, 74*, 431–461.

Liberman, I. Y., & Liberman, D. (1979). Speech, the alphabet and teaching to read. In L. B. Resnick & P. A. Weiner (Eds.), *Theory and practice in early reading* (Vol. 2, pp. 109–132). Hillsdale, NJ: Erlbaum.

Liberman, I. Y., Shankweiler, D., Fischer, F. W., & Carter, B. (1974). Explicit syllable and phoneme segmentation in the young child. *Journal of Experimental Child Psychology, 18*, 201–212.

Lonigan, C. J. (2006). Conceptualizing phonological processing skills in prereaders. In D. K. Dickinson & S. B. Neuman (Eds.), *Handbook of early literacy research* (pp. 77–89). New York: Guilford.

Lonigan, C. J., Burgess, S. R., & Anthony, J. L. (2000). Development of emergent literacy and early reading skills in preschool children: evidence from a latent-variable longitudinal study. *Developmental Psychology, 36*(5), 596–613.

Lonigan, C. J., Burgess, S. R., Anthony, J. L., & Barker, T. A. (1998). Development of phonological sensitivity in 2- to 5-year-old children. *Journal of Educational Psychology, 90*(2), 294–311.

Lundberg, I., Frost, J., & Petersen, O. (1988). Effects of an extensive program for stimulating phonological awareness in preschool children. *Reading Research Quarterly, 23,* 264–284.

MacGinitie, W. H., & MacGinitie, R. K. (1992). *Gates-MacGinitie reading tests* (2nd Canadian ed.). Toronto, Canada: Nelson Canada.

MacLean, M., Bryant, P., & Bradley, L. (1987). Rhymes, nursery rhymes, and reading in early childhood. *Merrill-Palmer Quarterly, 33,* 255–281.

Mason, J. M. (1980). When do children begin to read: An exploration of four year old children's letter and word reading competencies. *Reading Research Quarterly, 15*(2), 203–225.

Mason, J. M. (1984). Early reading from a developmental perspective. In P. D. Pearson, R. Barr, M. L. Kamil, & P. Mosenthal (Eds.), *Handbook of reading research* (Vol. 1, pp. 505–544). New York: Longman.

Masonheimer, P. E., Drum, P. A., & Ehri, L. C. (1984). Does environmental print identification lead children into word reading? *Journal of Reading Behavior, 16*(2), 257–271.

McBride-Chang, C. (1995). What is phonological awareness? *Journal of Educational Psychology, 87,* 179–192.

McBride-Chang, C. (1999). The ABCs of the ABCs: The development of letter-name and letter-sound knowledge. *Merrill-Palmer Quarterly, 45*(2), 285–308.

McGee, L. M., & Richgels, D. J. (1989). "K is Kristen's": Learning the alphabet from a child's perspective *The Reading Teacher, 43,* 216–225.

McKeown, M. G., & Beck, I. (2006). Taking advantage of read-alouds to help children make sense of decontextualized language. In A. van Kleech, S. A. Stahl, & E. B. Bauer (Eds.), *On reading books to children* (pp. 159–176). Mahwah, NJ: Erlbaum.

Metsala, J. L. (1999). Young children's phonological awareness and nonword repetition as a function of vocabulary development. *Journal of Educational Psychology, 91*(1), 3–19.

Metsala, J. L., & Walley, A. C. (1998). Spoken vocabulary growth and the segmental restructuring of lexical representations: Precursors to phonemic awareness and early reading ability. In J. L. Metsala & L. C. Ehri (Eds.), *Word recognition in beginning literacy* (pp. 89–120). Hillsdale, NJ: Erlbaum.

Mills, J. R., & Jackson, N. E. (1990). Predictive significance of early giftedness: The case of precocious reading. *Journal of Educational Psychology, 82,* 410–419.

Morphett, M. V., & Washburne, C. (1931). When should children begin to read? *Elementary School Journal, 31,* 496–503.

Morris, D., Bloodgood, J. W., Lomax, R., & Perney, J. (2003). Developmental steps in learning to read: A longitudinal study in kindergarten and first grade. *Reading Research Quarterly, 38*(3), 302–328.

Morrow, L. M., & Schickedanz, J. A. (2006). The relationship between sociodramatic play and literacy development. In D. K. Dickinson & S. B. Neuman (Eds.), *Handbook of early literacy research* (Vol. 2, pp. 269–280). New York: Guilford.

Morrow, L. M., & Weinstein, C. S. (1986). Encouraging voluntary reading: The impact of a literature program on children's use of library centers. *Reading Research Quarterly, 21,* 330–346.

Muter, V., Hulme, C., & Snowling, M. (1997). *Phonological abilities test.* London: The Psychological Corporation.

Muter, V., Hulme, C., & Snowling, M. & Stevenson, J. (2004). Phonemes, rimes, vocabulary, and grammatical skills as foundations of early reading development: Evidence from a longitudinal study. *Developmental Psychology, 40*(5), 665–681.

Nagy, W. E., & Scott, J. A. (2000). Vocabulary processes. In M. L. Kamil, P. B. Mosenthal, P. D. Pearson, & R. Barr (Eds.), *Handbook of reading research* (Vol. III, pp. 269–284). Mahwah, NJ: Erlbaum.

National Institute for Literacy. (2008). *Developing early literacy: Report of the National Early Literacy Panel.* Retrieved from http://www.nifl.org

National Institutes of Childhood Development (NICHD) Early Child Care Research Network. (2005). Pathways to reading: The role of oral language in the transition to reading. *Developmental Psychology, 41,* 428–442.

National Society for the Study of Education. (1925). *Report of the National Committee on Reading.*

Twenty-fourth Year Book of the National Society for the Study of Education. Bloomington, IL: Public School Publishing Company.

Neuman, S. B. (2006). The knowledge gap: Implications for early education. In D. K. Dickinson & S. B. Neuman (Eds.), *Handbook of early literacy research* (Vol.2, pp. 29–40). New York: Guilford.

Neuman, S. B., & Roskos, K. A. (1993). Access to print for children of poverty: differential effects of adult mediation and literacy-enriched play settings on environmental and functional print tasks. *American Educational Research Journal, 30,* 95–122.

Neuman, S. B., & Roskos, K. A. (1997). Literacy knowledge in practice: Contexts of participation for young writers and readers. *Reading Research Quarterly, 32,* 10–32.

Neuman, S. B. (1990). Assessing inferencing strategies: In J. Zutell & S. McCormick (Eds.), *Literacy theory and research* (pp. 267–274). Chicago: National Reading Conference.

Newcomer, P. L., & Hammill, D. D. (1988). *Test of language development-primary* (2nd ed.). Austin, TX: Pro-Ed.

O'Connor, R. E., Jenkins, J. R., & Slocum, T. A. (1995). Transfer among phonological tasks in kindergarten: Essential instructional content. *Journal of Educational Psychology, 87,* 202–217.

Olson, S. L., Bates, J. E., & Bayles, K. (1984). Mother-infant interaction and the development of individual differences in children's cognitive competence *Developmental Psychology, 20,* 166–179.

Ouellette, G. P. (2006). What's meaning got to do with it: The role of vocabulary in word reading and reading comprehension. *Journal of Educational Psychology, 98*(3), 554–566.

Pan, B., Rowe, M., Singer, J., & Snow, C. (2005). Maternal correlates of growth in toddler vocabulary production in low-income families. *Child Development, 76*(4), 763–782.

Paratore, J. R. (1993). Influence of an intergenerational approach to literacy on the practice of literacy of parents and their children. In C. Kinzer & D. Leu (Eds.), *Examining central issues in literacy, research, theory, and practice* (pp. 83–91). Chicago: National Reading Conference.

Paratore, J. R., Melzi, G., & Krol-Sinclair, B. (1999). *What should we expect of family literacy? Experiences of Latino children whose parents participate in an intergenerational literacy program.* Newark, DE: International Reading Association.

Paris, S. G. (2005). Reinterpreting the development of reading skills. *Reading Research Quarterly, 40*(2), 184–202.

Paris, A., & Paris, S. (2007). Teaching narrative comprehension strategies to first graders. *Cognition and Instruction, 25*(1), 1–44.

Peck, L., & McGlothlin, L. E. (1940). Children's information and success in first-grade reading. *Journal of Educational Psychology, 31,* 653–664.

Phillips, G., McNaughton, S., & MacDonald, S. (2004). Managing the mismatch: Enhancing early literacy progress for children with diverse language and cultural identities in mainstream urban schools in New Zealand. *Journal of Educational Psychology, 96*(2), 309–323.

Piaget, J. T. (1954). *The construction of reality in the child* (M. Cook, Trans.). New York: Ballantine Books.

Piaget, J. T. (1963). *The origins of intelligence in children* (M. Cook, Trans.). New York: Norton.

Pressley, M., & Afflerbach, P. (1995). *Verbal protocols of reading: The nature of constructively responsive reading.* Hillsdale NJ: Erlbaum.

Pressley, M., Wood, E., Woloshyn, V. E., Martin, V. E., King, A., & Menke, D. (1992). Encouraging mindful use of prior knowledge: Attempting to construct explanatory answers facilitates learning. *Educational Psychologist, 27,* 91–110.

Price, L. H., van Kleeck, A., & Huberty, C. J. (2009). Talk during book sharing between parents and preschool children: A comparison between storybook and expository book conditions. *Reading Research Quarterly, 44*(2), 171–194.

Psychological Corporation. (1989a). *The Stanford Achievement Test* (8th ed.). Orlando, FL: Harcourt Brace Jovanovich.

Psychological Corporation. (1989b). *Stanford Early School Achievement Test* (3rd ed.). San Antonio, TX: Harcourt Brace Jovanovich.

Purcell-Gates, V. (1995). *Other people's words: The cycle of illiteracy.* Cambridge, MA: Harvard University Press.

Purcell-Gates, V. (1996). Stories, coupons, and the TV guide: relationships between home literacy experiences and emergent literacy knowledge. *Reading Research Quarterly, 31,* 406–428.

Reese, E., Cox, A., Harte, D., & McAnally, H. (2003). Diversity in adults' styles of reading books to children. In A. van Kleek, S. A. Stahl, & E. B. Bauer (Eds.), *On reading books to children: Parents and teachers* (pp. 37–57). Mahwah, NJ: Erlbaum.

Reutzel, R., Fawson, P., Young, J., Morrison, T., & Wilcox, B. (2003). Reading environmental print: What is the role of concepts about print in discriminating young readers' responses? *Reading Psychology, 24*, 123–162.

Reynell, J. K., & Gruber, C. P. (1977). *Reynell developmental language scales.* Los Angeles: Western Psychological Services.

Rimm-Kaufman, S., Pianta, R. C., & Cox, M. (2000). Teachers' judgments of problems in children's transition to school. *Early Childhood Research Quarterly, 15*, 147–166.

Roth, F. P., Speece, D. L., & Cooper, D. H. (2002). A longitudinal analysis of the connection between oral language and early reading. *The Journal of Educational Research, 95*(5), 259–272.

Roth, F. P., Spekman, N. J., & Fye, E. C. (1995). Reference cohesion in the oral narratives of students with learning disabilities and normally achieving students. *Learning Disability Quarterly, 18,* 25–40.

Rowe, M. L., Levine, S. C., Fisher, J. A., & Goldin-Meadow, S. (2009). Does linguistic input play the same role in language learning for children with and without early brain injury? *Developmental Psychology, 45*(1), 90–102.

San Felipe-Del Rio Consolidated Independent School District. (1975). Del Rio English story comprehension test. Del Rio, Texas.

Scarborough, H. S., & Dobrich, W. (1994). On the efficacy of reading to preschoolers. *Developmental Review, 14*, 245–302.

Schatschneider, C., Fletcher, J., Francis, D., Carlson, C., & Foorman, B. (2004). Kindergarten prediction of reading skills: A longitudinal comparative analysis. *Journal of Educational Psychology, 96*(2), 265–282.

Schickedanz, J. A. (1990). *Adam's writing revolutions: One child's literacy development from infancy through grade one.* Portsmouth, NH: Heinemann.

Schickedanz, J. A. (1998). What is developmentally appropriate practice in early literacy? Considering the alphabet. In S. B. Neuman & K. A. Roskos (Eds.), *Children achieving: Best practices in early literacy* (pp. 20–37). Newark: DE: International Reading Association

Schickedanz, J. A. (2001). Learning new words through books. *Scholastic Early Childhood Today, 15*(7), 14–15.

Schickedanz, J. A., & Casbergue, R. M. (2004). *Writing in preschool: Learning to orchestrate meaning and marks.* Newark, DE: International Reading Association.

Semel, E., Wiig, E., & Secord, W. (1987). *Clinical Evaluation of Language Fundamentals—Revised.* San Antonio, TX: The Psychological Corporation.

Sénéchal, M. (1997). The differential effect of storybook reading on preschoolers' acquisition of expressive and receptive vocabulary. *Journal of Child Language, 24*, 123–138.

Sénéchal, M., & Cornell, E. H. (1993). Vocabulary acquisition through shared reading experiences. *Reading Research Quarterly, 28*, 360–374.

Sénéchal, M., & LeFevre, J. (2002). Parental involvement in the development of children's reading skill: A five-year longitudinal study. *Child Development, 73*(2), 445–460.

Sénéchal, M., Ouellette, G., & Rodney, D. (2006). The misunderstood giant: On the predictive role of early vocabulary to future reading. In D. K. Dickinson & S. B. Neuman (Eds.), *Handbook of early literacy research* (Vol. II, pp. 173–182). New York: Guilford.

Share, D. L. (1999). Phonological recoding and orthographic learning: a direct test of the self-teaching hypothesis. *Journal of Experimental Child Psychology, 72*(2), 95–129.

Share, D. L., & Gur, T. (1999). How reading begins: a study of preschoolers' print identification strategies. *Cognition and Instruction, 17*(2), 177–213.

Smith, L. (1941). Measurement of the size of general English vocabulary through the elementary grades and high school. *General Psychology Monographs, 24*, 311–345.

Snow, C. E. (1991). The theoretical basis for relationships between language and literacy development. *Journal of Childhood Education, 6*(1), 5–10.

Snow, C. E., Burns, M. S., & Griffin, P. (1998). *Preventing reading difficulties in young children.* Washington, DC: National Academy Press.

Snow, C. E., & Kurland, B. F. (1996). Sticking to the point: Talk about magnets as a context for engaging in scientific discourse. In D. Hicks (Ed.), *Discourse, learning, and schooling* (pp. 189–221). New York: Cambridge University Press.

Sonnenschein, S., Brody, G., & Munsterman, K. (1996). The influence of family beliefs and practices on children's early reading development. In L. Baker, P. Afflerbach, & D. Reinking (Eds.), *Developing engaged readers in school and home communities* (pp. 3–20). Mahwah, NJ: Erlbaum.

Spira, E. G., Bracken, S. S., & Fischel, J. (2005). Predicting improvement after first-grade reading difficulties: The effects of oral language, emergent literacy and behavior skills. *Developmental Psychology, 41*(1), 225–234.

Stanovich, K. E., Cunningham, A. E., & Cramer, B. (1984). Assessing phonological awareness in kindergarten children: Issues of task comparability. *Journal of Experimental Child Psychology, 38,* 175–190.

Stipek, D., & Miles, S. (2008). Effects of aggression on achievement: Does conflict with the teacher make it worse? *Child Development, 79*(6), 1721–1735.

Storch, S. A., & Whitehurst, G. J. (2002). Oral language and code-related precursors to reading: Evidence from a longitudinal structural model. *Developmental Psychology, 38*(6), 934–947.

Tabors, P. O., Beals, D. E., & Weizman, Z. O. (2001). You know what oxygen is: Learning new words at home. In D. K. Dickinson & P. O. Tabors (Eds.), *Beginning literacy with language: Young children learning at home and at school* (pp. 93–110). Baltimore, MD: Brookes.

Tabors, P. O., Roach, K. A., & Snow, C. (2001). Home language and literacy environment. In D. K. Dickinson & P. O. Tabors (Eds.), *Beginning literacy with language: Young children learning at home and school* (pp. 111–138). Baltimore, MD: Brookes.

Tamis-LeMonda, C. S., Bornstein, M. H., & Baumwell, L. (2001). Maternal responsiveness and children's achievement of language milestones. *Child Development, 72,* 748–767.

Templin, M. C. (1957). *Certain language skills in children.* Minneapolis: University of Minnesota Press.

Torgesen, J. K. (2000). Individual differences in response to early interventions in reading: The lingering problem of treatment resisters. *Learning Disabilities Research and Practice, 15,* 55–64.

Treiman, R. (1985). Onsets and rimes as units of spoken syllables: evidence from children. *Journal of Experimental Child Psychology, 39,* 161–181.

Treiman, R. (1994). Use of consonant letter names in beginning spelling. *Developmental Psychology, 30,* 567–580.

Treiman, R., & Broderick, V. (1998). What's in a name: children's knowledge about the letters in their own names. *Journal of Experimental Child Psychology, 70*(2), 97–116.

Treiman, R., Cohen, J., Mulqueeny, K., Kessler, B., & Schechtman, S. (2007). Young children's knowledge about printed names. *Child Development, 78*(5), 1458–1471.

Treiman, R., Broderick, V., & Tincoff, R. (1998). Children's phonological awareness: confusions between phonemes that differ only in voicing. *Journal of Experimental Child Psychology, 68*(1), 3–21.

Tunmer, W. E. (1989). The role of language-related factors in reading disability. In D. Shankweiler & I. Liberman (Eds.), *Phonology and reading disability: Solving the reading puzzle* (pp. 91–132) Ann Arbor: University of Michigan Press.

Valdez-Menchaca, M. C., & Whitehurst, G. J. (1992). Accelerating language development through picture book reading: a systematic extension to Mexican day care. *Developmental Psychology, 28,* 1106–1114.

Velting, O., & Whitehurst, C. (1997). Inattention-hyperactivity and reading achievement in children from low-income families: A longitudinal model. *Journal of Abnormal Child Psychology, 25,* 321–331.

Wagner, R. K., Torgesen, J. K., & Laughon, P., Simmons, K., & Rachotte, C. A. (1993). Development of young readers' phonological processing abilities. *Journal of Educational Psychology, 85,* 83–103.

Wagner, R. K., Torgesen, J. K., & Rashotte, C. A. Hecht, S. A., Barker, T. A., Burgess, S.R., et al. (1997). Changing relations between phonological processing abilities and word-level reading as children develop from beginning to skilled readers: A 5-year longitudinal study. *Developmental Psychology, 33,* 468–479.

Walley, A. C. (1993). The role of vocabulary development in children's spoken word recognition and segmentation ability. *Developmental Review, 13,* 286–350.

Walley, A. C., Metsala, J. L., & Garlock, V. M. (2003). Spoken vocabulary growth: Its role in the development of phoneme awareness and early reading ability. *Reading and Writing: An Interdisciplinary Journal, 16,* 5–20.

Wasik, B. A., Bond, M. A., & Hindman, A. (2006). The effects of a language and literacy intervention on Head Start children and teachers. *Journal of Educational Psychology, 98*, 63–74.

Weizman, Z. O., & Snow, C. E. (2001). Lexical input as related to children's vocabulary acquisition: effects of sophisticated exposure and support for meaning. *Developmental Psychology, 37*(2), 265–279.

Wells, G. (1985). *The meaning makers: Children learning language and using language to learn.* Portsmouth, NH: Heinemann.

Wentzel, K. (1997). Student motivation in middle school: The role of perceived pedagogical caring. *Journal of Educational Psychology, 89*, 411–419.

Whitehurst, G. J., Arnold, D. S., Epstein, J. N., Angell, A. L., Smith, M., & Fischel, J. F. (1994). A picture book reading intervention in day care and home for children from low-income families. *Developmental Psychology, 30*(5), 679–689.

Whitehurst, G. J., & Lonigan, C. J. (2002). Emergent literacy: Development from prereaders to readers. In S. B. Neuman & D. K. Dickinson (Eds.), *Handbook of early literacy research* (Vol. 1, pp. 11–29). New York: Guilford.

Wigfield, A., & Asher, S. R. (1984). Social and motivational influences on reading. In P. D. Pearson, R. Barr, M. L. Kamil, & P. Mosenthal (Eds.), *Handbook of reading research* (pp. 423–452). New York: Longman.

Wiig, E. H., & Secord, W. (1988). *Test of language competence-expanded.* San Antonio, TX: The Psychological Corporation.

Witty, P., & Kopel, D. (1936). Preventing reading disability: The readiness factor. *Educational Administration and Supervision, 28*, 401–418.

Woloshyn, V. E., Paivio, A., & Pressley, M. (1994). Using elaborative interrogation to help students acquire information consistent with prior knowledge and information inconsistent with prior knowledge. *Journal of Educational Psychology, 86*, 79–89.

Woodcock, R. W. (1987). *Woodcock reading mastery tests—revised.* Circle Pines, MN: American Guidance Services.

Woodcock, R. W., & Johnson, M. B. (1989). Woodcock-Johnson psycho-educational battery—revised. Allen, TX: DLM Teaching Resources.

Woodcock, R. W., & Mather, N. (1989). WJ-R-R tests of cognitive ability standard battery: Examiner's manual. In R. W. Woodcock & M. B. Johnson (Eds.), *Woodcock-Johnson psycho-educational battery—revised.* Allen, TX: DLM Teaching Resources.

Woodcock, R. W., & Mather, N. (1989–1990). WJ-R-R tests of achievement: Examiner's manual. In R. W. Woodcock & M. B. Johnson (Eds.), *Woodcock-Johnson psycho-educational battery—revised.* Allen, TX: DLM Teaching Resources.

Woodward, A., Markham, E., & Fitzsimmons, C. (1994). Rapid word learning in 13–18-month-olds. *Developmental Psychology, 30*, 553–566.

Worden, P. E., & Boettcher, W. (1990). Young children's acquisition of alphabet knowledge. *Journal of Reading Behavior, 22*, 277–293.

Yaden, D. B., Rowe, D. W., & MacGillivray, L. (2000). Emergent literacy: A matter (polyphony) of perspectives. In M. L. Kamil, P. B. Mosenthal, P. D. Pearson, & R. Barr (Eds.), *Handbook of reading research* (Vol. III, pp. 425–454). Mahwah, NJ: Erlbaum.

Yopp, H. K. (1988). The validity and reliability of phoneme awareness tests. *Reading Research Quarterly, 23*, 159–177.

Zevenbergen, A. A., & Whitehurst, G. J. (2006). Dialogic reading: A shared picture book intervention for preschoolers. In A. van Kleech, S. A. Stahl, & E. B. Bauer (Eds.), *On reading books to children* (pp. 177–202). Mahwah, NJ: Erlbaum.

Zimmerman, I. L., Steiner, V. G., & Pond, R. E. (1979). *Preschool language scale—Revised edition.* San Antonio, TX: The Psychological Corporation.

7 Primary Grade Reading

Barbara R. Foorman and Carol M. Connor

Florida State University

During the first decade of the 21st century, a national focus on primary grade reading has been mandated by the Reading First component of the No Child Left Behind (NCLB) Act of 2001. NCLB is the result of a bipartisan effort to strengthen accountability requirements of the Elementary and Secondary Education Act (ESEA, 1965) and to achieve its goal of reducing the achievement gap between students living in poverty and their more affluent peers. To accomplish this goal, a target of reaching 100% proficiency by 2014 was established for all students and disaggregated data were used to determine Annual Yearly Progress (AYP) towards that deadline. Additionally, teachers were required to meet the federal definition of highly qualified as having at least a bachelor's degree and certification in the subject area in which they teach. The Reading First component of NCLB also required that instructional strategies in kindergarten through third grade be based on scientifically-based reading research.

In this chapter we will first review the instructional recommendations from the reading research on which the Reading First component of NCLB was based, in particular the National Reading Panel (NRP; National Institute of Child Health and Human Development, 2000). We will also review subsequent consensus documents that have informed primary reading instruction, such as the 2009 Framework for the National Assessment of Educational Progress (NAEP; National Assessment Governing Board, 2007). Second, we will summarize basic reading research conducted during this decade that has instructional implications, such as the mapping of oral language to word reading development and features of text that affect reading comprehension. Third, we will review recent studies of reading instruction that address the question of the conditions under which primary-grade students become successful readers. In this section, we will discuss both classroom-based studies and interventions.

RESEARCH REVIEWED IN CONSENSUS DOCUMENTS THAT INFORM READING POLICY

National Reading Panel Report (NICHD, 2000)

In 1997 the U.S. Congress asked the directors of the National Institute for Child Health and Human Development (NICHD) and the U.S. Department of Education to convene a committee to determine the readiness of applying reading research to classroom practice. The agreed upon methodology was that of a meta-analysis of relevant research studies from PsycInfo and ERIC databases from the last 30 years with the stipulation that each study met these criteria: published in English in a refereed journal; focused on children's reading development in the age/grade range from preschool to Grade 12; and used an experimental or quasi-experimental design with a control group or a multiple-baseline method. Curricular topics studied by the NRP were: alphabetics (phonemic awareness and phonics), fluency, vocabulary, and comprehension. The only topic for which the committee felt a meta-analysis could be conducted was alphabetics (the other areas, such as comprehension, vocabulary, and fluency were converted to best evidence syntheses), and those results were subsequently published in two peer-reviewed journal articles (Ehri, Nunes, Stahl, & Willows, 2001; Ehri, Nunes, Willows, Schuster, et al., 2001).

NRP Findings and Instructional Recommendations.   With respect to phonemic awareness, meta-analyses revealed that: (a) phonemic awareness causes improvement in students' phonemic awareness, reading, and spelling (with effect sizes in spelling for students with reading disabilities being weak); and (b) phonemic awareness instruction is most effective when (i) alphabetic letters are included, (ii) there are fewer rather than more manipulations of phonemic units, and (iii) instruction is conducted in small groups. These findings received widespread acceptance in new curriculum materials and have impacted instruction in kindergarten and Grade 1 (e.g., Connor, Jakobsons, Crowe, & Granger, 2009).

In the area of phonics, meta-analyses revealed that: (a) systematic phonics instruction produces significant benefits for students in kindergarten through Grade 6 and for students with reading disabilities, regardless of socioeconomic status; (b) the impact is strongest in kindergarten and Grade 1; and (c) phonics should be integrated with instruction in phonemic awareness, fluency, and comprehension.

Conclusions based on a descriptive, best-evidence synthesis of fluency results were: (a) repeated oral reading with guidance from teachers, peers or parents had a significant, positive impact on word reading, fluency, and comprehension across grade levels; (b) no multi-year studies of the relation between guided oral reading and the development of fluency were available; (c) there was an insufficient number of good studies available to address whether independent, silent reading is causally related to reading outcomes; and (d) among the few relevant studies the panel was able to locate, independent silent reading did not prove an effective practice when used as the only type of reading instruction to develop fluency and other reading skills, particularly with students who have not yet developed critical alphabetic and word reading skills. The effect of the latter conclusion was for educators to question the large amounts of time spent in sustained silent reading.

From the best-evidence synthesis of vocabulary research, the NRP committee concluded that: (a) the research base is inadequate to determine the best method for teaching vocabulary; and (b) multiple approaches to teaching vocabulary are advised (e.g., direct, indirect, multiple exposures, computer use). In the area of comprehension, again from a best-evidence synthesis, the committee concluded that: (a) teaching a combination of techniques assists in recall, question answering and generation, and summarization of texts; and (b) more research is needed in (i) teacher training, (ii) on which strategies for which ages, which genres, and what level of text difficulty, and on (iii) teaching comprehension in the content areas.

Controversy around the Phonics Meta-Analysis.   As indexed by the response of the educational research community, only the phonics meta-analysis proved controversial. Two re-analyses of the NRP phonics meta-analysis have questioned the conclusion that systematic phonics instruction is more effective than other forms of phonics instruction (Camilli, Vargas, & Yurecko, 2003; Camilli, Wolfe, & Smith, 2006; Hammill & Swanson, 2006). However, using the coding of the NRP studies posted by Camilli et al. (2003; 2006), Stuebing, Barth, Cirino, Fletcher, and Francis (2008) conducted regression analyses showing that Camilli et al.'s findings are not inconsistent with those of the NRP. The NRP examined the treatment effect of phonics by averaging effects of (a) systematic phonics instruction versus unsystematic phonics instruction and (b) systematic phonics versus no phonics instruction ($d = 0.41$). Camilli et al. (2003; 2006) addressed a different question—the incremental value of adding language activities and tutoring over and above phonics; in doing so, they dropped several studies from the corpus and included other moderators. However, their coding can be reconstructed to yield virtually the same effect sizes in comparing effects of systematic phonics versus the combined effects of unsystematic phonics and no phonics (d = 0.39), or, alternatively, the difference between systematic phonics versus no phonics (0.443) and systematic phonics versus some phonics (d = 0.188) or a difference of d = 0.316. Although these effect sizes of d = 0.316-0.41 are conventionally described as small to moderate (Cohen, 1988), Stuebing et al. challenge Hammill and Swanson's (2006) claim that small to moderate effect sizes are not meaningful. They point out that when the base rate of struggling readers is high and the cost of treatment relative to the benefit of reduction in incidence is low, the utility of explicit instruction in the alphabetic principle is apparent. Finally, Stuebing et al. (2008) replicated Camilli et al.'s (2003; 2006) analyses and showed that adding tutoring and systematic language activities to systematic phonics yields larger effects (d = 1.34), thereby reinforcing the benefits of comprehensive reading instruction. Just as the NRP concluded that phonics must be integrated with instruction in phonemic awareness, fluency, and comprehension, Camilli et al. showed that the addition of language activities and tutoring to phonics produced larger effects than any of these components in isolation. Thus, comprehensive programs that integrate reading and language arts and provide tutoring to increase intensity are more effective than programs that isolate these elements. This is a constructive way to view balanced reading instruction.

Other Relevant Syntheses over the Last Decade

The *Reading Framework for the 2009 National Assessment of Educational Progress* (NAEP, National Assessment Governing Board, 2007) lays out the design of the NAEP reading assessment—the national reading comprehension test designed to provide a report card on proficiency levels for students in grades 4, 8, and 12. Proficiency levels in reading have remained flat since 1992 when the previous reading framework was published. In 2007, 33% of fourth graders performed below the basic level on NAEP reading, which has been interpreted by the National Assessment Governing Board to mean that fourth graders lack the skills to access grade level text (National Center for Education Statistics, 2007). Among minorities the percentages are even more alarming: at grade 4, 53% of Blacks and 50% of Hispanics are below basic. These results have prompted standards-based reform at federal and state levels and were instrumental in promoting the strict accountability provisions in NCLB, including the requirement to disaggregate data for minority groups. In fact, with the passage of NCLB, the NAEP reading and math tests became required at Grades 4 and 8, and results were compared to states' standards-based tests to encourage states to raise their standards and to realign their tests (Porter, 2007).

Several significant changes in the 2009 NAEP reading framework have implications for primary grade reading instruction. First, vocabulary is measured explicitly by measuring word meanings in context. The goal is to report useful information on the extent of vocabulary knowledge. Second, separate subscales are reported for literary and informational text, as has been done on international assessments of reading, and, for the first time, poetry is assessed in Grade 4. Research on text structures shows that texts contain organizational patterns (or grammars) that alert readers to the meaning (e.g., Goldman & Rakestraw, 2000; Graesser, Golding, & Long, 1991; Pearson & Camperell, 1994). Third, cognitive targets of locate/recall, integrate/interpret, and critique/evaluate are defined and distinguished by text type. For example, literary text may require the inference of inferring mood or tone, whereas informational text may require the inference of distinguishing facts from opinions. To measure these cognitive processes, students will respond to both multiple choice and constructed response questions, with the distribution of these question types equal in Grade 4 and the proportion of constructed responses increasing in grades 8 and 12. Fourth, different standards for grade level expectations will be established (see Table 7.1 for Grade 4). Fifth, 12th-grade NAEP achievement levels will be anchored in the reading and analytic skills necessary for success in college and the workplace. Finally, passage

Table 7.1   Preliminary Achievement Levels for the 2009 NAEP Reading Assessment

Grade 4		
Achievement Level	Literary	Informational
Advanced	Grade 4 Students at the *Advanced* level should be able to: • Interpret figurative language • Make complex inferences • Identify point of view • Evaluate character motivation • Describe thematic connections across literary texts	Grade 4 Students at the *Advanced* level should be able to: • Make complex inferences • Evaluate the coherence of a text • Explain the author's point of view • Compare ideas across texts
Proficient	Grade 4 Students at the *Proficient* level should be able to: • Infer character motivation • Interpret mood or tone • Explain theme • Identify similarities across texts • Identify elements of author's crafts	Grade 4 Students at the *Proficient* level should be able to: • Identify author's implicitly stated purpose • Summarize major ideas • Find evidence in support of an argument • Distinguish between fact and opinion • Draw conclusions
Basic	Grade 4 Students at the *Basic* level should be able to: • Locate textually explicit information, such as plot, setting, and character • Make simple inferences • Identify supporting details. • Describe character's motivation • Describe the problem • Identify mood	Grade 4 Students at the *Basic* level should be able to: • Find the topic sentence or main idea • Identify supporting details • Identify author's explicitly stated purpose • Make simple inferences

selection will be based on a combination of expert judgment plus the use of at least two research-based readability formulas.

To understand the fourth grade expectations delineated in Table 7.1, a brief review of NAEP proficiency levels is required. The advanced level denotes superior performance. The proficient level signifies solid academic performance for the grade level assessed. The basic level represents partial mastery of prerequisite knowledge and skills necessary for proficiency at the grade level assessed. In discussing proficiency levels for vocabulary, the 2009 NAEP reading framework describes basic vocabulary as concrete and below grade level, with word meaning assessment limited to the most familiar definition for any given word. At the proficient level, a reader has a sizeable, flexible, and often above grade level vocabulary with depth of meaning beyond the most common definition of a word. These expectations for proficient fourth-grade readers exceed those delineated in many states' standards. For example, in Table 7.1, NAEP's basic fourth-grade reader's expectations to find the main idea, identify supporting details and the author's purpose, and make simple inferences are those expected by proficient, but not basic, readers in many states. With NCLB using NAEP performance as a yardstick against which state standards and state tests are evaluated, grade-level expectations for primary reading are likely to rise, and instructional strategies are likely to change in turn—to more use of informational text (e.g., Duke, 2000; Duke & Pearson, 2003), more emphasis on vocabulary instruction (e.g., Beck, McKeown, & Kucan, 2002, 2008), more emphasis on engagement and comprehension strategies (e.g., Guthrie et al., 2004), and more emphasis on classroom book reading followed by student-teacher discussion (Block, Parris, Reed, Whiteley, & Cleveland, 2009; Nystrand, Wu, Gamoran, Zeiser, & Long, 2003).

RECENT BASIC RESEARCH ON READING WITH IMPLICATIONS FOR PRIMARY GRADE READING

In the past decade there has been significant progress in understanding the contributions of oral language to reading—both to word recognition and to comprehension. In addition, advances have been made in delineating and measuring text difficulty.

Mapping of Oral Language to Word Reading

Researchers agree that a child learning to read English must master the alphabetic system in order to grasp the meaning of what is read (e.g., National Research Council, 1998; Rayner, Foorman, Perfetti, Pesetsky, & Seidenberg, 2001), and that mastery of the alphabetic system requires access to phoneme-level units (Ehri, 1998; Liberman et al., 1974; Perfetti, 1992). The disagreement for researchers comes at verifying the level of mapping of phonological units and orthographic units during the acquisition process. According to Walley, Metsala, and Garlock's (2003) Lexical Restructuring Model, growth in oral vocabulary leads to increasingly well-specified phonological representations, which, in turn, promote reading development. For theorists who espouse a phase or stage theory of reading such as Ehri (1999, 2005), the mapping occurs at the level of phoneme and grapheme, and as beginning readers recode printed words the letters and their sequence are "amalgamated" to their pronunciation in speech. Ziegler and Goswami's (2005) psycholinguistic grain size theory posits that "phonological structure, phonological and orthographic neighborhood characteristics, and the transparency of spelling-sound mappings act together to determine the units and mappings that play a role in the amalgamation process in different orthographies" (p. 21). In shallow (i.e., transparent and consistent mapping) orthographies, such as Finnish, Italian, Spanish, German, and Greek, grapheme-phoneme mappings are readily accessible and efficient and word reading accuracy is near ceiling by the middle of first grade (Seymour et al., 2003). However, in a deep (opaque and inconsistent mapping) orthography such as English where vowel pronunciations may yield multiple spellings (e.g., "long *a*" in *mate, rain, play, baby, eight, vein, great,* and *they*), there is a mismatch in grain size between phonology and orthography, and word reading accuracy is much slower (e.g., an accuracy rate of 40% in first grade in Seymour et al., 2003).

Because of the grain size mismatch in English, researchers argue that multiple recoding strategies are necessary, supplementing grapheme-phoneme correspondences with spelling rimes and whole-word recognition (e.g., Ehri & Wilce, 1983; Ziegler & Goswami, 2005). These three recoding strategies are typically represented in instructional approaches to teaching reading in English and the debate revolves around the order or balance of the strategies (Rayner et al., 2001). Whole-word strategies have been shown to lead to slower reading success (e.g., Chall, 1967; Evans & Carr, 1985; NICHD, 2000). No differences between the grapheme-phoneme strategy or the rime spelling strategy are apparent in experimental studies of normally developing readers (Haskell, Foorman, & Swank, 1992; NICHD, 2000; P. Walton, L. Walton, & Felton, 2001); however, there does appear to be a benefit in grapheme-phoneme instruction over spelling rime instruction with beginning readers who have poor phonemic awareness and struggle with reading (Foorman, Francis, Fletcher, Schatschneider, & Mehta, 1998). For readers of any age, phoneme awareness is typically acquired reciprocally with learning to read and relatively quickly if the orthography is consistent. However, across alphabetic orthographies, there are children with phonological difficulties at the level of the phoneme who require direct instruction in grapheme-phoneme recoding, but, even then, some continue to struggle to reach a stage in which word recognition is automatic (Rayner et al., 2001; Ziegler & Goswami, 2005).

Nonstage, incremental theories (Seidenberg & McClelland, 1989; Perfetti, 1992; Plaut, 2005; Share, 1995) stand in contrast to phase or stage based theories of reading (e.g., Chall, 1983, Gough, Juel, & Griffith, 1992; Ehri 1999). Stage or phase theories emphasize cognitive structures that guide thinking during a particular phase of development. For example, for Ehri (2005) there are pre-alphabetic, partial alphabetic, full alphabetic, and consolidated alphabetic phases. In a nonstage, incremental approach, beginning readers learn words because of the weighted connections among phonology, orthography, and semantics computed by learning previous words. The original Seidenberg and McClelland (1989) model illustrated computations of the connections between phonology and orthography in learning to read and was applied to beginning reading instruction by Adams (1990, 2001) and by Foorman (1994). Thus, exposure to *have* prior to *save* may weight the orthography-phonology connections towards the less regular pronunciation of *–ave*. This is not the same as saying that *have* is an irregular word and must be learned by a visual route. It is important to remember that the onset of *have* — /h/ — generalizes to the pronunciation of the initial phonemes in words such as *hot*, *has*, and *happy*. Thus, words such as *have* (and *pint*, *laugh*, and *said*) are quasi-regular and learning to read is an example of learning in a quasi-regular domain where rules are allowed to deviate from central tendencies (Seidenberg & McClelland, 1989). But with the addition of a semantic node (see Figure 7.1), computational models activate knowledge of word meanings that mediate the phonological-orthographic pathway so that the correct pronunciation is computed (Harm & Seidenberg, 2004;

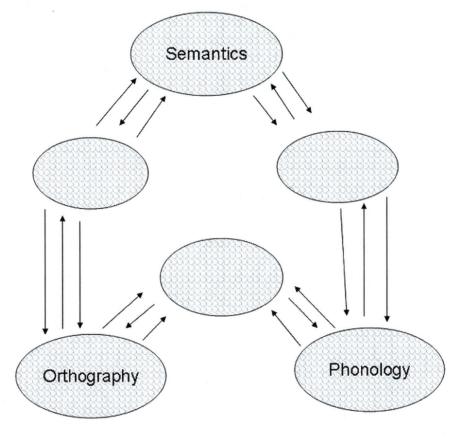

Figure 7.1 The triangle model after Seidenberg & McClelland (1989) and Plaut, McClelland, Seidenberg, & Patterson (1996).

Plaut, McClelland, Seidenberg, & Patterson, 1996). This computational model is similar to Share's (1995) self-teaching hypothesis, which proposes that partial decoding coupled with top-down oral vocabulary provides children with a mechanism for recognizing visual configurations.

Inherent in connectionist models and Share's self-teaching hypothesis is the notion of feedback to correct errors. In computational models, the feedback is through "back propagation" programming; in human behavioral situations, parents or teachers provide the feedback. The phrase "guided reading" or "scaffolding" captures this contextualized feedback. The question of how directive feedback needs to be is important and will vary depending on the needs of the beginning reader (e.g., Juel & Minden-Cupp, 2000). Often teacher prompts and feedback are more prescriptive than responsive because of the emphasis on (a) whole-class instruction rather than on differentiated instruction (e.g., Mathes et al., 2005; Rayner et al., 2001) and on (b) phonologically impaired (i.e., dyslexic) students rather than on typically developing students. Ziegler and Goswami (2005) argue for the development of new connectionist models that better capture (a) available levels of phonological representations across languages prior to and resulting from reading, and (b) the different instructional environments available to different orthographies.

Also inherent in connectionist models and Share's self-teaching hypothesis is the notion of item-based learning, which is word and neighborhood specific. Thus, with respect to beginning reading instruction, the sequence of words in the curricula matters, especially for students whose learning opportunities are limited to school. In other words, it matters if *have* is presented before or after *save*, whether the reader has phoneme identify for /h/ and /s/, and the size and breadth of the reader's oral vocabulary. Over 20 years ago, Juel and Roper-Schneider (1985) examined the frequency with which adjacent pairs of letters occurred in words in basal text and suggested that: "The types of words which appear in beginning reading texts may well exert a more powerful influence in shaping children's word identification strategies than the method of reading instruction" (p. 151).

Connectionist models and item-based theories of word learning (e.g., Share, 1995) also have implications for reading assessment. Jenkins, Hudson, and Johnson (2007) point out that screens in first and second grade that employ word reading tasks as predictors of end-of-year outcomes in reading have good specificity. That is, they identify as not-at-risk individuals who later perform satisfactorily on a future criterion measure (i.e., true negatives). The reason why certain word-level screens, such as those used in the early reading assessment in Texas (TPRI; Foorman, Fletcher, & Francis, 2004) and in Florida (Florida Department of Education, 2009–2010), have good specificity is not because they consist of an inventory of phonics rules or lists of high frequency words. Rather, the item difficulty of the words, empirically determined through Item Response Theory, reflects those orthographic features (e.g., frequency, sound-spelling predictability and consistency) that predict the alphabetic knowledge tapped by benchmark word lists and passages. In this way, accuracy and fluency on well-designed word-level screens generalize to characteristics of words, not of readers, and can be said to reflect item-based learning rather than stage-based reading development. Thus, the question becomes, "On what population of words is this student accurate or fluent?" rather than "Is this student an accurate or fluent reader?"

Mapping of Oral Language to Reading Comprehension

Recent longitudinal research has helped us understand how oral language and reading development are intertwined. Phonological awareness and rapid naming predict reading comprehension in second grade but oral language skills account for an additional 13.8% of the variance (Catts, Fey, Zhang, & Tomblin, 1999). In a structural analysis of longitudinal data from preschool through fourth grade, Storch and Whitehurst (2002) found that strong relations among code-related and oral language skills in preschool decreased over the grades. In first and second grades code-related skills strongly predicted reading comprehension, but by third and fourth grades, reading accuracy and comprehension were separable. Reading accuracy was predicted by decoding skill, whereas reading comprehension was predicted by prior and current reading accuracy as well as oral language skills. In a longitudinal analysis of children ages 7–11, Oakhill, Cain, and Bryant (2003) found that early skills in inference, story structure, and comprehension monitoring all predicted later global comprehension independent of earlier comprehension skill. Thus, it is possible that oral language skills lie dormant during the development of beginning reading skills but reemerge as these skills service the larger goal of understanding written language. However, it is also possible that early comprehension measures differ so much from later measures that the differential correlations obtained primarily reflect measurement bias.

The dimensionality of literacy is also important to consider. We tend to use the term "literacy" to refer to written and oral language skills but no one had tested whether in fact these skills were unidimensional. Mehta, Foorman, Branum-Martin, and Taylor (2005) did just this in multilevel confirmatory factor analyses of reading and language outcomes, utilizing data from 1,342 students in 127 classrooms in grades 1–4 in 17 high poverty schools. Results supported a unitary literacy factor for word reading, reading comprehension, and spelling, with the role of phonological awareness as an indicator of literacy diminishing over the grades. Writing was the least related to the literacy factor but the most impacted by teacher effects. In fact, sheer time spent teaching writing positively predicted writing outcomes. Language competence, as measured by receptive vocabulary and verbal IQ tasks, was distinct at the student level but perfectly correlated with literacy at the classroom level. Thus, oral and written language skills appear to be so interrelated with reading skills that they form a single construct, raising the possibility that they deserve equal instructional attention.

Conceptualizing and Measuring Text Difficulty

What makes text difficult to read for 6- to 11-year-old students? In answering this question, it is helpful to refer to the framework established by the RAND Reading Study Group (2002): Reading comprehension is an *interaction* among reader characteristics, text features, and the activity or socio-cultural context in which the text is situated. A reader's interest in the topic and motivation to read is critically important (e.g., Guthrie & Wigfield, 2000). Research from cognitive psychology has shown the kind of inferences and mental models that skilled readers make when reading text and the kind of comprehension monitoring necessary to ensure consistency in meaning as text is read. Individual differences in working memory place constraints on these cognitive processes in children as well as adults. Working memory constraints are also apparent in syntactic processing of complex structures such as embedded phrases, anaphora, and cohesive ties. In addition to syntactic demands, the semantic demands imposed by the vocabulary used in a text can impede reading comprehension. If a reader has difficulty grasping the meaning of words in sentences, then he or she will struggle with the meaning of sentences, paragraphs, and the text as a whole.

To address the demands on readers of primary grade text, Foorman, Francis, Davidson, Harm, and Griffin (2004) developed a relational database to analyze all the text in the student edition of six first-grade basal reading programs published between 1995 and 2000. The composition of text differed across the six programs with respect to length, grammatical complexity, the number of unique and total words, repetition of words, and coverage of important vocabulary. Potential decoding accuracy rates were computed and found to vary widely across the six programs and often depended heavily on holistically taught words. Moreover, the vast majority of words (i.e., a median of 70%) appeared only once in each 6-week instructional block across the year. The one existing study that looked at the number of repetitions necessary for word learning in average beginning readers found that four to six repetitions of relatively unfamiliar words had a positive effect on the speed of reading the same words again a few days later (Reitsma, 1983).

Hiebert (2005) points out that prior to the 1990s, basals had "controlled vocabulary" text. From the 1930s through the 1950s, the "control" was in the form of printed word frequencies, with careful attention to the number of repetitions needed to induce learning (Gates & Russell, 1939). In the 1960s, the notion of control shifted from word frequency to sublexical features of words. Beginning text consisted largely of the accumulating set of letter-sound correspondences taught. However, by the mid-1980s, the attempt to control the nature and number of words in basal text began to disappear. Hiebert (2007) sees this loss of control on lexical features as instrumental in creating dysfluent readers. To promote greater fluency among readers, Hiebert espouses a word zone fluency curriculum that controls words for printed word frequency and orthographic and morphological structure.

It is beyond the scope of this chapter to describe recent work on characterizing the cognitive and linguistic demands of texts above the primary grades, but it is important to acknowledge the development of computational models that allow for improved readability formulae (e.g., Lexiles; Stenner, Sanford, & Burdick, 2006), measurement of semantic complexity (e.g., Latent Semantic Analysis; Landauer, 1998), and measurement of coherence relations (e.g., Coh-Metrix; Graesser, McNamara, Louwerse, & Cai, 2004). As our capacity to use the power of computers to store and analyze text and to predict comprehension expands, we are likely to develop increasing sophistication in our ability to literally engineer more pedagogically useful texts for beginning readers as they move along their continuum of development.

CLASSROOM-BASED STUDIES AND INTERVENTIONS

An encouraging trend over the past decade is that more—and more rigorous—reading research is being conducted in classrooms. This is important because the classroom setting has many more unmeasured and unmeasurable (or at least hard to measure) variables than are found in carefully constructed studies conducted in laboratories or pull-out intervention settings in which highly trained researchers can monitor and control contextual variation. Classroom-based research provides important insights into how we can better serve students in classrooms and prepare teachers to provide more effective instruction.

School-Level Reform

Increasingly, it is understood that literacy instruction occurs in the context of a larger system and that home and community have an impact on classroom literacy through their influence on children's entering skills (see chapters in this volume, for effects on literacy of parenting, the home learning environment, and preschool). Classroom literacy exists within a school context and the school provides the proximal environment for classrooms, teachers and students, and strongly influences what happens in classrooms (Coburn, 2004; Taylor, Pearson, Clark, & Walpole, 2000). Qualitative research that compares effective schools with less effective schools, based on either nomination or student outcomes, shows that there are common characteristics that consistently provide students with an effective learning environment. (Pressley et al., 2001; Taylor & Pearson, 2002; Taylor et al., 2000; Wharton-McDonald, Pressley, & Hampston, 1998). These characteristics include: Strong leadership; high expectations for student achievement; emphasis on academics; safe and orderly environment; a dedicated block of time (about 90–120 minutes) devoted to literacy instruction; frequent use of assessment to evaluate student progress; and in the classroom, use of small homogeneous literacy skill-based groups in the classroom; and good classroom management (Pressley, Raphael, Gallagher, & DiBella, 2004; Wharton-McDonald et al., 1998).

School reform initiatives have incorporated many of these findings into their protocols and there is increasing quasi-experimental support that by changing school environments, student outcomes can be improved. For example, Tivnan and Hemphill (2005) compared four school reform models with differing pedagogy, philosophies, and implementation protocols. These differences mirrored some of the Reading Wars tensions (basic skills versus more holistic meaning-focused approaches). Nevertheless, all of these reform efforts incorporated key characteristics found in the effective schools literature. The specific reform initiatives compared were: Building Essential Literacy; Developing Literacy First; Literacy Collaboration; and Success for All. The researchers found that, overall, there were no significant differences in students' literacy outcomes among the four reform packages; all of the reforms were associated with improved student literacy skills, especially word reading and phonological awareness (a high proportion of children reached grade expectations). However, they were all less successful in their effect on vocabulary and reading comprehension. A key finding was that implementation of the reform protocol varied substantially among teachers, as did the instruction children received in their classrooms (see also Taylor, Pearson, & Rodriguez, 2003, who report similar findings).

Classroom Intervention

Increasingly, we are appreciating the important role of the climate and social/emotional support provided by effective teachers. For example, Hamre and Pianta (2005) showed that classrooms that were high in instructional support as well as social/emotional support, based on classroom observations using the CLASS, were systematically associated with stronger student literacy and social outcomes, especially for children who had the weakest skills in kindergarten. Children with greater behavior problems in kindergarten, based on teacher report, were less likely to have conflicts with their first-grade teachers when observers reported high levels of classroom social/emotional support. At the same time, children with similar kindergarten behaviors continued to demonstrate high levels of conflict with their first-grade teachers when observers reported low levels of social/emotional support. Student engagement and motivation also contribute to students' literacy development (e.g., Connor et al., 2009; Guthrie et al., 2004).

Nonetheless, it is the amount and type of literacy instruction children receive in the classroom that is consistently and systematically associated with their literacy skill growth, when climate and motivation are held constant. Teachers tend to report providing a balance of code-based and meaning-based instructional strategies. For example, Xue and Meisels (2004), using the ECLS kindergarten data, found that teachers (n = 2690) did not assume an either-or approach to phonics and integrated literature (i.e., whole language). Moreover, both strategies were effective with students (n = 13,608) and the more teachers reported using both a phonics and an integrated literature approach, the stronger was students' performance on standardized tests and their motivation to learn. Other recent studies examined instruction globally at the classroom level and compared fairly balanced instructional regimes that varied in emphasizing more code- and skill-based instructional strategies as compared with emphasizing more holistic and meaning-based instructional strategies (Craig, 2006; Mathes et al., 2005; Roberts & Meiring, 2006). For example, Craig (2006) randomly assigned 87 kindergarteners to either an interactive writing (holistic and more meaning-focused) or a metalinguistic games-plus (more skill-based and explicitly focused on decoding) intervention designed to improve students' phonological awareness, spelling, and early reading development. Both groups made similar gains on all measures with large effect sizes. Although there was some evidence of an advantage for the interactive writing on students' reading comprehension, these differences were small.

Mathes et al. (2005) found similar results when they randomly assigned 298 first graders who were at risk of academic failure to one of 3 conditions: (a) enhanced classroom instruction (EC), (b) EC plus the Proactive Reading intervention, and (c) EC plus the Responsive Reading intervention. Both of the interventions were small-group, pull-out tutorials that had comprehensive lesson plans. Proactive was based on a direct instruction model with a scripted lesson plan, carefully designed scope and sequence, and decodable text. Responsive was a guided reading intervention that spent about 20% of the time in explicit but unscripted instruction in phonics elements and used leveled readers rather than decodable text. They found that, in general, students who received either intervention in addition to EC made greater progress than did students who received only EC. Moreover, the effect sizes were highly similar for the two interventions— similar to Craig's finding. The authors did find that the Responsive Reading intervention was more effective for children who began the study with higher vocabulary skills than it was for children who began with weaker vocabulary skills.

Connor, Morrison, and colleagues examined the effect of instruction, across multiple dimensions, and found specific child characteristic by instruction interactions for preschoolers (Connor, Morrison, & Slominski, 2006), first graders (Connor, Morrison, & Katch, 2004), second graders (Connor, Morrison, & Underwood, 2007b), and third graders (Connor, Morrison, & Petrella, 2004), and for multiple outcomes including word reading, reading comprehension, vocabulary, and background knowledge. Moreover, these correlational studies have been replicated with different samples of children (Connor et al., 2009) across kindergarten through third grade and by other researchers (Al Otaiba et al., 2008; Foorman et al., 1998; Foorman et al., 2006; Juel & Minden-Cupp, 2000). Taken together, these results show that the effects of particular literacy instructional strategies may depend on the language and literacy skills children bring to the learning opportunity. Generally, children with weaker skills in a particular area (e.g., word reading) appear to show greater progress when they receive more time in explicit instruction on that target outcome, whereas the same instructional strategy may be negatively associated with or have little effect on growth for children with stronger skills. At the same time, children with stronger skills tend to demonstrate greater progress when provided more opportunities in higher-order meaning-focused instructional activities (e.g., comprehension strategies or opportunities to read books independently) or more advanced code-focused skills (e.g., morphological awareness) when compared with students with weaker skills. Overall, children with stronger vocabulary skills learn from a wider range of learning opportunities than do children with weaker vocabulary skills, who, by contrast, tend to show greater progress when instruction is more explicit and targeted toward ameliorating their assessed weaknesses.

The idea of child by instruction interactions is not new. Introduced by Cronbach and Snow in 1957 (Bracht, 1970; Cronbach, 1957; Cronbach & Snow, 1969), aptitude by treatment interactions (ATI) featured prominently in Barr's handbook chapter (Barr, 1984). However, the research evidence for ATIs as defined at the time was equivocal and the research largely abandoned (Cronbach & Snow, 1977; Cronbach & Webb, 1975). With the advent of new research on the specific constructs that predict reading (e.g., phonological awareness, word reading, vocabulary, etc.), more nuanced views of reading instruction, better classroom observation techniques, and stronger statistical analytic strategies, such as Hierarchical Linear Modeling (HLM; Raudenbush & Bryk, 2002), these child by instruction interactions are found consistently across studies and samples.

While compelling, virtually all of the studies that find child by instruction interactions are descriptive and correlational. Thus the causal implications of this line of work have been unclear. Recently, however, Connor, Morrison, Fishman, Schatschneider, and colleagues (2007a, 2009) conducted a randomized control field trial to test the effect of individualizing first-grade reading instruction, taking into account the child by instruction interaction literature. In this study, schools (n = 10) and teachers (n = 47) were randomly assigned to an intervention or waitlist business-as-usual control condition. Teachers in the intervention condition were provided with Assessment to Instruction software (A2i) that computed recommended amounts and types of instruction for each student using dynamic system forecasting models (i.e., algorithms), which are analogous to models used by meteorologists to forecast weather. Children's assessed vocabulary and reading scores were entered into the software and used to compute the recommended amounts and types of instruction required to help children reach their target reading score. This target score was based on district norms and was, essentially, reading at grade level or achieving a year's worth of growth by the end of first grade. As more research is conducted, algorithms will be refined to provide more effective recommendations. Teachers were trained in the use of the software and on how to individualize instruction in the classroom to meet the recommended amounts for each student. This included the use of small homogeneous skill-based groups based on findings from the previously discussed research on effective schools (Taylor et al., 2000) and differentiated content and presentation of instructional materials.

Teachers were also trained to use a multidimensional framework that indexed their core literacy curriculum across two dimensions—code- versus meaning-focused activities and teacher- versus child-managed activities (Connor et al., 2009). The former captures the content of the instruction and follows from the Simple View of Reading (Hoover & Gough, 1990) and other more complex models (Adams, 2001; Rayner et al., 2001). The latter, not to be confused with teacher-directed versus child-centered instruction (Bredekemp & Copple, 1997), asks who is focusing the students' attention on the learning activity at hand, the teacher and child jointly, or the student. Thus teacher-managed instruction may be highly interactive and child-centered, including coaching (Taylor et al., 2003) and scaffolding, whereas child-managed instruction includes activities where children are expected to work independently (e.g., seat work) or with peers (e.g., buddy reading). These dimensions operate simultaneously so that virtually any research-based literacy activity can be coded across these dimensions. Thus, the teacher reading aloud to the class and discussing aspects of the book would be a teacher-managed meaning-focused activity. Children reading silently in the library corner would be a child-managed meaning-focused activity. The teacher explaining how to blend or segment phonemes into words would be a teacher-managed code-focused activity. Researchers consistently find that teachers provide a variety of literacy instruction activities that cross all four activity types in English-only classrooms (Foorman et al., 2006; Xue & Meisels, 2004) as well as in bilingual classrooms (Foorman, Goldenberg, Carlson, Saunders, & Pollard-Durodola, 2004). The results of the Connor et al. (2009) classroom observations, which recorded the instruction each target child received in the fall, winter and spring, confirmed this finding and showed that teachers consistently provided all four types of instruction but in differing proportions.

Using these multidimensional instructional categories, the A2i software recommended greater amounts of teacher-managed code focused instruction for students who had weaker word reading skills (i.e., below grade expectations) and less for students with stronger skills in a non-linear relation, where exponentially increasing amounts of teacher-managed code focused instruction was recommended as students' reading scores fell below grade expectations. Algorithms recommended greater amounts of child-managed meaning-focused instruction all year long for children with stronger vocabulary skills. However, for children with weaker vocabulary skills, the software recommended less child-managed meaning-focused instruction in the fall with increasing amounts over the school year. The recommendations were based on the child by instruction interactions observed in an earlier correlational study (Connor et al., 2004) and are depicted in Figure 7.2. Note that more time in child-managed meaning-focused instruction (top) is associated with lower spring word reading scores for children with higher vocabulary skills and just the opposite effect is observed for students with weaker vocabulary skills.

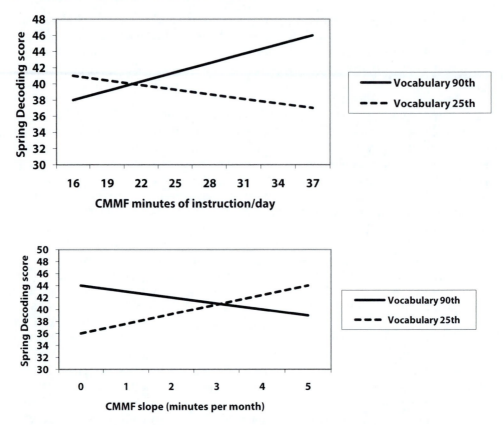

Figure 7.2 Top. First graders' spring word reading skills, holding fall skills constant at the mean, as a function of the amounts of child-managed meaning-focused instruction provided during the school year. The
lines contrast growth for children with fall vocabulary skills falling at the 90th percentile on the Peabody
Picture Vocabulary Test (solid line) versus children with fall vocabulary skills falling at the 25th percentile
in the fall (dashed line).
      Bottom. Showing the effect of changing amounts of child-managed meaning-focused instruc-
tion from fall to spring (slope). For children with stronger fall vocabulary skills (90th percentile), steady
amounts all year long (slope = 0) are associated with stronger word reading growth whereas for students
with weaker vocabulary skills (25th percentile), small amounts in the fall with increasing amounts in the
spring (slope = 5) are associated with stronger word reading skill growth.

The researchers found a significant effect of individualizing instruction in favor of children
in the intervention classrooms compared to children in the control classrooms on their reading
comprehension skills, about a 2 month difference (effect size (d) = .27, Connor et al., 2007a).
Additional analyses revealed that total amounts of instruction did not predict students' reading
scores, but the precision with which teachers taught recommended amounts did predict student
word reading and reading comprehension outcomes (Connor et al., 2009).

Taking together the experimental, quasi-experimental and correlational findings, the impact
of individualizing or differentiating literacy instruction in the classroom is compelling, with
implications not just for struggling readers but for all children. Although most research described
has focused on students at risk for academic underachievement, emerging research suggests that
children who are fairly to very proficient readers may be underserved (Neal & Schanzenbach,
2007; Viadero, 2007). Taking into account child by instruction interactions offers the potential
to insure reading skill progress for all children.

Response to Intervention (RTI)

As Mathes and colleagues (2005) demonstrated, for children struggling to learn how to read, simply improving general classroom instruction is not enough to bring them to grade level performance. Students who started first grade with weaker reading skills showed more progress when they received additional small group interventions, regardless of the focus (e.g., Proactive versus Responsive interventions described above). Response to Intervention (RTI) models provide a systematic school or district-wide method to help children who are struggling with reading before they experience academic failure with a joint aim of prevention and, lacking that, early identification of reading difficulties.

Historically, children with reading disabilities (RD) have been identified for services using the IQ-achievement discrepancy model, which requires students to demonstrate up to two standard deviations of difference between their IQ and their reading achievement (e.g., Fletcher & Foorman, 1994; Stanovich & Siegel, 1994; Stuebing, Fletcher, LeDoux, Lyon, Shaywitz, & Shaywitz, 2002; Vaughn & Fuchs, 2003). The Individuals with Disabilities Educational Improvement Act of 2004 provides RTI as an alternative to the discrepancy model. This means that a local education agency "may use a process that determines if the child responds to scientific, research-based intervention as a part of the evaluation procedures" (Pub. L. No. 108-446 § 614 [b][6][A]; § 614 [b] [2 & 3]). In addition, districts are allowed to use up to 15% of special education funds for prevention and early intervention. This shift in federal law allows districts to use funds to provide intervention to struggling readers *before* they fail to meet grade-level achievement standards and was meant to work in concert with the Reading First component of NCLB (Foorman, Kalinowski, & Sexton, 2007).

Proponents of RTI criticize the IQ-achievement discrepancy model for several reasons: (a) there is a documented increase in the numbers of students with reading disabilities (RD; US Department of Education, 2004); (b) there are important differences across states and districts in their definitions of RD (US Department of Education, 2004); (c) there are a disproportionate number of children living in poverty and children of color among those labeled RD (Donovan & Cross, 2002); (d) there is a growing recognition that the instructional needs of students labeled RD are not substantially different from children who have not been identified (Fletcher & Foorman, 1994); and finally (e) that without the diagnosis, many children who would benefit from early systematic and intensive intervention, especially children from high poverty families, do not receive the amounts and types of literacy instruction they need.

RTI is an emerging concept and thus there are a number of models described in the literature. Nevertheless, the models share a number of similarities. They utilize a multilevel or tiered system, which starts with high quality classroom instruction (e.g., Connor et al., 2007a, 2009; Denton, Foorman, & Mathes, 2003; Mathes et al., 2005, Gersten et al., 2008). For example, individualized classroom instruction may be considered the first level or tier. Children who do not respond to high quality classroom instruction are then identified and provided more intensive small group instruction, which is either highly structured and scripted using evidence-based interventions (e.g., McMaster, Fuchs, Fuchs, & Compton, 2005; Torgesen, Rashotte, & Alexander, 2001; Torgesen et al., 1999) or that addresses students' difficulties by further individualizing instruction based on a problem-solving model (Deno et al., 2002; Marston, Muyskens, Lau, & Center, 2002; Reschly, Tilly, & Grimes, 1999). There are also models that combine aspects of both of these, beginning with evidenced-based strategies and then increasingly tailoring instruction based on progress monitoring (Case, Speece, & Molloy, 2003; O'Connor, Fulmer, Harry, & Bell, 2005; Speece & Case, 2001; Vaughn, Linan-thompson, & Hickman, 2003). Across models, children who still fail to respond to this more intensive intervention are then referred for one-on-one special services provided by a reading specialist or other professional—a third tier or level.

There is no research to date that clearly identifies one model as more effective than another and research is ongoing even as states begin to implement RTI models (see the chapter on RTI in this volume for further information).

Summary of Classroom Studies and Interventions

Increasingly, research is showing that global school and curriculum reforms will probably not meet the goal of NCLB—all children reading proficiently by fourth grade. Such interventions tend to under-serve children who are able readers as well as those that are struggling. Instead, new research is showing that classroom instruction that is dynamic and responsive to the instructional and social/emotional needs of individual students, that is based on ongoing assessment of skills and is tailored, based on these assessments, and that conceptualizes literacy instruction multidimensionally rather than as either-or (e.g., phonics versus whole language) will be more successful. However, the research called for is demanding and incorporates experimental designs, careful classroom observation tools, and stronger partnerships between researchers and schools.

CONCLUSIONS AND FUTURE DIRECTIONS

As the U.S. Congress works on the reauthorization of No Child Left Behind act in the Obama administration, the role of federal government in education is a constant theme (Foorman et al., 2007). From its inception, the Elementary and Secondary Education Act of 1965 has forbidden the federal government from mandating curriculum and instruction (PL 89-10, 79 *Stat.* 27, section 604). Even so, some continuity across administrations seems highly likely. For example, by all accounts and appearances, accountability for achievement gains for disaggregated groups will remain, with more flexibility provided to capture growth: more and more states will be allowed to use growth models rather than counting the number of students achieving a particular performance standard. And the teacher quality agenda of NCLB is likely to be further expanded than in the previous administration. The reassessments of the NRP phonics meta-analysis and other recent research underscores the importance of a comprehensive reading/language arts approach where mastery of the alphabetic system is integrated with opportunities to read engaging books and to write. Classroom studies will continue to address the teacher-level variables that moderate the relation between the abilities students bring to the classroom in the fall and their achievement outcomes at the end of the year. In this fashion, we will better understand the complex interactions between students' abilities and teachers' allocation of time to various content areas in order to meet the needs of individual students.

REFERENCES

Adams, M. J. (1990). *Beginning to read*. Cambridge, MA: MIT Press.

Adams, M. J. (2001). Alphabetic anxiety and explicit, systematic phonics instruction: A cognitive science perspective. In S. B. Neuman & D. K. Dickinson (Eds.), *Handbook of early literacy research* (Vol. I, pp. 66–80). New York: Guilford.

Al Otaiba, S., Connor, C. M., Kosanovich, M., Schatschneider, C., Dyrlund, A. K., & Lane, H. (2008). Reading First kindergarten classroom instruction and students' phonological awareness and decoding fluency growth. *Journal of School Psychology, 48*, 281–314.

Barr, R. (1984). Beginning reading instruction: From debate to reformation. In P. D. Pearson, R. Barr, M. L. Kamil, & P. Mosenthal (Eds.), *Handbook of reading research* (Vol. I, pp. 545–581). New York: Longman.

Beck, I. L., McKeown, M. G., & Kucan, L. (2002). *Bringing words to life: Robust vocabulary instruction.* New York: Guilford.

Beck, I. L., McKeown, M. G., & Kucan, L. (2008). *Creating robust vocabulary instruction: Frequently asked questions and extended examples.* New York: Guilford.

Block, C. C., Parris, S. R., Reed, K. L., Whiteley, C. S., & Cleveland, M. (2009). Instructional approaches that significantly increase reading comprehension. *Journal of Educational Psychology, 101*(2), 262–281.

Bracht, G. H. (1970). Experimental factors related to aptitude-treatment interactions. *Review of Educational Research, 40*(5), 627–645.

Bredekemp, S., & Copple, C. (Eds.). (1997). *Developmentally appropriate practice in early childhood programs.* Washington DC: National Association for the Education of Young Children.

Camilli, G., Vargas, S., & Yurecko, M. (2003). Teaching children to read: The fragile link between science and federal education policy. *Education Policy Analysis Archive, 11*(15). Retrieved May 26, 2008, from http://epaa.asu.edu/epaa/v11n15/

Camilli, G., Wolfe, P. M., & Smith, M. L. (2006). Meta-analysis and reading policy: Perspectives on teaching children to read. *The Elementary School Journal, 107,* 27–36.

Case, L. P., Speece, D. L., & Molloy, D. E. (2003). The validity of a response-to-instruction paradigm to identify reading disabilities: A longitudinal analysis of individual differences and contextual factors. *School Psychology Review, 32*(4), 557–582.

Catts, H. W., Fey, M. F., Zhang, X., & Tomblin, J. B. (1999). Language basis of reading and reading disabilities: Evidence from a longitudinal investigation. *Scientific Studies of Reading, 3,* 331–361.

Chall, J .S. (1967/1983). *Learning to read: The great debate.* Fort Worth, TX: Harcourt Brace.

Coburn, C. E. (2004). Beyond decoupling: Rethinking the relationship between the institutional environment and the classroom. *Sociology of education, 77*(3), 211–244.

Cohen, J. (1988). Statistical power analysis for the behavioral sciences (2nd ed.). Hillsdale, NJ: Erlbaum.

Connor, C. M., Jakobsons, L. J., Crowe, E., & Granger, J. (2009). Instruction, differentiation, and student engagement in Reading First classrooms. *Elementary School Journal, 109*(3), 221–250.

Connor, C. M., Morrison, F. J., Fishman, B., Ponitz, C. C., Glasney, S., Underwood, P., et al. (2009). The ISI classroom observation system: Examining the literacy instruction provided to individual students. *Educational Researcher, 38*(2), 85–99.

Connor, C. M., Morrison, F. J., Fishman, B. J., Schatschneider, C., & Underwood, P. (2007a). The early years: Algorithm-guided individualized reading instruction. *Science, 315*(5811), 464–465.

Connor, C. M., Morrison, F. J., & Katch, E. L. (2004). Beyond the reading wars: The effect of classroom instruction by child interactions on early reading. *Scientific Studies of Reading, 8*(4), 305–336.

Connor, C. M., Morrison, F. J., & Petrella, J. N. (2004). Effective reading comprehension instruction: Examining child by instruction interactions. *Journal of Educational Psychology, 96*(4), 682–698.

Connor, C. M., Morrison, F. J., & Slominski, L. (2006). Preschool instruction and children's literacy skill growth. *Journal of Educational Psychology, 98*(4), 665–689.

Connor, C. M., Morrison, F. J., & Underwood, P. (2007b). A second chance in second grade? The independent and cumulative Impact of first and second grade reading Instruction and students' letter-word reading skill growth. *Scientific Studies of Reading, 11*(3), 199–233.

Connor, C. M., Piasta, S. B., Fishman, B., Glasney, S., Schatschneider, C., Crowe, et al. (2009). Individualizing student instruction precisely: Effects of child by instruction interactions on first graders' literacy development. *Child Development, 80*(1), 77–100.

Craig, S. A. (2006). The effects of an adapted interactive writing intervention on kindergarten children's phonological awareness, spelling, and early reading development: A contextualized approach to instruction. *Journal of Educational Psychology, 98*(4), 714–731.

Cronbach, L. J. (1957). The two disciplines of scientific psychology. *American Psychologist, 12,* 671–684.

Cronbach, L. J., & Snow, R. E. (1969). *Individual differences in learning ability as a function of instructional variables* (ERIC Document reproduction service no. ED 029 001). Stanford, CA: Stanford University, School of Education.

Cronbach, L. J., & Snow, R. E. (1977). *Aptitudes and instructional methods: A handbook for research on interactions.* New York: Irvington.

Cronbach, L. J., & Webb, N. (1975). Between-class and within-class effects in a reported aptitude X treatment interaction: Reanalysis of a study by G. L. Anderson. *Journal of Educational Psychology, 67*(6), 717–724.

Deno, S. L., Espin, C. A., Fuchs, L. S., Shinn, M. R., Walker, H. M., & Stoner, G. (2002). Evaluation strategies for preventing and remediating basic skill deficits. In Anonymous (Ed.), *Interventions for academic and behavior problems II: Preventive and remedial approaches* (pp. 213–241). Washington, DC: National Association of School Psychologists.

Denton, C., Foorman, B., & Mathes, P. (2003). Schools that 'Beat the Odds': Implications for reading instruction. *Remedial and Special Education, 24*, 258–261.

Donovan, M. S., & Cross, C. T. (2002). *Minority students in special and gifted education.* Washington, DC: National Academy Press.

Duke, N. K. (2000). 3.6 minutes per day: The scarcity of informational texts in first grade. *Reading Research Quarterly, 35*(2), 202–224.

Duke, N. K., & Pearson, P. D. (2003). Effective practices for developing reading comprehension. In A. E. Farstrup & S. J. Samuels (Eds.), *What research has to say about reading instruction* (3rd ed., pp. 205–242). Newark, DE: International Reading Association.

Ehri, L. C. (1998). Grapheme-phoneme knowledge is essential for learning to read words in English. In J. Metsala & L. Ehri (Eds.), *Word recognition in beginning literacy* (pp. 3–40). Mahwah, NJ: Erlbaum.

Ehri, L. C. (1999). Phases of development in learning to read words. In J.V. Oakhill & R. Beard (Eds.), *Reading development and the teaching of reading: A psychological perspective* (pp. 79–108). Oxford, UK: Blackwell.

Ehri, L. C. (2005). Development of sight word reading: Phases and findings. In M. J. Snowling & C. Hulme (Eds.), *The science of reading: A handbook* (pp. 135–154). Oxford, UK: Blackwell.

Ehri, L. C., Nunes, S., Stahl, S., & Willows, D. (2001). Systematic phonics instruction helps students learn to read: Evidence from the National Reading Panel's meta-analysis. *Review of Educational Research, 71*, 393–447.

Ehri, L. C., Nunes, S., Willows, D., Schuster, B., Yaghoub-Zadeh, Z., & Shanahan, T. (2001). Phonemic awareness instruction helps children learn to read: Evidence from the National Reading Panel's meta-analysis. *Reading Research Quarterly, 36*, 250–287.

Ehri, L., & Wilce, L. (1983). Development of word identification speed in skilled and less skilled beginning readers. *Journal of Educational Psychology, 75,* 3–18.

Elementary and Secondary Education Act of 1965, Pub. L. No. 89-10, 79 Stat. 27 (1965).

Evans, M. A., & Carr, T. H. (1985). Cognitive abilities, conditions of learning, and the early development of reading skill. *Reading Research Quarterly, 20,* 327–350.

Fletcher, J. M., & Foorman, B. R. (1994). Issues in definition and measurement of learning disabilities: The need for early intervention. In G. R. Lyon (Ed.), *Frames of reference for the assessment of learning disabilities: New views on measurement issues* (pp. 185–200). Baltimore, MD: Brookes.

Florida Department of Education. (2009–2010). Florida asessments for Instruction in reading. Tallahassee, FL: Author.

Foorman, B. R. (1994). The relevance of a connectionist model of reading for "The Great Debate." *Educational Psychology Review, 6*(1), 25–47.

Foorman, B. R., Francis, D. J., Fletcher, J. M., Schatschneider, C., & Mehta, P. (1998). The role of instruction in learning to read: Preventing reading failure in at risk children. *Journal of Educational Psychology, 90*, 37–55.

Foorman, B .R., Fletcher, J. M., & Francis, D. J. (2004). Early reading assessment. In W. M. Evers & H. J. Walberg (Eds.), *Testing student learning, evaluating teaching effectiveness* (pp. 81–125). Stanford, CA: The Hoover Institution.

Foorman, B. R., Francis, D. J., Davidson, K., Harm, M., & Griffin, J. (2004). Variability in text features in six grade 1 basal reading programs. *Scientific Studies in Reading, 8*(2), 167–197.

Foorman, B. R., Goldenberg, C., Carlson, C., Saunders, W., & Pollard-Durodola, S. D. (2004). How teachers allocate time during literacy instruction in primary-grade English language learner classrooms. In M. McCardle & V. Chhabra (Eds.), *The voice of evidence: Bringing research to the classroom* (pp. 289–328). Baltimore, MD: Brookes.

Foorman, B. R., Kalinowski, S. J., & Sexton, W. L. (2007). Standards-based educational reform is one important step toward reducing the achievement gap. In A. Gamoran (Ed.), *Standards-based reform and the poverty gap: Lessons from "No Child Left Behind."* Washington, DC: Brookings.

Foorman, B. R., Schatschneider, C., Eakin, M. N., Fletcher, J. M., Moats, L. C., & Francis, D. J. (2006). The impact of instructional practices in grades 1 and 2 on reading and spelling achievement in high poverty schools. *Contemporary Educational Psychology, 31*, 1–29.

Gates, A. I., & Russell, D. H. (1939). Types of materials, vocabulary burden, word analysis, and other factors in beginning reading. *Elementary School Journal, 39*, 27–35, 119–128.

Gersten, R., Compton, D., Connor, C. M., Dimino, J., Santoro, L., Linan-Thompson, S., et al. (2008). *Assisting students struggling with reading: Response to Intervention and multi-tier intervention for reading in the primary grades. A practice guide.* Washington, DC: National Center for Education Evaluation and Regional Assistance, Institute of Education Sciences, U.S. Department of Education.

Goldman, S., & Rakestraw, J. (2000). Structural aspects of constructing meaning from text. In R. Barr, M. Kamil, P. Mosenthal, & P. D. Pearson (Eds.), *Handbook of reading research* (Vol. III, pp. 311–335). New York: Longman.

Gough, P. B., Juel, C., & Griffith, P. L. (1992). Reading, spelling, and the orthographic cipher. In P. B. Gough, L. C. Ehri, & R. Treiman (Eds.), *Reading acquisition* (pp. 35–48). Hillsdale, NJ: Erlbaum.

Graesser, A., Golding, J. M., & Long, D. L. (1991). Narrative representation and comprehension. In R. Barr, M. L. Kamil, P. B. Mosenthal, & P. D. Pearson (Eds.), *Handbook of reading research* (Vol. II, pp. 171–205). White Plains, NY: Longman.

Graesser, A. C., McNamara, D. D., Louwerse, M. M., & Cai, Z. (2004). Coh-Metrix: Analysis of text on cohesion and language. *Behavior Research Methods, Instruments, & Computers, 36*, 193–202.

Guthrie, J. T., & Wigfield, A. (2000). Engagement and motivation in reading. In M. L. Kamil, P. B. Mosenthal, P. D. Pearson, & R. Barr (Eds.), *Handbook of reading research* (Vol. III, pp. 403–422). Mahwah, NJ: Erlbaum.

Guthrie, J. T., Wigfield, A., Barbosa, P., Perencevich, K. C., Taboada, A., Davis, M. H., et al. (2004). Increasing reading comprehension and engagement through concept-oriented reading instruction. *Journal of Educational Psychology, 94*(3), 403–423.

Hammill, D. D., & Swanson, H. L. (2006). The National Reading Panel's meta-analysis of phonics instruction: Another point of view. *The Elementary School Journal, 107*, 17–26.

Hamre, B. K., & Pianta, R. C. (2005). Can instructional and emotional support in the first-grade classroom make a difference for children at risk of school failure? *Child Development, 76*(5), 949–967.

Harm, M. W., & Seidenberg, M. S. (2004). Computing the meanings of words in reading: Cooperative division of labor between visual and phonological processes. *Psychological Review, 111*(3), 662–720.

Haskell, D. W., Foorman, B. R., & Swank, P. R. (1992). Effects of three orthographic/phonological units on first grade reading. *Remedial and Special Education, 13*, 40–49.

Hiebert, E. H. (2005). State reform policies and the reading task for first graders. *Elementary School Journal, 105*, 245–266.

Hiebert, E. H. (2007). The fluency curriculum and text elements that support it. In P. Schwanenflugel & M. Kuhn (Eds.), *Fluency instruction for shared reading: Two whole class approaches* (pp. 36–54). New York: Guilford.

Hoover, W. A., & Gough, P. B. (1990). The simple view of reading. *Reading and Writing, 2*(2), 127–160.

Individuals with Disabilities Education Improvement Act of 2004 (IDEA), Pub. L. No. 108-446, 118 Stat 2647-2808 (2004).

IRA Commission on Response to Intervention. (2009). IRA Commission on RTI: Working draft of guiding principles. *Reading Today, 26*(4), 1, 4–6.

Jenkins, J. R., Hudson, R. F., & Johnson, E. S. (2007). Screening for at-risk readers in a response-to-intervention (RTI) framework. *School Psychology Review, 36*, 582–600.

Juel, C., & Minden-Cupp, C. (2000). Learning to read words: Linguistic units and instructional strategies. *Reading Research Quarterly, 35*(4), 458–492.

Juel, C., & Roper-Schneider, D. (1985). The influence of basal readers on first-grade reading. *Reading Research Quarterly, 20*, 134–152.

Landauer, T. K. (1998). Learning and representing verbal meaning: The latent semantic Aaalysis theory. *Current Directions in Psychological Science, 7*, 161–164.

Liberman, I. Y., & Shankweiler, D., Fischer, F. W., & Carter, B. (1974). Explicit syllable and phoneme segmentation in the young child. *Journal of Experimental Child Psychology, 18*, 201–212.

Marston, D., Muyskens, P., Lau, M., & Center, A. (2002). Problem solving model for decision-making with high-incidence disabilities. *Learning Disabilities Research & Practice, 18*, 187–200.

Mathes, P. G., Denton, C. A., Fletcher, J. M., Anthony, J. L., Francis, D. J., & Schatschneider, C. (2005). The effects of theoretically different instruction and student characteristics on the skills of struggling readers. *Reading Research Quarterly, 40*(2), 148–182.

McMaster, K. L., Fuchs, D., Fuchs, L. S., & Compton, D. L. (2005). Responding to nonresponders. An experimental field trial of identification and intervention methods. *Exceptional Children, 71*, 445–563.

Mehta, P., Foorman, B. R., Branum-Martin, L., & Taylor, W. P. (2005). Literacy as a unidimensional multilevel construct: Validation, sources of influence, and implications in a longitudinal study in grades 1–4. *Scientific Studies of Reading, 9*(2), 85–116.

National Assessment Governing Board. (2007). *Reading framework for the 2009 National assessment of educational progress.* Washington, DC: Author.

National Center for Educational Statistics (NCES). (2007). *NAEP 2005 reading: A report card for the nation and the states.* Washington, DC: U.S. Department of Education.

National Institute of Child Health and Human Development. (2000). *National Reading Panel–Teaching children to read: Reports of the subgroups* (NIH Pub. No. 00-4754). Washington, DC: U.S. Department of Health and Human Services.

National Research Council. (1998). *Preventing reading difficulties in young children.* Committee on the Prevention of Reading Difficulties in Young Children, Committee on Behavioral and Social Science and Education, C. E. Snow, M. S. Burns, & P. Griffin (Eds.). Washington, DC: National Academy Press.

No Child Left Behind Act of 2001, Pub. L. No. 107-110, 115 Stat. 1425 (2001).

Neal, D., & Schanzenbach, D. W. (2007). Left behind by design: Proficiency counts and test-based accountability. Retrieved July 2007, from http://www.aei.org/docLib/20070716_NealSchanzenbachPaper.pdf

Nystrand, M., Wu, L. L., Gamoran, A., Zeiser, S., & Long, D. (2003). Questions in time: investigating the structure and dynamics of unfolding classroom discourse. *Discourse Processes, 35*, 135–198.

Oakhill, J. V., Cain, K. E., & Bryant, P. E. (2003). The dissociation of word reading and text comprehension: Evidence from component skills. *Language and Cognitive Processes, 18*, 443–468.

O'Connor, R., Fulmer, D., Harry, K. R., & Bell, K. M. (2005). Layers of reading intervention in kindergarten through third grade: Changes in teaching and student outcomes. *Journal of Learning Disabilities, 39*(5), 440–456.

Pearson, P. D., & Camperell, K. (1994). Comprehension of text structures. In R. B. Ruddell, M. R. Ruddell, & H. Singer (Eds.), *Theoretical models and processes of reading* (4th ed., pp. 448–468). Newark, DE: International Reading Association.

Perfetti, C. A. (1992). The representation problem in reading acquisition. In P. Gough, L. Ehri, & R. Treiman (Eds.), *Reading acquisition* (pp. 107–143). Hillsdale, NJ: Erlbaum.

Plaut, D. C. (2005). Connectionist approaches to reading. In M. J. Snowling & C. Hulme (Eds.), *The science of reading: A handbook* (pp. 24–38). Oxford, UK: Blackwell.

Plaut, D. C., McClelland, J. L., Seidenberg, M. S., & Patterson, K. (1996). Understanding normal and impaired word reading: Computational principles in quasi-regular domains. *Psychological Review, 103*, 56–115.

Porter, A. C. (2007). NCLB lessons learned: Implications for reauthorization. In A. Gamoran (Ed.), *Standards-based reform and the poverty gap: Lessons from "No Child Left Behind"* (pp. 286–324). Washington, DC: Brookings.

Pressley, M., Raphael, L., Gallagher, J. D., & DiBella, J. (2004). Providence-St. Mel School: How a school that works for African American students works. *Journal of Educational Psychology, 96*(2), 216–235.

Pressley, M., Wharton-McDonald, R., Allington, R., Block, C. C., Morrow, L., Tracey, D., et al. (2001). A study of effective first-grade literacy instruction. *Scientific Studies of Reading, 5*(1), 35–58.

RAND Reading Study Group. (2002). *Reading for understanding.* Santa Monica, CA: RAND.

Raudenbush, S. W., & Bryk, A. S. (2002). *Hierarchical linear models: Applications and data analysis methods* (2nd ed.). Thousand Oaks, CA: Sage.

Rayner, K., Foorman, B. R., Perfetti, C. A., Pesetsky, D., & Seidenberg, M. S. (2001). How psychological science informs the teaching of reading. *Psychological Science in the Public Interest, 2*(2), 31–74.

Reitsma, P. (1983). Printed word learning in beginning readers. *Journal of Experimental Child Psychology, 36*, 321–339.

Reschly, D. J., Tilly, W. D., III, & Grimes, J. P. (1999). *Special education in transition: Functional assessment and noncategorical programming.* Frederick, CO: Sopris West.

Roberts, T. A., & Meiring, A. (2006). Teaching phonics in the context of children's literature or spelling: Influences on first-grade reading, spelling, and writing and fifth-grade comprehension. *Journal of Educational Psychology, 98*(4), 690–713.

Seidenberg, M., & McClelland, J. L. (1989). A distributed, developmental model of word recognition and naming. *Psychological Review, 96*, 523–568.

Seymour, P. H. K., Aro, M., & Erskine, J. M. (2003). Foundation literacy acquisition in European orthographies. *British Journal of Psychology, 94*, 143–174.

Share, D. L. (1995). Phonological recoding and self-teaching: Sine qua non of reading acquisition. *Cognition, 55*, 151–218.

Speece, D. L., & Case, L. P. (2001). Classification in context: An alternative approach to identifying early reading disability. *Journal of Educational Psychology, 93*, 735–749.

Stanovich, K. E., & Siegel, L. S. (1994). Phenotypic performance profile of children with reading disabilities: A regression-based test of the phonological-core variable-difference model. *Journal of Educational Psychology, 86*, 24–53.

Stenner, A. J., Sanford, E. E., & Burdick, D. S. (2006). How accurate are lexile text measures? *Journal of Applied Measurement, 7*(3), 307–322.

Storch, S. A., & Whitehurst, G. J. (2002). Oral language and code-related precursors to reading: Evidence from a longitudinal structural model. *Developmental Psychology, 38*, 934–947.

Stuebing, K. K., Barth, A., Cirino, P., Fletcher, J. M., & Francis, D. J. (2008). A response to recent re-analyses of The National Reading Panel Report: Effects of systematic phonics instruction are practically significant. *Journal of Educational Psychology, 100*, 123–134.

Stuebing, K. K., Fletcher, J. M., LeDoux, J. M., Lyon, G. R., Shaywitz, S. E., & Shaywitz, B. A. (2002). Validity of IQ-discrepancy classifications of reading disabilities: A meta-analysis. *American Educational Research Journal, 39*(2), 469–518.

Taylor, B. M., & Pearson, P. D. (Eds.). (2002). *Teaching reading: Effective schools, accomplished teachers*. Mahwah, NJ: Erlbaum.

Taylor, B. M., Pearson, P. D., & Rodriquez, M. C. (2003). Reading growth in high-poverty classrooms: The influences of teacher practices that encourage cognitive engagement in literacy learning. *Elementary School Journal, 104*, 3–28.

Taylor, B. M., Pearson, P. D., Clark, K., & Walpole, S. (2000). Effective schools and accomplished teachers: lessons about primary-grade reading instruction in low-income schools. *Elementary School Journal, 101*(2), 121–165.

Taylor, B. M., Pearson, P. D., & Rodriquez, M. C. (2003). Reading growth in high-poverty classrooms: The influences of teacher practices that encourage cognitive engagement in literacy learning. *Elementary School Journal, 104*, 3–28.

Tivnan, T., & Hemphill, L. (2005). Comparing four literacy reform models in high-poverty schools: Patterns of first-grade achievement. *Elementary School Journal, 105*(5), 419–441.

Torgesen, J. K., Rashotte, C. A., & Alexander, A. (2001). Principles of fluency instruction in reading: Relationships with established empirical outcomes. In M. Wolf (Ed.), *Dyslexia, fluency, and the brain* (pp. 333–355). Parkton, MD: York Press.

Torgesen, J. K., Wagner, R. K., Rashotte, C. A., Rose, E., Lindamood, P., Conway, T., et al. (1999). Preventing reading failure in young children with phonological processing disabilities: Group and individual responses to instruction. *Journal of Educational Psychology, 91*, 579–593.

U.S. Department of Education. (2004). Twenty-sixth annual report to Congress on the implementation of the Individuals with Disabilities Education Act. Retrieved October 1, 2006, from http://www.ed.gov/about/reports/annual/osep/2004/index.html

Vaughn, S., & Fuchs, L. S. (2003). Redefining learning disabilities as inadequate response to instruction: The promise and potential problems. *Learning Disabilities Research and Practice, 18*(3), 137–146.

Vaughn, S., Linan-thompson, S., & Hickman, P. (2003). Response to instruction as a means of identifying students with reading/learning disabilities. *Exceptional Children, 69*, 391–409.

Viadero, D. (2007, July 16). NCLB seen as curbing low, high achievers' gains. Retrieved from http://lnk.edweek.org/edweek/index.html?url=/ew/articles/2007/07/16/43nclb_web.h26.html&tkn=HN0YoGR4vSrb8IGv%2FEqP44BxjGf7b%2BBy

Walley, A. C., Metsala, J. L., & Garlock, V. M. (2003). Spoken vocabulary growth: Its role in the development of phoneme awareness and early reading ability. *Reading and Writing: An Interdisciplinary Journal, 16,* 5–20.

Walton, P. D., Walton, L. M., & Felton, K. (2001). Teaching rime analogy or letter recoding reading strategies to prereaders: Effects on prereading skills and word reading. *Journal of Educational Psychology, 93,* 160–180.

Wharton-McDonald, R., Pressley, M., & Hampston, J. M. (1998). Literacy instruction in nine first-grade classrooms: Teacher characteristics and student achievement. *Elementary School Journal, 99*(2), 101–128.

Xue, Y., & Meisels, S. J. (2004). Early literacy instruction and learning in kindergarten: Evidence from the early childhood longitudinal study — kindergarten class of 1998–1999. *American Educational Research Journal, 41*(1), 191–229.

Ziegler, J. C., & Goswami, U. (2005). Reading acquisition, developmental dyslexia, and skilled reading across languages: A psycholinguistic grain size theory. *Psychological Bulletin, 131,* 3–29.

8 Adolescents as Readers

Patricia A. Alexander and Emily Fox
University of Maryland

One of the undeniable trends in the domain of literacy is the rising interest in adolescent readers. Evidence of this trend is apparent not only in the number of empirical and theoretical studies focusing on middle school and high school students within leading literacy and psychological journals, but also in the expanded grant opportunities for those researching adolescent readers (e.g., the Adolescent Literacy Network [U.S. Department of Education, 2006a] and the Striving Readers Initiative [U. S. Department of Education, 2006b]). Much of this heightened regard is due to the growing concern for middle school and high school students who remain at risk in terms of their performance on high-stakes measures of reading; that is, struggling adolescent readers (Cassidy & Cassidy, 2007; Cassidy, Garrett, & Barrera, 2006). Indeed, a primary focus in a number of recent reviews, books, and chapters has been on adolescents as endangered readers and, thus, endangered learners (e.g., Alvermann, 2002; Biancarosa & Snow, 2004; Franzak, 2006; Phelps, 2005; Snow & Biancarosa, 2003).

Of course, one need not scour recent publications or investigate current federal initiatives to discern changing attitudes toward adolescent readers. Such a shift can be observed in an analysis of the contributions to prior volumes of the *Handbook of Reading Research*, both in terms of the prevalence of this topic and the particular attention paid to adolescents and their reading. Specifically, in the inaugural volume of the *Handbook* (Pearson, Barr, Kamil, & Mosenthal, 1984), no chapter was expressly dedicated to adolescent reading or adolescent readers, although there was discussion of studying as a specific form of reading especially required of middle school and high school students (Anderson & Armbruster, 1984). Although there was a greater presence for adolescents in Volume II of the *Handbook* (Barr, Kamil, Mosenthal, & Pearson, 1991), those chapters still targeted the reading demands in the secondary classroom (e.g., Alvermann & Moore, 1991; Hegarty, Carpenter, & Just, 1991; Weaver & Kintsch, 1991), rather than the characteristics of those engaged in such reading. The chapter centered on literacy acts at the secondary level (Guthrie & Greaney, 1991) did, however, include discussion of the independent (out-of-school) reading behaviors of secondary students. Even within Volume III of the *Handbook*, relevant chapters still emphasized expository reading or reading to learn (Alexander & Jetton, 2000; Bean, 2000), text structure (Goldman & Rakestraw, 2000), college studying (Nist & Simpson, 2000), and the role of text in classroom learning (Wade & Moje, 2000). However, Wade and Moje concluded their chapter by urging an expanded perspective on what counts as text and learning from text, particularly for adolescents.

In this chapter, we take Wade and Moje's (2000) message to heart by considering both in- and out-of-school reading and "text" as broadly configured. However, we have a secondary purpose. Specifically, we proffer this brief historical backdrop as a preparation for laying out an orientation toward adolescent reading alternative to that seen in prior volumes of the *Handbook*. Rather than concentrate on content-area, expository reading, or expository texts typically read within schools, we have chosen to explore the topic of adolescent reading from a developmental perspective. We will consider the biophysical, cognitive, and psychosocial attributes of adolescents as a way to approach the nature of and ecology for reading for this population. Rather than foreground subject-matter texts and content-area pedagogy, we foreground the adolescent, confronting certain developmental issues or transitions and this particular stage of development's relation with reading.

We argue that their developmental issues and transitions are what make adolescents an interesting and challenging population with regard to such questions as: What do adolescents read? Why do adolescents read? How do adolescents read? We concur that the problem of struggling adolescent readers is of paramount importance and worthy of the empirical, pedagogical, and monetary interest it currently engenders. Both the long-term study of content-area reading and the nature of struggling adolescent readers, however, can be enriched and extended by taking the critical step of conceptualizing adolescence as a stage in lifelong reading development (Moje, 2002).

WHO ARE ADOLESCENTS?

> Adolescence is a stage of life distinct from either childhood or adulthood. This is true not just for human beings but for other species as well, especially primates. This observation strongly suggests that it is a time during which certain tasks need to be completed, among them becoming physically and sexually mature, acquiring skills needed to carry out adult roles, gaining increased autonomy from parents, and realigning social interconnections with members of both the same and the opposite sex. (Elliott & Feldman, 1990, p. 3)

It probably goes without saying that adolescents constitute a unique developmental population, particularly in modern, post-industrial societies. Nonetheless, within much of the reading literature, the characteristics of adolescents are often assumed rather than explicated. This pertains even to the simplest marker of adolescence—age. For the sake of clarity, we will restrict our consideration in the present chapter to those between the ages of 12 and 18.

Outside the parameter of age, adolescents are typically viewed as being in transition to adulthood. Developmental research tends to consider this transition, as having four aspects: physical development, cognitive development, changes in self/social relationships, and a changing context (Elliott & Feldman, 1990; Mertz, 1975; Santrock, 1999; Wigfield, Byrnes, & Eccles, 2006). For this chapter we conduct an interpretative analysis of the research on adolescent readers around those four aspects, organized by the empirically-based premises that adolescence constitutes a period of: (a) biophysiological development, including transformations in brain structure and organization, as well as those changes associated with puberty; (b) cognitive development, including increased reasoning ability and comfort with abstract thought; (c) development in identity and social relationships, including greater autonomy and heightened orientation toward peers; and (d) shifting school contexts and educational expectations.

In light of the vastness of the developmental literature, it is our intention to delimit examination to those dimensions of development most directly pertinent to the processing of written or oral texts and to related pedagogical practice. Moreover, it is essential to note that the aspects of human growth and maturation we discuss under each developmental category are, in reality, intricately intertwined. For instance, this is apparent in the ensuing discussions of biophysiological and cognitive changes, since observable differences in the cognitive processing of adolescent readers are, in part, attributable to neurobiological maturation. Finally, within the developmental literature the concepts of maturation and growth have distinct and important meanings, which we will honor. Maturation refers to those modifications that principally result from one's genetic or biological makeup (e.g., increased height), whereas growth or development can refer to changes arising largely from experience and environmental circumstances (e.g., social reading patterns). Maturation and growth are also often overlapping and co-relational.

BIOPHYSIOLOGICAL DEVELOPMENT

The external physical transformations associated with the adolescent period are unmistakable (e.g., more adult-like stature, and primary or secondary sexual characteristics). Nonetheless, the relevance of these physical developments to reading may not be so transparent. Conversely, the internal neurophysiological changes that are part of biophysiological development, while generally considered more significant to reading, are less transparent to the casual observer. Here we will elaborate on issues related to puberty and brain development and their potential relation to adolescents and their reading (see Table 8.1).

Puberty and the Adolescent Reader

What potential relations between the sexual maturation of youth and their reading merit attention? As one consequence of these physical changes—along with associated factors, such as greater self-awareness, increased importance of social comparisons, and exploration of gender identity—adolescents experience a heightened sense of body image, along with interest in learning how to navigate the new terrain of sexual feelings and behavior (Brooks-Gunn & Reiter,

Table 8.1   Biophysiological and Cognitive Changes in Adolescence and Related Reading Outcomes

Aspect of Adolescence	Possible Manifestation in Adolescents	Possible Relation to Adolescent Reading	Overview of Research Findings
Biophysiological: Puberty—Sexual and skeletal maturation, changes in hormonal levels	Changes in body size and shape, increased awareness of and interest in sexuality	Body image and magazine reading; interest in reading about sex/romance; dissemination of health information	Adolescent readers may be vulnerable to pressure conveyed by magazines to conform to 'ideal' body types; adolescent girls read to explore their developing sexuality; likely to get reinforcement of cultural norms and social pressures.
Biophysiological: Brain development— Changes in density of grey/white matter in frontal/parietal regions of brain	Development of self-regulatory capacity, including monitoring, attention, working memory; development of social cognition, including self-awareness, perspective-taking, empathy.	Increased capacity for self-regulation, ability to monitor; increased working memory capacity and efficiency; increased ability to understand perspective of others, respond empathetically	Adolescents appear to have improved capacity for monitoring; greater working memory capacity likely to be related to improved reading comprehension, construction of more elaborated mental representations.
Cognitive: Increased capability for abstract, logical, multidimensional thought. Greater content knowledge, automaticity, strategic repertoire, strategic flexibility. Increased self-awareness.	Ability to move away from literal, to identify logical structure of text and to reason from it, to link across distant or disparate text elements. Flexible, appropriate, and somewhat automated use of multiple resources for making meaning.	General reading achievement; inferential and elaborative comprehension; recognition and use of text structure to build comprehension; building understanding across multiple texts; beliefs about written and oral text.	Aspects of inferential and elaborative comprehension develop during/beyond adolescence. More able to use text structure and features to support comprehension; some types of text may require extensive exposure and practice.

1990; Mertz, 1975; Santrock, 1999). Adolescents' reading appears to come into play in facing this sexual maturation in two general ways. For one, texts, broadly configured, become a conduit for adolescents' learning about their emerging sexuality and bodily changes, as evidenced by reading habits and topical interests (Hidi & Baird, 1986; Hopper, 2005)—a point to which we will return later. For another, the texts with which adolescents engage may contribute to the sexual mores and physical ideals that these still impressionable minds internalize. The research findings suggest, however, that the outcomes of these print engagements may not always be positive or desirable.

For example, Tiggemann (2006) collected longitudinal questionnaire data from 214 adolescent females to investigate the role of media exposure (e.g., magazines and television) in their body images. Tiggemann determined that both the amount of exposure and the type of processing these adolescent females reported over time were important predictors of body dissatisfaction and a drive for thinness for participants. She also concluded that particular groups of girls were seemingly more vulnerable to the messages and images in these popular media. Similarly, Thomsen, Weber, and Brown (2002) explored the relation between reading women's beauty and fashion magazines and the use of dangerous dieting methods among 502 high school females. Even when controlling for anxiety about weight and frequency of regular exercise, the authors detected a weak but significant association between reading and certain risky behaviors, such as taking appetite suppressants and restricting calories.

Others have found this link between popular press media and adolescents' emerging body image intriguing. For instance, relying largely on sociodemographic methodologies, Botta (2003), Utter, Neumark-Sztainer, Wall, and Story (2003) and others (Carson, Rodriguez, & Audrain-McGovern, 2005; Kaplan & Cole, 2003) identified meaningful relations between adolescent males' and females' reading of popular press about dieting/weight loss, fashion, and emerging sexuality and their decreased psychosocial well-being and increased engagement in weight control behaviors. Of course, these data were almost exclusively self-report and correlational, making any causal determinations inappropriate. Nonetheless, such patterns in the research suggest that what these adolescents read may exert an effect, desirable or not, on their identities and body images.

NEUROLOGICAL CHANGES

Adolescent brain development is a relatively recent area of research that has opened up since the advent of newer brain imaging techniques (Berninger & Corina, 1998; Berninger & Richards, 2002). From this growing body of work, it appears that adolescents show differential changes in the white matter and grey matter in particular regions of the brain. There appears to be a steady increase in the white matter in the frontal and parietal regions of their brains (Blakemore & Choudhury, 2006; Giedd et al., 1999). White matter (myelin) is an insulating material that speeds the rate of transmission of neural impulses. In addition, adolescents show a reduction of grey matter density in the frontal and parietal lobes, possibly reflecting increased myelination along with synaptic reorganization and pruning following an increase in grey matter in these regions immediately prior to puberty (Blakemore & Choudhury, 2006; Giedd et al., 1999).

Such changes presumably contribute to efficiency of brain activity in these areas, and may be associated with the development of certain cognitive functions during adolescence, including the self-regulatory functions controlled by the frontal lobes: selective attention, decision-making, impulse control, and working memory (Blakemore & Choudhury, 2006; Luna et al., 2001; Yurgelun-Todd, 2007). In addition, certain aspects of social cognition are believed to be associated with this frontal region, including self-awareness, perspective taking and empathy (Blakemore & Choudhury, 2006; Yurgelun-Todd, 2007). Here we will consider findings related to cognitive monitoring or regulation, given the long established importance of these mental processes to efficient and effective reading performance (Garner, 1987; Hacker, 2004; Pressley & Afflerbach, 1995). We will also discuss related studies of memory that can inform observed patterns in monitoring and regulation.

Cognitive Monitoring or Regulation.   The comprehension of text, especially at a non-superficial level, requires readers to be aware of their cognitive performance and sensitive to internal inconsistencies as well as to potential conflicts between their existing knowledge and the content of the text (Garner, 1987). Competent readers also must be able to regulate their reading so as to maximize performance and enhance understanding (Baker, 2002; Pressley & Afflerbach, 1995). Here we weigh the possible associations between brain development and adolescents' monitoring or regulation of their reading. In so doing, we find some evidence of a linkage in the research of Grabe, Antes, Kahn, and Kristjanson (1991) and Hacker (1997).

In their research, Grabe et al. (1991) compared the error detection of early adolescent (age 12) and adult readers. They saw that performance varied depending on whether the inserted errors represented internal inconsistencies or external contradictions. Specifically, while adolescents and adults did not differ with regard to the detection of contradictions between the text and prior knowledge (external), the young adolescents were significantly poorer at identifying internal inconsistencies than the adults. Hacker (1997) also used an error detection methodology to investigate text monitoring. In his study, seventh, ninth, and eleventh graders searched three times through a given text. Hacker determined that monitoring on lexical, syntactic, and semantic levels was positively associated with age and reading ability. He found that even when some adolescents had the knowledge necessary to identify more errors, they still failed to apply that knowledge in detecting errors.

Related Memorial Processing.   The ability to engage in text monitoring or error detection may be understood in relation to what Roberts (1989) described as voluntary and involuntary memory, processes that manifest differently from childhood to adolescence. Both processes involved the use of semantic elaboration to enhance memory (e.g., writing a sentence about a character in a story), but voluntary memory also involved the explicit intent of elaborating in order to remember better (e.g., writing such a sentence in order to remember what was read). Specifically, Roberts concluded that the activation of involuntary memory processes during reading was seemingly more effective than voluntary memory for younger students. Roberts also surmised that the ability to effectively use voluntary memory processes to comprehend text appeared to develop between the ages of 10 and early adolescence (i.e., 12 to 14). In general, involuntary processing appeared to result in more organization and better recall for younger individuals and voluntary memory strategies were more effective on the same material for older students.

Cain (2006), Holsgrove and Garton (2006), and Oberauer, Weidenfeld, and Hörnig (2006) also found links between reading performance and adolescents' working memory. For example, Holsgrove and Garton investigated the performance of sixty 13-year-olds on tasks measuring phonological processing, syntactic processing, and reading comprehension, along with several measures of working memory hypothesized to be related to the phonological loop (measuring storage of phonologically encoded information and the ability to maintain a list of orally presented words) and the central executive (measuring ability to focus attention and overcome interference in a recall task). The processing of 13-year-olds was of particular interest in this investigation, as they were hypothesized to be at a stage in reading development at which phonological and syntactic processing would both contribute uniquely to reading comprehension performance. The researchers found that both phonological and syntactic processing predicted reading comprehension, and that the presence or absence of syntactic processing distinguished good from poor readers. Further, the phonological loop, but not the central executive, played a small but significant role in processes involved in reading comprehension for 13-year-olds, although the authors argued that a greater role for the central executive might be observed with different measures of working memory and of comprehension.

Although the focus of their research was high school students' handling of ambiguous spatial descriptions, Oberauer et al. (2006) also reported significant effects as a result of working memory capacity. Here, however, no specific rationale for studying adolescents per se was given, and the findings are likely to apply to adults as well. This study directed adolescents to comprehend or detect errors in spatial descriptions. Participants with high or low working memory capacity differed mainly in the probability of constructing an adequate mental model of the content, but they were similar in their probability of detecting an ambiguity in the spatial description they read. Consequently, the authors posited that working memory capacity was less of a constraint in readers' general comprehension of text than when they were dealing with complex structural representations.

COGNITIVE DEVELOPMENT

Under the heading of cognitive development (see Table 8.1), we explore changes in mental processing that manifest in the adolescent reader. What distinguishes these developments from those previous addressed (e.g., puberty) is that they may be reflective not only of maturation but also of prior experience. These cognitive transformations include qualitative shifts in reasoning ability and an increasing comfort with abstraction, bringing adolescents into the realm of what Piaget termed formal operations or hypothetico-deductive thought (1964/1967).

> From early adolescence on, thinking tends to involve abstract rather than merely concrete representations; to become multidimensional rather than limited to a single issue; to become relative rather than absolute in the conception of knowledge; and to become self-reflective and self-aware. (Keating, 1990, p. 64)

Such developments allow adolescents to benefit from their exposure to literacy experiences and to the knowledge those experiences afford, in a manner not typical for younger children (Keating, 1990; Wigfield et al., 2006). For instance, adolescents become more able to consider multiple viewpoints (Chall, 1983; Mertz, 1975), and to think hypothetically (Mertz, 1975), abstractly (Keating, 1990; Mertz, 1975; Santrock, 1999), and logically (Mertz, 1975; Santrock, 1999). In addition, Keating found that adolescents' cognitive processing may benefit from having automated procedures that may have required deliberate thought for younger children. Adolescents are likely to have accumulated a larger repertoire of strategies for problem solving, and to be able to use them with greater control and flexibility (Keating, 1990).

These developments in cognitive capability are likely to be associated with how adolescents read and how well they read. We found support for this contention in the research studies investigating adolescent reading in terms of building understanding of text using inferential and elaborative comprehension (e.g., Nippold & Martin, 1989). There are also studies pertaining to adolescent readers' recognition and use of text structure and text features (e.g., van den Broek, Lynch, Naslund, Ievers-Landis, & Verduin, 2003), which we consider further. In addition—while beyond the scope of this chapter—there is relevant research on achievement (e.g., Evans, Floyd, McGrew, & Leforgee, 2001), intertextuality (e.g., Hartman, 1995), and beliefs about the nature of text (e.g., Horowitz, 1994), that also highlights connections between adolescents' cognitive capabilities and how they read.

Inferential and Elaborative Comprehension. Getting into a text and comprehending it well demands inferential and elaborative processing (Graesser, Millis, & Zwaan, 1997; Kintsch & Rawson, 2005; Pressley & Afflerbach, 1995). For example, building coherent meaning from extended or complex text requires anaphoric ties, articulating and sustaining multiple processing goals, and interpreting idiomatic or metaphoric language. There is evidence in the literature that these processes show improvement during the adolescent period.

According to Chapman (1983), for instance, the ability to deal with anaphoric references is still being acquired late in secondary school. Assessing reading by means of cloze procedure, Chapman found that average scores for pronoun cloze completion increased with age for children ages 8, 11, and 14, although the 14-year-olds were still not fully competent at this process. Nippold and her colleagues have also studied response to idioms, proverbs, and adverbial conjuncts and documented an age-related trend. For instance, Nippold and Martin (1989) examined idiom interpretation with a cross-sectional sample of 14- to 17-year-olds and determined that overall accuracy improved with age. As in the Chapman study, however, even the oldest adolescents had not mastered idiomatic interpretation. Nippold, Martin, and Erskine (1988) compared fourth, sixth, eighth, and tenth graders' proverb comprehension and production, and ascertained that performance steadily improved across the grades. The oldest group showed the least variability on the tasks. Similarly, Nippold, Schwartz, and Undlin (1992) compared adolescents and young adults (ages 12, 16, 19, and 24) on their use and understanding of adverbial conjuncts (e.g., nevertheless, however, or similarly). Data showed an increasing ability by age to use and understand conjuncts, with the young adults demonstrating the mastery of understanding (but not use) of these words that eluded the adolescents.

Recognition and Use of Text Structure/Features. With maturation and experience, adolescents not only develop in their ability to reason inferentially or with abstract or metaphoric language, but also in terms of their recognition of text structures and features (Chambliss, 1995; Kletzien, 1992). This pattern is apparent in the work of van den Broek et al. (2003) who compared third, sixth, ninth, and eleventh graders' comprehension of main ideas in narratives in which the position of character goal statements and their connections to other statements were varied within the text structure. Although even the youngest students in this study could identify main ideas, they were not as consistently successful as the adolescents, suggesting that this reading ability develops during the school years.

Moore and Scevak (1997) identified a similar developmental trend in fifth, seventh, and ninth graders' comprehension and recall of history and science content that included graphic aids (e.g., tables or diagrams). Moore and Scevak found a grade effect for the science texts, such that younger students attended more to details and focused less on main idea, theme, and the connection of text and graphics for those texts. They concluded that the younger students may have had less background knowledge of both content and structure for science texts. In their study of fifth, seventh, and ninth graders' and adults' reading of social studies texts, Ohlhausen and Roller (1988) also came to the conclusion that the improved performance in identifying important information in social studies passages for older adolescents and adults might be related to their greater knowledge of domain-specific content as well as more familiarity with typical structures for domain-related texts.

PSYCHOSOCIAL DEVELOPMENT

Especially during the last quarter century, researchers and practitioners have become increasingly aware that reading is a social act (Alexander & Fox, 2004). This awareness has been fostered

by the influence of social cognitive and sociocultural theories of human learning and development (Lave & Wenger, 1991; Rogoff, 2000; Vygotsky 1934/1986) and by pedagogical practices
intended to build collaborative, engaged learning communities (reviewed in Perry, Turner, &
Meyer, 2006). Our purpose here is to consider the social aspects of reading for adolescents in
light of what we understand about adolescents' psychosocial development.

For instance, we know that during adolescence, individuals engage in active, conscious self-
construction and experience changes in their social relationships and roles, including increased
autonomy and orientation toward peers (Santrock, 1999). Adolescents face the developmental
task of preparing for adulthood (Erikson, 1959/1980), and weigh aspects of their eventual adult
identity, including vocation, gender, ideology, sexual orientation, and religion, while integrating
those aspects into a coherent self (Harter, 1990; Santrock, 1999). As part of this preparation for
adulthood, adolescents also work on situating and understanding themselves in relation to their
peers, moving themselves more outside their family network of roles and responsibilities in a
widening social network (Wentzel, 2000).

Adolescents are typically engaged in active experimentation with roles and values, and get
vicarious information from peer and adult models, as well as from text (Franzak, 2006; Harter,
1990; Neilsen, 2006). They are concerned about conformity to social and peer norms, and interested in finding out the standards that exemplify the roles and values they are exploring. They
typically begin to assume more responsibilities and operate somewhat more independently from
direct adult or parental supervision; more activities are available to them and they have more
discretion in their choice of activities (Moje, 2002; Steinberg, 1990; Wigfield et al., 2006). Peers
constitute an important social support network by means of cliques, and an important source of
normative information in the form of crowds (Brown, 1990).

When we turned to the literature to see how adolescents' explorations of self and development
of peer-based social networks might have been investigated in relation to adolescents' reading
behaviors, we found research in two main areas: reading habits and interests, and construction
of identity and of social roles associated with that identity (see Table 8.2).

Reading Habits and Interests.   In Chall's (1983) model of reading development, she held that
high school students at Stage 4 were distinguished from those at the lower Stage 3 partly by their
reading habits and interests, in that they read more globally, although not with full assimilation
or integration. More recently, Irwin (2003) speculated on the reasons why some adolescents
and adults read voluntarily and many others do not. It was Irwin's contention that adolescents'
engagement in reading was reflective of their conceptions of themselves as readers. Moreover,
this conception was seen as related to adolescents' understanding of gender (e.g., reading seen
as a feminine activity), their perceived competence, and their understanding of the purpose
and nature of reading (e.g., as work, as a social activity, or as high-risk), along with influence of
parents' attitudes and behaviors.

The empirical literature also shows evidence of age-related reading patterns. For instance,
Hopper (2005) surveyed 11- to 15-year-olds in England and found that adolescents chose to read
books that their peers were reading or that family members recommended. The role of family
recommendations found here echoed that seen in case-study research by Chandler (1999) with
American high school juniors. Many of Hopper's participants reported reading non-book materials (e.g., newspapers), particularly magazines. Girls read more magazines dealing with fashion,
sex, love, romance, and health, whereas boys read specialty interest magazines (e.g., computer/
technology, sports, or cars). Not surprisingly, the adolescents also reported considerable reading of Internet material. Nippold, Duthie, and Larsen (2005) surveyed sixth to ninth graders
on their pleasure reading, giving students a list of possible materials including poems, short
stories, plays, novels, comics, technical books, newspapers, and magazines. What is particularly relevant to the focus of this chapter is that interest in pleasure reading was seen to decline

Table 8.2　Psychosocial and Ecological Changes in Adolescence and Related Reading Outcomes

Aspect of Adolescence	Possible Manifestation in Adolescents	Possible Relation to Adolescent Reading	Overview of Research Findings
Psychosocial: Identity—working on figuring out a number of aspects of eventual adult identity, such as vocation, gender, ideology, sexual orientation, and religion, and integrating these into a coherent self	Concern about conformity to social and peer norms; interest in finding out the norms that are associated with the roles and values they are exploring; peers form important source of normative information	Reading to learn about possible roles and aspects of identity; perception of self as reader, and of meaning and uses of reading; gender as a factor in reading identity and choices.	Adolescents use text as part of active exploration of possible/ideal selves, source of information about social norms. May need scaffolding and appropriate texts. Important role for magazines and other non-book texts, providing perceived useful and valued information. They construct understandings of themselves as readers and of what counts as reading, possible gender differences.
Psychosocial: Self/social development —working on situating and understanding themselves in relation to peers, moving more outside family network of roles and responsibilities	Peers become important social support network; adolescents somewhat more independent from direct adult or parental supervision; more activities available to them and more discretion in choice of activities	Role of supportive reading community, both peers and family; choice and uses of reading materials, including magazines; distinction between school-based and other reading.	Social networks can act as supports for reading, book clubs or sharing and discussing reading with friends and family, can also discourage certain types of reading, particularly for boys. Adolescents may separate enjoyment of and competence for reading outside of school from reading associated with the classroom.
Ecological: Move from elementary school to middle/junior high/intermediate school to high school.	Larger, more heterogeneous, more impersonal school structure; many teachers, departmentally organized; often tracked; performance oriented; focus on content area instruction.	Decreased motivation for reading as "school" reading; increased role for textbook /lecture/ regurgitation of content area information; expectation that students know how to learn from reading, grasp appropriate content-area reading behaviors; developing understanding of appropriate disciplinary discourse and practices.	Adolescents take textbooks as authoritative sources, prefer oral or digital information over print, focus on immediate task rather than building conceptual understanding. When solving problems related to their own interests, had skills and strategies for getting needing information from relevant texts. Making connections to text supported deeper comprehension, but requires accurate and relevant connections.

across this age group, with males more likely to report that they spent no time reading for pleasure. Such a decline could possibly be due to increased time spent socializing, competition from other activities, or an increase in school-related reading. Nippold et al. determined that overall reading was moderately popular as a leisure activity, with popular reading materials including magazines, novels, and comics.

Others have contributed to the literature on the frequency and character of adolescents' reading habits and interest, addressing topics such as reading of manga by Japanese adolescents (Allen & Ingulsrud, 2005) and out-of-school book discussion groups (Alvermann, Young, Green, & Wisenbaker, 1999), as well as the in- and out-of-school reading contexts, reading interests, and reading materials of adolescents in an urban midwestern community (Moje, Overby, Tysvaer, & Morris, 2008). In an investigation of possible gender effects, Smith and Wilhelm (2004) conducted interviews with 49 middle and high school males to explore their out-of-school literacy activities. These males did not see literacy as "feminine," but rather as "schoolish." Overall, Smith and Wilhelm concluded that "home literacies were characterized by the boys' use of texts that were appropriately challenging in ways that extended their competence in actual use; school literacy was characterized by the boys' encountering texts that they found too difficult for reasons that remained obscure to them" (p. 460).

Identity and Social Roles.   Within the reading research, there are studies that discuss the portrayal of adolescents within literature, as well as studies that document adolescents' engagement with such literary works (e.g., Neilsen, 2006). With regard to the portrayal of adolescents within literature, D'Angelo (1989) conducted a content analysis of prize-winning novels for young adults, chosen by committees for a variety of prestigious literary awards including the Newbery, *Hornbook*, and National Book Awards. D'Angelo argued that such award-winning books are highly likely to be among those studied in class or recommended to adolescent readers by teachers and librarians. She located ten novels set within the United States (1945–1985) that featured a female adolescent character. From this analysis, D'Angelo described a shifting portrayal of those female characters over time to female protagonists working at developing intellectual skills, accepting and using the body, and achieving emotional independence of parents and adults.

The research is also useful in understanding the reciprocal relation between adolescents' identity and social roles and their reading engagement, and cultural influence on both what is read and what perceptions of self are formed. In one interesting study, for example, Carnell (2005) investigated British adolescents' reading of *Full On* magazine. *Full On* was a magazine created primarily for 14- to 16-year-old boys as an intervention to encourage their reading and challenge negative aspects of "lad culture." Participants were surveyed, and data from interviews were also used. Interestingly, girls appeared to read the magazine as much as boys. Boys did report that they enjoyed reading about role models and how they overcame problems, and found some of the presented information (e.g., preparing for exams) interesting and useful. The young males who were surveyed and interviewed professed that reading in public (other than the *Full On* magazine) was a difficult social act for them to carry off. Finders (1996) also reported cultural norms in adolescents' reading of certain print materials. In this case, the author documented the communal reading of teen magazines as a cultural practice, an initiation rite, engaged in by the seventh-grade girls studied.

Marsh and Stolle (2006) focused their ethnographic lens on two adolescent girls' construction of their racial/gender identities during book club discussion. The girls differed in the degree to which they used the discussion space to actively explore and reconstruct their identities. Overall, Marsh and Stolle found that Carlie, a White seventh grader, was beginning to reconstruct her ideas of gender and gender stereotypes, building upon her reading of *The True Confessions of Charlotte Doyle*. In contrast, Elsa, a ninth-grade Mexican immigrant who was discussing *The*

House on Mango Street, used the discussion space to reconfirm her prior beliefs and ideas about race and racial identities. The authors surmised that both girls were somewhat naïve about the ability to choose one's racial or gender identity, seeing it as a matter of personal choice and not recognizing the power of social contexts and structures.

Discussion also proved to be a mechanism for exploring social identities in Vyas's (2004) qualitative study of seven Asian American high school students participating in an after-school literature club. Overall, the students' reading and discussion brought some issues of identity to consciousness and gave them exposure to alternative ways of dealing with situations, allowing them to try out the choices and decisions they were making about their own bicultural identities. Interestingly, the four males in the group remained more peripheral participants. Students discussed literature-revealed and personally salient issues related to their bicultural identities as they provided rationales for characters' intentions and exposed their personal beliefs by passing judgments. Even though Neilsen (2006) explored more mainstream cultural identities, her in-depth interviews of an 11th-grade male and female also showed that experiencing texts was an opportunity for these teens to project themselves into the portrayed roles and attributes and try them on for size.

Given researchers' strong reliance on more qualitative investigations, we find that understanding the role of reading in the development of adolescents' self-identities and social roles remains highly speculative. As logical as it seems that well-crafted or powerful narratives or biographies can allow adolescents, struggling with their sense of self and place in the world, to try on different characters and scenarios, more empirical and causal studies are clearly needed.

CHANGING SCHOOL CONTEXTS AND EDUCATIONAL EXPECTATIONS

As they move into adolescence, students typically move from elementary school to middle school, and then on to high school. With this movement comes radical change in school contexts and educational expectations. In contrast to elementary school, for example, the higher grade levels, particularly at the high school level, are larger, more impersonal, and more heterogeneous in terms of interactions with both teachers and peers (Entwisle, 1990; Wigfield, 2004; Wigfield et al., 2006). Instruction is typically departmentally organized, focused on content area learning, tracked by ability level, and may be geared toward high-stakes assessments (Wigfield, 2004). Students are expected to acquire content-specific disciplinary knowledge, often delivered by the transmission model via teacher and authoritative textbooks (Alvermann, 2002; Hynd & Stahl, 1998; O'Brien, Stewart, & Moje, 1995; Wigfield et al., 2006).

In terms of literacy and reading instruction, students typically do not have reading instruction after about the sixth grade. Language arts and English classes address comprehension of and response to literary texts, but reading in the content areas is often not addressed (Biancarosa & Snow, 2004; O'Brien et al., 1995; Vacca, 2002). Students are expected to develop the knowledge, skills, and interests that apply across domains, as well as the domain-specific knowledge, skills, and interests pertaining to each content area, to learn effectively from text (Alexander & Jetton, 2000, 2003; Biancarosa & Snow, 2004).

When we turned to the literature to see how changing school contexts and expectations have been investigated in relation to adolescents' reading behaviors, we found research in two broad areas: domain-specific or content-area reading, and student engagement or affect. These findings are summarized in Table 8.2.

Domain-Specific or Content-Area Reading.   Here we focus specifically on adolescents' reading practices in content-area classrooms; Moje (this volume) addressed the complementary issue of how teachers use texts in such classrooms. Chall (1983) offered one of the earliest developmental characterizations of reading, articulating various stages framed by growing content area demands. For example, in Stage 4 of Chall's model, accommodation "takes place when the reading tasks, particularly those in school, cover a multiplicity of knowledge—facts, ideas, opinions, views—with discussions and written assignments designed to force the student to grapple with that multiplicity. Most content areas in the secondary school lend themselves well to providing the needed challenge and practice…" (pp. 50–51). Even though more recent models have offered a more integrated and complex portrayal of reading development, principled domain knowledge has remained a critical facet of emerging competence or expertise (Alexander, 2003).

Research by Moje et al. (2004) and others (Behrman, 2003; Paxton, 2002; Wineburg, 1991) adds credence to the importance of domain-related reading during the adolescent period. For example, Moje and Dillon (2006) used two female high school students from a chemistry class and a biology class as informants in a study of the literacy environments within content areas. In biology, the targeted adolescent was given study guides and questions and was expected to skim text to find the answers, which would then support project completion. That project was undertaken in a small group in which the girl often did the reading, and the boys did the hands-on work. In chemistry, the target adolescent read from a textbook and concentrated on organizational skills with emphasis on accuracy, precision, and organization. In this environment, the textbook and teacher were seen as authoritative sources of knowledge, with little room for questioning or confusion, or for student activity and engagement. Overall, the findings raised questions about how reading and writing should ideally be positioned in content-area classes.

Paxton's research (1997, 2002) also brought attention to the role of texts and reading within high school classes. One key finding from Paxton's studies concerned the consequences of viewing school texts as authorless or anonymous constructions. When historical text was read with a visible author, students tended to show greater engagement and to give personal thought to the information. Students reading the visible author text also engaged in more dialogue with the text authors, tended to make judgments about those authors and their motives, and thought more about history than those reading the anonymous versions. In the 2002 study, adolescents with the visible author texts also wrote longer essays, showed greater personal agency, and exhibited more awareness of audience than those with the anonymous texts.

A broader perspective on texts and learning from texts in the content-area classroom motivated the study by Moje et al. (2004) of the varied funds of knowledge that students bring to content-area discourse in science classrooms. In this research, the students, ages 12 to 15, were from predominantly Latino communities and the data involved observations and interviews with students, teachers, community leaders, and parents. As we have seen in other studies, Moje et al. reported that these adolescents preferred to read magazines, with young women frequently choosing fan magazines, while the young men reported reading magazines about cars. Echoing the findings of Carnell's (2005) study of British youth, Moje et al. noted that the males, in contrast to females, did not make their magazine reading a public activity. Further, the adolescents did consult print news media for specific information and appeared to be competent at identifying and using appropriate texts to get the information they needed to fulfill self-generated goals.

Engagement and Affect.   Two expanding areas of research that would seem particularly fruitful for the study of adolescent readers are learner engagement or involvement and the relation between cognition and emotion. Waning engagement in reading beginning with the middle school years has been well documented (Wigfield, 2004), and adolescents' increased negative emotions and emotionality, likely associated with hormonal changes, have long been noted (Brooks-Gunn & Reiter, 1990). To date, however, much of the focus on engagement has been within the elementary or early middle school grades and has not specifically targeted adolescents or high school classrooms (e.g., the CORI program of research of Guthrie et al., 2004). Nonetheless, the research on adolescents does offer some insights into the benefits of enticing or welcoming these sometimes-reluctant participants to get engaged in classroom-based literacy activities (e.g., Reed & Schallert, 1993; Turner et al., 1998).

For example, Spires and Donley (1998) examined the effects of increasing engagement with informational text by encouraging their ninth-grade participants to make personal connections to the text. Students either activated their personal knowledge or experience or attempted to discern the main idea of the given social studies text. In Study 1, the treatment group outperformed controls on application-level questions but not literal-level ones. In a second study, both the groups focused on personal knowledge and those seeking the main idea performed higher on application-level questions and had more positive attitudes toward reading than controls. Spires and Donley concluded that making personal connections during reading fostered high-level thinking about informational texts, and that activating students' personal knowledge was more motivating than concentrating on the main idea. In this study, going beyond the text with their personal thoughts was not only appropriate but also highly valued, and privileged the adolescents' personal knowledge within the instructional context. Of course, as Pressley (2004) would caution, personal knowledge activation is only helpful when there is relevant *and* accurate knowledge to relate to the text or task at hand.

Ainley, Corrigan, and Richardson (2005) explored the role of emotions in how adolescents read. They investigated 12- to 15-year-olds' reading of popular-culture and popular-science texts in terms of the adolescents' emotional responses and persistence. In this study, adolescents read texts about dolphins, Formula 1 racing, body image, and U2 in Africa. The texts were read in sections on computer. At the end of each section, participants chose to read on or quit, and selected an icon expressing an affective response and its intensity at that point. Patterns of persistence indicated that texts were not able to maintain and hold the students' attention sufficiently for many of them to read the entire text, even though young adolescents frequently consume materials and sources of that type. The researchers found that students' reported individual interest in the broader domain significantly influenced the decision to persist. Although the topic itself played a role in triggering some interest, that situational interest was not necessarily sustained across the entire text.

Pitcher et al. (2007) also assessed adolescents' motivation to read with a version of the Motivation to Read Profile revised to be suitable for that population. Based on data from a diverse sample, the authors determined that females valued reading more than males did, and their valuing of reading increased with grade. In contrast, interest in and valuing of reading for males declined during adolescence. There were no significant differences on reading self-concept ascertained for grade, gender, or ethnicity. Pitcher et al. found that participants' self-concepts as readers and how much they valued reading was associated with their general enjoyment of reading and specific reading choices.

Relevant to our prior discussion, Pitcher et al. (2007) also determined from subsequent interviews that these adolescents' definitions of reading did not always include reading magazines, e-mail, games, or such non-academic, alternative texts, a finding echoed by Moje et al. (2008). Moreover, reading interests often did not seem to include any form of academic reading, but suggested rather the importance of personal connections to a topic and pursuit of individual interests, again in line with the findings of Moje et al. (2008). As seen also by Chandler (1999), Pitcher et al. (2007) reported that friends and family members influenced adolescents' reading choices, although choices also reflected books discussed in class or recommended by other students in literature circles. Respondents also tended to place high value on being allowed to choose what to read for school.

LESSONS LEARNED

How does this developmental sojourn into the world of the adolescent provide a roadmap that might guide future educational research and instructional practice? There are innumerable lessons derivable from what is known about the biophysiological, cognitive, psychosocial, and ecological aspects of this unique period of human development. Here we wish to highlight four empirically grounded conclusions and consider their implications for reading.

The Biophysiological Bases of the Literacy Experience Cannot Be Overlooked

Inundated with discussions of high-stakes assessment, reading standards, or curricular innovations, reading researchers and practitioners can sometimes forget that adolescents face dramatic biological and physiological changes in their transition into adulthood. Those changes can relate directly to what adolescents choose to read, why they read, and how they read, as well as how they apply what is learned through their encounters with text. Thus, it would seem appropriate for those conceptualizing reading research or proposing literacy interventions to weigh the viability of such designs and interventions in terms of what is known about this particular population. For instance, does developmental evidence support a researcher's decision to study metacognition or self-regulation among 12-year-old readers, or justify a perception that 14-year-olds are capable of judging the validity of authors' arguments in persuasive discourse? It is common to encounter research studies in which the target population is identified in terms of age, gender, ethnicity, and general reading abilities or disabilities. What is often lacking, however, is a rationale for why this particular age of reader was suitably chosen for this particular exploration or intervention. Not only should such a justification be present, but it should also embrace the biological and physical attributes of the adolescent reader.

Expanded Visions of Adolescence Should be Mirrored in Expanded Views of "Struggling" Adolescent Readers

To date, the pillars of reading that have defined emergent literacy have largely framed the concept of the struggling adolescent reader (Cassidy & Cassidy, 2007). Thus, those who have not mastered the graphophonemic foundations of English or whose reading is halting or unexpressive are among those perceived as endangered readers. However, as this brief developmental portrait has suggested, adolescents face literacy challenges not confined by those often-discussed literacy pillars (Alexander, 2006; Alvermann, 2002). Those who do not have basic conceptual knowledge in history, mathematics, science, or other academic domains; those who do not have the requisite strategies to cope with the increasingly abstract concepts or complex content; those whose self-concept as a reader is based on perceptions of reading as schoolish; and those who have no heart to read or the will to engage—all belong to the ranks of the struggling adolescent reader.

Limited or Narrowly Conceived Literacy Programs or Interventions May Exacerbate Rather than Ameliorate Reading Problems for Adolescents

From the broad developmental literature and the pertinent literacy studies, it becomes apparent that experiences are foundational to adolescents' growth as readers. The linguistic predispositions that are part of our biophysical makeup (e.g., ability to remember) are elaborated or enriched through formal and informal learning opportunities. Given the rises in linguistic abstraction, conceptual load, and domain-specific applications that routinely confront adolescent readers, many direct literacy experiences would benefit this population. Yet, even as the need for such relevant instruction grows—instruction that could be embedded in the subject-matter domains in which much of school reading occurs—its presence significantly dwindles. Without a reconceptualization of reading as a lifelong learning endeavor that requires on-going and continual nurturance, there is a good chance that essential experiential opportunities will be missed, and along with them any developmental augmentations that might be realized.

Keys to Reading Motivation for Adolescents Might be Found in Nontraditional or Alternative Texts Processed in Out-of-School Settings

We repeatedly encountered studies that showed that adolescents may well live literate lives if we are willing and able to conceptualize reading and texts liberally. For instance, when the materials are magazines or other forms of popular press, or when the topics are about adolescents and the problems they face or the interests they possess, voluntary print engagement has been documented (e.g., Moje et al., 2008; Pitcher et al., 2007). It is also evident that adolescents are comfortable in the world of technology, where browsing the Internet, chatting on line, or text messaging are commonplace print-based activities. As Moje (2002) and others have suggested, adolescents' existing literacy experiences and capabilities, along with their out-of-school interests and hobbies, could be invaluable conduits to more traditional, schooled reading and associated competencies.

We acknowledge that this idea of building bridges between individuals' existing talents and interests and new or unrealized processes is nothing new. The writings of Dewey (1900/1990) and James (1899/1992) are replete with admonitions to use individuals' interest and experiences as the starting point for meaningful learning. Yet, it seems that these are suggestions or admonitions whose time has come again.

In addition to a starting point, an ending point or goal is also essential. For adolescents to take advantage of the bountiful opportunities reading offers, they—and we—must have a clear and convincing vision of their real possibilities as readers.

REFERENCES

Ainley, M., Corrigan, M., & Richardson, N. (2005). Students, tasks, and emotions: Identifying the contribution of emotions to students' reading of popular culture and popular science texts. *Learning and Instruction, 15*, 433–447.

Alexander, P. A. (2003). The development of expertise: The journey from acclimation to proficiency. *Educational Researcher, 32*(8), 10–14.

Alexander, P. A. (2006). The path to competence: A lifespan developmental perspective on reading. *Journal of Literacy Research, 37*, 413–436.

Alexander, P. A., & Fox, E. (2004). A historical perspective on reading research and practice. In R. B. Ruddell & N. Unrau (Eds.), *Theoretical models and processes of reading* (5th ed., pp. 33–68). Newark, DE: International Reading Association.

Alexander, P. A., & Jetton, T. L. (2000). Learning from text: A multidimensional and developmental perspective. In M. L. Kamil, P. B. Mosenthal, P. D. Pearson, & R. Barr (Eds.), *Handbook of reading research* (Vol. III, pp. 285–310). Mahwah, NJ: Erlbaum.

Alexander, P. A., & Jetton, T. L. (2003). Learning from traditional and alternative texts: New conceptualization for an information age. In A. Graesser, M. Gernsbacher, & S. Goldman (Eds.), *Handbook of discourse processes* (pp. 199–241). Mahwah, NJ: Erlbaum.

Allen, K., & Ingulsrud, J. E. (2005). Reading manga: Patterns of personal literacies among adolescents. *Language and Education, 19*, 265–280.

Alvermann, D. E. (2002). Effective literacy instruction for adolescents. *Journal of Literacy Research, 34*, 189–202.

Alvermann, D. E., & Moore, D. W. (1991). Secondary school reading. In R. Barr, M. L. Kamil, P. B.

Mosenthal, & P. D. Pearson (Eds.), *Handbook of reading research* (Vol. II, pp. 951–983). White Plains, NY: Longman.

Alvermann, D. E., Young, J. P., Green, C., & Wisenbaker, J. M. (1999). Adolescents' perceptions and negotiations of literacy practices in after-school read and talk clubs. *American Educational Research Journal, 36*, 221–264.

Anderson, T. H., & Armbruster, B. B. (1984). Studying. In P. D. Pearson, R. Barr, M. L. Kamil, & P. Mosenthal (Eds.), *Handbook of reading research* (Vol. I, pp. 657–679). White Plains, NY: Longman.

Baker, L. (2002). Metacognition in comprehension instruction. In C. C. Block & M. Pressley (Eds.), *Comprehension instruction: Research-based best practices* (pp. 77–95). New York, NY: Guilford Press.

Barr, R., Kamil, M. L., Mosenthal, P. B., & Pearson, P. D. (1991). *Handbook of reading research* (Vol. II). White Plains, NY: Longman.

Bean, T. W. (2000). Reading in the content areas: Social constructivist dimensions. In M. L. Kamil, P. B. Mosenthal, P. D. Pearson, & R. Barr (Eds.), *Handbook of reading research* (Vol. III, pp. 629–644). Mahwah, NJ: Erlbaum.

Behrman, E. H. (2003). Reconciling content literacy with adolescent literacy: Expanding literacy opportunities in a community-focused biology class. *Reading Research and Instruction, 43*, 1–30.

Berninger, V. W., & Corina, D. (1998). Making cognitive neuroscience educationally relevant: Creating bidirectional collaborations between educational psychology and cognitive neuroscience. *Educational Psychology Review, 10*, 343–354.

Berninger, V. W., & Richards, T. L. (2002). *Brain literacy for educators and psychologists*. San Diego, CA: Academic Press.

Biancarosa, G., & Snow, C. E. (2004). *Reading next-A vision for action and research in middle and high school literacy: A report from Carnegie Corporation of New York*. Washington, DC: Alliance for Excellent Education.

Blakemore, S., & Choudhury, S. (2006). Development of the adolescent brain: Implications for executive function and social cognition. *Journal of Child Psychology and Psychiatry, 47*, 296–312.

Botta, R. A. (2003). For your health? The relationship between magazine reading and adolescents' body image and eating disturbances. *Sex Roles, 48,* 389–399.

Brooks-Gunn, J., & Reiter, E. O. (1990). The role of pubertal processes. In S. S. Feldman & G. R. Elliott (Eds.), *At the threshold: The developing adolescent* (pp. 16–53). Cambridge, MA: Harvard University Press.

Brown, B. B. (1990). Peer groups and peer cultures. In S. S. Feldman & G. R. Elliott (Eds.), *At the threshold: The developing adolescent* (pp. 171–196). Cambridge, MA: Harvard University Press.

Cain, K. (2006). Children's reading comprehension: The role of working memory in normal and impaired development. In S. J. Pickering (Ed.), *Working memory and education* (pp. 61–91). San Diego, CA: Academic Press.

Carnell, E. (2005). Boys and their reading: Conceptions of young people about the success of the "Full On" magazine. *The Curriculum Journal, 16*, 363–389.

Carson, N. J., Rodriguez, D., & Audrain-McGovern, J. (2005). Investigation of mechanisms linking media exposure to smoking in high school students. *Preventive Medicine, 41*, 511–520.

Cassidy, J., & Cassidy, D. (2007). What's hot, what's not for 2007. *Reading Today, 24*(4), 1, 10–12.

Cassidy, J., Garrett, S. D., & Barrera, E. S. (2006). What's hot in adolescent literacy 1997–2006. *Journal of Adolescent & Adult Literacy, 50*, 30–36.

Chall, J. (1983). *Stages of reading development*. New York, NY: McGraw-Hill.

Chambliss, M. J. (1995). Text cues and strategies successful readers use to construct the gist of lengthy written arguments. *Reading Research Quarterly, 30*, 778–807.

Chandler, K. (1999). Reading relationships: Parents, adolescents, and popular fiction by Stephen King. *Journal of Adolescent & Adult Literacy, 43*, 228–239.

Chapman, J. (1983). *Reading development and cohesion*. London, England: Heinemann Educational Books.

D'Angelo, D. A. (1989). Developmental tasks in literature for adolescents: Has the adolescent female protagonist changed? *Child Study Journal, 19*, 219–237.

Dewey, J. (1990). *The school and society*. Chicago, IL: The University of Chicago Press. (Original work published 1900)

Elliott, G. R., & Feldman, S. S. (1990). Capturing the adolescent experience. In S. S. Feldman & G. R. Elliott (Eds.), *At the threshold: The developing adolescent* (pp. 1–13). Cambridge, MA: Harvard University Press.

Erikson, E. K. (1980). *Identity and the life cycle.* New York, NY: W. W. Norton. (Original work published 1959)

Entwisle, D. R. (1990). Schools and the adolescent. In S. S. Feldman & G. R. Elliott (Eds.), *At the threshold: The developing adolescent* (pp. 197–224). Cambridge, MA: Harvard University Press.

Evans, J. J., Floyd, R. G., McGrew, K. S., & Leforgee, M. H. (2001). The relations among measures of Cattell-Horn-Carroll (CHC) cognitive abilities and reading achievement during childhood and adolescence. *School Psychology Review, 31,* 246–262.

Finders, M. J. (1996). Queens and teen zines: Early adolescent females reading their way toward adulthood. *Anthropology & Education Quarterly, 27,* 71–89.

Franzak, J. A. (2006). *Zoom:* A review of the literature on marginalized adolescent readers, literacy theory, and policy implications. *Review of Educational Research, 76,* 209–248.

Garner, R. (1987). *Metacognition and reading comprehension.* Westport, CT: Ablex.

Giedd, J. N., Bluementhal, J., Jeffries, N. O., Castellanos, F. X., Liu, H., Zijdenbos, A., et al. (1999). Brain development during childhood and adolescence: A longitudinal MRI study. *Nature Neuroscience, 2,* 861–863.

Goldman, S. R., & Rakestraw, J. A. (2000). Structural aspects of constructing meaning from text. In M. L. Kamil, P. B. Mosenthal, P. D. Pearson, & R. Barr (Eds.), *Handbook of reading research* (Vol. III, pp. 311–335). Mahwah, NJ: Erlbaum.

Grabe, M., Antes, J., Kahn, H., & Kristjanson, A. (1991). Adult and adolescent readers' comprehension monitoring performance: An investigation of monitoring accuracy and related eye movements. *Contemporary Educational Psychology, 16,* 45–60.

Graesser, A. C., Millis, K. K., & Zwaan, R. A. (1997). Discourse comprehension. *Annual Review of Psychology, 48,* 163–189.

Guthrie, J. T., & Greaney, V. (1991). Literacy acts. In R. Barr, M. L. Kamil, P. B. Mosenthal, & P. D. Pearson (Eds.), *Handbook of reading research* (Vol. II, pp. 68–96). White Plains, NY: Longman.

Guthrie, J. T., Wigfield, A., Barbosa, P., Perencevich, K. C., Taboada, A., Davis, M. H., Scafiddi, N. T., & Tonks, S. (2004). Increasing reading comprehension and engagement through Concept-Oriented Reading Instruction. *Journal of Educational Psychology, 96,* 403–423.

Hacker, D. J. (1997). Comprehension monitoring of written discourse across early-to-middle adolescence. *Reading and Writing: An Interdisciplinary Journal, 9,* 207–240.

Hacker, D. J. (2004). Self-regulated comprehension during normal reading. In R. B. Ruddell & N. Unrau (Eds.), *Theoretical models and processes of reading* (5th ed., pp. 755–779). Newark, DE: International Reading Association.

Harter, S. (1990). Self and identity development. In S. S. Feldman & G. R. Elliott (Eds.), *At the threshold: The developing adolescent* (pp. 352–387). Cambridge, MA: Harvard University Press.

Hartman, D. K. (1995). Eight readers reading: The intertextual links of proficient readers reading multiple passages. *Reading Research Quarterly, 30,* 520–561.

Hegarty, M., Carpenter, P. A., & Just, M. A. (1991). Diagrams in the comprehension of scientific text. In R. Barr, M. L. Kamil, P. B. Mosenthal, & P. D. Pearson (Eds.), *Handbook of reading research* (Vol. II, pp. 641–668). White Plains, NY: Longman.

Hidi, S., & Baird, W. (1986). Interestingness: A neglected variable in discourse processing. *Cognitive Science, 10*(2), 179–194.

Holsgrove, J. V., & Garton, A. F. (2006). Phonological and syntactic processing and the role of working memory in reading comprehension among secondary students. *Australian Journal of Psychology, 58,* 111–118.

Hopper, R. (2005). What are teenagers reading? Adolescent fiction reading habits and reading choices. *Literacy, 39,* 113–120.

Horowitz, R. (1994) Adolescent beliefs about oral and written language. In R. Garner & P. Alexander (Eds.), *Beliefs about text and instruction with text* (pp. 1–24). Hillsdale, NJ: Erlbaum.

Hynd, C. R., & Stahl, S. A. (1998). What do we mean by knowledge and learning? In C. R. Hynd (Ed.), *Learning from text across conceptual domains* (pp. 15–44). Mahwah, NJ: Erlbaum.

Irwin, N. (2003). Personal constructs and the enhancement of adolescent engagement in reading. *Support for Learning, 18*, 29–34.

James, W. (1992). Talks to teachers on psychology and to students on some of life's ideals. In W. James, *Writings 1878–1899* (pp. 705–887). New York, NY: The Library of America. (Original work published 1899)

Kaplan, E. B., & Cole, L. (2003). "I want to read stuff on boys": White, Latina, and black girls reading *Seventeen* magazine and encountering adolescence. *Adolescence, 38*, 141–159.

Keating, D. P. (1990). Adolescent thinking. In S. S. Feldman & G. R. Elliott (Eds.), *At the threshold: The developing adolescent* (pp. 54–89). Cambridge, MA: Harvard University Press.

Kintsch, W. & Rawson, K. A. (2005). Comprehension. In M. J. Snowling & C. Hulme (Eds.), *The science of reading: A handbook* (pp. 209–226). Oxford, England: Blackwell Publishing.

Kletzien, S. B. (1992). Proficient and less proficient comprehenders' strategy use for different top-level structures. *Journal of Reading Behavior, 24*, 191–215.

Lave, J., & Wenger, E. (1991). *Situated learning: Legitimate peripheral participation.* Cambridge, England: Cambridge University Press.

Luna, B., Thulborn, K. R., Munoz, D. P., Merriam, E. P., Garver, K. E., Minshew, N. J., Keshavan, M. S., Genovese, C. R., Eddy, W. F., & Sweeney, J. A. (2001). Maturation of widely distributed brain function subserves cognitive development. *NeuroImage, 13*, 786–793.

Marsh, J. P., & Stolle, E. P. (2006). Re/constructing identities: A tale of two adolescents. In D. E. Alvermann, K. A. Hinchman, D. W. Moore, S. F. Phelps, & D. R. Waff (Eds.), *Reconceptualizing the literacies in adolescents' lives* (2nd ed., pp. 47–63). Mahwah, NJ: Erlbaum.

Mertz, M. P. (1975). Understanding the adolescent reader. *Theory into Practice, 14*, 179–185.

Moje, E. B. (2002). Re-framing adolescent literacy research for new times: Studying youth as a resource. *Reading Research and Instruction, 41*, 211–228.

Moje, E. B., Ciechanowski, K. M., Kramer, K., Ellis, L., Carrillo, R., & Collazo, T. (2004). Working toward third space in content area literacy: An examination of everyday funds of knowledge and Discourse. *Reading Research Quarterly, 39*, 38–70.

Moje, E. B., & Dillon, D. R. (2006). Adolescent identities as demanded by science classroom discourse communities. In D. E. Alvermann, K. A. Hinchman, D. W. Moore, S. F. Phelps, & D. R. Waff (Eds.), *Reconceptualizing the literacies in adolescents' lives* (2nd ed., pp. 85–106). Mahwah, NJ: Erlbaum.

Moje, E. B., Overby, M., Tysvaer, N., & Morris, K. (2008). The complex world of adolescent literacy: Myths, motivations, and mysteries. *Harvard Education Review, 78*, 107–154.

Moore, P. J., & Scevak, J. J. (1997). Learning from texts and visual aids: A developmental perspective. *Journal of Research in Reading, 20*, 205–223.

Neilsen, L. (2006). Playing for real: Texts and the performance of identity. In D. E. Alvermann, K. A. Hinchman, D. W. Moore, S. F. Phelps, & D. R. Waff (Eds.), *Reconceptualizing the literacies in adolescents' lives* (2nd ed., pp. 5–27). Mahwah, NJ: Erlbaum.

Nippold, M. A., Duthie, J. K., & Larsen, J. (2005). Literacy as a leisure activity: Free-time preferences of older children and young adolescents. *Language, Science, and Hearing Services in Schools, 36*, 93–102.

Nippold, M. A., & Martin, S. T. (1989). Idiom interpretation in isolation versus context: A developmental study with adolescents. *Journal of Speech & Hearing Research, 32*, 59–66.

Nippold, M. A., Martin, S. A., & Erskine, B. J. (1988). Proverb comprehension in context: A developmental study with children and adolescents. *Journal of Speech & Hearing Research, 31*, 19–28.

Nippold, M. A., Schwartz, I. E., & Undlin, R. A. (1992). Use and understanding of adverbial conjuncts: A developmental study of adolescents and young adults. *Journal of Speech & Hearing Research, 35*, 108–118.

Nist, S. L., & Simpson, M. L. (2000). College studying. In M. L. Kamil, P. B. Mosenthal, P. D. Pearson, & R. Barr (Eds.), *Handbook of reading research* (Vol. III, pp. 645–666). Mahwah, NJ: Erlbaum.

Oberauer, K., Weidenfeld, A., & Hörnig, R. (2006). Working memory capacity and the construction of spatial mental models in comprehension and deductive reasoning. *Quarterly Journal of Experimental Psychology, 59*, 426–447.

O'Brien, D. G., Stewart, R. A., & Moje, E. B. (1995). Why content literacy is difficult to infuse into the secondary school: Complexities of curriculum, pedagogy, and school culture. *Reading Research Quarterly, 30*, 442–463.

Ohlhausen, M. M., & Roller, C. M. (1988). The operation of text structure and content schemata in isolation and in interaction. *Reading Research Quarterly, 23,* 70–88.

Paxton, R. J. (1997). "Someone with a life wrote it": The effects of a visible author on high school history students. *Journal of Educational Psychology, 89,* 235–250.

Paxton, R. J. (2002). The influence of author visibility on high school students solving a historical problem. *Cognition and Instruction, 20,* 197–248.

Pearson, P. D., Barr, R., Kamil, M. L., & Mosenthal, P. (1984). *Handbook of reading research* (Vol. I). White Plains, NY: Longman.

Perry, N. E., Turner, J. C., & Meyer, D. K. (2006). Classrooms as contexts for motivating learning. In P. A. Alexander & P. H. Winne (Eds.), *Handbook of educational psychology* (2nd ed., pp. 327–348). Mahwah, NJ: Erlbaum.

Phelps, S. (2005). *Ten years of research on adolescent literacy, 1994–2004: A review* (Report for Institute of Education Sciences). Naperville, IL: Learning Point Associates.

Piaget, J. (1967). The mental development of the child. In *Six psychological studies* (A. Tenzer, Trans.), pp. 3–73. New York, NY: Random House. (Original work published 1964)

Pitcher, S. M., Albright, L. K., DeLaney, C. J., Walker, N. T., Seunarinesingh, K., Mogge, S., et al. (2007). Assessing adolescents' motivation to read. *Journal of Adolescent & Adult Literacy, 50,* 378–396.

Pressley, M. (2004). The need for research on secondary literacy education. In T. L. Jetton & J. A. Dole (Eds.), *Adolescent literacy research and practice* (pp. 415–432). New York, NY: The Guilford Press.

Pressley, M., & Afflerbach, P. (1995). *Verbal protocols of reading.* Hillsdale, NJ: Erlbaum.

Reed, J. H., & Schallert, D. L. (1993). The nature of involvement in academic discourse tasks. *Journal of Educational Psychology, 85,* 253–266.

Roberts, T. A. (1989). Developmental aspects of activating voluntary and involuntary memory processes during reading. *Contemporary Educational Psychology, 14,* 1–11.

Rogoff, B. (2000). *Culture and development.* New York, NY: Oxford University Press.

Santrock, J. W. (1999). *Life-span development* (7th ed.). New York, NY: McGraw-Hill.

Smith, M., & Wilhelm, J. D. (2004). "I just like being good at it": The importance of competence in the literate lives of young men. *Journal of Adolescent & Adult Literacy, 47,* 454–461.

Spires, H. A., & Donley, J. (1998). Prior knowledge activation: Inducing engagement with informational texts. *Journal of Educational Psychology, 90,* 249–260.

Snow, C. E., & Biancarosa, G. (2003). *Adolescent literacy and the achievement gap: What do we know and where do we go from here?* (Adolescent Literacy Funders Meeting Report). New York, NY: Carnegie Corporation.

Steinberg, L. (1990). Autonomy, conflict, and harmony in the family relationship. In S. S. Feldman & G. R. Elliott (Eds.), *At the threshold: The developing adolescent* (pp. 255–276). Cambridge, MA: Harvard University Press.

Thomsen, S. R., Weber, M. W., & Brown, L. B. (2002). The relationship between reading beauty and fashion magazines and the use of pathogenic dieting methods among adolescent females. *Adolescence, 37,* 1–18.

Tiggemann, M. (2006). The role of media exposure in adolescent girls' body dissatisfaction and drive for thinness: Prospective results. *Journal of Social and Clinical Psychology, 25,* 523–541.

Turner, J. C., Meyer, D. K, Cox, K. E., Logan, C., DiCintio, M., & Thomas, C. T. (1998). Creating contexts for involvement in mathematics. *Journal of Educational Psychology, 90,* 730–745.

U.S. Department of Education. (2006a). *Adolescent Literacy Research Network.* Retrieved June 18, 2007, from http://www.ed.gov/about/offices/list/ovae/pi/hs/adollit.html

U.S. Department of Education. (2006b). *Striving Readers.* Retrieved June 18, 2007, from http://www.ed.gov/programs/strivingreaders/index.html

Utter, J., Neumark-Sztainer, D., Wall, M., & Story, M. (2003). Reading magazine articles about dieting and associated weight control behaviors among adolescents. *Journal of Adolescent Health, 32,* 78–82.

Vacca, R. T. (2002). From efficient decoders to strategic readers. *Educational Leadership, 60,* 6–11.

van den Broek, P., Lynch, J. S., Naslund, J., Ievers-Landis, C. E., & Verduin, K. (2003). The development of comprehension of main ideas in narratives: Evidence from the selection of titles. *Journal of Educational Psychology, 95,* 707–718.

Vyas, S. (2004). Exploring bicultural identities of Asian high school students through the analytic window of a literature club. *Journal of Adolescent & Adult Literacy, 48,* 12–23.

Vygotsky, L. S. (1986). *Thought and language.* (A. Kozulin, Trans.). Cambridge, MA: MIT Press. (Original work published in 1934)

Wade, S. E., & Moje, E. B. (2000). The role of text in classroom learning. In M. L. Kamil, P. B. Mosenthal, P. D. Pearson, & R. Barr (Eds.), *Handbook of reading research* (Vol. III, pp. 609–627). Mahwah, NJ: Erlbaum.

Weaver, C. A., & Kintsch, W. (1991). Expository text. In R. Barr, M. L. Kamil, P. B. Mosenthal, & P. D. Pearson (Eds.), *Handbook of reading research* (Vol. II, pp. 230–245). White Plains, NY: Longman.

Wentzel, K. R. (2000). What is it that I'm trying to achieve? Classroom goals from a content perspective. *Contemporary Educational Psychology, 25,* 105–115.

Wigfield, A. (2004). Motivation for reading during the early adolescent and adolescent years. In D. S. Strickland & D. E. Alvermann (Eds.), *Bridging the literacy achievement gap Grades 4–12* (pp. 56–69). New York, NY: Teachers College Press.

Wigfield, A., Byrnes, J. P., & Eccles, J. S. (2006). Development during early and middle adolescence. In P. A. Alexander & P. H. Winne (Eds.), *Handbook of educational psychology* (2nd ed., pp. 87–113). Mahwah, NJ: Erlbaum.

Wineburg, S. S. (1991). Historical problem solving: A study of the cognitive processes used in the evaluation of documentary and pictorial evidence. *Journal of Educational Psychology, 83,* 73–87.

Yurgelun-Todd, D. (2007). Emotional and cognitive changes during adolescence. *Current Opinion in Neurobiology, 17,* 251–257.

9   Adult Literacy (Age 18 and Beyond)

Greg Brooks
University of Sheffield, UK

This chapter summarizes some of the research on adult literacy, and covers: the scale of the problem; a sketch of the background information and theory needed to contextualize the topic; the amount of progress adult literacy learners make; factors that appear to affect their progress (or not), especially confidence-building and computer-assisted instruction; the rigor or otherwise of the research designs used; what works for adult basic skills in the workplace; how long it takes adult learners to achieve educationally significant progress; and whether their progress also brings financial benefit. Along the way some historical information is presented, and finally some implications are drawn for theory, policy, practice, and research.

First, however, since an entire further handbook could be written on this topic, some limits on the scope of this chapter should be mentioned: (a) 'Literacy' is defined as 'the ability to read and write', so that coverage is not extended to oracy (listening and speaking skills), numeracy (except where evidence on literacy and numeracy is bundled together in the literature), or metaphorical collocations such as emotional, financial, visual, etc., literacy—but it should immediately be pointed out that most of the literacy evidence is for reading and there is precious little for writing; (b) Topics already covered for the literacy of children and which do not materially differ for adults have been omitted; (c) The minute literature on literacy for adults with learning disabilities (see, e.g., Corley & Taymans, 2002) and the defective literature on developmental dyslexia in adults (see the critique in Rice with Brooks, 2004) are not addressed; (d) Nor are the specialized literatures on literacy and health, formative and summative assessment, and the preparation of adult literacy teachers; (e) Only research from predominantly English-speaking countries is used—in fact mainly from Britain and the United States—and only passing reference is made to other countries, especially less developed ones; (f) Family literacy, though its adult provision is obviously relevant, is covered in a separate chapter in this volume. However, some evidence on instruction in English as a second language (ESL, called ESOL, English for speakers of other languages, in Britain) is included; (g) Most attention is given to research-based findings on the *teaching* of literacy to adults.

THE SCALE OF THE PROBLEM

As Vincent (2000) shows, by about 1900 the most industrialized countries in Europe (and this is also true of such countries elsewhere) had achieved mass literacy, in the sense that almost all adults could read and write, at least to a basic level—so why, just over a century later, is adult literacy such a concern for governments in so many developed countries? During both world wars, the British and US governments were dismayed to discover how many men in their armed forces had poor literacy. Sticht (2002) documents efforts by the US armed forces over a long period to remedy this, and Burt (1945), in Britain, similarly reported attempts to teach 'illiterate men' in the British army. It seems to have been assumed even then for many years that decades of universal education had eliminated the problem in the civilian population, leaving only the army and prisons to tackle their clients' problems—yet there must have been sufficient concern in the USA to warrant the setting up of the current Adult Education and Literacy System in 1964, and in Britain a survey in 1972 claimed that 2 million adults (out of a population of about 53 million) needed help with literacy (Haviland, 1973).

Earlier estimates of adult literacy levels had been based on experts' opinions or (in Britain) on the proportion of brides and grooms who signed their names on their wedding certificates (as opposed to marking a mark), so there was clearly a need for more sophisticated and objective evidence. Apart from a stray survey of the reading abilities of 26-year-olds in Britain in 1972 (Rodgers, 1986), direct performance surveys of the actual literacy abilities of adults may be said to begin with the Young Adult Literacy Survey of 1985 and National Adult Literacy Survey (NALS; Kirsch, Jungeblut, Jenkins, & Kolstad, 1993) of 1992 in the USA, the survey of 'Literacy Skills Used in Daily Activities' in Canada in 1989, and two surveys of reading attainment covering various age groups carried out in Britain in 1991–94.

These culminated in the International Adult Literacy Survey (IALS) of 1994–98. This was the first attempt to estimate levels of literacy internationally using tests which were intended to be equivalent across languages and cultures (UNESCO figures for literacy rates in various member states from 1970 onwards were based on experts' and administrators' estimates). Participants were asked to tackle three out of seven blocks of tasks which covered three domains of literacy: prose (continuous text, e.g. newspaper articles), document (non-continuous text, e.g. graphs, timetables), and quantitative (arithmetical problems embedded in text, this domain being a proxy for numeracy). Items were ranked on a 0–500 scale depending on the success of participants in getting them right, and each participant was attributed the score of the item they had an 80% chance of getting right, so that their scores were ranked on the same scale. From examination of the data, items and participants were classified into five levels; the criteria for each level in prose and document literacy are shown in Table 9.1, and those for quantitative literacy in Table 9.2.

IALS Level 2 (called Level 1 in Britain) is generally considered to be the threshold of functional literacy and numeracy, so that adults with only Level 1 (UK Entry level) skills may be thought to have difficulty in meeting the literacy and numeracy demands of everyday life, whether as citizens, employees, family members or private individuals. Indeed the Level 1 descriptions in Tables 9.1 and 9.2 betoken such basic skills that people at that level would indeed struggle with many demands.

Australia, Britain, Canada, Ireland, New Zealand and the USA were the (mainly) English-speaking countries among the 23 which took part in IALS, and the governments of all six were dismayed at their populations' poor showing. The proportions of adults with scores in Level 1 were mainly just above 20%, implying about 40 million functionally illiterate/innumerate adults in the USA, over 7 million in Britain, over 4 million in Canada, and correspondingly high numbers in other English-speaking countries; the estimates were much higher than for many developed non-English-speaking countries. (However, the figure for France was nearer 40%, and the French government was so appalled that it refused to let the result be published, officially—but it appeared in *Libération* newspaper anyway.)

There have been disputes over the methodology of IALS—see especially Sticht (1999), who criticized the practice of attributing individuals the score for the item they had an 80% chance of getting right. He pointed out that setting the criterion at 50% would have produced much lower estimates of the numbers of adults with poor skills, and that these would seem much more in tune with people's intuitions about how many of their fellow citizens have poor literacy than the possibly alarmist estimates produced by the 80% criterion. Also, Hamilton and Barton (2000) called in question the validity of the IALS framework, which sampled only certain restricted forms of reading, and ignored writing. Powerful longitudinal research (Barton & Hamilton,

Table 9.1   Descriptions of the Five Levels of Proficiency in Prose and Document Piteracy in IALS 1994–98

Level	Prose literacy	Document literacy
IALS/ international Level 5 (UK Level 4)	Some tasks in this level require the respondent to search for information in dense text which contains a number of plausible distractors. Others ask respondents to make high-level inferences or use specialized background knowledge. Some tasks ask respondents to contrast complex information.	Tasks in this level require the respondent to search through complex displays that contain multiple distractors, to make high-level text-based inferences, and to use specialized knowledge
IALS/ international Level 4 (UK Level 3)	These tasks require respondents to perform multiple-feature matches and to integrate or synthesize information from complex or lengthy passages. More complex inferences are needed to perform successfully. Conditional information is frequently present in tasks at this level and must be taken into consideration by the respondent.	Tasks in this level, like those at the lower levels, ask respondents to perform multiple-feature matches, cycle through documents, and integrate information; however, they require a greater degree of inferencing. Many of these tasks require respondents to provide numerous responses but do not designate how many responses are needed. Conditional information is also present in the document tasks at this level and must be taken into account by the respondent.
IALS/ international Level 3 (UK Level 2)	Tasks in this level tend to require respondents to make literal or synonymous matches between the text and information given in the task, or to make matches that require low-level inferences. Other tasks ask respondents to integrate information from dense or lengthy text that contains no organizational aids such as headings. Respondents may also be asked to generate a response based on information that can be easily identified in the text. Distracting information is present, but is not located near the correct information.	Some tasks in this level require the respondent to integrate multiple pieces of information from one or more documents. Others ask respondents to cycle through rather complex tables or graphs which contain information that is irrelevant or inappropriate to the task.
IALS/ international Level 2 (UK Level 1)	Some tasks in this level require respondents to locate a single piece of information in the text; however, several distractors or plausible but incorrect pieces of information may be present, or low-level inferences may be required. Other tasks require the respondent to integrate two or more pieces of information or to compare and contrast easily identifiable information based on a criterion provided in the question or directive.	Tasks in this level are more varied than those in Level 1 (UK Entry level). Some require the respondents to match a single piece of information; however, several distractors may be present, or the match may require low-level inferences. Tasks in this level may also ask the respondent to cycle through information in a document or to integrate information from various parts of a document.
IALS/ international Level 1 (UK Entry level)	Most of the tasks in this level require the respondent to read relatively short text to locate a single piece of information which is identical to or synonymous with the information given in the question or directive. If plausible but incorrect information is present in the text, it tends not to be located near the correct information.	Tasks in this level tend to require the respondent either to locate a piece of information based on a literal match or to enter information from personal knowledge onto a document. Little, if any, distracting information is present.

Source: Desjardins et al. (2005)

Table 9.2   Descriptions of Performance at Five Levels of 'Quantitative Lteracy', IALS 1994–98

IALS/international Level 5 (UK Level 4)	Tasks in this level require respondents to understand complex representations and abstract and formal mathematical and statistical ideas, possibly embedded in complex texts. Respondents may have to integrate multiple types of mathematical information, draw inferences, or generate mathematical justification for answers.
IALS/international Level 4 (UK Level 3)	Tasks at this level require respondents to understand a broad range of mathematical information of a more abstract nature represented in diverse ways, including in texts of increasing complexity or in unfamiliar contexts. These tasks involve undertaking multiple steps to find solutions to problems and require more complex reasoning and interpretation skills, including comprehending and working with proportions and formulas or offering explanations for answers.
IALS/international Level 3 (UK Level 2)	Tasks in this level require the respondent to demonstrate understanding of mathematical information represented in a range of different forms, such as in numbers, symbols, maps, graphs, texts and drawings. Skills required involve number and spatial sense, knowledge of mathematical patterns and relationships, and the ability to interpret proportions, data and statistics embedded in relatively simple texts where there may be distractors. Tasks commonly involve undertaking a number of processes to solve problems.
IALS/international Level 2 (UK Level 1)	Tasks in this level are fairly simple and relate to identifying and understanding basic mathematical concepts embedded in a range of familiar contexts where the mathematical content is quite explicit and visual with few distractors. Tasks tend to include one-step or two-step processes and estimations involving whole numbers, benchmark percents and fractions, interpreting simple graphical or spatial representations, and performing simple measurements.
IALS/international Level 1 (UK Entry level)	Tasks in this level require the respondent to show an understanding of basic numerical ideas by completing simple tasks in concrete, familiar contexts where the mathematical content is explicit with little text. Tasks consist of simple, one-step operations such as counting, sorting dates, performing simple arithmetic operations, or understanding common and simple percents such as 50%.

Source: Desjardins et al. (2005)

1998) has been done in the city of Lancaster in England on the role of writing in adults' lives. Gillespie (2001, p. 72) summarizes:

> … the results of this … study… [R]esearchers noted that when people talked about writing, they imbued it with power. Some adults felt frustration at the inadequacy of their written work; they knew what they wanted to say but could not find the words to express their thoughts. But others preferred writing to reading or felt they could express themselves better by writing than by speaking. They took great pleasure in writing and felt empowered by it.

The general lack of attention to adults' writing in research and surveys needs to be addressed.

A successor to IALS, the Adult Literacy and Lifeskills (ALL) survey, was carried out in 2003. Numeracy was treated as a separate domain, so that literacy estimates were nearer to measures of reading comprehension ability. Many new items were included, but the framework was very similar to IALS. Six countries took part, including Canada and the USA; their estimates for adults with Level 1 literacy were 15% and 20% respectively (Desjardins, Murray, Clermont, &Werquin, 2005). Britain did not take part; instead, in 2002–03 England (alone) mounted a national survey of need, which produced an estimate of 16% of adults aged 16-65, or about 5.8 million people, having literacy attainment within Level 1 (UK Entry level) (Williams, with Clemens, Oleinikova, & Tarvin, 2003). This was lower than the IALS estimate; whether the change represented a real reduction or an artifact of using different instruments and methods (IALS was paper-and-pencil; the England survey in 2002–03 was computer-administered) is disputed.

What is clear from the British evidence (the two surveys mentioned and several others), however, is that there is a lifecourse trend: the proportion of people with poor literacy declines up to about the age of 30, remains low for a decade or so, then rises continuously in later middle age and the retirement years, such that for people in their 60s and 70s it is higher than for those in their 20s. The last point probably entails that, for older adult literacy students, maintaining their skills may be a more realistic goal than trying to improve them, but this does not sit easily with Western governments' rhetoric on the necessity to improve skills in the competitive global market.

However, regardless of arguments over the validity, reliability and comparability of surveys of adult literacy and numeracy levels, the perception is abroad that even many developed, industrialized countries with long histories of universal education have a problem: too many adults whose life chances are blighted by inadequate skills. What can be done? What theory do we need?

First, the problem needs to be understood. Adult literacy learners are by definition people who did not acquire sufficient literacy when they were children, so a theory of why they are in the position they are in, and of how to help them, would require theories of: the essential conditions for successful acquisition of literacy; what could have gone wrong; any differences between children and adults which might make learning to read and write different and/or more difficult for adults; and what might be effective in helping adult learners achieve better literacy.

A minimum specification of the essential conditions for children's successful acquisition of literacy would include: adequate intelligence, normal or corrected-to-normal vision and hearing, normal brain function, sufficient access to printed material in a language which they speak natively or have learnt, a supportive family/community, sufficient exposure to opportunities to learn to read and write, and effective teaching. Most of these specifications have been the topic of research, as have theories about what causes difficulties in learning to read and write (though I will shortly add to the factors that should be dealt with in relation to adults), but two aspects of theory listed above exist only in embryo.

In addition to the problems children might have in learning to read and write, adults might have had intermittent or inadequate schooling, and possibly undiagnosed problems with sight, hearing or dyslexia. Also, they might be so demotivated by their earlier failure that they convince themselves that they can't learn, and the fact that they are adults, with many years' more life experience than children, might mean that materials and methods appropriate for children would be unsuitable.

Since the early 1970s attempts have been made to produce theories of adult learning that take account of the perceived differences between children and adults that might make literacy learning distinctive and/or more difficult for adults, under the label of 'andragogy' (see especially Knowles, 1973). [Incidentally, though now hallowed in the literature, this neologism is etymologically sexist. Where the parallel term 'pedagogy' means in origin 'child-leading' and the Greek 'ped-' element is gender-neutral, 'andragogy' means 'man-leading' with 'man' implying 'adult human male'. But the etymologically gender-neutral term meaning 'adult person-leading' would have to be 'anthropagogy', which is if anything even clumsier and more offputting than 'andragogy'.]

Tusting and Barton (2003, p. 19) summarize the essential tenets of andragogy as follows:

> [It] consists primarily of a set of assumptions about the adult learner. Knowles claimed that adults have to know why they need to learn something before they undertake to learn it. They must move from a dependent self-concept to a self-directing one. They have accumulated more experience, and experiences of a different quality, than children, and their

readiness to learn is linked to the tasks associated with their social role and stage of life. Adults engage in problem-centred, rather than subject-centred, learning and are driven by internal rather than external motivation… In the pedagogical model, which Knowles identifies as having been linked historically with teacher-directed education of children, these assumptions are reversed.

Tusting and Barton (2003, pp. 21–22) also report critiques of andragogy (e.g. that it overstates differences between adults and children in terms of learning) and later developments which have attempted to meld certain aspects of it, especially the need for adults to be self-directed learners, with a more general notion of all learners, of whatever age, as requiring individualized instruction.

It is true of many adult learners that they have negative memories of their schooling. This has led some educators of adults to avoid trying to teach aspects of literacy that they believe to have been particularly boring or counter-productive (because failure-inducing) in adult learners' schooling, especially phonics. This seems also to have been in tune with the downplaying of phonics in the teaching of children during the reading skirmishes. Yet if, as the research evidence increasingly suggests (Ehri, Nunes, Stahl, & Willows, 2001; Torgerson, Brooks, & Hall, 2006), systematic phonics instruction enables children to make better progress in learning to read than unsystematic or no phonics instruction, and is thus an essential element of effective teaching of literacy, it would seem at least plausible that phonics might be helpful to adults too.

However, research evidence on what works for adult learners is noticeably sparse, and practice has been based almost entirely on professional judgment—so what has adult literacy provision looked like?

A BRIEF HISTORY OF ADULT LITERACY PROVISION

Although Sticht (2002) traces antecedents back to 1778, the current Adult Education and Literacy System in the USA dates from 1964, and Sticht also documents the vast scale of the enterprise now. In Britain, following small-scale community efforts in the 1960s, a national *Right to Read* campaign was launched in 1973, followed by the establishment of the Adult Literacy Resources Agency (later the Basic Skills Agency) in 1974, and an influential BBC television series, *On the Move*, in 1975–76. This was the first adult literacy campaign mounted in a Western European country (Hamilton & Merrifield, 2000), and also led to a huge expansion of provision. Australia (Australian Council on Adult Literacy, date of establishment unknown), Canada (National Literacy Secretariat, established 1987), Ireland (National Adult Literacy Agency, established 1980) and New Zealand (Literacy Aotearoa, established 1982) also set up adult literacy agencies and initiatives. Thus all these agencies were in place even before IALS confirmed the ongoing need for them.

Hamilton and Merrifield (2000) chronicled the liberal, humanistic, 'social service' ethos of the provision in Britain in the 1970s and 1980s—all the tutors were volunteers, and often worked with learners one-on-one in the learners' homes. Gradually this was replaced by a professional, paid service (though many tutors are still on poorly-paid, part-time, insecure contracts), and the ethos changed to one promoted (by the British government, at least) as serving the economic interests of the country. Much of this change of emphasis appears to be true also of other countries, and to have been reinforced by a step change around the turn of the millennium.

The reaction to IALS in the USA culminated in the calling of the National Literacy Summit in February 2000 and the publication of its manifesto, *From the Margins to the Mainstream*, and of a new National Reporting System. The British government set up a commission of inquiry which produced its report, *A Fresh Start: Improving Literacy and Numeracy* (Department for

Education and Employment, 1999), in 1999; this gave rise to the *Skills for Life* initiative aimed at improving adult literacy, language (i.e. spoken English for speakers of other languages) and numeracy from 2001, the development of national tests of adult literacy and numeracy, and the 2002–03 survey mentioned above. The costs of the initiatives are huge: Sticht (2002) gives estimates for the USA, and *Skills for Life* has received unprecedented amounts of funding: £500 million a year, and this largely continues.

What teaching and learning were actually like in adult literacy classrooms has, however, to an extent remained a secret garden—but see below.

A BRIEF HISTORY OF RESEARCH ON ADULT LITERACY

Adult literacy seems to have attracted virtually no research attention before the 1970s. Formal research (as distinct from developing materials, methods and tests) may be said to date from the evaluations of the US Army's FLIT (Functional Literacy) programs in 1966–75 (Sticht, Sticht, Armstrong, Hickey, & Caylor, 1987), and in Britain with evaluations of the *Right to Read* campaign (Gorman, 1981; Gorman & Moss, 1979; Jones & Charnley, 1978).

Though both countries already had relevant research and development organizations (National Institute for Literacy, Basic Skills Agency) carrying out small-scale programs of both R and D, in the wake of IALS each set up an additional organization: the National Center for the Study of Adult Learning and Literacy (NCSALL, established 1996, wound up 2007) in the USA, and the National Research and Development Centre for adult literacy and numeracy (NRDC, established 2002) in England. Again, this was accompanied by unprecedented levels of funding: £2.5 million a year core funding for NRDC, for example. The work of NCSALL and NRDC and their counterparts elsewhere provides the bulk of the evidence for this chapter. It is probably true to say that more research and development work has been done in this field in the years 1996–2008 than in all previous history.

STUDENTS' PROGRESS: HOW MUCH DO THEY IMPROVE THEIR SKILLS?

From the surveys the scale of need is abundantly clear, and longitudinal studies (e.g. Parsons and Bynner, 1998, 2007; Bynner & Parsons, 1997, 2006a, b) have shown that the effects of poor skills on people's lives are pervasively bad—but do adult literacy programs actually enable students to improve their skills? Torgerson and colleagues (Torgerson, Porthouse, & Brooks, 2003; Torgerson et al., 2004) found just enough evidence from randomized controlled trials (all of it from the USA) to demonstrate rigorously in a meta-analysis that receiving adult literacy (and numeracy) instruction does produce more progress than not receiving it. Though this finding is intuitively obvious, this was the first time it had been rigorously demonstrated. If the finding had not been positive, questions would have had to be raised about whether provision should continue.

Alongside that must be set the evidence that adults' average progress in literacy is modest. For the USA Sticht and Armstrong (1994) summarized evidence from over 30,000 students attending a large number of programs, all of which had shown statistically significant gains (but, given that providers have a strong financial incentive not to report non-significant results, and an even stronger one not to report negative ones, this suggests publication bias); the gains ranged between a half and 1½ grade levels, following amounts of instruction ranging between 1 and 229 hours. Beder (1999) appears to have set a stricter criterion for the quality of the research he summarized, and based his conclusions on just two attempted national studies (one was the National Evaluation of Adult Education Programs carried out in 1990–94) and six local ones, plus a secondary analysis of data from the NALS of 1992. None of the studies reported data on writing, and only four on numeracy; all tested reading. Because of serious attrition, neither national study provided reliable data. In their re-analysis of NALS data, Sheehan-Holt and Smith (2000, p. 227) were able to compare adults 'at the lower end of the literacy skills continuum' within the survey who had participated in adult literacy provision in the previous year with directly comparable people who had not. The main finding was that 'no association was found between participation in [basic skills] programs and literacy skills'. The local studies provided mixed results. Beder's (1999, p. 5) conclusion from all the evidence he analyzed was that 'As measured by tests, the evidence is insufficient to determine whether or not participants in adult … education gain in basic skills.'

The evidence for modest gains by learners in England comes from three studies. In 1998–99 Brooks, Davies, et al. (2001) measured the progress of 1200+ adult literacy students in reading and 700+ in writing. About half the reading items were drawn from the least difficult tasks in IALS (they were supplemented by even simpler tasks from British sources), and the statistical model used was that used to analyze IALS data. The average gain in reading was 3 percentile points, from the 19th to the 22nd percentile on the IALS scale. The average gain in writing was tiny: an increase in the average number of words written from 19 to 21, with no significant change in sentence length, accuracy of grammar or spelling, or handwriting. In 2004–05, in the Effective Practice in Reading study (for more detail see below), Brooks, Burton, Cole, and Szczerbiński (2007a, b) tracked the progress of 179 adult literacy students; their average gain was equivalent to about half of one IALS level. Brooks and Pilling (in press; summaries in Rhys Warner et al., 2008 and Vorhaus, Howard, Brooks, Bathmaker, & Appleby, 2009) report the progress in numeracy of adult numeracy learners and in reading and writing of adult literacy and ESOL learners after 3 to 6 months of instruction (typically one 2-hour session a week) in 2004–06. Adult literacy learners' gain in writing was non-significant; the other four gains were statistically significant, but all represented about one third of (the British equivalent of) one IALS level.

Reasons for the modest progress may include: low participation rates (only a few per cent of adults with poor skills are receiving instruction at any one time); low starting points (see the survey evidence above); substantial numbers of students with mother tongues other than English; the fact that many tutors are on part-time, insecure contracts; relatively high drop-out rates (routinely around 50% in a year); and insufficient attention to effective teaching strategies.

As an example of the last point, Besser et al. (2004) in England explored 53 students' capabilities in the following areas: word identification, comprehension (explicit and implicit), phonological awareness, decoding, and spelling. Most exhibited the scattered pattern of strengths and weaknesses well known to practitioners as 'spiky profiles'. There were fewest difficulties with word identification, most with spelling. Three groups, or reader profiles, emerged, each with distinct teaching requirements:

1. A small subgroup of competent readers with no discernible difficulties in any of the areas investigated. They appeared to be attending to improve their writing.
2. A rather larger subgroup who appeared to have difficulties only in the phonological area, including spelling. These students might well have benefited from close attention to phonological awareness (including phonics) in the context of meaningful reading and writing.
3. The majority, who had difficulties in several areas. Very few had difficulties in every area—rather, this is the group with classic 'spiky profiles'—but it seems clear that, if they were to make progress, teaching should address both their areas of strength and their areas of weakness across all the subskills of reading and spelling.

A wide range of strategies was being used to address the students' reading difficulties, but there appeared to be a less than perfect match between their difficulties and the teachers' teaching strategies. Whilst teaching was observed that targeted some of the identified difficulties, intensive, focused reading instruction did not comprise a significant amount of the teaching that occurred. In particular, little work at sentence level or on comprehension beyond the literal was seen. Most of the students had poor phonological awareness, but much of the phonics teaching was done on the spur of the moment rather than systematically, and there were instances of tutors' inadequate grasp of phonetics leading to inaccurate phonics teaching.

RESEARCH DESIGNS: THE 'GOLD STANDARD' AND ALTERNATIVES TO IT FOR ANSWERING DIFFERENT QUESTIONS

But in order to investigate teaching strategies that might be more effective, reliable methods appropriate to the research questions asked must be used, since what counts as evidence depends on what the research question is. If the research question is 'What factors in teaching *cause* adult students to make progress in literacy?', it can be argued that the 'gold standard' research design is the randomized controlled trial (also known as an experimental study). RCTs have the potential to provide robust evidence because they purport to control all possible extraneous causes of measured progress.

It is still legitimate, however, to ask what findings can be derived from other forms of evidence addressing different research questions in the field, for example:

- 'What factors in teaching adult students are *known to correlate* with better progress in literacy?'
- 'Does students' confidence improve, and is this a prerequisite for progress?'
- 'What evidence is there that computer-assisted instruction enables adults to make better progress?'
- 'What works for adult literacy in the workplace?'
- 'How much instructional time do students need to make educationally significant progress?'
- 'Do adult basic skills students benefit financially from improving their skills?'

The first of these follows logically from considering RCTs as the gold standard; the 'silver standard' would then be quasi-experimental but still quantitative designs such as matched-groups studies (also called non-randomized controlled trials). By definition these cannot investigate *causation* because they do not control for all possible confounding factors, but they can provide strong evidence of *correlation* between instructional and other contextual variables on the one hand and students' progress in basic skills, or changes in their attitudes and self-confidence, on the other. Such correlations then provide some evidence towards better instruction, and for more rigorous investigation through RCTs.

The other five questions listed above are admittedly something of a hotchpotch, but they are frequently addressed in the literature, are of interest to policy-makers as well as researchers and practitioners, and have all been the subject of at least a modicum of quantitative research—including, in the case of computer-assisted instruction, a few RCTs.

FINDINGS FROM RANDOMIZED CONTROLLED TRIALS

Kruidenier (2002) in the USA and Torgerson et al. (2003, 2004) in Britain carried out systematic reviews of relevant RCTs. Among those analyzed by Torgerson et al. were several that had individual positive findings. Taking single studies as reliable entails making the assumption that other studies on the same topic with null or negative results do not exist—a very hazardous assumption given the possibility of publication bias and the presence of one definite negative finding (see below). However, if this assumption is made and the single studies are taken as reliable at least until further studies show otherwise, then the following three individual trials provide positive findings for adult literacy instruction:

- Reciprocal teaching (see Palincsar, 1982, 1986; Palincsar & Brown, 1984) had positive effects on reading comprehension (Rich & Shepherd, 1993). Of all the pedagogical findings in the field, this is the one with the strongest evidence. Also, according to Torgerson et al.'s quality appraisal, this was the highest quality study of all. There has been a large amount of research on the technique in North America, but scarcely any elsewhere, and very little at adult level. However, Rosenshine and Meister (1994) did a meta-analysis on the 16 most rigorous studies at school level and found a (small) effect size of 0.32 on standardized tests.
- A 'diagnostic prescriptive' approach had positive effects on reading comprehension, but not on word identification (Cheek & Lindsey, 1994). The approach involved formal and informal diagnostic procedures to identify adults' strengths and weaknesses, and use of the diagnoses to develop individual educational prescriptions—very much the traditional liberal, humanistic approach, in fact.
- For inmates at a US prison, a 'community-building group process' accompanied by the SRA reading program had a positive effect on reading (Roberts & Cheek, 1994). This appears to parallel the finding at school level in Britain that working on children's self-esteem and reading in parallel has definite potential (see Lawrence, 1985, 1988, and summary in Brooks, 2002, 2007).

However, if these positive findings from single trials are accepted, then there is also one negative finding that should also be accepted. In this study there was a statistically significant advantage for the *control* group, that is, the intervention had the opposite of the intended effect:

- The aim of the study (Dietrich, 1994) was to investigate the effectiveness of auditory perception training on the reading ability of adult poor readers at a community college. The experimental group received a phonological skills approach, while the control group received a traditional metacognitive approach. The results showed no difference on an auditory perception test or a word naming test, but the control group made more progress on a word identification test. Since the auditory test results suggested that auditory perception training was ineffective, perhaps the negative result for word naming meant that the control group was making better use of the time available.

Since Kruidenier (2002) and Torgerson et al. (2003, 2004) carried out their reviews, only one more RCT has been carried out (as far as is known). In January–June 2005, Brooks et al. (2008) investigated whether offering adult literacy students a financial incentive to attend would impact on either attendance or attainment. Attainment was not affected (neither the treatment nor the control group's average score changed between pre- and post-test), but there was a perverse effect on attendance: the treatment group's average attendance was slightly but significantly *lower* than the control group's. This was attributed to some students being discouraged from attending by feeling they were being bribed to do something they were already intrinsically motivated to do.

Kruidenier (2002) cast his net much wider than RCTs and listed dozens of findings. They were based on both adult- and school-level (K–12) research, and distinguished between 'principles' based on 'more than one' experimental study and 'trends', 'ideas' and 'comments' based on only one experimental study or on indirect evidence (mainly from K–12 research). Here only the principles based on adult-level research are listed. They are reproduced *verbatim*, hence the tentative tone (pp. 20–30):

- Phonemic awareness and/or word analysis instruction may lead to increased achievement in other aspects of reading for adult beginning readers.
- Word analysis may be taught using approaches that include direct instruction in word analysis along with instruction in other aspects of reading.
- Fluency [meaning greater speed, accuracy and expressiveness in reading aloud] may be taught to adult basic education students and fluency practice may lead to increases in reading achievement.
- Fluency may be taught using approaches that include the repeated reading of passages of text, words from texts, and other text units.
- Providing explicit instruction in reading comprehension strategies may lead to increased reading comprehension achievement.
- Combining comprehension instruction with instruction in various other components of reading may lead to increased reading comprehension achievement.

Behind the cautious wording this seems to mean that phonics, fluency and explicit comprehension instruction are all promising approaches. In two small-scale non-experimental studies, Burton (2007) and Burton, Davey, Lewis, Ritchie, & Brooks (2008) indeed found that practicing oral reading fluency enhanced students' progress, and the latter study found the same for phonics instruction. However, apart from Rich and Shepherd (1993) cited above, there appears to be little or no rigorous research on the direct teaching of comprehension to adults.

FACTORS *KNOWN TO CORRELATE* WITH BETTER PROGRESS

As already indicated, these findings are based on quantitative but not RCT investigations. Basic Skills Agency (2000) summarized quantitative evidence showing that effective programs have high expectations of students' achievements, and enable students to gain credit and accreditation for their learning and move into further study if they wish.

In the Brooks et al. (2001b) study cited above, factors associated with better progress in reading (none were found for writing) were:

- All the tutors in an area having qualified teacher status;
- Tutors having assistance in the classroom;
- Regular attendance by students.

In 1999–2001 Condelli, Wrigley, Yoon, Cronen, & Seburn (2003) collected data from 495 adult ESL students in 39 classes in 13 programs in seven US states. This was a correlational study (it provided the inspiration for the Effective Practice in Reading study and several others conducted subsequently in England) which aimed to uncover factors in teachers' classroom practices which were related to students' progress in literacy and/or spoken English. Its method was essentially quantitative generalization from qualitative observation of what went on in classrooms. Virtually the only instructional variable found to correlate with growth in literacy was teachers making connections to the 'outside' or real world. It is worth noting that this and the study mentioned in the next paragraph are among the very few to have systematically gathered qualitative evidence about what actually goes on in adult literacy (including ESL) classrooms—much more needs to be known about this.

In the Effective Practice in Reading study, Brooks et al. (2007a, b) also used a correlational design, aiming to relate students' progress in reading and/or changes in their attitudes on the one hand, to (on the other) the teaching strategies their tutors were observed using in the classroom in about 470 hours of teaching; again the observational side used a qualitative-to-quantitative approach. Since the average amount of progress made was modest (see above), it is not surprising that rather few factors were found to correlate with it: regular attendance, students working less on their own in class (this also emerged in the Besser et al., 2004 study), students working more in pairs in class, students engaging in more self-study between classes. However, several approaches which the literature suggests are effective were rarely seen:

- encouragement of fluent oral reading
- reciprocal teaching
- explicit comprehension strategies
- accurate phonics teaching
- language experience, which a generation ago was the standard approach (Gillespie, 1991, 2001; Mace, 1995; Morley & Worpole, 1982).

The invisibility of phonics and fluency instruction led directly to the two studies by Burton mentioned above.

DOES STUDENTS' CONFIDENCE IMPROVE, AND IS THIS A PREREQUISITE FOR PROGRESS?

Yes and no, respectively. Many adult literacy tutors seem to have it as an article of faith that they must first boost learners' self-confidence before improvement in basic skills can occur. Beder (1999, see especially pp. 5, 69) analyzed the wider benefits of the 23 'most credible' adult basic skills evaluations in the United States up till then, and concluded that participation in adult education had a positive effect on learners' self-image (6 studies out of the 8 measuring this), but a comparison of those data with his data on progress carried out by Brooks, Giles, et al. (2001, pp. 129–130) showed no convincing correlation. Brooks et al. (2007a, b) found that students' self-confidence and reading both improved, but that the two were not correlated, and Burton et al. (2008) had similar findings. Grief, Meyer, and Burgess (2007a, b) found that students' writing improved, but that their confidence improved as a *result* of attending a course. The implication would seem to be that adult education tutors should work on their students' skills as a means to improving their self-confidence, rather than *vice versa*, which in turn would mean that they should concentrate more on effective instruction methods.

WHAT EVIDENCE IS THERE THAT COMPUTER-ASSISTED INSTRUCTION ENABLES ADULTS TO MAKE BETTER PROGRESS?

CAI (known in Britain as ICT, Information and communications technology) did show some benefit for students at Entry levels 2 and 3 (the upper two-thirds of IALS Level 1) in a study in Britain conducted for Ufi (formerly known as the University for Industry) (Mellar & Kambouri, 2001)—but this was a single-group pre-test/post-test study. In Torgerson et al.'s (2003, 2004) systematic review of RCTs, a meta-analysis of the two most relevant studies showed no benefit of CAI over conventional instruction. Apparently on the basis of the same two RCTs (both conducted in US prisons), Kruidenier (2002) expressed the finding more optimistically as: 'In general,… CAI is at least as effective as non-CAI in increasing reading comprehension achievement' (p. 30). However, the further analysis of non-randomized controlled trials by Torgerson et al. (2004, 2005) again found no convincing evidence of benefits from CAI over conventional instruction.

In total, Torgerson et al.'s (2004, 2005) two systematic reviews found three RCTs and 16 other controlled trials (that is, matched-groups quasi-experiments) relevant to CAI and adult literacy and/or numeracy. All three RCTs (one of which was not used in the meta-analysis because its subjects were not prisoners) had non-significant results. Of the 16 other controlled trials, three had no clear result, seven were non-significant, and four had at least one statistically significant finding in favour of CAI, but two had statistically significant results in favour of the traditionally taught control group, that is, against the use of CAI.

A previous US systematic review (Rachal, 1995) comparing computer-assisted and traditional approaches in adult reading achievement included 21 studies dating between 1979 and 1995, and also broadly found little benefit of CAI—but the further back the study, the less relevant the computer technology is today. Although today it is desirable for all adults to understand and use computers, and they should therefore learn to do this, using computers with adult students in the hope of boosting their literacy remains a forlorn hope—though more precisely focused approaches may produce better results, since much 'computer-assisted instruction' belies that description: it seems to consist of letting students sit at computers and find their own way through programs, rather than their teachers using the computers as instructional tools by setting precise tasks and goals.

Other technologies may hold more promise. NALA in Ireland has reported considerable success with using distance teaching via radio and television, but no quantitative data to support this.

WHAT WORKS FOR ADULT BASIC SKILLS IN THE WORKPLACE?

As will quickly become apparent, there is very little useful quantitative evidence on this question. The US Army's FLIT programs, which focused on training job-related reading quickly, produced not only greater gains for job-related reading than general literacy programs, but also gains in general reading that were on average better than those delivered by general literacy programs (Sticht et al., 1987). Similarly, research in England on embedding basic skills instruction in vocational training found that attainment tended to increase in line with higher degrees of embeddedness (Casey et al., 2006). This suggests a fruitful approach for students who are in work, but many adult literacy students are not.

A detailed and rigorous study of workplace basic skills was started at the University of London Institute of Education and King's College London in 2003, and was due to report in 2009. One of its early outputs addressed the widespread belief that giving employees training to improve their basic skills encourages them to change their jobs, thus depriving their employers of the benefit of their investment. This belief not only betrays a grudging attitude to other people's skills (employers and managers would vehemently resist any cut-backs in their professional development, however often they might change jobs), but also probably explains employers' widespread reluctance to pay for such training and their demands that governments should pay. But a review of the research evidence on the benefits to employers of improving workplace basic skills (Ananiadou, Jenkins, & Wolf, 2003) showed that employees who received training were actually more likely to stay with their employer than those who did not. Perhaps employers remember trained people who leave more acutely than those who stay.

A more substantive finding from the study is that most workplace basic skills programs in England provide no more than 30 hours' instruction, and that students on average make no progress in that time (Hodgson & Wolf, 2008; Vignoles, 2009)—which is directly relevant to the next topic.

HOW MUCH INSTRUCTIONAL TIME DO STUDENTS NEED TO MAKE EDUCATIONALLY SIGNIFICANT PROGRESS?

Comings (2003) summarized the US evidence on this. Students need to attend at least 100 hours of instruction to make progress equivalent to one US grade level (after 150 hours, the probability of making this much progress is 75 per cent), but the average student stays in provision for fewer than 70 hours in a year. Even that average is probably too high because those who enroll but leave after just a few hours' attendance are not counted (this is true also in Britain). In the Effective Practice in Writing study in England (Grief et al., 2007a, b), students who attended for about 50 hours made more progress than those who attended less. In the Brooks, Davies, et al. (2001) study students who attended at least 50 hours of provision between pre- and post-test made the most progress in reading, and regular attendance has been correlated with more progress in reading in two later studies in England (Brooks et al., 2007a, b; Burton et al., 2008).

But time on task should perhaps be defined more carefully, in two ways. First, it is not necessarily the case that all time spent in an adult literacy classroom is spent on literacy. Besser et al. (2004) noted that not enough class time was spent on reading activities, and therefore students were not making sufficient progress. In the Effective Practice in Reading study, Brooks et al. (2007a, b) found that, on average, only 37% of class time (44 minutes of a standard 120-minute session) was spent on active reading instruction or practice, and that the most frequent activity was students reading silently.

Secondly, if students engage in self-study outside class, this should obviously be counted as time on task. Reder and Strawn (2001) found that many of the 1000 people in the Longitudinal Study of Adult Learning (LSAL) in Portland, Oregon engaged in self-study, and that this was true both of those attending literacy classes and those not attending. Several years on, Reder (2005) was able to show that students who reported more self-study between classes made better progress. This also emerged as an important factor in the Effective Practice in Reading study in England. However, there is an important contextual difference between the two national systems. In the USA, the GED sets an important target for students, and this may well explain the amounts of self-study they engage in. There is no equivalent in Britain, and the self-study effect is much weaker (see Brooks et al., 2007a, p. 32). LSAL has also shown that persistence in learning leads to cumulative gains.

DO ADULT BASIC SKILLS STUDENTS BENEFIT FINANCIALLY FROM IMPROVING THEIR SKILLS?

Yes, in many cases. Tyler (2001a, b; Tyler, Murnane, & Willett, 2000) reviewed all the relevant evidence from the USA, and showed that acquiring the GED could have a substantial impact on the earnings of at least some adult students, particularly those who had low skills or passed the GED with very low scores, who could earn between 5% and 25% more than comparable people without a GED. He also showed that the pay-off in the form of increased earnings was more likely to show up over time than immediately after acquiring the GED—this effect is also apparent in results from LSAL.

The evidence for Britain comes from lifetime cohort studies. Dearden, McIntosh, Myck, & Vignoles (2000, see p. 6 especially) reported the first detailed analysis for the UK of the economic returns to individuals of basic skills qualifications. In general, they found that literacy and numeracy qualifications at UK Level 1 (IALS Level 2) or above returned earnings several per cent higher than qualifications below that level. The most recent study focused on a cohort of people born in 1970 and studied at age 34 in 2004. The main findings (Vignoles, de Coulon, & Marcenaro-Gutierrez, 2007, pp. 1–2) were:

- Literacy and numeracy have a strong and similar association with individuals' earnings. When the researchers controlled for an individual's ability and family background, an additional standard deviation in literacy resulted in approximately 14% higher earnings, whilst an additional standard deviation in numeracy resulted in 12% higher earnings.
- Overall, the authors found literacy and numeracy effects on earnings that were over and above any general effect on earnings from a person having higher cognitive ability.
- They also found that having better basic skills was significantly associated with the likelihood of being in employment and full-time employment at age 33/34.
- Just under 10% of the variation in earnings could be explained by differences in literacy and numeracy skills.

CONCLUSIONS: PEDAGOGY—GENERAL OR SPECIFIC?

Clearly, time on task (as always) is a key determinant of progress. Beyond that, there are some factors that help, such as well-qualified staff, but few are actually forms of teaching strategy. Most of the correlates of progress mentioned above are more to do with general teaching skills than with specifics. General teaching skills include classroom organization, relating teaching to the real world, embedding the teaching of skills in a rich curriculum, not relying on technology for progress in literacy (though of course adult students, like everyone else, need to learn how to use computers), providing plenty of opportunities for student involvement, giving praise and encouragement, etc. In their ESL study, Condelli et al. (2003) used a detailed checklist of such general strategies, and it was from this that their finding about relating teaching to the outside world emerged. Using aggregated data from almost exactly the same instrument, Burton et al. (2008) found that teachers' scores for general strategies correlated well with their students' progress.

But what of teaching specific skills, such as comprehension, phonics or fluency? Reciprocal teaching would seem to score highly both as a specific strategy and as inherently requiring intensive student engagement, so it is perhaps not surprising that the strongest individual pedagogical finding mentioned here related to this technique. However, Burton et al. (2008) used a checklist for rating teachers' compliance with the techniques they had been trained to use, and found that their phonics teachers' scores on this also correlated well with their students' progress. Perhaps after all both good general teaching skills and close attention to teaching specific skills are needed.

IMPLICATIONS FOR THEORY, PRACTICE, AND POLICY

Models of adult literacy learning need to be developed beyond the point where they seem to treat adults as wholly different from children simply because adults have lived longer, know more about the world, and are hardly ever true beginners in literacy. This seems to have created a reluctance to draw on models of child learning, even where they might be relevant. Debate on the implications of this for theory has scarcely begun.

Western governments currently expend a great deal of rhetoric on the need for 21st-century skills, as though it were clear what these are and certain that acquiring or improving them is the key to sustaining developed countries' places in the economic pecking order. They place less emphasis, but should place more, on the need for good basic skills as a human right so that everyone can fulfill their potential and therefore take a full role as private individuals, citizens, family members and employees—and probably earn more.

Teachers of adult basic skills need to have both good generic teaching skills and good subject-specific teaching skills. For adult literacy, the latter include, but are not limited to, knowing how to teach phonics, oral reading fluency, comprehension and appreciation of what is read, and how to apply these and other skills to texts on both paper and screen.

Therefore those who train teachers of adult basic skills need to have not only all the skills just mentioned but also knowledge of how to model them for those in training, and knowledge of the research basis for their recommendations.

IMPLICATIONS FOR RESEARCH

But as this review shows, the research base is still pretty thin. In particular, there have been far too few intervention studies, i.e. those seeking to determine rigorously whether various teaching strategies are actually effective in raising students' achievement, the one honorable exception being reciprocal teaching and its benefits for comprehension. There are fleeting indications in the literature that systematic phonics instruction (especially, perhaps, systematic synthetic phonics instruction) might benefit adult learners as much as it has been shown to benefit children, but this awaits convincing demonstration. Similarly, there is ample evidence for the benefits of fluency instruction for children's progress in reading, but hardly any on the use of this strategy with adults. In just over a century of research on whether formal instruction in grammar benefits students' writing, the only aspect ever to have shown results is the technique known as sentence combining—and here there is an almost complete dearth of evidence both at school level and with adults. All these single aspects of teaching strategy (and others) would benefit from well-designed RCTs. The field would also benefit from studies comparing the effectiveness of different approaches—and to date there appear to have been no such studies at all. There is ample scope for the next generation of researchers.

REFERENCES

Ananiadou, K., Jenkins, A., & Wolf, A. (2003). *The benefits to employers of raising workforce basic skills levels: A review of the literature.* London: National Research and Development Centre for Adult Literacy and Numeracy.

Barton, D., & Hamilton, M. (1998). *Local literacies: Reading and writing in the community.* New York: Routledge.

Basic Skills Agency. (2000). *Effective basic skills provision for adults.* London: Basic Skills Agency.

Beder, H. (1999). *The outcomes and impacts of adult literacy education in the United States (NCSALL Report 6).* Cambridge, MA: Harvard Graduate School of Education, National Center for the Study of Adult Learning and Literacy.

Besser, S., Brooks, G., Burton, M., Parisella, M., Spare, Y., Stratford, S., & Wainwright, J. (2004). *Adult students' difficulties with reading: An exploratory study.* London: National Research and Development Centre for Adult Literacy and Numeracy.

Brooks, G. (2002). *What works for children with literacy difficulties? The effectiveness of intervention schemes* (Research Report no. RR380). London: Department for Education and Skills.

Brooks, G. (2007). *What works for pupils with literacy difficulties? The effectiveness of intervention schemes* (3rd ed.). London: Department for Children, Schools and Families.

Brooks, G., Burton, M., Cole, P., Miles, J., Torgerson, J., & Torgerson, D. (2008). Randomised controlled trial of incentives to improve attendance at adult literacy classes. *Oxford Review of Education, 34*(5), 493–504. Retrieved from http://www.informaworld.com/smpp/content~content=a787091318~db=all~ order=pubdate

Brooks, G., Burton, M., Cole, P., & Szczerbiński, M. (2007a). *Effective teaching and learning: Reading.* London: National Research and Development Centre for Adult Literacy and Numeracy.

Brooks, G., Burton, M., Cole, P., & Szczerbiński, M. (2007b). *Effective teaching and learning: Reading. Summary report.* London: National Research and Development Centre for Adult Literacy and Numeracy.

Brooks, G., Giles, K., Harman, J., Kendall, S., Rees, F., & Whittaker, S. (2001). *Assembling the fragments: A review of research on adult basic skills* (Research Report no. 220). London: Department for Education and Employment.

Brooks, G., Davies, R., Duckett, L., Hutchison, D., Kendall, S., & Wilkin, A. (2001). *Progress in adult literacy: Do students learn?* London: Basic Skills Agency.

Brooks, G., & Pilling, M. (in press). *The impact of Skills for Life on adult literacy, language and numeracy learners. Final report on analysis of new quantitative data.* London: National Research and Development Centre for Adult Literacy and Numeracy.

Burt, C. (1945, February). The education of illiterate men in the army. *British Journal of Educational Psychology, 15,* 20–27.

Burton, M. (2007). *Oral reading fluency for adults.* London: National Research and Development Centre for Adult Literacy and Numeracy.

Burton, M., Davey, J., Lewis, M., Ritchie, L., & Brooks, G. (2008). *Improving reading: phonics and fluency. Practitioner guide.* London: National Research and Development Centre for Adult Literacy and Numeracy.

Bynner, J., & Parsons, S. (1997). *It doesn't get any netter: The impact of poor basic skills on the lives of 37 year olds.* London: Basic Skills Agency.

Bynner, J., & Parsons, S. (2006a). *New light on literacy and numeracy.* London: National Research and Development Centre for Adult Literacy and Numeracy.

Bynner, J., & Parsons, S. (2006b). *New light on literacy and mumeracy: Summary report.* London: National Research and Development Centre for Adult Literacy and Numeracy.

Casey, H., Cara, O., Eldred, J., Grief, S., Hodge, R., Ivanič, R., et al. (2006). *"You wouldn't expect a maths teacher to teach plastering..." Enbedding literacy, language and numeracy in post-16 vocational programmes — the impact on learning and achievement.* London: National Research and Development Centre for Adult Literacy and Numeracy.

Cheek, E. H., & Lindsey, J. D. (1994). The effects of two methods of reading instruction on urban adults' word identification and comprehension abilities. *Journal of Vocational and Technical Education, 11,* 14–19.

Comings, J. (2003, March). *Evidence-based education: A perspective from the United States.* Paper presented at NRDC/CCER International Conference, Nottingham, UK.

Condelli, L., Wrigley, H. S., Yoon, K., Cronen, S., & Seburn, M. (2003). *What works study for adult ESL literacy students* (draft final report). Washington, DC: U.S. Department of Education, Office of the Under Secretary.

Corley, M. A., & Taymans, J. M. (2002). Adults with learning disabilities: A review of the literature. In J. Comings, B. Garner, & C. Smith,(Eds.), *Annual review of adult learning and literacy, vol. 3* (pp. 44–83). San Francisco: Jossey-Bass.

Dearden, L., McIntosh, S., Myck, M., & Vignoles, A. (2000). *The returns to academic, vocational and basic skills in Britain.* London: Department for Education and Employment.

Department for Education and Employment. (1999). *A fresh start: Improving literacy and numeracy (The Moser Report).* London: Department for Education and Employment.

Desjardins, R., Murray, S., Clermont, Y., & Werquin, P. (2005). *Learning a living: First results of the adult literacy and life skills survey.* Ottawa and Paris: Statistics Canada and OECD. Retrieved from http:// www.statcan.ca/english/freepub/89-603-XIE/2005001/pdf/89-603-XWE-part1.pdf

Dietrich, J. A. (1994). *The effect of auditory perception training on the reading ability of adult poor readers.* Kingston: University of Rhode Island.

Ehri, L. C., Nunes, S. R., Stahl, S. A., & Willows, D. M. (2001). Systematic phonics instruction helps students learn to read: Evidence from the National Reading Panel's meta-analysis. *Review of Educational Research, 71*(3), 393–447.

Gillespie, M. K. (1991). *Becoming authors: the social context of literacy for adult beginning writers.* Unpublished doctoral dissertation, University of Massachusetts, Amherst.

Gillespie, M. K. (2001). Research in writing: implications for adult literacy education. In J. Comings, B. Garner, & C. Smith (Eds.), *Annual review of adult learning and literacy, vol 2* (pp. 63–110). San Francisco: Jossey-Bass.

Gorman, T. P. (1981). A survey of attainment and progress of learners in adult literacy schemes. *Educational Research, 23*(3), 190–198.

Gorman, T., & Moss, N. (1979). *Survey of attainment and progress in adult literacy schemes.* Slough, UK: National Foundation for Educational Research.

Grief, S., Meyer, B., & Burgess, A. (2007a). *Effective teaching and learning: Writing.* London: National Research and Development Centre for Adult Literacy and Numeracy.

Grief, S., Meyer, B., & Burgess, A. (2007b). *Effective teaching and learning: Writing. Summary report.* London: National Research and Development Centre for Adult Literacy and Numeracy.

Hamilton, M., & Barton, D. (2000). The international adult literacy survey: What does it really measure? *International Review of Education, 46*(5), 377–389.

Hamilton, M., & Merrifield, J. (2000). Adult learning and literacy in the United Kingdom. In J. Comings, B. Garner, & C. Smith (Eds.), *Annual review of adult learning and literacy, vol 1* (pp. 243–303). San Francisco: Jossey-Bass.

Haviland, R. (1973). *Survey of provision for adult illiteracy in England.* Reading, UK: Centre for the Teaching of Reading, University of Reading.

Hodgson, A., & Wolf. A. (2008). *Adult learning, policy and accreditation.* Paper presented at Economic and Social Research Council Teaching and Learning Research Programme conference, London, 25 November.

Jones, H. A., & Charnley, A. H. (1978). *Adult literacy: A study of its impact.* Leicester, UK: National Institute of Adult Education.

Kirsch, I. S., Jungeblut, A., Jenkins, L., & Kolstad, A. (1993). *Adult literacy in America: A first look at the results of the national adult literacy survey.* Princeton, NJ: Educational Testing Service.

Knowles, M. (1973). *The adult learner: A neglected species.* Houston, TX: Gulf Publishing.

Kruidenier, J. (2002). *Research-based principles for adult basic education reading instruction.* Jessup, MD: National Institute for Literacy.

Lawrence, D. (1985). Improving self-esteem and reading. *Educational Research, 27*(3), 195–200.

Lawrence, D. (1988). *Enhancing self-esteem in the classroom.* London: Paul Chapman.

Mace, J. (1995). *Literacy, language and community publishing: Essays in adult education.* Clevedon, UK: Multilingual Matters.

Mellar, H., & Kambouri, M. (2001). *Basic skills and ICT: A report to Ufi.* London: University of London Institute of Education.

Morley, D., & Worpole, K. (Eds.). (1982). *Republic of letters: Working class writing and local publishing.* London: Comedia.

Palincsar, A. S. (1982*). Improving the reading comprehension of junior high school students through the reciprocal teaching of comprehension-monitoring strategies.* Unpublished doctoral dissertation, University of Illinois at Urbana-Champaign.

Palincsar, A. S. (1986). The role of dialogue in providing scaffolded instruction. *Educational Psychology, 21,* 73–98.

Palincsar, A. S., & Brown, A. L. (1984). Reciprocal teaching of comprehension-fostering and comprehension-monitoring activities. *Cognition and Instruction, 1*(2), 117–172.

Parsons, S., & Bynner, J. (1998). *Influences on adult basic skills: Factors affecting the development of literacy and numeracy from birth to 37.* London: Basic Skills Agency.

Parsons, S., & Bynner, J. (2007). *Illuminating disadvantage: Profiling the experiences of adults with entry level literacy or numeracy over the lifecourse.* London: National Research and Development Centre for Adult Literacy and Numeracy.

Rachal, J. R. (1995). Adult reading achievement comparing computer-assisted and traditional approaches: A comprehensive review of the experimental literature. *Reading Research and Instruction, 34,* 239–258.

Reder, S. (2005, September). Literacy and the life course. *Reflect, 2,* 16–17.

Reder, S., & Strawn, C. (2001, April). Program participation and self-directed learning to improve basic skills. *Focus on Basics, 4*(D), 15–18.

Rhys Warner, J., Vorhaus, J., Appleby, Y., Bathmaker, A-M., Brooks, G., Cole, P., et al. (2008). *The Learner study: The impact of the Skills for Life strategy on adult literacy, language and numeracy learners. Summary report.* London: National Research and Development Centre for Adult Literacy and Numeracy. Retrieved from http://www.nrdc.org.uk/publications_details.asp?ID=158

Rice, M. with Brooks, G. (2004). *Developmental dyslexia in adults: A research review.* London: National Research and Development Centre for Adult Literacy and Numeracy.

Rich, R., & Shepherd, M. J. (1993). Teaching text comprehension strategies to adult poor readers. *Reading and Writing, 5,* 387–402.

Roberts, R. E., & Cheek, E. H. (1994). Group intervention and reading performance in a medium-security prison facility. *Journal of Offender Rehabilitation, 20,* 97–116.

Rodgers, B. (1986). Change in the reading attainment of adults: a longitudinal study. *British Journal of Developmental Psychology, 4*(1), 1–17.

Rosenshine, B., & Meister, C. (1994). Fostering literacy learning in supportive contexts. *Review of Educational Research, 64*(4), 479–530.

Sheehan-Holt, J. K., & Smith, C. S. (2000). Does basic skills education affect adults' literacy proficiencies and reading practices? *Reading Research Quarterly, 35*(2), 226–243.

Sticht, T. G. (1999). How many low-literacy adults are there in Canada, the U.S. and the U.K.? Should the IALS estimates be revised? *Literacy across the CurriculuMedia Focus, 14*(3–4), 21–22.

Sticht, T. G. (2002). The rise of the adult education and literacy system in the United States: 1600–2000. In J. Comings, B. Garner, & C. Smith (Eds.), *Annual Review of Adult Learning and Literacy, vol. 3* (pp. 10–43). San Francisco: Jossey-Bass,

Sticht, T. G., & Armstrong, W. B. (1994). *Adult literacy in the United States: A compendium of qualitative data and interpretive comments.* San Diego, CA: Applied Behavioral and Cognitive Sciences Inc. and San Diego Community College District.

Sticht, T. G., Armstrong, W. B., Hickey, D. T., & Caylor, J. S. (1987). *Cast-off youth: Policy and training methods from the military experience.* New York: Praeger.

Torgerson, C. J., Brooks, G., & Hall, J. (2006). *A systematic review of the research literature on the use of phonics in the teaching of reading and spelling.* London: Department for Education and Skills Research Report 711. Retrieved http://www.dfes.gov.uk/research/data/uploadfiles/RR711_.pdf

Torgerson, C., Brooks, G., Porthouse, J., Burton, M., Wright, K., & Watt, I. (2004). *Adult literacy and numeracy interventions and outcomes: A review of controlled trials.* London: National Research and Development Centre for Adult Literacy and Numeracy.

Torgerson, C. J., Porthouse, J., & Brooks, G. (2003). A systematic review and meta-analysis of randomised controlled trials evaluating interventions in adult literacy and numeracy. *Journal of Research in Reading, 26*(3), 234–255.

Torgerson, C., Porthouse, J., & Brooks, G. (2005). A systematic review and meta-analysis of controlled trials evaluating interventions in adult literacy and numeracy. *Journal of Research in Reading, 28*(2), 87–107.

Tusting, K., & Barton, D. (2003). *Models of adult learning: A literature review.* London: National Research and Development Centre for Adult Literacy and Numeracy.

Tyler, J. H. (2001a). *So you want a GED? Estimating the impact of the GED on the earnings of dropouts.* Cambridge, MA: National Center for the Study of Adult Learning and Literacy.

Tyler, J. H. (2001b). *What do we know about the economic benefits of the GED: A synthesis of the evidence from recent research.* Providence, RI: Brown University Press.

Tyler, J. H., Murnane, R. J., & Willett, J. B. (2000). *Estimating the impact of the GED on the earnings of young dropouts using a series of natural experiments.* Cambridge, MA: National Center for the Study of Adult Learning and Literacy.

Vignoles, A. (2009). *The returns to investments to adult skills in the UK, and the effectiveness of policies aimed at improving them.* Paper presented at Institute for Fiscal Studies Conference, Cambridge, UK, April 3.

Vignoles, A., de Coulon, A., & Marcenaro-Gutierrez, O. (2007). *The value of basic skills in the British labour market* (No. CEE02-07). London: Centre for the Economics of Education, London School of Economics and Department for Education and Skills.

Vincent, D. (2000). *The rise of mass literacy: Reading and writing in modern Europe.* Oxford, UK: Polity Press.

Vorhaus, J., Howard, U., Brooks, G., Bathmaker, A-M., & Appleby, Y. (2009). The impact of the "Skills for Life" infrastructure on learners: a summary of methods and findings. In S. Reder & J. Bynner (Eds.), *Tracking adult literacy and numeracy skills: Findings from longitudinal research* (pp. 200–221). New York: Routledge.

Williams, J., with Clemens, S., Oleinikova, K., & Tarvin, K. (2003). *The skills for life survey: A national needs and impact survey of literacy, numeracy and ICT skills.* Norwich, UK: The Stationery Office. Retrieved from http://www.dfes.gov.uk/research/data/uploadfiles/RR490

Part 3

Process of Reading

10 The Development of Comprehension

Nell K. Duke
Michigan State University

Joanne Carlisle
University of Michigan

BACKGROUND

The Importance of Understanding the Development of Comprehension

Understanding the development of comprehension foregrounds the challenges that children face in learning to understand written texts at different ages and grade levels (Snow, Griffin, & Burns, 2005). It is important for teachers, especially, to understand the nature of comprehension development so that they can understand both the common pathways and the individual differences in their students' development of comprehension, and have a sound basis for selecting instructional goals, materials, and approaches that foster students' language and literacy development (Gersten, Fuchs, Williams, & Baker, 2001).

Comprehension development has not been the focus of any chapter in the three previous volumes of the *Handbook of Reading Research*, although it has been the focus of reviews elsewhere (e.g., Oakhill & Cain, 2007). Earlier editions included chapters that addressed particular aspects of comprehension development, processes related to comprehension, or pedagogical practices designed to improve reading comprehension. Perhaps most closely related to the topic of this chapter is discussion of the relation of language and literacy in the classroom in Wilkinson and Silliman (2000). These researchers documented the contribution of a sociolinguistic approach for understanding classroom language. They began by articulating a common assumption, namely that children come to school with a basic system of oral communication (including sound structure, syntax, and meaning). They argued that children develop deeper knowledge about language through exposure to discourse structures and subject matter content in the classroom. Language and literacy acquisition in schools mutually reinforce each other.

In this chapter, we expand on this perspective through examination of research on developmental trends and factors that affect students' comprehension in both oral and written language contexts. We limit the scope of our treatment of this enormous topic to early development, from birth through the elementary years. We do not discuss the impact of specific interventions designed to foster reading comprehension development, as this topic is addressed in Wilkinson and Son (this volume) and, as we indicated, in many previous *Handbook of Reading Research* chapters.

COMPREHENSION PROCESSES

Before we can turn to discussion of the development of comprehension processes, it is important to clarify what we mean by language and reading comprehension. Language is the knowledge and use of a set of symbols to represent ideas and intentions. Language is used to convey meanings, and to do so, members of a language culture use agreed-upon conventions that affect the forms and meanings of words, word sequences, and so on. Language is used for communication, for exchanges of ideas and information; comprehension refers to the listener or reader's understanding of the message expressed by the speaker or writer (RAND Reading Study Group, 2002). In this respect, listening comprehension and reading comprehension are not different—both are focused on accessing the meaning of a message communicated by someone else. Listeners/readers and speakers/writers are partners in the communication process.

We define comprehension as the act of constructing meaning with oral or written text. This is truly a constructive process. Meaning does not reside in the oral or written text, which Spiro (1980) calls but "a skeleton, a blueprint for the creation of meaning" (p. 245). Rather, in our view of comprehension, the listener/reader creates and adjusts a mental representation of the meaning of the text (Kintsch, 1998; McNamara, Miller, & Bransford, 2000), using multiple interacting factors, including the text (its language, content, structure, purpose, and features), the listener or reader (her existing knowledge base, views, purposes, processes, strategies, and skills), and the context in which the communication occurs (RAND Reading Study Group, 2002). In reading, theorists believe these factors work together to build meaning in the following way: the reader accesses the meaning of words in text, processes the syntax of clauses and sentences, relates clauses and sentences to one another to build local coherence (e.g., by inferring what pronouns refer to), and relates larger pieces of text to build global coherence (e.g., by inferring how one portion of the text is relevant to another), in the end building a situation model of the text (Kintsch, 1998; Perfetti, 2007). This typically no longer includes memory of the specific clauses or sentences within the text, but rather is the overall meaning made of the text through the interaction of reader, text, and context factors. The profound impact of these multiple interacting factors makes characterizing comprehension development quite complex.

In characterizing comprehension development, three preliminary distinctions are helpful. First, we need to distinguish between mastery constructs and growth constructs (Afflerbach, Pearson, & Paris, 2008). Mastery constructs are those that can be learned to mastery, 100%. For example, alphabet knowledge is a mastery construct—we can have essentially perfect knowledge of letter names, shapes, and associated sounds. In contrast, growth constructs are those that can never really be mastered. We can always become better at a growth construct, as we can continue to develop in that area throughout our lifetimes. Comprehension is a quintessential growth construct. As adults, we might still be developing our ability to comprehend some kinds of text (e.g., the IRS Manual) and some content (e.g., studies in neuropsychology), and we might be refining the practices we use to comprehend text (e.g., searching text ever more effectively). As such, an account of comprehension development does not bring readers to an end point, to 100% mastery—another indication of what makes characterizing comprehension development so complex.

A second distinction, suggested by Brown (1980), is between deliberate, conscious, strategic interventions during reading and other intelligent processing that goes on below the level of conscious introspection. As educators, we think in terms of teaching students strategies, activities used deliberately (e.g., strategies to identify an unfamiliar word). As they become fluent in basic processes of reading, what were once deliberate actions to aid comprehension are carried out largely automatically. Nonetheless, even proficient readers, who can read on automatic pilot (Brown's 1980 phrase), can still encounter problems that require deliberate activities ("debugging" activities, as Brown called them) to figure out what has gone wrong and to address these problems. Afflerbach, Pearson, and Paris (2008) suggested calling these more deliberate actions "strategies" and the more automatic, smooth-running processes "skills." It is important to bear in mind that activity can shift from skill to strategy, in these terms, and back again in an instant. For example, a reader who ordinarily processes aspects of story structure without consciously looking for them (skillful reading) might find herself lost in reading a story thus needing to revert to deliberately rereading the opening of the story to identify the setting. Thus, while more experienced and effective comprehenders may employ skills more often and strategies less often than developing comprehenders, at times all comprehenders engage in acts best characterized as "strategies" (Pressley & Afflerbach, 1995).

A third distinction important to reading this chapter is between development and instruction. Development refers to change over time, in this case in the ability to comprehend oral and written text. Some aspects of comprehension change gradually, whether the child receives instruction in that area or not. For example, children learn new words and word meanings through interacting with other children and adults. However, instruction can influence comprehension development (e.g., Duke & Pearson, 2002; Gersten, Fuchs, Williams, & Baker, 2001). For example, children who receive instruction in vocabulary will develop larger vocabularies faster than those who do not. And indeed, we will refer to the role of instruction repeatedly in our discussion of comprehension development. That said, this chapter is not a review of research on comprehension instruction. Wilkinson and Son (this volume) among many others have covered this ground. Thus, our references to instruction as an influence on comprehension development will be relatively general and brief. This should in no way be taken as a slight to the critical role that instruction can play.

Finally, it is important to note that in educational research, comprehension is often presented as a product or outcome, most often determined by performance on a test that requires reading and responding to passages. Good comprehenders are seen as those who perform well on such a test. However, we must remember that comprehension is a receptive language process. We cannot know what meaning a reader constructed from a given passage or set of passages until that reader says or does something (e.g., summarizes the passage, answers questions about the passage)—and even then we are only able to make inferences about the meaning the reader constructed.

Listening and Reading Comprehension

While we have emphasized commonality in listening and reading comprehension, there are also striking differences in the two processes. Most obviously, written language requires the reader to decode written symbols. These symbols make written text stable, whereas oral texts, unless recorded, lack permanence. Thus, there are processes, such as controlling the pace of comprehension, rereading, skimming, and navigating a text for information, that are possible (and important) with written text but not with oral texts (Sticht, 1982).

Oral and written texts are also presented with different conventions, which in turn place different processing demands on the reader. Written texts mark sentences and paragraphs, use paralinguistic cues such as italicization, and provide other forms of visual representation of ideas and information (e.g., pictures, graphs). These affordances interact with the readers' experience using them to aid comprehension. The texts themselves tend to be quite different. The texts in oral communication tend to be more context-embedded, as the speaker and listener are likely to be talking about a topic or event familiar to both; written language is more likely to be more context-reduced, as the author is not likely to know to the same degree of specificity with whom he or she is communicating, in what time and place, and for what purpose. The writer therefore needs to make an effort to write in such a way that the message will be understood across by a wide variety of readers and contexts. Indeed, researchers who have studied listening and reading comprehension typically conclude that there are many differences, as well as similarities, between these processes. Danks and End (1987), for example, reviewed research identifying similarities and differences across five categories: speech perception and print decoding, lexical access, clause and sentence integration, discourse understanding, and comprehension monitoring.

Important for our purposes in this chapter is not so much how listening and reading comprehension are similar and different, but that they are developmentally intertwined. For example, a child's developing listening vocabulary certainly affects her word recognition and comprehension of written text. At the same time, as a child reads, she learns new words and ways of expressing ideas that are subsequently available to her not only for reading comprehension but for listening comprehension as well. In the years when students are first learning to read, they typically can comprehend more challenging passages when listening than when reading, because of limitations in their word recognition (Sticht & James, 1984). By the middle schools years, the pattern is often reversed: students' performance on challenging passages is better by reading than by listening. This is because readers can pace themselves, reread sentences, and carry out other strategic activities to construct their understanding of the text. Such activities are not possible when listening to passages of the kind that are typically used in written texts. Because of the developmental shift in comprehension of passages by listening and reading, listening comprehension tests should not be used as a "benchmark" for the optimal development of a student's reading comprehension. This is especially true for students with language or reading disabilities because of underlying difficulties processing oral or written language (Carlisle, 1989; Carver & Clark, 1998).

With the premise that oral and written language and their development are inextricably linked but also distinct in developmentally important ways, we turn now to discussing what is known, and yet to be known, about the development of language and reading comprehension. We divide our discussion into three sections: comprehension development from birth to kindergarten entry, comprehension development in the early elementary school years, and comprehension development in the later elementary school years. In each section we consider what is developing during that period, some home and school influences on development during that period, and in what ways development during that period predicts later reading comprehension. We conclude with a discussion of the implications of our review for further study.

INTERPRETIVE ANALYSIS

Comprehension Development in the First Years of Life

Birth to kindergarten entry is an explosive period in oral language and cognitive development. Early on, long before babies understand words, they learn to interpret the meanings of vocal patterns and intonations, facial expressions, and the like. They learn to communicate with caregivers through gestures, crying, and verbal utterances that are not words at all. Thus, their ability to communicate intentions and feelings develops long before language. However, language develops quickly, too; before they start school, they can understand almost everything that adults say to them, although their ability to express themselves develops more slowly than their comprehension (Gleason, 2001).

Language interaction in the home setting influences children's language development. The number and quality of interactions with others significantly influence development of language. For example, Hart and Risley (1995) found that by age 3, children's vocabulary was related to the language parents directed at them, which varied considerably from parent to parent. In fact, the nature and style of parents' communication with their child(ren) (e.g., feedback tone, guidance style) was more closely related to the child's performance on a standardized vocabulary measure (PPVT) than was the child's IQ.

Specific language processes developing from birth to five interact in various ways and affect children's overall language development. One such process involves phonology—that is, phonological perception and processing tends to be holistic when children are first learning words. Gradually as they learn words that differ in one phonemic feature (e.g., nap and map), they begin to process words in a more segmental manner (Fowler, 1991). This process supports the development of phonemic awareness, so that in the preschool years children are able to recognize and produce rhymes and to match words that have the same first sound. Their processing of sounds in words is related to the development of their vocabulary (Metsala & Walley, 1998). Associations of sound and meaning help build representations of words in memory—and lexical representations are used to map sounds and spellings after the preschool years, as children learn to decode and spell words. Strong links among the phonological, orthographic, and semantic features of words build high quality lexical representations of words, which in turn facilitate written word recognition later on (Reichle & Perfetti, 2003). Word recognition is, in turn, strongly related to reading comprehension (e.g., Snow, Porche, Tabors, & Harris, 2007; Vellutino, Tunmer, Jaccard, & Chen, 2007).

Before they attend school, many children develop an interest in and awareness of words—and, in fact, of other aspects of language as well (Clark, 2003). In this period, children usually do not have conscious awareness of the relation of structure and meaning and have limited abilities to reflect on, analyze, or manipulate language; nonetheless, many do learn to enjoy simple jokes that involve a play on word meanings, alliterative names, and so on. Even such implicit understandings of language forms and meanings serve children well as they learn to read and write (Lyster, 2002). The beginning of more explicit awareness is fostered by such experiences as learning nursery rhymes, talking about words, and learning to make and understand puns. Early aspects of linguistic awareness are believed to contribute substantially to children's vocabulary and comprehension development (Bryant, Bradley, Maclean, & Crossland, 1989).

Cognitive capabilities that are developing in the period from birth to kindergarten entry influence children's understanding and use of language (Nelson, 1996). For example, children are developing their ability to engage in analogical and causal reasoning—kinds of reasoning that are needed to understand oral and written language once students begin school (e.g., Cain & Oakhill, 1999). Even in the toddler years children are developing certain habits of mind and ways of thinking, such as inferring (e.g., Graham & Kilbreath, 2007), that could be viewed as a foundation for the skills and strategies of later reading comprehension.

Features of the home environment and activities that involve books and writing materials affect preschool children's vocabulary development and their ability to comprehend texts, written or oral (Dickinson & Tabors, 2001). Exposure to text through parents' own reading and their reading to children provide models that suggest the value and purposes of books and reading (Baker, Scher, & Mackler, 1997; Purcell-Gates, 1996; Weigel, Martin, &

Bennett, 2005). Reading books to children not only helps them acquire concepts of print but also introduces them to discourse patterns in books and basic meaning-making strategies (e.g., linking information from pictures and words) (DeTemple, 2001). Children begin to understand the genres of written language. For example, by kindergarten, children who have been read to can employ the kinds of words, syntax, and discourse patterns found in texts of specific genres, such as fairy tales or information books (Duke & Kays, 1998; Pappas, 1993; Purcell-Gates, 1988; Sulzby, 1985). To the extent that the books read to preschoolers provide new concepts and information, children also have opportunities to learn about the world and to acquire knowledge about particular topics (what Hirsch, 2003, and Neuman, 2006, have regarded as domain knowledge). This knowledge base will contribute to development of their reading comprehension over time.

Of course, not all reading to children is equally supportive of their language and literacy development. For example, engaging children in the discussion of text appears to contribute more to comprehension development than simply reading aloud (e.g., Whitehurst et al., 1988). Substantial variation in parent-to-child reading practices is related to parental SES, race, ethnicity, and cultural background, the parent-child relationship, and text genre (e.g., Bus, 2001; Pellegrini, Perlmutter, Galda, & Brody, 1990; Raikes et al., 2006). Other factors include whether an early childhood education intervention is involved and what that intervention entails (e.g., Lonigan, Shanahan, & Cunningham with the National Early Literacy Panel, 2008), although these factors fall outside the scope of this chapter.

Like the home environment, the preschool environment can contribute enormously to language development as well as to reading comprehension. In language-rich preschools, children learn to participate in a variety of literacy-related activities (e.g., play with letters and writing tools, listening to stories read aloud). They learn to participate in talk about books (Wilkinson & Son, this volume). Extensive language learning opportunities, including talk during play activities and snack time, are associated with gains in vocabulary (Cote, 2001). In a general way, researchers have found that preschool attendance prepares children for literacy in school and has been related to achievement in school (Duncan et al., 2007).

Predictors of Later Reading Comprehension

To what extent do early language development, cognitive development, and home and preschool literacy opportunities contribute to the development of reading comprehension, once children go to school? In a recent meta-analysis, researchers (Lonigan et al., 2008) found five constructs, measured prior to kindergarten entry, that were shown in three or more studies to predict later reading comprehension: phonological short-term memory (mean correlation 0.51), alphabet knowledge (0.45), visual perception (0.41), oral language (0.40), and phonological awareness (0.36). The dominance of word and sub-word level skill (3 of 5 outcomes) and the only moderate relationship of oral language to later reading comprehension may be explained in part by the fact that most of the studies did not follow children very far into schooling, when oral language becomes increasingly related to reading comprehension and word and sub-word level skills become decreasingly so (see later discussion). As noted earlier, the particular measures (and characteristics of these measures) are also likely to influence these findings. In particular, limitations of extant reading comprehension assessments for young children might have played a role in the results of these studies.

Lonigan and colleagues (2008) conducted a secondary analysis in which they examined aspects of oral language that were assessed in each of the studies. The results show that some measures of oral language were strongly predictive of later reading comprehension, even in the relatively small window of time in which many of these studies were conducted, while others are far less so. In particular, broader measures—overall language comprehension, expressive, and receptive language comprehension—were highly correlated with later reading comprehension (mean correlations of 0.70, 0.63, and 0.59, respectively; note that this analysis included kindergarten students). Other researchers have also found that variation in oral language development, even early in life, is strongly related to reading comprehension years later. For example, Craig, Connor, and Washington (2003) found that syntactic complexity in preschoolers who speak African American English was predictive of reading comprehension achievement through third grade. In a particularly long-ranging study, Rescorla (2005) compared children who were late talkers (i.e., age 24 to 31 months) to matched peers with typical language development and found that the late talkers had poorer reading comprehension at age 13 with an effect size of the difference being 0.84.

Although far less studied, inferencing ability in the preschool years also seems to be predictive of later reading comprehension. Kendeou et al. (2006) examined preschool children's ability to make inferences related to the causal structure of narratives presented via video and aurally. For one cohort, children's comprehension on these tasks at age 4 predicted their performance on these tasks at age 6; for a second cohort, performance in these tasks at age 6 predicted reading comprehension at age 8. In the parlance of reading comprehension skills and strategies presented earlier, inferencing is usually a skill, that is, automatic, but sometimes a strategy, that is, quite deliberate. This research suggests the roots of this type of reasoning, so important to reading comprehension, are laid quite early.

Finally, various characteristics of a child's experiences at home and at school during the preschool years have also been found to predict later reading comprehension directly and indirectly. Various home literacy practices in the preschool years are related to later language and reading development (e.g., Landry, Smith & Swank, 2003). In a 3-year longitudinal study, Hood, Conlon, and Andrews (2008) found that, after controlling for age, gender, memory, and nonverbal ability, parental teaching of letters and words was related to the children's performance on a measure of letter and word identification in grades 1 and 2, and parent-child reading was related to vocabulary growth in Grade 1; both word identification and vocabulary were, in turn, related to reading comprehension. Snow, Porche, Tabors, and Harris (2007) found that maternal extended discourse and support for literacy in the home predicted reading comprehension growth in grades 4, 7, and 10, where maternal extended discourse is comprised of the percentage of nonimmediate talk in book reading, the percentage of fantasy talk in toy play, the percentage of explanatory and narrative talk at mealtime, and the percentage of science process talk in magnet play.

Similarly, preschool teachers' extended discourse and the extent to which their classroom exposed children to rare words predicted children's reading comprehension growth in grades 4, 7, and 10 (Snow, Porche, Tabors, & Harris, 2007), where teachers' extended discourse was measured by their group focusing talk, cognitive extending talk during group time, percentage of book analysis talk during book reading, and percentage of extending talk during free play. Teachers' book readings have also been found to predict children's comprehension, as well as their vocabulary, several years later (Dickinson & Smith, 1994).

Before leaving this section on predictors of later reading comprehension, we remind readers that our account is necessarily limited by the potential predictors researchers have examined and how they have examined them. There may be strong predictors of reading comprehension that have not yet been identified because researchers have not yet looked at them or have done so with inadequate measures. For example, it is possible that the degree to which parents and preschool teachers model comprehension strategies is highly predictive of later reading comprehension, but, to our knowledge, research has not yet examined that possibility.

Also important is the reminder that just because a construct predicts later reading comprehension does not mean that we should therefore teach or foster development of that construct. To take an example from mathematics, one predictor of later achievement is the ability to count to 100. As a result, we know of preschool programs rushing to teach children to count to 100. In one case we are aware of, teachers in a math project chose not to teach number sense to their preschool children, reasoning that their program needed to focus only on teaching children to count to 100 (J. Sarama and D. Clements, personnel communication, May, 26, 2009). Of course, the problem is that counting to 100 is very likely a proxy for a number of things that better position that child for stronger later math achievement rather than the cause of stronger later math achievement. This suggests the need to be quite cautious in applying findings about predictors of reading comprehension directly to instructional practice.

Reading Comprehension in the Early Elementary School Years

In the early elementary school years, schooling emerges as a pervasive influence on children's reading comprehension development. Even children with similar demographic and individual characteristics can show very different courses of reading comprehension development, depending on the classroom context in which they are learning (e.g., Taylor, Pearson, Clark, & Walpole, 2000; Tivnan & Hemphill, 2005). This variation is not attributable simply to the specific interventions or instructional methods teachers use to address reading comprehension but appears also to be influenced by such factors as the time devoted to instruction, the aspects of language and reading that are emphasized, the availability of materials, and the instructional activities used by the teacher (e.g., Taylor et al., 2000; Tivnan & Hemphill, 2005; Valencia, Place, Martin & Grossman, 2006; Wilkinson & Son, this volume).

Numerous teacher, classroom, and school factors affect comprehension development (see the Wilkinson & Son chapter for a review of pedagogical factors). However, we leave these broader issues aside now in order to focus on aspects of language development that influence the development of reading comprehension in the early school years. These include linguistic awareness and the language and discourses of schooling. Students develop some language capabilities through involvement in literacy activities (such as the production of narratives) at the same time that language capabilities influence the student's interactions with literacy. Language and literacy are likely to reinforce one another synergistically (e.g., Catts, Fey, Tomblin, & Zhang, 2002). According to Snowling, "learning to read demands an interplay of different language skills that may interact to an extent yet to be determined. Reading acquisition is a dynamic process that draws differentially on different language resources in different developmental phases" (2005, p. 70). Individual differences in cognitive skills and experiential factors also mediate developmental changes in students' language and literacy (Vellutino, Scanlon, Sipay, et al., 1996).

Much of the language development that occurs in kindergarten through Grade 3 is incidental, in the sense that students are learning through exposure to and imitation of the words, expressions, and patterns of language use they observe others using. Children are likely to learn words and phrases that seem relevant to them in a particular context, but what they learn depends on the meaning they can derive from the discourse situation (Nelson, 1996). Incidental word learning accounts for a large percentage of all new words learned. Estimates are that each year children learn on average 3,000 words, only about 300 of which are explicitly taught to them in school (Beck & McKeown, 1991). Similarly, gradual learning of increasingly complex syntactic structures occurs less through direct instruction than through exposure to adult discourse and the language of books, as seen through studies of students' retellings and renderings of stories and informational texts (Morrow, 1985; Pappas, 1993; Purcell-Gates, McIntyre, & Freppon, 1995).

Children are acquiring metalinguistic capabilities that are critical for language and literacy development in the early elementary years and beyond (e.g., phonemic awareness, syntactic awareness—see Gombert 1992). In fact, Nagy (2007) argued that reading comprehension development is largely dependent on children's metalinguistic ability. Explicit or conscious awareness of language gradually emerges in the early elementary years. For example, students are not yet very adept at using word parts to read and understand unfamiliar words, as the ability to do so requires attention to the relation between form or structure and meaning (Carlisle & Fleming, 2003). Similarly, Anglin (1993) found that when compared to third or fifth graders, first graders were limited in their ability to figure out the possible meaning of unfamiliar words with familiar parts, such as *treelet*.

Two other aspects of language are developing rapidly in the early elementary years. First, students become increasingly able to convey ideas clearly to one another (i.e., referential communication; Lloyd, 1990). Second, they are learning the language and discourse patterns of schooling. Teachers play a role in fostering language development through the ways that they elicit responses from students and foster sharing and discussion of ideas. Such language functions are important for students for whom language learning presents particular challenges, such as English language learners and students with learning disabilities (e.g., August et al., 2006; Boyd & Rubin, 2006). While students are, in essence, learning "talking to learn" (Wallach & Ehren, 2004), early elementary students need considerable adult guidance for successful small-group literacy discussions, as students' peer status and literacy development can influence their participation and collaboration (Matthews & Kesner, 2003).

Students' development of oral communicative capabilities (listening and speaking) influences literacy acquisition in a number of ways. Participation in conversations and discussions prepares students to engage in learning to read and write and to use reading and writing for various communicative purposes. Students' ability to understand instructional discourse and to engage in the social networking around learning in the classroom are critical in forming habits of mind that are necessary for the development of proficiency in reading comprehension. Perhaps not surprisingly, language and academic success go hand in hand (Fey, Catts, & Larrivee, 1995).

In the early elementary years, language becomes the content as well as the medium for learning. In particular, there is a prevailing view that learning academic language is critical for successful literacy and academic achievement, both for monolingual English speakers and students who are English language learners (August & Shanahan, 2006). Academic language includes the many abstract terms and expressions used to talk about literacy (e.g., *theme, summarize, glossary*), as well as the grammatical structures and formulations that convey information and ideas in different content areas (Halliday, 1993; Schleppegrell, 2004).

Through the early elementary years, students are exposed to a greater variety of genres and types of texts and are increasingly expected to learn from texts (Palincsar & Duke, 2004). Children's knowledge of both narrative and informational text language and structures develops substantially during the early elementary years (e.g., Donovan & Smolkin, 2002; Kamberelis, 1999; Purcell-Gates, Duke, & Martineau, 2007). Again, teachers play a critical role. As Schleppegrell (2004) has pointed out, the cognitive demand that characterizes learning from books is a function of the relation of the task and the learner rather than inherent in the text itself. The teacher's choice of tasks, ways of fostering language use in talking about texts, and ability to scaffold children's understanding of the discourse structures in texts are important determinants of children's literacy development.

While phonemic awareness has long been seen as important in preparing students for reading, in recent years researchers have stressed the interplay of phonology and semantics in language development (Scarborough, 2005; Tunmer & Chapman, 1998). More specifically, vocabulary growth has been shown to contribute to a change in the nature of phonological representations in that they become more segmental in form (Metsala & Walley, 1998). Thus, deficits in phonemic awareness might go hand in hand with slow vocabulary development. A related aspect of cognitive development is students' ability to simultaneously consider phonological and semantic information—an index of cognitive flexibility. Development of cognitive flexibility has been linked to reading comprehension, above and beyond decoding skill, verbal ability, and the broader ability to simultaneously consider multiple aspects of stimuli (Cartwright, 2002).

Rapid development of letter-sound knowledge, word reading, and decoding strategies also characterizes the early elementary period, in which word recognition is the major instructional emphasis. Performance on tests of word reading or decoding are typically strongly correlated with performance on reading comprehension measures in the early elementary years (see discussion below). In part, this strong association reflects the need to develop fast and accurate word recognition capabilities, which are the cornerstone of fluent reading and critical to reading comprehension. Fluent reading involves reading texts accurately and with appropriate rate and expression, fostered in large measure by extensive practice reading texts and by some programs or instructional methods targeting fluency (Rasinski & Hoffman, 2003; Rasinski, this volume). In the early elementary years children display widely varying levels of fluency; many studies have found that fluent reading of connected text is related to reading comprehension, even above and beyond fluent word reading (e.g., Jenkins, Fuchs, van den Broek, Espin, & Deno, 2003). Fluency is so important to reading comprehension because it reduces demands on the reader at every level—letter, word, and text—allowing the reader to devote greater cognitive resources to meaning-making (LaBerge & Samuels, 1974; Logan, 1997).

The early elementary years are also an important time for growth in the use of reading comprehension skills and strategies. Certainly, young students are developing the ability to make various kinds of inferences (e.g., Barnes, Dennis, & Haefele-Kalvaitis, 1996; Casteel & Simpson, 1991) and to monitor comprehension (e.g., Kinnunen, Vauras, & Niemi, 1998). At least if provided with instruction, they develop in their ability to think about their own approach to text comprehension (e.g., Paris & Jacobs, 1984; Brown, Pressley, Van Meter, & Schuder, 1996). If taught specific reading comprehension strategies or repertoires of strategies, early elementary children become increasingly able to apply these as they read, demonstrating ownership and independent use of methods to improve their understanding of texts (see Pearson & Duke, 2002; Roberts & Duke, 2010; and Stahl, 2004, for reviews). Thus, comprehension strategies can be part of what develops in comprehension development in the early elementary grades, although the relative rarity of comprehension instruction in these years might undermine that possibility (Pressley, 2002; Westby, 2004).

Unfortunately, the research base does not yet permit a detailed account of the course of development of reading comprehension strategies in the early elementary grades. Very likely, research will never reveal an invariant order in which strategies are learned and applied, but rather will reveal that strategy deployment at any age depends on the interaction of characteristics of the reader (including basic processes and background knowledge), the text, and the context (RAND Report, 2002). Researchers have shown that young readers are more able to make some kinds of inferences (e.g., "in the text" connections) than others (e.g., integration of information across texts). However, recent research suggests that these findings may be more a function of the instructional opportunities afforded to children than to true developmental differences in strategy acquisition (e.g., Oyler & Barry, 1996; Sipe, 2000).

Finally, in the early elementary years many children begin to engage in extensive independent reading, and others, sadly, do not. By fourth grade, Guthrie (2004) found that students reading at grade level engaged in an average of 60 minutes per day of reading during free time and homework and another 60 minutes per day during teacher-guided instruction. Fourth graders reading at the second grade level engaged in only 10 minutes per day of reading during free time and homework and spent only 20 in teacher-guided instruction. The amount of reading in these early years has been found to predict reading comprehension years later, even after controlling for previous reading comprehension (Cunningham & Stanovich, 1997). Clearly, reading experience matters in developing fluent and strategic reading, but it is also likely to contribute to student's vocabulary, knowledge about the world, and understanding of the features, and ways of engaging with, different kinds of written texts.

Predictors of Reading Comprehension

With respect to predicting children's reading comprehension in these early years of schooling, one persistent finding is the strong links between word recognition, fluency, and reading comprehension (e.g., Berninger, Abbott, Vermeulen, & Fulton, 2006; Catts, Hogan, & Fey, 2003; Speece, Roth, Cooper, & de la Paz, 1999; Vellutino et al., 2007; Rupley, Willson, & Nichols, 1998; for a review for kindergarten specifically, see Lonigan et al., 2008). Phonological awareness is part of the story too, because it plays a supporting role in the development of word recognition (e.g., Catts et al., 1999). That is, the relationship of phonological awareness and reading comprehension appears from fairly early on to operate primarily through word recognition (e.g., Demont & Gombert, 1996; Speece et al., 1999).

Word recognition and fluency aside, oral language capabilities of various kinds predict reading comprehension in the early elementary grades. However, as we document later in the chapter, this relationship appears even stronger in the later elementary years, perhaps because there is less variance in word reading ability still extant to predict reading comprehension and/or because the texts on the tests are more complex, relying on more sophisticated language knowledge. Catts and colleagues found that language impairment evidenced in kindergarten portends reading comprehension difficulties as early as Grade 2 and into Grade 4 (Catts et al., 2002; Catts et al., 1999). Listening comprehension in kindergarten has been found to predict reading comprehension in Grade 2 (Lepola, Niemi, Kuikka, & Hannula, 2005). Similarly, listening comprehension in Grade 1 predicted reading comprehension by Grade 3 (de Jong & van der Leij, 2002), and listening comprehension at 8.5 years (roughly Grade 3) predicted reading comprehension then and at age 13 (Nation & Snowling, 2004). Whether syntactic knowledge is predictive of reading comprehension development is a matter of some debate. Some studies have found performance on measures of syntactic knowledge to be predictive in early elementary and beyond (e.g., Craig et al., 2003; Demont & Gombert, 1996), while other studies have not (e.g., Gottardo, Stanovich, & Siegel, 1996; Roth, Speece, & Cooper, 2002; Vellutino et al., 2007). It is possible that the conception of syntactic awareness and the particular designs of the studies contributed to these disparate results.

Vocabulary in the early elementary years has been found to be predictive of reading comprehension (Nation & Snowling, 2004; Seigneuric & Ehrlich, 2005; Vellutino et al., 2007), and various vocabulary-related abilities in kindergarten (e.g., word retrieval, ability to define words) predicted, with print awareness, reading comprehension by Grade 2 (Roth et al., 2002). Tannenbaum, Torgesen, and Wagner (2006) demonstrated that breadth as well as depth of vocabulary knowledge (with depth including speed of word retrieval) predicted reading comprehension in third grade, with breadth somewhat more predictive.

Surprisingly few studies have examined the relationship of specific comprehension skills and strategies in the early elementary grades to reading comprehension then or in later schooling. One exception is a study carried out by Cain, Oakhill, and Bryant (2004) in which they examined the relation of reading comprehension to the ability to make inferences, knowledge of story structure, and comprehension monitoring. In the earliest grade studied (third grade), they observed relationships between reading comprehension and each of these abilities, with each of them accounting for unique variance in reading comprehension, above and beyond word reading ability, vocabulary and general verbal ability. In another study, comprehension monitoring was found to predict listening comprehension as early as first grade (Kinnunen et al., 1998). These findings suggest the potential value of further research, designed to examine the complex array of factors that influence reading comprehension development.

The relation of early elementary children's genre knowledge to later reading comprehension is another under-researched area. Kendeou et al. (2006) found performance on tasks of comprehending narratives presented aurally and via video at age 6 to be predictive of performance on reading comprehension measures at age 8. However, Roth et al. (2002) did not find narrative discourse capabilities in kindergarten to be related to reading comprehension at Grade 2. To our knowledge, researchers have not yet examined the relationship of competence with other genres, such as informational genres, to later reading comprehension performance.

Home factors in the early elementary years continue to predict reading comprehension. Sénéchal (2006) found that parent reports of frequency of storybook reading, which Sénéchal terms "informal" literacy experiences, predicted, indirectly, children's Grade 4 reading comprehension (as well, directly, as their vocabulary and child reports of reading for pleasure). Interestingly, parent reports of teaching about literacy to children, which Sénéchal has termed "formal" literacy experiences, were associated with kindergarten alphabetic knowledge and Grade 4 reading fluency but not reading comprehension. This work helps to illustrate the non-unitary nature of the home environment (e.g., Iverson & Wahlberg, 1982), with some home characteristics important to reading comprehension development and others not.

Another study of home factors as predictors of reading comprehension development in the early elementary years (and beyond) examined both home and school experiences of a ethnically diverse group of low-income students originally in grades 2, 4, and 6 over a 2-year period (Snow, Barnes, Chandler, Goodman, & Hemphill, 1991). The researchers were able to identify parsimonious models of home and school factors predicting word recognition and vocabulary, but found a far wider range of factors associated with reading comprehension growth. These factors included literacy practices in the home, educational expectations for the child, parental involvement in schooling, family income, the number of outings with adults the child experienced in week, and the degree to which the amount and content of television viewing in the home was restricted (with greater restriction predicting greater growth in reading comprehension). That such a range of variables proved to predict reading comprehension is consistent with our assertion at the outset of the chapter about the relative complexity and multifaceted nature of reading comprehension, and thus the challenge of measuring it, the many factors that contribute to it, and its development over time.

As a part of this complexity, it is critical to understand that in the elementary years home and school factors interact to predict the course of reading comprehension development. In this respect, the Snow, Porche, Tabors, and Harris (2007) study is again instructive. Students whose home environments were rated low nonetheless made expected gains in reading comprehension when their classrooms were rated in 2 consecutive years as high with respect to instruction, the emotional climate, and the literacy environment. However, only 25% of students whose home environments were rated low made expected gains if one of their two classrooms was rated low; none made expected gains when both classrooms were rated low.

Instructional factors have proven to be predictors of reading comprehension in other studies as well, although again we refer the reader to Wilkinson and Son (this volume) for a more complete treatment of this topic. For example, Taylor, Pearson, Peterson, and Rodriguez (2003) found that reading comprehension growth during the school year in grades 2 through 5 was predicted by a greater degree of higher-level questioning, a greater degree of classroom time on task, a lesser degree of comprehension skill instruction, and a lesser degree of passive responding. Connor, Morrison, and Petrella (2004) found that students who entered third grade with average or low reading comprehension showed greater growth over the course of the year if their classrooms provided more teacher-managed reading comprehension instructional activities, and less growth in classrooms with more child-managed reading comprehension activities. Yet the results of a study by Smith, Lee, and Newmann (2001) suggest that teacher-managed should not be interpreted as referring to didactic instruction. They found greater reading growth ("reading" as measured by the Iowa Test of Basic Skills) in grades 2 through 8 classrooms in which teachers engaged in more interactive rather than didactic instruction. Among other things, in didactic instruction the primary approach to teaching was lecture combined with asking single right-answer questions. In contrast, interactive instruction was characterized by the teacher acting as guide or coach; discussion, interpretation, and application were the primary focus of teaching. Finally, as explained earlier, a number of specific instructional interventions designed to teach reading comprehension strategies in the early elementary grades are associated with greater growth in reading comprehension than is seen in study control or comparison groups (see Pearson & Duke, 2002; Roberts & Duke, 2010; and Stahl, 2004, for reviews). Thus, we end this section very much as we started it, with the critical role that opportunities to learn in school play in reading comprehension development in the early elementary years.

Comprehension in the Later Elementary School Years

In the later elementary years, we see a continuation of the development of language and literacy found in the early school years, but these are accompanied by shifts in emphasis. Capabilities in various aspects of language development, knowledge development, and strategy use associated with content area learning become ever more important. Instruction and the instructional context continue to shape development, with more curricular attention paid to reading comprehension.

Language development continues in the upper elementary years (Nippold, 2007). Students are developing not only language but also aspects of linguistic awareness that are particularly related to their reading and spelling, including syntactic awareness (Scott, 2004) and morphological awareness (Carlisle, 2000; Singson, Mahoney, & Mann, 2000). Morphological awareness contributes to reading comprehension in the later elementary years more than in the early elementary years (Carlisle, 2000; Singson et al., 2000). Anglin (1993) found that between third- and fifth-grade, students became increasingly competent at inferring the meanings of morphologically complex words (e.g., *priesthood*) by analysis of word structure. Fifth graders can also learn to infer word meanings from context (Baumann et al. 2002). These two vocabulary-learning strategies work together well as students encounter unfamiliar words in texts (Baumann et al., 2002; Nagy & Scott, 2000). Importantly, students won't think to use these strategies if they are not monitoring their comprehension enough to realize that a particular word, or its meaning in that context, is unfamiliar to them. This illustrates the larger point that multiple capabilities interact in comprehension.

Comprehension skill and strategy use are certainly continuing to develop in this period. More so than in the early elementary years, students are able to make inferences based not just on textual information (e.g., the motive of a character) but also through use of background knowledge (Cain, Oakhill, & Lemmon, 2004; Casteel & Simpson, 1991). They also become increasingly skillful in forming and explaining generalizations. Anderson and his colleagues (e.g., Clark et al., 2003) have shown that fourth-grade students can learn to formulate an argument and find information in texts to support generalizations. They can learn effective argumentation by modeling the discourse of adults or other students, a process Anderson and his colleagues refer to as *collaborative argumentation*. In addition, as they progress from the early to the later elementary years, they are increasingly able to monitor their own reading for understanding and engage in strategic reading (Cain et al., 2004; Paris & Cross, 1988). By fifth or sixth grade, comprehension monitoring and effective use of word and text comprehension strategies are more important in predicting text comprehension than word reading (Willson & Rupley, 1997). This reveals the importance of strategy acquisition in reading comprehension development and portends the benefits of strategy instruction at this age, discussed later in the section.

The content areas receive greater instructional emphasis in the late elementary years, although some have argued this emphasis should be present from much earlier on (e.g., Duke, 2003; Hirsch, 2003). By the end of the elementary grades, children who have been struggling with reading comprehension score lower on assessments of science and math as well as English language arts (Cain & Oakhill, 2006), suggesting the importance of reading comprehension for content area learning, which is undoubtedly influenced by students' foundational reading skills and content-area knowledge. With greater emphasis on content area learning comes the necessity for students to be able to understand features of content area texts and ways that information is conveyed, verbally and otherwise. For example, students need to learn to navigate text to find the information they want or need (Dreher, 2002; Symons, MacLatchy-Gaudet, Stone, & Reynolds, 2001). Similarly, the ability to navigate and comprehend hypertext takes on greater importance in school tasks (Eagleton, Dobler, & Leu, 2006). By sixth grade, according to one study, good Internet readers engage in a wide range of strategies and practices, some of which go beyond those required in print-based reading, such as use of Web-based search engines and informational website structures, rapid cycles of information-seeking, and intertwining cognitive strategies and physical reading actions (Coiro & Schmar-Dobler, 2007; see also Leu et al., 2008).

For at least some students, the late elementary years see a deepening knowledge of narrative and expository genres. Students demonstrate increasing understanding of the structure of stories and increasing ability to identify their main ideas (McKeough & Genereux, 2002; van den Broek, Lynch, Naslund, Ievers-Landis, & Verduin, 2003). As documented later in the chapter, understanding of the characteristics of narratives is a strong predictor of reading comprehension in these years. Greater exposure to and experience with expository text in the late elementary grades leads some readers to become more aware of and knowledgeable about expository text structure (e.g., Englert & Thomas, 1987; McGee, 1982), although readers can develop this knowledge earlier if given instruction (Williams et al., 2005). Notably, there is an interaction between knowledge of text structure and knowledge of content related to the text, with text structure knowledge more important when the reader knows less about the text (Roller, 1990). Again, this underscores that multiple capabilities interact in reading comprehension.

The classroom context continues to have a profound impact on children's comprehension development in the later elementary years. Not surprisingly given the greater emphasis on content area learning in the later elementary years, how the teacher handles teaching comprehension of content area text appears to be influential for development. Instruction in strategies for reading expository text yields substantial gains in reading comprehension for struggling readers in the later elementary grades (see Martin & Duke, in press, for a review). Situating comprehension instruction within science instruction, with strong attention to fostering motivation to read, appears to be very powerful for comprehension development (Guthrie, McRae, & Klauda, 2007; Romance & Vitale, 2001). Notably, reading and writing, accompanied by hands-on experiences, appear to enhance, rather than detract from, content area learning (Anderson & Guthrie, 1999; Romance & Vitale, 2001; Wang, 2005).

Talk in the classroom is also influential for reading comprehension development. The nature of teacher talk not only can affect students' engagement but also offers opportunities for improvement of students' ability to explain ideas and share information (Berry, 2006). The nature of student-to-student talk can also be influential. Teachers are likely to use more routines and methods of making-meaning from reading that involve small group discussion, such as literature discussion groups (Almasi, 1995; Goatley, Brock & Raphael, 1995). These small group discussions appear to have the potential to impact comprehension-related constructs, such as students' vocabulary and use of comprehension strategies (Kong & Fitch, 2002/2003). Effective involvement in discussions, whether led by students or teachers, becomes increasingly important for participation in learning, not only in language arts but in other content areas as well. Quality discussion in classrooms is linked to gains in reading comprehension (Murphy, Wilkinson, Soter, Hennessey, & Alexander, 2009; Wilkinson & Son, this volume).

Other aspects of the classroom affect students' opportunities to develop comprehension. One is exposure to a rich literacy environment. The availability of reading materials (type, quantity, and quality) used to promote comprehension and interest in reading was related to elementary students' reading comprehension growth (Hoffman, Sailors, Duffy, & Beretvas, 2004). The literacy environment in the later elementary years is also marked by increasing access to electronic media in a wide variety of forms (McKenna & Walpole, 2007); research on the explosion of text types used in the late elementary years is an emerging field (Leu, Kinzer, Coiro, & Cammack, 2004). Another important factor is the extent to which students are actually spending time reading, whether during instructional events or independently (Anderson, Wilson, & Fielding, 1988; Guthrie, 2004). In the late elementary years, students benefit from having a wealth of opportunities to read and write, and the quality and extensiveness of these opportunities has been associated with noteworthy gains in reading comprehension (e.g., Allington, 2002; Taylor, Pearson, Peterson, & Rodriguez, 2003).

Finally, an important influence on students' reading comprehension development is interest in reading. In a large-scale, national survey, McKenna, Kear, and Ellsworth (1995) found that students' interest in both academic and recreational reading dropped off precipitously across the elementary years with modest declines only among the high ability readers. Efforts to build interest and motivation, such as giving students the opportunity to pick books to read or topics for papers, promotes interest in reading, which in turn promotes the development of reading comprehension (Guthrie, Hoa, et al., 2007).

Predictors of Reading Comprehension

In the later elementary years, word recognition and fluency become less potent predictors of reading comprehension, while language development gains predictive power. Vellutino et al. (2007) found that semantic skills are more important determinants of reading comprehension for sixth and seventh graders than for second and third graders. In a longitudinal study of Dutch elementary students, Verhoeven and Van Leeuwe (2008) found that word decoding had a large relationship to early reading comprehension but only a small effect on later comprehension. Catts, Hogan, and Adlof (2005) found a shift similar to that noted by other researchers; in this study, word decoding accounted for a decreasing amount of the variance in reading comprehension, while language comprehension accounted for an increasing amount of variance in reading comprehension between the second and eighth grades. Vocabulary, in particular, is very highly correlated with reading comprehension in the upper elementary years (Anderson & Freebody, 1981; Baumann, 2009). For example, Wagner, Muse, and Tannenbaum (2007) found that for fourth graders, the correlation of vocabulary and reading comprehension was 0.86. Morphological awareness, measured by knowledge of meanings of words with suffixes, was a stronger predictor of reading comprehension than the ability to read aloud such words; this pattern was evident in the fifth but not the third grade (Carlisle, 2000).

While there is convergence of these findings, it is important to recognize that language development may only *seem* more important to reading comprehension in the later than the earlier elementary years. Language is developing rapidly in the early elementary years, and that development undoubtedly affects comprehension of oral and written texts in the earlier elementary years. However, as discussed earlier, by the later elementary years there is less variance in word reading ability still extant to predict reading comprehension and the texts on assessments are far more linguistically sophisticated. In any case, for students who are able to read most of the words in their grade-level texts, language development (or aspects thereof, such as vocabulary) becomes the major factor in identifying sources of variation in reading comprehension performance in the later elementary grades (e.g., Cain, 2009; Catts et al., 2005; Curtis, 1980).

Other important predictors of reading comprehension in the later elementary grades involve the use of comprehension skills and strategies. By fifth or sixth grade, comprehension monitoring and effective use of other word and text comprehension strategies are strong predictors of reading comprehension, and more important predictors than word reading (Willson & Rupley, 1997). Several studies discussed in the section on Predictors of Comprehension in the Early Elementary Grades apply here as well. For example, Cain et al.'s (2004) study extends into the later elementary grades, where findings indicate that the ability to make inferences, knowledge of story structure, and comprehension monitoring all predict reading comprehension above and beyond verbal ability and word recognition. Somewhat similarly, Paris and Jacobs (1984) found that 8- and 10-year-olds who reported greater awareness of strategies such as previewing and rereading performed better on tests of reading comprehension.

Various home and school factors also serve as predictors of reading comprehension in the later elementary school years. Some of the studies of home and school influences on reading comprehension reviewed in the section on the early elementary years extend into the later elementary grades, including the work of Snow and colleagues (Snow et al., 1991), in which a wide range of home and school variables were predictive of reading comprehension growth during these years.

Reading Comprehension Beyond the Elementary Years

While our discussion of research on comprehension development stops at the end of the elementary years, we would be remiss if we did not remind readers that comprehending written texts is a critical factor in the academic success of middle school, high school, and post-secondary education students—and that proficiency in text comprehension carries over into the workplace, affecting the quality of life of adults (Cunningham & Stanovich, 1997; Venezky, 2000). As industries and businesses invest in more and more technological advances, greater demands for both print and computer literacy are placed on the employees. In their lives outside of the workplace, as well, adults need to be able to read and understand complex information in different types of written texts, such as directions to complete tax returns. To function independently in the United States today, adults need not only basic instruction in reading and writing skills that are typically taught in schools but also experience with a wide variety of types of texts read for different purposes.

Multiple Paths of Reading Comprehension Development

While it is clear that comprehension develops, it is also clear that there is not a single path to comprehension development. This is largely because there are myriad reader factors, text factors, and context factors that all impact reading comprehension (RAND Reading Study Group, 2002). Scarborough (2001) has described a process in which different developing components of language and literacy become intertwined over time, mutually strengthening bonds among them, and in doing so contributing to the development of students' reading comprehension. Comprehension is affected by individual differences in students' capabilities and experiences as they interact with the quality of the opportunities they have at home and school to develop language and literacy (e.g., Connor et al., 2004). There is no single set of stages or linear trajectory on which readers can be placed.

One result of these different pathways is that students may reach the same level of development in reading comprehension, at least as measured by a test, and yet have very different profiles of strengths and weaknesses in comprehension-related abilities. In a study by Buly and Valencia (2002), a diverse group of 108 fourth graders who all scored "below proficiency" on the Washington Assessment of Student Learning (WASL) were administered a battery of reading-related assessments that formed three factors: word identification, fluency, and meaning (which was comprised of vocabulary knowledge and responses to comprehension questions for a series of narrative and expository passages from an informal reading inventory). Results revealed at that although students' level of reading comprehension on the WASL was similar, they exhibited very different profiles of strength and weakness. For example, 18% of students were what the researchers termed "automatic word callers"; they had relatively high word identification and fluency, but scored relatively poorly in the meaning factor (vocabulary, passage comprehension). Notably, a number of these students were English Language Learners; learning to read in a second language is yet another factor that affects the course of reading comprehension development (August & Shanahan, 2006; Proctor, August, & Carlo, 2006; Proctor, Carlo, August, & Snow, 2005). Another 18% of students in the Buly and Valencia study showed an inverse profile—they scored relatively well on the meaning factor (though still below grade level expectations) but had relatively poor fluency and word recognition (Buly & Valencia, 2002, called them "word stumblers"). While performing at similar levels of reading comprehension on the WASL, these students are progressing along different paths in developing the capabilities and experiences they need to understand written texts.

Another indication of multiple paths to reading comprehension development comes from looking at studies that have differentiated reading comprehension assessment by genre. For example, the Progress in International Reading-Literacy Study (PIRLS; Mullis, Martin, Kennedy, & Foy, 2007) of predominately 9-year-old children from 45 nations revealed that some students have substantially stronger comprehension when reading for literary experience, whereas others demonstrate higher comprehension when reading to acquire and use information, with still others demonstrating comparable skill across these two purposes for reading (Park, 2008). Different students are likely to have had different opportunities to learn about genre-influenced aspects of reading comprehension and are likely to have benefited from the opportunities differently (e.g., depending on their language and reading capabilities).

As we have shown through discussion of language and other factors that influence reading comprehension development in the preschool, early elementary and late elementary years, students' developing language and cognitive capabilities, their reading experience and knowledge about the world, the language they are surrounded with at home and in schools, the reading and other literacy-related materials they have access to, and the assistance and instruction of their teachers all interact to shape the developmental trajectory of their reading comprehension capabilities.

IMPLICATIONS

The research reviewed in this chapter provides many insights about the development of comprehension in the preschool through elementary school years. That said, the review reveals a number of areas in which additional research is needed. We discuss six of these in the paragraphs that follow.

How Can We Foster Language Development in the Classroom in Ways that Develop Comprehension?

Experts have been concerned for some time about the lack of attention to students' language development in the preschool and early elementary school classroom. One explanation is that teachers, like parents (Sénéchal, LeFevre, Thomas, & Daley, 1998), have not been taught to understand children's language learning and have limited ideas about what to do in their classrooms to foster language development (Adger, Snow, & Christian, 2002). An important area for research is how to help teachers foster the language development of their students. Are there more and less effective methods for teachers to develop language-rich classrooms? How can teachers provide opportunities for students to communicate with one another and with their teacher around literacy? How can we help teachers develop students' linguistic awareness—their ability to reflect on, analyze, and manipulate linguistic elements—such as finding a different way to state an idea or identifying two meanings of polysemous words such as *bat*. Most importantly for the purposes of this chapter, what is the impact of creating such classrooms and instruction on children's reading comprehension development? The literature reviewed in this chapter suggests that there should be marked benefits for students' developing comprehension capabilities, but this is an assumption worth testing. In fact in general the field would benefit from more studies that simultaneously examine oral and written language outcomes.

How Can We Enhance Attention to Reading Comprehension in the Early Years?

It is clear from the literature reviewed here that we should be concerned about the development of reading comprehension from very early on, long before children can read text themselves. Because from very early on some children are not developing apace with their peers, we should be trying early on to intervene in such cases. Unfortunately, too often the development of comprehension isn't given instructional priority until students have become fluent readers. Reports suggest that there is little comprehension instruction in the early school years (Connor et al., 2004; Pressley, 2002) even though we have at least some idea of kinds of comprehension instruction in grades K to 3 that can improve comprehension (Pearson & Duke, 2002; Roberts & Duke, 2010; Stahl, 2004).

Because correlations between word recognition and fluency in the early elementary years are so strong, it is tempting to think that these aspects of reading should be the primary focus of research and instruction in the early elementary years. But to the extent that this focus detracts from students' developing comprehension capabilities, that is a mistake. As we saw, a number of other factors in the early elementary school years also influence and predict development of reading comprehension, and interplay with word recognition and fluency in important ways. Moreover, factors that predict reading comprehension well later on—for example, vocabulary and inferencing—are not so easily developed that we can neglect them for a period of time. Further, there is considerable evidence that simultaneous attention to word recognition, fluency, and comprehension works synergistically to improve outcomes. For example, interventions for at risk children in the early elementary grades that provide reading comprehension as well as code instruction show impressive results (e.g., Berninger et al., 2003; Vellutino, Scanlon, Small, & Fanuele, 2006, see also Hiebert and Taylor, 2000, for a review). In short, more research should examine in the same study the relation of instruction and development of a broad range of contributors to reading comprehension development.

What Are the Developmental Progressions of the Reasoning Abilities that Underlie Reading Comprehension?

We know a great deal about the course of development of some contributors to reading comprehension, such as word recognition and fluency. We know far less about the development of other contributors, such as the ability to monitor or draw inferences. How does readers' ability to monitor comprehension or draw inferences in particular contexts develop from the preschool through the elementary years? How do individual differences and home and school contexts affect the development of reasoning in reading? Questions such as these require considerable investigation. Further, while teaching some comprehension strategies, such as visualization and summarization, has been shown to be effective at improving comprehension, we know little about their development or contribution to reading comprehension over time.

While many think of these reasoning abilities as specific to reading comprehension, they are quite similar to those used in other domains, such as science (e.g., Cervetti, Pearson, Bravo, & Barber, 2006). Thus, our understanding of their development in the context of reading might be informed by understanding the development of reasoning skills more generally. Indeed, as has long been noted (e.g., Thorndike, 1917), reading is reasoning in many respects. And, like reading, it is influenced by innate characteristics, prior knowledge and experience, affective dimensions, and home and school contexts. Understanding the influence and interaction of these over time as they shape the development of the reasoning involved reading comprehension offers a world of possibilities for research.

How Can We Differentiate Reading Comprehension Instruction?

The research reviewed for this chapter reveals that children differ from one another in the many areas that affect comprehension development, including (but not limited to) innate capabilities, experiences (at home and in school), opportunities to learn, and interests. Assuming that it is critical to design instruction to address individual needs, the important question facing the field is how to differentiate reading comprehension instruction, taking into account individual differences in these areas of development. For example, how can we differentiate instruction for Buly and Valencia's (2002) "word callers" versus "word stumblers"? How important is it to pay attention to differential abilities in listening and reading comprehension (Carlisle, 1989)? How can we differentiate instruction for students who fit the five profiles of narrative reading comprehension in struggling second- to ninth-grade readers identified by Wade (1990)? How can we differentiate instruction for students who have rich background knowledge but fail to monitor their comprehension? How should instruction for these students be different from that provided to students who monitor their comprehension but find it so often breaking down because they lack the background knowledge to make meaning with the text? We would benefit substantially from more research on both how to identify these different comprehension profiles (see our next point) and how we might differentiate instruction more profitably for them.

How Can We Better Assess Reading Comprehension in Young Children?

Our understanding of comprehension development is necessarily limited by the comprehension assessments available for research. This review suggests some challenges for future research and development in comprehension assessment. One challenge is assessing comprehension meaningfully before children can read words well. We found relatively few studies examining listening and reading comprehension in the preschool and kindergarten years, perhaps in part because of the lack of suitable measures of comprehension during these periods. We found more studies examining listening and reading comprehension in the early elementary years, but these studies were often restricted to comprehension of simplistic texts because of the limitations of children's word recognition ability. Further, as noted earlier, the dependence of assessment performance in this period on word recognition ability may be overwhelming our ability to identify other contributors to reading comprehension (Lonigan et al., 2008).

The results of one study show that reading comprehension assessments vary in how much word reading and oral language contribute to the overall score (Cutting & Scarborough, 2006). As a result, early comprehension assessments that do not require word reading are of particular interest. In narrative, Paris and Paris (2003) and Kendeou et al. (2006) have developed promising approaches. Promising assessments of comprehension of informational texts that do not require word reading have also been developed recently (Billman et al., 2008; Hall, Markham, Culatta, 2005; Hilden et al., 2008; Palincsar, Magnusson, Pesko, & Hamlin, 2005).

We also would benefit from assessments that help us learn more about students' comprehension of narrative and informational texts, as well as texts that are representative of other genre (e.g., poetry). Such assessments are needed because comprehension of different genres of text involves different processes and develop at different rates. For example, some students show stronger comprehension of literary text than informational text and others show the inverse pattern (Park, 2008; see Duke & Roberts, 2010, for a review). Thus, a challenge for researchers is development of methods to assess students' comprehension of different types of texts.

An even more fundamental challenge facing comprehension assessment is the ability to examine the processes as well as the products of reading comprehension. Many of the assessments used in studies reviewed for this chapter resulted in a single score that compared a student's performance relative to his age or grade peers, based on ability to answer multiple choice questions following the reading of short passages. Our understanding of comprehension development would be well served by more assessments and systems of assessment that examine the processes of students' comprehension. For example, we would benefit from valid and reliable assessments that measure students' efforts to bring comprehension strategies to bear when encountering unfamiliar vocabulary and concepts.

Do Different Factors Affect Development of Comprehension of Hypermedia Texts?

The vast majority of studies reviewed for this chapter used unillustrated printed texts, most of them read linearly and in their entirety. In contrast, much of the reading that adults, and increasingly, students, do involves reading highly visual digital texts nonlinearly and selectively (e.g., Greenhow, Robelia, & Hughes, 2009). As noted earlier, there is overlap in the skills and strategies required for this kind of reading, but there are also differences (Duke, Schmar-Dobler, & Zhang, 2006). This raises the possibility that different factors affect development of comprehension of hypermedia text.

As with the approach we have taken to examining the development of reading comprehension in this chapter, research on the development of hypermedia comprehension, research needs to focus on both home and school influences on this development. Children vary widely in the experiences they have learning on a computer as well as accessing information and communicating information through web-based technologies (see Greenhouse et al., 2009). Might these experiences affect the development of processes they use in reading printed texts? Further, does variation in students' use of online texts relate to the kinds of learning activities and instruction in on-line reading they receive in school? We continue to need studies that help us understand the development of skills and strategies used in on-line reading, as compared to those used in reading printed text—for example, does on-line reading lead to greater skill at problem-based inquiry (Coiro & Schmar-Dobler, 2007; Leu, O'Byrne, Zawilinski, McVerry, & Everett-Cacopardo, 2009)?

It is increasingly clear that research in this area is a critically needed in order to better understand comprehension development in today's schools (Leu, Coiro, Castek, Hartman, Henry & Reinking, 2008).

Summary

The roots of reading comprehension are laid very early. Children's innate characteristics and their home and school environments affect the development of comprehension in a complex interplay that changes over time. Many different aspects of language and cognitive development contribute to, and are in turn affected by, comprehension development. Schooling has a tremendous influence. Schooling has the potential to provide students with a wide range of opportunities for meaningful use of written text for learning and personal pleasure, opportunities that contribute to the development of their comprehension. In addition, high quality instruction is critical for the development of comprehension skills that students need for academic success and quality of life after schooling. Research has much to say, although there is also much left to learn, about the development of reading comprehension.

References

Adger, C. T., Snow, C. E., & Christian, D. (2002). *What teachers need to know about language.* McHenry. IL: Delta Systems.

Afflerbach, P., Pearson, P. D., & Paris. S. G. (2008). Clarifying differences between reading skills and reading strategies. *The Reading Teacher, 61,* 364–373.

Allington, R. L. (2002). What I've learned about effective reading instruction from a decade of studying exemplary elementary classroom teachers. *Phi Delta Kappan, 83,* 740–747.

Almasi, J. F. (1995). The nature of fourth graders' sociocultural conflicts in peer-led and teacher-led discussions of literature. *Reading Research Quarterly, 30,* 314–351.

Anderson, E., & Guthrie, J. T. (1999, April). *Motivating children to gain conceptual knowledge from text: The combination of science observation and interesting texts.* Paper presented at the Annual Meeting of the American Educational Research Association, Montreal, Canada.

Anderson, R. C., & Freebody, P. (1981). Vocabulary knowledge. In J. T. Guthrie (Ed.), *Comprehension and teaching: Research reviews* (pp. 77–117). Newark, DE: International Reading Association.

Anderson, R. C., Wilson, P. T., & Fielding, L. G. (1988). Growth in reading and how children spend their time outside of school. *Reading Research Quarterly, 23,* 285–303.

Anglin, J. M. (1993). Vocabulary development: A morphological analysis. *Monographs of the Society for Research in Child Development, 58,* 1–186.

August, D., & Shanahan, T. (Eds.). (2006). *Developing literacy in second-language learners: Report of the National Literacy Panel on language-minority children and youth.* Mahwah, NJ: Erlbaum.

August, D., Snow, C., Carlo, M., Proctor, C. P., Francisco, A. R., Duursma, E., & Szuber, A. (2006). Literacy development in elementary school second-language learners. *Topics in Language Disorders, 26,* 351–364.

Baumann, J. F. (2009). Vocabulary and reading comprehension: The nexus of meaning. In S. E. Israel & G. G. Duffy (Eds.), *Handbook of research on reading comprehension* (pp. 323–346). New York: Routledge.

Baumann, J. F., Edwards, E. C., Font, G., Tereshinski, C. A., Kame'enui, E. J., & Olejnik, S. F. (2002). Teaching morphemic and contextual analysis to fifth-grade students. *Reading Research Quarterly, 37,* 150–176.

Baker, L., Scher, D., & Mackler, K. (1997). Home and family influences on motivations for reading. *Educational Psychologist, 32*(2), 69–82.

Barnes, M. A., Dennis, M., & Haefele-Kalvaitis, J. (1996). The effects of knowledge availability and knowledge accessibility on coherence and elaborative inferencing in children from six to fifteen years of age. *Journal of Experimental Child Psychology, 61,* 216–241.

Beck, I. L., & McKeown, M. G. (1991). Conditions of vocabulary acquisition. In R. Barr, M. L. Kamil, P. B. Mosenthal, & P. D. Pearson (Eds.), *Handbook of reading research* (Vol 2, pp. 789–814). New York: Longman.

Berninger, V. W., Abbott, R. D., Vermeulen, K., & Fulton, C. M. (2006). Paths to reading comprehension in at-risk second-grade readers. *Journal of Learning Disabilities, 39,* 334–351.

Berninger, V., Vermeulen, K., Abbott, R., McCutchen, D., Cotton, S., Cude, J., et al. (2003). Comparison of three approaches to supplementary reading instruction for low achieving second grade readers. *Language, Speech, and Hearing Services in Schools, 34,* 101–116.

Berry, R. A. W. (2006). Teacher talk during whole-class lessons: Engagement strategies to support the verbal participation of students with learning disabilities. *Learning Disabilities Research and Practice, 21,* 211–232.

Billman, A. K., Duke, N. K., Hilden, K. R., Zhang, S., Roberts, K., Halladay, J. L., et al. (2008). Concepts of Comprehension Assessment (COCA). Retrieved June 18, 2008, from http://www.msularc.org/html/project_COCA_main.html

Boyd, M., & Rubin, D. (2006). How contingent questioning promotes extended student talk: A function of display questions. *Journal of Literacy Research, 38,* 141–169.

Brown, A. (1980). Metacognitive development and reading. In R. J. Spiro, B. C. Bruce, & W. F. Brewer (Eds.), *Theoretical issues in reading comprehension: Perspectives from cognitive psychology, linguistics, artificial intelligence, and education* (pp. 453–482). Hillsdale, NJ: Erlbaum.

Brown, R., Pressley, M., Van Meter, P., & Schuder, T. (1996). A quasi-experimental validation of transactional strategies instruction with low-achieving second grade readers. *Journal of Educational Psychology, 88,* 18–37.

Bryant, P. E., Bradley, L. L., Maclean, M., & Crossland, J. (1989). Nursery rhymes, phonological skills and reading. *Journal of Child Language, 16,* 407–428.

Buly, M. R., & Valencia, S. W. (2002). Below the bar: Profiles of students who fail state reading assessments. *Educational Evaluation and Policy Analysis, 24,* 219–239.

Bus, A. G. (2001). Joint caregiver-child storybook reading: A route to literacy development. In S. B. Neuman & D. K. Dickinson (Eds.), *Handbook of early literacy research* (pp. 179–191). New York: Guilford.

Cain, K. (2009). Making sense of text: Skills that support text comprehension and its development. *Perspectives on language and literacy, 35*(2), 11–14.

Cain, K., & Oakhill, J. V. (1999). Inference making ability and its relation to comprehension failure in young children. *Reading and writing: An interdisciplinary Journal, 11,* 489–503.

Cain, K., & Oakhill, J. (2006). Profiles of children with specific reading comprehension difficulties. *British Journal of Educational Psychology, 76,* 683–696.

Cain, K., Oakhill, J., & Bryant, P. (2004). Children's reading comprehension ability: Concurrent prediction by working memory, verbal ability, and component skills. *Journal of Educational Psychology, 96,* 31–42.

Cain, K., Oakhill, J., & Lemmon, K. (2004). Individual differences in the inference of word meanings from context: The influence of reading comprehension, vocabulary knowledge, and memory capacity. *Journal of Educational Psychology, 96,* 671–681.

Carlisle, J. F. (2000). Awareness of the structure and meaning of morphologically complex words: Impact on reading. *Reading and Writing: An Interdisciplinary Journal, 12,* 169–190.

Carlisle, J. F. (1989). Diagnosing comprehension deficits through listening and reading. *Annals of Dyslexia, 39,* 159–176.

Carlisle, J. F., & Fleming, J. (2003). Lexical processing of morphologically complex words in the elementary years. *Scientific Studies of Reading, 7,* 239–253.

Carver, R. P., & Clark, S. W. (1998). Investigating reading disabilities using the Rauding diagnostic system. *Journal of Learning Disabilities, 31,* 453–471, 481.

Cartwright, K. B. (2002). Cognitive development and reading: The relation of reading-specific multiple classification skill to reading comprehension in elementary school children. *Journal of Educational Psychology, 94,* 56–63.

Casteel, M. A., & Simpson, G. B. (1991). Textual coherence and the development of inferential generalization skills. *Journal of Research in Reading, 14,* 116–129.

Catts, H. W., Fey, M. E., Tomblin, J. B., & Zhang, X. (2002). A longitudinal investigation of reading outcomes in children with language impairments. *Journal of Speech, Language, and Hearing Research, 45*, 1142–1157.

Catts, H. W., Fey, M. E., Zhang, X., & Tomblin, B. (1999). Language basis of reading and reading disabilities: Evidence from a longitudinal investigation. *Scientific Studies of Reading, 3*, 331–361.

Catts, H. W., Hogan, T. P., & Adlof, S. M. (2005). Developmental changes in reading and reading disabilities. In H. W. Catts & A. G. Kamhi (Eds.), *The connections between language and reading disabilities* (pp. 25–40). Mahwah, NJ: Erlbaum.

Catts, H. W., Hogan, T., & Fey, M. E. (2003). Subgrouping poor readers on the basis of individual differences in reading-related abilities. *Journal of Learning Disabilities, 36*, 151–164.

Cervetti, G., Pearson, P. D., Bravo, M. A., & Barber, J. (2006). Reading and writing in the service of inquiry-based science. In R. Douglas, M. Klentschy, & K. Worth (Eds.), *Linking science and literacy in the K-8 classroom* (pp. 221–244). Arlington, VA: NSTA Press.

Clark, E. V. (2003). *First language acquisition*. Cambridge,UK: Cambridge University Press.

Clark, A., Anderson, R. C., Kuo, L., Kim, I., Archodidou, A., & Nguyen-Jahiel, K. (2003). Collaborative reasoning: Expanding ways for children to talk and think in school. *Educational Psychology Review, 15*, 181–198.

Coiro, J., & Schmar-Dobler, E. (2007). Exploring the online reading comprehension strategies used by sixth-grade skilled readers to search for and locate information on the internet. *Reading Research Quarterly, 42*, 214–257.

Connor, C. M., Morrison, F. J., & Petrella, J. N. (2004). Effective reading comprehension instruction: Examining child by instruction interactions. *Journal of Educational Psychology, 96*, 682–698.

Cote, L. R. (2001). Language opportunities during mealtimes in preschool classrooms. In D. K. Dickinson & P. O. Tabors (Eds.), *Beginning literacy with language* (pp. 205–221). Baltimore: Paul H. Brookes.

Craig, H. K., Connor, C. M., & Washington, J. A. (2003). Early positive predictors of later reading comprehension for African American students: A preliminary investigation. *Language, Speech, and Hearing in Schools, 34*, 31–43.

Cunningham, A. E., & Stanovich, K. E. (1997). Early reading acquisition and its relation to reading experience and ability 10 years later. *Developmental Psychology, 33*, 934–945.

Curtis, M. E. (1980). Development of components of reading skill. *Journal of Educational Psychology, 72*, 656–669.

Cutting, L. E., & Scarborough, H. H. (2006). Prediction of reading comprehension: Relative contributions of word recognition, language proficiency, and other cognitive skills can depend on how comprehension is measured. *Scientific Studies of Reading, 10*, 277–299.

Danks, J. H., & End, L. J. (1987). Processing strategies for reading and listening. In R. Horowitz & S. J. Samuels (Eds.), *Comprehending oral and written language* (pp. 271–294). San Diego: Academic Press.

de Jong, P. F., & van der Leij, A. (2002). Effects of phonological abilities and linguistic comprehension on the development of reading. *Scientific Studies of Reading, 6*, 51–77.

Demont, E., & Gombert, J. E. (1996). Phonological awareness as a predictor of recoding skills and syntactic awareness as a predictor of comprehension skills. *British Journal of Educational Psychology, 66*, 315–332.

DeTemple, J. (2001). Parents and children reading books together. In D. K. Dickinson & P. O. Tabors (Eds.), *Beginning literacy with language* (pp. 31–51). Baltimore: Paul H. Brookes.

Dickinson, D. K., & Smith, M. W. (1994). Long-term effects of preschool teachers' book readings on low income children's vocabulary and story comprehension. *Reading Research Quarterly, 29*, 104–122.

Dickinson, D. K., & Tabors, P. O. (2001). *Beginning literacy with language*. Baltimore: Paul H. Brookes.

Donovan, C. A., & Smolkin, L. B. (2002). Children's genre knowledge: An examination of K–5 students' performance on multiple tasks providing differing levels of scaffolding. *Reading Research Quarterly, 37*, 428–465.

Dreher, M. J. (2002). Children searching and using information text. In C. C. Block & M Pressley, (Eds.), *Comprehension instruction: Research-based best practices* (pp. 289–304). New York: Guilford.

Duke, N. K. (2003). Reading to learn from the very beginning: Information books in early childhood. *Young Children, 58*(2), 14–20.

Duke, N. K., & Kays, J. (1998). "Can I say 'once upon a time'?": Kindergarten children developing knowledge of information book language. *Early Childhood Research Quarterly, 13*, 295–318.

Duke, N. K., & Pearson, P. D. (2002). Effective practices for developing reading comprehension. In A. E. Farstrup & S. J. Samuels (Eds.), *What research has to say about reading instruction* (3rd ed., pp. 205–242). Newark, DE: International Reading Association.

Duke, N. K., & Roberts, K. L. (2010). The genre-specific nature of reading comprehension and the case of informational text. In D. Wyse, R. Andrews, & J. Hoffman (Eds.), *The international handbook of English language and literacy teaching* (pp. 74–86). London: Routledge.

Duke, N. K., Schmar-Dobler, E., & Zhang, S. (2006). Comprehension and technology. In M. C. McKenna, L. D. Labbo, R. D. Kieffer, & D. Reinking (Eds.), *International handbook of literacy and technology, Volume II* (pp. 317–326). Mahwah, NJ: Erlbaum.

Duncan, G. J., Dowsett, C. J., Claessens, A., Magnuson, K., Hustun, A., Kebanov, P., et al. (2007). School readiness and later achievement. *Developmental Psychology,* 1428–1446.

Eagleton, M. B., Dobler, E., & Leu, D. J. (2006). *Reading the web: Strategies for internet literacy.* New York: Guilford.

Englert, C. S., & Thomas, C. C. (1987). Sensitivity to text structure in reading and writing. A comparison between learning disabled and non-learning disabled students. *Learning Disability Quarterly, 10,* 93–105.

Fey, M. E., Catts, H. W., & Larrivee, L. S. (1995). Preparing preschoolers for the academic and social challenges of school. In M. E. Fey, J. Windsor & S. F. Warren (Eds.), *Language intervention: Preschool through the elementary years* (pp. 3–37). Baltimore: Paul H. Brookes.

Fowler, A. E. (1991). How early phonological development might set the stage for phoneme awareness. In S. A. Brady & D. P. Shankweiler (Eds.), *Phonological processes in literacy: A tribute to Isabelle Y. Liberman* (pp. 97–118). Hillsdale, NJ: Erlbaum.

Gersten, R., Fuchs, L. S., Williams, J. P., & Baker, S. (2001). Teaching reading comprehension strategies to students with learning disabilities: A review of research. *Review of Educational Research, 71,* 279–320.

Gleason, J. B. (Ed.). (2001). *The development of language,* 5th ed. Boston: Allyn & Bacon.

Goatley, V. J., Brock, C. H., & Raphael, T. E. (1995). Diverse learners participating in regular education "Book Clubs." *Reading Research Quarterly, 30,* 352–380.

Gombert, J. E. (1992). *Metalinguistic development.* Chicago: University of Chicago Press.

Gottardo, A. Stanovich, K. E., & Siegel, L. S. (1996). The relationships between phonological sensitivity, syntactic processing and verbal working memory in the reading performance of third-grade children. *Journal of Experimental Child Psychology, 63,* 563–582.

Graham, S. A., & Kilbreath, C. S. (2007). It's a sign of the kind: Gestures and words guide infants' inductive inferences. *Developmental Psychology, 43,* 1111–1123.

Greenhow, C., Robelia, B., & Hughes, J. E. (2009). Learning, teaching, and scholarship in a digital age. *Educational Researcher, 38,* 246–259.

Guthrie, J. T. (2004). Teaching for literacy engagement. *Journal of Literacy Research, 36,* 1–30.

Guthrie, J. T., Hoa, L. W., Wigfield, A., Tonks, S. M., Humenick, N. M., & Littles, E. (2007). Reading motivation and reading comprehension growth in the later elementary years. *Contemporary Educational Psychology, 32*(3), 282–313.

Guthrie, J. T., McRae, A., & Klauda, S. L. (2007). Contributions of Concept-Oriented Reading Instruction to knowledge about interventions for motivations in reading. *Educational Psychologist, 42,* 237–250.

Hall, K. M., Markham, J. C., Culatta, B. (2005). The development of the Early Expository Comprehension Assessment (EECA): A look at reliability. *Communication Disorders Quarterly, 26*(4), 195–206.

Halliday, M. A. K. (1993). Towards a language-based theory of learning. *Linguistics and Education, 5,* 93–116.

Hart, B., & Risley, T. R. (1995). *Meaningful differences in the everyday experience of young American children.* Baltimore: Paul H. Brookes.

Hiebert, E. H., & Taylor, B. M. (2000). Beginning reading instruction: Research on early interventions. In M. Kamil, P. Mosenthal, R. Barr, & P. D. Pearson (Eds.), *Handbook of reading research* (Vol. 3, pp. 455–482). Mahwah, NJ: Erlbaum.

Hilden, K. R., Duke, N. K., Billman, A. K., Zhang, S., Halladay, J. L., Schaal, A. M., et al. (2008). *Informational Strategic Cloze Assessment (ISCA).* Retrieved June 18, 2008, from http://www.msularc.org/html/project_ISCA_main.html

Hirsch, E. D., Jr. (2003). Reading comprehension requires knowledge — of words and the world. *American Educator, 27*(1), 10–13, 16–22, 28–29, 48.

Hoffman, J. V., Sailors, M., Duffy, G. G., & Beretvas, S. N. (2004). The effective elementary classroom literacy environment: Examining the validity of the TEX-IN3 observation system. *Journal of Literacy Research, 36,* 303–334.

Hood, M., Conlon, E., & Andrews, G. (2008). Preschool home literacy practices and children's literacy development: A longitudinal analysis. *Journal of Educational Psychology, 100,* 252–271.

Iverson, B. A., & Walberg, H. J. (1982). Home environment and school learning: A quantitative synthesis. *Journal of Experimental Education, 50,* 144–151.

Jenkins, J. R., Fuchs, L. S., van den Broek, P., Espin, C., & Deno, S. L. (2003). Sources of individual differences in reading comprehension and reading fluency. *Journal of Educational Psychology, 95,* 719–729.

Kamberelis, G. (1999). Genre development and learning: Children writing stories, science reports, and poems. *Research in the Teaching of English, 33,* 403–460.

Kendeou, P., Lynch, J. S., van den Broek, P., Espin, C., White, M., & Kremer, K. E. (2006). Developing successful readers: Building early narrative comprehension skills through television viewing and listening. *Early Childhood Education Journal, 33,* 91–98.

Kinnunen, R., Vauras, M., & Niemi, P. (1998). Comprehension monitoring in beginning readers. *Scientific Studies of Reading, 2,* 353–376.

Kintsch, W. (1998). *Comprehension: A paradigm for cognition.* New York: Cambridge University Press.

Kong, A., & Fitch, E. (2002/2003). Using Book Club to engage culturally and linguistically diverse learners in reading, writing, and talking about books. *The Reading Teacher, 56,* 352–362.

Landry, S. H., Smith, K. E., & Swank, P. R. (2003). The importance of parenting during early childhood for school-age development. *Developmental Neuropsychology, 24,* 559–591.

LaBerge, D., & Samuels, S. J. (1974). Toward a theory of automatic information processing in reading. *Cognitive Psychology, 6,* 293–323.

Lepola, J., Niemi, P., Kuikka, M., & Hannula, M. M. (2005). Cognitive-linguistic skills and motivation as longitudinal predictors of reading and arithmetic achievement: A follow-up study from kindergarten to grade 2. *International Journal of Educational Research, 43*(4–5), 250–271.

Leu, D. J., Coiro, J., Castek, J., Hartman, D. K., Henry, L. A., & Reinking, D. (2008). Research on instruction and assessment in the new literacies of online reading comprehension. In C. C. Block & S. Parris (Eds.), *Comprehension instruction: Research-based best practices* (pp. 321–345). New York: Guilford.

Leu, D. J., Jr., Kinzer, C. K., Coiro, J., & Cammack, D. (2004). Toward a theory of new literacies emerging from the Internet and other information and communication technologies. In R. B. Ruddell & N. Unrau (Eds.), *Theoretical models and processes of reading* (5th ed., pp. 1568–1611). Newark, DE: International Reading Association.

Leu, D. J., O'Byrne, W. I., Zawilinski, J., McVerry, G., & Everett-Cacopardo, H. (2009). Expanding the new literacies conversation. *Educational Research, 38,* 264–269.

Lloyd, P. (1990). Children's communication. In R. Grieve & M. Hughes (Eds.), *Understanding children* (pp. 51–70). Cambridge, MA: Basil Blackwell.

Logan, G. D. (1997). Automaticity and reading: Perspectives from the instance theory of automatization. *Reading & Writing Quarterly, 13,* 123–147.

Lonigan, C. J., Schatschneider, C., Westberg, L., & the National Early Literacy Panel. (2008). Identification of children's skills and abilities linked to later outcomes in reading, writing, and spelling. In *Developing early literacy: Report of the National Early Literacy Panel* (pp. 55–106). Louisville, KY: National Center for Family Literacy.

Lonigan, C. J., Shanahan, T., & Cunningham, A., with the National Early Literacy Panel. (2008). Impact of shared-reading interventions on young children's early literacy skills. In *Developing early literacy: Report of the National Early Literacy Panel* (pp. 153–172). Washington, DC: National Institute for Literacy and National Center for Family Literacy.

Lyster, S. H. (2002). The effects of morphological versus phonological awareness training in kindergarten on reading development. *Reading and Writing, 15,* 261–294.

Martin, N. M., & Duke, N. K. (in press). Interventions to enhance informational text comprehension. In R. Allington & A. McGill-Franzen (Eds.), *Handbook of reading disabilities research.* London: Routledge.

Matthews, M. W., & Kesner, J. (2003). Children learning with peers: The confluence of peer status and literacy competence within small-group literacy events. *Reading Research Quarterly, 38,* 208–234.

McGee, L. M. (1982). Awareness of text structure: Effects on children's recall of expository text. *Reading Research Quarterly, 17,* 581–590.

McKenna, M. C., Kear, D. J., & Ellsworth, R. A. (1995). Children's attitudes toward reading: A national survey. *Reading Research Quarterly, 30,* 934–956.

McKenna, M. C., & Walpole, S. (2007). Assistive technology in the reading clinic: Its emerging potential. *Reading Research Quarterly, 42,* 140–145.

McKeough, A., & Genereux, R. (2002). Transformations in narrative thought during late childhood and adolescence: A comparison of average and exceptional story writers. In F. J. Mönks & H. Wagner (Eds.), *Development of human potential: Investment into our future, Proceedings of the 8th conference of the European Council for High Ability (ECHA)* (pp. 38–41). Bad Honnef, Germany: Verlag Karl Heinrich Bock.

McNamara, T., Miller, D., & Bransford, J. D. (2000). Mental models and reading comprehension. In R. Barr, M. L. Kamil, P. B. Mosenthal, & P. D. Pearson (Eds.), *Handbook of reading research* (Vol. 2, pp. 490–511). New York: Longman.

Metsala, J. L., & Walley, A. C. (1998). Spoken vocabulary growth and the segmental restructuring of lexical representations: Precursors to phonemic awareness and early reading ability. In J. L. Metsala & L. C. Ehri (Eds.), *Word recognition in beginning literacy* (pp. 89–120). Mahwah, NJ: Erlbaum.

Morrow, L. M. (1985). Retelling stories: A strategy for improving children's comprehension, concept of story structure, and oral language complexity. *The Elementary School Journal, 85,* 647–661.

Mullis, I. V. S., Martin, M. O., Kennedy, A. M., & Foy, P. (2007). *PIRLS 2006 international report: IEA's progress in international reading literacy study in primary schools in 40 countries.* Chestnut, MA: International Study Center, Boston College.

Murphy, P. K., Wilkinson, I. A. G., Soter, A. O., Hennessey, M. N. & Alexander, J. F. (2009). Examining the effects of classroom discussion on students' high-level comprehension of text: A meta-analysis. *Journal of Educational Psychology, 101,* 740–764.

Nagy, W. E. (2007). Metalinguistic awareness and the vocabulary-comprehension connection. In R. K. Wagner, A. E. Muse, & K. R. Tannenbaum (Eds.), *Vocabulary acquisition: Implications for reading comprehension* (pp. 52–77). New York: Guilford.

Nagy, W. E., & Scott, J. A. (2000). Vocabulary processes. In M. L. Kamil, P. Mosenthal, P. D. Pearson, & R. Barr (Eds.), *Handbook of reading research* (Vol. 3, pp. 269–284). Mahwah, NJ: Erlbaum.

Nation, K., & Snowling, M. J. (2004). Beyond phonological skills: Broader language skills contribute to the development of reading. *Journal of Research in Reading, 27,* 342–356.

Nelson, K. (1996). *Language in cognitive development: Emergence of the mediated mind.* Cambridge, UK: Cambridge University Press.

Neuman, S. B. (2006). The knowledge gap: Implications of leveling the playing field for low-income and middle-income children. *Reading Research Quarterly, 41,* 176–201.

Nippold, M. A. (2007). *Later language development: School-age children, adolescents, and young adults* (3rd ed.). Austin, TX: PRO-ED.

Oakhill, J., & Cain, K. (2007). Introduction to comprehension development. In J. Oakhill & K. Cain (Eds.), *Children's comprehension problems in oral and written language: A cognitive perspective* (pp. 3–40). New York: Guilford.

Oyler, C., & Barry, A. (1996). Intertextual connections in read-alouds of information books. *Language Arts, 73,* 324–329.

Palincsar, A. S., & Duke, N. K. (2004). The role of text and text-reader interactions in young children's reading development and achievement. *The Elementary School Journal, 105,* 183–197.

Palincsar, A. S., Magnusson, S. J., Pesko, E., & Hamlin, M. (2005). Attending to the nature of subject matter in text comprehension assessments. In S. G. Paris & S. A. Stahl (Eds.), *Children's reading comprehension and assessment* (pp. 257–278). Mahwah, NJ: Erlbaum.

Pappas, C. (1993). Is narrative "primary"? Some insights from kindergarteners' pretend readings of stories and information books. *Journal of Reading Behavior, 25,* 97–129.

Paris, S. G., & Cross, D. R. (1988). The zone of proximal development: Virtues and pitfalls of a metaphorical representation of children's learning. *Genetic Epistemologist, 16,* 27–37.

Paris, S. G., & Jacobs, J. E. (1984). The benefits of informed instruction for children's reading awareness and comprehension skills. *Child Development, 55,* 2083–2093.

Paris, A. H., & Paris, S. G. (2003). Assessing narrative comprehension in young children. *Reading Research Quarterly, 38,* 36–76.

Park, Y. (2008). *Patterns in and predictors of elementary students' reading performance: Evidence from the* data of the *Progress in International Reading Literacy Study 2006*. Unpublished doctoral dissertation, Michigan State University.

Pearson, P. D., & Duke, N. K. (2002). Comprehension instruction in the primary grades. In C. C. Block & M. Pressley (Eds.), *Comprehension instruction: Research-based best practices* (pp. 247–258). New York: Guilford.

Pellegrini, A. D., Perlmutter, J. C., Galda, L., & Brody, G. H. (1990). Joint reading between black Head Start children and their mothers. *Child Development, 61,* 443–453.

Perfetti, C. (2007). Reading ability: Lexical quality to comprehension. *Scientific Studies of Reading, 11,* 357–383.

Pressley, M. (2002). Comprehension strategies instruction: A turn-of-the-century status report. In C. C. Block & M. Pressley, (Eds.), *Comprehension instruction: Research-based best practices* (pp. 11–27). New York: Guilford.

Pressley, M., & Afflerbach, P. (1995). *Verbal protocols of reading: The nature of constructively responsive reading*. Hillsdale, NJ: Erlbaum.

Proctor, C. P., August, D., & Carlo, M. S. (2006). The intriguing role of Spanish language vocabulary knowledge in predicting English reading comprehension. *Journal of Educational Psychology, 98,* 159–169.

Proctor, C. P., Carlo, M., August, D., & Snow, C. E. (2005). Native Spanish-speaking children reading in English: Toward a model of comprehension. *Journal of Educational Psychology, 97,* 246–256.

Purcell-Gates, V. (1988). Lexical and syntactic knowledge of written narrative held by well-read-to kindergarteners and second graders. *Research in the Teaching of English, 22,* 128–160.

Purcell-Gates, V. (1996). Stories, coupons, and the TV Guide: Relationships between home literacy experiences and emergent literacy knowledge. *Reading Research Quarterly, 31,* 406–428.

Purcell-Gates, V., Duke, N. K., & Martineau, J. A. (2007). Learning to read and write genre-specific text: Roles of authentic experience and explicit teaching. *Reading Research Quarterly, 42,* 8–45.

Purcell-Gates, V., McIntyre, E., & Freppon, P. A. (1995). Learning written storybook language in school: A comparison of low-SES children in skills-based and whole language classrooms. *American Educational Research Journal, 32,* 659–685.

Raikes, H., Pan, B. A., Luze, G., Tamis-LeMonda, C. S., Brooks-Gunn, J., Constantine, J. Tarullo, H., Raikes, A., & Rodriguez, E. T. (2006). Child bookreading in low-income families: Correlates and outcomes during the first three years of life. *Child Development, 77,* 924–953

RAND Reading Study Group. (2002). *Reading for understanding: Toward an R & D program in reading comprehension*. Santa Monica, CA: RAND.

Rasinski, T. V., & Hoffman, J. V. (2003). Oral reading in the school literacy curriculum. *Reading Research Quarterly, 38,* 510–522.

Reichle, E. D., & Perfetti, C. A. (2003). Morphology in word identification: A word-experience model that accounts for morpheme frequency effects. *Scientific Studies of Reading, 7,* 219–237.

Rescorla, L. (2005). Age 13 language and reading outcomes in late-talking toddlers. *Journal of Speech, Language, and Hearing Research, 48,* 459–472.

Rupley, W. H., Willson, V. L., & Nichols, W. D. (1998). Exploration of the developmental components contributing to elementary children's reading comprehension. *Scientific Studies of Reading, 2,* 143–158.

Roberts, K., & Duke, N. K. (2010). Comprehension in the primary grades: A review of the research. In K. Ganske and D. Fisher (Eds.), *A comprehensive look at reading comprehension* (pp. 23–45). New York: Guilford.

Roller, C. M. (1990). The interaction between knowledge and structure variables in the processing of expository prose. *Reading Research Quarterly, 25,* 79–89.

Romance, N. R., & Vitale, M. R. (2001). Implementing an in-depth expanding science model in elementary schools: Multi-year findings, research issues, and policy implications. *International Journal of Science Education, 23,* 373–404.

Roth, F. P., Speece, D. L., & Cooper, D. H. (2002). A longitudinal analysis of the connection between oral language and early reading. *Journal of Educational Research, 95*(5), 259–272.

Scarborough, H. S. (2001). Connecting early language and literacy to later reading (dis)abilities: Evidence, theory and practice. In S. B. Neuman & D. K. Dickinson (Eds.), *Handbook of early literacy research* (pp. 97–110). New York: Guilford.

Scarborough, H. S. (2005). Developmental relationships between language and reading: Reconciling a beautiful hypothesis with some ugly facts. In H. W. Catts & A. G. Kamhi (Eds.), *The connections between language and reading disabilities* (pp. 3–24). Mahwah, NJ: Erlbaum.

Schleppegrell, M. J. (2004). Characterizing the language of schooling. In M. J. Schleppegrell, *The language of schooling: A functional linguistics perspective* (pp. 1–20). Mahwah, NJ: Erlbaum

Scott, C. M. (2004). Syntactic contributions to literacy learning. In C. A. Stone, E. R. Silliman, B. J. Ehren, & K. Apel (Eds.), *Handbook of language and literacy* (pp. 340–362). New York: Guilford.

Seigneuric, A., & Ehrlich, M. F. (2005). Contribution of working memory capacity to children's reading comprehension: A longitudinal investigation. *Reading and Writing: An Interdisciplinary Journal, 18,* 617–656.

Sénéchal, M. (2006). Testing the home literacy model: Parent involvement in kindergarten is differentially related to grade 4 reading comprehension, fluency, spelling, and reading for pleasure. *Scientific Studies of Reading, 10,* 59–87.

Sénéchal, M., LeFevre, J., Thomas, E. M., & Daley, K. E. (1998). Differential effects of home literacy experiences on the development of oral and written language. *Reading Research Quarterly, 33,* 96–116.

Singson, M., Mahoney, D., & Mann, V. (2000). The relation between reading ability and morphological skills: Evidence from derivational suffixes. *Reading and Writing: An Interdisciplinary Journal, 12,* 219–252.

Sipe, L. R. (2000). Those two gingerbread boys could be brothers": How children use intertextual connections during storybook readalouds. *Children's Literature in Education, 31*(2), 73–90.

Smith, J. B., Lee, V. E., & Newmann, F. E. (2001, January). *Instruction and achievement in Chicago elementary schools.* Chicago: Chicago Consortium on School Research.

Snow, C. E., Barnes, W., Chandler, J., Goodman, I., & Hemphill, L. (1991). *Unfulfilled expectations: Home and school influences on literacy.* Cambridge, MA: Harvard University Press.

Snow, C. E., Griffin, P., & Burns, M.S. (2005). *Knowledge to support the teaching of reading: Preparing teachers for a changing world.* San Francisco: Jossey-Bass.

Snow, C. E., Porche, M. V., Tabors, P. O., & Harris, S. R. (2007). *Is literacy enough? Pathways to academic success for adolescents.* Baltimore: Paul H. Brookes.

Snowling, M. J. (2005). Literacy outcomes for children with oral language impairments: Developmental interactions between language skills and learning to read. In H. W. Catts, & A. G. Kamhi (Eds.), *The connections between language and reading disabilities* (pp. 55–75). Mahwah, NJ: Erlbaum.

Speece, D. L., Roth, F. A., Cooper, D. H., & de la Paz, S. (1999). The relevance of oral language skills to early literacy: A multivariate analysis. *Applied Psycholinguistics, 20,* 167–190.

Spiro, R. J. (1980). Constructive processes in prose comprehension and recall. In R. J. Spiro, B. C. Bruce, & W. E. Brewer (Eds.), *Theoretical issues in reading comprehension* (pp. 245–278). Hillsdale, NJ: Erlbaum.

Stahl, K. A. D. (2004). Proof, practice, and promise: Comprehension strategy instruction the primary grades. *The Reading Teacher, 57,* 598–610.

Sticht, T. G. (1982). Literacy at work. *Advances in Reading/Language Research, Vol 1* (pp. 219–243). Greenwich, CT: JAI Press.

Sticht, T. G., & James, J. H. (1984). Listening and reading. In P. D. Pearson, R. Barr, M. L. Kamil, & P. Mosenthal (Eds.), *Handbook of reading research* (Vol. 2, pp. 293–317). Mahwah, NJ: Erlbaum.

Sulzby, E. (1985). Children's emergent reading of favorite storybooks: A developmental study. *Reading Research Quarterly, 20,* 458–481.

Symons, S., MacLatchy-Gaudet, H., Stone, T. D., & Reynolds, P. L. (2001). Strategy instruction for elementary students searching informational text. *Scientific Studies of Reading, 5,* 1–33.

Tannenbaum, K. R., Torgesen, J. K., & Wagner, R. K. (2006). Relationships between word knowledge and reading comprehension in third-grade children. *Scientific Studies of Reading, 10,* 381–398.

Taylor, B. M., Pearson, P. D., Clark, K., & Walpole, S. (2000). Effective schools and accomplished teachers: Lessons about primary-grade reading instruction in low-income schools. *The Elementary School Journal, 101,* 121–165.

Taylor, B. M., Pearson, P. D., Peterson, D. S., & Rodriguez, M. C. (2003). Reading growth in high-poverty classrooms: The influence of teacher practices that encourage cognitive engagement in literacy learning. *The Elementary School Journal, 104,* 3–28.

Thorndike, E. L. (1917). Reading as reasoning. *Journal of Educational Psychology, 8,* 323–332.

Tivnan, T., & Hemphill, L. (2005). Comparing four literacy reform models in high-poverty schools: Patterns of first-grade achievement. *The Elementary School Journal, 105,* 419–441.

Tunmer, W. E., & Chapman, J. W. (1998). Language prediction skill, phonological recoding ability, and beginning reading. In C. Hulme & M. Joshi (Eds.), *Reading and spelling: Development and disorders* (pp. 33–67). Mahwah, NJ: Erlbaum.

Valencia, S. W., Place, N. A., Martin, S. D., & Grossman, P. L. (2006). Curriculum materials for elementary reading: Shackles and scaffolds for four beginning teachers. *The Elementary School Journal, 107,* 93–120.

van den Broek, P., Lynch, J.S., Naslund, J., Ievers-Landis, C. E., & Verduin, K. (2003). The development of comprehension of main ideas in narratives: Evidence from the selection of titles. *Journal of Educational Psychology, 95,* 707–718.

Vellutino, F. R., Scanlon, D. M., Sipay, E. R., Pratt, A., Chen, R., & Denckla, M. B. (1996). Cognitive profiles of difficult-to-remediate and readily remediated poor readers: Early intervention as a vehicle for distinguishing between cognitive and experiential deficits as basic causes of specific reading disability. *Journal of Educational Psychology, 88,* 601–638.

Velluntino, F. R., Scanlon, D. M., Small, S., & Fanuele, D. P. (2006). Response to intervention as a vehicle for distinguishing between children with and without learning disabilities: Evidence for the role of kindergarten and first-grade interventions. *Journal of Learning Disabilities, 39,* 157–169.

Vellutino, F. R., Tumner, W. E., Jaccard, J. J., & Chen, R. (2007). Components of reading ability: Multivariate evidence for a convergent skills model of reading development. *Scientific Studies of Reading, 11,* 3–32.

Venezky, R. L. (2000). The origins of the present-day chasm between adult literacy needs and school literacy instruction. *Scientific Studies of Reading, 4,* 19–39.

Verhoeven, L., & Van Leeuwe, J. (2008). Prediction of the development of reading comprehension: A longitudinal study. *Applied Cognitive Psychology, 22,* 407–423.

Wade, S. E. (1990). Using think alouds to assess comprehension. *The Reading Teacher, 43,* 442–451.

Wagner, R. K., Muse, A. E., & Tannenbaum, K. R. (2007). Promising avenues for better understanding: Implications of vocabulary development for reading comprehension. In R. K. Wagner, A. E. Muse & K. R. Tannenbaum (Eds.), *Vocabulary acquisition: Implications for reading comprehension* (pp. 276–292). New York: Guilford.

Wallach, G. P., & Ehren, B. J. (2004). Collaborative models of instruction and intervention: Choices, decisions, and implementation. In E. R. Silliman & L. C. Wilkinson (Eds.), *Language and literacy learning in schools* (pp. 39–59). New York: Guilford.

Wang, J. (2005). *Evaluation of seeds of science/Roots of reading project: Shoreline science and terrarium investigations.* Los Angeles, CA: National Center for Research on Evaluation, Standards, and Student Testing (CRESST).

Weigel, D. J., Martin, S. S., & Bennett, K. K. (2005). Ecological influences of the home and the child-care center on preschool-age children's literacy development. *Reading Research Quarterly, 40,* 204–233.

Westby, C. (2004). A language perspective on executive functioning, metacognition, and self-regulation in reading. In C. A. Stone, E. R. Silliman, B. J. Ehren, & K. Apel (Eds.), *Handbook of language and literacy* (pp. 398–427). New York: Guilford.

Whitehurst, G. J., Falco, F., Lonigan, C. J., Fischel, J. E., DeBaryshe, B. D., Valdez-Menchaca, M. C., et al. (1988). Accelerating language development through picture-book reading. *Developmental Psychology, 24,* 552–558.

Wilkinson, L. C., & Silliman, E. R. (2000). Classroom language and literacy learning. In M. L. Kamil, P. B. Mosenthal, P. D. Pearson, & R. Barr (Eds.), *Handbook of reading research* (Vol. 3, pp. 337–360). Mahwah, NJ: Erlbaum.

Williams, J. P., Hall, K. M., Lauer, K. D., Stafford, K. B., DeSisto, L. A., & deCani, J. S. (2005). Expository text comprehension in the primary grade classroom. *Journal of Educational Psychology, 97,* 538–550.

Willson, V. L., & Rupley, W. H. (1997). A structural equation model for reading comprehension based on background, phonemic and strategy knowledge. *Scientific Studies of Reading, 1,* 45–63.

11 Word Recognition

Theresa A. Roberts, Catherine Christo, and John A. Shefelbine
California State University, Sacramento

INTRODUCTION

In 1986 Benjamin Bloom published an article titled "Automaticity: The Hands and Feet of Genius" in which he discussed the results of 5 years of research examining the characteristics of those who were experts in their fields. In describing the importance of practice and the development of automaticity critical to reaching mastery in any field, Bloom referred back to the work of Bryan and Harper and an 1899 article from their work with Morse code operators. The quote is as relevant today to a discussion of word recognition as it was in the late 1800s to the development of proficiency in sending and receiving Morse code:

> The learner must come to do with one stroke of attention what now requires half a dozen, and presently in one still more inclusive stroke what now requires thirty-six. He must systematize the work to be done and must acquire a system of automatic habits corresponding to the system of tasks. When he has done this he is the master of the situation in his (occupational, professional) field...Finally, his whole array of habits is swiftly obedient to serve in the solution of new problems. Automatism is not genius, it is the hands and feet of genius. (Bryan & Harper, cited in Bloom, 1986, p. 72)

In the first volume of the *Handbook of Reading Research,* Gough (1984) also underscored the importance of word recognition: "Word recognition is the foundation of the reading process" (p. 225). Likewise, when discussing word recognition processes for the second volume of the handbook, Stanovich (1991) cited this quotation from Gough and confirms its continued importance: "Skill at word recognition is so central to the reading process that it can serve as a proxy diagnostic for instructional methods" (p. 418). The last decades of reading research have confirmed the primacy of word recognition in skilled reading. Within this same time period, many of the previous debates about the nature of word recognition have been continued and new ones initiated, often at a level of discussion that hones in on very precise elements of the word recognition process.

In order to take full advantage of a text, the reader must reach the level of word recognition proficiency noted by Bloom. Rapid word recognition frees up mental resources for thinking about the writer's intent and the meaning of the text rather than what word the print represents. Rapid word recognition is a necessary component of skilled reading across all alphabetic languages and thus a full understanding of its nature and acquisition is a foundational component of any general or language-specific theory of reading (Share, 2008a).

A lack of automaticity in word recognition is considered the most salient impediment to English reading for students with reading disorders (Fletcher, Lyon, Fuchs, & Barnes, 2007; Vellutino, Fletcher, Snowling, & Scanlon, 2004). In addition, fluency measures, whether assessing the speed and/or accuracy with which one reads individual words or reads text, are highly correlated with overall reading competence (Fuchs, Fuchs, Hosp, & Jenkins, 2001; Hasbrouck & Tindal, 2006) and, in the primary grades, are strong predictors of students who are likely to have reading difficulties (Good, Simmons, & Kame'euni, 2001). Promoting the development of accurate, automatic word recognition is also foundational in the development of proficient readers (Ehri, 2005). It is important in second language reading as well (da Fontura & Siegel, 1995; Geva, Wade-Woolley, & Shany, 1997; Geva, Yaghoub-Zadeh, & Schuster, 2000).

In discussing automaticity of word recognition processes, however, it is important to revisit Stanovich's (1991) distinction between obligatory execution, resource use, and conscious attention. Word recognition is obligatory for those who are skilled readers (even in the beginning stages of skill development)—but it is not resource free. Although word recognition can occur when attention is directed elsewhere, it still uses mental resources. Stanovich notes that "obligatory execution of word recognition processes develops quite rapidly, but the speed and efficiency of execution...continue to develop" (p. 426). Skilled word recognition is often described as automatic and effortless (Guttentage & Haith, 1978; LaBerge & Samuels, 1974), and emerging for many children by the end of Grade 1, but recent evidence has shown that in both emerging and skilled reading, spelling-sound conversion obligates central attention (O'Malley, Reynolds, Stolz, & Besner, 2008; Peereman, Brand, & Rey, 2006). Theories of word recognition must account for the obligatory nature of word recognition and its early emergence in beginning readers while also accounting for the speed and efficiency that develops in skilled readers. The term automatic is typically used to refer to the obligatory nature of word recognition.

CHAPTER OVERVIEW

The topic of "visual word recognition processes" has one of the largest literatures in cognitive psychology (Lupker, 2005). For this reason, any research review will necessarily be selective. The chapter focuses on word recognition in English. However, this focus on English word recognition carries with it an important caveat. English has one of the most opaque or deep orthographies of all the world's languages and is characterized by complex and variable relationships between spoken and written language (Katz & Frost, 1992; Share, 2008b; Ziegler & Goswami, 2005). This feature of the relationship between oral and written English has pervasive and significant influences on (a) word recognition processes and the word representations that interact with them, (b) theories and models that explain word recognition, (c) the developmental trajectory and character of word recognition and the instruction designed to teach it, (d) the measurement of it and, (e) understanding of the contextual factors such as word characteristics and lexical knowledge that influence it. English word recognition processes must be understood in this broader context.

Due to the complexity of word recognition, the diversity in how it has been studied, and the rich variation in theoretical frameworks to explain it, the chapter examines word recognition from diverse angles that together yield a clearer understanding of the nature of word recognition and highlight important issues that continue to engage researchers. One angle focuses on research methods. We describe three different word recognition research methodologies and approaches: behavioral, computational, and neuroscientific. A second perspective examines how word recognition is conceptualized within five theoretical frameworks. These five theoretical perspectives are:

- grain size theory (Ziegler & Goswami, 2005),
- strong phonological theories (Frost, 1998; Van Orden, Pennington, & Stone, 1990),
- the dual route theory of reading aloud (Coltheart, 2005, 2006; Coltheart, Rastle, Perry, Langdon, & Ziegler, 2001),

- triangle connectionist models of reading (Harm & Seidenberg, 2004; Plaut, 2005; Seidenberg & McClelland, 1989), and
- connectionist dual process models (Perry, Ziegler, & Zorzi, 2007).

Grain size theory is treated first because it appropriately situates English word recognition within the context of the size and consistency of its orthographic units and in so doing establishes that English is an outlier orthography (Share, 2008). Strong phonological theory is considered next as it emphasizes how phonology is an essential element of word recognition across languages via its ever present, but varying relationship with orthography. Share (2008) has described the involvement of phonology in word recognition as "the first linguistic universal or, more precisely, phonological universal of writing systems" (p. 603). The next three theoretical models are those that are most constrained to English, although they have been enormously influential in reading science, both historically and currently.

Following review of the five theoretical frameworks, the development of word recognition, word recognition in dyslexia, and second language word recognition are briefly examined. Consideration of development is necessary because empirical data and theory indicate that the transition from novice to expert in word recognition provides important insight into the nature of word recognition (Ziegler & Goswami, 2006). Accounting for dyslexia has been an important focus in testing the premises of theories and models of word recognition, particularly dual route theory and connectionist models. Consideration of word recognition in second language learners addresses an important educational concern in contexts where many children for whom English is a second language are learning to read in English, including the United States, Canada, and the United Kingdom. This discussion also helps to frame understanding of English word recognition into its broader context as an atypical written language. The four-part processor model described in Adams (1990) will be used as a basic typology for discussing the major topics within the chapter: methodological approaches, theoretical perspectives, development, reading difficulty, and English-as-second language word recognition.

The Four-Part Processor Model

In her landmark book, *Beginning to Read: Thinking and Learning about Print,* Adams (1990), building on work of others dating back to 1977 (Baron, 1977), identifies three primary processors that work together in reading words (see Figure 11.1). These three primary processors can also be thought of as representing the three types of information contained in or conveyed by written words: (a) *orthographic* information, the processing of sequences of letters in text, (b) *meaning* (or *semantic*) information, which includes vocabulary knowledge, and (c) *phonological* information, the speech segments embedded in spoken and written words. A fourth component of Adam's scheme is the *context processor* that is responsible for constructing the meaning of the text. Word recognition relies on the dynamic interaction of these various sources of information. Much of the word recognition literature has been concerned with the interface between the phonological and orthographic processors. Investigation of the semantic processor and contextual information has been much more limited, although the most recent work shows increased attention to these two dimensions. In the Adams (1990) model, the context processor refers to the linguistic/semantic context associated with reading words in connected text. Integrating the full scope of the word recognition literature indicates that additional and critical features of context include the particular language in which word recognition is being learned (Share, 2008; Ziegler & Goswami, 2006), the task demands of different word recognition experimental paradigms (Adelman, Brown, & Quesada, 2006; van Orden & Kloos, 2005), and the nature of instructional support in learning to read words (Hutzler, Ziegler, Perry, Wimmer, & Zorzi, 2004; Ziegler & Goswami, 2006). A complete theory of word recognition must explain the nature and

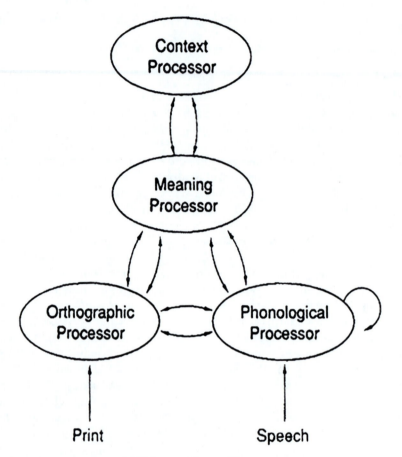

Figure 11.1 Four-part processor model (Adams, 1990, p. 158).

management of information within each of the three main processors, how and when each is activated, and how they interact. It must also explain how variation in language, semantics, task, and instructional context shapes word recognition.

Research Approaches

Three major methodological approaches used in word recognition research are behavioral, computational, and neuroscientific approaches. These three methodologies vary in the degree to which they build an understanding of visual word recognition through sensitivity to within-individual factors or to contextual features of learning, task demands, and word stimuli.

Manipulating the conditions under which words are to be processed and/or the features of the words themselves permits examination of a variety of variables involved in word recognition.

Behavioral Approaches.   In studies utilizing behavioral measures, child or adult participants are most frequently asked to perform one of two tasks. In **word naming** tasks, researchers measure how accurately and/or quickly participants can pronounce a word visually presented for varying periods of time that may last only a few milliseconds, perhaps in a variety of contexts. These contextual manipulations include, for example, flashing another stimulus word before (*forward masks*) or after (*backward masks*) the target word or pairing (**priming**) target words with other words that vary in their phonological, orthographic, or semantic relationship to the target.

Words may also be presented with part of the visual configuration degraded, with interferences, or with fractionating of the stimulus. These manipulations are designed to shape, slow down, or control the sequencing of word recognition processes. For example, there has been extensive interest in using variation in word naming procedures to determine whether word recognition processes occur serially or in parallel (e.g.. Alario, De Cara, & Ziegler, 2007; Rastle & Coltheart, 2006). These naming tasks can be implemented with words presented in isolation, with other words, in sentences, or in text, although single word presentation is dominant in the literature. The majority of the English language studies have examined oral pronunciation of individual words rather than silent reading (Share, 2008).

A second major behavioral approach to studying English word recognition in experimental settings involves *lexical decision* tasks where participants decide whether a visually presented word is a real word. There are advantages and disadvantages to both *naming* and *lexical decision* tasks that have longstanding recognition (Gough, 1984). *Naming* directly involves word recognition but does not require processing the word's meaning (*lexical access*) and boosts phonological involvement due to oral pronunciation of words. *Lexical decision* is more likely to ensure lexical processing but is affected by the character of pseudowords (*foils*) and chance errors resulting from "yes/no" responses.

These manipulations of task context allow researchers to determine how variations in word characteristics and word clusters related to the three processors (phonological, orthographic, semantic) facilitate or impede word recognition. In so doing, researchers aspire to uncover foundational processes and the features of word representations that are involved in word recognition. These variations also permit testing of competing theoretical explanations for the influence and timing of various processing components and word representation features involved in recognizing words.

Behavioral approaches to word recognition also entail formal and informal measurement and descriptions of the reading behaviors of beginning and mature readers as well as proficient and disabled readers under conditions of looser control. These types of studies are more likely to occur in the context of instructional settings (e.g., Coyne, Kame'euni, & Simmons, 2001). Children may be asked to orally read words from lists or to read connected text. A major interest in these types of studies is to determine the level of word recognition skill in developing or mature readers for assessing educational progress in reading. A particularly significant area of study in this regard involves fluency assessment (Fuchs et al., 2001) and the attendant variables involving accuracy and rate of word reading. Possible implications for intervention can be gauged in these studies when participants read words differing in characteristics such as regularity, irregularity and word or pseudoword status from lists, or when the word reading errors they make while reading connected text are qualitatively analyzed for diagnostic purposes. Thus, there is less interest in or possibility of uncovering the subtle, detailed, and time-sensitive processes and word representation features that are of interest in the psychological experimental studies that constitute the bulk of the behavioral word recognition literature.

A common feature of both the experimental and more educationally embedded studies is that they rely heavily on oral rather than silent reading and on single word reading, which leads to specific consequences (Coltheart, Curtis, Atkins, & Haller, 1993; Coltheart et al., 2001; Edfeldt, 1960; Perry et al., 2007; Seidenberg & McClelland, 1989; Zorzi, Houghton, & Butterworth, 1998a, 1998b). These consequences include greater interest in accuracy than rate, increased reliance on phonology, and failure to account for complex interactions among lexical items, syntax and the broader linguistic environment of connected text. Table 11.1 and Table 11.2 show the major word characteristics and important context effects on word recognition.

Computational Approaches.   Computational approaches to the study of word recognition use computer programs written to simulate the cognitive processes humans rely on when reading or

Table 11.1　Word Characteristic Variables in Word Recognition

Word Characteristic Variables in Word Recognition	
Variable(s)	*Example*
1. Word frequency	*cake* faster than *sake*
2. Word versus nonword	*log* faster than *pog*
3. Word length x real word versus nonword	*nad* faster than *strend*, but *stand* about as fast as *cat*
4. Spelling regularity	*like* faster than *laugh*
5. Frequency x regularity	low frequency regular faster than low frequency irregular (*snuff* versus *rough*), but the difference between high frequency regular/irregular (*run* versus *done*) is not as great
6. Irregularity x position	irregularities at the beginning of a word faster than irregularities at the end (*knife* versus *though*)
7. Pseudohomophone	*brane* (pseudohomophone) faster than *brene* (nonword)
8. Frequency x pseudohomophones	*hazz* faster than *glew*
9. Orthographic neighborhood x nonword versus pseudohomophone	*zace* faster than *zuce*, but *brane* no faster than *noze*

learning to read words. These computational approaches have been rigorously and extensively used to test differing views of how word recognition occurs. Connectionist parallel distributed processing theories (e.g., Harm & Seidenberg, 2004; Seidenberg & McClelland, 1989) and dual route theories (e.g., Coltheart, 2005) are being vigorously compared through computational modeling. Computational approaches seek to verify or falsify theoretical postulates about the nature of word recognition by evaluating whether or not word reading effects generated by behavioral studies (such as priming, homophone, and neighborhood effects) are outputted by computational simulations with different algorithms derived from a particular theory's assertions about how word recognition operates (e.g., Coltheart, 2005). Computational studies have produced a prolific and nuanced array of results that depend on very specific aspects of stimulus words and experimental procedures (Lukatela & Turvey, 1999; vanOrden & Kloos, 2005).

For example, Powell, Plaut, and Funell (2006) collected word recognition data from British children during their first year of learning to read. They found the simulated connectionist network was not as successful as children at reading pseudowords and did not match children's lexical and non-lexical error patterns. In a second simulation where training of grapheme-phoneme correspondences was added to the computer program, pseudoword reading outputted by the model improved sharply and now closely matched the performance of real students. The authors argued that their study showed the importance of specific grapheme-phoneme correspondence rules in learning to read.

Neuroscientific Approaches.　Though still relatively new, neuroimaging research examines the areas of the brain that are activated during word reading using a variety of neuroscientific methods (Palmer, Brown, Peterson, & Shlaggar, 2004; Shaywitz, 2003). Other studies are refining understanding of the brain-based foundations of the semantic, orthographic, and phonological processors and the distribution of labor that occurs among them during word recognition (Frost, Mencl, et al., 2005; Pugh et al., 2000). Neuroscientific studies have provided information about the different activity patterns among beginning and mature readers as well as proficient and disabled readers (Papanicolaou et al., 2003). They have also yielded promising evidence

Table 11.2   Broader Context Variables in Word Recognition

Broader Context Variables	
Variable(s)	*Example*
1. Language (consistency)	
▪ Orthographic transparency (consistency)	Spanish and Italian are more transparent than English
▪ Orthography x phonological units	transparent orthographies encourage phonemic units while opaque orthographies such as English encourage larger units such as onset and rime
2. Instruction	
▪ Instructional context	focus on grapheme-phoneme conversion (GPC) rules or larger units (onset and rime) or sight words; use of decodable or non-decodable text
▪ Orthography x instructional context	transparent orthographies are mastered more easily and quickly and with less explicit instruction
3. Task demands	
▪ Oral versus silent reading	oral increases phonological effects, complete phonological and serial processing
▪ Lexical decision versus naming	different word reading effects due to overt pronunciation and/or differing lexical access
▪ Monosyllabic versus polysyllabic words	monosyllabic ignores complex syllable juncture and morphological effects
▪ Single words versus connected text	word meaning, sentence, discourse, and other meanings within text

regarding beneficial changes in brain activity in response to effective intervention (Berninger et al., 2003; Richards et al., 2006; Richards & Berninger, 2008; Simos et al., 2006.). All three of the reviewed methodological approaches to the study of word recognition are utilized in studies with differing theoretical frameworks. We now shift the lens to examining word recognition from a theoretical perspective.

Five Theoretical Views of Word Recognition

The following section describes five different theoretical perspectives on word recognition. While there are several other important theories or models of word recognition, we have selected these five because they highlight different yet crucial aspects of word reading and have also significantly shaped investigation within the field.

First, we review Ziegler and Goswami's (2005) *grain size* theory that links differences in word recognition processing strategies to variations in the nature of word representations across languages and in how these language structures map onto the written language. In terms of the four-part processor model, the emphasis within grain size theory is how the availability, consistency, and size of orthographic units interact with phonological processing and consequently word recognition.

We then consider *"strong" phonological* theory that emphasizes and describes the critical role of the phonological processor in word recognition. Phonological processing is considered the "default procedure" in word recognition within "strong" phonological theory and, as such, can accommodate "most findings in visual word perception" (Frost, 1998, p. 72). Studies utilizing behavioral, computational, and neuroscientific approaches have all devoted attention to the role of phonology in word recognition.

Next we discuss *dual route and connectionist* models. These models differ in specifying how the orthographic, phonological, and semantic processors interact when reading familiar versus unfamiliar and regular versus irregular words. Dual route theories posit that there is a direct "route" between the orthographic and semantic processors for reading familiar and irregular words, while the phonological processor is also necessary for reading unfamiliar, regular words, and pseudowords. Connectionist models, on the other hand, maintain that all three processors are activated and interactive when reading all kinds of words, with the relationships amongst the three processors distributed across a mental neural network. These models also differ in how they specify word representations. These two models are the foundation for much of the computational research.

The fifth and final theory is a *connectionist dual-process* model that incorporates the uniform computational style of parallel distributed processing but avoids any strict commitment to a single route. This hybridized approach to word recognition incorporates the orthographic, phonological, and semantic processors.

Psycholinguistic Grain Size Theory

Grain size theory (Ziegler & Goswami, 2005) examines differences in sound-symbol relationships across languages and how these variations affect the reading strategies of skilled readers, the development of word recognition within beginning readers, and the incidence and nature of dyslexia. "Grain size" or *granularity* refers to the size of phonological and orthographic units; typical units are syllables (/pic/ + /nic/), onset and rimes (/m/ + /an/), and phonemes (/s/ + /a/ +/t/). Bigger grain sizes require readers to master more orthographic units. Spelling-sound mappings differ in *consistency*. For example, orthographic symbols may represent more than one phoneme, as does the /ow/ in *cow* and *crow,* and phonemes may be represented by more than one orthographic unit, as in *meet* and *meat.* Yet another factor involves the *availability* of orthographic units for representing all the phonological units in a word. Hebrew script, for example, may leave out vowel sounds (Frost, 2006). Relationships between grain size and consistency vary across languages. In English, smaller grain sizes are less consistent, while the opposite is true for Spanish and Italian.

Much of Ziegler and Goswami's (2005) grain size theory focuses on accounting for variations in the development of word recognition across languages. While beginning readers may utilize different kinds of orthographic units depending on the consistency (or transparency) of how spoken language maps on to orthography, skilled readers of alphabetic languages ultimately "gain access to" phoneme-size units. The smaller grain sizes are less reliable in English and therefore children must become more adept at using additional sources of information at a larger grain size for word recognition, although debate remains about the degree to which larger grain sizes such as the rime are influential. These other sources of information include semantic knowledge, vocabulary, morphology, syntax, and text context, There is evidence that larger grain sizes are particularly useful for puzzling out the irregular words that plague English orthography (e.g., Nation & Snowling, 1998; Ricketts, Nation, & Bishop, 2007; Share, 1995; Stanovich, 1980; Tunmer & Chapman, 1998, 2006). For example, Goswami, Ziegler, Dalton, and Schneider (2001) found that English-speaking children were more affected by whole-word phonology when reading pseudowords than were German-speaking children for whom orthography is more consistent. Knowledge of whole-word phonology implicates word knowledge. Thus, evidence revealed by grain size theory highlights the importance of the semantic processor in English word recognition.

Grain size theory, consistent with other theories of word recognition, has focused on monosyllabic words. Other evidence has shown that vocabulary knowledge plays an important role in polysyllabic word recognition (e.g., Shefelbine, 1990; Shefelbine, Lipscomb, & Hern, 1989). Polysyllabic word recognition may be particularly vexing in less consistent (more opaque) orthographies like English (Ferrand & New, 2003). The syllable boundaries in English polysyllabic words are often ambiguous, particularly in those with VCV patterns such as *o/pen* and *mel/on*. Because the division can "legally" occur before or after the consonant, readers deduce the correct pronunciation by making a match with a word in their lexicon. Pseudowords such as *pitok* are difficult to pronounce because no lexical match is available. The complexity of polysyllabic decoding in English has not received sufficient attention in grain size research or research conducted within other theoretical frameworks.

For languages with a more consistent orthography, context and other linguistic skills such as vocabulary and syntax influence word recognition to a lesser degree (Geva & Siegel, 2000; Nikolopoulos, Goulandris, Hulme, & Snowling, 2006). An interesting extension of this idea is that opaque orthographies, such as English, may be more likely to require a lexical route to word recognition than would transparent orthographies where phonological recoding would suffice for lexical access.

Strong Phonological Theory

Frost (1998) proposes a *"strong" phonological* theory of word recognition based on the premise that words in the mental lexicon are stored in their phonological form and that prelexical phonological recoding is the norm rather than the exception during lexical access to meaning. In fact, according to the strong phonological theory, the assembly of a prelexical phonological representation from print is a *mandatory* process (Frost, 1998, p. 89).

Frost (1998) maintains that three dimensions of the strong phonological model (processing speed, orthographic unit size, and lexical access efficiency) can explain the visual perception of words by skilled readers. While dual route models assume that phonological recoding is slower than direct access to word representations, there is evidence that, at least in English, the first cycle of phonological computation is very rapid because it uses an *impoverished phonological representation* consisting of consonants that are quickly and automatically identified (Berent & Perfetti, 1995). In a slower and more attention-demanding cycle that follows, vowels are identified using lexical information. With increased practice, the speed of generating skeletal phonological structures becomes even faster. Skilled readers quickly process the more complex orthographic spellings that are characteristic of deeper orthographies. These complex spellings include the many vowel sounds in English represented by two or more letters (/ea/ as in *eat*) and phonemic clusters such as /ight/ in *night*. Finally, skilled readers can efficiently achieve lexical access with an impoverished phonological representation while beginning readers require more phonological detail.

Frost (1998) also contends that evidence of attenuated phonology effects for phonologically complex words does not imply its absence because a detailed phonological analysis of each word is not required. Even when phonological elements are irregular, such as the i in *pint,* a rapid search of the mental lexicon occurs. Regular elements, in this case p, n, and t, provide phonological information that dramatically reduces possible words and renders the ambiguity of "i" less important.

Phonological effects in word recognition are robustly reported in studies utilizing behavioral, computational and neuroscientific approaches or some combination among the three. They have been found for both alphabetic and non-alphabetic languages, particularly those with more transparent or shallow orthographies (Berent & Perfetti, 1995; Berninger et al., 2006; Folk, 1999; Frost, 1994; Harm & Seidenberg, 2004; Hu & Catts, 1998; Mulatti, Reynolds & Besner, 2006; Perfetti & Bell, 1991; Pollatsek, Rayner, & Lee, 2000).

However, there continues to be theoretical and empirical debate about the relative strength of phonology's influence, the timing of its influence (either early or late in the word reading process; Perfetti, Bell, & Delaney, 1988), whether phonological processing occurs in parallel or serially (Alario et al., 2007), and the size of the phonological elements that are most attended to (Muter, Hulme, Snowling, & Stevenson, 2004; Ziegler & Goswami, 2005). These issues have been raised in both studies with adults and studies with children. Van Orden and Kloos (2005) maintain that *context sensitivity* has been a hidden factor behind many contradictory findings related to phonology.

An artifact of the almost exclusive reliance on oral reading as compared to silent reading in the study of English word recognition is that it may inflate the role of phonology due to articulatory demands or because naming tasks require complete serial processing of phonemes (see Share, 2008). This processing that occurs during speech production is different in kind from the partial phonological assembly argued for in strong phonological theory (de Jong & Share, 2007; Poeppel, 2001).

Dual Route Theory

An essential premise of the dual route model is the presence of two internal processes for word recognition (Coltheart et al., 1993; see Figure 11.2). Similar to early models of word recognition, there is one route, "the lexical route," that is used for recognizing real words that are familiar to the reader (Coltheart, 2006). This route uses graphemic information to access the word's meaning and pronunciation via a mental lexicon of known words. When a familiar word is seen, the orthographic lexicon recognizes the word and directly accesses both meaning and phonology. The other, "non-lexical route" is used to access grapheme-phoneme conversion (GPC) rules that are applied to render a pronunciation of (decode) words that are not well represented in the mental lexicon (Coltheart, 2006). These words include unfamiliar words, words with incomplete

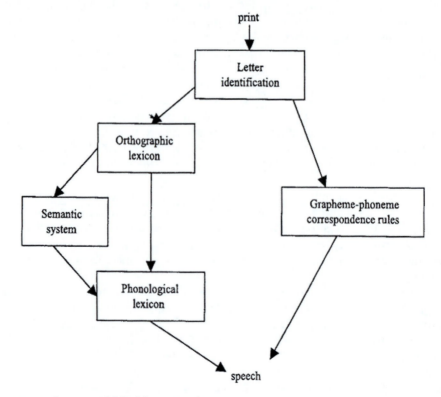

Figure 11.2 Dual route model (Coltheart, 2006).

representations, or pseudowords with regular spellings. What determines which route will be used is the reader's familiarity with a word's orthographic form.

This theory posits a *localist* representation for words in a mental lexicon, where each word the reader has learned in its printed form has an individual entry. There is also a mental storehouse of grapheme-phoneme conversion rules that can be used in decoding printed words into their spoken form (Coltheart et al., 1993). Furthermore, it is hypothesized that these GPC rules are serially, rather than simultaneously, applied. An expectation from the hypothesized, non-lexical GPC route is that word length effects and serial position effects should be found when reading unknown words or pseudowords because phonological information is hypothesized to proceed letter by letter in a sequence. Studies have both supported and challenged this hypothesis.

Coltheart expanded on earlier dual route models (Forster & Chambers, 1973) that were based on behavioral data and proposed a computational explanation, the dual route cascaded model (DRY) (Coltheart, Rastle, Perry, Langdon, & Ziegler, 2001). Within this computer-implemented model there are three routes to reading a word aloud: "the lexical semantic route, the lexical non-semantic route and the grapheme-phoneme correspondence (GPC) route" (Coltheart et al., 2001, p. 213). Within the DRC model, the interactions that occur between and among units and layers within the word recognition system are defined by a priori structures specified in the computer program. While information is feeding forward (from orthographic lexicon to the phonological lexicon, it is also feeding backward (from the phonological lexicon to the orthographic lexicon) with either inhibitory or excitatory consequences, for a particular pronunciation candidate. This feedback serves to make the system more accurate and quicker at recognizing common letter-sound patterns (e.g., /ar/). The dual route model can account for the majority of the word effects found in the behavioral data with human participants (see Table 11.1).

Connectionist Models

Within most connectionist models, information about words is assumed to be stored in a distributed manner across different information units that align with the phonological, orthographic and semantic components of the four-part processor model. Word recognition occurs as a result of a pattern of activation across and within these units reaching a threshold level of "excitation" that results in an accurate pronunciation of the word. Thus, all information about a word is linked through a neural network and activation in any one part of the network produces activation in related parts, where the critical parts represent phonological, orthographic, and semantic information.

Unlike dual route models that propose a discreet mental entry representing a word, separate paths for familiar and unfamiliar words, and the sequential activation of the different processors, connectionist models describe a "dynamical system that settles into a stable pattern of semantic activation over several time steps, based on continuous but time-varying input" (Harm & Seidenberg, 2004, p. 669). Orthographic units function as parts of the representation of many different words. For example, /at/ is a part of the representations for *rat, mat, rattle,* and *format.*

Repeated exposure to words causes the network to read words based on the relationships between patterns in word forms an individual has encountered in print. Through experience with printed words, connections between different units in the network are formed, with more exposure to a word leading to stronger weighting. Word recognition skill evolves as a result of learning within the network regarding the "frequency and consistency of correspondences between orthography and phonology" (Seidenberg, 1993b, p. 299). These connections are stored and feedback about their efficiency that is obtained both during and as a result of word recognition attempts serves to strengthen, weaken, and/or inhibit possible reader responses. Word recognition is then essentially statistical learning. During word reading, these statistically derived connections are activated simultaneously (in parallel). Experience with print serves to strengthen or weaken connections in the appropriate directions. Thus, connectionist models account for how word recognition develops, and this learning procedure is instantiated in connectionist computational models. On the other hand, in the dual route cascaded model the procedures used by a skilled reader are specified in the computational model's architecture; it does not learn.

While often called *triangle models* because they specify that word representations are distributed amongst the phonological, orthographic, and semantic processors (Seidenberg & McClelland, 1989), until recently connectionist models have focused primarily on the interaction between orthography and phonology. Harm and Seidenberg (2004) created and tested a computational model to address the question of how word meaning is accessed within a connectionist model. Meaning occurs due to activation from all three sources (orthographic, phonemic, and semantic; see Figure 11.3).

Additional studies have demonstrated that training in one type of processing will improve functioning in others, thereby documenting the cross-processor connections that develop as children learn to read (Berninger, 2007). This evidence is also consistent with the interconnected network proposed by the distributed (amongst the three processors), parallel (occurring all at once) processing in connectionist models. For example, training in morphological processing reduces energy use in phonological processing centers (Richards et al., 2002) and behaviorally can lead to better performance on phonologically based tasks (Torgesen, Wagner, & Rashotte, 1997). Connectionist models have accounted for behavioral data observed in children learning to read, and a variety of effects associated with word characteristics such as homophones and pseudohomophones, regularity, and neighborhood effects (Seidenberg, Petersen, MacDonald, & Plaut, 1996; Seidenberg, Waters, Barnes, & Tanenhaus, 1984; see Table 11.1).

Table 11.3 compares two critical dimensions of dual route and connectionist models of word recognition: the mental representation of words and processes for reading words. The table shows that in addition to important differences, both models have two different processes for reading different kinds of words. More recent models blend elements of both dual route and connectionist theories, an example of which is described in the next section.

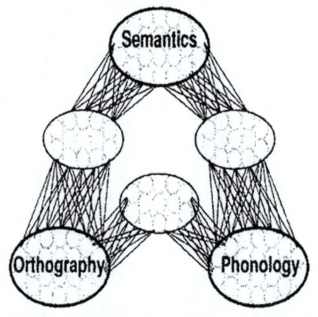

Figure 11.3 A connectionist network based on the "triangle" framework (Seidenberg & McClelland, 1989). From Plaut, 2005, p. 25.

Table 11.3   Comparison of Word Representation, Mechanisms for Reading Words, and How Development is Explained within Dual Route and Connectionist Models of Word Recognition

Dual Route	Connectionist
Mental Representation of Word Units	
Word units are locally stored in the mental lexicon; this includes knowledge of the words' spelling and pronunciation	Representations of "units" are distributed across the processors and involve spelling units smaller than the word itself
Processes for Reading	
Grapheme-phoneme conversion (GPC) system operates serially and is built into the architecture	Statistical pattern extraction with varying degrees of feedback and with parallel processing or operation
Both have 2 processes for reading:	

- a process for phonological recoding, necessary for reading non-word and regular words
- a process for accessing lexical representations, regular sight words, and irregular words

Explains Learning Processes	
no	yes

Connectionist Dual Process Model

Zorzi et al. (1998a, 1998b) developed a *connectionist dual process* (*CDP*) model of reading that explains word recognition as resulting from computational instantiations of parallel distributed processing but without rigid commitment to a single route for word recognition. Their model was developed to build on the strengths of dual route and connectionist models while avoiding their weaknesses. The latest version of this approach, the new connectionist dual process (CDP+) model (Perry et al., 2007), is based on a methodological strategy called *nested modeling*, where the new model is first tested against previous models with the same data sets used by the previous models. The original CDP model was "highly sensitive" to the statistical consistency of spelling-sound relationships across different grain sizes and was "reasonably" close to the pseudoword reading performance found in behavioral studies (Perry et al., 2007, p. 276). However, the model regularized the pronunciation of irregular words and was insensitive to some aspects of word frequency.

The CDP+ model addresses these limitations by adding a lexical route similar to that of the dual-route cascade model discussed earlier (Coltheart, 2005) and the earlier interactive model of McClelland and Rumelhart (1981). The model's performance in reading pseudowords was improved by using graphemes (individual letters or letter combinations representing an individual phoneme) as orthographic input rather than individual letters only (Perry et al., 2007). These grapheme units or spelling patterns, such as /ee/ and /th/, as well as onsets and rimes, are processed serially, similar to how the grapheme-phoneme conversion (GPC) rules in dual route models are applied. Word recognition is again seen to be essentially statistical learning, derived from associations between the orthographic, phonological, and semantic processors.

A criticism of some theoretical accounts of learning to read is that they are not sufficiently related to more general theories of learning. Zorzi et al. (1998b) maintain that connectionist network models have brought general *associative learning* rules or algorithms into the "mainstream of cognitive psychology" (p. 367). Their model relies on a simple associative learning rule upported in studies of animal and human learning to demonstrate that exposure to a very small set of words can lead to the successful decoding of new words.

Similarly, Van Orden, Pennington, and Stone (1990) propose that how readers learn the relationships between spelling and phonology is "analogous to general treatments of language learning" (p. 500). Instead of subscribing to the grapheme-phoneme correspondence (GPC) rules of dual route models, Van Orden et al. utilize a *covariate learning hypothesis* to describe how sounds are mapped onto letters. Initially, letter-sound relationships are stimulus specific. However, as students encounter other words with some of the same orthographic-phonological correspondences, statistical regularity effects result in rule-like knowledge that can be applied to new words. Similarly, the many vowels with multiple spellings (*ray, rate, rain*) and irregular spellings (*through, though, thought*) explain why students often rely more on consonants than vowels. Placing word recognition within the context of learning in general is an important theoretical reminder embedded in the CDP+ model.

The CDP+ model has succeeded in simulating Coltheart et al.'s (1993) results from a dual route model and was able to address problems within both connectionist and dual route models: consistency effects for words and pseudowords (dual route), serial effects and the additive effects of regularity and frequency (connectionist), word length effects (original connectionist dual process), and sensitivity to item level variance (all three previous models). The authors note that adding the lexical route adapted from the dual-route cascade model improved the reading of pseudowords and irregular words but still provided a minor contribution to the new model's "success in simulating a broad range of phenomena in written word naming" (Perry et al., 2007, p. 279).

Development of Word Recognition

Behavioral studies with children, studies utilizing computational models, and studies examining the neuroscientific bases of learning to read words show that connecting units in speech with the related units in printed words is the fundamental task. The dependency of word recognition processes upon phonology pressures and necessitates attention to phonological elements—such as individual phonemes, syllables, or morphemes—for linking phonology and orthography, particularly early in reading acquisition and when printed words are new or not well-known. All three types of studies also support the development of word recognition as an interaction between learner cognition and print experiences, and the context of learning, especially characteristics of orthography and instruction. At different points in development, different aspects of phonological and orthographic processing are more relevant, rendering the association between phonological and orthographic competencies and word recognition a dynamic one (Wagner et al., 1997). In addition, for all beginning readers all written words are unfamiliar.

Over the course of word recognition development, children develop diverse constellations of related and integrated processes that they use to recognize words. These constellations are formed of a number of important basic learning mechanisms, some of which are explicitly embedded in the theories covered in this chapter. Statistically based pattern extraction and pattern weighting between pronunciations and spellings (Harm & Seidenberg, 2004; Perry et al., 2007; Seidenberg & McClelland, 1989), self-teaching (Share, 2004), association learning of grapheme-phoneme pairings (Hutzler et al., 2004; Perry et al., 2007; Van Orden et al., 1990), and memory for whole word spellings (Ehri, 2005) are among the most important of these learning mechanisms.

In addition to the influence of individual differences in learning mechanisms, individual phonological and orthographic processing competencies have a strong relationship with word recognition at many different points in word recognition development. These influences derive from the key involvement of both speech and orthography in word recognition. Alphabet knowledge (e.g., Ehri, 1987, 1998, 2005; Ehri & Wilce, 1985; Frith, 1985; Gough & Hillinger, 1980; Scanlon & Vellutino, 1996; Treiman & Rodriguez, 1999), phonological recoding (Share, 1995), phonemic awareness (Liberman, Shankweiler, & Liberman, 1989; Torgesen & Burgess, 1998; Share, 2008; Wagner & Torgesen, 1987; Wagner et al., 1997), and ability to analyze word structure including segmenting and blending (Ehri, 2005; Liberman et al., 1989; Lundberg,

Olofsson, & Wall, 1980; Perfetti, Beck, Bell, & Hughes, 1987) are among the most significant of these influences. Consistent but arguably less powerful influences have been found for other cognitive skills related to phonological and orthographic processing (e.g., Cardoso-Martins, & Pennington, 2004). These effects include rapid automatic naming (RAN) (Wolf, 1991) and verbal memory (Baddeley, 1986). Learning to recognize words is dependent on learning to orchestrate these multiple cognitive and linguistic skills into a word recognition system that is effective, efficient, and fast.

Behavioral Approaches. Models of the development of word recognition have typically been conceptualized within the context of the English language. The most influential of these models propose a stage or phase-based progression from novice to skilled reader. Phonological and orthographic influences on the development of word recognition are specified in these models (Ehri, 1995; Frith, 1985; Gough & Hillinger, 1980; Morton, 1989; Rack, Hulme, Snowling, & Wightman, 1994; Stuart & Coltheart, 1988). Ehri's (1998) phase theory has played a pivotal role in behavioral studies revealing that the development of children's word recognition in the deep orthography of English progresses through four phases. These four phases are the pre-alphabetic, partial alphabetic, full alphabetic, and consolidated alphabetic phases. Children initially rely on partial information about graphemes, analogous to the statistical pattern extraction from activations among the phonological, orthographic, and semantic processors that explain learning within connectionist triangle models. Grapheme-phoneme knowledge is inconsistently and/or partially applied in the pre-alphabetic phase, when children's have only partial understanding of the system of graphemic and phonemic pairings. Full alphabetic readers systematically attend to all the speech and print relationships in words, yet they have not mastered morphological patterns and multiple spelling patterns for the same phoneme. Phoneme blending is a crucial skill in becoming an alphabetic reader (Lundberg, Olofsson, & Wall, 1980; Perfetti et al., Hughes, 1987). In the final phase of word reading development, readers consolidate the grapheme-phoneme connections in words into larger units. Spellings of rimes, syllables, morphemes, and whole words are unitized and promote efficient memory for word spellings. Speech-print knowledge that begins with very small grain sizes grows into a system that relies on larger grain sizes to amalgamate spellings and internally stored word pronunciations. This process promotes what Ehri (2005) refers to as "sight word reading," where word reading is mediated by memory for whole word spellings. This procedure appears to be similar to the lexical procedures specified in both dual route and connectionist models of word recognition.

Yet an important issue related to Ehri's and other stage or phase models of English word recognition is whether or not the pre-alphabetic and partial alphabetic phases capture the developmental progression of readers learning to read in orthographies that are more consistent than English. In these languages, novices very quickly progress to full alphabetic and consolidated alphabetic word reading (Mannhaupt, Jansen, & Marx, 1997). Another point is that instruction may influence the patterns of progression (Landerl, 2000; Share & Gur, 1999).

Experiments where words are read aloud by beginners show a slow sound-by-sound process (Frith, 1998; Goswami, 2001, 2003) that is consistent with using GPC rules within the dual-route cascaded model or firing of emerging and as yet insufficiently weighted connections between orthographic, phonological, and semantic units in connectionist models. This pattern is more striking with pseudowords than with real words. Yet in experimental conditions where the influence of phonology is gauged with methodologies that activate phonology implicitly, evidence of fast, early, and parallel use of phonological information in word reading is found even in beginners (Alario et al., 2007; Booth, Perfetti, & MacWhinney, 1999), consistent with the strong phonology theoretical arguments.

Language context influences the development of word recognition. The length of time needed for word recognition to become automatic and fluent is highly dependent on the transparency of phonology and orthography relationships (Durgonglu & Oney, 1999; Seymour, Aro, & Erskine, 2003). Children learning to read in transparent orthographies, such as Greek, Finnish, or German, achieved real and pseudoword reading scores between 93% and 98% correct by the end of one year of phonics instruction, while their Scottish and English counterparts learning to read less transparent orthographies scored 34% and 29%, respectively (Seymour et al., 2003). The pattern-seeking nature of word recognition processes as conceptualized within word recognition theories suggests that word recognition in less consistent orthographies such as English may be enhanced by presenting beginning students with spelling patterns that are controlled enough to mimic shallow, consistent orthographies (which are much easier to master), yet with sufficient variety to generalize knowledge to novel patterns.

Other behavioral studies have examined relationships among individual cognitive characteristics hypothesized to be involved in recognizing words (e.g., Cardoso-Martins & Pennington, 2004; Metsala & Walley, 1998; Scarborough, 1998; Vellutino, Tunmer, Jaccard, & Chen, 2007; Wagner et al., 1997; Wolf, Bowers, & Biddle, 2000). Precursors, correlates, and casual influences on the development of word recognition have been identified in these studies. Alphabet knowledge (letter names, letter sounds), phonological awareness, rapid automatic naming (speed in naming continuous lists of numbers, letters, pictured objects and colors), memory, and vocabulary size influence the development of word recognition.

Developing readers' advantage in reading real words, more familiar words, more meaningful words, and words that occur more frequently implicate semantic influences and individual differences in print exposure. Although there is more than one factor that contributes to these word effects, semantics is an obviously relevant one (Powell et al., 2006). The interface of vocabulary (and other semantic sources) and word recognition has received little attention in research on the development of word recognition research in spite of the representation of semantics as a key component in the four processor model presented by Adams and in theories and models of word recognition.

Computational Approaches. Computational approaches have yielded less understanding of the development of word recognition than behavioral studies. In fact one strand of debate within the computational literature is the limitations of connectionist models in mirroring the developmental data on children's word learning. Children learn to read regular words much more quickly with far fewer exposures and perform better earlier on pseudoword reading than do computational models (Zorzi et al., 1998b). In computational approaches, a corpus of 3,000 whole words is input into the computational network during the learning phase while children are incrementally exposed to a more limited number of words when they first begin to read. In an important recent study, Powell et al. (2006) adjusted the connectionist computational model of Plaut, McClelland, Seidenberg, and Patterson (1996) to be more in line with both the learning tools available to children and their print and instructional experience. They introduced a training strand to the model where individual grapheme-phoneme conversion rules in both initial and final position were weighted more heavily than digraphs to model early word recognition instruction. Words drawn from children's reading materials were introduced incrementally. In this case, children's performance and the performance of the model were highly similar, suggesting the potential fruitfulness of computational approaches that model the effect of instructional context.

Neuroscientific Approaches. The neuroscientific evidence on word recognition in beginning readers is broadly consistent with theoretical accounts emphasizing the interplay of phonological processing and orthography with developmental change toward an increasingly integrated and flexible system with faster processing capable of responding to the constraints imposed by the oral and written language in which word recognition is learned (Parvianen, Helensiu, Poskiparta,

Niemi, & Salmelin, 2006; Shaywitz, 2003). This developmental pattern provides another demonstration of individual-context interactions in word recognition. Beginning readers rely on a cortical system that is widely distributed and includes right hemisphere tempoparietal and frontal regions, with certain regions showing greater involvement, integration, and diffusion as word recognition skill increases (Price, 2000). With increasing skill, the left hemisphere ventral system becomes centrally involved in fluent word recognition (Booth et al., 1999; Shaywitz et al., 2002). This left hemisphere ventral system has semantic (Fiebach, Friederici, Mueller, & von Cramon, 2002), linguistic (Pugh, Sandak, Frost, Moore, & Mencl, 2005), and possibly visual word form functions (Cohen et al., 2002), suggesting increasing interaction of meaning, language, and orthography in the brain with word recognition development. Neuroscientific understanding of word recognition development is not complete.

Problems in Word Recognition

Both the International Dyslexia Association (IDA, 2007) and the National Institutes of Child Health and Development (2007) identify difficulties with word recognition as the most distinguishing behavioral feature in dyslexia or specific reading disability (Lyon, Shaywitz, & Shaywitz, 2003). According to Fletcher, Lyon, Fuchs, and Barnes (2007), "word level reading disability (WLRD) is synonymous with 'dyslexia'" (p. 85). Though students may have difficulty comprehending text for reasons other than deficits in word recognition (for example, language processing difficulties, poor reasoning skills), in English, children with basic word recognition problems are those most likely to be identified as dyslexic or having a specific reading disability. Evidence from neuroimaging and behavioral research, as discussed below, consistently identifies that problems in rapid word recognition distinguish between normally developing and impaired readers. These data also support the importance of linking phonological and orthographic information in word recognition acquisition.

Behavioral Approaches. Typically, students with dyslexia have relataively stronger oral language and relatively weaker reading skills, although very recent studies suggest more pervasive oral language challenges. For example, such children frequently are (a) stronger in oral comprehension than in reading comprehension, (b) stronger in comprehension of connected text than in reading single words, and (c) stronger in reading real words than in reading pseudowords (Christo, Davis, & Brock, 2008). Further evidence of word recognition problems as the fundamental disorder in dyslexia is found in intervention studies. Interventions that lead to improved word recognition target basic word recognition skills and underlying phonological processing (Denton & Mathes, 2003: Foorman, 2003; Haager, Klinger, & Vaughn, 2007; Uhry & Clark, 2004).

Thus, there is a wealth of evidence (supported by both behavioral and neuroimaging studies) indicating that failure to develop automatic word recognition is a primary cause of reading disability. However, it is less clear what impedes the development of automatic word recognition. Clearly, there is strong evidence to support the role of adequate phonological processing in learning to read and deficits in phonological processing as a core problem for struggling readers (Adams, 1990; Catts, 1989; Liberman et al., 1989; Lyon et al., 2003; Wagner & Torgesen, 1987). Visual processing (Talcott et al., 2007), temporal processing (Tallal, 2006), and the ability to rapidly access name codes (RAN; Wolf et al., 2000) are additional potential problems. It is likely that there is more than one factor that can impede the development of linkages between orthographic, phonological, and semantic processors.

Computational Approaches. Proponents of both dual route and connectionist models have elaborated how their respective models account for reading disability and have had some success in their computational algorithms outputting word recognition performance similar to that of impaired readers. The effectiveness of different models to yield the word recognition results for reading disability found in behavioral studies has been an important facet of model testing. For example, Coltheart et al. (1993) suggest that different subtypes of developmental dyslexia arise due to difficulties in developing one or more of the various modules needed for efficient reading. Children with "phonological dyslexia" have difficulty acquiring the grapheme-phoneme rule system while those with "developmental surface dyslexia" have difficulty "acquiring the lexical procedure for reading." This distinction is based on the premise that there are two distinct forms of developmental dyslexia. Evidence tends to support the primacy of what Coltheart describes as phonological dyslexia (Adams, 1990; Calfee, Lindamood, & Lindamood, 1973; Liberman et al., 1989; Lyon et al., 2003; Wagner & Torgesen, 1987), evidence that again attests to the influence of phonology in word recognition within impaired readers. The core problem for most poor readers seems to be in developing a readily accessible system of grapheme-phoneme connections. Though children may score relatively better on norm-referenced tests when applying phonics rules to accurately decode pseudowords than they are at recognizing real words, they are generally still slower than their peers at both (Christo et al., 2008; Vellutino et al., 2004). In other words they have developed knowledge of the grapheme-phoneme system and can use it accurately but they have not developed fast, automatic retrieval of these codes nor the connections that allow them to use the codes to create the "word forms" that foster quick recognition of real words.

Seidenberg (1993a) reports that computational models based on connectionist theories resemble the behaviors that are seen in struggling readers. When phonological information is represented imprecisely in the model, reading of real words tends to remain intact while reading of pseudowords diminishes. When more complete phonological representations were incorporated in the model, reading of pseudowords improved (Harm & Seidenberg, 1999). This behavior is in line with the definition of dyslexia put forth by the IDA and NICHD that places the cause of dyslexia primarily in phonological processes. Seidenberg (2005) also outlines findings that corroborate behavioral studies on reading. For example, when designing feedback to the computational model that mimics two different approaches to teaching reading, it was found that the absence of information on pronunciation led to poorer performance. This finding is in line with current research supporting an instructional approach that incorporates phonics (NICHD, 2007).

Dual route theories have been particularly successful in accounting for acquired dyslexia. The presence of two routes for accessing words can account for the two types of acquired dyslexia: phonological dyslexia in which the reader has difficulty using decoding skills to read real or pseudoword words and surface dyslexia in which the reader has intact decoding skills but cannot read real words that do not follow common phonics patterns. Dual route cascaded models are also able to account for word effects such as frequency, regularity and homophone priming.

Neuroscientific Studies.   Neuroimaging data has confirmed that dyslexic children engage areas of their brain that differ from typical children while performing word-reading tasks (Hoeft et al., 2007; Shaywitz et al., 2004). There is greater reliance on left frontal (Broca's area) activity and right frontal processing (visual memory) than in proficient readers. In addition, there is reduced activity in the area of the brain that has been identified as the "word form area" (Fletcher et al., 2007; Shaywitz, 2003). This area, located within the occipital-parietal region becomes more active as children learn to read and gain skill at automatic word recognition (Fletcher et al., 2007). As the word from area becomes more involved during reading, other areas of the brain show reduced activity. Berninger and Richards (2002) describe this area as the meeting place of the occipital cortex and the "phonological loop". It is within this association area that orthographic and phonological information become linked. These linkages then lead to the fluent word recognition critical to skilled reading. Subcortical auditory function involved in the representation of acoustic features of speech has also been implicated in reading impairment (Banai et al., 2009). Intervention studies have shown that the brain activation profiles of struggling readers can be normalized following intensive interventions (Shaywitz et al., 2004; Simos et al., 2002).

English as a Second Language Word Recognition

It is estimated that roughly 60% of the world's population is bilingual. In contexts in which English is the dominant language such as the United States, Canada, and the United Kingdom, there have been striking increases in the number of children who speak a primary language other than English and are thus learning to read English as a second language. These educational circumstances motivate the scientific study of English second language word recognition in these countries. Studying second language word recognition more broadly allows for cross linguistic comparisons with the potential to provide theoretical insight into the language-universal and language-specific features of word recognition and the lexical representations that both derive from them and direct them (Frost, Kugler, Deutsch, & Forster, 2005; Velan & Frost, 2007).

Theories and models of word recognition that have been productive in understanding English first language word recognition are being tested and adapted to simulate second language reading. These studies have shown that first (L1) and second (L2) languages are involved in word recognition, that word frequency effects are intensified in deep orthographies, and that both orthographic and phonological neighbors influence word recognition within each language and between the two languages (Brysbaert, Van Dyck, & Van de Poel, 1999; Cuetos & Barbón, 2006; Duyck, 2005; Frost, Katz, & Bentin, 1987; Lemhöfer, Dijkstra, Schriefers, Baayen, & Grainger, 2008; van Wijnendaele & Brysbaert, 2002). The significance of orthographic depth and phonological processing for second-language word reading is verified by these studies. Orthographic depth and phonological processing are important considerations in grain size theory and strong phonological theory, respectively. Computational approaches to second language word recognition are beginning to appear, as are related behavioral studies that draw on connectionist models or the dual-route cascaded model of word recognition (Hutzler et al., 2004; van Wijnendaele & Brysbaert, 2002). Neuroimaging studies related to second- language word recognition are also emerging and contribute to understanding the complex relationships among phonology, orthography, and semantics in second language word recognition (e.g., Pugh et al., 2005).

Behavioral Approaches. Behavioral studies have yielded strong evidence that word recognition skill in emerging second language readers in English and other languages is related to individual differences in phonology-related skills in both the first and second language (Comeau, Cormier, Grandmaison, & Lecroix, 1999; Dijkstra, Grainger, & van Heuven, 1999; Dufva & Voeten, 1999; Durgunoglu, Nagy, & Hancin-Bhatt, 1993; Geva, Yaghoub-Zadeh, & Schuster, 2000; Lipka & Siegel, 2007). Articulation accuracy, phonological awareness, and, to a less consistent degree, phonological memory and rapid automatic naming in a first or second language are associated with second language word recognition (Chiappe, Siegel, & Wade-Woolley, 2002; Gottardo, 2002;Perfetti, 1999; Roberts, 2005; Quiroga, Lemos-Britton, Mostafapour, Abbott, & Berninger, 2002; Verhoeven, 1990). These findings are largely compatible with the emphasis of the strong phonological theory.

Recent studies detail complexities among the salience of different sizes of phonemic structure in a language, orthographic representations of these units, and how the degree of similarity in these features across L1 and L2 influence cross-language effects (Bialystok, McBride-Chang, & Luk, 2005; Geva, Wade-Woolley, & Shany, 1997; Gottardo, Yan, Siegel, & Wade-Woolley, 2001; Lindsey, Manis, & Bailey, 2003). These studies document language and orthography specific relationships that are consistent with grain size theory (Bialystok et al., 2005; Frith, Wimmer,

& Landerl, K., 1998; Perfetti, Zhang, & Berent, 1992; Velan & Frost, 2007; Ziegler & Goswami, 2005). Greater cross-linguistic effects are found when there are closer relationships between first and second language orthography or between first and second language phonology. In addition, second language beginning readers can develop word reading skill to a level commensurate with that of children learning to read in their first language with strong evidence of this capability in English second language reading, particularly when children receive sufficient phonics instruction (Chiappe & Siegel, 1999; Geva, Yaghoub-Zadeh, & Schuster, 2000; Geva & Siegel, 2000; Geva & Wade-Woolley, 1998; Lesaux & Siegel, 2003).

Computational Approaches.   Computational approaches to second language word recognition are beginning to appear, as are related studies that draw on connectionist models or the dual-route cascaded model of word recognition (Hutzler et al., 2004; Mulatti et al., 2006; van Wijnendaele & Brysbaert, 2002). Results from the studies using computational modeling of second language word recognition, like the behavioral studies, point to the significance of phonology and reveal influences of both first and second language phonology (Pugh et al., 2006).

Neuroscientific Approaches.   Neuroscientific studies suggest that the neuroscientific foundation for both spoken and written language is remarkably similar across languages. Speech perception and production across languages have similar brain organization (Indefrey & Levelt, 2004; Perfetti et al., 1992). Indeed, studies on fluent bilinguals have reported overlapping L1 and L2 systems for spoken language with evidence of greater L1 and L2 integration for those with higher levels of L2 oral proficiency (Kim, Relkin, Lee, & Hirsch, 1997; Klein, Milner, Zadora, Meyer, & Evans, 1995; Perani et al., 1998; Price, Green, & von Studnitz, 1999). At later points of word recognition development, disruption in left hemisphere ventral cortex is associated with reading disability in bilinguals, similar to what has been found in first language word recognition (Paulesu et al., 2001; Rumsey et al., 1997; Salmelin, Service, Kisila, Uutela, & Salonen, 1996; Shaywitz, 2002).

TOWARD THE FUTURE

We suggest two future directions for word recognition research. The first of these is for more research that examines and systematically takes into account the contextual influences on word recognition that have been discussed within this chapter: language in which word recognition is being studied, instructional variation, and task demands. The second suggestion is for a greater focus on demarcating the interactions among the semantic, phonological, and orthographic processors.

Contextual Influences

Language in which Word Recognition is Being Studied.   The relationship between oral language structure and its representation in written language has been shown to exert a strong influence in word recognition. The consistency, simplicity, and degree to which mappings between phonemes in speech and graphemes in words are represented in a language's orthography shape word recognition processes. While studies of the English language dominate the word recognition literature, there is little doubt that English, with its deep orthography, yields a view of word recognition processes and the nature of word representations that is substantially skewed by its peculiarities. Theories and research should therefore be clearly contextualized and informed by an understanding of the nature of the particular language in which they are situated. Further, the study of word recognition across languages that vary in how their orthography is structured will illuminate processes that are central to the development of word recognition across languages and those that are peculiar to particular languages. Such information would be useful in the development of reading instruction and interventions.

Instructional Context.   Learning to read is dependent upon tutelage over a period of time ranging from months to years (Byrne, 1992; Gough, 1993; Gough & Hillinger, 1980; Gough & Juel, 1991; Liberman, 1992; Liberman & Liberman, 1990; Seymour & Elder, 1986). Accounting for how variability in the context of "learning to read experiences" shapes word recognition processes and word representation is crucial to document and understand (Hutzler et al., 2004; Stuart, 1999; Stuart, Masterson, & Dixon, 2000; Ziegler & Goswami, 2005; Ziegler & Goswami, 2006). For example, some forms of "systematic, explicit" instruction in English reading address problems associated with a less transparent orthography by carefully controlling the sequencing of spelling-sound relationships in teaching and the availability of different spellings in text. Grain size theory also suggests that a combination of small and larger grain size instruction might be useful for initial instruction in opaque transparencies like English, as children learning to read in English show evidence of using whole-word phonology early in reading acquisition (Walton & Walton, 2002; Walton, Walton, & Felton, 2001; Ziegler & Goswami, 2006).

Yet studies on the effects of different types of instruction in learning to read English have tended to capture only broad variations in instructional experience (NICHD, 2009). Similarly, studies examining instructional variation in second language word recognition have also tended to be based on rather global levels of differentiation, comparing for example, language of instruction, and different curricula (see Cheung & Slavin, 2005, for a discussion). Questions in second language word recognition involve the optimal level of generality, specificity, and variation needed within instructional programs teaching word recognition based on potential areas of L1 to L2 facilitation and responding to potential sources of difficulty between L1 and L2 oral languages and orthographies. Neuroscientific evidence from intervention studies for impaired readers showing how instructional experience appears to shape brain function supports the importance of carefully crafted instructional contexts for promoting accurate and efficient word reading (Shaywitz et al., 2004). Grain size theory (Ziegler & Gozwami, 2005) and Perry et al.'s (2007) new connectionist dual process model have been used to show the promise of existing theories and models of word recognition for elucidating and testing instructional influences on word recognition processes and word representations.

Studies examining word recognition under different types of instruction designed with sensitivity to the details of what is understood about word recognition are needed. Experimental instructional studies that carefully manipulate multiple variables discussed within this chapter as well as studies examining overall approaches and programs carefully crafted to include several factors known to influence word recognition are suggested. A related area of research involves exploring the instructional variables that are likely to influence automaticity, such as the variation in grapheme-phoneme patterns, grain size of units, and amount of "practice" that optimize it.

Task Demands.   Throughout this chapter, word recognition has been seen to depend on characteristics of the words to be read. These characteristics modulate word recognition processes in terms of speed and accuracy. Differences between overt word naming and making a decision about whether or not a stimulus is indeed a real word are consistently reported. Monosyllabic and polysyllabic words are also likely to activate different aspects of word recognition and to require some modulation of word recognition strategies, particularly in language contexts where there is significant overlap of syllabic and morphological structure. Yet the studies of word recognition rely far more heavily on monosyllabic than polysyllabic stimulus words.

Oral or silent reading of words is another aspect of task demands influencing word recognition performance, particularly in regards to phonology and the activation of serial or parallel processing. Oral and silent reading also differ in their ecological connection to actual reading. Reading words singularly or in connected text modulates word recognition processes. Word recognition processes are highly reactive to task demands. This reactivity is an important methodological consideration for designing empirical studies and research results must be tempered by the context of the task demands under which they were obtained (Adelman, Brown, & Quesada, 2006). One instructional implication of this reactivity is the importance of carefully considering how words encountered in text or used for teaching word recognition may ease or stress word recognition efficiency.

Interaction of Semantic, Phonological, and Orthographic Influences

All of the theories and models of word recognition examined in this chapter and most others recognize the importance of semantic, phonological, and orthographic influences in word recognition. In spite of this, there has been surprisingly little attention to the semantic processor. Increasing attention to the influence of the semantic processor and sharpening the critical conceptual dimensions of semantic influences is important. In computational studies, semantic features of individual words are the basis for operationalizing the semantic component. Interesting emerging work suggests that an important aspect of semantic influences may be episodic memory traces for words (Perfetti, Lui, & Tan, 2005; Perfetti, Wlotko, & Hart, 2005). To maximize external validity to actual reading, phrase, sentence, and discourse level semantic influences on word recognition should be considered. The interface of word knowledge and other semantic sources with word recognition is a particularly important area of study in the development of word recognition and second language word recognition for obvious reasons.

FINAL WORDS

We hope in the future to see existing theories/models of word recognition adapted as needed and new ones emerge that systematically incorporate context effects—including language, instructional, and task demand contexts. We also hope to see word recognition science that accounts more fully for the interaction among semantics, phonology, and orthography. While these efforts are complex and challenging to be sure, accounting for how word recognition operates in reading meaningful text would seem to demand them. Recent studies grounded in grain size theory, strong phonological theory, the dual route cascaded model, connectionist triangle models, and the connectionist dual processes model indicate movement in these directions.

REFERENCES

Adams, M. J. (1990). *Beginning to read: Thinking and learning about print.* Cambridge, MA: MIT Press.
Adelman, J. S., Brown, G. A., & Quesada, J. F. (2006). *Psychological Science, 17*(9), 814–823.
Alario, F. X., De Cara, B., & Ziegler, J. C. (2007). Automatic activation of phonology in silent reading is parallel: Evidence from beginning and skilled readers. *Journal of Experimental Child Psychology, 97,* 205–219.
Baddeley, A. D. (1986). *Working memory.* Oxford, UK: Oxford University Press.
Banai, K., Hornickel, J., Skos, E., Nicol, T., Zecker, S., & Kraus, N. (2009). Reading and subcortical auditory function. *Cerebral Cortex Advance Access* published March 17, 2009, doi:10.1093/cercor/bhp024 .
Baron, J. (1977). Mechanisms for pronouncing printed words: Use and acquisition. In D. LaBerge & S. J.

Samuels (Eds.), *Basic processes in reading: perception and comprehension* (pp. 175–216). Hillsdale, NJ: Erlbaum.

Berent, I., & Perfetti, C. A. (1995). A rose is a REEZ: The two-cycles model of phonology assembly in reading English. *Psychological Review, 102,* 146–184.

Berninger, V. W. (2007). *Process assessment of the learner II.* San Antonio, TX: Harcourt Assessment.

Berninger, V. W., Abbott, R. D., Thomson, J., Wagner, R., Swanson, H. L., Wijsman, E. M., et al. (2006). Modeling phonological core deficits within a working memory architecture in children and adults with developmental dyslexia. *Scientific Studies of Reading, 10*(2), 165–198.

Berninger, V., Nagy, W., Carlisle, J., Thomson, J., Hoffer, D., Abbott, S., et al. (2003). Effective treatment for children with dyslexia in grades 4–6: Behavioral and brain evidence. In B. Foorman (Ed.), *Preventing and remediating reading difficulties: Bringing science to scale* (pp. 381–417). Timonium, MD: York Press.

Bialystok, E., McBride-Chang, C., & Luk, G. (2005). Bilingualism, language proficiency and learning to reading in two writing systems. *Journal of Educational Psychology, 97,* 580–590.

Bloom, B. S. (1986). "The hands and feet of genius": Automaticity. *Educational Leadership, 43*(5), 70–77.

Booth, J. R., Perfetti, C. A., & MacWhinney, B. (1999). Quick, automatic and general activation of orthographic and phonological representations in young readers. *Developmental Psychology, 35,* 3–19.

Brysbaert, M., Van Dyck, G., & Van de Poel, M. (1999). Visual word recognition in bilinguals: Evidence from masked phonological priming. *Journal of Experimental Psychology: Human Perception and Performance, 25,* 137–148.

Byrne, B. (1992). Studies in the acquisition procedure for reading: Rationale, hypotheses, and data. In P. Gough, L. Ehri, & R. Treiman (Eds.), *Reading acquisition* (pp. 1–34). Hillsdale, NJ: Erlbaum.

Cardoso-Martins, C., & Pennington, B. F. (2004). The relationship between phoneme awareness and rapid serial naming skills and literacy acquisition: The role of developmental period and reading ability. *Scientific Studies of Reading, 8*(1), 27–52.

Calfee, R. C., Lindamood, P. & Lindamood, C. (1973). Acoustic-phonetic skills and reading-kindergarten. *Journal of Educational Psychology, 64*(3), 293–298.

Cheung, H., & Slavin, A. (2005). Effective reading programs for English Language Learners and other language-minority students. *Bilingual Research Journal, 29*(2), 241–267.

Chiappe, P., & Siegel, L. S. (1999). Phonological awareness and reading acquisition in English- and Punjabi-speaking Canadian children. *Journal of Educational Psychology, 91*(1), 20–28.

Chiappe, P., Siegel, L. S., & Wade-Woolley, L. (2002). Linguistic diversity and the development of reading skills: A longitudinal study. *Scientific Studies of Reading, 6*(4), 369–400.

Christo, C., Davis, J. & Brock, S. (2008). *Identifying, assessing and treating dyslexia at school.* New York: Springer.

Cohen, L., Lehericy, S., Chochon, F., Lemer, C., Rivaud, S., & Dehaene, S. (2002). Language specific tuning of visual cortex? Functional properties of the Visual Word Form Area. *Brain, 125,* 1054–1069.

Coltheart, M. (2005). Modeling reading: The dual route approach. In M. J. Snowling & C. Hulme (Eds.), *The science of reading: A handbook* (pp. 6–23). Malden, MA: Blackwell.

Coltheart, M. (2006). Dual route and connectionist models of reading: An overview. *London Review of Education, 4*(1), 5–17.

Coltheart, M., Curtis, B., Atkins, P., & Haller, M. (1993). Models of reading aloud: Dual-route and parallel-distributed-processing approaches. *Psychological Review, 100*(4), 589–608.

Coltheart, M., Rastle, K., Perry, C., Langdon, R., & Ziegler, J. (2001). DRC: A dual route cascaded model of visual word recognition and reading aloud. *Psychological Review, 108,* 204–256.

Comeau, L., Cormier, P., Grandmaison, E., & Lacroix, D. (1999). A longitudinal study of phonological processing skills in children learning to read in a second language. *Journal of Educational Psychology, 91*(1), 29–43.

Coyne, M. D., Kame'enui, E. J., & Simmons, D. C. (2001). Prevention and intervention in beginning reading: Two complex systems. *Learning Disabilities Research & Practice, 16*(2), 62–73.

Cuetos, F., & Barbón, A. (2006). Word naming in Spanish. *European Journal of Cognitive Psychology, 18,* 415.

da Fontoura, H. A., & Siegel, L. S., (1995). Reading, syntactic, and working memory skills of bilingual, Portuguese-English Canadian children. *Reading and Writing: An Interdisciplinary Journal, 7,* 139–153.

de Jong, P. F., & Share, D. L. (2007). Orthographic learning during oral and silent reading. *Scientific Studies of Reading, 11,* 55–71.

Denton, C., & Mathes, P. (2003). Intervention for struggling readers: Possibilities and challenges. In B. Foorman (Ed.), *Preventing and remediating reading difficulties: Bringing science to scale* (pp. 229–252). Baltimore, MD: York Press.

Dijkstra, T., Grainger, J., & van Heuven, W. J. (1999). Recognition of cognates and interlingual homographs: The neglected role of phonology. *Journal of Memory and Language, 41,* 496–518.

Dufva, M., & Voeten, M. J. (1999). Native language literacy and phonological memory as prerequisites for learning English as a foreign language. *Applied Psycholinguistics, 20*(3), 329–348.

Durgunoglu, A. Y., Nagy, W., & Hancin-Bhatt, B. J. (1993). Cross-language transfer of phonological awareness. *Journal of Educational Psychology, 85*(3), 453–465.

Durgunoglu, A. Y., & Oney, B. (1999). A cross-linguistic comparison of phonological awareness and word recognition. *Reading and Writing, 11*(4), 281–299.

Duyck, W. (2005). Translation and associative priming with cross-lingual pseudohomophones: Evidence for nonselective phonological activation in bilinguals. *Journal of experimental Psychology: Learning, Memory, and Cognition, 31,* 1340–1359.

Edfeldt, A. W. (1960). *Silent speech and silent reading.* Chicago: The University of Chicago Press.

Ehri, L. C. (1987). Learning to read and spell words. *Journal of Reading Behavior, 19,* 5–31.

Ehri, L. C. (1995). Phases of development in learning to read words by sight. *Journal of Research in Reading, 18,* 116–125.

Ehri, L. C. (1998). Grapheme-phoneme knowledge is essential for learning to read words in English. In J. L. Metsala & L. C. Ehri (Eds.), *Word recognition in beginning literacy* (pp. 3–40). Mahwah, NJ: Erlbaum.

Ehri, L. C. (2005). Learning to read words: Theory, findings, and issues. *Scientific Studies of Reading, 9*(2), 167–188.

Ehri, L. C., & Wilce, L. S. (1985). Movement into reading: Is the first stage of printed word learning visual or phonetic? *Reading Research Quarterly, 20*(2), 163–179.

Ferrand, L., & New, B. (2003). Syllabic length effects in visual word recognition and naming. *Acta Psychologica, 113,* 167–183.

Fiebach, C. J., Friederici, A. D., Mueller, K., & von Cramon, D. Y. (2002). FMRI evidence of dual routes to the mental lexicon in visual word recognition. *Journal of Cognitive Neuroscience, 14,* 11–23.

Fletcher, J. M., Lyon, G. R., Fuchs, L. S., & Barnes, M. A. (2007). *Learning disabilities: From identification to intervention.* New York: Guilford.

Folk, J. R. (1999). Phonological codes are used to access the lexicon during silent reading. *Journal of Experimental Psychology: Learning, Memory, and Cognition, 25,* 892–906.

Foorman, B. R. (2003). Preventing and remediating reading difficulties: *Bringing science to scale.* Baltimore: York Press.

Forster, K. I., & Chambers, S. M. (1973). Lexical access and naming time. *Journal of Verbal Learning and Verbal Behavior, 12,* 627–635.

Frith, U. (1985). Beneath the surface of developmental dyslexia. In K. E. Patterson, J. C. Marshall, & M. Coltheart (Eds.), *Surface dyslexia* (pp. 301–322). London: Erlbaum.

Frith, U., Wimmer, H., & Landerl, K. (1998). Differences in phonological recoding in German- and English-speaking children. *Scientific Studies of Reading, 2*(1), 31–54.

Frost, R. (1994). Prelexical and postlexical strategies in reading: Evidence from a deep and a shallow orthography. *Journal of Experimental Psychology: Learning, Memory, and Cognition, 20,* 116–129.

Frost, R. (1998). Toward a strong phonological theory of visual word recognition: True issues and false starts. *Psychological Bulletin, 123*(1), 71–99.

Frost, R. (2006). Becoming literate in Hebrew: The grain size hypothesis and Semitic orthographic systems. *Developmental Science, 9*(5), 439–440.

Frost, R., Katz, L., & Bentin, S. (1987). Strategies for visual word recognition and orthographical depth: A multilingual comparison. *Journal of Experimental Psychology: Human Perception and Performance, 13,* 104–115.

Frost, R., Kugler, T., Deutsch, A., & Forster, K. I. (2005). Orthographic structure versus morphological structure: Principles of lexical organization in a given language. *Journal of Experimental Psychology: Learning, Memory, and Cognition, 31,* 1293–1326.

Frost, S. J., Mencl, W. E., Sandak, R., Moore, D. L., Rueckl, J. G., Katz, L., et al. (2005). A functional magnetic resonance imaging study of the tradeoff between semantics and phonology in reading aloud. *NeuroReport, 16*, 621–624.

Fuchs, L. S., Fuchs, D., Hosp, M. K., & Jenkins, J. R. (2001). Oral reading fluency as an indicator of reading competence: A theoretical, empirical, and historical analysis. *Scientific Studies of Reading, 5*(3), 239–256.

Geva, E., & Siegel, L. S. (2000). Orthographic and cognitive factors in the concurrent development of basic reading skills in two languages. *Reading and Writing: An Interdisciplinary Journal, 12*(1-2), 1–30.

Geva, E., & Wade-Woolley, L. (1998). Component processes in becoming English-Hebrew biliterate. In A. Y. Durgunoglu & L. Verhoeven (Eds.), *Literacy development in a multilingual context: Cross-cultural perspectives* (pp. 85–110). Mahwah, NJ: Erlbaum.

Geva, E., Wade-Woolley, L., & Shany, M. (1997). Development of reading efficiency in first and second language. *Scientific Studies of Reading, 1*, 119–144.

Geva, E., Yaghoub-Zadeh, Z., & Schuster, B. (2000). Understanding individual differences in word recognition skills of ESL children. *Annals of Dyslexia, 50*, 123–154.

Good, R. H., III, Simmons, D. C., & Kame'enui, E. J. (2001). The importance and decision-making utility of a continuum of fluency-based indicators of foundational reading skills for third-grade high-stakes outcomes. *Scientific Studies of Reading, 5*(3), 257–288.

Goswami, U., Ziegler, J. C., Dalton, L., & Schneider W. (2001). Pseudohomophone effects and phonological recoding procedures in reading development in English and German. *Journal of Reading and Language, 45*(4), 648–664.

Gottardo, A. (2002). The relationships between language and reading skills in bilingual Spanish-English speakers. *Topics in Language Disorders, 22*(5), 46–70.

Gottardo, A., Yan, B., Siegel, L. S., & Wade-Woolley, L. (2001). Factors related to English reading performance in children with Chinese as a first language: More evidence of cross-language transfer of phonological processing. *Journal of Educational Psychology, 93*(3), 530–542.

Gough, P. B. (1984). Word recognition. In P. D. Pearson (Ed.), *Handbook of reading research* (pp. 225–254). New York: Longman.

Gough, P. (1993). The beginning of decoding. *Reading and Writing: An Interdisciplinary Journal, 5*, 181–192.

Gough, P. B., & Hillinger, M. L. (1980). Learning to read: An unnatural act. *Annals of Dyslexia*, 179–196.

Gough, P. B., & Juel, C. (1991). The first stages of word recognition. In L. Rieben & C. Perfetti (Eds.), *Learning to read: Basic research and its implications* (pp. 47–56). Hillsdale, NJ: Erlbaum.

Guttentage, R., & Haith, M. (1978). Automatic processes as a function of age and reading ability. *Child Development, 49*, 707–716.

Haager, D., Klingner, J., & Vaughn, S. (Eds.). (2007). *Evidence-based reading practices for response to intervention*. Baltimore: Paul H. Brookes.

Harm, M. W., & Seidenberg, M. S. (1999). Phonology, reading acquisition, and dyslexia: Insights from connectionist models. *Psychological Review, 106*, 491–528.

Harm, M., & Seidenberg, M. S. (2004). Computing the meanings of words in reading: Division of labor between visual and phonological processes. *Psychological Review, 111*, 662–720.

Hasbrouck, J. & Tindal, G. A. (2006). Oral reading fluency norms: A valuable tool for reading teachers. *The Teading Teacher, 59*, 636–644.

Hoeft, F., Meyler, A., Glover, G. H., Kobayashi, N., Mazaika, P., Jo, B., et al. (2007). Prediction of children's reading skills using behavioral, functional, and structural neuroimaging measures. *Behavioral Neuroscience, 121*(3), 602–613.

Hu, C. F., & Catts, H. W. (1998). The role of phonological processing in early reading ability: What we can learn from Chinese. *Scientific Studies of Reading, 2*(1), 55–79.

Hutzler, F., Ziegler, J. C., Perry, C., Wimmer, H., & Zorzi, M. (2004). Do current connectionist learning models account for reading development in different languages? *Cognition, 91*, 273–296.

Indefrey, P., & Levelt, W. J. M. (2004). The spatial and temporal signatures of word production components. *Cognition, 92*, 101–144.

International Dyslexia Association. (2007). Dyslexia basics fact sheet. Retrieved September 30, 2007, from http://www.interdys.org/ewebeditpro5/upload/Dyslexia_Basics_FS_-_final_81407.pdf

Katz, L., & Frost, R. (1992). The reading process is different for different orthographies: The orthographic depth hypothesis. In R. Frost & L. Katz (Eds.), *Orthography, phonology, morphology, and meaning* (pp. 67–84). Amsterdam, The Netherlands: North-Holland.

Kim, H. S., Relkin, N. R., Lee. K. M., & Hirsch, J. (1997). Distinct cortical areas associated with native and second languages. *Nature, 388*, 171–174.

Klein, D., Milner, B., Zadora, R. J., Meyer, E. & Evans, A. C. (1995). The neural substrates underlying word generation: A bilingual functional imaging study. *Proceeding of the National Academy of Science, 92*, 2899–2903.

LaBerge, D., & Samuels, S. J. (1974). Toward a theory of automatic information processing in reading. *Cognitive Psychology, 6*, 293–323.

Landerl, K. (2000). Influences of orthographic consistency and reading instruction on the development of nonword reading skills. *European Journal of Psychology of Education, 15*, 239–257.

Lemhöfer, K., Dijkstra, T., Schriefers, H., Baayen, R. H., Grainger, J., & Zwitserlood, P. (2008). Native language influences on word recognition in a second language: A megastudy. *Journal of Experimental Psychology: Learning, Memory, and Cognition, 34*(1), 12–31.

Lesaux, N. K., & Siegel, L. S. (2003). The development of reading in hildren who speak Enlgish as a second language. *Develomental Psychology, 39*, 1005–1019.

Liberman, A. M. (1992). The relation kf sleech to reading and wiring . In R. Frost & L. Katz (Eds.), *Orthography, phonology, morphology, and meanng* (pp. 167–178). Amsterdam, The Netherlands: Elsevier.

Liberman, I. Y., & Liberman, A. M. (1990). Whole language vs. code emphasis: Underlying assumptions and their implication for reading instruction. *Annals of Dyslexia, 40*, 51–76.

Liberman, I. Y., Shankweiler, D., & Liberman, A. M. (1989). The alphabetic principle and learning to read. In A. M. Liberman & D. Shankweiler (Eds.), *Phonology and reading disability: Solving the reading puzzle.* Ann Arbor: University of Michigan Press.

Lindsey, K. A., Manis, F. R., & Bailey, C. E. (2003). Prediction of first-grade reading in Spanish-speaking English-language learners. *Journal of Educational Psychology, 95*(3), 482–494.

Lipka, O., & Siegel, L. S. (2007). The development of reading skills in children with English as a second language. *Scientific Studies of Reading, Vol. 11*(2), 105–131.

Lundberg, I., Olofsson, A., & Wall, S. (1980). Reading and spelling skills in the first school years predicted from phonemic awareness skills in kindergarten. *Scandinavian Journal of Psychology, 21*, 159–173.

Lupker, S. J. (2005). Visual word recognition: Theories and findings. In M. Snowling & C. Hulme (Eds.), *The science of reading: A handbook* (pp. 39–60). Malden, MA: Blackwell.

Lukatela, G., & Turvey, M. T. (1998). Reading in two alphabets. *American Psychologist, 53*, 1057–1072.

Lyon, G. R., Shaywitz, S. E., & Shaywitz, B. A. (2003). Defining dyslexia, comorbidity, teachers' knowledge of language and reading: A definition of dyslexia. *Annals of Dyslexia, 53*, 1–14.

Mannhaupt, G., Jansen, H., & Marx, H. (1997). Cultural influences on literacy development. In C. K. Leong & R. M. Joshi (Eds.), *Crosslanguage studies of learning to read and spell: Phonologic and orthographic processing* (pp. 161–173). Dordrecht, The Netherlands: Kluwer.

McClelland, J. L., & Rumelhart, D. E. (1981). An interactive activation model of context effects in letter perception: Part 1. An account of basic findings. *Psychological Review, 88*, 375–407.

Metsala, J. L., & Walley, A. C. (1998). Spoken vocabulary growth and the segmental restructuring of lexical representations: Precursors to phonemic awareness and early reading ability. In J. L. Metsala & L. C. Ehri (Eds.), *Word recognition in beginning literacy* (pp. 89–120). Hillsdale, NJ: Erlbaum.

Morton, J. (1989). An information-processing account of reading acquisition. In A. M. Galaburda (Ed.), *From reading to neurons* (pp. 43–66). Cambridge, MA: MIT Press.

Mulatti, C., Reynolds, M. G., & Besner, D. (2006). Neighborhood effects in reading aloud: New findings and new challenges for computational models. *Journal of Experimental Psychology: Human Perception and Performance, 32*(4), 799–810.

Nation, K., & Snowling, M. (1998). Individual differences in contextual facilitation: Evidence from dyslexia and poor reading comprehension. *Child Development, 69*, 96–111.

National Institute of Child Health & Development. (2007). *Learning disabilities: What are learning disabilities?* Retrieved December 15, 2007, from http://www.nichd.nih.gov/health/topics/learning_disabilities.cfm

National Reading Panel. (2000). *Teaching children to read: An evidence-based assessment of the scientific research literature on reading and its implications for reading instruction.* Washington, DC: National Institute of Child Health and Development.

Nikolopoulos, D., Goulandris, N., Hulme, C., & Snowling, M. J. (2006). The cognitive bases of learning to read and spell in Greek: Evidence from a longitudinal study. *Journal of Experimental Child Psychology, 94*, 1–17.

O'Malley, S., Reynolds, M. G., Stolz, J. A., & Besner, D. (2008). Reading aloud: Spelling-sound translation uses central attention. *Journal of Experimental Psychology: Learning, Memory, and Cognition, 34*(2), 422–429.

Palmer, E., Brown, T., Peterson, S., & Shlaggar, B. (2004). Investigation of the functional neuroanatomy of single word reading and its development. *Scientific Studies of Reading, 8*(3), 203–223.

Papanicolaou, A. C., Simos, P. G., Breier, J. I., Fletcher, J. M., Foorman, B. R., Francis, D., et al. (2003). Brain mechanisms for reading in children with and without dyslexia: A review of studies of normal development and plasticity. *Developmental Neuropsychology, 24*(2/3), 593–612.

Parviainen, T., Helensiu, P., Poskiparta, E., Niemi, P., & Salmelin, R. (2006). Cortical sequence of word perception in beginning readers. *The Journal of Neuroscience, 26*(22), 6052–6061.

Paulesu, E., DeMonet, J. F., Fazio, F., McCrory, E., Chanoine, V., Brunswick, N., et al. (2001). Dyslexia: Cultural diversity and biological unity. *Science, 291*, 2165–2167.

Peereman, R., Brand, M., & Rey, A. (2006). Letter-by-letter processing in the phonological conversion of multiletter graphemes: Searching for sounds in printed pseudowords. *Psychonomic Bulletin & Review, 13*(1), 38–44.

Perani, D., Paulseu, E., Galles, N. S., Dupoux, E., Dehaene, S., Bettinardo, V., et al. (1998). The bilingual brain: Proficiency and age of acquisition of the second language. *Brain, 67*, 19–32.

Perfetti, C. A. (1999). Comprehending written language: A blueprint of the reader. In C. Brown & P. Hagoot (Eds.), *The neurocognition of language* (pp. 167–208). New York: Oxford University Press.

Perfetti, C. I., Beck, I., Bell, L., & Hughes, C. (1987). Phonemic knowledge and learning to read are reciprocal: A longitudinal study of first grade children. *Merrill-Palmer Quarterly, 33*, 283–319.

Perfetti, C. A., & Bell, L. C. (1991). Phonemic activation during the first 40 ms of word identification: Evidence from backward masking and priming. *Journal of Memory and Language, 30*, 473–485.

Perfetti, C. A., Bell, L., & DeLaney, S. (1988). Automatic phonetic activation in silent word reading: Evidence from backward masking. *Journal of Memory and Language, 27*, 59–70.

Perfetti, C. A., Liu, Y., & Tan, L. H. (2005). The lexical constituency model: Some implications of research on Chinese for general theories of reading. *Psychological Review, 112*, 43–59.

Perfetti, C., Wlotko, E. W., & Hart, L. A. (2005). Word learning and individual differences in word learning reflected in event-related potentials. *Journal of Experimental Psychology, 31*(6), 1281–1292.

Perfetti, C. A., Zhang, S., & Berent, I. (1992). Reading in English and Chinese: Evidence for a "universal" phonological principle. In R. Frost & L. Katz (Eds.), *Orthography, phonology, morphology and meaning* (pp. 227–248). Oxford, UK: North-Holland.

Perry, C., Ziegler, J. C., & Zorzi, M. (2007). Nested incremental modeling in the development of computational theories: The CDP+ model of reading aloud. *Psychological Review, 114*(2), 273–315.

Plaut, D. C. (2005). Connectionist approaches to reading. In M. J. Snowling & C. Hulme (Eds.), *The science of reading: A handbook* (pp. 24–38). Malden, MA: Blackwell.

Poeppel, D. (2001). New approaches to the neural basis of speech sound processing: Introduction to special section on brain and speech. *Cognitive Science, 25*, 659–661.

Pollatsek, A., Rayner, K., & Lee, H. W. (2000). Phonological coding in word perception and reading. In A. Kennedy, R. Radach, D. Heller, & J. Pynte (Eds.), *Reading as a perceptual process* (pp. 399–429). Amsterdam, The Netherlands: Elsevier.

Powell, D., Plaut, D., & Funnell, E. (2006). Does the PMSP connectionist model of single word reading learn to read in the same way as a child? *Journal of Research in Reading, 29*, 229–250.

Price, C. J. (2000). The anatomy of language: Contribution from functional neuroimaging. *Journal of Anatomy, 3*, 335–359.

Price, C. J., Green, D. W., & von Studnitz, R. (1999). A functional imaging study of translation and language switching. *Brain, 122*, 2221–2235.

Pugh, K. R., Mencl, W. E., Jenner, A. R., Katz, L., Frost, S. J., Lee, J. R., et al. (2000). Functional neuroimaging studies of reading and reading disability (developmental dyslexia). *Mental Retardation and Developmental Disabilities Research Reviews, 6*, 207–213.

Pugh, K. R., Sandak, R., Frost, S. J., Moore, D., & Mencl, W. E. (2005). Examining reading development and reading disability in English Learners: Potential contributions from functional neuroimaging. *Learning Disabilities Research and Practice, 20*(1), 24–30.

Pugh, K. R., Sandak, R., Frost, S. J., Moore, D., Rueckl, J. G., & Mencl, W. E. (2006). Neuroscientific studies of skilled and impaired reading: A work in progress. In G. D. Rosen (Ed.), *The dyslexic brain: New pathways in neuroscience discovery* (pp. 21–48). Mahwah, NJ: Erlbaum.

Quiroga, T., Lemos-Britton, Z., Mostafapour, E., Abbott, R. D., & Berninger, V. (2002). Phonological awareness and beginning reading in Spanish-speaking ESL first graders: Research into practice. *Journal of School Psychology, 40*(1), 85–111.

Rack, J. P., Hulme, C., Snowling, M. J., & Wightman, J. (1994). The role of phonology in young children learning to read words: The direct-mapping hypothesis. *Journal of Experimental Child Psychology, 57,* 42–71.

Rastle, K., & Coltheart, M. (2006). Is there serial processing in the reading system and are there local representations? In S. Andrews (Ed.), *From Inmarks to Ideas: Current issues in lexical processing* (pp. 3–24). Hove, UK: Psychology Press.

Richards, T. L., Aylward, E. H., Berninger, V. W., Field, K. M., Grimme, A. C., Richards, A. L., et al. (2006). Individual fMRI activation in orthographic mapping and morpheme mapping after orthographic or morphological spelling treatment in child dyslexics. *Journal of Neurolinguistics, 19*(1), 56–86.

Richards, T. L., & Berninger, V. W. (2008). Abnormal fMRI connectivity in children with dyslexia during a phoneme task: Before but not after treatment. *Journal of Neurolinguistics, 21*(4), 294–304.

Richards, T., Berninger, V., Aylward, E., Richards, A., Thomson, J. B., Nagy, W., et al. (2002). Reproducibility of proton MR spectroscopic imaging (PEPSI): Comparison of dyslexic and normal-reading children and effects of treatment on brain lactate levels during language tasks. *American Journal of Neuroradiology, 23,* 1678–1685.

Ricketts, J., Nation, K., & Bishop, D. V. M. (2007). Vocabulary is important for some, but not all reading skills. *Scientific Studies of Reading, 11,* 235–257.

Roberts, T. (2005). Articulation accuracy and vocabulary size contributions to phonemic awareness and word reading in English Language Learners. *Journal of Educational Psychology, 97,* 601–616.

Rumsey, J. M., Nace, K., Donohue, B., Wise, D., Maisog, J. M., & Andreason, P. (1997). A positron emission tomographic study of impaired word recognition and phonological processing in dyslexic men. *Archives of Neurology, 54,* 562–573.

Salmelin, R., Service, E., Kisila, P., Uutela, K., & Salonen, O. (1996). Impaired visual word processing in dyslexia revealed with magnetoencephalophy. *Annals of Neurology, 40,* 157–162.

Scanlon, D. M., & Vellutino, F. R. (1996). Prerequisite skills, early instruction and success in first grade reading: Selected results from a longitudinal study. *Mental Retardation and Developmental Disabilities Research Reviews, 2,* 54–63.

Scarborough, H. (1998). Early identification of children at risk for reading disabilities: Phonological awareness and some other promising predictors. In B. Shapiro, P. Accardo, & A. Capute (Eds.), *Specific reading disability: A view of the spectrum* (pp. 77–121). Timonium, MD: York Press.

Seidenberg, M. S. (2005). Connectionist models of word reading. *Current Directions in Psychological Science, 14,* 238–242.

Seidenberg, M. S. (1993a). A connectionist modeling approach to recognition and dyslexia. *American Psychological Society, 4*(5), 299–304.

Seidenberg, M. S. (1993b). Connectionist models and cognitive theory. *American Psychological Society, 4*(4), 228–235.

Seidenberg, M. S., & McClelland, J. L. (1989). A distributed, developmental model of word recognition and naming. *Psychological Review, 96,* 523–568.

Seidenberg, M. S., Petersen, A., MacDonald, M. C., & Plaut, D. C. (1996). Pseudohomophone effects and models of word recognition. *Journal of Experimental Psychology: Learning, Memory, and Cognition, 22*(1), 48–62.

Seidenberg, M. S., Waters, G. S., Barnes, M. A., & Tanenhaus, M. K. (1984). When does irregular spelling or pronunciation influence word recognition? *Journal of Verbal Learning and Verbal Behavior, 23,* 383–404.

Seymour, P. H. K., Aro, M., & Erskine, J. M. (2003). Foundation literacy acquisition in European orthographies. *British Journal of Psychology, 94,* 143–174.

Seymour, P. H., & Elder, L. (1986). Beginning reading without phonology. *Cognitive Neuropsychology, 3,* 1–36.

Share, D. L. (1995). Phonological recoding and self-teaching: Sine qua non of reading acquisition. *Cognition, 55,* 151–218.

Share, D. L. (2004). Orthographic learning at a glance: On the time course and developmental onset of self-teaching. *Journal of Experimental Child Psychology, 87*(4), 267–298.

Share, D. (2008a). On the Anglocentricities of current reading research and practice: The perils of overreliance on an "outlier" orthography. *Psychological Bulletin, 134*(4), 584–615.

Share, D. L. (2008b). Orthographic learning, phonological recoding, and self-teaching. In R. Kail (Ed.), *Advances in child development and behavior* (Vol. 36, pp. 31–82). Amsterdam, The Netherlands: Elsevier.

Share, D. L., & Gur, T. (1999). How reading begins: A study of preschoolers' print identification strategies. *Cognition and Instruction, 17,* 177–213.

Shaywitz, S. E. (2003). *Overcoming dyslexia: A new and complete science-based program for reading problems at any level.* New York: Knopf.

Shaywitz, B., Shaywitz, S. E., Blachman, B., Pugh, K. R., Fulbright, R., Skudlarski, P., et al. (2004). Development of left occipitotemporal systems for skilled reading following a phonologically based intervention in children. *Biological Psychiatry, 55,* 926–933.

Shaywitz, B., Shaywitz, S. E., Blachman, B., Pugh, K. R., Mencl, W. E., Fulbright, R., et al. (2002). Disruption of posterior brain systems for reading in children with developmental dyslexia. *Biological Psychiatry, 52,* 101–110.

Shaywitz, S. E., Shaywitz, B. A., Pugh, K., R., Fulbright, R. K., Constable, R. T., Mencl, W. E., et al. (1998). Functional disruption in the organization of the brain for reading in dyslexia. *National Academy of Sciences, 95,* 2636–2641.

Shefelbine, J. A. (1990). A syllabic-unit approach to teaching decoding of polysyllabic words to fourth- and sixth-grade disabled readers. In J. Zutell & S. McCormick (Eds.), *Literacy theory and research: Analyses from multiple paradigms* (pp. 223–229). Chicago: National Reading Conference.

Shefelbine, J., Lipscomb, L., & Hern, A. (1989). Variables associated with second-, fourth-, and sixth-grade students' ability to identify polysyllabic words. In S. McCormick & J. Zutell (Eds.), *Cognitive and social perspectives for literacy research and instruction* (pp. 145–154). Chicago: National Reading Conference.

Simos, P. G., Fletcher, J. M., Bergman, E., Breier, J. I., Foorman, B. R., Castillo, E. M., et al. (2002). Dyslexia-specific brain activation profile becomes normal following successful remedial training. *Neurology, 58,* 1203–1213.

Simos, P. G., Fletcher, J. M., Denton, C., Sarkari, S., Billingsley-Marshall, R., & Papanicolaou, A. C. (2006). Magnetic source imaging studies of dyslexia interventions. *Developmental Neuropsychology, 30*(1), 591–611.

Stanovich, K. E. (1980). Toward an interactive-compensatory model of individual differences in the development of reading fluency. *Reading Research Quarterly, 16,* 32–71.

Stanovich, K. (1991). Changing perspectives on word recognition. In D. Pearson, R. Barr, M. Kamil, & M. Mosenthal (Eds.), *Handbook of reading research* (pp. 418–452). New York: Longman.

Stuart, M. (1999). Getting ready for reading: Early phoneme awareness and phonics teaching improves reading and spelling in inner-city second language learners. *British Journal of Educational Psychology, 69,* 587–605.

Stuart, M., & Coltheart, M. (1988). Does reading develop in a sequence of stages? *Cognition, 30,* 139–181.

Stuart, M., Masterson, J., & Dixon, M. (2000). Spongelike acquisition of sight vocabulary in beginning readers? *Journal of Research in Reading, 23,* 12–27.

Tallal, P. (2006). Process faster, talk earlier, read better. In G. D. Rosen (Ed.), *The dyslexic brain: New pathways in neuroscience discovery* (pp. 49–74). Mahwah, NJ: Erlbaum.

Talcott, J. B., Hansen, P. C., Willis-Owen, C., McKinnell, I. W., Richardson, A. J., & Stein, J. F. (1998). Visual magnocellular impairment in adult developmental dyslexics. *Neuro-Ophthalmology, 20*(4), 187–201.

Torgesen, J. K., & Burgess, S. R. (1998). Consistency of reading-related phonological processes throughout early childhood: Evidence from longitudinal-correlational and instructional studies. In J. Metsala & L. Ehri (Eds.), *Word recognition in beginning reading* (pp. 161–168). Hillsdale, NJ: Erlbaum.

Torgesen, J. K., Wagner, R. K., & Rashotte, C. A. (1997). Prevention and remediation of severe reading disabilities: Keeping the end in mind. *Scientific Studies of Reading, 1*(3), 217–234.

Treiman, R., & Rodriguez, L. (1999). Young children use letter names in learning to read words. *Psychological Science, 10*(4), 334–339.

Tunmer, W., & Chapman, J. W. (1998). Language prediction skills, phonological recoding ability, and beginning reading. In R. M. Joshi & C. Hulme (Eds.), *Reading and spelling: Development and disorders* (pp. 33–67). Hillsdale, NJ: Erlbaum.

Uhry, J. K., & Clark, D. B. (2004). *Dyslexia: Theory & practice of instruction* (3rd ed.). Austin, TX: Pro-Ed.

Van Orden, G. C., & Kloos, H. (2005). The question of phonology and reading. In M. J. Snowling & C. Hulme (Eds.), *The science of reading: A handbook* (pp. 24–38). Malden, MA: Blackwell.

Van Orden, G. C., Pennington, B. F., & Stone, G. O. (1990). Word identification in reading and the promise of subsymbolic psycholinguistics. *Psychological Review, 97*(4), 488–522.

Van Wijnendaele, I., & Brysbaert, M. (2002). Visual word recognition in bilinguals: Phonological priming from the second to the first language. *Journal of Experimental Psychology: Human Perception and Performance, 28*(3), 616–627.

Velan, H., & Frost, R. (2007). Cambridge University versus Hebrew University: The impact of letter transposition on reading English and Hebrew. *Psychonomic Bulletin & Review, 14*(5), 913–918.

Vellutino, F. R., Fletcher, J. M., Snowling, M. J., & Scanlon, D. M. (2004). Specific reading disability (dyslexia): What have we learned in the past four decades? *Journal of Child Psychology and Psychiatry, 45*(1), 2–40.

Vellutino, F. R., Tunmer, W. E., Jaccard, J. J., & Chen, R. (2007). Components of reading ability: Multivariate evidence for a convergent skills model of reading development. *Scientific Studies of Reading, 11*(1), 3–32.

Verhoeven, L. T. (1990). Acquisition of reading in a second language. *Reading Research Quarterly, 25*(2), 90–111.

Wagner, R. K., & Torgesen, J. K. (1987). The nature of phonological processing and its causal role in the acquisition of reading skills. *Psychological Bulletin, 101,* 192–212.

Wagner, R. K., Torgesen, J. K., Rashotte, C. A., Hecht, S. A., Barker, T. A., Burgess, S. R., et al. (1997). Changing relations between phonological processing abilities and word level reading as children develop from beginning to skilled readers: A 5-year longitudinal study. *Developmental Psychology, 33*(3), 468–479.

Walton, P. D., & Walton, L. M. (2002). Beginning reading by teaching in rime analogy: Effects on phonological skills, letter-sound knowledge, working memory, and word-reading strategies. *Scientific Studies of Reading, 6,* 79–115.

Walton, P. D., Walton, L. M., & Felton, K. (2001). Teaching rime analogy or letter recoding reading strategies to prereaders: Effects on prereading skills and word reading. *Journal of Educational Psychology, 93,* 160–180.

Wolf, M. (1991). Naming speed and reading: The contribution of the cognitive neurosciences. *Reading Research Quarterly, 26,* 123–140.

Wolf, M., Bowers, P. G., & Biddle, K. (2000). Naming-speed processes, timing, and reading: A conceptual review. *Journal of Learning Disabilities, 33*(4), 387–407.

Ziegler, J. C., & Goswami, U. (2005). Reading acquisition, developmental dyslexia, and skilled reading across languages: A psycholinguistic grain size theory. *Psychological Bulletin, 131,* 3–29.

Ziegler, J. C., & Goswami, U. (2006). Becoming literate in different languages: Similar problems, different solutions. *Developmental Science, 9*(5), 429–436.

Zorzi, M., Houghton, G., & Butterworth, B. (1998a). Two routes or one in reading aloud? A connectionist dual-process model. *Journal of Experimental Psychology: Human Perception and Performance, 24,* 1131–1161.

Zorzi, M., Houghton, G., & Butterworth, B. (1998b). The development of spelling-sound relationships in a model of phonological reading. *Language and Cognitive Processes, 13,* 337–371.

12 Orthographic Processing in Models of Word Recognition

Anne E. Cunningham, Ruth G. Nathan,
and Katie Schmidt Raher
University of California, Berkeley

INTRODUCTION

Automaticity with word recognition plays a fundamental role in facilitating comprehension of text and, thus, is a primary determinant of reading achievement throughout schooling. The greater a child's facility with word identification, the better his or her chances of comprehension and general proficiency in reading (Cunningham & Stanovich, 1997; Juel, 1988). As a result, developing our collective understanding of the causes of individual differences in the acquisition of fluent word recognition is critical for the prevention and remediation of reading difficulties. Although there is general agreement in the field that rapid word recognition is a marker of skilled reading and necessary for higher order processes (see review in Pearson, Dole, Duffy, & Koehler, 1992; Stanovich, 2000), a more complete explanation of the processes by which fluent word recognition develops is needed. Research has consistently demonstrated the importance of phonological processing skills in reading acquisition (National Institute of Child Health and Human Development [NICHD], 2000; Share, 1995; Stanovich, 1986, 2000). However, it is increasingly apparent that phonological processes cannot single-handedly explain all of the reliable variance in word recognition skill. Recent attention has focused on orthographic processing as an additional source of variance (Cunningham, Perry, & Stanovich, 2001).

The purpose of the current chapter is to review the evidence suggesting the importance of orthographic processing, and to describe how such fit into current models of word recognition have traditionally emphasized phonological processing and alphabetic coding skill. After outlining new trends and analyses on the relationship between orthographic processing and word recognition, we will review the fundamental role of phonological decoding in the cognitive formation, storage, and quick access of orthographic representations necessary for developing fluent word recognition. Implications and recommendations for classroom practice, public policy, and future research will also be discussed.

THE CRUCIAL ROLE OF FAST, AUTOMATIC WORD RECOGNITION IN SKILLED READING

Children differ in their ability to learn how to read and read fluently (e.g., Snowling & Hulme, 2005; Stanovich, 1982a, 1982b). Although some children acquire reading skill quite easily, reading difficulties and disabilities are an unfortunate reality for many individuals (e.g., McGill-Franzen, Ward, Goatley, & Machado, 2002; Ralph & Patterson, 2005; Stanovich, 1982c; Vellutino & Fletcher, 2005). Students without fluent word recognition struggle to accomplish the primary purpose of reading, namely to comprehend and gain meaning from the texts they encounter throughout school and beyond. There are strong theoretical and empirical accounts of the fundamental relationship between fluent word recognition and reading comprehension.

Theoretical Accounts of Word Recognition and Reading Comprehension

All current interactive models of skilled reading, from dual-route models (e.g., Coltheart, 1994, 2005) to connectionist frameworks (e.g., Seidenberg, 2005; Seidenberg & McClelland, 1989), as well as all current developmental models of reading emphasize the need for fast, automatic word recognition (e.g., Ehri, 2005a). (For a complete discussion of models of word recognition, see Roberts, Christo, & Shefelbine, and Tunmer & Nicholson in this volume.) Although these theoretical frameworks differ in their explanations of the cognitive processes involved in reading, they all assume that word recognition moves from a highly demanding, intentional process requiring constant, laborious symbol-sound translation to a less demanding, direct process which incorporates the automatic recognition of letters and immediate identification of specific words through their lexical quality (Perfetti, 2007). For example, lexical quality is relevant in understanding and pronouncing the word *record* in "You need a *record* of the transaction" and "They can't *record* the conversation" (Perfetti, 2007, p. 359). In fact, *lexical quality* — precision in mental representations of form (i.e., which include variations in phonology and orthography) and flexibility in representations of meaning (e.g., appropriate definitional interpretation in cases of multiple word meanings or homophonic pair selection)—is critical to understanding and pronouncing numerous complex form-meaning pairings. Whereas low lexical quality can hinder the word-related processes necessary for successful reading comprehension, high lexical quality facilitates automaticity of word recognition (Perfetti, 2007).

Automaticity with word recognition, the ability to read words accurately, quickly, and effortlessly (i.e., without conscious attention to the process; Logan, 1997; Stanovich, Cunningham, & West, 1981; Stroop, 1935), allows cognitive resources to be allocated almost entirely to reading comprehension, comprehension monitoring, and other higher-order processes (LaBerge & Samuels, 1974; Muter, Hulme, Snowling, & Stevenson, 2004; Neves & Anderson, 1981; Perfetti, 1985, 1992; Perfetti & Hart, 2001; Schwanenflugel et al., 2006). When word recognition is not yet automatized, the reader experiences significant cognitive demands while decoding text. As a reader matures, and the demands of conceptually more difficult texts require the use of complex thinking strategies, a reduction in conscious attention is necessary at the word recognition level to free up cognitive energy required for comprehension (Perfetti, 2007; Rayner, Foorman, Perfetti, Pesetsky, & Seidenberg, 2001). Overall, in order to reduce the cognitive load involved in processing alphabetic orthographies and increase the resources allocated toward comprehension, readers must obtain explicit knowledge and effortless use of the alphabetic code (Perfetti, 1985; Vellutino, Tunmer, Jaccard, & Chen, 2007).

Empirical Evidence for the Role of Automatic Word Recognition in Reading Comprehension

In addition to the theoretical accounts of the crucial role of fast, automatic word recognition, the empirical research is replete with evidence that fluent word recognition is the strongest predictor of reading comprehension from first through at least third grade (Adams, 1990; NICHD, 2000; Vellutino et al., 2007) and accounts for a high degree of variance in comprehension throughout schooling (e.g., Adolf, Catts, & Little, 2006; Cunningham, Stanovich, & Wilson, 1990; Cutting & Scarborough, 2006; Francis, Shaywitz, Stuebing, Shaywitz, & Fletcher, 1996; Juel, 1988; Juel, Griffith, & Gough, 1986; Scarborough, Ehri, Olson, & Fowler, 1998; Stevenson & Newman, 1986). For instance, Juel (1988) provided longitudinal evidence on the reading and writing development of 54 children from first through fourth grade. She reported a high probability (.88) of difficulty with reading comprehension by the end of fourth grade for students who could not fluently read grade-appropriate text by the end of first grade (i.e., students with slow speed of word recognition) and, conversely, a low probability (.12) of reading comprehension difficulties for those students who could read with ease by the end of first grade (i.e., students with rapid speed of word recognition). Interestingly, of the 24 children who remained poor readers through fourth grade, only two had average decoding skills, indicating the strong role of phonological skill in word identification. Similarly, in their longitudinal study, Cunningham and Stanovich (1997) found that first-grade word identification skills (specifically decoding skills) strongly predicted eleventh-grade reading comprehension, even after partialing out cognitive ability, as indexed by oral receptive vocabulary and spatial reasoning.

Across a wide array of empirical studies, findings demonstrate the powerful relationship between early word recognition ability and future reading development and ability (Cunningham & Stanovich, 1997; Stanovich, 2000). Given this critical relationship between rapid, automatic word recognition and reading comprehension, researchers interested in facilitating children's comprehension and preventing reading difficulties have generated a vast amount of reading research concerned with the psychological processes underlying fluent word recognition over the last 30 years (e.g., Blachman, 2000; Goswami, 2000; Metsala & Walley, 1998; Stanovich, 1982a; Vellutino, 1979; also see Roberts et al., and Tunmer & Nicholson in this volume). We now turn to a discussion of these processes.

ORTHOGRAPHIC PROCESSES IN RECENT MODELS OF READING ACQUISITION

Orthographic Processing as a Unique Secondary Contributor to Variance in Word Recognition

An abundant amount of research has determined that *phonological awareness*, one's sensitivity to and ability to manipulate the sound structure of language (and more specifically, *phonemic awareness,* one's ability to distinguish and manipulate *phonemes,* the smallest unit of linguistic sound) constitutes the most potent causal factor in the acquisition of word recognition in the primary grades (for a review, see Blachman, 2000; Bradley & Bryant, 1983; Byrne & Fielding-Barnsley, 1995; Cunningham, 1990; Ehri et al., 2001; Hatcher, Hulme, & Ellis, 1994; Kjeldsen, Niemi, & Olofsson, 2003; Lundberg, Frost, & Peterson, 1988; NICHD, 2000; Stanovich, 1986), with deficits in the phonological processing arena being core to reading disability (Stanovich, 2000; Vellutino & Scanlon, 1987; For additional information, see Roberts et al. and Tunmer & Nicholson in this volume.) Nevertheless, although the variance in word recognition ability accounted for by phonological awareness and other phonological processes is quite high, there is still some reliable variance left unaccounted for (Cunningham et al., 2001; Cunningham & Stanovich, 1993; Stanovich, Cunningham, & Cramer, 1984; Stanovich & West, 1989; Vellutino et al., 2007; Wagner, 1988; Wagner & Torgesen, 1987). Indeed, some investigators argue that although the development of a minimal level of phonological awareness is necessary for efficient word recognition, it is not sufficient, and additional factors should be considered (Anthony & Francis, 2005; Blachman, 2000; Juel et al., 1986; Snow, Burns, & Griffin, 1998; Torgesen & Hudson, 2006; Tunmer & Nesdale, 1985). Consequently, considerable attention has been given to the exploration of other cognitive processes that may contribute to word recognition skill. One area of investigation that has been explored and refined over time has entailed processes in the visual/orthographic domain.

In the early literature on the role of visual processes in word recognition, it was postulated that deficits in the general processing of visual information were the major contributors to difficulties with reading acquisition. For instance, case studies of adults with acquired surface dyslexia (Patterson, Marshall, & Coltheart, 1985) and clinical studies of children with developmental surface dyslexia (e.g., Castles & Coltheart, 1996) suggested a subtype of poor readers with unique difficulties in maintaining the visual representations of words.[1] However, substantial empirical evidence, including numerous controlled studies, served to undermine this visual deficit hypothesis as a major cause of reading disability or a major determinant of variability in reading ability (Mitchell, 1982; Rutter, 1978; Stanovich, 1982a, 1986; for a review see Vellutino, 1979). In fact, enough is now known to conclude that even if a real phenomenon is uncovered, global visual deficits, such as visual memory or the ability to maintain visual representations, will not be the dominant cognitive locus of reading disability (Stanovich, 1992).

Although it was determined that general deficits in visual processing do not lead to reading difficulties, some researchers began to suggest that problems in visual processing are indeed real, but are of a more subtle and localized nature. More specifically, studies of individual differences suggested that children show marked variance in their tendency to utilize *print-specific information* (i.e., *orthographic information*) when recognizing words (Baron & Treiman, 1980; Booth, Perfetti, MacWhinney, & Hunt, 2000; Bryant & Impey, 1986; Freebody & Byrne, 1988; Share & Shalev, 2004; Treiman, 1984). This variation may explain why some children with adequate phonological awareness still lag behind in the development of word recognition efficiency (Castles & Coltheart, 1996; Patterson et al., 1985). Investigators began to suspect that this more specified class of visual information processing, namely *orthographic processing*, might explain additional variance in word recognition beyond the contribution of phonological skills and alphabetic knowledge. Reitsma (1983), and Stanovich and West (1989) argued that orthographic processing was another "sticking point" in word recognition and, thus, a second critical locus of variance.

Over the past two decades, research has left little doubt that these subtle orthographic processing skills are just such a "sticking point," and indeed explain significant unique variance in reading and spelling ability (Badian, 2001; Barker, Torgesen, & Wagner, 1992; Cunningham et al., 2001; Cunningham & Stanovich, 1990, 1993). For example, in an early study with third- and fourth-grade children, Cunningham and Stanovich (1990) found that orthographic processing ability, as measured by two orthographic measures, accounted for 10% of the variance in word recognition skill after statistically controlling variance due to the phonological processing composite (which accounted for 20% of the variance). This demonstrated that orthographic processing is also a key factor in individual differences in word recognition. Further, Barker and colleagues (1992) found observed that orthographic processing ability accounted for unique variance on five different reading tasks (nonword reading, untimed isolated word identification, timed word identification, and oral and silent reading rates for texts) above and beyond what was accounted for by phonological processing or general cognitive abilities. In a longitudinal investigation of children from first through third grade, Cunningham and colleagues (2001) found that a composite measure of six orthographic processing tasks predicted additional invariance in word recognition after variance accounted for by the phonological processing measures had been statistically controlled. Overall, these convergent results make a compelling case for the secondary contribution of orthographic processes to fluent word recognition.

Difficulties with Defining Orthographic Processing

Although in general agreement that orthographic processing could be a determinant of variability in word recognition, the field has not always converged on how it defines (for reviews see Wagner & Barker, 1994). Orthographic processes have been defined as either involving *procedural* or *declarative* knowledge (Berninger, 1994), with the tasks used to measure orthographic processes focusing on either *process* or *products,* respectively (Geva & Willows, 1994). In other words, orthographic processes have been defined "in terms of the operations occurring on orthographic representations (orthographic operations), or as the representations themselves (orthographic knowledge)" (Hagiliassis, Pratt, & Johnston, 2006, p. 236). For instance, Reitsma (1983), and Stanovich and West (1989) used a *procedural* notion when defining orthographic processing as the ability to form, store, and access orthographic representations. On the other hand, utilizing the idea of *declarative* orthographic knowledge, orthographic processing has been defined as a reader's knowledge about permissible letter patterns, such as how English does not permit the letter "v" as the last letter in a one-syllable word (Cassar & Treiman, 1997; Cummings, 1988; Perfetti, 1985; Treiman, 1993) and as a reader's word-specific knowledge, such as knowledge of real word spellings (Ehri, 1980).

Although the literature thus far appears to represent orthographic processes as two concurrent concepts, one of procedural orthographic operations and the other of declarative orthographic knowledge, we believe it is best to utilize a definition that incorporates *both* components in the future (e.g., Siegel, Share, & Geva, 1995). Therefore, for the purposes of this review, we have employed an operational definition that includes both procedural and declarative components: Orthographic processing is the ability to form, store, and access orthographic representations, which (a) specify the allowable order of letters within the orthography of a specific language, and (b) are themselves tightly linked to phonological, semantic, morphological, and syntactic information within the language in which they operate (Cassar & Treiman, 1997; Ehri, 1980; Perfetti, 1992; Reitsma, 1983; Share, 1995; Stanovich & West, 1989).

Evidence substantiating our more comprehensive definition of orthographic processing comes from recent examinations of the validity of the construct (Cunningham et al., 2001; Hagiliassis et al., 2006). These studies, which have included a range of important measures (see Table 12.1), tapping both the procedural and declarative components, have revealed robust evidence for a

Table 12.1   Tasks Employed to Measure Orthographic Processes

Task	Research	Skills Required
Orthographic Choice	Olson et al., 1994; Olson, Wise, Conners, Rack, & Fulker, 1989	Children view pairs of phonologically similar letter strings on paper (e.g., *rain-rane, sammon-salmon*) and choose the correctly spelled word
Orthographic Verification	Hagiliassis et al., 2006; Manis, Szeszulski, Holt, & Graves, 1990	Children listen to a word (e.g., *street*) and verify if the visual stimulus presented on a screen is an accurate orthographic representation of what was heard (e.g., *street* or *streat*)
Homophone Choice	Stanovich & West, 1989	Children view phonologically identical but orthographically different words in print (e.g., *ate-eight*), and when asked a question (e.g., *which is a number?*), they must decide which word is correct
Homophone Verification	Hagiliassis et al., 2006	Children listen to a word (e.g., *week*) and sentence (e.g., *Monday is the first day of the week*) and verify if the visually-presented stimulus (e.g., *week* or *weak*) matches the correct use in the sentence
Nonlexical Choice (Letter String Choice)	Treiman, 1993; Cassar & Treiman, 1997	Children select the item that looks most like it could be a real word when presented with pairs of letter strings (e.g., *beff-ffeb, filv-filk*)
Irregular Word Reading (exception word reading or sight word reading)	Coltheart & Leahy, 1996	Children read words that violate grapheme-phoneme correspondence rules (e.g., *answer*)
Irregular Word Spelling	Manis, Custodio, & Szeszulski, 1993	Children listen to an irregular word and its use in a meaningful sentence, and then recall and spell the word
Peabody Individual Achievement Test (PIAT) spelling subtest	Dunn & Markwardt, 1970	Children listen to regular and irregular word stimuli (e.g., *cow*) and select the correct spelling from four options (e.g., *cou, cau, caw, cow*)

single construct. As described, Cunningham et al. (2001), through correlational and principal components analysis, found that six different orthographic measures (three variations of the letter string choice task, two orthographic choice tasks, and a homophone choice task) moderately correlated with one another and loaded on a single factor, suggesting that they tap the same construct. Similarly, Hagiliassis et al. (2006) found that various orthographic processing tasks were tapping a related construct. Furthermore, the findings from both of these studies suggest that the most commonly used orthographic processing measures—orthographic choice/verification, homophone choice/verification, nonlexical choice, and spelling—are measuring the same underlying processes.

Orthographic Processing as a Separable Construct from Phonological Processing

Despite the existence of measures that can capture the same underlying construct, researchers have occasionally questioned whether the tasks that measure phonological or orthographic processing are ever able to purely measure their unique contribution (for varied reviews of this debate, see Burt, 2006; Foorman, 1994; Wagner & Barker, 1994). Essentially, isolating individual differences in orthographic processing is problematic because there is little doubt that the development of orthographic processing skill must be somewhat dependent on phonological processing abilities (Barron, 1986; Ehri, 1984, 1995, 1997; Cunningham & Stanovich, 1990; Juel et al., 1986; Share, 1995; Stanovich & West, 1989). Nonetheless, given that no psychological process is ever isolated with complete purity by its operational measures, this does not present an insoluble problem for advancing knowledge of the orthographic processing concept. It is only necessary that tasks have *differential* weighting on phonological and orthographic processes. Advantageously, research has begun to resolve the theoretical issues by illuminating and refining the relationships among the various tasks that are termed measures of orthographic and phonological processing (see reviews throughout Berninger, 1994; also see Vellutino, Scanlon, & Tanzman, 1994).

For example, Hagiliassis and colleagues' (2006) factor analysis revealed that orthographic and phonological processing tasks load primarily on separate factors when evaluating children's *accuracy* of performance on a range of measures, providing evidence for the construct validity of both types of processing. However, this did not generalize to findings from the *response-time* results (the timed speed of children's responses). It is possible that a general speed factor was obscuring the factor structure of these tasks. It was nevertheless noted that accuracy on tasks may be a more pure assessment of orthographic processing than response times, for which orthographic processing becomes more entangled with underlying phonological processing skills. Additionally, the findings from this study suggest that orthographic verification and homophonic verification tasks most purely measured orthographic processing, while nonlexical choice was the least pure measure. This is likely due to the fact that tasks such as orthographic and homophonic verification/choice eliminate to a significant degree the phonological interference by presenting participants with written word pairs which sound identical when phonologically recoded (e.g., *rain/rane, ate/eight*).

As it is unlikely that any *one* task will ever be an entirely pure measure of orthographic processes, selecting a range of the most appropriate tasks and analyses for the specific goals of a study and interpreting the results accordingly are critical for advancing the field (see Berninger, 1994; Geva & Willows, 1994, for additional methodological precautions). Overall, given that orthographic processing has been found to be a unique and separable construct, and that it accounts for a significant amount of individual variance in word recognition, it is appropriate to turn our conversation to how orthographic processing develops and leads to reading fluency.

ORTHOGRAPHIC PROCESSING AND THE SELF-TEACHING HYPOTHESIS

Fluency, the ability to recognize words quickly and accurately (NICHD, 2000), depends on the acquisition of word-specific orthographic representations (Booth, Perfetti, & MacWhinney, 1999; Perfetti, 1985, 2007) that are linked to phonological, semantic, morphological, and syntactic information (Share, 1995). While a substantial body of research has been dedicated to examining the development of phonological awareness in beginning reading (e.g., Bus & van IJzendoorn, 1999; NICHD, 2000), relatively little research has been conducted on the development of stable orthographic processing. This disparity in the literature has been noted by investigators interested in modeling children's acquisition and facility in word recognition (e.g., Foorman, 1994). Given the recently established significance of orthographic processing skills in reading, researchers have begun to posit theoretical frameworks for the development of this secondary source of variance in word recognition (Badian, 2001; Barker et al., 1992; Cunningham et al., 2001; Cunningham & Stanovich, 1990, 1993; Share, 1995). Share's (1995) *self-teaching hypothesis* is one such framework. Empirical investigations of this hypothesis have advanced the field in clarifying the mechanisms underlying the development of stable orthographic representations, or rather *orthographic learning*.

The *self-teaching hypothesis* (Jorm, 1979; Jorm & Share, 1983; Share, 1995) postulates that the detailed orthographic representations necessary for fast, efficient word recognition are primarily self-taught during independent reading. Phonological recoding (i.e., decoding via translation of a printed letter string into its spoken form) is the mechanism or self-teacher that enables a reader to independently acquire an autonomous orthographic lexicon. Upon encountering unfamiliar words, the reader "self-teaches" by applying previous knowledge of grapheme-to-phoneme correspondences to generate candidate target pronunciations which are then matched with known words in the reader's oral vocabulary (Share, 1995). A successful decoding encounter with an unfamiliar word provides the reader with an opportunity to acquire word-specific orthographic information, such as order and identity of letters. This exhaustive grapheme-by-grapheme decoding (en route to a correct pronunciation) will result in the formation of well-specified orthographic representations. In typical readers, a small number of subsequent successes with the same word are sufficient for the word to be added to the child's orthographic lexicon (Share, 1999, 2004). Eventually, the amalgamation of phonological and orthographic representations in memory fosters the rapid fluency of word identification (Ehri, 2005a, 2005b; Ehri & Saltmarsh, 1995).

Originally, Share (1995) proposed three key components of the self-teaching function of phonological recoding. First, self-teaching evokes both phonological and orthographic processes, both of which are assumed to make independent contributions to the acquisition of fluent word recognition. The phonological component—the ability to use knowledge of spelling-sound relationships to identify unfamiliar words—is considered to be the primary means for acquiring orthographic representations (Share, 1995). Yet over and above this phonological ability, there are individual differences in the ability to form, store, and retrieve word-specific orthographic information (Badian, 2001; Barker et al., 1992; Cunningham et al., 2001; Cunningham & Stanovich, 1990, 1993). Therefore, although such differences in orthographic processing can determine how quickly and accurately orthographic representations are acquired, they fundamentally depend on the proficient employment of the phonological component.

Second, the self-teaching hypothesis adopts an item-based approach, in that word recognition processes will fundamentally rely on the frequency of exposure to a word and the nature of success with the item's identification. Many theories of reading development assume that children learn to read by progressing through a series of stages defined by different types of decoding strategies (e.g., Chall, 1983; Ehri, 1991, 2005a; Ehri & McCormick, 1998; Frith, 1985;

Gough & Hillinger, 1980). In contrast, the self-teaching hypothesis contends that the way a reader attempts to read a word depends on the particular word, rather than on a particular stage (or phase) of development. If the word is familiar, the reader will read it automatically. If the word is unfamiliar, the reader will phonologically recode it. Because readers of all skill levels encounter low-frequency words, phonological recoding is thus a powerful mechanism used throughout life, not only in beginning reading. The feedback from phonological recoding gradually results in the formation of an orthographic representation of specific words, which will eventually become a part of the reader's automatic sight vocabulary. Thus, automaticity, according to the self-teaching model, is characteristic of specific words, not readers.

Third, as discussed previously, the process of phonological recoding becomes increasingly "lexicalized" throughout reading development, such that orthographic representations become fully specified over time. Some rudimentary self-teaching skills exist before the beginning reader has even established conventional decoding skills. With some basic letter-sound knowledge, phonological awareness, and utility of context—such as appropriate stress (re'/ cord vs. rec' /ord) or pronunciation (/red/ vs. /read/)—to elucidate exact word pronunciations from preliminary phonological recoding, early self-teaching may ensue. As orthographic knowledge increases, "simple one-to-one letter-sound correspondences become modified in light of new lexical constraints [among other constraints, such as morphological knowledge] imposed by a growing body of orthographic knowledge" (Share, 1995, p. 156). For example, there are two common sounds for the letter *c* (/k/ and /s/). The sound selection, however, is specified by the vowel that follows *c* as in the words *city* and *cat*. In these examples, the vowels dictate the sound-symbol correspondence. With increased print exposure, the reader is alerted to regularities beyond the level of simple one-to-one correspondences, such as positional (final versus initial *y*), context-sensitive (soft and hard *g* and *c*), and morphemic constraints (*missed* rather than *mist*). According to Share (2008), this leads to an "ever-changing and self-refining process that at first appears to be very 'bottom-up,' with little sensitivity to higher order regularities but over the course of print experience becomes increasingly attuned ('lexicalized') to the given orthography in a two-way interplay between decoding abilities and orthographic knowledge" (pp. 12–13). This process of "lexicalization" ultimately results in decoding skill that is much more sophisticated than simple knowledge of sound-symbol correspondence.

Investigations of the Self-Teaching Hypothesis

In recent years, various researchers have set out to directly test and refine the theoretical arguments set forth by Share's (1995) self-teaching model. Through these cross-linguistic investigations, converging evidence for the self-teaching hypothesis has emerged. The evidence has spanned multiple languages, from shallow orthographies such as Hebrew (Share, 1995, 1999, 2004), to Dutch (de Jong & Share, 2007; Reitsma, 1983), which entails morphophonemic elements (Bosman, de Graaff, & Gijsel, 2006), to the complex and deep orthography of English (e.g., Bowey & Muller, 2005; Cunningham, 2006; Cunningham, Perry, Stanovich, & Share, 2002; Ehri & Saltmarsh, 1995; Kyte & Johnson, 2006; Nation, Angells, & Castles, 2007).

Elegant research designs have been employed to disentangle the inherent complexity of children's instantiations of print. Most studies examining the self-teaching hypothesis involve children reading aloud short passages embedded with target pseudowords that require phonological recoding. Subsequently, researchers use post-test measures to determine whether children have self-taught each target word's orthography. The most commonly used measure is a type of *orthographic choice task* that taps a child's ability to correctly identify the orthographic representations of novel stimuli. More specifically, the reader chooses between the pseudoword target (e.g., *surn*) and several foils, including a homophonic alternative (e.g., *sern*), a visually similar pseudoword (e.g., *sarn*), and a letter transposition alternative (e.g., *srun*). The assumption is that children who recognize the target words over homophones must be doing so on the basis of functional orthographic representations, given that both words sound the same when they are phonologically recoded. Thus, investigators are able to directly tap children's orthographic processes above and beyond phonological processes. In some experiments (Cunningham, 2006; Share, 2004, Experiment 3) investigators employed targets that were real words in children's oral vocabulary (e.g., homophonic choices were *chews, chooze*). Since pilot studies ensured that same-grade children were equally likely to choose correctly and incorrectly spelled words, investigators were still able to model children's orthographic learning, rather than simply their existing orthographic knowledge.

Naming tasks are also employed to examine if children are able to more accurately and quickly name, or read, targets than homophonic alternatives. Presentation of the target word in the naming task is assumed to activate orthographic representations linked with information regarding pronunciation, whereas presentation of an untaught homophone alternate would require phonological recoding, slowing its naming time. It should be noted that naming tasks have not always been found to be sensitive to differences in orthographic learning (Bowey & Miller, 2007; Cunningham et al., 2002; Share, 1999, 2004). Measuring the time it takes to name an entire list of pseudowords, rather than naming onset latencies, seems to be more reflective of children's errors and hesitations across items and thus may better account for children's actual acquisition of novel orthographic representations (Bowey & Muller, 2005).

Finally, a post-test for *spelling* reproduction accuracy is used as another index of strength of orthographic learning of the target (pseudo)word that children have formerly read. This task, which demands production rather than just recognition, has occasionally been found to be too difficult to detect orthographic learning (Cunningham, 2006; Share, 2004; Treiman, 1984). Nevertheless, Perfetti (1985) has argued that spelling ability represents the most precise and robust index of a child's instantiation of a word—as can be seen in the progressive developmental spelling inventory for the word "ship" in *s, sp, shp, sep, shep, ship* (Bear, Invernizzi, Templeton, & Johnston, 2004, p. 307).

Some theorists have critiqued the use of these three tasks, arguing that a certain ordering of post-test measures may create priming which could influence subsequent performance (e.g., Nation et al., 2007). For instance, it is possible that requiring children to spell and name nonword targets before completing an orthographic choice task may increase performance in the orthographic choice task, leading orthographic learning to be enhanced. However, a number of studies that have employed these measures with varied counterbalancing methods and orders have resulted in similar findings (e.g., Bowey & Muller, 2005; Cunningham, 2006; Cunningham et al., 2002; Kyte & Johnson, 2006; Share, 1999, 2004), suggesting that the order of presentation does not create a confound.

Overall, through the creative employment of the self-teaching experimental design, researchers have been able to successfully investigate the key tenets of the self-teaching hypothesis. First and foremost, a number of studies have found a critical relationship between phonological recoding and orthographic learning (Bowey & Muller, 2005; Cunningham, 2006; Cunningham et al., 2002; de Jong & Share, 2007; Kyte & Johnson, 2006; Share, 1999, 2004; Sprenger-Charolles, Siegel, & Bonnet, 1998; Wesseling & Reitsma, 2000). Share (1999) carried out a series of experiments to directly test his hypothesis using the highly regular, or shallow, Hebrew orthography. Three days after exposure to novel stimuli, second-grade children were more able to correctly identify, quickly name, and accurately spell the targets than alternative homophonic pseudowords. Four exposures were sufficient to generate this substantial orthographic learning. Furthermore, when phonological processing was minimized through concurrent articulation in a subsequent experiment, orthographic learning decreased significantly. Another experiment revealed that this attenuation in learning was not attributable to brief visual exposures or the loss of contextual support, clearly demonstrating the need for phonological factors in orthographic learning.

Share's study substantiated Reitsma's (1983) much earlier findings of quick orthographic learning in Dutch by extending the notion of self-teaching to unaided reading of connected text, which requires independent phonological recoding by the child.

Cunningham and colleagues (2002) examined English-speaking second-grade children's ability to self-teach after reading target homophonic pseudowords (e.g., *slurst/slirst*) in the context of real stories. Convergent with Share's findings in Hebrew, they found that young readers of a much deeper orthography also evidenced significant orthographic learning of targets, as indicated by performance on orthographic choice, naming, and spelling tasks. Cognitive abilities and rapid naming were not able to account for this robust orthographic learning once decoding accuracy had been partialed out. Additionally, in another study Cunningham (2006) utilized real words that would be known orally but not in print to examine children's ability to self-teach varied homophonic forms of stimuli (e.g., *prince/prinse*) when embedded within cohesive or scrambled texts. Three days after reading English passages, the participating first graders correctly identified targets over homophonic alternates at a significantly greater rate, regardless of context. Further, children's accuracy of phonological recoding during story reading across both studies was reliably and significantly correlated with their orthographic learning (r = .52, r = .66, respectively), as purported by the self-teaching hypothesis and convergent with Share's (1999) previous experimental findings. It should be noted that the use of context and meaningful words in experimental investigations has not necessarily generated *more* significant self-teaching (Cunningham, 2006; Landi, Perfetti, Bolger, Dunlap, & Foorman, 2006; Nation et al., 2007; Share, 2004, Experiment 3). That is, despite more accurate phonological recoding with connected and meaningful text, children have also demonstrated the ability to reliably self-teach with unconnected text for which they had a generally harder time decoding (Cunningham, 2006). This suggests that although context can support children in their reading, it does not necessarily hinder phonological recoding, as needed for orthographic learning of novel words.

In a later study examining English-speaking fourth and fifth graders' acquisition of orthographic representations, Kyte and Johnson (2006) again demonstrated the critical role played by phonological recoding in such orthographic learning. To enhance Share's (1999) design, a within-subject comparison was employed, whereby children were asked to make lexical decisions while engaged in either a read aloud condition promoting the use of phonological recoding or a concurrent articulation condition, presumed to attenuate the use of decoding. Children showed significantly more orthographic learning with the read aloud condition, and although this effect was only small to medium and some orthographic learning emerged from the concurrent articulation condition, the authors suggest that this was due to the fact that "residual phonological processing" still occurred despite concurrent articulation (Kyte & Johnson, 2006, p. 180). Nevertheless, the accuracy of decoding the pseudoword targets during the learning phase was moderately correlated with the orthographic learning composite, providing additional evidence for the critical self-teaching role of phonological recoding in the acquisition of skilled reading.

Cross-linguistic evidence supports the proposition that children self-teach through phonological recoding while reading text *silently* as well. In silent reading, children could potentially acquire orthographic representations without phonological recoding. However, Bowey and Muller (2005) employed a silent reading design that provided additional evidence for the self-teaching function of phonological recoding. While the English-speaking third-grade children's ability to accurately identify significantly more target pseudowords than homophonic or visually similar alternatives on posttests indicated that orthographic learning had occurred, their capacity for naming the targets significantly faster established that phonological recoding within their silent reading had indeed mediated their rapid acquisition of the orthographic representations. Through a similar investigation that revealed a significant relationship between phonological recoding efficiency and orthographic learning, Bowey and Miller (2007) once again warranted support for the possibility of self-teaching during silent reading. Dutch-speaking children who were asked to silently read expository texts in their slightly more orthographically shallow language also showed evidence of self-teaching (de Jong & Share, 2007). Silent and oral reading generated comparable orthographic learning, as indicated by children's ability to more accurately identify and spell targets; however, de Jong and Share (2007) found that oral reading did produce somewhat stronger orthographic representations according to naming latencies. Bowey and Muller (2005) employed a more sensitive naming measure, a naming task assessing children's reading speed of the entire pseudoword list rather than just the onset latencies, such as was employed in de Jong and Share's (2007) work.

Although future research with optimally sensitive measures will need to be completed to clarify the differential orthographic learning benefits that oral versus silent reading affords, silent reading nevertheless appears to provide opportunities for children to acquire the orthographic representations necessary for efficient reading. These orthographic learning opportunities through silent reading offer potential specification for how print exposure, which contributes unique variance to both word recognition and orthographic processing, beneficially fosters reading acquisition (Cunningham et al., 2001; Cunningham & Stanovich, 1993). The opportunity for self-teaching provided by silent reading is important, in that children will most likely engage in this type of meaningful reading with connected texts. In the remainder of this section we will describe how children self-teach and acquire orthographic representations *beyond* what is afforded by phonological recoding.

Additional Factors Related to Children's Self-Teaching.   While much of the work above has demonstrated the fundamental self-teaching role played by phonological recoding, orthographic processes are not entirely parasitic on phonological processing skills (Barker et al., 1992; Cunningham, 2006; Cunningham et al., 2002; Cunningham & Stanovich, 1990). First, some studies have revealed that *prior* orthographic knowledge contributes unique variance to children's capacity to self-teach beyond what is accounted for by phonological recoding of text. In the 1980s, Reitsma (1983) demonstrated that Dutch children are able to quickly learn orthographic forms of words and suggested that prior orthographic knowledge may contribute to orthographic learning. Moreover, Cunningham's recent work with English speakers (Cunningham, 2006; Cunningham et al., 2002) has provided further evidence for this hypothesis, such that children's prior orthographic knowledge (as indicated by orthographic choice, letter-string, and homophone choice tasks) predicted orthographic learning above and beyond variance predicted by accurate phonological recoding. Similarly, from the end of first grade, French-speaking children's orthographic *and* phonological skills accounted for later differences in orthographic skills at the end of fourth grade (Sprenger-Charolles, Siegel, Béchennec, & Serniclaes, 2003).

Additionally, several studies suggest that print exposure likely contributes to orthographic learning, beyond the self-teaching accounted for by the phonological recoding of text (Barker et al., 1992; Braten, Lie, Andreassen, & Olaussen, 1999; Cunningham & Stanovich, 1990; Chateau & Jared 2000; McBride-Chang, Manis, Seidenberg, Custodio, & Doi, 1993; Olson, Forsberg, Wise, & Rack, 1994). For instance, Cunningham and Stanovich (1990) discovered that individual differences in orthographic processing are in part due to differences in print exposure. Third- and fourth-grade children were administered a number of assessments, including orthographic choice and homophone choice tasks as measures of orthographic processing and the Title Recognition Test as a measure of print exposure. Hierarchical regression analyses demonstrated that even after partialing out phonological processing ability, print exposure contributes significant variance to orthographic processing. Assessing first-grade children with an even larger battery of phonological and orthographic processing variables, Cunningham and colleagues (2001) replicated this finding and confirmed the potential effect of print exposure on the development of orthographic processing.

Kyte and Johnson (2006) also suggest that orthographic learning may possibly occur through "visual processing of unfamiliar words," given the slight levels of orthographic learning that occurred in their condition with concurrent articulation (p. 181). They argue that Cunningham et al.'s (2002) finding of a strong relationship between prior orthographic knowledge and orthographic learning provides indirect evidence for the role of such visual processes. They also posit that deaf children's ability to achieve some degree of reading skill clearly indicates visual processing's role in orthographic learning. However, more work must be conducted to delineate the multiple factors that account for the acquisition of orthographic representations necessary for reading fluency.

Some theorists have proposed that phonological retrieval, the efficiency of access to phonological codes for lexical items in long-term memory as measured by rapid automatized naming (RAN) tasks, contributes to the acquisition of orthographic representations (Bowers, Sunseth, & Golden, 1999; Bowers & Wolf, 1993; Wolf, Bally, & Morris, 1986; Wolf, Bowers, & Biddle, 2000). Theoretically, Bowers and Wolf (1993) have argued that "slow letter (or digit) naming speed may signal disruption of the automatic processes which support induction of orthographic patterns, which, in turn, result in quick word recognition" (p. 70). Consequently, Cunningham et al. (2002) discussed the relevance of understanding the potential role of RAN in orthographic processing independent of decoding accuracy and testing this hypothesis. Despite this theoretical prospect, Cunningham et al.'s (2002) empirical study found that a composite of RAN measures did not significantly predict orthographic learning in second graders once target decoding accuracy had been partialed out in hierarchical regression analyses. In another study examining a group of younger students, Cunningham (2006) again found that a strong effect of RAN was not observed for orthographic learning once decoding ability was accounted for. Whatever effect RAN has in producing individual differences in orthographic learning, at least in these particular studies, the effect appeared to be masked and/or overwhelmed by the potent effects of decoding accuracy. Likewise, Torgesen, Wagner, Rashotte, Burgess, and Hecht (1997), in a study of second- to fourth-grade reading subskill growth, found that RAN did not predict fourth-grade orthographic processing after partialing out word reading accuracy.

Despite these convergent findings, some research suggests that further work remains to better understand the potentially mediating role of naming speed. In Cunningham and colleagues' (2002) sub-analysis, somewhat more variance was explained by a rapid naming score that solely included alphanumeric stimuli, yet the effect remained insignificant. Bowey and Muller (2005) similarly found alphanumeric naming speed, but not non-symbol naming speed, to be significantly correlated with orthographic learning. However, alphanumeric naming speed was again not significantly predictive of orthographic learning after other phonological and orthographic variables were partialed out in regression analyses. Bowey and Muller suggest that different processes may underlie these differential naming speed skills, and Cunningham et al. (2002) maintained that additional investigations with larger sample sizes are necessary to clarify these issues. Thus, future work, with populations representing children with and without a reading disability, and with larger sample sizes, will likely be needed to shed light on the specificity of the RAN variable's connection to orthographic processing.

Nuances across Orthographic Depth.   While the findings concerning self-teaching above provide convergent evidence that unassisted phonological recoding facilitates children's orthographic learning, it is also clear that the factors involved in orthographic learning have not been entirely resolved. Beyond factors such as prior orthographic knowledge, print exposure, and RAN, results have often been mixed regarding the effects of differing amounts of exposure, durability or length of retention of learning, and developmental onset of self-teaching. These additional mixed results appear to be due to the fact that readers of shallow and deep orthographies may process words differently (Frost, 2005; Goswami, Ziegler, Dalton, & Schneider, 2001; Seymour,

2005), and because of differences in irregular grapheme-to-phoneme correspondences. Such nuances across the cross-linguistic research have continued to shed light on the theoretical tenets of the self-teaching model.

When studying third-grade children reading pointed Hebrew, Share (2004) found that the most significant self-teaching resulted from only one exposure to a target, with diminishing orthographic learning resulting from subsequent exposures. Similarly, in Dutch—a language that is less shallow than pointed Hebrew, de Jong and Share (2007) found that two exposures generated robust and significant orthographic learning while six exposures provided no additional benefits for third graders. Share (2004) argues that "more 'effort' appears to be invested in decoding at the very first encounter with a novel string," hence generating the strongest learning on initial trials (p. 278). On the contrary, when examining second- and third-grade children's orthographic learning of English text, investigators found that four exposures were optimal for reliable self-teaching (Bowey & Muller, 2005; Nation et al., 2007). Although some orthographic learning resulted from one trial, four exposures in this deep orthography led to significantly more self-teaching (Nation et al., 2007). However, eight exposures in English did not necessarily lead to better results (Bowey & Muller, 2005). Still, it appears that in a deep orthography, such as English, more exposures are required for self-teaching among second and third-grade students.

Furthermore, to examine the durability of orthographic learning, which involves the storage and subsequent access of orthographic processing, Share (2004) evaluated orthographic learning of target stimuli after 1, 7, and 30 days from initial exposure. He found that third-grade Hebrew speakers demonstrated the highest level of learning after seven days with only a slight decline after 30 days. Results from children exposed to English texts, however, revealed that orthographic learning was most robust after one day, with only modest self-teaching evident after six (Bowey & Muller, 2005) or seven days (Nation et al., 2007). Thus, due to the relatively inconsistent relationship between the spoken and written forms of language, the acquisition of orthographic representations in English may not be quite as durable as observed in more shallow orthographies or may require additional repetition over time.

The majority of findings discussed thus far have emerged from studies with participants who were at the end of second grade or beyond. Empirical evidence from younger children reading different languages reveals further insights into the conceptualization and developmental onset of self-teaching. Regardless of the number of exposures or use of meaningful words, Share (2004, Experiments 2 & 3) discovered that first-grade readers of Hebrew did not demonstrate any significant orthographic learning; however, he suggested that there were "glimmerings" of orthographic learning after eight exposures. This lack of self-teaching was evident despite even greater accuracy on phonological recoding than achieved by his previous sample of third graders. Similar results were reported with early second-grade beginning readers, and with normal and disabled fourth through sixth graders (Share, 2004; Share & Shalev, 2004). These results have generated counterevidence to the fundamental role of phonological recoding in self-teaching, but they have not generalized to other more orthographically deep languages. A very different outcome emerged with first graders in English (Cunningham, 2006), who demonstrated reliable self-teaching after decoding targets six times in passages, with or without the support of context. Likewise, first-grade children demonstrated quick orthographic learning in other studies in English (Ehri & Saltmarsh, 1995) and in Dutch (Reitsma, 1983).

Current Trends in the Self-Teaching Hypothesis: Progress Toward a Hybrid Model.   Share (2004) provides some possibilities for the mixed findings in his own research and across orthographies. While the first-grade children in his studies demonstrated higher levels of decoding accuracy with pointed Hebrew, it was a laborious process, and they did not necessarily read the words automatically and fluently. Students were thus unable to amalgamate the orthographic and phonological representations to generate self-teaching. Thus, he argues that decoding accuracy may not actually be sufficient to evoke orthographic learning, but rather automaticity and how efficiently children phonologically recode may play a more critical role in facilitating self-teaching. This hypothesis is consistent with findings in other studies of reading in shallow orthographies where decoding speed is a more salient feature of reading disability than decoding accuracy (Breznitz, 1997; Wimmer, 1993; Ziegler, Perry, Ma-Wyatt, Ladner, & Schulte-Körne, 2003).

Moreover, for the first-grade students in Share's (2004) study, there was no need to attend to word specific orthography due to the high level of decodability or shallowness of the orthography. This need to attend may fundamentally contribute to a child's reliable self-teaching. From the end of second grade onward, children learning to read Hebrew may process word-specific orthographic detail differently than they did in first grade. A print-specific processing advantage, rather than a difference in skill, may emerge over the second-grade year (Share, 2004), during which Hebrew classrooms move to a "read to learn" instructional focus. With massively larger amounts of texts at children's disposal, this print-specific processing advantage is acquired via extensive print exposure. Share calls this the *orthographic sensitivity hypothesis*, which "assumes that a critical volume of print exposure brings about a fundamental change in orthographic sensitivity," eventually enabling "the more experienced reader to develop a sensitivity to ortho-graphic detail that is beyond the grasp of the novice" (Share, 2004, p. 291). Given that "simple one-to-one letter-sound relationships have such far-reaching utility" in the early stages of read-ing languages as shallow as Hebrew, there is no need to attend to the word-specific orthography of text (Share, 2004, p. 292). Indeed, Martens and de Jong's (2006) research suggests that both beginning and advanced readers in Dutch (a somewhat deeper orthography than Hebrew) rely on multi-letter features in word recognition, and the speed with which orthographic learning occurs may result from children's capacity for depending on such multi-letter features. In deeper orthographies, readers do not often have the luxury of simple one-to-one correspondences, and they are thus obliged to look beyond "low-level phonology and consider higher-order regularities that are often word-specific" (Share, 2004, p. 292). As a result, children reading more complex orthographies may develop orthographic sensitivity and a greater reliance on large, multi-letter orthographic units sooner, and therefore demonstrate self-teaching as early as the first grade, despite the less extensive print exposure. Nonetheless, as discussed previously, print exposure appears to have a potential effect on the ongoing development of orthographic processing, even in orthographically complex languages.

Research on the role of orthographic processes in reading disability has also begun to lend credence to the orthographic sensitivity hypothesis. In the past, some research suggested that children with disabilities require more print exposure (Booth et al., 2000; Ehri & Saltmarsh, 1995) and/or intensity in phonological awareness and decoding training (Lovett et al., 2000; Torgesen, 2005; Torgesen et al., 2001; Wise, Sevcik, Morris, Lovett, & Wolf, 2007) than non-disabled readers to achieve accurate and fluent word representations. Other research suggested that children with disabilities actually have compensatory processes that facilitate greater suc-cess with orthographic learning relative to younger non-disabled readers (Siegel et al., 1995), with children with reading difficulties seeming to have orthographic abilities commensurate with their level of word recognition (i.e., they were not different from reading-age controls; Stanovich & Siegel, 1994). More recently, however, Share and Shalev's (2004) findings appeared to support a so-called *hybrid* view, which combines and broadens these previous perspectives. They conducted a self-teaching study in which they examined dyslexic, garden-variety poor, and adequately achieving readers' self-teaching in Hebrew. Their investigation strengthened the argument for the orthographic sensitivity hypothesis, such that some poor readers appeared at an early age to have surface-like symptoms of dyslexia—that is, facility with phonological concepts but great difficulty with whole word recognition, but that such behavior faded over time possibly as a result of increased sensitivity to orthographic patterns afforded by numerous decoding encounters with extensive amounts of print. Therefore, poor readers may develop a specialized print-specific orthographic processing advantage which materializes from voluminous print exposure, suggesting quantitative rather than qualitative weaknesses in self-teaching among disabled Hebrew readers.

Overall, the self-teaching hypothesis, refined in part due to the empirical evidence described above, has now been conceptualized in a broader and more universalistic framework (Share, 2008). That is, Share's conceptualization has transitioned from a purely item-based hypothesis to a hybrid model that includes phases of the development of self-teaching and skilled word identification—moving from an imperfect, yet nevertheless functional and independent approach to decoding, to a more refined heuristic. Regardless of the complexity and depth of the orthography, every alphabetic code provides the opportunity and algorithm for such movement. More specifically, there is a shift from early decoding of unfamiliar words to the automatic recognition of these items as familiar. Further, the independent identification of words via decoding facilitates the increasing establishment of such autonomous orthographic representations and thus sets the stage for the skilled reader's expertise in word recognition in any orthography. Share clarifies that while one could think of the progression of strategies or modes employed to decode at the item level as "stage-like," his broadened conceptualization is not necessarily aligned with traditional stage theories, which are focused at the level of reading in general. However, he notes that the tenet of lexicalization in his hypothesis still allows a concurrent emphasis on item-level changes and developmental changes in the *process* of word identification. Overall, in this broader framework, "this 'unfamiliar-to-familiar' transition (seen from the perspective of individual items) or 'novice-to-expert' transition (from the reader's perspective) represents a fundamental and overarching duality in word reading that applies to *all* words in *all* possible orthographies" (p. 8).

Share's recent dual conceptualization (item-reader) derives from two advantages he sees over the traditional dual-route approach's processing distinction between regular and irregular words: (a) the dualism in reading words is common to all skilled learning—the transition from slow, unskilled performance to automatic, one-step performance; and (b) the broader novice/expert or unfamiliar/familiar converges with the "dualistic nature of an efficient orthography" (pp. 9–10) where, for example, the spelling of a word is a compromise between the needs of the novice (decipherability) and the expert (automaticity)—as in "magician" spelled thus (where print to meaning is more direct due to the retention of the base morpheme's spelling), as opposed to "magishin" spelled phonetically. An effective orthography must (a) allow both experts and novices to recode a word independently (print to sound translation must be rule-governed to some extent), and (b) provide experts with distinctive visual-orthographic configurations required for automazation, and thus morphemes should ideally be constant (e.g., *magic/magician*; *compose/ composition*). As new data on the underlying mechanisms of word recognition come to the fore, models of reading development and skilled reading will become ever more refined. At this writing, it appears that Share's hybrid model of lexicalization accounts best for the extant data on the development of orthographic representations.

IMPLICATIONS

A number of tentative recommendations for educational practice and policy can be offered based on the research outlined in this chapter. First, it has become apparent that beyond the development of phonological processes and an understanding of the alphabetic principle (see chapters in this volume by Foorman & Connor, Tunmer & Nicholson, and Roberts et al.), progress towards learning to read includes the establishment of rich lexical instantiations of orthographic patterns and their associated pronunciations (Ehri, 2005b; Share, 1995, 2008). Because children need multiple and varied opportunities to self-teach (e.g., Cunningham et al., 2002; Share, 1999), providing children sufficient time to phonologically recode words on their own during instructional moments (e.g., paired or small group reading) will contribute to their development of automaticity (Share, 1995). That is, when a child hesitates to attempt decoding due to difficulties, it will be important for teachers to refrain from immediately supplying the word and rather to provide enough wait time to allow an adequate opportunity for a child to completely attempt phonological recoding. Even unitary attempts to phonologically recode may facilitate some level of orthographic learning for the child.

Second, to the extent that the practices of reading and spelling are similar, in that they both rely on rich orthographic representations of printed word forms (Perfetti, 1985, 2007), learning to spell words using their exact graphemic structure is a potentially powerful way to improve the quality of such representations (Shahar-Yames & Share, 2008). In effect, "spelling should help reading more than practice at reading helps spelling" (Perfetti, 1997, p. 31). Not only does accurate spelling developed through instruction facilitate reading (Berninger, Abbott, Abbot, Graham, & Richards, 2002; Shanahan & Lomax, 1986, 1988) and vocabulary growth (Rosenthal & Ehri, 2008), but it also facilitates writing. That is, attention demands that are needed for composition are not drained by resources directed toward accurate spelling (Torrance & Galbraith, 2006). Given the significance of knowledge of accurate spelling for reading and writing development, teachers should certainly devote time to spelling instruction.

Third, as a student's knowledge of the linkages between orthography and phonology increases due to instruction and self-teaching opportunities, wide reading experience within and beyond the classroom can afford children increased opportunities to encounter unique and rare words that can be incorporated into their lexicon (Booth et al., 1999; Cunningham & Stanovich, 1997, 1998; Stanovich, 1992). With such reading experience, the recognition of novel words becomes possible, and the development of automaticity more probable (Ehri, 2005b; Samuels, 2006). That is, print exposure provides students the opportunity to acquire information beyond sound-symbol correspondences such as morphologic and syntactic knowledge (Chliounaki & Bryant, 2007; Lavric, 2007; Perfetti, 2007), hence allowing the phonological, orthographic, semantic, and morphological representations to become amalgamated in memory (Ehri, 2005b). The quality of this fusion is critical for the development of automaticity in word recognition and in turn facility with comprehension. Therefore, in English, explicit and advanced instruction in the structure of the language, including syntactic constraints (e.g., the regular past tense, regardless of pronunciation, is spelled *ed*) and morphological relationships (root preservation, as in *magic/magician*), is warranted for children who do not readily acquire this knowledge on their own (Ehri, 2005b; Moats, 2000; Perfetti, 2007; Rayner et al., 2001).

Fourth, in regard to learning to read in a language other than one's first, educators must remember that orthographies vary in their level of transparency—from deep (e.g., English and Dutch) to shallow (e.g., pointed Hebrew, Serbo-Croatian, Spanish, German, or Greek). Bilingual students learning to read in English, for example, where the reader's first language is more transparent, requires a shift in stance toward letter-phoneme conversion; it must be shown that some graphemes represent several phonemes (g*ym*/g*e*t; m*ea*t/br*ea*d/gr*ea*t) and some phonemes are represented by multiple spelling variants (*f*riend/pu*ff*/enou*gh*/*ph*one). This is not an easy task and must be recognized by teachers of children acquiring dual literacy (Moats, 2000), especially where the difference in orthographic transparency is great. In such situations, sound-symbol correspondence instruction needs to be particularly explicit in the teaching of reading (August & Vockley, 2002) as well as in spelling (Peréz Cañado, 2005). In addition, alternative languages usually differ in the number of phonemes represented (e.g., Spanish has 27; English has 44), which suggests that certain practices at the oral language level, such as extended opportunities to speak using the target language, are warranted (Tabors & Snow, 2002). Noting the National Research Council report (Snow et al., 1998), Tabors and Snow (2002) explicitly point out that learners of a second language must not only have grasped, but stabilized, the "phonetic distinctions" that characterize the target language in order to make sense of grapheme-phoneme designations (p. 174).

Fifth, as policymakers adopt textbooks for reading instruction, they might give more strategic consideration to the words themselves. Many current textbooks—with low levels of word repetition and numerous low-frequency and unfamiliar words—pose complex challenges for beginning readers (Hiebert, 2005). The nuanced research on self-teaching should be considered, so that the texts provided for students are more supportive of the orthographic learning necessary for automatic word recognition. For instance, while four exposures may allow normally developing readers of English to self-teach, this number is insufficient for robust maintenance over time (Nation et al., 2007), or for children with reading disabilities who may require many more exposures to achieve enough decoding success for meaningful orthographic learning (Share & Shalev, 2004). Thus, children who read orthographically complex English texts will likely need numerous exposures to items *within* and *across* texts to ensure accurate formation, durable storage, and quick access of orthographic representations (Nation et al., 2007). Readers of other languages may need multiple exposures to words at certain points in development but not as many at other points in time (Share, 1999, 2004; Share & Shalev, 2004). Finally, emphasizing multiple exposures not to just any words in text, but also to the most frequent words in the language may further support beginning and struggling readers' word recognition as well as vocabulary development.

CONCLUSIONS AND FUTURE RESEARCH

There is abundant theoretical and empirical support demonstrating that automatic word recognition facilitates higher level reading processes. As discussed throughout this chapter, the well-established central component of word recognition fluency is phonological processing, which is in turn facilitated by alphabetic knowledge. Yet we have also demonstrated in this review that orthographic processing should be viewed as a second crucial "sticking point" in word recognition. Thus, both phonological processes that reflect redundant, word-specific information including context-sensitive grapheme-phoneme information (e.g., *jumped* is pronounced / jumpt/), and orthographic processes that are fully specified and consistent, contribute to lexical quality when working efficiently. That is, word identity can be reliability retrieved, activated, and available for building comprehension when proficient phonological and orthographic processes are both well established (Perfetti, 2007).

Progress in understanding orthographic processes continues to contribute to more detailed models of word recognition. Fortunately, the field is moving toward a more refined definition of orthographic processing that accounts for both procedural operations (e.g., recognizing a word automatically) and declarative knowledge (e.g., permissible letter patterns). Further, progress has also been made in showing that orthographic processing is most likely a separate factor. That is, although there is a conceptual link between phonological and orthographic processes, it appears that to some degree the two constructs can be separated both theoretically and empirically (e.g., Cunningham et al., 2001; Hagiliassis et al., 2006). The knowledge gained about orthographic processing will additionally continue to clarify models of skilled reading, as well as reading development. For example, while dual-route and connectionist models of skilled word recognition differ, researchers seem to agree that experience gained through both instruction and reading practice work to specify lexical entries over time. We are learning more about the properties and consequences of high-quality orthographic representations within the lexicon (for example, how redundancy is a factor in developing high-quality orthographic representations as seems to be the case in phonological representations). Developmental models will also become more refined as a result of this knowledge. For instance, stage-based models that relied on dual-route theory have given way to phase-based models that assume more of a connectionist architecture via a "visual route that is paved with phonological information" (see Ehri, 1992, 2005b for more information about the evolution and nuances of these models).

The research of Share and his associates (e.g., Share, 1995, 2004), in acknowledging the role of orthographic representations in word reading efficiency, has popularized a paradigm now used by many researchers across languages to study how orthographic processing develops. It has become apparent that phonological recoding most likely works as a self-teaching mechanism—on a word-by-word and reader-by-reader basis—that enables an individual to independently acquire an autonomous orthographic lexicon that is used during the act of reading to facilitate word recognition without depleting available attention.

Of course, there is still much work to be done. Across languages of varying orthographic depth and syllabic complexity, the acquisition of orthographic representations presents a challenge for researchers who study developmental and individual differences. While the phonological recoding function of self-teaching may play a fundamental role in orthographic learning, other variables—such as prior orthographic knowledge and print exposure, which likely provide opportunities for developing orthographic sensitivity to larger orthographic units—may also be significant aspects of development. The field will need to continue to explore how orthographic processes develop over time and across languages. In order to investigate developing orthographic processes, however, continued refinement of measurement tools and conceptualizations of orthographic processing will be key in the success of future investigations.

The potential role of naming speed and decoding fluency in self-teaching is another important area for future research. It is conceivable that slow speed of processing could impact the ability to self-teach by interfering with the integration of a novel word's phonological and/or orthographic features with stored orthographic, phonological, syntactic, and semantic representations. Smooth operation of self-teaching might require that phonological and orthographic aspects be synthesized within a certain time frame for effective encoding. This is a theoretically plausible conjecture but the necessary empirical support has not yet been produced. Regardless of the outcome of the debate about the role of rapid naming, there is no question that slow, effortful decoding diminishes available cognitive resources needed for higher-level reading goals. The failure to achieve such fluency and automaticity in word recognition is the hallmark of the remediated dyslexic (Torgesen, 2005). That is, although the remediated student has most likely learned sound-symbol correspondences, his or her lack of reading experience has prevented fluency development at the word level. With a more nuanced explication of how automaticity in word recognition is acquired, the field will be one step closer to understanding how to assist struggling students to become more fluent readers.

Finally, although there is still much to learn about orthographic processes in the development of reading, the implications of the research discussed in this chapter have been historically, and are currently, addressed in teaching practices across the philosophical divide between whole language and phonics approaches (Juel & Minden-Cupp, 2000). Reading and spelling (including attempts at writing words) have been, and are, seen as complementary processes. There is a long tradition within the field linking the teaching of reading and spelling (Clay, 1985; Francis, 1982), including the teaching of phonemic awareness and spelling (Ball & Blachman, 1991), and the role of spelling knowledge in the development of word recognition fluency (Berninger et al., 2002; Cunningham & Cunningham, 1992; Ehri, 1997; Perfetti, 1985, 1997; Shanahan, 1984, 2006). More recent research is further detailing how the linkages between spelling and reading are formed (e.g., Coltheart, 2005; Ehri, 2005b; Plaut, 2005), and why both reading and spelling processes are ultimately so vital to comprehension of text and the development of life-long readers (Perfetti, 2007; Samuels, 2006).

Therefore, implications from this chapter should serve to emphasize the importance and continued use of practices that link reading and spelling (and early writing) development. However, we agree with Juel and Minden-Cupp (2000): "Rather than a broad brush, either/or instructional approach that is applied to all children in a classroom, word recognition instruction is likely to be most effective if there is an emphasis on different linguistic units at different levels of reading development" (p. 488). That is, specific objectives in relation to the developmental level and characteristics of the child need to shape the unit of phonological exploration (e.g., alternatives such as sound-by-sound decoding /c/ /a/ /t/ vs. onset and rime decoding /c/ /at/). Such choice on the part of teachers bodes well in light of the ongoing refinement of the self-teaching hypothesis. While it is appealing to know that words can be identified if they have been directly taught as whole word units, or even identified on the basis of context and the utilization of sound-symbol knowledge (albeit imperfect), the ability to independently decode novel strings through phonological recoding, such that rich orthographic representations can be formed, stored, and used, is perhaps the most valuable skill for learning orthographic representations of words (Share, 2008).

We began with a review of the research demonstrating that automatic word recognition is necessary for successful reading comprehension. We conclude with the argument that although much of what a reader ultimately has to do is *read*, there are significant advantages in encouraging a student to develop a proclivity toward phonologically recoding novel words (sounding them out on the path to automatic word recognition). Furthermore, the assistance of trained teachers who understand the intricacies of language and reading development, and instruct with attention to the complexities of the languages their students hear, speak, and write, is priceless.

NOTE

1. Based on a dual-route framework of reading, phonological dyslexia involves a core deficit in processing the phonological rules that relate graphemes to phonemes, whereas surface dyslexia involves difficulty with the visual-orthographic component of, or direct access during, word recognition (Castles & Coltheart, 1993). That is, those with phonological dyslexia have more trouble decoding pseudowords (which follow regular phoneme-grapheme rules) than irregular words (which do not follow regular phoneme-grapheme rules), whereas those with surface dyslexia exhibit the opposite pattern. Most with developmental dyslexia have difficulty in both areas, with greater proficiency likely affected by print exposure. Moreover, these different profiles may just be due to differences in severity of disability, and surface dyslexia may simply be an unstable subtype with a transient delay in reading development, whereby phonological deficits tend to be evident for all with developmental dyslexia and maintained long-term (Stanovich, 2000). (For a review see Fletcher, Lyon, Fuchs, & Barnes, 2006.) The double deficit hypothesis of dyslexia (Wolf & Bowers, 1999) posits that deficits in both phonological and naming-speed (i.e., phonological retrieval) are two separable sources of reading impairment, with greater reading difficulties present in children with both deficits as compared to children with one or neither deficit.

REFERENCES

Adams, M. (1990). *Beginning to read: Thinking and learning about print.* Cambridge, MA: Massachusetts Institute of Technology.

Adolf, S. M., Catts, H. W., & Little, T. (2006). Should the simple view of reading include a fluency component? *Reading and Writing, 19,* 933–958.

Anthony, J. L., & Francis, D. J. (2005). Development of phonological awareness. *Current Directions in Psychological Science, 14,* 255–259.

August, D., & Vockley, M. (2002). *From Spanish to English: Reading and writing for English language learn-*

ers, kindergarten through third grade. Washington DC: National Center on Education and the Economy and the University of Pittsburgh.

Badian, N. A. (2001). Phonological and orthographic processing: Their roles in reading prediction. *Annals of Dyslexia, 51,* 179–202.

Ball, E., & Blachman, B. (1991). Does phonemic awareness training in kindergarten make a difference in early word recognition and developmental spelling? *Reading Research Quarterly, 26,* 49–66.

Barker, T. A., Torgesen, J. K., & Wagner, R. K. (1992). The role of orthographic processing skills on five different reading tasks. *Reading Research Quarterly, 27,* 334–345.

Baron, J., & Treiman, R. (1980). Some problems in the study of differences in cognitive processes. *Memory and Cognition, 8,* 313–321.

Barron, R. W. (1986). Word recognition in early reading: A review of the direct and indirect access hypotheses. *Cognition Special Issue: The Onset of Literacy, 24,* 93–119.

Bear, D., Invernizzi, M., Templeton, S., & Johnston, F. (2004). *Words their way: Word study for phonics, vocabulary, and spelling instruction* (3rd ed.). Englewood Cliffs, NJ: Prentice Hall.

Berninger, V. W. (1994). Introduction to the varieties of orthographic knowledge I: Theoretical and developmental issues. In V. W. Berninger (Ed.), *The variety of orthographic knowledge I: Theoretical and developmental issues* (pp. 1–25). Dordrecht, Netherlands: Kluwer.

Berninger, V. W., Abbott, R. D., Abbot, S. P., Graham, S., & Richards, T. (2002). Writing and reading: Connections between language by hand and language by eye. *Journal of Learning Disabilities, 35,* 39–56.

Blachman, B. A. (2000). Phonological awareness. In M. L. Kamil, P. B. Mosenthal, P. D. Pearson, & R. Barr (Eds.), *Handbook of reading research, Vol. III* (pp. 483–502). Mahwah, NJ: Erlbaum.

Booth, J. R., Perfetti, C. A., & MacWhinney, B. (1999). Quick, automatic, and general activation of orthographic and phonological representations in young readers. *Developmental Psychology, 35,* 3–19.

Booth, J. R., Perfetti, C. A., MacWhinney, B., & Hunt, S. B. (2000). The association of rapid temporal perception with orthographic and phonological processing in children and adults with reading impairment. *Scientific Studies of Reading, 4,* 101–132.

Bosman, A., de Graaff, S., & Gijsel, M. (2006). Double Dutch: The Dutch spelling system and learning to spell in Dutch. In R. M. Joshi & P. G. Aaron (Eds.), *Handbook of orthography and literacy* (pp. 135–150). Mahwah, NJ: Erlbaum.

Bowers, P. G., Sunseth, K., & Golden, J. (1999). The route between rapid naming and reading progress. *Scientific Studies of Reading, 3,* 31–53.

Bowers, P. G., & Wolf, M. (1993). Theoretical links among naming speed, precise timing mechanisms and orthographic skill in dyslexia. *Reading and Writing: An Interdisciplinary Journal, 5,* 69–85.

Bowey, J. A., & Miller, R. (2007). Correlates of orthographic learning in third-grade children's silent reading. *Journal of Research in Reading, 30,* 115–128.

Bowey, J. A., & Muller, D. (2005). Phonological recoding and rapid orthographic learning in third-graders' silent reading: A critical test of the self-teaching hypothesis. *Journal of Experimental Child Psychology, 92,* 203–219.

Bradley, L., & Bryant, P. E. (1983). Categorizing sounds and learning to read: a causal connection. *Nature, 301,* 419–421.

Braten, I., Lie, A., Andreassen, R., & Olaussen, B. S. (1999). Leisure time reading and orthographic processes in word recognition among Norwegian third- and fourth-grade students. *Reading and Writing: An Interdisciplinary Journal, 11,* 65–88.

Breznitz, Z. (1997). The effect of accelerated reading rate on memory for text among dyslexic readers. *Journal of Educational Psychology, 89,* 287–299.

Bryant, P. E., & Impey, L. (1986). The similarities between normal readers and developmental and acquired dyslexics. *Cognition Special Issue: The Onset of Literacy, 24,* 121–137.

Burt, J. S. (2006). What is orthographic processing skill and how does it relate to word identification in reading? *Journal of Research in Reading, 29,* 400–417.

Bus, A., & van IJzendoorn, M. (1999). Phonological awareness and early reading: A meta-analysis of experimental training studies. *Journal of Educational Psychology, 91,* 403–414.

Byrne, B., & Fielding-Barnsley, R. (1993). Evaluation of a program to teach phonemic awareness to young children: A 1-year follow-up. *Journal of Educational Psychology, 85,* 104–111.

Byrne, B., & Fielding-Barnsley, R. (1995). Evaluation of a program to teach phonemic awareness to young children: A 2- and 3-year follow-up and a new preschool trial. *Journal of Educational Psychology, 87,* 488–503.

Cassar, M., & Treiman, R. (1997). The beginnings of orthographic knowledge: Children's knowledge of double letters in words. *Journal of Educational Psychology, 89,* 631–644.

Castles, A., & Coltheart, M. (1993). Varieties of developmental dyslexia. *Cognition, 47,* 149–180.

Castles, A., & Coltheart, M. (1996). Cognitive correlates of developmental surface Dyslexia: A single case study. *Cognitive Neuropsychology, 13,* 25–50.

Chall, J. S. (1983). Literacy: Trends and explanations. *Educational Researcher, 12,* 3–8.

Chateau, D., & Jared, D. (2000). Exposure to print and word recognition process. *Memory & Cognition, 28,* 143–153.

Chliounaki, K., & Bryant, P. (2007). How children learn about morphological spelling rules. *Child Development, 78,* 1360–1373.

Clay, M. (1985). *The early detection of reading difficulties* (3rd ed.). Auckland, New Zealand: Heinemann.

Coltheart, M. (1994). *Treating reading difficulties caused by brain damage.* Carlton South VIC, Australia: Australian Psychological Society.

Coltheart, M. (2005). Modeling reading: The dual-route approach. In M. J. Snowling & C. Hulme (Eds.), *The science of reading: A handbook* (pp. 6–23). Malden, MA: Blackwell.

Coltheart, M., Curtis, B., Atkins, P., & Haller, M. (1993). Models of reading aloud: Dual-route and parallel-distributed processing approaches. *Psychological Review, 100,* 589–608.

Coltheart, M., & Leahy, J. (1996). Assessment of lexical and nonlexical reading abilities in children: Some normative data. *Australian Journal of Psychology, 48,* 136–140.

Cummings, D. (1988). *American English spelling.* Baltimore, MD: Johns Hopkins Press.

Cunningham, A. E. (1990). Explicit vs. implicit instruction in phonemic awareness. *Journal of Experimental Child Psychology, 50,* 429–444.

Cunningham, A. E. (2006). Accounting for children's orthographic learning while reading text: Do children self-teach? *Journal of Experimental Child Psychology, 95,* 56–77.

Cunningham, A. E., Perry, K. E., & Stanovich, K. E. (2001). Converging evidence for the concept of orthographic processing. *Reading and Writing, 14,* 549–568.

Cunningham, A. E., Perry, K. E., Stanovich, K. E., & Share, D. L. (2002). Orthographic learning during reading: Examining the role of self-teaching. *Journal of Experimental Child Psychology, 82,* 185–199.

Cunningham, A. E., & Stanovich, K. E. (1990). Assessing print exposure and orthographic processing skill in children: A quick measure of reading experience. *Journal of Educational Psychology, 82,* 733–740.

Cunningham, A. E., & Stanovich, K. E. (1993). Children's literacy environments and early word recognition subskills. *Reading and Writing, 5,* 193–204.

Cunningham, A. E., & Stanovich, K. E. (1997). Early reading acquisition and its relation to reading experience and ability 10 years later. *Developmental Psychology, 33,* 934–945.

Cunningham, A. E., & Stanovich, K. E. (1998). The impact of print exposure on word recognition. In J. M. Metsala & L. C. Ehri (Eds.), *Word recognition in beginning literacy* (pp. 235–262). Mahwah, NJ: Erlbaum.

Cunningham, A. E., Stanovich, K. E., & Wilson, M. R. (1990). Cognitive variation in adult college students differing in reading ability. In T. H. Carr & B. A. Levy (Eds.), *Reading and its development: Component skills approaches* (pp. 129–159). New York: Academic Press.

Cunningham, P. M., & Cunningham, J. W. (1992). Making words: Enhancing the invented spelling-decoding connection. *Reading Teacher, 46,* 106–115.

Cutting, L. E., & Scarborough, H. S. (2006). Prediction of reading comprehension: Relative contributions of word recognition, language proficiency, and other cognitive skills can depend on how comprehension is measured. *Scientific Studies of Reading, 10,* 277–299.

de Jong, P. F., & Share, D. L. (2007). Orthographic learning during oral and silent reading. *Scientific Studies of Reading, 11,* 55–71.

Dunn, L. M., & Markwardt, F. C. (1970). *Peabody Individual Achievement Test.* Circle Pines, MN: American Guidance Service.

Ehri, L. C. (1980). The development of orthographic images. In U. Frith (Ed.), *Cognitive processes in spelling* (pp. 311–338). San Diego, CA: Academic.

Ehri, L. C. (1984). How orthography alters spoken language competencies in children learning to read and spell. In J. Downing & R. Valtin (Eds.), *Language awareness and learning to read* (pp. 119–147). New York: Springer-Verlag.

Ehri, L. C. (1991). Learning to read and spell words. In C. A. Perfetti (Ed.), *Learning to read: Basic research and its implications* (pp. 57–73). Hillsdale, NJ: Erlbaum.

Ehri, L. C. (1992). Reconceptualizing the development of sight word reading and its relationship to recoding. In P. Gough, L. C. Ehri, & R. Treiman (Eds.), *Reading acquisition* (pp. 107–143). Hillsdale, NJ: Erlbaum.

Ehri, L. C. (1995). Phases of development in learning to read words by sight. *Journal of Research in Reading, 18,* 116–125.

Ehri, L. C. (1997). Learning to read and spell are one and the same, almost. In C. A. Perfetti, L. Rieben, & M. Fayol (Eds.), *Learning to spell: Research, theory, and practice* (pp. 237–269). Mahwah, NJ: Erlbaum.

Ehri, L. C. (2005a). Development of sight word reading: Phases and findings. In M. J. Snowling & C. Hulme (Eds.), *The science of reading: A handbook* (pp. 135–154). Malden, MA: Blackwell.

Ehri, L. C. (2005b). Learning to read words: Theory, findings, and issues. *Scientific Studies of Reading, 9,* 167–188.

Ehri, L. C., & McCormick, S. (1998). Phases of word learning: Implications for instruction with delayed and disabled readers. *Reading and Writing Quarterly, 14,* 135–163.

Ehri, L. C., Nunes, S., Willows, D., Schuster, B., Yaghoub-Zadeh, Z., & Shanahan, T. (2001). Phonemic awareness instruction helps children learn to read: Evidence from the National Reading Panel's Meta-analysis. *Reading Research Quarterly, 36,* 250–287.

Ehri, L. C., & Saltmarsh, J. (1995). Beginning readers outperform older disabled readers in learning to read words by sight. *Reading and Writing, 7,* 295–326.

Fletcher, J. M., Lyon, G. R., Fuchs, L. S., & Barnes, M. A. (2006). *Learning disabilities: From identification to intervention.* New York: Guilford Press.

Foorman, B. R. (1994). Phonological and orthographic processing: Separate but equal? In V. W. Berninger (Ed.), *The variety of orthographic knowledge I: Theoretical and developmental issues* (pp. 321–358). Dordrecht, Netherlands: Kluwer.

Francis, H. (1982). *Learning to read: Literate behavior and orthographic knowledge.* London: George Allen & Unwin.

Francis, D. J., Shaywitz, S. E., Stuebing, K., Shaywitz, B. A., & Fletcher, J. M. (1996). Developmental lag versus deficit models of reading disability: A longitudinal, individual growth curve analysis. *Journal of Educational Psychology, 88,* 3–17.

Freebody, P., & Byrne, B. (1988). Word-reading strategies in elementary school children: Relations to comprehension, reading time, and phonemic awareness. *Reading Research Quarterly, 23,* 441–453.

Frith, U. (1985). Beneath the surface of developmental dyslexia. In K. Patterson, J. Marshall, & M. Coltheart (Eds.), *Surface dyslexia* (pp. 301–330). London: Erlbaum.

Frost, R. (2005). Orthographic systems and skilled word recognition processes in reading. In M. J. Snowling & C. Hulme (Eds.), *The science of reading: A handbook* (pp. 272–295). Malden, MA: Blackwell.

Geva, E., & Willows, D. (1994). Orthographic knowledge is orthographic knowledge is orthographic knowledge. In V. W. Berninger (Ed.), *The variety of orthographic knowledge I: Theoretical and developmental issues* (pp. 359–380). Dordrecht, Netherlands: Kluwer.

Goswami, U. (2000). Phonological and lexical processes. In M. Kamil, P. B. Mosenthal, P. D. Pearson, & R. Barr (Eds.), *The handbook of reading research: Volume III* (pp. 251–268). Mahwah, NJ: Erlbaum.

Goswami, U., Ziegler, J. C., Dalton, L., & Schneider, W. (2001). Pseudohomophone effects and phonological recoding procedures in reading development in English and German. *Journal of Memory and Language, 45,* 648–664.

Gough, P. B., & Hillinger, M. L. (1980). Learning to read: An unnatural act. *Bulletin of the Orton Society, 30,* 179–196.

Hagiliassis, N., Pratt, C., & Johnston, M. (2006). Orthographic and phonological processes in reading. *Reading and Writing, 19,* 235–263.

Hatcher, P. J., Hulme, C., & Ellis, A. W. (1994). Ameliorating early reading failure by integrating the teaching of reading and phonological skills: The phonological linkage hypothesis. *Child Development, 65,* 41–57.

Hiebert, E. H. (2005). State reform policies and the task textbooks pose for first-grade readers. *The Elementary School Journal, 105,* 245–266.

Jorm, A. F. (1979). The cognitive and neurological basis of developmental dyslexia: A theoretical framework and review. *Cognition, 7,* 19–33.

Jorm, A. F., & Share, D. L. (1983). Phonological recoding and reading acquisition. *Applied Psycholinguistics, 4,* 103–147.

Juel, C. (1988). Learning to read and write: A longitudinal study of 54 children from first through fourth grades. *Journal of Educational Psychology, 80,* 437–447.

Juel, C., Griffith, P. L., & Gough, P. B. (1986). Acquisition of literacy: A longitudinal study of children in first and second grade. *Journal of Educational Psychology, 78,* 243–255.

Juel, C., & Minden-Cupp, C. (2000). Learning to read words: Linguistic units and instructional strategies. *Reading Research Quarterly, 35,* 458–492.

Kjeldsen, A., Niemi, P., & Olofsson, Å. (2003). Training phonological awareness in kindergarten level children: Consistency is more important than quantity. *Learning and Instruction, 13,* 349–365.

Kyte, C. S., & Johnson, C. J. (2006). The role of phonological recoding in orthographic learning. *Journal of Experimental Child Psychology, 93,* 166–185.

LaBerge, D., & Samuels, S. J. (1974). Toward a theory of automatic information processing in reading. *Cognitive Psychology, 6,* 293–323.

Landi, N., Perfetti, C. A., Bolger, D. J., Dunlap, S., & Foorman, B. R. (2006). The role of discourse context in developing word form representations: A paradoxical relation between reading and learning. *Journal of Experimental Child Psychology, 94,* 114–133.

Lavric, A. (2007). ERP evidence of morphological analysis from orthography: A masked priming study. *Journal of Cognitive Neuroscience, 19,* 866–877.

Logan, G. D. (1997). Automaticity and reading: Perspectives from the instance theory of automatization. *Reading and Writing Quarterly, 13,* 123–146.

Lovett, M. W., Lacerenza, L., Borden, S. L., Frijters, J. C., Steinbach, K. A., & De Palma, M. (2000). Components of effective remediation for developmental reading disabilities: Combining phonological and strategy-based instruction to improve outcomes. *Journal of Educational Psychology, 92,* 263–283.

Lundberg, I., Frost, J., & Peterson, O. (1988). Effects of an extensive program for stimulating phonological awareness in preschool children. *Reading Research Quarterly, 23,* 263–284.

Manis, F. R., Custodio, R., & Szeszulski, P. A. (1993). Development of phonological and orthographic skill: A 2-year longitudinal study of dyslexic children. *Journal of Experimental Child Psychology, 56,* 64–86.

Manis, F. R., Szeszulski, P. A., Holt, L. K., & Graves, K. (1990). Variation in component word recognition and spelling skills among dyslexic children and normal readers. In T. H. Carr & B. A. Levy (Eds.), *Reading and its Development: Component Skills Approaches* (pp. 207–259). San Diego, CA: Academic Press.

Martens, V. E. G., & de Jong, P. F. (2006). The effect of visual word features on the acquisition of orthographic knowledge. *Journal of Experimental Child Psychology, 93,* 337–356.

McBride-Chang, C., Manis, F. R., Seidenberg, M. S., Custodio, R. G., & Doi, L. M. (1993). Print exposure as a predictor of word reading and reading comprehension in disabled and nondisabled readers. *Journal of Educational Psychology, 85,* 230–238.

McGill-Franzen, A., Ward, N., Goatley, V., & Machado, V. (2002). Teachers' use of new standards, frameworks, and assessments: Local cases of NYS elementary grade teachers. *Reading Research and Instruction, 41,* 127–148.

Metsala, J. L., & Walley, A. C. (1998). Spoken vocabulary growth and the segmental restructuring of lexical representations: Precursors to phonemic awareness and early reading ability. In J. L. Metsala & L. C. Ehri (Eds.), *Word recognition in beginning literacy* (pp. 89–120). Mahwah, NJ: Erlbaum.

Mitchell, D. (1982). *The process of reading: A cognitive analysis of reading and learning to read.* New York: Wiley.

Moats, L. C. (2000). *Speech to print: Language essentials for teachers.* Baltimore, MD: Paul H. Brookes.

Muter, V., Hulme, C., Snowling, M. J., & Stevenson, J. (2004). Phonemes, rimes, vocabulary, and grammatical skills as foundations of early reading development: Evidence from a longitudinal study. *Developmental Psychology, 40,* 665–681.

Nation, K., Angells, P., & Castles, A. (2007). Orthographic learning via self-teaching in children learning to read English: Effects of exposure, durability, and context. *Journal of Experimental Child Psychology, 96,* 71–84.

NICHD: National Institute of Child Health and Human Development, NIH, DHHS. (2000). *Report of the National Reading Panel: Teaching Children to Read.* Washington, DC: U.S. Government Printing Office.

Neves, D. M., & Anderson, J. R. (1981). Knowledge compilation: Mechanisms for the automatization of cognitive skills. In J. R. Anderson (Ed.), *Cognitive skills and their acquisition* (pp. 57–84). Hillsdale, NJ: Erlbaum.

Olson, R., Forsberg, H., Wise, B., & Rack, J. (1994). Measurement of word recognition, orthographic and phonological skills. In G. R. Reid (Ed.), *Frames of reference for the assessment of learning disabilities: New views on measurement issues* (pp. 243–268). Sydney, Australia: Paul H. Brookes.

Olson, R., Wise, B., Conners, F., Rack, J., & Fulker, D. (1989). Specific deficits in component reading and language skills: Genetic and environmental influences. *Journal of Learning Disabilities, 22,* 339–348.

Patterson, K., Marshall, J., & Coltheart, M. (1985). *Surface dyslexia.* London: Erlbaum.

Peréz Cañado, M. L. (2005). English and Spanish spelling: Are they really different? *The Reading Teacher, 58,* 522–530.

Pearson, P. D. Dole, J. A., Duffy, G. G., & Koehler, L. R. (1992). Developing expertise in reading comprehension. In A. Farstup & J. Samuels (Eds.), *What research has to say about reading instruction* (2nd ed., pp. 145–199). Newark, DE: International Reading Association.

Perfetti, C. A. (1985). *Reading ability.* New York: Oxford University Press.

Perfetti, C. A. (1992). The representation problem in reading acquisition. In P. B. Gough, L. C. Ehri, & R. Treiman (Eds.), *Reading acquisition* (pp. 145–174). Hillsdale, NJ: Erlbaum.

Perfetti, C. A. (1997). The psycholinguistics of spelling and reading. In C. A. Perfetti, L. Rieben, & M. Fayol (Eds.), *Learning to spell: Research, theory, and practice across languages* (pp. 21–38). Mahwah, NJ: Erlbaum.

Perfetti, C. A. (2007). Reading ability. *Scientific Studies of Reading, 11,* 357–383.

Perfetti, C. A., & Hart, L. (2001). The lexical quality hypothesis. In L. Vehoeven, C. Elbro, & P. Reitsma (Eds.), *Precursors of functional literacy* (pp. 189–214). Amsterdam: John Benjamins.

Plaut, D. C. (2005). Connectionist approaches to reading. In M. J. Snowling & C. Hulme (Eds.), *The science of reading: A handbook* (pp. 24–38). Malden, MA: Blackwell.

Ralph, M. A. L., & Patterson, K. (2005). Acquired disorders of reading. In M. J. Snowling & C. Hulme (Eds.), *The science of reading: A handbook* (pp. 413–430). Malden, MA: Blackwell.

Rayner, K., Foorman, B. R., Perfetti, C. A., Pesetsky, D., & Seidenberg, M. S. (2001). How psychological science informs the teaching of reading. *Psychological Science in the Public Interest, 2,* 31–74.

Reitsma, P. (1983). Printed word learning in beginning readers. *Journal of Experimental Child Psychology, 36,* 321–339.

Rosenthal, J., & Ehri, L. C. (2008). The mnemonic value of orthography for vocabulary learning. *Journal of Educational Psychology, 100,* 175–191.

Rutter, M. (1978). Prevalence and types of dyslexia. In A. Benton & D. Pearl (Eds.), *Dyslexia: An appraisal of current knowledge* (pp. 5–28). New York: Oxford University Press.

Samuels, J. (2006). Toward a model of reading fluency. In A. Farstrup & S. J. Samuels (Eds.), *What research has to say about fluency instruction* (pp. 24–46). Newark, DE: International Reading Association.

Scarborough, H. S., Ehri, L. C., Olson, R. K., & Fowler, A. E. (1998). The fate of phonemic awareness beyond the elementary school years. *Scientific Studies of Reading, 2,* 115–142.

Schwanenflugel, P. J., Meisinger, E. B., Wisenbaker, J. M., Kuhn, M. R., Strauss, G. P., & Morris, R. D. (2006). Becoming a fluent and automatic reader in the early elementary school years. *Reading Research Quarterly, 41,* 496–522.

Seidenberg, M. S. (2005). Connectionist models of word reading. *Psychological Science in the Public Interest, 14,* 238–242.

Seidenberg, M. S., & McClelland, J. L. (1989). A distributed, developmental model of word recognition. *Psychological Review, 96,* 523–568.

Seymour, P. H. K. (2005). Early reading development in European orthographies. In M. J. Snowling & C. Hulme (Eds.), *The science of reading: A handbook* (pp. 296–315). Malden, MA: Blackwell.

Shahar-Yames, D., & Share, D. L. (2008). Spelling as a self-teaching mechanism in orthographic learning. *Journal of Research in Reading, 31*, 22–39.

Shanahan, T. (1984). Nature of the reading-writing relation: An exploratory multivariate analysis. *Journal of Educational Psychology, 76*, 466–477.

Shanahan, T. (2006). *Relations among oral language, reading, and writing development.* New York: Guilford Press.

Shanahan, T., & Lomax, R. G. (1986). An analysis and comparison of theoretical models of reading-writing relationships. *Journal of Educational Psychology, 78*, 116–123.

Shanahan, T., & Lomax, R. G. (1988). The reading-writing relationship: Seven instructional principles. *Reading Teacher, 41*, 636–647.

Share, D. L. (2008). Orthographic learning, phonological recoding, and self-teaching. In R. V. Kail (Ed.) *Advances in child behavior and development, Vol. 36* (pp. 31–82). San Diego, CA: Elsevier Academic Press.

Share, D. L. (1995). Phonological recoding and self-teaching: Sine qua non of reading acquisition. *Cognition, 55*, 151–218.

Share, D. L. (1999). Phonological recoding and orthographic learning: A direct test of the self-teaching hypothesis. *Journal of Experimental Child Psychology, 72*, 95–129.

Share, D. L. (2004). Orthographic learning at a glance: On the time course and developmental onset of self-teaching. *Journal of Experimental Child Psychology, 87*, 267–298.

Share, D. L., & Shalev, C. (2004). Self-teaching in normal and disabled readers. *Reading and Writing, 17*, 769–800.

Siegel, L. S., Share, D., & Geva, E. (1995). Evidence for superior orthographic skills in dyslexics. *Psychological Science, 6*, 250–254.

Snow, C. E., Burns, M. S., & Griffin, P. (Eds.). (1998). *Preventing reading difficulties in young children.* Washington, DC: National Academy Press.

Snowling, M. J., & Hulme, C. (2005). Learning to read with a language impairment. In M. J. Snowling & C. Hulme (Eds.), *The science of reading: A handbook* (pp. 397–412). Malden, MA: Blackwell.

Sprenger-Charolles, L., Siegel, L. S., Béchennec, D., & Serniclaes, W. (2003). Development of phonological and orthographic processing in reading aloud, in silent reading, and in spelling: A four-year longitudinal study. *Journal of Experimental Child Psychology, 84*, 194–217.

Sprenger-Charolles, L., Siegel, L. S., & Bonnet, P. (1998). Reading and spelling acquisition in French: The role of phonological mediation and orthographic factors. *Journal of Experimental Child Psychology, 68*, 134–165.

Stanovich, K. E. (1982a). Individual differences in the cognitive processes of reading: 1. Word decoding. *Journal of Learning Disabilities, 15*, 485–493.

Stanovich, K. E. (1982b). Individual differences in the cognitive processes of reading: 2. Text-level processes. *Journal of Learning Disabilities, 15*, 549–554.

Stanovich, K. E. (1982c). Word recognition skill and reading ability. In M. Singer (Ed.), *Competent reader, disabled reader: Research and application* (pp. 81–102). Hillsdale, NJ: Erlbaum.

Stanovich, K. E. (1986). Matthew effects in reading: some consequences of individual differences in the acquisition of literacy. *Reading Research Quarterly, 21*, 360–406.

Stanovich, K. E. (1992). Speculation on the causes and consequences in individual differences in early reading acquisition. In P. Gough, L. Ehri, & R. Treiman (Eds.), *Reading acquisition* (pp. 307–342). Hillsdale, NJ: Erlbaum.

Stanovich, K. E. (2000). *Progress in understanding reading: Scientific foundations and new frontiers.* New York: Guilford Press.

Stanovich, K. E., Cunningham, A. E., & Cramer, B. (1984). Assessing phonological awareness in kindergarten children: Issues of task and comparability. *Journal of Experimental Psychology, 38*, 175–190.

Stanovich, K. E., Cunningham, A. E., & West, R. F. (1981). A longitudinal study in the development of automatic recognition skills in first graders. *Journal of Reading Behavior, 13*, 57–74.

Stanovich, K. E., & Siegel, L. S. (1994). Phenotypic performance profile of children with reading disabilities: A regression-based test of the phonological-core variable-difference model. *Journal of Educational Psychology, 86*, 24–53.

Stanovich, K. E., & West, R. F. (1989). Exposure to print and orthographic processing. *Reading Research Quarterly, 24,* 402–433.

Stevenson, H. W., & Newman, R. S. (1986). Long-term prediction of achievement and attitudes in mathematics and reading. *Child Development, 57,* 646–659.

Stroop, J. R. (1935). Studies of interference in serial verbal reactions. *Journal of Experimental Psychology, 18,* 643–662.

Tabors, P. O., & Snow, C. E. (2002). Young bilingual children and early literacy development. In S. Neuman & D. K. Dickinson (Eds.), *Handbook of early literacy research* (pp. 159–178). New York: Guilford Press.

Torgesen, J. K. (2005). *Recent discoveries on remedial interventions for children with dyslexia.* Malden, MA: Blackwell.

Torgesen, J. K., Alexander, A. W., Wagner, R. K., Rashotte, C. A., Voeller, K. K. S., & Conway, T. (2001). Intensive remedial instruction for children with severe reading disabilities: Immediate and long-term outcomes from two instructional approaches. *Journal of Learning Disabilities, 34,* 33–58.

Torgesen, J. K., & Hudson, R. F. (2006). Reading fluency: Critical issues for struggling readers. In S. J. Samuels & A. E. Farstrup (Eds.), *What research has to say about fluency instruction* (pp. 130–158). Newark, DE: International Reading Association.

Torgesen, J. K., Wagner, R. K., Rashotte, C. A., Burgess, S., & Hecht, S. (1997). Contributions of phonological awareness and rapid automatic naming ability to the growth of word-reading skills in second- to fifth-grade children. *Scientific Studies of Reading, 1,* 161–185.

Torrance, M., & Galbraith, D. (2006). The processing demands of writing. In C. A. MacArthur, S. Graham, & J. Fitzgerald (Eds.), *Handbook of writing research* (67–80). New York: Guilford Press.

Treiman, R. (1984). Individual differences among children in spelling and reading styles. *Journal of Experimental Child Psychology, 37,* 463–477.

Treiman, R. (1993). *Beginning to spell.* New York, NY: Oxford University Press.

Tunmer, W. E., & Nesdale, A. R. (1985). Phonemic segmentation skill and beginning reading. *Journal of Educational Psychology, 77,* 417–427.

Vellutino, F. R. (1979). *Dyslexia: Theory and research.* Cambridge, MA: MIT Press.

Vellutino, F. R., & Fletcher, J. M. (2005). Developmental dyslexia. In M. J. Snowling & C. Hulme (Eds.), *The science of reading: A handbook* (pp. 362–378). Malden, MA: Blackwell.

Vellutino, F. R., & Scanlon, D. M. (1987). Phonological coding, phonological awareness, and reading ability: Evidence from a longitudinal and experimental study. *Merrill-Palmer Quarterly, 33,* 321–363.

Vellutino, F. R., Scanlon, D. M., & Tanzman, M. S. (1994). *Components of reading ability: Issues and problems in operationalizing word identification, phonological coding, and orthographic coding.* Baltimore, MD: Paul H. Brookes.

Vellutino, F. R., Tunmer, W. E., Jaccard, J. J., & Chen, R. (2007). Components of reading ability: Multivariate evidence for a convergent skills model of reading development. *Scientific Studies of Reading, 11,* 3–32.

Wagner, R. K. (1988). Causal relations between the development of phonological processing abilities and the acquisition of reading skills: A meta-analysis. *Merrill-Palmer Quarterly, 34,* 261–279.

Wagner, R. K., & Barker, T. A. (1994). The development of orthographic processing ability. In V. W. Berninger (Ed.), *The variety of orthographic knowledge I: Theoretical and developmental issues* (pp. 243–276). Dordrecht, Netherlands: Kluwer.

Wagner, R. K., & Torgesen, J. K., (1987). The nature of phonological processing and its causal role in the acquisition of reading skills. *Psychological Bulletin, 101,* 192–212.

Wesseling, R., & Reitsma, P. (2000). The transient role of explicit phonological recoding for reading acquisition. *Reading and Writing, 13,* 313–336.

Wimmer, H. (1993). Characteristics of developmental dyslexia in a regular writing system. *Applied Psycholinguistics, 14,* 1–33.

Wise, J. C., Sevcik, R. A., Morris, R. D., Lovett, M. W., & Wolf, M. (2007). The relationship among receptive and expressive vocabulary, listening comprehension, pre-reading skills, word identification skills, and reading comprehension by children with reading disabilities. *Journal of Speech, Language, and Hearing Research, 50,* 1093–1109.

Wolf, M., Bally, H., & Morris, R. (1986). Automaticity, retrieval processes, and reading: A longitudinal study in average and impaired readers. *Child Development, 57,* 988–1000.

Wolf, M., Bowers, P. G., & Biddle, K. (2000). Naming-speed processes, timing, and reading: A conceptual review. *Journal of Learning Disabilities, 33,* 387–407.

Ziegler, J. C., Perry, C., Ma-Wyatt, A., Ladner, D., & Schulte-Körne, G. (2003). Developmental dyslexia in different languages: Language-specific or universal? *Journal of Experimental Child Psychology, 86,* 169–193.

13   Reading Fluency

Timothy V. Rasinski
Kent State University

D. Ray Reutzel
Utah State University

David Chard
Southern Methodist University

Sylvia Linan-Thompson
University of Texas at Austin

BACKGROUND: DEFINING READING FLUENCY

Fluency as a key construct in reading research appeared very early in the literature about reading development. As early as 1886, Cattell described the importance to reading of learners recognizing words nearly automatically. Shortly thereafter, Huey (1968) noted that automaticity with the details of print allowed a reader to focus attention on the content of what is read. In the 1970s, LaBerge and Samuels (1974) posited a theory of automaticity that suggested that mastery of the sublexical components of reading (i.e., letter-sound correspondences, blending, word recognition) contributed to fluency. More recently, the focus has shifted to fluency as a critical stage that learners pass through in their attainment of reading proficiency (Chall, 1983; Ehri, 2005; Ehri & Wilce, 1983; Samuels, 2002). The National Reading Panel (2000) again emphasized reading fluency noting that neglect of fluency in classroom instruction belied the fact that it is a "critical component of skilled reading" (p. 32). Though attention paid to the topic of reading fluency has increased over the past few years, consensus has not yet been achieved on how to define it.

Breznitz (2006) noted that existing definitions of reading fluency can be categorized in three distinct ways: (a) as a measurable consequence of learning pre-skills to reading, (b) as a linguistic and developmental outcome, and (c) as a systemic processing outcome. These categories are clearly interrelated and their distinctions reflect specific researchers' theoretical or conceptual perspectives on the role of fluency in reading development. From a measurement perspective, reading fluency is typically defined as including reading rate and accuracy (Torgesen, Rashotte, & Alexander, 2001). This perspective focuses on a definition of fluency as the quality of oral reading that allows for its objective measurement as correct words read per unit of time (e.g., minutes) and reflects the use of fluency as a dependent variable in research studies and program evaluations.

Expanded definitions of fluency frequently go beyond rate and accuracy to include an aspect of understanding the text. For example, Harris and Hodges (1985) emphasized fluency's relationship to comprehension by defining it as "freedom from word identification problems that might hinder comprehension" (p. 85). Others have offered similar definitions clearly linking word and text level reading with meaning (Chard, Pikulski, & McDonagh, 2006; Hudson, Mercer, & Lane, 2000; Schreiber, 1980). In most cases, these definitions depend largely on theoretical models that conceive of fluency as a synthesis of linguistic and cognitive skills that develop with time and instruction. Thus, fluent readers are able to simultaneously automatically process text and simultaneously understand and reflect the syntactic and semantic features of the text by reading with prosody (LaBerge & Samuels, 1974; Perfetti, 1977, 1985).

A final approach to defining fluency combines the development of linguistic and cognitive systems combined with biological systems associated with executive functioning for coordinating the other systems (Berninger, 2001). In other words, it attempts to encompass how children's language and thinking develop within the sensory and neurological systems. This systemic perspective suggests that because the various linguistic and cognitive systems function at different speeds during word reading (i.e., some students are able to read words faster than others), each student's processing speed and reading fluency is limited by the brain's ability to coordinate language and cognition (Breznitz, 2003, 2006). Slower readers have a slower speed of processing that could be attributed to anyone of the contributing systems and results in a reader struggling to understand the author's message.

For the purposes of this chapter, we define fluency as a characteristic of reading that occurs when readers' cognitive and linguistic systems are developed to the extent that they can read with sufficient accuracy and rate to allow for understanding the texts and reflecting its prosodic features. We have chosen to characterize fluent reading as having two specific features: automaticity and prosody. We feel these features reflect both a historic and contemporary knowledge base on fluency and fluency instruction. They also help us to understand the relationship between reading fluency and readers' comprehension of texts. The next sections of this chapter describe in greater detail the state of the current knowledge base for each of these features.

READING FLUENCY: AN HISTORICAL PERSPECTIVE

Reading fluency has its roots in oral reading. Oral reading held a dominant place in early American reading, in and out of the classroom. According to reading historians (Hyatt, 1943; Smith, 1965), in many early American homes there often was only one person who could read. Thus, if reading was to occur, someone had to read aloud. Because of its prominence in people's daily lives for entertainment and sharing information, oral reading was considered a primary focus for classroom instruction (Hyatt, 1943). Authors of some of the earliest textbooks for reading, for example, identified oral reading as the mode of choice for instruction (McGuffey, 1879; Newell, 1880).

The development of "eloquent oral reading" became the focus of reading instruction in this period (Smith, 1965). Authors of reading texts of the time identified the goal of reading instruction in the following way:

> A just delivery consists in a distinct articulation of words pronounced in proper tones, suitably varied to the sense, and the emotions of the mind; with due attention to accent, to emphasis, in its several gradations; to rests or pauses of the voice, in proper places... (Lyman Cobb, cited in Smith, 1965)

Schools of the time employed a form of oral recitation that focused on elocution (Hoffman & Segel, 1983; Hoffman, 1987) over comprehension. The recitation lesson usually involved the teacher orally reading a text followed by the students orally practicing the passage on their own. Then, after a sufficient period of practice, the students orally read or recited the passage for the teacher and students. Students' readings were judged by the teacher on the quality of their oral reading and their recall of what they had read. Toward the end of the 19th century, oral reading had become such an ingrained and perceived necessary part of American education that philosopher William James (1892, as cited in Hoffman & Segel, 1983) indicated that the teacher's success in teaching reading was based upon the quality of students' oral reading.

Oral Reading in Decline

Near the end of the 19th century, the acceptance of oral reading as the primary mode of instruction in reading began to wane. As psychologists began to learn more about the inner workings of the mind, there began an era in which the development of educational methods were informed by more sophisticated understandings of the mental processes employed by readers as they read. Education scholars in Europe and the United States began to question the role of oral reading in the classroom (Hyatt, 1943). They argued that oral reading gave priority to elocution over comprehension and was a major cause of problems in reading instruction of the time (Hyatt, 1943; Parker, 1884). Horace Mann (1891) claimed that over 90% of students in reading classes do not understand what they read.

Moreover, as reading material became more easily accessible, the need for oral reading for imparting information to others declined. Individual silent reading became a more common feature of family and community life. Thus, it was argued, schools should aim their efforts to teaching and using silent reading, which was emerging as the more ubiquitous form of reading in society in the late 19th century.

Science and scientific inquiry began to have an impact on reading education around the turn of the century. Reading scholars, such as Huey (1968), noted that oral reading had become a task that was found only in schools. In everyday life, silent reading predominated. The focus on abstracting meaning from text should be the focus of reading instruction, and silent reading should be the primary instructional mode for teaching reading comprehension (Parker, 1884; Rasinski, 2003).

Reading scholars of the time noted that the number of books, magazines, newspapers, and other materials available for adults and children began to expand at a rapid pace (Hyatt, 1943). In order for students and teachers to take advantage of and cover this expanding body of print, silent reading, which was inherently more efficient than oral reading, needed to be emphasized.

The standardized testing movement, which began in the early 20th century, also supported the shift away from oral reading and toward silent reading. Group-administered reading achievement tests in a silent reading format became more common. William S. Gray, a highly influential scholar in reading, used these tests in a series of school evaluation studies in the early 1900s that demonstrated that students who practiced reading silently performed best on the assessments (Hoffman, 1991). Fuchs, Fuchs, Hosp, and Jenkins (2001) have noted the ongoing decline of reading tests that incorporated a fluency component, both oral and silent, from the 1920s through the 1990s.

Thus, during this period silent reading began to supplant oral reading as the primary mode of reading during reading instruction (e.g., Buswell & Wheeler, 1923). Silent reading focused readers' attention on the apprehension of meaning, the goal of reading, while instruction in oral reading tended to focus attention on word perfect, accurate recitation of the text. Silent reading was also felt to maximize student engagement in reading and text coverage. Silent reading instruction aimed at student understanding of the text with the first and only reading, thus increasing the opportunity to read many texts; oral reading instruction aimed at expressiveness in reading through intensive practice of a limited number of texts (Hoffman & Segel, 1983). Volume of reading was necessarily limited as one student read orally at a time. Silent reading, on the other hand, could easily be done by multiple students simultaneously.

By the 1920s, silent reading was well entrenched in American schools. According to Smith (1965), schools seemed to become obsessed with the notion of silent reading for improving comprehension and reading speed. Silent reading became such a focus of instruction that a program that emphasized silent reading exclusively was adopted in some of the Chicago schools in the late 1930s through the early 1940s. To support the approach known as the "non-oral" method of reading instruction, experts claimed that proficient reading occurs when meaning is gained directly from printed symbols, involving only the eyes and the central nervous system, without any inner speech (McDade, 1937, 1944; Rohrer, 1943). In the "non-oral" method silent reading that involved internal sounding of words was discouraged. Although severely criticized (Rohrer, 1943) and eventually abandoned, the emergence of the "non-oral" method demonstrates the extent to which oral reading was viewed as unnecessary and, in some cases, detrimental to success in learning to read.

Although silent reading has continued to maintain a dominant position in classroom instruction, scholars and teachers have recognized that oral reading does play an important role in reading instruction. In her 1966 essay identifying significant reading skills for the primary grades, Durkin states emphatically that "… silent reading is what we are trying to teach at all stages of reading development and at all grade levels. Such an emphasis… should not suggest, of course, that oral reading be eliminated from reading programs" (p. 33).

Nevertheless, Rasinski and Zutell (Rasinski, 1989; Rasinski & Zutell, 1996; Zutell & Rasinski, 1991) report that by the later part of the 20th century, even textbooks for training teachers in reading instruction provided little, if any, in-depth focus on defining, teaching, or assessing oral reading fluency. This historical trend in reading instruction and assessment in the United States demonstrates a gradual but sustained movement away from oral reading fluency instruction.

Round-Robin Reading

The demise of oral reading as a goal for reading instruction in the 20th century and the arguments for an emphasis on comprehension and silent reading as the best tools to lead students to high levels of success, however, did not lead to the disappearance of oral reading in classrooms. Research into classroom instructional practices (e.g., Austin & Morrison, 1963) revealed that oral reading continued as a mainstay of classroom practice. Despite criticisms, round-robin reading (unrehearsed oral reading, with turn-taking) persisted throughout the latter half of the 20th century as a ubiquitous form of reading practice. Oral reading was used primarily as a method of checking students' word recognition after silent reading (Eldredge, Reutzel, & Hollingsworth, 1996). This change in the use of oral reading from reading for fluent expression to reading for checking word recognition became the genesis of round-robin reading. Integrated into the basal reading programs that assumed the preeminent position in elementary reading instruction from the early 1950s to the present (Hoffman, 1987; Hoffman & Segel, 1983), round-robin reading has become one of the most ubiquitous forms of reading in American classrooms. Despite its pervasive use (Hoffman, 1987; Howlett & Weintraub, 1979), round-robin reading has never been widely advocated nor endorsed by scholars of reading (Beach, 1993).

More Recent Developments in Fluency

Over the past three decades significant advances in our understanding of reading have caused reading scholars to look more closely at reading fluency. In their seminal volume on reading, Gibson and Levin (1975) make mention of oral reading, expressive reading, and reading rate, but fail to elucidate a strong connection between these aspects of reading and overall proficiency in reading. Indeed, they state that, "Reading aloud in the early grades probably has little justification other than to give the teacher some insight into the child's progress" (Gibson & Levin, 1975, p. 105).

One of the more important milestones in contemporary conceptions of reading fluency came with the publication of LaBerge and Samuels's (1974) theory of automatic information processing in reading. This was perhaps the first modern theoretical basis offered for the importance of fluency, and its operation. LaBerge and Samuels argued that the surface-level processing of words in reading (visual perception, sounding, phrasing words together, etc.) should ideally be done at an automatic level, a level that requires minimal attention or cognitive capacity. In doing so, readers are able to reserve their finite cognitive resources for the more important task in reading—comprehension. LaBerge and Samuels hypothesized that poor comprehension for many readers could be explained by their having to invest too much of their cognitive resources in the surface-level aspects of reading—slow, laborious, conscious-filled decoding of words. This diversion of resources depleted or exhausted what could be invested in comprehension.

Stanovich (1980) later refined this theory into what he termed the "interactive compensatory" explanation of reading fluency. Stanovich reasoned that a major difference between good and poor readers was in the way they processed text while reading. Poor readers are less able than good readers to employ automatic, attention-free bottom-up processes in decoding while reading. Rather, they compensate for their difficulty in using the more efficient automatic word-decoding processes by employing more context-bound strategies that require significant amounts of cognitive resources for word decoding. In doing so, they have fewer cognitive resources available for comprehension—a task in reading that requires top-down, contextually dependent, and conscious processing of the text. Such readers are characterized by their slow, laborious, monotone, and unenthusiastic oral reading. Good readers, on the other hand, are quite able to use automatic, attention-free, bottom-up processes for word decoding and thus reserve their limited top-down, contextually dependent processes for comprehending what they read. These readers are characterized by their accurate and nearly effortless word reading with appropriate phrasing and meaningful expression

Samuels (1979) put the theory of automatic information processing in reading to a test. He hypothesized that automaticity for readers, as for athletes and musicians, is developed through repeated practice. Yet, he observed that in classrooms of the day teachers tended to cover the reading curriculum at a pace that was too fast for students to develop conscious mastery (accuracy) or automaticity of critical reading skills.

Thus, he asked students to read short passages of approximately 250 words in length repeatedly until they achieved a reading speed of 95 words per minute. Samuels found that this method of repeated readings lead to improvements in passage reading across a variety of dimensions, including word decoding accuracy, reading speed, and expression. Moreover, he found that when students moved on to new texts their initial readings of the new passages were better than their initial readings of the earlier passages, and the number of repetitions required to achieve the criterion reading rate diminished. Samuels explained his findings in terms of automatic information processing in reading. He argued that through their practiced or repeated readings of texts, readers were developing automaticity in word decoding and word processing. Significantly, this automaticity was generalized to new passages that the students had not previously read.

Carol Chomsky (1976) tested a similar method for improving reading—a method that involved repeated reading but also included an adaptation of an approach first developed by Heckelman (1969) called the Neurological Impress Method (Hollingsworth, 1978; Hoskisson, 1975a, 1975b). Today, this approach is referred to as assisted reading or reading while listening. Chomsky asked struggling readers to repeatedly read texts while simultaneously listening to audio taped versions of the same texts read fluently until they thought they could read the texts fluently. Like Samuels, Chomsky reported remarkably positive results for students on texts practiced, on new texts never before read, and in students' attitude toward and confidence in their reading.

Schreiber (1980, 1991; Schreiber & Read, 1980) offered an alternative explanation for the positive results from repeated readings. He argued that through practice students developed a greater awareness of the prosodic features of oral reading and speech. That is, through repeated readings they were learning to embed in their reading the expressive and intonational features of oral speech that help to mark phrase boundaries within and between sentences and convey meaning. Dysfluent readers tend to read in a slow, word-by-word manner that does not lend itself well to prosodic and syntactically appropriate phrased reading that carries meaning. Through repeated readings, even dysfluent readers are more able to capture the prosodic and syntactic essence of the text, thus improving the surface-level processing of the passage as well as text comprehension.

Both conceptualizations of reading fluency, automatic processing of the surface-level features of text and the ability to attend to the prosodic and syntactic features of text while reading, appear compelling and are considered central elements of contemporary conceptions of reading fluency (Kuhn & Stahl, 2000).

Relying on this groundbreaking work of the 1970s and early 1980s, Allington (1983) argued that reading fluency appears to be an important aspect of the reading process that holds great promise for improving the reading performance of many struggling readers. Equally important, Allington also noted that the reading community had largely ignored fluency.

Allington's article (1983) began a slow but increasing awareness of the contribution of reading fluency to proficient reading. Subsequent research on oral reading has pointed to an association between oral reading and reading achievement (e.g., Stallings, 1980; Wilkinson, Wardrop, & Anderson, 1988). Pinnell et al. (1995), however, found that simply the amount and frequency of reading aloud in the classroom was not associated with reading improvement. The authors suggested that it is not the sheer quantity of oral reading that takes place in the classroom but the type of oral reading that makes the difference in student reading achievement – instruction in oral reading that is aimed at improving reading fluency. In a study of students referred for reading intervention services, Rasinski and Padak (1998) found that referred students exhibited larger discrepancies from normal achievement levels on measures of fluency than on measures of word recognition accuracy or comprehension.

Finally, the publication of the report of the National Reading Panel (2000), as well as other scholarly publications of and reviews of reading fluency (e.g. Kuhn, Schwanenflugel, & Meisinger, 2010; Rasinski & Hoffman, 2003; Samuels & Farstrup, 2006), has returned reading fluency (and oral reading) to a preeminent position in the reading curriculum. The panel indicated that sufficient empirical evidence exists for identifying fluency as critical to students' success in learning to read. Thus, policy initiatives at the beginning of the 21st century aimed at improving reading instruction in the United States have included reading fluency as a key component.

RESEARCH INTO THE AUTOMATICITY COMPONENT OF FLUENCY

Automaticity of word identification is a defining feature of reading fluency. To understand automaticity's role in reading, it is instructive to review prominent theories of automaticity. In their seminal article on automaticity, LaBerge and Samuels (1974) argued that human beings were limited in their capacity to attend to more than one cognitive demand at a time unless the individual alternates between activities (e.g., reading and watching a documentary) or the person learns how to do one of the activities automatically. The limited capacity argument was subsequently supported by others who suggested that in addition to limited attention, readers who were not decoding automatically faced limited memory capacity for more complex linguistic requirements in comprehension (Perfetti & Hogaboam, 1975).

The theory of automaticity proposed by LaBerge and Samuels (1974) was later applied to information processing models that suggest that some activities (e.g., making inferences) require conscious control, active attention and cognitive capacity, while other activities can become automatic (e.g., word recognition) requiring little active attention and cognitive capacity and are difficult to modify once learned (Perfetti & Hogaboam, 1975; Posner & Snyder, 1975). Moreover, these information processing models lent support to the notion that those activities that could be governed by automatic processes did so through practice under consistent conditions leading to increased efficiency (Mackay, 1982; Perfetti, 1985; Schiffrin & Schneider, 1977). With increased experience, connections that result from the automatic processes grow stronger leading to increased automaticity (Anderson, 1992; Cohen, Dunbar, & McLelland, 1990).

Automaticity in Reading

Perfetti's (1985) "verbal efficiency theory" highlights the importance of lower level lexical skills in reading and explains the impact of processing information at multiple levels of reading comprehension. He suggests that lower level processes (e.g., word identification) must reach a minimum performance level before higher level processes can be performed simultaneously during reading. When lower level processes are performed inefficiently, higher order processes attempt to compensate. Perfetti's theory assumes that resource demands can be reduced through learning and practice and efficiency may be enhanced through careful allocation of resources.

Stanovich (1990) also contributed to the contemporary focus on automaticity. Where limited capacity models of automaticity focus on the cognitive demands of each particular task, Stanovich takes a modularity approach emphasizing the efficiency of processing. In Stanovich's view, efficient processing allows a reader to create high quality word representations in memory. A reader's level of automaticity is then dependent on the quality of these representations. Readers who have a rich store of high quality word representations are able to read more fluently, independent of context (Ehri, 2005; Nicholson, 1991; Stanovich, 1986). Less skilled readers, those who do not have a rich store of word representations, rely more on context to predict unfamiliar words (Nicholson & Tan, 1999).

Logan (1988) developed a related memory-based theory of fluency entitled the "instance theory of automatization." Logan's theory is based on three conceptual assumptions: (a) obligatory encoding, (b) obligatory retrieval, and (c) instance representation (Logan, 1997). Obligatory encoding involves focusing attention on a stimulus (e.g., a word) and storing details of that stimulus in memory. Obligatory retrieval suggests that attending to a stimulus is sufficient to retrieve previous exposures or similar stimuli from memory. Instance representation refers to the coding and storage of each memory trace of experiences with a stimulus in memory. Key to this theory is the notion that each memory trace is coded and stored separately regardless of prior experience with the stimulus.

Logan (1988) contends that information recall is automatic when it relies on retrieval of stored instances from memory, theoretical memory traces laid down in the brain each time a task is executed. Logan (1997) later suggested that automaticity develops as a consequence of the "power law" which states that the reaction time to a stimulus decreases as a result of practice and repetition. The level of automaticity developed is dependent on the amount of practice, the level of consistency in the task environment, and the number of relevant instances of the task recorded in memory. As the reader's knowledge base expands and becomes accurate, performance becomes reliant on memory retrieval, rather than the more time consuming task of problem solving. Stanovich's model of modular processing and Logan's power law result in the same implications for instruction; specifically, if a word is read frequently enough, the cumulative practice results in an increased likelihood that the word will be recognized upon further exposures and that recognition latency will decrease.

RESEARCH INTO THE PROSODIC COMPONENT OF FLUENCY

Prosody is an area of phonology that focuses on the rhythmical and tonal features of speech that are layered upon individual phonological segments and include stress, pitch, and duration

(Schreiber, 1991). Stress involves the prominence that is placed on individual syllables within words. Intonation is the rise and fall of voice pitch during speech or oral reading. Duration is the length of time employed in pronouncing a word or part of a word.

In reading, prosody refers to the ability to make oral reading sound like authentic oral speech. Referring to prosody in reading, Martin (1966) has stated that "much of the meaning of the sentence is in its sound, not necessarily in the words themselves" (p. 13). Prosody or prosodic reading has been identified by a number of reading scholars as an essential component of reading fluency (e.g., Allington, 1983; Kuhn & Stahl, 2000; National Reading Panel, 2000; Rasinski & Hoffman, 2003) However, it has not garnered the same level of research attention as has the automaticity component of fluency (Dowhower, 1991).

Prosody can aid speakers and readers in constructing meaning in several ways. For example, prosody can be used to emphasize certain words or mark phrase or sentence boundaries in texts. Prosody can also be used to mark a sentence as an interrogative or exclamation. According to Schreiber (1980, 1987, 1991) and others (Coots, 1982; Dowhower, 1991), a very significant role that prosody plays in oral and written language comprehension is to assist the reader in segmenting or chunking text into syntactically appropriate and meaningful phrasal groupings of words. Phrasing plays an important role in oral language production and comprehension (Epstein, 1961; Johnson, 1965; Cooper & Paccia-Cooper, 1980). Schreiber (1991) argues that the ability to chunk or phrase text into syntactically appropriate and meaningful multi-word units is an important aspect of learning to read. In general, some but not all phrase boundaries in written text are marked by punctuation. When phrase boundaries are not explicitly marked in written texts readers must employ their prosodic sensitivity to parse written text into appropriate phrases. Research has shown that younger and less able readers are less able to employ prosodic elements in phrasing written texts (Clay & Imlach, 1971; Dowhower, 1987; Schreiber, 1980, 1987, 1991; Schreiber & Read, 1980).

Although prosody and its role in text chunking fit well into a conceptual definition of fluency, a limited amount of research has examined its empirical position in reading fluency. Two questions are central to clarifying prosody's role in reading fluency and overall reading achievement. First, is there a relationship between prosody during oral reading and readers' overall reading proficiency? And, second, if a relationship does exist, to what extent does instruction in prosody lead to improvements in fluency and overall reading achievement.

Most of the limited research on prosody has examined the relationship between prosody and overall reading achievement. Prosody is most commonly measured by qualitative assessments of a reader's use of prosody during oral reading, using a quantitative rubric as a guide for measuring prosody. Using such a protocol, Rasinski (1985) found significant and substantial correlations between measures of prosody on a six-point rubric and performance on a standardized test of silent reading comprehension for third- ($r = .74$) and fifth-grade ($r = .73$) students. In oral reading studies sponsored by the National Assessment of Educational Progress, Pinnell et al. (1995) and Daane, Campbell, Grigg, Goodman, and Oranje (2005) also found substantial correlations between measures of phrasing and expression (prosody) and fourth graders' performance on a silent reading comprehension test. In both studies, students who were ranked highest on a four-point oral prosody rubric tended to have the highest scores on a standardized silent reading comprehension assessment. Lower scores on prosody were associated with poorer silent reading comprehension. In a more recent study, Rasinski, Rikli, and Johnston (2009) found significant correlations between assessments of oral reading prosody and performance on a standardized silent reading comprehension test for third-, fifth-, and seventh-grade students. Moreover, the magnitude of the correlations between grade levels did not change substantially from lower to higher grade levels.

While qualitative and subjective measures of oral reading prosody, such as the ones used in the previously mentioned studies, are valid and recommended for classroom use (Miller & Schwanenflugel, 2006), the restricted range of prosody rubrics limits the precision of the assessment and the potential for capturing the robustness of potential relationships. Moreover, such assessments tend to be intercorrelated with reading rate, thus suggesting a possible confounding with measures of automaticity.

Whalley and Hansen (2006) studied the relationship between fourth-grade students' word and phrase level prosodic sensitivity and reading ability. Word level prosodic sensitivity was assessed objectively by having students distinguish between identical compound words and phrases that differed only by prosodic features. Phrase level prosody was assessed objectively by students matching a spoken phrase with a phrase that substituted the words with nonsense syllables but retained the prosodic features of the spoken phrase. After controlling for phonological awareness and general rhythmic sensitivity, students' prosodic word and phrase sensitivity predicted unique variation in word-reading accuracy and reading comprehension. Phrase-level prosodic sensitivity predicted unique variation in reading comprehension after controlling additionally for word reading accuracy. The authors argue that these results suggest that prosodic skills play an important part in students' overall reading development.

Using spectrographic analyses of 80 third-grade students, Miller and Schwanenflugel (2006) reported a significant relationship between measures of readers' basic declarative sentence declinations and pitch rises following yes-no questions (both objective and quantitative measures of prosody) and reading comprehension as measured by standardized assessments. The researchers argue that these results provide support for the notion that prosody emerges once accurate and automatic text reading occurs and that prosody contributes to comprehension beyond the contributions of automatic and accurate word recognition. In a more recent study, the same authors (Miller and Schwanenflugel, 2008) found that developing an adult-like intonation contour (pitch) in early elementary students' reading is associated with later comprehension development. Aspects of prosody seem related to students' overall reading achievement.

Other studies have suggested relationships between prosody, syntactic structure in written texts, and reading comprehension (e.g., Goldman-Eisler, 1972; Gottardo, Stanovich, & Siegel, 1996; Koriat, Greenburg, & Kreiner, 2002; Leikin & Assayag-Bouskila, 2004; Muter, Hulme, Snowling & Stevenson, 2004; Young & Bowers, 1995). An accumulating body of evidence, then, suggests a significant relationship between prosody and reading achievement, and that prosody plays an important role in students' reading development over and beyond other factors, including phonological awareness, word recognition accuracy and automaticity, and general rhythmic sensitivity. Whether prosody is a precursor or an outcome of reading comprehension has yet to be fully established. Nevertheless, it seems clear that a substantial relationship exists between some aspects of prosody in reading and reading comprehension.

ASSESSING READING FLUENCY

Fluency consists of three major components—accuracy and automaticity in word recognition, and prosody in oral textual reading. Accuracy in word recognition refers to the ability of readers to decode the words in texts.

Assessments of readers' ability to recognize words accurately abound. Informal reading inventories (IRI), in use for decades, have employed decoding accuracy as a key benchmark for assessing reading achievement (Johnson, Kress, & Pikulski, 1987; Pikulski, 1990). Accuracy is determined by the percentage of words a reader can read correctly; it has been shown to be a valid measure of reading proficiency (Fuchs, Fuchs, & Deno, 1982).

Although various indices for word recognition accuracy on informal reading inventories exist, generally a 99% accuracy level on a text is indicative of independent reading; 95% indicates instructional level; and accuracy levels at or below 90% are considered frustration level. A normal achieving reader is able to read grade level passages with a word recognition accuracy level that falls within the instructional range. Although these criteria are not universally recognized (e.g., Powell, 1971), research does lend support to the understanding that readers' comprehension degrades when the percentage of words read accurately falls below 95%, and that a 95% word recognition accuracy level agreed with estimates of instructional level performance by teachers and standardized tests of reading (Fuchs et al., 1982; Homan & Klesius, 1985).

Reading rate provides a way of determining students' level of word recognition automaticity. The assumption is that quick reading is a reflection of automaticity in word recognition. Reading rate, as a measure of reading proficiency, has been studied since at least the early 20th century (Starch, 1915). More recently, recognizing the need to develop a reading assessment that was time efficient, reliable, and valid, Deno (1985) developed an approach referred to as Curriculum Based Measurement (CBM) in reading. (Because this measurement approach is focused on reading fluency, it is often referred to as Oral Reading Fluency [ORF] assessment.) This CBM/ORF approach to assessment, like informal reading inventories, requires readers to read grade level text orally; the CBM/ORF score is operationally defined as the number of words read correctly in one minute. Readers' scores are then compared against grade level norms (e.g., Edformation, 2008; Hasbrouck & Tindal, 1992, 2005, 2006) for analysis. Readers who perform at or near the 50 percentile norms are considered to be progressing adequately in automaticity. Readers who are significantly and consistently below the norm for their grade level and time of year may be at risk in their reading fluency development.

Although only fairly recently developed, the CBM/ORF fluency assessment has been validated through a number of studies in which CBM/ORF correlates significantly with other measures of reading achievement and reading comprehension. Correlations ranging in magnitude from r =.45 to .91 have been reported for students in first through secondary grades (e.g., Deno, Mirkin, & Chiang, 1982; Fuchs, Fuchs, Hosp, & Jenkins, 2001; Fuchs, Fuchs, & Maxwell, 1988; Good, Simmons, & Kame'enui, 2001; Marston, 1989; Rasinski et al., 2005; Riedel, 2007). Other studies using a more general measure of reading rate have found significant correlations between rate and silent reading comprehension for third-, fourth-, and fifth-grade students (Daane et al., 2005; Pinnell et al., 1995; Rasinski, 1985).

Despite the strong associations between reading rate and more general measures of reading achievement, some scholars have raised concerns about the use of reading rate as a reading assessment (e.g., Deno, Mirkin, & Chiang, 1982). Critics argue that measures of reading rate emphasize reading speed rather than comprehension and that reading rate becomes the defacto primary instructional focus in some classrooms (Goodman, 2006; Pressley, Hilden, & Shankland, 2005; Rasinski, 2006; Samuels, 2006, 2007). Samuel (2007) further argues that measures of automaticity that involve only reading rate are not true measures of fluency, as fluency involves decoding and comprehension while reading, not simply quick word decoding.

Prosody or expressiveness in oral reading is the third component of fluency. Since prosody while reading does not lend itself easily to precise quantification, scholars have turned to qualitative rubrics or rating scales to guide assessment; oral reading rubrics that focus on prosody range from well-phrased and expressive reading to word-by-word, monotonic reading. Miller and Schwanenflugel (2006) argue that such qualitative approaches to assessing prosody are valid and appropriate for classroom use.

The use of a rubric is simple. A reader reads a grade level passage while a rater listens to the reading for as little as 60 seconds. At the end of the listening period, the rater consults the rubric and assigns a score that most closely aligns with prosodic characteristics of the oral reading. In using a rubric, teachers and other raters need to have a well-established sense of what constitutes appropriate phrasing and expressiveness in reading for their assigned grade level.

Several fluency rubrics have been developed and found to work well in assessing fluency and overall reading proficiency (e.g., Allington, 1983; Allington & Brown, 1979; Rasinski, 1985).

Using a six-point rubric with third- and fifth-grade students, Rasinski found that the instrument was highly reliable (test-retest reliability = .90) and was significantly correlated with the students' performance on a standardized test of reading proficiency. Similarly, in two large scale studies of fourth graders' oral reading fluency sponsored by the National Assessment of Educational Progress (NAEP) Pinnell et al. (1995) and Daane et al. (2005) found that ratings of fourth-grade students' oral reading performance were strongly associated with their silent reading comprehension.

Using a multi-dimensional 12-point prosody rubric (Zutell & Rasinski, 1991), a consortium of school districts in eastern Nebraska (Johnston, 2006) have used prosody as the primary measure of reading fluency and have reported high levels of reliability in the use of the rubric with large numbers of students over a span of several years (Johnston, 2006; Rasinski et al., 2009). One study employing the multi-dimensional rubric with over 1,200 elementary and middle school students in an urban school district reported substantial and significant correlations (r > .50) with a standardized test of reading comprehension for students in grades 3, 5, and 7 (Rasinski et al., 2009). Although it may seem that the impressionistic nature of rating oral reading fluency may challenge the reliability of such measures, a brief training period for teachers in which they have the opportunity to listen to, discuss, and rate a range of students' oral reading results in teacher ratings that have a high level of consistency (Rasinski et al., 2009).

Although prosody rubrics may not be as precise as assessments of decoding accuracy and reading rate, in the hands of knowledgeable teachers, they provide practitioners with tools for informing their own instruction and students with a method for guiding their own personal fluency development. To that extent, prosody rubrics may be an ideal assessment tool—they provide assessment information that can also directly guide instruction. Readers who are rated poorly on a prosody rubric, can use the descriptors on the rubric itself to guide their improvement.

Frequent assessments of readers' fluency allows teachers to make informed data-based instructional decisions that can lead to better teaching and improved learning (Deno, 1997). Instruction that is guided by frequent, quick, reliable, valid, and curriculum-based assessment has the potential to lead to improved teacher decision making and instruction, and student performance in reading (Fuchs, Deno, & Mirkin, 1984; Fuchs & Fuchs, 1986; Marston & Magnusson, 1985). For example, if a teacher has set fluency goals for a classroom of readers and some students are not making progress toward those goals, the teacher may decide that those students need additional and intensive reading fluency instruction. Some reading experts, however, have raised concerns that this type of informed and focused instruction may be too narrowly focused on secondary aspects of students' oral reading (e.g., reading rate) and may lead to instructional decisions that are not sufficiently sensitive to students' other instructional needs in reading (Rasinski, 2006; Samuels, 2007).

RESEARCH ON INSTRUCTIONAL PRACTICES FOR TEACHING READING FLUENCY

In the past, the role of reading fluency has been characterized as "neglected" or "intellectually spasmodic" with "periods of great effort and creativity, followed by fallow periods of relative disinterest" (Allington, 1983; Wolf & Katzir-Cohen, 2001, p. 211). However, with the publication of the National Reading Panel's (NRP) Report (2000), reading fluency has taken center stage in classrooms across the United States (Pikulski & Chard, 2005). The NRP (2000) declared reading fluency to be "an essential part of reading" (p. 328). There are those, however, who challenge the centrality of reading fluency in today's reading curriculum (Altwerger, Jordan, & Shelton, 2007). In this section, research findings related to six areas of reading fluency instruction and practice are reviewed: (a) integrated reading fluency lessons; (b) independent reading; (c) assisted reading; (d) prosody instruction; (e) reading for performance; and (g) family/home fluency programs.

Integrated Reading Fluency Lessons

Integrated reading fluency lessons provide group instruction, teacher modeling, repeated, assisted, and wide readings, as well as reading as performance. Research focused upon integrated reading fluency lessons includes approaches such as: (a) Fluency Oriented Reading Instruction (FORI), (b) Wide Reading (WR), (c) Oral Recitation Lesson (ORL), (d) Fluency Development Lesson (FDL), (e) Shared Book Experience (SBE), and (f) Retrieval, Automaticity, Vocabulary, Engagement, and Orthography (RAVE-O).

Fluency Oriented Reading Instruction (FORI).   Fluency Oriented Reading Instruction (FORI) was designed for primary-grade reading and content area reading instruction using core reading program selections (Kuhn & Schwanenflugel, 2006; Stahl, Heubach, & Holcomb, 2005). Students read a selected text orally and repeatedly over the course of a week. On the first day of a FORI lesson, the teacher reads a selected text aloud while the students follow along with their own copy. After reading, a teacher-led discussion alerts students' attention to the important ideas to comprehend the text. Over subsequent days, students orally read the selected text several times using echo-, choral-, and partner-reading. Students also practice the text at home for an additional 15 to 30 minutes per day. The final day of a FORI lesson culminates with extension activities.

Stahl, Heubach, and Cramond (1997) and Stahl (2004) report studies in which FORI was implemented by four teachers in two schools during the first year, and by 10 teachers in three schools the second year, for a total of 14 classrooms and five schools. In both years, students made average gains of nearly 2 years on an informal reading inventory. Ninety-eight percent of 105 struggling readers were reading on grade level or higher by the end of the second-grade year. Unfortunately, these early FORI studies were conducted without the benefit of a control or a comparison group.

Stahl and Heubach (2005) conducted a multi-year study of FORI in which the performance of the FORI group was compared to the expectation of a year's growth on the Qualitative Reading Inventory (QRI; Leslie & Caldwell, 1988). Results showed that first and second-grade students in the FORI group made average gains from 1.77 to 1.88 years in a single year's time. Growth in rate and accuracy was greatest between November and January.

In a follow-up study, Kuhn et al. (2006) compared the effects of FORI to wide reading (WR), a form of repeated reading, and a control group in which students received traditional reading instruction. Results showed that high- and low-skilled readers were equally and positively affected by FORI and WR. Long-term use of the FORI intervention significantly increased students' sight word reading and reading comprehension as compared to a control group. FORI represents an effective integrated reading fluency lesson for improving fluency instruction in classroom settings.

Wide Reading (WR).   Wide reading involves reading a range of new books with fewer repetitions than is found in traditional implementations of repeated reading practice. In repeated reading practice, a single text may be read and reread for multiple days. In wide reading, repeated reading of text is usually confined to a single day, lesson or sitting before moving onto a new book the next day. Wide reading, like repeated reading, also incorporates assisted reading facilitated by teachers and peers into the lesson structure (Kuhn, 2004, 2005).

Homan, Klesius, and Hite (1993) compared "non-repetitive" teacher-assisted oral reading to paired student repeated readings of texts with close teacher monitoring. Results of this research found no differences among sixth-grade below-average readers' reading errors or reading rate. Significant growth in reading comprehension as measured by oral retellings resulted from using both repeated and "non-repeated" reading practice.

Kuhn (2000, 2004, 2005) found children who repeatedly read a different book each day outperformed children who read one book repeatedly over several days. Kuhn (2004, 2005) investigated the effect of using wide reading compared to repeated reading with 24 struggling second-grade readers in three randomly assigned classrooms. Performance in these intervention groups were contrasted with students in a control and a listening-only comparison group. The instructional treatment involved 18 sessions with each session lasting 15–20 minutes per day three times per week for 6 weeks. Because of the small number of participants in the study, 18 total students, and the short study duration, only descriptive statistics were reported. Results indicated that struggling readers in both repeated reading and wide reading groups demonstrated greater than expected gains in isolated word recognition, prosodic reading, and text oral reading rate compared to students in the control or a listening-only group. The wide reading intervention group also demonstrated larger than expected gains in comprehension.

In the previously described Kuhn et al. (2006) study, long-term use of wide reading significantly increased second-grade students' sight word reading, oral reading rates, and reading comprehension over controls and was roughly equivalent to the effects of using FORI (Kuhn & Woo, 2008).

The Oral Recitation Lesson (ORL).   The Oral Recitation Lesson (ORL) was developed as an instructional alternative to the traditionally presented basal reading program (Hoffman, 1987; Hoffman & Crone, 1985). Teachers read a text aloud while students followed along with their own copy of the text. Then, students practiced their assigned part of the text together and independently in preparation for a recitation before the class. Although Hoffman (1987) reported the ORL to be effective, no statistical evidence was provided. The effectiveness of ORL was examined in a series of two studies with second-graders (Reutzel & Hollingsworth, 1993; Reutzel, Hollingsworth, & Eldredge, 1994). In the first study, ORL was compared to Round Robin (RRR) reading in four second-grade classrooms in two schools over 4 months. The time spent reading was equal in both treatments. Results indicate that ORL was superior on measures of fluency and researcher-designed measures of reading comprehension. In a second study, Reutzel et al. (1994) compared the effects of ORL with Holdaway's (1979) Shared Book Experience (SBE). In this study, the ORL group made significantly fewer oral reading errors than did the SBE group.

Shared Book Experience (SBE).   Eldredge, Reutzel, and Hollinsworth (1996) compared the effectiveness of 30-minute lessons using SBE to Round Robin (RRR) reading on students' reading fluency development over 4 months. The SBE lesson consisted of a teacher-led introductory discussion, group guided reading and a discussion of the contents of the book. Students repeatedly read the book as a class, in pairs, or independently. Results indicate that the SBE group significantly outperformed the RRR reading group in word recognition, fluency, and comprehension.

The Fluency Development Lesson (FDL).   The Fluency Development Lesson (FDL) was conceived as a 10- to 15-minute fluency focused augmentation to the regular classroom reading lesson (Rasinski, Padak, Linek, & Sturtevant, 1994). In the FDL each student reads a new 50–150 word text each day with a planned review of previously read texts, culminating in a repertoire of practiced texts. The texts to be practiced were selected using three criteria—

content, predictability, and rhythm. An FDL begins with the teacher introducing the text and inviting student predictions, followed by the teacher modeling a fluent reading of the text to the class. After modeling, the teacher leads a discussion focused on comprehending the text and evaluating the qualities of fluent reading including rate, phrasing, and expression. Students are then paired for practicing the text of the day. Student pairs exchange roles of reader and listener with the listener providing feedback to the reader. After paired reading, the whole class reconvenes to listen to individuals, pairs, or small groups perform the text. At the conclusion of the lesson, students place the daily text into a folder with other previously read texts and are encouraged to reread these texts during the day and at home for more practice.

Results showed no statistically significant difference between the control condition (in which students read the same texts orally and silently along with discussion, summarizing, and artistic responses to the texts) and students in the FDL treatment, with the notable exception of a statistically significant difference in second-grade oral reading rate favoring the FDL treatment. In mean comparisons between FDL and the controls, all FDL means were greater than the controls and yielded effect sizes from .133 to .962. There was a consistent trend favoring the FDL over the control groups. In addition, teachers in the study were interviewed and consistently reported positive responses for using the FDL in their regular reading lessons.

Retrieval, Automaticity, Vocabulary Elaboration, Orthography (RAVE-O). The Retrieval, Automaticity, Vocabulary Elaboration, Orthography (RAVE-O) fluency intervention was designed as an intensive, pull-out, small group intervention for highly at-risk second and third grade students (Wolf, Miller, & Donnelly, 2000). The program is designed around three goals: (a) development of fluency in reading, (b) a focus on developing sub-lexical and lexical reading skills, and (c) an evolving sense of success due to acquisition of necessary cognitive tools and strategies aimed at decoding and retrieving words. Students receive 30 minutes of phonological training along with 30 minutes of RAVE-O. In the RAVE-O lesson, children learn several core words around a particular rime. After discussing the meanings of the words, the words are taught on rime cards with separable onsets that are color coded. Children learn to segment and compose a set of about 5 words each week while learning to also recognize other words containing the same rime. They play a computerized game and other activities with these words to increase automaticity. Word recognition is paired with writing to bring automaticity in decoding and word recognition to a higher level. Knowing multiple meanings of the core words is also an important part of the RAVE-O intervention. To assist with retrieval, children participate in various multi-modality (listening, handling objects) and cognitive-monitoring activities (question answering games—Starts with, Sounds like, Similar to, words). Preliminary data on the RAVE-O program for 200 second- and third-grade children with severe reading impairments indicated significant gains in word attack, word identification, oral reading rate and accuracy, and passage comprehension (Wolf & Katzir-Cohen, 2001).

Research on Independent Reading Practice

Conventional wisdom asserts that reading fluency is developed primarily through practice. Consequently, one might expect to find a robust and extensive body of experimental research examining the effects of practice on the acquisition of students' reading fluency. At the turn of the millennia, the authors of the National Reading Panel (2000) lamented the lack of such a body of research when they stated " that most of the evidence linking up input variables such as amount read and output variables such as reading ability is correlational" (p. 310). It should go without saying that correlation evidence is insufficient to establish causality or the direction/sequence of relationships, but given the preponderance of research showing this relationship some have been tempted in the absence of a robust and extensive body of experimental research examining the effects of practice on the acquisition of students' reading fluency to assume a cause and effect relationship. Fortunately, in the past decade, increased attention has been devoted to conducting and reporting experimental studies addressing the effects of various forms of practice on the development of students' reading fluency.

The National Reading Panel (2000) sparked considerable controversy with the conclusion that evidentiary support is lacking that demonstrates positive effects of encouraging independent reading practice on reading fluency or achievement (Allington, 2002; Coles, 2000; Cunningham, 2001; Edmondson & Shannon, 2002; Krashen, 2002). The role of independent reading in classroom instruction and its effects on fluency and overall reading achievement is certainly an area ripe for further research.

Hiebert (2006, p. 208) noted the need for fluency interventions that provide "opportunities for students to transfer their skills to silent reading." Scaffolding of silent reading involves the teacher setting up supports, guidelines, procedures, deadlines, and accountability for students. Manning and Manning (1984) suggested scaffolding include such practices as setting a purpose and a deadline for reading. Several recent studies have begun to address ways to scaffold silent reading effectively and have demonstrated some promise in improving fluency and overall reading achievement (Kelley & Clausen-Grace, 2006; Kim & White, 2008; Reutzel, Jones, Fawson, & Smith, 2008.

Assisted Reading Practice

Reading fluency can be developed through a process termed assisted reading (Rasinski & Hoffman, 2003). Assisted reading is defined as a student's "oral reading of text while simultaneously listening to a fluent rendering of the same text" (Rasinski & Hoffman, 2003, p. 514). Assisted reading can be performed by an adult teacher or tutor who reads with the student or by the use of various technological media Assisted reading fluency practice includes: (a) Guided Repeated Oral Reading with Feedback (GRORF), (b) round-robin reading, (c) reading partner assisted, and (d) technology assisted.

Guided Repeated Oral Reading with Feedback (GRORF).   Early researchers (Dahl & Samuels, 1979; Dowhower, 1987, 1994; O'Shea, Sindelar, & O'Shea, 1985, 1987; Rashotte & Torgesen, 1985; Samuels, 1979) found that students who engaged in repeated readings of single texts made gains in reading rate and word recognition accuracy on the passage practiced and on passages not previously read. Kuhn and Stahl (2004) found 33 studies examining the effects of repeated reading without support on fluency development. Fifteen of these studies assessed the effects of repeated reading using a control group. The results were mixed with repeated reading significantly outperforming the control group in 28 to 40% of the comparisons.

GRORF involves repeated readings with help and feedback from a more able adult or peer. This often takes the form of a teacher or tutor modeling appropriate aspects of fluent oral reading followed by various forms of guided practice including choral reading or paired reading with subsequent verbal feedback from the teacher, peers, or tutors (Vadasy, Sanders, & Peyton, 2005). The National Reading Panel (2000) analyzed 51 studies involving GRORF across categories of immediate effects, group experiments, single subject, and methods comparison studies. They reported a mean effect size of 0.41 for GRORF on students' acquisition of reading speed and accuracy.

Kuhn and Stahl (2004) found that many repeated reading studies did not use performance criterion levels to evaluate the effectiveness of repeated readings. Kuhn and Stahl found in 6 of 11 studies that children benefited more from reading slightly challenging materials at or above their instructional levels than from reading materials below their instructional levels. Stahl and

Heubach (2006) argued that the appropriate (instructional) level for any given student's reading fluency practice is best characterized by an inverse function of the amount of support or scaffolding that is readily available to the student. Where there is less available support, the level of text difficulty should be easier. Where there is more available support, the text difficulty can be more challenging, even up to and including frustration level. Kuhn and Stahl (2004) also found that when repeated readings of texts resulted in increased reading fluency, there was frequently an increase in students' reading comprehension (Kuhn & Stahl, 2004).

Repeated reading research has examined repeated reading with Elkonin boxes (Devault & Joseph, 2004), with previewing, phrase drill error correction, and syllable-segmentation and blending (Daly, Bonfiglio, Mattson, Perampierie, & Foreman-Yates, 2006), and with scaffolded and unscaffolded texts (Compton, Appleton & Hosp, 2004 Hiebert, 2005, 2006). All of these studies demonstrated positive effects for repeated reading practice with guidance, scaffolding, and feedback.

In conclusion, guided repeated reading of texts with feedback (GRORF) has been shown to be effective in promoting fluency growth among a variety of students across differing reading levels and text levels. Scaffolding the texts so that they contain relatively low percentages of rare words when students engage in repeated reading practice has also been shown to promote reading fluency gains.

Round Robin Reading (RRR).   Although rightfully fading in popularity in many classrooms, round robin reading (RRR), which involves one student reading aloud while other students follow along silently, nevertheless continues to be used in some classrooms today. Past criticisms of RRR have focused on the negative effects of solo reading upon struggling readers' self-concepts or reading enjoyment. Stahl (2004) contends, in addition to the negative effects just mentioned, that RRR limits valuable practice time since students spend time waiting for others to read rather than practicing reading themselves. Research seems to support Stahl's (2004) contention that RRR constrains students' reading practice time.

Gambrell, Wilson, and Gnatt (1981) observed that in reading groups where round robin reading was the predominant method of practice all students read an average of 6 minutes per day and that struggling readers read only 2 minutes per day. To systematically investigate the effects of RRR on second-grade students' reading achievement growth, Eldredge, Reutzel & Hollingsworth (1996) conducted a study comparing RRR to a shared reading approach where groups of children chorally read along in large print books with their teachers. It is important to note that the time spent in reading practice was equal for both groups, 30 minutes of practice per day. Shared reading was found to be superior to round-robin reading in reducing children's oral reading errors, improving their reading fluency, increasing their vocabulary acquisition, and improving their reading comprehension. Clearly, there are reading approaches more efficient and effective than RRR.

Reading Partner Assisted Fluency Practice.   Neurological Impress Method (NIM), and other modifications of NIM, live on in classrooms today as teachers model fluent reading and then assist students in various types of choral readings, i.e., echoic, unison, and antiphonal (Kuhn & Stahl, 2004). Gestalt psychologists believed that the neural processes active during original perceptual events endured beyond the moment in a subdued form called a memory trace (Bower & Hilgard, 1981). A memory trace continued to exist as an active neural process after the original perceptual event had passed but was of too low an intensity to enter consciousness. In the use of the Neurological Impress Method (NIM) it was assumed the neurological pathways in the mind of a struggling reader were trained to imitate those of more able readers (Heckelman, 1969). Through simultaneously seeing the printed word and hearing the word spoken as pointed to and uttered by a more able reader, it was assumed that a neurological memory trace would be established in the mind of the less able reader similar to the one that existed in the mind of the more able reader.

Heckelman (1969) found a mean gain of 1.9 years growth on oral reading fluency and comprehension for using NIM. Hollingsworth (1978) found significant differences between the two groups on a standardized test of reading comprehension with the modified NIM students making 1 year growth compared to the control's .04 year's growth. Eldredge and Quinn (1988) and Eldredge (1990) studied the effects of a modified NIM with more fluent peers serving as partners for struggling second grade readers reading texts slightly above their independent reading levels. In these studies, students in the modified NIM group consistently outperformed students in the control basal reader group on measures of reading comprehension. Flood, Lapp, & Fisher (2005) conducted two studies of a modified version of NIM that included a reading comprehension component. Results showed statistically significant gains from pre to post measurement for all students on measures of oral and silent reading fluency and reading comprehension. Other research has found similarly positive effects for using NIM and other NIM-like procedures (Chomsky, 1978; Henk, Helfeldt, & Platt,1986; Langford, Slade, & Burnett, 1974; Mathes, Simmons, & Davis, 1992; Mefferd & Pettegrew, 1997; Mikkelsen, 1981; Feazell, 2004).

Paired or partner reading is another version of fluency practice assisted by others. Paired reading is non-repeated, child selected, and adult guided with the student occasionally signaling a desire to read "solo" until an error is made and then the adult model takes over the reading again (Topping, 1987a, 1987b, 1989). Morgan & Lyon (1979) investigated the effects of paired reading over a 12– to 13-week period of time in which children read with their parents. Children made gains of nearly a year in both word recognition and comprehension with a range of gains between 10 and 13 months. Rasinski (1994) reported similar results for paired reading when used by adult tutors in classrooms.

Partner reading involves pairs of peer-aged students reading aloud to one another. Koskinen and Blum (1986) found that students in a partner reading condition significantly outperformed a comparison study strategy group on fluency measures. Mathes and Fuchs (1993) investigated a repeated reading treatment in which students alternated the roles of tutor and tutee reading three different passages three times each for nine minutes. Students in a sustained reading group read the basal reader continuously for nine minutes. Results were mixed. The sustained students performed better than the control students on a measure of fluency but not comprehension. The repeated reading students did not differ significantly from the controls or the sustained reading group.

Similarly, Vaughn et al. (2000) compared eight classrooms of third-grade students' reading fluency growth using two interventions: partner reading, and collaborative strategic reading to increase comprehension. Both interventions demonstrated utility on the fluency growth of low to average achieving students. King et al. (2001) researched a peer assisted learning strategy (PALS) where pairs of students completed phonics activities along with repeated readings of a shared text. Results indicated PALS increased these first graders' reading fluency and comprehension.

Meisinger, Schwanenflugel, Bradley, and Stahl (2004) investigated the quality of interactions during partner reading. When students were allowed to choose their partners, social cooperation was better than in student pairs where the teacher selected partners. Stahl and Heubach (2005) also found that allowing students to select their reading partners increased fluency practice among first and second graders, especially among lower-achieving students. When the tasks or texts for reading practice were either too difficult or not difficult enough for the partner pairings, partners evidenced significant off-task behaviors. Pairings of low readers with low readers, and high readers with high readers were found to be less effective in promoting quality interactions during partner reading.

Labbo and Teale (1990) showed that cross-age tutoring, where an older student reader is paired with a younger student reader, significantly increased fluency growth for both partners over students practicing in basal reading groups or art project partners. Similar findings have been reported in other studies involving cross-age tutoring (Fuchs, Fuchs, Mathes, & Simmons, 1997; Greenwood & Delquadri, 1995; Sutton, 1991; Wright & Cleary, 2006).

In conclusion, reading with a tutor, partner, buddy, or peer appears to have beneficial effects for developing students' reading fluency. Students increase their engagement in reading practice when they select their partners and when the texts to be practiced are of appropriate difficulty for the pair of students. Research demonstrates that reading practice assisted by older students working with younger students is also effective.

Technology Assisted Reading Practice.   Students' reading fluency practice can be assisted through the use of various types of currently available technologies. In tape assisted fluency practice, students read a passage while simultaneously listening to a pre-recorded fluent recording of the passage (Chomsky, 1978; Pluck, 1995). Carbo's (1978a) talking books provided tape assisted reading at a slower reading pace which clearly emphasized phrasing and indicated when to turn pages. Small groups of struggling readers in Carbo's (1978b) study made better than average gains in word recognition. Rasinski (1990a) replicated these findings with third-grade students. Beimiller and Shany (1995) found that students who participated in tape assisted readings did as well on measures of reading comprehension as did students in teacher led repeated reading practice.

Koskinen, Wilson, and Jensema (1985) used closed-caption television to increase the reading performance of 35 second- through sixth-grade struggling readers in a summer reading clinic. In a subsequent experimental study using closed caption television with seventh- and eighth-grade English language learners, Neuman and Koskinen (1992) found that students in the closed caption television experimental group outperformed students in TV only, textbook reading only, and reading along and listening to a text on measures of word knowledge and recall of information in science texts.

The National Reading Panel (2000) found only six studies that examined the use of computers and speech recognition software to improve students' reading. Such programs also often provide back highlighting of words, pronunciation of unknown words, and multiple ways of representing a word's meaning if requested by the user. One the most used and well-known computer-based reading fluency practice programs is Read Naturally (Ihnot, Mastoff, Gavin, & Hendricksen, 2001). Read Naturally has been shown to increase oral reading fluency in English-speaking (Hasbrouck, Ihnot, & Rogers, 1999) and in Spanish-speaking students (De la Colina, Parker, Hasbrouck, & Alecio, 2001), and in students with persistent reading problems (Denton, Fletcher, Anthony, & Francis, 2006). Biggs, Homan, Dedrick, Minick, and Rasinski (2008) reported significant gains in reading comprehension among students using a computer-based singing program that employed guided repeated reading of song lyrics. Seventh- and eighth-grade struggling readers using the program for 30 minutes three times per week for 9 weeks made significantly greater gains in reading comprehension over a matched control group. Students in the experimental treatment demonstrated gains of 7 months. Moreover, a delayed post-test 4 months after the end of the study demonstrated that students had retained their initial gains. With advances in computer technology, it is likely that greater potential benefits for guiding students' reading practice toward increased reading fluency will result. In conclusion, fluency practice which uses various types of existing technologies including audio tapes, closed caption television, and computer-based programs with speech recognition have shown beneficial effects for developing students' reading fluency.

Prosody Instruction

As prosody appears to be a discrete fluency variable that may contribute independently to reading achievement, examining the role of instruction in prosody in overall reading development is appropriate. Instruction in prosody, to make oral reading sound like language and make sense (Aulls, 1977; Dowhower, 1991), should theoretically aid readers in comprehending text, and specifically should assist readers in phrasing text into meaningful units. Although reading instruction has traditionally focused on teaching word decoding skills, textual phrasing or chunking "has rarely if ever been taught" (Schreiber, 1991, p. 162).

Schreiber (1991) explains that repeated and assisted reading are the main instructional methods for using exploiting students' prosodic knowledge to assist in textual phrasing while reading. According to Schreiber, through repeated and assisted reading readers are more likely to attend to and embed prosody in their reading. This embedding of prosody leads to more appropriate phrasing or chunking of texts which leads to improved fluency and comprehension. Ongoing instruction in repeated and assisted reading leads readers to rely on other cues such as morphological markers and function words that mark phrases and are embedded in written texts.

The difficulty with examining this prosodic approach for fluency, however, is that the very same methods advocated for improving prosody, repeated and assisted readings, are also advocated for improving word recognition automaticity. In the following sections we explore the effects of repeated and assisted reading on students reading development. The extent to which any improvements from these methods in overall reading achievement as are due to improvements in automaticity or prosody has yet to be determined. Nevertheless, given the emerging evidence on the relationship between prosody and overall reading achievement, it is reasonable to assume that methods for improving reading fluency (i.e., repeated and assisted reading) should have embedded within them an instructional emphasis on prosody as well as word recognition accuracy and automaticity.

Some studies have examined directly the impact of fluency instructions on prosody. Dowhower (1987) and Herman (1985) found that repeated reading instruction lead to significant improvements in prosody during story reading. Dowhower (1987) also reported that repeated readings lead to improvements in reading comprehension.

Text segmenting (Dowhower, 1991) refers to explicitly marking phrase boundaries in written texts to assist readers in phrasing texts meaningfully and applying prosody during oral reading. Although research on the role of phrasing does not seem to be currently in vogue, Rasinski's (1990b, 1994) review of research on instruction focused on text phrasing suggests that a focus on phrasing has substantial potential for delivering positive outcomes on word recognition, fluency, and comprehension.

It is well established that prosodic reading and sensitivity is associated with proficient reading. More proficient readers tend to employ prosody in their oral reading—to segment text into meaningful phrases and perhaps in other ways to construct meaning. Methods used for developing readers' prosody and text segmenting skills are known and have been shown to be effective in improving reading achievement. The extent to which such gains are due to improvements in prosody and/or automaticity are less clear. Further research into the nature and instructional place of prosody in the reading curriculum is called for.

Reading as Performance

Readers' theater is a motivating and effective approach for increasing students' reading fluency, especially prosody (Rasinski, 2008; Worthy & Prater, 2002) in which students rehearse (repeated read) a script in order to prepare for a later performance for peers or other audiences. Students are assigned parts or roles for performing the reading of the scripted text. Recitations and radio readings are often folded in as alternative ways to perform texts similar to readers' theater. Martinez, Roser, and Strecker (1999) researched the effects of readers' theater compared to a control group over a period of 10 weeks in two second-grade classrooms. Results showed an average 17 wpm gain in readers' theater compared to the control group's 6.9 wpm gain. The readers' theater group gained an average of 1.4 grade levels on an informal reading inventory compared to the control group's average gain of .7 grade levels. Expressive reading was improved for all of the readers' theater students except 4 while only 10 of 28 students in the control group improved reading expressiveness. Finally, readers' theater students wrote in their writing journals about their enthusiasm for performing readers' theaters.

Griffith and Rasinski (2004) reported striking results for using readers' theater to increase fourth grade readers' fluency. Three years of data indicated that fourth-grade students made over 2 years of gain in reading achievement during a single year when readers' theater was regular part of the classroom reading program. Reading rates were similarly affected with average student gains nearly doubling the expected yearly gains of 30 wpm. These students likewise found readers' theater to be an engaging and motivating way to practice reading to fluent levels. From these results, one can conclude that engaging students in various forms of reading practice that results in performing readings of texts for an audience is inherently motivating and effective in promoting reading fluency.

Family/Home Fluency Programs

Rasinski and Stevenson (2005) describe the results of implementing a home-based, parent-tutoring program for use with first-grade students called Fast Start. This program provides a 10- to 15-minute daily lesson guide for parents in which parents read a brief text to and with their children repeatedly, proactively listen to their child read, and engage them in a brief word-study activity. Thirty beginning first-grade students, representing a wide range of early reading abilities, were randomly assigned to experimental or control conditions for an implementation period of 11 weeks. Students most at-risk in reading were found to make significantly greater gains on measures of letter/word recognition and reading fluency than students in the control condition. Students in the Fast Start program had reached the January fluency benchmarks by November and reported personal enjoyment from engaging in the program.

Much has been learned in the past two decades about the nature of effective reading fluency practice and instruction in classrooms, clinics, and homes (e.g., Chard, Vaughn, & Tyler, 2002; Kuhn & Stahl, 2000; National Reading Panel, 2000; Rasinski & Hoffman, 2003; Therrien, 2004). Research has shown that a variety of practices ranging from integrated whole class fluency lessons to independent reading practice to teacher, peer, and technology assisted practice and fluency performances can be used effectively to help children develop fluent reading. Despite these advances, many questions about effective reading fluency instruction and practice remain. In the years ahead, researchers will need to unravel the intricacies of the complex interactions among the social, cognitive, and text-based factors that play a part in developing children's reading fluency in support of the ultimate aims of all reading instruction – readers who want to read and comprehend what they read.

FLUENCY AND ELLS

As mentioned previously, LaBerge and Samuels' (1974) framework for reading fluency explains that we are only able to attend to one thing at a time, therefore we alternate our attention between activities when we have to attend to two or more activities. However, if one activity is so well learned that it becomes automatic, we are able to attend to a second activity simultaneously. Given this framework, we would assume that each time we add an activity; we would have to revert to alternating attention until one task becomes automatic. This framework helps us understand the challenges faced by ELLs as they attempt to build reading fluency in a second or sometimes third language.

To be fluent, all readers, regardless of language proficiency, must possess automatic word recognition skills, must be able to read a large number of high-frequency words, and to use other cues to identify words in text (Tunmer & Chapman, 1995). They must also be able to hold information in working memory while constructing meaning from text (Francis, Rivera, Lesaux, Kieffer, & Rivera, 2006). Working memory may be further taxed by the fact that ELLs may also be translating words read to their home language to access their meaning.

Language skills play a significant role in reading fluency; familiarity with syntax, morphology, and word meanings impact students' reading fluency and in turn comprehension Students unfamiliar with English syntax, phrasing, and vocabulary are less able to anticipate upcoming text in a sentence and therefore, approach each word as an independent word rather that as part of a sentence with meaning.

Other factors that may impact ELLs reading fluency are familiarity of the topic and the readability level of the text. Of these two factors, familiarity with the topic is more dependent on language proficiency. A student who is familiar with a topic is more likely to understand the concepts and vocabulary associated with those concepts and read with good comprehension.

Research with ELLs indicates that many ELLs are able to develop word-level decoding skills; however, they continue to lag behind their peers on measures of reading fluency and comprehension (Chiappe & Siegel, 1999; Vaughn et al., 2006). Some EL learners lack reading fluency for many of the same reasons as non-ELLs: lack of decoding skills and lack of automatic recognition of words. Other students have adequate reading fluency, they can decode accurately and automatically, and they often read with prosody, but they do not comprehend what they have read. Reasons for this are inadequate background knowledge, and difficulty with English syntax, grammar, and vocabulary. Follow-up with reading comprehension measures is advised.

Although intervention research with ELLs is scant, two studies were identified by the Report of the National Literacy Panel on Language-Minority Children and Youth (August & Shanahan, 2006). These two studies demonstrate that students benefit from fluency instruction in English (Denton, 2000) and for Spanish-speaking students, in Spanish (De la Colina et al., 2001). Although the results from these studies have to be interpreted with caution due to design issues, they do indicate that time spent on building reading fluency is beneficial for ELLs.

Guided repeated reading activities in its many forms are beneficial for several reasons. First, they provide students with models of fluent reading and of the pronunciation of words that they may have heard but are not familiar with in their written form. Second, oral reading forces students to attend to each word (Francis et al., 2006). Third, corrective feedback cues students to their mispronunciations and provides an additional model for words they are unable to read.

Although the research base for determining the effectiveness of reading fluency instruction for ELLs is weak, there is no reason to believe that ELLs would not benefit from the fluency instruction described earlier in this chapter.

READING FLUENCY IN THE FUTURE—RESEARCH AND INSTRUCTION

Many issues associated with developing reading fluency remain unsettled. The National Reading Panel (2000) defined the elements of reading fluency as "accuracy, rate, and expression" but most of the studies the panel reviewed focused exclusively on rate and accuracy. More research is needed to determine how rate and accuracy function separately and in combination to affect children's reading fluency and comprehension developmentally and longitudinally. The unexplored labyrinth of expressive or prosodic reading needs much more research attention. We simply do not adequately understand how reading prosody affects or is affected by reading accuracy, rate, or comprehension. In addition, the connection between fluency and reading comprehension needs to be clarified. We do not know if or under which conditions fluency precedes comprehension, is a consequence of comprehension, or occurs simultaneously and interactively with comprehension. S. J. Samuels (2007), a member of the National Reading Panel, asserts that fluent readers not only read accurately, expressively, and with appropriate rate but they also simultaneously comprehend what they read.

Paris and Stahl (2005) and Altwerger et al. (2007) call into question long-standing assumptions about the relationship between reading fluency and reading comprehension. These researchers have highlighted a diminishing relationship between fluent reading and reading comprehension as readers develop over time. Paris and Stahl (2005) label the relationship between fluency and comprehension "spurious" because the relationship is unstable over time. Altwerger et al. (2007) demonstrate low correlations of fast, accurate reading with measures of reading comprehension among readers at varying grade levels. Pikulski and Chard (2005) raise the prospect that vocabulary rather than fast, accurate reading may be more highly related to reading comprehension as children encounter more difficult content texts in later grades. It is often stated that fluency is the bridge from decoding to comprehension. We need a better definition of, theories about, and research on how the relationship between reading fluency and decoding, vocabulary, and comprehension change over time and why.

As schools and teachers cope with a substantial influx of ELL students into classrooms nationally, more research is needed to understand how ELL students develop reading fluency in English (August & Shanahan, 2006; Fitzgerald, Amendum, & Guthrie, 2008; Shanahan & Beck, 2006). Recent evidence by Fitzgerald, Amendum, and Guthrie (2008) suggest that ELL students develop reading fluency over time in much the same way as do monolingual English students, but, clearly, more research is needed to understand the nature of support that ELL students need to develop reading fluency on a similar trajectory to mono-lingual English students.

Similarly, the appropriate role of reading fluency among older students is an issue that requires further investigation. Most models of reading position reading fluency as a competency that is developed in the primary grades (e.g., Chall, 1983). Nevertheless, some studies have found that fluency (or the lack of fluency) is a factor that may constrain the development of reading achievement among upper elementary, middle and secondary school students (Rasinski et al., 2009; Rasinski et al., 2005; Worthy & Broadus, 2002).

Research has shown that the type, structure, and content of texts affect the development of reading fluency. Recent research suggests that deliberately planned and controlled text elements can provide optimal practice and learning conditions for developing reading fluency (Hiebert, 2006; Menon & Hiebert, 2005). We need research that addresses what word frequency is optimal within and between texts to lead to early fluency development. More research is needed to determine the number of new words that should be introduced in new texts as students develop their reading fluency to higher and higher levels in more and more difficult texts. We need to know how word counts and frequencies as well as new word meanings affect students' fluency development over time. Current research leaves open the questions of which levels of text difficulty are optimal for independent practice as compared to group or individual instructional practice with and without feedback. Similarly, when fluency is achieved in one text type such as narrative text, how well does narrative fluency affect or transfer to reading other text types? Much more work is needed to explore what types of texts lend themselves most appropriately to fluency development. For example, the utility of poetry, song, rhetoric, and other rhythmical texts for increasing students' reading fluency has largely gone unexamined.

The purposes and aims of fluency practice are coming under increasing scrutiny as fast, accurate reading appears to be displacing a focus upon reading comprehension. Repeatedly reading texts of low interest and literary quality raises questions about undermining students' reading motivation (Rasinski, 2008). Few researchers have systematically studied the claimed motivational value (both positive and negative) of repeated readings and reading performance. Researchers have also yet to systematically study how repeated readings for performance and other authentic purposes develops students' oral reading expression and their confidence in reading.

Several studies have shown that oral reading practice is preferable to silent reading practice as a means for developing early fluency (Rasinski & Hoffman, 2003). On the other hand, for nearly a century silent reading has been preferred over oral reading when reading comprehension is the goal (Allington, 1983). In view of this fact, Hiebert (2006) asserted that researchers need to determine when and how to help students transfer their oral reading fluency to silent reading. We need longitudinal research that explores if oral and silent reading processes are developmental in nature portending a sequential or staged use of these two practice modes by younger students.

Stahl (2004) criticized various types of silent, independent reading practice approaches, chief among these, Silent Sustained Reading (SSR). Recent research has shown that effective silent, independent reading practice includes specific characteristics. Although recent research seems to indicate that conditions for effective silent reading practice are similar to those found with oral reading practice, we need more studies that determine characteristics that are necessary to render silent, independent reading practice efficacious for all students. Although repeated reading has been shown to be effective in promoting students' reading accuracy and reading rate, we need future research that determines at what point in a student's reading development repeated or wide reading is more or less beneficial. We should focus on answering questions such as, at what point in fluency development should reading practice transition from repeated readings of a single text to wide reading. We need research that examines whether or not a variety of text types and content foci are more or less effective in promoting reading fluency. Alternatively, we need to determine if repeated and wide readings can be simultaneously used in effective fluency practice.

We need research that focuses on reading fluency as a dependent variable. This is particularly true if we examine fluency developmentally. Although fluency instruction and practice may initially focus on increasing students' accuracy, rate, and expression, the interaction of text difficulty and reader intentions and relative level of proficiency must be examined as a part of what is meant by the term fluent reading as readers mature and develop. Research and classroom experiences dictate that fluent reading is related to text difficulty and the purposes for which the reader is reading. This may mean that fluent reading as a variable is defined and measured differently when expert readers read challenging text to be remembered and used later than when novice readers read instructional or independent level texts for the purposes of immediately demonstrating speed and accuracy. We also need research that examines when fluency as a dependent variable is most influenced by a student's decoding abilities as compared with a student's vocabulary and comprehension abilities. The situated nature of the fluency variable itself calls for much more research that developmentally examines the "fluent reading" of novice and expert readers.

Given its situated position as a link between word decoding and reading comprehension, we also need more research that examines fluency as an independent variable. It is not enough for fluency instruction and interventions to show improvements in measures of reading fluency alone. The ultimate aim of all reading instruction is to improve students' ability to comprehend text and their overall reading achievement. Research into reading fluency instruction must, in the end demonstrate improvements in students' reading comprehension and reading achievement.

Most recent fluency research has controlled the amount of practice time of treatment conditions as compared with control conditions. But the issue of time is another variable related to fluency that requires considerably more research attention (National Reading Panel, 2000). We do not know from current research how much instructional/practice time is needed to increase students' reading fluency in groups or as individuals, nor are we absolutely certain that differential gains in various reading achievement are due to the uniqueness of the fluency instruction or to the fact that students are simply spending greater amounts of time in engaged reading, when compared with control treatments.

Research has yet to determine how much time is needed respectively for instruction of fluency as compared with practice. Is there an optimal proportion of time allocated to instruction and practice? The issue of engaged and allocated time has yet to be fully explored in relation to student practice for fluency under differing practice conditions and with differing levels of text difficulty. It is clear that the variable of "time" in relation to fluency development is critical to examine in future reading fluency research.

It should be noted that the 2008 evaluation study of Reading First (Gamse, Bloom, Kemple, & Jacob, 2008) found that less than 5 minutes per day was devoted to reading fluency instruction in both Reading First classrooms (classrooms in which fluency instruction was mandated) and non-Reading First classrooms. Of the major components of reading instruction that were measured (word recognition, fluency, vocabulary, and comprehension), fluency was given the least amount of instructional time by teachers. In our opinion fluency instruction in the primary grades requires substantially more than five minutes per day. Perhaps one reason for the disappointing results noted in the report is due to the relative lack of attention given to reading fluency in all classrooms.

Finally, the contentious issue of reading fluency assessment needs considerable research attention. The consequential validity of current reading fluency assessments is a concern of primary importance. Many researchers and classroom teachers worry that current reading fluency assessments, such as the DIBELS ORF, are narrowing and restricting classroom fluency instruction and practice to reading for accuracy and rate and neglecting reading comprehension. Are current reading fluency assessment tools and procedures acting to inhibit necessary attention to reading comprehension in classrooms? Questions abound about fluency assessment. Can readers sustain one minute reading rates over longer time periods when reading longer texts? Although some researchers have shown a strong relationship between 1-minute reading rates and reading comprehension subtest scores on standardized, norm-referenced reading tests, does the relationship between fluency and comprehension remain stable when readers consciously slow down to comprehend more difficult texts? At what point does inaccurate reading interfere with reading comprehension? There have been no efforts to develop assessments that determine the role of vocabulary knowledge and how it affects students' fluency development. Are current fluency assessment tools of sufficient quality to allow educators to make informed judgments about which instructional interventions are best for inaccurate or slow readers? How are educators using current fluency assessments to decide interventions for struggling readers? Should slow reading always be treated as a source of concern? If not, when? Despite the tremendous increases in our understanding of reading fluency in recent years and the recognition of fluency's potential for improving instruction, there is much that still needs to be learned. Much research is yet needed for teachers to use reading fluency instruction and practice to fulfill the promise of it becoming the link between students' decoding, comprehension, and motivation.

REFERENCES

Allington, R.L. (1983). Fluency: The neglected reading goal. *The Reading Teacher, 36,* 556–561.

Allington, R. L. (2002). What I've learned about effective reading instruction. *Phi Delta Kappan,* 740–747.

Allington, R. L. (2002). *Big brother and the national reading curriculum: How ideology trumped evidence.* Portsmouth, NH: Heinemann.

Allington, R. L., & Brown, S. (1979). *Fact: A multi-media reading program.* Milwaukee, WI: Raintree.

Altwerger, B., Jordan, N., & Shelton, N. R. (2007). *Reading fluency: Process, practice, and policy.* Portsmouth, NH: Heinemann.

Anderson, J. R. (1992). Automaticity and the ACT*Theory. *American Journal of Psychology, 105*(2), 165–180.

August, D., & Shanahan, T. (2006). *Developing literacy in second-language learners: Report of the National Literacy Panel on language-minority children and youth.* Mahwah, NJ: Erlbaum.

Aulls, M. W. (1977). *The acquisition of reading fluency by skilled and less skills readers in grades, one, two, and three.* Paper presentation, New Orleans, Louisiana: 27th National Reading Conference. (ERIC Document Reproduction Service No. 150538)

Austin, M., & Morrison, C. (1963). *The first R: the Harvard report on reading in elementary schools.* New York: Macmillan.

Beach, S. A. (1993). Oral reading instruction: Retiring the bird in the round. *Reading Psychology, 14,* 333–338.

Beimiller, A., & Shany, M. T. (1995). Assisted reading practice: Effects on performance for poor readers in grades 3 and 4. *Reading Research Quarterly 30,* 382–295.

Berninger, V. W. (2001). Understanding the "lexia" in dyslexia: A multidisciplinary team approach to learning disabilities. *Annals of Dyslexia, 51,* 23–48.

Biggs, M. C., Homan, S. P., Dedrick, R., Minick, V., & Rasinski, T. (2008). Using an interactive singing software program: A comparative study of struggling middle school readers. *Reading Psychology, 29*(3), 195–213.

Bower, G. H., & Hilgard, E. R. (1981). *Theories of learning* (5th ed.). Englewood Cliffs, NJ: Prentice-Hall.

Breznitz, Z. (2003). Speed of phonological and orthographic processing as factors in dyslexia: Electro-physiological evidence. *Genetic, Social, and General Psychology Monographs, 129*(2), 183–206.

Breznitz, Z. (2006). *Fluency in reading: Synchronization of processes.* Mahwah, NJ: Erlbaum.

Buswell, G. T., & Wheeler, W. H. (1923). *The silent reading hour. Teacher's manual for the third reader.* Chicago: Wheeler.

Carbo, M. (1978a). Teaching reading with talking books. *The Reading Teacher, 32,* 267–273.

Carbo, M. (1978b). A word imprinting technique for children with severe memory disorders. *Teaching Exceptional Children, 11,* 3–5.

Cattell, M. (1886). The time it takes to see and name objects. *Mind, 2,* 63–85.

Chall, J. S. (1983). *States of reading development.* New York: McGraw-Hill.

Chard, D. J., Pikulski, J. J., & McDonagh, S. (2006). Fluency: The link between decoding and comprehension for struggling readers. In T. Rasinski, C. Blachowicz, & K. Lems (Eds.), *Teaching reading fluency* (pp. 39–61). New York: Guilford.

Chard, D. J., Vaughn, S., & Tyler, B. (2002). A synthesis of research on effective interventions for building fluency with elementary students with learning disabilities. *Journal of Learning Disabilities, 35,* 386–406.

Chiappe, P., & Siegel, L. S. (1999). Phonological awareness and reading acquisition in English- and Punjabi-speaking Canadian children. *Journal of Educational Psychology, 91*(1), 20–28.

Chomsky, C. (1976). After decoding: What? *Language Arts, 53,* 288–296.

Chomsky, C. (1978). When you still can't read in third grade. After decoding, what? In S. J. Samuels (Ed.), *What research has to say about reading instruction* (pp. 13–30). Newark, DE: International Reading Association.

Clay, M. M., & Imlach, R. H. (1971). Juncture, pitch, and stress as reading behavior variables. *Journal of Verbal Learning and Verbal Behavior, 10,* 133–139.

Cobb, L. (1835). *The North American reader.* New York: B. & S. Colins.

Cohen, J. D., Dunbar, K., & McLelland, J. L. (1990). On the control of automatic processes: A parallel distributed processing account of the Stroop effect. *Psychological Review, 97,* 332–361.

Coles, G. (2000). *Misreading reading: The bad science that hurts students.* Portsmouth, NH: Heinemann.

Compton, D. L., Appleton, A. C., & Hosp, M. K. (2004). Exploring the relationship between text-leveling systems and reading accuracy and fluency in second-grade students who are average and poor decoders. *Learning Disabilities Research, 19*(3), 176–184.

Cooper, W. E., & Paccia-Cooper, J. (1980). *Syntax and speech.* Cambridge, MA: Harvard University Press.

Coots, J. H. (1982). Reading comprehension: Instructional implications of SWRL research (Tech Reports 052 and 120). Los Alamitos, CA: Southwest Regional Laboratory (ERIC Document Reproduction Service No. 241-902)

Cunningham, J. W. (2001). The National Reading Panel Report. *Reading Research Quarterly, 30*(3), 326–335.

Dahl, P. R., & Samuels, S. J. (1979. An experimental program for teaching high speed word recognition and comprehension skills. In J. E. Button, T. Lovitt, & T. Rowland (Eds.), *Communications research in learning disabilities and mental retardation* (pp. 33–65). Baltimore, MD: University Park Press.

Daly III, E. J., Bonfiglio, C. M., Mattson, T., Persampieri, M., & Foreman-Yates, K. (2006). Refining the experimental analysis of academic skills deficits: Part II. Use of brief experimental analysis to evaluate reading fluency treatments. *Journal of Applied Behavior Analysis, 39*(3), 323–331.

Daane, M. C., Campbell, J. R., Grigg, W. S., Goodman, M. J., & Oranje, A. (2005). *Fourth-grade students reading aloud: NAEP 2002 special study of oral reading.* Washington, DC: U.S. Department of Education, Institute of Education Sciences.

De la Colina, M. G., Parker, R. I., Hasbrouck, J. E., & Alecio, R. (2001). Intensive intervention in reading fluency for at-risk beginning Spanish readers. *Bilingual Research Journal, 25,* 503–538.

Deno, S. L. (1985). Curriculum-based measurement: The emerging alternative. *Exceptional Children, 52,* 219–232.

Deno, S. S. (1997). Whether thou goest…Perspectives on progress monitoring. In J. L. Lloyd, E. J. Kameenui, & D. Chard (Eds.), *Issues in educating students with disabilities* (pp. 77–99). Mahwah, NJ: Erlbaum.

Deno, S. L., Mirkin, P., & Chiang, B. (1982). Identifying valid measures of reading. *Exceptional Children, 49,* 36–45.

Denton, C.A. (2000). The efficacy of two English reading interventions in a bilingual education program. Unpublished doctoral dissertation. Texas A&M University, College Station.

Denton, C. A., Fletcher, J. M., Anthony, J. L., & Francis, D. J. (2006). An evaluation of intensive intervention for students with persistent reading difficulties. *Journal of Learning Disabilities, 39*(5), 447–466.

Devault, R., & Joseph, L. M. (2004). Repeated readings combined with word boxes phonics technique increases fluency levels of high school students with severe reading delays. *Preventing School Failure, 49*(1), 22–27.

Dowhower, S. L. (1987). Effects of repeated reading on second-grade transitional readers' fluency and comprehension. *Reading Research Quarterly, 22,* 389–407.

Dowhower, S. L. (1991). Speaking of prosody: Fluency's unattended bedfellow. *Theory into Practice, 30,* 165–175.

Dowhower, S. L. (1994). Repeated reading revisited: Research into practice. *Reading and Writing Quarterly, 10,* 343–358.

Durkin, D. (1966). Identifying significant reading skills in kindergarten through grade three. In H. A. Robinson (Ed.), *Reading: Seventy-five years of progress. Proceedings of the annual conference on reading held at The University of Chicago* (pp. 33–36). Chicago: University of Chicago Press.

Edformation. (2008). AIMSweb™: A research based formative assessment system, 2008. [Data file]. Retrieved March 30, 2008, from http://www.edformation.com/

Edmondson, J., & Shannon, P. (2002). The will of the people. In R. L. Allington (Ed.), *Big brother and the national reading curriculum: How ideology trumped evidence* (pp. 224–231). Portsmouth, NH: Heinemann.

Ehri, L. C. (2005). Learning to read words: Theories, findings, and issues. *Scientific Studies of Reading, 9*(2), 167–188.

Ehri, L. C., & Wilce, L. S. (1983). Development of word identification speed in skilled and less skilled beginning readers. *Journal of Educational Psychology, 75*, 3–18.

Eldredge, J. L. (1990). Increasing reading performance of poor readers in the third grade by using a group assisted strategy. *Journal of Educational Research, 84*, 69–77.

Eldredge, J. L., & Quinn, W. (1988). Increasing reading performance of low-achieving second graders by using dyad reading groups. *Journal of Educational Research, 82*, 40–46.

Eldredge, J. L., Reutzel, D. R., & Hollingsworth, P. M. (1996). Comparing the effectiveness of two oral reading practices: Round-robin reading and the shared book experience. *Journal of Literacy Research, 28*, 201–225.

Epstein, W. (1961). The influence of syntactical structure on learning. *American Journal of Psychology, 74*, 80–85.

Feazell, V. S. (2004). Reading acceleration program: A schoolwide intervention. *The Reading Teacher, 58*(1), 66–72.

Fitzgerald, J., Amendum, S., & Guthrie, K. (2008). Young Latino students' reading growth in all-English classrooms. *Journal of Literacy Research, 40*(1), 59–94.

Flood, J., Lapp, D., & Fisher, D. (2005). Neurological impress method plus. *Reading Psychology, 26*, 147–160.

Francis, D. J., Rivera, M., Lesaux, N., Kieffer, M., & Rivera, H. (2006). *Practical guidelines for the education of English language learners: Research-based recommendations for instruction and academic interventions.* Portsmouth, NH: RMC Research Corporation.

Fuchs, D., Fuchs, L. S., Mathes, P., & Simmons, D. (1997). Peer-assisted learning strategies: Making classrooms more responsive to student diversity. *American Educational Research Journal, 34*, 174–206.

Fuchs, D., Fuchs, L, Yen, L., McMaster, K., Svenson, E., Yang, N., et al. (2001). Developing first-grade reading fluency through peer mediation. *Teaching Exceptional Children 34*(2), 90–93.

Fuchs, L, Deno, S. L., & Mirkin, P. (1984). The effects of frequent curriculum-based measurement and evaluation on pedagogy, student achievement, and students' awareness of learning. *American Educational Research Journal, 21*, 449–460.

Fuchs, L. S., & Fuchs, D. (1986). Effects of systematic formative evaluation: A meta-analysis. *Exceptional Children, 53*, 199–208.

Fuchs, L. S., Fuchs, D., & Deno, S. (1982). Reliability and validity of curriculum-based informal reading inventories. *Reading Research Quarterly, 18*, 6–26.

Fuchs, L. S., Fuchs, D., Hosp, M. K., & Jenkins, J. R. (2001). Oral reading fluency as an indicator of reading competence: A theoretical, empirical, and historical analysis. *Scientific Studies of Reading, 5*, 239–256. doi:10.1207/S1532799XSSR0503_3

Fuchs, L. S., Fuchs, D., & Maxwell, L. (1988). The validity of informal reading comprehension measures. *Remedial and Special Education, 9*(2), 20–28.

Gambrell, L. B., Wilson, R. M., & Gnatt, W. N. (1981).Classroom observations of task-attending behaviors of good and poor readers. *Journal of Educational Research, 74*, 400–404.

Gamse, B. C., Bloom, H. S., Kemple, J. J., & Jacob, R. T. (2008). *Reading First impact study: Interim report.* Washington DC: National Center for Education Evaluation and Regional Assistance, U.S. Department of Education.

Gibson, E. J., & Levin, H. (1975). *The psychology of reading.* Cambridge, MA: MIT Press.

Goldman-Eisler, F. (1972). Pauses, clauses, sentences. *Language & Speech, 15*, 103–113.

Good, R. H., & Kaminski, R. A. (2002). *Dynamic indicators of basic early literacy skills* (6th ed.). Eugene, OR: Institute for the Development of Educational Achievement. Retrieved from http://dibels.uoregon.edu

Good, R. H., Simmons, D. C., & Kame'enui, E. J. (2001). The importance and decision-making utility of a continuum of fluency-based indicators of foundational reading skills for third-grade high stakes outcomes. *Scientific Studies of Reading, 5*, 257–288. doi:10.1207/S1532799XSSR0503_4

Goodman, K. S. (2006). A critical review of DIBELS. In K. S. Goodman (Ed.), *The truth about DIBELS: What it is, what it does* (pp. 1–39). Portsmouth, NH: Heinemann.

Gottardo, A., Stanovich, K. E., & Siegel, L. S. (1996). The relationships between phonological sensitivity, syntactic processing, and verbal working memory in the reading performance of third-grade children. *Journal of Experimental Child Psychology, 63*, 563–582.

Greenwood, C. R., & Delquadri, J. (1995). Class-wide peer tutoring and the prevention of school failure. *Preventing School Failure, 39,* 21–25.

Griffith, L. W., & Rasinski, T. V. (2004). A focus on fluency: How one teacher incorporated fluency with her reading curriculum. *The Reading Teacher, 58*(2), 126–137.

Harris, T., & Hodges, R. (1985). *The literacy dictionary.* Newark, DE: International Reading Association.

Hasbrouck, J. E., Ihnot, C., & Rogers, G. (1999). Read naturally: A strategy to increase oral reading fluency. *Reading Research and Instruction, 39,* 27–37.

Hasbrouck, J. E., & Tindal, G. (1992). Curriculum-based oral reading fluency norms for students in Grades 2 through 5. *Teaching Exceptional Children, 24,* 41–44.

Hasbrouck, J., & Tindal. G. (2005). Oral reading fluency: 90 years of assessment (BRT Technical Report No. 33), Eugene, OR: Author. Retrieved March 30, 2008, from http://brt.uoregon.edu/techreports/

Hasbrouck, J., & Tindal, G. A. (2006). Oral reading fluency norms: A valuable assessment tool for reading teachers. *The Reading Teacher, 59*(7), 636–644.

Heckelman, R. G. (1969). A neurological impress method of reading instruction. *Academic Therapy, 4,* 277–282.

Herman, P. A. (1985). The effect of repeated reading on reading rate, speech pauses, and word recognition accuracy. *Reading Research Quarterly, 20,* 553–564.

Homan, S. P., & Klesius, J. P. (1985). A re-examination of the IRI: Word recognition criteria. *Reading Horizons, 26,* 54–61.

Hiebert, E. H. (2005). The effects of text difficulty on second graders' fluency development. *Reading Psychology, 26,* 1–7.

Hiebert, E. H. (2006). Becoming fluent: Repeated reading with scaffolded texts. In S. J. Samuels & A. E. Farstrup (Eds.), *What research has to say about fluency instruction* (pp. 204–226). Newark, DE: International Reading Association.

Hoffman, J. V. (1987). Rethinking the role of oral reading in basal instruction. *Elementary School Journal, 87,* 367–373.

Hoffman, J. V. (1991). Teacher and school effects in learning to read. In R. Barr, M. Kamil, P. Mosenthal, & P. D. Pearson (Eds.), *Handbook of reading research* (Vol. 2, pp. 911–950). White Plains, NY: Longman.

Hoffman, J. V., & Crone, S. (1985). The oral recitation lesson: A research-derived strategy for reading in basal texts. In J. A. Niles & R. V. Lalik (Eds.), *Issues in literacy: A research perspective, 34th yearbook of the National Reading Conference* (pp. 76–83). Rockfort, NY: National Reading Conference.

Hoffman, J. V., & Segel, K. (1983). *Oral reading instruction: A century of controversy (1880–1980).* Paper presented at the annual meeting of the International Reading Association, Anaheim, CA. (ERIC Document Number: ED 239-237)

Holdaway, D. (1979). *The foundations of literacy.* Sydney, Australia: Ashton Scholastic.

Hollingsworth, P. M. (1978). An experimental approach to the impress method of teaching reading. *The Reading Teacher, 31,* 624–626.

Homan, S. P., Klesius, J. P., & Hite, C. (1993). Effects of repeated readings and non-repetitive strategies on students' fluency and comprehension. *Journal of Educational Research, 87*(2), 94–100.

Hoskisson, K. (1975a). The many facets of assisted reading. *Elementary English, 52,* 312–315.

Hoskisson, K. (1975b). Successive approximation and beginning reading. *The Elementary School Journal, 75*(7), 442–451.

Howlett, N., & Weintraub, S. (1979). Instructional procedures. In R. C. Calfee & P. Drum (Eds.), *Teaching reading in compensatory classes* (pp. 87–103). Newark, DE: International Reading Association.

Hudson, R., Mercer, C. D., & Lane, H. (2000). *Exploring reading fluency: A paradigmatic over-view.* Unpublished manuscript, University of Florida, Gainesville.

Huey, E. B. (1968). *The psychology and pedagogy of reading.* Boston: MIT Press. (Original work published 1908)

Hyatt, A. V. (1943). *The place of oral reading in the school program: Its history and development from 1880–1941.* New York: Teachers College, Columbia University.

Ihnot, C., Mastoff, J., Gavin, J., & Hendrickson, L. (2001). *Read naturally.* St. Paul, MN: Read Naturally.

James, W. (1892). *Psychology.* New York: Holt.

Johnson, D. S. (1996). *Assessment for the prevention of early reading problems: Utility of dynamic indicators of basic early literacy skills for predicting future reading performance.* Unpublished doctoral dissertation, University of Oregon, Eugene.

Johnson, M. S., Kress, R., A., & Pikulski, J. J. (1987). *Informal reading inventories.* Newark, DE: International Reading Association.

Johnson, N. (1965). The psychological reality of phrase-structure rules. *Journal of Verbal Learning and Verbal Behavior, 4,* 469–475.

Johnston, S. (2006). The fluency assessment System: Improving oral reading fluency with technology. In T. Rasinski, C. Blachowicz, & K. Lems (Eds.), *Fluency instruction* (pp. 123–140). New York: Guilford.

Kame'enui, E. J. (2002). *An analysis of reading assessment instruments for K–3.* Eugene, OR: Institute for the Development of Educational Achievement.

Kelley, M., & Clausen-Grace, N. (2006). R5: The sustained silent reading makeover that transformed readers. *The Reading Teacher, 60*(2), 148–157.

Kim, J. S., & White, T. G. (2008). Scaffolding voluntary summer reading for children in grades 3 to 5: An experimental study. *Scientific Studies of Reading, 12*(1), 1–23.

King, S., Yoon, E., Jernigan, M., Jaspers, J., Gilbert, T., Morgan, P., et al. (2001). Developing first-grade fluency through peer mediation. *Teaching Exceptional Children, 34*(2), 90–93.

Koskinen, P. S., Wilson, R. M., & Jensema, C. (1985). Closed-caption television: A new tool for reading instruction. *Reading World, 24*(4), 1–7.

Koriat, A., Greenberg, S. N., & Kreiner, H. (2002). The extraction of structure during reading: Evidence from reading prosody. *Memory & Cognition, 30*(2), 270–280.

Koskinen, P. S., & Blum, I. H. (1984). Repeated oral reading and acquisition of fluency. In J. A. Niles & L. A. Harris (Eds.), *Changing perspectives on research in reading/language processing and instruction, Thirty-third yearbook of the National Reading Conference* (pp. 183–187). Rochester, NY: National Reading Conference.

Koskinen, P. S., & Blum, I. H. (1986). Paired repeated reading: A classroom strategy for developing fluent reading. *The Reading Teacher, 40,* 70–75.

Krashen, S. (2002). More smoke and mirrors: A critique of the National Reading Panel Report on Fluency. In R. L. Allington (Ed.), *Big brother and the national reading curriculum: How ideology trumped evidence* (pp. 112–124). Portsmouth, NH: Heinemann.

Kuhn, M. R. (2000). *A comparative study of small group fluency instruction.* Unpublished doctoral dissertation, University of Georgia, Athens.

Kuhn, M. R. (2004). Helping students become accurate, expressive readers: Fluency instruction for small groups. *The Reading Teacher, 58*(4), 338–344.

Kuhn, M. R. (2005). A comparative study of small group fluency instruction. *Reading Psychology, 26*(2), 127–146.

Kuhn, M. R., & Schwanenflugel, P. J. (2006). Fluency-oriented reading instruction: A merging of theory and practice. In K. A. D. Stahl & M. C. McKenna (Eds.), *Reading research at work: Foundations of effective practice* (pp. 205–213). New York: Guilford.

Kuhn, M. R., Schwanenflugel, P. J., & Meisinger, E. B. (2010). Review of research: Aligning theory and assessment of reading fluency: Automaticity, prosody, and definitions of fluency. *Reading Research Quarterly, 45*(2), 230–251.

Kuhn, M. R., Schwanenflugel, P. J., Morris, R. D., Morrow, L. M., Woo, D. G., Meisinger, E. B., et al. (2006). Teaching children to become fluent and automatic readers. *Journal of Literacy Research, 38*(4), 357–387.

Kuhn, M. R., & Stahl, S. A. (2000). *Fluency: A review of developmental and remedial practices* (CIERA Rep. No. 2-008). Ann Arbor, MI: Center for the Improvement of Early Reading Achievement.

Kuhn, M. R., & Stahl, S. A. (2004). Fluency: A review of developmental and remedial practices. In R. B. Ruddell & N. J. Unrau (Eds.), *Theoretical models and processes of reading* (5th ed., pp. 412–451). Newark, NJ: International Reading Association.

Kuhn, M. R., & Woo, D. G. (2008). Fluency oriented reading: Two whole-class approaches. In M. R. Kuhn & P. J. Schwanenflugel (Eds.), *Fluency in the classroom* (pp. 17–35). New York: Guilford.

Labbo, L. D., & Teale, W. H. (1990). Cross age reading: A strategy for helping poor readers. *The Reading Teacher, 43,* 363–369.

LaBerge, D., & Samuels, S. A. (1974). Toward a theory of automatic information processing in reading. *Cognitive Psychology, 6,* 293–323.

Langford, K., Slade, B., & Burnett, E. (1974). An examination of impress techniques in remedial reading. *Academic Therapy, 9,* 309–319.

Leikin, M., & Assayag Bouskila, O. (2004). Expression of syntactic complexity in sentence comprehension: A comparison between dyslexic and regular readers. *Reading and Writing, 17*(7/8), 801–822.

Leslie, L., & Caldwell, J. (1988). *Qualitative reading inventory.* New York: HarperCollins.

Logan, G. D. (1997). TI: Automaticity and reading: Perspectives from the instance theory of automatization. *Reading and Writing Quarterly, 13*(2), 123–146.

Logan, G. D. (1988). Toward an instance theory of automatization. *Psychological Review, 95,* 492–527.

Mackay, D. G. (1982). The problem of flexibility, fluency, and speed-accuracy trade off in skilled behavior. *Psychological Review, 89,* 483–506.

Mann, H. (1891). Second annual report of the secretary of the board of education–1838. In *Life and works of Horace Mann, II* (pp. 531–532). Boston: Lee and Shephard.

Manning, G. L., & Manning, M. (1984). What models of recreational reading make a difference. *Reading World, 23,* 375–380.

Marston, D. (1989). A curriculum-based measurement approach to assessing academic performance: What it is and why do it. In M. R. Shinn (Ed.), *Curriculum-based measurement: Assessing special children* (pp. 18–78). New York: Guilford.

Marston, D., & Magnusson, D. (1985). Implementing curriculum-based measurement in special and regular education settings. *Exceptional Children, 52,* 266–276.

Martin, B. (1966). *Sounds of language* (teachers edition). New York: Holt Rinehart & Winston.

Martinez, M., Roser, N., & Strecker, S. (1999). "I never thought I could be a star": A readers theatre ticket to reading fluency. *The Reading Teacher, 52,* 326–334.

Mathes, P. G., & Fuchs, L. S. (1993). Peer-mediated reading instruction in special education resource rooms. *Learning Disabilities Research and Practice, 8*(4), 233–243.

Mathes, P. G., Simmons, D. C., & Davis, B. I. (1992). Assisted reading techniques for developing reading fluency. *Reading Research and Instruction, 31*(4), 70–77.

McDade, J. E. (1937). A hypothesis for non-oral reading: Argument, experiment, and results. *Journal of Educational Research, 30,* 489–503.

McDade, J. E. (1944). Examination of a recent criticism of non-oral beginning reading. *Elementary School Journal, 44,* 343–351.

McGuffey, W. H. (1879). *McGuffey's second eclectic reader.* New York: American Book Company.

Mefferd, P. E., & Pettegrew, B. S. (1997). Fostering literacy acquisition of student with developmental disabilities: Assisted reading with predictable trade books. *Reading Research and Instruction, 36,* 177–190.

Meisinger, E. B., Schwanenflugel, P. J., Bradley, B., & Stahl, S. A. (2004). Interaction quality during partner reading. *Journal of Literacy Research, 36*(2), 111–140.

Menon, S., & Hiebert, E. H. (2005). A comparison of first-graders' reading with little books or literature-based basal anthologies. *Reading Research Quarterly, 40*(1), 12–38.

Mikkelsen, V. P. (1981). *The effects of a modified neurological impress method on developing decoding skills.* Paper presented at East Carolina University, Greenville, NC. (ERIC Document Reproduction Service No. ED 209638)

Miller, J., & Schwanenflugel, P. J. (2006). Prosody of syntactically complex sentences in the oral reading of young children. *Journal of Educational Psychology, 98,* 839–853.

Miller, J., & Schwanenflugel, P. J. (2008). A longitudinal study of the development of reading prosody as a dimension of oral reading fluency in early elementary school children. *Reading Research Quarterly, 43*(4), 336–354.

Morgan, R., & Lyon, E. (1979). Paired reading: A preliminary report on a technique for parental tuition of reading-retarded children. *Journal of Child Psychology and Psychiatry and Allied Disciplines, 20,* 151–160.

Morris, D., & Nelson, L. (1992). Supported oral reading with low achieving second graders. *Reading Research and Instruction, 32,* 49–63.

Muter, V., Hulme, C., Snowling, M. J., & Stevenson, J. (2004). Phonemes, rimes, vocabulary, and grammatical skills as foundations of early reading development: Evidence from a longitudinal study. *Developmental Psychology, 40,* 665–681.

National Institute of Child Health and Human Development. (2000). *Report of the National Reading Panel. Teaching children to read: An evidence-based assessment of the scientific research literature on reading and its implications for reading instruction: Reports of the subgroups* (NIH Publication No. 00-4754). Washington, DC: U.S. Government Printing Office.

National Reading Panel. (2000). *Report of the National Reading Panel: Teaching children to reading. Report of the subgroups.* Washington, DC: U.S. Department of Health and Human Services, National Institutes of Health.

Neuman, S. B., & Koskinen, P. S. (1992). Captioned television as comprehensible input: Effects of incidental word learning from context for language minority students. *Reading Research Quarterly, 27*(1), 94–106.

Newell, M. A. (1880). *Newell's fourth reader.* Baltimore, MD: John B. Piet and Co.

Nicholson, T. (1991). Do children read words better in context or in lists? A classic study revisited. *Journal of Educational Psychology, 83,* 444–450.

Nicholson, T., & Tan, A. (1999). Proficient word identification for comprehension. In G. B. Thompson & T. Nicholson (Eds.), *Learning to read: Beyond phonics and whole language* (pp. 150–173). Newark, DE: International Reading Association.

O'Shea, L. J., Sindelar, P. T., & O'Shea, D. (1985). The effects of repeated readings and attentional cues on reading fluency and comprehension. *Journal of Reading Behavior, 17,* 129–142.

O'Shea, L. J., Sindelar, P. T., & O'Shea, D. (1987). The effects of repeated readings and attentional cues on the reading fluency and comprehension of learning disabled readers. *Learning Disabilities Research, 2,* 103–109.

Paris, S. G., & Stahl, S. A. (2005). *Children's reading comprehension and assessment.* Mahwah, NJ: Erlbaum.

Parker, F. W. (1884). *Talks on pedagogics.* New York: Barnes and Co.

Perfetti, C. A. (1977). Language comprehension and fast decoding: Some psycholinguistic prerequisites for skilled reading comprehension. In J. T. Guthrie (Ed.), *Cognition, curriculum and comprehension* (pp. 20–41). Newark, DE: International Reading Association.

Perfetti, C. (1985). *Reading ability.* New York: Oxford University Press.

Perfetti, C. A., & Hogaboam, T. (1975). The relationship between single word decoding and reading comprehension skill. *Journal of Educational Psychology, 67,* 461–469.

Pikulski, J. J. (1990). Informal reading inventories. *The Reading Teacher, 11,* 514–516.

Pikulski, J. J., & Chard, D. J. (2005). Fluency: Bridge between decoding and reading comprehension. *The Reading Teacher, 58*(6), 510–519.

Pinnell, G. S., Pikulski, J. J., Wixson, K. K., Campbell, J. R., Gough, P. B., & Beatty, A. S. (1995). *Listening to children read aloud.* Washington, DC: Office of Educational Research and Improvement, U. S. Department of Education.

Pluck, M. (1995). Rainbow Reading Programme: Using taped stories. *Reading Forum, 1,* 25–29.

Posner, M. I., & Snyder, C. R. R. (1975). Attention and cognitive control. In R. L. Solso (Ed.), *Information processing and cognition: The Loyola symposium* (pp. 669–681). Hillsdale, NJ: Erlbaum.

Powell, W. R. (1971). The validity of instructional reading level. In R. E. Liebert (Ed.), *Diagnostic viewpoints in reading* (pp. 121–133). Newark, DE: International Reading Association.

Pressley, M., Hilden, K., & Shankland, R. (2005). *An evaluation of end-grade-3 Dynamic Indicators of Basic Early Literacy Skills (DIBELS): Speed reading without comprehension, predicting little* (Tech. Rep.). East Lansing: Michigan State University, Literacy Achievement Research Center.

Rashotte, C. A., & Torgeson, J. K. (1985). Repeated reading and reading fluency in learning-disabled children. *Reading Research Quarterly, 20,* 180–188.

Rasinski, T. V. (1985). *A study of factors involved in reader-text interactions that contribute to fluency in reading.* Unpublished doctoral dissertation, The Ohio State University, Columbus.

Rasinski, T. V. (1989). Fluency for everyone: Incorporating fluency instruction in the classroom. *The Reading Teacher, 43,* 690–693.

Rasinski, T. V. (1990a). Effects of repeated reading and listening-while-reading on reading fluency. *Journal of Educational Research, 83,* 147–150.

Rasinski, T. V. (1990b). *The effects of cued phrase boundaries in texts.* Bloomington, IN: ERIC Clearinghouse on Reading and Communication Skills. (ERIC Document Reproduction Service No. ED 313689)

Rasinski, T. V. (1994). Developing syntactic sensitivity in reading through phrase-cued texts. *Intervention in School and Clinic, 29,* 165–168.

Rasinski, T. V. (2003). *The fluent reader.* New York: Scholastic.

Rasinski, T. V. (2004). *Assessing reading fluency.* Honolulu: Pacific Resources for Education and Learning. Retrieved from http://www.prel.org

Rasinski, T. V. (2006). Reading fluency instruction: Moving beyond accuracy, automaticity, and prosody. *The Reading Teacher, 59,* 704–706.

Rasinski, T. V. (2008). Teaching fluency artfully. In R. Fink & S. J. Samuels (Eds.), *Inspiring reading success: Interest and motivation in an age of high-stakes testing* (p. 117–140). Newark, DE: International Reading Association.

Rasinski, T .V., & Hoffman, T. V. (2003). Theory and research into practice: Oral reading in the school literacy curriculum. *Reading Research Quarterly, 38,* 510–522.

Rasinski, T. V., & Padak, N. D. (1998). How elementary students referred for compensatory reading instruction perform on school-based measures of word recognition, fluency, and comprehension. *Reading Psychology: An International Quarterly, 19,* 185–216.

Rasinski, T. V., Padak, N., Linek, W., & Sturtevant, E. (1994). The effects of fluency development instruction on urban second grader readers. *Journal of Educational Research, 87,* 158–164.

Rasinski, T., Padak, N., McKeon, C., Krug,-Wilfong, L., Friedauer, J., & Heim, P. (2005). Is reading fluency a key for successful high school reading? *Journal of Adolescent and Adult Literacy, 49,* 22–27.

Rasinski, T. V., Rikli, A., & Johnston, S. (2009). Reading fluency: More than automaticity? More than a concern for the primary grades? *Literacy Research and Instruction, 48,* 350–361.

Rasinski, T. V., & Stevenson, B. (2005). The effects of *Fast Start* reading: A fluency-based home involvement reading program, on the reading achievement of beginning readers. *Reading Psychology, 26*(2), 109–125.

Rasinski, T. V., & Zutell, J.B. (1996). Is fluency yet a goal of the reading curriculum? In E. G. Sturtevant, & W. M. Linek (Eds.), *Growing literacy* (18th yearbook of the College Reading Association) (pp. 237–246). Harrisonburg, VA: College Reading Association.

Reutzel, D. R., Fawson, P. C., & Smith, J.A. (2008). Reconsidering silent sustained reading: An exploratory study of scaffolded silent reading (ScSR). *Journal of Educational Research, 102*(1), 37–50.

Reutzel, D. R., & Hollingsworth, P. M. (1993). Effects of fluency training on second grader's reading comprehension. *Journal of Educational Research, 86*(6), 325–331.

Reutzel, D. R., Hollingsworth, P. M., & Eldredge, J. L. (1994). Oral reading instruction: The impact upon student reading development. *Reading Research Quarterly, 29*(1), 40–62.

Reutzel, D. R., Jones, C. D., Fawson, P. C., & Smith, J. A. (2008). Scaffolded silent reading (ScSR): An alternative to guided oral repeated reading that works! *The Reading Teacher, 62,* 194–207.

Riedel, B. R. (2007). The relation between DIBELS, reading comprehension, and vocabulary in urban first-grade students. *Reading Research Quarterly, 42,* 546–567.

Rohrer, J. H. (1943). An analysis and evaluation of the "non-oral" method of reading instruction. *Elementary School Journal, 43,* 415–421.

Samuels, S. J. (1979). The method of repeated reading. *The Reading Teacher, 32,* 403–408.

Samuels, S. J. (2002). Reading fluency: Its development and assessment. In A. E. Farstrup & S. J. Samuels (Eds.), *What research has to say about reading instruction* (3rd ed., pp.166–183). Newark, DE: International Reading Association.

Samuels, S. J. (2006, May). *Introduction to reading fluency.* Paper presented at the annual meeting of the International Reading Association, Chicago.

Samuels, S. J. (2007). The DIBELS tests: Is speed of barking at print what we mean by fluency? *Reading Research Quarterly, 42,* 563–566.

Samuels, S. J. & Farstrup, A. E. (2006). *What research has to say about fluency instruction.* Newark, DE: International Reading Association.

Schiffrin, R. M., & Schneider, W. (1977). Controlled and automatic processing: II. Perceptual learning, automatic, attending, and a general theory. *Psychological Review, 84,* 127–190.

Schreiber, P. A. (1980). On the acquisition of reading fluency. *Journal of Reading Behavior, 12,* 177–186.

Schreiber, P. A. (1987). Prosody and structure in children's syntactic processing. In R. Horowitz & S. J. Samuels (Eds.), *Comprehending oral and written language* (pp. 243–270). New York: Academic Press.

Schreiber, P. A. (1991). Understanding prosody's role in reading acquisition. *Theory into Practice, 30,* 158–164.

Schreiber, P. A., & Read, C. (1980). Children's use of phonetic cues in spelling, parsing, and – maybe – reading. *Bulletin of the Orton Society, 30,* 209–224.

Shanahan, T., & Beck, I. (2006). Effective literacy teaching for English language learners. In D. August & T. Shanahan (Eds.), *Developing literacy in second-language learners* (pp. 415–488). Mahwah, NJ: Erlbaum.

Smith, N. B. (1965). *American reading instruction.* Newark, DE: International Reading Association.

Stahl, S. (2004). What do we know about fluency? In P. McCardle & V. Chhabra (Eds.), *The voice of evidence in reading research* (pp. 187–211). Baltimore, MD: Paul H. Brookes.

Stahl, S. A., & Heubach, K. (2006). Fluency-oriented reading instruction. In K. A. D. Stahl & M. C. McKenna (Eds.), *Reading research at work: Foundations of effective practice* (pp. 177–204). New York: Guilford.

Stahl, S. A., Heubach, K., & Cramond, B. (1997). *Fluency-oriented reading instruction* (Reading research report no. 79). Athens, GA and College Park, MD: National Reading Research Center.

Stahl, S., Heubach, K., & Holcomb, A. (2005). Fluency-oriented reading instruction. *Journal of Literacy Research, 37,* 25–60.

Stallings, J. (1980). Allocated academic learning time revisited, or beyond time on task. *Educational Researcher, 9*(2), 11–16.

Stanovich, K. E. (1980). Toward an interactive-compensatory model of individual differences in the development of reading fluency. *Reading Research Quarterly, 16,* 32–71.

Stanovich, K. E. (1986). Matthew effects in reading: Some consequences of individual differences in the acquisition of literacy. *Reading Research Quarterly, 21,* 360–407.

Stanovich, K. E. (1990). Concepts in developmental theories of reading skill: Cognitive recourses, automaticity, and modularity. *Developmental Review, 10*(1), 72–100.

Starch, D. (1915). The measurement of efficiency in reading. *Journal of Educational Psychology, 6,* 1–24.

Sutton, P. A. (1991). *Strategies to increase oral reading fluency of primary resource students.* East Lansing, MI: National Center for Research on Teacher Learning. (ERIC Document Reproduction Service No. 233328)

Therrien, W. (2004). Fluency and comprehension gains as a result of repeated reading: A meta-analysis. *Remedial and Special Education, 25,* 252–261.

Topping, K. (1987a). Paired reading: A powerful technique for parent use. *The Reading Teacher, 40,* 604–614.

Topping, K. (1987b). Peer tutored paired reading: Outcome data from ten projects. *Educational Psychology, 7,* 133–145.

Topping, K. (1989). Peer tutoring and paired reading. Combining two powerful techniques. *The Reading Teacher, 42,* 488–494.

Torgesen, J., Rashotte, C., & Alexander, A. (2001). The prevention and remediation of reading fluency problems. In M. Wolf (Ed.), *Dyslexia, fluency and the brain* (pp. 333–335). Cambridge, MA: York Press.

Tunmer, W. E., & Chapman, J. W. (1995). Context use in early reading development: Premature exclusion of a source of individual differences? *Issues in Education, 1,* 97–100.

Vadasy, P. F., Sanders, E. A., & Peyton, J. A. (2005). Relative effectiveness of reading practice or word-level instruction in supplemental tutoring: How text matters. *Journal of Learning Disabilities, 38*(4), 364–380.

Vaughn, S., Chard, D. J., Bryant, D. P., Coleman, M., Tyler, B. J., Linan-Thompson, S., et al. (2000). Fluency and comprehension interventions for third grade students. *Remedial and Special Education, 21*(6), 325–335.

Vaughn, S., Mathes, P., Linan-Thompson, S., Cirino, P., Carlson, C., Pollard-Durodola, S., et al. (2006). Effectiveness of an English intervention for first-grade English language learners at risk for reading problems. *The Elementary School Journal, 107,* 153–180.

Whalley, K., & Hansen, J. (2006). The role of prosodic sensitivity in children's reading development. *Journal of Research in Reading, 29,* 288–303.

Wilkinson, I., Wardrop, J. L., & Anderson, R. C. (1988). Silent reading reconsidered: Reinterpreting reading instruction and its effects. *American Educational Research Journal, 25,* 127–144.

Wolf, M., & Katzir-Cohen, T. (2001). Reading fluency and its intervention. *Scientific Studies of Reading, 5*(3), 211–229.

Wolf, M., Miller, L., & Donnelly, K. (2000). Retrieval, automaticity, vocabulary, elaboration, orthography (RAVE-O): A comprehensive, fluency-based reading intervention program. *Journal of Learning Disabilities, 33*(4), 375–386.

Worthy, J., & Broadus, K. (2002). Fluency beyond the primary grades: From group performance to silent, independent reading. *The Reading Teacher, 55*(4), 334–343.

Worthy, J., & Prater, K. (2002). "I thought about it all night": Readers Theater for reading fluency and motivation. *The Reading Teacher, 56,* 294–297.

Wright, J., & Cleary, K. S. (2006). Kids in the tutor seat: Building a schools' capacity to help struggling readers through a cross-age peer-tutoring program. *Psychology in the Schools, 43*(1), 99–107.

Young, A., & Bowers, P. G. (1995). Individual differences and text difficulty determinants of reading fluency and expressiveness. *Journal of Experimental Child Psychology, 60,* 428–454.

Zutell, J., & Rasinski, T. V. (1991). Training teachers to attend to their students' oral reading fluency. *Theory into Practice, 30,* 211–217.

14 Oral Discourse and Reading

Joshua F. Lawrence and Catherine E. Snow[1]

Harvard Graduate School of Education

In 1923, Walter Barnes, then Head of the English Department at Fairmont State Normal School in West Virginia, published a brief volume called *The New Democracy in the Teaching of English*, in which he argued that much of what went on in English classes was ineffective, and thus undemocratic, because it failed to motivate students or to prepare them for lives of reading or using English in any but high literary ways. He argued that students should be given a wide array of books to read, not just the classics, and that they should be encouraged to read "for life, not art," in other words, quickly and for the story rather than studiously for the literary craft. He also argued for deleting the rhetorical forms of narration, description, exposition, and argumentation from writing instruction, in favor of focus on useful oral and written language forms—conversation, discussion, explanation, informal argument, speech-making, story-telling, and letter-writing.

Barnes' provocative little volume, which makes its case without the distraction of a single reference to empirical work or others' writings, posits major educational challenges that continue to face teachers today—what is the role for oral discourse in the classroom? What oral discourse skills should students be taught, or given a chance to practice, as part of their instruction? How should we define "reading" in English class—as reading for enjoyment, reading to learn how authors think, or reading for discussion of the text? What should we emphasize in teaching writing—real-life forms like letters or school-based forms like literary analysis essays? To the dilemmas Barnes posed we could add several that have the same nature: Should students be expected to read challenging science or history texts, or can they learn those subject matters better by hearing about them from teachers who understand them? Should students be expected to focus on reading original sources in the disciplines they study, or do simplified synthetic presentations of the material suffice? Should students be trained to give oral presentations about their learning, or to participate in debates and discussions of content-matter related topics? What is the role of talk in the learning and the reading we expect of students?

Stimulated by questions like these, we review in this chapter research relevant to the question of oral discourse in the classroom, in an attempt to synthesize evidence about its relevance to literacy outcomes as well as to learning of content matter, vocabulary, and of oral discourse skills themselves. A number of different relationships have been posited between oral discourse and reading, each with its own theoretical and instructional implications:

- Skill in oral language is a developmental precursor to reading acquisition, implying that supporting oral language skills in early childhood will lead directly to better literacy performance (precursor skill perspective).
- Skill in oral language is a prerequisite to reading with comprehension, as specified for example in the "simple view of reading," implying that supporting oral language skills in early and later childhood contributes to later comprehension skills (component skill perspective).
- Skill in oral language is crucial to participating in instructional interactions that lead to effective learning of vocabulary and comprehension skills (background knowledge, con-

text, understanding of argument structure, support for aspects of a situation model and/or enhance motivation as a precursor to and support for reading). This aspect of oral language is thought to be especially important in the years before children can read independently with ease, or when children are reading especially challenging texts (scaffolding of component skills perspective).

- Participation in oral discourse, taught and practiced in pedagogical approaches such as Questioning the Author (QtA) or Reciprocal Teaching, is a mechanism for learning to experience and internalize responses to text that will eventually lead to greater independent reading comprehension skill (scaffolding of comprehension processes perspective).
- Participation in oral discourse, in programs like Collaborative Reasoning, is a mechanism for practicing the perspective-taking and reasoning skills crucial to comprehension and writing (appropriation perspective).
- Learning through modeling and practice to produce oral discourse of a sophisticated sort (academic language) is, in addition to being a route to better literacy skills, itself a goal of education closely related to literacy and a marker of full literacy development (autonomous goal perspective).

The first three of these justifications for the inclusion of discussion in the classroom might be grouped under a literacy skills perspective and the next two as Vygotskian in nature, emphasizing opportunities for the scaffolded, interactive, oral development of skills that will ultimately be deployed autonomously, privately, and in literate encounters.

It is notable that some of these hypotheses about the relationship between oral discourse and reading outcomes have been formulated based mostly on data from a limited stage of reading development—the literacy skills relationships have been tested with primary and early elementary grade readers, while the argument that oral discourse skill is a goal in itself pertains mostly to more advanced learners acquiring more sophisticated reading skills. Only the Vygotskian claim, that oral discourse is a context for practicing, learning, and appropriating comprehension skills, has been posited as valid across ages and levels of reading skill. In this chapter we review the literature on how oral discourse relates to literacy within a developmental framework, so as to articulate more clearly (a) any relationship among these various hypotheses, (b) claims related to their developmental limits, and (c) the dynamic linking oral to literate skills as broadly as possible, across as wide a range of developmental stages as possible.

HISTORICAL BACKGROUND

There has been an increasingly explicit focus on oral discourse in the work of reading researchers since Walter Barnes' 1923 book, as demonstrated by the increasing attention devoted to the topic in successive editions of this handbook. Much of the research that laid the ground for current perspectives on classroom discussion and discourse are found in chapters focused on metacognition, reading comprehension, and strategy instruction in the first two editions. In the first edition, research programs intended to help students appropriate reading comprehension skills and strategies are described as being influenced by Vygotsky (1978, 1986), who argued that higher order cognitive processes were often the internalization of communicative events that were initially interactive and scaffolded by experts. For example, Baker and Brown (1984) reviewed Palinscar and Brown's Training Studies and provided a brief overview of how conversational turn taking was used in that program to support reading. In their chapter on research on teaching reading comprehension Tierney and Cunningham (1984) also reviewed discussion as one tool in developing background knowledge and supporting comprehension before, during, and after reading. They reviewed student-centered approaches to supporting reading comprehension, including Stauffer's (1959) Directed Reading-Thinking Activity, Manzo's (1969) ReQuest Procedure, and Palinscar and Brown's (1984) Reciprocal Teaching. Clearly, when the first edition was published there were several theoretical perspectives and empirical studies which suggested that oral discussion could play an important role in reading comprehension. However, it is clear in each of these chapters that oral discourse was understood primarily as a facilitator of student acquisition of specific comprehension strategies; these studies did not emphasize forms of oral discourse as essential in changing how we think about classroom instruction.

The second edition reviewed more research on oral discussion. In their chapter on comprehension instruction Pearson and Fielding (1991) described a model of explicit instruction aimed at "the gradual release of responsibility," i.e., shifting responsibility over time from teachers modeling comprehension to students' independent application of the reading strategy or skill (based on Campione, 1981). Oral discourse has been taken up by many researchers and practitioners as one of the essential ways to move from modeling to application, and the gradual release of responsibility model has been widely cited in research, professional development literature, and in guides for teachers and volunteers (Block & Parris, 2008; Chandler-Olcott & Hinchman, 2005). Pearson and Fielding also provided a review of research on student-teacher dialogue (including teachers' use of inferential, predictive, summative and interpretive questions) and research on peer interaction and tutoring programs. Many of these themes were echoed in the chapter on teachers' instructional actions (Roehler & Duffy, 1991), which provided a review of research on teacher explanations, modeling (including think-alouds), questions, and the gradual release of responsibility. They also reviewed research from two programs that carefully manipulated classroom teacher-student and peep-peer discourse to support learning: Reciprocal Teaching, and the Kamehameha Early Education Program. Alvermann and Moore (1991) described the experimental research on reading practices in their chapter on secondary school reading, and reviewed some studies that emphasize oral discourse as a support for reading comprehension, but they did not explicitly focus on differences in oral discourse in the programs they review. The description they provided of actual secondary reading practices, however, highlighted the essential role of lecture and discussion in secondary schools. The second handbook clearly reflected advances in our understanding of the importance of teacher discourse and peer-to-peer conversation in supporting reading, and in recognition that text and discourse support and reinforce each other in schools.

The third volume of the *Handbook of Reading Research* acknowledged the importance of oral discourse with a chapter dedicated to classroom language and literacy learning (Wilkinson & Silliman, 2000). Wilkinson and Silliman reviewed a wide range of research on classroom language, including careful descriptive studies of contextualized language use, summarized theoretical perspectives on classroom communication, and provided a taxonomy of how oral discourse is conceptualized as supporting reading comprehension. Recognizing the strengths of this chapter, it is not our intention to cover this ground again, but to provide a more detailed review of correlational and quasi-experimental studies relating oral discourse to literacy outcomes, with an emphasis on more recent research.

Current Trends and Issues

Definition of Oral Discourse

A first issue to clarify is whether we are focusing in this chapter on oral discourse as a skill accomplished by the learner, or as a context for learning. Of course, if oral discourse is a context for learning, then the level of discourse skill a student requires in order to participate in the learning opportunities classroom discourse affords must be taken into account. When viewed as a skill, oral discourse can be taken to mean many things, and since language develops with enormous alacrity, the actual phenomena being referred to change qualitatively across the developmental span under consideration here (preschool through 12th grade). Claims have been made that many different aspects of oral discourse skill relate to reading: telling stories, comprehending stories, using academic language forms like definitions, producing extended discourse, producing effective arguments with warrants for claims, comprehending multiple perspectives in making or countering arguments, and so on (e.g., Snow, Porche, Tabors, & Harris, 2007; Snow, Tabors, & Dickinson, 2001; Tabors, Roach, & Snow, 2001)

A crucial question that can only be definitively answered with further research is whether there is any specific oral discourse form or skill that accounts for the relationship to literacy, either predictively or in process, or whether these extended discourse skills are simply parasitic on oral language skills in general, and vocabulary in particular, which of course has recurrently been shown to have a robust relationship to literacy (Nagy & Scott, 2000).

For purposes of this chapter, we define *oral discourse* as extended oral productions, whether monologic or multi-party, centered around a topic, activity, or goal (see Ninio & Snow, 1996; Ninio & Snow, 1999). We define *oral discourse development* as acquiring the skills uniquely required for participation in oral discourse, i.e., setting aside the acquisition of grammar, vocabulary, and pragmatics skills needed for casual conversation, but including the grammar, vocabulary, and pragmatics skills required for lengthier, topic-focused interactions, or for certain genres of monologue (definition, explanation) even if relatively brief. When reviewing the literature on children up through the primary grades, we focus on oral discourse as an activity—a context for learning—rather than primarily as a skill. When reviewing the literature on older children, we do consider oral discourse as both an outcome and a context for learning, acknowledging that sophisticated oral discourse skills no doubt develop through participation in oral discourse activities, but they may by enriched as well by reading. It is unlikely that the oral skills of great orators, for example, reflect only the language they have heard with no influence from the language they have read.

The research relating oral discourse to literacy comes in two forms: correlational and prospective research showing that children with high oral discourse skills tend to learn literacy skills with ease, and instructional or intervention studies that inject support for oral discourse (often oral discourse focused precisely on comprehension and vocabulary learning) into the classroom, and seek impacts on comprehension outcomes. Each of these different kinds of research has its own advantages; the first has high ecological validity and is informative about normal development, whereas the second allows for causal inferences but may have limited utility in guiding wide scale instructional improvement. Thus, we attempt in the review that follows to come to conclusions that reflect knowledge acquired from both types of research.

Oral Discourse During Emergent and Early Reading

The presumed importance of oral discourse as a preparation for literacy is emphasized by the ubiquity of attention to talking and reading with young children in parenting advice. There is considerable correlational evidence to support the value of this advice. Frequency of shared reading during the preschool period, for example, is a good predictor of school readiness in analyses of large scale, nationally representative data sets such as the NCES birth cohort study (e.g., Barrueco, Lopez, & Miles, 2007). Smaller, more focused observational studies amplify the information about this relationship. For example, in the Home-School Study of Language and Literacy Development children in low-income, English-speaking families were observed in the home and at preschool at ages three and four, and tested for language and literacy outcomes regularly starting at age five. One of the major predictors of later reading outcomes reflecting experiences in the home during the preschool period was exposure to extended discourse, a composite made up of several specific oral discourse genres: engaging in pretend-play talk during toy play, discussing information that went beyond that present in text or pictures during book-reading, and participation of narratives and explanations during dinner table conversations (Tabors et al., 2001). Extended discourse was also a major predictor among the children's preschool classroom experiences, where it was defined as frequency of engagement in cognitively challenging talk during group activities such as bookreading or morning circle time.

Numerous correlational studies show that the frequency and quality of book-reading interactions during the preschool years predict vocabulary outcomes (e.g., Dickinson & Smith, 1994; Torr, 2004; van Kleeck, 2003; Weizman & Snow, 2001) which in turn predict later reading outcomes (Sénéchal, Ouellette, & Rodney, 2006). A small set of experimental studies offers robust experimental evidence relating book-reading talk to vocabulary outcomes, if the talk is explicitly structured as 'dialogic,' i.e., involving rich opportunities for the children to respond to open-ended questions and ultimately to take over much of the responsibility for telling the story (Hargrave & Sénéchal, 2000; Lonigan & Whitehurst, 1998; Valdez-Menchaca & Whitehurst, 1992; Whitehurst, Arnold, et al., 1994; Whitehurst, Epstein, et al., 1994).

Text Talk is another procedure for increasing the richness of oral discourse around texts read to or with young children (now developed into a curriculum published by Scholastic for use in grades K–3) (Beck & McKeown, 2001, 2007). Text Talk is designed primarily as a vocabulary enhancement procedure, but in fact the instructional strategies embedded in the program promote student involvement in answering open-ended questions and in offering high-level interpretations of the text as well as in vocabulary learning. Though Text Talk has not been subject of a full-scale evaluation, the quasi-experimental study reported by Beck and McKeown (2007) suggests it is effective in promoting learning of the words taught.

It is striking that procedures like Dialogic Reading and Text Talk have been largely discussed, evaluated, and marketed as vocabulary interventions, when in fact these same activities can reasonably be analyzed as promoting deep comprehension. Learning to retell a story autonomously, the ultimate goal of the dialogic reading interactions, or to respond to probing comprehension questions by citing textual evidence, as in Text Talk, both constitute direct instruction in comprehension of written text, delivered to children at an age before they typically are reading those texts. Useful examples of classroom activities that lead to opportunities for rich oral language related to literacy, and of the levels of oral discourse skill children can be expected to display in the preschool and primary grades, is available in Resnick and Snow (2009).

Oral Discourse as Related to Conventional Reading

Once children have been taught basic decoding skills (or while they are acquiring them), classroom discourse in the early elementary grades is typically focused on assessing and ensuring comprehension. Since the texts read in these early grades are often designed to teach decoding rather than primarily to engage interest or challenge comprehension, such oral activities can be reduced to rather routine IRE sequences. There is considerable evidence, though, that expanding such discussions to include specific features can improve students' comprehension skills. The list of discourse features that have been shown to promote comprehension even in the primary grades includes:

- Establishing a purpose for reading
- Activating relevant background knowledge
- Posing open-ended questions that require deep processing
- Responding to student initiatives
- Promoting peer interaction

The features on this list are present across a variety of programs which have generated some evidence of success, including the KEEP model, instructional conversations, collaborative reasoning, Reciprocal Teaching, and Questioning the Author, though each of these programs also has specific features that distinguish it. Reciprocal Teaching and Questioning the Author are discussed in the next section, as they have been used primarily with somewhat older students.

KEEP Model and Instructional Conversations

A body of work that emerged from the innovations introduced in the Kamehameha School in the 1970s (Au & Jordan, 1981; Tharp & Gallimore, 1991) developed over various cycles of implementation (e.g., in the Rough Rock school in Arizona, Jordan, 1995) and research into an emphasis on the importance of "instructional conversations." A key aspect of instructional conversation developed to allow students more freedom of turn-taking and greater access to peer talk, based on observations that teacher-controlled IRE-dominated talk was counterproductive in classrooms serving native Hawaiian and native-American children (Au & Mason, 1981). Thus, specific aspects of instructional conversations might vary in response to cultural norms, but a central notion is that new knowledge is built through participation in topic-focused talk in which students and teachers have equal participation rights, teachers play the role of guide or facilitator rather than the expert, shared background knowledge is taken as a starting place, and open-ended questions are frequent (Goldenberg, 1991; Goldenberg & Patthey-Chavez, 1995; Saunders, Goldenberg, & Hamann, 1992; Tharp & Gallimore, 1991). The developers of the ideas around instructional conversation acknowledge that considerable professional development is needed to ensure its implementation (Goldenberg & Gallimore, 1991). This model of talk has been studied systematically primarily in classrooms serving ethnic- and language-minority children, where positive effects on reading comprehension have been shown (Goldenberg, 1991).

Collaborative Reasoning

Another line of research that has developed around a set of procedures to enrich classroom discussion is referred to as "collaborative reasoning." One of the principal assumptions of this explicitly Vygotskian research program is that participation in argumentation and discussion produces critical thinking skills, specifically an understanding of argument schemas, that are useful in reading and in writing. Researchers set out to understand the patterns of argumentative discourse in classroom settings, and subsequently to teach those forms of discourse explicitly as a preparation for reading and writing more sophisticated texts (Reznitskaya et al., 2008).

Collaborative reasoning promotes argumentation by introducing engaging topics or big questions or interesting dilemmas based on stories read. The discussions occur in peer groups, guided by teachers who might prompt students to state their positions clearly, challenge students with counterarguments, sum up good student arguments, and model good reasoning processes. A variety of studies have shown that student discourse reveals more sophisticated reasoning when collaborative reasoning procedures are used (Chinn, Anderson, & Waggoner, 2001), and that there are positive effects of participation in collaborative reasoning on written arguments, among U.S. fourth and fifth graders (Reznitskaya et al., 2001) as well as students in China and Korea (Dong, Anderson, Kim, & Li, 2006). Essays written by students who had experienced collaborative reasoning contained more supporting reasons, more anticipatory counterarguments, more rebuttals, and more arguments than those in the standard teaching condition.

Oral Discourse During Middle and Secondary Grades

Correlational Studies

There is a long tradition of research into correlations between features of classroom practices and reading outcomes, including many features of oral discourse. In the 1960s and 1970s, process-product researchers tried to examine a wide range of classroom practices and look for correlations with improved reading achievement (Fisher et al., 1978; Soar, 1973). Unfortunately, correlational methods may lead to misinterpretations of nonlinear relationships between classroom practices and student outcomes. At the time these studies were conducted, it was not technically possible to describe how classroom instruction predicted student reading growth (Singer & Willett, 2003) or capture variation between classrooms and schools when modeling relationships (Bryk & Raudenbrush, 1988; Bryk & Raudenbush, 1992). These studies have also been criticized for not paying enough attention to theory or the research literature in selecting which relationships to explore, but instead exploring relationships across all the collected data, inevitably resulting in Type I error (Berliner, 1979; Gage & Needels, 1989). Although these findings need to be treated cautiously, they were reviewed in the first version of this handbook (Rosenshine & Stevens, 1984). Some of the strongest relationships in the data were the positive correlations between classroom discussion and reading achievement, especially in secondary schools. More recent correlational research also supports these early findings.

Gamoran and Nystrand (1991) analyzed data from English and social studies classes in 16 midwestern schools to predict improvement in each class controlling for a host of background variables. They found that discussion occurred less than 1 minute a day in typical English and social studies classes in their sample, whereas 8 to 10 minutes were spent lecturing, and 12 to 14 minutes were spent in question and answer format in English and social studies classes respectively. In a series of regression analyses, they showed that amount of time engaged in discussion was the strongest predictor of achievement scores, followed by time allocated to question and answer, and then the time spent in teacher lecturing. In another analysis of these data, Nystrand and Gamoran (1991) found that discussion time and small-group time correlated with incidence of authentic reading and writing tasks and class time allotted to contiguous reading and writing. In a series of regressions, these variables and others (authenticity of teacher questions, uptake, high evaluation of oral response and writing) were compared to models that only included variables that captured student disengagement or procedural engagement. Results demonstrated that while procedural engagement did predict improved achievement, it did so less well than the substantive engagement variables associated with discussion and small-group work.

Applebee, Langer, Nystrand, and Gamoran (2003) looked at classroom discussion in 19 schools, including both middle and high schools with a total of 1,412 students in 64 classes. Observers used the class observation system (Nystrand, 1999) to code many features of classroom conversation, including authentic teacher questions, open discussion, questions with uptake, evidence of envisionment building, extended curricular conversations, and high academic standards. Results demonstrated that fewer than 2 minutes per 60-minute class were typically allotted to open discussion, with students in lower tracks participating in even less open discussion than higher-track peers. A principal component analysis of observation variables identified two components to be used in predictive analyses. Discussion-based approaches (Component 1) included authentic teacher questions, open discussion, curricular conversations and emphasis on envisionment building activities (for which see Langer, 1985); this component predicted spring literacy scores controlling for baseline data and a range of background variables. High academic demands (Component 2) consisted of emphasis on revision of mechanics and content as well as hours of English homework per week and did not predict spring scores once academic track was included. This series of studies demonstrated that classroom discussion is an important predictor of literacy achievement, and that there is remarkably little rich discussion in many classrooms, especially those that serve the low-track students who need the most support.

Paideia Seminars are a format in which all participants, including the teacher and the students, have read rich and complex texts in advance of the class and come prepared to discuss predetermined questions. The teacher introduces each question and then facilitates student responses, taking notes and summarizing student discussion if it loses focus or cogency. Although students need to be prepared to cite textual evidence for claims, students are not intended to reach consensus in their discussion and teachers are expected to let conversation run its course without praising "correct" answers. Instead, teachers are expected to act as facilitators, encouraging student turn taking, eye contact, and active listening (Adler, 1982).

Billings and Fitzgerald (2002) examined Paideia Seminars in the classes of a veteran teacher using the technique with her 11th-grade English classes. Analysis of transcribed classroom discourse focused on who talked, the purpose of the talk and the form of the talk. These analyses demonstrated that, even though the teacher had used this method and believed in the importance of student talk, she tended to hold the floor far longer ($M = 45.6$ minutes) than the students did ($M = 25.9$ minutes) across the three sessions. Discourse analysis demonstrated that neither students nor teacher read from the text often (usually not at all) but that they tended to reference the text often. When the teacher was asked to reflect on her facilitation of the sessions she acknowledge that the session did not conform to the expectation of the Paideia Seminars in key ways, an interesting finding given evidence that teachers do not share beliefs about good classroom discussion or have a good capacity to self-evaluate facilitation of discussion in secondary classrooms without well defined discourse expectations (Alvermann, O'Brien, & Dillon, 1990).

Experimental and Quasi-Experimental Studies

Many of the quasi-experimental studies focused on classroom discourse evaluated effectiveness of tools and resources developed to support teachers in generating lengthier and richer classroom discussions. Each of the tools and studies focuses on its unique method for packaging the promotion of extended discourse, but we try in this chapter to emphasize the similarities among them.

RECIPROCAL TEACHING

Although the Reciprocal Teaching model developed out of a research program into comprehension-fostering and comprehension-monitoring activities, it is the interactive training component that has had the most significant influence on research in oral discourse. In their pilot study, Brown and Palinscar (1982) developed an intervention based in part on the work of Manzo (1969), in which the teacher modeled specific reading comprehension responses (summarizing, questioning, clarifying, and predicting) and elicited student participation. The results from this study were impressive: students improved from a baseline performance of 15% correct to 85% correct after training.

In their follow-up study, Palinscar and Brown (1984) used the Reciprocal Teaching intervention with six students who had been matched with students who were placed in a variety of comparison conditions. All students in the Reciprocal Teaching intervention were seventh graders who demonstrated at least minimum acceptable levels of coding fluency, but performed poorly on reading comprehension measures. Students in the Reciprocal Teaching group discussed reading in either the peer teacher or student role, with the adult teacher helping to facilitate the peer teachers' use of the reading comprehension strategies in guiding discussion. Coded transcriptions of the discussion from the Reciprocal Teaching classes demonstrated increase in correctly stated main idea questions, quality summary statements and main idea summaries.

Students in Reciprocal Teaching groups showed dramatic improvement in their performance on the daily reading comprehension task relative to the control groups, and also demonstrated improved reading comprehension of social studies and science reading.

Reciprocal Teaching has been a widely disseminated and replicated form of instruction, perhaps stimulated by the original authors' interest in replication in regular classrooms. In the second study reported by Palinscar and Brown (1984), a classroom teacher at the research site facilitated the reciprocal instruction conversations with sixth- and eighth-grade students. In other regards the procedures for this study were the same as those in the first, and many of the same outcomes were obtained: there was a marked improvement in the quality of student dialogue, improvement on daily comprehension tests and evidence of transfer to content-area reading.

Researchers have used a wide range of standardized and researcher-developed tests to determine the effects of Reciprocal Teaching with students from grades 3 and up (Rosenshine & Meister, 1994). Studies have generated both significant and non-significant effects at all grade levels except third grade, for which only non-significant results have been obtained. Not surprisingly, each of these studies adopts some but not all of the instructional moves described by Palinscar and Brown (1984). Indeed, Palinscar and Brown themselves modified Reciprocal Teaching by introducing the strategies in whole class instruction before launching oral discussion, for instance (Palincsar, Brown, & Martin, 1987). That being said, there also seems to have been a tendency for professional developers and publishers of instructional texts to apply the term *Reciprocal Teaching* to strategy instruction that may or may not include careful attention to student dialogue and classroom discourse (in some cases resulting in a lethal mutations as defined in Brown & Campione, 1996).

QUESTIONING THE AUTHOR

Like Reciprocal Teaching, Questioning the Author is a program of instructional moves that have been developed to help students focus on the meaning of their reading by paying special attention to how teachers respond to reading orally and then model and facilitate classroom discourse. The central conceptual theme of these tools is that teachers want to provide a format through which students can converse with the author. As such, students need to think of authors as fallible, and as bringing their own perspectives and biases to their writing. An emphasis on these aspects of reading demands an instructional focus on meaning making and comprehension strategies, and careful attention to student talk to facilitate rich discussion (Beck & McKeown, 2006; Beck, McKeown, & Hamilton, 1997).

Beck and colleagues (2006; 1997) argue that question-driven discussion that follows the IRE model and treats texts as the repository for correct answers is not sufficient for supporting a conversation about meaning. QtA teachers devise queries rather than questions, and require students to provide elaborate responses in their own language and engage with other students to determine and co-create meaning. QtA teachers are also provided with a range of suggested "talk moves" to help teachers sustain conversation and model tools for students to do the same (these will be described more extensively below).

Beck and colleagues evaluated classroom interactions in an urban fourth grade classroom implementing QtA relative to baseline data before QtA implementation (Beck, McKeown, Sandora, Kucan, & Worthy, 1996). They found that there were changes in the kind of questions used by both social studies and English Language Arts teachers; information retrieval questions dropped from 77% to 12% and 43% to 12.5% of teacher questions in each classroom respectively. They also found changes in social studies revoicing moves, and a doubling of student talk in QtA classrooms compared to baseline. They found a significant change in how students engaged with text on a researcher-created constructing meaning task; there was a large increase in the numbers of students whose responses gave evidence in their own words of having created a complete situation model of the text.

ACCOUNTABLE TALK

Wolf, Crosson, and Resnick (2004) conducted an evaluation of instructional quality including the extent to which classwork is rigorous, the teacher's expectations are clear, and specific elements of classroom discourse are present, elements which together define Accountable Talk. Specifically, Accountable Talk requires evidence of participation, linking ideas (from both students and teachers), asking and providing knowledge, and asking for and modeling rigorous thinking. Analysis was conducted on observational data from 21 reading lessons in elementary and middle schools. The classroom discourse from each lesson was rated by the degree to which it was accountable to the learning community, accountable to accurate knowledge, and accountable to standards of reasoning (Michaels, O'Connor, & Resnick, 2008). In addition, discourse analysis of teachers' talk moves and patterns of classroom interaction were conducted. When elements of the Accountable Talk rubric were used to predict academic rigor in stepwise regression analyses, only rubric categories that captured evidence of student discussion (providing knowledge and showing rigorous thinking) remained as significant predictors in the final model, accounting for 81% of the variation in observed academic rigor. Similarly, use of Accountable Talk in math lessons has been shown to be effective in raising math scores for low-income students (Chapin, O'Connor, & Anderson, 2003). One of the explicit implications from this work is that more needs to be done to help teachers become aware of the use of talk moves to support classroom discussion.

WORD GENERATION

Word Generation (WG) is an initiative that focuses on helping students develop vocabulary and academic language skills by ensuring recurrent exposure to frequently occurring academic words across various disciplinary contexts. The model for this instruction involves teachers across the curriculum (English language arts, science, math, social studies) who coordinate with each other to ensure approximately 15 minutes of Word Generation instruction per day for every student. Although academic vocabulary is the explicit target of instruction, a wide range of literacy and classroom discussion activities and protocols are used, which provide opportunities for classroom discussion and for hearing and using the new words in engaging contexts. Each week's words are presented in a paragraph that sets up a controversial topic or theme such as immigration, school uniforms, or the status of pop musicians as role models. Each week's activities culminate in a classroom debate and a brief written 'taking a stand' essay. During the second year of Word Generation data was collected from over one thousand students in five participating schools and three comparison schools (Snow, Lawrence, & White, 2009). Regression analysis was used to determine if participation in WG predicted improved vocabulary outcomes for students controlling for pretest measures. The results of this analysis demonstrated that treatment was a significant predictor of word learning for all students, although word learning gains were small. More importantly for the purposes of this review, words learned by students in the treatment schools predicted improved results on the state standardized assessment of English language arts and reading. These results suggest that the relatively small number of words learned were not responsible for improvement on the global measure, but rather that improvement reflected the level of student participation and involvement in classroom activities, daily discussion, and rigorous debate, which in turn was reflected in improved literacy achievement.

Components of Discourse-Rich Programs

As noted above, the various specific programs or procedures designed to generate classroom discussion share many features. We summarize those in this section, under the categories of teacher talk and parameters of discussion.

Teacher Talk

Teacher talk has an extremely important and broad set of functions in any classroom which we want to acknowledge before examining specific talk moves that teachers make. First, we need to consider that the world of school discourse is socially constructed by specific historical conditions (Gee, 2001, 2006). In the particularly context of the United States that means that certain kinds of knowledge that students bring with them to school will be valued, while other kinds, particularly the knowledge shared by language and cultural minority students, may not be (Moje et al., 2004; Moll, 1992). Teacher discourse is one of the central tools that teachers use to explicitly address the perceived disjuncture between students' personal and social knowledge base and what is being expected of them by text. As is clear from the Reading Apprenticeship framework, social and personal dimension are readily compatible with the cognitive and knowledge building functions of teacher talk (Greenleaf, Schoenbach, & Cziko, 2001; Schoenbach, Greenleaf, Cziko, & Hurwitz, 1999).

Some of the specific teacher moves that have been examined include the following:

- **Modeling**. Teachers who model how they handle the reading challenges they encounter by "thinking aloud" help students understand what skilled readers do as they are reading, and thus provide explicit guidance to students on how to do the same (Collins & Smith, 1982; Kucan & Beck, 1997).
- **Direct explanation.** In addition to demonstrating how to attack problems, teachers name specific strategies and talk about when they should be employed. There is evidence that this move improves student use of strategies over the modeling of the strategy alone (Bereiter & Bird, 1985).
- **Marking**. Marking is a strategy described in Questioning the Author in which the teacher responds to a student question or comment in a way that highlights specific aspects of the text. Turning back is a similar move described in QtA in which the teacher turns the conversation back to the text by asking students "what does the author say about that?"
- **Verifying and clarifying student understandings.** Revoicing is a move in which the teacher rewords a student comment (or asks another student to do so), in some cases reformulating its meaning, and asks the student if that is what was intended (O'Connor, 2001; O'Connor & Michaels, 1996). Asking students to clarify their meaning with questions like "what do you mean" challenges students to articulate the full extent of their understanding (Heyman, 1983).

Parameters of Discussion Protocols

The generally positive findings from researchers evaluating the effectiveness of programs like Reciprocal Teaching, Questioning the Author, Word Generation, and Accountable Talk suggest that attention to student discourse is especially important in supporting student literacy. Clearly, these programs have similarities in focusing teacher attention specifically on the quality and amount of student talking during the class period. By being explicit about expectations for classroom discourse, teachers also draw student attention to certain aspects of school talk that may go unnoticed in most classrooms. Not all aspects of classroom discourse are changed by any program or all at once, but the following are some of the dimensions highlighted in these programs:

- **Interpretive authority.** Most of these programs encourage students to take a large role in interpreting the text, although a gradual transition from teacher to student roles as official arbiters of meaning is often prescribed. The Paideia Seminars are very explicit about teachers being facilitators, perhaps because it is designed for high school students. Almasi and Gambrell (1997) note that students assume authority more easily in peer-peer than in teacher-student discussions. A diverse range of perspectives can result in stimulating intellectual conflict (Johnson & Johnson, 2009).
- **Control over turns (order, air time).** Teachers implementing Reciprocal Teaching have reported being very deliberate about choosing which students they select to be the peer-teacher, and there are specific instructions about sharing the floor in many if not all of these programs. That being said, it is interesting how little research has focused on discussion formats that dictate order and air time explicitly; these elements have been manipulated more extensively in adult discussion protocols such as Final Word and the Constructivist Learning Groups Protocol (Garmston & Wellman, 1994; McDonald, Mohr, Dichter, & McDonald, 2003).
- **Control over topic.** A widely recognized feature of productive discussion is that it be topic-focused and coherent (Almasi, O'Flahavan & Arya, 2001). Approaches to guiding student discussion topics include formulating specific questions for groups to answer, assigning specific reading strategies for students to use when interpreting textual meaning, and specifying to what degree conversation should be tied directly to the text and to what degree students can instead discuss connections to other texts and experiences.
- **Open-ended and genuine questions.** A key strategy in launching authentic discussion is to start from genuine and stimulating questions, often ones worthy of discussion and ones on which opinions can legitimately differ. This strategy is central to the design of collaborative reasoning, Word Generation, and Paideia Seminars; discussions focused on ensuring correct comprehension of text (Reciprocal Teaching, Questioning the Author) are meant to start with genuine questions, but also questions to which the correct answers can be found in the text.

Implications for Practice, Policy, and Future Research

Practice

Research reviewed here strongly supports the claim that when students have extended time for engaged conversation about text, they are likely to comprehend what they read better, and to build autonomous comprehension and writing skills. It also seems to be the case that by attending to their talk moves and how they set up student discussion routines, teachers can provide the scaffolding for students to have rich discussion using a range of reading strategies and techniques. Although there are important differences in what topics and strategies would be appropriate for younger and older readers, the qualities of rich discussion are very similar across grade levels:

- they start from worthy questions
- students and teachers share both authority and participation rights
- time for peer interaction is available
- an explicit goal for the discussion has been established
- rules about appropriate contributions to the discussion are known to all participants.

Though evidence is consistent in suggesting the value of these practices, we must also confront the fact that genuine discussion is remarkably infrequent and brief in U.S. classrooms. Even when lip service is given to the importance of discussion in literacy programs or professional development for literacy, the resultant practice is often unrecognizable as discussion, often subverted by the focus on vocabulary or strategy instruction rather than by the big ideas and important questions that generate genuine discussion. There is considerable evidence that the professional development needed to support genuine classroom discussion is neither brief nor easy (Goldenberg & Gallimore, 1991), and even teachers who are highly skilled at it may not succeed in every class.

The research reviewed here provides some general support for the range of practices known as book clubs or literature circles (Alvermann, Young, Green, & Wisenbaker, 1999; Goatley, Brock, & Raphael, 1995; Paratore & McCormack, 1997; Stien & Beed, 2004). Literature circles create opportunities to discuss books, which is one of the features indexing compliance with the early literacy standard called habits of reading (Resnick & Hampton, 2009). Literature circles share features with the programs reviewed here, in that they emphasize rich student discourse and provide a range of tools for teachers to think about how to help students maintain academic discussion. Unlike the specific programs offered here, however, book clubs do not necessarily have specific instructional topics. One result is that there is huge variation in how students and teachers conduct book clubs or literature circles, making it extremely difficult to describe the strengths and weaknesses of this collection of approaches. To the degree that these formats provide students with models for how to attack text and opportunities for rich discussion, these practices probably support and strengthen student literacy, although there is some evidence that non-struggling readers benefit from this approach but weaker readers do not (Marshall, 2006).

Further Research

Despite the widespread agreement that classroom discussion contributes to important literacy skills and to content-area learning, there is remarkably little research focused on it (Murphy, Wilkinson, Soter, Hennessey, & Alexander, 2009). Many practices, such as book clubs, have been widely adopted with no research confirming their effectiveness. We need to understand which features of book clubs and other such procedures support student learning.

Research that provides guidelines for the use of discussion with students at different ages and in different learning settings is also needed. There is no explicitly developmental study of classroom discussion; the research reviewed in this chapter suggests strongly that many of the features of good classroom discussion in secondary classrooms can be replicated in the primary grades, but systematic study is needed to explore whether that is true and if so what adjustments are needed for younger participants.

Microgenetic research on discussion is also needed. Groups that engage regularly in classroom conversation develop in different ways (Almasi et al., 2001). It would be extremely valuable to know if groups meet typical milestones in their ability to sustain academic discussion, and how the sequence of the groups' ability to sustain academic discourse is similar or different for classes using different programs. Similarly, more information about the affordances and effects of peer-peer versus teacher-led discussion is needed, and about the optimal mechanisms for preparing students to engage in productive discussion.

A major issue that needs research attention is implementation. How are teachers best prepared to lead, launch, and facilitate discussion, and then to evaluate the value of the discussions for student learning and the quality of student contributions to the discussion?

Finally, the relation of discussion to outcomes needs more study. Precisely what features of classroom discussion account for its positive effects on student learning? Are formats other than face-to-face discussion (e.g., written responses to genuine questions, on-line discussions) equally productive, or is the social engagement crucial to the effects (see Kim, Anderson, Nguyen-Jahiel, & Archodidou, 2007)?

Policy Perspectives

A focus within accountability systems implemented at state, district, or school level on easily testable skills can reduce teachers' willingness to invest time in classroom discussion. More robust evidence showing that engagement in classroom discussion leads to comprehension advances, to improved writing across a variety of genres, and to more efficient learning in content areas will be needed if we are to make a place for discussion in poorly performing schools. In addition, adding participation in debate, oral argument, and discussion as a standard that secondary students should meet would increase emphasis on opportunities for students to learn these discourse skills as an end in itself rather than only as a means to better literacy outcomes.

NOTES

1. Work on this chapter has been greatly influenced by the authors' collaborations with Claire White, M. Catherine O'Connor, and members of the Strategic Education Research Partnership (SERP) Boston Field Site Design Team, with funding to SERP from the Spencer Foundation, the William and Flora Hewlett Foundation, and the Carnegie Corporation of New York. In addition, Joshua Lawrence was supported during the writing of this chapter by a Spencer Foundation Senior Scholar Award to Catherine Snow.

REFERENCES

Adler, M. (1982). *The Paideia proposal: An educational manifesto.* New York: Macmillan.

Almasi, J., & Gambrell, L. B. (1997). Conflict during classroom discussions can be a good thing. In J. R. Paratore & R. McCormack (Eds.), *Peer talk in the classroom: Learning from research.* Newark, DL: International Reading Association.

Almasi, J., O'Flahavan, J. F., & Arya, P. (2001). A comparative analysis of student and teacher development in more and less proficient discussions of literature. *Reading Research Quarterly, 36*(2), 96–120.

Alvermann, D., & Moore, D. W. (1991). Secondary School Reading. In R. Barr, M. L. Kamil, P. B. Mosenthal, & P. D. Pearson (Eds.), *Handbook of reading research* (Vol. II, pp. 951–983). New York: Longman.

Alvermann, D., O'Brien, D., & Dillon, D. (1990). What teachers do when they say they're having discussions of content area reading assignments: A qualitative analysis. *Reading Research Quarterly, 25*(4), 296–322.

Alvermann, D., Young, J. P., Green, C., & Wisenbaker, J. M. (1999). Adolescents' perceptions and negotiations of literacy practices in after-school read and talk clubs. *American Educational Research Journal, 36*(2), 221–264.

Applebee, A., Langer, J., Nystrand, M., & Gamoran, A. (2003). Discussion-based approaches to developing understanding: Classroom instruction and student performance in middle and high school English. *American Educational Research Journal, 40*(3), 685–730.

Au, K. H., & Jordan, C. (1981). Teaching reading to Hawaiian children: Finding a culturally appropriate solution. In G. Trueba, G. Guthrie, & K. H. Au (Eds.), *Culture and the bilingual classroom* (pp. 139–152). Rowley, MA: Newbury House.

Au, K. H., & Mason, J. (1981). Social organizational factors in learning to read: The balance of rights hypothesis. *Reading Research Quarterly, 17*(1), 115–152.

Baker, L., & Brown, A. L. (1984). Metacognitve skills and reading. In D. Pearson, R. Barr, M. L. Kamil, & P. B. Mosenthal (Eds.), *Handbook of reading research* (Vol. 1, pp. 353–394). Mahwah, NJ: Erlbaum.

Barnes, W. (1923). *The new democracy in the teaching of English.* Chicago: Rand McNally & Company.

Barrueco, S., Lopez, M., & Miles, J. (2007). Parenting behaviors in the first year of life: A national comparison of Latinos and other cultural communities. *Journal of Latinos and Education, 6*(3), 253–265.

Beck, I., & McKeown, M. (2001). Text Talk: Capturing the benefits of read-aloud experiences for young children. *The Reading Teacher, 55*(1), 1–20.

Beck, I., & McKeown, M. (2006). *Improving comprehension with questioning the author: A fresh and expanded view of a powerful approach.* New York: Scholastic.

Beck, I., & McKeown, M. (2007). Increasing young low-income children's oral vocabulary repertoires through rich and focused instruction. *The Elementary School Journal, 107*(3), 251–271.

Beck, I., McKeown, M., & Hamilton, R. (1997). *Questioning the author: An approach for enhancing student engagement with text.* Newark, DE: International Reading Association.

Beck, I., McKeown, M., Sandora, C., Kucan, L., & Worthy, J. (1996). Questioning the author: A year-long classroom implementation to engage students with text. *The Elementary School Journal, 96*(4), 385–414.

Bereiter, C., & Bird, M. (1985). Use of thinking aloud in identification and teaching of reading comprehension strategies. *Cognition and instruction, 2*(2), 131–156.

Berliner, D. (1979). Tempus educare. In P. Peterson & H. J. Walberg (Eds.), *Research on teaching.* Berkely, CA: McCutchan.

Billings, L., & Fitzgerald, J. (2002). Dialogic discussion and the paideia seminar. *American Educational Research Journal, 39*(4), 907–941.

Block, C. C., & Parris, S. R. (2008). *Comprehension instruction: Research-based best practices.* New York: Guilford.

Brown, A. L., & Campione, J. C. (1996). Psychological theory and the design of innovative learning environments: On procedures, principles, and systems. In L. Schauble & R. Glaser (Eds.), *Innovations in learning: New environments for education* (pp. 288–325). Mahwah, NJ: Erlbaum.

Brown, A. L., & Palinscar, A. S. (1982). Inducing strategic learning from texts by means of informed, self-control training. *Topics in Learning and Learning Disabilities, 2*(1), 1–17.

Bryk, A., & Raudenbrush, S. (1988). Toward a more appropriate conceptualization of research on school effects: A three-level hierarchical linear model. *American Journal of Education, 97*, 65–108.

Bryk, A., & Raudenbush, S. (1992). *Hierarchical linear models: Applications and data analysis methods.* Nebury Park, CA: Sage.

Campione, J. C. (1981). *Learning, academic achievement, and instruction.* Paper delivered at the Second Annual Conference on Reading Reserch of the Study of Reading, New Orleans.

Chandler-Olcott, K., & Hinchman, K. A. (2005). *Tutoring adolescent literacy learners: A guide for volunteers.* New York: Guilford Press.

Chapin, S., O'Connor, M., & Anderson, N. (2003). *Classroom disucssions: Using math talk to help students learn: Grades 1–6.* Sausalito, CA: Math Solutions Publications.

Chinn, C., Anderson, R., & Waggoner, M. (2001). Patterns of discourse in two kinds of literature discussion. *Reading Research Quarterly, 36*(4), 378–411.

Collins, A., & Smith, E. (1982). Teaching the process of reading comprehension. In D. K. Detterman & R. J. Sternberg (Eds.), *How and how much can intelligence be increased* (pp. 173–189). Norwod, NJ: Ablex.

Dickinson, D. K., & Smith, M. W. (1994). Long-term effects of preschool teachers' book reading on low-income children's vocabulary and story comprehension. *Reading Research Quarterly, 29*(2), 104–122.

Dong, T., Anderson, R., Kim, I., & Li, Y. (2006). Collaborative reasoning in Asia: Discourse mismatch reconsidered. Unpublished manuscript.

Fisher, C. W., Filby, N. N., Marliave, R., Cahen, L. S., Dishaw, M. M., Moore, J. E., et al. (1978). *Teaching behaviors, academic learning time, and student achievement: Final report of phase III-B, beginning teacher evaluation study.* San Francisco: Far West Educational Laboratory for Educational Research and Development.

Gage, N. L., & Needels, M. C. (1989). Process-product research on teaching: A review of criticisms. *The Elementary School Journal, 89*(3), 253–300.

Gamoran, A., & Nystrand, M. (1991). Background and instructional effects on achievement in eighth-grade English and social studies. *Journal of Research on Adolescence, 1*(3), 277–300.

Garmston, R., & Wellman, B. (1994). Insights from constructivist learning theory. *Educational Leadership, 51*(7), 84–85.

Gee, J. (2001). Reading as situated language: A sociocognitive perspective. *Journal of Adolescent & Adult Literacy, 44*(8), 714–725.

Gee, J. (2006). *Social linguistics and literacies: Ideology in discourses.* Abingdon, UK: Routledge.

Goatley, V. J., Brock, C. H., & Raphael, T. E. (1995). Diverse learners participating in regular education "book clubs." *Reading Research Quarterly, 30*(3), 352–380.

Goldenberg, C. (1991). *Instructional conversations and their classroom application.* Washington, DC: The National Center for Research on Cultural Diversity and Second Language Learning.

Goldenberg, C., & Gallimore, R. (1991). Changing teaching takes more than a one-shot workshop. *Educational Leadership, 49*(3), 69–72.

Goldenberg, C., & Patthey-Chavez, G. (1995). Discourse processes in instructional conversations: Interactions between teacher and transition readers. *Discourse Processes, 19*(1), 57–74.

Greenleaf, C. L., Schoenbach, R., & Cziko, C. (2001). Apprenticing adolescent readers to academic literacy. *Harvard Educational Review, 71*(1), 79–130.

Hargrave, A. C., & Sénéchal, M. (2000). A book reading intervention with preschool children who have limited vocabularies: The benefits of regular reading and dialogic reading. *Early Childhood Research Quarterly, 15*(1), 75–90.

Heyman, R. (1983). Clarifying meaning through classroom talk. *Curriculum Inquiry, 13*(1), 23–42.

Johnson, D. W., & Johnson, R. T. (2009). Energizing learning: The instructional power of conflict. *Educational Researcher, 38*(1), 37–51.

Jordan, C. (1995). Creating cultures of schooling: Historical and conceptual background of the KEEP/ Rough Rock collaboration. *Bilingual Research Journal, 19*(1), 83–100.

Kim, I., Anderson, R., Nguyen-Jahiel, K., & Archodidou, A. (2007). Discourse patterns during children's collaborative online discussions. *The Journal of the Learning Sciences, 16*(3), 333–370.

Kucan, L., & Beck, I. (1997). Thinking aloud and reading comprehension research: Inquiry, instruction, and social interaction. *Review of Educational Research, 67*(3), 271–282.

Langer, J. (1985). Levels of questioning: An alternative view. *Reading Research Quarterly, 21*(5), 586–602.

Lonigan, C. J., & Whitehurst, G. J. (1998). Relative efficacy of parent and teacher involvement in a shared-reading intervention for preschool children from low-income backgrounds. *Early Childhood Research Quarterly, 12*(2), 263–290.

Manzo, A. V. (1969). The request procedure. *Journal of Reading, 13,* 123–126.

Marshall, J. (2006). *The effects of participation in literature circles on reading comprehension.* University of Miami, Coral Gables, Florida.

McDonald, J. P., Mohr, N., Dichter, A., & McDonald, E. (2003). *The power of protocols: An educator's guide to better practice.* New York: Teachers College Press.

Michaels, S., O'Connor, C., & Resnick, L. (2008). Deliberative discourse idealized and realized: Accountable talk in the classroom and in civic life. *Studies in Philosophy and Education, 27*(4), 283-297.

Moje, E. B., Ciechanowski, K. M., Kramer, K., Ellis, L., Carrillo, R., & Collazo, T. (2004). Working toward third space in content area literacy: An examination of everyday funds of knowledge and Discourse. *Reading Research Quarterly, 39*(1), 38–70.

Moll, L. C. (1992). Literacy research in community and classrooms: A sociocultural approach. In R. Beach, J. L. Green, M. L. Kamil, & T. Shanahan (Eds.), *Multidisciplinary perspectives on literacy research* (pp. 179–207). Urbana, IL: National Council of Teachers of English.

Murphy, P., Wilkinson, I., Soter, A., Hennessey, M., & Alexander, J. (2009). Examining the effects of classroom discussion on students' comprehension of text: A meta-analysis. *Journal of Educational Psychology, 101*(3), 740–764.

Nagy, W., & Scott, J. A. (2000). Vocabulary processes. In M. Kamil, P. B. Mosenthal, P. D. Pearson, & R. Barr (Eds.), *Handbook of reading research* (Vol. III). Mahwah NJ: L. Erlbaum.

Ninio, A., & Snow, C. (1996). *Pragmatic development.* Boulder, CO: Westview Press.

Ninio, A., & Snow, C. (1999). The development of pragmatics: Learning to use language appropriately. In T. K. Bhatia & W. C. Ritchie (Eds.), *Handbook of language acquisition* (pp. 347–383). New York: Academic Press.

Nystrand, M. (1999). Classroom language assessment system (CLASS 3.0). Madison, WI: Center on English Learning and Achievement.

Nystrand, M., & Gamoran, A. (1991). Instructional discourse, student engagement, and literature achievement. *Research on the Teaching of English, 25*(3), 261–290.

O'Connor, M. (2001). "Can any fraction be turned into a decimal?"A case study of a mathematical group discussion. *Educational Studies in Mathematics, 46*(1), 143–185.

O'Connor, M., & Michaels, S. (1996). Shifting participant frameworks: Orchestrating thinking practices in group discussion. In D. Hicks (Ed.), *Discourse, learning, and schooling* (pp. 63–103). New York: University of Cambridge Press.

Palinscar, A. S., & Brown, A. L. (1984). Reciprocal teaching of comprehension-fostering and comprehension-monitoring strategies. *Cognition & Instruction, 1*(2), 117–175.

Palincsar, A. S., Brown, A. L., & Martin, S. M. (1987). Peer interaction in reading comprehension instruction. *Educational Psychologist, 22*(3/4), 231.

Paratore, J. R., & McCormack, R. (Eds.). (1997). *Peer talk in the classroom: Learning from research.* Newark, DE: International Reading Association.

Pearson, D., & Fielding, L. G. (1991). Comprehension instruction. In R. Barr, M. L. Kamil, P. B. Mosenthal, & P. D. Pearson (Eds.), *Handbook of reading research* (Vol. II, pp. 815–860). New York: Longman.

Resnick, L., & Hampton, S. (2009). *Reading and writing grade by grade.* Newark, DE: National Center on Education and the Economy and University of Pittsburgh.

Resnick, L., & Snow, C. (2009). *Speaking and listening for preschool through third grade.* Newark, DE: New Standards/International Reading Association.

Reznitskaya, A., Anderson, R., Dong, T., Li, Y., Kim, I., & Kim, S.-Y. (2008). Learning to think well: Application of argument schema theory to literacy instruction. In C. C. Block, S. R. Parris, & L. Morrow (Eds.), *Comprehension instruction: Research-based best practices* (pp. 196–213). New York: Guilford Press.

Reznitskaya, A., Anderson, R., McNurlen, B., Nguyen-Jahiel, K., Archodidou, A., & Kim, S. (2001). Influence of oral discussion on written argument. *Discourse Processes, 32*(2&3), 155–175.

Roehler, L., & Duffy, G. (1991). Teachers' Instructional Actions. In R. Barr, M. L. Kamil, P. B. Mosenthal, & P. D. Pearson (Eds.), *Handbook of reading research* (Vol. II, pp. 861–884). New York: Longman.

Rosenshine, B., & Meister, C. (1994). Reciprocal teaching: A review of the research. *Review of Educational Research, 64*(4), 479–530.

Rosenshine, B., & Stevens, R. (1984). Classroom instruction and reading. In D. P. Pearson, R. Barr, M. L. Kamil, & P. B. Mosenthal (Eds.), *Handbook of reading research* (Vol. I). Mahwah, NJ: Erlbaum.

Saunders, W., Goldenberg, C., & Hamann, J. (1992). Instructional conversations beget instructional conversations. *Teaching and Teacher Education, 8*(2), 199–218.

Schoenbach, R., Greenleaf, C., Cziko, C., & Hurwitz, L. (1999). *Reading for understanding.* San Francisco: Jossey-Bass.

Sénéchal, M., Ouellette, G., & Rodney, D. (2006). The misunderstood giant: On the predictive role of early vocabulary to future reading. In D. K. Dickinson & S. Neuman (Eds.), *Handbook of early literacy research* (Vol. II, pp. 173–182). New York: Guildford Press.

Singer, J., & Willett, J. (2003). *Applied longitudinal data analysis: Modeling change and even occurrence.* New York: Oxford University Press.

Snow, C., Lawrence, J., & White, C. (2009). Generating knowledge of academic language among urban middle school students. *Journal of Research on Educational Effectiveness, 2*(4), 325–344.

Snow, C., Porche, M. V., Tabors, P., & Harris, S. (2007). *Is literacy enough?: Pathways to academic success for adolescents.* Baltimore, MD: Paul H. Brookes.

Snow, C., Tabors, P., & Dickinson, D. K. (2001). Language development in the preschool years. In D. K. Dickinson & P. Tabors (Eds.), *Beginning Literacy with Language* (pp. 1–25). Baltimore, MD: Paul H. Brookes.

Soar, R. S. (1973). *Follow-through classroom process measurement and pupil growth (1970–1971): Final report.* Gainesville: Institute for Development of Human Resources, College of Education, University of Florida.

Stauffer, R. G. (1959). A directed reading-thinking plan. *Education, 79,* 527–532.

Stien, D., & Beed, P. (2004). Bridging the gap between fiction and nonfiction in the literature circle setting: Literature circles can Be a valuable tool for engaging students with nonfiction texts. *The Reading Teacher, 57*(6), 510–519.

Tabors, P., Roach, K., & Snow, C. (2001). Language development in the preschool years. In D. K. Dickinson & P. Tabors (Eds.), *Beginning Literacy with Language* (pp. 111–138). Baltimore, MD: Paul H. Brookes.

Tharp, R., & Gallimore, R. (1991). *The instructional conversation: Teaching and learning in social activity. Research Report: 2.* Washington, DC: National Center for Research on Cultural Diversity and Second Language Learning, Center for Applied Linguistics.

Tierney, R. J., & Cunningham, J. (1984). Research on teaching reading comprehension. In D. Pearson, R. Barr, M. L. Kamil, & P. B. Mosenthal (Eds.), *Handbook of reading research* (Vol. 1, pp. 609–656). Mahwah, NJ: Erlbaum.

Torr, J. (2004). Talking about picture books: The influence of maternal education on four-year-old children's talk with mothers and pre-school teachers. *Journal of Early Childhood Literacy, 4*(2), 181–210.

Valdez-Menchaca, M. C., & Whitehurst, G. J. (1992). Accelerating language development through picture book reading: A systematic extension to Mexican day care. *Developmental Psychology, 28*(6), 1106–1114.

van Kleeck, A. (2003). Research on book sharing: Another critical look. In A. van Kleeck, S. A. Stahl, & E. Bauer (Eds.), *On reading books to children: Parents and teachers* (pp. 259–306). Mahwah, NJ: Erlbaum.

Vygotsky, L. S. (1978). *Mind in society: The development of higher psychological processes* (M. Cole, Trans.). Cambridge, MA: Harvard University Press.

Vygotsky, L. S. (1986). *Thought and language* (A. Kozulin, Trans.). Cambridge, MA: MIT Press.

Weizman, Z. O., & Snow, C. E. (2001). Lexical input as related to children's vocabulary acquisition: Effects of sophisticated exposure and support for meaning. *Developmental Psychology, 37*(2), 265–279.

Whitehurst, G. J., Arnold, D. S., Epstein, J. N., Angell, A. L., Smith, M., & Fischel, J. (1994). A picture book reading intervention in day care and home for children from low-income families. *Developmental Psychology, 30*(5), 679–689.

Whitehurst, G. J., Epstein, J. N., Angell, A. L., Payne, A. C., Crone, D. A., & Fischel, J. (1994). Outcomes of an emergent literacy intervention in Head Start. *Journal of Educational Psychology, 86*(4), 542–555.

Wilkinson, L. C., & Silliman, E. R. (2000). Classroom language and literacy learning. In M. Kamil, P. B. Mosenthal, P. D. Pearson, & R. Barr (Eds.), *Handbook of reading research* (Vol. III, pp. 337–360). Mahwah NJ: Erlbaum.

Wolf, M., Crosson, A., & Resnick, L. (2004). Classroom talk for rigorous reading comprehension instruction. *Reading Psychology, 26*(1), 27–53.

Part 4
Teaching and Learning of Reading

15 Locating Struggling Readers in a Reconfigured Landscape

A Conceptual Review

Linda Kucan
University of Pittsburgh

Annemarie Sullivan Palincsar
University of Michigan

The opportunity to prepare a chapter for the *Handbook of Reading Research* is—at once—daunting and invigorating. In the process of crafting a chapter for this volume, authors join intellectual forerunners in representing and shaping that portion of the field that has been placed in their care. For us, those forerunners include Johnston and Allington (1991), Wixson and Lipson (1991), and Klenk and Kibby (2000), each of whom provided well-crafted historical accounts of policy as well as descriptions of instructional interventions for students identified as learning disabled or requiring remedial reading instruction.

In considering how to meet our charge of building on that work, we considered how best to characterize our efforts. Kennedy (2007) made a useful distinction between two types of literature review. She proposed that a *systematic* review is one that focuses on a specific empirical question "often posed in a cause-and-effect form, such as 'To what extent does A contribute to B?'" (p. 139). In contrast, she described a *conceptual* review as an attempt to gain "new insights into an issue" (p. 139); for example, by describing how researchers frame and investigate a problem or topic. We elected to prepare a conceptual review, the goal of which was to survey research for insights into how struggling readers are currently being located or positioned in a landscape that is itself being reconfigured or reshaped. To achieve this goal, we adopted an approach that Barr (2001) used in writing a review of research on reading instruction. She surveyed current research, identified four active areas of inquiry, and selected exemplars of work that reflected important research efforts from different perspectives in those areas. In this way, she mapped the terrain of reading instruction research, focusing on particular sites of activity.

Like Barr, we limit our areas of focus, considering topics related to struggling readers in four major areas: policy, classroom and school-wide interventions, perspectives on basic reading processes, and theories of identity and engagement. In each case, we provide a limited sampling. We chose these topics after conducting a sweeping survey of reading research, consulting the field's premier journals, and also attending to the larger sociopolitical context in which research occurs. The studies we selected are framed by a variety of theoretical perspectives, employ diverse methodologies, and consider a broad array of units of analysis. Given the prominent role that policy, particularly at the federal level, has come to play in the study and education of struggling readers, we begin there.

POLICY SPECIFIC TO STRUGGLING READERS

The period following World War II saw an expansion in policy-driven efforts to reform U.S. public schooling, especially at the federal level (Ravitch, 1985). Notable among these efforts were the National Defense Education Act of 1958 (which launched curriculum reform in mathematics and science in response to Sputnik) and the Elementary and Secondary Education Act of 1965 (which, as part of the War on Poverty, sought to improve education for poor students). However, policy-driven reform soon became a problem in and of itself. Researchers characterized the U.S. public education system as a sprawling array of weakly coordinated agencies and organizations, both public (e.g., local, state, and national education agencies) and non-public (e.g., professional associations, publishers, universities and colleges, and interest groups). This sprawling array of organizations functioned as a source of weakly coordinated, policy-driven reform initiatives, most of which provided little guidance for school-level change and most of which were backed by minimal authority (Cohen, 1982; Cohen & Spillane, 1991). Rather than fostering improvement, one unintended consequence was the reproduction of system-level incoherence within schools themselves, as leaders and teachers sought to respond to a blizzard of incoherent and ever-churning environmental expectations for improvement. This incoherence was particularly apparent in the vast array of uncoordinated programs and services for at-risk students (Allington & Johnston, 1989).

By the early 1990s, recognition of policy incoherence as an obstacle to reform led to a systemic reform movement: a logic of improvement focused on using a small set of policy instruments (e.g., content standards, performance standards, and accountability assessments) to coordinate system-wide reform activity (Smith & O'Day, 1991; Fuhrman, 1991). The logic of systemic reform was instrumental in shaping a series of federal policies that sought to effect coordinated, integrated improvements throughout the system, from classrooms through state and federal agencies: the reauthorization of ESEA as the Improving America's Schools Act of 1994; the Obey-Porter Comprehensive School Reform Demonstration Act of 1997; the Reading Excellence Act of 1998; and the reauthorization of the Improving America's Schools Act as the No Child Left Behind Act of 2002 (NCLB). One of the cornerstone programs of NCLB was the Reading First (RF) Program (which used the Reading Excellence Act as its foundation). NCLB has been widely recognized as the most ambitious federal intervention into K–12 schooling in the history of U.S. public education, with operational implications for states, districts, and schools. For this reason, and because it has played such a significant role in shaping the landscape specific to struggling readers, we focus on the Reading First (RF) Program.

Reading First

The Reading First Program sought to promote instructional practices that have been validated by scientific research, which was explicitly defined in the legislation (No Child Left Behind Act, 2001). NCLB legislated that RF funding was to be used for: (a) reading curricula and materials that focus on the five essential components of reading instruction, as identified by the National Reading Panel (2000): (i) phonemic awareness, (ii) phonics, (iii) vocabulary, (iv) fluency, and (v) comprehension; (b) professional development and coaching for teachers regarding how to use scientifically-based reading practices, and how to work with struggling readers; and (c) diagnosis and prevention of early reading difficulties through student screening, interventions for struggling readers, and monitoring of student progress. States were permitted some flexibility with regard to allocating resources across these three categories, and local decisions could be made regarding specific choices within the categories (i.e., which curricula, assessments, models of professional development would be used). The RF grants were made available to states between July 2002 and September 2003. By April of 2007, states had awarded subgrants to 1,809 school districts, which had provided funds to 5,880 schools. By design, districts and schools demonstrating the greatest need, as measured by student reading proficiency and poverty status, were to receive the highest funding priority.

As this chapter was being prepared, the final report of the *Reading First Impact Study* was published (Gamse, Jacob, Horst, Boulay, & Unlu, 2008). This study used a regression discontinuity design which enabled the investigators to control statistically for all systematic pre-existing differences between the two groups of schools being compared in the study: those that received RF funds, and those that were eligible for funding, but did not receive funds. In this manner, non-RF schools were to play the same role as control schools would play in a randomized experiment. There were 18 study sites, 17 school districts, and 1 state-wide program.

Direct observations and surveys to assess instruction and program implementation revealed that RF produced a positive and significant impact on the amount of instructional time spent on the five essential components in grades 1 and 2. The impact was equivalent to an effect size of 0.33 standard deviations in Grade 1 and 0.46 in Grade 2. In addition, RF produced a positive and significant impact on multiple practices promoted by the program, including professional development, support from coaches, amount of reading instruction, and supports for struggling readers. RF produced a positive and significant impact on decoding (using the Test of Silent Word Reading Fluency) among first graders tested in one school year (spring, 2007), with an effect size of 0.17 standard deviations. However, RF did not produce a significant impact on student reading comprehension test scores (measured using the Stanford Achievement Test) in grades 1, 2, or 3.

The failure to find any effect of RF on reading comprehension is, of course, a disappointing outcome, considering the $6 billion investment RF represents. On the other hand, there are lessons to be learned from this initiative that have important implications for future large-scale efforts to improve instruction for struggling readers. While RF did change the amount of time dedicated to reading instruction, as well as the nature of teacher practices, RF had no statistically significant impact on student engagement with print; it has long been recognized that opportunities for students to read self-selected text, and to read widely, has a significant effect on reading achievement (e.g., Nagy, Herman, & Anderson, 1985). Furthermore, the RF impact study found no evidence of differentiated instruction for struggling readers; research by Connor, Morrison, and Katch (2004) speaks to the importance of differentiation of reading instruction to optimize student achievement.

In addition, the National Reading Panel report (2000), which shaped the architecture of RF interventions, represented comprehension instruction in terms of the teaching of individual strategies, noting seven strategies in particular. A number of reading researchers have expressed concern regarding the appropriate place of strategy instruction in the teaching of reading comprehension (e.g., Beck & McKeown, 1998; McKeown, Beck, & Blake, 2009; Palincsar, 2007; Pressley et al., 1992). When first conceived, strategy instruction was designed to engage readers in monitoring how well they were understanding text, and support them in regulating their reading of text for the purpose of building meaning. Strategies were designed to be a means to an end—comprehension—and not an end in and of themselves. The RF Impact study was not designed to assess the quality of comprehension instruction; hence, a hypothesis to be explored in future work is whether teachers engaged in forms of comprehension instruction that did not promote understanding and learning from text. Related to this point is the fact that the focus on language arts instruction, legislated by RF, reduced the amount of time that primary grade students spent learning science and social studies content. Research by Guthrie, Wigfield, and their colleagues (2006), as well as Vitale and Romance (2007) suggests that content instruction is an important means of improving reading comprehension.

Perhaps an additional explanation for the disappointing finding regarding comprehension is that the primary measure of reading deployed across districts implementing RF was the *Dynamic Indicators of Basic Early Literacy Skills* (DIBELS, Good & Kaminski, 2002), a measure that places a premium on reading speed, rather than comprehension. Finally, the National Reading Panel report, as well as RF, were virtually silent on the instruction of English language learners.

In closing, RF changed the struggling reader landscape; despite its limitations, it focused attention on the need for teachers to receive professional development specific to early reading instruction and struggling readers; in addition, it acknowledged that classroom level change in curriculum and instructional practice is key to improving the performance of struggling readers. The challenge to the reading community is to use the lessons of RF to advance a research agenda that systematically explores the multiple hypotheses identified above, investigating the relative contributions of: student engagement with print, differentiated instruction, the quality of instruction, and attention to the needs of English language learners in enhancing early literacy achievement among struggling readers.

Response to Intervention

A second policy initiative that is changing the contours of the landscape specific to struggling readers was introduced with the 2004 reauthorization of the Individuals with Disabilities Education Act (IDEA). This law designates that schools are no longer required to determine that a student is eligible for special services based on a significant disparity between academic potential (as typically measured by an intelligence test) and academic achievement. Instead, educators may use an alternative approach in which they ascertain how students, who are referred for special services, respond first to research-based practices carried out in the context of classrooms, and then to interventions tailored to the needs of the student. After receiving one or more tailored interventions, students who do not show evidence of progress are referred for an evaluation for a specific learning disability. This approach has been labeled Response to Intervention (RTI).

Before describing research on RTI, we describe the impetus for this legislation. How learners are "sorted" for the purposes of planning and enacting instruction has long been a thorny issue for the field of education. The process of identifying students as "atypical" is particularly germane to the reading community because there has been a 200% increase in the number of students identified as learning disabled since this category was first conceived, 80% of whom have been characterized as reading disabled (Lyon, 1995).

Mehan, Hertweck, and Meihls (1986) documented the vagaries by which certain children qualified for special education services, while others did not. They found that the designation of a child as "educationally handicapped," was frequently determined by organizational, fiscal, and legal constraints, rather than by attributes of the child. Artiles (2004) and McDermott. Goldman, and Varenne (2006) offer more recent analyses of the same phenomenon; documenting the "cultural work" that is entailed in noticing and diagnosing children with learning difficulties as learning disabled. The over-representation of students of color and students who speak a first language other than English in programs for "identified" children and youth is of particular concern, given the evidence that "struggling readers" may be denied access to instructional opportunities that promote proficient and advanced levels of academic achievement (Sunderman, Kim, & Oerfield, 2005). For example, Rentner et al. (2006) documented that struggling readers in the districts they studied, received twice the amount of basic skill instruction in reading and mathematics instruction received by their typically achieving peers, and were denied content instruction that would advance comprehension and learning from text. Valli and Buese (2007) further argue that, it is not only the curriculum that is being constrained for students who are identified as struggling, but also the range of teaching methods, which, ultimately, denies these students access to opportunities to attain the kinds of thinking skills called for by 21st-century demands. Unfortunately, these studies point to some aspects of the landscape for struggling readers that have remained unchanged. It has long been recognized that differential instructional opportunities are provided struggling readers that do not work in their best interest; for example, practicing components of reading without experiencing reading in a holistic manner (Allington, Stuetzel, Shake, & Lamarche, 1986), experiencing fewer opportunities to read informational text than do good readers (Allington, 1984), and experiencing fewer opportunities to use reading to advance building understanding (Collins, 1988).

RTI represents a paradigm shift to the extent that making judgments about who is an atypical learner no longer focuses exclusively on within-student factors, but takes into account the instructional context; that is, RTI operationalizes the "exclusionary clause" suggesting that a learner's disability cannot be the consequence of poor instructional opportunity. In addition, RTI was designed to redress the problem that, traditionally, students needed to essentially fail before they were entitled to additional academic support; that is, they needed to demonstrate a disparity between their grade level placement and academic attainment. The provisions of RTI call for only those students who fail to respond to a tailored intervention to be identified as learning disabled. Furthermore, RTI legislation permits 15% of special education funds to be spent on early intervention activities.

The federal guidelines emphasize that there is no one model of or approach to RTI; the spirit of the law is to optimize instruction for students who are struggling, and identify and support these students before their difficulties become more serious. One model of RTI is referred to as "the three-tier model." In this model, the first tier is quality instruction and ongoing monitoring in the general education classroom. The second tier is the provision of intensive intervention for students who have not made adequate progress in the core program of the classroom. When students do not respond to the second tier of intervention, they qualify for special education services, or for an evaluation to determine if they should receive special education—third tier—services.

A study by Vaughn, Linan-Thompson, and Hickman (2003) is illustrative of an RTI investigation. In this study, 45 second-grade students, identified as at-risk for reading problems, received 50, 35-minute sessions of instruction. The participants were those who were in the second quartile or below in their reading ability; teacher nomination was followed by formal assessment to confirm reading abilities and challenges. The 45 students were largely Hispanic/Latino and included 15 English language learners.

The intervention sessions were planned in increments; that is, after 10 weeks of supplementary instruction, the students were assessed to determine the success with which they met pre-established criteria; those who met criteria no longer continued in the intervention, whereas those who did not were enrolled in another 10-week session. Core reading instruction continued in the classroom throughout this time. The intervention focused on: phonemic awareness, mastery of letter-sound relationships and word families, fluency, instructional level reading and comprehension, and spelling. At the end of 10 weeks of instruction, 10 students met the exit criteria. Instruction was then modified to provide more intensive instruction in word study and fluency, and less focus on phonological awareness. In addition, the researchers added an inventory to assess the quality of the instructional time assessing student engagement and positive support for learning; this inventory permitted the researchers to report that the quality of instruction was high, with little time off-task.

At the end of 20 weeks of instruction, another 14 students met criteria. At the end of 30 weeks of instruction, another 10 students met criteria. This resulted in 11 students (i.e., 24% of the total sample) who did not meet criteria, after 30 sessions. The researchers continued to monitor the reading achievement of students dismissed from the intervention program, and determined that 70% continued to "thrive" in the general education setting. Further analyses indicated that the students who responded to the intervention outperformed those who did not make adequate response on the pre-assessment measures of fluency, passage comprehension, and rapid naming, while measures of word attack and phonological awareness were not predictive of who would qualify to exit the intervention.

The researchers argued that by establishing a-priori criteria for success, as well as a maximum amount of time for supplemental instruction, it was possible to identify a distinct group of students who required the kind of intensive and sustained support that is suggestive of special education support; furthermore, the cohort who required additional support did, in fact, yield a different profile on the pre-assessments than did those students who responded to the intervention. Replications of this finding would contribute to the field's capacity to be more accurate in identifying who should be eligible for early and sustained intervention.

While findings regarding the use of RTI models, such as those presented above, as well as those reported by O'Connor (2002) and Speece, Case, and Molloy (2003) are promising, research on RTI is still in its infancy. Most of the research has been conducted with students in the first 3 years of schooling. Typically, the interventions have been implemented by researchers, rather than teachers. Another current limitation regarding the usefulness of RTI is the limited range of valid instruments to which the field has access; we have psychometrically robust ways of assessing phonemic awareness, sound-symbol correspondence, and fluency, but no efficient screening measures for oral language problems, or problems with listening and reading comprehension that may well predict reading problems (Jenkins, Hudson, & Johnson, 2007; Scarborough, 2005). Given that, the field needs to ensure that teachers are including vocabulary instruction, listening comprehension instruction, and reading comprehension instruction in the curriculum and then monitoring the progress of students across these areas, just as teachers would monitor the performance of students on measures of phonemic awareness and reading fluency.

RESEARCH ON CLASSROOM CURRICULUM AND INSTRUCTION

Just as Reading First and Response to Intervention focus on curriculum and instruction within classrooms, increasingly, researchers' attentions have focused on the classroom in an effort to understand and improve reading achievement, especially for struggling readers. While there are now a number of literacy-specific observational systems available to researchers who are studying literacy instruction in classrooms (Edmunds & Briggs, 2003; Estrada, 2004; Foorman & Schnatschneider, 2003; Greenwood, Abbott, & Tapia, 2003; Juel & Minden-Cupp, 2000), these systems yield frequency counts, and are used to characterize categories of activities (e.g., teaching phonics, use of low-level or higher-order questions). These efforts have not been designed to assess the quality of instruction, nor to assess the appropriateness of instruction for particular groups of students.

In contrast, an example of research designed to evaluate the quality of instruction in classrooms, and to plan efficacious curriculum and instruction based on student data, is a study by Connor, Morrison, and Katch (2004). In their study of 42 first-grade classrooms, using measures of vocabulary and decoding (with 108 children)—in hand with measures of instructional practice—the researchers found that there were specific patterns of instructional practice that predicted decoding skill growth. Children's growth in decoding skill in first grade was affected by both their initial levels of vocabulary and decoding skills, as well as by the type of instruction they received, which was identified as either teacher-managed or child-managed.

Decoding skill was measured through assessing alphabet recognition, letter-sound correspondence, and single word decoding. These authors argue that attempting to group teachers simply by their focus on code-based or meaning-based instruction may inadequately capture differences in learning opportunities. They characterized learning opportunities in terms of their explicitness, as well as whether the instruction was managed by the teacher or student. The instruction was regarded as explicit if attention were directed to components of word decoding strategies, in contrast to exposing children to word lists that have similar spelling—sound correspondences. The instruction was described as child-managed if the student were responsible for his or her own learning (such as, in the course of completing worksheets independently). In addition, the researchers studied instruction and development over time, at three points during the school year.

The findings revealed that there were changes in amount and type of instruction in classrooms over the course of a school year. Teachers provided significant amounts of each of the types of instruction that were coded; furthermore, they changed the amount of each type of instruction over time. In general, the researchers documented more teacher-managed explicit and child-managed explicit at the beginning of the year. They also observed differences in the total amount of time language arts instruction occurred across a school term.

The type of instruction had a significant—but complex—effect on achievement; an effect that was dependent upon the children's fall vocabulary and decoding skills, with entering scores accounting for 70% of the variance that was detected in the spring reading decoding scores. Children who began the year with higher vocabulary and decoding scores achieved higher spring scores. Children who fell below the 25th percentile, on vocabulary and decoding measures, showed greater growth in decoding in classrooms with more teacher-managed explicit instruction and less growth in classrooms with less teacher-managed explicit instruction. Furthermore, the more child-managed implicit instruction they received (e.g., individual sustained silent reading), the less growth they demonstrated in decoding and the less child-managed implicit instruction they received the more growth they exhibited. However, if students entered first grade with high vocabulary and decoding skills (i.e., fell at the 90th percentile), there was a contrasting pattern; these children thrived in classrooms in which there were higher amounts of child-managed implicit instruction and did not fare as well in classrooms in which there were lower amounts of child-managed implicit instruction. Clearly, this research suggests that it is better to ask about effective instruction for individual students, than to ask about high- or low-quality instruction in classrooms.

While the research reported above was conducted in the primary grades, Slavin, Cheung, Groff, and Lake (2008) conducted a best-evidence synthesis regarding reading programs with students in grades 6–12, and similarly concluded that the most powerful interventions are those that change the nature of instruction, rather than those that change the nature of curricula.

COGNITIVE PROFILES OF STRUGGLING READERS INFORMED BY EMERGING THEORETICAL CONSTRUCTS

In this section, we consider research that is informing highly specified cognitive profiles of struggling readers; that is, the identification of discrete features of the processing in which struggling readers engage that affect their decoding and comprehension. Researchers in this area draw upon well-specified theoretical constructs informed by empirical data secured from behavioral experimentation, eye-movement research, computational modeling, and neuro-imaging. This research provides insights into the traditional areas of reading research—decoding, vocabulary, and comprehension—and suggests instructional implications for struggling readers. In the sections that follow, we address each of these areas, highlighting the work of researchers who are extending theoretical boundaries by using innovative methodologies.

Decoding

Typical trajectories for developing readers involve a number of important accomplishments including insights related to the alphabetic principle. Attaining the alphabetic principle enables readers to map individual letter/sound relationships; attaining a concept of word allows readers to recognize the boundaries of words in connected text (Flanigan, 2007; Morris, 1993; Morris, Bloodgood, Lomax, & Perney, 2003). Building on these insights, beginning readers can engage in decoding, using their knowledge of letter/sound relationships to "sound out" words.

A study by McCandliss, Beck, Sandak, and Perfetti (2003) investigated a possible source of difficulty for children who are learning to decode. The goal of the study was to "develop a cognitive profile of children who had been in regular reading classrooms but had failed to acquire adequate decoding skills" (p. 76). Theoretical notions informing the study (Ehri, 1991; Perfetti, 1991) suggested that "the quality of a child's word representations in reading can by improved by focusing on every letter within printed words" (p. 78).

McCandliss et al. (2003) identified first graders who were successful in decoding the initial consonant in a word but who were less successful in deciphering subsequent vowels and consonants. These students participated in an instructional intervention called Word Building. During Word Building sessions, students manipulated letter cards to build a linked set of words formed by changing one letter, an exercise in "progressive minimal contrasts" (p. 78). After each change, the student decoded the word. A typical beginning sequence included these words: *sat, sit, sat, at, it, sit, sat, sit* (Beck, 2006). After 20 hours of Word Building sessions over a period of 4 months, Word Building students significantly outperformed control group students on tests of decoding as measured by an experimental pseudo-word test as well as the Woodcock Reading Mastery Test—Revised (1998).

The McCandliss et al. (2003) study identified a specific aspect of decoding that challenged beginning readers and showed the positive impact of an intervention targeted to address that challenge. A subsequent study by Harm, McCandliss, and Seidenberg (2003) made use of computational modeling to analyze the cognitive processes affected by the Word Study intervention. The authors noted: "Computational simulations of reading have now reached a level of development that allows them to be applied to questions concerning the effectiveness of interventions for disabled readers. The strengths of such simulations complement empirical studies of reading interventions....By tightly linking the training conditions, intervention method, and evaluation metrics of a computational model to established empirical studies, analysis of the model can provide leverage for understanding behavioral effects" (p. 157).

Harm and colleagues (2003) developed a connectionist model to compare the effects of the learning that results from focusing on phonological representations compared to the learning that results from focusing on specific letter-sound mappings, or orthographic-phonological relationships. These researchers wanted to investigate empirical findings demonstrating that "the effectiveness of interventions that target phonological representations through speech activities declines sharply once exposure to print has begun" (p. 176). Their findings suggested that the positive impact of the Word Building intervention could be attributed to the learning that resulted from attending to the smallest components of a word—letters—and to the sequence of those letters—spelling. According to Harm and colleagues (2003), "If knowledge of phonemic structure is critical to skilled reading, and this knowledge is normally acquired mainly through the pairing of orthography and phonology, then teaching methods and remedial interventions that emphasize this pairing should be effective" (p. 179).

Vocabulary

Skilled readers are able to access accurate phonological and orthographic representations of words, but such representations are not sufficient for comprehension. According to Perfetti (2007), "[W]ord meanings can be considered the interface between word identification and comprehension" (p. 380). The characteristics of this interface are specified in his Lexical Quality Hypothesis (LQH). A fundamental tenet of the LQH is that reading is an integrative process that proceeds word by word. "As each word is read its meanings are accessed (automatically) and pruned to fit into the context, which the reader must represent as part of an understanding of the text (i.e., a mental model of the situation described by the text) (Perfetti, Yang, & Schmalhofer, 2008, p. 304). The Lexical Quality Hypothesis describes the knowledge that readers need about the features of words to facilitate the processes of accessing and pruning. Specifically, this knowledge includes orthography, phonology, grammar, and meaning, as well as connections or bindings that "secure coherence among the constituents, the orthographic, phonological, and semantic representations, which together are the word's identity" (p. 360). Skilled readers have high- quality representations of words; less skilled readers have low-quality representations.

In experiments to test aspects of the Lexical Quality Hypothesis, Perfetti and his colleagues designed tasks to assess the consequences of high-quality and low-quality lexical representations. For example, skilled and less-skilled comprehenders were presented two words in succession and had to decide if the words were related. Sample word pairs included: *wails-dolphins, whales-cries*, and *night-armor, knight-evening*. Skilled comprehenders demonstrated faster decision-making than less-skilled comprehenders.

The Lexical Quality Hypothesis with its emphasis on the multifaceted quality of lexical representations—phonological, orthographic, and semantic—contrasts with prevailing deficit hypotheses that focus on discrete deficits in phonological processing, naming speed, and semantic processing. According to Perfetti (2007), these deficit hypotheses "seem to be about mechanisms that are not functioning properly. In contrast, the LQH is about knowledge that has not been acquired or practiced to a high-enough level" (p. 380). The problems of most struggling readers "cut across meaning, orthographic, and phonological knowledge" (p. 380). Thus, instruction for struggling readers should promote knowledge-building and practice that supports their development of high-quality lexical representations, including phonological, orthographic, and semantic word features, as well as an understanding of how these features work together to create a word's coherent and robust identity.

Comprehension

Increasingly well-specified theoretical constructs such as the Lexical Quality Hypothesis are helping researchers and educators to understand readers' lexical and sublexical knowledge, and their ability to apply that knowledge in decoding and accessing word meanings. Parallel developments are taking place related to the higher-order processes that underlie reading comprehension.

Current models of text comprehension such as the Landscape Model of Reading (van den Broek, Young, Tzeng, & Linderholm, 1998), which extends Kintsch's Construction Integration model of text comprehension (Kintsch & van Dijk, 1978), suggest that the process of comprehending text involves the construction of a coherent mental representation. One way to depict this mental representation is as a network of connected nodes, with each node corresponding to specific content units and each connection between nodes depicting the relationships between the content units (van den Broek & Kremer, 2000). The connections between nodes are established when readers infer relationships between content or information. Of particular importance are two categories of meaningful connections: referential and causal-logical (Graesser, McNamara, & Louwerse, 2003). In order to establish referential relations, readers need to connect people and objects mentioned in a text and subsequent references to them, which are often in the form of pronouns, synonyms, or paraphrases. In order to establish causal-logical relations, readers need to link events that depend on or cause each other. Inferring these relationships can pose difficulties for readers when they are "numerous and complex, extending over long distances in the text, involving extensive background knowledge, and requiring coordination of multiple pieces of information" (Rapp, van den Broek, McMaster, Kendeou, & Espin, 2007, p. 292).

Rapp and his colleagues (2007) designed a study to investigate how struggling, average, and good readers in fourth, seventh, and ninth grades, draw inferences while reading, using eye-tracking (Rayner, 1998; Rayner, Chace, Slattery, & Ashby, 2006) and think aloud (Ericcson & Simon, 1984) methods. The eye-tracking records allowed the researchers to know when readers backtracked to reread or slowed down to read particular text segments. The think-aloud protocols allowed the researchers to find out what readers were focusing their attention on as they read.

Across the three grade levels (fourth, seventh, and ninth), two processing patterns emerged for struggling readers. One pattern exhibited by the struggling readers was to constrain their processing by focusing on the current text segment being read, rereading or closely paraphrasing the text information. Another pattern was for struggling readers to think about information beyond the text segment they were reading by calling upon background knowledge that was not useful in building a representation of text ideas.

Both groups of struggling readers performed similarly on measures of recall and oral reading fluency, as well as scores on standardized reading comprehension measures. The two profiles were only detected by investigating the during-reading processing of the readers. According to Rapp and his colleagues (2007), "the utility of these profiles will be the degree to which they help guide the development and application of interventions to remediate subgroup difficulties" (p. 305).

Interventions that focus on inferencing processes require an understanding of readers' processing profiles as well as features of text that support inferencing in the service of establishing coherence. Research in these areas is an emerging enterprise. According to Graesser and his colleagues (2003), "Very few teachers are aware of the broad landscape of coherence relations, because the field of discourse processes has only a 25-year history. Most researchers who have studied text coherence have not yet considered the implications of coherence for teaching reading" (p. 95).

Research on the Fourth-Grade Slump

We conclude this section with two studies that were designed to inform the field's understanding of the fourth-grade slump. While the preponderance of research specific to understanding reading disabilities has been conducted with children in the primary grades, it has long been recognized that some children begin to reveal reading challenges in the fourth grade (Chall, 1983). Leach, Scarborough, and Rescorla (2003) compared the literacy, language, and cognitive skills of fourth and fifth graders, 35 of whom had early identified reading disabilities, 31 of whom had late-identified, garden variety, reading disabilities (following third grade), and 95 of whom were typical students.

We sample a few of the significant findings from this study. Students with late-emerging reading difficulties showed less severe word-level processing deficits than did the early emerging group. Students with late-identified reading deficits were heterogeneous; 66% struggled with comprehension; of these, 64% also demonstrated word-level processing deficits, suggesting that word recognition, decoding, and spelling continue to impede progress in reading achievement beyond the primary grades. However, for both the early and late emerging students, the correlations between word recognition and reading comprehension scores was much higher in third than in fourth and fifth grades. These findings (among others) led the researchers to conclude that some children's reading disabilities appear not just to be identified relatively late in their school careers (i.e., overlooked by educators), but, in fact, are actually late-emerging. Hence, teachers need to continue to be vigilant monitoring the acquisition and development of reading skills as children matriculate through the grades. Furthermore, the heterogeneous nature of the reading profiles of the identified students in this sample, points to the need for teachers to have command of a broad repertoire of specific interventions appropriate to the profiles of readers.

The fourth-grade slump can also be examined from a contextual perspective. While children in the primary grades experience a preponderance of narrative text, the reading diet of upper elementary students generally consists of healthy doses of informational text (Duke, 2000). The vocabulary, structural, and conceptual demands associated with informational text may well contribute to depressed reading achievement.

Best, Floyd, and McNamara (2008) designed a study to investigate the role of decoding skills and world knowledge on third graders' comprehension of narrative and expository texts. There were 61 third-grade participants in this study, all of whom demonstrated age-appropriate reading abilities on measures of comprehension and vocabulary. The students read both a narrative and expository passage (counterbalanced for order of presentation) and completed three tasks immediately following the reading of each: a free recall, a cued recall, and 12 multiple-choice questions. Across each of these measures, the children's scores were significantly higher for the narrative than informational texts. Correlational analyses indicated that, for the narrative text, cued recall and accuracy with the multiple choice questions were significantly and moderately correlated with both world knowledge and decoding skills. For the expository text, all three comprehension measures were significantly and moderately correlated with world knowledge. In fact, once decoding skills were controlled for, world knowledge added approximately 14% to the prediction of comprehension as measured by multiple-choice responses, and 21% to the prediction of comprehension as measured by cued recall, while decoding skills demonstrated lower and inconsistent relationships with the understanding of expository text. Drawing upon the Landscape Model identified above, the authors concluded that children with less prior knowledge struggle to form coherent mental representations of text because of their challenges generating the inferences that informational text often demands. Recalling the finding of Rapp and colleagues (2007), the situation becomes more complex; deep comprehension is not possible in the absence of some background knowledge. Hence, students need extended practice learning to learn from instructional texts that are well-matched with their prior knowledge so that they can develop robust situation models, which will then support future learning, *and* they need opportunities to learn how to monitor the relationship between the situation model they are developing and the textbase; checking, for example, that they are not being hampered by incorrect or incomplete conceptions of the content they are encountering in the text. This is a tall order, particularly since the field does not yet have a way of characterizing how much one must know about a topic to advance one's learning about that topic. Nevertheless, the critical role that prior knowledge plays in supporting comprehension speaks to the urgency of redressing the narrowing of the curriculum; the significant reduction of instructional time on content instruction in science, social studies, and art (Sunderman et al., 2005) will only serve to exacerbate the challenges faced by struggling readers.

IDENTITY AND THE STRUGGLING READER

Identity is a significant focus of attention in psychology, anthropology, sociology, and cultural studies (e.g., Holland, Lachiocotte, Skinner, & Cain, 1998). It is also becoming an important theoretical perspective in educational research (e.g., Alvermann, 2001; Franzak, 2004, 2007; Gee, 2000–2001; Guthrie & Wigfield, 2000; McCarthey & Moje, 2002; Wortham, 2004). An emerging application of identity theory relates specifically to struggling readers—how they are identified and positioned, as well as how they identify and position themselves in various contexts.

Perspectives on Identity

Two important themes in identity research can be located in the work of George Herbert Mead, founder of social psychology as it developed in the United States (Menand, 2001). Mead foregrounded the notions that the self is socially constructed, and that discourse and participation in discursive communities play critical roles in mediating that construction.

According to Mead (1934), "The self...is a social structure, and it arises in social experience" (p. 140). As Gee (2000–2001) has described it, an individual is shaped by and constructs an identity through social interactions and performances, ultimately becoming recognized as a certain "kind of person" (p. 99). The discourses in which people participate are an essential aspect of identity formation: "Discourses are ways of being 'certain kinds of people'" (Gee, p. 110). They are ways of acting in the world, ways of thinking, and ways of knowing. They are also ways of being perceived and understood. So, for example, students who identify themselves as struggling readers may participate in classes in particular ways to hide that identity. They may act out to divert attention from their lack of understanding, or remain silent to avoid notice. Teachers who identify students as struggling readers may ascribe certain characteristics to them and modify their interactions accordingly. They may request that students be removed from their class and attend alternative sessions where more support or control can be provided.

Participation in—or exclusion from—a discursive community has profound consequences on a person's identity. According to Mead (1934):

> A person learns a new language and, as we say, gets a new soul. He puts himself into the attitude of those that make use of that language. He cannot read its literature, cannot converse with those that belong to that community, without taking on its particular attitudes. He becomes in that sense a different individual. (p. 283)

Wortham (2004) underscored the impact of the specific kinds of learning afforded by participation in a discursive community, noting: "If learning involves changing participation in social activities across time, learners become different kinds of people as they learn—because they shift their positions with respect to other people and/or with respect to socially defined activities" (p. 731).

Students make decisions about their participation or engagement in classroom activities that involve reading based not only on their cognitive abilities, but also on what they want to acquire or achieve, on their goals and desires. As Guthrie and Wigfield (2000) suggested, a reader "has wants and intentions that enable reading processes to occur. That is, a person reads a word or comprehends a text not only because she can do it, but because she is motivated to do it" (pp. 403–404).

In the sections that follow, we foreground the work of researchers who use perspectives on identity, motivation, and engagement to investigate the decisions and attitudes of struggling readers, and their related consequences.

Struggling Readers in Content Area Classrooms: Understanding the Silence

Hall's dissertation (2006) involved a year-long investigation of three struggling readers in specific classroom contexts: Sarah, a sixth-grade student in social studies class; Alisa, a seventh grader in science class; and Nicole, an eighth-grade student in mathematics class. Hall used a descriptive case study approach to collect and interpret data from questionnaires, interviews, and observations to consider these readers, their teachers, and their classroom experiences. In a cross-case analysis, she discovered that all three students were noticeably silent during class activities related to reading and talking about text, rarely if ever asking questions, or volunteering to respond to teacher questions. Based on an analysis of student comments from interviews and questionnaires, as well as field notes documenting their classroom participation, Hall concluded that the students deliberately chose to remain silent in class in order to meet their personal goals. These goals centered on preventing others from identifying them as poor readers, projecting a possible identity as a good reader, and carefully listening and observing others in order to gather information about text content and how to complete assignments.

An understanding of Hall's cases can be informed by the co-regulation model developed by McCaslin (2004). McCaslin used the co-regulation (CR)construct to foreground the expert-novice roles that exist within a Zone of Proximal Development (Vygotsky, 1962, 1978). For example, in a classroom, students are experts in matters related to their social worlds; whereas, teachers are generally novices in understanding that world. However, teachers are experts related to the world of learning and success in school—a world in which students are the novices. McCaslin (2009) drew attention to the impact of social and cultural influences on the choices that students make related to their participation in school activities. And, like Hall, she suggested that teachers who are aware of these influences can much better provide students with the kind of support and encouragement that will mediate their motivation and achievement in school settings.

Struggling Readers in Alternative School Settings Engaged in Alternative Tasks

While Hall has focused her attention on middle school students in traditional classroom settings engaged in traditional print-based tasks, O'Brien has investigated high school and middle school students in alternative school-based settings. According to Wortham (2004),"[W]e must follow people across contexts and observe how they pursue new possibilities in new contexts, how they take what Dreier (2000) calls 'new angles.' A new angle is a different way of thinking or acting in a given context that allows participants to pursue previously unavailable alternatives" (p. 725).

In a 4-year study with high school students, O'Brien (2001) worked with two teachers to develop a project-based curriculum that came to be known as the Literacy Lab. The Literacy Lab provided opportunities for students identified as at-risk to engage in literate practices related to electronic media. In case studies of struggling readers at work in the lab setting, O'Brien found that students who had decoding and comprehension problems were able to use media resources to construct interesting and sophisticated multimedia artifacts such as documentaries. O'Brien explained that, although the students "still struggled with print, they overcame some of the struggles when print served as one media text among many" (p. 4). O'Brien (2003) maintained that, given the opportunity to explore self-selected topics and to make use of multimedia resources, struggling high school readers displayed behaviors that were not characteristic of disengaged students. On the contrary, O'Brien pointed out that "The contrast in how these kids and their peers in the Literacy Lab are positioned within the dominant print-based curriculum and how they are repositioned and reposition themselves as capable, interested students is compelling" (p. 9).

The notion of interest and its relationship to identity has been explored by a number of researchers including Renninger (2009). Renninger noted that *interest* most commonly refers to a state of "heightened affect that accompanies engagement with particular content, in a given context, at a particular point in time" (p. 106). Hidi and Renninger (2006) interrogated this notion to articulate how interest develops and what conditions support its development. They foregrounded the impact on student interest of choice—choices about setting goals, selecting goal-related activities, and allocating time to meet those goals. Hidi and Renninger emphasize the important role of teachers in providing contexts (such as the Literacy Lab) that elicit and support student interest and effort.

CONCLUSION

It is our hope that the traversal of the struggling readers landscape described in this chapter has provided insights into the complexities of the terrain, as well as promising pathways for future exploration. As we view the contours of this landscape, we are encouraged by the research and theoretical refinements that are yielding more carefully specified accounts of those individual, developmental, and contextual differences that characterize students for whom reading is an effortful enterprise. We also recognize the challenge that these developments pose. Specifically, we see the need for assessments that provide detailed information about what struggling readers are struggling with. These assessments need to take into account trajectories of reading development and concomitant changes in context (e.g., changes in the characteristics of the texts with which students are interacting, and changes in the nature of the demands for learning from text).

We need to focus our efforts on minimizing the bottle-neck effects of the decoding problems experienced by some struggling readers to ensure that these learners are supported to engage with rich ideas and continue to develop their capacity to think and reason with language. We need to focus our efforts on the teaching of comprehension, even as young children are learning to decode text, to reduce the later emergence of reading comprehension problems.

Research informed by perspectives on identity reveals additional contours to the struggling readers landscape. Insights from this research make it necessary to expand the description of *struggling* to include not only those who have been assessed as lacking in the skills that readers use in making meaning from text, but also those who deliberately disengage from traditional text-based meaning-making. Our interventions need to attend more carefully to this dynamic.

We also acknowledge the need for making accessible to teachers and teacher educators the theoretical information that can inform the design of curriculum and instruction to address the challenges struggling readers face. Without current and complete information about what aspects of literacy development cause students to struggle and why, teachers will not be able to develop the specialized content and pedagogical content knowledge that will allow them to assess and mediate their students' efforts.

We are heartened by policy makers and researchers who view the classroom as the preeminent context for investigations focusing on the quality of instruction and its consequences from both teacher and learner perspectives. Of particular interest are the funded grant programs for investigating interventions for striving adolescent readers (Office of Elementary and Secondary Education, 2006), and supporting research into comprehension processes, interventions, and assessments (Institute of Education Sciences, 2009).

We believe that there will always be a *Handbook* chapter about struggling readers, but we also believe that ongoing research and information-sharing efforts will inform those chapters and provide teachers with increasingly helpful ways to understand and support those students who struggle with reading.

REFERENCES

Allington, R. L. (1984). Content coverage and contextual reading in reading groups. *Journal of Literacy Research, 16*(2), 85–96.

Allington, R. . & Johnston, P. (1989). Coordination, collaboration, and consistency: The design of compensatory and special education interventions. In R. E. Slavin, N. L. Karweit, & N. A. Madden (Eds.), *Effective programs for students at risk* (pp. 320–354). Boston: Allyn and Bacon.

Allington, R.L. Stuetzel, H., Shake, M., and Lamarche, S. (1986). What is remedial reading? A descriptive study. *Reading Research and Instruction, 24,* 15–30.

Alvermann, E. (2001). Reading adolescents' reading identities: Looking back to see ahead. *Journal of Adolescent and Adult Literacy, 44*(8), 676–690.

Artiles, A. (2004). The end of innocence: Historiography and representation in the discursive practice of LD. *Journal of Learning Disabilities, 37,* 550–555.

Barr, R. (2001). Research on the teaching of reading. In V. Richardson (Ed.), *Handbook of research on teaching* (4th ed., pp. 390–415). Washington, DC: American Educational Research Association.

Beck, I. L. (2006). *Making sense of phonics: The hows and whys.* New York: Guilford Press.

Beck, I. L. & McKeown, M. G. (1998). Comprehension: The sine qua non of reading. *The keys to literacy* (pp. 40–52). Washington, DC: Council for Basic Education.

Best, R. M., Floyd, R. G., & McNamara, D. S. (2008). Differential competencies contributing to children's comprehension of narrative and expository texts. *Reading Psychology, 29,* 137–164.

Chall, J. (1983). *Learning to read: The great debate.* New York: Wiley.

Cohen, D. K. (1982). Policy and organization: The impact of state and federal educational policy on school governance. *Harvard Educational Review, 52,* 474–499.

Cohen, D. K., & Spillane, J. P. (1991). Policy and practice: The relations between governance and instruction. In S. H. Fuhrman (Ed.), *Designing coherent education policy: Improving the system* (pp. 35–95). San Francisco: Jossey-Bass.

Collins, J. (1988). Language and class in minority education. *Anthropology & Education Quarterly, 19*(4), 299–326.

Connor, C. M., Morrison, F. J., & Katch, E. L. (2004). Beyond the reading wars: Exploring the effect of child-instruction interaction on growth in early reading. *Scientific Studies of Reading, 8,* 305–336.

Dreier, O. (2000). Psychotherapy in clients' trajectories across contexts. In C. Mattingly & L. Garro (Eds.), *Narrative and the cultural construction of illness and healing* (pp. 237–258). Berkeley: University of California Press.

Duke, N. (2000). For the rich, it's richer. Print environments and experiences offered to first-grade students in very low- and very high SES school districts. *American Educational Research Journal, 37,* 456–457.

Edmunds, M., & Briggs, K. (2003). The instructional content emphasis instrument: Observations of reading instruction. In S. R. Vaughn & K. L. Briggs (Eds.), *Reading in the classroom: Systems for observing teaching and learning* (pp. 31–52). Baltimore, MD Paul Brookes.

Ehri, L. C. (1991). Development of the ability to read words. In R. Barr, M. L. Kamil, P. Mosenthal, & P. D. Pearson (Eds.), *Handbook of reading research* (Vol. 2, pp. 383–417). White Plains, NY: Longman.

Ericsson, K. A., & Simon, H. A. (1984). *Protocol analysis: Verbal reports as data.* Cambridge, MA: Bradford Books/MIT Press.

Estrada, P. (2004). Patterns of language arts instructional activity and excellence in first- and fourth-grade culturally and linguistically diverse classrooms. In H. C. Waxman, R. G. Tharp, & R. S. Hilberg (Eds.), *Observational research in U.S. classrooms: New approaches for understanding cultural and linguistic diversity* (pp. 122–143). Cambridge, UK: Cambridge University Press.

Flanigan, K. (2007). A concept of word in text: A pivotal event in early reading acquisition. *Journal of Literacy Research, 39*(1), 37–70.

Foorman, B., & Schnatschneider, C. (2003). Measuring teaching practice during reading/language arts instruction and its relation to student achievement. In S. R. Vaughn & K. L. Briggs (Eds.), *Reading in the classroom: Systems for observing teaching and learning* (pp. 73–104). Baltimore, MD: Paul Brookes.

Franzak, J. K. (2004). Constructing struggling readers: Policy and the experiences of eighth grade readers. In J. Worthy, B. Maloch, J. V. Hoffman, D. L. Schallert, & C. M. Fairbanks (Eds.), *53rd yearbook of the National Reading Conference* (pp. 189–217). Oak Creek, WI: National Reading Conference.

Franzak, J. K. (2007). *Zoom:* A review of the literature on marginalized adolescent readers, literacy theory, and policy implications. *Review of Educational Research, 76*(2), 209–248.

Fuhrman, S. H. (Ed.). (1991). *Designing coherent education policy: Improving the system.* San Francisco: Jossey-Bass.

Gamse, B. C., Jacob, R. T., Horst, M., Boulay, B., & Unlu, F. (2008). *Reading First impact study final report* (NCEE 2009-4039). Washington, DC: National Center for Education Evaluation and Regional Assistance, Institute of Education Sciences, US Department of Education.

Gee, J. P. (2000–2001). Identity as an analytic lens for research in education. *Review of Research in Education, 25,* 99–125.

Good, R. H., & Kaminski, R. A. (2002). *Dynamic indicators of basic early literacy skills* (6th ed.). Eugene. OR: Institute for the Development of Educational Achievement.

Graesser, A. C., McNamara, D. S, & Louwerse, M. M., (2003). What do readers need to learn in order to process coherence relations in narrative and expository text? In A. P. Sweet & C. E. Snow (Eds.), *Rethinking reading comprehension* (pp. 82–98). New York: Guilford Press.

Greenwood, C. R., Abbott, M., & Tapia, Y. (2003). Ecobehavioral strategies: Observing, measuring, and analyzing behavior and reading interventions. In S. R. Vaughn & K. L. Briggs (Eds.), *Reading in the classroom: Systems for observing teaching and learning* (pp. 53–82). Baltimore, MD: Paul Brookes.

Guthrie, J. T., & Wigfield, A. (2000). Engagement and motivation in reading. In M. L. Kamil, P. B. Mosenthal, P. D. Pearson, & R. Barr (Eds.), *Handbook of reading research* (Vol. III, pp. 403–422). Mahwah, NJ: Erlbaum.

Guthrie, J. T., Wigfield, A., Humernick, N. M., Perencevich, K. C., Taboada, A., & Barbosa, P. (2006). Influences of stimulating tasks on reading motivation and comprehension. *Journal of Educational Research, 99*, 232–245.

Hall, L. A. (2006). IRA Outstanding Dissertation Award for 2006: Anything but lazy: New understandings about struggling readers, teaching, and text. *Reading Research Quarterly, 41*(4), 424–426.

Harm, M. W., McCandliss, B. D., & Seidenberg, M. S. (2003). Modeling the successes and failures of interventions for disabled readers. *Scientific Studies of Reading, 7*(2), 155–182.

Hidi, S., & Renninger, K. A. (2006). The four-phase model of interest development. *Educational Psychologist, 41*, 111–127.

Holland, D., Lachicotte, W., Skinner, D., & Cain, C. (1998). *Identity and agency in cultural worlds.* Cambridge, MA: Harvard University Press.

Institute of Education Sciences. (2009). *Reading for understanding.* Retrieved from http://ies.ed.gov/funding/ncer_rfas/reading.asp

Jenkins, J. R., Hudson, R. F., & Johnson, E. S. (2007). Screening for at-risk readers in a response to intervention framework. *School Psychology Review, 36*(4), 582–600.

Johnston, P., & Allington, R. (1991). Remediation. In R. Barr, M. L. Kamil, P. B. Mosenthal, & P. D. Pearson (Eds.), *Handbook of reading research* (Vol. 11, pp. 984–1012). New York: Longman.

Juel, C., & Minden-Cupp, C. (2000). Learning to read words: Linguistic units and instructional strategies. *Reading Research Quarterly, 35*, 458–492.

Kennedy, M. M. (2007). Defining a literature. *Educational Researcher, 36*(3), 139–147.

Kintsch, W., & van Dijk, T. A. (1978). Toward a model of text comprehension and production. *Psychological Review, 85*(5), 363–394.

Klenk, L., & Kibby, M. W. (2000). Re-mediating reading difficulties: Appraising the past, reconciling the present, constructing the future . In M. L. Kamil, P. B. Mosenthal, P. D. Pearson, & R. Barr (Eds.), *Handbook of reading research* (Vol. III, pp. 667–690). Mahwah, NJ: Erlbaum.

Leach, J. M., Scarborough, H. S., & Rescorla, L. (2003). Late-emerging reading disabilities. *Journal of Educational Psychology, 95*(2), 211–224.

Lyon, G. R. (1995). Research in learning disabilities: Contributions from scientists supported by the National Institute of Child Health and Human Development. *Journal of Child Neurology, 10*, S120–S126.

McCandliss, B., Beck, I., Sandak, R., & Perfetti, C. (2003). Focusing attention on decoding for children with poor reading skills: A study of the Word Building intervention. *Scientific Studies of Reading, 71*(1), 75–105.

McCarthey, S. J., & Moje, E. B. (2002). Conversations: Identity matters. *Reading Research Quarterly, 37*(2), 228–238.

McCaslin, M. (2004). Co-regulation of opportunity, activity, and identity in student motivation: Elaborations on Vygotskian themes. In D. McInerney & S. Van Etten (Eds.), *Big theories revisited: Vol. 4. Research on sociocultural influences on motivation and learning* (pp. 249–274). Greenwich, CT: Information Age.

McCaslin, M. (2009). Co-regulation of student motivation and emergent identity. *Educational Psychologist, 44*(2), 137–146.

McDermott, R., Goldman, S., & Varenne, H. (2006). The cultural work of learning disabilities. *Educational Researcher, 35*(6), 12–17.

McKeown, M. G., Beck, I. L., & Blake, R. G.K. (2009). Rethinking reading comprehension instruction: A comparison of instruction for strategies and content approaches. *Reading Research Quarterly, 44*(3), 218–253.

McNamara, D., O'Reilly, T., & de Vega, M. (2007). Comprehension skill, inference making, and the role of knowledge. In F. Schmalhofer & C. A. Perfetti (Eds.), *Higher level language processes in the brain: Inference and comprehension processes* (pp. 233–251). Mahwah, NJ: Erlbaum.

Mead, G. H. (1934). *Mind, self, and society from the standpoint of a social behaviorist.* Chicago: University of Chicago Press.

Mehan, H., Hertweck, A., & Meihls, J. L. (1986). *Handicapping the handicapped: Decision making in students' educational careers.* Stanford, CA: Stanford University Press.

Menand, L. (2001). *The metaphysical club: A story of ideas in America.* New York: Farrar, Strauss, and Giroux.

Morris, D. (1993). The relationship between children's concept of word in text and phoneme awareness in learning to read: A longitudinal study. *Research in the Teaching of English, 27,* 133–154.

Morris, D., Bloodgood, J., Lomax, R., & Perney, J. (2003). Developmental steps in learning to read: A longitudinal study in kindergarten and first grade. *Reading Research Quarterly, 38,* 2–24.

Nagy, W. E., Herman, P. A., & Anderson, R. C. (1985). Learning words from context. *Reading Research Quarterly, 20,* 233–253.

National Institute of Child Health and Human Development. (2000). *Report of the National Reading Panel: Teaching children to read: An evidence-based assessment of the scientific research literature on reading and its implications for reading instruction. Reports of the subgroups.* Washington, DC: U.S. Department of Health and Human Services, NIH Pub. No 00-4754.

No Child Left Behind Act of 2001, ESEA, 2001, Title I, Part B, Subpart I.

O'Brien, D. (2001, June). "At-risk" adolescents: Redefining competence through the multiliteracies of intermediality, visual arts, and representation. *Reading Online, 4*(11). Retrieved http://www.readingonline.org/newliteracies/lit_index.asp?HREF= /newliteracies/ obrien/index.html

O'Brien, D. (2003, March). Juxtaposing traditional and intermedial literacies to redefine the competence of struggling adolescents. *Reading Online, 6*(7). Retrieved http://www.readingonline.org/newliteracies/lit_index.asp?HREF=obrien2/

O'Connor, R. E. (2002). Increasing the intensity of intervention in kindergarten and first grade. *Learning Disabilities Research & Practice, 15,* 43–54.

Office of Elementary and Secondary Education. (2006). *Striving Readers.* Retrieved from http://www.ed.gov/print/programs/strivingreaders/award.html

Palincsar, A. S. (2007). The role of research, theory, and representation in the transformation of instructional research. *National Reading Conference Yearbook, 67,* 41–52.

Perfetti, C. A., (1991). Representation and awareness in the acquisition of reading competence. In L. Richen & C. A. Perfetti (Eds.), *Learning to read: Basic research and its implications* (pp. 33–44). Hillsdale, NJ: Erlbaum.

Perfetti, C. (2007). Reading ability: Lexical quality to comprehension. *Scientific Studies of Reading, 11*(4), 357–383.

Perfetti, C., Yang, C-L., & Schmalhofer, F. (2008). Comprehension skill and word-to-text integration processes. *Applied Cognitive Psychology, 22,* 303–318.

Pressley, M., El-Dinary, P. B., Gaskins, I., Schuder, T., Bergman, J. L., Almasi, J., et al. (1992). Beyond direct explanation: Transactional instruction of reading comprehension strategies. *Elementary School Journal, 92*(5), 513–555.

Rapp, D. N., van den Broek, P., McMaster, K. L., Kendeou, P., & Espin, C. A. (2007). Higher-order comprehension processes in struggling readers: A perspective for research and intervention. *Scientific Studies of Reading, 11*(4), 289–312.

Ravitch, D. (1985). *The troubled crusade: American education, 1945–1980.* New York: Basic Books.

Rayner, K. (1998). Eye movements in reading and information processing: 20 years of research. *Psychological Bulletin, 85,* 618–660.

Rayner, K., Chace, K. H., Slattery, T. J., & Ashby, J. (2006). Eye movements as reflections of comprehension processes in reading. *Scientific Studies of Reading, 10,* 241–255.

Renninger, K. A. (2009). Interest and identity development in instruction: An inductive model. *Educational Psychologist, 44*(2), 105–118.

Rentner, D. S., Scott, C., Kober, N., Chudowsky, N., Chudowsky, V., Joftus, S., et al. (2006). *From the capital to the classroom: Year 4 of the No Child Left Behind Act.* Washington, DC: Center on Education Policy. Retrieved April 1, 2006, from http://www.cep-dc.org/nclb/Year4/Press/

Scarborough, H. S. (2005). Developmental relationships between language and reading: Reconciling a beautiful hypothesis with some ugly facts. In H. W. Catts & A. G. Kamhi (Eds.), *The connections between language and reading disabilities* (pp. 3–24). Mahwah, NJ: Erlbaum.

Slavin, R. E., Cheung, G., Groff, C., & Lake, C. (2008). Effective reading programs for middle and high schools: A best-evidence synthesis. *Reading Research Quarterly, 43*(3), 290–322.

Smith, M. S., & O'Day, J. (1991). Systemic school reform. In S.H. Fuhrman and B. Malen, (Eds.), *The politics of curriculum and testing: The 1990 Yearbook of the Politics of Education Association* (pp. 233–267). New York: The Falmer Press.

Speece, D. L., Case, L. P., & Molloy, D. E. (2003). Responsiveness to general education instruction as the first gate to learning disabilities identification. *Learning Disabilities Research & Practice, 18*(3), 147–156.

Sunderman, G. L., Kim, J. S., & Orfield, G. (2005). *NCLB meets school realities: Lessons from the field.* Thousand Oaks, CA: Corwin Press.

Valli, L., & Buese, D. (2007). The changing roles of teachers in an era of high-stakes accountability. *American Educational Research Journal, 44*(3), 519–558.

van den Broek, P., & Kremer, K. E. (2000). The mind in action: What it means to comprehend during reading. In B. M. Taylor, M. F. Graves, & P. van den Broek (Eds.), *Reading for meaning: Fostering comprehension in the middle grades* (pp. 1–31). Newark, DE: International Reading Association.

van den Broek, P., Young, M., Tzeng, Y., & Linderholm, T. (1998). Integrating memory-based and constructionist processes in accounts of reading comprehension. *Discourse Processes, 39*, 299–316.

Vaughn, S., Linan-Thompson, S., & Hickman, P. (2003). Response to instruction as a means of identifying students with reading/learning disabilities. *Exceptional Children, 69*(4), 391–409.

Vitale, M. R., & Romance, N. R. (2007). A knowledge-based framework for unifying content-area reading comprehension and reading comprehension strategies. In D. McNamara (Ed.), *Reading comprehension strategies: Theory, interventions, and technologies* (pp. 1–30). Mahwah, NJ: Erlbaum.

Vygotsky, L. S. (1962). *Thought and language.* Cambridge, MA: MIT Press.

Vygotsky, L. S. (1978). *Mind in society: The development of higher psychological processes.* Cambridge, MA: Harvard University Press.

Wixson, K. K., & Lipson, M. Y. (1991). Perspectives on reading disability research. In R. Barr, M. L. Kamil, P. B. Mosenthal, & P. D. Pearson (Eds.), *Handbook of reading research* (Vol. 11, pp. 609–570). New York: Longman.

Woodcock, R. N. (1998). *Woodcock reading mastery tests-revised.* Circle Pines, MN: American Guidance Services.

Wortham, S. (2004). The interdependence of social identification and learning. *American Educational Research Journal, 41*(3), 715–750.

16 A Dialogic Turn in Research on Learning and Teaching to Comprehend

Ian A. G. Wilkinson and Eun Hye Son
The Ohio State University

[Understanding a paragraph] consists in selecting the right elements of the situation and putting them together in the right relations, and also with the right amount of weight or influence or force for each. The mind is assailed as it were by every word in the paragraph. It must select, repress, soften, emphasize, correlate and organize, all under the influence of the right mental set or purpose or demand.

(Thorndike, 1917, p. 431)

Comprehending is a dynamic and context sensitive process. The RAND Reading Study Group (2002) defined reading comprehension as "the process of simultaneously extracting and constructing meaning" (p. 11) that involves an interplay between the knowledge and capabilities of the reader, the demands of the text, the activities engaged in by the reader, and the sociocultural context in which reading occurs. By this account, the product of comprehension—meaning—is not stable. Changing one element, for example, by increasing the knowledge or motivation of the reader, altering the text, or asking the reader a question, changes the interaction between the reader, text, and activity and hence the meaning the reader constructs (cf. Harrison, 2004). It is not too farfetched to say that the product of comprehension changes day-by-day, hour-by-hour, and moment-by-moment (Pearson, 2001).

This view of comprehension has considerable precedent. It is reminiscent of Thorndike's (1917) view of understanding espoused in the quotation at the beginning of this chapter. It is compatible with Spiro's (2001) cognitive flexibility theory as applied to the learning and teaching of reading. According to Spiro, skilled readers need to be flexible and adaptive in their interactions with text to construct an understanding that is responsive to the needs of a new situation and demands of a new text. It is also compatible with Kintsch's (1998) construction-integration model of comprehension. According to Kintsch, skilled readers comprehend text by constructing a representation of the words and ideas and their interrelations (the text base), and integrating this information with relevant prior knowledge and goals (the knowledge base) to form an understanding of the text (the situation model). By this account, knowledge construction and understanding are dynamic, constantly fluctuating phenomena. The reader's prior knowledge informs the construction of the text base and the interconnections with the situation model, and the new knowledge acquired becomes part of the reader's long-term store of knowledge for use in new situations for understanding new texts. In Pearson's (2006) words, "knowledge begets comprehension begets knowledge."

Despite considerable precedent for this view of reading comprehension, the report of the National Reading Panel (National Institute of Child Health and Human Development [NICHD], 2000) did little to advance a perspective on comprehension as a dynamic and context sensitive process. The report focused on text and reader variables as the sole sources of variability in the comprehension process. Under the heading of comprehension instruction, the report listed seven comprehension strategies that members of the panel identified as having adequate research support—comprehension monitoring, cooperative learning (though this is a teaching strategy, not a cognitive process), constructing graphic and semantic organizers, question answering, question generation, using story structure, and summarizing—the implication being that good teaching of comprehension involved teaching these seven strategies (Pressley, 2006). Hence, the impression created by the report was that comprehension and comprehension instruction were relatively static, stable phenomena.

Prior reviews of research on comprehension instruction laid the foundation for the view of comprehension and comprehension instruction we advance in this chapter. Tierney and Cunningham (1984), writing in the first volume of the *Handbook of Reading Research*, anticipated some of the problems with the explicit teaching of comprehension. They expressed concerns about the mechanistic character of much comprehension strategies instruction and noted the goal of such instruction might be misdirected:

> We have serious reservations about the degree to which many of the studies assume the worth of explicit teaching of strategies (Pearson & Gallagher, 1983). Teaching children our theories about how they think in order to get them to think better seems to us to be fraught with danger. It is true that we should be concerned with process, but to the extent that comprehension is like gardening, we must be more interested in the vegetables produced than the tools in the shed. Student understanding is more important than tacit or meta-understanding. (p. 634)

These concerns were echoed by Carver (1987), who argued that the efficacy of explicit teaching of strategies might be due simply to the increased amounts of time students spent reading, and by Resnick (1987), who argued that the construct validity of the strategies was not yet established (do good readers actually use discrete strategies?). Pearson and Dole (1987) raised concerns about what explicit strategy instruction might mean for the curriculum in terms of what should be taught to improve comprehension. All these writers questioned whether strategies actually helped students acquire the habits of mind to transfer to new texts and novel situations.

Pearson and Fielding (1991), writing in the second volume of the *Handbook*, reiterated some of these concerns. They noted that the danger with explicit instruction is that the explanations and self-reflections might "become more complicated than the task itself, leading to the possibility that students will become trapped in introspective nightmares" (p. 851). They go on to speculate that teachers might be able to eliminate the need for explicit instruction by focusing on the content of the text itself. Their review is noteworthy because it heralded the social turn in research and instruction in comprehension, noting the potential effects of peer interaction and dialogue on students' comprehension and the benefits of giving students more responsibility for meaning making and more interpretive authority in discussions about text. This social turn was given emphasis in Kucan and Beck's (1997) review of research on thinking aloud and reading comprehension in which they speculated that collaborative discussion might provide a new direction for research on teaching comprehension.

Pressley (2000b), writing in the third volume of the *Handbook*, took a more expansive approach to reviewing research on comprehension instruction. He noted that strategies instruction needed to be richer and more flexible to promote students' self-regulated use of strategies. New to this review was coverage of research on transactional strategies instruction, a flexible, responsive approach to teaching strategies in the context of discussion to stimulate dialogue about text. Not long after, Gersten, Fuchs, Williams, and Baker (2001), in their review of research on teaching comprehension strategies to students with learning disabilities, documented the shift towards more flexible frameworks for comprehension instruction and the role of dialogue about text.

The purpose of the present chapter is to describe what we see as a dialogic turn in research on the learning and teaching of reading comprehension and to encourage those working in the field to think about the topic in a slightly new way. The focus is on comprehension instruction beyond the word level. We do not consider research on decoding and vocabulary, even though these are central enabling skills of comprehension (see Pressley, 2000b; Duke & Carlisle, this volume). Our thesis is that if comprehending is a dynamic, context sensitive process, then instruction needs to be more dynamic and flexible. In this chapter, we describe the current state of research on dialogic approaches to teaching comprehension that, we believe, offer more dynamic, flexible approaches to instruction.

Scholars use the term "dialogic" in a variety of ways. For some it means dialogue, for some it means giving students voice or agency, and for some it means collaborative inquiry among teachers and students and the co-construction of knowledge and understanding through dialogue. We use this term to denote all these things but, in particular, we use it according to Bakhtin (1981, 1986) to emphasize that the construction of meaning is a dynamic and relational process. In Bakhtin's terms, language and the ideas it embodies are continually structured by heteroglossia—multiple voices that produce tension, sometimes conflict, within and between participants, as one voice "refracts" another (Nystrand, 1997). This tension arises from the juxtaposition of relative perspectives and helps shape discourse and understanding. In this sense of the term dialogic, the interaction among different voices is the foundation for comprehension; meaning emerges "when different perspectives are brought together in a way that allows them to inter-animate or 'inter-illuminate' each other" (Wegerif, 2006, p. 146).

We employed a two-pronged approach to locate literature for this review. First, we located all reviews of research on the topic of teaching reading comprehension. We conducted searches of the ERIC and PsycINFO databases using the subject identifier "reading comprehension" and the keywords "teaching" or "instruction," limiting the search to literature reviews and meta-analyses that had been published in journals. We read the abstracts and selected relevant reviews, favoring those directly related to strategy instruction and those that were more recent. We read chapters on the topic in previous volumes of the *Handbook*, searched other edited books for review chapters, and located additional reviews that were cited in these sources. In total, we located over 60 reviews of research on teaching reading comprehension. Second, we conducted searches of ERIC and PsycINFO to locate articles reporting empirical studies of teaching reading comprehension that had been published since 1999 (to pick up where the previous *Handbook* chapter left off), again using the subject identifier "reading comprehension" and the keywords "teaching" or "instruction," limiting the search to articles that had been published in journals. We independently read the abstracts and selected articles that were relevant to the present review: those that were empirical studies, involved students in grades K–12, and focused on teaching reading comprehension (rather than simply measuring reading comprehension as a dependent variable). Our percent agreement in identifying relevant articles was 85%. All disagreements were resolved through discussion. We also conducted targeted searches of articles by scholars whom we knew were conducting programs of research on the topic and talked with colleagues about relevant sources.

The structure of the chapter is as follows. First, we reprise the three waves of research on comprehension strategies instruction described by Pressley (1998). Studies published since 1999 are incorporated, as appropriate, to provide an update on this research. Second, we problematize comprehension strategies instruction. Third, we describe what might be characterized as the fourth wave of research on comprehension instruction—research on approaches that can be grouped under the heading of dialogic. This includes research on content-rich instruction, discussion, argumentation, and intertextuality. Fourth, we conclude by considering the implications for theory, research, and practice.

THREE WAVES OF RESEARCH ON COMPREHENSION STRATEGIES INSTRUCTION (WITH AN UPDATE)

Michael Pressley characterized research on teaching comprehension strategies in terms of three waves of studies. The best description of these three waves can be found in Pressley (1998). Similar accounts of the evolution of research on strategy instruction can be found in Pressley, Brown, El-Dinary, and Afflerbach (1995) and Pressley (2000a, 2000b, 2001, 2002a, 2002b, 2006).

First Wave: Single Strategy Instruction

The first wave of studies, conducted in the 1970s and early 1980s, focused on the effects of teaching students individual comprehension strategies. These were laboratory and classroom-based studies. Researchers taught students in an experimental group to use a strategy, while students in a comparison group received no instruction in the strategy. Researchers typically measured outcomes on experimenter-developed tests of comprehension specific to the texts employed in the studies. Results showed effects on comprehension in favor of students in the experimental groups and researchers interpreted these effects as evidence that students could be taught to use a strategy and that it benefited students' comprehension. Strategies shown to be effective in such studies included: activating prior knowledge, generating questions during reading, constructing mental images of the text, summarizing, and analyzing stories into story grammar components. These studies were reviewed by Tierney and Cunningham (1984), Pearson and Dole (1987), Haller, Child, and Walberg (1988), Pressley, Johnson, Symons, McGoldrick, and Kurita (1989), and Pearson and Fielding (1991).

Researchers have continued to investigate the effects of teaching students individual comprehension strategies. Since 1999, researchers have investigated the effects of teaching students strategies of main idea identification (Jitendra, Hoppes, & Xin, 2000), story theme identification (Wilder & Williams, 2001; Williams et al., 2002), self-regulation (Haddad et al., 2003), semantic mapping (Pappa, Zafiropoulou, & Metallidou, 2003), use of expository text structure (Hall, Sabey, & McClellan, 2005; Williams, 2005; Williams, Hall, & Lauer, 2004; Williams et al., 2005; Williams et al., 2007; Williams, Stafford, Lauer, Hall, & Pollini, 2009), and use of mental imagery (Joffe, Cain, & Maric, 2007). Most of these studies have targeted special populations of students who were at risk for academic failure or who were learning English as a second language.

Second Wave: Multiple Strategies Instruction

The second wave, conducted in the 1980s, focused on the effects of teaching students multiple strategies. The best-known instructional approach studied at this time was reciprocal teaching, an approach where teachers taught students to apply strategies of questioning, clarifying, summarizing, and predicting (Palincsar & Brown, 1984). During the second wave, the direct explanation approach to strategy instruction came to the fore (Duffy et al., 1987). Teachers explained to students in the experimental groups how to use a small repertoire of strategies, modeled the use of the strategies, and engaged students in guided and independent practice of the strategies. Students in the comparison groups did not receive strategy instruction. Results showed sizeable effects on experimenter-developed tests of comprehension and, sometimes, smaller but statistically significant effects on standardized tests of reading comprehension relative to students in the comparison groups. Researchers again interpreted these gains as evidence that students could be taught to use multiple strategies and that they produced fairly robust benefits for students' comprehension. These studies were reviewed by Pearson and Fielding (1991) and Rosenshine and Meister (1994).

Researchers have also continued to investigate the effects of teaching students small reper-toires of strategies in a manner consistent with Pressley's second wave research. Most of the strategy instruction studies published since 1999 fall into this category. Many of the studies have investigated reciprocal teaching or some variant thereof (e.g., Johnson-Glenberg, 2000), and many have again targeted special populations of students such as those with disabilities (e.g., Faggella-Luby, Schumaker, & Deshler, 2007; Mastropieri et al., 2001) or those for whom English is a second language (e.g., Fung, Wilkinson, & Moore, 2003).

Noteworthy is a series of studies, dating back to 1996, conducted by Vaughn, Klingner, and colleagues evaluating the effectiveness of Collaborative Strategic Reading (CSR; Kim et al., 2006; Klingner & Vaughn, 1996, 2000; Klingner, Vaughn, Arguelles, Hughes, & Leftwich, 2004; Klingner, Vaughn, Hughes, & Arguelles, 1999; Klingner, Vaughn, & Schumm, 1998; Vaughn et al., 2000; Vaughn, Hughes, Schumm, & Klingner, 1998). CSR combines elements of recipro-cal teaching and cooperative learning to help students with learning disabilities and English language learners in elementary school make sense of content-area texts. Teachers first model for the class how to use four comprehension strategies: brainstorming and predicting, monitor-ing understanding, identifying main ideas, and generating questions and reviewing key ideas. Students then engage in further modeling and practice. The students then employ the strate-gies while working in pairs or small, heterogeneous, peer-led groups. Students in groups are assigned different roles (e.g., leader, reporter) to foster cooperative work. CSR has also been combined with other reading instruction approaches to meet the diverse needs of students in middle school (Bryant, Ugel, Thompson, & Hamff, 1999; Bryant et al., 2000). As with the earlier second wave research, most studies of CSR and of other approaches to multiple strategy instruc-tion have shown beneficial effects on experimenter-developed and standardized tests of reading comprehension.

Third Wave: Transactional Strategies Instruction

The third wave, which began in 1989, was a program of research that Pressley and his colleagues conducted focused on a more flexible approach to teaching students multiple strategies. Press-ley and colleagues studied school-based, teacher-developed implementations of comprehension strategies instruction (e.g., Pressley et al., 1992) and developed an approach they called "transac-tional strategies instruction" (TSI), so called because it emphasized transactions between read-ers and text, transactions among participants (students and teacher), and joint construction of understanding. Students were taught, usually within the context of a content-rich curriculum, a small repertoire of strategies that typically included predicting based on prior knowledge, gen-erating questions, clarifying confusions, constructing mental images, relating text content to prior knowledge, and summarizing. Brown, Pressley, Van Meter, and Schuder (1996) conducted a year-long, quasi-experimental study of the effects of TSI with low-achieving Grade 2 students. Results showed robust effects on experimenter-developed measures of strategy awareness, strat-egy use, and comprehension, as well as on standardized measures of reading achievement in favor of students receiving TSI.

Pressley regarded two other studies as providing evidence of the effects of strategy instruc-tion that was consistent with the TSI approach. These were true experiments conducted by Col-lins (1991) with grades 5 and 6 students and by Anderson's (1992; see also Anderson & Roit, 1993) with middle school and high school students. Both studies also showed substantial effects on standardized measures of reading comprehension.

During the development and evaluation of TSI, evidence accrued in support of the validity of comprehension strategies. Wyatt et al. (1993) conducted a verbal protocol analysis of the reading of 15 skilled readers (professors from the University of Maryland) and Pressley and Afflerbach (1995) compiled a synthesis of results from over 40 verbal protocol studies in which readers were asked to think aloud as they read. According to Presley and Afflerbach, findings from the studies converged on the notion that skilled readers were "constructively responsive readers" and deployed a range of strategies fluidly, on a moment-to-moment basis, in response to the demands of the text, the needs of the situation, and their cognitive and metacognitive capabilities. Pressley et al. (1995) claimed that these strategies were the same ones that were taught in TSI. For those who believed the data from verbal protocol studies, these findings addressed the concerns of scholars who doubted the validity of comprehension strategies. Here was evidence that good readers used comprehension strategies.

We identified only two recent studies of TSI (some of the more dialogic approaches to comprehension instruction might also be considered examples of TSI, but we discuss these in a later section). Reutzel, Smith, and Fawson (2005) compared TSI with an approach to comprehension instruction where teachers taught a series of strategies one-at-a-time (single strategy instruction, SSI). This was a true experiment where 80 Grade 2 students were randomly assigned to the two treatments. Teachers taught students to use strategies with science information big books over a semester. Results showed no differences in comprehension between the TSI and SSI groups as measured by recall of main ideas from transfer passages and a norm-referenced, standardized test of comprehension. But there were significant and substantial differences in favor of the TSI students in recall of details from the transfer passages, performance on a curriculum-based test of comprehension, and science content knowledge. This is one of the few studies demonstrating the viability of multiple strategy instruction with children in the early grades (for reviews of strategy instruction in the early grades, see Pearson & Duke, 2002; Stahl, 2004). In another recent study of TSI, Hilden and Pressly (2007) conducted a case study of five middle school teachers as they participated in a yearlong professional development program in TSI. The authors documented the challenges and successes the teachers experienced as they encouraged students' self-regulated use of comprehension strategies.

In summary, research on strategy instruction has evolved from laboratory and classroom-based studies of single-strategy instruction, to studies of the teaching small repertoires of strategies, to studies of teaching these repertoires in more flexible ways in more collaborative contexts. There is now no doubt that instruction in small repertoires of comprehension strategies, when implemented well, produces robust effects on measures of comprehension, including standardized tests (e.g., Anderson, 1992; Brown et al., 1996; Collins, 1991). This seems to be especially the case for students with learning disabilities (Gersten et al., 2001; see also Faggella-Luby & Deshler, 2008). What remain in doubt are why this happens, whether this instruction yields the generative, flexible comprehension students need, and whether the effects are sustainable in the classroom.

PROBLEMS WITH STRATEGIES INSTRUCTION

Why Does Teaching Strategies Improve Students' Comprehension?

It is still not clear why teaching strategies improves students' comprehension. As noted earlier, Pressley et al. (1995) argued that teaching strategies enabled students to emulate what skilled readers do and that the strategies were directly responsible for enhancing students' comprehension. However, early in the development of strategy instruction, Resnick (1985) argued that the speed and automaticity with which skilled readers comprehend text made it unlikely that they deliberately devoted attention to asking questions, constructing summaries, and so on. Rosenshine and Meister's (1994) review of research on reciprocal teaching cast further doubt on whether strategies were indeed directly related to comprehension. They found that students' comprehension was generally the same regardless of the kinds and number of strategies taught (see also Rosenshine, Meister, & Chapman, 1996). Moreover, among those studies that enabled researchers to study the ability of students to use one of the strategies, generating questions, they found no relationship between ability to use the strategy and students' reading comprehension. Sinatra, Brown, and Reynolds (2002) argued that the deliberate allocation of attention to strategies might even undermine students' comprehension because it diverts their cognitive resources away from understanding the text. They also pointed out that researchers were still hard pressed to identify the most effective strategies.

There are at least two alternative explanations for the effect of teaching strategies. One alternative explanation is that teaching strategies promotes students' active engagement with text. Kintsch and Kintsch (2005) noted that a feature of all strategies is that they promote the active construction of meaning during reading, and the linking of the text with reader's prior knowledge and experience (see also Willingham, 2007). Another alternative explanation is that strategies are vehicles that enable students to engage in dialogue about text. There are various perspectives on what the dialogue affords—a collaborative scaffold (Palincsar, 1986), a think aloud that enables students to learn from each other about the processes of constructing meaning (Kucan & Beck, 1997), or a means of giving students voice (Palincsar, 2006). The latter explanation and perspectives privilege the social rather than individual aspects of learning (see Gersten et al., 2001).

At the time of writing, we know of only two studies that directly address the issue of alternative explanations for the effects of strategy instruction. McKeown, Beck, and Blake (2009) compared multiple strategies instruction with a version of Questioning the Author (QtA), an approach that eschews the teaching of strategies in favor of having students focus on text content in response to general, meaning-based questions (Beck & McKeown, 2006; Beck, McKeown, Sandora, Kucan, & Worthy, 1996). McKeown and colleagues also included a control group that received instruction from a modified basal program. They conducted two experiments with fifth grade students in a low-performing school, using scripted instruction to standardize coverage of the texts. The first study was a quasi-experiment, and the second was a true experiment involving random assignment of students. Results showed significant differences between students in the two conditions in favor of QtA on open-ended or probed recall of instructed texts and marginal differences in favor of QtA on recall of transfer texts read without instructional support. However, performance of students in the QtA condition was not significantly greater than that of students in the basal control condition.

Garcia, Taylor, Pearson, Stahl, and Bauer (2007) conducted a quasi-experimental study comparing multiple strategies instruction with instruction that emphasized responsive engagement with text. The responsive engagement instruction drew on Saunders and Goldenberg's (1999) Instructional Conversations and incorporated additional features intended to promote high-level discussions of text. There was also a control group that received vocabulary instruction. The study involved students in grades 2/3 and 4/5 in 12 low-income schools in four sites. Results for grades 4/5 varied by site but overall showed no significant differences between students in the strategy and responsive engagement conditions in comprehension of an instructed text. A transfer text was used at one of the sites and results again showed no significant differences in comprehension between the strategy and responsive engagement groups. On both instructed and transfer passages, students in the two conditions significantly outperformed those in the control condition. Results for grades 2/3 also varied by site though they were more difficult to interpret.

Neither the McKeown et al. (2009) study nor the Garcia et al. (2007) study permits an unambiguous interpretation of the benefits of strategy instruction. Instructing students in strategies might be a way of promoting sustained, active engagement with the ideas in a text, and/or of fostering dialogue about the text. Nevertheless, the results of the two studies are compatible with the notion that it is not the strategies *per se* that are responsible for improvement in students' comprehension.

Does Teaching Strategies Yield the Generative, Flexible Comprehension Students Need?

Another problem with strategies is that instruction can become too mechanical. Shortly after the first wave of strategy instruction research, scholars voiced concerns that strategies can become an end-point of instruction rather than a means to an end (Baker, 1994, 2002; Beck, McKeown, Hamilton, & Kucan, 1997; Brown & Campione, 1998; Moats, 2004; Paris & Winograd, 1990; Tierney & Cunningham, 1984).

These concerns were warranted because they have been realized. Hacker and Tenent (2002) noted the tendency of some teachers to overemphasize the four strategies of reciprocal teaching to the detriment of students' engagement in meaningful dialogue about text (see also, Coley, DePinto, Craig, & Gardner, 1993; Marks et al., 1993). Similarly, Reutzel et al. (2005) noted that teachers in their SSI condition tended to focus on learning and applying a strategy rather than focusing on it as a vehicle to acquire science content knowledge. Garcia et al. (2007) noticed that teachers who were taught to implement strategy instruction during a year of professional development tended to "get stuck," overemphasizing strategies even as they were to trying to foster students' more responsive engagement with text. The risk of instruction becoming too mechanical is that the interactions among teacher and students become highly structured to the point where they inhibit generative learning and students' flexible, self-regulated use of strategies (cf. Cohen, 1994; King, 1999).

Is the Teaching of Strategies Sustainable in the Classroom?

Yet another problem with strategies is that they are difficult for teachers to sustain in the classroom. Despite the wealth of evidence in support of the effectiveness of strategies, observations of reading and language arts instruction in elementary schools in different regions of the United States indicate that the teaching of strategies is not very common. Pressley, Wharton-McDonald, Mistretta-Hampton, and Echevarria (1998) observed language arts instruction in 10 fourth- and fifth-grade classrooms in upstate New York over a school year. They saw very little comprehension strategy instruction; what they saw instead was a great deal of comprehension assessment. More recently, Taylor, Pearson, Clark, and Walpole (2000) observed instruction in first- through third-grade classrooms in 14 high-poverty schools in Virginia, Minnesota, Colorado, and California and reported seeing little strategies instruction. Taylor, Pearson, Peterson, and Rodriguez (2003, 2005) also reported observing little strategy instruction in grades 1–5 in high-poverty schools in various parts of the United States. Connor, Morrison, and Petrella (2004), in a study of 43 third-grade classrooms in the Midwest, noted that teachers spent an average of less than 1 minute per day explicitly instructing strategies. These findings are all too reminiscent of Durkin's (1978/1979) finding that what masqueraded for comprehension instruction in the 1970s was little more than either oral or written comprehension quizzes.

A likely explanation for the apparent dearth of strategies instruction is that teachers find it hard to learn and hard to do. Pressley, Goodchild, Fleet, Zajchowski, and Evans (1989) and Deshler and Schumaker (1993) argued that strategy instruction posed many challenges for teachers. El-Dinary and Schuder (1993) provided empirical support for this argument, documenting the difficulties experienced by seven teachers as they attempted to become TSI teachers. They reported that by the end of the year, only two of the seven teachers were committed to comprehension strategies instruction (see also El-Dinary, 1994; 2002; Pressley & El-Dinary, 1997). Similarly, Brown and Coy-Ogan (1993) and Duffy (1993) documented that learning to teach strategies required a long-term commitment from teachers.

Recent studies have confirmed the challenges strategy instruction poses for teachers of reading (Hilden & Pressley, 2007; Klingner et al., 2004; Klingner et al., 1999; Mason, 2004; Taylor et al., 2005). All of these recent studies have shown that teaching strategies can take several years for teachers to learn to do well, requires considerable amount of classroom time, and may conflict with teachers' prior beliefs and practices.

DIALOGIC APPROACHES TO LEARNING AND TEACHING TO COMPREHEND: THE FOURTH WAVE

The fourth wave of research on comprehension instruction emphasizes approaches that might be grouped under the heading of dialogic. The dialogic turn in research on learning and teaching to comprehend was motivated, in part, by the concerns about strategies instruction outlined above and by the recognition that comprehension was a more fluid, context sensitive process that required more a dynamic, flexible approach to instruction. In this section, we review research on four such approaches: content-rich instruction, discussion, argumentation, and intertextuality. We characterize research on these more dialogic approaches as the 'fourth wave' of research on comprehension instruction.

Pressley's third wave of studies of TSI and the attendant theory of constructively responsive reading probably set the stage for these more dialogic approaches to learning and teaching of reading comprehension. Pressley and Afflerbach's (1995) review of verbal protocol studies revealed that comprehension was an active, moment-by-moment process affected by complex interactions among an array factors. Such a view of comprehension necessitated a more complex view of teaching (Pressley et al. 1995). In TSI, there is an emphasis on dialogue, on giving students more control over their own learning, and on collaborative inquiry as a mean of constructing knowledge and understanding. These features are also found in the approaches considered in the fourth wave. However, what is key to these more dialogic approaches is the juxtaposition of relative perspectives or discourses that gives rise to tension and sometimes conflict among different voices. From a dialogic perspective, it is from the interaction and struggle among different, even competing, voices that meaning and understanding emerge.

Content-Rich Instruction

In recent years, there has been increasing interest in studies of strategy instruction embedded within specific content domains such as science or social studies to promote comprehension. The National Reading Panel (NICHD, 2000) referred to such studies as "curriculum-plus-strategies" studies, noting that they constituted a promising line of inquiry. Recent research in this area is marked by a high degree of integration of strategy instruction and subject-matter teaching and the richness of the subject-matter content. One rationale for bringing together these two endeavors is that strategies provide the tools to help students make sense of the content, and the content gives meaning and purpose to the strategies—in other words, the two inter-animate or inter-illuminate each other. The strategies might be content general, applicable in a range of contexts, or they might be specific to the demands of the domain in which students are working.

One program of research that exemplifies this trend is research on Concept-Oriented Reading Instruction (CORI; Guthrie, Wigfield, & Perencevich, 2004). CORI is an instructional program to develop upper elementary students' comprehension, motivation for reading, and understanding of science (see http://www.cori.umd.edu/). It involves teaching the comprehension strategies of activating background knowledge, questioning, searching for information, summarizing, and organizing information graphically. These strategies are taught in the usual sequence of modeling, scaffolding, and guided and independent practice. What is key to CORI is that strategies are taught within a rich context of collaborative inquiry in science, where students establish knowledge goals and make real-world connections through hands-on experiences and other activities. This context, in combination with other instructional features, provides the impetus for students' development of strategies and motivation. Research on CORI began with Guthrie et al.'s (1996) demonstration that CORI enhanced third and fifth graders' literacy engagement and motivation over the course of one year. Since then, Guthrie and colleagues have conducted 10 quasi-experimental studies comparing the effects of CORI with those of traditional instruction and more conventional strategy instruction with students in grades 3, 4, and 5 (e.g., Guthrie, Anderson, Alao, & Rinehart, 1999; Guthrie et al., 1998; Guthrie et al., 1996; Guthrie, Wigfield, Barbosa et al., 2004; Guthrie et al., 2006; Guthrie, Wigfield, & VonSecker, 2000; Wigfield, Guthrie, Tonks, & Perencevich, 2004)). In a meta-analysis of these studies, Guthrie, McRae, and Klauda (2007) reported mean effects sizes in favor of CORI ranging from 0.65 to 0.93 on researcher-developed tests of comprehension and 0.91 on standardized tests of comprehension. The meta-analysis also showed mean effect sizes of 1.34 on measures of students' science knowledge and of 1.00 and 1.20 on measures of students' motivation for reading.

Another program of research in this area is research on In-Depth Expanded Application of Science (IDEAS; Romance & Vitale, 1992, 2001). The IDEAS model embeds reading and language arts instruction within a daily 2-hour block of in-depth science concept instruction. The assumption is that, by contextualizing reading and language arts instruction within the knowledge-building activities of science, students' learning of reading comprehension skills and strategies (e.g., concept mapping, relating new knowledge to prior knowledge) is more meaningful and purposeful. Romance and Vitale (2001) summarized the results of four quasi-experimental studies comparing the effects of IDEAS with those of traditional instruction with students in grades 2 through 5. Results of most studies showed significantly greater performance in comprehension as measured by standardized tests, as well as greater performance in science achievement and more positive attitudes towards reading and science.

Research on Reading Apprenticeship by Greenleaf, Schoenbach, and colleagues (Greenleaf, Schoenbach, Cziko, & Mueller, 2001; Jordan, Jensen, & Greenleaf, 2001; Jordan & Schoenbach, 2003; Schoenbach, Braunger, Greenleaf, & Litman, 2003; Schoenbach & Greenleaf, 2000) provides insight into what content-rich strategy instruction might look like in middle and high schools. Reading Apprenticeship is an instructional framework in which teachers apprentice students into reading by serving as a "master" reader of subject-area texts in science, social studies, math, or English (Schoenbach, Greenleaf, Cziko, & Hurwitz, 1999). Teachers model their own strategies for reading and making sense of challenging texts in their disciplines and give students opportunities for guided and independent practices in using the strategies embedded in authentic content-area reading experiences. An important feature of the model is the use of "metacognitive conversations" in which teachers and students make visible their discipline-based comprehension strategies and processes in group discussions and other collaborative learning environments. In a single-group pretest-posttest design study, Greenleaf and Mueller (2003) showed that ninth-grade students who engaged in an academic literacy course based on Reading Apprenticeship made greater than expected gains over a school year on a standardized test of reading comprehension. A large-scale, randomized control trial conducted as part of an evaluation by the U.S. Institute of Education Sciences (Corrin, Somers, Kemple, Nelson, & Sepanik, 2008; Kemple et al., 2008), showed that a similar yearlong course in academic literacy, used as a supplementary literacy program for struggling ninth-grade readers, produced small but statistically significant benefits relative to a control condition on standardized tests of students' reading comprehension, at least in schools with high levels of program implementation. It should be noted that none of these studies provides a direct test of Reading Apprenticeship embedded in the teaching of specific subject-areas, but they do provide support for the general instructional framework.

These and other programs of research (see the work on integrating science and literacy instruction by Hapgood, Magnusson, & Palincsar, 2004; and Palincsar & Magnusson, 2001; on Seeds of Science/Roots of Reading by Pearson and Barber at http://seedsofscience.org; and the edited collection of papers in Saul, 2004) attest to the benefits of bringing strategy instruction, and comprehension instruction in general, into dialogic relationship with subject-matter teaching. This research highlights the benefits of content-rich instruction for both students' reading comprehension and content knowledge.

As is evident in the research reviewed, most studies in this area have been conducted in elementary school. A challenge for future research is learning how to help teachers integrate comprehension instruction into content-area teaching in middle and high schools where the subject-matter demands are more complex (Conley, 2008). The work of Greenleaf, Schoenbach, and colleagues (e.g., Greenleaf et al., 2001) on Reading Apprenticeship provides some direction in this regard. Another program of research in this area is the work of Deshler, Schumaker, and colleagues (e.g., Deshler & Schumaker, 2006; Hock, Brasseur, & Deshler, 2008) on the Strategic Instruction Model designed to help middle and high school students with learning disabilities comprehend complex content in their subject-matter classes. More research in this area is needed.

Discussion

Research on the role of classroom discussion as means of promoting reading comprehension is not new; it has been the subject of investigation since the early 1960s. What is new is the level of attention being paid to the effects of discussion on students' comprehension and the proliferation of approaches to conducting high-quality discussions about text. There are now a large number of discourse-intensive pedagogies that disrupt the I-R-E (Initiation-Response-Evaluation) pattern of traditional classroom discourse in favor of more open-ended, collaborative exchanges of ideas among participants for the purpose of improving students' understanding and interpretation of texts.

The theory underlying the use of discussions to improve comprehension derives from cognitive, sociocognitive, sociocultural, and dialogic perspectives on learning and teaching. From a cognitive perspective, discussion promotes active engagement in making meaning from a text (McKeown et al., 2009). From a sociocognitive perspective, discussion enables students to make public their perspectives on issues arising from the text, consider alternative perspectives proposed by peers, and attempt to reconcile conflicts among opposing points of view (Almasi, 1995). From a sociocultural perspective, discussion enables students to co-construct knowledge and understandings about the text and internalize ways of thinking that foster the knowledge, skills, and dispositions needed to transfer to the reading of new texts (Wells, 2007). And from a dialogic perspective, the tension and conflict between relative perspectives and competing voices in discussion about a text helps shape the discourse and students' comprehension (Nystrand, 2006).

The major approaches to conducting discussion can be distinguished in terms of the degree of control exerted by the teacher versus the students and the dominant stance toward the text (cf. Chinn, Anderson, & Waggoner, 2001). The degree of control exerted by the teacher versus the students depends on who has control of the topic of discussion, who has interpretive authority, who controls the turns, and who chooses the text. The dominant stance toward the text depends largely on the teacher's goals for the discussion and can be categorized in terms of an aesthetic, efferent, or critical-analytic stance. An aesthetic, or more appropriately expressive (see Soter, Wilkinson, Connors, Murphy, & Shen, 2010), stance refers to a reader-focused response to the text. In this stance, the discussion gives prominence to the reader's affective response to the text, to the readers' spontaneous, emotive connection to all aspects of the textual experience (Rosenblatt, 1978). An efferent stance refers to a more text-focused response in which the discussion gives prominence to reading to acquire and retrieve information. The focus is on "the ideas, information, directions, conclusions to be retained, used, or acted on after the reading event" (Rosenblatt, 1978, p. 27). A critical-analytic stance refers to a more objective, critical response in which the discussion gives prominence to interrogating or querying the text in search of the underlying arguments, assumptions, worldviews, or beliefs (cf. Wade, Thompson, & Watkins, 1994).

These two dimensions of text-based discussions—degree of control exerted by the teacher versus the students and the dominant stance toward the text—are related (Wilkinson & Reninger, 2005). Discussions in which students have the greatest control tend to be those that give prominence to an aesthetic or expressive stance toward the text. These approaches include Book Club (Raphael & McMahon, 1994), Grand Conversations (Eeds & Wells, 1989), and Literature Circles (Short & Pierce, 1990). Conversely, discussions in which teachers have the greatest control tend to be those that give prominence to an efferent stance. These approaches include Instructional Conversations (Goldenberg, 1992/1993), Questioning the Author (Beck & McKeown, 2006; Beck et al., 1997), and Junior Great Books Shared Inquiry (Great Book Foundation, 1987). Discussions in which students and teachers share control tend to give prominence to a critical-analytic stance. In these approaches, the teacher has considerable control over text and topic, but students have considerable interpretive authority and control of turns. Approaches that fall into this category include Collaborative Reasoning (Anderson, Chinn, Chang, Waggoner, & Nguyen, 1998), Paideia Seminars (Billings & Fitzgerald, 2002), and Philosophy for Children (Sharp, 1995).

There are other approaches to text-based discussion although they are less easy to categorize, in part because there is less research on them. These other approaches include Conversational Discussion Groups (O'Flahavan, 1989), Dialogical-Thinking Reading Lessons (Commeyras, 1993), Idea Circles (Guthrie & McCann, 1996), and Point-Counterpoint (Rogers, 1990). There are also various instantiations of literature discussion groups based on reader-response theory (see Gambrell & Almasi, 1996), discussion-based envisionments of literature (Langer, 1993; 1995, 2001), and instructional integrations of writing, reading, and talk (Nystrand, Gamoran, & Carbonaro, 2001; Sperling & Woodlief, 1997).

Evidence on the role of discussion in improving students' comprehension comes from correlational, single-group, and multiple-group design studies. Nystrand and Gamoran (Gamoran & Nystrand, 1991; Nystrand, 1997; Nystrand & Gamoran, 1991) conducted possibly the largest correlational study ever of the relationship between discussion and students' comprehension. They observed the instructional practices in 58 eighth-grade and 54 ninth-grade language arts and English classes in eight midwestern communities in the United States. They observed each class four times a year and assessed students understanding and interpretation of literature at the end of each year, collecting data on over 1,895 students. Their results indicated that features of whole-class discussion were positively related to students' reading comprehension, as measured by both recall and depth of understanding, as well as response to aesthetic aspects of literature. These features included sustained, open exchange of ideas among students; teachers asking authentic questions (i.e., questions where the answer was not prespecified), provided they were related to the literature under discussion; and uptake (i.e., questions where the teacher incorporated and built on students' comments). Nystrand (1997, 2006) argued out that these features of discourse served an epistemic role in discussion by giving students more voice and agency in construction of their learning and understanding.

These results were largely replicated in a follow-up correlational study by Applebee, Langer, Nystrand, and Gamoran (2003) of 974 students in 64 middle and high school English classrooms. Their results confirmed that open discussion, authentic questions, and uptake, used in the context of academically challenging tasks, were positively related to students' reading comprehension and literature achievement.

Similar results have been reported in other correlational studies. Langer (2001) studied the instructional practices associated with student achievement in 25 middle and high schools, involving 44 teachers and 88 classes. This was a nested, multiple-case design comparing practices in schools with higher-than-expected achievement in literacy with those in more typically performing schools; hence it was essentially a causal-comparative study. Langer found that whole-class and small-group discussion was one of the characteristics of instruction in the higher-performing schools. Taylor et al.'s (2000) observational study was similar in design in that they compared the instructional practices of first- through third-grade teachers in 14 schools categorized as most, moderately, or least effective in promoting student reading achievement. They showed that asking higher-level, aesthetic-response questions in discussions about text was a feature of instruction of the most accomplished teachers and teachers in the most effective schools (see also, Taylor, Pearson, Clark, & Walpole, 1999). In subsequent school change work, to promote the cognitive engagement of students in grades 1-5 in diverse array of high-poverty schools, Taylor et al. (2002, 2003, 2005) again found that higher-level questions predicted students' end-of-year achievement in reading (though not always in comprehension).

Murphy, Wilkinson, Soter, Hennessey, and Alexander (2009) conducted a meta-analysis of 42 single-group and multiple-group studies that examined the effects of different approaches to text-based discussions on measures of teacher and student talk and individual student comprehension and learning outcomes. Results showed that the approaches were differentially effective in promoting comprehension. Many of the approaches were effective at promoting students' literal and inferential comprehension especially those that had a more efferent stance toward the text, namely Questioning the Author, Instructional Conversations, and Junior Great Books Shared Inquiry. Some of the approaches were particularly effective at promoting students' critical-thinking, reasoning, and argumentation about text, namely Collaborative Reasoning and Junior Great Books Shared Inquiry. Only a small number of studies documented effects of discussion on standardized measures using multiple-group designs. Among these studies, Lipman (1975) reported the strongest effect on students' comprehension after three years of instruction with Philosophy for Children, producing an effect size of 0.55 on the Iowa Test of Basic Skills. The effect sizes for the other studies averaged approximately 0.20. Another finding from Murphy et al.'s meta-analysis was that increases in student talk did not necessarily result in concomitant increases in student comprehension. Rather, a particular kind of talk was necessary to promote comprehension. This is consistent with observations from other research that the success of discussion hinges not on increasing the amount of student talk per se, but in enhancing the quality of the talk (Wells, 1989). Results of the meta-analysis also suggested that the approaches exhibited greater effects for students of below-average ability than for students of average or above-average ability.

An important finding from the body of research on text-based discussions is that discussion can benefit English Language Learners (ELLs). Saunders and Goldenberg (1999) conducted an experimental study of the effects of Instructional Conversations in combination with literature logs on 116 fourth and fifth grade ELL and English-proficient students. Results showed both ELL and English-proficient students who participated in the Instructional Conversations + Literature Logs condition scored significantly higher in literal and inferential comprehension of narrative texts than did students in other conditions (literature logs only, Instructional Conversations only, and a reading plus study control condition). The ELL students in the Instructional Conversations + Literature Logs condition also scored significantly higher on measures of theme explanation and exemplification than did students in the other conditions. Other studies have shown similar effects of discussions for ELL students (see Nystrand, 2006).

Although there is a convergence of theory and data suggesting that high-quality discussions can improve students' comprehension, more research is necessary. Much of the research involves correlational and single-group pretest-posttest designs, and uses indices of discourse as proxy measures of comprehension. More experimental and quasi-experimental studies are needed that include individual outcome measures of students' comprehension. It is especially important to assess students' comprehension of texts outside of the discussion to gauge whether students acquire the habits of mind to transfer their abilities to new texts and novel situations. Another limitation of research in this area is that the bulk of studies have focused on discussions of literary texts. It is important to examine the conduct and effects of high-quality discussions with informational texts in the content areas.

Argumentation

Studies of argumentation about issues raised by text might be considered a subset of research on discussion but we believe such studies warrant special attention because they have an explicit focus on teaching the knowledge and skills of argumentation. Research on learning and teaching to argue has a rich intellectual tradition especially in science education (see Chinn, 2006). Argumentation is "discourse in which learners take positions, give reasons and evidence for their positions, and present counterarguments to each other's ideas when they have different views" (Chinn, 2006, p. 355). Hence, by definition, almost all research on argumentation as an instructional tool can be categorized as dialogic. The studies of argumentation reviewed in this section also exemplify the dialogic turn in research on learning and teaching of reading comprehension in that argumentation is embedded in the context of discussions about and around text and/or within content-rich instruction.

Argumentation is an explicit feature of the Collaborative Reasoning approach to discussion mentioned in the previous section. Anderson and colleagues believe that knowing the form and function of an argument is important for readers if they are to adopt a critical-analytic stance toward text (Reznitskaya & Anderson, 2002). In Collaborative Reasoning, students are encouraged to take a position on an issue, support it with reasons and evidence from the text, and challenge other students with counterarguments and rebuttals. These rhetorical moves can be broken down into a number of "argument stratagems" that provide the building block for an "argument schema" that students internalize as they participate in the discussions. Support for this theory comes from a study by Anderson et al. (2001) in which they showed that, once a student successfully used a particular argument stratagem, other students in the group adopted it for use in their arguments in a process of social propagation that Anderson and colleagues called the *snowball phenomenon*. Moreover, Anderson and colleagues have shown that once students internalize the argument schema from oral group discussions, they are able demonstrate transfer to written argumentation performed individually and independently. In a number of quasi-experimental studies with fourth and fifth-grade students, they showed that students who participated in anywhere from 4 to 10 Collaborative Reasoning discussions wrote persuasive essays that contained a greater number of arguments, counterarguments, and rebuttals than essays of students in control conditions who received regular classroom reading instruction (Dong, Anderson, Kim, & Li, 2008; Kim, 2001; Reznitskaya, Anderson, & Kuo, 2007; Reznitskaya et al., 2001). The magnitude of the effects on the total number of argument components in the persuasive essays was moderate to large with effect sizes ranging from 0.45 to 0.68 (Reznitskaya et al., 2008).

Another approach to classroom talk that foregrounds skills of argumentation is Accountable Talk. Developed by Resnick and colleagues (Michaels, O'Connor, & Resnick, 2008; Michaels, O'Connor, Hall, & Resnick, 2002; Resnick, 1999; Resnick & Hall, 1998), Accountable Talk is an approach to conducting academically productive classroom talk across a range of content areas. It is premised on the Vygotskian notion that talk and social interaction are fundamental to learning (Wertsch, 1991) and that particular forms and norms of discourse are needed to promote learning in academic contexts. Resnick and colleagues argue that, for classroom talk to promote learning, it must be accountable—to the learning community, to accurate and appropriate knowledge, and to standards of reasoning. In other words, it must be responsive to and build on what others have said; it must have a basis in evidence from text or other sources; and it must follow the norms of good reasoning. When students engage in Accountable Talk, they consider each other's ideas and collectively explore a topic, challenge each other's ideas and opinions, and provide reasons and evidence to support their claims and arguments. Empirical studies suggest that it has potential for promoting reading comprehension (Matsumura et al., 2006; Wolf, Crosson, & Resnick, 2005) although, at the time of writing, we know of no studies that provide a direct test of the impact of Accountable Talk on students' comprehension.

Argumentation has been much studied as means of promoting conceptual change in science. Syntheses of research from both reading education and science education suggest that an effective approach to changing students' alternative conceptions is by reading and discussing refutational expository text, preferably under teacher guidance, in ways that promote cognitive conflict (Guzzetti, 2000; Guzzetti, Snyder, Glass, & Gamas, 1993). Discussion is key to the benefits of this approach because it encourages students to support their views with evidence from the text. Noteworthy is the Discussion Web (Alvermann, Hynd, & Qian, 1995), a technique in which students, under guidance of the teacher and using a graphic aid, are encouraged to choose positions on an issue, list reasons for their positions, and support their opinions with evidence.

Argumentation is also fundamental to the process of scientific inquiry (Duschl & Osborne, 2002). Students need to learn how to seek evidence and reasons for the ideas or knowledge claims that they draw from experimentation in science. Hand and colleagues have developed an approach to teaching scientific argument through the use of what they call the Science Writing Heuristic (SWH; Burke, Greenbowe, & Hand, 2006; Hand, 2007). The SWH is an instructional framework to guide students' discussions, thinking, and writing in science in ways that parallel the discussions, reasoning, and writing of "real" scientists. The development of argumentation is embedded within science inquiry processes where students learn to makes claim, provide evidence to support their claims, and reflect on how their ideas change. In a number of experimental studies of various configurations of the SWH in different fields of science (e.g., chemistry, biology), Hand and colleagues have shown that students across a range of ages produced science texts showing greater evidence of argumentation and the language of science than found in texts of students who received traditional science instruction (Akkus, Gunel, & Hand, 2007; Hand, Prain, Lawrence, & Yore, 1999; Hand, Wallace, & Yang, 2004; Hand, Prain, & Yore, 2001; Rudd, Greenbowe, & Hand, 2007).

Another instructional model to enhance argumentation in science comes from the work of Krajcik and colleagues (McNeill, Lizotte, Krajcik, & Marx, 2006; Moje et al., 2004) on project-based instruction in science. Krajcik and colleagues developed a "scientific explanation" framework to help middle school students construct scientific explanations (i.e., arguments) about phenomena. To make scientific explanations more easily accessible and practical for students, they adapted Toulmin's (1958) model of argumentation by breaking down the task of scientific explanation into the three components of *claim*, *evidence*, and *reasoning* (to justify why the evidence supports the claim). Studies by McNeill, Lizotte, and Krajcik (2005), McNeill et al. (2006) and McNeill and Krajcik (2007) have examined the efficacy of this model and the extent and nature of teacher modeling and scaffolding needed to enhance middle school students' ability to construct scientific explanations.

For the purposes of this chapter, a limitation of the research reviewed in this section is that most of the approaches to teaching argumentation focus largely on text production rather than text comprehension. The primary outcome measure was the quality of written responses to writing prompts rather than a standardized test of reading comprehension (see also Moje, 2007). In part, this is because of the difficulties researchers encountered in finding suitable measures to assess students' critical-reflective thinking about and around text and, in part, it is because the focus of the research has been on writing-to-learn strategies. Nevertheless, in the absence of more direct studies of students' comprehension, this research provides a reasonable account of the extent to which dialogic approaches to instruction enabled students to internalize the schema for a well-formed argument and to acquire the disposition to reason critically and reflectively about text as well as other sources of information (cf. Reznitskaya et al., 2008).

Intertextuality

Intertextuality, arising from the juxtaposition of text in relation to other texts, is an important intellectual resource for making meaning (Lemke, 1992), and might be regarded as the sine qua non of dialogic approaches to teaching comprehension. Nevertheless, making connections across texts, at least in the sense of texts as written objects, seems to be rare in elementary classroom instruction (Short, 1992; Soter, Connors, & Rudge, 2008; Varelas & Pappas, 2006). Available research suggests that even adolescents in the higher grades seldom engage in intertextual processing when faced with the task of comprehending information from multiple texts (Goldman, 2004).

Most studies of intertextuality have involved students reading multiple passages for research tasks at a single point in time, and have focused on the nature of students' cognitive processing and representation of texts (e.g., Hartman, 1995; Wolfe & Goldman, 2005). There have been few studies investigating the classroom environments or instructional practices that promote intertextual connections, how the connections change over time, or their effect of the connections on students' comprehension (work on intertextuality is described in the edited collection of papers in Shuart-Faris & Bloome, 2004).

One recent program of research in this area is a series of studies by Pappas, Varelas and colleagues (Pappas, Varelas, Barry, & Rife, 2003; Varelas & Pappas, 2006; Varelas, Pappas, & Rife, 2006). They investigated the intertextual connections made by first- and second-grade students and their teachers in two classrooms during read-alouds of information books in an integrated science-literacy unit. The studies were part of a collaborative school-university action research project in which Pappas and Varelas worked with two teachers who taught a unit on States of Matter over the course of seven read-alouds. The instruction was dialogic in that it was content-rich, and involved many opportunities for hands-on explorations and extensive discussion in which teachers encouraged and valued students' ideas.

In each of the studies, the researchers conducted qualitative and quantitative analyses of the discourse of the read-alouds. In their first study, Pappas et al. (2003) developed a taxonomy of intertextual connections and examined the roles they played in supporting students' engagement with texts. They defined intertextual connections as instances where students or teachers attempted to make sense of a text being read or discussed by means of other texts that students and teachers instantiated in particular read-aloud sessions, where 'text' was defined broadly according to Wells (1999) as any "representation of meaning using a conventional symbolic system" (p. 378). Their taxonomy of connections included links to:

- written texts, other texts that were orally shared, other media, or prior classroom discourse (e.g., "We're going to read a book called 'Flash, Crash, Rumble, and Roll' and that one has some stuff about lightening");
- hands-on explorations in science (e.g., "Now ... one half of the class yesterday was up here in front of the class and we were heating up the teapot and we were seeing the exact same thing, right?");
- recounts of previous events that students or the teacher had experienced or heard about (e.g., "Last time I poured cold water in my plate ... cause ... I was gonna use my mom's water and I seen air coming up"); and

- implied generalized events that students or the teacher had experienced or heard about (e.g., "Like when you leave your milk, when you leave your milk for a long time in the refrigerator, it will become thick").

Pappas et al. (2003) noticed that these intertextual links seemed to support students' understanding and learning in a variety of ways. Particularly important was the epistemic role the intertextual connections played in supporting students' tentative exploration of ideas raised by the texts. In a later study, Varelas and Pappas (2006) conducted an analysis focused on the learning opportunities afforded by the intertextual connections. They documented how the intertextual links made by students changed over time as they appropriated the language of science to talk about ideas from the texts. In another analysis, focused on the second-grade students' discourse, Varelas et al. (2006) showed how the students made sense of important scientific concepts of evaporation, boiling, and condensation. The researchers identified the intertextual links that accompanied children's acquisition of these concepts, and showed how the links provided opportunities for them to further their understanding of the concepts. Because of the nature of the design of these studies and the lack of outcome measures, it is impossible to tell whether the intertextual connections played a causal role in shaping students' comprehension as the construct is conventionally defined and measured. Taken together, however, the studies provide a compelling case that intertextuality was instrumental in advancing students' understanding and thinking about the texts.

There has been other recent research on the instructional conditions that promote intertextual connections. These include studies of literature discussions by Lenski (1999, 2001) and studies of storybook read-alouds by Sipe (1996, 1998, 2000, 2001). However, similar to the above studies, most have not included measures of individual students' reading comprehension. In the few classroom studies that have assessed students' comprehension across multiple texts (e.g., VanSledright & Kelly, 1998), intertextuality has been implicit rather than explicit in the analyses (see Goldman, 2004).

An agenda for future research is for instructional studies to focus explicitly on intertextuality and to include individual outcome measures. Both design experiments and traditional experimental studies are needed to examine the instructional conditions and practices that promote intertextual connections, how the connections change over time as students' are enculturated into such practices, and the effects of the connections on students' comprehension. We need to know more about the affordances of juxtaposing different types of texts and experiences and of alternative orderings of the texts and experiences for teachers' and students' engagement in intertextuality, and we need to know more about the roles played by the different types of intertextual connections.

IMPLICATIONS

We conclude by considering the implications of the dialogic turn in learning and teaching of reading comprehension for theory, research, and practice. For theory, a dialogic perspective calls into question the adequacy of some theoretical models of reading comprehension. For example, Kintsch's (1998) construction-integration model provides an elaborate account of how readers comprehend a single text. Although it captures some of the dynamic aspects of knowledge construction and understanding, as described at the beginning of this chapter, it does not provide an entirely adequate account of how readers make sense of multiple texts and diverse sources of information. If the construction of meaning is a dynamic and context-sensitive process and meaning resides in the relations among diverse perspectives (cf. Bakhtin, 1981, 1986), then we need theoretical models of comprehension that provide an account of how readers construct more elaborate and flexible representations of their understanding of text. One possibility for such a model is cognitive flexibility theory (Spiro, 2001), which provides an account of how readers construct a flexible, adaptive understanding of texts in terms of a "criss-crossing" of the topical landscape from multiple and diverse perspectives. Another possibility is a more multi-layered account of the mental representation formed in comprehension along the lines of the documents model proposed by Perfetti and colleagues (Britt, Perfetti, Sandak, & Rouet, 1999; Perfetti, Rouet, & Britt, 1999). The documents model is an extension of Kintsch's construction-integration model that posits a layer of representation that captures the intertextual connections among multiple sources (Bråten, Strømsø, & Britt, 2009; see also Goldman, 2004). Theoretical models like these, that provide an account of the construction of meaning as a dynamic and relational process, are needed to capture the dialogic quality of comprehension.

For research, the jury is still out on the effects of some of the more dialogic approaches to comprehension instruction. The research on content-rich instruction is compelling in showing that it yields benefits both for students' reading comprehension and their content knowledge. Research on this issue should continue to be a fruitful area of inquiry, particularly as researchers consider how to integrate comprehension instruction into more discipline-specific teaching in middle and high schools. By contrast, the research on discussion, argumentation, and instruction related to intertextuality is less convincing. There are not yet enough empirical studies of sufficient quality to conclude that these approaches might supplant explicit instruction in comprehension strategies. As we have indicated, there is consensus that instruction in small repertoires of comprehension strategies can produce robust benefits for students' comprehension, especially for students with learning disabilities, and that the benefits can transfer to new texts and novel situations. If more dialogic approaches to teaching comprehension are to gain traction in classroom instruction, more and better research is needed concerning their impact on comprehension. It is especially important to show that discussions about text or instruction related to intertextuality can help foster the habits of mind to enhance comprehension of texts when students read independently.

Researchers studying more dialogic approaches to comprehension instruction should be encouraged to employ measures of comprehension that more adequately reflect the dynamic and context-sensitive nature of the construct. Much of the research reviewed under the heading of dialogic has employed traditional experimenter-developed and commercially available standardized assessments—involving immediate or delayed recall, reading for gist understanding, or comprehension of single, brief passages at one point in time. These kinds of measures restrict what researchers can say about the role of dialogic approaches in shaping students' comprehension. As indicated in our review, some researchers have analyzed the students' discourse in the context of discussion, argumentation, and so forth, in place of using individual outcome measures, in the hope that discursive practices provide a richer, more sensitive accounting of the quality of students' understanding and interpretation of text. While this approach has merit, it is worth considering what kinds of individual outcome measures might best inform researchers and teachers about students' understanding and learning in classrooms that include more dialogic experiences around text. The RAND Reading Study Group (2002) report called for new kinds of assessments that reflect the dynamic and context-sensitive nature of comprehension and Sweet (2005) recently reiterated this call. The research reviewed in this chapter suggests that we have a long way to go before such measures become a reality.

For classroom practice, dialogic approaches might provide more appropriate contexts for students to develop the automatic, fluid articulation of strategies necessary for generative and flexible comprehension. Just as encouraging students' flexible application of comprehension strategies has been found to provide a vehicle for "coordinating dialogue about text" (Pressley, 1998, p. 120), so too the more dialogic approaches probably provide a natural vehicle for students' use of strategies. Many scholars have noted that high-quality discussions create authentic opportunities for students to use comprehension strategies such as prediction, summarization, imagery, or comprehension monitoring without much explicit instruction from the teacher (e.g., Almasi, 2002; Applebee et al., 2003; Reninger, 2007; Taylor, Pearson, Garcia, Stahl, & Bauer, 2006). Moreover, descriptions of the conduct of text-based discussions sometimes include recommendations to explain or highlight comprehension strategies (Kamil et al., 2008; Vogt, 1996; McKeown et al., 2009). Thus strategy instruction and the more dialogic approaches to instruction might be more closely linked in actual classroom practice and may complement, rather than compete with, each other. Research is needed on the intersections between the two "types" of comprehension instruction.

Dialogic approaches might also be more amenable to teachers wanting to incorporate strategies instruction into their teaching. Shortly before his death, Michael Pressley (2006) decried the lack of comprehension strategies instruction in U.S. elementary schools and expressed interest in making comprehension strategies instruction more appealing for teachers. Dialogic approaches to comprehension instruction might offer teachers ways of teaching strategies that are easier to implement and more sustainable in the classroom.

ACKNOWLEDGMENTS

We thank David Bloome, Nell Duke, Georgia Garcia, John Guthrie, William Nagy, Annemarie Palincsar, Barbara Taylor, and Alina Reznitskaya for their assistance with references for this chapter and for sharing their ideas on the topic. We also thank P. David Pearson and Peter Afflerbach for their suggestions and forbearance. Any errors of interpretation are ours.

REFERENCES

Akkus, R., Gunel, M., & Hand, B. (2007). Comparing an inquiry based approach known as the Science Writing Heuristic to traditional science teaching practices: Are there differences? *International Journal of Science Education, 29*(14), 1745–1765.

Almasi, J. F. (1995). The nature of fourth graders' sociocognitive conflicts in peer-led and teacher-led discussions of literature. *Reading Research Quarterly, 30*(3), 314–351.

Almasi, J. F. (2002). Research-based comprehension practices that create higher-level discussions. In C. C. Block, L. B. Gambrelli & M. Pressley (Eds.), *Improving comprehension instruction: Rethinking research, theory, and classroom practice* (pp. 229–242). San Francisco, CA: Jossey-Bass.

Alvermann, D., Hynd, C., & Qian, G. (1995). The effects of interactive discussion and text type on the learning of counter-intuitive science concepts. *Journal of Educational Research, 88*(3), 146–153.

Anderson, R. C., Chinn, C., Chang, J., Waggoner, J., & Nguyen, K. (1998). Intellectually stimulating story discussions. In F. J. L. Osborn (Ed.), *Literacy for all: Issues in teaching and learning* (pp. 170–186). New York: Guilford Press.

Anderson, R. C., Nguyen-Jahiel, K., McNurlen, B., Archodidou, A., Kim, S.-y., Reznitskaya, A., et al. (2001). The snowball phenomenon: Spread of ways of talking and ways of thinking across groups of children. *Cognition and Instruction, 19*(1), 1–46.

Anderson, V. (1992). A teacher development project in transactional strategy instruction for teachers of severely reading-disabled adolescents. *Teaching & Teacher Education, 8*, 391–403.

Anderson, V., & Roit, M. (1993). Planning and implementing collaborative strategy instruction for delayed readers in grades 6-10. *Elementary School Journal, 94*, 121–137.

Applebee, A. N., Langer, J. A., Nystrand, M., & Gamoran, A. (2003). Discussion-based approaches to developing understanding: Classroom instruction and student performance in middle and high school English. *American Education Research Journal, 40*(3), 685–730.

Baker, L. (1994). Fostering metacognitive development. *Advances in Child Development and Behavior, 25*, 201–239.

Baker, L. (2002). Metacognition in comprehension instruction. In C. C. Block & M. Pressley (Eds.), *Comprehension instruction: Research-based best practices* (pp. 77–95). New York: Guilford Press.

Bakhtin, M. M. (1981). *The dialogic imagination: Four essays*. Austin: University of Texas Press.

Bakhtin, M. M. (1986). *Speech genres and other late essays*. Austin: University of Texas Press.

Beck, I. L., & McKeown, M. G. (2006). *Improving comprehension with Questioning the Author: A fresh and expanded view of a powerful approach*. New York: Scholastic.

Beck, I. L., McKeown, M. G., Hamilton, R., & Kucan, L. (1997). *Questioning the author: An approach for enhancing student engagement with text*. Newark, DE: International Reading Association.

Beck, I. L., McKeown, M. G., Sandora, C., Kucan, L., & Worthy, J. (1996). Questioning the Author: A year-long implementation to engage students with text. *Elementary School Journal, 96*(4), 387–416.

Billings, L., & Fitzgerald, J. (2002). Dialogic discussion and the Paideia Seminar. *American Educational Research Journal, 39*(4), 907–941.

Bråten, I., Strømsø, H. I., & Britt, M. A. (2009). Trust matters: Examining the role of source evaluation in students' construction of meaning within and across multiple texts. *Reading Research Quarterly, 44*, 6–28.

Britt, M. A., Perfetti, C. A., Sandak, R., & Rouet, J. F. (1999). Content integration and source separation in learning from multiple texts. In S. R. Goldman, A. C. Graesser, & P. van den Broek (Eds.), *Narrative comprehension, causality, and coherence: Essays in honor of Tom Trabasso* (pp. 209–233). Mahwah, NJ: Erlbaum.

Brown, A. L., & Campione, J. C. (1998). Designing a community of young learners: Theoretical and practical lessons. In N. M. Lambert & B. L. McCombs (Eds.), *How students learn: Reforming schools through learner-centered education* (pp. 153–186). Washington, DC: American Psychological Association.

Brown, R., & Coy-Ogan, L. (1993). The evolution of transactional strategies instruction in one teacher's classroom. *Elementary School Journal, 94*, 221–233.

Brown, R., Pressley, M., Van Meter, P., & Schuder, T. (1996). A quasi-experimental validation of transactional strategies instruction with low-achieving second-grade readers. *Journal of Educational Psychology, 88*(1), 18–37.

Bryant, D. P., Ugel, N., Thompson, S., & Hamff, A. (1999). Instructional strategies for content-area reading instruction. *Intervention in School and Clinic, 34*, 293–302.

Bryant, D. P., Vaughn, S., Linan-Thompson, S., Ugel, N., Hamff, A., & Hougen, M. (2000). Reading outcomes for students with and without reading disabilities in general education middle-school content area Classes. *Learning Disability Quarterly, 23*(4), 238–252.

Burke, K. A., Greenbowe, T. G., & Hand, B. M. (2006). Implementing the science writing heuristic in the chemistry laboratory. *Journal of Chemical Education, 83*, 1032–1038.

Carver, R. P. (1987). Should reading comprehension skills be taught? In J. E. Readence & R. S. Baldwin (Eds.), *Research in literacy: Merging perspectives (Thirty-sixth Yearbook of the National Reading Conference)* (pp. 115–126). Rochester, NY: National Reading Conference.

Chinn, C. (2006). Learning to argue. In A. M. O'Donnell, C. Hmelo-Silver, & G. Erkens (Eds.), *Collaborative learning, reasoning, and technology* (pp. 355–383). Mahwah, NJ: Erlbaum.

Chinn, C. A., Anderson, R. C., & Waggoner, M. A. (2001). Patterns of discourse in two kinds of literature discussion. *Reading Research Quarterly, 36*, 378–411.

Cohen, E. G. (1994). Restructuring the classroom: Conditions for productive small groups. *Review of Educational Research, 64*(1), 1–35.

Coley, J., DePinto, T., Craig, S., & Gardner, R. (1993). From college to classroom: Three teachers' accounts of their adaptations of reciprocal teaching. *The Elementary School Journal, 94*, 255–266.

Collins, C. (1991). Reading instruction that increases thinking abilities. *Journal of Reading, 34*(7), 510–516.

Commeyras, M. (1993). Promoting critical thinking through dialogical-thinking reading lessons. *The Reading Teacher, 46*(6), 486–494.

Conley, M. (2008). *Content area literacy: Learners in context*. Boston, MA: Allyn and Bacon.

Connor, C. M., Morrison, F. J., & Petrella, J. N. (2004). Effective reading comprehension instruction: Examining child x instruction interactions. *Journal of Educational Psychology, 96*(4), 682–698.

Corrin, W., Somers, M.-A., Kemple, J. J., Nelson, E., & Sepanik, S. (2008). *The enhanced reading opportunities study: Findings from the second year of implementation* (NCEE 2009-4036). Washington, DC:

National Center for Education Evaluation and Regional Assistance, Institute of Education Sciences, U.S. Department of Education.

Deshler, D. D., & Schumaker, J. B. (1993). Strategy mastery by at-risk students: Not a simple matter. *Elementary School Journal, 94*(2), 153–167.

Deshler, D. D., & Schumaker, J. B. (2006). Teaching adolescents to be strategic learners. In D. D. Deshler & J. B. Schumaker (Eds.), *Teaching adolescents with disabilities: Accessing the general education curriculum* (pp. 121–156). New York: Corwin Press.

Dong, T., Anderson, R. C., Kim, I., & Li, Y. (2008). Collaborative reasoning in China and Korea. *Reading Research Quarterly, 43,* 400–424.

Duffy, G. (1993). Rethinking strategy instruction: Four teachers' development and their low achievers' understanding. *Elementary School Journal, 93,* 231–247.

Duffy, G. G., Roehler, L. R., Sivan, E., Rackliffe, G., Book, C., & Meloth, M. S. (1987). Effects of explaining the reasoning associated with using reading strategies. *Reading Research Quarterly, 22,* 347–368.

Durkin, D. (1978/1979). What classroom observations reveal about reading comprehension instruction. *Reading Research Quarterly, 14,* 481–533.

Duschl, R., & Osborne, J. (2002). Supporting and promoting argumentation discourse in science education. *Studies in Science Education, 38,* 39–72.

Eeds, M., & Wells, D. (1989). Grand conversations: An exploration of meaning construction in literature study groups. *Research in the Teaching of English, 23,* 4–29.

El-Dinary, P. B. (1994). *Teachers learning, adapting and implementing strategies-based instruction in reading.* Unpublished doctoral dissertation, University of Michigan, Ann Arbor.

El-Dinary, P. B. (2002). Challenges of implementing transactional strategies instruction for reading comprehension. In C. C. Block & M. Pressley (Eds.), *Comprehension instruction: Research-based best practices* (pp. 201–215). New York: Guilford Press.

El-Dinary, P. B., & Schuder, T. (1993). Seven teachers' acceptance of transactional strategies instruction during their first year using it. *Elementary School Journal, 94,* 207–219.

Faggella-Luby, M., & Deshler, D. (2008). Reading comprehension in adolescents with LD: What we know; what we need to learn. *Learning Disabilities Research & Practice, 23*(2), 70–78.

Faggella-Luby, M., Schumaker, J. S., & Deshler, D. D. (2007). Embedded learning strategy instruction: Story-structure pedagogy in heterogeneous secondary literature classes. *Learning Disability Quarterly, 30*(2), 131–147.

Fung, I. Y. Y., Wilkinson, I. A. G., & Moore, D. W. (2003). L1-assisted reciprocal teaching to improve ESL students' comprehension of English expository text. *Learning and Instruction, 13*(1), 1–31.

Gambrell, L. B., & Almasi, J. F. (Eds.). (1996). *Lively discussions! Fostering engaged reading.* Newark, DE: International Reading Association.

Gamoran, A., & Nystrand, M. (1991). Background and instructional effects on achievement in eighth-grade English and social studies. *Journal of Research on Adolescence, 1,* 277–300.

Garcia, G. E., Taylor, B. T., Pearson, P. D., Stahl, K. A. D., & Bauer, E. B. (2007). *Final report: Instruction of reading comprehension: cognitive strategies or cognitive [responsive] engagement?* Submitted to the Institution of Educational Sciences, US Department of Education, WDC (Grant R305G030140). Champaign: University of Illinois.

Gersten, R., Fuchs, L. S., Williams, J. P., & Baker, S. (2001). Teaching reading comprehension strategies to students with learning disabilities: A review of research. *Review of Educational Research, 71*(2), 279–320.

Goldenberg, C. (1992/1993). Instructional conversations: Promoting comprehension through discussion. *The Reading Teacher, 46*(4), 316–326.

Goldman, S. R. (2004). Cognitive aspects of constructing meaning through and across multiple texts. In N. Shuart-Ferris & D. M. Bloome (Eds.), *Uses of intertextuality in classroom and educational research* (pp. 313–347). Greenwich, CT: Information Age.

Great Book Foundation. (1987). *An introduction to Shared Inquiry.* Chicago: The Great Books Foundation

Greenleaf, C., Schoenbach, R., Cziko, C., & Mueller, F. (2001). Apprenticing adolescent readers to academic literacy. *Harvard Educational Review, 71*(1), 79–129.

Greenleaf, C. L., & Mueller, F. L. (2003). *Impact of the pilot academic literacy course on ninth grade students' reading development: academic year 1996–1997.* San Francisco, CA: Stuart Foundations

Guthrie, J. T., Anderson, E., Alao, S., & Rinehart, J. (1999). Influences of Concept-Oriented Reading Instruction on strategy use and conceptual learning from text. *Elementary School Journal, 99*(4), 343–366.

Guthrie, J. T., & McCann, A. D. (1996). Idea circles: Peer collaboration for conceptual learning. In L. B. Gambrell & J. F. Almasi (Eds.), *Lively discussions! Fostering engaged reading* (pp. 87–105). Newark, DE: International Reading Association.

Guthrie, J. T., McRae, A., & Klauda, S. L. (2007). Contributions of Concept-Oriented Reading Instruction to knowledge about interventions for motivations in reading. *Educational Psychologist, 42*, 237–250.

Guthrie, J. T., Van Meter, P., Hancock, G. R., Alao, S., Anderson, E., & McCann, A. (1998). Does Concept-Oriented Reading Instruction increase strategy-use and conceptual learning from text? *Journal of Educational Psychology, 90*(2), 261–278.

Guthrie, J. T., Van Meter, P., McCann, A. D., Wigfield, A., Bennett, L., Poundstone, C. C., et al. (1996). Growth of literacy engagement: Changes in motivations and strategies during concept-oriented. *Reading Research Quarterly, 31*(3), 306–332.

Guthrie, J. T., Wigfield, A., Barbosa, P., Perencevich, K. C., Taboada, A., Davis, M. H., et al. (2004). Increasing reading comprehension and engagement through concept-oriented reading instruction. *Journal of Educational Psychology, 96*(3), 403–423.

Guthrie, J. T., Wigfield, A., Humenick, N. M., Perencevich, K. C., Taboada, A., & Barbosa, P. (2006). Influences of stimulating tasks on reading motivation and comprehension. *Journal of Educational Research, 99*(4), 232–245.

Guthrie, J. T., Wigfield, A., & Perencevich, K. C. (Eds.). (2004). *Motivating reading comprehension: Concept-oriented reading instruction.* Mahwah, NJ: Erlbaum.

Guthrie, J. T., Wigfield, A., & VonSecker, C. (2000). Effects of integrated instruction on motivation and strategy use in reading. *Journal of Educational Psychology, 92*(2), 331–341.

Guzzetti, B. J. (2000). Learning counter-intuitive science concepts: What have we learned from over a decade of research? *Reading and Writing Quarterly, 16*, 89–98.

Guzzetti, B. J., Snyder, T. E., Glass, G. V., & Gamas, W. S. (1993). Promoting conceptual change in science: A comparative meta-analysis of instructional interventions from reading education and science education. *Reading Research Quarterly, 28*, 117–159.

Hacker, D. J., & Tenent, A. (2002). Implementing reciprocal teaching in the classroom: Overcoming obstacles and making modifications. *Journal of Educational Psychology, 94*(4), 699–718.

Haddad, F. A., Garcia, Y. E., Naglieri, J. A., Grimditch, M., McAndrews, A., & Eubanks, J. (2003). Planning facilitation and reading comprehension: Instructional relevance of the pass theory. *Journal of Psychoeducational Assessment, 21*(3), 282–289.

Hall, K. M., Sabey, B. L., & McClellan, M. (2005). Expository text comprehension: Helping primary-grade teachers use expository texts to full advantage. *Reading Psychology, 26*(3), 211–234.

Haller, E. P., Child, D. A., & Walberg, H. J. (1988). Can comprehension be taught? A quantitative synthesis of "metacognitve" studies. *Educational Researcher, 17*(9), 5–8.

Hand, B. (Ed.). (2007). *Science inquiry, argument and language: A case for the science writing Heuristic.* Rotterdam, The Netherlands: Sense.

Hand, B., Prain, V., Lawrence, C., & Yore, L. D. (1999). A writing-in-science framework designed to improve science literacy. *International Journal of Science Education, 21*, 1021-1035.

Hand, B., Wallace, C. S., & Yang, E. M. (2004). Using the Science Writing Heuristic to enhance learning outcomes from laboratory activities in seventh grade science: Quantitative and qualitative aspects. *International Journal of Science Education, 26*, 131–149.

Hand, B. M., Prain, V., & Yore, L. D. (2001). Sequential writing tasks' influence on science learning. In P. Tynjälä, L. Mason, & K. Lonka (Eds.), *Writing as a learning tool: Integrating theory and practice* (pp. 105–129). Dordrecht, The Netherlands: Kluwer.

Hapgood, S., Magnusson, S. J., & Palincsar, A. S. (2004). Teacher, text, and experience mediating children's learning of scientific inquiry. *Journal of the Learning Sciences, 13*(4), 455–506.

Harrison, C. (2004). *Understanding reading development.* London: Sage.

Hartman, D. K. (1995). Eight readers reading: The intertextual links of proficient readers reading multiple passages. *Reading Research Quarterly, 30*(3), 520–561.

Hilden, K. R., & Pressley, M. (2007). Self-regulation through transactional strategies instruction. *Reading & Writing Quarterly, 23*(1), 51–75.

Hock, M., Brasseur, I., & Deshler, D. (2008). Comprehension instruction in action: The at-risk student. In C. Block & S. Parris (Eds.), *Comprehension instruction: Research based practices* (2nd ed., pp. 271–294). New York: Guilford Press.

Jitendra, A. K., Hoppes, M. K., & Xin, Y. P. (2000). Enhancing main idea comprehension for students with learning problems: The role of a summarization strategy and self-monitoring instruction. *Journal of Special Education, 34*(3), 127–139.

Joffe, V. L., Cain, K., & Maric, N. (2007). Comprehension problems in children with specific language impairment: Does mental imagery training help? *International Journal of Language & Communication Disorders*(6), 648–664.

Johnson-Glenberg, M. C. (2000). Training reading comprehension in adequate decoders/poor comprehenders: Verbal versus visual strategies. *Journal of Educational Psychology, 92*(4), 772–782.

Jordan, M., Jensen, R., & Greenleaf, C. (2001). 'Amidst familial gatherings': Reading apprenticeship in a middle school classroom. *Voices from the Middle, 8*(4), 15–24.

Jordan, M., & Schoenbach, R. (2003). Breaking through the literacy ceiling: Reading is demystified for secondary students in reading apprenticeship classrooms, where students "can read to learn" in all their subject areas. *Leadership, 33*(2), 8–13.

Kamil, M. L., Borman, G. D., Dole, J., Kral, C. C., Salinger, T., & Torgesen, J. (2008). *Improving adolescent literacy: Effective classroom and intervention practices: A practice guide* (NCEE #2008-4027). Washington, DC: National Center for Education Evaluation and Regional Assistance, Institute of Education Sciences, U.S. Department of Education

Kemple, J., Corrin, W., Nelson, E., Salinger, T., Herrmann, S., & Drummond, K. (2008). *The enhanced reading opportunities study: Early impact and implementation findings* (NCEE 2008-4015). Washington, DC: National Center for Education, Evaluation and Regional Assistance, Institute of Education Sciences, U.S. Department of Education.

Kim, A.-H., Vaughn, S., Klingner, J. K., Woodruff, A. L., Reutebuch, C. K., & Kouzekanani, K. (2006). Improving the reading comprehension of middle school students with disabilities through computer-assisted collaborative strategic reading. *Remedial and Special Education, 27*(4), 235–249.

Kim, S.-y. (2001). *The effects of group monitoring on transfer of learning in small group discussions.* Unpublished doctoral dissertation, University of Illinois at Urbana-Champaign, Urbana-Champaign.

King, A. (1999). Discourse patterns for mediating peer learning. In A. M. O'Donnell & A. King (Eds.), *Cognitive perspectives on peer learning* (pp. 87–115). Mahwah, NJ: Erlbaum.

Kintsch, W. (1998). *Comprehension: A paradigm for cognition.* New York: Cambridge University Press.

Kintsch, W., & Kintsch, E. (2005). Comprehension. In S. G. Paris & S. A. Stahl (Eds.), *Children's reading comprehension and assessment* (pp. 71–92). Mahwah, NJ: CIERA.

Klingner, J. K., & Vaughn, S. (1996). Reciprocal teaching of reading comprehension strategies for students with learning disabilities who use English as a second language. *Elementary School Journal, 96,* 275–293.

Klingner, J. K., & Vaughn, S. (2000). The helping behaviors of fifth graders while using collaborative strategic reading during ESL content classes. *TESOL Quarterly, 34*(1), 69–98.

Klingner, J. K., Vaughn, S., Arguelles, M. E., Hughes, M. T., & Leftwich, S. A. (2004). Collaborative strategic reading: "Real-world" lessons from classroom teachers. *Remedial and Special Education, 25*(5), 291–302.

Klingner, J. K., Vaughn, S., Hughes, M. T., & Arguelles, M. E. (1999). Sustaining research-based practices in reading: A 3-year follow-up. *Remedial and Special Education, 20*(5), 263–274.

Klingner, J. K., Vaughn, S., & Schumm, J. S. (1998). Collaborative strategic reading during social studies in heterogeneous fourth-grade classrooms. *Elementary School Journal, 99*(1), 3–22.

Kucan, L., & Beck, I. L. (1997). Thinking aloud and reading comprehension research: Inquiry, instruction, and social interaction. *Review of Educational Research, 67*(3), 271–299.

Langer, J. (1993). Discussion as exploration: Literature and the horizon of possibilities. In G. E. Newell

& R. K. Durst (Eds.), *Exploring texts: The role of discussion and writing in the teaching and learning of literature* (pp. 23–43). Norwood, MA: Christopher-Gordon.

Langer, J. A. (1995). *Envisioning literature: Literary understanding and literature instruction.* Newark, DE: International Reading Association.

Langer, J. A. (2001). Beating the odds: Teaching middle and high school students to read and write well. *American Educational Research Journal, 38,* 837–880.

Lemke, J. (1992). Intertextuality and educational research. *Linguistics and Education, 4,* 257–268.

Lenski, S. D. (1999). The Directed Reading-Connecting Activity (DR-CA): A strategy to promote connections across texts. *Journal of Reading Education, 24,* 9–14.

Lenski, S. D. (2001). Intertextual connections during discussions about literature. *Reading Psychology, 22,* 313–335.

Lipman, M. (1975). *Philosophy for children.* Monclair, NJ: Monclair State College.

Marks, M., Pressley, M., Coley, J. D., Craig, S., Gardner, R. I., DePinto, T., et al. (1993). Three teachers' adaptations of reciprocal teaching in comparison to traditional reciprocal teaching. *Elementary School Journal, 94,* 267–283.

Mason, L. H. (2004). Explicit self-regulated strategy development versus reciprocal questioning: Effects on expository reading comprehension among struggling readers. *Journal of Educational Psychology, 96*(2), 283–296.

Mastropieri, M. A., Scruggs, T., Mohler, L., Beranek, M., Spencer, V., Boon, R. T., et al. (2001). Can middle school students with serious reading difficulties help each other and learn anything? *Learning Disabilities Research & Practice, 16*(1), 18–27.

Matsumura, L. C., Slater, S. C., Junker, B., Peterson, M., Boston, M., Steel, M., et al. (2006). *Measuring reading comprehension and mathematics instruction in urban middle schools: A pilot study of the Instructional Quality Assessment* (CSE Report 681). Los Angeles, CA: University of Los Angeles, National Center for Research on Evaluation, Standards and Student Testing

McKeown, M. G., Beck, I. L., & Blake, R. G. K. (2009). Rethinking reading comprehension instruction: A comparison of instruction for strategies and content approaches. *Reading Research Quarterly, 44*(3), 218–253.

McNeill, K. L., & Krajcik, J. (2007). Middle school students' use of appropriate and inappropriate evidence in writing scientific explanations. In M. Lovett & P. Shah (Eds.), *Thinking with data* (pp. 233–265). New York: Taylor & Francis Group.

McNeill, K. L., Lizotte, D. J., & Krajcik, J. (2005). *Identifying teacher practices that support students' explanations in science.* Paper presented at the annual meeting of the American Educational Research Association, Montreal, Canada.

McNeill, K. L., Lizotte, D. J., Krajcik, J., & Marx, R. W. (2006). Supporting students' construction of scientific explanations by fading scaffolds in instructional materials. *The Journal of the Learning Sciences, 15*(2), 153–191.

Michaels, S., O'Connor, C., & Resnick, L. (2008). Reasoned participation: Accountable talk in the classroom and in civic life. *Studies in Philosophy and Education, 27*(4), 283–297.

Michaels, S., O'Connor, M. C., Hall, M. W., & Resnick, L. B. (2002). *Accountable talk: Classroom conversation that works* (3 CD-ROM set). Pittsburgh, PA: University of Pittsburgh.

Moats, L. C. (2004). Science, language, and imagination in the professional development of reading teachers. In P. McCardle & V. Chhabra (Eds.), *The voice of evidence in reading research* (pp. 269–287). Baltimore, MD: Brookes.

Moje, E. B. (2007). Developing socially just subject-matter instruction: A review of the literature on disciplinary literacy. In L. Parker (Ed.), *Review of research in education* (pp. 1–44). Washington, DC: American Educational Research Association.

Moje, E. B., Peek-Brown, D., Sutherland, L. M., Marx, R. W., Blumenfeld, P., & Krajcik, J. (2004). Explaining explanations: Developing scientific literacy in middle-school project-based science reforms. In D. Strickland & D. E. Alvermann (Eds.), *Bridging the gap: Improving literacy learning for preadolescent and adolescent learners in grades 4–12* (pp. 227–251). New York: Teachers College Press.

Murphy, P. K., Wilkinson, I. A. G., Soter, A. O., Hennessey, M. N., & Alexander, J. F. (2009). Examining the effects of classroom discussion on students' high-level comprehension of text: A meta-analysis. *Journal of Educational Psychology, 101,* 740–746.

National Institute of Child Health and Human Development [NICHD]. (2000). *Report of the National Reading Panel. Teaching children to read: An evidence-based assessment of the scientific research literature on reading and its implications for reading instruction* (No. 00-4769). Washington, DC: U.S. Government Printing Office.

Nystrand, M. (1997). *Opening dialogue: Understanding the dynamics of language and learning in the English classroom.* New York Teachers College Press.

Nystrand, M. (2006). Research on the role of classroom discourse as it affects reading comprehension. *Research in the Teaching of English, 40*(4), 392–412.

Nystrand, M., & Gamoran, A. (1991). Instructional discourse, student engagement, and literature achievement. *Research in the Teaching of English, 25*(3), 261–290.

Nystrand, M., Gamoran, A., & Carbonaro, W. (2001). On the ecology of classroom instruction: The case of writing in high school English and social studies. In P. Tynjala., L. Mason, & K. Lonka (Eds.), *Writing as a learning tool: Integrating theory and practice* (pp. 57–81). Dordrecht, The Netherlands: Kluwer.

O'Flahavan, J. F. (1989). *Second graders' social, intellectual, and affective development in varied group discussions about literature: An exploration of participation structure.* Unpublished doctoral dissertation, University of Illinois at Urbana-Champaign, Urbana-Champaign.

Palincsar, A. S. (1986). The role of dialogue in providing scaffolded instruction. *Educational Psychologist, 21*(1-2), 73–98.

Palincsar, A. S. (2006). *RT '82 to '06: The role of research, theory, and representation in the transformation of instructional research.* Paper presented at the National Reading Conference, Los Angeles, CA.

Palincsar, A. S., & Brown, A. L. (1984). Reciprocal teaching of comprehension-fostering and comprehension-monitoring activities. *Cognition and Instruction, 1*(2), 117–175.

Palincsar, A. S., & Magnusson, S. J. (2001). The interplay of first-hand and second-hand investigations to model and support the development of scientific knowledge and reasoning. In S. M. Carver & D. O. Klahr (Eds.), *Cognition and instruction: Twenty-five years of progress* (pp. 151–193). Mahwah, NJ: Erlbaum.

Pappa, E., Zafiropoulou, M., & Metallidou, P. (2003). Intervention on strategy use and on motivation of Greek pupils' reading comprehension in English classes. *Perceptual and Motor Skills, 96*(3), 773–786.

Pappas, C. C., Varelas, M., Barry, A., & Rife, A. (2003). Dialogic inquiry around information texts: The role of intertextuality in constructing scientific understandings in urban primary classrooms. *Linguistics and Education, 13*(4), 435–482.

Paris, S. G., & Winograd, P. (1990). How metacognition can promote learning and instruction. In B. F. Jones & L. Idol (Eds.), *Dimensions of thinking and cognitive instruction* (pp. 15–52). Hillsdale, NJ: Erlbaum.

Pearson, P. D. (2001). Life in the radical middle: A personal apology for a balanced view of reading. In R. F. Flippo (Ed.), *Reading researchers in search of common ground* (pp. 78–83). Newark, DE: International Reading Association.

Pearson, P. D. (2006). *A new framework for teaching reading comprehension in the upper elementary grades.* Paper presented at the north region summer conference of America's Choice, Saratoga Springs, NY.

Pearson, P. D., & Dole, J. A. (1987). Explicit comprehension instruction: A review of research and a new conceptualization of instruction. *Elementary School Journal, 88,* 151–165.

Pearson, P. D., & Duke, N. K. (2002). Comprehension instruction in the primary grades. In C. C. Block & M. Pressley (Eds.), *Comprehension instruction: Research-based best practices* (pp. 247–258). New York: Guilford Press.

Pearson, P. D., & Fielding, L. (1991). Comprehension instruction. In R. Barr, M. L. Kamil, P. B. Mosenthal, & P. D. Pearson (Eds.), *Handbook of reading research* (Vol. 2, pp. 815–860). White Plains, NY: Longman.

Pearson, P. D., & Gallagher, M. C. (1983). The instruction of reading comprehension. *Contemporary Educational Psychology, 8,* 317–344.

Perfetti, C. A., Rouet, J. F., & Britt, M. A. (1999). Toward a theory of documents representation. In H. van Oostendorp & S. R. Goldman (Eds.), *The construction of mental representations during reading* (pp. 99–122). Mahwah, NJ: Erlbaum.

Pressley, M. (1998). Comprehension strategies instruction. In J. Osborn & F. Lehr (Eds.), *Literacy for all: Issues in teaching and learning* (pp. 113–133). New York: Guilford Press.

Pressley, M. (2000a). Comprehension instruction in elementary school: A quarter-century of research progress. In B. M. Taylor, M. F. Graves, & P. van den Broek (Eds.), *Reading for meaning: Fostering comprehension in the middle grades* (pp. 132–151). New York: Teachers College Press.

Pressley, M. (2000b). What should comprehension instruction be the instruction of? In M. L. Kamil, P. B. Mosenthal, P. D. Pearson, & R. Barr (Eds.), *Handbook of reading research* (Vol. 3, pp. 545–561). Mahwah, NJ: Erlbaum.

Pressley, M. (2001). Comprehension instruction: What makes sense now, what might make sense soon. *Reading Online, 5*(2). Retrieved from http://www.readingonline.org/articles/art_index. asp?HREF=handbook/pressley/index.html

Pressley, M. (2002a). Comprehension strategies instruction: A turn-of-the-century status report. In C. C. Block & M. Pressley (Eds.), *Comprehension instruction: Research-based best practices* (pp. 11–27). New York: Guilford Press.

Pressley, M. (2002b). Metacognition and self-regulated comprehension. In A. E. Farstrup & J. S. Samuels (Eds.), *What research has to say about reading instruction* (3rd ed., pp. 291–309). Newark, DE: International Reading Association.

Pressley, M. (2006). *What the future of reading research could be.* Paper presented at the International Reading Association Reading Research conference, Chicago, IL.

Pressley, M., & Afflerbach, P. (1995). *Verbal protocols of reading: The nature of constructively responsive reading.* Hillsdale, NJ: Erlbaum.

Pressley, M., Brown, R., El-Dinary, P., & Afflerbach, P. (1995). The comprehension instruction that students need: Instruction fostering constructively responsive reading. *Learning Disabilities Research & Practice, 10*(4), 215–224.

Pressley, M., & El-Dinary, P. B. (1997). What we know about translating comprehension-strategies instruction research into practice. *Journal of Learning Disabilities, 30*(5), 486–488, 512.

Pressley, M., El-Dinary, P. B., Gaskins, I., Schuder, T., Bergman, J., Almasi, L., et al. (1992). Beyond direct explanation: Transactional instruction of reading comprehension strategies. *Elementary School Journal, 92*(5), 513–555.

Pressley, M., Goodchild, F., Fleet, J., Zajchowski, R., & Evans, E. D. (1989). The challenges of classroom strategy instruction. *Elementary School Journal, 89*(3), 301–342.

Pressley, M., Johnson, C. J., Symons, S., McGoldrick, J. A., & Kurita, J. A. (1989). Strategies that improve children's memory and comprehension of what is read. *Elementary School Journal, 89,* 3–32.

Pressley, M., Wharton-McDonald, R., Mistretta-Hampton, J. M., & Echevarria, M. (1998). The nature of literacy instruction in ten grade 4/5 classrooms in upstate New York. *Scientific Studies of Reading, 2,* 159–194.

RAND Reading Study Group. (2002). *Reading for understanding.* Santa Monica, CA: Rand Corporation.

Raphael, T. E., & McMahon, S. I. (1994). Book Club: An alternative framework for reading instruction. *The Reading Teacher, 48*(2), 102–116.

Reninger, K. B. (2007). *Intermediate-level, lower-achieving readers' participation in and high-level thinking during group discussions about literary texts.* Unpublished doctoral dissertation, The Ohio State University, Columbus.

Resnick, L. (1999, June 16). Making America smarter. *Education Week, 8,* 38–40.

Resnick, L. B. (1985). Cognition and instruction: Recent theories of human competence. In B. L. Hammonds (Ed.), *Psychology and learning: The master lecture series* (Vol. 4, pp. 127–186). Washington, DC: American Psychological Association.

Resnick, L. B. (1987). *Education and learning to think.* Report. Washington, DC: National Academy Press

Resnick, L. B., & Hall, M. W. (1998). Learning organizations for sustainable education reform. *Daedalus, 127,* 89–118.

Reutzel, D. R., Smith, J. A., & Fawson, P. C. (2005). An evaluation of two approaches for teaching reading comprehension strategies in the primary years using science information texts. *Early Childhood Research Quarterly, 20*(3), 276–305.

Reznitskaya, A., & Anderson, R. C. (2002). The argument schema and learning to reason. In C. C. Block & M. Pressley (Eds.), *Comprehension instruction: Research-based best practices* (pp. 319–334). New York: Guilford Press.

Reznitskaya, A., Anderson, R. C., Dong, T., Li, Y., Kim, I.-H., & Kim, S.-Y. (2008). Learning to think well:

Applications of argument schema theory. In C. C. Block & S. Parris (Eds.), *Comprehension instruction: Research-based best practices* (pp. 196–213). New York: Guilford Press.

Reznitskaya, A., Anderson, R. C., & Kuo, L.-J. (2007). Teaching and learning argumentation. *Elementary School Journal, 107,* 449–472.

Reznitskaya, A., Anderson, R. C., McNurlen, B., Nguyen-Jahiel, K., Archodidou, A., & Kim, S.-y. (2001). Influence of oral discussion on written argument. *Discourse Processes, 32*(2-3), 155–175.

Rogers, T. (1990). A point, counterpoint response strategy for complex short stories. *Journal of Reading, 34*(4), 278–282.

Romance, N. R., & Vitale, M. R. (1992). A curriculum strategy that expands time for in-depth elementary science instruction by using science-based reading strategies: Effects of a year-long study in grade four. *Journal of Research in Science Teaching, 29*(6), 545–554.

Romance, N. R., & Vitale, M. R. (2001). Implementing an in-depth expanded science model in elementary schools: Multi-year findings, research issues, and policy implications. *International Journal of Science Education, 23*(4), 373–404.

Rosenblatt, L. (1978). *The reader, the text, and the poem: The transactional theory of the literature work.* Carbondale: Southern Illinois University Press.

Rosenshine, B., & Meister, C. (1994). Reciprocal teaching: A review of the research. *Review of Educational Research, 64*(4), 479–530.

Rosenshine, B., Meister, C., & Chapman, S. (1996). Teaching students to generate questions: A review of the intervention studies. *Review of Educational Research, 66*(2), 181–221.

Rudd, J. A., Greenbowe, T. J., & Hand, B. M. (2007). Using the Science Writing Heuristic to improve students' understanding of general equilibrium. *Journal of Chemical Education, 84*(12), 2007–2012.

Saul, E. W. (Ed.). (2004). *Crossing borders in literacy and science instruction: Perspectives on theory and practice.* Newark, DE: International Reading Association.

Saunders, W. M., & Goldenberg, C. (1999). Effects of instructional conversations and literature logs on limited- and fluent-English-proficient students' story comprehension and thematic understanding. *Elementary School Journal, 99,* 277–301.

Schoenbach, R., Braunger, J., Greenleaf, C., & Litman, C. (2003). Apprenticing adolescents to reading in subject-area classrooms. *Phi Delta Kappan, 85*(2), 133–138.

Schoenbach, R., & Greenleaf, C. (2000). *Tapping teachers' reading expertise: Generative professional development with middle and high school content-area teachers.* Paper presented at the Secondary Reading Symposium. Washington, DC: Office of Educational Research and Innovation. (Report No. ED-99-CO-0154, B-5).

Schoenbach, R., Greenleaf, C., Cziko, C., & Hurwitz, L. (1999). *Reading for understanding: A guide to improving reading in middle and high school classrooms.* San Francisco, CA: Jossey-Bass.

Sharp, A. M. (1995). Philosophy for Children and the development of ethical values. *Early Child Development and Care, 107,* 45–55.

Short, K. (1992). Researching intertextuality within collaborative classroom learning environments. *Linguistics and Education, 4,* 313–334.

Short, K. G., & Pierce, K. M. (Eds.). (1990). *Talking about books: Creating literate communities.* Portsmouth, NH: Heinemann.

Shuart-Faris, N., & Bloome, D. (Eds.). (2004). *Uses of intertextuality in classroom and educational research.* Greenwich, CT: Information Age.

Sinatra, G. M., Brown, K. J., & Reynolds, R. E. (2002). Implications of cognitive resource allocation for comprehension strategies instruction. In C. C. Block & M. Pressley (Eds.), *Comprehension instruction: Research-based best practices* (pp. 62–76). New York: Guilford Press.

Sipe, L. (1996). *The construction of literary understanding by first and second graders in response to picture storybook read-alouds.* Unpublished doctoral dissertation, The Ohio State University, Columbus.

Sipe, L. (1998). Individual literary response styles of first and second graders. In T. Shanahan & F. V. Rodriguez-Brown (Eds.), *47th Yearbook of the National Reading Conference* (pp. 76–89). Chicago: National Reading Conference.

Sipe, L. (2000). The construction of literary understanding by first and second graders in oral response to picture storybook read-alouds. *Reading Research Quarterly, 35,* 252–275.

Sipe, L. (2001). A palimpsest of stories: Young children's intertextual links during readalouds of fairytale variants. *Reading Research and Instruction, 40*(4), 333–352.

Soter, A. O., Connors, S., & Rudge, L. (2008). Use of a coding manual when providing a meta-interpretation of internal-validity mechanisms and demographic data used in qualitative research. *Journal of Ethnographic and Qualitative Research, 2,* 269–280.

Soter, A. O., Wilkinson, I. A. G., Connors, S., Murphy, P. K., & Shen, V. (2010). Deconstructing "aestheitc response" in small-group discussions about literature: A possible solution to the "aesthetic response" dilemma. *English Education, 42,* 204–225.

Sperling, M., & Woodlief, L. (1997). Two classrooms, two writing communities: Urban and suburban tenth graders learning to write. *Research in the Teaching of English, 31,* 205–239.

Spiro, R. (2001). Principled pluralism for adaptive flexibility in teaching and learning to read. In R. F. Flippo (Ed.), *Reading researchers in search of common ground* (pp. 92–97). Newark, DE: International Reading Association.

Stahl, K. A. D. (2004). Proof, practice and promise: Comprehension strategy instruction in the primary grades. *Reading Teacher, 57,* 598–609.

Sweet, A. P. (2005). Assessment of reading comprehension: The RAND reading study group vision. In S. G. Paris & S. A. Stahl (Eds.), *Children's reading comprehension and assessment* (pp. 3–12). Mahwah, NJ: Erlbaum.

Taylor, B. M., Pearson, P. D., Clark, K. F., & Walpole, S. (1999). Effective schools/accomplished teachers. *The Reading Teacher, 53,* 156–159.

Taylor, B. M., Pearson, P. D., Clark, K., & Walpole, S. (1999). Effective schools and accomplished teachers: Lessons about primary grade reading instruction in low-income schools. *Elementary School Journal, 101,* 121–165.

Taylor, B. M., Pearson, P. D., Garcia, G. E., Stahl, K., & Bauer, E. (2006). Improving students' reading comprehension. In K. Stahl (Ed.), *Seeking understanding in how to teach reading: Selected works by Steven Stahl* (pp. 303–315). New York: Guilford Press.

Taylor, B. M., Pearson, P. D., Peterson, D. P., & Rodriguez, M. C. (2003). Reading growth in high-poverty classrooms: The influence of teacher practices that encourage cognitive engagement in literacy learning. *Elementary School Journal, 104*(1), 3–28.

Taylor, B. M., Pearson, P. D., Peterson, D. P., & Rodriguez, M. C. (2005). The CIERA school change framework: An evidenced-based approach to professional development and school reading improvement. *Reading Research Quarterly, 40*(1), 40–69.

Taylor, L. K., Alber, S. R., & Walker, D. W. (2002). The comparative effects of a modified self-questioning strategy and story mapping on the reading comprehension of elementary students with learning disabilities. *Journal of Behavioral Education, 11*(2), 69–87.

Thorndike, E. L. (1917). Reading as reasoning: A study of mistakes in paragraph reading. *Journal of Educational Psychology, 8,* 425–434.

Tierney, R. J., & Cunningham, J. W. (1984). Research on teaching reading comprehension. In P. D. Pearson, R. Barr, M. L. Kamil, & P. Mosenthal (Eds.), *Handbook of reading research* (Vol. 1, pp. 609–655). Mahwah, NJ: Erlbaum.

Toulmin, S. (1958). *The uses of argument.* Cambridge, UK: Cambridge University Press.

VanSledright, B. A., & Kelly, C. (1998). Reading American history: The influence of using multiple sources on six fifth graders. *Elementary School Journal, 98,* 239–265.

Varelas, M., & Pappas, C. C. (2006). Intertextuality in read-alouds of integrated science-literacy units in urban primary classrooms: Opportunities for the development of thought and language. *Cognition and Instruction, 24*(2), 211–259.

Varelas, M., Pappas, C. C., & Rife, A. (2006). Exploring the role of intertextuality in concept construction: Urban second graders make sense of evaporation, boiling, and condensation. *Journal of Research in Science Teaching, 43*(7), 637–666.

Vaughn, S., Chard, D. J., Bryant, D. P., Coleman, M., Tyler, B.-J., Linan-Thompson, S., et al. (2000). Fluency and comprehension interventions for third-grade students. *Remedial and Special Education, 21,* 325–335.

Vaughn, S., Hughes, M. T., Schumm, J. S., & Klingner, J. K. (1998). A collaborative effort to enhance reading and writing instruction in inclusion classrooms. *Learning Disability Quarterly, 21,* 57–74.

Vogt, M. E. (1996). Creating a response-centered curriculum with literature discussion groups. In L. B. Gambrell & J. F. Almasi (Eds.), *Lively discussions: Fostering engaged reading* (pp. 181–193). Newark, DE: International Reading Association.

Wade, S. E., Thompson, A., & Watkins, W. (1994). The role of belief systems in authors' and readers' construction of text. In R. Garner & P. A. Alexander (Eds.), *Beliefs about text and instruction with text* (pp. 265–293). Hillsdale, NJ: Erlbaum.

Wegerif, R. (2006). A dialogic understanding of the relationship between CSCL and teaching thinking skills. *International Journal of Computer Supported Collaborative Learning, 1*(1), 143–157.

Wells, G. (1989). Language in the classroom: Literacy and collaborative talk. *Language and Education, 3*, 251–273.

Wells, G. (1999). *Dialogic inquiry: Toward a sociocultural practice and theory of education.* Cambridge, UK: Cambridge University Press.

Wells, G. (2007). Semiotic mediation, dialogue and the construction of knowledge. *Human Development, 50*(5), 244–274.

Wertsch, J. V. (1991). *Voices of the mind: A sociocultural approach to mediated action.* Cambridge, MA: Harvard University Press.

Wigfield, A., Guthrie, J. T., Tonks, S., & Perencevich, K. C. (2004). Children's motivation for reading: Domain specificity and instructional influences. *Journal of Educational Research, 97*(6), 299–309.

Wilder, A. A., & Williams, J. P. (2001). Students with severe learning disabilities can learn higher-order comprehension skills. *Journal of Educational Psychology, 93*, 268–278.

Wilkinson, I. A. G., & Reninger, K. B. (2005). *What the approaches look like: A conceptual framework for discussions.* In M. Nystrand (Chair), Making sense of group discussions designed to promote high-level comprehension of texts. Symposium presented at the annual meeting of the American Educational Research Association, Montreal, Canada.

Williams, J. P. (2005). Instruction in reading comprehension for primary-grade students: A focus on text structure. *The Journal of Special Education, 39*(1), 6–18.

Williams, J. P., Hall, K. M., & Lauer, K. D. (2004). Teaching expository text structure to young at-risk learners: Building the basics of comprehension instruction. *Exceptionality, 12*, 129–144.

Williams, J. P., Hall, K. M., Lauer, K. D., Stafford, K. B., DeSisto, L. A., & deCani, J. S. (2005). Expository text comprehension in the primary grade classroom. *Journal of Educational Psychology, 97*(4), 538–550.

Williams, J. P., Lauer, K. D., Hall, K. M., Lord, K. M., Gugga, S. S., Bak, S.-J., et al. (2002). Teaching elementary school students to identify story themes. *Journal of Educational Psychology, 94*, 235–248.

Williams, J. P., Nubla-Kung, A. M., Pollini, S., Stafford, K. B., Garcia, A., & Snyder, A. E. (2007). Teaching cause-effect structure through social studies content to at-risk second graders. *Journal of Learning Disabilities, 40*, 111–120.

Williams, J. P., Stafford, K. B., Lauer, K. D., Hall, K. M., & Pollini, S. (2009). Embedding reading comprehension training in content-area instruction. *Journal of Educational Psychology, 101*(1), 1–20.

Willingham, D. T. (2007). How we learn. Ask the cognitive scientist: The usefulness of brief instruction in reading comprehension strategies. *American Educator, 30*(4), 39–50.

Wolf, M. K., Crosson, A. C., & Resnick, L. B. (2005). Classroom talk for rigorous reading comprehension instruction. *Reading Psychology, 26*(1), 27–53.

Wolfe, M. B. W., & Goldman, S. R. (2005). Relations between adolescents' text processing and reasoning. *Cognition & Instruction, 23*(4), 467–502.

Wyatt, D., Pressley, M., EI-Dinary, P., Stein, S., Evans, P., & Brown, R. (1993). Reading behaviors of domain experts processing professional articles that are important to them: The critical role of worth and credibility monitoring. *Learning and individual differences, 5*, 49–72.

17 Toward a Theory of Word Selection

William E. Nagy
Seattle Pacific University

Elfrieda H. Hiebert
University of California, Berkeley

Which words should a teacher teach? There is general agreement that some vocabulary must be taught (NICHD, 2000), but there are far too many potentially unfamiliar words in the texts used in schools to teach them all (Nagy & Anderson, 1984). This gap between the number of words not known and the number that can be taught is further exacerbated by factors such as the time-intensive nature of high-quality vocabulary instruction (Stahl & Fairbanks, 1986), the existence of huge individual differences in vocabulary size (Hart & Risley, 1995), and the linguistic and socioeconomic diversity of the American student population (Douglas-Hall, Chau, & Koball, 2006). For the students whose exposure to academic language occurs almost exclusively in the school context, the instructional choices that are made from the tens of thousands of words in English will determine the extent to which these students acquire the vocabulary of academic texts. It is essential for educators and policy-makers to have a principled basis for identifying the words that should be targeted for vocabulary instruction. (Note that by vocabulary instruction we are referring to teaching word *meanings*—not to helping students with words already in their oral vocabularies that they might find difficult to decode.)

The purpose of this chapter is to move us closer to a principled basis for choosing words to teach. The ultimate goal—a theory of word selection—is clearly beyond us at this point; research on many of the foundations necessary for such a theory is still limited. One task that we believe is critical in a review—and one that we have taken to heart—is to identify research that needs to be done if informed choices are to be made on solid evidence. However, we already possess substantial bodies of research that can inform and constrain any attempt to build such a theory. We review much of that research in this synthesis.

A theory of word selection has at least three components, the first of which is to identify the relevant features of words. What attributes of words need to be taken into account when one is selecting words for instruction? We identified eight features that have been used or proposed for use in selecting vocabulary for instruction. We have further parsed these eight candidates according to four roles or contexts of words. These appear in Table 17.1.

A second component of a theory of word selection is a framework for assigning relative weight to different features of vocabulary and for determining how features can be used in combination. Among our features are both word frequency and familiarity. If one is to take both of these features into account, it must be determined what relative priority should be given to each. Furthermore, it becomes apparent that taking multiple criteria into account involves more than simply assigning priorities: We need to understand how the criteria interact. To take a simple example, one could propose a theory of word selection based not just on frequency and familiarity, but also on a frequency-familiarity discrepancy. That is, one might consider it most important to teach words whose familiarity to students is disproportionately low, given their frequency in text. This is just one example of the ways that a theory of word selection might require one to consider the interaction of multiple criteria, rather than simply weighting them. We take up the prioritization and combining of criteria in the last section of this chapter, where

Table 17.1 Factors Impacting Choice of Words for Instruction

Role in the Language	Frequency: How often does this word occur in text?
	Dispersion: How does the frequency of this word differ for different genres, topics, or subject areas?
Role in the Lexicon	Morphological relatedness: How many words are part of the word's morphological family?
	Semantic relatedness: How is this word related to other words that the students know, or need to know?
Role in Students' Existing Knowledge	Familiarity: Is this word already known to students and, if so, to what degree?
	Conceptual difficulty: To what extent can the meaning of this word be explained to students in terms of words, concepts, and experiences with which they are already familiar?
Role in the Lesson	Role in the particular text: Does the student need to know this word in order to understand the text?
	Role in the larger curriculum: Will this word be encountered again in reading? Should students be able to use this word in their writing?

we consider the function of words in texts and content areas, and address the ways that a model of word selection must distinguish between informational and narrative texts.

There is a third part of a theory of word selection, one that we have chosen not to address in this chapter—the goals and roles of different participants in shaping a vocabulary curriculum. Publishers of core reading programs have different aims in choosing words than students who are reading particular texts or their teachers who are instructing them to read these texts. Giving students a choice in the words they study can have powerful motivational benefits (Ruddell & Shearer, 2002), but the role of students in word selection is beyond the scope of this chapter. As a field, we are at the early stages in the development of a theory of word selection. This third component will have to wait until more basic work is completed. Our goal in this chapter is to identify fundamental issues in selecting vocabulary for large-scale curricular and instructional programs.

THE ROLE OF WORDS IN THE LANGUAGE

Frequency

Words occur with substantially different frequencies in written language, and different types of words tend to be characteristic of different frequency ranges. A small group of words, including articles (*a, the*), conjunctions (e.g., *and, but*), prepositions (e.g., *in, for*), and pronouns (e.g., *it, you*) occur very frequently in most connected texts. At the other end of the frequency spectrum, low frequency words are more likely to be morphologically complex (i.e., derived from more basic words via prefixation, suffixation, or compounding), more likely to be nouns, more likely to be specific to a particular domain of discourse, and more likely to have only a single meaning.

Perhaps the most salient—and important—fact about word frequency is the dramatic drop-off at the front end of the frequency spectrum. The word *the*, the most frequent word in the language, occurs more than 68,000 times in a million words of text. The next word, *of*, occurs less than half as often, and the tenth word less than a sixth as often. This same pattern—a steep decline in frequency at the higher-frequency end of the list—remains constant as one looks over larger intervals. For example, the 1,000th most frequent word in the language (*separate*) occurs 92 times in a million words of text, the 2,000th word (*classroom*) occurs 41 times, and the 3,000th word (*bitter*) only 24 times (Zeno, Ivens, Millard, & Duvvuri, 1995).

There are two key consequences to this pattern of frequency distribution of words in written English. One is that the bulk of text, counted in terms of tokens (running words), is made up of a relatively small core of words. For example, the most frequent 100 words make up almost 50% of the running words in text, and 5,600 words account for approximately 80% of the words in texts read by adolescents and adults (Zeno et al., 1995) and 90% of the word in texts read by children (Carroll, Davies, & Richman, 1971). A second consequence is that, once one gets past a relatively small core of high frequency words, the marginal benefits of learning any additional individual word are minimal, at least in terms of text coverage.

Word frequency has been one of the most thoroughly investigated areas in vocabulary-related research, and data on word frequencies have had a substantial impact on reading instruction (Clifford, 1978). Beginning in 1921, Thorndike provided rankings of the frequency of the most common words. These rankings were used for the selection of words for graded or basal readers, at least those at the initial levels. The graded readers, in turn, were used to validate readability formulas. Since readability formulas were used to select and create middle and high school texts, policies of vocabulary control based on frequency had a far-reaching impact.

Since the 1980s (Davison & Green, 1988), there has been a backlash against the emphasis on frequency as a basis for instructional decision-making. Some of this reaction stems from inherent limitations of word frequency. Because data on word frequencies is relatively easy to obtain, frequency has often been used as a stand-in for other word properties such as conceptual difficulty or familiarity. However, the frequency of a word in written language (which is what is represented in most current databases) may be a poor representation of these constructs. Highly frequency words are not necessarily the easiest to learn and define (e.g., *the*) nor are words rare in print necessarily difficult to learn (e.g., *fireman, t-shirt*). The lack of correspondence between frequency and familiarity is also exacerbated by the fact that the frequency of a particular form of a word may be less relevant than the frequency of its parts. The word *sleeplessness* is a relatively rare word (occurring about once per two million words of text (Zeno et al., 1995)), but it is not a difficult word for the students who understand that it is formed from a familiar stem and common suffixes. Perhaps the most serious limitation of most frequency counts is that the frequencies, being compiled by computer rather than by hand, ignore distinctions of meaning. The frequency of *bear* listed in a database (e.g., Zeno et al., 1995), for example, does not indicate how many occurrences referred to the animal, how many meant "endure," or how many meant "carry."

However, when frequency is taken as representing what it actually measures—how frequently students are likely to encounter a given word form in text, and not as a convenient stand-in for harder-to-measure word properties such as conceptual difficulty—it offers information that is essential for effective selection of words. Word frequency is especially important in the case of students such as English Language Learners for whom there may be substantial gaps within the core of 5,000 or so frequent words that are essential for understanding a wide variety of school texts (Nation, 2001).

Dispersion

Dispersion is an index of the degree to which a word occurs across texts with different content emphases. An index developed by Carroll et al. (1971) ranges from 0 for a word that appears only in a single subject area to 1 for a word that appears equally often in all subject areas. Words that exemplify a range of dispersion indices are *adverb* (.03), *Afghanistan* (.20), *alloy* (.40), *ace* (.60), *adoption* (.80), and *a* (.998) (Zeno et al., 1995).

The more frequent the word, the more likely it is that it will appear across a variety of content areas. Most words among the 1,000 most-frequent words (e.g., *do, must, after*) occur frequently in all content areas. Words in the low-frequency zones (occurring less than once in a million words of text) typically have low dispersion indices (e.g., *combustible*, D = .04; *rambunctious*, D = .000). These are words that are limited in their use even in a single subject, whether it be literature or a content area. Among words that occur with moderate frequency (i.e., 10–99 times per million), however, the relationship between dispersion and frequency can vary considerably. Some words have moderate frequency but relatively high dispersion indices (e.g., *origin*, D = .94), meaning that these words appear in numerous subject areas (though perhaps with different meanings). Other words within the moderate-frequency group have low dispersion indices, which means that they are specific to a particular content area (e.g., *noun*, D = .22; *equator*, D = .51, *chromosomes*, D = .52; *circuit*, D = .28).

All other things being equal, a high dispersion index indicates that a word is used across a variety of domains and, hence, has high utility and is a good candidate for instruction. Such words are important to teach, not only because they are used across a wide variety of subject areas, but also because, for that very reason, teachers in any given area may assume that someone else has the responsibility of making sure that students know them.

Coxhead's (2000) Academic Word List is a good example of the use of dispersion as a criterion for word selections. From words not in the General Service List (West, 1953)—essentially, words not among the 2,000 most frequent words in the language—Coxhead selected those that were used across a variety of domains in college-level texts. The goal was to identify words of broad utility, words that any learner of English would need in order to read academic language in any domain. The resulting list of 570 headwords (along with numerous inflected and affixed relatives), though developed in New Zealand, and originally intended for non-English-speaking students planning to attend universities in English-speaking countries, is probably the best available attempt at identifying essential academic vocabulary. (It must be kept in mind, of course, that this list does not include items already in the General Service List, which itself also contains words that could be considered academic vocabulary, such as *agriculture, application, calculate, classify*, and *confidential*.)

We would agree that dispersion is one factor—among many—that should be taken into account when selecting words for instruction. However, two points of caution are also in order. First, the fact that a word has a low dispersion index does not mean it is unimportant. The words *numerator, denominator*, and *quotient* have an extremely restricted sphere of application, but within that sphere, they are essential. Second, since dispersion indices, like frequencies, are normally calculated without regard to distinctions in meaning, a high dispersion index may cloak substantial specialization for various senses of a word. The word *table*, for example, has a relatively high dispersion index (0.88), indicating that it is used across a variety of subject areas. However, individual meanings of the word (e.g., a visual display of information, or to postpone discussion) are likely to be much more restricted in their distribution.

THE ROLE IN THE LEXICON

The properties of words that have been discussed to this point—frequency and distribution—provide information at a global level about how words relate to the corpus of texts in which they occur. However, there is another dimension of words' role in the language that must be taken into account—how a given word is related to other words in the language. We consider two specific types of relationships here—morphological and semantic.

Morphological Relationships

A *morpheme* is defined as the linguistic unit of meaning that cannot be divided into smaller meaningful parts. For example, the words *brave* and *stone* each consist of single morphemes, while the words *bravely* and *stones* each consist of two morphemes—a root and a suffix. Words that are related morphologically are connected in some way in the internal lexicon (that is, in the representation of word knowledge in memory). Encounters with any one member of such a family (e.g., *corporate, incorporate,* or *corporation)* impacts how well one knows and how quickly one will recognize other members (Nagy, Anderson, Schommer, Scott, & Stallman, 1989). Nagy and Anderson (1984) estimated that more than 60% of the new words that readers in grades 3–9 encounter in print could be analyzed into parts that obviously contribute to the meaning of the whole word, and the majority of words that children learn after the early elementary grades are morphologically complex (Anglin, 1993).

The everyday concept of "word" takes morphological relationships into account. We consider *walk, walks, walked,* and *walking* to be different forms of "the same word." While inflectional suffixes as represented in the last sentence do not make fundamental changes in the meaning of the word or part of speech, prefixes and derivational suffixes create new (though related) words, sometimes with substantially different meanings and often of a different part of speech. *Unhappy* is the opposite of *happy. Standardize* is a verb, but *standardization* is a noun. Compounding, another type of morphological relationship, is used to create new words that can have meanings quite different than the constituent root words (e.g., *carpool, runway*).

Decisions about morphological relationships are made, whether implicitly or explicitly, whenever words are selected for instruction. In the primary grades, most students can generalize their learning of root words to other inflected forms of that word (e.g., *walk, walks, walking, walked)* (Anglin, 1993). Hence, when one selects words for instruction, one is not selecting individual words, but sets or families of morphologically related forms. The only question is where one draws the boundaries to the family. While the role of inflections in word choice is uncontroversial, things become more complicated with derivational relationships. First is the issue of generalizability of learning: If the word *respect* has been taught, not much further instruction should be needed for *respectful*; but it is unclear how much of learning would automatically transfer to the word *respective*. Then there is the issue of computing word frequencies: should the frequency of the word *walk* include the frequency of *walker*?

We would certainly agree that capitalizing on morphological relationships can lead to more efficient vocabulary instruction. However, proposals for vocabulary instruction that assume the benefits of capitalizing on morphological relationships among words need to deal with some possible pitfalls. First, many morphological relationships are far from transparent semantically. Words such as *vision, visual, visible, visualize,* and *visage* emanate from the same Latin word *(visus)* but the meanings of these words have diverged considerably from the original meaning of look, sight, appearance. An understanding of *vision* as *eyesight* will not aid greatly in understanding *visage* as *countenance*.

Second, morphological relationships are often obscured by differences in pronunciation and sometimes in spelling as well. Adding a suffix to a word often changes the stress pattern of a word, which in turn can impact the pronunciation of the vowels in a word (e.g., *divine/divinity*). Sometimes the spelling of consonants stays the same but the pronunciation is changed (e.g., *resign/resignation*); in other cases, both the spelling and the pronunciation of the consonant are affected by the suffix (e.g., *opaque/opacity*). Unfortunately, the weakest readers appear to be most affected by such phonological or orthographic irregularities and least likely to spontaneously notice seemingly obvious relationships among words (Carlisle, 2003).

The main implication of morphological relatedness for choosing words is that all other things being equal (which, of course, is not always the case), it is better to choose words that belong to a set of morphologically related words. For example, though the words *impress* and *throng* occur with roughly the same frequency in print, the word *impress,* besides having associated inflectional forms *(impressed, impresses, impressing)* affords the opportunity to study the relationships among *impress* and words such as *impression, impressive,* and *impressionable.* The word *throng*, on the other hand, has no relatives besides the inflectional variants *thronged*, *throngs*, and *thronging*. Teaching morphological families of words not only leads to greater efficiency of instruction—more words covered at less instructional cost per word—but also provides students with numerous examples of morphological relationships, increasing the likelihood that they can independently capitalize on such relationships in their reading.

Semantic Relationships among Words

The fact that human beings are able to access the meanings of words they know so quickly—usually in a fraction of a second—means that memory for word meanings must be highly structured. Various forms of evidence have contributed to our understanding of how word knowledge is represented in memory, including research on word association (e.g., Entwisle, 1966), semantic priming (e.g., Levelt, Roelofs, & Meyer, 1999), slips of the tongue, speech disorders, brain scans, and large linguistic corpora (Aitchison, 2003). In particular, research on word associations has provided insight into ways in which words are related in memory. Most common responses involve coordination of members of a common semantic class (e.g., *boots/shoes*), collocation of words that commonly are used together (e.g., *absent/minded*), superordination (e.g., *brass/metal)*, and synonyms (e.g., *absent/missing)*. Other relationships apparent in responses are part-whole (*branch/tree*), instrumental (*broom/floor*), and scriptal (*hospital/nurse*) (Moss, Ostrin, Tyler, & Marslen-Wilson, 1995).

Semantic priming studies tend to reveal similar types of relationships, though priming effects have been found for semantically related words (e.g., *sheep/cow*) that are not related in word association tasks (Devitto & Burgess, 2004). The picture of the mental lexicon that emerges from various research paradigms is that of a richly interconnected network, reflecting a variety of types of relationships among word meanings. It would seem plausible, then, that semantic relatedness among words should be taken into account in some way when selecting words for instruction. But although there is an extensive and diverse body of research on the structure of the mental lexicon, there is little bridging research documenting the effectiveness of instructional methods that attempt to take the structure of the mental lexicon into account.

One instructional approach is based on a proposed isomorphism between instruction and internal representations—if words are stored in groups, they should be taught in groups (Beck, McKeown, & McCaslin, 1983; Finkbeiner & Nicol, 2003). There are also more substantive reasons for this approach. One is the efficiency of explanation. For example, since explanations of the words *cumulus*, *cirrus*, and *stratus* require reference to shared concepts (e.g., *water vapor, temperature, altitude*), it is more economical to teach these words together. A related argument is efficiency of the curriculum; especially in foreign language study, it is useful to work with sets of words related to a common theme (e.g., weather, shopping for groceries, asking directions). It is also hypothesized that learning words in semantically related groups leads to more precise knowledge, insofar as the meaning of a word lies in the ways that it contrasts with words of similar meaning. An empirical motivation for teaching words in semantically related groups is the well-replicated finding that lists of words are better remembered when the words are grouped semantically rather than randomly (Tulving & Psotka, 1971).

However, as Finkbeiner and Nicol (2003) point out, memorizing lists of known words is a substantially different task than learning new words. To date, research on instruction where words are taught in semantically related groups has produced, at best, mixed results. Stahl, Burdge, Machuga, and Stecyk (1992) found no difference in students who received rich instruction (Beck et al., 1983) with semantically versus randomly grouped words. Both Tinkham (1993) and Waring (1997), examining sparser paired-associate vocabulary instruction, reported a significant negative effect for teaching words in semantic sets.

In a subsequent investigation, Tinkham (1997) examined how the type of semantic relationship influenced learning. When all members of a set were defined by a single superordinate (e.g., types of metal—*tin, bronze, iron*), learning was substantially worse than for a set of unrelated words. When all words were associated with a common theme but not necessarily similar to each other in meaning (e.g., *frog, hop, slimy, pond, croak*), there was a slight facilitation of learning relative to a set of unrelated words. Finkbeiner and Nicol (2003) found detrimental effects of semantic grouping even using relatively broad semantic sets such as animals, kitchen utensils, furniture, or body parts.

One important distinction implied by the research just described is between semantic relatedness and semantic similarity. Semantic relatedness is a potential asset for learning, whereas semantic similarity is a distinct liability. Thus, words with highly similar meanings (e.g., *peach, apricot, nectarine*) should not be introduced at the same time since too much similarity is likely to lead to confusion. Not all semantic relationships, however, involve similarity. Pairs such as *law/police, leaf/tree*, and *learn/school* are strongly associated, but the meanings in each pair are not similar to each other. Tinkham's (1997) findings suggest that grouping words on the basis of such thematic relationships could have a modest positive impact on learning.

Recognizing the importance of relatedness among words has implications for word choice. First, the negative effects of similarity appear to be associated with introducing words that are simultaneously novel and highly similar in meaning. An alternative is to introduce similar words in a staggered manner with a known member of a semantic set serving as an anchor for introducing related words (Marzano & Marzano, 1988). Second, the importance of semantic relatedness in the organization of the mental lexicon reminds us that our goal is teaching concepts, not just words, and that concepts consist of relationships. Ultimately, vocabulary instruction aims to strengthen and deepen students' knowledge of semantic fields—that is, to develop students' knowledge of concepts and of the relationships among these concepts—not just to teach individual words. Increasing one's knowledge of a familiar but only partially known word supports the learning of related words, and learning related words is the primary means of deepening one's knowledge of partially known words.

One specific way that recognizing this type of interdependence among words affects word choice is that the utility of a word must be understood as a function, not just of that individual word, but of the semantic field to which it belongs. For example, at least with respect to narratives, Marzano and Marzano's (1988) superclusters "Feelings/Emotions," "Mental Actions/Thinking," and "Difficulty/Danger" would have more general utility than "Animals," "Transportation," and "Texture/Durability."

THE ROLE OF WORDS IN STUDENTS' EXISTING KNOWLEDGE

Word selection also needs to take students' prior knowledge into account. Prior knowledge includes both whether students know the specific words to be taught (familiarity) and how familiar they are with the concepts to which words refer (conceptual difficulty).

Familiarity

In an analysis of the studies on which the National Reading Panel (NRP; NICHD, 2000) based their conclusions about vocabulary instruction, Scott, Lubliner, and Hiebert (2006) reported that the familiarity of words was the most frequent criterion for selecting (or rejecting) words for inclusion in research studies. How do we determine what words students do or don't know? Do we pretest students? With what types of items? Or do we appeal to existing databases about student word knowledge, such as Dale and O'Rourke's (1981) *Living Word Vocabulary* (*LWV*)? This latter response has been the most frequent; the typical source for establishing familiarity of words in the studies reviewed by Scott et al. was the *LWV*.

One of the appeals of the *LWV* is that, unlike most frequency databases, it provides separate data for different meanings of words. However, the continued use of the *LWV* as a database for word familiarity points to a disturbing gap in the research. The demographics of the student population have changed substantially since the data for the *LWV* were collected (late 1950s and early 1960s); students chose the meaning best associated with a word from among only three choices, the sample was a convenience sample, and little is known about the construction or administration of the tests.

Creating an up-to-date and psychometrically sound remake of the *LWV* would be a major service to the field, but the task is fraught with theoretical as well as practical pitfalls. What it means to know a word is complex (Nagy & Scott, 2000), in ways that go beyond the capacities of available assessments. For example, it would be difficult to assess the subtle difference in tone evoked by the use of the term *sashayed* rather than *walked, moved,* or *perambulated*. Further, choices about word familiarity need to be informed by goals for use. For example, is it students' ability to use the word in a discussion that determines knownness or their ability to recognize the gist of the meaning in a story? In addition, even if a criterion for knownness could be assumed, there are different perspectives on how that information should be put to use. Some have argued that a major problem with current practice is that words selected for instruction are too familiar, that is, too likely to be known by students. Others have argued that vocabulary instruction would be more effective if aimed at partially known, rather than completely unknown, words.

Gates (1962) raised the first perspective when he reported that second graders knew over 80% of the second-grade words that were targeted for instruction and, additionally, knew over 75% of the third- and fourth-grade words that were to be taught in these subsequent grades. Stallman et al. (1990) replicated this study with a more comprehensive set of measures that addressed different levels of vocabulary knowledge and with fifth graders as well as second graders. They reported that second- and fifth-grade cohorts knew over 75% of grade level words and over 70% of the words from the next two grade levels. We have found no evidence that any subsequent basal reading program has employed recent or systematic data on students' knowledge of vocabulary to select words for instruction.

The second perspective is that of Biemiller (Biemiller & Boote, 2006; Biemiller & Slonim, 2001) who has suggested a developmental continuum of words. He has gathered data supporting this continuum by testing approximately 2,870 word meanings and rating another 1,760 meanings from the *LWV*. From this group, Biemiller has identified some 1,860 root-word meanings that are "worth teaching" in the primary grades. This criterion reflects the words known by 40% to 80% of students at the end of a grade. The assumption is that, other things being equal, students are likely to acquire these words in roughly the order of their knownness. Thus, interventions for students with smaller vocabularies would focus on the words already known by the majority of the other students at that grade level. In theory, this basis for word selection would identify the words that would most easily be learned, help students with smaller vocabularies catch up with their peers, and hopefully, put them on a more level playing field for future vocabulary learning.

This assumption, however, has not been put to a test. Are words at the growing edge of one's vocabulary really easier to learn than words further removed from one's current vocabulary level? Do students indeed learn the words of the next grade level more easily when they have been remediated in the words of the previous level? These questions illustrate what we consider to be an area especially in need of research.

Conceptual Difficulty

Some words are harder to learn than others. In some cases, the problem lies in the form. Some words are simply too long to take in easily and don't have any obvious meaningful parts (e.g., *sesquipedalian*). In other cases, the difficulty has something to do with the meaning. There are a number of interrelated factors that have been found to be related to the speed with which words are processed, and the relative age at which words are acquired, including concreteness versus abstractness, imageability, and context availability (see Schwanenflugel, 1991, for a discussion). That is, words can be processed more quickly, and tend to be acquired at a younger age, if they are concrete, if it is easier to form a mental image of the referent of the word, or if it is easier to think of a context or situation in which the word might be apply. Many studies have explored the effects of concreteness, imageability, and context availability on processing time (e.g., in a lexical decision task), and for the most part have found significant effects (e.g., Altarriba, Bauer, & Benvenuto, 1999; Schwanenflugel, Akin, & Luh, 1992). Others have examined the effects of these factors on word learning (e.g., de Groot & Keijzer, 2000), and likewise found significant results.

The factors that make words difficult to learn tend to be confounded with each other – concrete words are typically higher in imageability and context availability (Schwanenflugel et al., 1992) and with other factors as well. For example, Reilly and Kean (2007) report that words lower in imageability tend to be longer and more morphologically complex. Furthermore, abstract nouns are likely to occur in the longer and more complex noun phrases typical of the academic register, but foreign to conversational language (Fang, 2008).

Although it does not appear that the various characteristics that underlie word difficulty can be reduced to a single factor (Schwanenflugel et al., 1992), Schwanenflugel (1991) argued that the effects of concreteness and imageability—and the fact that these effects often disappear when supportive verbal contexts are provided—can be explained, at least in part, in terms of context availability. That is, what makes a word difficult to process or to learn is to a great extent the ease with which individuals can find—or create—links between the word's meaning and their existing knowledge base.

In the literature on vocabulary instruction, Graves (2000) has distinguished among the different types of word-learning tasks that students face, including: (a) learning to read known words, (b) learning new words representing known concepts, (c) learning new words representing new concepts, and (d) learning new meanings for known words. Along similar lines, Nagy, Anderson, and Herman (1987) operationalized difficulty of word meaning, or conceptual difficulty, in terms of the relationship of a new word's meaning to students' existing knowledge, with the key distinction being between words that are new labels for concepts already known to the learner (e.g., *apologize* for the known concept saying you're sorry) and words which require the acquisition of new factual information or a new system of concepts to learn (e.g., *divide* as the boundary between river systems).

Nagy et al. (1987) found that conceptual difficulty was the factor that most strongly influenced whether students learned a given word from context while reading a text. Other word features that did not have a significant impact on learning from context in this study were word length, part of speech, morphological transparency, and proportion of students who reported knowing the word before reading. There was no evidence of incidental learning from context for words at the highest level of conceptual difficulty. At the level of texts, proportion of conceptually difficult words was also a significant predictor of word learning.

Thus, both theory and a variety of research efforts support the idea that how hard it is to learn a word depends to a large extent on the relationship of the meaning of that word to the learner's existing stock of concepts and experiences. For example, within the three-tier model of word developed by Beck, McKeown, and Kucan (2002), conceptual difficulty plays an important role. Within this model, the words chosen for instruction should be ones "for which students understand the general concept but provide precision and specificity in describing the concept." (p. 19). Beck et al.'s (2002) advice—to choose words that are "just right" in terms of conceptual difficulty, just as one would aim for words that are "just right" in terms of frequency in the language—seems completely sensible. However, it will not work for content-area text, where the most conceptually difficult words are also likely to be the most important words for students to learn. The fact that content area vocabulary tends to be conceptually difficult poses a number of challenges for learning and instruction. One is the presence of polysemous vocabulary that students have come to know in everyday language or in another content area—words such as *force* and *energy*. Such terms have technical and precise meaning in content areas that may need to be addressed within the content area instruction. Further, there are many physical and social phenomena about which students may have perceptions and beliefs that conflict with the meanings of the vocabulary in the content area (Posner, Strike, Hewson, & Gertzog, 1982).

Relatedness among word meanings is another critical part of conceptual difficulty: A word can be conceptually difficult because it is part of a system of related meanings that is new, not simply because its meaning is unknown. These systems of related words become the unit of instruction, rather than individual words. While the unknown words in a narrative text are, for the most part, unlikely to be encountered again, the new terms of one topic in a content area are likely to be the foundation for the new concepts of the next topic.

THE ROLE OF THE WORD IN THE LESSON

In the previous section of this chapter, we considered how selecting words for instruction is impacted by the relationship of words to knowledge that students already possess. In this fourth section we consider the impact of how words relate to the knowledge that students are supposed to be gaining—that is, the role of the word in the particular text students are reading or are going to read, and the role of the word in the larger curriculum that they are encountering. In this section, we also address the second aspect of building a theory of word selection—the priority given to each of the factors that impact the choice of words—because this second step to a theory of word selection cannot be separated from the goals, content, and contexts of instruction.

The Role of the Word in the Text

The details of word selection are likely to be driven primarily by the words that occur in specific texts. In reading/language arts programs, publishers typically identify five to seven words from a text (e.g., *immense, grizzly, payroll, dismay, cord, lumberjack*), the criteria for word choice presumably being assumed unfamiliarity of the words to students and the importance of these words in the text.

Both these criteria are problematic. We have already discussed the fact that words selected for instruction are often not actually unfamiliar to students. It is also unclear whether the words typically selected are in fact important to understanding the text, and how their importance might be verified. We would agree with Beck et al. (2002) that words which are necessary for, or which would enrich, the comprehension of a text are, as such, reasonable candidates for instruction, assuming that they are not already familiar to the students. However, not all unfamiliar words in a text are potential obstacles to comprehension; Freebody and Anderson (1983) found that as many as one content word in six could be replaced by a more difficult synonym without significantly decreasing students' understanding of text. It is far from certain, then, that all of the words selected for instruction in a typical lesson are actually necessary for students to know in order to understand that particular text.

Furthermore, the sorts of instructional activities described in the teacher's guide—looking the words up in a glossary or responding to questions (e.g., which of these is a grizzly? A bear or an ant?) are seldom if ever of the kinds or amounts that are documented to improve comprehension. As Beck and her colleagues have demonstrated (e.g., Beck et al., 1983), instruction of sufficient quality to ensure gains in comprehension must be rich and time-intensive. Hence, insofar as the goal of vocabulary instruction is to improve comprehension of a text, word selection must be very strategic—identifying the few words that are most crucial for comprehension of the text. However, we know of no research directly testing any criteria for establishing which specific words are most important for the comprehension of a given text, nor of research on teachers'—or publishers'—ability to identify such words.

It must also be recognized that teaching the meanings of unfamiliar words is not the only option available for improving students' comprehension of text containing unfamiliar words. Instruction in comprehension strategies has a strong track record (NICHD, 2000; Palincsar & Brown, 1984). Other ways of improving comprehension of text containing unfamiliar words include providing glosses for unfamiliar words (Abraham, 2008) and paraphrasing difficult segments of text. Certainly one wants to provide students with some form of assistance in reading a text in which there are potentially unfamiliar words that are crucial to successfully constructing the meaning. However, the kind of time- and labor-intensive instruction required to bring a word firmly into a student's reading vocabulary is not the only form of assistance that can aid comprehension.

There is no question that having students understand the texts they read is one of teachers' highest priorities; hence, we include the role of the word in text as one factor in a model of word selection. However, if this were the only factor to be taken into account, we believe that very few words in narratives would end up being selected for vocabulary instruction, because there should be relatively few unfamiliar words that are absolutely essential for the comprehension of a well-chosen text. (This observation would not apply to informational texts, as we illustrate in the next section.) Our aim in this chapter—a review that examines the foundations for a model of word selection in large-scale curricular and instructional efforts—means that our focus has not been limited to guidelines for teachers in selecting words from specific narratives for particular students. Several frameworks have been developed for that purpose (e.g., Beck et al., 2002; Graves, 2000). In designing vocabulary curricula on a large-scale, the other factors we have discussed must be considered; and the relative weight assigned to these factors depends on how words relate to the broader goals of instruction.

The Role of the Word in the Curriculum

To address the role of the word in the curriculum adequately, we must take distinctions among content areas into consideration: The role that difficult or new words play in the texts of science, mathematics, and social studies is often very different from the role they play in typical reading/language arts texts.

Differences across Content Areas.   Linguists (Biber, 1988) and educators (Duke, 2004) have recognized the extensive differences between narrative and informational texts. Armbruster and Nagy (1992) identified two dimensions on which the unique vocabulary of reading/language arts and content-area lessons differ: (a) the kinds of words and (b) the role of these words in texts. With respect to the kinds of words, a reasonable hypothesis is that the distribution of words from Marzano and Marzano's (1988) superordinate clusters differs as a function of genre. In a biology class, the relative importance of the superclusters "Animals" and "Feelings/ Emotions" would be the reverse of that in a literature class.

But genre differences impact not only which clusters are important, but also the nature and structure of the clusters. The relationship among emotion terms, for example, will include instances of differences of degree (*happy/ecstatic*) and opposites (*happy/sad*), but will not include the elaborate taxonomic relationships found in biology. It is likely that individual informational texts contain more words semantically related to each other than narratives, and that the semantic relationships among words in informational texts tend to be more domain-specific. If the narrative and expository texts analyzed by Nagy et al. (1987) can be taken as anything like representative, more of the unfamiliar words are more likely to be conceptually difficult (i.e., unknown concepts embedded in a network of unfamiliar concepts) in informational text (40%) than in narratives (10%).

The roles that these words have in texts may also differ. The rare or unfamiliar vocabulary may tend to be used to describe or embellish ideas in narrative texts, while content area vocabulary often represents major concepts that are essential to comprehending the text and learning the content area. But it is not only the words and their roles that differ across different content areas: The relative importance of the factors impacting word selection depends on the content area as well.

As we have already argued, the general frequency of a word in the language is an important factor to be considered in selecting words and, in general, low-frequency words should not be taught unless other criteria strongly support their choice. However, each content area has words important to specific domains that, though they may be frequent enough in a particular area, have low overall frequencies (e.g., *equation, vowel, melody*). Their low frequency in the language in general should not exclude them from receiving attention. Likewise, a high dispersion index is generally an indication that a word is worth teaching, but a low dispersion index—indicating that a word's use is confined to a specific domain—certainly does not mean it is not worth teaching.

Dispersion does, however, alert us to a distinction between two kinds of words that can be important in content areas: words such as those just mentioned whose use is confined to a specific domain and general academic vocabulary which appear across many content areas such as those on the Academic Word List (e.g., *process, observe, communicate*) (Coxhead, 2000). General academic vocabulary poses at least two instructional problems. One is that no one may end up teaching them because these words (e.g., *format, minimal*) are not unique to any specific content area. As they are not typically literary words, English teachers may not see them as their responsibility either. Another problem posed by words that occur across a variety of domains is that their meanings are sometimes domain-specific. The words *function* and *positive*, for example, have different meanings in mathematics than they do in other domains.

Words in Reading/Language Arts Lessons.   In many content areas, there is at least some consensus about the core content to be covered, and most decisions about vocabulary follow from the necessity of having terminology for essential concepts. Defining core content in reading/language arts lessons is more problematic. The vocabulary that Marzano (2004) identified within standards documents for English/language arts emphasized words such as *acronym, dictation,* and *narrator*—words that are used in instruction rather than words such as *roundup, coyote, spurs,* and *bawling* that appear in a narrative. Standards documents cannot identify a core grade-level vocabulary for narrative text, we propose, because of the vast differences in the vocabulary used by narrative writers, and the fact that the unfamiliar words in narrative are not always directly related to the central ideas of the text.

We are not suggesting by any stretch that there are no concepts in literature. We would argue, however, that simplistic reliance on only two factors—familiarity of words to students and importance to the text—will not result in effective selection of words for instruction in reading/language arts lessons. The need for attending to semantic relationships among words in reading/language arts lessons is just as great as in other domains, even if not as immediately obvious. Words should be selected that relate to important themes and ideas and that increase students' ability to make and articulate distinctions among important sets of words. Hence, the importance of a given word should be determined, not just on how much that word contributes to getting the gist of that text, but on the extent to which it helps refine students' knowledge of a semantic domain. Developing depth of word knowledge—which is inseparable from understanding relationships among words within a domain—is as important as introducing students to unfamiliar words. The word *argue*, for example, might be overlooked as a candidate for teaching, because students are already familiar with this word, at least in the sense of *quarrel*. However, if the word is used in a slightly different sense—to make a case for or against—it belongs to a semantic field (i.e., words such as *assert, affirm, suggest, claim, imply, convince, assume, presume,* and *suppose*) that contains critical conceptual distinctions. Most of these words may be partially familiar to students, but the distinctions among them may be murky.

CONCLUSION

Developing students' ability to understand and produce academic language is central to the mission of the educational system. With this mission in mind, our main goal in this chapter has been to outline the essential components of a theory of word selection.

Though unanimity among scholars in any field is rare enough, we do not believe that the list of features impacting word selection that we have offered would be especially controversial. For example, one currently influential framework for selecting words for instruction proposed by Beck et al. (2002) includes almost all of the features of words we have mentioned. As previously stated, vocabulary is parsed into three tiers within this framework with the second tier identified as the focus of reading/language arts instruction. The term "Tier 2" in this framework is defined in terms of frequency—words that are not so frequent as to be known by almost all students (Tier 1), or so infrequent as to be seldom seen by students, or limited to specific domains (Tier 3). However, Beck et al.'s (2002) framework utilizes other criteria as well—dispersion: "Words that ...appear frequently across a variety of domains" (p. 19); familiarity: "Words that are characteristic of mature language users" (p. 19); conceptual difficulty: "Words for which students understand the general concept but provide precision and specificity in describing the concept" (p. 19); relationships among words: "How does the word relate to other words, to ideas that students know or have been learning?" (p. 29); role in the text: "What does the word bring to a text or situation?" (p. 29); and role in the curriculum: "Does it directly relate to some topic of study in the classroom?" (p. 29). Thus, with the exception of morphological relatedness, all of the criteria that appear in Table 17.1 have been addressed and, while Beck et al. do not specifically mention morphological relatedness, it could easily be added as a factor to take into consideration.

We expect disagreements not about the list of features, but about how they are operationalized. For example, Beck et al. (2002) do not operationalize frequency in terms of any specific objective measures While this has the advantage of allowing teachers flexibility in their choice of words, a lack of any firm frequency limits allows the selection of words that are known by most mature language users, but which occur relatively infrequently in print (less than 5 times per million words of text)—for example, *benevolent, sinister, despise, mumble, valet, decent,* and *sullen.* Such words are indeed colorful and interesting. However, there is as yet no firm evidence that the teaching of such words leads to any benefits beyond the knowledge of those specific words. If 200 such words were taught over the course of a year—an ambitious goal for any program of vocabulary instruction—the proportion of words in text known by students would increase by only one-tenth of 1%.

We expect an even greater degree of disagreement, however, about how the features are prioritized, if for no other reason than the relative weight given to the features depends to a large extent on one's understanding of the long-term goals of education. The weighting of features also depends on the nature of the text, and the purposes for reading it, and hence must be, at least in part, genre-specific. For example, as we have pointed out, we believe that Beck et al.'s use of dispersion and conceptual difficulty as criteria are more appropriate for narrative than for informational text.

Another ground for disagreement about prioritization of features is lack of information. A secondary goal of this chapter has thus been to point out some of the most serious gaps in the research foundations necessary for such a theory. Crucial questions still need to be addressed concerning all of the factors that impact word selection. Information about word frequency from vast and increasingly diverse corpora of written language is becoming available, but there is less information about frequency based on oral language and even less based on students' writing at various grade levels. Data on the frequencies of specific meanings of words, though it would be harder to attain, would make frequency counts immeasurably more valuable. Data on familiarity is likewise scarce, as evidenced by the fact that researchers are still appealing to the outdated and psychometrically deficient *LWV*.

We are also lacking research on some fundamental assumptions that underlie the process of word selection. For example, research is needed to establish the existence and strength of zone of proximal development effects in vocabulary learning: Are students really better at learning words that are on the growing edges of their vocabularies? Likewise, we need to know more about the facilitation and/or interference that is associated with different types of semantic relationships among words. Perhaps the most glaring need is further refinement of the construct of conceptual difficulty. This is arguably one of the most important factors but also one of the most difficult to operationalize. Almost nothing has been done to determine how well teachers, or researchers, can rate this trait, and how well it actually predicts the learnability of words.

Despite the gaps in the research base, we are still confident in outlining some foundations for a theory of word selection. We have argued, first of all, that *all* of the features in our list need to be taken into consideration. A one-criterion process (i.e., looking only at frequency, or only at familiarity, or only at the role of a word in a particular text) will not succeed. A second major point we want to re-emphasize is that the relative weight of features depends on the genre of text: The principles of word choice for informational text cannot be identical to those for narratives.

Frequency has been one of the most prominent factors in word selection, with an almost unavoidable pendulum swing between simplistic overuse and neglect. Insofar as the goal of vocabulary instruction is to increase the overall proportion of words in text know to students, it is absolutely necessary to take frequency into account when selecting words to teach, especially for students most in need of increased vocabulary growth. Selecting words on the basis of frequency alone does carry with it certain risks—for example, unnatural and uninteresting texts—but we believe that these negative effects can be minimized by understanding frequency as necessarily informing, but not determining, word choice.

Familiarity has likewise, implicitly or explicitly, been a major factor in word selection. The point we want to stress most strongly is that familiarity must be understood in an incremental rather than absolute sense. That is, the question is not whether students know a word, but how well they know it. The fact that students are superficially familiar with a word does not mean that it doesn't need to be taught.

Relatedness among words has probably been the most neglected factor in word selection. Morphological relatedness is important because increasing students' generative word knowledge is as important as increasing their knowledge of specific individual words. By giving priority to words that belong to rich morphological families, one can further both goals. Semantic relatedness is important because ultimately, word knowledge is about interrelated sets of words, not isolated units.

We conclude with an acknowledgement of the need for educators to attend to the third and last component of a theory of word selection—who gets to make the choices, or, better said, how the task of selecting words should be divided up among responsible parties. Our goal was to present scholarship on a framework for the selection of words, recognizing throughout the chapter numerous areas where current knowledge is insufficient for guiding large-scale instructional implementations. The question of how different constituencies might collaborate in using this information to make the best selections goes considerably beyond the scope of this chapter. It is a question that needs to be addressed by a variety of constituents, including, although not necessarily limited to, teachers, school-, district-, and state-level literacy specialists, authors and publishers of textbooks and assessments, and policy-makers who establish state and national standards and assessments. Researchers have an ongoing and critical role in providing these various constituents the best possible information.

REFERENCES

Abraham, L. B. (2008). Computer-mediated glosses in second language reading comprehension and vocabulary learning: A meta-analysis. *Computer Assisted Language Learning, 21*(3), 199–226.

Aitchison, J. (2003). *Words in the mind: An introduction to the mental lexicon* (3rd ed.). London: Blackwell.

Altarriba, J., Bauer, L. M., & Benvenuto, C. (1999). Concreteness, context-availability, and imageability ratings and word associations for abstract, concrete, and emotion words. *Behavior Research Methods, Instruments, & Computers, 31*, 578–602.

Anglin, J. M. (1993). Vocabulary development: A morphological analysis. *Monographs of the Society for Research in Child Development, 58*(10), Serial #238.

Armbruster, B. B., & Nagy, W. E. (1992). Vocabulary in content area lessons. *The Reading Teacher, 45*(7), 550–551.

Beck, I. L., McKeown, M. G., & McCaslin, E. S. (1983). Vocabulary development: All contexts are not created equal. *The Elementary School Journal, 83*(3), 177–181.

Beck, I. L., McKeown, M. G., & Kucan, L. (2002). *Bringing words to life: Robust vocabulary instruction.* New York: Guilford.

Biber, D. (1988). *Variation across speech and writing.* Cambridge, UK: Cambridge University Press.

Biemiller, A., & Boote, C. (2006). An effective method for building meaning vocabulary in primary grades. *Journal of Educational Psychology, 98*(1), 44–62.

Biemiller, A., & Slonim, N. (2001). Estimating root word vocabulary growth in normative and advantaged populations: Evidence for a common sequence of vocabulary acquisition. *Journal of Educational Psychology, 93*, 498–520.

Carlisle, J. F. (2003). Morphology matters in learning to read: A commentary. *Reading Psychology, 24*, 291–322.

Carroll, J. B., Davies, P., & Richman, B. (1971). *The American Heritage word frequency book.* Boston: Houghton Mifflin.

Clifford, G. J. (1978). Words for schools: The applications in education of the vocabulary researches of Edward L. Thorndike. In P. Suppes (Ed.), *Impact of research on education: Some case studies* (pp. 107–198). Washington, DC: National Academy of Education.

Coxhead, A. (2000). A new academic word list. *TESOL Quarterly, 34*(2), 213–238.

Dale, E., & O'Rourke, J. (1981). *Living word vocabulary.* Chicago: World Book/Childcraft.

Davison, A., & Green, G.M. (Eds.). (1988). *Linguistic complexity and text comprehension: Readability issues reconsidered.* Hillsdale, NJ: Erlbaum.

de Groot, A., & Keijzer, R. (2000). What is hard to learn is easy to forget: The roles of word concreteness, cognate status, and word frequency in foreign language vocabulary learning and forgetting. *Language Learning, 50*(1), 1–56.

Devitto, Z., & Burgess, C. (2004). Theoretical and methodological implications of language experience and vocabulary skill: Priming of strongly and weakly associated words. *Brain and Cognition, 55*, 295–299.

Douglas-Hall, A., Chau, M., & Koball, H. (2006). *Basic facts about low-income children.* New York: National Center for Children in Poverty.

Duke, N. K. (2004). The case for information text. *Educational Leadership, 61*(6), 40–43.

Entwisle, D. (1966). *Word associations of young children.* Baltimore, MD: Johns Hopkins University Press.

Fang, Z. (2008). Going beyond the fab five: Helping students cope with the unique linguistic challenges of expository reading in intermediate grades. *Journal of Adolescent & Adult Literacy, 51*(6), 476–487.

Finkbeiner, M., & Nicol, J. (2003). Semantic category effects in second language word learning. *Applied Psycholinguistics, 24*, 369–383.

Freebody, P., & Anderson, R. C. (1983). Effects on text comprehension of differing proportions and locations of difficult vocabulary. *Journal of Reading Behavior, 15*(3), 19–39.

Gates, A. I. (1962). The word recognition ability and the reading vocabulary of second and third grade children. *The Reading Teacher, 15*(6), 443–448.

Graves, M. F. (2000). A vocabulary program to complement and bolster a middle-grade comprehension program. In B. M. Taylor, M. F. Graves, & P. van den Broek (Eds.), *Reading for meaning: Fostering comprehension in the middle grades* (pp. 116–135). New York: Teachers College Press.

Hart, B., & Risley, T. (1995). *Meaningful differences in everyday parenting and intellectual development in young American children.* Baltimore, MD: Brookes.

Levelt, W. J .M., Roelofs, A., & Meyer, A. S. (1999). A theory of lexical access in speech production. *Behavioral and Brain Sciences, 22*, 1–38.

Marzano, R. J. (2004). *Building background knowledge for academic achievement.* Alexandria, VA: Association for Supervision and Curriculum Development.

Marzano, R. J., & Marzano, J. S. (1988). *A cluster approach to elementary vocabulary instruction.* Newark, DE: IRA.

Moss, H. E., Ostrin, R. K., Tyler, L. K., & Marslen-Wilson, W. D. (1995). Accessing different types of lexical semantic information: Evidence from priming. *Journal of Experimental Psychology: Learning, Memory, and cognition, 21*(4), 863–883.

Nagy, W. E., & Anderson, R. C. (1984). How many words are there in printed school English? *Reading Research Quarterly, 19*, 304–330.

Nagy, W. E., Anderson, R. C., & Herman, P. A. (1987). Learning word meanings from context during normal reading. *American Educational Research Journal, 24*, 237–270.

Nagy, W.E., Anderson, R. C., Schommer, M., Scott, J.A., & Stallman, A.C. (1989). Morphological families in the internal lexicon. *Reading Research Quarterly, 24*(3), 262–282.

Nagy, W., & Scott, J. (2000). Vocabulary processing. In M. Kamil, P. Mosenthal, P. D. Pearson, & R. Barr (Eds.), *Handbook of reading research* (Vol. 3, pp. 269–284). Mahwah, NJ: Erlbaum.

Nation, I. S. P. (2001). *Learning vocabulary in another language.* Cambridge, UK: Cambridge University Press.

National Institute of Child Health and Human Development (NICHD). (2000). *Report of the National Reading Panel: Teaching children to read: An evidence-based assessment of the scientific research literature on reading and its implications for reading).* Washington, DC: U.S. Government Printing Office.

Palincsar, A. S., & Brown, A. L. (1984). Reciprocal teaching of comprehension-fostering and comprehension-monitoring activities. *Cognition and Instruction, 1*(2), 117–175.

Posner, G. J., Strike, K. A., Hewson, P. W., & Gertzog, W. (1982). Accommodation of a scientific conception: Toward a theory of conceptual change. *Science Education, 66*(2), 211–227.

Reilly, J., & Kean, J. (2007). Formal distinctiveness of high- and low-imageability nouns: Analyses and theoretical implications. *Cognitive Science, 31*(1), 157–168.

Ruddell, M. R., & Shearer, B. A. (2002). "Extraordinary," "tremendous," "exhilarating," "magnificent": Middle school at-risk students become avid word learners with the vocabulary self-collection strategy. *Journal of Adolescent & Adult Literacy, 45*, 352–363.

Schwanenflugel, P. J., Akin, C., & Luh, W. (1992). Context availability and the recall of abstract and concrete words. *Memory & Cognition, 20*, 96–104.

Schwanenflugel, P. J. (1991). Why are abstract concepts hard to understand? In P. Schwanenflugel (Ed.), *The Psychology of Word Meanings* (pp. 223–250). Mahwah, NJ: Erlbaum.

Scott, J. A., Lubliner, S., & Hiebert, E. H. (2006). Constructs underlying word selection and assessment tasks in the archival research on vocabulary instruction. In J. V. Hoffman, D. L. Schallert, C. M. Fairbanks, J. Worthy, & B. Maloch (Eds.), *55th Yearbook of the National Reading Conference* (pp. 264–275). Oak Creek, WI: NRC.

Stahl, S. A., Burdge, J. L, Machuga, M. B., & Stecyk, S. (1992). The effects of semantic grouping on learning word meanings. *Reading Psychology, 13*(1), 19–35.

Stahl, S. A., & Fairbanks, M. M. (1986). The effects of vocabulary instruction: A model-based meta-analysis. *Review of Educational Research, 56*, 72–110.

Stallman, A. C., Commeyras, M., Kerr, B., Meyer Reimer, K., Jiménez, R., Hartman, D. K., et al. (1990). Are "new" words really new? *Reading Research and Instruction, 29*(2), 12–29.

Thorndike, E. L. (1921). *The teacher's word book.* New York: Columbia University Press.

Tinkham, T. (1993). The effect of semantic clustering on the learning of second language vocabulary. *System, 21*, 371–380.

Tinkham, T. (1997). The effects of semantic and thematic clustering on the learning of second language vocabulary. *Second Language Research, 13*(2) 138–163.

Tulving, E., & Psotka, J. (1971). Retroactive inhibition in free recall: Inaccessibility of information available in the memory store. *Journal of Experimental Psychology, 87*, 1–8.

Waring, R. (1997). The negative effects of learning words in semantic sets: A replication. *System, 25*(2), 261–274.

West, M. (1953). *A general service list of English words.* London: Routledge.

Zeno, S. M., Ivens, S. H., Millard, R. T., & Duvvuri, R. (1995). *The educator's word frequency guide.* New York: Touchstone Applied Science Associates.

18 The Development and Teaching of Word Recognition Skill

William E. Tunmer and Tom Nicholson
Massey University

In a recent review Snow and Juel (2005) drew attention to the long history of conflict about the most effective way to teach English-speaking children how to read, a conflict that has been described as the "great debate" (Chall, 1967/1983/1996) or, when emotions run high, the "reading wars" (Connor, Morrison, & Katch, 2004). They noted, for example, that from Huey's (1979) book, *The Psychology and Pedagogy of Reading*, first published in 1908, "we learn that all the various approaches to teaching reading current today had been developed by 1870, and that complaints standard today... about effectiveness of instruction were voiced in response to every reform of reading methods" (p. 504). In one form or another the debate over reading methods has raged for more than a century, with the pendulum swinging back and forth between approaches that emphasize the development of alphabetic coding skills, or phonics, and those that do not, such as the whole-word method or, more recently, whole language. But this raises an important question: Why has the debate gone on for so long? One would think that after all this time the teachers themselves might have discovered the most effective approach to teaching literacy by gradual refinements of existing methods, leaving it to the academics to provide a more detailed explanation for why the favored approach works best.

In the following sections we argue that there is indeed an explanation for the persistence of the conflict over methods and it comes from cognitive science. The source of the conflict stems largely from the failure to distinguish between the questions of how children learn to read and how children should be taught to read. The first question is concerned with the cognitive developmental processes involved in learning to read, whereas the second focuses on what parents and teachers can do to facilitate the acquisition of reading skills. Although the two questions are clearly interrelated, they are conceptually distinct. A thorough understanding of how children acquire reading skills would certainly help parents and professionals assist children in the task of learning to read. But if a child learned to read by a particular approach to *teaching* reading, it does not follow that the child *learned* to read according to the theory of reading acquisition underpinning the approach. As Liberman and Liberman (1992) argued, most children (perhaps up to 75%) will independently discover the skills necessary for learning to read in an alphabetic orthography no matter how unhelpful the method of instruction. Consistent with this claim, evidence reviewed by the National Reading Panel (2000) indicated that although explicit instruction in phonics was more effective than more implicit approaches (e.g., embedded phonics), there was substantial overlap in the distributions of word reading accuracy scores between the two approaches. The majority of children taught by reading methods that place little or no emphasis on the explicit and systematic teaching of letter-sound patterns do in fact learn to read. The central claim of this chapter is that the search for the "best method" for teaching reading is fundamentally misguided, as the most effective approach used with any given child depends crucially on the reading-related knowledge, skills, and experiences the child brings to the task of learning to read.

The chapter is divided into three sections. In the first section we discuss shortcomings of both the whole language and phonics approaches to teaching word recognition skill. In the second section we present an alternative approach to beginning reading instruction, examine current trends in research on the development and teaching of word recognition skill, and suggest directions for future research. In the third section we describe possible implications of recent research for preservice teacher training and educational practice.

"A POX ON BOTH YOUR HOUSES"

In a paper so entitled, Gough (1996) argued that the underlying theoretical assumptions of both traditional phonics and whole language are partially correct and partially incorrect, and as a consequence an unacceptably large number of children fail to learn to read by the use of either approach. He expressed skepticism over suggestions that as many as 20% of children are learning disabled or dyslexic, arguing that the majority of children labelled "reading disabled" have failed to learn to read because they have not received adequate reading instruction, a claim supported by research (e.g., Vellutino et al., 1996; Vellutino, Scanlon, & Jaccard, 2003). Gough further suggested that much of the confusion over reading methods, and, ultimately, the basis of a false dichotomy between phonics and whole language, arises from misunderstandings surrounding the constructivist view of learning, which is most closely associated with whole language.

Pedagogical constructivism is based on the theory of learning that emphasizes the active construction of knowledge (Tracey & Morrow, 2006). Learning is seen as the natural by-product of active mental engagement. As Stanovich (1994) noted, this instructional approach assumes "that self-discovery is the most efficacious mode of learning, that most learning can be characterized as 'natural', and that cognitive components should never be isolated/fractionated during the learning process" (p. 264). Challenging students to construct their own solutions to "authentic" problems in information-rich settings is considered to be the most effective teaching strategy for bringing about desired learning outcomes, such as learning to read.

Related to issues concerning constructivist views of learning is the recent theoretical work of Byrne (2002, 2005). In developing a conceptual framework for theories of learning to read, Byrne introduced the notion of *division of labor*, which assumes that any act of learning is the joint product of the learner and the environment. He argued that different acts of learning can be located at different points along a continuum representing the division of labor between the learner and the environment. One end of the continuum represents acts of learning requiring only meager and fragmentary environmental input for learning to occur, whereas the other end represents learning that requires rich and highly structured input from the environment. For example, because spoken language is part of the biological heritage of humans, acquiring one's native language requires little more than exposure to a speech community in the first years of life. During this period children attempt to understand the purpose (meaning) of individual speech acts by interpreting the situation as a whole, while their brains attend to relationships between structural features of utterances and features of the situations in which they occur to induce the syntax of the language (Pinker, 1994). In contrast, learning how to use calculus to solve problems in engineering or physics requires a great deal of highly structured environmental input. Learning to read falls somewhere between these two extremes, but the question remains of *where* along the division of labor continuum is reading acquisition most appropriately located, or, if reading can be analyzed into component processes, what are the relative contributions of the learner and the environment to each component over time (Byrne, 2005)? Snow and Juel (2005) underscored the importance of answering this question by pointing out that the century-old conflict about how to teach literacy has centered around two issues: first, what unit of language should be used in teaching reading and writing, and second, "to what degree can we trust children to induce an adequate understanding of the system themselves, without explicit instruction about its character?" (p. 505).

Objections to Whole Language

Whole language was derived largely from "Psycholinguistic Theory" (Tracey & Morrow, 2006, pp. 57–61) and has been variously described as a philosophy of how children learn, a belief system about literacy learning, an attitude toward teaching, and a set of instructional strategies for facilitating literacy development in children (Bergeron, 1990). However, core assumptions of whole language can be identified. Gough (1996) argued that whole language is based on two fundamental misconceptions, one relating to how we learn to read and the other to how we read.

Is Learning to Read Natural?   Regarding the first misconception, whole language has followed a predominantly constructivist approach to literacy education that assumes that learning to read is essentially like learning to speak, where both abilities are thought to develop "naturally" (Smith & Elley, 1994, p. 81). From the assumption that the ability to read evolves naturally and spontaneously out of children's pre-reading experiences with "environmental print" (commonly occurring environmental labels accompanied by context or logos, such as the word *stop* appearing on an octagonally shaped sign), whole language theorists concluded that literacy teaching should be modelled on first-language acquisition, where the focus is on meaning construction, not the abstract structural units that provide the basis for mapping print onto spoken language. Because it is assumed that children are naturally predisposed to learn written language, reading problems are thought to result from methods of instruction that conflict with the natural purpose of language, which is the communication of meaning. Explicit instruction in word-level skills and strategies (e.g., phonological awareness, alphabetic coding skills) is therefore downplayed or discouraged. If children are immersed in a print-rich environment in which the focus is on the construction of meaning, they will readily induce the spelling-sound relations necessary for learning to read; letter-sound patterns are "caught, not taught." Word analysis activities, if any, arise primarily from the child's responses during text reading and typically focus on boundary letters (i.e., initial and final letters). The focus of this approach, then, is on learning to read by reading, with minimal attention being given to the development of phonemically-based, word-level skills and strategies. As Smith and Elley (1994), two leading proponents of whole language in New Zealand, claimed, "children learn to read themselves; direct teaching plays only a minor role" (p. 87). In terms of Byrne's (2005) conceptual framework, this approach to reading instruction assumes that the processes of learning to read are highly *learner dependent*, with children relying on induction to a very large degree.

This view of learning to read as a subset of more general language learning faces an immediate difficulty when we examine school systems or countries that have adopted the whole language approach to literacy education, such as New Zealand (for detailed descriptions of the New Zealand version of whole language, see Connelly, Johnston, & Thompson, 2001; Nicholson, 2000, 2002; Smith & Elley, 1994; Tunmer & Chapman, 2002). If children do indeed "learn to read themselves" with only a limited amount of direct instruction being required (because they need only use the same underlying strategies and mental capacities that enabled them to acquire spoken language), we would not expect to find that 15%–20% of all 6-year-old children in New Zealand require expensive, intensive, one-to-one Reading Recovery tutoring (a nationally implemented early intervention program developed by Clay, 1985) after having been immersed in a print-rich environment for an entire year. Most of these children have made little or no progress toward gaining independence in reading during their first year of schooling (Chapman, Tunmer, & Prochnow, 2001). Moreover, given that the world is awash in print, we would also not expect so few children to learn to read before going to school, with those who do typically having received a considerable amount of instruction and/or encouragement and support in literacy-related activities in their home prior to school entry (Nicholson, 1999). The most likely explanation for these apparent contradictions of a key assumption of whole language is that learning to read is not natural (Gough, 1996; Gough & Hillinger, 1980; Liberman & Liberman, 1992; Perfetti, 1991). As Perfetti (1991) argued, "learning to read is not like acquiring one's native language, no matter how much someone wishes it were so" (p. 75). Spoken language is acquired with a large biological contribution and is universal among human communities, whereas written language is a culturally transmitted artifact that is far from universal.

Supporting these claims is a considerable amount of research indicating that environmental print experiences alone do not enable children to learn to read. Later stages of beginning reading are not continuous extensions of the kind of spontaneous word learning that results from exposure to environmental print, where children learn to "read the environment" rather than the word (e.g., Greaney & Ryder, 2005; Masonheimer, Drum, & Ehri, 1984). In the second volume of the *Handbook of Reading Research*, Juel (1991) presented arguments and evidence in support of a basic discontinuity in the acquisition of word recognition skill. According to this view, beginning readers quickly learn to recognize dozens of words through the natural strategy of selective association, the pairing of a partial stimulus cue to a response. Any cue that will distinguish the word may be used by the child, such as something in the immediate environment in which the word appears (e.g., a thumbprint; Gough, 1993), a single character or a matching pair of characters, the font in which the characters appear, the names of some of the letters if the child knows some letter names, or possibly a property of the whole word (e.g., its color, its length, or the resemblance of the whole word to a familiar object).

Studies by Byrne (1992) and Gough (1993) provided evidence in support of a partial-cue reading stage in early reading development. Byrne (1992) reported the results of a series of experiments demonstrating that pre-readers are largely ignorant of phonological segments in spoken words, adopting instead a non-analytic strategy in which new words are learned by associating some distinguishing feature of the printed word with its spoken counterpart as a whole. Pre-school children with no knowledge of reading or the sounds of individual letters could be taught to discriminate FAT from BAT, but this did not enable them to discriminate FUN from BUN at a level above chance. Byrne concluded that the failure of pre-readers to develop analytic links between print and speech results from the extension of the more natural non-analytic strategy of using partial cues to recognize words.

Beginning readers who continue to learn to read words this way will face two major problems (Gough, Juel, & Griffith, 1992). First, although the hypothesis of selective association predicts that the beginning reader will easily acquire a few words on the basis of visually distinct cues, it also predicts that the child's natural strategy of associating a familiar spoken word with some feature or attribute of the word's printed form will eventually break down. Each new word will become increasingly harder to acquire because of the difficulty of finding a unique cue to distinguish it from those that have already been learned. For example, if the child selects the presence of a squiggly character (i.e., the letter *s*) to recognize the word *stop*, then difficulties will arise when attempts are made to use this same character to recognize the words *tops*, *post*, and *pots* (in this example the selection of *any* character as a distinguishing cue, such as the cross-shaped figure, will fail). Beginning readers will make an ever-increasing number of errors and become confused and frustrated unless they discover or are led to discover an alternative strategy for establishing the relationship between the written and spoken forms of the language.

Second, the strategy of selective association based on distinctive visual cues is developmentally limiting because it is not generative; it does not provide a means for identifying words not seen before. This is an important consideration because most of the words that beginning readers encounter in print are novel (Share, 1995). Beginning reading materials typically employ upwards of 1,500 words, each of which must be encountered a first time. Moreover, when a new word does appear in print it does not suddenly begin appearing with great frequency. Approximately 35%–40% of the words used in beginning reading materials appear only once (Jorm & Share, 1983). Thus beginning readers are continually encountering words that they have not seen before and may not set eyes on again for some time.

Gough et al. (1992) argued that normal progress in learning to read can only occur if the child makes the transition to the next stage of reading acquisition, the *cipher* stage. Entering this stage requires that the child becomes conceptually aware of the interrelatedness of the visual patterns and sounds shared by different words. Unlike the first stage, where the child naturally (and nonconsciously) associates a spoken word with some particularly salient visual cue in the corresponding written word, the cipher stage is not natural. Rather, it is characterized by fully analytic processing which requires an explicit and conscious awareness of the relationship that exists between alphabetic shapes and phonological segments, referred to as the *alphabetic principle*. According to this view, then, reading skill is not picked up simply through exposure to print but almost always requires adult intervention to facilitate the development of analytic processing. Following Byrne (2005), the processes of learning to read are, at least to some degree, *environment dependent*.

For progress to occur in learning to read beyond the initial partial-cue reading stage, the beginning reader must acquire *phonological recoding ability*, the ability to translate letters and letter patterns into phonological forms (Juel, 1991). Making use of letter-sound relationships to identify unfamiliar words is the basic mechanism for acquiring word-specific knowledge (i.e., knowledge of specific letter sequences), including knowledge of irregularly spelled words (Adams, 1990; Adams & Bruck, 1993; Ehri, 1992, 1997, 2005; Gough & Walsh, 1991; Harm & Seidenberg, 1999; Hulme, Snowling, & Quinlan, 1991; Perfetti, 1992; Share, 1995; Tunmer & Chapman, 1998, 2006). Taking advantage of the systematic mappings between subcomponents of written and spoken words enables beginning readers to identify unknown words which, in turn, results in the formation of sublexical, visuophonological connections between printed words and their spoken counterparts in lexical memory. This process provides the basis for constructing the detailed orthographic representations required for the automatization of word recognition (or what Ehri, 2005, calls *sight word* knowledge), thus freeing up cognitive resources for allocation to sentence comprehension and text integration processes (Jenkins, Fuchs, van den Broek, Espin, & Deno, 2003; Perfetti, 1985; Pressley, 2006; Share, 1995; Tan & Nicholson, 1997).

For beginning readers who continue to rely mostly on partial visual cues and contextual guessing at the expense of phonological information, there is little interaction between the subcomponents of written and spoken words. As Adams and Bruck (1993) pointed out, "without the mnemonic support of the spelling-to-sound connections, the visual system must eventually become overwhelmed: the situation in which [these children] are left is roughly analogous to learning 50,000 telephone numbers to the point of perfect recall and instant recognition" (p. 130). The word recognition skills of these children therefore remain relatively weak because they do not develop as rich a network of sublexical connections between orthographic and phonological representations in lexical memory as do normally developing readers. Consequently, these children experience progressive deterioration in their rate of reading comprehension development as they grow older, because word recognition processes that are inefficient and capacity draining make understanding text more difficult (Byrne, Freebody, & Gates, 1992).

Evidence supporting a basic discontinuity in the acquisition of word recognition skill comes from two studies reviewed by Juel (1991). In these studies (Gough, Juel, & Roper-Schneider, 1983; Juel, Griffith, & Gough, 1985) beginning readers were identified as either cue or cipher readers according to their ability to pronounce pseudowords correctly (e.g., *buf, cleef*), a commonly used measure of phonological recoding ability. Not only did the cipher readers (who performed well on the pseudoword reading test) read and spell words better than the cue readers (who were unable to read pseudowords), they also used qualitatively different reading and spelling strategies, as indicated by striking differences between the two groups in the kinds of reading and spelling errors they made. The text reading errors of cue readers were usually substitutions, and the substitutions tended to be words they had previously encountered in text. When reading words in isolation, like *rain*, their errors contained only some of the letters in the unknown word (e.g., *ring, in, with, are, ran*). The spelling errors of cue readers suggested that they recalled some of the letters in the target word and the word's approximate length, and then filled in the unrecalled letters with random letters. For example, when asked to spell *rain*, their spelling errors included *weir, rach, fen ramt,* and *ran*. In contrast, the reading errors of cipher readers were fewer in number and the few substitutions they made were rarely drawn from earlier text. Moreover, their errors were more graphemically similar to the words in text, often resulting in nonsense words (e.g., *rannin* for *rain*). The spelling errors of cipher readers tended to be driven by the phonological form of the word, typically resulting in either "invented" spellings or homophonous nonword versions of the target word (e.g., *raine* and *rane* for *rain*).

Whole language proponents have often argued that explicit, systematic instruction in letter-sound patterns is not only unnecessary but will likely impede reading development by diverting children's attention from the natural purpose of engaging written language, which is the construction of meaning (Goodman, 1986). Evidence against this claim comes from the results of a study by Connelly et al. (2001) comparing the reading comprehension performance of two groups of beginning readers matched on age, time in school, and word recognition. One group (from Scotland) was taught by the phonics approach to teaching reading, and the other group (from New Zealand) by the whole language approach. Although the whole language taught children had faster reaction times to familiar words and read connected text at a faster rate, they scored less well than the phonics taught children on measures of phoneme segmentation, nonword reading, and reading comprehension. Compared with the whole language group, the phonics group spent more time identifying unknown words, made more spoken attempts at reading unknown words, produced more contextually appropriate errors, and produced a higher proportion of contextually appropriate errors that were graphemically similar to the target word. Connelly et al. (2001) attributed the higher reading comprehension performance of the phonics taught children to this approach to word identification:

> This procedure may encourage them to think about the story as they sound out words and check that their responses match the context. The procedure would lead to greater rehearsal of content of the story as reading proceeds. Hence, although the phonics taught children are slower in their reading they comprehend and remember more about the story. (p. 452)

Connelly et al. (2001) concluded from their findings that heavy phonics instruction during the early years of schooling does not impede the development of age appropriate comprehension skills in reading. If anything, the acquisition of rudimentary alphabetic coding skills actually promotes the development of reading comprehension ability because early partial decoding attempts of unknown words in text encourage the use of context cues to help select an appropriate sounding word that makes sense in the story. Meaning construction is not unique to whole language, as the goal of any literacy program must be to help children derive meaning from print and express meaning in print. The question is how best to do it.

Multiple Cuing Systems.   The second misconception of whole language identified by Gough (1996) concerns how we read. Whole language theorists have assumed that skilled reading is a process in which minimal word-level information is used to confirm predictions about the upcoming words of text based on multiple sources of information (Clay, 1991; Goodman, 1967; Smith, 1978). Clay, for example, claimed that "in efficient rapid word perception the reader relies mostly on the sentence and its meaning and some selected features of the forms of words.

Awareness of the sentence context (and often the general context of the text as a whole) and a glance at the word enables the reader to respond instantly" (p. 8). Goodman and Smith argued that unlike fluent readers, poor and beginning readers are less able to make use of contextual redundancy in ongoing sentence processing.

From these assumptions whole language proponents concluded that reading acquisition is largely a process in which children learn to use multiple cues in identifying words in text, with text-based cues (picture cues, semantic sources of information, syntactic sources of information, preceding passage context, prior knowledge activated by the developing meaning of the text) being used mostly to generate hypotheses about the text yet to be encountered and letter-sound information generally being used for confirmation and self-correction (Snow & Juel, 2005; Tracey & Morrow, 2006). Smith and Elley (1994) argued that because language follows a predictable pattern, children "learn to read with minimal input from the text, predicting and confirming and making sense as they go" (p. 142). Children in whole language programs are therefore urged to use sentence context cues as the primary source of information in identifying unfamiliar words, with letter-sound cues being used only very sparingly and mainly to confirm language predictions (Cambourne, 1988; Clay, 1998; Smith & Elley, 1994). As Clay (1998) put it, beginning readers "need to use their knowledge of how the world works; the possible meanings of the text; the sentence structure; the importance of order of ideas, or words, or of letters; the size of words or letters; special features of sound, shape and layout; and special knowledge from past literary experiences *before* they resort to left to right sounding out of chunks or letter clusters or, in the last resort, single letters" (p. 9, emphasis added).

The major shortcoming of this instructional philosophy, however, is that it stresses the importance of using information from many sources in identifying unfamiliar words without recognizing that skills and strategies involving phonological information are of primary importance in beginning literacy development (Perfetti, 1985; Pressley, 2006; Shankweiler & Fowler, 2004). Pressley (2006) argued that "the scientific evidence is simply overwhelming that letter-sound cues are more important in recognizing words…than either semantic or syntactic cues" (p. 21). Aside from the scientific evidence, the validity of this claim becomes almost self-evident when one considers learning to read in a non-alphabetic orthography like Japanese kanji, which is based on borrowed or modified Chinese logographs. It takes 10 to 12 years of devoted study to learn to recognize 1,000 to 2,000 logographs, whereas the average high school student who has learned to read an alphabetic orthography can recognize quickly and accurately 25,000 words or more (Akamatsu, 2006; Gough & Hillinger, 1980). This begs the question of what is the source of this enormous difference? The Japanese student presumably has access to all the same cues (picture cues, word shape cues, sentence context cues, preceding passage content, activated prior knowledge, etc.) as the child learning to read an alphabetic orthography, save one: letter-sound cues. The latter cues clearly make a huge difference in learning to read.

A major difficulty with the theoretical underpinnings of whole language is the assumption that the words of text are highly predictable as a consequence of the developing meaning of text. Research by Gough (1983) has demonstrated that the words that can be predicted in text are typically frequently occurring function words that children can already recognize rather than less frequently occurring but more meaningful content words. The average predictability of content words (nouns, verbs, adjectives) in running text is less than 10%, compared to about 40% for function words (articles, prepositions, conjunctions, pronouns). To illustrate this point, Adams (1991) divided the words of a passage from a typical school text into frequent words (e.g., *when, you, an, to, the, and, he, some*) and infrequent words (e.g., *infection, doctor, penicillin, medicine, discovered, mold, bacteria, disease*) and then asked, "Given a passage constructed of these words, how good would your comprehension be if you read only the frequent while ignoring the infrequent?" (p. 49). Because the information conveyed by words varies inversely with their frequency, the teaching approach recommended by whole language proponents presents us with the following dilemma: while children are taught to rely on the meaning of the passage to infer the meanings of its less familiar words, the meaning of the passage depends disproportionately on the meanings of its *least* familiar and *least* predictable words. A further disadvantage of relying heavily on context to predict words is that not only will this strategy result in missed learning opportunities when context is insufficient to make a prediction, but it will also result in *misleading* learning trials when a prediction is contextually appropriate but nevertheless incorrect. Deficient and misleading data will almost certainly impede progress.

Contrary to Goodman (1967) and Smith's (1978) claim that poor and beginning readers are less able to use sentence context to recognize words as they read, research using discrete-trial reaction tasks (in which children are asked to name words preceded by either congruous, incongruous, or neutral contexts) has shown that the effect of context on speed of word recognition during reading decreases with increasing age, grade level, reading ability, word familiarity and stimulus quality (see Stanovich, 1980, 1984, 1986, for reviews). Studies that have examined accuracy of recognizing words in isolation and in context report a similar pattern of results. Nicholson (1991), for example, found that context aids weaker, younger readers, but is not helpful for better, older readers. These findings suggest that poor readers compensate for their deficient decoding skills by relying more on sentence context to facilitate word recognition (Stanovich, 1980). In contrast, good readers are less reliant on syntactic and semantic information because they are more proficient in using word-level information. Pressley (2006) stated that "perhaps the most disturbing conclusion that comes from this research is that teaching children to decode by giving primacy to semantic-contextual and syntactic-contextual cues over graphemic-phonemic cues is equivalent to teaching them to read the way weak readers read!" (p. 164).

Instruction in the use of letter-sound patterns is usually discouraged or downplayed in whole language programs because English orthography is thought to contain so many irregularities that focusing too much attention on teaching alphabetic coding skills will not only waste valuable time but possibly even confuse children and impede progress (Cambourne, 1988; Smith & Elley, 1994). Smith and Elley (1994) argued that teaching orthographic patterns "is a difficult, unnecessary and largely fruitless activity, creating distorted ideas about the nature and purpose of reading" (p. 143). With regard to orthography-phonology relationships in alphabetic writing systems, English does in fact lie at the low end of the consistency continuum (Ziegler & Goswami, 2005).

In response to the claim that English orthography is too irregular to be of much use, researchers have argued that no word in English is completely phonologically opaque (Gough & Hillinger, 1980; Share, 1995; Tunmer & Chapman, 1998). Even irregularly spelled words like *stomach, castle,* and *spinach* provide accurate phonological cues to the word's identity. Learning to read would certainly be a much more difficult task if spoken words like *stomach* were represented in the orthography as a random sequence of letters (e.g., *omtshca*) rather than as irregular spellings. When beginning readers apply their developing knowledge of spelling-to-sound relationships to unfamiliar irregular words, the result will often be close enough to the correct phonological form that sentence context can be used to arrive at a correct identification, provided that the word is in the child's listening vocabulary (Gough & Hillinger, 1980; Share, 1995).

Evidence in support of this claim comes from a series of studies reported by Tunmer and Chapman (1998, 2006) on the role of context in learning to read. The purpose of the first study was to determine the *potential* contribution of letter-sound knowledge and sentence context to identifying irregularly spelled words and words containing polyphonic spelling patterns (such as *ost* as in *most* and *lost*). Beginning readers achieved an average score of 25% when asked to correct the regularized pronunciations of content words containing irregular or polyphonic spelling patterns (e.g., *stomach* pronounced as *stow-match*). However, when the same mispronounced words were orally presented in (underdetermining) sentence contexts (e.g., "The football hit him in the *stow-match*") in a later test session, the children's average performance more than doubled (66%), suggesting that the letter-sound information contained in irregularly spelled words is potentially very useful, especially when combined with sentence context cues.

In two further studies Tunmer and Chapman investigated the relative contributions of phonological recoding ability and contextual facilitation to early literacy achievement. Share (1995) hypothesized that phonological recoding functions as a self-teaching mechanism that enables beginning readers to acquire word-specific orthographic knowledge after phonologically recoding words a few times. Tunmer and Chapman (1998, 2006) proposed that in addition to phonological recoding ability, beginning readers also use the constraints of sentence context in conjunction with gradually improving phonological recoding skills to identify unfamiliar words in text. In this view the use of sentence context to confirm hypotheses about what unfamiliar words might be, based on incomplete information from partial decoding attempts, results in correct word identifications which, in turn, facilitate the development of sight word (i.e., word-specific) knowledge. Tunmer and Chapman further hypothesized that two cognitive prerequisites are required to make use of these word identification strategies. The ability to use mappings between spelling patterns and sound patterns requires sensitivity to the subcomponents of spoken words (i.e., *phonological sensitivity*), and the ability to use sentence context to supplement information from partial decodings, or to select the correct target among a set of candidate pronunciations generated from polyphonic or irregular spellings, requires sensitivity to the semantic and syntactic constraints of sentence contexts (i.e., *grammatical sensitivity*).

In support of these claims, path analyses of data from a 3-year longitudinal study of factors associated with beginning reading development indicated that the ability to use letter-sound patterns and the ability to use sentence context made the strongest independent contributions to variance in early reading achievement; that the use of letter-sound patterns exerted a stronger influence on reading achievement than the use of sentence context; and that when extraneous variables and autoregressive effects were controlled, phonological sensitivity was the major factor influencing the ability to use letter-sound patterns, and grammatical sensitivity was the major factor influencing the ability to use sentence context. Tunmer and Chapman also found that in addition to obtaining the expected positive correlation ($r = .78$) between phonological recoding ability (as measured by the ability to read pseudowords) and word-specific knowledge (as measured by the ability to read exception words), a scatterplot of the data revealed that there were many children who performed reasonably well on the pseudoword reading test but recognized few exception words (most likely because a few positive learning trials are required to cement the orthographic representations of words in lexical memory; Cunningham, Perry, Stanovich, & Share, 2002; Share, 1995, 1999). However, there were no children who performed poorly on the pseudoword reading test and well on the exception word reading test. These results suggest that phonological recoding ability is necessary (but not sufficient) for the development of word-specific knowledge. A similar pattern of results was reported by Gough and Walsh (1991), who also found that beginning readers with higher levels of phonological recoding skill required fewer trials to learn unfamiliar exception words than did children with lower levels of phonological recoding ability.

A contingency analysis of the data further indicated that not only is letter-sound knowledge necessary for acquiring word-specific knowledge, but it is even necessary for taking advantage of the constraints of sentence context in identifying unfamiliar words in text. Only children who had begun to acquire phonological recoding ability were able to benefit from sentence context. For children with limited phonological recoding ability, context provided little or no help in identifying unfamiliar words, as the words were largely unanalyzed. Beginning readers with good alphabetic coding skills also did not need to rely on context as often as less skilled decoders because of their superior ability to recognize words in isolation, but when they did rely on context to assist them in identifying unknown words, they were much more likely to identify the words than less skilled decoders. That is, beginning readers who were able to generate the regularized pronunciation "stow-match" when presented with the irregular word *stomach* were more likely to identify the word when it appeared in the underdetermining sentence context, "The football hit him in the _____" than children who failed to identify any of the sounds of the word, or perhaps only the sound of the first letter or boundary letters (e.g., "statch").

An important implication of these findings is that instead of teaching children to use sentence context cues as the primary strategy for recognizing unfamiliar words in text (with letter-sounds cues only being used to confirm language predictions), beginning readers should be encouraged to look for familiar spelling patterns first, and to use sentence context cues to confirm hypotheses about what unfamiliar words might be, based on available word-level information. Context should only be used to supplement word-level information, not to substitute for it.

Objections to Phonics

As well as questioning the key theoretical assumptions of whole language, Gough (1996) argued that traditional phonics programs are also based on fundamental misconceptions about the reading acquisition process.

Is Learning to Read Largely Environment Dependent?   Most phonics programs assume that children can only acquire the letter-sound patterns of English orthography (i.e., phonological recoding skill) through direct transmission models of instruction in which the teaching of letter-sound correspondences is explicit and systematic. In this highly structured and teacher-supported approach to instruction the processes of learning to read are assumed to be largely *environment dependent* (Byrne, 2005).

Most traditional phonics programs were developed during the heyday of behaviourism. From the assumptions that learning proceeds in a quantitative fashion according to the basic laws of learning, and that all children acquire skills in essentially the same manner (although at different rates), it followed that children should be taught (i.e., stimulated) in the same way. The challenge for educational researchers was to discover the "best" way. Consequently, early phonics programs focused primarily on the curriculum, which typically included scope and sequence charts, a heavy emphasis on teaching word analysis skills in isolation and in a particular sequence, graded reading materials based on controlled vocabulary and sentence structure, workbook activities, and an overall lock-step, "skill-and-drill" approach to instruction (Calfee & Drum, 1986). Pedagogical constructivism was not a prominent feature of these programs.

In rejecting the underlying assumptions of traditional phonics programs, Gough (1996) argued that there are simply too many letter-sound relationships for children to acquire by direct instruction, probably several hundred (Gough & Hillinger, 1980). Phonological recoding skill, or cipher knowledge, includes not only knowledge of correspondences between single letters or digraphs (e.g., *sh, oa*) and single phonemes, correspondences between groups of letters (e.g., *tion*) and groups of phonemes (e.g., /shun/), and polyphonic spelling patterns (e.g., *ear* as in *bear* and *hear, own* as in *clown* or *flown*), but also knowledge of more complex conditional rules whose application depends on position-specific constraints or the presence of "marker" letters. Cipher knowledge also draws upon morphophonemic rules that speakers of English know implicitly, such as that regular noun plural inflection is realized as /s/ when it follows a voiceless stop consonant, as in *cats*, and as /z/ when it follows a voiced phoneme, as in *dogs*.

Although Gough (1996) strongly held the view that learning to read is not entirely natural, he did agree with whole language proponents in part:

> I think they are partly right, that the child must do a major part of reading acquisition by himself. Indeed, I do agree with them that the child learns to read mainly by reading. As I see it, the main engine of reading acquisition, beyond its beginning, is reading itself. Why

do I say this? As I see it, there are too many spelling-sound correspondences to be taught; we can only teach a small subset of them. The child must induce the rest on her own. (p. 7)

As the reading attempts of beginning readers with a firm understanding of the alphabetic principle become more successful, the orthographic representations of more words become established in lexical memory from which additional spelling-sound relationships can be induced without explicit instruction, a process called *lexicalized phonological recoding* (Thompson, Fletcher-Flinn, & Cottrell, 1999). Once children have reached this point in reading development, they are able to take greater advantage of the positive (rich-get-richer) Matthew effects of reading achievement (Stanovich, 1986), including greater practice opportunities for building fluency and for facilitating implicit learning of additional letter-sound patterns, both of which foster further growth in reading by enabling children to cope with more difficult materials. At this stage of reading development, the most effective way children can become better readers, according to Gough (1996), is by reading. In Gough's view, then, the processes of learning to recognize words are initially *environment dependent* but necessarily become increasingly *learner dependent*.

A prerequisite for the initiation of the process of making greater independent use of letter-sound information to identify unknown words in text is a firm grasp of the alphabetic principle. Gough (1996) argued that "despite its intentions, phonics does not install the cipher; at best, it instills it. It helps many children to discover it" (p. 14). Some explicit phonics instruction may therefore go "a long way" in facilitating the process by which children induce untaught spelling-sound relationships (Juel, 1991, p. 783). As Snow and Juel (2005) put it, "phonics may be useful to children not because of the specific letter-sound relations taught, but because a phonics approach gives children the chance to discover the alphabetic principle, and provides practice looking closely at word spelling" (p. 516). In support of this claim is a considerable amount of evidence that explicit, systematic instruction in the code relating spellings to pronunciations contributes to students' growth in reading (Adams, 1990; Christensen & Bowey, 2005; Oakhill & Beard, 1999; National Reading Panel, 2000; Snow, Burns, & Griffin, 1998). On the basis of an examination of findings from a wide range of sources (e.g., studies of reading development, specific instructional practices, and effective teachers and schools), Snow and Juel (2005) concluded that explicit attention to alphabetic coding skills in early reading instruction is helpful for all children and crucial for some.

The reason that teaching phonics fails to implant the cipher (the spelling-sound relations actually used by fluent readers) is that the rules of phonics bear little or no resemblance to the sublexical relations induced by lexicalized phonological recoding. There are at least four differences between phonics rules and cipher rules (Gough, 1996; Gough & Hillinger, 1980). First, the rules of phonics are explicit (i.e., articulable), whereas the "rules" of the cipher are implicit. Second, the rules taught in phonics are relatively few, whereas cipher rules number in the hundreds. Third, phonics rules are largely context-free, whereas cipher rules are mostly context-sensitive (i.e., depend on position-specific constraints and the presence of other letters). Fourth, phonics rules are slow and laborious to apply, whereas cipher rules operate very quickly and (seemingly) effortlessly. These differences between phonics rules and cipher knowledge draw attention to the need for further research on phonics instruction that investigates "sounding out as problem-solving versus sounding out as an increasingly automatic process that eventually gives way to sight word recognition" (Pressley, Graham, & Harris, 2006, p.12). Pressley et al. suggested that phonics instruction might affect each of these processes differently at different points in instruction.

Evidence in support of the formation of induced sublexical relations (ISRs) by children learning to read comes from research by Thompson and colleagues (Fletcher-Flinn & Thompson, 2004; Thompson, Cottrell, & Fletcher-Flinn, 1996; Thompson & Fletcher-Flinn, 2006; Thompson,

Fletcher-Flinn, & Cottrell, 1999). Consistent with Gough's (1996) claims about the nature of the cipher, they reported that not only were ISRs sensitive to position within the word (e.g., the letter *b* in final position) but also to position-specific constraints and contextual factors. For example, among 6-year-olds, the ISR for the grapheme *y* in final position of 2-syllable words (e.g., *baby, happy*) was distinguished from two other ISRs for *y*, one that depended on position (e.g., *y* in *yes, you*) and the other on context (e.g., *y* in single open syllable words such as *by, my*).

Thompson and colleagues claimed that the nonconscious induction of sublexical relations occurs almost from the outset of learning to read, arguing that this is what must have occurred in New Zealand, where until recently, beginning reading instruction did not include the teaching of explicit phonics or any other systematic instruction in letter-sound relations. In this view the processes of learning to recognize words are largely *learner dependent*, as in whole language. But this assumes that children who learn to read in a whole language setting and who acquire ISRs do not have explicit knowledge of the alphabetic principle when this may not be the case. Based on his own extensive research on this issue, Byrne (2005) expressed doubt that implicit induction of letter-sound mappings can be part of children's earliest contributions to reading development before they have acquired an explicit awareness of the alphabetic principle.

Supporting Byrne's position is research carried out in New Zealand by Tunmer and Chapman (2002) examining the relation of beginning reader's reported strategies for identifying unknown words in text to future reading achievement. Five-year-old beginning readers participating in a 3-year longitudinal study were divided into two groups according to their responses to the following question: "When you are reading on your own and come across a word that you don't know, what do you do to try to figure out what the word is?" The majority of children reported using word-based strategies (e.g., sound it out, think of the sounds, say the letters, do the sounds of it, make the sounds, hear all the letters, listen to what the letters are, you try and get the letters right, you hear the letters, say out the letters, say the sounds in the word, sound it out, dad says so) rather than text-based strategies (e.g., guess, think, guess what the word is, read it over again, read on, have a look at the picture, keep on going, then go back and see what the word is, I leave it, think about the word, try to guess what it is). From these results Tunmer and Chapman concluded, as did Liberman and Liberman (1992), that the instructional approach to teaching reading followed in the classroom (i.e., whole language) is not necessarily reflected in the word identification strategies that the vast majority of children actually use in learning to read. Consistent with this suggestion, the results further showed that the children whose responses indicated a conceptual awareness of the alphabetic principle became the better readers. The beginning readers who reported using word-based strategies outperformed the children who reported using text-based strategies on all reading and reading-related measures taken in the middle of Year 3. Moreover, these children were six times less likely to require Reading Recovery in Year 2 than the children who relied on text-based strategies in Year 1 (6% vs. 37%).

Attention to Phonemic Awareness.   Gough (1996) argued that another major shortcoming of traditional phonics programs (and whole language programs as well) is that insufficient attention is devoted to the development of phonemic awareness, the ability to reflect on and manipulate the phonemic elements of spoken words. To discover mappings between spelling patterns and sound patterns, children must be able to segment spoken words into subcomponents. New school entrants who experience ongoing difficulties in detecting phonemic sequences in words will not be able to fully grasp the alphabetic principle and discover spelling-to-sound relationships. Without specific intervention, the development of word recognition skill in these children will be impeded, resulting in negative (poor-get-poorer) Matthew effects in reading achievement (Stanovich, 1986). Stanovich (1996) succinctly described the causal chain of events leading to reading problems: "Impaired language segmentation skills lead to difficulties in phonological coding which in turn impede the word recognition process which underpins reading comprehension" (p. 155).

Many beginning readers find it extraordinarily difficult to detect phonemic sequences in spoken words, even though they are clearly capable of discriminating between speech sounds and using phonemic contrasts to signal meaning differences (Liberman, 1999). The reason is that "explicit awareness of phonemic structures depends on metalinguistic abilities that do not come free with the acquisition of language" (Shankweiler & Crain, 1986, p. 142). Using a phonemic contrast to signal a meaning difference (e.g., *pig* vs. *big*), which is done intuitively and at a subconscious level, is not the same as the metalinguistic act of consciously reflecting on and manipulating the phonemic elements of speech. Gaining conscious access to phonemic segments is much more difficult for children because there is no simple physical basis for recognizing phonemes in speech (Liberman, Cooper, Shankweiler, & Studdert-Kennedy, 1967). Because phonemic segments do not exist in the acoustic signal per se but must be constructed from it, children must develop the ability to perform cognitive operations on the products of the mental mechanism responsible for converting the speech signal into a sequence of phonemes.

These considerations provide a likely explanation for why many children who have begun formal reading instruction fail to benefit from either letter-name knowledge or letter-sound knowledge in learning to recognize words, and why traditional phonics-based approaches have been repeatedly abandoned over the years in an attempt to find alternative approaches with lower rates of reading failure. Because there is no one-to-one correspondence between phonemes and segments of the acoustic signal, most letter sounds and letter names are only imprecise physical analogues of the phonemes in spoken words. Whether children learn to associate the sound "buh" or the name "bee" or both with the letter *b*, they must still be able to segment the sound or name to make the connection between *b* and the abstract phoneme /b/, which cannot be pronounced in isolation. In support of these claims is a considerable amount of research indicating that training in phonemic awareness during or before reading instruction produces significant experimental group advantages in reading achievement, especially when combined with letter-sound training (Blachman, 2000; Ehri, Nunes, Willows, Schuster, Yaghoub-Zadeh, & Shanahan, 2001; Gillon, 2004; Goswami, 2001; Pressley, 2006; Shankweiler & Fowler, 2004), and including whole language settings (Castle, Riach, & Nicholson, 1994).

Teacher-Centered Instruction and Lock-Step Curricula.   Gough (1996) also criticized traditional phonics programs for being overly teacher-centered and having a curriculum that is typically rigid, fixed, and lock-step, with the same lesson given to every child. The difficulty with such an approach is that children differ in the amount of reading-related knowledge, skills, and experiences they bring to the classroom, in the explicitness and intensity of instruction they require to learn skills and strategies for identifying words, and in where they are located along the developmental progression from prereader to skilled reader. Regarding the latter, learning to read is a process that takes place over time, involves qualitatively different (but perhaps overlapping) phases, and may break down at different points. Developmental theories of how children acquire automaticity in word recognition specify the critical cognitive skills and learning strategies (phonemic awareness, letter knowledge, understanding of the alphabetic principle, use of alphabetic coding skills, exposure to print, etc.) required to progress from one phase of word learning to the next, and provide frameworks for identifying the different learning needs of children according to the phase of reading development they have reached.

Ehri (2005) provided a synopsis of eight developmental theories of learning to read, including her own, which includes four phrases of sight word learning. The *pre-alphabetic* phase involves the use of partial and arbitrary visual cues, or global visual features, to identify words (see previous discussion); the *partial-alphabetic* phase involves connections between more salient letters and sounds; the *full-alphabetic* phase involves complete connections between all the graphemes in words and phonemes in pronunciations; and the *consolidated alphabetic* phase involves connections formed from subword units larger than individual graphemes (e.g., rimes, syllables, morphemes).

An example of how developmental theories of reading acquisition can be used to inform educational practice comes from Iversen, Tunmer, and Chapman (2005). They suggested that a developmental theory such as Ehri's (2005) provides the basis for a likely explanation of the differential effectiveness of Reading Recovery (RR), a popular early intervention program used in several countries. The program appears to be beneficial for some struggling readers but not others, as indicated by the high percentage (up to 30%) of RR students who do not complete the program but, instead, are referred on by their RR tutor for further assessment and possible additional remedial assistance (Elbaum, Vaughn, Hughes, & Moody, 2000).

Iversen et al. (2005) argued that delayed readers who have managed to acquire a working knowledge of the major grapheme-phoneme correspondences and possess a reasonable degree of phonemic awareness are able to execute phonological recoding operations, but only very slowly and laboriously. According to Ehri (2005), these struggling readers have just entered the full-alphabetic phase of word learning and are described as "gluing to print" because they painstakingly sound out and blend letter-sound associations when reading words. For children who have progressed to this increasingly *learner-dependent* phase of reading development, the heavy emphasis on text reading in RR lessons provides them with additional opportunities to apply their developing phonological recoding skills to identifying words. As their reading attempts become more successful, these delayed readers will begin making greater independent use of letter-sound information to identify unfamiliar words in text from which additional spelling-sound relationships can be induced by means of lexicalized phonological recoding. The extra practice in reading provided in RR is therefore likely to be beneficial in helping these struggling readers catch up with their peers.

A large proportion of struggling readers, however, operate at even lower phases of word learning, which Ehri (2005) described as the pre-alphabetic and partial-alphabetic phases. Delayed readers who are still in these phases of development typically have limited or severely limited phonemic awareness and alphabetic coding skills. As noted previously, children who experience ongoing difficulties in detecting phonological sequences in words will not be able to fully grasp the alphabetic principle and discover spelling-to-sound relationships. For these children, more intensive and systematic training in phonemic awareness and phonemically-based decoding strategies is likely to be required than what is typically provided in RR lessons.

Evidence in support of this claim comes from two studies. Iversen and Tunmer (1993) found that the effectiveness of RR could be improved considerably by incorporating into the program more intensive and explicit instruction in phonological awareness and the use of letter-sound relationships (especially orthographic analogies), in combination with strategy training on how and when to use this knowledge to identify words while reading text and to spell words while writing messages. Chapman et al. (2001) found in a longitudinal study of RR that the students who failed to achieve significant progress in the program, and were referred on as a consequence, showed the most severe deficits on all phonological processing measures taken at the beginning of the program, during the year preceding entry into the program, and during the year following referral from the program.

In summary, Gough's (1996) central claim is that both exposure to explicit instruction in phonemic awareness and alphabetic coding skills to engender a firm understanding of the alphabetic principle, and the use of inductive/constructivist processes to acquire implicit knowledge of spelling-sound patterns (i.e., cipher knowledge), are important in learning to read. Although traditional phonics programs have tended to assume that the processes of learning to read are largely *environment dependent* and have therefore adopted more rigid, teacher-centered approaches to instruction, teaching phonics need not be in conflict with constructivist views of learning (Snow & Juel, 2005).

Phonics and whole language both have positive features that can be combined to produce a more effective approach to beginning reading instruction. In teaching word analysis skills, for example, there needs to be a balance between activities designed to facilitate the acquisition of letter-sound knowledge and activities designed to foster an understanding of how to use such knowledge in identifying unknown words in text. In whole language programs, word analysis skills are usually taught as the need arises during instructional reading. However, there are two major advantages in providing beginning and struggling readers with explicit instruction in orthographic patterns and word identification strategies outside the context of reading connected text rather than relying only on "mini-lessons" given in response to children's oral reading errors during text reading. First, instruction in word analysis skills that is deliberately separated from meaningful context allows children to pay full attention to the letter-sound patterns being taught, as well as avoid having their text reading overly disrupted (Morris, Tyner, & Perney, 2000). Second, isolated word study helps to ensure that beginning readers see the importance of focusing on word-level cues as the most useful source of information in identifying words, and to overcome any tendency they may have to rely primarily on sentence context cues in identifying unfamiliar words rather than using context to supplement word-level information.

Providing beginning readers with explicit, systematic teaching of word analysis skills does not mean adopting a rigid skill-and-drill approach in which word identification skills are taught largely in isolation with little or no connection to actual reading. Although beginning readers should receive explicit instruction in letter-sound patterns outside the context of reading connected text, they should also be taught how and when to use this information during text reading through demonstration, modelling, direct explanation, and guided practice. It cannot be assumed that beginning readers who are successful in acquiring word analysis skills will automatically transfer them when attempting to read connected text (Lyon & Moats, 1997). Rather, beginning readers need to be encouraged to become active problem solvers with regard to graphic information in text (Juel, 1991). This includes adopting a set for diversity in which they learn to use irregular and polyphonic spelling patterns and partial decoding attempts to generate alternative pronunciations of target words until one is produced that matches a word in their spoken vocabulary and is appropriate to the sentence context.

Supporting these claims are the results of two studies demonstrating that a balance in the content of supplemental reading programs between out of context training in word analysis skills and opportunities to practice and receive feedback on applying the newly acquired skills during text reading, is more important than the particular approach to teaching reading adopted in the programs (Hatcher et al., 2006; Mathes et al., 2005). Both studies reported similar positive outcomes when comparing the effects of programs based on more highly structured, direct transmission models of instruction with those based on less structured, cognitive strategy-oriented models where the ultimate goal was teaching students to apply the strategies independently. As Mathes et al. (2005) concluded on the basis of their results:

> Perhaps the most important finding of this research is that supplemental intervention approaches derived from different theoretical perspectives were both effective... Both interventions provided for instruction in key reading skills, balanced with opportunities to apply reading and writing skills in connected text... (p. 179)

CURRENT TRENDS AND DIRECTIONS FOR FUTURE RESEARCH

Although children must rely on induction to acquire the phonological recoding skills necessary for learning to read, the amount of explicit instruction in phonemic awareness and phonemically-based decoding strategies needed to "kick-start" the processes of self-teaching (Share, 1995, 1999, 2004) and lexicalized phonological recoding (Thompson & Fletcher-Flinn, 2006) appears to vary considerably across children (Byrne, 2005). For some beginning readers, the processes of acquiring literacy skills are highly *learner dependent*. As Snow and Juel (2005) put it, "many children 'get the point' after having had only a few spelling-sound correspondences taught explicitly" (p. 519). In contrast, for other children the learning processes are more *environment dependent*, with the children requiring a fairly structured and teacher-supported introduction to reading. For children experiencing difficulty in developing the ability to perceive intuitively the systematic connections between speech and print as a by-product of more general reading (Gough, 1996), more intensive instruction in phonemic awareness and alphabetic coding skills is likely to be necessary (Torgesen, 2004, 2005).

What causes such individual differences in literacy learning processes is unclear. Although possible intrinsic factors have been identified (Byrne, 2005), a more likely candidate is differences in essential reading-related knowledge, skills, and experiences (collectively referred to as *literate cultural capital*) at school entry that stem largely from social class/cultural differences in home literacy environment (Pressley, 2006, pp. 126–127). *Literate cultural capital* is a generic term referring to reading-related factors (e.g., letter knowledge) at school entry that are an outgrowth of activities in the home environment that support early literacy development (Tunmer, Chapman, & Prochnow, 2003, 2004, 2006). These *cognitive entry behaviours* (the existing knowledge, skills, and experiences that students have at the outset of learning something new, like reading) vary greatly at school entry (Whitehurst & Lonigan, 2001) and include oral language (promoted by verbal interaction in the home); familiarity with "book" or "decontextualized" language and basic understanding of concepts and conventions of printed language (promoted by adult storybook reading); knowledge of letter names and sounds (developed by exposure to ABC books and games); ability to produce preconventional spellings of words (developed by manipulating movable letters to form "invented" spellings; e.g., writing *color* as KLR, or *fairy* as FRE); sensitivity to the subcomponents of spoken words, or phonological awareness (promoted by playing rhyming and sound analysis games, being read books that increase phonological sensitivity, encouraging use of invented spellings, and exposure to alphabet materials and games; e.g., pig Latin, I spy, nursery rhymes, Dr. Seuss books, ABC books); and sensitivity to the semantic and syntactic constraints of sentence contexts, or grammatical awareness (promoted by verbal interaction in the home, playing language games, engaging in linguistic humor, and being read storybooks).

Children who have such preschool experiences are much better prepared for reading instruction than are children who come to school from language-impoverished environments (Pressley, 2006; Whitehurst & Lonigan, 2001). Weakness in oral language, for example, places an upper limit on reading comprehension (Hoover & Gough, 1990), which would account for research showing that in addition to phonological factors (e.g., phonological awareness), non-phonological oral language factors (e.g., expressive vocabulary, sentence or story recall) are predictive of long-term reading outcomes (Leach, Scarborough, & Rescorla, 2003; Scarborough, 2005). Oral language comprehension becomes more important at later stages of learning to read after children have begun to master basic word identification skills, and when children's reading materials have become more advanced in components of language that are common to both oral language comprehension and reading comprehension (e.g., semantics, syntax, pragmatics).

Vocabulary knowledge, a component of oral language, influences early literacy development in at least two ways. First, vocabulary growth during the preschool years plays a major role in the development of preliterate phonological sensitivity by causing lexical representations to become more segmental (Carroll, Snowling, Hulme, & Stevenson, 2003). Because deficiencies in vocabulary growth are accompanied by more poorly specified phonological representations of spoken words, the development of phonemic awareness is likely to be impaired in children with poorly developed vocabulary knowledge at school entry. Second, children with poorly developed vocabulary knowledge will have trouble identifying and assigning appropriate meanings to unknown printed words, especially partially decoded or irregularly spelled words, if the corresponding spoken words are not in their listening vocabulary (Ricketts, Nation, & Bishop, 2007). This in turn will limit the development of their phonological recoding skills, as additional spelling-sound relationships can be induced from words that have been correctly identified.

During the early stages of reading development, two metalinguistic abilities are required to make use of the two major learning strategies for identifying unfamiliar words in text. As noted previously, the ability to use mappings between spelling patterns and sound patterns requires sensitivity to the subcomponents of spoken words (or phonological awareness), and the ability to use sentence context to supplement information from partial decodings, or to select the correct target among a set of candidate pronunciations generated from polyphonic or irregular spellings, requires sensitivity to the semantic and syntactic constraints of sentence contexts (or grammatical awareness).

Letter-name knowledge is one of the best predictors of beginning reading achievement and appears to contribute to early literacy development in three ways (Foulin, 2005). First, letter-name knowledge serves as a bridge towards understanding the alphabetic principle, as reflected in children's invented spellings (e.g., *da* for *day*, *bl* for *bell*), where the names of letters are used to represent sounds in words. Second, letter-name knowledge acts as a precursor to letter-sound knowledge because the names of most letters contain the phoneme to which the letter normally refers (e.g., the first phoneme of the letter-name /bi/ is /b/). Third, letter-name knowledge facilitates the development of phonological sensitivity, especially when children are exposed to alphabet books and games that increase knowledge of letter names and their relation to sounds in words (e.g., "s" is for snake). Bowey (2005) argued that the influence of letter knowledge and phonological sensitivity on learning to read is inextricably linked, with both serving as *co-determinants* of the acquisition of the alphabetic principle and the development of early word reading.

Children who possess higher levels of these cognitive entry abilities at the beginning of school profit more from reading instruction, learn to read sooner, and read better than children who do not (Whitehurst & Lonigan, 2001). Supporting this claim is a large body of research showing substantial predictive relationships between preschool measures of reading-related skills and later reading achievement (Bowey, 2005; Catts, Fey, Zhang, & Tomblin, 1999; Elbro & Scarborough, 2004; Muter & Snowling, 1998; Scarborough, 2001). In a 7-year longitudinal study, Tunmer, Chapman, and Prochnow (2006) found that a composite measure of literate cultural capital (comprising two measures of phonological awareness, two measures of grammatical awareness, letter-name knowledge, and receptive vocabulary) at the start of school (when the mean age of the children was 5 years, 1 month) accounted for almost 50% of the variance in Year 7 reading comprehension performance after the effects of all other school entry variables were controlled (phonological memory, SES, ethnicity). For the children in the bottom quartile of the literate cultural capital scores at school entry, all were at least one year behind in reading age in Year 7. The average deficit was 2 years, 4 months. The results further indicated that children from low-income and/or culturally diverse backgrounds had considerably less literate cultural capital when they arrived at school than did children from more advantaged backgrounds.

Regarding the latter findings, children from low-income backgrounds seem particularly susceptible to early reading difficulties because they often lack the necessary preschool exposure to the kinds of language play activities and early literacy experiences that promote the development of literate cultural capital. Supporting this claim is research indicating that children from low-income backgrounds begin school with significantly lower levels of literacy-related skills and experiences than children from more advantaged backgrounds (Goldenberg, 2001; Nicholson, 1997, 2003; Phillips & Lonigan, 2005; Snow et al., 1998; Whitehurst & Lonigan, 2001). Home literacy environment appears to be the major contributing factor to these differences in entry-level prereading skills (Hart & Risley, 1995; Korat, Klein, & Segal-Drori, 2007; Morrison

& Cooney, 2002; Nicholson, 1999; Snow et al., 1998). Korat et al. (2007), for example, found that both SES and richness of the home literacy environment were positively associated with children's emergent literacy skills. Sénéchal (2006) argued that the influences of SES and home literacy experiences on early literacy development are best understood in terms of proximal and distal causes, with SES seen as a more distal cause that operates through parenting and home literacy environment.

Although further research is required, the location of children on Byrne's (2005) division of labor continuum at school entry appears to depend largely on the amount of literate cultural capital they possess, with *learner-dependent* children (typically from more advantaged backgrounds) having higher levels of essential reading-related knowledge, skills, and experiences, and *environment-dependent* children (typically from low-income backgrounds) having more limited amounts. A predominantly constructivist, "book experience" approach to reading instruction with a major emphasis on reading of trade books and writing of text (and some incidental teaching of word analysis skills during text reading) is therefore likely to be more suitable for *learner-dependent* children than heavy code-emphasis approaches. However, at-risk, *environment-dependent* children will almost certainly benefit more from reading instruction that includes explicit, systematic teaching of phonemic awareness and phonemically-based decoding strategies outside the context of reading connected text in combination with plenty of opportunities to practice and receive feedback on using these skills during text reading. If these children are not provided with explicit instruction to overcome their weaknesses in school entry reading-related skills, especially phonological awareness, they will likely be forced to rely increasingly on ineffective word identification strategies, such as using picture cues, partial word-level cues, and contextual guessing, which if uncorrected, will ultimately result in negative Matthew effects in reading.

Consistent with these suggestions is research indicating that systematic phonics instruction is particularly beneficial for low SES children (Chall, 1967; National Reading Panel, 2000; Xue & Meisels, 2004). Jeynes and Littell (2000) carried out a meta-analysis of studies examining the effects of whole language instruction on the literacy achievement of children from low-income backgrounds. Overall, the results indicated that less-advantaged children benefited less from whole language instruction than from more skills-oriented, basal instruction, leading the authors to conclude that "using a whole language approach with low-SES children could widen the gap between advantaged and disadvantaged students" (p. 31). Supporting this conclusion are the results of a study by Foorman, Francis, Fletcher, Scatschneider, and Mehta (1998) of the effects of different methods of beginning reading instruction on the reading growth of beginning readers from low-income backgrounds. They found that the degree of explicitness of instruction in the alphabetic code and related skills was positively associated with the amount of improvement in reading, and that more explicit instruction in alphabetic coding resulted in less disparity between students in reading achievement at the end of the year than less explicit approaches to teaching spelling-sound patterns. Hatcher, Hulme, and Snowling (2004) reported that providing supplementary training in phonological awareness to beginning readers in code-oriented classrooms was helpful in enhancing the subsequent reading skills of at risk children (those who entered school with poor vocabulary and poor phonological awareness), but made no difference for children not at risk, suggesting that these children already had sufficient levels of literate cultural capital at school entry to benefit from reading instruction.

Relatedly, Tunmer, Chapman, and Prochnow (2003, 2004) investigated the hypothesis that a comparatively high percentage of reading failures can be triggered by a largely "one size fits all," constructivist approach to beginning reading instruction that fails to respond adequately to differences in essential reading-related skills and knowledge at school entry. In the first of two studies, they found that incorporating into classroom whole language programs supplementary materials and procedures designed to help children develop awareness of sound sequences in spoken words and make greater use of letter-sound patterns in identifying unfamiliar words, produced significantly greater gains in reading achievement than the standard whole language approach to literacy instruction in New Zealand, especially for children from low-income, culturally diverse backgrounds. In the second study they analyzed data from the Progress in International Reading Literacy Study (PIRLS) 2001 (Mullis, Martin, Gonzalez, & Kennedy, 2003) and found that for specified differences in literate cultural capital possessed by children at school entry (as assessed by the Early Home Literacy Activities Index, the Index of Home Educational Resources, and the Index of Parents' Attitudes Toward Reading), the New Zealand whole language approach to literacy education was consistently associated with much larger differences in future reading achievement than most other participating countries. Tunmer and Prochnow (2009) analyzed data from the PIRLS 2006 study (Mullis, Martin, Kennedy, & Foy, 2007) and obtained a very similar pattern of results. Overall, the results of these studies suggest that the literature-based, constructivist approach to teaching literacy in New Zealand is generally beneficial to children with an abundance of literate cultural capital at school entry, but disadvantageous to children with limited amounts of literate cultural capital.

In support of a possible interaction between school entry reading-related skills (high vs. low literate cultural capital) and method of teaching reading (constructivist vs. explicit approaches) are the results of a study by Juel and Minden-Cupp (2000) examining the effects of different instructional emphases on children possessing varying amounts of literacy-related skills at the beginning of school. They found that "children who entered first grade with few literacy skills benefited from a heavy dose of phonics," whereas children who entered first grade with comparatively high levels of literacy and literacy-related skills "did exceptionally well in a classroom that included a less structured phonics curriculum and more reading of trade books and writing of text" (p. 484). Children with limited school entry literacy skills (i.e., *environment-dependent* children) benefited more from explicit, code-emphasis approaches to beginning reading instruction than from whole language/book experience approaches, whereas the opposite pattern occurred with children who had high levels of literacy-related abilities at the beginning of school (i.e., *learner-dependent* children). Perhaps most importantly, Juel and Minden-Cupp reported that "the classroom… that had the very highest success both overall and with the low group had considerably different instruction across the groups" (p. 482).

IMPLICATIONS FOR PRACTICE

This latter finding has important implications for the teaching of reading and preservice teacher training. Rather than focusing on the curriculum (i.e., constructivist vs. explicit approaches) as the key to improving the effectiveness of beginning reading instruction, greater attention may need to be placed on differential (or individualized) instruction, where teachers use research-based assessment procedures and instructional strategies to cater to the differing skill needs of beginning readers from the outset of schooling, with particular attention focused on ensuring the development of phonemically-based word-level skills and strategies by *all* children during the early stages of reading acquisition. Here *skills* refer to declarative, or factual, knowledge, such as that a particular letter or letter sequence makes a particular sound, whereas *strategies* refer to (self-improving) procedural, or "how to" knowledge, which includes understanding how and when to apply letter-sound knowledge in actively solving problems regarding graphic information in text. The ability to determine what instructional approach works best for which children will require high levels of teacher knowledge and professionalism, including knowledge of a conceptual framework for implementing differential instruction in which a cognitive-developmental model of reading acquisition (of the sort described by Ehri, 2005) provides the basis for systematic assessment, the results of which point to appropriate instructional strategies for students with particular needs.

Significant progress in investigating child-by-instruction interactions and the effectiveness of implementing differential instruction in the classroom has been made by Connor and colleagues (Connor, Morrison, & Katch, 2004; Connor, Morrison, Fishman, Schatschneider, & Underwood, 2007; Connor, Morrison, & Petrella, 2004; Connor, Morrison, & Slominski, 2006; Connor, Morrison, & Underwood, 2007). For example, Connor, Morrison, and Katch (2004) found that children who began first grade with below-average reading-related skills made larger reading gains in classrooms that provided greater amounts of teacher-managed, code-focused instruction throughout the year than in classrooms that provided greater amounts of child-managed, meaning-focused instruction. In contrast, for children with higher reading-related skills at school entry, greater growth in reading was achieved in classrooms that provided lesser amounts of teacher-managed, code-focused instruction and greater amounts of child-managed, meaning-focused instruction. On the basis of these and other similar findings, Connor, Morrison, Fishman, et al. (2007) concluded that instructional strategies that may be effective with some students may be ineffective when applied to other students with different skills. In support of this claim, Connor et al. reported that children in first-grade classrooms that individualized reading instruction by taking into account child-by-instruction interactions made greater gains in reading achievement than children in control classrooms.

Although more work needs to be done, a possible outcome of this research is a greater degree of integration of classroom reading programs and programs designed for the prevention and identification of reading disability, such as the recently developed response-to-intervention (RTI) model (Fuchs & Fuchs, 2006; Tunmer, 2008; Tunmer & Greaney, in press). RTI operationalizes "unexpected underachievement" (historically, the central defining feature of the reading disability construct) in terms of both low performance on reading and reading-related measures, and poor response to high quality instruction. Unlike the "wait-to-fail" approach associated with discrepancy-based assessment procedures, the RTI assessment procedure provides the basis for the early identification of students at risk for reading failure. RTI uses evidence-based instruction and continuous progress monitoring across multiple tiers (usually three, see Denton & Mathes, 2003) to provide early intervention for at-risk children and to develop a more reliable procedure for identifying students with reading disability. Regular classroom instruction represents the primary intervention (first tier), small-group tutoring for students demonstrating unsatisfactory progress in the primary intervention represents the more intensive secondary intervention (second tier), and intensive special education for students who respond poorly to the secondary intervention represents the tertiary intervention (third tier). The first tier of RTI models typically involves "enhanced classroom instruction" (Denton & Mathes, 2003, p. 233) where literacy teaching in the earliest years of school addresses the *individual* needs of all of the children in the classroom, especially those experiencing early literacy difficulties.

CONCLUSIONS

In summary, the weight of recent research on the development and teaching of word recognition skill points toward a resolution of the great debate. Whole language and traditional phonics instruction both have serious limitations. Neither approach has been successful in teaching all children to read even though both approaches claim to be the one best size for all. As Gough (1996) has bravely pointed out, it may be time to say "a pox on both your houses." We need to find a better way to teach reading that begins from the very start of schooling. All the evidence suggests that waiting for children to fail is exactly the wrong thing to do. Our interventions do not enable children to catch up (Torgesen, 2005) which makes it imperative that we get it right from Grade 1, or as nearly right as we possibly can.

A key problem facing both whole language and phonics in Grade 1 is that children may not respond to either approach without some phonemic awareness skills, or awareness of the alphabetic principle. We need to address this issue in our provision of classroom instruction by including the teaching of phonemic awareness. We could even teach phonemic awareness before schooling begins so as to create a more level playing field in terms of levels of literate cultural capital among children starting Grade 1. Another problem is that neither whole language nor phonics on its own has the capability to give the right balance of learner-dependent and environment-dependent instruction. Whole language provides plenty of opportunity for children to read but is weak on teaching the alphabetic principle. It is beneficial for children at the learner-dependent end of Byrne's (2005) continuum of learning processes, most of whom are from higher-income backgrounds, but disadvantageous for children at the environment-dependent end. Likewise, phonics gives lots of practice in learning the alphabetic principle but does not provide much opportunity for putting the alphabetic principle into practice through actual reading of text. Phonics is good for children at the environment-dependent end of the continuum, typically children from lower-income backgrounds, but it is weak at the learner-dependent end of continuum, in that it does not give children sufficient opportunity to learn to read by reading.

The research covered in the present chapter suggests that neither whole language nor phonics is suitable for "real world" classrooms that almost always include both learner-dependent and environment-dependent children. Each method in itself is too restrictive but within both methods we have the seeds of an even better one. This new method would not be whole language or phonics. What it would do is enable teachers to draw on the key elements of both approaches to provide instruction that best suits the needs of individual children. How best to do this is the challenge that lies ahead. Whole language and phonics both have excellent features but we need something better, like "whole phonics," a method that can be adjusted to fit the different needs of learners, that will teach all children how to read, no matter whether they are rich or poor, and inspire them to become readers.

REFERENCES

Adams, M. J. (1990). *Beginning to read: Thinking and learning about print*. Cambridge, MA: MIT Press.

Adams, M .J. (1991). Why not phonics and whole language? In W. Ellis (Ed.), *All language and the creation of literacy* (pp. 40–53). Baltimore, MD: Orton Society.

Adams, M. J., & Bruck, M. (1993). Word recognition: The interface of educational policies and scientific research. *Reading and Writing, 5,* 113–139.

Akamatsu, N. (2006). Literacy acquisition in Japanese-English bilinguals. In M. Joshi & P.G. Aaron (Eds.), *Handbook of orthography and literacy* (pp. 481–496). Mahwah, NJ: Erlbaum.

Bergeron, B. S. (1990). What does the term Whole Language mean? Constructing a definition from the literature. *Journal of Reading Behavior, 22,* 301–329.

Blachman, B. A. (2000). Phonological awareness. In M. L. Kamil, P. B. Mosenthal, P. D. Pearson, & R. Barr (Eds.), *Handbook of reading research* (Vol. 3, pp. 483–502). Mahwah, NJ: Erlbaum.

Bowey, J. A. (2005). Predicting individual differences in learning to read. In M. J. Snowling & C. Hulme (Eds.), *The science of reading: A handbook* (pp. 155–172). Oxford, UK: Blackwell.

Byrne, B. (1992). Studies in the acquisition procedure for reading: Rationale, hypotheses, and data. In P. B. Gough, L. Ehri, & R. Treiman (Eds.), *Reading acquisition* (pp. 1–34). Hillsdale, NJ: Erlbaum.

Byrne, B. (2002). The process of learning to read: A framework for integrating research and educational practice. In R. Stainthorpe & P. Tomlinson (Eds.), *Learning and teaching reading. British Journal of Educational Psychology Monograph Series II; Psychological Aspects of Education — Current Trends, 1,* 29–43.

Byrne, B. (2005). Theories of learning to read. In M. J. Snowling & C. Hulme (Eds.), *The science of reading: A handbook* (pp. 104–119). Oxford, UK: Blackwell.

Byrne, B., Freebody, P., & Gates, A. (1992). Longitudinal data on the relations of word-wording strategies to comprehension, reading time, and phonological awareness. *Reading Research Quarterly, 27,* 141–151.

Calfee, R., & Drum, P. (1986). Research on teaching reading. In M.C. Wittrock (Ed.), *Handbook of research on teaching* (pp. 804–849). New York: Macmillan.

Cambourne, B. (1988). *The whole story: Natural learning and the acquisition of literacy in the classroom.* Auckland, New Zealand: Ashton Scholastic.

Carroll, J. M., Snowling, M. J., Hulme, C., & Stevenson, J. (2003). The development of phonological awareness in preschool children. *Developmental Psychology, 39,* 913–923.

Castle, J. M., Riach, J., & Nicholson, T. (1994). Getting off to a better start in reading and spelling: The effects of phonemic awareness instruction within a whole language program. *Journal of Educational Psychology, 86,* 350–359.

Catts, H. W., Fey, M., Zhang, X., & Tomblin, B. (1999). Language basis of reading and reading disabilities: Evidence from a longitudinal investigation. *Scientific Studies of Reading, 3,* 331–361.

Chall, J. S. (1967/1983/1996). *Learning to read: The great debate.* Fort Worth, TX: Harcourt Brace.

Chapman, J. W., Tunmer, W. E., & Prochnow, J. E. (2001). Does success in the Reading Recovery program depend on developing proficiency in phonological processing skills? A longitudinal study in a whole language instructional context. *Scientific Studies of Reading, 5,* 141–176.

Christensen, C. A., & Bowey, J. A. (2005). The efficacy of orthographic rime, grapheme-phoneme correspondence, and implicit phonics approaches to teaching decoding skills. *Scientific Studies of Reading, 9,* 327–349.

Clay, M. M. (1985). *The early detection of reading difficulties* (3rd ed.). Auckland, New Zealand: Heinemann.

Clay, M. M. (1991). *Becoming literate: The construction of inner control.* Auckland, New Zealand: Heinemann.

Clay, M. M. (1998). *An observation survey of early literacy achievement.* Auckland, New Zealand: Heinemann.

Connelly, V., Johnston, R., & Thompson, G. B. (2001). The effects of phonics instruction on the reading comprehension of beginning readers. *Reading and Writing, 14,* 423–457.

Conner, C. M., Morrison, F. J., Fishman, B. J., Schatschneider, C., & Underwood, P. (2007). Algorithm-guided individualized reading instruction. *Science, 315,* 464–465.

Connor, C. M., Morrison, F. J., & Katch, L. E. (2004). Beyond the reading wars: Exploring the effect of child-instruction interactions on growth in early reading. *Scientific Studies of Reading, 8,* 305–336.

Connor, C. M., Morrison, F. J., & Petrella, J. N. (2004). Effective reading comprehension instruction: Examining child X instruction interactions. *Journal of Educational Psychology, 96,* 682–698.

Connor, C. M., Morrison, F. J., & Slominski, L. (2006). Preschool instruction and children's literacy skill growth. *Journal of Educational Psychology, 98,* 665–689.

Connor, C. M., Morrison, F. J., & Underwood, P. S. (2007). A second chance in second grade: The independent and cumulative impact of first- and second-grade reading instruction and students' letter-word reading skill growth. *Scientific Studies of Reading, 11,* 199–233.

Cunningham, A. E., Perry, K. E., Stanovich, K., & Share, D. (2002). Orthographic learning during reading: Examining the role of self-teaching. *Journal of Experimental Child Psychology, 82,* 185–199.

Denton, C. A., & Mathes, P. G. (2003). Intervention for struggling readers: Possibilities and challenges. In B. R. Foorman (Ed.), *Preventing and remediating reading difficulties: Bringing science to scale* (pp. 229–251). Baltimore, MD: York Press.

Ehri, L. C. (1992). Reconceptualizing the development of sight word reading and its relationship to recoding. In P. Gough, L. C. Ehri, & R. Treiman (Eds.), *Reading acquisition* (pp. 107–143). Hillsdale, NJ: Erlbaum.

Ehri, L. C. (1997). Sight word learning in normal readers and dyslexics. In B. Blachman (Ed.), *Foundations of reading intervention and dyslexia: Implications for early intervention* (pp. 163–189). Mahwah, NJ: Erlbaum.

Ehri, L. C. (2005). Development of sight word reading: Phases and findings. In M. J. Snowling & C. Hulme (Eds.), *The science of reading: A handbook* (pp. 135–154). Oxford, UK: Blackwell.

Ehri, L. C., Nunes, S. R., Willows, D. M., Schuster, B. V., Yaghoub-Zadeh, Z., & Shanahan, T. (2001). Phonemic awareness instruction helps children learn to read: Evidence from the National Reading Panel's meta-analysis. *Reading Research Quarterly, 36*, 250–287.

Elbaum, B., Vaughn, S. Hughes, M., & Moody, S. (2000). How effective are one-to-one tutoring programs in reading for elementary students at risk for reading failure? A meta-analysis of the intervention research. *Journal of Educational Psychology, 92*, 605–619.

Elbro, C., & Scarborough, H. S. (2004). Early identification. In T. Nunes & P. Bryant (Eds.), *Handbook of children's literacy* (pp. 339–359). Dordrecht, The Netherlands: Kluwer.

Fletcher-Flinn, C. M., & Thompson, G. B. (2004). A mechanism of implicit lexicalized phonological recoding used concurrently with underdeveloped explicit letter-sound skills in both precocious and normal reading development, *Cognition, 90*, 303–335.

Foorman, B. R., Francis, D. J., Fletcher, J. M., Schatschneider, C., & Mehta, P. (1998). The role of instruction in learning to read: Preventing reading failure in at-risk children. *Journal of Educational Psychology, 90*, 37–55.

Foulin, J. N. (2005). Why is letter-name knowledge such a good predictor of learning to read? *Reading and Writing, 18*, 129–155.

Fuchs, D., & Fuchs, L. S. (2006). Introduction to Response to Intervention: What, why, and how valid is it? *Reading Research Quarterly, 41*, 93–99.

Gillon, G. T. (2004). *Phonological awareness: From research to practice.* New York: Guilford.

Goldenberg, C. (2001). Making schools work for low-income families in the 21st century. In S. B. Neuman & D. K. Dickson (Eds.), *Handbook of early literacy research* (pp. 211–231). New York: Guilford Press.

Goodman, K. S. (1967). Reading: A psycholinguistic guessing game. *Journal of the Reading Specialist, 6*, 126–135.

Goodman, K. S. (1986). *What's whole in whole language: A parent-teacher guide.* Portsmouth, N.H: Heinemann.

Goswami, U. (2001). Early phonological development and the acquisition of literacy. In S. B. Neuman & D. K Dickinson (Eds.), *Handbook of early literacy research* (pp. 111–125). New York: Guilford.

Gough, P. B. (1983). Context, form and interaction. In K. Rayner (Ed.), *Eye movements in reading: Perceptual and language processes* (pp. 203–211). San Diego, CA: Academic Press.

Gough, P. B. (1993). The beginning of decoding. *Reading and Writing, 5*, 181–192.

Gough, P. B. (1996, February). *A pox on both your houses.* Paper presented to symposium on integrated direct instruction in reading, sponsored by the Language Arts Foundation of America and Oklahoma City Schools, Oklahoma City.

Gough, P. B., & Hillinger, M. L. (1980). Learning to read: An unnatural act. *Bulletin of the Orton Society, 30*, 179–196.

Gough, P. B., Juel, C., & Griffith, P. L. (1992). Reading, spelling, and the orthographic cipher. In P. B. Gough, L. C. Ehri, & R. Treiman (Eds.), *Reading acquisition* (pp. 35–48). Hillsdale, NJ: Erlbaum.

Gough, P. B., Juel, C., & Roper-Schneider, D. (1983). A two-stage model of initial reading acquisition. In J. A. Niles & L. A. Harris (Eds.), *Searches for meaning in reading/language processing and instruction* (pp. 207–211). Rochester, NY: National Reading Conference.

Gough, P. B., & Walsh, M. A. (1991). Chinese, phoenicians, and the orthographic cipher. In S. A. Brady & D. Shankweiler (Eds.), *Phonological processes in literacy: A tribute to Isabelle Y. Liberman* (pp. 199–209). Hillsdale, NJ: Erlbaum.

Greaney, K. T., & Ryder, J. (2005). Evidence of phonological-based word identification deficits among children with difficulties. *Set: Research information for teachers, 1*, 2–6.

Hart, B., & Risley, T. R. (1995). *Meaningful differences in the everyday experience of young American children.* Baltimore, MD: Brookes.

Hatcher, P. J., Goetz, K., Snowling, M. J., Hulme, C., Gibbs, S., & Smith, G. (2006). Evidence for the effectiveness of the Early Literacy Support programme. *British Journal of Educational Psychology, 76*, 351–367.

Hatcher, P. J., Hulme, C., & Snowling, M. J. (2004). Explicit phonological training combined with reading instruction helps young children at risk of reading failure. *Journal of Child Psychology and Psychiatry, 45,* 338–358.

Harm, M. W., & Seidenberg, M. S. (1999). Phonology, reading acquisition and dyslexia: Insights from connectionist models. *Psychological Review, 106,* 491–528.

Hoover, W. A., & Gough, P. B. (1990). The simple view of reading. *Reading and Writing, 2,* 127–160.

Huey, E. B. (1908/1979). *The psychology and pedagogy of reading.* Cambridge, MA: MIT Press.

Hulme, C., Snowling, M. J., & Quinlan, P. (1991). Connectionism and learning to read: Steps toward a phonologically plausible model. *Reading and Writing, 3,* 159–168.

Iversen, S. A., & Tunmer, W. E., (1993). Phonological processing skill and the Reading Recovery program. *Journal of Educational Psychology, 85,* 112–125.

Iversen, S., Tunmer, W. E., & Chapman, J. W. (2005). The effects of varying group size on the Reading Recovery approach to preventative early intervention. *Journal of Learning Disabilities, 38,* 456–472.

Jenkins, J. R., Fuchs, L. S., van den Broek, P., Espin, C. & Deno, S. L. (2003). Sources of individual differences in reading comprehension and reading fluency. *Journal of Educational Psychology, 95,* 719–729.

Jeynes, W. H., & Littell, S. W. (2000). A meta-analysis of studies examining the effect of whole language instruction on the literacy of low-SES students. *The Elementary School Journal, 101,* 21–33.

Jorm, A., & Share, D. (1983). Phonological recoding and reading acquisition. *Applied Psycholinguistics, 4,* 103–147.

Juel, C. (1991). Beginning reading. In R. Barr, M. L. Kamil, P. D. Pearson, & P. Mosenthal (Eds.), *Handbook of reading research* (Vol. 2, pp. 759–788). New York: Longman.

Juel, C., Griffith, P. L., & Gough, P. B. (1985). Reading and spelling strategies of first-grade children. In J. A. Niles & R. Lalik (Eds.), *Issues in literacy: A research perspective* (pp. 306–309). Rochester, NY: National Reading Conference.

Juel, C., & Minden-Cupp, C. (2000). Learning to read words: Linguistic units and instructional strategies. *Reading Research Quarterly, 35,* 458–492.

Korat, O., Klein, P., & Segal-Drori, O. (2007). Maternal mediation in book reading, home literacy environment, and children's emergent literacy: A comparison between two social groups. *Reading and Writing, 20,* 361–398.

Leach, J. M., Scarborough, H. S., & Rescorla, L. (2003). Late-emerging reading disabilities. *Journal of Educational Psychology, 95,* 211–224.

Liberman, A. M. (1999). The reading researcher and the reading teacher need the right theory of speech. *Scientific Studies of Reading, 3,* 95–112.

Liberman, A. M., Cooper, F. S., Shankweiler, D. P., & Studdert-Kennedy, M. (1967). Perception of the speech code. *Psychological Review, 74,* 431–461.

Liberman, I. Y., & Liberman, A. M. (1992). Whole language versus code emphasis: Underlying assumptions and their implications for reading acquisition. In P. Gough, L. Ehri, & R. Treiman (Eds.), *Reading acquisition* (pp. 343–366). Hillsdale, NJ: Erlbaum.

Lyon, G. R., & Moats, L. C. (1997). Critical conceptual and methodological considerations in reading intervention research. *Journal of Learning Disabilities, 30,* 578–588.

Masonheimer, P., Drum, P., & Ehri, L. C. (1984). Does environmental print identification lead children into word reading? *Journal of Reading Behaviour, 16,* 257–272.

Mathes, P. G., Denton, C. A., Fletcher, J. M., Anthony, J., Francis, D. J., & Schatschneider, C. (2005). The effects of theoretically different instruction and student characteristics on the skills of struggling readers. *Reading Research Quarterly, 40,* 148–182.

Morris, D., Tyner, T., & Perney, J. (2000). Early steps: Replicating the effects of a first-grade reading intervention program. *Journal of Educational Psychology, 92,* 681–693.

Morrison, F. J., & Cooney, R. (2002). Parenting and academic achievement: Multiple paths to early literacy. In J. Borkowski, S. Ramey Landesman, & M. Bristol-Power (Eds.), *Parenting and the child's world: Influences on academic achievement and social-emotional development* (pp. 141–160). Mahwah, NJ: Erlbaum.

Mullis, I. V. S., Martin, M. O., Gonzalez, E. J., & Kennedy, A. M. (2003). *PIRLS 2001 International Report.* Boston: International Study Center, Lynch School of Education, Boston College.

Mullis, I. V. S., Martin, M. O., Kennedy, A. M., & Foy, P. (2007). *PIRLS 2006 International Report.* Boston: International Study Center, Lynch School of Education, Boston College.

Muter, V., & Snowling, M. (1998). Concurrent and longitudinal predictors of reading: The role of metalinguistic and short-term memory skills. *Reading Research Quarterly, 33,* 320–335.

National Reading Panel. (2000). *Teaching children to read. An evidence-based assessment of the scientific research literature on reading and its implications for reading instruction.* Washington, DC: National Institute for Child Health and Human Development.

Nicholson, T. (1991). Do children read words better in context or in lists? A classic study revisited. *Journal of Educational Psychology, 83,* 444–450.

Nicholson, T. (1997). Closing the gap on reading failure: Social background, phonemic awareness, and learning to read. In B. A. Blachman (Ed.), *Foundations of reading acquisition and dyslexia: Implications for early intervention* (pp. 381–407). Mahwah, NJ: Erlbaum.

Nicholson, T. (1999). Literacy in the family and society. In G. B. Thompson & T. Nicholson (Eds.), *Learning to read: Beyond phonics and whole language* (pp. 1–22). New York: Teachers College Press.

Nicholson, T. (2000). *Reading the writing on the wall: Debates, challenges and opportunities in the teaching of reading.* Palmerston North, New Zealand: Dunmore Press.

Nicholson, T. (2002). The social and political contexts of reading: Contempory literacy policy in Aotearoa New Zealand. In P. Adams & H. Ryan (Eds.), *Learning to read in Aotearoa New Zealand* (pp. 22–50). Palmerston North, New Zealand: Dunmore Press.

Nicholson, T. (2003). Risk factors in learning to read. In B. Foorman (Ed), *Preventing and remediating reading difficulties: Bringing science to scale* (pp. 165–193). Timonium, MD: York Press.

Oakhill, J., & Beard, R. (1999). *Reading development and the teaching of reading.* Oxford, UK: Blackwell.

Perfetti, C. A. (1985). *Reading ability.* New York: Oxford University Press.

Perfetti, C. A. (1991). The psychology, pedagogy, and politics of reading. *Psychological Science, 2,* 70–76.

Perfetti, C. A. (1992). The representation problem in reading acquisition. In P. Gough, L. Ehri, & R. Treiman (Eds.), *Reading acquisition* (pp. 107–143). Hillsdale, NJ: Erlbaum.

Phillips, B. M., & Lonigan, C. J. (2005). Social correlates of emergent literacy. In M. J. Snowling & C. Hulme (Eds.), *The science of reading: A handbook* (pp. 173–187). Oxford, UK: Blackwell.

Pinker, S. (1994). *The language instinct: How the mind creates language.* New York: Harper Perennial.

Pressley, M. (2006). *Reading instruction that works: The case for balanced teaching.* New York: Guilford Press.

Pressley, M., Graham, S., & Harris, K. (2006). The state of educational intervention research as viewed through the lens of literacy instruction. *British Journal of Educational Psychology, 76,* 1–19.

Ricketts, J., Nation, K., & Bishop, D. V. M. (2007). Vocabulary is important for some, but not all reading skills. *Scientific Studies of Reading, 11,* 235–357.

Scarborough, H. S. (2001). Connecting early language and literacy to later reading (dis)abilities: Evidence, theory, and practice. In S. B. Neuman & D. K. Dickinson (Eds.), *Handbook of early literacy research* (pp. 97–110). New York: Guilford.

Scarborough, H. (2005). Developmental relationships between language and reading: Reconciling a beautiful hypothesis with some ugly facts. In H. W. Catts & A. G. Kamhi (Eds.), *The connections between language and reading disabilities* (pp. 3–24). Mahwah, NJ: Erlbaum.

Sénéchal, M. (2006). Testing the home literacy model: Parent involvement in kindergarten is differentially related to Grade 4 reading comprehension, fluency, spelling, and reading for pleasure. *Scientific Studies of Reading, 10,* 59–87.

Shankweiler, D., & Crain, S. (1986). Language mechanisms and reading disorder: A modular approach. *Cognition, 24,* 139–168.

Shankweiler, D., & Fowler, A. E. (2004). Questions people ask about the role of phonological processes in learning to read. *Reading and Writing, 17,* 483–515.

Share, D. L. (1995). Phonological recoding and self-teaching: *Sine qua non* of reading acquisition. *Cognition, 55,* 151–218.

Share, D. L. (1999). Phonological recoding and orthographic learning: A direct test of the self-teaching hypothesis. *Journal of Experimental Child Psychology, 72,* 95–129.

Share, D. L. (2004). Orthographic learning at a glance: On the time course and developmental onset of self-teaching. *Journal of Experimental Child Psychology, 87,* 267–298.

Smith, F. (1978). *Understanding reading.* New York: Holt, Rinehart & Winston.

Smith, J. W. A., & Elley, W. B. (1994). *Learning to read in New Zealand.* Auckland, New Zealand: Longman Paul.

Snow, C. E., Burns, M. S., & Griffin, P. (1998). *Preventing reading difficulties in young children.* Washington, DC: National Academy Press.

Snow, C. E., & Juel, C. (2005). Teaching children to read: What do we know about how to do it? In M. J. Snowling & C. Hulme (Eds.), *The science of reading: A handbook* (pp. 501–520). Oxford, UK: Blackwell.

Stanovich, K. (1980). Toward an interactive-compensatory model of individual differences in the development of reading fluency. *Reading Research Quarterly, 16,* 32–71.

Stanovich, K. (1984). The interactive-compensatory model of reading: A confluence of developmental, experimental and educational psychology. *Remedial and Special Education, 5,* 11–19.

Stanovich, K. E. (1986). Matthew effects in reading: Some consequences of individual differences in the acquisition of literacy. *Reading Research Quarterly, 21,* 340–406.

Stanovich, K. E. (1994). Constructivism in reading education. *The Journal of Special Education, 28,* 259–274.

Stanovich, K. E. (1996). Toward a more inclusive definition of dyslexia. *Dyslexia, 2,* 154–166.

Tan, A., & Nicholson, T. (1997). Flashcards revisited: Training poor readers to read words faster improves their comprehension of text. *Journal of Educational Psychology, 89,* 276–288.

Thompson, G. B., Cottrell, D., & Fletcher-Flinn, C. (1996). Sublexical orthographic-phonological relations early in the acquisition of reading: The knowledge sources account. *Journal of Experimental Child Psychology, 62,* 190–222.

Thompson, G. B., & Fletcher-Flinn, C. M. (2006). Lexicalised implicit learning in reading acquisition: The Knowledge Sources theory. In C. M. Fletcher-Flinn & G. M. Haberman (Eds.), *Cognition and language: Perspectives from New Zealand* (pp. 141–156). Bowen Hills, Queensland: Australian Academic Press.

Thompson, G. B., Fletcher-Flinn, C. M., & Cottrell, D. S. (1999). Learning correspondences between letters and phonemes without explicit instruction. *Applied Psycholinguistics, 20,* 21–50.

Torgesen, J. K. (2004). Lessons learned from research on interventions for students who have difficulty learning to read. In P. McCardle & V. Chhabra (Eds.), *The voice of evidence in reading research* (pp. 355–382). Baltimore, MD: Brookes.

Torgesen, J. K. (2005). Recent discoveries on remedial interventions for children with dyslexia. In M.J. Snowling & C. Hulme (Eds.), *The science of reading: A handbook* (pp. 521–537). Oxford, UK: Blackwell.

Tracey, D. H., & Morrow, L. M. (2006). *Lenses on reading: An introduction to theories and models.* New York: Guilford.

Tunmer, W. E. (2008). Recent developments in reading intervention research: Introduction to the Special Issue. *Reading and Writing, 21,* 299–316.

Tunmer, W. E., Chapman, J. W. (1998). Language prediction skill, phonological recoding ability and beginning reading. In C. Hulme & R. M. Joshi (Eds.), *Reading and spelling: Development and disorder* (pp. 33–67). Hillsdale, NJ: Erlbaum.

Tunmer, W. E., & Chapman, J. W. (2002). The relation of beginning readers' reported word identification strategies to reading achievement, reading-related skills, and academic self-perceptions. *Reading and Writing, 15,* 341–358.

Tunmer, W. E., & Chapman, J. W. (2006). Metalinguistic abilities, phonological recoding skills, and the use of sentence context in beginning reading development: A longitudinal study. In R. M. Joshi & P. G. Aaron (Eds.), *Handbook of orthography and literacy* (pp. 617–635). Mahwah, NJ: Erlbaum.

Tunmer, W. E., Chapman, J. W., & Prochnow, J. E. (2003). Preventing negative Matthew effects in at-risk readers: A retrospective study. In B. Foorman (Ed.), *Preventing and remediating reading difficulties: Bringing science to scale* (pp. 121–163). Timonium, MD: York Press.

Tunmer, W.E ., Chapman, J. W., & Prochnow, J. E. (2004). Why the reading achievement gap in New Zealand won't go away: Evidence from the PIRLS 2001 international study of reading achievement. *New Zealand Journal of Educational Studies, 39,* 127–145.

Tunmer, W. E., Chapman, J. W., & Prochnow, J. E. (2006). Literate cultural capital at school entry predicts later reading achievement: A seven year longitudinal study. *New Zealand Journal of Educational Studies, 41,* 183–204.

Tunmer, W. E., & Greaney, K. T. (2010). Defining dyslexia. *Journal of Learning Disabilities, 43,* 229–243.

Tunmer, W. E., & Prochnow, J. E. (2009). Cultural relativism and literacy education: Explicit teaching based on specific learning needs is not deficit theory. In R. Openshaw & E. Rata (Eds.), *The politics of conformity in New Zealand* (pp. 154–190). Auckland, New Zealand: Pearson.

Vellutino, F. R., Scanlon, D. M., & Jaccard, J. (2003). Toward distinguishing between cognitive and experiential deficits as primary sources of difficulty in learning to read: A two year follow-up of difficult-to-remediate and readily remediated poor readers. In B. Foorman (Ed.), *Preventing and remediating reading difficulties: Bringing science to scale* (pp. 73–120). Baltimore, MD: York Press.

Vellutino, F. R., Scanlon, D. M., Sipay, E. R., Small, S. G., Pratt, A., Chen, R. S., et al. (1996). Cognitive profiles of difficult to remediate and readily remediated poor readers: Early intervention as a vehicle for distinguishing between cognitive and experiential deficits as basic causes of specific reading disability. *Journal of Educational Psychology, 88*, 601–638.

Whitehurst, G. J., & Lonigan, C. J. (2001). Emergent literacy: Development from prereaders to readers. In S. B. Neuman & D. K. Dickinson (Eds.), *Handbook of early literacy research* (pp. 11–29). New York: Guilford Press.

Xue, Y., & Meisels, S. J. (2004). Early literacy instruction and learning in kindergarten: Evidence from the early childhood longitudinal study – kindergarten class of 1998–1999. *American Educational Research Journal, 41*, 191–229.

Ziegler, J. C., & Goswami, U. (2005). Reading acquisition, developmental dyslexia, and skilled reading across languages: A psycholinguistic grain size theory. *Psychological Bulletin, 131*, 3–29.

19 The Teaching and Learning of Critical Literacy

Beyond the "Show of Wisdom"

Peter Freebody
The University of Sydney, Australia

Jill M. Freiberg
Griffith University, Queensland, Australia

> Literacy in any society is not just a matter of who could read and write, but one of how their skills function, and of the adjustments—mental, emotional, intellectual, physical and technological—necessary to accommodate it.
>
> (McKitterick, 1990, p. 5)

INTRODUCTION: RULES, STANDARDS, AND IRRITATIONS

Critical literacy is a term that covers a range of attempts on the part of educators to prepare young people for societies that conduct much of their daily business via texts—not only much of their information exchange and training, but also much of their governance, organisation, and ethical and moral acculturation. These societies rely on texts and widespread literacy capabilities to liberate and oppress, to inform and obscure. They generally prefer to conduct and legitimate much of their day-to-day politics, orderliness, conciliation, and violence via textual practices. In McKitterick's terms, it is necessary to accommodate, formally, through education, to these distinctively contemporary uses of literacy.

In this chapter we briefly introduce the idea of critical literacy, contrast it with other forms of literacy and literacy education, and give some illustrations of research that point both to the need for some version of critical literacy education and to some of its more promising forms. Our chapter pursues the idea that the most productive view of critical literacy is that it refers to a distinct and growing body of technical knowledge about textuality. This comprises knowledge of texts in a range of modalities, textual interpretation, construction and evaluation, and critical understandings about the reflexive relationship of interpretation to both textual and social practices and structures. We argue here that critical literacy educators and their students need to work toward building this cumulative, integrated body of knowledge.

We begin our discussion with one of Western culture's icons of critical inquiry. In his extensive introduction to the early dialogues conducted by Socrates, Saunders (1987) pointed out that Socrates used to insist on a number of conditions before engaging in any dialogue about the qualities of human behaviour. First and, for Socrates, foremost, was that, when responding to his queries and comments, his interlocutors must tell the truth, including all the relevant truth, as best they could. Second, Socrates insisted that speakers not merely dwell on specific instances of a human quality but also attempt to come to terms with general concepts, continuously working the relationship between anecdotal specificities and abstract generalities. Socrates worked on the principles that ethical, moral, social, ideological, and political issues could be systematically analysed and, further, that such systematic analyses, rather than pastimes, were an integral part of the good private and public life. In the end, these principles came at a high price:

Socrates did not die just because he was an irritating conversationalist … He died at least partly because of his philosophy. Many ancient Greeks, like many people today, believed i) that in technical matters there are indeed fixed rules and standards, which depend on a body of exact knowledge, possessed by various practitioners; ii) that this is not the case in moral, social and political questions, in which one man's opinion and standards are in principle as valid as another's, so that individuals and states may legitimately adopt whatever moral principles and practices convenience or exigency dictates … Socrates agreed with (i), but used it to undermine (ii). (Saunders, 1987, pp. 33–34)

Literacy educators are often taken aback to learn that Socrates saw the written word as an obstacle to this project, a project he regarded as resolutely dialogic in nature: The give-and-take of disputation, however difficult, was a necessary component of the cause of promoting deeper understanding. Socrates could not read or write, nor could he see how the written word could advance his program for subjecting human behavior—its ethics, morality, ideology, and politics—to the "rules and standards" of analysis:

Writing will produce forgetfulness in the minds of those who learn to use it … you give your students not truth, but only the appearance of truth; they will read many things and will have learned nothing; they will therefore seem to know many things, when they are, for the most part, ignorant and hard to get along with, having the show of wisdom without the reality. (Socrates in dialogue with Phaedrus, Sections 275e–276b, reported by Plato, 360 BCE)

Teachers, researchers, and policy makers seriously engaging the literacy-dependency of present-day societies and their schools confront, in one way or another, Socrates' warning about the written word. Critical literacy educators have invested effort in trying to spell out that concern, and to find ways of having students learn how to work explicitly with ethical, moral, social, ideological, and political questions as part of how they learn to read and write.

In most contemporary societies, much of the heavy duty of teaching and learning reading and writing occurs in schools and other similar institutional settings. These institutions, along with the societies that sustain them, have become seriously text dependent. A generation of literacy researchers ago, the eminent educational psychologist David Olson roundly declared, "schooling is a matter of mediating the relationship between children and the printed text" (1977, p. 66). At issue in literacy debates are the nature, purposes, and boundaries of such mediations. Schools typically provide settings for students to re-articulate what they read in such a way that this re-articulation passes as an accurate and, in some settings, an authentic personal expression. Teachers' reliance on set textual materials is foundational to most contemporary schooling, and yet the real currency-exchange for students' achievement in schools is the acceptability of their apparently accurate and personal re-renderings of those textual materials.

So a chapter such as this needs to concern itself not just with various definitions and versions of critical literacy, but also with the nature of the educational settings into which such a notion finds its way: How can an apparently undomesticated notion such as critical literacy function in educational settings, especially formal settings such as schools? Whatever else they may be, schools are places in which everyday talk, written texts, social structures, and institutional imperatives are generally so seamlessly coordinated that the ways in which they benefit and constrain teachers and students and their activities seem natural—not, at first glance, a habitat conducive to a collection of interruptive knowledge, practices, and dispositions that might come under the heading of critical literacy. But the position we outline in this chapter is that schools need to do with critical literacy what they do best—(a) develop it as a body of coherent, cumulative knowledge focused on the nature and evaluation of interpretation of text, and (b) revisit this knowledge in a spiralling manner across curriculum domains and through the school years.

BACKGROUND: VERSIONS OF LITERACY

Treating literacy as a cultural technology itself constitutes the beginnings of a critical perspective. Such a recognition immediately brings with it an appreciation that there are majority and minority answers to questions such as: what is literacy? What it is for? What other personal or community attributes are associated or enabled by literacy? How do schooled versions of literacy differ from unschooled versions, and so on (Freebody & Freiberg, 2008)? It also becomes clear, as we ask such questions, that not all kinds of literacy users get to research, teach, and set policy about literacy. So a perennial issue for literacy educators, most notably curriculum designers, is the accommodations made by those who do not have access to decisions about publicly acceptable definitions of literacy and its benefits and uses. For instance, when Levinson (2007) encountered hostility toward school-based literacy education among English Gypsies, in light of the usually invisible and often secret knowledge, understandings, and practices of communities that underpin reading and writing activities, he was led to "speculate as to the alternative literacies that we have all forfeited" (p. 33).

In what terms does an inquiry into critical literacy proceed? Fundamentally, why are there different forms of literacy and where have they come from? How do scholars and educators currently distinguish between different forms of literacy teaching and learning? Here we summarize three approaches to developing a vocabulary for describing and debating different kinds of literacy: definitional, disciplinary, and paradigm approaches. We outline these dimensions of variability in literacy to place critical literacy in this broader conceptual setting and thereby give some sense of what kind of descriptor it is.

Definitions of Literacy

Here is a collection of influential definitions of literacy.

1. A person is literate when he [*sic*] has acquired the essential knowledge and skills which enable him to engage in all those activities in which literacy is required for effective functioning in his group and community, and whose attainments in reading, writing and arithmetic make it possible for him to continue to use these skills towards his own and the community's development. (cited in Oxenham, 1980, p. 87)
2. Literacy is a characteristic acquired by individuals in varying degrees from just above none to an indeterminate upper level. Some individuals are more literate or less literate than others, but it is really not possible to speak of literate and illiterate persons as two distinct categories. (UNESCO, 1957, p.18)
3. The concepts "functional literacy" and "functional illiteracy" were introduced to distinguish the higher-order level of abilities that separates those who are barely able to read and write ("basic illiterates") from those who are able to use their skills to function fully in the workplace, the community, and at home ("functional literates"). (Center for Educational Research and Innovation, OECD, 1992, p. 18)
4. Following the regional hearings, the [US National Reading] Panel considered, discussed, and debated several dozen possible topic areas and then settled on the following topics for intensive study:
Alphabetics
    Phonemic Awareness Instruction
    Phonics Instruction
Fluency
Comprehension
    Vocabulary Instruction

Text Comprehension Instruction

Teacher Preparation and Comprehension Strategies Instruction

Teacher Education and Reading Instruction

Computer Technology and Reading Instruction (US National Reading Panel Summary, 2002)

5. Effective literacy is intrinsically purposeful, flexible and dynamic and involves the integration of speaking, listening and critical thinking with reading and writing. (Department of Employment, Education and Training, 1991, p. 5)

6. Literacy refers to an individual's ability to read, write, speak in English, compute and solve problems at levels of proficiency necessary to function on the job, in the family of the individual and in society. (US Department of Labor, Employment and Training, *Workforce Investment Act*, 1998)

7. Using printed and written information to function in society, to achieve one's goals, and to develop one's knowledge and potential. This definition [of literacy] attempts to encompass a broad set of information processing skills that adults may use in performing different types of tasks at work, at home, or in their communities. Some other types of knowledge and skill (including teamwork, interpersonal skills, and other communication skills) were also recognized as being important but could not be measured with the resources available. (Murray, Kirsch, & Jenkins, 1996, p. 17)

8. Literacy is a complex set of abilities needed to understand and use the dominant symbol systems of a culture—alphabets, numbers, visual icons—for personal and community development ... In a technological society, literacy extends beyond the functional skills of reading, writing, speaking and listening to include multiple literacies such as visual, media and information literacy. These new literacies focus on an individual's capacity to use and make critical judgments about the information they encounter on a daily basis. [L]iteracy ... is an essential foundation for learning through life, and must be valued as a human right. (Center for Literacy, Quebec, Canada, 2008)

9. Literacy is a shorthand for the social practices and conceptions of reading and writing. (Street, 1984, p. 1)

10. While the search for a single, universal definition of literacy is based on misguided premises, there is value in seeking to elucidate the distinctive features of particular *literacies*. (Roberts, 1995, p. 230)

It is commonplace to note changes in definitions of literacy (Resnick & Resnick, 1977; Venezky, 1984). These changes have been related to differing times and cultural settings (Kaestle, 1991), differing technologies of literacy (Lankshear, Green, & Snyder, 2000), the differing functions of literacy in any given society (McKitterick, 1990), and the changing significance of literacy for individuals and collectives (Harris, 1989).

In scanning the definitions above, we can also note some critical variations concerning literacy: as one part of a dichotomy or a continuum; as a collection of personal attributes and skills or social practices. Some of these definitions are in fact open-textured, relying on context, in particular those that give pride of place to such attributes as effectiveness, functioning, appropriateness, personal goals, and so on. It is also informative to consider these definitional variations in terms of how well they allow their authors to pursue some practical action—teaching, testing, writing a curriculum, or implementing a policy. Definition number 7 is most overt in this regard, acknowledging the relevance of "other types" of features and then setting those aside as unmeasurable. Clearly, the contexts of practical activity in which these definitions were produced offered both opportunities and constraints. In light of the comment on defining literacy shown in number 10, we need to regard any definition of such an open-textured collection of cultural technologies and processes not just as a description but also as both a pragmatic starting point and an intervention in practice, research, and policy.

Disciplinary Variations in Concepts of Literacy

Disciplines of study provide another setting in which differences in the concept of literacy can be seen. Practitioners of different disciplines have worked up a literacy that is best suited to their particular conceptual and methodological crafts (see Freebody, 2008, for a more detailed description of these differences).

Examinations of earlier volumes of this and similar collections show that the mainstream approaches to reading, writing, and literacy used to be housed within Psychology. Many productive contributions continue to emerge from that setting. Much of the work drawn together under the US National Reading Panel (2000), for instance, shows that, while there are varieties in methodological approaches evident in the research summarized, these tend to reflect differences in approaches among the practitioners of psychology—experimentalists, psychometricians, cognitivists, developmentalists, learning theorists of various schools, and so on. Psychological approaches tend to view reading and writing as essentially internal mental processes whose explication can help teachers operate more effectively. Linguistic and cultural diversity tend not to clutter psychological accounts too much, although some recent collections on reading and diversity (Bernhardt, 2003; Joshi & Aaron, 2006) take some serious account of these.

Significant advances have been made since the early 1980s in developing the potential contribution of linguistics to literacy education. These advances have included: (a) a strong and effective critique of the dominance of narrative in literacy education (Martin, 1989); (b) literacy, language and classrooms pedagogy (Christie & Martin, 2007; Gee, 1991, 2005; Kucer, 2005); and (c) curriculum literacies in classrooms (Kress, Jewitt, Ogborn, & Tsatsarelis, 2001; Unsworth, 2004). Linguistics has also informed critical literacy education through a connection with critical discourse analysis, especially those forms and techniques developed through the sustained analytic work of Fairclough (e.g., Fairclough, 2001, Fairclough & Chouliaraki, 1999; Fairclough, Pardoe, & Szerszynski, 2006).

Major input into the development of the concept of critical literacy has come from educators working in the critical traditions of sociology. Sociologists are fundamentally concerned with questions about social order: how it is to be understood, how it is possible, and how it is maintained or disrupted. In that regard, many critical sociologists have called for approaches to literacy education that inform learners of the role of particular texts, texts in general, and literacy in general in those ordering processes. The specific nature of the critique provided by these educators has shaped the kinds of analyses of and recommendations for literacy education that they have provided. Emphasized have been the roles played by literacy education in the development of an economically and politically preferred citizenry (e.g., A. Luke, 1988; Uhlmann, 2008), in the production of a historically new set of discourses about childhood (C. Luke, 1989), in gender relations (Lee, 1996; Luttrell, 1996; Smith, 1999), and in race relations (Greene & Abt–Perkins, 2003; Willis, 2008).

Similarly, historians have documented the uses and spread of literacy across various timespans and geographic regions, such as ancient Greece and Rome (Harris, 1989; Robb, 1994), medieval Europe (McKitterick, 1990) and 20th-century North America (Graff, 1995; Kaestle, 1991). Graff has argued that important lessons from the history of literacy include caution concerning claims about its psychological, societal, and economic benefits, a realistic understanding of how readily educational practices can be changed in contemporary institutional settings, and an empirically adequate account of the diversity of literacy practices (Graff, 2001). He warned about the consequences of marginalizing historical studies of literacy:

The limits imposed by a neglect of the quietly present past mark their records as impressively as their achievements. Repetition is least among the costs of failing to learn from history; if only we might repeat the course! (p. 10)

Anthropological approaches to the study of literacy have similarly focused on the contrast between, on the one hand, the diversity of literacy practices in both mainstream and minority subcultures and, on the other, the restrictive range of literacy practices taught and assessed in educational institutions (Heath & Street, 2008; Prinsloo & Breier, 1996; Rogers, 2003; Stein & Mamabolo, 2005), along with more general anthropological analyses of literacy in action in daily life (e.g., Barton & Hamilton, 1998; Heath, 1983; Street, 1984).

Each of these disciplines of study recasts a workable notion of literacy into an object amenable to its conceptual and methodological preferences. Each affords a distinctive cut beneath the surface of a concept deeply taken for granted in most contemporary societies, particularly by the speakers of the prestigious dialects of those societies and those who have access to adequate educational provision. Each definition thereby continues to develop its own contribution to our understandings of literacy and the inter-relationships among interpretation, textuality and texts, and social practices and structures.

Orientations to Literacy

Work within and across each of these informing disciplines can be further clustered into particular orientations surrounding the nature, functions, and special benefits of literacy. In examining influential texts and teaching practices in the area, drawing from across a range of disciplines, it is possible to identify three general orientations (after Gilbert, 1989) that have shaped the institutionalized study of literacy: (a) literacy for growth, (b) cultural heritage literacy, and (c) a variety of approaches under the heading responsive literacy, which we describe below as *correct literacy*, *appropriate literacy*, and *critical literacy*. By the middle of the 20th century, the term *literacy* was not prominent as a topic or organizer of research and teaching. Much that was researched and written about literacy came generally under three other headings: English, reading, and composition. (*Adult literacy* was generally used to refer to workplace training, remedial reading and composition, or English reading and composition for speakers of languages other than the language of instruction.) The orientations we summarize here reflect this.

Informed primarily by the traditions of teaching subject English in schools and universities are a range of ideas about literacy that can be grouped together under the heading of *cultural heritage literacy*. This position holds that the fundamental function of literacy is to provide a guided exposure to the valued literary works of that language's history, works that are motivated by an orientation to aesthetic experience and the aim of exploiting the imaginative capacity of language. Teaching young people to read and write fundamentally is taken here to be about cultivating a particular kind of psychological reaction. Literacy here affords access to this heritage and these forms of responsiveness, however construed, as a way of establishing a notion of cultural level, and countering the potentially coarsening effects of popular culture and functional human existence. An influential report to the British government shortly after World War I and the Bolshevik revolution in Russia made the case most forcefully:

We claim that no personality can be complete, see life steadily and see it whole, without that unifying influence, that purifying of the emotions which art and literature can alone bestow. It follows then from what we've said above, that the bulk of our people, of whatever class, are unconsciously living starved existences. (Newbolt Report, 1921, p. 257, cited in Mellor & Patterson, 2005, p. 466)

A member of the committee that wrote that report later commented on the significance of a literature-based education for the maintenance of social order in Britain:

> Deny to working-class children any common share in the immaterial and presently they will grow into the men who demand with menaces a communism of the material. (Sampson, 1925, p. x)

The "immaterial" that could tame "men who demand with menaces" was embodied in a slowly evolving, safely "historical" canon of works. Toward the middle of the 20th century, the idea of the canon was under challenge from a number of sources, initially in Anglophone countries, from a form of liberal humanism. This informed the development of a version of literacy education that may be termed *literacy for growth*. In this orientation, literacy was seen as providing students with an arena in which they could explore the social and psychological worlds in which they live, and grow and develop their personal understandings and sensitivities to that world. This was taken to occur principally through guided encounters with texts tailored to afford such understandings and sensitivities (Dixon, 1967). The focus here is on the development of deeper and more finely nuanced psychological interiors that function to offer individuals sources of understanding that can guide their activities and relationships, through a heightened sense of self, itself a product of an ideology of feeling. The notion of literacy's role as developing such individuals via a moral and aesthetic program is a notion we now see to have been transitional between the importance of the literary canon and a growing sense of *student-centeredness* in education.

A third orientation has developed alongside these from sources generally outside subject English. This we may term the *responsive* orientation because it has as its centerpiece the proposition that the purposes, contents, and processes of teaching literacy are finally justified by reference to some set of demands that the society presents to adults. Educational discourses currently show three forms of this. The first of these comprises skills-based training approaches, and sets of atomistic skills relating to the consumption and production of texts are the focus. The skills found in this body of work (e.g., Adams, 1990; Snow, Burns & Griffin, 1998) have to do with managing the variety of conventions for the production of written texts: spelling, punctuation and layout conventions, for example. This includes skills to do with the understanding and use of conventional grammatical formations and even conventional textual macro-structures, such as the learning of narrative or expository text-types or genres (e.g., Meyer et al., 2002). The essential response to the language and literacy demands that face an individual is the response of correctness in the management of the graphic product, as a reader or writer. The product of this first form of responsive literacy education we may therefore term *correct literacy*.

A second version of the responsive orientation places the varying social and cultural functions of literacy at the center of the domain of study. In this respect, correctness is re-embedded in social and cultural appropriateness. The proficient user of text is now a person with a broad lexical, grammatical and textual repertoire, along with a heightened sensitivity to the variations of genre and register called for in different communicative situations. The product of this form literacy education we may term *appropriate literacy*. Several of the definitions listed above have a core notion of appropriate functioning in the various contexts of literacy societies:

> The possession of skills perceived as necessary by particular persons and groups to fulfil their own self-determined objectives as family and community members, citizens, consumers, job-holders, and members of social, religious, or other associations of their choosing. This includes the ability to obtain information they want and to use that information for their own and others' well-being; the ability to read and write adequately to satisfy the requirements they set for themselves as being important for their own lives; the ability to

deal positively with demands made on them by society; and the ability to solve the problems they face in their daily lives. (Hunter & Harmon, 1979, p. 7)

Central here is dealing with the texts encountered and called for by the practical social and cultural contexts in which they play a part (Martin, 2007; Martin & Rothery, 1981). Specific forms of textual practice, oral and written, are evaluated in terms of their efficacy and the breadth and flexibility of their application, as instances of socio-cultural practice:

> One cannot understand text without understanding the system from which it derives, and one cannot measure success without considering the kind of language that is appropriate in different types of context. Good writing is writing whose grammar, lexis, and discourse structure realise the kind of communication demanded by a given register. (Martin, 1980, p. 29)

A third variant of the responsive paradigm is the focus of this chapter, critical literacy. That is, we see critical literacy as an extension of a general orientation to literacy that we call here responsive, in that it is called for by the material realities of human experience and by the social, ideological, and linguistic processes by which those realities are understood and addressed. Here correctness and appropriateness are put to this form of responsiveness.

ELABORATING CRITICAL LITERACY

For school students, literacy is high stakes; much of their success is achieved through the production of texts, mostly in print and graphic formats based generally on texts they have read. A question that arises is: Can some genuine version of critical literacy take place in educational settings? In these settings students do not actually need to believe what they read, but they do need to display that they can produce a "believing writer" as an act of assessable interpretation. That is, they need to display a version of themselves as readers compliant within the terms of the specific curriculum area at hand, questioning reading materials only when, and in the ways, that a history- or mathematics- or fine-arts-conscious reader would question them. Their talk and their writing need to re-embody the beliefs of the text as evidenced in the discourses, topics, and resources of the text. By and large, however questionable the textual materials used in schooling may be, their selection is aimed at affording pedagogies and assessments that do not call for multiple interpretations—even in curricula incorporating some form of critical literacy (Mellor & Patterson, 2005).

For purposes of this discussion, we divide the various educators working with critical literacy education into four families, reflecting emphases on (a) developing dispositions and habits, (b) providing pedagogy and procedure, (c) encouraging ideology critique, and (d) developing coherent bodies of technical knowledge about interpretation and textual mechanisms for shaping and constraining interpretive possibilities.

Critical Literacy as Dispositions and Habits

In an influential exposition on critical literacy, Shor (1992) gave the following description of its key features:

> Habits of thought, reading, writing, and speaking which go beneath surface meaning, first impressions, dominant myths, official pronouncements, traditional clichés, received wisdom, and mere opinions, to understand the deep meaning, root causes, social context,

personal ideology, and personal consequences of any action, event, object, process, organization, experience, text, subject matter, policy, mass media, or discourse. (p. 129)

We can note a number of issues about this approach, issues that will recur in the following discussion. First, critical literacy is seen here as a resolutely personal, individualized attribute. Second, its activation is needed because of suspicions about the validity of everyday experience. Finally, it is about habits of mind, rather than about the development and application of knowledge about texts and their social and ideological significance.

The literate person here is fundamentally a reader and writer whose capabilities are designed to protect against the regulative work done by and through the technologies of language, especially writing. It is clear that such approaches derive from a theorization of the literacy demands the educated person will face. But these demands are now recast: They are no longer merely technical or sociocultural, but rather, fundamentally and effectively, nothing but ideological. The essential response to these literacy demands is one of awareness of and potential resistance to the ideological work done by texts.

The nature and significance of these demands was described most compellingly by the South American adult literacy educator who has become associated with the foundations of the modern critical literacy movement:

> In accepting the illiterate as a person who exists on the fringe of society, we are led to view him as a sort of "sick man," for whom literacy would be the "medicine" to cure him, enabling him to "return" to the "healthy" structure from which he has become separated. Educators would be benevolent counsellors, scouring the outskirts of the city for the stubborn illiterates, runaways from the good life, to restore them to the forsaken bosom of happiness by giving them the gift of the word ... These men, illiterate or not, are, in fact, not marginal ... the solution to their problem is not to become "beings inside of," but men freeing themselves; for, in reality, they are not marginal to the structure, but oppressed men within it. Alienated men, they cannot overcome their dependency by "incorporation" into the very structure responsible for their dependency ... the illiterate is no longer a person living on the fringe of society, a marginal man, but rather a representative of the dominated strata of society. (Freire, 1972, p. 28)

Unlike Shor, Freire worked with a collective rather than an individuated notion of human agency through literacy practice. Nonetheless, both began with a view that managing texts is always potentially both problematic and liberating, and always reflects the workings of politicized cultural experience (e.g., Freire & Macedo, 1987; Seigel & Fernandez, 2000). Guiding, through reading, and production, through writing, of interpretive possibilities are viewed here as relational processes, always entailing relations of power and generally interested in disguising, naturalizing, or neutralizing those relations. The emphasis here, the "primary unit of analysis" (Morgan & Ramanathan, 2005), is the identity of the reader as he or she encounters the discourses constituting the text.

Critical Literacy as Pedagogy and Procedure

The argument has also been developed that working with texts and textual practices is necessary but not sufficient in delivering the aspirations of most forms of critical literacy (e.g., Iyer, 2007). Rather, critical literacy needs, in this formulation, to be viewed as essentially a pedagogy of inclusion (and see Pennycook, 2001), and in contrast, some text-bound forms of critical literacy can be counterproductive in the case of many of the students in classrooms. Iyer argued that it is in the pedagogies in which they participate that students have most at stake in terms of their identities, not just in the texts they work with or what they might come to understand about those texts.

The notion that critical literacy is at its heart a feature of pedagogy has also been developed by Lewison, Flint, and Van Sluys (2002), who examined lessons in school subject English (Darvin, 2007, studied lessons in mathematics and science with a similar orientation). For Lewison et al., critical literacy in the classroom can be analyzed into the following four dimensions of criteria: (a) disrupting the commonplace, (b) interrogating multiple viewpoints, (c) focusing on sociopolitical issues, and (d) taking action and promoting social justice. While these things are taken to happen around texts, the kinds of specifically textual practices that emerge as the portable knowledge from the educational experiences remain unclear.

Critical Literacy as Ideology Critique

The early provenance of critical literacy lies in political awareness and action among adult literacy students (as in Freire & Macedo, 1987), and a simultaneously emerging dissatisfaction with the perception that language and literacy can be considered and thus taught as neutral, merely technical competencies. This combination of activism and dissatisfaction opened up, from their various disciplinary outlooks, the notion that texts and teaching practices both reflect and sustain class structures, along with the gendered, racialized, and cultural environments in which they operate (Devine, Savage, Scott, & Crompton, 2005). The position was well articulated by Hagood (2002):

> What is central to critical literacy that focuses on identity is the influence of the text and specifically of identities in texts on the reader. The text, imbued with societal and cultural structures of race, class, and gender, marks the site of the struggle for power, knowledge, and representation. (pp. 250–251)

In drawing these various approaches together, Janks (2000) identified four inter-related lines of ideology work in critical literacy education, focusing on (a) the role of literacy education in analyses of cultural and political domination; (b) access to powerful ways of knowing and communicating; (c) understanding the significance of linguistic, dialectical, and cultural diversity; and (d) learning the role of literate communication in the design of learners' personal and social futures. These preoccupations have evolved differently in different disciplinary and professional sites. Advocates and practitioners have included writers, teachers, and policy makers in universities, colleges and schools, grouped generally under the banners of social, linguistic, humanities, and cultural studies. Active as well have been policy makers, curriculum developers and evaluators in education-oriented civil-service units.

A question arises concerning how teachers and educational researchers may act on the complexity and potential importance of this outline of critical literacy education. How can students be resourced to contribute meaningfully to such issues? What knowledge bases might be developed such that some viable exchange about, say, race, class, and gender, can actually take place in ways that provide portable knowledge with which to avoid defeat in subsequent combative encounters with texts?

Further questions concern the outcomes of seeing texts as sites of "the struggle for power" and interpretations as expressions of self-identity. First, there is an implication here that interpretation can be "won," clinched by one or another set of members of a category of race, class, and gender. While texts have been used routinely this way, and still are in many cultural and political settings, it seems to us that, although it may be this realization that motivates teachers and learners to engage in some form of critical activity, it does not constitute doing critical literacy or becoming critically literate. It may animate the learning, but what that learning may actually comprise remains unaccounted for. Second, the characterization of interpretation as an expression of self-identity has serious implications for critical evaluations of those interpretations. Both of these implications ignore the effort that matters and is portable, which is the development of resources for both the production and evaluation of multiple situated interpretations.

A SELECTION OF ILLUSTRATIVE RESEARCH ON THE TEACHING AND LEARNING OF CRITICAL LITERACY

Current debates and research programs in many countries center on the place of critical literacy within educational institutions and programs, the relationship between the forms of literacy education needed in new cultural, political, economic, and technological conditions, and the ways in which literacy education practices are implicated in processes of identity construction. Three examples of research projects associated with these debates are briefly outlined below. The goal here is to supplement recent summaries and reviews (Beach, Green, Michael, & Shanahan, 2005; Franzak, 2006; Freebody, 2008; Siegel & Fernandez, 2000), and to broaden the purview to include productive instances of research activity around the question of the teaching and learning of critical literacy.

A more specific intention is to provide some examples of research in and around the issue of the qualitative distinctions between kinds of literacy education experiences and programs as a way of (a) documenting the need for the systematic development of a range of resources, and (b) demarcating the kinds of resources we may regard as comprising a critical literacy program, even when the researchers themselves do not use this term.

Critical Theoretical Knowledges and Practices

In an extensive and distinctive review of research and policy literature, Franzak (2006) attempted to show the relationships among four questions about contemporary literacy education:

1. What theoretical paradigms currently influence literacy education practices in language/literacy classrooms?
2. What does qualitative research show about the reading habits and values of adolescent readers?
3. What inferences can be drawn, therefore, about the experiences of students struggling with reading at school?
4. How do reading policies address struggling adolescent readers?

Franzak (2006) reviewed U.S. empirical studies and significant policy documents from the major research databases, including studies that documented literacy learners' experiences. One of his key conclusions was that the research literature strongly suggests that marginalized adolescent readers tend to read "submissively" (and see Moje, Young, Readence, & Moore, 2000), which is to say, they give the text authority, expecting it to provide its meanings unequivocally and effortlessly, rather than engaging in an active, dialogic exchange with the text. This may be described as a dispositional practice, but two questions arise: What reliable knowledge about a text, texts in general, or reading and writing makes this apparently unacceptable "submissiveness" a problem? What do writers and text designers do to make submissiveness a plausible reading attitude in the first place? That is, some basic, reliable technical knowledge is needed even to begin questioning the appropriateness of "submission" from occasion to occasion.

Franzak's (2006) review demonstrated the theoretical, practical, and policy value of the realization that the real literacy question concerns the kinds of literacy on offer, not how much.

It also mounts a strong argument about young people as the targets and products of policy. But for the most part, what is striking is that Franzak's review of the body of work on marginalized adolescent readers showed that the studies and their recommendations were virtually all missing any reference to a coherent theory of knowledge—knowledge about literacy, texts, and interpretation and the relationships among them. Instead, studies focused on explaining success of failure in literacy learning:

1. As a result of individual culture-based attitudes and dispositions or inherent person-based abilities or aptitudes, what Alvermann (2001) deemed to be the "deprivation approach."
2. As a result of the breadth of textual experience and therefore, interpretive schemata or procedures for making sense of texts.
3. As an effect of curriculum, especially of text selection.
4. As an effect of pedagogy and the degree to which pedagogical practices (a) enhance individuals' abilities to "take ownership" of the reading process, (b) ensure effective levels of student engagement, and (c) enhance portable knowledge of reading strategies and procedures, and the likelihood of their sustained and flexible use.

Franzak's (2006) review revealed a broadly based perspective that views literacy and literacy pedagogy as personal mastery of a set of procedures and practices, and critical literacy as a set of more cognitively complex procedures and practices, rather than a coherent body of disciplinary knowledge.

Critical Technical Knowledges

In an inquiry into the impact of a secondary language arts program in the United States, Hobbs and Frost (2003) used a field experiment to study students' reading, listening ,and viewing comprehension, writing, and message-analysis skills. Participating in the study were Year 11, predominantly White students, some of whom made up a control group matched for socioeconomic status and parental occupation. The control group undertook a conventional media literacy course of study designed by their teachers. Hobbs and Frost were interested in whether or not a program explicating the nature of information representation in text—visual, spoken and written—could impact on their analytic responses to multimodal media texts. They collected data on the students' pre- and post-tests on comprehension of audio news commentaries and print magazine articles, a sample of the students' writing about these texts, and students' answers to analytical questions on a brief media message.

Briefly, Hobbs and Frost (2003) found that, after controlling for the two groups' differences in overall grade averages, the intervention group scored significantly higher than the control group on the reading comprehension measures, locating main ideas and identify key details; that they also performed reliably higher on listening and viewing comprehension in the multimodal sessions; and, importantly for our purposes, that they also were reliably better at recognizing how authors used such techniques as revealing point of view and omitting information to achieve their purposes in writing.

This study did not examine teachers' specific instructional techniques, but it does indicate the immediate effects of the explication of technical knowledge about how interpretation is influenced by strategic moves on the part of authors of multimodal texts:

> This study finds that students who received media-literacy instruction were more likely to recognize the complex blurring of information, entertainment, and economics that are present in contemporary nonfiction media. (Hobbs & Frost, 2003, p. 351)

Critical Procedural Knowledges

Finally, we turn to a review by Kuiper, Volman, and Terwel (2005). They reviewed a large number of empirical and theoretical studies in the research literature from 1997 to 2003 from major educational databases. Their focus was on the demands that the use of the Web as an information resource makes on the support and supervision of students' learning processes. Their impression was that many educationalists took it for granted that young adolescents' apparent familiarity and fluency with digital technologies implied a commensurate degree of intellectual and literacy capability. The educationalists turned out to be wrong.

The conclusions of Kuiper et al. (2005), from the vantage of an interest in critical literacy, were sobering. They found, for instance, that the children and adolescents studied often had difficulty locating information, lacked skills in exploring Websites, and focused on trying to find one answer to each question; that they rarely looked at the reliability or authority of the information they had found; and that, in a profound sense, these young people lacked the skills to decipher the vast amounts of information they were able to find. Kuiper et al. argued on this basis that young people must be helped to acquire search skills and the skill to make some purposeful judgements about the information they find.

From these findings and recommendations, we might conclude that new technologies and the growing use of online learning environments can increase rather than diminish the urgency of critical literacy education. They provide a warrant for education that maximizes opportunities for dialogic, educative reflection on the validity of interpretations of the materials found on the Internet, in a sense bringing Socrates' complaint about the "show of wisdom" forward a couple of millennia into the digital age. It seems that such a critical literacy program needs to go well beyond focusing on basic reading and writing training, reading resistantly, or locating the gaps and silences in a text. Though certainly relying on developed knowledge of linguistic, structural, and ideational technologies of texts, it also needs to focus on critical evaluations of situated, motivated texts and interpretative productions, using those same technical knowledge resources.

These three studies establish at least the plausibility of themes running through many literacy research circles around the concept of bodies of knowledge: that this knowledge does not come free with the acquisition of speaking and listening, or with basic reading and writing skills, but rather calls for active, extended effort on the part of educators. A future for critical literacy can be envisaged only in terms of a renewed commitment to the development, coordination, and curricular animation of such bodies of knowledge, and to making it known that those bodies of knowledge are now available, that they are contestable, and that they are amenable to curricular organization.

CRITICAL LITERACY AS A BODY OF TECHNICAL KNOWLEDGE: STUDYING INTERPRETATION

Here we briefly outline our preferred position: that critical literacy needs now to be productively viewed as a distinct and growing body of technical knowledge about textuality and texts, as artifacts of literate social practices. This body of knowledge provides critical knowledge and processes for interrogating specific, situated interpretations as motivated and purposeful productions.

Bernstein (2000) explored the characteristics of *hierarchical knowledge structures* that build and integrate knowledge over time and *horizontal knowledge structures* in which new ideas are segmentally aggregated, rather than integrated. This notion of segmented versus cumulative learning has provided a strong source for critiquing curriculum and schooling more generally. We take the equity implications of integrated, cumulative learning to relate to educational equity as well as to expertise and economic and cultural well-being (Bernstein, 2000).

Here we outline some of the components we believe should make up an integrated curriculum on the topic of critical literacy, candidate bodies of vertical knowledge that can offer a serious program of literacy education over extended periods, are (a) textual forms and technologies; texts and interpretations as analysable productions' (b) textual and literate practices as social practices: texts and interpretations as context-relevant, motivated social actions; and (c) reflexivity: texts and interpretations as productive.

TEXTUAL FORMS AND TECHNOLOGIES: TEXTS AND INTERPRETATIONS AS ANALYZABLE PRODUCTIONS

Here we include knowledge about different forms of communication and how they can variously build and obscure their semantic commitments in a range of modalities (e.g., Fairclough, 2001). Lemke (1998, 2002), for instance, has inquired into the significance of different forms of meaning-making for different kinds of communication: different resources provide different strengths and weaknesses. In particular, Lemke (2002) drew a distinction between resources relating to typological (meaning by kind) and topological (meaning by degree). Each category of resources is organized around a certain type of meaning-making. Language, Lemke showed, is a typologically oriented resource, especially good at formulating difference and describing relationships, essentially at making categorical distinctions, and chaining together causes and effects. Other visual semiotic resources, he showed, are better at "formulating degree, quantity, gradation, continuous change, continuous co-variation, non-integer ratios, varying proportionality, complex topological relations of relative nearness or connectedness" (Lemke, 1998, p. 87). Lemke showed that in reading and writing, it is in the interplay between modalities that crucial categorizations about the social and material world are made, and made as natural and unproblematic affordances of meaning.

Textual and Literate Practices as Social Practices: Texts and Interpretations as Context-Relevant, Motivated Social Actions

Historians and sociologists with an interest in historical forms of literacy education have documented the effects of the changing purposes to which the technologies of literacy have been put (e.g., Kaestle, 1991) and will be put in the years ahead (Warschauer, 2003). Many of these effects can be conceptualized in terms of the relationship between the production of a certain type of readerships and social structures.

Active participation in a literacy-saturated society involves an understanding of literacy's special role in socialization, that is, in the particular ways in which a society strives systematically to conjoin private, individual interests, motivations, and concerns with public, organizational and administrative interests and structures. Literacy has a special part to play in making the public personal and vice versa. For individuals and communities, therefore, encountering the texts around them involves, among other things, drawing them into relations of ruling and being ruled, and aligns their interests with particular formations within social organization (Smith, 1987). Texts are integral to the operation of many everyday settings, such as people's contractual, civic commitments and their dealings with government and other public institutions; because of that, along with practical work, texts simultaneously organize social relations, and, thereby, do ideological, moral, and political work. In contemporary societies, the need is for the production and need for a critical citizen-reader and -writer, as well as a reading citizenry:

Challenges such as climate change call for more and even more capable environmental scientists; perhaps more critically in democratic societies ... they call for voters who understand the role of science ... a discipline-aware populace that constitutes a more sophisticated "lay" readership, better positioned to make personal, community, and political choices. (Freebody, Martin, & Maton, 2008, p. 199)

Viewing literacy as an open-textured, variable concept raises questions about the qualities of human ability and practice: What *kinds* of literate citizens and workers does a society encourage and equip through its educational systems? How do these qualities of capacity and disposition compare to what that society wants and needs? Contemporary societies present particular tensions between individual agency, community participation, and social responsibility. In literacy-dependent societies, it is the ways in which people learn to read and write, and what they learn about reading and writing, that are consequential for how these tensions might be ignored, intensified, or resolved.

Reflexivity: Texts and Interpretations as Productive

A variety of research programs have shown ways in which both texts and interpretive activities are productive of social practices and structures. Freebody and Zhang (2008), for instance, used recently developed forms of image analysis (Kress & van Leeuwen, 2006) to examine the interrelationship of image and language in the very first school reading books given to beginning students in the People's Republic of China. Their interest was partly in the contrast between the contents of these readers and the materials given to beginning school students in the West. One of their conclusions was that the Western materials remained concerned with images and language that was resolutely everyday (Freebody & Baker, 1985). The potentially remarkable was made unremarkably relevant to the apparent lives of the young children. The contrast with the Chinese materials was striking in this regard:

> In the Chinese corpus we find an apprenticeship that entails revisiting the "everyday" and restructuring it in particular ways, in this case, as "extraordinary," so that extraordinary phenomena, such as the flag-ceremony, Tiananmen Square, ancient scenes and texts, become ordinary, ritualised, predictable parts of the new public world afforded by learning to read. The materials of the mundane are re-encountered via the crafting of words and images that re-invest the everyday with gravity and transcendence; beginning readers, as part of learning to read, learn to invest their families, their games, their schooling, and their "being Chinese" with a monumental and luminous quality. (Freebody & Zhang, 2008, p. 44)

The structures of images and language and the juxtaposition of ancient and modern, near and far, and everyday and remarkable, all afforded these interpretations from the most elementary, and yet most informative, school texts. As in the texts studied by Freebody and Baker (1985), these patterns indicate the programmatic nature of literacy acculturation.

Stuckey, a researcher and adult literacy educator, documented, in her *The Violence of Literacy* (1991), how researchers and policy makers claimed that illiteracy was a cause rather than a consequence of institutionalized poverty and social injustice. For Stuckey, the ways in which literacy education is provided now implicated literacy in the myth of a classless society, at the expense of poor and disenfranchised groups. Many literacy research and implementation programs, she argued, merely served to deflect attention away from the real barriers to social mobility. Stuckey's experience as a literacy worker, her research on the impact of adult literacy programs, and her analysis of the conditions of teaching adult literacy led her to an ideological conclusion similar to that of Freire, but with a more direct and pragmatic focus on the economic conditions of all concerned. She found that adult literacy programs usually failed to take serious account of the basic realities of the lives of their clients, that most of these programs were developed and sourced from outside the target communities, and that they typically had transient volunteers as staff.

Similarly, Graff's (1995) analysis of the literacy myths indicated the ways in which literacy is used as a talisman of modernity and progress, or at least the aspiration of progress. This is not new. As Harris (1989) described, in the high period of the Roman Empire literacy was a code term for morality, respectability, and, to put it as bluntly as Cicero, speaking Latin correctly. It is a small step to literacy league tables that produce rankings of students, teachers, schools, educational jurisdictions, and even nations.

CONCLUSION

Advocates and practitioners of critical literacy are critical of conventional literacy education, the neutral, purely technical version of literacy it reflects, and the propositions it refuses to entertain. Six refusals characterize conventional, individualized, naturalized understandings of literacy and literacy education (cf. Luke & Freebody, 1997):

1. The refusal of the idea of a fully literate person as anything other than technically competent. Corollary to this are (a) the refusal to recognize the emergence of anything other than perceptual and cognitive competence in learners, and (b) the refusal to dismiss a child-like nostalgia for correct literacy as necessary and sufficient for functioning in modern societies.
2. The refusal of literacy teaching as anything other than a technical challenge, and its key resources, semiotic objects, as neutral media for communication.
3. The refusal of discipline- and curriculum-specific forms of literacy as anything other than topical and shallow procedural variations on a basic, generic literacy.
4. The refusal to acknowledge the significance of the reading-writing relationship in developing membership of a literate society. Corollary to this are (a) the equation of literacy with reading (as in the Australian National Inquiry into the Teaching of Literacy, 2005), and (b) a refusal of literacy as entailing agency—production and participation—as well as consumption of texts.
5. A refusal of the collective force of forms of interpretation in reading and writing and of collective literacy activity as a political, civil, and vocational resource.
6. A refusal of the sociological concept of a readership, a community of interpretation, and communities that contest interpretation.

We have tried to locate critical literacy among its near relatives, to give some understanding of its place in the broader educational effort. Further, we have located our own position within a set of ideas about critical literacy. We have tried to point to what we see as the next direction, rather than to simply summarize the valuable work that has gone before. The argument we put here is that the term *critical literacy* covers a distinctive body of curricular knowledge, with application across a broad range of current school subjects, on the matter of knowledge about textual practices to do with reading, constructing, analysing, and evaluating texts and interpretations of texts. Further, this body of knowledge is the most significant and portable knowledge a learner can take from educational experiences. Its significance lies in the increasingly complex and powerful ways in which learners can learn to evaluate interpretation and thus reflexively read their own personal histories of interpretation into the varying accounts they encounter of the structures of the social and material world around them. One implication of this position is that debates about whether teachers and learners should focus on critical literacy, basic functional skills, or—not and—literary and cultural heritage are deeply irrelevant to the question of why schools should consider addressing and committing to the teaching and learning of this distinct body of knowledge.

To take on the question "What kind of literacy education?" is to confront the potentially restrictive effects of institutionalized education, and of socialization more broadly; it is to be forced to find grounds for asserting the intellectually, culturally, and morally constitutive consequences of literacy. Our point here has been that these grounds are to be found not only in the enabling resources of literacy for heritage and personal growth, of correctness and appropriateness in literacy. They are also found in the valuable, systematic accumulation of knowledge about the interpretation of texts, in an understanding of the ways in which interpretation connects personal to public interests, and in an appreciation of the fact that the dissemination of this knowledge is a key project for societies with truly democratic aspirations. McKitterick concluded a study of literacy in medieval Europe with this comment:

> It would be idle to pretend that what we have uncovered necessarily permeated unchanged to the lowest levels of society in any one of the various communities we have studied, or even that it did so in similar ways. Nevertheless, we do maintain that no person in society remained unaffected by the activities of those groups able to make the most of the opportunities afforded them by acquisition of the technical skills of reading and writing associated with literacy and of knowledge of the written word and all that that implied. (McKitterick, 1990, p. 333)

"All that that implied" is the aspiration of a program of critical literacy education: over and above fluency and active participation in important literacy activities, a robust, knowledgeable sociological understanding of literacy as individual and collective resource. For the most part, these aspects of literacy are currently ignored or trivialized in many classrooms, curricula, literacy policies, and literacy research programs.

We have argued here that many responses to the need for a critical form of literacy education have foregrounded ideology critiques and pedagogical routines without a clear sense of the bodies of knowledge that might make the issues raised in such activities portable across time, cultural setting, and epistemological domain. It is the ways in which textual formations afford interpretations that we take to be the educational point here, a point that needs to be revisited across knowledge domains and educational levels. The persistent educational question is this: With what resources (linguistic, cognitive, sociological, ethical, ideological) might we lead students to be able to compare and evaluate their own and others' interpretations of texts? Those resources need to be continuously developed, marshalled, co-ordinated, sequenced, and disseminated through educational effort.

The programs thereby envisaged extend beyond reader-response approaches because they devote attention to the semiotic affordances of texts, and they challenge supposedly natural and authentic reactions to texts. They also go beyond metalinguistic or language-awareness programs because they target the variability of situated interpretation as an object of study and scrutiny, rather than working toward a decisive, linguistically defensible reading.

This revisitation of critical literacy sets its aim at developing, across the major school curriculum areas, increasingly defensible, valid and reliable ways of evaluating interpretations, including ideologically motivated interpretations, through the study of situated textual practices in the building of knowledge, identity, and community. One of the goals is to allow learners to come to evaluate their own apparently idiosyncratic individual and collective productions of interpretations of texts. This is important so that they can come to see societies as products of interpretive traditions, and so that they can build up the means to exert individual and collective agency as they use and adapt those traditions.

In a recent attack on relativism, the leader of the Catholic Church in Australia levelled this charge at proponents of critical literacy:

> Schools that abandoned traditional English programs in favour of "critical literacy" are trying to make students agents of social change. (Pell, 2005)

Seen as a set of habits or dispositions, or as an instinct or compulsion for scepticism, critical literacy is indeed open to this charge. But seen as a curriculum rather than a cause, critical literacy becomes a set of useful resources for learners who may choose to pursue a cause—religious, relativistic, or otherwise—and maybe even a cause not endorsed by their teachers.

REFERENCES

Adams, M.J. (1990). *Learning to read: Thinking and learning about print.* Cambridge, MA: MIT Press.

Alvermann, D. E. (2001). Reading adolescents' reading identities: Looking back to see ahead. *Journal of Adolescent & Adult Literacy, 44,* 676–690.

Australian National Inquiry into the Teaching of Literacy. (2005). *Teaching reading.* Canberra: Department of Education, Science and Training.

Barton, D., & Hamilton, M. (1998). *Local literacies: A study of reading and writing in one community.* London: Routledge.

Beach, R., Green, J., Michael, M., & Shanahan, T. (Eds.). (2005). *Multidisciplinary perspectives on literacy research* (2nd ed.). Cresskill, NJ: Hampton Press.

Bernhardt, E. (2003). Challenges to reading research from a multilingual world. *Reading Research Quarterly, 38,* 112–117.

Bernstein, B. (2000). *Pedagogy, symbolic control and identity.* Oxford, UK: Rowman & Littlefield.

Center for Educational Research and Innovation (OECD). (1992). Retrieved March 28, 2008, from http://www.oecd.org/department/0,3355,en_2649_35845581_1_1_1_1_1,00.html

Center for Literacy. (2008). Rretrieved November 3, 2008 from http://www.centreforliteracy.qc.ca/def.htm

Christie, F., & J. R. Martin (Eds.). (2007). *Language, knowledge and pedagogy: Functional linguistic and sociological perspectives.* London: Continuum.

Darvin, J. (2007). Teaching critical literacy principles to math and science educators. *Teaching Education, 18,* 245–256.

Department of Employment, Education and Training (DEET). (1991). *Australia's language, The Australian language and literacy policy.* Canberra: Government Printing Office.

Devine, F., Savage, M., Scott, J., & Crompton, R. (Eds.). (2005). *Rethinking class: Cultures, identities and lifestyles.* London: Palgrave, Macmillan.

Dixon, J. (1967). *Growth through English.* Oxford, UK: Oxford University Press.

Fairclough, N. (2001). *Language and power.* London: Longman.

Fairclough, N., & Chouliaraki, L. (1999). *Discourse in late modernity: Rethinking critical discourse analysis.* Edinburgh: Edinburgh University Press.

Fairclough, N., Pardoe, S., & Szerszynski, B. (2006). Critical discourse analysis and citizenship. In H. Hausendorf & A. Bora (Eds.). *Analyzing citizenship talk* (98–123). Amsterdam: John Benjamins.

Franzak, J. K. (2006). Zoom: A review of the literature on marginalized adolescent readers, literacy theory, and policy implications. *Review of Educational Research, 76,* 209–248.

Freebody, P. (2008). Critical literacy education: On living with 'innocent language.' In B. V. Street & N. Hornberger (Eds.), *Encyclopedia of language and education, Volume 2: Literacy* (98–123). Heidelberg, Germany: Springer.

Freebody, P., & Baker, C. D. (1985). Children's first reading books: Introductions to the culture of literacy. *Harvard Educational Review, 55,* 381–398.

Freebody, P., & Freiberg, J. (2008). Globalized literacy education: Intercultural trade in textual and cultural practice. In M. Prinsloo & M. Baynham, (Eds.), *The new literacy studies: Advances in research and theory* (pp 17–34). Amsterdam: John Benjamins.

Freebody, P., Martin, J. R., & Maton, K. (2008). Talk, text, and knowledge in cumulative, integrated learning. *Australian Journal of Language and Literacy, 31*, 188–201.

Freebody, P., & Zhang, B. (2008). The designs of culture, knowledge, and interaction on the reading of language and image. In L. Unsworth (Ed.), *New literacies and the English curriculum: Multimodal perspectives* (pp. 17–34). London: Continuum (pp. 23–46).

Freire, P., (1972). *Pedagogy of the oppressed* (Trans. Myra Bergman Ramos). Harmondsworth, UK: Penguin.

Freire, P., & Macedo, D. (1987). *Literacy: Reading the word and the world*. South Hadley, MA: Bergin and Garvey.

Gee, J. P. (1991). *Social linguistics and literacies: Ideology in discourses*. London: Falmer Press.

Gee, J. P. (2005). *Introduction to discourse analysis*. London: Routledge.

Gilbert, P. (1989). *Writing, schooling and deconstruction: From voice to text in the classroom*. London: Routledge.

Graff, H. J. (1995). *The labyrinths of literacy: Reflections on literacy past and present*. Pittsburgh, PA: University of Pittsburgh Press.

Graff, H. J. (2001). Literacy's myths and legacies: From lessons from the history of literacy to the question of critical literacy. In P. Freebody, S. Muspratt, & B. Dwyer (Eds.), *Difference, silence, and textual practice: Studies in critical literacy* (pp. 1–30). Cresskill, NJ: Hampton Press.

Greene, S., & Abt–Perkins, D. (2003). How can literacy research contribute to racial understanding? Making race visible: Literacy research for cultural understanding. In S. Greene & D. Abt–Perkins (Eds.), *Making race visible: Literacy research for racial understanding* (pp. 1–31). New York: Teachers College Press.

Hagood, M. C. (2002). Critical literacy for whom? *Reading Research and Instruction, 41*, 247–266.

Harris, W. V. (1989). *Ancient literacy*. Cambridge, MA: Harvard University Press.

Heath, S. B. (1983). *Ways with words: Language, life, and work in communities and classrooms*. New York: Oxford University Press.

Heath, S. B., & Street, B. V. (2008). *On ethnography: Approaches to language and literacy research*. New York: Teachers' College Press.

Hobbs, R., & Frost, R. (2003). Measuring the acquisition of media-literacy skills. *Reading Research Quarterly, 38*, 330–355.

Hunter, C., & Harmon, D. (1979). *Adult illiteracy in the United States: A report to the Ford Foundation*. New York: McGraw Hill.

Iyer, R. (2007). Negotiating critical, postcritical literacy: The problematic of text analysis. *Literacy, 41*, 161–168.

Janks, H. (2000). Domination, access, diversity and design: A synthesis for critical literacy education. *Educational Review, 52*, 175–186.

Joshi, R. M., & Aaron, P. G. (Eds.). (2006). *Handbook of orthography and literacy*. Mahwah, NJ: Erlbaum.

Kaestle, C. F. (1991). *Literacy in the United States*. New Haven, CT: Yale University Press.

Kress, G., Jewitt, C., Ogborn, J., & Tsatsarelis, C. (2001). *Multimodal teaching and learning: The rhetorics of the science classroom*. London: Continuum.

Kress, G., & van Leeuwen, T. (2006). *Reading images: The grammar of visual design*. London: Routledge.

Kucer, S. B. (2005). *Dimensions of literacy: A conceptual base for teaching reading and writing in school settings* (2nd ed.). Mahwah, NJ: Erlbaum.

Kuiper, E., Volman, M., & Terwel, J. (2005). The web as an information resource in K-12 education: strategies for supporting students in searching and processing information. *Review of Educational Research, 75*, 285–328.

Lankshear, C., Green, B., & Snyder, I. (2000). *Teachers and technoliteracy: managing literacy, technology and learning in schools*. St. Leonards, Australia: Allen & Unwin.

Lee, A. (1996). *Gender, literacy, curriculum: Re-writing school geography*. London: Taylor & Francis.

Lemke, J. L. (1998). Multiplying meaning: Visual and verbal semiotics in scientific text. In J. R. Martin & R. Veel (Eds.), *Reading science: Critical and functional perspectives on discourses of science* (pp. 87–113). London: Routledge.

Lemke, J. L. (2002). Multimedia genres for science education and scientific literacy. In M. Shleppegrell & M. C. Colombi, *Developing advanced literacy in first and second languages* (pp. 21–44). Mahwah, NJ: Erlbaum.

Levinson, M. P. (2007). Literacy in English gypsy communities: Cultural capital manifested as negative. *American Educational Research Journal, 44,* 5–39.

Lewison, M., Flint, A. S., & van Sluys, K. (2002). Taking on critical literacy: The journey of newcomers and novices. *Language Arts, 79,* 382–392.

Luke, A. (1988). *Literacy, textbooks and ideology: Postwar literacy instruction and the mythology of Dick and Jane.* London: Falmer Press.

Luke, A., & Freebody, P. (1997). The social practices of literacy. In S. Muspratt, A. Luke, & P. Freebody (Eds.), *Constructing critical literacies: Teaching and learning textual practice* (pp. 185–226). Cresskill, NJ: Hampton Press.

Luke, C. (1989). *Pedagogy, printing, Protestantism: The discourse on childhood.* Albany: State University of New York Press.

Luttrell, W. (1996). Taking care of literacy: One feminist's critique. *Educational Policy, 10,* 342–365.

Martin, J. R. (1980). Writing project: paper 2. In J. R. Martin & J. Rothery (Eds.), *Writing Project report 1980.* Sydney, Australia: Linguistics Department, University of Sydney.

Martin, J. R. (1989). *Factual writing: Exploring and challenging social reality.* Oxford, UK: Oxford University Press.

Martin, J. R. (2007). Construing knowledge: a functional linguistic perspective. In F. Christie & J. R. Martin (Eds.), *Language, knowledge and pedagogy: Functional linguistic and sociological perspectives* (pp. 34–64). London: Continuum.

Martin, J. R., & Rothery, J. (1981). *Writing Project report 1981.* Sydney, Australia: Linguistics Department, University of Sydney.

McKitterick, R. (1990). *The uses of literacy in medieval Europe.* Cambridge, UK: Cambridge University Press.

Mellor, B., & Patterson, A. (2005). Theory, pedagogy and the historical imperative. In R. Beach, J. Green, M. Michael, & T. Shanahan (Eds.), *Multidisciplinary perspectives on literacy research* (2nd ed., pp. 455–480). Cresskill, NJ: Hampton Press.

Meyer, B .J. F., Middlemiss, W., Theodorou, E., Brezinski, K. L., McDougall, J., & Bartlett, B J. (2002). Effects of structure strategy instruction delivered to fifth-grade children via the Internet with and without the aid of older adult tutors. *Journal of Educational Psychology, 94,* 486–519.

Moje, E. B., Young, J. P., Readence, J. E., & Moore, D. W. (2000). Reinventing adolescent literacy for new times: Perennial and millennial issues. *Journal of Adolescent & Adult Literacy, 43,* 400–410.

Morgan, B., & Ramanathan, V. (2005). Critical literacies and language education: Global and local perspectives. *Annual Review of Applied Linguistics, 25,* 151–169.

Murray, T. S., Kirsch, I. S., & Jenkins, L. B. (Eds.). (1996). *Adult Literacy in OECD countries: Technical report on the First International Adult Literacy Survey.* Washington, DC: National Center for Education Statistics, Office of Educational Research and Improvement.

Newbolt Report. (1921). *The teaching of English in England.* London: Government Printer.

Olson, D. R. (1977). The language of instruction: The literate bias of schooling. In R. C. Anderson, R. J. Spiro, & W. E. Montague (Eds.), *Schooling and the acquisition of knowledge* (pp. 65–89). Hillsdale, NJ: Erlbaum.

Oxenham, J. (1980). *Literacy: writing, reading and social organisation.* London: Routledge and Kegan Paul.

Pell, G. (2005). *The dictatorship of relativism.* Address to the National Press Club, Canberra, Australia. Retrieved March 26, 2008, from http://www.sydney.catholic.org.au/Archbishop/Addresses/2005921_1181.shtml

Pennycook, A. (2001). *Critical applied linguistics: A critical introduction.* Mahwah, NJ: Erlbaum.

Plato. (n.d.). *Phaedrus* (Trans. B. Jowett). Retrieved April 30, 2007. from http://ccat.sas.upenn.edu/jod/texts/phaedrus.html

Prinsloo, M., & Breier, M. (1996). *The social uses of literacy: Theory and practice in contemporary South Africa.* London: Multilingual Matters/Sached Books.

Resnick, D. P., & Resnick, L. B. (1977). The nature of literacy: An historical exploration. *Harvard Educational Review, 47,* 370–387.

Robb, K. (1994). *Literacy and Paideia in ancient Greece*. Oxford, UK: Oxford University Press.

Roberts, P. (1995). Defining literacy: paradise, nightmare or red herring? *British Journal of Educational Studies, 43*, 412–432.

Rogers, R. (2003). *A critical discourse analysis of family literacy practices: Power in and out of print*. Mahwah, NJ: Erlbaum.

Sampson, G. (1925). *English for the English*. Cambridge, UK: Cambridge University Press.

Saunders, T. J. (1987). Introduction to Socrates. In *Plato, Early Socratic Dialogues* (pp. 13–36). London: Penguin.

Shor, I. (1992). *Empowering education: Critical teaching for social change*. Chicago: University of Chicago Press.

Siegel, M., & Fernandez, S. (2000). Critical approaches. In M. Kamil, R. Barr, P. D. Pearson, & P. Mosenthal (Eds.), *Handbook of reading research* (Vol. 3, pp. 141–152). Mahwah, NJ: Erlbaum.

Smith, D. E. (1987). *The everyday world as problematic: A feminist sociology*. Toronto: University of Toronto Press.

Smith, D. E. (1999). *Writing the social: Critique, theory and investigations*. Toronto: University of Toronto Press.

Snow, C. E., Burns, M. S., & Griffin, P. (Eds.). (1998). *Preventing reading difficulties in young children*. Washington, DC: National Academy Press.

Stein, P., & Mamabolo, T. (2005). 'Pedagogy is not enough': Early literacy practices in a South African school. In B. V. Street (Ed.), *Literacies across educational contexts: Mediating teaching and learning* (pp. 25–42). Philadelphia: Carlson Press.

Street, B. (1984). *Literacy in theory and practice*. Cambridge, UK: Cambridge University Press.

Stuckey, J. E. (1991). *The violence of literacy*. Portsmouth, NH: Boyton/Cook.

Uhlmann, A. J. (2008). The field of Arabic instruction in the Zionist state. In J. Albright & A. Luke (Eds.), *Pierre Bourdieu and literacy education* (pp. 95–112). London: Routledge.

UNESCO. (1957). *World illiteracy at mid-century*. Paris: UNESCO.

Unsworth, L. (2004). Comparing school science explanations in books and computer-based formats: The role of images, image/text relations and hyperlinks. *International Journal of Instructional Media, 31*, 283–301.

US Department of Labor, Employment and Training (1998). Workforce Investment Act. Retrieved March 26, 2008 from http://www.doleta.gov/usworkforce/wia/wialaw.txt

US National Reading Panel. (2000). *Teaching children to read: An evidence-based assessment of the scientific research literature on reading and its implications for reading instruction*. Washington, DC: U.S. Government Printing Office.

US National Reading Panel Summary. (2002). Retrieved March 26, 2008, from http://www.nichd.nih.gov/publications/nrp/intro.cfm

Venezky, R. L. (1984). The history of reading research. In P. D. Pearson, R. Barr, M. L. Kamil, & P. Mosenthal (Eds.), *Handbook of reading research* (pp. 3–38). NY: Longman.

Warschauer, M. (2003). *Technology and social inclusion: Rethinking the digital divide*. Cambridge, MA: MIT Press.

Willis, A. I. (2008). Critical race theory and literacy. In B. V. Street & N. H. Hornberger (Eds.), *Encyclopedia of language and education, Volume 2: Literacy* (pp. 15–28). Heidelberg, Germany: Springer.

20 The Role of Text in Disciplinary Learning

Elizabeth Birr Moje, Darin Stockdill,
Katherine Kim, and Hyun-ju Kim
University of Michigan

Over the past 30 years of literacy research, developments in sociocultural theories of literate practice have turned many reading researchers from viewing text as the driver of literacy processes and practices toward understanding who readers are and how contexts mediate text comprehension and production. This turn to readers and contexts has been extremely useful in advancing understandings of how and why people read texts differently in and for different contexts and purposes. At the same time, however, recent literacy theories and research studies have not accounted as fully as they might for how text use and comprehension differ as a function of domains of academic disciplines (e.g., history, mathematics, art, etc.) or of everyday life (e.g., homes, communities, churches, etc.). Researchers have attended to features of different genres of text that might shape people's comprehension (e.g., Graesser, McNamara, & Louwerse, this volume), but we know less, as a field, about how texts are actually used in different domains. This gap is particularly noteworthy when considering the discouraging data on young people's comprehension of the complex texts of the secondary and postsecondary levels of schooling (ACT, 2006; Lee, Grigg, & Donahue, 2007). As literacy scholars conduct research to enhance the literacy proficiencies of older readers and ready them for postsecondary and workplace settings, it is critical that they attend to the demands of academic, or disciplinary, texts because such texts are key ingredients of disciplinary work and of human interaction, more broadly conceived.

In this review, then, we examine what counts as text, generally speaking, and then turn to two disciplinary domains to examine the varieties of text types, uses, and associated literacy practices in those domains. We limit our review to two disciplinary domains out of necessity: There are not enough pages to review even just the four major academic disciplines, globally construed (i.e., natural sciences, social sciences, mathematics and literature/composition), let alone all the sub-disciplines those four areas entail. To offer a broad view, however, we have chosen two domains that, at least on the surface, appear distinctly different: history and mathematics.

History is an area in which some research has been done on text by members of the disciplines and by members of school subject-areas, most likely because texts figure rather prominently in the production of historical accounts and in school history learning. Mathematics, until recently, has seen less research done on text use by mathematicians or by members of mathematics classrooms. However, recent curricular changes have prompted a greater focus on text and text demands in mathematics teaching and learning, thus justifying a focus on the role of texts in mathematics. Finally, we follow in the footsteps of the two past *Handbook on Reading Research* reviews (Alexander & Jetton, 2000; Wade & Moje, 2000), whose authors used history/ social studies and mathematics as points of contrasts to illustrate disciplinary text differences.

For each of these disciplinary domains, we examine (a) what counts as text, (b) the variety of text types studied within those categories, (c) the processes and practices associated with those texts in the work of the disciplines and associated professions, and (d) how texts are used in subject-matter classrooms. In the cases of both history and mathematics, we limited these portions of the review to classroom-based, or subject-matter, research conducted at the upper elementary grades, secondary school, and postsecondary settings. It could legitimately be argued that attention to disciplinary text learning should begin at the elementary grades, but for the sake of maintaining a reasonable scope for this review, we confine our review to studies conducted at the upper grades and beyond. For clarity, we refer to the *disciplines* when examining the work of professionals and researchers who engage in disciplinary study, and to *subject-matter areas* when examining how teachers and students think about the texts of learning in school. These distinctions, and our rationale for looking at the relationship between the two, rest on the idea that the nature of a discipline contributes to how subject-areas are framed in schools and to what occurs in classroom teaching and learning (Alexander, 1998; Stodolsky, 1988; Stodolsky & Grossman, 1995; Siskin, 1994; Wade & Moje, 2000).

Because our review of classroom text use suggests a recent emphasis on expanding what counts as a classroom text from the traditional view of textbooks as dominant to the inclusion of primary and real-world sources, we conclude with a section that examines the research on the developing relationship between the texts typically privileged in classroom disciplinary learning and the texts young people privilege in their everyday lives, outside of school. This portion of the review includes studies that have implications for how the texts that youth read and write outside of school might be used to further disciplinary learning.

Finally, we offer a synthesis of these three areas by highlighting questions that remain unaddressed by the extant research on the role of text in disciplinary knowledge production and school learning. The synthesis offers possibilities for future research and the continued development of textual theories.

OVERVIEW OF TEXT THEORIES AND RESEARCH

To situate ourselves in various literatures on text and on classroom learning and to provide a general overview on past perspectives on text-based research, we consulted the most relevant chapters from a past volume of the *Handbook of Reading Research,* one on learning from text (Alexander & Jetton, 2000) and one on the role of text in classroom learning (Wade & Moje, 2000). To provide additional background, we also examined research on text analysis and text processing (Graesser, McNamara, & Rus, in press; Kintsch & Van Dijk, 1978; Mandl, Stein, & Trabasso, 1984), learning from text (Alexander, Kulikowich, & Jetton, 1994; Alexander, Kulikowich, & Schulze, 1994a, 1994b) and studies that analyzed the quality of textbooks (Anderson & Armbruster, 1984; Armbruster & Anderson, 1985; Chambliss & Calfee, 1998). These reviews and studies were not, however, the focus of our review; rather, they provided background on the range of work done on or related to text, thus helping us to define what counts as text and to examine trends in research on text.

WHAT COUNTS AS TEXT IN READING AND LITERACY RESEARCH

In an attempt to address the question of what counts as text, the Wade and Moje (2000) *Handbook of Reading Research* review summarized various theoretical and epistemological perspectives on text, writ large. Wade and Moje outlined five different perspectives, each with distinct sub-categories: (a) cognitive and sociocognitive perspectives, (b) literary perspectives, (c) linguistic perspectives, (d) social and cultural perspectives, and (e) critical perspectives. These perspectives offer definitions of text that range from published print to any "textualized" (Bloome & Egan-Robertson, 1993) interaction. Anything, according to Bloome and Egan-Robertson, can be textualized if it can be interpreted or is seen as carrying meaning. From this perspective, almost anything in a classroom could count as text, including oral classroom discourse, symbols written by hand on a Smartboard, published textbooks, routinized gestures or body language, newspapers, student notes, or classroom arrangements (cf. Alexander & Jetton, 2000; Dillon, Brien, & Volkman, 2001).

More recently, many scholars (Alvermann & Hagood, 2000a; Gee, 2004; New London Group, 1996; Kress, 2003; Luke, 2003) have argued that definitions of literacy and text in an era of advanced technology must be reexamined and expanded in accordance with the world outside schools. Kress, for example, argued that text can be perceived as "the result of the social semiotic action of representation" (p. 84), which comprises a variety of modes (audio, visual, aural, gesture, alphabet letters, etc.) and a variety of media (the Internet, TV, video, etc.). Research on out-of-school literacy practices, and some studies of in-school practices, have thus explored "multiple forms of representation" (Eisner, 1994) in which children and youth engage, such as online reading, multimedia text productions (e.g., video clips, blogs, homepages, fanfiction writing, etc.), and text messaging.

For our purposes, we take a relatively broad view of what counts as text. Much of the research we reviewed focused on written (i.e., encoded symbols of some sort) texts, but we recognize that what counts as a text is dependent on the social and cultural situation in which the text is offered, taken up, and interpreted, and that views of text may change from one context or domain to another. Furthermore, a broad perspective on text cannot ignore the ways that visual, performed, and spoken texts have an impact on the reading and use of written texts in disciplinary learning. We also acknowledge the important role that media (e.g., paper or digital) for producing and storing texts play in accessing texts for classroom instruction. Finally, we draw from the work of critical theorists to argue that texts can serve as tools or as commodities through which knowledge—and thus, power and social control—can be bought, sold, and controlled in the marketplace of knowledge and ideas (Wade & Moje, 2000). Germane to disciplinary knowledge production and subject matter learning, texts in disciplines and subject areas control, to some extent, what can be known and learned. They provide the artifacts of past knowledge production and mediational tools for learning. The conventions for producing and using texts provide the grounds by which new knowledge can be produced, communicated, and learned. Consequently, knowing how texts are used and made sense of by teachers and students is especially meaningful in reading research.

PAST RESEARCH ON THE ROLE OF TEXT IN CLASSROOM LEARNING

Whereas this review examines the role of text in particular subject area classrooms, Wade and Moje (2000) chose to focus on generic classroom text practices, distinguishing between the roles of text in two different pedagogical approaches, specifically transmission and participatory approaches to learning, arguing that what and how texts were used depended in large part on the nature of instruction. According to Wade and Moje, in classrooms that relied on a transmission approach to teaching and learning, the official text was the textbook, but teacher lecture (and either written teacher or student notes) served as the dominant, albeit unofficial, texts of instruction. As such, the role of text in a transmission approach was, unsurprisingly, to transmit information from the teacher or textbook to the students. By contrast, participatory approaches, documented most often in English and science classrooms, employed a range of texts, including textbooks, newspaper articles, music lyrics, and other "real-world" texts. Moreover, the research reviewed showed that teachers and students used texts for many purposes, such as augmenting investigations, offering alternative viewpoints, expressing ideas in unique ways, or communicating understandings and/or findings of inquiry.

Although Wade and Moje (2000) focused on the differences between these generic instructional approaches, they also included a limited review of research on disciplinary differences in classroom practices. Specifically, they noted that a small number of studies have documented differences in subject-matter areas in terms of how the subject matter is defined and, as a consequence, how text materials are used. Teacher and students considered subject areas such as mathematics and foreign language to be highly sequential and well defined, and those texts tended to be followed sequentially, whereas subjects such as English, social studies, and natural sciences (Stodolsky & Grossman, 1995) were considered more open-ended, with vaguely defined content boundaries. As a result, curricular materials were used in less sequential and predictable ways. Science and foreign language teachers, perceived as specialists, reported that they were allowed the most control over the selection of instructional materials, followed by social studies and English teachers, whose subject areas were considered less sequential and less defined. Math teachers reported they had less control and autonomy over curricular content, and received more consensus on what should be covered, more control by state and district assessment programs and curriculum guides, and more press for coverage (Stodolsky & Grossman, 1995). Wade and Moje (2000) further documented that students' beliefs, values, and views of the subject areas influence teachers' practice as well as the students' learning from text, and presented a number of different studies that documented how students thought about the subject matter, if not the texts of those subjects. In general, students' beliefs about subject areas reflected their teachers (and broader societal conceptions) in the sense that mathematics and the sciences were often taken more seriously than other subject areas (Ball & Lacey, 1984).

Alexander and Jetton (2000) expanded on the importance of considering subject-area or disciplinary domains when considering learning from text in their *Handbook of Reading Research* review. They examined a number of different studies that demonstrated the role of different kinds of knowledge necessary to comprehend domain-specific texts. Goldman and colleagues (Goldman, 1997; Goldman & Varma, 1995), for example, demonstrated that text comprehension requires knowledge of text structures and genres (cf. Chambliss, 1995; Graesser et al., in press; McNamara & Kintsch, 1996), and that these genres and structures reflect and reproduce disciplinary differences. Alexander and Jetton also reviewed a host of studies that made clear how other kinds of knowledge (particularly knowledge of the domains and related topics in those domains) intersect with interest and strategy use when reading domain-specific texts (Alexander, 1998; Alexander & Judy, 1988; Alexander, Kulikowich, & Schulze, 1994a, 1994b; Kintsch, 1988). When viewed as a set, these studies suggested that how people learn from domain-specific texts is shaped in part by the texts themselves, together with what people know when they enter the domains and the text learning opportunities available once there.

Each of these findings of how people learn from text, how texts are structured, and how texts are used in different participation structures begs the question of just how texts are being used to advance learning in the different domains of secondary schools (i.e., the subject areas). Although a number of studies have examined text comprehension experimentally (e.g., Anderson & Pearson, 1984; Graesser, McNamara, Louwerse, & Cai, 2004; Graesser et al., in press; Kintsch, 1988, 1998; McNamara & Kintsch, 1996) and have studied different approaches to teaching text comprehension (e.g., McKeown, Beck, & Blake, 2009), less was written prior to 2000 about the particular ways secondary school subject-area teachers and students use texts, think about texts, or make sense of the texts they use on an everyday basis. Our present review suggests that, indeed, little has been published to that effect since that year.

Recently, Lee and Spratley (2010) analyzed the complex knowledge required for reading academic texts, demonstrating the ways in which disciplinary epistemologies produce syntactical/grammatical, structural, rhetorical, and discursive practices represented in academic texts, although they are often misrepresented or turned into a hybrid of disciplinary and school discourse. As useful as that analysis is, the Lee and Spratley piece does not represent empirical work on how teachers use texts in the subject areas or on what teachers expect and students are able to do with those texts. In addition, despite a longstanding tradition of research on adolescent/secondary school literacy and more recent calls for attention to disciplinary learning from text, the field appears to have only scattered documentation of how texts are used by members of disciplines. What we were able to find in the literature, however, provides some glimpses into assumptions about text and about text practices, thus serving as a useful spur for further research around these questions.

THE ROLE OF TEXT IN THE WORK OF HISTORIANS, HISTORY TEACHERS, AND HISTORY LEARNERS

The discipline of history provides an excellent opportunity for examining the role of text in both disciplinary and classroom applications. Historical research relies heavily upon examination of the past through the analysis of diverse written texts. Likewise, texts play a key role in history classrooms, where schools and teachers seek to develop understanding of the world and its past through history instruction. Nevertheless, the uses of text by historians and by teachers and students of history often vary in important ways. In the practice of history, texts are generally used in order to answer a question or analyze an historical problem, yet in classroom instruction the process is often reversed, with questions used to assess student comprehension of the text. An exploration of these and other differences can help provide a deeper understanding of the roles of text in history practice and learning.

This line of inquiry is extremely important for both historians and educators concerned with youth reading and engagement in historical practice. History educators argue that understanding, analyzing, and evaluating information and texts from the past and the present is crucial to people's participation in civic society (NCSS, 2007). Texts are also heavily used in most social studies classrooms (Wineburg & Martin, 2004). However, in 2005, only 35% of 12th graders scored at or above proficient in general reading comprehension (Perie, Grigg, & Donahue, 2005) and in 2006, only 14% of 12 graders assessed in the National Assessment of Educational Progress (NAEP) exam scored at the proficient or advanced level in history (Lee & Weiss, 2007). Literacy is crucial to social studies education, yet students, especially those in urban schools, struggle in their attempt to interpret historical texts and have difficulty judging the quality of the information they encounter (Wineburg, 2001). Many students view history texts as voices of authority and accept their conclusions without question, but they also find the texts disconnected from their lives (Bain, 2006). Comparing differing accounts or engaging in intertextual learning in history is difficult for large numbers of high school students (Afflerbach & VanSledright, 2001).

Taken together, these data suggest that more attention should be given to how texts are used in history classrooms. It is also worth asking about the various ways texts might be used in history classrooms. To these ends, this section addresses the nature of texts in the discipline of history and in history classrooms, how they are used in both domains (the discipline and the classroom), and their differing demands in historical practice and in school learning.

Search procedures for the review on the use of text in history instruction began with a broad query using Google Scholar and terms such as "text use in social studies" and "social studies text." We followed with a more focused search using electronic databases such as PscyINFO, JSTOR, and ERIC. Search terms varied across combinations of "history," "social studies," "text," and "text use." In addition, we looked to articles and scholars we had utilized in past work relating to disciplinary literacy in the social studies. Our focus was on articles printed in the last 10 years in peer-reviewed journals, although we also referred to a limited set of older works. We then selected those which focused most directly on how different forms of texts are used in secondary history instruction, although we drew on important work on younger students when relevant. The search was challenging, in that much work in this area is either practice-based or theoretical. In addition, there appears to be less focus on how texts are used and more on the texts themselves.

To look at how historians use text in a disciplinary context, we consulted *The Journal of American History Online* and *The Historical Journal* to find articles in which historians explicitly made use of diverse texts in their research. In this part of the search, we noticed that the use of text by historians seems to be assumed, and thus there is little discussion among them as to the actual thinking and reading practices in which they engage as they work with texts. We offer, nevertheless, our review of what we could ascertain about text use in the discipline of history in the following section.

The Role of Texts in the Discipline of History

To begin looking at how historians use text, and at the demands of the texts they use, we present examples of historical studies and analyze the role of texts in this work. These studies do not represent the entire field, but rather serve to elucidate the complex functions and roles of text in the field of history. There are few analyses of how texts function in historical study or of how historians read documents to construct meanings. The focus of historians is most often on the outcome of their interpretation of texts, not upon the processes they use or the structures of the texts themselves. Even so, when they engage with text in their practice, historians do so purposefully and with specific epistemological and disciplinary approaches. Ford (2008), for example, demonstrated historical analysis of multiple texts as she compared how politicians in the upper South and lower South tried to reconfigure slavery in their respective regions in the face of growing sociopolitical instability between 1787 and 1838, using evidence from diverse documents to warrant her claims. She utilized public debate transcripts, first person narratives, newspaper articles, congressional reports, and other primary documents from the time period and also consulted the secondary analyses of other historians.

An interesting contrast between disciplinary practice and history teaching emerged with respect to this article on the website of the *Journal of American History* (www.journalofameri-canhistory.org), in a section titled "Teaching the JAH." This site provides teaching resources for articles published in the journal, including the article by Ford. It includes a link to Ford's article, to several of the primary documents used, and to six "exercises" for teaching with the article. There is also a "Teaching the Article" commentary by Ford, which contains no historical questions, but rather a summary of the article. Moreover, although the six exercises provide links to documents and individual questions about each, they do not encourage synthesis or connection across the questions and the documents, even though the author provides extensive synthesis— the work of an historian—in the historical analysis represented in the article.

Historical practices such as corroboration or cross-text analysis, absent in the "Teaching the Article" exercise discussed above, are nevertheless crucial to the practice and epistemology of history. This is especially true given the broad array of text types utilized in the field. Indeed, the range of what counts as an historical text is wide and includes everything from personal letters to legal documents to secondary historical analyses. In one instructional history unit, for example, Bain (2006) included 40 different primary sources, such as woodcuts, papal bulls, stained glass windows, and first person accounts, suggesting that what counts as a text in the discipline of history seems limited only by the presence of encoded symbol systems from which meaning can be made. Furthermore, the range and accessibility of these texts is only growing greater as the area of what some call "digital history" expands and develops. Massive archives of historical documents, both primary and secondary, are available online to the public. These documents span the range discussed above and include scanned originals, transcriptions of documents, timelines, and an array of other secondary accounts and interpretations (*Journal of American History*, 2008).

Although what counts as text is broad in the study of history, it can be argued that historians do privilege printed texts. Given the prominence of print texts, historians also wrestle with the limitations of printed documents as evidence. Care must be taken to view historical documents not as history themselves but as accounts which provide evidence for a range of possible interpretations. Historians need sufficient prior knowledge to read across documents and connect them to prior study, and they often deal with technical and sometimes antiquated vocabulary and jargons in a wide range of genres. They consistently consider the source of historical documents, considering bias and positionality of both themselves and the authors of documents. Historians, it appears, face many challenges and textual demands in this respect, yet they seldom discuss these challenges but rather assume that they and other historians have the necessary skills to make meaning from text.

How then do historians actually use such a potentially broad array of texts? As exemplified in the work of Dawson (2000), historians must critically approach texts as evidence for historical arguments, not as history in and of themselves. Dawson examined some of the scholarly work around the life and diary of Samuel Pepys, an English Member of Parliament in the late 1600s who kept a detailed diary about his life that has become an important account of life in 17th-century England. Dawson essentially argued that many historians have tried to interpret the diary of Pepys through the lens of what they know about Pepys as an individual. This, however, is problematic because most of what is known about him comes from the diary. Dawson posited that the text itself should be the focus of analysis, and that more can be learned about Pepys by focusing on the discourse of the text in conjunction with analysis of other texts he left.

Dawson's (2000) argument implied that historical texts can be confused with history itself; what is written may be construed to represent what actually happened. To avoid this, he discussed how the historian must always attempt to contextualize any primary historical account as a piece of evidence, one aspect of a larger puzzle that helps to explain at a minimum how the authors of the past interpreted events around them. From Dawson's perspective, any historical document must be interpreted at multiple levels; the historian should remember that all texts are written with a purpose and an audience, and the story of how a text was created is as much a part of history as the story it tells.

In this type of work with texts, historians generally analyze documents in reference to a particular historical problem or research question, which guides their selection and use of text. Moreover, scholars engaging in this process usually begin with significant background knowledge of both content and methodology already in place. For example, Steele (2008) used a wide variety of texts in an exploration of Thomas Jefferson's views on gender and sexuality. To structure his inquiry, it appears that Steele first generated a problem or question, that of Jefferson's actual views on gender relations, and then gathered textual resources to help him explore this topic. In his references he cited an extensive list of primary documents authored by Jefferson, including letters, articles, essays, and legal decisions, as well as additional secondary analyses by other historians. Weaving together elements of evidence from all of these documents, Steele constructed his case, adding in his own interpretation of each document and synthesizing them into a series of conclusions.

Using think-aloud strategies to make visible the epistemologies and analytical processes employed by historians, Wineburg (1998, 2001) explored the cognitive processes and disciplinary practices of historians as they engage in their work and related them to instructional practice. He has also extended this work by comparing historical thinking to typical classroom practice. In one study, Wineburg (1998) interviewed and observed two historians reading and analyzing texts about Abraham Lincoln while they thought aloud about their reading. Both were academic historians, but one had engaged in significant scholarship on Lincoln whereas the other had different specialized knowledge and experience. The historian with less prior knowledge struggled with inconsistencies in information about Lincoln, yet he worked through his confusion and used the skills of a historian—questioning, analyzing, re-visiting information, and trying out different interpretations—to make up for his lack of prior knowledge. In this instance a single text did not contain the answers to this historian's questions. He could not learn new information by simply remembering details, especially when some of the information was contradictory to what he may have already known. Instead, the text served as a resource for investigation to be corroborated through comparison and contrast with other texts. The text also had to be questioned with respect to the author's position and purpose ("sourced," in Wineburg's words), and then deconstructed and contextualized. By contrast, the second historian utilized his prior knowledge but also relied upon similar historical heuristics to engage with the texts. Although prior knowledge made it easier for one historian to process the text, both historians were able to deeply analyze the texts and produce reasoned arguments because they were able to engage in the reading practices critical to the discipline. Wineburg (2001) argued that these analytical approaches to reading and thinking about texts in order to answer questions or propose solutions to historical problems are crucial components of historical practice, and should be taught to all people as they learn history/social studies.

The Role of Texts in History Classrooms

Classroom learning of history, however, often has a different focus than disciplinary practice in history, and the use of text is reflective of this difference. As described above, historians engage with and produce histories, yet in the classroom students are generally expected to learn history, rather than produce it, and traditionally these have not been the same practices. Historical learning in schools generally entails review of basic chronology and historical information, and schools have tended to utilize the history textbook as the primary resource in this effort. In 1994, Britt, Rouet, Georgi, and Perfetti drew from a review of previous studies to assert that textbooks were the dominant form of text in instruction. Bain (2006) concurred over 12 years later when he wrote, "the textbook continues to form the bedrock of history teaching, the foundation upon which most teachers build their curriculum. The National Center for Education Statistics reports that over 84% of 12th-grade U.S. history students claim to read a textbook at least once a week, and 44% say they read from the textbook 'about everyday'" (p. 2081).

Beyond these frequency reports and the NAEP survey data, however, few data exist on what and how texts are used in history classrooms of the 21st century. Indeed, of the two main types of research reviewed here, the majority of studies focus on the texts themselves or on how students process texts independently (i.e., outside of instruction), often in relation to an experimental text. Specifically, we review the following two types of social studies/history text-related research: (a) studies of the structure of textbooks, including experimental modifications to structure and analyses of students' comprehension of modified textbook passages, and (b) qualitative studies of teaching and learning with text in history/social studies classrooms.

Examining the Structure of Social Studies Textbooks to Enhance Student Learning from Text

Given the reported dominance of the textbook in history, it is no surprise that much of the research done on text in this area has documented the deficiencies of textbooks and sought to improve them. In groundbreaking work, Beck and colleagues (e.g., Beck, McKeown, & Gromoll, 1989; Beck, McKeown, and Worthy, 1995), for example, argued that although social studies textbooks are often poorly written and lack cohesion and clarity, they can be written to be more comprehensible and could be salvaged as a social studies learning tool. Similarly, Chambliss and Murphy (2002) studied 65 fourth and fifth graders' representations of arguments as encountered in grade-appropriate social studies texts, looking at how students did or did not use discourse structures and/or topics from the texts to develop their own understandings of the presented arguments. Over two-thirds of the subjects were able to recall hierarchical structures of arguments from the text (main point supported by details), although some children only reproduced lists of details. Prior knowledge, developmental factors, and the vividness of the text's language and imagery affected recall. This study, as an examination of reading processes, looked at how students engage with the texts of social studies classrooms, but did not address the type of subject-area learning expected, the disciplinary reading practices required for the textbook passages, or how these texts were used as part of regular classroom instruction. This last point seems critical in considering the results of all studies of readers' processes when engaged with the texts of history instruction; without more information about how teachers mediate text comprehension, it is difficult to assess the role that these texts play in subject-area learning and in disciplinary literacy learning.

Crawford and Carnine (2000) also examined textbook organization, comparing the effect of a conceptually organized history textbook on student learning to the effect of a traditional textbook. History textbooks are typically organized by chronology and, within particular time periods, by topic, rather than concept. Conceptually organized texts, by contrast, are organized by historical concepts, such as how changes in industrialization might have affected immigration patterns or the effects of regional or world conflicts on economic production. The concepts are addressed chronologically (because to address cause-effect relationships without a sense of what came before in a different historical period would not advance conceptual understanding), but the chronology is not presented as a list of events.

Crawford and Carnine (2000) enacted the study with 81 eighth-grade students in four United States history classrooms. Two regular classroom teachers were involved; each taught one class with the conceptually organized textbook and one class with the conventional textbook. Content learning was assessed with an objective test (multiple choice, matching, chronology) and an essay test. Students using the conceptually organized text performed significantly better than the control group on the objective test measures, but there was no significant difference between the groups on the essay test (the low overall writing performance was perhaps a factor). This study did not alter the typical text usage pattern of conventional classrooms, but sought to improve the status quo with a better textbook.

Twyman and Tindal (2006) carried out a similar study, but used a computer-adapted text in comparison to the traditional textbook in special education classes. They analyzed the effect of each text on the development of content-related comprehension and problem-solving skills over a three-week history unit in two self-contained social studies special education classes in a rural Pacific Northwest high school. They found no significant differences between the groups using the paper textbook and the computer-adapted text on multiple-choice measures, although the authors did present a "near-significant" difference on the essays, with students in the experimental group scoring higher. The study did not provide convincing evidence that the computer-adapted text was more effective than the conventional textbook. Both the computer and paper texts took the form of authoritative, secondary historical resources, presenting students with summarized information typical of contemporary textbooks. More important, perhaps, the difference between the two texts in this study was not based in text content or purpose, but rather in the supports provided to readers and the manner of navigation through the text itself. Further investigation is needed in this area, with larger samples and more varied approaches to actual text content and language, and future research with digital textbooks should take these considerations into account.

Porat (2004) exemplifies one of the few studies of how students took up and made sense of history textbook content. Porat addressed how students interpreted texts, challenging the notion that textbooks shape students' historical conceptions and arguing that students' pre-existing ideas and prior knowledge dramatically shape their reading and understanding of the textbook. In his study, Porat examined the text interpretations of 11 Israeli high school students with respect to a textbook account of an important event in the Israeli-Palestinian conflict. The students were split between two very different high schools, one in a largely secular, liberal, and middle-class community and one in a predominantly religious, conservative, and rural community. The event, the Tel Hai incident, is part of national narratives around heroism and struggle, and has a popular "legendary" version, which presents Jewish settlers as heroes and protagonists and places blame for the event on the Palestinians. An "accidental" version of the narrative, presented in the textbook, portrays the event as having accidental antecedents and places no blame on either party.

Initially, the students were asked by the researcher to write an historical account, based upon their prior knowledge, of the event, in which Palestinian Arabs killed several Jewish settlers in 1920. The students were then interviewed to flesh out their historical accounts. Following the interviews, students read a textbook version of the event and orally summarized their view of it. Finally, 1 year later, the same students wrote an account of the event from memory.

Porat found that prior to reading, the students at the secular school tended to take a moderate view of the conflict, recognizing some claims of both parties. Specifically, the researcher interpreted initial student accounts from the secular school as more neutral. Students at the religious school tended to side with the Israeli right-wing and settlement movements and viewed the Israeli-Arab conflict through the lens of Israeli nationalism and Zionism, presenting, according to Porat, versions of the legendary narrative. More important, even after reading the account, the two schools responded differently. Students from the secular school tended to adopt the textbook account of the event, whereas students from the more religious school maintained primary components of the legendary account, only taking up ideas from the textbook that could be used to support that position.

Although this study examined how students interacted with a textbook, Porat (2004) relied upon a researcher-constructed text passage and did not analyze how the text was used instructionally or how instruction might have mediated students' understanding of the text or the concepts represented in the text. Thus, Porat demonstrated that students' perspectives shaped their reading of historical accounts, but did not examine how teacher mediation of the text or the use of multiple textual sources might have reshaped perspectives.

Two additional types of work on social studies textbooks have been conducted outside of reading research. Paxton (1999, 2002) studied the problems of secondary level history textbooks, but challenged the notion that textbook problems are all about text structure. Although Paxton acknowledged the importance of well-structured texts, he argued that typical conceptions of considerateness overlook a key dimension of history textbooks in particular: the lack of historian's authorial voice. Paxton pointed out that history textbooks have often been criticized for being incorrect, broad, difficult to understand, and dull, which he attributed to the lack of historian's voice. More important, from Paxton's perspective, the lack of historian's voice not only produces less engaging texts, but also masks the work that historians do in producing historical accounts. Given research on the importance of understanding who produced accounts, what sources were used, and the strength of evidentiary warrant (Bain, 2006; Wineburg, 1998, Paxton's critique raised important concerns for the role of history textbooks in history learning.

To test his argument, Paxton (2002) carried out a study in which 30 high school students were divided into two groups and asked to read different textbook passages. One group read a passage that was an unaltered excerpt from a textbook, anonymously written in third person; the second group worked with a passage rewritten in first person to present a clear authorial voice. Students wrote essays in response to the texts, and a sub-sample of 6 students, 3 from each group, engaged in think-aloud protocols while reading. Paxton analyzed the essays and think-aloud data to explore students' recognition and use of an "authorial presence." He found that the students reading anonymous texts seemed less likely to think about the author as a historical source, less likely to make evaluations of possible author bias, and demonstrated a lack of critical reading in written responses to questions. Students reading texts written with a "visible author" were able to write response essays with more "personal agency and awareness of audience" (p. 197). Based on these conclusions, Paxton called for the inclusion of a wider variety of documents in instruction, a greater recognition that history is made of differing accounts, and the development of more effective print resources.

Building on Paxton's (1999, 2002) work, as well as classroom-based work by Bain (2005, 2006), Lee (2007) developed what she termed "Visible Inquiry Text" for use in history instruction. The texts Lee produced included historical content, but were also accompanied by clear references to processes of historical inquiry integrated into the text. The overall goal was to create a considerate text that students could follow in which historical inquiry was not hidden but made visible and comprehensible. Researching the effectiveness of this approach with 12 high school history students, Lee found that students using these texts were better able to grasp and then use certain inquiry strategies of the discipline than students using conventional classroom history textbooks. The small sample size made the results of the study suggestive, rather than definitive, but the in-depth analyses Lee conducted in this exploratory work provided an important example and future direction for similar studies.

Finally, Schleppegrell, Achugar, and Oteíza (2004) used systemic functional linguistics to deconstruct the language of social studies textbooks. Their research demonstrated that making explicit how the language of social studies textbooks functioned to communicate particular ideas could support students' text comprehension. This research, although focused primarily on comprehension gains, suggested that the role of text in history classroom learning is central and that it should not be left to students to decipher texts. It should be noted, however, that like most of the reading research studies already reviewed, Schleppegrell et al. focused on history textbooks only, rather than on the wide array of texts that could be used in many history classrooms.

Overall, the existing research on texts in history classrooms, then, appears to assume that textbooks are actually used in history classrooms. And, overall, regardless of the text type focused on in the study, few studies have looked at how the texts are used, how students comprehend the texts, or the impact of these other texts on students' history learning. One exception to that critique is found in a study conducted by Afflerbach and VanSledright (2001). The authors analyzed history textbooks with a focus on how students interpreted embedded texts in the book. These embedded texts generally include primary source excerpts, literature excerpts, pictures, charts, and other supplementary resources. They argued that little research had been done on how students read across or them or on how teachers can effectively use them. Thus they analyzed the "challenges that … embedded texts present[ed] to middle-grade students and the strategies and stances that student readers use[d] in relation to these challenges" (p. 698). The study involved a detailed analysis of the reading of an ethnically- and gender-mixed purposive sample of seven fifth-grade, competent readers. Students were presented with two texts, and asked to read a chapter from "an innovative United States history textbook series (Hakim, 1993) that contained two embedded texts: a diary excerpt and a poem" (p. 699). They also read a chapter from a more conventional textbook; both sections were about American colonization and Jamestown. As they read, students engaged in think-alouds, providing verbal reports of their meaning-making processes.

Some students were challenged by the diary entry and its archaic vocabulary and syntax, yet these elements were engaging for the better readers. Students who had had greater exposure to such texts had less difficulty and developed more connections to the text. Students with less prior experience and knowledge were frustrated by the excerpt and did not connect to it. Similarly, the embedded poem was long and contained difficult vocabulary. It, too, helped develop understanding of the topic among better readers, but more average readers struggled, and the genre of poetry puzzled some as it did not match their expectations for historical text.

Although the text features presented comprehension advantages for stronger readers, few of the students in the study compared across texts; indeed, only one student showed evidence of reading across text. The students also failed to source texts as they read. However, some students did call upon prior knowledge from the Disney movie *Pocahontas* when they engaged with this topic. The film appeared to have shaped the historical thinking and text engagement of some respondents. Afflerbach and VanSledright (2001) concluded that embedded texts have potential for history instruction; they can enrich students' understandings of and connections to text, yet they may also confuse or be of less use to certain students. Thus, when using these resources, teachers need to consider how to introduce and scaffold the material. To that end, Afflerbach and VanSledright called for more research on how students understand and see these texts, rather than just whether they engage in particular practices associated with strong or weak reading comprehension, as well as more research on how such texts are actually used in classrooms. Afflerbach and VanSledright's argument builds on work by text researchers who argue that how students understand differences in text genre and argument structure may shape how they take up and comprehend text ideas (see Graesser et al., in press; McNamara, Kintsch, Butler Songer, & Kintsch, 1996).

Text Use in History Teaching and Learning

Of the studies we located that focused on the everyday use of text in history classrooms, all were focused on texts other than the standard textbook and all were conducted by researchers in history and social studies education, rather than by reading researchers. This pattern seems important, because despite the prominence of their presence in schools and in research, history textbooks are not the only resources used in classrooms. At the same time, history and social studies educators caution against the superficial or uncritical use of primary sources. Bain (2006), for example, addressed the use of primary sources as a way to challenge the authority of the textbook. He noted that his students saw the textbook as the historical authority, and he sought to develop a "transformation in [his] students' relationships to the books, to the historical content in the books, and to the authors who wrote them" (p. 2084).

Working with his own classes, Bain (2006) carried out a case study of three classrooms with a total of 76 students across a 3-week unit on the plague in 14th century Africa, Europe, and Asia. As he taught, he collected archival, ethnographic, and observational data on his students. In addition to reading and analyzing multiple primary sources, "Students also used data compiled by historians, including population estimates, mortality rates, and economic indicators." (p. 2087). They used these diverse resources to construct their own accounts of the plague, and only then did they engage with the textbook. They compared their accounts to that of the book, and then wrote letters to the text authors questioning their choices with respect to evidence and focus in the book. The students were also encouraged to question Bain's own construction of the text set.

In this process, the students developed varying ranges of understanding and knowledge about the Plague and the use of primary sources in history. Bain (2006) provided evidence of varying levels of complexity of student reading; some students did not question sources or read across documents whereas others did a better job. More successful students connected authors and documents to a historical context and used their own accounts to judge the quality of the textbook. As these students questioned the decisions made by the textbook authors and by their teacher, they began to shift the authority from the book to the evidence found in their own analyses, thus approaching more authentic historical practice. In this study, Bain effectively demonstrated how diverse historical texts can be used and made clear how students' assumptions about and relationships to text as authority might shape their comprehension of the main concepts of history, but did not focus explicitly on the reading demands of such texts. He also did not delve deeply into the factors which led some students to be successful and others to struggle; future research could take up these questions.

Saye and Brush (2002) explored the use of digital texts in classroom historical inquiry through their design of an "integrated hypermedia learning environment," which they called Decision Point. This tool was an "interactive database of multimedia content resources" related to themes of instruction, in this case the Civil Rights Movement. Decision Point included organizational tools to help students collect, analyze, and question historical evidence and also to develop their own historical arguments. Historical information was presented through timelines, photographs, audio, video, and primary and secondary text documents. The researchers used Decision Point in a design study in one secondary United States history classroom with 21 students to explore its application. They found certain challenges inherent to the use of the "embedded scaffolds" of the application. Students needed significant support in historical thinking in order to engage effectively with the tool, and thus the teacher needed to be a master teacher familiar with disciplinary thinking. Despite the difficulties, they found that students did show an improved ability from pre- to post-instruction in using data from a variety of sources to support an argument, a key aspect of historical inquiry with text.

Summarizing the Research on Text in History and History Classrooms

Looking across these studies, the primary difference between the nature of text in historical practice and school-based learning perhaps begins with the textbook. Although historians do frequently refer to secondary historical analyses, they do not accord them the authority given the textbook in a classroom. Moreover, with the exception of two studies described previously (Bain, 2006; Saye & Brush, 2002), most work around texts in history instruction has examined the text or the interaction of text and individual reader (as measured in student outcome data), rather than the use or role of text in history instruction itself. The use of historical inquiry to guide text interaction is seldom mentioned, let alone examined. In addition, while historians use primary documents extensively and social studies educators advocate such documents (Bain, 2005; Wineburg & Martin, 2004), the existing evidence does not make clear how often or to what extent primary sources are used in history classrooms. Finally, although classroom observational research on historical literacy (Bain, 2006; Moje & Speyer, 2008) suggests that at least some history teachers use instructional resources such as photographs, audio recordings, and video in their teaching, these media are generally not discussed in research focused on the use of text in history classrooms. An investigation of the role of such texts in history teaching and learning, and specifically of how these other media shape the comprehension of print media, seems long overdue.

Text use in history classrooms is perhaps beginning to change with the advent of new technologies. Although resources like Decision Point are still not widely used, increasing Internet access is making a wide variety of resources more accessible. The ease of finding and obtaining documents may in time change actual patterns of use. According to Lee (2002), "digital history" is made up of "electronically reproduced primary source texts, images, and artifacts as well as the constructed historical narratives, accounts, or presentations that result from digital historical inquiry" (p. 504). Such resources are often stored in electronic collections and provide greater ease of access and use of a variety of texts. For example, the "American Memory Project" of the United States Library of Congress has a collection of over 3,000 documents about slavery, including interviews with and documents about ex-slaves carried out during the WPA and the Federal Writer's Project, 1936–1940. Numerous similar collections exist, with the potential to provide teachers and students with access to digital reproductions of diaries, newspapers, letters, maps, official documents, and other such resources. The databases and websites available could serve as valuable tools for instruction because they are easy to search, well organized, and can be used in a variety of ways and settings.

Given the vast array of resources available, educators must be careful to assess the quality and authenticity of such resources before they use them with students. The evidence reviewed by Lee (2002), however, suggests that digital history has had a limited impact so far in secondary school classrooms. Some teachers appear to be using digital history effectively, but many more teachers appear to need more support and training on how best to utilize these resources. Our own review of the literature found few current studies that examine how teachers and students are using the Internet-based resources in history learning, suggesting another potentially fruitful line of inquiry on the role of text in disciplinary learning.

Finally, students who read any of these historical texts face numerous challenges. As Wineburg (2001) pointed out, much of the meaning in such documents lies in the "subtext, a text of hidden and latent meanings" involving the motivations, rationale and goals of the author. Furthermore, many historical texts, by definition, originated in past eras and present the reader with new vocabulary and language usage which must be comprehended and placed into context in order to gain meaning from the document (Afflerbach & VanSledright, 2001). In addition, historical accounts are often narratives, and problems can arise when students confuse one narrative for official history and consequently dismiss alternative narratives as necessarily false (Barton & Levstik, 2004). Historians, by virtue of their training, are aware of these challenges and address them as part of their work; teachers and students then can learn from disciplinary practice in order to address the difficulties more effectively, but more research needs to be done on how historians use texts, and how teachers currently teach from and teach about such texts.

The differences in the role of text between the practice of history and learning history in school stem in part from differing goal structures and social contexts. In the practice of history, questions drive the use of text, whereas in history classrooms, the text often drives and produces the questions. Practicing historians use texts to research questions of interest to them, and in the process they typically utilize a variety of text types and engage in corroboration, sourcing, and contextualization. History teachers and learners in elementary and secondary schools, however, tend to use textbooks, and primary documents to a lesser degree, to summarize large patterns of history and review factual information.

A robust body of research addresses the problems of history and social studies textbooks, but researchers do not appear to have studied the extent to which textbooks are used and the nature of the use in classrooms. One of the primary shortcomings in much of this work done around text is that the research often assumes that current conventional usage patterns of text are appropriate; in other words, most studies that have sought to improve history textbooks have not focused upon their use, but upon their structure. Bain (2006) focused on the use of the textbook, but in turn did not address its structure; these areas can be integrated in productive ways. Furthermore, although several studies did examine the structure of texts, there was little evidence of analyses of textual content, of the role and nature of the historical information texts presented, or of how, as Afflerbach and Vansledright (2001) argued, students actually take up different texts in classroom situations. There has also been little work done comparing the use of textbooks to the use of primary documents. Although primary documents are currently popular in the instructional literature, few studies have compared content learning and literacy outcomes across the different text types.

In addition to shifting the research focus from problems with textbooks (or even with primary texts), it appears that new methods of conducting research on the role of text in history learning are needed. Looking across the classroom studies profiled above, we noted that few studies on text use and historical literacy look beyond one school or even a few classrooms. Reading research could thus benefit from large-scale observational and survey research to document and analyze text use and instructional patterns around text in a broad array of history classrooms in different regions, different school types (rural, suburban, exurban, urban), and among different grade levels.

Finally, much of the extant work, which is valuable, was undertaken in the 1990s; significantly less work has been done since 2000. The field needs more research into how new text types, including digital resources, are and can be used in the history classroom. The challenge in the field of historical and literacy education, in a time when history and social studies research appear to be taking a back seat to an emphasis on reading, mathematics, and science learning, is to find rigorous and meaningful ways to conduct this research.

In the next section, we turn to one of those foregrounded disciplinary/subject matter areas: mathematics. As we have done in the review of historical text use, here we review the available literature on how texts are used by practicing mathematicians and contrast those uses with the uses of text in mathematics classrooms, as represented by the extant literature.

THE ROLE OF TEXT IN THE WORK OF MATHEMATICIANS AND MATHEMATICS TEACHERS AND LEARNERS

Despite reform efforts and rhetoric directed toward improving the mathematics achievement of U.S. public school graduates, students are not achieving at the levels they should be, whether the ultimate beneficiary of public education is the national economy; the field of mathematics; the individual pursuit of life, liberty, and happiness; or the democratic foundations of our nation. More important, achievement differences among students continue to reflect differences in social class, race, and poverty. Given this state of affairs, the fundamental nature of classroom learning, and the undeniable importance of text in all classroom activity, we examine the role of texts in the discipline of mathematics and in mathematics classrooms. Specifically, given the weight of algebra in the mathematics curriculum—approximately 60% of the questions on the ACT test concern algebra, for example (Gilman, Saydak, & Vlk, 2005)—we look here at the role of text in the practice of mathematics, as it can be discerned in mathematical studies, and in the teaching and learning of algebra, as indicated by studies of actual middle and high school classrooms.

METHODS OF THE REVIEW

Driven by the need to understand the present situation and to yield understandings strong enough to support the weight of considerable future research and reform efforts, this review is limited to work published since 2000 in peer-reviewed journals. This review also does not consider work on cognitive issues in the processing of algebraic text, linguistic analysis of classroom texts, or the theoretical or ideological issues related to mathematics teaching and learning. Instead, we examine studies that reveal something about the role of text in the discipline of algebraic mathematics or in mathematics classrooms, particularly algebra classrooms. Like our review of the role of text use in history classrooms, we found that the available literature on actual mathematics text use is scant, and we thus draw from and attempt to extend the findings of related studies.

Data collection began with searches of the leading educational electronic databases (ERIC, PsycINFO, Education Abstracts, ISI Web of Science, and ProQuest Dissertation Abstracts), along with searches of general databases like ArticleFirst and Google Scholar. Formulating searches was something of a challenge. Terms such as reading, writing, literacy, and text yielded thousands of false hits; terms such as algebra and textbook, or even text, seemed too limiting. Search terms were therefore narrowed and expanded selectively to include items such as instructional practices, curricular materials, teaching, learning, mathematics, and algebraic concepts, such as *functions*. The search results were then culled. It is important that no recent studies seem to have been conducted specifically concerning the role of text in algebra classrooms of adolescent students. The research profiled here therefore deals secondarily or perhaps only peripherally with text, and the findings that do not relate to text are not discussed.

The general trends revealed in the data are both disheartening and encouraging; disheartening because of the dearth of quality research addressing this foundational question of what is going on with text in algebra classrooms, yet encouraging because the need for further research is unquestionable. In terms of research on text use in the practice of mathematics, little exists.

In studies that do consider the use of text in mathematics learning at all, there is a tendency to equate the mathematics curriculum with the curricular materials. This may be most clearly reflected in the fact that when schools consider ways to improve or otherwise revise the mathematics education they provide, talk often turns to changing the textbook. As we illustrate in this review, however, studies of algebra classrooms show that this approach is not likely to succeed because the role of text is complicated, variability among teachers is significant, factors such as access to technology can also shape how text serves teaching and learning, and analyzing or changing textbooks is not enough.

What Counts as Text in Mathematics and Mathematics Learning?

Wallace and Clark (2005) identified three types of texts in their framework for thinking about the potential roles of text in mathematics classrooms: problems, mathematics, and life. "Problems" as texts appear to be the primary focus of research on algebra teaching and learning. This work looks closely at both symbolic expressions and verbal word problems, in textbooks and in student work, to explore the cognitive demands of comprehending and constructing algebra. Although such research may further the field's understanding of how algebraic thinking develop and of the role of text in that development, it tends to stay out of classrooms, with most such research done in laboratory or other controlled settings. Moreover, this relatively large body of research evidences a narrow characterization of algebra as problems and procedures, possibly indicating the persistent and still powerful legacy of a transmission-based, rather than constructivist or inquiry-based, stance on algebra learning and on the uses of algebra texts.

The second and third types of text outlined by Wallace and Clark (2005) are more expansive. When they labeled "mathematics" itself as a kind of text, Wallace and Clark referred to the body of knowledge and sets of tasks typically rendered in formal schooling. This view of text in mathematics includes the problems to be read and solved from textbooks, worksheets and other classroom materials and adds "seeking solutions to real-life problems, examining multiple sources of text, in-depth discussion, use of multiple formats, and justification of a solution,... [utilizing] textbooks (and other classroom materials), trade books, articles, etc." (p. 69). The mathematical text of "life" includes the texts of mathematics as a discipline and places them in real time (junk mail advertisements, for example), positioning the discipline of mathematics "as a language of power necessary to take part in a democratic society" (p. 69). The difference is subtle, but significant, and bears restating: Although "mathematics" texts may be realistic, they are not typically real-life, as illustrated in the following mathematics textbook excerpt analyzed by Gerofsky (1996):

> Every year (but it has never happened), Stella (there is no Stella) rents a craft table at a local fun fair (which does not exist) ... She reduces the price of each additional sweater (and there are no sweaters) by 10% of the price of the previous sweater that the person bought (and there are no people, or sweaters, or prices). (p. 41)

Although the work of mathematicians may not revolve around the sorts of real-time, real-life texts discussed by Wallace and Clark (2005), it does unquestionably deal with issues and problems that have real import for the field currently. Research tends to focus on formal mathematics texts, reflecting the recent push toward constructivist theories of learning as espoused by influential organizations such as the National Council of Teachers of Mathematics (NCTM), but little if any attention has been paid to actual life texts related to mathematics. Thus, while the stated goal of recent reform efforts is to apprentice students into the work of mathematicians and other everyday practitioners, recent studies do not seem to support the goal by examining the mathematics texts of real mathematicians (which might be best represented by Wallace and

Clark's conception of texts as problems) or of everyday life situations (e.g., the junk mail advertisement). In other words, although what counts as mathematical text is broad, in Wallace and Clark's view, what gets counted as text in most research studies of mathematics learning is narrow, typically confined to the texts of schooling.

Public school social studies curricula have been criticized for failing to incorporate primary documents, thereby denying children the opportunity to engage meaningfully with history as a discipline, but there appears to be no corollary in mathematics education. That is, there are few studies that make serious recommendations to bring primary mathematical documents into classrooms (Love & Pimm, 1996). Calls to bring outside or real-world texts into the algebra classroom are arguably deceptive, for often they are not about real-world texts at all (consider the above example offered by Gerofsky, 1996). Moreover, the opportunity to read and write real mathematical texts, those that deal with real-life mathematics, is generally reserved for doctoral-level studies. Given that the educational background of most secondary teachers does not reach this level, it may be no wonder that the role of text in their classrooms is not truly mathematical. This is not to say that texts are not used, of course, although we might in fact come to such a fantastic conclusion, judging by contemporary research.

What Is the Role of Text in the Discipline of Mathematics?

Mathematics is a language, and algebra in adolescent classrooms, where symbolic notation may be confronted seriously for the first time, is as much about the language as the ideas expressed by it. Clearly, the mathematics is being communicated and constructed somehow, and the primary means must be textual, but the ubiquity of text may render it invisible, and this carries over into analyses of the work of mathematicians. Mason, Burton, and Stacey (1985) and Burton (1999) analyzed mathematical thinking, with a focus on how mathematicians come to know and conceive of their subject, but the role of text in these processes was not mentioned. The same can be said when examining the role of text in mathematics learning, for that matter: Boaler and Staples' (2008) impressive 5-year study of 700 students and their teachers at three California high schools is another good example. One would guess that, in all the lecturing, questioning, discussing, justifying, and collaborating around and about mathematics, texts were ever present, but texts somehow did not appear in the research report in any substantial form. Whether in the working lives of mathematicians or in the learning lives of mathematics students, texts seem to be almost invisible.

Perhaps such practices reflect the nature of mathematical discourse, where the convention is not to state the obvious. The texts are the mathematics, however. It is through language that mathematics is expressed, communicated, and created (Bass, 2006). Burton and Morgan (2000) studied mathematicians' writing, investigating whether and how published research papers might reveal information about authors' epistemological stances, identities, and ways of representing mathematical activity. Applying discourse analytic theories of Kress (2003) and Halliday and Matthiessen (2004), and using the Mathematical Association of America's (MAA) *Mathematical Writing* (Knuth, Larrabee, & Roberts, 1989) as a point of comparison, Burton and Morgan analyzed 53 published mathematics research papers, finding, for example, that, whereas the MAA advocated the use of "we" both to encourage a more active, agentive voice and to attempt to include the reader, practicing mathematicians tended to avoid personal pronouns and to use the passive voice. The mathematicians appeared, in other words, to write neutrally and anonymously. They also tended to use absolute verbal modality (particularly the case with female authors), reflecting a view that mathematics is about certainty.

In a follow-up study, Morgan (2005) applied systemic functional linguistics to compare how definitions were treated in two trigonometry textbooks (one lower level, one higher level) and one example of published academic research. (Although trigonometry is not algebra, we include Morgan's study because it may be unique.) The lower-level math textbook tended to present definitions as a one-to-one relationship between a word and a concept, presented as absolute, unchallengeable fact. In the higher-level texts, on the other hand, the treatment of definitions seemed much more complex. Words and concepts were open to multiple definitions, where choice of one definition was driven by the author's purpose; definitions did more than just name concepts, functioning as key elements of the mathematical rhetoric that, in essence, is the math; and there was, as a consequence, greater recognition of definitions as socially constructed, "though it is not always clear whether this is the construction of new objects or naming of pre-existing objects" (p. 111).

Bass (2006), an algebra scholar, offered a more explicit stance on the role of text in mathematical knowledge production and the learning of mathematics in an essay on the role of oral and written language in knowledge generation in mathematics:

> For one thing, mathematics does involve substantial amounts of conventional text, not least in the form of dreaded word problems, but also in its extensive use of ordinary language, in both informal and technical ways. Further, mathematical relations and equations, even when expressed with technical notation (symbols, diagrams, etc.), are themselves a form of text, meaningful and articulable propositions, and their comprehension demands skills of literacy not entirely unlike those required for other kinds of textual sense making. Indeed, literacy for the student of mathematics entails being able to navigate flexibly back and forth between two or more language systems—academic mathematics language, school language, and common out-of-school languages (including one's home language). (p. 1)

Bass (2006) continued in his essay to argue that words, symbols, and diagrams are the grist of mathematical text; these three forms of representation are fundamental to communication of mathematical knowledge, and thus are fundamental aspects of using mathematical texts. But equally important, argued Bass, is understanding two epistemological imperatives in mathematics. First is that the nature of knowledge in mathematics is dependent on deductive mathematical proof rather than on empirical evidence rendered by nature or on human social constructs. A second and related imperative is that the means of proving must be shared and thus must be rendered with utmost precision. Thus, argued Bass, "The practices of doing mathematics are in significant measure the practices of precise and supple use of language, in a variety of forms" (p. 3). Taken together, these two epistemological imperatives produce a quality of language unique to mathematics: the compression of concepts via the use of symbols and the provision of alternate representations such as diagrams and graphs. Each of these forms produces texts that serve not only to communicate ideas in mathematics, but also to do mathematics itself. The role of text in the production of mathematical knowledge (i.e., the doing of mathematics) thus appears to be central and unique to the work itself, and yet may be taken-for-granted by those who do mathematics on a daily basis.

What Is the Role of Text in Mathematics (Algebra) Classrooms?

Our review suggests that the tensions uncovered between what counts as text and how it is used in the practice of mathematics and what counts as text and how it is used in classrooms may parallel the tensions between reform and traditional orientations toward mathematics teaching and learning in schools. Organizations such as the NCTM and the MAA urge participants to think of mathematics as a human phenomenon, culturally and socially mediated, but they face a long historical positioning of mathematics as autonomously, anonymously, and authoritatively impersonal (Burton & Morgan, 2000). In an analysis of textbooks, bolstered by teacher and student interviews and teacher observations, Haggarty and Pepin (2002) investigated differences in opportunities to learn presented by mathematics textbooks in the United Kingdom, France, and Germany. They examined the nature of the mathematics made available in textbooks, how teachers mediated the math in textbooks, and the access pupils had to textbooks. The researchers concluded that both cultural and educational traditions may influence what happens in classrooms. For example, texts that represented mathematics as highly skills-based or linguistic appeared to lead teachers to represent mathematics as skills-based and linguistic in their instruction. That is, students in such classrooms were expected to learn mathematics primarily through skills practice or symbolic manipulation. Moreover, Haggarty and Pepin suggested that the selection of particular text types were mediated in broader cultural traditions of countries and regions, thus suggesting that a study of mathematics text use in disciplinary domains needed to account for differences among countries and cultural groups.

Regardless of how and why the nature of mathematics texts has evolved, scholars working from a disciplinary literacy perspective (Lee & Spratley, 2010; Moje, 2007a, 2008a; Shanahan & Shanahan, 2008) argued that apprenticeship into the practices of mathematicians should involve apprenticeship into the ways in which mathematicians use language, which might include, for example, using words, symbols, and diagrams with a high degree of precision, as described by Bass (2006). Mathematics textbooks currently in use may not be conducive to this focus on language, however, as illustrated by some of the implications of Morgan's (2005) findings:

1. Students may not learn how or why mathematicians use particular words;
2. Students may not learn how mathematicians arrive at particular definitions and language;
3. Opportunities to learn "the powerful and productive role that definitions can play in mathematics" may be limited to higher-level students; and
4. National standards and other cultural forces emphasizing vocabulary and driving the publication of such textbooks may present "a restricted image of the nature of mathematical language itself ... [which] consists of more than just specialist vocabulary" and in which constructing definitions and using them rhetorically are fundamental activities (p. 115).

There may be instructionally sound reasons why the texts used and the ways in which they are used by students and mathematicians differ, however. Some perspectives would call for very different types of texts in learning mathematics from those used in doing mathematics, for example. In addition, adolescents may not be developmentally ready to use text like mathematicians, who have mastered their unnatural discourse through years of practice.

The research of Nathan, Long, and Alibali (2002) underscored these findings by analyzing ten popular pre-algebra and algebra textbooks to determine how the texts seemed to scaffold algebra learning, that is, whether they gave precedence to symbolic or more narrative language. Not surprisingly, they found that the texts privileged symbolic language, although the algebra texts did so to a larger degree than the pre-algebra texts, and the more recently published texts had fewer sections made up exclusively of symbol language (reflecting reform). Considered in that light, Nathan and Koedinger's (2000) finding that students were more successful solving word problems than symbolic problems may seem predictable, yet it ran contrary to the beliefs of many high school teachers and, perhaps, the general population, who characterize word problems as the bane of K–12 mathematics. Based on their research, Nathan et al. (2002) called for greater understanding of the development of algebraic thinking, recognition of multiple paths in its development, closer attention to texts as influential upon students and teachers, and more research on educators' beliefs about students, algebra, curricular materials, teaching, and learning. Nevertheless, very little research appears to have been conducted in mathematical literacy or mathematics education on text use, other than the role of curricular materials in leading teachers into certain kinds of mathematical teaching practices.

Teachers' Uses of Curricular Materials and Classroom Texts

Despite the need for more information about how students use and make sense of classroom texts in mathematics, the dominant trend in studies of algebra education is a focus on teachers' uses of classroom texts. Remillard (2005) reviewed research conducted since 1980 on teachers' use of mathematics curricular materials like textbooks to investigate how scholarship has treated foundational constructs such as what counts as curricular materials and what is the teacher's role with respect to them. She did not focus on any particular branch of mathematics, and thus her findings have general significance for algebra as a central part of secondary mathematics. Remillard (2005) noted that, perhaps spurred by the shifts in theoretical stance among educational scholars, a number of researchers over the last 25 years have looked at teacher use of curricular resources. She concluded, however, that instead of increasing our understanding of how curriculum is enacted in actual classrooms, this body of work only seems to reveal how little we know. There simply appears to be too much variability: "Findings from these studies, however, have not been consolidated to produce reliable, theoretically grounded knowledge on teachers' interactions with curriculum materials that might guide future research or the design or implementation of curricula" (p. 212).

Herbel-Eisenmann, Lubienski, and Id-Deen's (2006) year-long case study of Jackie, an algebra teacher, is interesting to consider in this context. Jackie taught in a school district that offered students a choice between a more traditional and a more reform-oriented mathematics curriculum and, despite having zealously promoted NCTM-related changes in her district's math program, she consciously and clearly tailored her instruction according to the class she was teaching, whether algebra or "integrated" mathematics. When pushed for specific examples, Jackie explained that ideas such as the Pythagorean Theorem are simply given to students in the algebra text and then students are asked to apply them. In contrast, the integrated mathematics materials posed problems to help students discover the theorem and to connect it to their previous knowledge. She explained that connections among algebraic representations were emphasized more in the integrated materials, she found it easier to discuss "how tables, graphs, and equations are related to each other," and graphing calculator explorations of these ideas were integrated throughout the materials. In the Algebra I class, the ideas and representations were treated separately: "In Algebra there are separate chapters for these things with fewer connections between them ... connections are not easily made by students" (pp. 332–333).

Although Jackie acknowledged the textbook as one of the factors driving the changes in her teaching practices and text use, she additionally cited the impact of parents, who had purposefully chosen a curricular stance, and students, who expected a certain curricular stance (although they might not talk about it as such). The authors concluded that research examining only one part of a teacher's day or only one aspect of a teacher's practice, such as use of curricular materials, may miss a great deal of important information. The authors also found that most studies of secondary school classrooms do just that. Ultimately, Herbel-Eisenmann et al. (2006) argued for an increased awareness of the situated, or "local," nature of mathematics teaching and the many factors that affect it.

Additional examples of variability in the ways texts are used in classrooms include Tarr and colleagues' studies of teachers (Tarr, Chavez, Reys, & Reys, 2006; Tarr et al., 2008), some using a reform-oriented curriculum designed by the National Science Foundation and others using a more traditional curriculum. In one study (Tarr et al., 2006) of nearly 40 teachers, they found that, regardless of the nature of the texts, teachers make significant decisions on a day-to-day basis about what topics to teach and how to teach them. Based on these findings, Tarr et al. argued that, unless the role of text in classrooms is somehow normalized, students' opportunities to learn mathematics are likely to be inequitable. Moreover, attempts to increase student achievement, simply by changing the classroom texts, may be futile because how the texts are used appears to matter as much as what is available in them.

Implicit in this recommendation for normalization is the notion that text use can be shaped in broad ways, despite the individuality of teachers or their situated practices. In addition to teacher training, one important influence that has been studied but needs to be better understood is technology. Just as literacy matters in all content areas, the complications embodied by so-called 21st-century literacy also matter in algebra. For example, Graham and Thomas's (2000) study of nearly 200 adolescents, in which graphing calculators were the experimental text for a three-week-long unit about letters as algebraic variables, found that achievement was greater for the students who read and wrote electronically (cf. Ellington, 2006).

Without question, the landscape is changing and, with it, the role of text in algebra teaching and learning. Navigating these changes successfully depends largely upon having a secure understanding of the terrain. As Remillard (2005) found, however, this understanding is lacking. Her recommendation, which seems to be echoed by the field of secondary mathematics education generally, was to be attentive to teaching as a complex, situated practice. Regarding the role of text, this approach may explain the trend in recent research to focus on language, both in classroom discourse and in textbooks. Even the work on methodology by and large seems to reflect a particular emphasis on language, advocating systemic functional linguistics to analyze mathematics textbooks, semiotics, and classroom activity (e.g., Radford, 2000; Zolkower & Shreyar, 2007). Although attention to context and language functions is certainly needed, something essential may yet be missing. One key missing ingredient in the puzzle of the role of text in mathematics learning is the student. Unlike the review of text use in history classrooms, our review documented only two close studies of how students make sense of the texts of mathematics classrooms, let alone of how texts are used every day.

Student-Text Interactions in Mathematics Classrooms

Hall (2007) used a year's worth of bi-weekly observations, student questionnaires and interviews, student comprehension assessments, and student work, to demonstrate how one student and her teacher interacted around the texts of a mathematics classroom. The student was identified as a struggling reader, whereas her teacher was identified as exemplary. Hall concluded that this one student engaged in behaviors that hid her struggle to read, thus leading the teacher to assume that she did not understand the mathematics, when, in fact, the text appeared to pose problems for her.

Lubienski's (2000) study is another rare instance of a study that concerns the role of text for adolescent students, although it does not discuss the text per se in great detail. As a trainer in a Connected Mathematics pilot school, Lubienski spent 1 year teaching seventh graders and collecting data on her students' attitudes and achievement with the new curriculum. Her interest was in class differences, and indeed she found them. Like the readers Heath (1983) documented in her study of the relationship between social class and reading practices, the students of middle to high socioeconomic status in Lubienski's mathematics study tended to prefer and do better with the open, contextualized problems of the new curriculum, whereas students of low socioeconomic status tended to want clearer directions, fewer words, better scores, and a different book. Thus, it seems that different cultural and social class practices also have implications for ways with mathematics learning. Such findings suggest that close research on how students of different backgrounds and experiences use and make sense of classroom texts could contribute to instructional interventions designed to improve both disciplinary literacy and mathematics learning, especially where texts are involved.

In addition, these findings should serve to remind disciplinary literacy researchers that texts are not simply linguistic artifacts or discursive tools to be understood in the context of classroom activity. Especially in schools, texts are the source of and inspiration for much of the learning that takes place, whether they are mentioned or not, and whether learning is cognitive, constructivist, or sociocultural. Simply stated, how texts are used in classrooms is at least as important as the content, organization, and wording of the text. And yet, most of the research we could locate on text and mathematics learning focused primarily on what texts said or on how texts might lead teachers to change their practice, that is, on how texts might be "educative" for teachers (Davis & Krajcik, 2005; Remillard, 2005).

Summarizing the Research on Text in Mathematics and Mathematics Classrooms

One motivation behind this chapter was a concern that current educational scholarship may be privileging the study of the social and cultural elements of teaching and learning, at the expense of examining how those texts represent and are mediated by social and cultural contexts. Having reviewed the research, we believe this concern is well founded, and it has led us to further concerns. No studies seem to have looked specifically at the role of text in algebra instruction. The peripheral discussions of text that we did find have treated it in an uncanny way, as a set of linguistic features without mention of what those features attach to, and calls for greater attention to text want to push scholarship even further in that direction. As Wallace and Clark (2005) noted, however, the content of texts largely shapes how they can and may be used. So, to the concerns about the disturbing absence of attention to how texts are used in studies of algebra instruction, we add the disturbing absence of text content, and we challenge scholars and practitioners alike to consider the implications of such dearth on the discussions about apprenticeship, relevance, and real-world, "everyday" mathematics. Synthesizing the current research, as sparse and variable as it may be, we conclude that these shortcomings must all be addressed if we are to develop the theoretical and practical understanding of algebra instruction that will allow schools to make gains in student achievement. It is more work, but it is important work. With that call, we turn to another area of text use we consider critical to disciplinary learning, that of young people's uses of texts in times and spaces outside of school.

THE ROLE OF YOUTHS' OUT-OF-SCHOOL TEXTS IN CLASSROOM DISCIPLINARY LEARNING

Based on expanded definitions of literacy and text as outlined previously in the chapter, literacy scholars—particularly those who study adolescents (e.g., Alvermann & Hagood, 2000b; Gee, 2003; Leander & Lovvorn, 2006; Lewis & Fabos, 2005; Steinkuehler, 2007)—have explored the literacy practices youth engage in outside of school, either informally or in out-of-school time literacy programs (Heath & McLaughlin, 1993; Morrell, 2002). These researchers have argued that young people read and write with competence in out-of-school (OOS) settings, especially as their engagements with texts move beyond the print-oriented literacy practices of school. This work emphasizes the different literacy practices mediated by diverse tools such as graphic novels, video games, instant messaging, and manga reading (Black, 2006, 2008; Chandler-Olcott, 2008; Chandler-Olcott & Mahar, 2003; Leander & McKim, 2003; Lewis, 2008).

Indeed, numerous small-scale studies of OOS literacies have demonstrated that participants were actively and often critically engaged in the community of practices which they voluntarily chose, in part, it seems, because they were already well aware of specific discourses and necessary knowledge required for their participation in various literacy communities (e.g., Alvermann, Young, Green, & Wisenbaker, 1999; Cowan, 2005; Finders, 1996a, 1996b; Gustavson, 2007; Mahiri, 1998; Moje, 2000). Despite these findings related to the literate practices of students outside of school, several important questions remain about the role of OOS texts in students' overall literacy learning. Specifically, the studies cited are uniformly, and necessarily, small in scale, and the field needs more detailed information about the text reading (and writing) of multiple groups of youth. More important, few studies have looked closely at the nature and complexity of OOS texts, at how youth use texts in their out-of-school experiences, or at how students' engagements with OOS texts might be leveraged to support or advance their in-school academic literacy learning.

Moreover, although the role of text in classroom learning has been attended to in previous editions of the *Handbook* (e.g., Alexander & Jetton, 2000; Wade & Moje, 2000), exploration of the role of OOS text on learning in the school disciplines seems not to be a primary focus in literacy research. However, current interest in disciplinary literacy (Alvermann, 2008; Lee & Spratley, 2010; Moje, 2007a, 2008a) that calls for attention to how youth navigate the multiple domain-specific practices in and out of school may prompt a new stage of research on OOS literacy practices in relation to disciplinary learning. In the spirit of promoting such a research agenda, we offer an analysis of the limited extant research on role of OOS (sometimes referred to as everyday) text in disciplinary learning. Here, however, we deviate from our prior focus on history and algebra as the disciplines under study for the simple reason that very little OOS research has made any explicit connection to any of the secondary school subject areas. Instead, our search criterion was to examine any OOS research that attempted to connect to academic or schooled literacy and text practices. Not surprisingly, the research we reviewed focused mainly on connections to the English Language Arts (cf. Moje, 2008b).

What Counts as Text Outside of School

For researchers to gain a better understanding of the role of OOS texts, it is important to clearly delineate their primary characteristics. This is a challenging task, however, because out-of-school texts encompass a variety of forms and modes, including still and moving images, sound, motion, and gesture as well as alphabet letters, and through these modes, texts can be produced in the Internet space, printed media, or television and movies. Furthermore, all of these media can be incorporated into one product designed to deliver its producer or author's message(s). That said, however, a few qualities have been described by researchers. First, many scholars argue that OOS texts are fluid and dynamic, often intersecting with other forms of texts. Second, many OOS texts are nonlinear, hyperlinked, multimodal, and interactive (Coiro, 2003); websites, for example, are among the most widely read text type outside of school (Moje, Overby, Tysvaer, & Morris, 2008; Roberts & Foehr, 2008), and clearly encompass each of these qualities. Third, even when published as paper texts, many OOS texts make explicit connections to other textual media. The Harry Potter book series, for example, extends far beyond the paper copies of the books, into movies, fanfiction texts, fan performances at media events, Internet sites, and more. Thus, what counts as text outside of school is a broad collection of text types and media, often linked by digital, media, and social networks. By contrast, many scholars have argued that in-school texts and accompanying literacy practices tend to be linear, isolated from other texts (except by the intertextual connections readers or teacher make), and fixed or static (Leander & Lovvorn, 2006) containers of information or ideas (Bowden, 1993; Ingalls, 2005), thus begging the question of how to make connections from the OOS texts youth read of their own volition or for social and work responsibilities and the in-school texts of the academic disciplines.

The Role of OOS Text in English Language Arts

In the early 1990s, noteworthy research studies were conducted in the area of writing and composition by employing OOS literacy practices of adolescents. Camitta (1993), as an on-site writing teacher, conducted a 3-year ethnographic research study in an urban high school on the East Coast, specifically examining students' writings prompted by any school activities, her own activity, and voluntary work done at home in order to explore adolescent vernacular writing as a set of texts and practices. Her findings through observation, interviews, and students' artifacts set the stage for many recent New Literacy Studies (NLS). She concluded that students were more actively engaged in writing when the chosen topics were closely linked into their own cultural and personal experiences (cf. Moll & Gonzalez, 1994).

Camitta (1993) also noted that her participants "document a tradition of writing that exists outside of the academy, is culturally significant, and will continue to exist influenced by, but not dependent upon, the conventions and practice of the academy" (p. 232). Finally, she emphasized the role of writing in transforming students' experience. She found that for her adolescent students, "writing, thinking, talking and feeling are interconnected activities, multiple channels and levels of discourse upon a topic" (p. 241). This multimodal aspect of literate practice is found in recent NLS research as well. For example, this view is closely aligned with the findings of Leander and Lovvorn (2006) in which they argue that literacy practices occurring inside or outside school should not be perceived with a dichotomized view, but as interrelated.

Similarly, Shuman (1993) conducted a 3-year ethnographic research on "Storytelling Rights," or "the use of writing and speaking in the everyday lives of urban adolescents" (p. 247). She found her high school participants challenged a dichotomous approach toward speaking and writing. They competently exchanged these two genres "for both distance and proximity" (p. 247). Also, she concluded similarly to Camitta (1993) in terms of multimodal channels through which their students should be allowed to pass in writing practices and in respect to the cultural context of their participants' everyday lives. In so doing, Camitta and Shuman acknowledged the importance of teaching so the students appropriated different forms of writing, particularly academic writing.

Lee (1993) paved the way for current mixed-methods research on the link between OOS and academic literacies via her study of the integration of African American vernacular discourse features as tools for text analysis in her English Language Arts classroom. She focused on one day of instruction with ninth graders and attempted to help the students connect their existing cultural knowledge with reading canonical texts in school. This is noteworthy because Lee (2001) brought everyday oral textual features into the study of texts in English Language Arts classrooms, while other researchers generally suggest implications for employing OOS texts in school in order to connect their findings to subject matter classes. Lee's (2001, 2007) current work on *cultural modeling* builds on the principles she established in the 1993 work wherein literate and discursive practices are connected to the analysis of text in school classrooms. Although her analyses did not explicitly attend to the nature or complexity of texts youth read outside of school, Lee provided an important model by drawing on important discourse practices and cultural knowledge that allow for complex text reading and communicative practice.

Moje et al. (2008) analyzed both OOS texts and students' readings of them in a large-scale study of youth literacy in and out of school. In one analysis drawing from the larger sample (Moje, 2007b), she used multiple data points to demonstrate that a male youth who appeared to be a poor reader in one context (a computer-administered reading diagnostic that used passages from adopted textbooks across the four academic domains), read skillfully and strategically in a different context (when reading a game magazine of his choosing). What made the analysis particularly compelling was the comparable linguistic complexity of the texts (although not necessarily comparable quality of writing, with the textbook losing out on that score). Moje argued that the young man's ability to read skillfully and strategically was bolstered by his knowledge of the content of the game magazine, together with his engagement in the text. This analysis, however, raises questions of what to do with such findings in terms of leveraging students' reading out of school to support the development of academic and critical text practices in disciplinary learning.

In a variation on Lee's (2007) work on the relationship between cultural and school literacy practices, Morrell (2002) emphasized the role of popular cultural texts as supplements to help students deconstruct dominant discourses and contend with oppressive practices in the hope of achieving a more egalitarian and inclusive society. However, some questions raised by many scholars of adolescent literacy remain unanswered in this study. For example, how did the popular cultural text promote students' learning of English? Although the text practices were used by the adolescent readers as an emancipating and critical tool in understanding the outside world, this study did not attempt to examine the participants' learning in relation to the discipline of English; Morrell's work did indicate, however, that the youth in his studies went on to postsecondary education at high rates, suggesting that simply valuing and incorporating OOS texts for in-school English—and, to some extent, social studies—learning, may make a difference in academic literacy development.

Indeed, in a later study, Morrell and Duncan-Andrade (2006) argued that the failure of many urban students to develop academic literacy skills derives from the inaccessibility of the school curriculum to students outside of the mainstream culture, rather than an intrinsic lack of intelligence on the part of the students. In their OOS literacy program, their participants were invited first to utilize their prior knowledge of familiar literacy forms such as hip-hop lyrics, films, and media (print or online newspapers and other media information) to optimize their learning of critical literacy skills and their application to an analysis of canonical texts. These everyday texts can be considered one form of funds of knowledge (Moll & Gonzalez, 1994) through which the participants were able to access the so-called academic texts.

In her dissertation on a similar topic of writing across academic and spoken-word genres, Ingalls (2005) analyzed data culled from observation of her participants' spoken-word performance and interviews on their academic and spoken-word writing practices. Again, based on the metaphor of containment she adopted from Bowden (1993), Ingalls argued that both in-school writing and OOS spoken-word writing texts are constrained in accordance with their own inherent rules. Significantly, the students Ingalls studied spent a much longer period revising the spoken-word text (e.g., poetry) and even employed a metadiscursive strategy more often and explicitly than they did when engaged in in-school writing assignments. As a college writing instructor, when she modified her writing assignment into a hybrid of spoken-word and traditional rhetorical writing paper similar to the cases of Camitta (1993) and Shuman (1993), she found that one of her participant students successfully and metadiscursively incorporated the two different genres into a meaningful text. The role of hybridity in this context allowed the student flexibility to employ genres in which she was already competent into an in-school assignment and to integrate her personal experiences into in-school writing. That said, not all students needed the opportunity to integrate OOS literacy practices into academic texts; at least one student involved in the case study demonstrated awareness of containment of the writing assignment without losing his excitement and engagement for the writing task.

The Role of OOS in Science, Social Studies, and Mathematics

We found even fewer studies focused on OOS text in relation to school-based science, social studies, or mathematics learning. Barton (1998), for example, conducted a study on an after-school science program for homeless children, focusing on three key participants of middle school age who lived with their single mothers in a homeless shelter. She conducted the study through interviewing and observing the students during and after her science class with a main question of "How are students' lived experiences used, manipulated, forced, pulled, and tugged to fit within the confines of science?" Through what she learned from her interviews, Barton designed her class curriculum in accordance to the young people's surroundings and familiar scientific experiences, with local pollution and food becoming main topics as these students tried to make a connection to their science inquiry project. This approach is similar to Morrell (2002) and Lee's (1993, 2007) studies mentioned above, in which students' everyday experiences are considered to be a scaffold to learning higher levels of disciplinary skills or strategies based on their prior knowledge and constructed through engaging them in their own cultural and social experiences. Barton argued that, "a significant piece of using lived experiences to create science is the decentering of science" (p. 389). Whether any OOS texts were employed in the service of in-school science learning was less clear from Barton's study; what is clear is that although working with text was critical to the work they did in school, texts were not closely analyzed in the study.

In another study explicitly linking the literacies of school science with those of young people's lives outside of school, Moje et al. (2004) studied 30 youth, ages 12–15 through classroom observation, surveys, and interviews. Moje et al. documented a range of texts that adolescents read outside of school, but noted that the reading of extended prose was not a major part of the adolescents' lives. Similar to Barton's (1998) and Lee's (2007) work, these researchers noted the relevance of students' existing knowledge for developing disciplinary knowledge. The authors argued that various kinds of texts, including popular cultural texts, which these students read and wrote on a daily basis, could be used to teach students academic literacies and science concepts while also teaching them to analyze and question the received knowledge available in academic texts. Like the Barton (1998) study, however, Moje et al. (2004) did not include a close analysis of classroom or OOS texts in this report.

In the case of social studies, Stockdill and Moje (2007) underscored the importance of everyday life issues and topics in the texts youth choose to read outside of school and the texts they were required to read in social studies classrooms. Part of a larger longitudinal research project, the study specifically examined the participants' attitudes toward social studies textbooks. Their typical response on the textbooks can be summarized in one word, "boring," due primarily to lack of connection to their real-world experiences. Surprisingly, the same participants who complained about the boring content of social studies textbooks stated that they were interested in reading OOS texts on the issues and themes related to social studies. This finding is aligned with those of aforementioned studies that demonstrated the important role of OOS text as a motivational or scaffolding tool to help adolescent students connect more meaningfully to content area texts.

In another social studies project, Squire, De Vane, and Durga (2008) designed a community of *Civilization III* gamers. *Civilization III* is a Massively Multiple Online Game, a digital game environment that allows a diverse group of gamers to come together virtually to play different kinds of games. In *Civilization III,* players find themselves in collaboration with, and sometimes up against, great leaders in world history as they try to build strong civilizations. The goal of the study was to analyze the game's potential to help disadvantaged upper elementary students develop fluency in both world history reading and problem-solving. The researchers traced trajectories of two core students culled from their larger research project of an after-school program. One of the most prominent findings of this research was the impact of engaging youth in designing and playing these world history games on the young people's academic practices. One of the core study participants, for example, was motivated to check out a relevant book from the library to investigate more information about his assigned country. Designing the game texts on their own, guided by an adult-expert (the researchers) apprenticeship, motivated the students to maintain their growing interest in world civilization and world history. Furthermore, participants who consistently participated in the whole year's program reported that their social studies grades improved dramatically from their grades of previous years.

It is important to note that this experience with producing OOS text attempted to bridge in- and out-of-school lives because "Civilization III contains vocabulary, concepts, and ways of thinking about world history with academic value" (Squire et al., 2008, p. 249). Explicit attention to such bridging is not often found in research studies on text use in disciplinary learning or in youth cultural studies. Such work thus illustrates the possibility of an OOS text being used to enhance academic literacy without diminishing students' motivation to engage or co-opting students' OOS experiences. However, although the study clearly implicates the possible role of both OOS and digital texts in disciplinary learning, the texts themselves were not the focus of analysis. The role that such texts play in disciplinary learning, together with the collection of more information about student learning outcomes on a variety of dimensions (engagement, world knowledge, domain knowledge, reading comprehension), could be important avenues of future research in linking OOS texts to classroom-based disciplinary learning.

Moje (2008b) argued that it is tempting to focus on adolescents' high literacy competence and metadiscursive capability across different media genres while overlooking the role that OOS texts play or might play in disciplinary learning in school and the demand they make on youth. Our review suggests that future research should examine the link between learning from diverse OOS texts and learning from corresponding disciplinary texts in school settings. Whether spoken-word genre or traditional writing, digital or paper texts, the participants described in the above-mentioned research studies were able to optimize their literacy skills and strategies when they were supported in choosing text genres and media that helped them engage in academic tasks.

In addition, OOS texts used in these research projects were all related to their participants' everyday life experiences. This important aspect might be easily overlooked since academic texts are often regarded as abstractions of everyday phenomena (Barton, 1998; Stockdill & Moje, 2007). There appears to be growing potential for OOS texts to be used as tools to connect students' experiences with disciplinary learning, help them navigate multiple disciplinary contexts, and support them in challenging and changing commonly held assumptions in myriad domains. More research, however, is needed on the nature and complexity of out-of-school texts and on points of overlap and difference between the texts youth enjoy reading outside of school and the texts they are asked to read in school.

Finally, the content of OOS text also should be examined. As Kress (2003) claims, newly developed multimedia and digital texts have not established their stability yet, particularly in the disciplines of school. In addition, the quality of the form and content of OOS texts, where a host of knowledge and epistemological discourses might be represented, has not been researched in deep and sustained ways. Given the clear role of various kinds of knowledge for proficiency in domain-specific reading and writing (Alexander & Judy, 1988), researchers need to document the kinds, nature, and extent of linguistic, world, domain, and topic knowledge youth might be learning via their reading and writing of texts outside of school. Although a great deal of OOS research focuses on how identities shape and are shaped by interactions with texts outside of school, few studies, to our knowledge, examine what youth learn about social, scientific, mathematical, and other concepts relevant to the disciplines.

CONCLUSIONS AND FUTURE DIRECTIONS

Our current review suggests that since the 2000 chapter in the *Handbook of Reading Research*, little research has been done to document specific uses of texts in disciplinary classrooms (i.e., where the text use was tied to the disciplinary learning goals) and even less has been conducted on students' thinking about or use of texts in classroom subject-matter learning, particularly across different disciplines. Similarly, little research has been conducted on possible connections between the texts youth read outside of school and the texts students are expected to read in school, despite arguments about the need to attend to youths' OOS literacy as a way to support in-school learning. In short, many claims are made about the text comprehension of children and youth, but less is known about what actually happens in terms of use of text and comprehension instruction in and out of school, especially for and with adolescents. Given the increased demand to improve reading and writing skills among adolescents, the changing nature of text media, and our growing knowledge of adolescents' literacy practices outside of school, it seems that such questions about specific uses of texts by teachers and students are especially worthy of study. Of particular interest are questions of how texts are actually used by members of the disciplines, how teachers use text in disciplinary teaching and learning, how and what sense students make of those texts, and how students learn from texts they read outside of school. And yet, as illustrated in the review, we noted several patterns in the existing research.

First, for both the disciplinary domains of history and mathematics, we found few studies of how texts are used by disciplinarians to produce or represent disciplinary knowledge. This is especially problematic given recent calls for attention to developing disciplinary literacy practices. We do know something about how social scientists such as historians and political theorists read single texts (see Shreiner, 2009; Wineburg, 1991, 1998), and Shanahan and Shanahan (2008) are developing studies of how various members of disciplines read, again, single texts. These are important springboards for further research on how members of different disciplines employ multiple texts in the service of producing knowledge in the discipline and related professions. For example, what are the reading practices necessary for synthesizing texts to produce an historical account? What are the writing practices most often used by historians to produce those texts? What do mathematicians care about when they read mathematics texts? That is, what is their purpose for reading? How do they know when and what to read? The list of possible research questions here is lengthy and represents a much-needed area for further study if we are to support young people and their teachers in using texts to learn in the disciplinary subject areas.

Second, a robust body of research in history and social studies examines textbooks. These studies uniformly find textbooks to be lacking organization, structural cues, and authorial voice. What's more, the language of textbooks is dense and merges some subject-specific vocabulary and discourse with terms, discourse, and narrative structures drawn from more everyday texts. Rewriting history/social studies textbooks and teaching youth to deconstruct the linguistic structures of these textbooks has proved to be productive. Still, we know little about whether and how textbooks are used in everyday social studies/history classrooms, and whether other types of texts could be used in conjunction with or more productively than standard textbooks.

Third, few studies of actual text use of any kind in history or mathematics classrooms are available. Studies of these subject-area classrooms were available (although less so for mathematics than for history/social studies), but despite being situated in subject-area classes, these studies of literacy were rarely discipline-specific, and they rarely focused on the texts themselves. Instead, they examined strategy instruction or other productive practices, usually with a focus on student comprehension outcomes of particular interventions or on the products of design experiments, but with less attention to the content and genres of the texts under study or to what students learned about subject-area concepts.

Fourth, particular to the subject-area of mathematics, we found that studies of text as curriculum driver abound. Specifically, studies of text in mathematics education emphasize how teachers might learn from *educative curricula* (Davis & Krajcik, 2005; Remillard, 2005) and thus adopt mathematics reforms. We found only two studies of how students read, make sense of, or use mathematics text, however, and these (Hall, 2007; Lubienski, 2000) focused on outcomes other than the students' comprehension of the texts. Even more important, we were not able to find studies that explicitly examined students' mathematical text reading practices in the service of mathematics learning or the practices students typically engaged when reading mathematics texts. Young people's reading of and attitudes toward mathematics texts is an area ripe for research, particularly as the text density of reform mathematics curricula continues to increase.

Fifth, few of the studies of texts read outside of school focused on the texts themselves, focusing instead on the literacy, identity, and social practices in which readers engaged when reading texts of choice outside of school or on how the texts motivated and engaged readers. In addition, few studies of youths' text choices or literacy practices outside of school make links to text use and/or learning in the disciplinary domains of school. Many scholars who study literacy outside of school argue that the study of youth OOS literacies and texts is legitimate in and of itself; these practices do not need to be tied to school learning. Although it is true that the field has learned a great deal from the contributions of these studies, literacy researchers could continue to learn by asking whether and how the texts and literacy practices youth value outside of school might be leveraged to support and extend disciplinary literacy and learning.

In sum, the study of the role of text in disciplinary learning is in early stages. Current studies focus largely on texts as separate from their readers (text analyses) or on the outcomes of students' text reading. Surveys and observational studies of subject-area and OOS text practices, coupled with experimental studies of how students read different text types specific to different disciplines, have much to offer the field.

REFERENCES

ACT, I. (2006). *Reading between the lines: What the ACT reveals about college readiness in reading.* Iowa City, IA: ACT.

Afflerbach, P., & B. VanSledright (2001). Hath! Doth! Middle graders reading innovative history text. *Journal of Adolescent & Adult Literacy, 44*(8), 696–707.

Alexander, P. A. (1998). The nature of disciplinary and domain learning: The knowledge, interest, and strategic dimensions of learning frm subject-matter text. In C. Hynd (Ed.), *Learning from text across conceptual domains* (pp. 263–287). Mahwah, NJ: Erlbaum.

Alexander, P. A., & Jetton, T. L. (2000). Learning from text: A multidimensional and developmental perspective. In M. Kamil, P. D. Pearson, R. Barr, & P. Mosenthal (Eds.), *Handbook of reading research* (pp. 285–310). Mahwah, NJ: Erlbaum.

Alexander, P. A., & Judy, J., E. (1988). The interaction of domain-specific and strategic knowledge in academic performance. *Review of Educational Research, 58*, 375–404.

Alexander, P. A., Kulikowich, J. M., & Jetton, T. L. (1994). The role of subject-matter knowledge and interest in the processing of linear and nonlinear and nonlinear texts. *Review of Educational Research, 64*, 201–252.

Alexander, P. A., Kulikowich, J. M., & Schulze, S. K. (1994a). How subject-matter knowledge affects recall and interest on the comprehension of scientific exposition. *American Educational Research Journal, 31*, 313–337.

Alexander, P. A., Kulikowich, J. M., & Schulze, S. K. (1994b). The influence of topic knowledge, domain knowledge, and interest on the comprehension of scientific exposition. *Learning and Individual Differences, 6*, 379–397.

Alvermann, D. E. (2008). Why bother theorizing adolescents' online literacies for classroom practice and research? *Journal of Adolescent & Adult Literacy, 52*, 8–19.

Alvermann, D. E., & Hagood, M. C. (2000a). Critical media literacy: Research, theory, and practice in" new times." *Journal of Educational Research, 93*, 193–205.

Alvermann, D. E., & Hagood, M. C. (2000b). Fandom and critical media literacy. *Journal of Adolescent & Adult Literacy, 43*, 436–446.

Alvermann, D. E., Young, J. P., Green, C., & Wisenbaker, J. M. (1999). Adolescents' perceptions and negotiations of literacy practices in after-school read and talk clubs. *American Educational Research Journal, 36*, 221–264.

Anderson, R. C., & Pearson, P. D. (1984). A schema-theoretic view of basic processes in reading comprehension. In P. D. Pearson, R. Barr, M. L. Kamil, & P. Mosenthal (Eds.), *Handbook of reading research* (Vol. 2, pp. 225–253). New York: Longman.

Anderson, T. H., & Armbruster, B. B. (1984). Content area textbooks. In R. C. Anderson, J. Osborne, & R. J. Tierney (Eds.), *Learning to read in American schools: Basal readers and content texts* (pp. 193–226). Hillsdale, NJ: Erlbaum.

Armbruster, B. B., & Anderson, T. H. (1985). Producing "considerate" expository text: Or easy reading is damned hard writing. *Journal of Curriculum Studies, 17*, 247–263.

Bain, R. B. (2005). 'They thought the world was flat?' HPL principles in teaching high school history. In J.

Bransford & S. Donovan (Eds.), *How students learn: History, mathematics, and science in the classroom* (pp. 179–214). Washington, DC: The National Academies Press.

Bain, R. B. (2006). Rounding up unusual suspects: Facing the authority hidden in the history classroom. *Teachers College Record, 108*, 2080–2114.

Ball, S., & Lacey, C. (1984). Subject disciplines as the opportunity for a group action: A measured critique of subject sub-cultures. In A. Hargreaves & P. Woods (Eds.), *Classrooms and staffrooms: The sociology of teachers and teaching* (pp. 234–244). Milton Keynes, UK: Open University Press.

Barton, A. C. (1998). Teaching science with homeless children: Pedagogy, representation, and identity. *Journal of Research in Science Teaching, 35*, 379–394.

Barton, K. C., & Levstik, L. S. (2004). *Teaching history for the common good*. Mahwah, NJ: Erlbaum.

Bass, H. (2006, April). *What is the role of oral and written language in knowledge generation in mathematics?* Paper presented at the Toward the Improvement of Secondary School Teaching and Learning: Integrating Language, Literacy, and Subject Matter.

Beck, I. L., McKeown, M. G., & Gromoll, E. W. (1989). Learning from social studies texts. *Cognition and Intruction, 6*, 99–158.

Beck, I. L., McKeown, M. G., & Worthy, J. (1995). Giving a text voice and improve students? understanding. *Reading Research Quarterly, 30*(2), 220–238.

Black, R. W. (2006). Language, literacy, and culture in online fanfiction. *E-Learning, 3*, 170–184.

Black, R. W. (2008). Just don't call them cartoons: The new literacy spaces of animé, manga, and fanfiction. In J. Coiro, M. Knobel, C. Lankshear, & D. J. Leu (Eds.), *Handbook of research in new literacies* (pp. 583–610). Mahwah, NJ: Erlbaum.

Bloome, D., & Egan-Robertson, A. (1993). The social construction of intertextuality in classroom reading and writing lessons. *Reading Research Quarterly, 28*, 304–333.

Boaler, J., & Staples, M. (2008). Creating mathematical future through an equitable teaching approach: The case of railside school. *Teachers College Record, 110*, 608–645.

Bowden, D. (1993). The limits of containment: Text-as-container in composition studies. *College Composition and Communication, 44*(3), 364–379.

Britt, M. A., Rouet, J., Georgi, M., & Perfetti, C. (1994). Learning from history texts: From causal analysis to argument models. In G. Leinhardt, I. L. Beck, & C. Stainton (Eds.), *Teaching and learning in history* (pp. 47–84). Hillsdale, NJ: Erlbaum.

Burton, L. (1999). Exploring and reporting upon the content and diversity of mathematicians' views and practices. *For the Learning of Mathematics, 19*(2), 36–37.

Burton, L., & Morgan, C. (2000). Mathematicians writing. *Journal for Research in Mathematics Education, 31*, 429–453.

Camitta, M. (1993). Vernacular writing: varieties of literacy among Philadelphia high school students. In B. V. Street (Ed.), *Cross-cultural approaches to literacy* (pp. 228–246). Cambridge, UK: The Press Syndicate of the University of Cambridge.

Chambliss, M. J. (1995). Text cues and strategies successful readers use to construct the gist of lengthy written arguments. *Reading Research Quarterly, 30*, 778–807.

Chambliss, M. J., & Calfee, R. (1998). *Textbooks for learning: Nurturing children's minds*. Boston, MA: Blackwell.

Chambliss, M. J., & Murphy, P. K. (2002). Fourth and fifth graders representing the argument structure in written texts. *Discourse Processes, 34*, 91–115.

Chandler-Olcott, K. (2008). Anime and manga fandom: Young people's multiliteracies made visible. In J. Flood, S. B. Heath, & D. Lapp (Eds.), *Handbook of research on teaching literacy through the communicative and visual arts* (Vol. 2, pp. 247–257). Newark, DE: International Reading Association.

Chandler-Olcott, K., & Mahar, D. (2003). "Tech-savviness" meets multiliteracies: Exploring adolescent girls' technology-mediated literacy practices. *Reading Research Quarterly, 38*, 356–385.

Cowan, P. M. (2005). Putting it out there: Revealing Latino visual discourse in the Hispanic academic summer program for middle school students. In B. V. Street (Ed.), *Literacies across educational contexts: Mediating learning and teaching* (pp. 145–169). Philadelphia: Caslon.

Coiro, J. (2003). Reading comprehension on the Internet: Expanding our understanding of reading comprehension to encompass new literacies. *The Reading Teacher, 56*, 458–464.

Crawford, D. B., & Carnine, D. (2000). Comparing the effects of textbooks in eighth-grade U.S. history: Does conceptual organization help? *Education and Treatment of Children, 23*, 387–422.

Davis, E., & Krajcik, J. (2005). Designing educative curriculum materials to promote teacher learning. *Educational Researcher, 34*(3), 3–14.

Dawson, M. S. (2000). Histories and texts: Refiguring the diary of Samuel Pepys. *The Historical Journal, 43,* 407–431.

Dillon, D. R., Brien, D. G. O., & Volkman, M. (2001). Reading and writing to get work done in one secondary biology classroom. In E. B. Moje & D. G. O. Brien (Eds.), *Constructions of literacy: Studies of teaching and learning in secondary classrooms* (pp. 51–75). Mahwah, NJ: Erlbaum.

Eisner, E. W. (1994). *Cognition and curriculum reconsidered.* New York: Teachers College Press.

Ellington, A. J. (2006). The effects of non-CAS graphing calculators on student achievement and attitude levels in mathematics: A meta-analysis. *School Science and Mathematics, 106*(1), 16–26.

Finders, M. J. (1996a). "Just girls": Literacy and allegiance in junior high school. *Written Communication, 13,* 93–129.

Finders, M. J. (1996b). Queens and teen zines: Early adolescent females reading their way toward adulthood. *Anthropology & Education Quarterly, 27,* 71–89.

Ford, L. (2008). Reconfiguring the old south: Solving the problem of slavery, 1787–1838. *Journal of American History, 95*(1), 99–122.

Gee, J. P. (2003). *What video games have to teach us about learning and literacy.* New York: Palgrave Macmillan.

Gee, J. P. (2004). New times and new literacies: Themes for a changing world. In A. Ball & S. Warshauer Freedman (Eds.), *Bakhtinian perspectives on language, literacy and learning* (pp. 279–303). Cambridge, UK: Cambridge University Press.

Gerofsky, S. (1996). A linguistic and narrative view of word problems in mathematics education. *For the Learning of Mathematics, 16*(2), 36–45.

Gilman, M. R., Saydak, V., & Vlk, S. (2005). *The ACT for dummies.* New York: Wiley.

Goldman, S. R. (1997). Learning from text: Reflections on the past and suggestions for the future. *Discourse Processes, 23,* 357–398.

Goldman, S. R., & Varma, S. (1995). CAPing the construction-integration model of discourse comprehension. In C. Weaver, S. Mannes & C. Fletcher (Eds.), *Discourse comprehension: Essays in honor of Walter Kintsch* (pp. 337–358). Hillsdale, NJ: Erlbaum.

Graesser, A. C., McNamara, D. S., Louwerse, M. M., & Cai, Z. (2004). Coh-metrix: Analysis of text on cohesion and language. *Behavior Research Methods, Instruments & Computers, 36*(2), 193–202.

Graesser, A. M., McNamara, D. S., & Rus, V. (in press). Computational modeling of discourse and comprehension. In M. Spivey, M. Joanisse & K. McRae (Eds.), *Cambridge handbook of psycholinguistics.* New York: Cambridge University Press.

Graham, A., & Thomas, M. O. J. (2000). Building a versatile understanding of algebraic variables with a graphic calculator. *Educational Studies in Mathematics, 41*(3), 265–282.

Gustavson, L. (2007). *Youth learning on their own terms.* New York: Routledge.

Haggarty, L., & Pepin, B. (2002). An investigation of mathematics textbooks and their use in English, French and German classrooms: Who gets an opportunity to learn what? *British Educational Research Journal, 28,* 567–590.

Hall, L. A. (2007). Bringing television back to the bedroom: Transactions between a seventh grade struggling reader and her mathematics teacher. *Reading Research and Instruction, 46,* 287–314.

Halliday, M. A. K., & Matthiessen, C. M. I. M. (2004). *An introduction to functional grammar* (3rd ed.). London: Arnold.

Heath, S. B. (1983). *Ways with words: Language, life, and work in communities and classrooms.* Cambridge, UK: Cambridge University Press.

Heath, S. B., & McLaughlin, M. W. (Eds.). (1993). *Identity and inner-city youth: Beyond ethnicity and gender.* New York: Teachers College Press.

Herbel-Eisenmann, B. A., Lubienski, S.T., & Id-Deen, L. (2006). Reconsidering the study of mathematics instructional practices: The importance of curricular context in understanding local and global teacher change. *Journal of Mathematics Teacher Education, 9,* 313–345.

Ingalls, R. L. (2005). *Taking a page from their books: Negotiating containment and resuscitating rhetoric in writing across academic and spoken-word genres.* Unpublished doctoral dissertation, University of Michigan, Ann Arbor.

Kintsch, W. (1988). The role of knowledge in discourse comprehension: A construction-integration model. *Psychological Review, 95,* 163–182.

Kintsch, W. (1998). *Comprehension: A paradigm for cognition.* New York: Cambridge University Press.

Kintsch, W., & Van Dijk, T. A. (1978). Toward a model of text comprehension and production. *Psychological Review, 85,* 363–394.

Knuth, D.E., Larrabee, T., & Roberts, P.M. (1989). *Mathematical writing.* Washington, DC: The Mathematical Association of America.

Kress, G. R. (2003). *Literacy in the new media age.* New York: Routledge.

Leander, K. M., & Lovvorn, J. (2006). Literacy networks: Following the circulation of texts, bodies, and objects in the schooling and online gaming of one youth. *Cognition & Instruction, 24,* 291–240.

Leander, K. M., & McKim, K. K. (2003). Tracing the everyday `sittings' of adolescents on the Internet: A strategic adaptation of ethnography across online and offline spaces. *Education, communication, & information, 3,* 211–240.

Lee, C. D. (1993). *Signifying as a scaffold for literary interpretation: The pedagogical implications of an African American discourse genre* (Vol. NCTE Research Report, No 26). Urbana, IL: National Council of Teachers of English.

Lee, C. D. (2001). Is October Brown Chinese? A cultural modeling activity system for underachieving students. *American Educational Research Journal, 38*(1), 97–141.

Lee, C. D. (2007). *Culture, literacy, and learning: Taking bloom in the midst of the whirlwind.* New York: Teachers College Press.

Lee, C. D., & Spratley, A. (2010). *Reading in the disciplines and the challenges of adolescent literacy.* New York: Carnegie Corporation of New York.

Lee, J. K. (2002). Digital history in the history/social studies classroom. *The History Teacher, 35,* 503–517.

Lee, J., Grigg, W., & Donahue, P. (2007). *The nation's report card: Reading 2007.* Washington, DC: National Center for Education Statistics, Institute of Education Sciences, U.S. Department of Education.

Lee, M. (2007). *Promoting historical inquiry using secondary sources.* Unpublished Dissertation, Dissertation Abstracts International, Ann Arbor.

Lee, J., & Weiss, A. (2007). *The nation's report card: U.S. history 2006* (NCES 2007-474). U.S. Department of Education, National Center for Education Statistics. Washington, DC: U.S. Government Printing Office.

Lewis, C. (2008). Internet communication among youth: New practices and epistemologies. In J. Flood, S. B. Heath, & D. Lapp (Eds.), *Handbook of research on teaching literacy through the communicative and visual arts* (Vol. 2, pp. 237–246). Newark, DE: International Reading Association.

Lewis, C., & Fabos, B. (2005). Instant messaging, literacies, and social identities. *Reading Research Quarterly, 40,* 470–501.

Love, E., & Pimm, D. (1996). 'This is so': A text on texts. In A. J. Bishop, K. Clements, C. Keitel, J. Kilpatrick, & C. Laborde (Eds.), *International handbook of mathematics education* (pp. 371–409). Dordrecht, The Netherlands: Kluwer.

Lubienski, S. T. (2000). Problem solving as a means toward mathematics for all: An exploratory look through a class lens. *Journal for Research in Mathematics Education, 31*(4), 454–482.

Luke, C. (2003). Pedagogy, connectivity, multimodality, and interdisciplinarity. *Reading Research Quarterly, 38,* 397–404.

Mahiri, J. (1998). *Shooting for excellence: African American and youth culture in new century schools.* Urbana, IL: NCTE.

Mandl, H., Stein, N. L., & Trabasso, T. (1984). *Learning and comprehension of text.* Hillsdale, NJ: Erlbaum.

Mason, J., Burton, L., & Stacey, K. (1985). *Thinking mathematically.* New York: Addison Wesley.

McKeown, M. G., Beck, I. L., & Blake, R. G. K. (2009). Rethinking reading comprehension instruction: A comparison of instruction for strategies and content approaches. *Reading Research Quarterly, 44,* 218–253.

McNamara, D. S., Kintsch, E., Butler Songer, N., & Kintsch, W. (1996). Are good texts always better? Interactions of text coherence, background knowledge, and levels of understanding in learning from text. *Cognition and Instruction, 14*(1), 1–43.

McNamara, D. S., & Kintsch, W. (1996). Learning from text: Effects of prior knowledge and text coherence. *Discourse Processes, 22,* 247–288.

Moje, E. B. (2000). To be part of the story: The literacy practices of gangsta adolescents. *Teachers College Record, 102,* 652–690.

Moje, E. B. (2007a). Developing socially just subject-matter instruction: A review of the literature on disciplinary literacy teaching. *Review of Research in Education, 31*(1), 1–44.

Moje, E. B. (2007b, May). *Reading the adolescent reader: Profiles of reader identities, knowledge, strategy, and skill.* Paper presented at the International Reading Association, Atlanta, GA.

Moje, E. B. (2008a). Foregrounding the disciplines in secondary literacy teaching and learning: A call for change. *Journal of Adolescent & Adult Literacy, 52,* 96–107.

Moje, E. B. (2008b). Youth cultures, literacies, and identities in and out of school. In S. B. Heath, J. Flood, & D. Lapp (Eds.), *Handbook of research on teaching literacy through the communicative and visual arts* (Vol. 2, pp. 207–220). Newark, DE: International Reading Association.

Moje, E. B., Ciechanowski, K. M. I., Kramer, K., Ellis, L., Carrillo, R., & Collazo, T. (2004). Working toward third space in content area literacy: An examination of everyday funds of knowledge and discourse. *Reading Research Quarterly, 39,* 38–70.

Moje, E. B., Overby, M., Tysvaer, N., & Morris, K. (2008). The complex world of adolescent literacy: Myths, motivations, and mysteries. *Harvard Educational Review, 78,* 107–154.

Moje, E. B., & Speyer, J. (2008). The reality of challenging texts in high school science and social studies: How teachers can mediate comprehension. In K. Hinchman & H. Thomas (Eds.), *Best practices in adolescent literacy instruction* (pp. 185–211). New York: Guilford.

Moll, L. C., & Gonzalez, N. (1994). Lessons from research with language-minority children. *Journal of Reading Behavior, 26,* 439–456.

Morgan, C. (2005). Words, definitions and concepts in discourses of mathematics, teaching and learning. *Language and Education, 19,* 103–117.

Morrell, E. (2002). Toward a critical pedagogy of popular culture: Literacy development among urban youth. *Journal of Adolescent & Adult Literacy, 46,* 72–77.

Morrell, E., & Duncan-Andrade, J. (2006). Popular culture and critical media pedagogy in secondary literacy classrooms. In M. Kalantzis & B. Cope (Eds.), *International Journal of Learning, 12.* Retrieved July 30, 2008, from http://www.ernestmorrell.com/images/International.Journal.Learning.2006.pdf

Nathan, M., & Koedinger, K. R. (2000). Teachers' and researchers' beliefs of early algebra development. *Journal for Research in Mathematics Education, 31,* 168–190.

Nathan, M. J., Long, S. D., & Alibali, M. W. (2002). The symbol precedence view of mathematical development: A corpus analysis of the rhetorical structure of textbooks. *Discourse Processes, 33,* 1–22.

National Council for the Social Studies (NCSS). (2007). *NCSS calls for change as the nation's report card predicts trouble ahead for the next generation and of citizens and a healthy democracy.* Retrieved May 21, 2007, from http://./www.ncss.org/newsItems/viewFullItem$1168

New London Group. (1996). A pedagogy of multiliteracies: designing social future. *Harvard Educational Review, 66,* 60–92.

Paxton, R. J. (1999). A deafening silence: History textbooks and the students who read them. *Review of Educational Research, 69*(3), 315–339.

Paxton, R. J. (2002). The influence of author visibility on high school students solving a historical problem. *Cognition and Instruction, 20*(2), 197–248.

Perie, M., Grigg, W. S., & Donahue, P. L. (2005). *The nation's report card: Reading 2005* (No. NCES 2006-451). Washington, DC: U.S. Government Printing Office.

Porat, D. (2004). It's not written here, but this is what happened: Students' cultural comprehension of textbook narratives on the Israeli-Arab conflict. *American Educational Research Journal, 41*(4), 963–996.

Radford, L. (2000). Signs and meanings in students' emergent algebraic thinking: A semiotic Analysis. *Educational Studies in Mathematics, 42,* 237–268.

Remillard, J. T. (2005). Examining key concepts in research on teachers' use of mathematics curricula. *Review of Educational Research, 75,* 211–246.

Roberts, D. F., & Foehr, U. G. (2008). Trends in media use. *The Future of Children: Children and Electronic Media, 18*(1), 11–37.

Saye, J., & Brush, T. (2000). Implementation and evaluation of a student-centered learning unit: A case study. *Educational Technology Research and Development, 48*(3), 79–100.

Schleppegrell, M. J., Achugar, M., & Oteíza, T. (2004). The grammar of history: Enhancing content-based instruction through a functional focus on language. *TESOL Quarterly, 38*(1), 67–93.

Shreiner, T. (2009). *Framing a model of democratic thinking to inform teaching and learning in civic education*. Unpublished Doctoral Dissertation, University of Michigan, Ann Arbor.

Shanahan, T., & Shanahan, C. (2008). Teaching disciplinary literacy to adolescents: Rethinking content-area literacy. *Harvard Educational Review, 78*(1), 40–61.

Shuman, A. (1993). Collaborative writing: appropriating power or reproducing authority? In B. Street (Ed.), *Cross-cultural approaches to literacy* (pp. 247–271). Cambridge, UK: The Press Syndicate of the University of Cambridge.

Siskin, L. S. (1994). *Realms of knowledge: Academic departments In secondary schools: academic departments In secondary schools*. London: Falmer Press.

Squire, K., De Vane, B., & Durga, S. (2008). Designing centers of expertise for academic learning through video games. *Theory into Practice, 47*, 240–251.

Steele, B. (2008). Thomas Jefferson's gender frontier. *The Journal of American History, 95*(1), 17–42.

Steinkuehler, C. (2007). Massively multiplayer online gaming as a constellation of literacy practices. *E-Learning, 4*, 297–318.

Stockdill, D., & Moje, E. B. (2007, April). *Adolescents as readers of culture, history, economics, and civics: The disconnect between student interest in their world and social studies schooling*. Paper presented at the American Educational Research Association, New York, NY.

Stodolsky, S. S. (1988). *The subject matters: Classroom activity in math and social studies*. Chicago: University of Chicago Press.

Stodolsky, S. S., & Grossman, P. (1995). The impact of subject matter on curricular activity: An analysis of five academic subjects. *American Educational Research Journal, 32*, 227–249.

Tarr, J. E., Chavez, O., Reys, R. E., & Reys, B. J. (2006). From the written to the enacted curriculum: The intermediary role of middle school mathematics teachers in shaping students' opportunity to learn. *School Science and Mathematics, 106*, 191–201.

Tarr, J. E., Reys, R. E., Reys, B. J., Chavez, O., Shih, J., & Osterlind, S. J. (2008). The impact of middle-grades mathematics curricula and the classroom learning environment on student achievement. *Journal for Research in Mathematics Education, 39*, 247–280.

Twyman, T., & Tindal, G. (2006). Using a computer-adapted, conceptually based history text to increase comprehension and problem-solving skills of students with disabilities. *Journal of Special Education Technology, 21*(2), 5–16.

Wade, S. E., & Moje, E. B. (2000). The role of text in classroom learning. In M. L. Kamil, P. B. Mosenthal, P. D. Pearson, & R. Barr (Eds.), *Handbook of reading research* (Vol. 3, pp. 609–627). Mahwah, NJ: Erlbaum.

Wallace, F. H., & Clark, K. K. (2005). Reading stances in mathematics: Positioning students and texts. *Action in Teacher Education, 27*(2), 68–79.

Wineburg, S. S. (1991). On the reading of historical texts: Notes on the breach between school and the academy. *American Educational Research Journal, 28*(3), 495–519.

Wineburg, S. S. (1998). Reading Abraham Lincoln: An expert/expert study in the interpretation of historical texts. *Cognitive Science, 22*(3), 319–346.

Wineburg, S. (2001). *Historical thinking and other unnatural acts*. Philadelphia: Temple University Press.

Wineburg, S. S., & Martin, D. (2004). Reading and rewriting history. *Educational Leadership, 62*(1), 42–45.

Zolkower, B., & Shreyar, S. (2007). A teacher's mediation of a thinking-aloud discussion in a 6th grade mathematics classroom *Educational Studies in Mathematics, 65*, 177–202.

21 The Classroom Assessment of Reading

Peter P. Afflerbach and Byeong-Young Cho
University of Maryland

In this chapter we examine the contributions that different traditions of research and inquiry make to the conceptualization and use of classroom reading assessment. Understandings of reading and assessment are informed by research in psychology and psychometrics, as well as sociology, discourse studies, politics, and economics. All of these disciplines provide lenses through which the usefulness of reading assessment can be examined. An overarching goal of the chapter is to make legitimate inferences about classroom assessment that enhances teaching and learning, just as assessment allows for the inference of student, teacher, and school achievement.

Classroom assessment should play a central role in describing and supporting students' reading development. Despite this role, classroom assessment has only recently been a focus of systematic investigation, and to complicate matters, there is disagreement as to the function and value of specific classroom assessments. In contrast to the unsettled state of research knowledge, there is the continuing need for research to inform theory and practice in classroom assessment of reading. We intend to address this disparity as we toggle between the extant research literature, current theories and practices of classroom assessment of literacy, and research and theory from related fields of inquiry.

Stiggins and Conklin (1992) observed that teachers' classroom assessment practices were of exceedingly varied quality, while noting that classroom assessment was rarely the focus of sustained school initiatives, teachers' professional development, or research itself. There is growing attention to formative classroom assessment in the last 20 years, with arguments for high quality classroom assessment (Crooks, 1989) and theoretical portrayals of how assessment can influence the educational enterprise (Pellegrino, Chudowsky, & Glaser, 2001). However, theories of effective assessment practice do not always inform the classroom. Calfee and Hiebert (1991), in the second edition of the *Handbook of Reading Research*, noted their misgivings about reviewing "research on the assessment of student performance based on teacher judgment." The hesitation is reflected in the following excerpt:

> On the one hand, several lines of development point to the importance of this topic…On the other hand, our preliminary forays into the literature discouraged us about the prospect of finding sufficient substance for a review. (p. 291)

Black and Wiliam (1998a) shared concerns about "the prospect of finding sufficient substance for a review," namely the availability of research evidence that described classroom assessment and its relation to teaching and learning. Their review did identify empirical research on classroom assessment that they believed demonstrated how enhanced formative assessment contributed to students' learning gains, yet the suitability of methodology of the studies that contributed to Black and Wiliam's review has been questioned (Dunn & Mulvenon, 2009).

CHAPTER PLAN

In designing the chapter, we use the work of Crooks (1989), Calfee and Hiebert (1991), and Black and Wiliam (1998a) as markers of increasing interest in classroom reading assessment, and of the need for ongoing research. We concentrate on research that describes formative classroom assessment in relation to student, teacher and school. Useful reading assessment is undergirded by careful description of both reading and assessment. Thus, we construct a construct of reading, and we provide an overview of the ongoing evolution of assessment, focusing on both psychometric and sociological aspects of useful assessment. We then discuss the situated nature of classroom assessment. We examine contexts for reading assessment, in which assessments are influenced by social, political and economic factors. In addition, we situate reading assessment in relation to the psychological, sociocultural, and physical/temporal spaces of the classroom. We then examine purposes and foci of classroom reading assessment. Based on the premise that classroom reading assessment is situated human activity, we describe seven characteristics of effective classroom reading assessment. We conclude the chapter with a consideration of future directions for the research of classroom assessments of reading.

THE EVOLVING CONSTRUCT OF READING

A preliminary task for any assessment project is to describe the nature of the construct to be assessed (Pellegrino et al., 2001). This description contributes to the consistent conceptualization of the construct, with which the suitability of classroom assessment materials and procedures may be examined. We note that there are competing conceptualizations of reading, reflecting diverse ideas about the nature of the act. We note also that particular perspectives on reading and reading assessment are privileged, sometimes through political power (United States Department of Education Office of the Inspector General, 2006), by economic influence (McDonnell, 2008), by habit and tradition (Rowan, 2002), or by default (Afflerbach, 2007).

Ideas about reading and literacy evolve. Across history, people have been assessed in relation to specific acts that represent socially important reading and literacy, including memorizing religious text, legibly writing one's name, following written directions, or answering multiple choice questions about text (Huey, 1908; Kaestle, 1991). Reading may be conceptualized in relation to the society and culture of which it is part (Scribner & Cole, 1981): as a force in modernization, a tool for negotiating understanding, a mechanism to stratify people within societies, or a road to emancipation (Freire, 1995). Reading and literacy refer to the specific social and cultural practices that people use to create and construct meaning from texts (Street, 1995). This historic and social situativity (Brown, Collins, & Duguid, 1989) suggests that reading practices will vary according to the contexts in which people live and interact, including school and community settings (Heath, 1983; Moll, Amanti, Neff, Gonzalez, 1992). Reading can involve decoding words, problem solving, constructing meaning from traditional and non-traditional texts (e.g., film, painting, the Internet; Kress, 2003; New London Group, 1996), and participating in real and virtual worlds (Palfrey & Gasser, 2008). Learning to read, in a broad sense, can be considered an apprenticeship: language learners become initiated into a community of practice (Lave & Wenger, 1991), and literacy involves becoming adept at using the knowledge that makes up a community's "ways of being in the world" (Gee, 2008). Each of the above conceptualizations enriches our understanding of reading and literacy, and also poses particular opportunities and challenges for classroom reading assessment.

In essence, the construct of reading (for this chapter, the "construct" of construct validity) is increasingly influenced by research and theory both from the core and from the periphery of where "reading" has been situated in the past. Change in the construct of reading can be illustrated by consideration of the evolution of acts that define the accomplished reader, from memorizing text to critically evaluating Internet websites. A potential benefit is the opportunity to consider assessment in the context of newer conceptualizations of reading, and the challenge is using assessments that honor both consensus and new conceptualizations.

Change in the conceptualization of reading is evident in recent reading and assessment policy and practice. Consider the definition of reading included in the National Assessment of Educational Progress 2009 Reading Framework (National Assessment Governing Board, 2008), a definition that guides the development of NAEP Reading tests, as well as many states' reading standards and assessment programs that are developed in relation to the NAEP Framework. The framework derives from expert consensus on the nature of reading and defines reading in the following manner:

Reading is an active and complex process that involves:
- Understanding written text
- Developing and interpreting meaning, and
- Using meaning as appropriate to type of text, purpose and situation (p. 2)

We have several related observations. First, this definition represents an innovative conceptualization of reading for such an influential, large-scale test. Second, and in contrast to the first point, when this definition of reading is compared with the recent conceptualizations of reading sketched in the previous pages, it appears constrained. This is necessary constraint—in the assessment development process there is often the artifice of making sure that how reading is defined is in alignment with what the assessment can assess. Third, the definition posits that the construction of meaning of text is but a midpoint, and not the terminus, of an act of reading. Meaning making is followed by the use of the meaning that is constructed. That the knowledge base about reading and literacy is continually evolving has critical implications for assessment. Construct validity (Messick, 1989) relates to how well a construct is understood and how well we transpose its essence into assessment form. There must be continual dialog between construct and assessment to establish and then maintain alignment. Too often, assessment underrepresents the construct of reading, resulting in "thin" assessment (Davis, 1998) that possesses validity, but only in relation to a portion of the construct.

While theory and research continue to contribute to rich accounts of reading, the reading environment in some classrooms is impoverished. Reading instruction most often focuses on students' reading skill and strategy development (Afflerbach, Pearson, & Paris, 2008) and learning from content areas texts, and classroom reading assessment follows suit. A result is that broad conceptualizations of reading and its uses do not make it through the classroom door. There is clear need to assess reading skill and strategy, but when they are the exclusive focus of assessment there is missed opportunity to more fully understand how students use and understand reading, and how students, their motivations, goals and diverse affective characteristics develop (Afflerbach, 2007).

A perennial challenge for the classroom assessment of reading is to achieve descriptive ability for both simple and complex learning related to reading. That is, research in reading demonstrates that accomplished readers use series of skills, strategies, and prior knowledge to achieve specific goals (Snow, 2002; van den Broek, Young, Tzeng, & Linderholm, 1998), and that developing readers progress through stages of increasing competence towards this accomplishment (Alexander, 2003). Readers monitor their work and progress (Hartman, 2001), and are influenced by myriad affective factors as they undertake reading tasks (Fredricks, Blumenfeld, & Paris, 2004). Readers use what they learn from reading to accomplish diverse tasks. Reading assessment must be developed to honor the construct of reading in its complexity, provide useful assessment information and be feasible in classrooms.

THE EVOLVING CONSTRUCT OF READING ASSESSMENT

Like reading, the field of educational measurement is continually evolving. Psychometric theories, tools and procedures are created and revised, reflecting change in the construct of assessment (Pellegrino et al., 2001). Across the last few decades, assessment practice and theory have been complemented by the emergence of consequential validity as a factor to consider in choosing and using assessment (Tittle, 1989), the idea that reliability and validity take on new meanings in formative classroom assessment (Moss, 2003), and increased understanding of the roles that assessment can play in contributing to student and teacher achievement (Black & Wiliam, 2006).

An evolving understanding of reading should contribute to assessment that seeks to best capture and describe reading in light of the new understanding (Valencia, Hiebert, & Afflerbach, 1994). Across the history of reading and reading assessment, if the goal of reading was to provide verbatim recall of text, then spoken or written recitation of text may be a valid measure. Likewise, if reading was equated with literal understanding, then multiple choice questions focused on literal content should possess construct validity (Pearson & Johnson, 1978). Following, if problem solving is considered part of the reading process, then asking students to apply what is learned from reading in a problem-solving performance represents assessment with increased alignment with the reading construct (Moskal, 2003). When students are required to participate in higher order thinking, the assessment must honor the complexity of the act, and relatively simple measures may provide diminishing returns (Afflerbach, Cho, & Kim, in press).

Pellegrino and colleagues (2001) offer a general model of assessment that specifies three critical components: *cognition, observation* and *interpretation*. According to their model, successful reading assessment will involve understanding and explicating the nature of students' reading behavior and achievement. For example, as we develop detailed understanding of the cognitive processes involved in summarizing a text (*cognition*), we are in the best position to construct classroom reading assessment that is valid measure of this important reading strategy. As we describe summarization, the nature of the strategy, the contexts in which it is useful, and the course of development for students who are learning to summarize, we provide details that can be used in developing the *observation*, or assessment materials and procedures. The assessment is then developed with close connection to the best understanding of the cognitive phenomenon to be measured. Confidence in the nature of our observation materials and procedures then allows us to make appropriate *interpretation*, or inferences from assessment results about the nature of students' reading and reading development.

We note that Pellegrino et al.'s (2001) model has an exclusive focus on cognition in learning—reflecting the goal of measuring and describing cognitive outcomes. Students' reading development and achievement are influenced by many factors (Stanovich, 1986), including readers' self-concept, self-esteem, attributions for performance, locus of control, attitude and motivation (e.g., Dweck, 1999; Corno, 1993; Guthrie & Wigfield, 2000; Pintrich, Marx, & Boyle, 1993). Research from the last two decades allows us to place, or situate, cognitive accounts of reading in affective and social milieu. The examination of the resulting interactions and dependencies provides evidence of the need to more broadly conceptualize reading, and what is assessed. Yet, it is the rare reading classroom in which assessment focuses on reader affect or social development.

Accompanying the ongoing evolution of educational assessment is increased understanding of consequential validity: what happens as a result of using assessment information (Tittle, 1989). While teachers and students have long understood the consequences of assessment, only recently has the phenomenon been formalized in educational measurement. Originally used in relation to test scores, consequential validity symbolizes the recognition that assessment has consequences. We believe that the idea of consequence should not be restricted to the use of test scores, and that anticipation of consequence should be a part of reading assessment development and use. For example, if classroom assessment information is used to determine the need for scaffolded reading strategy instruction (e.g., Palincsar & Brown, 1984), instruction that in turn contributes to students' strategic reading development, the assessment has positive consequential validity. However, if assessment results are used to label students, teacher, and schools as "failing," then possible negative consequences may include loss of self-esteem, diminished self-concept and poor motivation. In classroom discourse and with related assessment, sustaining and positive teacher feedback can have positive consequence, compared with terminal and negative feedback (Anderson, Evertson, & Brophy, 1979).

CHANGES IN THE CONCEPTUALIZATION OF VALIDITY AND RELIABILITY RELATED TO CLASSROOM READING ASSESSMENT

Classroom assessment of reading must be valid and reliable so that the meaning we construct from assessment information about students is accurate and useful. In addition, assessments should demonstrate fairness and close relation to the domain they assess. However, classroom reading assessment must be conducted with awareness of how specific goals of classroom assessment may reframe traditional measurement theory (Stobart, 2006). The psychometric concepts of validity and reliability that are used to judge assessment quality bear reconsideration when applied to formative classroom reading assessment (Brookhart, 2003), and the examination of the similarities and differences in reliability and validity for particular types of assessment is one of the more dynamic areas of research related to classroom assessment (Linn, Baker, & Dunbar, 1991; Messick, 1989). This work focuses on the development of measurement theory that accommodates alternative forms of assessment and positions the understanding of validity and reliability in relation to classroom assessment (Moss, 2003; Smith, 2003). For example, the majority of reading tests are standardized and involve only test-like reading (short texts, assuming general levels of student familiarity for content, do-able in a constrained timeframe), with the intention of producing scores that are comparable across contexts (Afflerbach, 2007). In contrast, classroom assessment of reading is often intended for interpretation within the context of instruction (Moss et al., 1992) and in relation to the teacher's detailed and evolving understanding of students' reading development. This is due to the fact that the boundary between classroom assessment and instructional experiences may be intentionally indistinguishable.

Validity informs "the degree to which evidence and theory support the interpretations of test scores entailed by proposed uses of the test" (AERA, APA, & NCME, 1999, p. 9). A test's construct validity is represented by the mapping of test items onto the domain, or the construct in which the student works and is assessed. Students' responses to items are coded, aggregated and transformed into a score, from which the student's performance is inferred. In this context, students' performances are interpreted without regard to classroom reading contexts, students' personal characteristics, or their ongoing learning experiences, in the name of standardization. In contrast, the goal of classroom assessment validity is to ensure that inferences about students' achievement in the classroom are appropriate, but in contrast to test validity, it aims at an integrative understanding of students' learning (Moss, 2003). We do well to interpret classroom reading assessment in light of other information about the student. Thus, the instructional context in which assessment is embedded is not to be ignored, and may be a primary consideration when examining validity of classroom assessment, as when student performance is considered in relation to personal progress, and not normative percentile rankings.

The conceptualization of reliability relates, in part, to the consistency of measurements used with a population of individuals or groups (AERA, APA, & NCME, 1999). Classic test reliability theory proposes that situational factors like assessment directions, times, items, and tasks may be sources of measurement error. Thus, standardization of assessment is intended to minimize the error variance and to yield comparable scores for ranking and categorizing students. In contrast, the reliability of classroom assessment is also about "consistency," but it is focused on how an assessment consistently informs teachers and students to foster student learning (Brookhart, 2003; Smith, 2003). A combination of reliable classroom assessments can be used by teachers and this integrated assessment information permits inferences about student learning, and also provide consistent feedback for students. In this conceptualization, the quality and value of assessment information, in these cases to inform instruction and learning in a predictable manner, is the focus (Moss, 2003).

HOW CLASSROOM ASSESSMENT CAN CONTRIBUTE TO STUDENT DEVELOPMENT

Assessment is intended to gather and report information on students' learning and development. As our understanding of effective assessment evolves, research and theory from affiliated fields suggest additional benefits of classroom reading assessment. Three examples illustrate the multiplicity of roles that classroom reading assessment can play. First, classroom assessment can foster students' metacognitive ability (Flavell, 1976; Garner, 1987). A hallmark of successful performance is independence, and independence in reading is related to the ability to set goals, monitor progress towards goals, and successfully undertake and complete acts of reading. Students can learn to be metacognitive through the models and explanations provided by teachers (Afflerbach & Meuwissen, 2005), and formative classroom assessment provides an appropriate venue for this learning (Black & Wiliam, 1998b).

Second, theories of human learning suggest that formative assessment is central to effective teaching. Vygotsky (1979) proposed the zone of proximal development, in which students can succeed at appropriate learning challenges. Teachers must be able to identify what learning is appropriate, and this is accomplished through regular and fine-grained formative assessment. Classroom reading assessment information is but one component of the complex thinking that is required of teachers who accurately identify and teach within students' zones of proximal development. The knowledge that teachers must combine dynamically in the zone of proximal development include knowledge of reading development, curriculum and instruction, individual students and their learning needs.

Third, excellence in teaching is a goal of the reflective practitioner (Schon, 1987), and formative classroom assessments of reading provide teachers with information that is regularly the focus of reflection. Each of the following questions can be answered through teacher reflection that is informed by classroom reading assessment: Is the conceptualization of student reading development accurate? Based on knowledge of general development of reading strategies and skills, is the student progressing to expectation? Is the assumption of student competence appropriate? Is the student's motivation concern impacting reading? Is the student able to apply what is learned from reading to the unit-long project? Is my classroom assessment program providing sufficient support for the student?

THE SITUATED NATURE OF CLASSROOM READING AND CLASSROOM READING ASSESSMENT

The continued updating of our understanding of reading and reading assessment does not guarantee effective classroom assessment practice. In reality, the evolution of reading and reading assessment suggest possibilities that may be realized only when the situated nature of classroom reading assessment is considered. Several models or frameworks demonstrate the need to consider assessment as situated in classrooms and communities (Black & Wiliam, 1998a; Liepzig &

Afflerbach, 2000). The CURRV (consequences, usefulness, roles and responsibilities, reliability and validity) model of reading assessment (Liepzig & Afflerbach, 2000) provides a means for determining the suitability of assessment for different audiences and purposes. While the CURRV model includes focus on classic psychometric characteristics of assessment (reliability and validity), it requires attention to situational variables of classroom assessment, including the consequences and uses of assessment, as well as the roles and responsibilities that particular assessments create for teachers and students. The CURRV model seeks to supplement consideration of the measurement characteristics of assessment with consideration of the real-world uses and consequences of assessment. For example, a classroom performance assessment must meet stringent psychometric criteria of validity and reliability for the assessment information to be worth our time and effort to use (Baxter & Glaser, 1998). In addition, a performance assessment may engage students in using rubrics, with the potential consequence of contributing to the development of self-assessment proficiency. The performance assessment may provide both formative and summative assessment information, as students use the rubric and scoring guide to chart a path to higher achievement. Finally, a performance assessment demands considerable activity from both teacher and students, thereby creating specific (and more prominent) roles and responsibilities in relation to the assessment.

The situativity of assessment and the importance of attention to the social and political contexts in which assessment is proposed and enacted is described by Black and Wiliam (2006). To increase the chances that classroom assessment reform programs in the United Kingdom would be supported, the researchers created an array of processes and products that introduced assessment change, demonstrated its usefulness, and was intended to help parents, administrators, and other concerned citizens understand and advocate for assessment change. This proactive "selling" of new assessment was perceived to be required, as assessment reform in the United Kingdom had experienced forward movement and backwards stepping, based seemingly on political agenda and power, rather than evidence and educator input. In fact,

> (formative assessment) was brushed aside by ministers and their advisers as either already in place, or as a dangerous fall back to discredited ideas on child centred learning; or as a mere nod towards teachers' classrooms work before focusing on the serious business of raising standards through national tests. (Black & Wiliam, 2006, p. 10)

Similarly, Shepard and Bliem (1995) describe the benefits introducing and providing detailed information about new assessments to parents and community members, to make tangible the benefits that accompany the assessments. Both the CURRV framework for determining the suitability of reading assessment, and the development of public relations documents and routines for new assessment programs signal that research alone may not be capable of bringing change to assessment. That classroom reading assessment is acted upon by factors in the school environment is further examined in the next section.

FACTORS THAT INFLUENCE CLASSROOM READING ASSESSMENT: A MODEL

The assessment of reading is situated in classrooms that are subject to outside influences of politics, economics, and society, and that are bounded further by three specific spaces within the classroom: sociocultural space, psychological space and physical/temporal space (Afflerbach, Cho, Kim, & Clark, 2010). These influences and spaces are represented in Figure 21.1. We note that this section includes focus on research and theory that explains why (or why not) assessment that is informed by current understandings of reading and that is useful to teachers and students is not always found in classrooms.

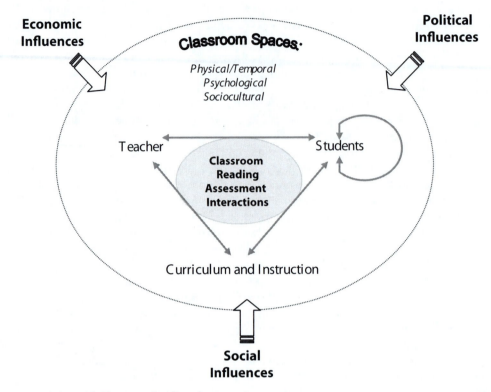

Figure 21.1 Situated Classroom Reading Assessment.

External Factors

Schooling is enacted in relation to the goals and ideologies of the larger society (Labaree, 2007), and classroom assessment is subject to the influence of economic, social, and political factors (Gipps, 1999; Hargreaves, Earl, & Schmidt, 2002). For example, political pressure (often realized through mandates) can require districts and schools to focus reading assessment efforts on summative, high-stakes tests (Frederiksen, 1984). This pressure may result in the enlistment of classroom assessment to serve as preparation for test-taking. Favoring assessment *of* learning over assessment *for* learning (Black & Wiliam, 1998a) means that classroom assessment may not be able to serve the purposes of informing teachers and students about ongoing levels of literacy achievement, helping students learn self-assessment, or encouraging reflective teacher practice.

Economic factors influence classroom reading assessment, and there is opportunity cost involved in choosing particular assessments over others. For example, the decision (or mandate) to spend funds on tests, test preparation, test scoring and test score reporting reduces (or removes) the option of using funds to support teachers' professional development (Stiggins & Bridgeford, 1985), training that is necessary for teachers to develop valid and reliable classroom reading assessment. Similarly, average class size within schools and districts is related to school resources and funding for schools, and the smaller the class, or more numerous the teaching assistants, the more effectively a teacher may gather, interpret, and use assessment information.

Social factors also influence classroom assessment. For example, traditions of assessment in classrooms and schools may become entrenched, uninformed by theory and unchanged in practice. Consider the most common discourse pattern in classrooms, initiate-evaluate-respond (IRE; Cazden, 2001), where the teacher begins with a question, students respond and the teacher evaluates the response. This discourse pattern, marked by frequent "question and answer" approaches to assessment, may be part of engaging reading classrooms, but it often restricts language use and assessment usefulness. When such routines maintain, unquestioned, they contribute to the maintenance of an assessment status quo. Opportunities to change discourse patterns that facilitate improved classroom assessments of reading, including the quality and quantity of student directed discussion (Black & Wiliam, 2006), may be lost.

The political influences on classrooms and assessment range from subtle to stark (Valencia & Wixson, 2000). Over time, particular expectations are made of reading assessment systems, and these systems develop in accordance with the relative power, preferences and needs of particular audiences (Rowan, 2002). For example, legislators demand summative test scores to judge the worth of schools, teachers and programs, while teachers need regular, formative assessment to inform instructional decision making (Gardner, 2006). An examination of how states assess reading, and the reach of these programs into daily school routines, demonstrates the preference given legislators in determining how assessment resources are used (Afflerbach, 2002). This skews attention and resources towards tests, arguably less helpful in the daily routines of the reading classroom. In other cases, particular reading assessments may maintain because they benefit certain people and organizations, a phenomenon known in economics as path dependency. Consider the reading test industry in light of the following:

> Major social policies create networks of vested interests that benefit from a policy and that develop operational rules and structures to protect it from political attacks and attempts to alter it. (McDonnell, 2008, p. 52)

The examination of classroom reading assessment from perspectives of economics, politics, and sociology illustrates that establishing and using effective classroom assessments of reading involves much more than the identification of reliable and valid assessments. It involves education and advocacy, and change in contexts where stasis may be imposed from without or within. Consideration of classroom assessments without examination of these possible influences limits the ability to correctly situate classroom assessment, to anticipate challenges to its effective use and to promote change that reflects current knowledge of reading and assessment.

Internal, Classroom-Related Factors

Classroom contexts influence reading and shape the nature of assessment (Gardner, 2006). Classrooms vary in terms of teacher, students, curriculum, and instruction, and their manner of interactions. Variables such as teacher expertise in assessment, the roles and responsibilities expected of teacher and student, the nature of curriculum, and educational goals influence the conceptualization and practice of classroom assessment (Crooks, 1989; Stiggins & Bridgeford, 1985). In this chapter, the classroom is conceptualized as existing of spaces: physical/temporal, sociocultural, psychological. Classroom reading assessment is enacted in relation to these classroom spaces, and future assessment may be designed in regard to them. We note that our conceptualization of three distinct spaces within classrooms may include some overlap (e.g., teacher dominated discourse relates, at once, to sociocultural and psychological spaces, and may be reflected in the physical layout of the classroom; Wells, 1989), but their possible influences on classroom reading assessment merit separate consideration. The development and use of effective classroom assessments depends on the careful appraisal and understanding of these spaces to determine, in essence, the situativity and related appropriateness of classroom reading assessment.

Physical/Temporal Space.   Classrooms involve physical space in which a teacher and students interact (Morrow, Reutzel, & Casey, 2006). Configurations of individual desks, workspaces, and communal areas situate students and enable or detract from specific reading and assessment practices. The position and the role of the teacher, fixed behind a desk or circulating amongst students, represents interaction in the physical space of the classroom. Group work, individual work, and classroom interactions, including assessment opportunities for teacher observations and peer discussions (Black & Wiliam, 2006), may be encouraged or discouraged by the physical space. Objects in classrooms represent another facet of physical space. Spaces that facilitate students' work may include collaborative stations, computer desks and reference areas. The number of books and computers influences student reading and reading choices, and the opportunity to assess reading in traditional and hypertext contexts (Leu et al., 2008).

Classrooms are also bound by time. The reading that students experience is impacted by time and how it is parceled out: teaching schedules, minutes allotted for instruction and assessment, and the time needed for students and teachers to transition from one classroom task to another (Creemers & Kyriakides, 2006). Reading lessons of 40 or 50 minutes are influenced by the fact that they must begin, develop, and conclude in such a time frame. Students' time on task, or engaged academic time will represent some subset of these minutes. Introducing, teaching and then assessing course material in a 50-minute lesson is often combined with a small number of summative assessment questions, and these combine to restrict the very learning that assessment seeks to describe. In contrast, if assessment is planned so that classroom reading assessment is an ongoing event, there are continuous opportunities for formative and summative assessment (Gardner, 2006).

Sociocultural Space.   The nature of daily discourse figures large in the sociocultural space of the classroom reading assessment. Discourse that is dominated by teacher talk and Initiate-Respond-Evaluate discourse patterns (Cazden, 1986) typically places students in the role of giving back information learned in class. It may restrict reading assessment to a classroom structured around dominant teacher talk that is characterized by often-rigid traditional learning routines (Mehan, 1979; Wells, 1989). In contrast, classrooms that include collaborative inquiry, individual problem finding and problem solving, or generating divergent answers to teachers' questions are marked by diverse discourses, and opportunities for assessment.

A further aspect of sociocultural space is the nature of relationships of teachers and students (Gipps, 1999). Shared decision making, or other-dominated decision making (be it the teacher or curriculum) will be factors in the suitability of roles and responsibilities that teachers and students assume. For example, the precedent for sharing, taking responsibility and turn-taking influences how well students adapt new assessment routines, including self and peer assessment.

Psychological Space.   Reading curricula primarily focus on student development of cognitive skills and strategies. However, the psychological space of a particular classroom involves much more than instruction that builds skills and strategies. All acts of reading demand particular levels of intellectual performance, and they involve students and teachers in their affective lives. The motivation that teachers and students bring to their work influences reading instruction and learning (Guthrie & Wigfield, 2000). Self-esteem and self-concept, as well as student and teacher attributions for reading outcomes and performances, are an important part of the conceptualization of the psychological space of the classroom (Olson, Banaji, Dweck, & Spelke, 2006). Curriculum and instruction may position students as individuals who must learn knowledge, construct knowledge, or both.

The psychological space of the classroom also influences students' life-long stances towards reading and knowledge. For example, students progressing through school must become increasingly self-reliant on their own assessment abilities (Black & Wiliam, 1998b). The metacognition required of successful, independent language users must be fostered in the classroom, where it contributes to students' sense of agency and volition (Corno, 1993). In addition, psychological space in classrooms figures greatly in the construction of meaning, how students conceptualize knowledge and their relationship to it—thus influencing the development of students' episte-mologies (Scherr & Hammer, 2009).

To sum, schools are influenced by prevailing social, economic, and political factors, and within the classroom, a second and related set of spaces impacts reading and its assessment. These factors interact to give each classroom idiosyncratic features. Understanding their related constraints and affordances is imperative for efforts that seek to create effective classroom read-ing assessment.

WHAT IS ASSESSED IN CLASSROOM ASSESSMENTS OF READING?

Earlier in this chapter it is noted that an overwhelming majority of reading assessment focuses on the cognitive strategies and skills involved in reading. Strategy, skill, and their development are a necessary focus of classroom reading assessment, but evolving conceptualizations of read-ing suggest that there is more to the equation (Moje et al., 2004). Motivation for reading, reader self-esteem, and the reader's stance towards knowledge are all important, assessable aspects of reading. However, not all factors that contribute to reading development and success are assessed. The reasons for ignoring particular aspects of students' successful reading are myriad: instruction and assessment have not traditionally attended to them (Anderson & Bourke, 2000), they are not enough of a focus in state and national standards documents and are therefore not assessed (Valencia & Wixson, 2000), they are not part of the model of reading from which instruction derives and on which assessment is based (Fredricks et al., 2004), they are not valued as highly as cognition when choices of what is assessed are influenced by politics and economics (Afflerbach et al., 2010), or they are considered "too subjective" to be usefully assessed. However, the sole focus on cognition in reading assessment is a misrepresentation of the construct of reading, and a comprehensive approach to classroom reading assessment will be more broadly focused.

Cognitive Strategies and Skills

If we were to infer from reading assessment what certifies the successful reader, strategy and skill would be our understanding. Traditionally, classroom reading assessment has focused on stu-dent readers' acquisition of reading strategies and skills, and the content area knowledge that is gained through successful reading (McKenna & Stahl, 2003). That strategy and skill are required for reading development and reading success is well-documented (Uhry & Ehri, 1999; van den Broek et al., 1998), and the advent of No Child Left Behind legislation and related instruction and assessment programs contributes to the primacy of strategy and skill, specifically phonemic awareness, phonics, fluency, vocabulary, and comprehension, as instruction and assessment foci. Classroom assessment of reading should focus, in part, on developmentally appropriate strategy and skill; in early grades, observation of a student attempting to read, listening to student discus-sions and analyzing writing can inform our understanding of the development of sound-symbol correspondence knowledge (Ziegler & Goswami, 2005). As readers develop further, assessment focuses on vocabulary knowledge and literal and inferential comprehension strategy develop-ment (Leslie & Caldwell, 2005). The use of strategies and skills contributes to comprehension, assessment describes this success, and the reader is certified as proficient or accomplished. This results in assessments that are focused on specific skill and strategy development and use, and end-of-reading questions intended to evaluate if students constructed meaning from text. How-ever, even with the hyper-focus on cognition, in the form of strategy and skill, much classroom reading assessment does not regularly sample students' higher order thinking in relation to reading and using reading (Afflerbach et al., in press).

Affective Characteristics

A second possible focus of classroom assessment is readers' affective characteristics (Verhoeven & Snow, 2001). Research describes the relationship between reading achievement and motivation (Guthrie & Wigfield, 1997), and suggests the importance of attending to self-concept (Bakan, 1971), self-esteem, volition, agency, and attributions. Readers' self-esteem and self-concept operate before, during, and after students read. Diminished self-esteem can lead students away from acts of reading, and this prevents positive experience and practice that are necessary for students to develop fluent reading (Stanovich, 1986). Through sets of experiences, readers develop positive or negative associations with reading (Hiebert, Winograd, & Danner, 1984). Individuals who make particular attributions for the outcomes of their work may determine that they are effortful, accomplished readers, or that they are "stupid," that reading is always difficult, that reading well involves good luck. However, attributions can be identified with assessment, and then re-trained with the effect of enhanced learning and performance (Dweck, 1999). Given the potential power of affect to influence reading development, assessment of affect should be a priority, yet it isn't. Existing assessments of affective characteristics, including measures of self-concept (Chapman & Tunmer, 1995), motivation (Gambrell, Palmer, Codling, & Mazzoni, 1996), and reading attitude (McKenna & Kear, 1990), represent forays into this important area.

Epistemologies and Stances Toward Learning and Knowledge

As students develop, reading may increasingly require that students make complex evaluative judgments about the quality of the texts they read (Bazerman, 1985), the trustworthiness of the author (VanSledright, 2002) and reliability of sources cited in texts (Leu et al., 2008). Being a critical reader demands critical reading skills, and it also assumes that a student is capable of taking a stance toward knowledge that allows for skepticism, criticism and investigation. Assessment that helps teachers understand students' emerging theories of knowledge, and the student reader's place in such reading are needed. However, a comparison of what is currently assessed and the construct of reading indicates that strategy and skill receive most (if not all) attention, and that readers' affective characteristics, known to have powerful influence on reading processes and products, remain largely unexamined. Finally, acts of assessment communicate importance to students: A consistent focus on strategy and skill enforces the idea that they are the ultimate reading goal. The neglect assessing affect in reading suggests to students that it is not valued.

THE PURPOSES OF CLASSROOM READING ASSESSMENT

While all classroom reading assessment should be conducted to foster student reading development, assessment materials and procedures are most effective when they are carefully matched to specific purposes. In the vast majority of cases, assessment serves a *reporting* function, bearing information about student performance or achievement. In addition to reporting, there are two important but relatively neglected purposes for classroom reading assessment: *supporting* and *teaching*. These purposes situate assessment in relation to "…motivating and encouraging students, and teaching students to do assessment for themselves" (Afflerbach, 2007; pp. 6–7), respectively.

Reporting: Students' Cognitive Strategy and Skill Development and Content Learning

Successful teachers create and consistently update mental models of their students: how they read, their strengths and weaknesses. Assessment information, in the form of test and quiz results (Fitt, Rafferty, Presner, & Heverly, 1999), reading inventories (Spector, 2005), questioning routines (Wolf, 1987), and performance assessments (Baxter & Glaser, 1998) reports on the status of student reading development. Teachers use the reported information to continually construct understandings of their individual students, a process akin to a reader's construction of meaning of text. Here, formative assessment plays a crucial role in supplying new information to teachers so that they may update their understandings of students: accomplishments, needs and suitable instruction. In other instances, assessment is then reported to students and parents, in the form of a grade, a rating, a score, or narrative report, in a discussion, meeting or report card.

The reporting function is also central to screening assessments used to determine what students might benefit from particular instruction, diagnostic assessment (which often follows screening) to provide more in depth understanding of the state of a student's reading, progress monitoring assessment to determine the nature of students' ongoing reading development, and outcome assessment, used to compare student learning with intended outcomes (University of Oregon, 2009). This approach to assessment, in which the reporting of cognitive skills and strategies is often the sole focus, is central in response to intervention (Fuchs & Fuchs, 2006) and curriculum based management (Deno, 1985) programs.

Supporting: Positive Student Affect towards Reading

Students construct meaning from classroom assessments of reading. The literal understanding of assessment can include the sense that students make of grades, scores and teachers' comments (e.g., "A" of "C," 60% or 95%, and "Needs improvement" or "Excellent"; Afflerbach & Moni, 1995). Students also use assessment to infer meaning about their status as readers, such as where on a continuum of "good reader" to "bad reader" they reside. Given the influence of self-concept and motivation on reading achievement (Guthrie & Wigfield, 2000), it is important that classroom reading assessment be used to provide a consistent and supportive signal to all readers, including those who are struggling. Labels such as "failing," "below average," or "treatment resistor" may accompany assessment information, yet classroom reading assessment results can be accompanied by comments such as "This is where you succeeded," or "This is where you gave great effort" (Johnston, 2005). Extending the sustaining, positive feedback from within a lesson to across the school year is a worthy goal, and formative assessment supplies the content of this feedback.

Teaching: The Development of Students' Self-Assessment

An additional and largely unrealized purpose of classroom reading assessment is to help students learn and practice self-assessment. Independent and successful readers continually self-assess: the ability to self-assess and its contribution to successful performance is well-demonstrated in the metacognitive literature (Pressley & Afflerbach, 1995; Winne & Perry, 2000). However, many classroom assessments are opaque: their workings and purposes are not fully understood, and students view assessment as a "black box" (Black & Wiliam, 1998b). This has several potentially negative effects. First, it may be that students lose the opportunity to learn and practice their own assessment routines, to develop independence in reading. Second, it removes the possibility of students feeling in control of acts of reading, thus the potential benefits of agency and being in control are lost. When student self-assessment of reading is conceptualized as consisting of strategies, the strategies may be modeled and explained by teachers, and the learning of self-assessment is an attainable instructional goal.

SITUATING THE FOCUS AND PURPOSE OF CLASSROOM READING ASSESSMENT

In this section we examine two representative forms of classroom reading assessment, performance assessment and portfolio assessment, with the intent of demonstrating their foci on particular student outcomes and achievements, and the manner in which they serve different purposes.

Performance Assessment

Performance assessment allows for both assessing and guiding students' reading. Performance assessment offers opportunities to observe and interpret how students learn from text and how they apply what is learned. Content area instruction, including history and science, may require that students critically read a variety of domain-related documents, beyond the acquisition of factual knowledge (Norris & Philips, 2003; Wineburg, 1991). For example, students who interpret and evaluate media reports of scientific research (Korpan, Bisanz, Bisanz, & Henderson, 1997; Norris, Philips, & Korpan, 2003; Phillips & Norris, 1999) can investigate findings from the research, the situation in which the research was conducted, and the media publishing of the research. In history classrooms, students perform intertextual construction of an argument from across a series of historical documents (VanSledright, 2002). Students deploy evaluative strategies in determining text provenance, age and authenticity. Performance assessments can describe the knowledge, skills and strategies, and related epistemology which students employ while conducting critical, domain-specific reading. These aspects of reading and reading development are often difficult to describe using more common assessments, such as multiple-choice questions.

Scoring rubrics are a key element in the process of developing and using performance assessments. A well-developed rubric is versatile in classroom assessment practice: it not only contributes to the validity of the measure, it can also contribute to students' learning. In particular, gradations of performance quality in rubrics provide teacher and student with opportunities to understand current levels of achievement, and the means to move towards future levels of achievement. This information may take a central role in teachers' formative feedback (Wiliam & Black, 1996). Rubrics are "instructional illuminators" (Popham, 1997) which highlight the critical goals and subgoals of instruction and learning. Over time, the continuing use of performance assessment rubrics helps students conceptualize both learned performance and assessment in relation to one another (Andrade, 2000; Popham, 1997; Tierney & Simon, 2004).

Consistent use of the language of assessment with scoring rubrics enhances students' metavocabularies for reading and learning (Tierney & Simon, 2004), which in turn supports metacognitive knowledge of classroom assessment actions. Thus, repeated interactions with well-specified rubrics promote students' understanding of goals and the means to attain those goals. This transparency of assessment (Frederiksen & Collins, 1989) benefits students working with rubrics and establishing understanding and ownership of assessment processes. Students understand not only the nature of performance that is expected, but also how to assess their own performance (Afflerbach, 2002; Andrade & Du, 2005; Cohen, Lotan, Abram, Scarloss, & Schults, 2002).

Brookhart and Durkin (2003) observed daily assessment in high school social studies classes and determined that students' perceived motivations to learn varied according to the type (and related task) of assessment activities, as well as their learning goals. Experiences with classroom-based performance assessment were positively related to students' motivation and the amount of effort spent on assessment tasks. Students with performance assessment experience used more active learning strategies and demonstrated clear goal orientations. Also noteworthy was that performance assessment stimulated "desires for competence" that bolstered students' will to learn and to master target skills and strategies.

Falk, Ort, and Moirs (2007) investigated hybridized assessment systems, developed for large-scale, state-wide use, but also used as classroom-based performance assessments of literacy for the early grades. The Early Literacy Profile (ELP) has two fundamental purposes: to monitor students' progress towards state standards (reporting purpose) and to provide teachers with instructionally useful information (teaching purpose). The ELP requires teachers to interview individual students, conduct diagnostic assessment, and evaluate students' reading responses. Teachers participating in the study had opportunities to learn about the ELP through professional development programs and used the assessment in their classroom instruction. Teachers reported challenges to implementing this assessment system, such that the time needed to assess individual students in interview sessions, and inconsistent observations of student reading among teachers. However, the majority of teachers reported that the ELP provided useful information that helped them identify their students' instructional needs. In addition, teachers indicated that the ELP information was effective for communicating assessment information with parents and the community, and so useful for accountability.

Portfolio Assessment

Herman, Gearhart, and Aschbacher (1996) define effective portfolios as the cumulative products of classroom instruction that include students' learning processes and accomplishments in specific and complex performances, with accompanying students' self-reflections on their own learning. Valid portfolios represent diverse dimensions of students' competency and literacy (Simon & Forgette-Giroux, 2000), including cognitive capacities, but also affective and social characteristics and students' self-assessment work.

A fully developed portfolio assessment can provide the evidentiary means to measure the development of students' content area knowledge, high-level thinking skills and strategies, and interests related to reading and learning. In a formative manner, portfolios may assist students in reviewing their accomplishments and evaluating their learning. Through analysis of portfolios, teachers may conduct continuous monitoring of students' progress and conduct ongoing revision of their mental model of students, learning, teaching, and classroom actions. These actions, in turn, help teachers identify future instructional foci. Moss et al. (1992) suggest that the portfolio assessment process is similar to classroom-based interpretive research. In a similar vein, Tierney and Clark (1998) label portfolio assessments as the "grounded evaluation" which enlists students' and teachers' classroom practices as primary evidence for the interpretation of students' learning.

Students' reflection on their learning is a key activity in portfolio assessment, yet encouraging and equipping students to self-evaluate their goals and progress is a challenging task for many teachers. Au and Carroll (1997) observed constructivist-oriented literacy classrooms where portfolios played central roles in instruction and assessment. New teachers, unfamiliar with portfolio assessments, did not reach the desirable level of assessment implementation by the end of the year. The researchers concluded that, in spite of an overall success in the promotion of students' ownership and self-esteem in literacy activities, classroom practice might have produced more positive effects on students' literacy achievements if teachers were supported to use portfolio assessment in connection with the constructivist-oriented instruction.

Underwood's (1998) year-long case study investigated whether school-wide portfolio assessment systems promoted students' literacy learning and motivational goal orientation at the classroom level. Teachers implemented portfolio assessment systems and provided students explicit instruction based on the criteria of the portfolio system. Students' works were evaluated by a teacher committee. Although there was no significant difference between the scores in direct writing tests of the control and experimental groups, the students in portfolio assessment classrooms performed significantly higher in open-ended reading tests than their counterparts in non-portfolio classrooms did. This study suggests that hybridized portfolio assessment systems may support individual teachers' formative use of portfolio assessments as well as student work in complex tasks.

Paratore, Hindin, Krol-Sinclair, and Duran (1999) observed parent-teacher conferences in elementary schools, and how family literacy portfolios work in parent-teacher collaborations toward understanding and promoting culturally diverse students' learning. Most participant parents in this study were recent immigrants, from low income households, or both. Parents received direct instructions on how to observe their child's literacy activities and how to collect artifacts used and produced in such activities. Participating parents shared their children's literacy portfolios with the teachers. Over time, teachers' and parents' discussions of home literacy artifacts contributed to understanding students' literacy abilities and performances. Although there was a mismatch of children's literacy performances between home and school contexts, it is noteworthy that some teachers modified their instructional approaches based on the evidence contained in the family portfolios. Using portfolio assessments for the teacher-parent conversation highlighted students' and parents' funds of knowledge, providing a perspective on home-school relationships (Moll et al., 1992), and offering the potential to bring together home and school literacies.

CHARACTERISTICS OF EFFECTIVE CLASSROOM READING ASSESSMENT

A synthesis of research in reading assessment, and affiliated fields that include instruction, learning, affective development, politics, and economics describes seven characteristics of effective classroom reading assessment: transparency and fostering participation in assessment, teacher and student reflection in relation to assessment, situated interpretation of student work, integration and flexibility of classroom assessment, validity and reliability, accountability and communicability of assessment, and serving diverse students. In this section we describe each characteristic, using research and theory from within and outside of reading and assessment research traditions.

Transparency and Fostering Participation in Assessment

Transparency of assessment and fostering students' participation in assessment relate directly to the socio-cultural nature of classroom reading assessment. Assessment is a social construction that requires students' knowledge and commitment to participate, as well as teachers' assumption of the role of expert guide (Gipps, 1999; Torrance & Pryor, 1998). In traditional assessment settings, students are relatively passive, yet classroom assessment can be used to place students in active roles, assessing and understanding their own reading and learning. Transparency, the degree to which assessment processes and goals are accessible and comprehensible to the students, is necessary for students to participate in classroom assessment practices. From a sociocultural perspective, transparency helps students access the core materials of learning and provides them with opportunities for situated learning in the community of practice (Lave & Wenger, 1991). Students have opportunities to participate in classroom assessment, as teachers help them construct understanding of the ways and means of assessment (Afflerbach & Meuwissen, 2005). Over time, assessment transparency allows students to inspect "inside the black box" of classroom assessment culture, a culture from which students are conventionally estranged (Black & Wiliam, 1998b). Transparency contributes to the transformation of an exclusive assessment culture into one of increasing student participation and competence with effective assessment practice (Black & Wiliam, 2006).

Assessment transparency is enhanced when assessment-related terms are discussed with students (Frederiksen & Collins, 1989). For example, as teachers pose questions, they can provide supporting narrative for those questions, including explanations of the purpose of the questions, and the relation of questions to classroom goals (Raphael & Au, 2005). Transparency is also enhanced by teacher-modeling and peer-collaboration that foster students' observations and reflections on how assessment works. Students' involvement in assessment includes discussion of the purposes of assessment, and devising ways of interpreting student works and performances. Teachers create transparency through their modeling and demonstrating these strategies while conducting classroom reading assessment.

In a longitudinal assessment project, Hickey and Zuiker (2005) investigated the GenScope assessment project, primarily to motivate lower achieving ninth-grade students' participation in science learning. A focus of the project was classroom assessment practices, specifically cycles of assessment activity that included formative questions used to check individual students' science conceptions, feedback rubrics used for peer-evaluation, and rubrics to foster and guide self-assessment. During feedback conversations, students reflected on their work, using detailed self-assessment rubrics. Students' learning was evaluated by their responses to open-ended and multiple choice assessments. Students in assessment-rich classrooms improved their understanding, as demonstrated by the two summative assessments. Assessment transparency and students' participation in the culture of classroom reading assessment requires an "open" culture, understandable materials and procedures, teacher modeling and a shift towards students' increasing responsibility to participate in assessment.

Teacher and Student Reflection in Relation to Assessment

Formative classroom assessment yields information that is used in teachers' and students' reflection on their classroom practices, and these reflective behaviors contribute to teacher and student growth (Black & Wiliam, 1998a). Formative classroom assessments serve as the external model for students who are learning to self-assess (Sadler, 1989). Students internalize assessment routines and goals through continual, engaged participation in the process of reading assessment. Eventually, students accurately appraise what they know and do, what resources are available, and how their knowledge and resources are to be used. These self-reflections mark the transfer from other-regulated (i.e., teacher) to metacognitive, self-regulated reading (Baker & Brown, 1984; Garner, 1987).

Using classroom assessment information, teachers can regularly identify student strengths and weaknesses. Based on iterative and recursive reflection, teachers identify students' zones of proximal development (Vygotsky, 1979). In the zone of proximal development, teachers use assessments to identify teachable moments and to inform instructional decision making. Teachers' reflection informs their perceptions of students. Simple alignment of assessment with instruction does not guarantee a successful implementation of classroom assessment. Success requires teachers' active and reflective use of assessment information to update teacher understanding and, so, instructional practices (Yin et al., 2008).

Student reflection is encouraged by the use of appropriate classroom assessments. To guide student learning, a checklist for student performance in a particular task reminds students what is needed and informs students of the nature of the performance. Based on a systematic and detailed checklist, students are assisted in planning, conducting, and evaluating their reading. The external model provided by the checklist can, over time and with practice, be internalized by the student, and used independently. Teacher feedback also plays central roles in class-room assessment for developing student self-reflective abilities (Crooks, 1989), and with timely instruction, student reflection can evolve along the route from teacher feedback through student self-assessment (Sadler, 1989).

Assessment and the Situated Interpretation of Student Work

Conventional reading assessments, including standardized tests, are based, in part, on a posi-tivist perspective that endorses objective measures of phenomena, as are used in the natural sciences. The "scientific" assessment of reading, as illustrated by standardized tests, assumes reading to be value-neutral: Reading skills and strategies are amenable to measure, divorced from the context in which they are normally used, and the interpretation of reading assessment results is ahistorical and decontextualized. In contrast, classroom assessments can provide for the situated interpretation of reading events, practices and accomplishments as they occur in student-environment interactions. Classroom assessment gains explanatory power when the context in which assessment occurs is considered. Just as researchers using interpretive inquiry are involved in the context of research and use their knowledge of the context in interpreting human and social realities from the data (Lincoln & Guba, 1985), teachers analyze and derive the meaning from classroom assessment, using knowledge of the classroom context (Moss et al., 1992; Moss, 2003).

Reading portfolios illustrate the nature and value of situated interpretation of assessment, as they are used to draw conclusions about student achievement when their contents are inter-preted in the context of classroom settings. Reading portfolios may include a range of student works from assignments and quizzes to reading logs and student self-reflections on their read-ing, and teachers apply interpretive strategies to assess students' reading portfolios. For exam-ple, teachers can code with a checklist and provide written and spoken comment in relation to the strengths and weakness of students' portfolio work. Teachers' narrative profiles of students reflect their knowledge of when, where, and how the works contained in the portfolio were produced, as they use context in the interpretation of student work. For example, they evaluate students in relation to both the goals of the marking period, and student growth—using both normative and individual frameworks for assessing the portfolio. These contextualized records become an evidentiary trail, understandable to teachers, students and audiences outside the classroom (Moss et al., 1992; Moss, 2003).

Integration and Flexibility of Classroom Assessment

Classroom reading assessment must be carefully integrated with curriculum, educational goals, and the broader school assessment program. As well, assessment must be flexible in its form, administration and application, so that the array of assessments used within a classroom is man-ageable and suited to different audiences and purposes (Liepzig & Afflerbach, 2000). Integration represents work to carefully match assessment with teaching and instruction, and single assess-ments with the larger assessment program. Consider the value of triangulation of data sources in experimental research, in which two or more sources provide unique information about the same person or event (Denzin, 1978). Triangulation allows for comparison of assessment results, with agreement of sources boosting confidence in judgments based on converging evidence, and disagreement suggesting the need for more information. While integration can make triangula-tion a possibility in classroom reading assessment, it is important that the efficiency factor of integration be determined. If we seek more than one data source about particular aspects of students' reading development, this adds to the assessment load. On the other hand, flexibility, as when a single assessment serves several purposes, is a possible antidote to this situation.

Flexibility signals that classroom reading assessment serves more than one purpose, and perhaps more than one audience. Such assessment should be a priority, given the resource constraints in classrooms. Flexibility also describes the assessment that remains consistent as assessment practice, but that is applicable to different classroom situations and phenomena. Consider the sixth-grade classroom in which students are expected to use performance assessments (e.g., Brookheart, Walsh, & Zientarski, 2006) across the school year, and across different subject areas. Within the particular school and district, assessment planning focuses on integration and flexibility, and one result is that performance assessment is used regularly, beginning in first grade. Sixth-grade students are well versed in performance assessment, given their extensive year-to-year experiences with it, and this reflects the school districts' long-term plan for integrating assessments across school years and subject areas. In conjunction with performance assessments, students are adept at using checklists that help guide students through the different challenges that the performance assessment presents. Across the school years, the checklists are scalable, with their contents reflecting increased complexity of schoolwork and assessment demand, as students move from elementary to middle and then high school.

Validity and Reliability of Classroom Assessment

The goal of classroom assessment validity is to ensure that inferences about students' learning, knowledge, and affective characteristics are appropriate (Afflerbach, 2007). Reliable classroom assessment provides consistent and accurate information that is useful for teachers and students. An account of validity and reliability and issues that are specific to classroom assessment is included in the earlier section, "Changes in the Conceptualization of Validity and Reliability Related to Classroom Reading Assessment." We refer the reader to that section for details on how validity and reliability are key characteristics of, and how they contribute to, effective classroom reading assessment.

Accountability and Communicability of Classroom Assessment

While assessment and accountability influence school reform, accountability systems and their attendant assessments sometimes sacrifice communicability and credibility for other purposes (Linn, 2000). The assessments used for accountability purposes are most often high-stakes standardized tests, which are easily and quickly administered and scored, relative to most classroom reading assessments. These tests yield raw scores and percentile rankings to present to assessment audiences, including policy makers, who seek accountability from teachers and schools. Accountability in this context is intended to influence teacher and school practice, but in most cases assessments implemented under the system are adopted without the consultation of important stakeholders like parents, teachers, and students (Afflerbach, 2007). In this system, the accountability information is presented numerically, widely used and traditionally accepted, but possessing minimal descriptive ability related to student growth. A discourse of accountability that privileges test results to carry meaning for politicians and taxpayers has little to say for school community members who want and need more regular, detailed information.

Two solutions are possible. First, high-stakes tests and other measures of accountability could become better representatives of all that reading development entails, continuing to report on the skill and strategy component of the reading construct, while incorporating reports of students' affective development. Second, classroom assessments of reading could assume greater role in demonstrating accountability, as performance assessments and portfolios are used in standardized manner, retaining the richness of report and the descriptions of the individual students, but adding comparability so that more trust is gained. Either of these approaches requires substantial changes, movement away from the status quo of one test determining accountability, and movement towards teacher expertise in assessment. When accountability is reconceptualized in the context of classroom assessment, it refers to "instructional aids and supports" for students learning (Linn, 1990). Such classroom reading assessment should be developed and used with consensus on how the assessment information is to be used to foster student development.

The communicative ability of assessment is as important a consideration as the validity and reliability ratings. Consider that reading assessment information that is not effectively communicated (or not fully understood) leaves the recipient of this information in the position of mis-constructing meaning about students, teachers, and reading programs. Thus, how and how well an assessment communicates is of paramount importance. Portfolio assessment is an appropriate frame in which to consider an assessment's ability to communicate. Portfolios contain students' work that is selected in relation to daily and long-term contexts. Students select and organize different artifacts and performances according to the particular goals of the portfolio assessment program. These might include vocabularies learned from reading, annotated bibliographies of texts read, and blog postings that summarize student responses to reading in and out of school. The contents of the portfolio is annotated, adding to the communicability of the portfolio: why the artifact was included, how it represents the student and reading accomplishment. Teachers check students' progress in the portfolio and share their reactions and suggestions with students: the portfolio becomes a context for assessment discussions. As a consequence of these classroom assessment activities and conversations, students' learning is guided and improved and their self-efficacy and self-assessment develop as they manage learning projects (Brookhart, 2001). Portfolio assessment information is shared in conferences with parents and with administrators. Detailed information and evidence of student learning is presented and communicated, offering useful information to parents and the community (Falk, Ort, & Moirs, 2007).

Serving Diverse Students and Their Assessment Needs

Classrooms are comprised of students with considerable individual differences. Currently, 20% of the student population in the United States is labeled learning disabled (LD) or English language learner (ELL), or both (Board on Testing and Assessment, 2004). Research on accommodation demonstrates that effective classroom reading assessment must follow specific guidelines for development and use so that all students are able to benefit from assessment, and that assessment provides the most accurate accounts of their development and achievement. An assessment accommodation must strive to maintain the validity of the assessment instrument and materials (Stretch & Osborne, 2005). As the maintenance of assessment validity is determined, accommodation for LD students may provide these students with a "differential boost" (Phillips, 1994) that lifts their performance more than the performance of unaccommodated students. Zuriff (2000) proposes that most unaccommodated students are already working at a maximum level of performance within the "normal" timeframe of a standardized test, noting that accommodated LD students perform significantly better on untimed tests than on tests with standardized time allotment.

The vast majority of research conducted with accommodation in assessment focuses on tests (Stansfield, 2002), and there is clear need for research that examines accommodation in classroom assessment. Nevertheless, findings from the test-centered accommodation research base are worthy of consideration. For example, surveys demonstrate the most common assessment accommodations for LD students include extended time to take tests, reading tests aloud to students, providing a scribe to take dictation from a student, paraphrasing test instructions and contents, and testing in small groups (Olson, Mead, & Payne, 2002). Assessment accommodation of ELL students includes extra time to take the assessment, the linguistic modification of test instructions and items (making the language of the assessment more understandable), and glossaries of key terms present in a test's reading selections (Abedi, Lord, & Plummer, 1997; Abedi, Lord, Hofstetter, & Baker, 2000).

While classroom assessments differ from standardized tests, research results in testing accommodations has implications for all assessments. The work of Abedi, his colleagues, and others suggests four foci that can guide the accommodation of assessment, including *validity, effectiveness, differential impact,* and *feasibility.* With *validity,* it is critical that the provision of an accommodation does not alter the construct—for example, when a reading test is read to a student, it is transformed into a listening test. If construct change does occur, the specifics of this change must be documented, to be used in careful interpretation of results. *Effectiveness* deals with the determination of what accommodations, or combinations of accommodations, best reduce the gap in performance between ELL and non-ELL students (or between LD and non-LD students). *Differential impact* allows for consideration of how an accommodation might place some students at disadvantage, as when the provision of extra time helps accommodated students, but gives them an advantage over unaccommodated students, and *feasibility* reminds that the requisite accommodations to be made to classroom assessments add a new layer of adjustment, administration and analysis to the assessment enterprise.

A final note on classroom assessment accommodation: LD and ELL students are entitled to receive assessment accommodation, based on laws and mandates. Upon meeting specific criteria for inclusion, students are accommodated. However, this process leaves considerable numbers of students who are deserving of some accommodation just beyond the reach of being accommodated (the student is not quite "LD enough," or "ELL enough"). In classroom assessment, these students, as well as their legally designated peers, can be accommodated in assessment routines that attend to individual differences. For example, the teacher who provides varies wait time for students answering questions, or repeats assessment instructions, based on an accurate appraisal of their current level of competence, is practicing accommodation.

CONCLUSIONS

The research and theory described in this chapter represent but the beginning of an immensely important body of work, work that situates classroom reading assessment at the center of instruction, learning, and achievement. However, theoretical arguments for centrality require concerted research efforts that continue to contribute to nuanced and detailed understanding of classroom reading assessment. In this chapter we presented classroom reading assessment from two situated perspectives: classroom reading in relation to research and theory from diverse, affiliated fields, and classroom reading in relation to complex classroom environments.

Consideration of affiliated literatures, including research on educational measurement, classrooms, and schools and society provides a robust account of the challenges to effective reading assessment, and the means to meet the challenges. As the research literature of classroom reading assessment continues to develop, attention to the evolving constructs of reading and reading assessment should be used to increase assessment validity. Classroom reading assessment, in both theory and practice, will be enriched by consideration of the political, economic, and social forces surrounding schools and classrooms. Classroom reading assessment itself is situated in complex school dynamics. Diverse students populate diverse classrooms, in which local and mandated goals vie for attention. In these classrooms, assessment must attend to different audiences and purposes. It must represent an informed balance of formative and summative approaches to assessment, and these must be linked for effectiveness.

As demonstrated by the reviewed research and theory, the situated nature of classroom assessment offers both promise and challenge. The promise relates to the availability of work in diverse fields to inform the development of classroom assessments. It is critical that the contexts in which reading assessment is used, the purposes, foci, and the internal and external factors that shape assessment are understood. The challenge includes coordination of the information that emanates from diverse areas of inquiry and the synthesis of this information in relation to evolving notions of reading and assessment. We presented a model of classroom reading assessment that describes a dynamic environment, subject to forces, sometimes supportive and sometimes opposite, that have subtle and stark influence on schooling and assessment. The model demonstrates that useful classroom reading assessment is not only a matter of developing valid and reliable assessment instruments and procedures; it demands, also, attention to situational variables.

FUTURE DIRECTIONS

Looking forward, classroom assessment will benefit from particular research foci. First, research in which the relationship between classroom reading assessment, students' reading achievement, and teacher efficacy is needed. The history of the relationship between reading assessment and research is one where assessment information (most frequently single test scores) serves as the dependent variable, reporting on the quality of instructional approaches and reading programs, and the results of experimental manipulations in teaching reading. In contrast, research is needed in which reading assessment is not the measure of significance, but the object of investigation.

As discussed in this chapter, investigation of classroom reading assessment and its relation to helping students learn how to conduct self-assessment for themselves is a worthy focus. This research will describe the benefits of assessment that serves both the reporting and teaching function. As well, examination of classroom assessment that provides consistent and positive messages of students who may struggle but who progress nevertheless, may describe assessment's role in fostering both cognitive and affective aspects of becoming a successful reader. That formative classroom assessment is at the center of effective teaching is an engaging suggestion. Theories of reflection in teaching and teaching students in their zones of proximal development implicate high quality formative classroom assessment, and research that provides details on how (and if) this is so are needed. Such investigation will provide detailed accounts of classroom assessment of reading in relation to learning goals, student reading growth and achievement, and levels of teacher expertise.

This chapter focuses on formative classroom reading assessment. Summative assessment, currently given much popular attention and school resources, must be carefully linked so that formative assessments anticipate summative assessments—not in the sense that classroom assessment helps train students to take summative tests, but in the sense that careful and consistent classroom reading assessment anticipates and predicts what students do on unit-end, marking period-end, and year-end tests. Research that demonstrates the value of linkages between formative and summative assessment will reinforce the idea that while accountability is measured by a single test on a single day, accountability is created by effective, daily classroom assessment and related instruction and learning.

The majority of research that focuses on formative classroom assessments describes how cognitive strategies and skills are assessed. It is rare to find assessment of student affective characteristics, characteristics that are proven to have enhancing or debilitating effect on students' reading development. The influence of affect on reading development and achievement is well established. Future research should focus on the usefulness of assessment of readers' affective characteristics, charting students' self-concepts and self-esteem, motivation and attributions for classroom outcomes, comparing such measures with students' ongoing reading achievement. As well, research should describe how assessment influences reader affect, in relation to the meaning that students construct from assessment information, and nature of assessment feedback.

As classroom reading assessment is closely aligned with instruction, we do well to remember that individual differences in learning figure largely in student success and failure. As many classroom assessments of reading share a border with instruction, and as many assessments demand increased responsibility and initiative on the part of students, research should focus on the suitability of particular classroom assessments for students, in relation to the demands they present, how well students understand them, the student's prior knowledge and experiences with such assessment, and the affective interactions that students have with assessment. Just as a student and reading curriculum may be mismatched, so too might a student be puzzled, bored, or overwhelmed by a particular assessment.

Finally, research can investigate classroom reading assessment as an agent of transformation, not as an appendage or an afterthought, but an integral component in how reading instruction and curricula are conceptualized and developed. The influence of assessment may be detrimental, as when the school experience is limited by teaching to the test. In contrast, classroom assessment can be transformative, and not reactionary, as it is conceptualized in relation to new ideas about reading and literacy, and new means of assessing them.

REFERENCES

Abedi, J., Lord, C., & Plummer, J. (1997). *Final report of language background as a variable in NAEP mathematics performance. CSE Technical Report 429.* Los Angeles: Center for the Study of Evaluation.

Abedi, J., Lord, C., Hofstetter, C., & Baker, E. (2000) Impact of accommodation strategies on English language learners' test performance. *Educational Measurement: Issues and Practice, 19,* 16–26.

AERA, APA, & NCME. (1999). *Standards for educational and psychological testing.* Washington, DC: Author.

Afflerbach, P. (2002). The road to folly and redemption: Perspectives on the legitimacy of high-stakes testing. *Reading Research Quarterly, 37,* 348–360.

Afflerbach, P. (2007). *Understanding and using reading assessment, K-12.* Newark, DE: International Reading Association.

Afflerbach, P., Cho, B., & Kim, J. (In press). The assessment of higher order thinking in reading. In G. Schraw (Ed.), *Assessment of higher order thinking skills.* Denver, CO: Information Age.

Afflerbach, P., Cho, B., Kim, J., & Clark, S. (2010). The classroom assessment of literacy. In D. Wycliffe (Ed.), *International handbook of English, language and literacy* (pp. 401–412). Cambridge, UK: Cambridge University Press.

Afflerbach, P., & Meuwissen, K. (2005). Teaching and learning self-assessment strategies. In S. E. Israel, C. C. Block, & K. Kinnucan-Welsch (Eds.), *Metacognition in literacy learning: Theory, assessment, instruction, and professional development* (pp. 141–164). Mahwah, NJ: Erlbaum.

Afflerbach, P., & Moni, K. (1995). The intended and interpreted meanings of teachers' evaluative feedback to students during reading lessons. *Yearbook of the National Reading Conference,* 137–147.

Afflerbach, P., Pearson, D., & Paris, S. (2008). Clarifying differences between reading skills and reading strategies. *The Reading Teacher, 61,* 364–373.

Alexander, P. (2003). The development of expertise: The journey from acclimation to proficiency. *Educational Researcher, 32,* 10–14.

Anderson, L., & Bourke, S. (2000). *Assessing affective characteristics in schools, 2/e.* Mahwah, NJ: Erlbaum.

Anderson, L., Evertson, C., & Brophy, J. (1979). An experimental study of effective teaching in first-grade reading groups. *Elementary School Journal, 79,* 193–223.

Andrade, H. (2000). Using rubrics to promote thinking and learning. *Educational Leadership, 57,* 13–18.

Andrade, H., & Du, Y. (2005). Student perspectives on rubric-referenced assessment. *Practical Assessment, Research & Evaluation, 10*(3). Retrieved January 20, 2007, from http://PAREonline.net/getvn.asp?v=10&n=3

Au, K., Carroll, J. H. (1997). Improving literacy achievement through a constructivist approach: The KEEP demonstration classroom project. *The Elementary School Journal, 97,* 203–221.

Bakan, R. (1971). Academic performance and self-concept as a function of achievement variability. *Journal of Educational Measurement, 8*, 317–319.

Baker, L., & Brown, A. L. (1984). Metacognitive skills and reading. In P. D. Pearson, R. Barr, M. L. Kamil, & P. Mosenthal (Eds.), *Handbook of reading research* (Vol. 1, pp. 353–394). New York: Longman.

Baxter, G., & Glaser, R. (1998). Investigating the cognitive complexity of science assessments. *Educational Measurement: Issues and Practice, 17*, 37–45.

Bazerman, C. (1985). Physicists reading physics: Schema-laden purposes and purpose-laden schema. *Written Communication, 2*, 3–24.

Black, P., & Wiliam, D. (1998a). Assessment and classroom learning. *Assessment in Education: Principles, Policy & Practice, 5*, 7–74.

Black, P., & Wiliam, D. (1998b). Inside the black box: Raising standards through classroom assessment. *Phi Delta Kappan, 80*, 139–148.

Black, P., & Wiliam, D. (2006). Developing a theory of formative assessment. In. J. Gardner (Ed.), *Assessment and learning* (pp. 81–100). London: Sage.

Board on Testing and Assessment. (2004). *Keeping score for all: The effects of inclusion and accommodation policies on large-scale educational assessment.* Washington DC: National Academy Press.

Brookhart, S. (2001). Successful students' formative and summative uses of assessment information. *Assessment in Education, 8*(2), 153–169.

Brookhart, S. (2003). Developing measurement theory for classroom assessment purpose and uses. *Educational Measurement: Issues and Practice, 22*, 5–12.

Brookhart, S., & Durkin, D. (2003). Classroom assessment, student motivation, and achievement in high school social studies classes. *Applied Measurement in Education, 16*, 27–54.

Brookhart, S., Walsh, J., & Zientarski, W. (2006). The dynamics of motivation and effort for classroom assessments in middle school science and social studies. *Applied Measurement in Education, 19*(2), 151–184.

Brown, J., Collins, A., & Duguid, P. (1989). Situated cognition and the culture of learning. *Educational Researcher, 18*, 32–42.

Calfee, R., & Hiebert, E. (1991). Classroom assessment of reading. In R. Barr, M. Kamil, P. Mosenthal, & P. Pearson (Eds.), *Handbook of reading research* (Vol. 2, 281–309). White Plains, NY: Longman.

Cazden, C. (1986). Classroom discourse. In M. Wittrock (Ed.), *Handbook of research on teaching* (3rd ed., pp. 432–462). New York: Macmillan.

Chapman, J., & Tunmer, W. (1995). Development of young children's reading self-concepts: An examination of emerging subcomponents and their relationship with reading achievement. *Journal of Educational Psychology, 87*, 154–167.

Cohen, E., Lotan, R., Abram, P., Scarloss, B., & Schults, S. (2002). Can groups learn? *Teachers College Record, 104*, 1045–1068.

Corno, L. (1993). The best laid plans: Modern conceptions of volition and educational research. *Educational Researcher, 22*, 14–22.

Creemers, B., & Kyriakides, L. (2006). Critical analysis of current approaches to modeling educational effectiveness; the importance of establishing a dynamic model. *School Effectiveness and School Improvement, 17*, 347–366.

Crooks, T. (1989). The impact of classroom evaluation practices on students. *Review of Educational Research, 58*, 438–481.

Davis, A. (1998). *The limits of educational assessment.* Oxford, UK: Blackwell.

Deno, S. (1985). Curriculum-based measurement: The emerging alternative. *Exceptional Children, 52*, 219–232.

Denzin, N. (1978) *Sociological methods: A sourcebook, 2e.* New York: McGraw Hill.

Dunn, K. E., & Mulvenon, S. W. (2009). A critical review of research on formative assessment: The limited scientific evidence of the impact of formative assessment in education. *Practical Assessment Research & Evaluation, 14*, 1–11.

Dweck, C. (1999). *Self theories: Their role in motivation, personality and development.* Philadelphia: Psychology Press.

Falk, B., Ort, S. W., & Moirs, K. (2007). Keeping the focus on the child: Supporting and reporting on teaching and learning with a classroom-based performance assessment system. *Educational Measurement, 12*, 47–75.

Fitt, D., Rafferty, K., Presner, M., & Heverly, M. (1999). *Improving the quality of teacher's tests.* Retrieved July 22, 2009, from http://www.highbeam.com/doc/1G1-55409981.html

Flavell, J. (1976). Metacognitive aspects of problem solving. In L. Resnick (Ed.), *The nature of intelligence* (pp. 231–235). Hillsdale, NJ: Erlbaum.

Fredricks, J., Blumenfeld, P., & Paris, A. (2004). School engagement: Potential of the concept, state of the art. *Review of Educational Research, 74,* 59–119.

Frederiksen, N. (1984). The real test bias: Influences of testing and on teaching and learning. [theoretical study]. *American Psychologist, 39*(3), 193–202.

Frederiksen, J. R., & Collins, A. (1989). A systems approach to educational testing. *Educational Researcher, 18,* 27–32.

Freire, P. (1995). *Pedagogy of hope: Reliving pedagogy of the oppressed.* New York: Continuum.

Fuchs, D., & Fuchs, L. (2006). New directions in research: Introduction to response to intervention: What, why, and how valid is it? *Reading Research Quarterly, 41,* 93–99.

Gambrell, L., Palmer, B., Codling, R., & Mazzoni, S. (1996). *Motivation to read profile (MRP).* Athens, GA: National Reading Research Center.

Garner, R. (1987). *Metacognition and reading comprehension.* Norwood, NJ: Ablex.

Gardner, J. (2006). *Assessment and learning.* London: Sage.

Gee, J. (2008). *Social linguistics and literacies: Ideology in discourses* (3rd ed.). New York: Routledge.

Gipps, C. (1999). Socio-cultural aspects of assessment. *Review of Research in Education, 24,* 355–392.

Greeno, J., and the Middle School Mathematics Through Applications Project Group. (1998). The situativity of knowing, learning and research. *American Psychologist, 53,* 5–26.

Guthrie, J. T., & Wigfield, A. (2000). Engagement and motivation in reading. In M. L. Kamil, P. B. Mosenthal, P. D. Pearson, & R. Barr (Eds.), *Handbook of reading research* (Vol. 3, pp. 403–422). Mahwah, NJ: Erlbaum.

Guthrie, J. T., & Wigfield, A. (Eds.). (1997). *Reading engagement: Motivating readers through integrated instruction.* Newark, DE: International Reading Association.

Hargreaves, A., Earl, L., & Schmidt, M. (2002). Perspectives on alternative assessment reform. *American Educational Research Journal, 39,* 69–95.

Hartman, H. (2001). *Metacognition in learning and instruction: Theory, research and practice.* Dordrecht, The Netherlands: Kluwer.

Heath, S. (1983). *Ways with words: Language, life, and work in communities and classrooms.* New York: Cambridge University Press.

Herman, J. L., Gearhart, M., & Aschbacher, M. (1996). Portfolios for classroom assessment: Design and implementation issues. In R. Calfee & P. Perfumo (Eds.), *Writing portfolios in the classroom: Policy and practice, promise and peril* (pp. 27–59). Mahwah, NJ: Erlbaum.

Hickey, D., & Zuiker, S. (2005). Engaged participation: A sociocultural model of motivation with implications for educational assessment. *Educational Assessment, 10,* 277–305.

Hiebert, E., Winograd, P., & Danner, F. (1984). Children's attributions for failure and success in different aspects of reading. *Journal of Educational Psychology, 76,* 1139–1148.

Huey, E. B. (1908/1968). *The psychology and pedagogy of reading: With a review of the history of reading and writing and of methods, texts, and hygiene in reading.* Cambridge, MA: M.I.T. Press.

Johnston, P. (2005). *Choice words.* Portland, ME: Stenhouse.

Kaestle, C. (1991). Studing the history of literacy. In C. Kaestle (Ed.), *Literacy in the United States: Readers and reading since 1880* (pp. 3–32). New Haven, CT: Yale University Press.

Korpan, C. A., Bisanz, G. L., Bisanz, J., & Henderson, J. M. (1997). Assessing literacy in science: Evaluation of scientific media news briefs. *Science Education, 81,* 515–532.

Kress, G. (2003). *Literacy in the new media age.* New York: Routledge.

Labaree, D. (2007). *Education, markets, and the public good: Selected works of David F. Labaree.* London: Routledge.

Lave, J., & Wenger, E. (1991). *Situated learning: Legitimate peripheral participation.* Cambridge, UK: Cambridge University Press.

Leslie, L., & Caldwell, J. (2005). *Qualitative reading inventory* (4th ed.). New York: Allyn and Bacon.

Leu, D., Jr., Coiro, J., Castek, J., Hartman, D. K., Henry, L., & Reinking, D. (2008). Research on instruction and assessment of the new literacies of online reading comprehension. In C. Block, & S. Parris (Eds.), *Comprehension instruction: Research-based best practices* (pp. 321–346). New York: Guilford.

Liepzig, D., & Afflerbach, P. (2000). Determining the suitability of assessments: Using the CURRV frame-work. In L. Baker, M. Dreher, & J. Guthrie (Eds.) *Engaging young readers* (pp. 159–187). New York: Guilford.

Lincoln, Y., & Guba. E. (1985). *Naturalistic inquiry.* Beverly Hills, CA: Sage.

Linn, R. (1990). Essentials of student assessment: From accountability to instructional aid. *Teachers College Record, 91,* 422–436.

Linn R. (2000). Assessments and accountability. *Educational Researcher, 29,* 4–16.

Linn, R., Baker, E., & Dunbar, S. (1991). Complex, performance-based assessment: Expectations and validation criteria. *Educational Researcher, 20,* 15–21.

McDonnell, L. (2008). The politics of educational accountability: Can the clock be turned back? In K. Ryan & L. Shepard (Eds.), *The future of test-based educational accountability* (pp. 47–67). New York: Routledge.

McKenna, M., & Kear, D. (1990). Measuring attitude towards reading: a new tool for teachers. *The Reading Teacher, 43,* 626–639.

McKenna, M., & Stahl, S. (2003). *Assessment for reading instruction.* New York: Guilford.

Mehan, H. (1979). *Learning lessons: Social organizaton in the classroom.* Cambridge, MA: Harvard University Press.

Messick, S. (1989). Validity. In R. Linn (Ed.), *Educational measurement* (3rd ed., pp. 12–103). London: Collier Macmillan.

Moje, E., McIntosh Ciechanowski, K., Kramer, K., Ellis, L., Carrillo, R., & Collazo, T. (2004). Working toward third space in content area literacy: An examination of everyday funds of knowledge and discourse. *Reading Research Quarterly, 39,* 38–71.

Moll, L., Amanti, C., Neff, D., & Gonzalez, N. (1992). Funds of knowledge for teaching: Using a qualitative approach to connect homes and classrooms. *Theory into Practice, 31,* 132–141.

Morrow, L., Reutzel, D., & Casey, H. (2006). Organization and management of language arts teaching: Classroom environments, grouping practices, and exemplary instruction. In C. Evertson & C. Weinstein (Eds.), *Handbook of classroom management: Research, practice, and contemporary issues* (pp. 559–581). Mahwah, NJ: Erlbaum.

Moskal, P. (2003). Recommendations for developing classroom perormance assessments and scoring rubrics. *Practical Assessment, Research and Evaluation.* Retrieved January 21, 2008, from http://pareonline.net/getvn.asp?v=8&n=14

Moss, P. (2003). Reconceptualizing validity for classroom assessment. *Educational Measurement: Issues and Practice, 22,* 13–25.

Moss, P., Beck, J., Ebbs, C., Matson, B., Muchmore, J., Steele, D. (1992). Portfolios, accountability, and interpretive approach to validity. *Educational Measurement: Issues and Practices, 11,* 12–21.

National Assessment Governing Board. (2008). *2009 NAEP reading framework.* Washington, DC: Author.

New London Group. (1996). A pedagogy of multiliteracies: Designing social futures. *Harvard Educational Review, 66,* 60–92.

Norris, S., & Philips, L. (2003). How literacy in its fundamental sense is central to scientific literacy. *Science Education, 87,* 224–240.

Olson, K., Banaji, M., Dweck, C., & Spelke, E. (2006). Children's biased evaluations of lucky vs, unlucky people and their social groups. *Psychological Science, 17,* 822–845.

Olson, B., Mead, R., & Payne, D. (2002). *A report of standard setting method for alternative assessments for students with significant disabilities.* Minneapolis: National Center on Educational Outcomes.

Palfrey, J., & Gasser, U. (2008). *Born digital: Understanding the first generation of digital natives.* New York: Basic Books.

Palincsar, A., & Brown, A. (1984). Reciprocal teaching of comprehension-fostering and monitoring activities. *Cognition and Instruction, 1,* 117–175.

Paratore, J., Hindin, A., Krol-Sinclair, B., & Duran, P. (1999). Discourse between teachers and Latino parents during conferences based on home literacy portfolio. *Education and Urban Society, 32,* 58–82.

Pearson, P., & Johnson, D. (1978). *Teaching reading comprehension.* New York: Holt, Rinehart & Winston.

Pellegrino, J., Chudowsky, N., & Glaser, R. (2001). *Knowing what students know: The science and design of educational assessment.* Washington, DC: National Academy Press.

Philips, L. M., & Norris, S. P. (1999). Interpreting popular reports of science: What happens when the reader's world meets the world on paper? *International Journal of Science Education, 21,* 317–327.

Phillips, S. (1994). High-stakes testing accommodations: Validity versus disabled rights. *Applied Measurement in Education, 7,* 93–120.

Pintrich, P., Marx, R., & Boyle, R. (1993). Beyond cold conceptual change: The role of motivational beliefs and classroom contextual factors in the process of conceptual change. *Review of Educational Research, 63,* 167–199.

Popham, W. J. (1997). What's wrong-and what's right-with rubrics. *Educational Leadership, 55,* 72–75.

Pressley, M., & Afflerbach, P. (1995). *Verbal reports of reading: The nature of constructively responsive reading.* Mahwah, NJ: Erlbaum.

Raphael, T., & Au, K. (2005). QAR: Enhancing comprehension and test taking across grades and content areas. *The Reading Teacher, 59,* 206–221.

Rowan, B. (2002). The ecology of school improvement: Notes on the school improvement industry in the United States. *Journal of Educational Change, 3,* 283–314.

Sadler, R. (1998). Formative assessment: Revisiting the territory. *Assessment in Education, 5,* 77–84.

Scherr, R., & Hammer, D. (2009). Student behavior and epistemological framing: Examples from collaborative active-learning activities in physics. *Cognition and Instruction, 27,* 147–174.

Schon, D. (1987). *The reflective practitioner: How professionals think in action.* New York: Basic Books.

Scribner, S., & Cole, M. (1981). *The psychology of literacy.* Cambridge, MA: Harvard University Press.

Shepard, L., & Bliem, C. (1995). Parents' thinking about standardized tests and performance assessments. *Educational Researcher, 24,* 25–32.

Simon, M., & Forgette-Giroux, R. (2000). Impact of a content selection framework on portfolio assessment at the classroom level. *Assessment in Education, 7,* 83–101.

Smith, J. (2003). Reconsidering reliability in classroom assessment and grading. *Educational Measurement: Issues and Practice, 22,* 26–33.

Snow, C. (2002). *Reading for understanding: Toward a research and development program in reading comprehension.* Santa Monica, CA: Rand Corporation.

Spector, J. (2005). How reliable are informal reading inventories? Psychology in the schools. Retrieved July 22, 2007, from http://www3.interscience.wiley.com/journal/110520731/abstract?CRETRY=1&SRETRY=0

Stanovich, K. (1986). Matthew effects in reading: Some consequences of individual differences in the acquisition of literacy. *Reading Research Quarterly, 21,* 360–407.

Stansfield, C. (2002). Linguistic simplification: A promising test accommodation for LEP students? *Practical Assessment, Research and Evaluation, 8.* Retrieved July 22, 2009, from http://pareonline.net/getvn.asp?v=8&n=7

Stiggins, R., & Bridgeford, N. (1985). The ecology of classroom assessment. *Journal of Educational Measurement, 22,* 271–286.

Stiggins, R., & Conklin, N. (1992). *In teachers' hands: Investigating the practices of classroom assessment.* Albany: State University of New York Press.

Stobart, G. (2006). The validity of formative assessment. In. J. Gardner (Ed.), *Assessment and learning* (pp. 133–146). London: Sage.

Street, B. (1995). *Social literacies.* London: Longmans.

Stretch, L., & Osborne, J. (2005). *Extended time test accommodation: Directions for future research and practice.* Retrieved March 22, 2008, from http://pareonline.net/pdf/v10n8.pdf

Tierney, R., & Clark, C. (with Fenner, L., Herter, R., Simpson, C., & Wiser, B.). (1998). Portfolios: Assumptions, tensions, and possibilities. *Reading Research Quarterly, 33,* 474–486.

Tierney, R., & Simon, M. (2004). What's still wrong with rubrics: Focusing on the consistency of performance criteria across scale levels. *Practical Assessment, Research & Evaluation, 9.* Retrieved January 20, 2007, from http://PAREonline.net/getvn.asp?v=9&n=2

Tittle, C. (1989). Validity: Whose construction is it in the teaching and learning context? *Educational Measurement: Issues and Practices, 8,* 5–13.

Torrance, H., & Pryor, J. (1998). *Investigating formative assessment: Teaching, learning and assessment in the classroom.* Philadelphia: Open University Press.

Uhry, J., & Ehri, L. (1999). Children's reading acquisition. In D. Wagner, R. Venezky, & B. Street (Eds.), *Literacy: An International Handbook.* Boulder, CO: Westview Press.

Underwood, T. (1998). The consequences of portfolio assessment: A case study. *Educational Assessment,* *5*, 147–194.

United States Department of Education Office of the Inspector General. (2006). *The Reading First grant* *application process.* Final inspection report. Washington, DC: Author.

University of Oregon. (2009). Big ideas in reading: The purposes of assessment. Retrieved June 3, 2009, from http://reading.uoregon.edu/assessment/assess_types.php

Valencia, S. W., & Wixson, K. K. (2000). Policy-oriented research on literacy standards and assessment. In M. J. Kamil, P. B. Mosenthal, P. D. Pearson, & R. Barr (Eds.), *Handbook of reading research* (Vol. III, pp. 911–935). Mahwah, NJ: Erlbaum.

Valencia, S., Hiebert, E., & Afflerbach, P. (1994). *Authentic assessment: Practices and possibilities.* Newark, DE: International Reading Association.

Van den Broek, P., Young, M., Tzeng, Y., & Linderholm, T. (1998). The landscape model of reading: Inferences and online construction of a memory representation. In H. van Oostendorp & S. Goldman (Eds.), *The construction of mental representations during reading* (pp. 71–98). Mahwah, NJ: Erlbaum.

VanSledright, B. (2002). *In search of America's past: Learning to read history in elementary school.* New York: Teachers College Press.

Verhoeven, L., & Snow, C. (2001). *Literacy and motivation: Reading engagement in individuals and groups.* Mahwah, NJ: Erlbaum.

Vygotsky, L. (1979). *Mind in society.* Cambridge, MA: Harvard University Press.

Wells, G. (1989). Language in the classroom: Literacy and collaborative talk. *Language and Education, 3,* 251–274.

Wiliam, D., & Black, P. (1996). Meanings and consequences: A basis for distinguishing formative and summative functions of assessment? *British Educational Research Journal, 23,* 537–548.

Wineburg, S. (1991). On the reading of historical texts: Notes on the breach between school and academy. *American Educational Research Journal, 28,* 495–519.

Winne, P., & Perry, N. (2000). Measuring self-regulated learning. In M. Boekarts, P. Pintrich, & M. Zeidner (Eds.) *Handbook of self-regulation* (pp. 532–566). Orlando, FL: Academic Press.

Wolf, D. (1987, Winter). The art of questioning. *Academic Connection,* 1–7.

Yin, Y., Shavelson, R., Ayala, C., Araceli Ruiz-Primo, M., Brandon, P., Furtak, E., et al. (2008). On the impact of formative assessment on student motivation, achievement, and conceptual change. *Applied Measurement in Education, 21,* 335–359.

Ziegler, J., & Goswami, U. (2005). Reading acquisition, developmental dyslexia, and skilled reading across languages: A psycholinguistic grain size theory. *Psychological Bulletin, 131,* 3–29.

Zuriff, G. (2000). Extra examination time for students with learning disabilities: An examination of the maximum potential hypothesis. *Applied Measurement in Education, 13,* 99–117.

22 The Role of Culture in Literacy, Learning, and Teaching

Guofang Li
Michigan State University

Social efficiency as an educational purpose should mean cultivation of power to join freely and fully in shared and common activities. This is impossible without culture, while it brings a reward in culture, because one cannot share in intercourse with others without learning—without getting a broader point of view and perceiving things of which one would otherwise be ignorant.

John Dewey, *Democracy and Education* (1916, p. 122)

In 2007, the U.S. Census Bureau reported that the number of people from ethnic or racial minorities in the United States had risen to more than 100 million, or around one-third of the population. The Hispanic population, now 44.3 million, was the fastest growing, at a rate of 3.4% between July 2005 and July 2006, and Asians were the second fastest-growing minority group at a rate of 3.2%, with their numbers standing at 14.9 million (Reuters, 2007). The growth in ethnic minorities has drastically changed the student compositions in U.S. schools. According to Myer, Madden, and McGrath (2005), from 1990 to 2001, the linguistically and culturally diverse student population has grown approximately 105%, whereas the general school population has grown only 12% (Meyer, 2004). There were approximately 1.3 million language minority or LEP (limited English proficient) students in 1990, accounting for approximately 3% of the school student population (Anstrom 1996). By 2004, this number had risen to 11%. It is projected that by 2015 about 30% of the school-aged population in the United States will be language minorities (Francis, M. Rivera, Lesaux, Kieffer, & H. Rivera, 2006).

These changing demographics pose unprecedented challenges for the public school system to accommodate a variety of needs for ethnic minority students, including their sociolinguistic, sociocultural, and socioemotional development. The majority of educators agree that to successfully address the increasingly diverse student populations and ensure language minority students' academic achievement, school instruction must be culturally responsive to students' linguistic and cultural backgrounds (Au, 1993; Gay, 2000; González, Moll, & Amanti, 2005; Ladson-Billings, 1994; Li, 2006; Moje & Hinchman, 2004; Moll & González, 1994). For literacy educators to be culturally responsive to students' diverse backgrounds, they must learn the role of culture in literacy learning and teaching.

While the chapter by Rueda (this volume) focuses on research and theory on cultural perspectives in reading research, this chapter reviews research on the role of culture in literacy teaching and learning by examining studies on culture and literacy in classrooms, schools, and out-of-school contexts. In the sections that follow, I first provide an overview of the process of literacy learning and cultural socialization. Next is a review of current trends and issues in research concerning the interplay between literacy and culture from both the learning and the teaching perspective. I conclude with suggestions for future lines of research.

LITERACY LEARNING AND CULTURAL SOCIALIZATION

The relationship between literacy and culture has been examined extensively in the literature (Au, 1993; Blount, 1982; Langer, 1987; Wagner, 1991). Though culture can be defined in many ways, it is often seen as "the forms of traditional behavior which are characteristics of a given society or a group of societies, or of a certain race, or of a certain area, or of a certain period of time" and "which has been developed by the human race and is successively learned by each generation" (Mead, 1951, p. 17). It "denotes an historically transmitted pattern of meanings embodied in symbols, a system of inherited conceptions expressed in symbolic forms by means of which men communicate, perpetuate, and develop their knowledge about and attitudes toward life" (Geertz, 1973, p. 89). Culture is also deeply rooted in the nexus of power relations that signifies the particular ways in which a social group lives out and makes sense of its given circumstances and conditions of life within the social structure in which various unequal social relations are produced (McLaren, 1998). Although a society's culture consists of the categories of knowledge that members of a society have to know or believe or use in order to organize their behaviors, it is not prescriptive for members' actions or ways of living. Rather, as Swidler (1986) points out, culture influences individual members' actions not by providing the ultimate values toward which actions are oriented, but by shaping a repertoire or "tool kit" of habits, skills, and styles from which people construct ways to organize their behavior in concrete situations. These ways of organizing behavior or "strategies of action" differ across individuals, groups, and circumstances depending on habits, moods, sensibilities, and views of the world (Geertz, 1973; Swidler, 1986).

Literacy, or the ability to identify, understand, interpret, create, communicate, compute, and use printed and written materials associated with varying contexts (UNESCO, 2004), is part of a culture. Literacy activities are embedded in the social, cultural, and historical contexts in which they occur. Shaped by different social and cultural norms, literacy acts—their functions, meanings, and methods of transmission—vary from one cultural group to another (Langer, 1987; Wagner, 1991). Becoming literate is a part of becoming acculturated in one's sociocultural worlds; literacy is seen as a means by which individuals conduct and construct their lives in the community and the society (Fishman, 1988, p. 143). Therefore, researchers suggest a broad approach to examine literacy within the sociocultural context in which it is acquired and learned, including factors associated with literacy learning and teaching such as language background, race, ethnicity, socioeconomic status, gender, and religion (Gunderson, 2008; Langer, 1987; Li, 2002; Street, 1995; Wagner, 1991).

One way to conceptualize the relationship between culture and literacy learning is to examine the functions of language in establishing and maintaining cultural practices. According to Gee (1989), a learner's social world can be categorized into two over-arching domains: the primary Discourse of the home and community, and the secondary Discourses of the public sphere—institutions such as the public schools. A Discourse is "a socially accepted association among ways of using language, other symbolic expressions, and artifacts, of thinking, feeling, believing, valuing and acting that can be used to identify oneself as a member of a socially meaningful group or 'social network'" (Gee, 1996, p. 131). The different social languages within the Discourses are seen as different cultural models embedded in the two different contexts (Gee, 1999). These cultural models represent the worldviews, beliefs, and values shared within the respective communities and groups (D'Andrade & Strauss, 1992; Quinn & Holland, 1987). According to Gee (1999), cultural models are "also variable, differing across different cultural groups, including different cultural groups in a society speaking the same language" (p. 60). In Gee's words, a cultural model is:

> [U]sually a totally or partially unconscious explanatory theory or "story line" connected to a word—bits and pieces of which are distributed across different people in a social group—

that helps to explain why the word has the different situated meanings and possibilities for the specific social and cultural groups of people it does. (1999, p. 44)

Gee (1996, 1999) theorizes that a cultural model not only defines what is normal and to be expected but also sets up what counts as non-normal and threatening in certain contexts. Therefore, cultural models often involve certain viewpoints about what is right and wrong and what can or cannot be done to solve problems in given situations. Such functions of setting up what count as right and normal, as Gee (1996) points out, often result in exclusionary actions, and create and uphold stereotypes.

Research has demonstrated that the dynamics and processes of different cultural models of literacy practices can have a significant impact on minority achievement and school reform (Gallimore & Goldenberg, 2001). Since cultural models carry within them values and perspectives about people and reality, cultural models from different cultures can "conflict in their content, in how they are used, and in values and perspectives they carry" (Gee, 1996, p. 90). For students from non-mainstream cultural backgrounds, the models of their home cultures can conflict seriously with those of mainstream culture (Gee, 1996). Studies on minority groups' literacy practices, for example, suggest that minority parents differ significantly in their cultural models of learning and their educated values, beliefs, and actions from their mainstream counterparts (e.g., Gallimore & Goldenberg, 2001; Goldenberg & Gallimore, 1995; Heath, 1983; Li, 2002, 2006; Valdés, 1996).

How do children acquire these different cultural models of literacy practices? Research on language socialization indicates that language and literacy learning is part of a process of socialization through which the learner acquires particular values and relationships in the sociocultural context where the learning takes place (Schieffelin & Ochs, 1986). Ochs (1986) posits that children acquire a worldview as they acquire a language. Since the process of acquiring language is deeply affected by the process of becoming a competent member of a community, language and literacy learning is intricately linked to the construction of social roles, cultural affiliations, beliefs, values, and behavioral practices (Schieffelin & Ochs, 1986). For learners who traverse two cultural worlds, the process of acquiring language(s) and literacies may involve the intersection of multiple/different cultural values and beliefs and multiple social contexts of socialization. For such learners, as Lam (2004) observed, it is important to note that language and literacy practices do not exist in isolation from each other, just as cultures and communities do not exist as discrete entities, but rather interact in various degrees of complementarity or conflict.

The multitude of interactions between different belief systems, and social and national languages define individual learners' sociocultural membership and shape what their voices can say (Wertsch, 1991). For example, power struggles between the primary Discourse and the secondary Discourse may affect a learner's choices of appropriating or "speaking" a particular social or national language and becoming a member of that sociocultural community. In some cases, learners are capable of repositioning themselves in contesting the official social languages and re/-creating their own social languages and identities (Gutiérrez, Rymes, & Larson, 1995). Therefore, literacy learning as a sociocultural practice emphasizes the relational interdependency of agent and world, persons-in-activity and situated action; learners' participation in learning is inherently "situated negotiation and renegotiation of meaning in the world" (Lave & Wenger, 1991, p. 51).

This dynamic process of literacy learning involves complex social relationships that a learner forms with other co-constructors of knowledge in their everyday literacy activities and events. These co-constructors are members of the learners' particular sociocultural contexts—teachers, peers, parents, and community members. Each of these co-constructors represents a voice of learning and knowing, and thus forms a multivoicedness in which multiple layers of values of knowing and learning are embodied (Bahktin, 1981, p. 272). In the following pages, I provide a review of research on culture and literacy learning that examines these complex social relationships within the learners' sociocultural world across the home, community and school contexts.

CULTURE AND LITERACY LEARNING

Four issues emerged from research concerning the links between literacy, culture, and learning: (a) culture and identity development derived from students' identification with their native language and culture, (b) culturally encoded gender roles that affect immigrant and minority students' literacy learning, (c) home and school cultural discontinuities in literacy, and (d) the impact of culturally marked notions of parental involvement on literacy learning.

Language, Culture, and Identity Development

Literacy researchers have discovered that children can develop an understanding of what literacy is and what it means from a young age (Wells, 1986, 1989). They can acquire not only the conventions of reading and writing, but also the sociocultural values attached to their particular literacy practices (Teale & Sulzby, 1986). Children's continuous development of literacy is related to their motivation to learn, and their beliefs, values, and goals about learning are crucial to their school achievement (Guthrie, McGough, Bennet, & Rice, 1996; Pintrich & Schrauben, 1992). Wigfield (1997) further argues that learners' engagement in learning involves personal investment, in that they not only exchange information with others, but also constantly re-read, reflect, and revisit a sense of who they are and how they are connected through complex social relationships with others in their everyday lives (Pierce, 1995). Therefore, learner identities—how learners see themselves and are seen by others in relation to their ethnic language and culture—have a significant impact on their learning and development (Harklau, 2008).

Conflicts between the heritage and mainstream cultures often result in cultural clashes and identity conflicts. Researchers have pointed out that the clash of values, behaviors, and attitudes between home and school culture often produces serious internal struggles for adolescents (Lam, 2003; P. W. Lee & Wong, 2002; Tran, 2002). For example, Vietnamese culture emphasizes obedience, discipline, and filial piety while mainstream American culture values autonomy and independence. For Vietnamese students, seeking to assimilate and striving for autonomy similar to that of their American peers often places them at risk of family conflict and internal disharmony (Lam, 2003). Many may feel the pressure to assimilate at the expense of their own cultural heritage, withdraw from and reject interactions with the mainstream, or act out and become apathetic to preserve their cultural identity (Suárez-Orozco & Suárez-Orozco, 2001; Zhou & Bankston, 1998). In her study of Hmong immigrant students, S. Lee (2005) discovered that students often construct their cultural identities against each other, and are pressured to adopt identities of either the "traditional" (those who identify with their heritage culture, obey their parents, dress conservatively, work hard, and stay out of trouble) or the Americanized (those who reject their heritage culture, disobey their parents, wear gang-style clothes, and skip school). Studies on Chinese students (Qin, 2009), Latino students (Flores-González, 2002), Arabic students (Sarroub, 2005), and East Indian students (Gibson, 1988) reported similar findings.

Conflicts between immigrant parents and their U.S.-born or -raised children are also found to be an important factor influencing the children's literacy learning and identity development. For many immigrant families, different life experiences between children and parents inevitably widen the generation gap, leading to intense bicultural conflicts that push children and parents into separate social worlds (Cheung & Nguyen, 2001; Zhou, 2001). The substantial language gap between parents and children, for example, is the most salient generational dissonance that creates acculturative stress. Children often learn the language more quickly and become acculturated at a faster rate than their parents, increasingly become family spokespersons, and assume the roles of interpreters, translators, and brokers due to the social isolation and limited language proficiency of the parents (see Centrie, 2004; Li, 2009a; Orellana, 2001). As children increasingly adopt parental roles, parents gradually lose control and the ability to exercise guidance, which often leads to intensified parent-child conflicts, role reversal, and ultimately loss of parental authority (Portes & Rumbaut, 1996; Zhou, 2001). As Harklau (2008) points out, these cultural conflicts and identity crises can ultimately lead to adverse "lifestage outcomes" (e.g., poor school achievement) and often result in a poorer sense of "personal efficacy" and a tendency to accept perceptions of limited social access rather than to challenge or circumvent them.

Culture, Gender Roles, and Literacy Learning

The cultural view of gender also plays a role in shaping students' literacy learning and engagement. For immigrant and minority students, the creation and recreation of gender roles in their daily interactions, especially in terms of intergenerational transmission of gender identities, often results in cultural conflicts and differences in literacy engagement. Findings from several studies (e.g., Baluja, 2002; Dion & Dion, 2001; Li, 2002, 2008; Qin, 2009; Valenzuela Jr., 1999) suggest that the immigrant parent generation tends to reconstruct the traditional gender roles in the host society—the domestic cultural code that defines women's domestic and childcare responsibilities and husbands' responsibilities for financial support and decision-making. The parents' culturally preferred version of gender roles usually shapes their expectations of their sons' and daughters' behavior and academic achievements. Daughters are often expected to follow the traditional gender role of their heritage culture (e.g., helping with household chores and raising younger siblings) while boys are expected to excel in school so that they have a good prospect to support the family.

In many immigrant households (e.g., those from Mexico and Asia), the older daughters take on various domestic roles such as tutors (when children serve as translators and teachers for their parents and younger siblings), advocates (when children intervene or mediate on behalf of their households during difficult transactions or situations), and surrogate parents (when children undertake nanny or parent-like activities) (Li, 2009b; Orellana, 2001; Valenzuela, Jr., 1999). Valenzuela, Jr. (1999), in his analysis of how girls and boys facilitate the establishment of permanent settlement in Mexican immigrant households, found that girls participated more than boys in tasks that required detailed explanations or greater responsibility; boys, despite their involvement in household activities, did not have the same responsibility roles as girls. Another example of culturally encoded gender roles affecting children's literacy learning is in Li's (2008) study of Vietnamese and Sudanese immigrant families. The two Vietnamese girls (Hanh and Nyen) in the study, for example, were expected to help with their younger brothers' school work in addition to completing their own school work, doing household chores, and translating or interpreting for their parents. Their brothers, however, even the older ones, were exempted from domestic duties and responsibilities. The boys also had fewer behavior restrictions—they could go out and socialize, whereas the girls were not allowed to do so. Hahn, for example, was not allowed to go anywhere except grocery shopping with her parents, or even to talk with her friends on the phone. Her brother, on the other hand, did not have these kinds of restrictions.

The double standards placed on the second generation have significant implications for their cultural translations between home and school, since the two Discourses have different codes for their expected behaviors. Unlike the home milieu, schools often do not differentiate gender expectations for boys and girls (Centrie, 2004). Whether they are able to negotiate the gender differences between school and home will significantly influence children's identity development, literacy engagement at home, and reading and writing practices in school (Hunt, 1995;

Li, 2009a; Orellana, 1995). In Hunt's (1995) study of Puerto Rican high school students' writing practices, and Orellana's (1995) study of Latino students' elementary literacy practices, for example, both found that the bilingual boys and girls had different preferences for their writing topics. Girls tended to write still-life portraits of friends, family, and the world; boys wrote more action-adventure stories. These studies suggest that social norms and cultural values shape the boys' and the girls' different literacy practices—both their construction and enactment in literacy (Orellana, 1995). Furthermore, as Dion and Dion (2001) note, the difference has potential implications not only for parent-child relations but also for the development of ethno-cultural identity among adolescents and young adults. For the girls, though the gendered tasks can help develop some literacy and bilingual skills (such as translation or paraphrasing) (Orellana & Reynolds, 2008), they often result in cultural conflicts and psychosocial stress (Li, 2009a; Qin, 2009). The a Vietnamese girl, Hanh, represented in Li (2009a), for example, struggled with the different gender expectations between school and home and between her and her brother. Her struggles caused her psychosocial stress in relationship with her father and in her self-perception as Vietnamese (Li, 2009a). Similar intergenerational conflicts are also observed in Qin's (2009) study of Chinese boys' and girls' gender identity formation. The boys in the study, in particular, often experienced difficulty communicating with their parents, who tended to hold more traditional gender expectations for them (such as "becoming dragon," which means becoming academically successful or becoming somebody) than their female peers. Under this pressure from home, these high-achieving students often experienced cultural conflicts in school because they were labeled as "nerds" and frequently experienced bullying and harassment from peers. Successful or not in the gender translation, as S. Lee (2005) points out, the struggle over gender roles is central to the stories of immigrant students.

Literacy, Culture, and Home and School Discontinuities

Though there are commonalities in literacy use across cultures, many factors such as cultural values, family socioeconomic backgrounds, and parental educational level influence how literacy is practiced in the home. In terms of cultural values, the distinctive world of literacy that exists in people's home surroundings and, in particular, their different ways of passing on the literacy values and skills their literacy practices embody, reflect the cultural experiences essential to their lives. Because literacy is a cultural practice, parents from different cultures have different beliefs about what it means to be literate, how to acquire literacy, and the role of schooling in achieving literacy (Compton-Lilly, 2003; Delgado-Gaitan, 1990; Heath, 1983; Li, 2002, Li, 2009b; Ogbu, 1982; Taylor & Dorsey-Gaines, 1988; Valdés, 1996). The diverse home literacy practices across families of Asian, Hispanic, African and African American, European American, and mixed-heritage backgrounds, for example, suggest cultural, linguistic and communication (e.g., discourse and interactional characteristics) discontinuities between school and home (see Goldenberg, Rueda, & August, 2006a, 2006b; Li, 2009b; Nieto, 1999).

Studies on interactional styles such the questioning rituals and cultural style of language use between school and home illuminate such discontinuities. In Heath's (1983) seminal study, *Ways With Words*, working-class African American children and adults' questioning styles, characterized by analogical comparisons and complex metaphors, were not congruent with mainstream school's emphasis on producing correct answers out of context. Cultural discontinuities are also found evident in different styles of interaction between school and home. In addition to the well-known studies on Native Hawaiian children's interactional differences by Au (1980) and Au and Mason (1981), studies on other ethnic groups have reached similar conclusions. For example, Boykin (1994) and Lee (1995) found that African American students in their studies frequently used "signifying," a form of "Afrocultural expression" in the African American community, that emphasizes spirituality, movement, verve, and oral tradition and is full of irony, double entendre, satire, and metaphorical language, were found to be incongruent with schooled literacy practices (see also Gunderson, 2008 and Tyler et al., 2008 for a review of values and styles of various ethnic groups). Similar findings were also observed in Latino families. Volk (1997), for example, examined two Puerto Rican kindergarteners' question use in lessons taught in both home and school activity settings, and discovered a web of discontinuities experienced by the children and their families in the two contexts. (For a review of values and styles of various ethnic groups, see also Gunderson, 2008 and Tyler et al., 2008.)

Another line of research on discontinuity between school and home literacy was developed from the perspective of cultural capital or high-status cultural signals (attitudes, preferences, formal knowledge, behaviors, goods, and credentials) that ultimately are to the owner's financial and social advantage (Bourdieu & Passeron, 1977; Coleman, 1988). Working from this perspective, in her study on Chinese immigrant families' home literacy practices, Li (2002, 2007) found that various forms of family cultural capital such as physical (economic), human (educational), and social capital (social networks and resources) interacted to have an impact on the children's home literacy practices, which were often different from mainstream practices. Applying a similar framework, Compton-Lilly (2007) examined how discontinuities of these forms of cultural capital in the contexts of school and home affected the success or failure of reading in two Puerto Rican families. She documented three different forms of reading cultural capital in the two families: embodied reading capital (dispositions of reading associated with accomplished readers and displayed through an allegiance to school-sanctioned reading norm), objectified reading capital (written or oral texts produced by students, demonstrating appropriate use of cultural resources, and officially recognized as evidence of reading proficiency), and institutionalized reading capital (qualifications, certifications, and credentials recognized as evidence of reading proficiency). Her analyses suggest that although the children in the study brought not only particular strengths to literacy classrooms but also particular ways of valuing and prioritizing among these strengths, these rich resources possessed by both children and families were often ignored, devalued, or denied in schools.

Literacy, Culture, and Parental Involvement in Literacy and Schooling

It is widely recognized that parental interest in and support of children's learning have a positive impact on students' academic achievement. Epstein (1992, 1995) theorizes that there are different levels of parental involvement ranging from involvement in the home, through participation in activities and events at school, to participation in the schools' decision-making process. Parental involvement at home includes attending to children's basic needs, discipline, preparing for school, and supporting school learning and/or engaging actively in homework. However, the degree and the ways of involvement vary from family to family and from culture to culture as families of different race, class, and religion backgrounds have different ways of transmitting and socializing literacy, different perceptions of families' and schools' roles in their children's education, and different ways of involvement in their children's academic learning.

Because literacy is a cultural practice, parents from different cultures have different beliefs about what it means to be literate, how to acquire literacy, and the role of schooling in achieving literacy. Several comparative studies in the United States have documented how the ways of learning and familial values are distinctively different among, for instance, African American, Hispanic, White, and Asian families (Rong & Grant, 1992; Steinberg, Dornbusch, & Brown, 1992; Steinberg, Lamborn, Darling, Mounts, & Dornbusch, 1994). Parental involvement in the Hispanic families often includes providing opportunities for children to learn through observation, to achieve gradual mastery of skills, to cooperate in tasks, and to collaborate in negotiating life's everyday trials (Carger, 1996; Lopez, 2001; Valdés, 1996). These practices differ from the White, middle-class families' emphasis on independent learning, and from the Asian families' preference for a direct instructional approach (Anderson & Gunderson, 1997; Blair, Blair, & Madamba, 1999; Chao, 1994; Li, 2005, 2006, 2009; Rong & Grant, 1992; Steinberg, Lamborn, Darling, Mounts and Dornbusch, 1994).

Cultural differences also shape how families make sense of their involvement in school settings. Many minority or immigrant parents, for example, consider themselves as important home-based educators, and their role is to support their children's education with involvement in their lives in the home; they view formal education as the school's responsibility and often are not active in parental participation in school settings (Goldenberg & Gallimore, 1995; Huss-Keeler, 1997; Li, 2006; Lopez, 2001; Zarate, 2007). These culturally different perceptions of parental involvement often result in school-home cultural discontinuities. In Huss-Keeler's (1997) study of the mainstream teachers' perceptions of Pakistani parental involvement, many Pakistani parents demonstrated interest in their children's education by supporting and assisting the children's studies at home but without being actively involved at school. Teachers perceived this, however, as "disinterest" in their children's education, and the children's learning and achievement consequently were frequently undermined. Similarly, Zarate (2007) in her study of Latino parental involvement in Miami, New York, and Los Angeles found that Latino parents and school teachers had culturally different perceptions on parental involvement. The parents understood their involvement in their children's education to mean monitoring the children's lives and providing moral guidance, regarding participation in their children's lives as complementary to their formal schooling. By contrast, the educators (teachers, counselors, and principals) considered parental involvement to require participation in formal parent-teacher organizations, back-to-school nights, open houses, and parent-teacher conferences.

These different perceptions of parental involvement have a profound influence on family-school relations and communication. Schools' communications and actions can convey positive, family-oriented attitudes, showing concern for family needs and perspectives, as well as negative attitudes (e.g., viewing differences as deficiencies or parents' active participation as over-involved or intrusive) (Christenson & Sheridan, 2001). According to Fine (1993), the latter attitude, which often places families in a powerless position, is detrimental to healthy family-school relationships and might increase the potential for conflict between school and parents. As Moles (1993) points out:

> Disadvantaged parents and teachers may be entangled by various psychological obstacles to mutual involvement such as misperceptions and misunderstandings, negative expectations, stereotypes, intimidation, and distrust. They may also be victims of cultural barriers reflecting differences in language, values, goals, methods of education, and definitions of appropriate roles. (p. 33)

One example of the effects of such cultural barriers is illustrated in Li's (2004, 2006) study of mainstream teachers and middle- and upper-class Chinese parents' perspectives in their children's literacy education. The Chinese parents considered their involvement at home to be monitoring and supervising homework and investing in their children's learning, for instance, by hiring tutors. In terms of school involvement, they seemed to have experienced barriers such as differences in language, values, goals, methods of education, and definitions of appropriate roles described above by Moles (1993). The teachers, on the other hand, viewed parental involvement as a shared activity, a task that should be completed through parent-child interactions at home. The teachers expected the parents' academic involvement at school and considered the "parenting" roles they brought to school as inappropriate. Similarly, in several studies on immigrant Latino's cultural models of literacy (Goldenberg, 1987, 1988; Goldenberg & Gallimore, 1995; Reese & Gallimore, 2000), researchers also found that the immigrant Latino parents shared a "bottom up" cultural schema or model of literacy development, in that children learned to read by learning the letters, corresponding sounds, and how the letters combine to form words. Reading and writing were to be taught explicitly. Reading, in particular, was viewed as something to be learned through repeated practice after children began formal schooling. Due to these particular cultural models of literacy, immigrant Latino parents did not accord much importance to pre-school literacy preparation. Early reading attempts by children were seen either as pretending to read, or not reading at all. These perceptions were fundamentally different from the "top-down" cultural models of literacy development and the emphasis on the importance of emergent literacy development common in the mainstream schools. These differences are important to the understanding of the cultural conflicts experienced between school and home by immigrants and minorities.

CULTURE AND LITERACY TEACHING

The emphasis in this section is research that attempts to integrate cultural practices into literacy instruction. The studies are unpacked according to three interrelated themes concerning cultural integration in literacy instruction that focus, respectively, on the teacher, the text, and the context.

Culture, Literacy Instruction, and the Teacher

Nieto (1999) argued that because teachers have a great deal to do with whether and how students learn, the role of the teacher as a cultural accommodator and mediator is fundamental in promoting students' learning. How teachers fulfill this role, however, is shaped by their beliefs, awareness of cultural differences, and their knowledge base in diverse approaches and practices that incorporate or make use of cultural experiences, knowledge, and practices in literacy instruction. Research on culturally responsive teachers has focused on two areas. One is documenting how teachers enact or "innovate" culturally responsive teaching in their literacy instruction (Gutiérrez et al., 1999; Ladson-Billings, 1992, 1994; Moje & Hinchman, 2004; Rivera, 2006; Sheets, 1995; Turner, 2005), and the other is training teachers to understand and incorporate culture in literacy instruction (González, Moll, & Amanti, 2005; Schmidt, 1998, 2003; Schmidt & Finkbeiner, 2006).

Research in the first area includes mostly qualitative studies of how teachers of various ethnic and cultural backgrounds teach literacy through cultural responsiveness in their classrooms. Au (1980) and Au and Mason (1981), for example, studied teachers who allowed native Hawaiian children to participate in reading lessons following rules similar to those in talk story, a Hawaiian community speech event. Au observed that in these talk story-like reading lessons, children's manner of speaking reflected the value many Hawaiian families attached to cooperation and working for the good of the group, rather than to individual achievement. These lessons were hybrid events that made connections to students' home culture and incorporated features of both community and school. Based on the studies of these innovative practices, Au (1993, 2007) concluded that literacy instruction must be "culturally responsive" to express respect for cultural values. That means that literacy teachers must appreciate students' home culture and attempt to build upon the use of language and literacy with which children are already familiar.

Ladson-Billings (1992) described an Italian American and an African American teacher who were successful teachers of African American students. Though one used a whole-language approach and the other adopted a basal text approach in literacy teaching, the two shared many commonalities in their teaching, and their students performed at grade level. Both teachers legitimated African American culture by making it a frame of reference for all texts, and did not shy away from issues of race and culture. In both classrooms, students were appreciated and celebrated both as individuals and members of a specific culture. The students' first language was also incorporated into their classroom conversations without reprimand or correction. Further, both teachers had high expectations for student achievement and spent a great deal of time building an atmosphere of academic achievement, support and trust among students, parents and themselves. Based on the practices of these exemplary teachers, Ladson-Billings (1994) advocated "a culturally relevant pedagogy" in which teachers empower students "intellectually, socially, emotionally, and politically by using cultural referents to impart knowledge, skills, and attitudes" (p. 381).

In a more recent study, H. J. Rivera (2006) conducted case studies of two preschool teachers' (one Jewish American female and one African American male) embodiment of culturally relevant teaching in an urban school. Similar to Ladson-Billings (1992), Rivera (2006) also found that although the teachers taught differently, many common factors characterized their enactment of culturally relevant teaching. Both teachers' philosophies of teaching had their roots in creating a learning environment with the influences of culture on curriculum and classroom context; both respected and appreciated everyone's culture; both fostered healthy social relations in the learning community of the classrooms and built a strong community of learners; and finally, both shared a strong sense of commitment to act on behalf of the children and families in the face of political concerns.

Whereas many studies described a holistic picture of the teachers' instructional practices, Gutiérrez, Banquedano-Lopez, and Tejeda (1999) explored a teacher's specific strategies in incorporating culture during class discussions in terms of third spaces or zones of proximal development. By analyzing examples from an ethnographic study of literacy instruction in one dual immersion elementary classroom, the researchers illustrated how the teacher used creative strategies in literacy instruction. These included incorporating students' local knowledge into the official curriculum (e.g., drawing on parallels between home and academic lexicon such as "busto" & "chi-chis"), using both ethnic and standard language varieties, and employing hybrid genres including cultural humor. These strategies created a culture of collaboration and third spaces that expanded students' learning.

In addition to documenting teachers' embodiment of culturally relevant pedagogy, another area of studies focused on the teacher includes studies on promoting cultural sensitivity among teachers (Edwards, 2004; Edwards, Pleasants, & Franklin, 1999; González, Moll & Amanti, 2005; Schmidt, 1998, 2003; Schmidt & Finkbeiner, 2006). Edwards (2004) and Edwards, Pleasants, and Franklin (1999) focused on helping teachers bridge literacy practices through understanding and listening to parents' stories, whereas Schmidt (1998, 2003) and Schmidt and Finkbeiner's (2006) "ABCs of cultural understanding and communication" model aimed to foster a sense of "knowing oneself and understanding others." The "ABCs of cultural understanding and communication" model consists of five steps. The first is autobiography, in which the teacher writes an autobiography that includes key events related to education, family, religious beliefs, etc. Next is biography, through interviews, the teacher constructs a biography of key events of a culturally different person. In the cross-cultural analysis step, the teacher studies the autobiography and biography and charts similarities and differences. After this comes appreciation of differences (the teacher writes an in-depth self-analysis of cultural differences). Finally, the teacher designs a year-long plan for connecting home, school and community for students' reading, writing, listening and speaking. Studies on the effects of using this model in domestic (see Schmidt, 1998, 2003) and international inservice and preservice teacher education contexts (see Schmidt & Finkbeiner, 2006) have reported positive results in fostering teachers' cross-cultural awareness and helping them become better cultural mediators and facilitators in their classrooms.

While the "ABCs of cultural understanding and communication" model focuses on promoting teacher cultural awareness and communication, González, Moll & Amanti's (2005) "funds of knowledge" approach trains teachers to be researchers and learners who conduct research on the families through home visits to document the funds of knowledge present at minority students' homes. Teachers then adjust literacy instruction based on their analyses of students' households (i.e., family history, routine practices of the household, parents' view about parenthood, school experiences, and language use for bilingual families). This approach has also suggested positive impacts on teachers as cultural mediators in their literacy instruction.

Culture, Literacy Teaching, and the Text

 Work on the interaction between culture and text in literacy teaching concerns mostly teachers' and students' use and choices of culturally relevant texts and materials, including oral, written, and popular cultural texts. Research suggests that literacy instruction that is not made personally meaningful to minority students will probably impede their reading development and that inappropriate teaching materials and content, such as worksheets or unfamiliar materials, may have adverse effects on reading development (Snow, Burns, & Griffin, 1998). Use of such materials, rather than multicultural literature that accurately depicts the experiences of diverse groups, will decrease students' motivation to read, and devalue their own life experiences as topics for writing (Au, 1998; Banks, 2002). Several studies on the use of culturally relevant materials and content suggest that culturally familiar materials have a positive impact on students' reading motivation and achievement (see also Goldenberg, Rueda, & August, 2006a, 2006b). For example, based on a long-term ethnographic study of the changes brought about through bilingual whole-language pedagogy, McCarty (1993) reported that Navajo children made gains on local and national tests following the classroom use of the Navajo language and thematic content prominent in Navajo daily life. Similar findings were also reported in studies on using culturally familiar materials for Latino (Jiménez, 1997), African American (Brooks, 2006), and for Arab students (Al-Hazza & Bucher, 2008).

Facilitating students' use of cultural tools or background knowledge in response to reading literature is also reported to be of critical importance to minority students' literacy learning in school. Based on her study of African American students' response to culturally conscious African American literature, Brooks (2006) argued for the importance of choosing texts with features closely tied to participants' social and cultural realities. In a similar vein, Kamberelis and Bovino (1999) emphasized the importance of scaffolding students' mastery over the forms, functions, rhetorical possibilities, and appropriateness of different genres or cultural artifacts in literacy instruction. In addition to paying attention to text choice and genre knowledge, Conrad, Gong, Sipp, and Wright (2004) also discussed the advantage of using text talk, that is, the use of challenging texts to improve students' oral language and comprehension abilities through a more focused approach with readalouds, as a gateway to support young children's literacy. In a study of how a Spanish immersion teacher used hybrid cultural and language practices to promote bilingual children's literacy interpretation, Gutiérrez, Banquedano-Lopez, and Tejeda (1999) stressed the use of multiple, diverse, and even conflicting mediational tools such as the use of diverse, alternative texts and codes (e.g., oral texts and vernacular language from home culture that is not legitimated in the curriculum), as well as ways of participating and sharing expertise to facilitate the emergences of third spaces or zones of proximal development to help expand literacy learning.

In addition to texts relevant to students' ethnic cultural backgrounds, popular cultural texts (such as superhero stories, Hip-hop, news media, digital media, and television) have also received increasing attention in research on literacy instruction, especially for urban minority students. A number of researchers argue for the power of integrating popular cultural texts in school literacy curriculum to promote academic literacy and critical consciousness (Dyson, 1997; Moje, 2002; Morrell & Duncan-Andrade, 2002, 2006; Sutherland, Botzakis, Moje, Alvermann, 2007;

Xu, 2004; Xu, Perkins, & Zunich, 2005). Based on an ethnographic study in an urban classroom of 7- to 9-year olds, Dyson (1997), for example, examined how young school children of various ethnic backgrounds used popular culture, especially superhero stories, in the unofficial peer social world and in the official school literary curriculum. The children reworked the popular cultural texts to represent the state of societal play, with its interrelated gender, racial, and class inequalities; mediated community dialogues with and through their characters; resisted the gendered nature of physical power; and negotiated social relations with others across societal divisions. Dyson, therefore, argued that children's unofficial use of diverse cultural materials can provide substance for official engagement and reflection in literacy learning, and that the literacy curricula teachers negotiate with children must be undergirded by an inclusive vision of cultural art forms as intertwined and produced in complex social relationships.

While Dyson (1997) examined young learners' use of cultural materials, a body of research explored using popular cultural materials with urban adolescents (Alvermann, Moon & Hagood, 1999; Moje, 2005; Morrell & Duncan-Andrade, 2002; 2005; Sutherland, Botzakis, Moje, Alvermann, 2007; Xu, 2004; Xu, Perkins, & Zunich, 2005). Xu (2004), for example, illustrated how the teacher of a 12th grade remedial English class with mostly African American students used the television show *Survivor: Africa* to provide a bridge to a literature unit using a novel, *Speak*. The use of multimodal texts and different challenging literacy activities (e.g., reviewing background of the show, comparing and contrasting the needs to survive, journal writing, and creating a performance art skit from the book) resulted in a hybrid space where the remedial students were able to engage in purposeful and meaningful literacy learning. The power of popular cultural texts was also reflected in Morrell and Duncan-Andrade's (2002) incorporation of Hip-hop music into a "traditional" senior English poetry unit, in which the poetry of the Elizabethan Age, the Puritan Revolution, and the Romantics were part of the district-mandated curriculum for 12th-grade English. Morrell and Duncan-Andrade began the unit with an overview of poetry in general, attempting to redefine poetry and the role of the poet in society. In the second major portion of the unit, students were asked to do group presentations of a canonical poem along with a Hip-hop text, preparing a justifiable interpretation of their texts, situating each within its specific historical and literary period, and analyzing the linkages between the two. Since Hip-hop was a cultural form students could relate to, they were able to generate some excellent interpretations as well as make interesting linkages between the canonical poems and the rap texts. These studies suggest that popular cultural media materials such as Hip-hop texts are literary texts and they can be used to scaffold and reinforce literary terms and concepts and ultimately foster literary interpretations (Morrell & Duncan-Andrade, 2006).

Culture, Literacy Instruction, and the Context

Studies on the context of literacy instruction focused on connections and disconnections between home and school discourses. Several researchers (e.g., Au, 1980, 1993, 2007; Ball, 1992, 1997; Moje et al., 2004; Orellana & Reynolds, 2008; Volk, 1997) have compared, from different perspectives, school literacy practices and the discourse patterns that students bring from home. All these studies pointed to the disconnection between school and home literacy practices and offered effective strategies or approaches to bridge these disconnections.

In their study of Latino/a students' content literacy in science in and out of school, Moje et al. (2004) found that although the youth possessed diverse funds of knowledge from home and community (e.g., skills gained from work in the home, environment and health funds from the community, knowledge from informal and formal peer activities, and knowledge gained by reading, writing, and talking about popular culture such as music, print magazines, news media, movies and television), they rarely volunteered this knowledge in classroom contexts. The researchers observed that as the young people moved from homes to schools to shopping malls and restaurants, they displayed knowledge of when and how to say, do, or write certain information. The researchers also noticed that the students were aware of audience and purpose during the interviews. These strategic uses of their everyday funds of knowledge were, however, often private and not accessible to other students or the teacher. Evidence of the students' private use of everyday funds of knowledge in the school and in multiple contexts offered hope to the researchers, who concluded that "the distance between everyday and academic Discourse is not as vast or as immutable as one might believe" (Moje et al., 2004, p. 5), and that educators need to construct third spaces in the classroom to allow students to draw upon their out-of-school funds in official content literacy learning.

Orellana and Reynolds (2008) illustrated similar school-home disconnection through their analysis of students' out-of-school translating and interpreting across languages or para-phrasing, and the cross-disciplinary school-based practice of paraphrasing or summarizing written texts. The researchers found that the everyday para-phrasing or translation activities performed by immigrant youth often entailed mixing different strategies (e.g., making choices about what to include in their translations and deciding when to render meanings explicit and when to maintain their ambiguity) driven largely by their goal of making sense of this material for their audiences, and with support from co-participants or adults. While home para-phrasing was often conducted at a discourse level, in contrast, school paraphrasing activities often focused on word level (including words and word phrases) and involved forms of wordplay (such as transforming the meaning of words via sound-play in Spanish) not specific to para-phrasing. In addition, teachers often maintained the right to determine how texts were appropriately paraphrased, while students' authority was secondary. Therefore, when the students paraphrased a text, their choices of "other words" were additionally constrained because they had to monitor themselves with an eye to what the teacher might presume they did not know. The disconnection between the two discourses often resulted in students' difficulty in completing school paraphrasing tasks. Similar to Moje et al. (2004), Orellana and Reynolds (2008) argued that many of the strategies that students used in para-phrasing outside of school can be bridged into classroom practices, and teachers need to find points of leverage or third spaces in the classroom to tap into students' repertoire of linguistic and cultural toolkits when engaging students in school literacy practices.

Similar research has also been conducted with African American learners' literacy practices in and out of school (Ball, 1992, 1997; Boykin, 1994; C. D. Lee, 1995, 1997, 2000, 2006). Lee (1995, 1997, 2000, 2006), for example, based on data collected through a mixed methods design, examined the relationship between African American students' use of vernacular English (such as signifying, proverb use, and narrative styles) and the demands of rich literary interpretation in school. Lee argued that African American students often use vernacular English outside school. The expertise that underlied such use can be applied to literary reading as well as subject-specific content literacy in school, because the cognitive strategies required for comprehension and interpretation of both were similar. Therefore, Lee posited that it was not enough to simply, "embrace and build upon the strengths of African American English and African American literature, but *more broadly to reconceptualize cultural variables and critical thinking as linked, teachable, and empowering*" (Lee, 1995, p. 625, italics original). Teachers must employ a "cultural apprenticeship model" to make explicit students' "cultural data sets" or cognitive strategies embedded in students' cultural practices outside of school, and to help the students to use these strategies to understand communication in print, especially highly specialized genres such as complex literature and content area learning.

Also focusing on African American students, Ball (1992, 1997) and Ball and Lardner (2005) examined the relationship between vernacular language use and writing practices. Ball examined the preferred patterns for the "organization of experience" or the text design patterns among African American adolescents. The results of her studies revealed that African American adolescents, in contrast to Hispanic American, Asian American, and European American adolescents, reported a strong preference for using vernacular-based patterns in academic writing tasks as they got older. This vernacular-based knowledge, however, was often not appreciated in writing and composition classrooms. Further, in her study of European American and African American teachers' assessment of minority students' written texts, Ball (1997) discovered that teachers of different cultural backgrounds had different views about the assessment of diverse students' written texts. Therefore, Ball and Lardner (2005) argued that teachers need to use culturally relevant strategies to unleash the potential of African American students and help them imagine new possibilities for their success as writers.

Taking a different focus, Li (2006) studied the contrasting pedagogical approaches to literacy instruction used by middle-class European Canadian teachers and Chinese immigrant parents in an elementary school in Canada. Whereas the Chinese parents in the study preferred a teacher-centered phonics instruction in which language, reading, and writing would be taught as discrete skills through repeated practice and with proper sequences, the teachers favored student-centered meaning-based approaches such as language experience and literature-based approaches, in which language and literacy teaching were embedded in an integrated curriculum. The dichotomous views held by the teachers and parents resulted in deep chasm between the two parties and cultural conflicts between school and home that had a negative impact on students' literacy learning in and out of school. Li suggested that to bridge the school-home disconnections, both teachers and minority parents need to adopt a "pedagogy of cultural reciprocity" whereby both parties acquire new cultural patterns. Through the process of cultural reciprocity, each can be endowed with new energy that changes the parent-school relations as well as producing new instructional practices that address students' learning needs. This reciprocal process of learning, Li argued, may enable both parties to understand each other's worldviews and cultural practices in literacy learning and instruction, and engage in meaningful dialogues to create hybrid practices that help students overcome the cultural and structural barriers that hinder their academic achievement.

CONCLUSIONS AND IMPLICATIONS FOR FUTURE RESEARCH

Clearly, the evidence suggests that culture plays a significant role in shaping literacy learning and teaching. For students and families from diverse backgrounds, cultural translation between home and school often results in various levels of displacement and fractures in their daily literacy experiences—from their language use and gender roles to home literacy practices, school expectations, and parental involvement. For teachers, this review of research on the role of culture in literacy instruction suggests a need to move beyond *just good teaching* narrowly focused on improving mainstream instructional strategies to acquire academic success (Au, 2007; Callins, 2004; Gay, 2000). Rather, literacy instruction needs to examine teachers' instructional beliefs and practices, the texts that they use, and the multiple contexts such as school and home in which literacy teaching and learning takes place. Taken as a whole, the research studies reviewed in the chapter support several practices for integrating culture in literacy instruction:

1. acknowledging the importance of students' cultural heritages, individual characteristics, and cultural identities;
2. recognizing cultural differences between students' home life and school literacy learning, and conflicts these differences may engender;
3. utilizing a wide array of instructional strategies that emphasize culturally relevant content, contexts and interactional structures; and

4. promoting the development of critical thinking abilities that can help students become better border crossers to tackle the broader contextual and societal factors in learning (Conrad, Gong, Sipp, & Wright, 2004; Gay, 2000; Ladson-Billings, 1994; Neuman, 1999; Schmidt & Finkbeiner, 2006).

This review suggests that helping minority students gain literacy abilities and skills that enable them to effectively cross various cultural borders in and out of school should take a critical place in minority literacy education (Li, 2008). As Apple and Weis (1983) insist, "Investigating the role [culture] plays and struggling to promote progressive elements of it becomes of great consequence" (p. 22). There is, however, much work to be done to explore the role of culture in literacy education. The following are suggestions for directions of future research.

Needed Research

Teacher Education and Teacher Professional Development. Though many teachers, as indicated in this review, are achieving success in their classrooms, the reality of many classrooms, especially in urban schools, has unfortunately not changed (Au & Raphael, 2000; Ladson-Billings, 2006). Two major challenges are the shortage of individuals of diverse backgrounds in the teaching force (Au & Raphael, 2000) and inadequate preparation of our in-service and pre-service teachers for teaching diverse learners (Ladson-Billings, 2006). The teacher population in the United States has remained largely homogeneous even though the student body is becoming increasingly diverse. According to a national survey of K–12 public school teachers conducted by the National Center for Education Information in 2005, 85% of the teaching force are middle class, White, and monolingual and 87.5% have no or little training in teaching linguistically and culturally diverse students (NCELA Newsline Bulletin, 2005). A recent survey conducted in California on the needs of teachers of English language learners (ELLs) (Gándara, Maxwell-Jolly, & Driscoll, 2005) found that the most commonly named challenges for them were their struggles to connect with language minority parents, to inform them of standards, expectations, and ways to help, and to communicate with and understand students of diverse cultural and academic backgrounds. Teachers of ELLs were also seriously challenged by a lack of teaching tools, including appropriate assessment materials and instruments.

The alarming under-preparedness of our teaching force for culturally diverse students and the largely unchanged nature of our classrooms suggest that more research is needed to explore effective ways of raising cultural awareness among inservice and preservice teachers and educating them about effective instructional approaches to integrate culture in their instruction. Future research needs to focus on building teacher competence in bridging cultures in their classrooms—"how to make positive, programmatic use of the insights they acquire about each child's family, cultural membership, families stories, language use, and home literacy practices" (Lapp, 2009, p. 272). Lapp suggests that teachers can be guided into contexts and situations that offer them opportunities to acquire authentic experience and knowledge about cultural diversity, and to develop competence in validating and linking home and school literacies in their instructional designs. Therefore, research on preparation for such teachers could focus on three areas:

1. how to help teachers know and reconcile with students' diverse home literacies and cultures;
2. what strategies and skills or competence they need to know to translate this knowledge into powerful tools in instructional design and practice that can bridge students' literacy and cultural discontinuities in and out of school; and

3. how to develop critical abilities that can transform teachers from mere cultural mediators and translators into change agents who tackle the issues of literacy displacement and fractures that are often based on race, gender, and/or class positions, and have adverse effects on children's learning experiences in and out of school.

Multiethnicity and Cultural Hybridity

Though the pedagogical practices and approaches reviewed in the previous section provide useful ways to improve instruction for specific ethnic groups, much of the research focused on students from one culture or cultural group. The different teaching approaches reviewed (e.g., culturally relevant teaching, culturally responsive instruction, funds of knowledge approach, pedagogy of cultural reciprocity), for example, often catered to a particular ethnic group or culture. Therefore, they are difficult for adaption and implementation in today's classrooms that are *multiethnic*, especially in economically disadvantaged urban centers (Au, 2007; Li, 2008). In reality, with the sudden influx of immigrant and minority students from diverse backgrounds, many teachers are not prepared to take on the role of teaching these students, and many do not have much contact with the diverse cultures of the minority students outside school (Clair, 1995; Huss-Keeler, 1997; Li, 2006) or know how to communicate with minority parents (Gándara et al., 2005). Addressing these multiple cultural practices in today's classroom is therefore an urgent task. Cole (1998) uses the term "polycultural" to describe the multiple cultures present in every classroom as well as the subcultures students create when they interact with each other. Future research therefore needs to explore effective approaches to help teachers address the polycultural nature of today's classrooms.

Li (2008) cautioned that inclusion of these multiple cultural practices cannot be achieved simply by adding ethnic content such as the foods, folkways, and holidays to school activities; rather, it needs to involve continual interface and exchange of cultural differences that in turn produce a mutual and mutable recognition and hybridity of these differences. It requires teachers (and students and parents alike) to develop competence in teaching literacy from an interstitial perspective that allows the emergence of cultural hybridities or third spaces (see Bhabha, 1994; Gutiérrez et al., 1999; Moje et al., 2004). To work from this perspective, as Li (2008) suggested, teachers may need to approach culture as children do—as genuine and natural explorers who are able to transform and be transformed by their cultural encounters and productively use methods of transcultural sensitization and reflective cultural analysis by paying particular attention to their own framework in cultural observation and interpretation. Teaching literacy through this interstitial perspective will transform students' lives and help them connect the present with the past and the future. In its deepest sense, "it concerns the opening of identities— exploring new ways of being that lie beyond our current state…. It places students on an outbound trajectory toward a broad field of possible identities" (Wenger, 1998, p. 263). More future research and practices are needed to focus on how to help teachers gain this interstitial perspective and become innovative in creating hybrid cultural spaces in their classrooms.

One direction towards such research is to study students' cultures as cultural practices or "repertoires of practice" that are socially and culturally organized and historically situated, not as individual cultural traits that are often static and overgeneralized (Cole, 1996, 1998, 2005; Gutiérrez, 2006; Gutiérrez, Morales, Martinez, 2009; Gutiérrez & Rogoff, 2003). According to Gutiérrez and her colleagues, treating culture as individual traits often conflates race/ethnicity with culture and promotes reductive or deficit views on these individuals who often come from minority communities. They suggest moving beyond this culture-as-traits assumption by

> focusing attention on variations in individuals' and groups' histories of engagement in cultural practices because the variations reside not as traits of individuals or collections of

individuals but as proclivities of people with certain histories of engagement with specific cultural activities. Thus, individuals' and groups' *experience* in activities—not their *traits*— become the focus of a cultural analysis. (Gutiérrez, 2006, p. 46)

This cultural historical perspective can help researchers identify students' language and literacy practices across different activity settings and a range of practices—"regularities in the ways cultural communities organize their lives as well as variations in the ways individual members of groups participate and conceptualize the means and ends of their communities' activities" (Gutiérrez & Rogoff, 2003, p. 22). To study "repertoires of practice" from a polycultural perspective, researchers also need to further their analyses through constant "confirmation or disconfirmation to extend what is known" (Gutiérrez & Rogoff, 2003, p. 23) across the cultural groups and their respective activity settings and practices.

Diverse Methods.   Though research has always pointed to the importance of culture in literacy learning and teaching, an emphasis on the interplay between literacy and culture can be difficult to maintain in an evidence-based and outcome-oriented approach to education (Gunderson, 2008; Gutiérrez et al., 2002; Ladson-Billings, 2006; Rupley, Nichols, & Blair, 2008). The National Literacy Panel's review of data on the role of culture in literacy education suggests that there is a need for more diverse methods of research. The studies discussed above are overwhelmingly qualitative in nature. Although culture is difficult to study by quantitative methods, future research on culture and literacy could productively bridge the qualitative/quantitative divide, and more research is needed using quantitative or mixed methods to investigate the links between literacy learning and culture. Several proposals in this direction have been made. Tyler et al. (2008) proposed a framework for investigating cultural discontinuities following a quantitative design. Tyler et al. suggested two important practices to measure or assess cultural discontinuities. One is to quantify behavioral manifestation of the specific cultural values held by ethnic minority students in out-of-school settings; the other is to record whether these same cultural value-based behaviors and activities found at home are discontinued once students enter the classroom in particular or the public school in general. The authors provided some specific steps to design such a study, including the need to construct a factor structure, corresponding variables, and factor-validated cultural activities scale to establish a cultural discontinuity score. Once a cultural discontinuity score has been established for a given ethnic minority group's cultural value-based behavior, additional questionnaires can determine if there is any association between cultural discontinuity scores and either school achievement or its psychological or cognitive antecedents (e.g., motivation, psychological well-being, school belongingness (Tyler et al., 2008). Though their methodology is yet to be tested and some of their suggested steps (e.g., establishing a score for cultural value-based behavior) may run the risk of essentializing people from a particular cultural group, similar theory building as well as application studies will yield important insights in the key role of culture in literacy learning and teaching.

REFERENCES

Al-Hazza, T. C., & Bucher, K. T. (2008). *Books about the Middle East: Selecting and using them with children and adolescents.* Columbus, OH: Linworth.

Alvermann, D. E., Moon, J. S., & Hagood, M. C. (1999). *Popular culture in the classroom: Teaching and researching critical media literacy.* Newark, DE: International Reading Association and the National Reading Conference.

Anderson, J., & Gunderson, L. (1997). Literacy learning outside the classroom. *The Reading Teacher, 50,* 514–516.

Apple, M., & Weis, L. (1983). Ideology and practice in schooling: A political and conceptual introduction. In M. Apple & L. Weis (Eds.), *Ideology and practice in schooling* (pp. 3–24). Philadelphia: Temple University Press.

Anstrom, K. (1996). Defining the Limited-English-Proficient student population [Electronic Version]. *Directions in Language and Education*, 1. Retrieved May 16, 2007, from http://www.ncela.gwu.edu/pubs/directions/09.htm

Au, K. H. (1980). Participation structures in a reading lesson with Hawaiian children: Analysis of a culturally appropriate instructional event. *Anthropology and Education Quarterly, 11*(2), 91–115.

Au, K. H. (1993). *Literacy instruction in multicultural settings.* Fort Worth, TX: Harcourt Brace.

Au, K. H. (1998). Socio-constructivism and the school literacy learning of students of diverse backgrounds. *Journal of Literacy Research, 30*(2), 297–319.

Au, K. H. (2007). Culturally responsive instruction: Application to multiethnic classrooms. *Pedagogies: An International Journal, 2*(1), 1–18.

Au, K., & Mason, J. M. (1981). Social organizational factors in learning to read: The balance of rights hypothesis. *Reading Research Quarterly, 17*(1), 115–152.

Au, K. H., & Raphael, T. E. (2000). Equity and literacy in the next millennium. *Reading Research Quarterly, 35*(1), 170–188.

Bahktin, M. (1981). Discourse in the novel. In C. Emerson & R. Rosaldo (Eds.), *The dialogic imagination: Four essays by M. Bakhtin* (pp. 259–422). Austin: University of Texas Press.

Ball, A. (1992). Cultural preference and the expository writing of African-American adolescents. *Written Communication, 9*(4), 501–532.

Ball, A. (1997). Expanding the dialogue on culture as a critical component when assessing writing. *Assessing Writing, 4*(2), 169–202

Ball, A., & Lardner, T. (2005). *African American literacies unleashed: Vernacular English and the composition classroom.* Carbondale: Southern Illinois University Press.

Baluja, K. F. (2002). Gender roles at home and abroad: The adaptation of Bangladeshi immigrants. New York: New Americans LFB Scholarly Publishing.

Banks, J. (2002). *An introduction to multicultural education.* Boston, MA: Allyn & Bacon.

Bhabha, H. K. (1994). *The location of culture.* New York: Routledge.

Blair, S. L., Blair, M. C., & Madamba, A. B. (1999). Racial/ethnic differences in high school students' academic performance: Understanding the interweave of social class and ethnicity in the family context. *Journal of Comparative Family Studies, 30*, 539–555.

Blount, B. G. (1982). Culture and the language socialization: Parental speech. In D. A. Wagner & H. W. Stevenson (Eds.), *Cultural perspectives on child development* (pp. 54–76). San Francisco: W. H. Freeman.

Bourdieu, P., & Passeron, J. C. (1977). *Reproduction in education, society and culture.* Beverly Hills, CA: Sage.

Boykin, A. W. (1994). Afrocultural expression and its implications for schooling. In E. R. Hollins, J. E. King, & W. C. Hayman (Eds.), *Teaching diverse populations: Forming a knowledge base* (pp. 243–266). Albany: State University of New York Press.

Brooks, W. (2006). Reading representations of themselves: Urban youth use culture and African American textual features to develop literary understandings. *Reading Research Quarterly, 41*(4), 372–393.

Callins, T. (2004). *Culturally responsive literacy instruction.* Practitioner Brief series. Washington, DC: National Center for Culturally Responsive Educational Systems.

Carger, C. (1996). *Of borders and dreams: A Mexican-American experience of urban education.* New York: Teachers College Press.

Centrie, C. (2004). *Identity formation of Vietnamese immigrant youth in an American high school.* New York: LFB Scholarly.

Chao, R. K. (1994). Beyond parental control and authoritarian parenting style: Understanding Chinese parenting through the cultural notion of training. *Child Development, 65*(4), 1111–1119.

Cheung, M., & Nguyen, S. M. H. (2001). Parent-child relationships in Vietnamese American families. In N. B. Webb (Ed.), *Culturally diverse parent-child and family relationships: A guide for social workers and other practitioners* (pp. 261–282). New York: Columbia University Press.

Christenson, S. L., & Sheridan, S. M. (2001). *Schools and families: Creating essential connections for learning.* New York: Guilford Press.

Clair, N. (1995). Mainstream classroom teachers and ESL students. *TESOL Quarterly, 29*, 189–196.

Cole, M. (1996). *Cultural psychology: A once and future discipline.* Cambridge, MA: Belknap Press of Harvard University Press.

Cole, M. (1998). Can cultural psychology help us think about diversity? *Mind, Culture, and Activity, 5*(4), 291–304.

Cole, M. (2005). Cross-cultural and historical perspectives on the developmental consequences of education. *Human Development, 48*, 195–216.

Coleman, J. S. (1988). Social capital in the creation of human capital. *American Journal of Sociology, 94*, 95–120.

Compton-Lilly, C. (2003). *Reading families: The literate lives of urban children.* New York: Columbia University.

Compton-Lilly, C. (2007). The complexities of reading capital in two Puerto Rican families. *Reading Research Quarterly, 42*(1), 72–98.

Conrad, N. K., Gong, Y., Sipp, L., & Wright, L. (2004). Using text talk as a gateway to culturally responsive teaching. *Early Childhood Education Journal, 31*(3), 187–192.

D'Andrade, R. G., & Strauss, C. (1992). *Human motives and cultural models. Publications of the society for psychological anthropology.* New York: Cambridge University Press.

Delgado-Gaitan, C. (1990). *Literacy for empowerment.* New York: The Falmer Press.

Dion, K. K., & Dion, K. L. (2001). Gender and cultural adaptation in immigrant families. *Journal of Social Issues, 57*(3), 511–521.

Dyson, A. H. (1997). *Writing superheroes: Contemporary childhood, popular culture, and classroom literacy.* New York: Teachers College Press.

Edwards, P. A. (2004). *Children's literacy development: Making it happen through school, family, and community involvement.* Boston: Allyn & Bacon.

Edwards, P. A., Pleasants, H., & Franklin, S. (1999). *A path to follow: Learning to listen to parents.* Portsmouth, NH: Heinemann.

Epstein, J. L. (1992). School and family partnerships. In. M. Alkin (Ed.), *Encyclopedia of educational research* (6th ed., pp. 1139–1151). New York: McMillan.

Epstein, J. L. (1995). School, family, community partnerships: Caring for the children we share. *Phi Delta Kappan, 76*, 701–712.

Fine, M. (1993). [Ap]parent involvement: Reflections on parents, power, and urban public schools. *Teachers College Record, 94*(4), 682–710.

Fishman, A. (1988). *Amish literacy: What and how it means.* Portsmouth, NH: Heinemann.

Flores-González, N. (2002). *School kids/street kids: Identity development in Latino students.* New York: Teachers College Press.

Francis, D. J., Rivera, M., Lesaux, N., Kieffer, M., & Rivera, H. (2006). *Practical guidelines for the education of English language learners: Research-based recommendations for instruction and academic interventions.* Retrieved May 8, 2007, from http://www.centeroninstruction.org/files/ELL1-Interventions.pdf

Gallimore, R., & Goldenberg, C. (2001) Analyzing cultural models and settings to connect minority achievement and school improvement research. *Educational Psychologist, 36*, 45–56.

Gándara, P., Maxwell-Jolly, J., & Driscoll, A. (2005). *Listening to teachers of English learners.* Santa Cruz, CA: Center for the Future of Teaching and Learning. Retrieved October 1, 2008, from http://lmri.ucsb.edu/publications/05_listening-to-teachers.pdf

Gay, G. (2000). *Culturally responsive teaching: Theory, research, and practice.* New York: Teachers College Press.

Gee, J. P. (1989). Literacy, discourse, and linguistics: Introduction. *Journal of Education, 171*(1), 5–17.

Gee, J. P. (1996). *Social linguistics and literacies: Ideology in discourse.* London: Taylor & Francis.

Gee, J. (1999). The new literacy studies and the "social turn." *Opinion Papers* (120). http://www.schools.ash.org.au/litweb/page300.html

Geertz, C. (1973). *The interpretation of cultures.* New York: Basic Books.

Gibson, M. (1988). *Accommodation without assimilation.* Ithaca, NY: Cornell University Press.

Goldenberg, C. (1987). Low-income Hispanic parents' contributions to their first-grade children's word-recognition skills. *Anthropology and Education Quarterly, 18*, 149–179.

Goldenberg, C. (1988). Methods, early literacy, and home-school compatibilities: A response to Sledge et al. *Anthropology and Education Quarterly, 19*, 425–432.

Goldenberg, C., & Gallimore, R. (1995). Immigrant Latino parents' values and beliefs about their children's education: Continuities and discontinuities across cultures and generations. In M. Maehr & P. R. Pintrich (Eds.), *Advances in motivation and achievement* (Vol. 9, pp. 183–228). Greenwich, CT: JAI.

Goldenberg, C., Rueda, R. S., & August, D. (2006a). Synthesis: Sociocultural contexts and literacy development. In D. August & T. Shanahan (Eds.), *Developing literacy in second-language learners: Report of the National Literacy Panel on language-minority children and youth* (pp. 249–268). Mahwah, NJ: Erlbaum.

Goldenberg, C., Rueda, R. S., & August, D. (2006b). Sociocultural influences on the literacy attainment of language-minority children and youth. In D. August & T. Shanahan (Eds.), *Developing literacy in second-language learners: Report of the National Literacy Panel on language-minority children and youth* (pp. 269–318). Mahwah, NJ: Erlbaum.

González, N. E., Moll, L., & Amanti, C. (2005). *Funds of knowledge: Theorizing practices in households, communities, and classrooms.* Mahwah, NJ: Erlbaum.

Gunderson, L. (2008). *ESL literacy instruction: A guidebook to theory and practice.* New York: Routledge.

Guthrie, J. T., McGough, K., Bennett, L., & Rice, M. E. (1996). Concept-oriented reading instruction: An integrated curriculum to develop motivations and strategies for reading. In L. Baker, P. Afflerbach, & D. Reinking (Eds.), *Developing engaged readers in school and home communities* (pp. 165–190). Hillsdale, NJ: Erlbaum.

Gutiérrez, K. (2006). *Culture matters: Rethinking educational equity.* New York: Carnegie Foundation.

Gutiérrez, K. D., Asato, J., Pacheco, M., Moll, L. C., Olson, K., Horng, E. L., et al. (2002). Conversations: "Sounding American": The consequences of new reforms on English language learners. *Reading Research Quarterly, 37*(3), 328–343

Gutiérrez, K. D., Baquedano-Lopez, P., Alvarez, H., & Chiu, M. (1999). Building a culture of collaboration through hybrid language practices. *Theory Into Practice, 38*(2), 87–93.

Gutiérrez, K. D., Baquedano-Lopez, P., & Tejeda, C. (1999). Rethinking diversity: Hybridity and hybrid language practices in the third space. *Mind, Culture, and Activity, 6*(4), 286–303.

Gutiérrez, K. D., Morales, P. Z., Martinez, D. C. (2009). Re-mediating literacy: Culture, difference, and learning for students from nondominant communities. *Review of Research in Education, 33*, 212–245.

Gutiérrez, K. D., & Rogoff, B. (2003). Cultural ways of learning: Individual traits and repertoires of practice. *Educational Researcher, 32*(5), 19–25.

Gutiérrez, K. D., Rymes, B., & Larson, J. (1995). James Brown vs. Brown v. The Board of Education: Script, counterscript, and underlife in the classroom. *Harvard Educational Review, 65*(3), 445–471.

Harklau, L. (2008). The adolescent English language learner: Identities lost and found. In J. Cummins & C. Davison (Eds.), *Handbook of English language teaching* (pp. 639–654). New York: Springer.

Heath, S. B. (1983). *Ways with words: Language, life, and work in communities and classrooms.* New York: Cambridge University Press.

Hunt, S. (1995). Choice in the writing class: How do students decide what to write and how to write it? *The Quarterly of the National Writing Project and the Center for the Study of Writing, 17*, 7–11.

Huss-Keeler, R. L. (1997). Teacher perception of ethnic and linguistic minority parental involvement and its relationships to children's language and literacy learning: A case study. *Teaching and Teacher Education, 13*(2), 171–182.

Jiménez, R. T. (1997). The strategic reading abilities and potential of five low-literacy Latino/a readers in middle school. *Reading Research Quarterly, 32*(3), 224–243.

Kamberelis, G., & Bovino, T. D. (1999). Cultural artifacts as scaffolds for genre development. *Reading Research Quarterly, 34*(2), 138–170

Ladson-Billings, G. (1992). Reading between the lines and beyond the pages: A culturally relevant approach to literacy teaching. *Theory into Practice, 31*(4), 312–320.

Ladson-Billings, G. (1994). *The dreamkeepers: Successful teachers of African American children.* San Francisco: Jossey-Bass.

Ladson-Billings, G. (2006). It's not the culture of poverty, it's the poverty of culture: The problem with teacher education. *Anthropology & Education Quarterly, 37*(2), 104–109.

Lam, B. T. (2003). *The psychological distress among Vietnamese American adolescents: Toward an ecological model*. Unpublished doctoral dissertation, Columbia University, New York.

Lam, W. S. E. (2004). Second language socialization in a bilingual chat room: Global and local considerations. *Language Learning & Technology, 8*(3), 44–65.

Langer, J. A. (Ed.). (1987). *Language and literacy and culture: Issues of society and schooling*. Norwood, NJ: Ablex.

Lapp, D. (2009). Say it today then say it differently tomorrow: Connecting home and school literacies. In G. Li (Ed.), *Multicultural families, home literacies, and mainstream schooling* (pp. 271–276). Greenwich, CT: Information Age.

Lave, J., & Wenger, E. (1991). *Situated learning: Legitimate peripheral participation*. Cambridge, UK: Cambridge University Press.

Lee, C. D. (1995). A culturally based cognitive apprenticeship: Teaching African American high school students skills in literary interpretation. *Reading Research Quarterly, 30*(4), 608–630.

Lee, C. D. (1997). Bridging home and school literacies: A model of culturally responsive teaching. In J. Flood, S. B. Heath, & D. Lapp (Eds.), *A handbook of research on teaching literacy through the communicative and visual arts* (pp. 875–884). New York: Macmillan.

Lee, C. D. (2000). Signifying in the zone of proximal development. In C. D. Lee & P. Smagorinsky (Eds.), *Vygotskian perspectives on literacy research: constructing meaning through collaborative inquiry* (pp. 191–225). New York: Cambridge University Press.

Lee, C. D. (2006). *Culture, literacy, and learning: Taking bloom in the midst of the whirlwind*. New York: Teachers College Press.

Lee, P. W., & Wong, S. L. (2002). At-risk Asian and Pacific American youths: Implications for teachers, psychologists and other providers. In E. H. Tamura, V. Chettergy, & R. Endo (Eds.), *Asian and Pacific Islander American education: Social, cultural, and historical contexts* (pp. 85–115). South El Monte, CA: Pacific Asia Press.

Lee, S. (2005). *Up against whiteness: Race, school and immigrant youth*. New York: Teachers College Press.

Li, G. (2002). *"East is east, west is west"? Home literacy, culture, and schooling*. New York: Peter Lang.

Li, G. (2004). Perspectives on struggling English language learners: Case studies of two Chinese-Canadian children. *Journal of Literacy Research, 36*(1), 29–70.

Li, G. (2005). Family as educator: A Chinese-Canadian experience of acquiring second language literacy. *Canadian Children, 30*(2), 9–16.

Li, G. (2006*). Culturally contested pedagogy: Battles of literacy and schooling between mainstream teachers and Asian immigrant parents*. Albany: State University of New York Press.

Li, G. (2007). Home environment and second language acquisition: The importance of family capital. *British Journal of Sociology of Education, 28*(3), 285–299.

Li, G. (2008). *Culturally contested literacies: America's "rainbow underclass" and urban schools*. New York: Routledge.

Li, G. (2009a). Behind the "model minority" mask: A cultural ecological perspective on a high achieving Vietnamese youth's identity and socio-emotional struggles. In C. Park, E. Endo, & X. L. Rong (Eds.), *New perspectives on Asian American parents, students, and teacher recruitment* (pp. 165–192). Greenwich, CT: Information Age.

Li, G. (Ed.). (2009b). *Multicultural families, home literacies, and mainstream schooling*. Greenwich, CT: Information Age.

Lopez, G. (2001). The value of hard work: Lessons on parent involvement from an (im)migrant household. *Harvard Educational Review, 71*(3), 416–437.

McCarty, T. (1993). Language, literacy, and the image of the child in American Indian classrooms. *Language Arts, 70*, 182–192.

McLaren, P. (1998). *Life in schools: An introduction to critical pedagogy in the foundations of education*. New York: Longman.

Mead, M. (1951). *The school in American culture*. Cambridge, MA: Cambridge University Press.

Meyer, D. (2004). *English language learner students in U.S. public schools: 1994 and 2000*. Washington, DC: National Center for Education Statistics, U.S. Department of Education, Institute of education Science.

Meyer, D., Madden, D., & McGrath, D. (2005). English language learner students in U.S. public schools: 1994 and 2000. *Education Statistics Quarterly, 6*(3). Retrieved from http://www.nces.ed.gov/programs/quarterly/vol_6/6_3/3_4.asp

Moje, E. B. (2002). But where are the youth? Integrating youth culture into literacy theory. *Educational Theory, 52*, 97–120.

Moje, E. B., Ciechanowski, K., Kramer, K., Ellis, L., Carrillo, R., & Collazo, T. (2004). Working toward third space in content area literacy: An examination of everyday funds of knowledge and discourse. *Reading Research Quarterly, 39*(1), 38–71.

Moje, E. B., & Hinchman, K. (2004). Culturally responsive practices for youth literacy learning. In J. Dole & T. Jetton (Eds.), *Adolescent literacy research and practice* (pp. 331–350). New York: Guilford Press.

Moles, O. C. (1993). Collaboration between schools and disadvantaged parents: Obstacles and openings. In N. F. Chavkin (Ed.), *Families and schools in a pluralistic society* (pp. 2–20). Albany: State University of New York Press.

Moll, L. C., & González, N. (1994). Lessons from research with language-minority children. *Journal of Reading Behavior, 26*(4), 439–456.

Morrell, E., & Duncan-Andrade, J. (2002). Toward a critical classroom discourse: Promoting academic literacy through engaging Hip-hop culture with urban youth. *English Journal, 91*(6), 88–92.

Morrell, E., & Duncan-Andrade, J. (2006). Popular culture and critical media pedagogy in secondary literacy classrooms. *International Journal of Learning, 12*(9), 273–280.

NCELA Newsline Bulletin, (2005). *NCES survey: Over 40% of the teachers teach LEPs.* Retrieved November 21, 2007, from http://www.ncela.gwu.edu/enews/2002/0611.htm

Neuman, S. B. (1999). Books make a difference: A study of access to literacy. *Reading Research Quarterly, 34*(3), 286–311.

Nieto, S. (1999). *The light in their eyes: Creating multicultural learning communities.* New York: Teachers College Press.

Ochs. E. (1986). *Culture and language acquisition: Acquiring communicative competence in a Western Samoan village.* New York: Cambridge University Press.

Ogbu, J. (1982). Cultural discontinuities and schooling. *Anthropology and Education Quarterly, 13*(4), 290–307.

Orellana, M. F. (1995). Literacy as a gendered social practice: Tasks, texts, talk, and take-up. *Reading Research Quarterly, 30*(4), 674–708.

Orellana, M. F. (2001). The work kids do: Mexican and Central American immigrant children's contribution to households and schools in California. *Harvard Educational Review, 71*(3), 366–389.

Orellana, M. F., & Reynolds, J. F. (2008). Cultural modeling: Leveraging bilingual skills for school paraphrasing tasks, *Reading Research Quarterly, 43*(1), 48–65.

Pierce, B. N. (1995). Social identity, investment, and language learning. *TESOL Quarterly, 29*(1), 9–31.

Pintrich, P. R., & Schrauben, B. (1992). Students' motivational beliefs and their cognitive engagement in classroom academic tasks. In D. H. Schunk & J. L. Meece (Eds.), *Student perceptions in the classroom* (pp. 149–183). Hillsdale, NJ: Erlbaum.

Portes, A., & Rumbaut, R. C. (1996). *Immigrant America: A portrait* (2nd ed.). Berkeley: University of California Press.

Qin, D. B. (2009). Being "good" or being "popular": Gender and ethnic identity negotiations of Chinese immigrant adolescents. *Journal of Adolescent Research, 24*(1), 37–66.

Quinn, N., & Holland, D. (1987). Culture and cognition. In D. Holland & N. Quinn (Eds.), *Cultural models in language and thought* (pp. 3–40). New York: Cambridge University Press.

Reese, L. J., & Gallimore, R. (2000). Immigrant Latinos' cultural model of literacy development: An alternative perspective on mome-school discontinuities. *American Journal of Education, 108*(2), 103–134.

Reuters. (2007). U.S. minority population tops 100 million: Hispanics are largest and fastest growing ethnic population, census reports. Retrieved May 10, 2008, from http:///id/18715129/from/ET/

Rivera, H. J. (2006). *A tale of two teachers: culturally relevant teaching case studies of theory and practice.* Unpublished doctoral dissertation, The Ohio State University, Columbus.

Rong, X. L., & Grant, L. (1992). Ethnicity, generation, and school attainment of Asians, Hispanics, and non-Hispanic whites. *The Sociological Quarterly, 33*(4), 625–636.

Rupley, W. H., Nichols, W. D., & Blair, T. R. (2008). Language and culture in literacy instruction: Where have they gone? *The Teacher Educator, 43*, 238–248.

Sarroub, L. K. (2005). *All American Yemeni girls: Being Muslim in a public school.* Philadelphia: University of Pennsylvania Press.

Schieffelin, B. B., & Ochs, E. (1986). *Language socialization across cultures.* Cambridge, UK: Cambridge University Press.

Schmidt, P. R. (1998). The ABC's model: Teachers connect home and school. In T. Shanahan & F. V. Rodriguez-Brown (Eds.), *National reading conference yearbook, 47* (pp. 194–208). Chicago: National Reading Conference.

Schmidt, P. R. (2003, February). *Culturally relevant pedagogy: A study of successful inservice.* Paper presented at the annual meeting of the National Reading Conference, Scottsdale, AZ.

Schmidt P. R., & Finkbeiner, C. (Eds.). (2006). *ABCs of cultural understanding and communication: National and international adaptations.* Greenwich, CT: Information Age.

Sheets, R. H. (1995). From remedial to gifted: Effects of culturally centered pedagogy. *Theory Into Practice, 34*(3), 186–193.

Snow, C., Burns, S., & Griffin, P. (1998). *Preventing reading difficulties in young children.* Washington, DC: National Academy Press.

Steinberg, L., Dornbusch, S. M., & Brown, B. B. (1992). Ethnic differences in adolescent achievement: An ecological perspective. *American Psychologist, 47*(6), 723–729.

Steinberg, L., Lamborn, S. D., Darling, N., Mounts, N. S., & Dornbusch, S. M. (1994). Over-time changes in adjustment and competence among adolescents from authoritative, authoritarian, indulgent, and neglectful families. *Child Development, 65*(3), 754–770.

Street, B. (1995). *Social literacies: Critical approaches to literacy in development, ethnography and education.* London: Longman.

Suárez-Orozco, C., & Suárez-Orozco, M. M. (2001). *Children of immigrants.* Cambridge, MA: Harvard University Press.

Sutherland, L. M., Botzakis, S., Moje, E. B., & Alvermann, D. E. (2007). Drawing on Youth Cultures in Content Learning and Literacy. In D. Lapp, J. Flood, & N. Farnan (Eds.), *Content area reading and learning instructional strategies* (3rd ed., pp.133–156). Mahwah, NJ: Erlbaum.

Swidler, A. (1986). Culture in action: Symbols and strategies. *American Sociological Review, 51*(2), 273–286.

Taylor, D., & Dorsey-Gaines, C. (1988). *Growing up literate: Learning from inner-city families.* Portsmouth: NH: Heinemann.

Teale, W. H., & Sulzby, E. (Eds.). (1986). *Emergent literacy: Writing and reading.* Norwood, NJ: Ablex.

Tran, A. N. (2002). *Acculturative stressors affecting Vietnamese American Adolescents and their parents.* Unpublished doctoral dissertation. Pacific Graduate School of Psychology, Palo Alto, California.

Turner, J. D. (2005). Orchestrating success for African American readers: The case of an effective third-grade teacher. *Reading Research and Instruction, 44,* 27–48.

Tyler, K. M., Uqdah, A. L., Dillihunt, M. L., Beatty-Hazelbaker., R., Conner, T., Gadson, N., et al. (2008). Cultural discontinuity: Toward a quantitative investigation of a major hypothesis in education. *Educational Researcher, 37*(5), 280–297.

UNESCO. (2004). The plurality of literacy and its implications for policies and programs: Position paper. Paris: United National Educational, Scientific and Cultural Organization. Retrieved May 10, 2009, from http://unesdoc.unesco.org/images/0013/001362/136246e.pdf

Valdés, G. (1996). *Con Respeto: Bridging the distance between culturally diverse families and schools: An ethnographic portrait.* New York: Teachers College Press.

Valenzuela, Jr., A. (1999). Gender roles and settlement activities among children and their immigrant families. *American Behavioral Scientist, 42*(4), 720–742.

Volk, D. (1997). *Questions in lessons: Activity settings in the homes and school of two Puerto Rican kindergartners.* Anthropology & Education, 28(1), 22–49.

Wagner, D. A. (1991). Literacy as culture: Emic and etic perspective. In E. M. Jennings & A. C. Purves (Eds.), *Literate systems and individual lives: Perspectives on literacy and schooling* (pp. 11–22). Albany: State University of New York Press.

Wells, G. (1986). *The meaning makers: Children learning language and using language to learn.* Portsmouth, NH: Heinemann.

Wells, G. (1989). Language in the classroom: Literacy and collaborative talk. *Language and Education, 3*(4), 251–273.

Wenger, E. (1998) *Communities of practice: Learning, meaning and identity.* Cambridge, UK: Cambridge University Press.

Wertsch, J. V. (1991). *Voices of the mind: A sociocultural approach to mediated action.* Cambridge, MA: Harvard Education Press.

Wigfield, A. (1997). Children's motivations for reading and reading engagement. In J. T. Gurthrie & A. Wigfield (Eds.), *Reading engagement* (pp. 14–33). Newark, DE: International Reading Association.

Xu, S. H. (2004). Teachers' reading of students' popular culture texts: The interplay of students' interests, teacher knowledge, and literacy curriculum. In C. M. Fairbanks, J. Worthy, B. Maloch, J. V. Hoffman, & D. L. Schallert (Eds.), *53rd yearbook of the National Reading Conference* (pp. 417–431). Oak Creek, WI: National Reading Conference.

Xu, S. H., Perkins, R. S., & Zunich, L. O. (2005). *Trading cards to comic strips: Popular culture texts and literacy learning in grades K–8.* Newark, DE: International Reading Association.

Zarate, M. E. (2007). *Understanding parental involvement: Perspectives, expectations and recommendations* (Policy report). Los Angeles: Tomas Rivera Policy Institute.

Zhou, M. (2001). Straddling different worlds: The acculturation of Vietnamese refugee children. In R. G. Rumbaut & A. Portes (Eds.), *Ethnicities: Children of immigrants in America* (pp. 187–228). Berkeley: University of California Press.

Zhou, M., & Bankston, C. L. III. (1998). *Growing up American: How Vietnamese children adapt to life in the United States.* New York: Russell Sage Foundation.

Part 5

Contexts of Reading

23 Popular Culture and Literacy Practices

Donna E. Alvermann
University of Georgia

Although the term popular culture may evoke notions of the ephemeral, literacy researchers' interest in this topic seems neither transient nor narrowly focused. Part of this interest stems no doubt from the increased visibility of research on social practices that involve reading and writing as well as other forms of communication (e.g., still and moving images, sounds, gestures, and embodied performances) within a popular culture context. Broadening the definition of text to include more than its linguistic features is another factor that accounts for increased attention to popular culture and literacy practices. Beyond these two influences are the ubiquitous technologies for transporting young and old alike into virtual worlds where the distinction between online and offline spaces is sometimes blurred to the point that popular culture texts produced and consumed in one space for fun and relaxation often become objects of intense study and work in another. The questions and sometimes full-scale debates that arise from popular culture's increased presence in the field of literacy education are prompting researchers to design studies aimed at better understanding the implications of this phenomenon and the directions in which it may go.

As a way into this literature, I begin with a brief historical overview of how the textual and social practices of popular culture connect to literacy practices. Next, I offer an interpretive analysis of three debates at the intersection of popular culture and literacy practices. Using that analysis, I conclude with a set of implications for theory, research, and classroom practice in literacy education.

HISTORICAL OVERVIEW: CONNECTING POPULAR CULTURE AND LITERACY PRACTICES

To understand how the textual and social practices of popular culture connect to literacy practices, it is useful to trace historically some of the ideological struggles that define both fields. In the case of popular culture, this tracing is anything but simple and straightforward. As a matter of fact, in the introductory chapter to their book, *Popular Culture: A Reader,* Guins and Cruz (2005) signaled by their choice of titles, "Entangling the Popular," that any careful consideration of popular culture's intellectual history would require a willingness to suspend all hope of a unified mindset, much less a definition.

Popular Culture

Studies of popular culture, at least as they have been conceptualized in the Western hemisphere, are largely products of work carried on in two academic fields: mass media studies and cultural studies. Beginning in the 1930s, scholars working within critical theory from a mass media perspective generally assumed that market forces associated with media production dominated working-class audiences' consumption of popular culture texts, largely through social engineering and psychological manipulation. For some, this assumption was validated in Horkheimer and Adorno's (1972) study of the culture industry and its mass culture products and processes. Along with other German intellectuals (e.g., Lowenthal, 1961; Marcuse, 1968) who were part of the Frankfurt Institute for Social Research, Horkheimer and Adorno described audiences as being easily taken in or "duped" by coercive power arrangements operating within the mass media establishment.

Benjamin (1936/1992), although associated with the Frankfurt School, was less distrustful of market forces. His work, in fact, caused a rupture in relations with his more pessimistic colleagues. In a seminal essay entitled "The Work of Art in the Age of Mechanical Reproduction," Benjamin outlined a greater participatory role for audiences—a view later taken up by an interdisciplinary group of British scholars who started the cultural studies movement at the Birmingham Centre for Contemporary Cultural Studies (CCCS). Although Hoggart (1957) is typically credited with founding the CCCS based on ideas expressed in his book, *The Uses of Literacy*, which endorsed opening up the canon (somewhat) by including a few elements of mass culture, it was Hall's (1981) theory of *production-in-use* that more clearly shaped the early intellectual life at Birmingham. According to Hall, the production-consumption process is dialogical in nature; that is, popular culture texts are neither inscribed with meaning guaranteed once and for all to reflect a producer's (author's, film director's) intentions, nor are they owned solely by creative and subversive audiences. Instead, *production-in-use* posits that producers and consumers of popular culture texts are in constant tension with each other. It is this tension between forces of containment and resistance, Hall argued that theoretically enables audiences to express meaning differently within different contexts at different points in time.

Concurrent with the growing influence of the cultural studies movement in the last decade of the 20th century—a time in which scholars with backgrounds in sociology, music, communications, film studies, media studies, history, philosophy, and economics focused largely on audiences' pleasures (Fiske, 1989)—a substantive critique began to form among some of the key figures in the movement. For instance, Kellner (1995) cautioned that "celebrating the audience and the pleasures of the popular, neglecting social class,... and failing to analyze ... the politics of cultural texts [would] make cultural studies merely another academic subdivision, harmless and ultimately of benefit primarily to the culture industries themselves" (p. 42). Other scholars, however, whose work in cultural studies focused on the Black diaspora (Gilroy, 1992), identity politics (McRobbie, 1994), and postcolonial hybridity (Bhabba, 1994), viewed the production of popular culture texts as a space in which to contest racialized, gendered, and universalized experiences.

On another front, Jenkins (1992) was studying television fans' behavior and theorizing participatory culture—a central concept in *Convergence Culture: Where Old and New Media Collide* (Jenkins, 2006). In Jenkins's view, convergence culture—or "the flow of content across multiple media platforms, the cooperation between multiple media industries, and the migratory behavior of media audiences who will go almost anywhere in search of the kinds of entertainment experiences they want" (p. 2)—offers a stance on audience that differs appreciably from earlier notions. Drawing from French cybertheorist Pierre Lévy's (1997) work on collective intelligence, Jenkins (2006) has argued that while individually we cannot know everything, collectively we can "pool our resources and combine our skills" in ways that make "collective intelligence... an alternative source of media power" (p. 4), albeit one that is unequally distributed between corporate media and consumers.

From Literacy to Literacies

Ongoing ideological struggles in the field of literacy, though seemingly not quite as entangled as those in popular culture, divide roughly into two competing models: the autonomous and the ideological views of literacy (Street, 1984, 1995). The autonomous model, according to Street (1984, 1995), characterizes reading and writing as neutral processes largely explained by individual variations in cognitive functioning and the motivation to achieve a literate status in life. It assumes a universal set of skills necessary for decoding and encoding primarily print text. Heath's (1983) work challenges this assumption in that her research showed it is *how* children are socialized into different literacies—their different *ways with words* and whether or not those ways match a school's approach to literacy instruction—that matters, and not the teaching of a universal set of skills per se.

In his critique of the autonomous model, Street (1995) drew from his earlier anthropological study of literacy in Iran during the 1970s. It was this fieldwork that led him to question the assumption that reading and writing are neutral processes and that literacy is singular in form. Street (1995) pointed out that the autonomous model "represents itself as though it is just natural" (p. 133) when in effect, all reading and writing processes (because they occur in larger social structures) "are always embedded in power relations" (p. 133). After calling into question the autonomous model's claim to objectivity, Street purposefully named his own model an ideological one. This model, known more widely for its view of literacy as a social practice inextricably linked to societal relations of power, is in direct competition with the autonomous model, which argues for a universal set of reading and writing skills that transcend social contexts and the uses to which people put their literacies.

A year after Street's (1995) critique of the autonomous model of literacy and 6 years after Gee's (1990) *Social Linguistics and Literacies: Ideology in Discourse* had appeared, an interdisciplinary group of scholars better known as the New London Group (1996) published its deliberations on the need to communicate using multiple modes of representation, not just language, in a world grown increasingly more diverse and dependent on new information communication technologies. The New London Group envisioned a design of literate futures that encompasses more than simply print-oriented literacy instruction. Thus, through a series of events that occurred mostly in the last decade of the 20th century, the notion of literacy "with a big 'L' and a single 'y'" (Street, 1995, p. 132) gradually gave way in some corners of the field to the plural form, *literacies*. Soon other related terms entered the lexicons of literacy researchers; for example, *multiliteracies* (New London Group, 1996) and *situated literacies* (Barton, Hamilton, & Ivanic, 2000) became commonplace in the burgeoning literature on what is called the *New Literacy Studies* (NLS).

A theory germane to any discussion of NLS, and particularly to the NLS research analyzed in this chapter, is one that addresses the social semiotics of multimodal literacy practices (Jewitt & Kress, 2003; Kress & van Leeuwen, 1996; Lemke, 1989). Concerned primarily with communication in its widest sense (visual, oral, aural, gestural, linguistic, musical, kinesthetic, and digital), social semiotic theory attempts to explain how people recruit various resources (or signs) to represent ideas they wish to communicate through a variety of modes across a range of media that are situated within shifting relations of power.

Connections

During the last decade or so of the 20th century, literacy researchers who were curious about children's and young people's engagement with popular culture (e.g., Alvermann, Moon, & Hagood, 1999; Beavis, 1998; Dyson, 1994; Knobel, 1999; Moje, 2000; O'Brien, 1998) drew from work in cultural and media studies (Ang, 1985; Buckingham, 1993; Buckingham & Sefton-Green, 1994; de Certeau, 1984; Green & Bigum, 1993; Luke, 1997; Robinson, 1997; Williams, 1961) that focused on audiences and their everyday uses of popular culture. By the first decade of the 21st century, literacy research on popular culture involving digital technologies was markedly more visible, at least among populations fortunate enough to have high-speed Internet access. This proliferation of digitalized popular culture, accompanied by an ever-increasing interest among literacy researchers in theorizing reading and writing as social practices, led to studies of online chat rooms (Merchant, 2001), fan fiction writing (Black, 2008), instant messaging (Lewis & Fabos, 2005), and mobile texting (Ito & Okabe, 2005).

Similarly, a growing interest in researching multimodal literacies led to inquiries into children's and young people's engagement with video and computer games, to the point that the term *game literacy* is now fairly common (Burn, 2007; Squire, 2008), though critiqued by some (e.g., Burn & Leach, 2004) for "implying that language has a kind of primary status as a mode of communication" (p. 155). More than a fashionable metaphor, game literacy refers not only to a game's multimodal properties but also to its peripheral literacies, such as writing scripts, researching a backstory (the history behind the game's plot), and designing walkthroughs (directions for playing the game). Game literacy may also involve participating in chat rooms, contributing to discussion boards, or joining communities of amateur Do-It-Yourself (DIY) game developers who "adhere to aesthetic guidelines influenced by but modified from those of the commercial market" (Camper, 2005, p. 79).

This cursory overview of literacy research in relation to the textual and social practices of popular culture does not begin to reflect the volume of work that is taking place in these connecting fields of study. For additional reviews of that literature, see the following: Beach and O'Brien (2008) on teaching popular culture texts; Bruce (2008) on multimedia production as composition; Hagood (2008) on popular culture, identities, and the new literacies; Jewitt (2008) on multimodality and literacy in school classrooms; Marsh (2008) on popular culture in the language arts classroom; Moje (2008) on youth cultures, literacies, and identities; Sefton-Green (2006) on youth, technology, and media cultures; and Tierney (2008) on meaning making across and within digital spaces.

THREE DEBATES AT THE INTERSECTION OF POPULAR CULTURE AND LITERACY PRACTICES

These debates fall roughly into three different, though not totally discrete, categories. One is the structure/agency debate that focuses on the degree to which mass media messages embedded in popular culture texts are negatively affecting children and young people, as opposed to evoking within them a sense of agency for interpreting such messages on their own terms. A second debate centers on whether or not children's and young people's participation in reading, viewing, listening to, and creating popular culture texts (especially digital texts) is an educational experience that has potential for transfer from informal to formal learning environments. A third debate calls into question an earlier approach to representing children's and young people's uses of popular culture and literacy practices; in short, it challenges researchers to view identity politics as sites of engagement for moving toward a more just and equitable world.

To locate research that might inform these debates, I conducted searches of electronic databases (e.g., JSTOR, EBSCO, GALILEO) as well as hand searches of journals and books in my personal collection. I also contacted colleagues worldwide to request their assistance in obtaining copies of in-press research reports. Of the 177 sources that I located and subjected to Maxwell's (2006) criteria for inclusion, only those references that appear at the end of this chapter were used in addressing the three debates. An earlier version of this chapter was presented at a one-day conference titled *Who Says Research Says? Research Syntheses in Reading*, which preceded the annual meeting of the 2007 National Reading Conference in Austin, Texas. Feedback from participants at the pre-conference led me to structure this review as a set of three debates, each of which has parallels in the history of the two fields—popular culture and literacy—and their overlapping textual and social practices.

Debate #1: A Question of Agency

As indicated at the start of this chapter, popular culture as a field of study is relatively ill defined. It has attracted scholars from a broad array of academic disciplines who have focused at various times on mass culture and cultural studies. During the 1990s a critique formed around the celebratory aspects of audience reception research. While some cultural studies scholars worried that a focus on audiences' pleasures threatened to neglect or mask the power differentials that keep certain racial, sexist, and postcolonial prejudices alive, other scholars viewed these same pleasures as sites at which to contest racialized, gendered, and universalized experiences. Controversy surrounding this issue, while not signaling a full-scale return to the critique of mass culture some 30 years earlier, nonetheless suggested that the structure/agency debate was far from resolved.

A similar structure/agency debate surfaced in the literacy field during the late 1990s when attention was called to the power differentials operating in the autonomous model of literacy instruction. For example, Luke and Freebody (1997) argued that "all language, all text, all discourse…'refracts' the world; bending, shaping, constructing particular versions and visions of the social and natural world that act in the interests of particular class, gender, and cultural groups" (p. 193). Increased awareness of textual positioning, coupled with changes in global markets and web technologies, continue to draw literacy researchers' attention to economic imperatives inherent in commercial media, the ways in which they filter through youth's encounters with popular culture, and the degree to which they are mediated in the filtering.

For example, in an analysis of ninemsn.com, an Australian web portal popular among school-age youth, Atkinson and Nixon (2005) drew on data available from a media marketing research firm to illustrate the tensions between youth-as-commodity and youth-as-consumer/user. Starting from the premise that "informal learning sites, technologies, texts, and literacies in consumer economies are significantly shaped in response to market forces and the discourses that support them" (p. 390), Atkinson and Nixon traced how the web portal's "site-produced personas" of targeted youth audiences became the property of advertisers—a practice that ultimately resulted in narrowing the kinds of popular culture texts available to youth. As the researchers pointed out, however, "actual child and teen media users [in contrast to their site-produced personas] do not necessarily take up the subject positions offered" (p. 404).

The idea that uses and meanings of textual and social practices in popular culture are negotiable and that media enterprises such as ninesmn.com cannot totally account for young people's "migratory behavior" (Jenkins, 2006, p. 2) can be seen in two studies reported by Moje and van Helden (2005). Drawing from her 5-year ethnography of Latino/a youth culture, identity, and literacy practices in one urban community, Moje's analysis of four young women's uses of popular culture texts showed that they negotiated the meanings of "mainstream" music, movies, and TV programs to produce texts that were more compatible with their ethnic, familial, religious, and educational backgrounds. Although not untouched by the niche advertising and entertainment markets that positioned them, these young women were "doing popular culture [by] playing at borders" (Moje & van Helden, 2005, p. 238); that is, they were shaping the available texts' meanings in ways that worked for them, while at the same time producing hybridized texts of their own identities. Similarly, van Helden reported that in his study the three young men who used their sexual identifications to "read" different meanings into Abercrombie & Fitch's advertisements "were aware of the popular meaning A&F carried, and they were aware that they were 'playing' with different meanings in their heads, and in their communications and behaviors" (Moje & van Helden, 2005, p. 228).

Evidence exists that the uses and meanings young people make of popular culture texts are never free of local/global structures (Carrington, 2003). In fact, these tensions are visible in how schools come to terms with students' out-of-school lives, as illustrated in Chan's (2006) interview study of Hong Kong youth and their production of short films and videos; in Grace and Tobin's (1998) participant-observation study of Hawaiian children's production of videos that transgressed school norms; and in Finders' (1996, 1997) ethnographic study of junior high school girls' uses of popular magazines (e.g., *Seventeen* and *YM*) that both challenged their school's institutional authority and solidified their own social friendship network. Findings from each of these studies suggest that similar to what Buckingham and Sefton-Green (2004) noted in their analysis of the *Pokémon* phenomenon, treating structure and agency as either/or conditions is generally unproductive, and at best, misleading.

Granting reciprocity to the two elements in the structure/agency binary is supported empirically in Kenway and Bullen's (2001) multi-year study of children growing up in a consumer culture, and in Leander and Lovvorn's (2006) ethnographic research on literacy networks. Specifically, Leander and Lovvorn examined the classroom literacy practices of one 13-year-old boy who was also heavily involved at home in a multiplayer online computer game called *Star Wars Galaxies: An Empire Divided* (LucasArts & Sony Entertainment, 2003). Using Latour's (1987) actor network theory to analyze how both classroom and gaming literacy practices produced and organized space-time relations, Leander and Lovvorn (2006) proposed that "becoming recruited (or enrolled) to use literacy, or assuming agency with literacy, or developing a particular identity through literacy is neither described through an individual's internal states nor socially attributed to larger structural orders" (pp. 293–294). Instead, they used their findings to argue for locating such practices within a literacy network that may make it possible to move beyond the current understanding of context-as-container, a notion that is central to the next debate.

Debate #2: A Question of Transfer

Whether or not children's and young people's participation in reading, viewing, listening to, and creating popular culture texts (especially digital texts) is an educational experience that has potential for transfer from informal to formal learning environments is a debate reflected in much of the current research on popular culture and literacy practices. One premise, though not always stated, is that the divide between informal and formal environments is "real" and that as such, it needs bridging. Another premise is that the type of learning assumed to take place in each locale is qualitatively different. Yet in a year-long study that focused on informal learning during computer gaming and chatting online among a group of boys and girls (9- to 13-year-olds) from low-income backgrounds in an out-of-school setting in the Shared Spaces Project (2003), Sefton-Green (2003) concluded that informal learning, while vague in terms of its pedagogic structure, "co-exists with formal learning rather than being in contradistinction to it" (p. 49). This co-existence is evident in studies of classrooms in which overlapping popular culture and literacy practices are taken for granted, even celebrated; it is less evident, however, in classrooms where students' informal experiences with popular culture are either questioned in terms of educational worth and/or viewed as being in need of bridging.

Perceived Educational Worth.   Perceptions of the educational merit of students' uses of popular culture vary considerably. Literacy practices that engage print-based popular culture texts are typically perceived as having greater transfer value (and perhaps greater educational worth) than practices that engage largely nonprint texts (O'Brien, 1998; O'Brien, Beach, & Scharber, 2007). An example is Skinner's (2007) case study of an adolescent girl's use of popular culture texts in an after-school writing club that included what Skinner referred to as mentor texts, or "print-based texts from which students have the explicit intention of learning and applying something about writing" (p. 345). Because mentor texts could be viewed as being more school-like than literacy practices associated with gaming (but see Beavis, 2007; Burn, 2007; Pahl, 2005), they could be said to also have greater transfer potential. The tendency to associate ease of transfer with educational worth, though perhaps not surprising, is difficult to explain in light of research that suggests peripheral literacies (Burn, 2007) commonly associated with computer games (e.g., researching a game's backstory, writing scripts, designing walkthroughs) actually promote the types of authentic, creative, and school-sanctioned literacies that educators purportedly value (Beavis, Nixon, & Atkinson, 2005; Burn, 2008; Gee, 2003; Steinkuehler, 2006; Warschauer & Ware, 2008).

Perceptions of the educational worth of popular culture texts permeate a range of study designs—from those that focus on teaching basic reading skills using multimedia (Reinking, 2005) and popular culture texts (Xu, 2004) to those that examine the sociocultural contexts into which such texts insert themselves, often at the expense of teacher comfort. For example, Rymes's (2004) 2-year case study of a young second language learner revealed how this student's competencies in learning with/through popular culture texts led to misunderstandings and undermined the discourse within which his teacher felt competent. Rymes illustrated this situation in a sociolinguistic analysis of the interactions among the focal student, one of his peers, and the teacher during a phonics lesson that involved the word *chancy* (as in the state of uncertainty) and *Chansey* (as in the name of a Pokémon character). In arguing for the need to develop a pedagogical awareness that takes into account the competencies and comfort zones of both students and teachers while at the same time challenging deficit lenses, Rymes's work parallels that of other researchers whose findings point to the role of children's and young people's peripheral literacies in legitimating a range of popular culture texts: comics (Bitz, 2008, Norton, 2003), films (Kist, 2008), video productions (Rogers, Winters, & LaMonde, in press), sports memorabilia (Mahiri, 1998), remixed music (Gustavson, 2008), raps (Kirkland, 2008b), digital images (McVee, Bailey, & Shanahan, 2008; Miller, 2008), instant messages (Lewis & Fabos, 2005), e-mails (Alvermann, 2006), mobile texts (Ito, Okabe, & Matsuda (2005), urban signage (Dutro & Zenkov, 2008), and tags (Moje, 2000).

Popular culture and literacy materials (whether print-based, multimodal, digital, or hyper-mediated) that can be integrated into meaningful hybrid curricula appear to stand a better chance of being considered educational worthy than materials that lack this integrative element (Xu, 2004). Research in support of this claim comes from the following studies: a class of 8- and 9-year-olds who compared *Red Riding Hood* to *Lara Croft*, a popular video game (Bearne & Wolstencroft, 2005); a kindergarten class in which children used their knowledge of superheroes to compose their own computer-generated stories (Labbo, 1996); a high school senior English class that incorporated hip-hop in a poetry unit (Morrell, 2004; Morrell & Duncan-Andrade, 2002); and an 8-year-old boy's use of video games as a source of subject matter and form in his own writing and drawing (Ranker, 2006). Teachers in each of these studies were supportive of students' uses of popular culture texts in their classrooms. In contrast, Leander's (2007) study of a school in which wired classrooms provided students with laptop access to an unprecedented world of texts, teachers were uncomfortable with students' multitasking online literacies (e.g., blogging, web browsing, remixing), especially when such activity led to the production of popular culture texts that threatened school-sanctioned learning and the teachers' authority. Perhaps the teachers in Leander's study, unlike those in the above mentioned studies (Bearne & Wolstencroft, Morrell & Duncan-Andrade, Labbo, and Ranker) perceived no meaningful curriculum into which popular culture texts and online literacy practices would fit.

Pedagogical challenges may also surface when discursive practices common to one more or less open social space are introduced into another, more closed, social space—especially one in which there is potential for threatening a teacher's authority. Yardi (2008) called attention to this set of circumstances in his study of the participatory culture of chat rooms. As he noted, chat rooms can become sites of contestation when students use backchanneling as a medium for communicating with each other:

> The potential success of peer-to-peer learning in a chat room is rooted in the theory of constructivist learning.... [That is] students are empowered to argue, debate, and discuss with one another, creating an environment in which they can take on as much power as they want.... [However] the backchannel may be perceived to be a medium that encourages transgression. Those who oppose it may argue that to participate in the backchannel is to purposefully upstage the teacher's role in the classroom. (pp. 139–152)

In addressing the debate about the educational worth and especially the challenges that result from introducing popular culture texts, such as zines, into formal learning environments, Beach and O'Brien (2008) sounded this cautionary note: "As soon as popular culture texts are imported into the classroom, they no longer retain their original meanings constituted by how they serve to resist school and authority" (pp. 796–797). This caution, while noteworthy, is further complicated by research (Lenhart, Madden, Macgill, & Smith, 2007) that suggests young people are less interested in resisting institutional authority than in creating content to share with their peers, although sharing for subversive purposes is well within the realm of possibilities (Guzzettti & Gamboa, 2004; Knobel & Lankshear, 2002).

Perceptions of the educational worth of popular culture texts are also colored by the contexts in which they are studied. For example, using fandom as her theoretical lens, Black (2007) conducted a 3-year ethnography of shared online writing among female English language learners (ELLs) who affiliated around a common interest in fanfiction—a term for stories that fans of an original work (e.g., *Harry Potter*) write by using the settings, characters, and plot from the original to imagine and create different situations that sometimes include curious remixes across genres and media. To give some indication of the diversity of the content, audience, and literacies involved at sites such as fanfiction.net, where writers review each other's work and request stories from their favorite fanfiction authors, Black (2007) wrote:

> While writing [fanfiction], the adolescent ELL may be carrying on several conversations at once via instant-messaging programs, chat rooms, and/or discussion boards [with other fanfiction writers] located in her former hometown in China, her new hometown in North America, and other such diverse places. She also may be drawing from her knowledge of academic forms of writing, different media genres, as well as her knowledge of English, Mandarin Chinese, and perhaps Japanese to construct the text. (p. 386)

Creating a space in which to interact around remixed texts with an appreciative audience was viewed as a highly desirable learning environment in Chandler-Olcott and Mahar's (2003) study of two adolescent girls whose shared interest in Japanese animation (anime) led to a series of anime-focused homepages and artwork that garnered knowledgeable feedback from anime listserv enthusiasts. Both girls demonstrated, as did the adolescents in Stone's (2007) research, that they knew how to attract and sustain people's attention in cyberspace—skills that are far from trivial in contemporary society where "attention, unlike information, is inherently scarce [with some economists predicting] that the human capacity to produce material things [will outstrip] the net capacity to consume the things that are produced" (Lankshear & Knobel, 2002, pp. 20-21).

Assumed Need for Bridging.   The permeable curriculum is a term that Dyson (1993) used to describe the space in which children's "unofficial" worlds—their knowledge of popular songs, movies, cartoons, comics, televised sports—and the relationships they formed with others around these visual and aural texts could seep into a school's curriculum and its officially sponsored written texts. It is a space in which "meaning is found, not in [texts] themselves, but in the social events through which those [texts] are produced and used" (Dyson, 1997, p. 181). Although the assumption that the divide between informal and formal environments is "real" and as such needs bridging is central to some of Dyson's (1997, 2003a, 2003b, 2003c) and Marsh and Millard's (2000, 2005) work on children's uses of popular culture in the classroom, the degree to which teachers actually accept, question, or resist this assumption has not been sufficiently studied (Lesley, 2008).

The existing research generally suggests reluctance on the part of teachers to recognize the classroom as a legitimate place for noncanonical texts that espouse ideological content deemed potentially at odds with the "official" curriculum (Marsh, 2006). For example, in a 3-year longitudinal study of preservice teachers' perceptions about the use of popular culture at the primary level of England's literacy curriculum, Marsh (2005) found that despite the prospective teachers' expressed approval of the use of popular culture in the literacy curriculum, during their field placements, they rarely if ever made use of their students' interests in popular culture. When they did, it was typically to connect students' interests to the school-sanctioned reading curriculum (e.g., using a Pokémon text to motivate them to read their schoolbooks). The prospective teachers' perceptions that popular culture texts were not to be engaged for their own personal worth is in direct opposition, interestingly, to what parents and caregivers of children up through the age of six reportedly value about their children's fascination with such texts (Marsh et al., 2005). In the Marsh et al. survey, 1,852 parents and caregivers reported that popular culture, in the form of comics, books related to TV shows, and websites featuring children's favourite characters from TV and films, determined to a large extent the kinds of books their children wanted to read or have read to them.

Contributing to the debate about transfer and the assumed need for bridging young people's uses of popular culture texts is Moje, Overby, Tysvaer, and Morris's (2008) large-scale, longitudinal study of predominantly Latino/a youth of middle- and high-school age. Based on a mixed methods analysis of first- and second-wave data sets, Moje et al. found that the students they surveyed and interviewed reported reading a wide range of popular culture texts in their leisure time; however, novel reading was the only literacy practice to have a statistically significant and positive relationship to students' English grades. Because novel reading was not that different from what young people in the study would have been expected to do in their English classes, it is possible that a reverse type of bridging occurred; that is, an in-school literacy practice may have seeped into their out-of-school leisure time activities, making the permeable curriculum perhaps more porous than Dyson (1997) originally imagined.

In another study of high school youth, a similar example of reverse bridging was noted. This time it occurred because one of the three participants in the study—a young woman named Saundra (pseudonym), who was deeply engaged in producing her own punk rock zines when Guzzetti and Gamboa (2004) initiated their multi-year ethnographic study—presumed the researchers needed special tutoring to appreciate the various social realities and literate practices in the world of punk rock. Acting on this presumption, Saundra designed a brochure and arranged tutorials that bore a striking resemblance to traditional classroom instruction. In fact, in recalling one particular tutorial, Guzzetti (2004) wrote:

> Saundra created a brochure for us, which she referred to as "a sort of *Punk Rock for Dummies*," in which she defined and explained the various genres, bands, and artists of punk rock, complete with a quiz to test our knowledge. She invited me to her apartment, where she had set up a seminar format at her kitchen table, with handouts of lyrics of punk rock songs, liner notes from CDs, and tape recordings she had made of various styles of punk rock. She had her stereo handy so that she could demonstrate the different genres as she explained them. (p. 10)

Similar linkages between informal and formal learning environments were observed in a study of LAN (Local Area Network) cafés in two Australian cities, where young people met regularly in *clans*, or teams, to play computer games (Beavis, Nixon, & Atkinson, 2005). An analysis of the data obtained in 16 interviews with LAN café owner-managers and their staffs revealed the somewhat ambiguous roles these individuals played in the young people's lives. Characterized by Beavis et al. as being somewhat akin to informal teachers, the owners and staff of the LAN cafés took a personal interest in facilitating games, such as *Counter-Strike*, and in providing a space where their young clientele could relax in relative safety. As was the case in Guzzetti and Gamboa (2004), the Beavis et al. study illustrates how, in a postmodern world, expertise and authority are collectively distributed, thereby blurring distinctions between teachers and learners (Jenkins, 2006; Lankshear & Knobel, 2007).

In sum, there is evidence to suggest that the co-existence of informal and formal learning environments facilitate the mingling of popular culture and literacy practices, and that the so-called transfer of learning may be bi-directional in flow, or perhaps even blurred. Evidence also exists to suggest that debates about the educational worth of popular culture texts and the view of context-as-container may take a backseat in the future.

Debate #3: A Question of Identity Politics

In questioning the adequacy of an earlier approach to representing children's and young people's uses of popular culture, Dolby (2003) challenged researchers to view the politics of identity construction as potential sites for working toward a more just and equitable world. Although her work focused on the intersection of popular culture and democratic practices, it parallels in several ways the research on popular culture and literacy practices in social (Bean, Bean, & Bean, 1999), political (Hoechsmann & Low, 2008), and economic (Spires, Lee, Turner, & Johnson, 2008) spheres of influence. In particular, Dolby was critical of research on popular culture that focuses solely on issues of representation, and called instead for studies that make identity politics both visible and engaging.

For instance, online social networking communities such as MySpace provide opportunities for young people to write, read, and speak their worlds into existence, as Kirkland (2008a) demonstrated in his portrayal of Derrick (pseudonym), a high school youth who created content in MySpace that belied his 12th-grade English teacher's description of him as someone who "could not write" and "did not [like to] write" (p. 2). Working from a critical perspective, Kirkland documented in a 3-year ethnography how Derrick's online compositions—remixes of digital audio and video technologies interspersed with stylized African American spellings—conveyed his identity as a socially conscious rapper and poet. In an interview with Kirkland, Derrick explained how social networking sites such as MySpace enabled him to identify as a writer:

> I be writing about my life mainly. It's like to say something really important, I got to get my story out there. It says a lot about our world—stuff that's fucked up and stuff that's not so fucked up. But it's my view... I don't usually tell my view by writing an essay. That's not my style. I can write like that, but I don't always want to write like that because I feel like I can get my point across better in a poem or in a rap. (Kirkland, 2008a, p. 5)

In other studies of identity construction as a site where youth can work toward reinventing themselves as the kinds of people they say they are (and want others to see them as), a common finding has been that popular culture tends to mobilize certain types of textual practices useful in acquiring social and cultural capital (Bourdieu, 1991/1982). For instance, Hagood (2004) documented the ways in which Tee (a pseudonym) and her group of friends were produced as a particular kind of youth by the religious accessories (texts) they wore—the W.S.F.J. (We Shine for Jesus) bracelets—and the Christian youth groups to which they belonged. At the same time, Tee pushed against certain assumptions other people were making about her and the music she listened to. In Tee's eyes, listening to CDs and radio stations that played non-Christian music did not negate her Christian identity. As Hagood noted, studying young people's attempts to "reshape the structures and identities that define them" (p. 159) can potentially inform age-old ways of thinking about popular culture and its uses.

Sutherland's (2005) study of how six 16-year-old Black girls used events in a class-assigned popular novel, *The Bluest Eye* (Morrison, 1994), to validate, modify, or contest particular identities that others have ascribed to them raises questions about a model of teaching multicultural literature that is prevalent in the United States. In analyzing the interviews she conducted with the girls, Sutherland found the model assumed an overly simplistic view of how students of color will respond to literature in which they supposedly see themselves represented. Her participants' responses (and in some instances their lack of response) hint at why popular novels used in conjunction with certain models of multicultural instruction may mediate identity construction in unintended ways.

Geographic locales, fan practices, and embodied performances are still other sites of identity construction that literacy researchers have explored in their attempt to show how young people's uses of popular culture texts can inform the larger social, political, and educational structures governing their lives. For instance, Dimitriadis (2001) found in his ethnography of a midwestern community center's youth program that two young men who participated in the program, and who were close friends from the same small town in Mississippi, relied on their idealized notion of "Southern" place to construct an identity for themselves in their new surroundings. Specifically, they used their knowledge of what constitutes a culture of southern rap music to achieve a partial sense of belonging in the Midwest. Using a geographic locale far removed from the site of the actual identity work being done (though not without some tension) provided the two friends a sense of social support initially, and just as importantly, offered local educators "data" for making the center's program more relevant.

Interviews with 12 life-long comic book readers afforded Botzakis (2008) entry into sites of identity construction among his participants that spanned childhood through young adulthood. Botzakis drew on Fiske's (1989) notion of popular culture being "found in its practices, not in its texts" (p. 45) and de Certeau's (1984) view of reading as a tactic to explain how the people in his study created literate identities for themselves once they realized their interests were not being met in school. The fan practices associated with comic book reading, according to Botzakis, call into question central tenets of school literacy instruction.

In a study of literacy practices involving 30 young adolescent girls and the avatars they created in an online role-playing community, Thomas (2007) used Butler's (1997) definition of performativity—"that aspect of a discourse that has the capacity to produce what it names" (pp. 111–112)—to explain the ways in which the girls used both words and embodied performances (the avatars) to author their online identities. This authoring more often than not resulted in what Thomas (2007) described as the "perfected being…a glamorous supermodel type avatar" (p. 36), which prompted her to ask what this might mean for a generation of children coming up. By articulating the flow between young girls' textual and corporal lives, Thomas uncovered the presence of several discourses operating in the politics of identity construction.

In sum, at least for the research reviewed here, studies of identity politics at the intersection of popular culture and literacy practices seem promising as sites for engaging young people in working toward a more just and equitable world. Although findings from these studies are but starting points along a continuum of possible change in the way young people's uses of popular culture are viewed, they nonetheless support the feasibility of focusing on sites of identity construction as opportunities for youth to speak their own truths into existence by combining words with images, sounds, gestures, and embodied performances (Fisher, 2007).

IMPLICATIONS FOR THEORY, RESEARCH, AND CLASSROOM PRACTICE

The following implications derive in large part from the interpretive analysis of the three debates just completed. In a few instances where additional evidence is required to flesh out a particular implication, I draw from additional sources to make my point.

Theory

To what end, as well as to where, productive tensions at the intersection of popular culture and literacy practices may lead are largely under theorized. Given the history of the debate surrounding the "push-pull" of the structure/agency divide in both popular culture and literacy research, it is likely that tensions resulting from this divide will continue. That said, it would still seem feasible to develop new theoretical frameworks for examining questions of agency in the context of negotiating the uses and meanings of textual and social practices in classrooms where popular culture and school-sanctioned literacies overlap.

Also under theorized are the principles behind the appropriation and leveraging of remix practices that increasingly motivate young people to create large quantities of online content for their own consumption and for others who appreciate their craft (Alvermann, 2008; Knobel & Lankshear, 2008). Remixing—the simple act of cutting and pasting from sound clips, images, video games, podcasts, message boards, newsgroups, blogs, and the like—can at times result in highly refined parodies. Critiques of online remix practices that claim they are trivial and lacking in creativity are easily challenged by Willis's (1990) earlier work on the vibrant symbolic life of youth in relation to TV viewing. This view of young people's symbolic creativity maps nicely onto Hall's (1981) earlier claim that audience consumerism is an active rather than a passive process. It also supports the notion that remix practices have educational worth and are perhaps not nearly as transgressive as current critiques might suggest.

Research

Research designs that are sensitive to the overlap in popular culture and literacy practices will of necessity give greater attention to the screen (Kress, 1998, 2003) as a legitimate space for studying children and young people's engagement with a wide range of texts, broadly defined. Such designs will also need to incorporate analytic procedures that are theoretically driven and make visible how young people's engagement with popular culture opens up opportunities for working toward a more just and equitable world, for identity politics achieved through popular culture texts do not skirt issues of race, ethnicity, gender, class, and other markers of difference.

One approach researchers might take would be to ask how popular culture texts work (along with other texts, people, objects, and technologies) to create and organize space-time relations in literacy networks that are relatively free of distinctions based on formal and informal learning arrangements (Leander & Lovvorn, 2006). To continue reifying distinctions between formal and informal literacy practices is to divorce them from the very spaces that give them meaning (Alvermann & Eakle, 2007). It also limits what researchers might learn from studies designed to treat contexts not as structured containers but as sieves through which social, cultural, institutional, economic, and political discourses animate one another and provide a sense of agency for both learners and teachers.

Research is needed that will lend explanatory power to why video games that contribute to learning in principled ways (Gee, 2003) are still largely rejected in the official school curriculum, as well as what might be done to change this state of affairs. Given that Vadeboncoeur's (2006) review of research on informal learning argues for asking not what counts as learning, but instead "How does a particular context contribute to learning?" (p. 272), studies are needed that systematically vary the conditions (school computer labs, LAN cafés, home entertainment centers) in which games are played and that ask if (and how) learning is accomplished differently in each. Ignoring the potential of games, especially those that evoke the collective intelligence of fans the world over, is to "save" young people from being recruited by a form of learning that for some, at least, equates to profound pleasure (Gee, 2007).

Increasingly, researchers are experiencing the effects of digitalized knowledge and net-worked communities, especially in terms of the questions that need asking and the methodologies and analytic tools required for answering their questions. As Luke (2003) predicted, researchers are generally finding it necessary to "play catch up with the unprecedented textual and social practices that students are already engaging with" (p. 402). Perhaps nowhere is the realization of the need to catch up with young people's uses of popular culture more visible than among English education researchers. In a recent and comprehensive review of that literature, Sperling and DiPardo (2008), wrote:

> Although much of the existing work on youth participation in digital literacies has taken place in out-of-school settings…, researchers have drawn on their findings to argue the need to integrate new media in classrooms in conceptually grounded and reflective ways (see Hull & Schultz, 2002: Stein, 2007). A recurrent theme in this work has been the need to foster criticality concerning the texts (and authors) that students encounter in their online travels. (p. 89)

Classroom Practice

With the exception of an eclectic body of research that focuses on issues such as students' spontaneous mentioning of popular culture texts in teacher-led discussions (Duff, 2004), there are few large-scale studies that examine the potential for connecting students' out-of-school interests in popular culture texts with classroom learning. One exception, as noted earlier, is a study by Moje et al. (2008) that provides evidence of a correlation between students' reading of popular novels outside of school and their in-school achievement, at least in the area of English language arts. Similar findings are reported in a study that assessed students' gains on school-like writing measures after having been exposed to certain kinds of films (Primary National Strategy and the United Kingdom Literacy Association, 2004).

Although there is some evidence that teaching for critical literacy using popular culture texts such as Tupac Shakur's (1999) poetry enhances young people's sense of agency in constructing literate identities (Kirkland, 2008b; Lesley, 2008), implications for critical classroom practice based on the body of literature reviewed in this chapter are largely absent. What is highlighted, however, is the question of identity politics and the need to create among youth "an awareness of how, why, and in whose interests particular texts might work" (Luke & Freebody, 1997, p. 218). Instructional frameworks for building this awareness include taking on alternative reading positions (Green, 1988), critiquing the media's impact on youthful consumers (Hobbs, 2007), developing a critical literacy pedagogy for working with youngsters (ages 3 to 8), and analyzing adolescent-directed uses of popular culture to identify relations of power that are then discussed with students (Heron-Hruby & Alvermann, 2009; Knobel & Lankshear, 2007).

Young children growing up today are likely to experience a world that is increasingly less dominated by linguistically bound texts. According to Mackey (2003), their universe will be comprised of "mutating literacies" (p. 403) and ever-changing "new" technologies. Children who create online content recognize that authorship is neither a solitary nor completely original enterprise. The implications of this for classroom practice are several. The practice of remixing provides an opportunity to discuss potential copyright infringements and websites that enable the legal use of licensed resources. Remixing also raises issues about grading and the need, perhaps, to rethink how classroom assignments are made. For instance, incorporating the concept of remixing into regular class assignments might involve students in creating new content that draws from their subject matter texts in combination with online resources and special techniques for producing new digital images. Black's (2008) point that youth who create derivative texts are "far from being 'mindless consumers' and reproducers of existing media" (p xiii) is an argument for encouraging students to actively engage with the ideological messages and materials of the original text. If the goal is to support students in becoming critical readers and writers, teachers need, of course, to provide class time for discussing the "new" texts. Similarly, student-designed websites might become (with the designer's permission) a launching point for social commentary and critique.

A PARTING THOUGHT

As illustrated in the literature reviewed here, children's and young people's uses of popular culture and literacy practices in both online and offline spaces provide numerous opportunities for theorizing and researching 21st-century literacy practices across media platforms that feature language as but one of several other modes of communication (imagery, sound, gesture, and performance). At the same time, students' uses of popular culture texts have led to creative and productive tensions in the field by rubbing up against some cherished and long-held beliefs about literacy instruction. My purpose in examining those tensions is motivated not by a desire to resolve them; nor is it fueled by a wish to bring closure to the debates surrounding them. Instead, I am attracted to the openings such debates offer for exploring further the textual and social practices that intersect popular culture and literacy research.

REFERENCES

Alvermann, D. E. (2006). Ned and Kevin: An online discussion that challenges the "not-yet-adult" cultural model. In K. Pahl & J. Rowsell (Eds.), *Travel notes from the new literacy studies* (pp. 39–56). Clevedon, UK: Multilingual Matters.

Alvermann, D. E. (2008). Commentary: Why bother theorizing adolescents' online literacies for classroom practice and research? *Journal of Adolescent & Adult Literacy, 52*, 8–19.

Alvermann, D. E., & Eakle, A. J. (2007). Dissolving learning boundaries: The doing, re-doing, and undoing of school. In D. Thiessen & A. Cook-Sather (Eds.), *International handbook of student experience in elementary and secondary school* (pp. 143–166). Dordrecht, The Netherlands: Springer.

Alvermann, D. E., Moon, J. S., & Hagood, M. C. (1999). *Popular culture in the classroom: Thinking and researching critical media literacy*. Newark, DE: International Reading Association and the National Reading Conference.

Ang, I. (1985). *Watching Dallas: Soap opera and the melodramatic imagination*. New York: Methuen.

Atkinson, S., & Nixon, H. (2005). Locating the subject: Teens online@ninemsn. *Discourse: Studies in the Cultural Politics of Education, 26*, 387–409.

Barton, D., Hamilton, M., & Ivanic, R. (Eds.). (2000). *Situated literacies: Reading and writing in context*. London: Routledge.

Beach, R., & O'Brien, D. (2008). Teaching popular culture texts in the classroom. In J. Coiro, M. Knobel, C. Lankshear, & D. J. Leu (Eds.), *The handbook of research on new literacies* (pp. 775–804). New York: Erlbaum/Taylor & Francis Group.

Bean, T. W., Bean, S. K., & Bean, K. F. (1999). Intergenerational conversations and two adolescents' multiple literacies: Implications for redefining content area literacy. *Journal of Adolescent & Adult Literacy, 42*(6), 438–448.

Bearne, E., & Wolstencroft, H. (2005). Playing with texts: The contribution of children's knowledge of computer narratives to their story writing. In J. Marsh & E. Millard (Eds.), *Popular literacies, childhood and schooling* (pp. 72–92). London: RoutledgeFalmer.

Beavis, C. (1998). Computer games, culture and curriculum. In I. Snyder (Ed.), *Page to screen* (pp. 234–255). London: Routledge.

Beavis, C. (2007). Writing, digital culture and English curriculum. *L1 – Educational Studies in Language and Literature, 7*(4), 23–44.

Beavis, C., Nixon, H., & Atkinson, S. (2005). LAN cafes: cafes, places of gathering, or sites of informal teaching and learning? *Education, Communication, & Information, 5*(1), 41–60.

Benjamin, W. (1992). *Illuminations.* (H. Arendt, Ed., H. Zohn, Trans.). London: Fontana. (Original work published in 1936)

Bhabba, H. K. (1994). *The location of culture.* New York: Routledge.

Bitz, M. (2008). The comic book project: Literacy outside (and inside) the box. In J. Flood, S. B. Heath, & D. Lapp (Eds.), *Handbook of research on teaching literacy through the communicative and visual arts: Volume II* (pp. 229–236). New York: Erlbaum/Taylor & Francis Group.

Black, R. W. (2007). Digital design: English language learners and reader reviews in online fiction. In M. Knobel & C. Lankshear (Eds.), *A new literacies sampler* (pp. 115–136). New York: Peter Lang.

Black, R. W. (2008). *Adolescents and online fan fiction.* New York: Peter Lang.

Botzakis, S. (2008). "I've gotten a lot out of reading comics": Poaching and lifelong literacy. *57th yearbook of the National Reading Conference* (pp. 119–129). Oak Creek, WI: National Reading Conference.

Bourdieu, P. (1991). *Language and symbolic power* (G. Raymond & M. Adamson, Trans.). Cambridge, MA: Harvard University Press. (Original work published 1982)

Bruce, D. L. (2008). Multimedia production as composition. In J. Flood, S. B. Heath, & D. Lapp (Eds.), *Handbook of research on teaching literacy through the communicative and visual arts: Volume II* (pp. 13–18). New York: Taylor & Francis.

Buckingham, D. (1993). *Children talking television: The making of television literacy.* London: Falmer Press.

Buckingham, D., & Sefton–Green, J. (Eds.). (1994). *Cultural studies goes to school: Reading and teaching popular media.* London: Taylor & Francis.

Buckingham, D., & Sefton-Green, J. (2004). Structure, agency, and pedagogy in children's media culture. In J. Tobin (Ed.), *Pikachu's global adventure* (pp. 12–33). Durham, NC: Duke University Press.

Burn, A. (2007). 'Writing' computer games: Game literacy and new-old narratives. *Educational Studies in Langue and Literature, 7*(4), 45–67.

Burn, A. (2008). The case of Rebellion: Researching multimodal texts. In J. Coiro, M. Knobel, C. Lankshear, & D. J. Leu (Eds.), *Handbook of research on new literacies* (pp. 151–178). New York: Erlbaum/Taylor & Francis Group.

Burn, A., & Leach, J. (2004). ICT and moving image literacy in English. In R. Andrews (Ed.), *The impact of ICT on literacy education* (pp. 153–179).

Butler, J. (1997). *Excitable speech: A politics of the performative.* London: Routledge.

Camper, B. (2005, December). Reveling in restrictions: Technical mastery and Game Boy advance homebrew software. *Proceedings of the 6th DAC conference: Digital experience: Design, aesthetics, practice* (pp. 79–88). Copenhagen, Denmark: University of Copenhagen.

Carrington, V. (2003). 'I'm in a bad mood. Let's go shopping': Interactive dolls, consumer culture and a 'glocalized' model of literacy. *Journal of Early Childhood Literacy, 3*(1), 83–98.

Chan, C. (2006). Youth voice? Whose voice? Young people and youth media practice in Hong Kong. *McGill Journal of Education, 41,* 215–225.

Chandler-Olcott, K., & Mahar, D. (2003). "Tech-savviness" meets multiliteracies: Exploring adolescent girls' technology-mediated literacy practices. *Reading Research Quarterly, 38,* 356–385.

de Certeau, M. (1984). *The practice of everyday life.* Berkeley: University of California Press.

Dimitriadis, G. (2001). "In the clique": Popular culture, constructions of place, and the everyday lives of urban youth. *Anthropology & Education Quarterly, 32*(1), 29–51.

Dolby, N. (2003). Popular culture and democratic practice. *Harvard Educational Review, 73,* 258–284.

Duff, P. A. (2004). Intertextuality and hybrid discourses: The infusion of pop culture in educational discourse. *Linguistics and Education, 14,* 231–276.

Dutro, E., & Zenkov, K. (2008). Urban students testifying to their own stories: Talking back to deficit perspectives. *57th Yearbook of the National Reading Conference* (pp. 172–186). Oak Creek, WI: National Reading Conference.

Dyson, A. H. (1993). *The social worlds of children learning to write in an urban primary school.* New York: Teachers College Press.

Dyson, A. H. (1994). The Ninjas, the X–Men, and the ladies: Playing with power and identity in an urban primary school. *Teacher College Record, 96,* 219–239.

Dyson, A. H. (1997). *Writing superheroes: Contemporary childhood, popular culture, and classroom literacy.* New York: Teachers College Press.

Dyson, A. H. (2003a). Popular literacies and the "all" children: Rethinking literacy development for contemporary childhoods. *Language Arts, 81,* 100–109.

Dyson, A. H. (2003b). *The brothers and sisters learn to write: Popular literacies in childhood and school cultures.* New York: Teachers College Press.

Dyson, A. H. (2003c). "Welcome to the jam": Popular culture, school literacy, and the making of childhoods. *Harvard Educational Review, 71,* 328–361.

Finders, M. J. (1996). Early adolescent females reading their way toward adulthood. *Anthropology and Education Quarterly, 28,* 467–492.

Finders, M. J. (1997). *Just girls: Hidden literacies and life in junior high.* New York: Teachers College Press.

Fisher, M. T. (2007). *Writing in rhythm: Spoken word poetry in urban classrooms.* New York: Teachers College Press.

Fiske, J. (1989). *Understanding popular culture.* New York: Routledge.

Gee, J. P. (1990). *Social linguistics and literacies: Ideology in discourses.* London: Falmer.

Gee, J. P. (2003). *What video games have to teach us about learning and literacy.* New York: Palgrave Macmillan.

Gee, J. P. (2007). Pleasure, learning, video games, and life: The projective stance. In M. Knobel & C. Lankshear (Eds.), *A new literacies sampler* (pp. 95–113). New York: Peter Lang.

Gilroy, P. (1992). Against ethnic absolutism. In L. Grossberg, C. Nelson, & P. Treichler (Eds.), *Cultural studies* (pp. 188–199). London: Routledge.

Grace, D. J., & Tobin, J. (1998). Butt jokes and mean-teacher parodies: Video production in the elementary classroom. In D. Buckingham (Ed.), *Teaching popular culture: Beyond radical pedagogy* (pp. 42–62). London: University College London Press.

Green, B. (1988). Subject-specific literacy and school learning: A focus on writing. *Australian Journal of Education, 32*(3), 156–179.

Green, B., & Bigum, C. (1993). Aliens in the classroom. *Australian Journal of Education, 37*(2), 119–141.

Guins, R., & Cruz, O. Z. (Eds.). (2005). *Popular culture.* Thousand Oaks, CA: Sage.

Gustavson, L. (2008). Influencing pedagogy through the creative practices of youth. In M. L. Hill & L. Vasudevan (Eds.), *Media, learning, and sites of possibility* (pp. 81–114). New York: Peter Lang.

Guzzetti, B. J. (2004, April). *Hanging out and around: Roles, relations, and realities of research in information settings.* Paper presented at the annual meeting of the American Educational Research Association, San Diego, CA.

Guzzetti, B. J., & Gamboa, M. (2004). Zines for social justice: Adolescent girls writing on their own. *Reading Research Quarterly, 39,* 408–436.

Hagood, M. C. (2004). A rhizomatic cartography of adolescents, popular culture, and constructions of self. In K. M. Leander & M. Sheehy (Eds.), *Spatializing literacy research and practice* (pp. 143–160). New York: Peter Lang.

Hagood, M. C. (2008). Intersections of popular culture, identities, and new literacies research. In J. Coiro, M. Knobel, C. Lankshear, & D. J. Leu (Eds.), *Handbook of research on new literacies* (pp. 531–551). New York: Erlbaum/Taylor & Francis Group.

Hall, S. (1981). Notes on deconstructing "the popular." In R. Samuel (Ed.), *People's history and socialist thought* (pp. 227–240). London: Routledge & Kegan Paul.

Heath, S. B. (1983). *Ways with words: Language, life, and work in communities and classrooms.* Cambridge, UK: Cambridge University Press.

Heron-Hruby, A., & Alvermann, D. E. (2009). Implications of adolescents' popular culture use for school literacy. In K. D. Wood & W. E. Blanton (Eds.), *Literacy instruction for adolescents: Research-based practices* (pp. 210–227). New York: Guilford.

Hobbs, R. (2007). *Reading the media: Media literacy in high school English.* New York: Teachers College Press.

Hoechsmann, M., & Low, B. E. (2008). *Reading youth writing:" New" literacies, cultural studies & education.* New York: Peter Lang.

Hoggart, R. (1957). *The uses of literacy.* New York: Oxford University Press.

Horkheimer, M., & Adorno, T. W. (1972). *Dialectic of enlightenment.* New York: Seabury.

Hull, G., & Schultz, K. (Eds.). (2002). *School's out: Bridging out-of-school literacies with classroom practice.* New York: Teachers College Press.

Ito, M., & Okabe, D. (2005). Intimate connections: Contextualizing Japanese youth and mobile messaging. In R. Harper, L. Palen, & A. Taylor (Eds.), *The inside text: Social, cultural and design perspectives on SMS* (pp. 127–146). Dordrecht, The Netherlands: Springer.

Ito, M., Okabe, D., & Matsuda, M. (Eds.). (2005). *Personal, portable, pedestrian: Mobile phones in Japanese life.* Cambridge, MA: The MIT Press.

Jenkins, H. (1992). *Textual poachers: Television fans and participatory culture.* London: Routledge.

Jenkins, H. (2006). *Convergence culture: Where old and new media collide.* New York: New York University Press.

Jewitt, C. (2008). Multimodality and literacy in school classrooms. In G. J. Kelly, A. Luke, & J. Green (Eds.), *Review of Research in Education, 32,* 241–267.

Jewitt, C., & Kress, G. (Eds.). (2003). *Multimodal literacy.* New York: Peter Lang.

Kellner, D. (1995). *Media culture.* New York: Routledge.

Kenway, J., & Bullen, E. (2001). *Consuming children: Education—entertainment—advertising.* Buckingham, UK: Open University Press.

Kirkland, D. (2008a). Shaping the digital pen: Media literacy, youth culture, and Myspace. *Youth Media Reporter.* Retrieved May 18, 2009, from http://www.youthmediareporter.org/2008/08/shaping_the_digital_pen_media.html

Kirkland, D. (2008b). "The rose that grew from concrete": Hip hop and the new English education. *The English Journal, 97*(5), 69–75.

Kist, W. (2008). Film and video in the classroom: Back to the future. In J. Flood, S. B. Heath, & D. Lapp (Eds.), *Handbook of research on teaching literacy through the communicative and visual arts: Volume II* (pp. 521–527). New York: Erlbaum/Taylor & Francis Group.

Knobel, M. (1999). *Everyday literacies.* New York: Peter Lang.

Knobel, M., & Lankshear, C. (2002). Cut, paste, and publish: The production and consumption of zines. In D. E. Alvermann (Ed.), *Adolescents and literacies in a digital world* (pp. 164–185). New York: Peter Lang.

Knobel, M., & Lankshear, C. (2007). Online memes, affinities, and cultural production. In M. Knobel & C. Lankshear (Eds.), *A new literacies sampler* (pp. 192–227). New York: Peter Lang.

Knobel, M., & Lankshear, C. (2008). Remix: The art and craft of endless hybridization. *Journal of Adolescent & Adult Literacy, 52,* 22–33.

Kress, G. (1998). Visual and verbal modes of representation in electronically mediated communication: The potentials of new forms of text. In I. Snyder (Ed.), *Page to screen: Taking literacy into the electronic age* (pp. 53–79). London: Routledge.

Kress, G. (2003). *Literacy in the new media age.* London: Routledge.

Kress, G., & van Leeuwen, T. (1996). *Reading images: The grammar of visual design.* London: Routledge.

Labbo, L. (1996). A semiotic analysis of young children's symbol making in a classroom computer center. *Reading Research Quarterly, 32,* 356–385.

Lankshear, C., & Knobel, M. (2002). Do we have your attention? New literacies, digital technologies, and the education of adolescents. In D. E. Alvermann (Ed.), *Adolescents and literacies in a digital world* (pp. 19–39). New York: Peter Lang.

Lankshear, C., & Knobel, M. (2007). Researching new literacies: Web 2.0 practices and insider perspectives. *E-Learning, 4*(3), 224–240.

Latour, B. (1987). *Science in action.* Cambridge, MA: Harvard University Press.

Leander, K. M., & Lovvorn, J. (2006). Literacy networks: Following the circulation of texts, bodies, and objects in the schooling and online gaming of one youth. *Cognition & Instruction, 24,* 291–340.

Lemke, J. (1989). Social semiotics: A new model for literacy education. In D. Bloome (Ed.), *Classrooms and literacy* (pp. 289–309). Norwood, NJ: Ablex.

Lenhart, A., Madden, M., Macgill, A. R., & Smith, A. (2007, December). Teens and social media. *PEW Internet & American Life Project*. Washington, DC: PEW Charitable Trusts. Retrieved October 15, 2008, from http://www.pewinternet.org/PPF/r/230/report_display.asp

Lesley, M. (2008). Access and resistance to dominant forms of discourse: Critical literacy and "at risk" high school students. *Literacy Research and Instruction, 47,* 174–194.

Lewis, C., & Fabos, B. (2005). Instant messaging, literacies, and social identities. *Reading Research Quarterly, 40,* 470–501.

Lévy, P. (1997). *Collective intelligence: Mankind's emerging world in cyberspace*. Cambridge, MA: Perseus Books.

Lowenthal, L. (1961). *Literature, popular culture and society*. Palo Alto, CA: Pacific Books.

LucasArts & Sony Online Entertainment. (2003). *Star Wars Galaxies: An empire divided*. [For a video review of this massively multiplayer online roleplaying game (MMORG) see http://www.gamespot.com/video/468222/6071089/star-wars-galaxies-an-empire-divided-video-review] [For background on the MMORG, see http://en.wikipedia.org/wiki/MMORPG]. Retrieved February 14, 2008.

Luke, A., & Freebody, P. (1997). Shaping the social practices of reading. In S. Muspratt, A. Luke, & P. Freebody (Eds.), *Constructing critical literacies: Teaching and learning textual practice* (pp. 185–225). Cresskill, NJ: Hampton.

Luke, C. (1997). Media literacy and cultural studies. In S. Muspratt, A. Luke, & P. Freebody (Eds.), *Constructing critical literacies: Teaching and learning textual practice* (pp. 19–49). Cresskill, NJ: Hampton.

Luke, C. (2003). Pedagogy, connectivity, multimodality, and interdisciplinarity. *Reading Research Quarterly, 38,* 397–403.

Mackey, M. (2003). Researching new forms of literacy. *Reading Research Quarterly, 38,* 403–407.

Mahiri, J. (1998). *Shooting for excellence: African American and youth culture in new century schools*. Urbana, IL: National Council of Teachers of English/Teachers College Press.

Marcuse, H. (1968). *One dimensional man*. London: Sphere.

Marsh, J. (2005). Tightropes, tactics and taboos: Preservice teachers' beliefs and practices in relation to popular culture and literacy. In J. Marsh & E. Millard (Eds.), *Popular literacies, childhood and schooling* (pp. 179–199). London: RoutledgeFalmer.

Marsh, J. (2006). Popular culture in the literacy curriculum: A Bourdieuan analysis. *Reading Research Quarterly, 41,* 160–174.

Marsh, J. (2008). Popular culture in the language arts classroom. In J. Flood, S. B. Heath, & D. Lapp (Eds.), *Handbook of research on teaching literacy through the communicative and visual arts: Volume II* (pp. 529–536). New York: Erlbaum/Taylor & Francis Group.

Marsh, J., Brooks, G., Hughes, J., Ritchie, L., Roberts, S., & Wright, K. (2005) *Digital beginnings: Young children's use of popular culture, media and new technologies*. Sheffield, UK: University of Sheffield. Retrieved November 20, 2007, from http://www.digitalbeginnings.shef.ac.uk

Marsh, J., & Millard, E. (2000). *Literacy and popular culture: Using children's culture in the classroom*. London: Paul Chapman.

Marsh, J., & Millard, E. (Eds.). (2005). *Popular literacies, childhood and schooling*. London: Routledge/Falmer.

Maxwell, J. A. (2006). Literature reviews of, and for, educational research: A commentary on Boote and Beile's "Scholars before researchers." *Educational Researcher, 35*(9), 28–31.

McRobbie, A. (1994). *Postmodernism and popular culture*. London: Routledge.

McVee, M. B., Bailey, N. M., & Shanahan, L.E. (2008). Using digital media to interpret poetry: Spiderman meets Walt Whitman. *Research in the Teaching of English, 43*(2), 112–143.

Merchant, G. (2001). Teenagers in cyberspace: An investigation of language use and language change in internet chatrooms. *Journal of Research in Reading, 24,* 293–306.

Miller, S. M. (2008). Teacher learning for new times: Repurposing new multimodal literacies and digital-video composing for schools. In J. Flood, S. B. Heath, & D. Lapp (Eds.), *Handbook of research on teaching literacy through the communicative and visual arts: Volume II* (pp. 441–453). New York: Erlbaum/Taylor & Francis Group.

Moje, E. B. (2000). "To be part of the story": The literacy practices of gangsta adolescents. *Teachers College Record, 102,* 652–690.

Moje, E. B. (2008). Youth cultures, literacies, and identities in and out of school. In J. Flood, S. B. Heath,

& D. Lapp (Eds.), *Handbook of research on teaching literacy through the communicative and visual arts: Volume II* (pp. 207–219). New York: Erlbaum/Taylor & Francis Group.

Moje, E. B., Overby, M., Tysvaer, N., & Morris, K. (2008). The complex world of adolescent literacy: Myths, motivations, and mysteries. *Harvard Educational Review, 78,* 107–154.

Moje, E. B., & van Helden, C. (2005). Doing popular culture: Troubling discourses about youth. In J. A. Vadeboncoeur & L. P. Stevens (Ed.), *Re/constructing "the adolescent": Sign, symbol, and body* (pp. 211–247). New York: Peter Lang.

Morrell, E. (2004). *Linking literacy and popular culture: Finding connections for lifelong learning.* Norwood, MA: Christopher-Gordon.

Morrell, E., & Duncan-Andrade, J. (2002). Toward a critical classroom discourse: Promoting academic literacy through engaging hip-hop culture with urban youth. *English Journal, 91*(6), 88–94.

Morrison, T. (1994). *The bluest eye.* New York: Plume/Penguin.

New London Group. (1996). A pedagogy of multiliteracies: Designing social futures. *Harvard Educational Review, 66,* 60–92.

Norton, B. (2003). The motivating power of comic books: Insights from Archie comic readers. *The Reading Teacher, 57,* 140–147.

O'Brien, D. (1998). Multiple literacies in a high-school program for "at-risk" adolescents. In D. E. Alvermann, K. A. Hinchman, D. W. Moore, S. F. Phelps, & D. R. Waff (Eds.), *Reconceptualizing the literacies in adolescents' lives* (pp. 27–49). Mahwah, NJ: Erlbaum.

O'Brien, D., Beach, R., & Scharber, C. (2007). "Struggling" middle schoolers: Engagement and literate competence in a reading writing intervention class. *Reading Psychology, 28,* 51–73.

Pahl, K. (2005). Narrative spaces and multiple identities: Children's textual explorations of console games in home settings. In J. Marsh (Ed.), *Popular culture, new media and digital literacy in early childhood* (pp. 126–145). London: RoutledgeFalmer.

Primary National Strategy (PNS)/United Kingdom Literacy Association (UKLA). (2004). *Raising boys' achievement in writing.* London: PNS/UKLA. Retrieved April 12, 2008, from http://www.standards.dfes.gov.uk/primary/publications/literacy/1094843/pns_ukla_boys094304report.pdf

Ranker, J. (2006). "There's fire magic, electric magic, ice magic, or poison magic": The world of video games and Adrian's compositions about *Gauntlet Legends. Language Arts, 84,* 21–33.

Reinking, D. (2005). Multimedia learning of reading. In R.E. Mayer (Ed.), *The Cambridge handbook of multimedia learning* (pp. 355–374). New York: Cambridge University Press.

Robinson, M. (1997). *Children reading print and television.* London: Falmer.

Rogers, T., Winters, K., & LaMonde, A. M. (in press). From image to ideology: Analyzing shifting identity positions of marginalized youth across the cultural sites of video production. *Pedagogies: An International Journal.*

Rymes, (B.). (2004). Contrasting zones of comfortable competence: Popular culture in a phonics lesson. *Linguistics and Education, 14,* 321–335.

Sefton-Green, J. (2003). Informal learning: Substance or style? *Teaching Education, 12,* 37–52.

Sefton-Green, J. (2006). Youth, technology, and media cultures. *Review of Research in Education, 30,* 279–306.

Shakur, T. (1999). *The rose that grew from concrete.* New York: MTV.

Shared Spaces Project. (2003). Center for the Study of Children, Youth and Media. Institute of Education, University of London. Retrieved January 28, 2008, from http://www.wac.co.uk/sharedspaces/index.php

Skinner, E. (2007). "Teenage addiction": Adolescent girls drawing upon popular culture texts as mentors for writing in an after-school writing club. *National Reading Conference Yearbook, 56* (pp. 345–361). Oak Creek, WI: National Reading Conference.

Sperling, M., & DiPardo, A. (2008). English education research and classroom practices: New directions for new times. *Review of Research in Education, 32,* 62–108.

Spires, H., Lee, J., Turner, K., & Johnson, J. (2008). Having our say: Middle grade student perspectives on school, technologies, and academic engagement. *Journal of Research in Techology on Education, 40,* 497–515.

Squire, K. (2008). Video-game literacy: A literacy of expertise. In J. Coiro, M. Knobel, C. Lankshear, & D. J. Leu (Eds.), *The handbook of research on new literacies* (pp. 635–669). New York: Erlbaum/Taylor & Francis Group.

Stein, P. (2007). *Multimodal pedagogies in diverse classrooms: Representation, rights and resources*. New York: Routledge.

Steinkuehler, C. A. (2006). Massively multiplayer online video gaming as participation in a discourse. *Mind, Culture, & Activity, 13*, 38–52.

Stone, J. C. (2007). Popular websites in adolescents' out-of-school lives: Critical lessons on literacy. In C. Lankshear & M. Knobel (Eds.), *A new literacies sampler* (pp. 49–65). New York: Peter Lang.

Street, B. V. (1984). *Literacy in theory and practice*. Cambridge, UK: Cambridge University Press.

Street, B. V. (1995). *Social literacies: Critical approaches to literacy in development, ethnography and education*. New York: Longman.

Sutherland, L.M. (2005). Black adolescent girls' use of literacy practices to negotiate boundaries of ascribed identity. *Journal of Literacy Research, 37*, 365–406.

Thomas, A. (2007). *Youth online: Identity and literacy in the digital age*. New York: Peter Lang.

Tierney, R. J. (2008). The agency and artistry of meaning makers within and across digital spaces. In S. E. Israel & G. G. Duffy (Eds.), *Handbook of research on reading comprehension* (pp. 261–288). New York: Erlbaum/Taylor & Francis Group.

Vadeboncoeur, J. A. (2006). Engaging young people: Learning in informal contexts. *Review of Research in Education, 30*, 239–278.

Warschauer, M., & Ware, P. (2008). Learning, change, and power: Competing frames of technology and literacy. In J. Coiro, M. Knobel, C. Lankshear, & D. J. Leu (Eds.), *The handbook of research on new literacies* (pp. 215–240). New York: Erlbaum/Taylor & Francis Group.

Williams, R. (1961). *The long revolution*. New York: Columbia University Press.

Willis, P. (1990). *Common culture: Symbolic work at play in the everyday cultures of the young*. Boulder, CO: Westview.

Xu, S. H. (2004). Teachers' reading of students' popular culture texts: The interplay of students' interests, teacher knowledge, and literacy curriculum. *53rd yearbook of the National Reading Conference* (pp. 417–431). Oak Creek, WI: National Reading Conference.

Yardi, S. (2008). Whispers in the classroom. In T. McPherson (Ed.), *Digital youth, innovation, and the unexpected* (pp. 143–164). (The John D. and Catherine T. MacArthur Foundation Series on Digital Media and Learning). Cambridge, MA: The MIT Press.

24 Reading Policy in the Era of Accountability

Cynthia E. Coburn, P. David Pearson, and Sarah Woulfin
University of California, Berkeley

The last two decades have witnessed a dramatic upsurge in policy making related to reading instruction. Several high profile policy initiatives place reading instruction squarely at the center of reform policy; moreover, those initiatives employ new policy mechanisms that reach down into the classroom in unprecedented ways. In the time since publication of the third edition of the *Handbook of Reading Research*, Congress passed No Child Left Behind, spreading high stakes accountability policy to states and districts across the nation. Since reading achievement sits at the core of many state accountability policies, NCLB has dramatically raised the stakes for student performance on standardized tests in reading, placing new pressure on teachers, schools, and districts to improve reading achievement.

In addition, many states and districts have responded to these accountability demands with their own policy making. For example, districts across the country have adopted new reading textbooks districtwide, linking them with pacing guides, increased professional development, and progress monitoring assessments. Finally, this time period has witnessed two federal initiatives specifically devoted to improving reading instruction: Reading Excellence Act and, more recently, Reading First. Reading First is distinctive in the history of educational policy making for the degree to which the federal government and states have specified appropriate instructional practice, focused on fidelity to curricular materials, and introduced extensive monitoring of teacher practice.

The increased policy attention on reading instruction and the use of new and aggressive policy instruments is bringing policy into classrooms as never before. Now, more than ever, the study of instructional policy is crucial for understanding the nature of reading instruction in our nation's public schools. To that end, this chapter provides a comprehensive review of empirical research on reading policy since publication of the third edition of the *Handbook of Reading Research*. After a brief review of recent trends in state and federal policy making in reading, we review studies related to elementary reading instruction in three parts: the dynamics of policy making in reading, the relationship between reading policy and teachers' classroom practice, and, ultimately, the impact of these policy initiatives on student achievement. In so doing, we trace the pathways from policy making through implementation and, finally, policy outcomes. Throughout, we paint a portrait of the state of research on reading policy as growing, but incomplete. We highlight key findings and point out areas that are ripe for future inquiry.

OVERVIEW OF READING POLICY

Policy makers have engaged in unprecedented efforts to use policy as a lever to improve teaching and learning in reading instruction in recent years. Throughout the 1990s, the country was in the midst of the evolving standards movement. Encouraged by federal Goals 2000 funds, state after state enacted new state standards in different content areas including reading and language arts. Based on the logic of systemic reform (Smith & O'Day, 1990), these standards tended to put forth ambitious visions of teaching and learning, which were then linked with state assessments to monitor progress and professional development to build teacher capacity. The basic idea was for states to put forth a vision of valued learning outcomes and use standardized tests to measure the degree to which schools met those outcomes, at the same time allowing local schools and districts the flexibility in deciding *how* to meet those outcomes (Cross, Riley, & Sanders, 2004). By 1995–1996, 48 states and the District of Columbia had developed academic standards and 42 states had implemented or were developing assessments aligned with academic standards (Gandal, 1996). For example, Michigan enacted a series of legislative mandates in the late 1980s and early 1990s that leveraged Goals 2000 funds to develop an academic core curriculum in key subject areas. The result was the Michigan English Language Arts Framework (MELAF), which developed integrated standards in English Language Arts. Those standards were intended to guide district efforts to develop a core curriculum as required by law (Birdyshaw, Pesko, Wixson, & Yochum, 2002; Borman & Cusick, 2002). The state subsequently used MELAF to guide revision of the state assessment—the Michigan Educational Assessment Program (MEAP)—so that state assessments were aligned with state standards. Finally, the state embarked on a program of professional development to local districts to build district and school capacity to enact the vision of ambitious teaching and learning embodied by the standards (Dutro, Fisk, Koch, Roop, & Wixson, 2002; Jennings, 1996).

At the same time that states were engaged in adopting standards in reading and other content areas, low reading scores on the 1992 and 1994 National Assessment of Educational Progress led to widespread perception of a crisis in reading instruction by the mid-1990s (Colvin, 1995). States responded by enacting additional legislation that focused specifically on early reading instruction. Most of these laws provided funds to support professional development for teachers and the purchase of instructional materials that focused on phonics and phonemic awareness. For example, in 1995, the state legislature in California adopted AB 170, which required that basic instructional materials in math and reading in grades 1–8 emphasized basic skills including phonics and spelling. Later, they adopted two additional bills (AB 3482 in 1996 and AB 1086 in 1997) that appropriated $89.4 million for professional development emphasizing phonics and phonemic awareness for K–3 and later 4–8 teachers throughout the state (California State Board of Education, 1999). By 1999, 36 states had bills that were passed or pending that promoted the use of phonics-based materials or provided professional development for teachers in instructional approaches to phonics or phonemic awareness (Pearson, 2004).

By the late 1990s, the federal government got in the action and began passing legislation specifically targeting reading instruction as well. In 1998, congress passed the Reading Excellence Act (P.L. 105-277) with the stated purpose of improving students' reading skills and teachers' instructional practice by using methods based in scientifically-based reading research (Edmondson, 2005; Mesmer & Karchmer, 2003). This legislation created a program of competitive state grants to provide staff development and tutorial assistance to low-performing and high-poverty districts. All professional development approaches and materials for children paid for under this grant program had to be supported by research that was considered "scientifically based." In this case, "scientifically based" was defined as employing systematic methods, using rigorous data analysis, valid and reliable measures, and being published in peer-reviewed publications. The legislation was significant because it was the first time that the federal government legislated a definition of reading instruction. It also marked the beginning of the press for "scientifically-based" research in federal legislation in education (Edmondson, 2005; Eisenhardt & Towne, 2003).[1] Like standards-based reform, this approach to policy making at the federal and state level tended to place its bets on impacting teachers' classroom practice and student learning by focusing on the materials that teachers used and building teacher capacity through professional development. However, these policies also tended to specify instructional practices with much greater precision than state standards and, in some cases, states linked funds with the use of specific curriculum materials, often those certified to be based on scientific research.

As the 1990s drew to a close, policy makers at the state, federal, and even district level began to shift toward a new policy strategy to improve reading instruction: test-based accountability. While state standards remained in place, this shift placed increased emphasis on testing by linking performance on standardized tests to a program of sanctions and rewards (Hamilton, Stecher, & Klein, 2002). Reading instruction was often at the center of these policy initiatives because most states include test scores in reading as a central part of their accountability formulae.

Several states led the way with high stakes accountability policies focused on reading instruction. For example, in 1993, the state legislature in Texas adopted their state accountability system. This system included the adoption of a statewide curriculum known as Texas Essential Knowledge and Skills (TEKS), a statewide assessment system, and the development of an extensive data system to monitor school and student progress (Haney, 2000; Vazquez Heilig, & Darling-Hammond, 2008). The accountability system was then updated in 1999 to better align TEKS with the state assessment, expand testing to all students in grades 3–8, and link passing the state test in reading and mathematics with promotion in grades 3, 5, and 8 (Texas Education Agency, 2002). A central feature of the accountability system in Texas was school performance ranking. All schools were assigned the rank of exemplary, recognized, acceptable, or unacceptable based on their test scores in reading and mathematics in elementary and middle school, dropout rates, and student attendance.[2] In a move that foreshadowed No Child Left Behind, student performance data were disaggregated by ethnicity and socioeconomic status, and school rankings were based on student performance in all categories. Schools were awarded cash awards for high performance and were subject to sanctions, including the possibility of school closure, if they missed performance targets for two years in a row (Haney, 2000).[3] Although each a bit different in design, Massachusetts, Kentucky, and Maryland were other early adopters of high stakes accountability policies as were some local school districts such as Chicago and Philadelphia (Mintrop & Trujillo, 2005).

High stakes accountability subsequently became the predominant policy strategy across the country with the passage No Child Left Behind (P.L. 107-110), which was signed into law in 2002 after receiving widespread bipartisan support in Congress. This sweeping federal legislation tied receipt of federal Title 1 funds to the development of a single statewide accountability system with annual tests in reading and mathematics (and, later, science) for students in grades 3–8. States were also required to set improvement targets such that all students reach proficiency by 2014. And, they were required to create a series of increasingly serious sanctions such as state takeover if schools failed to make improvement targets for all subgroups of children (Fuhrman, 2004; Stecher, Hamilton, & Gonzalez, 2003). This legislation brought high stakes accountability—heretofore present only in select states and districts—to all states across the country.

A final major policy strategy implicating reading instruction also emerged in the late 1990s and early part of the 21st century: mandated curricula. This policy strategy appears to have developed as local school districts in different regions of the country began to see mandated curricula as a strategy to improve reading achievement. Districts across the country not only began to mandate a single curriculum for the entire district, they began to link the curricula to pacing guides, progress monitoring assessments, and monitoring to ensure fidelity to the instructional approaches embodied in the chosen curriculum (Sloan, 2006; Snipes, Doolittle, & Herlihy, 2002; Achinstein & Ogawa, 2006).

This strategy subsequently gained a much higher profile when it was embedded in the federal Reading First policy. Reading First, part of NCLB (Title 1, Part B, Subpart 1), was a competitive state grant program intended to assist low-income, low-performing schools in raising student reading achievement (USED, Moss, Fountain, Boulay, Horst, et al., 2008). To receive funds, states had to develop plans for increasing teachers' use of scientifically-based instructional approaches through the adoption of scientifically-based curricular materials.[4] Drawing on the influential meta-study from the congressionally-mandated National Reading Panel (NRP), Reading First also focused attention on what has come to be called the "big five": phonemic awareness, phonics, fluency (instantiated as either guided reading instruction or independent reading), comprehension, and vocabulary.[5] Finally, Reading First emphasized diagnosis and prevention of early reading difficulties through the use of valid and reliable assessments, interventions for struggling students, and ongoing monitoring of struggling students (Gamse, Jacob, Horst, Boulay, & Unlu, 2008; United States Department of Education, 2002; United States Department of Education, 2004).

Like the Reading Excellence Act, Reading First provided funds for the use of "scientifically-based" materials and professional development to ensure that teachers used them as intended. But Reading First also intensified the policy intervention by linking the curricular materials to the use of progress monitoring assessment (for example, the DIBELS assessments, which were adopted by many states), providing stronger guidance about how curricular materials should be used, and instituting the use of school-based coaching to provide on-site professional development. Many states also stipulated that teachers in Reading First schools use the adopted curriculum and interventions with fidelity and put procedures in place to monitor teachers' instructional practice to ensure fidelity to implementation. For example, Massachusetts' Reading First program proposed a comprehensive instructional program, including state-selected core, supplemental, and intensive intervention programs, aligned with reading research as represented in the NRP report and the state's English Language Arts framework (Massachusetts Department of Education, 2005a, p. 3). To monitor implementation at the state, district, and school levels, the state department of education relied on their consistent assessment system and implementation evaluations. The state conducted school site visits, in part to monitor implementation of the use of core reading program, materials, and assessments (Massachusetts Department of Education, 2005b, p. 17). Reading First also unfolded in the context of high stakes accountability provided by NCLB, so the underperforming schools targeted by Reading First were often experiencing the increased sanctions associated with NCLB as well.

It is important to note that with Reading First, research played a new role in impacting policy, curriculum, and practice. In the past, research had been regarded as one among many information sources consulted in policy formation—including expert testimony from practitioners, information about school organization and finance, and evaluations of compelling cases. In the case of Reading First, scientific research was the driver of the system and the basis on which the standards for the primary policy levers—curriculum, assessment, and professional development—were established. This was not the benign, "sowing the seeds of knowledge" logic of marketplace of ideas. It was reform by mandate and monitoring. Above all, the enactment of Reading First in NCLB meant that research had become a full participant in the policy arena.

Three final things are worth noting about the policy-making activity during this time period. First, it was extensive. The last two decades has witnessed unprecedented policy attention to reading instruction as states and the federal government have become increasingly and actively involved in crafting policies and programs intended to improve student achievement in reading instruction. Second, it was layered. Each wave of policy activity, rather than supplanting earlier policy initiatives, tended to layer new policies on top of pre-existing ones. For example, the adoption of state standards during the standards movement in the late 1980s and early 1990s became linked to high stakes assessment at the dawn of the accountability movement in the mid 1990s (Fuhrman, 2004; Hamilton et al., 2002). Many districts responded to the accountability movement by mandating districtwide curriculum adoptions, which they then monitored with benchmark assessments and attention to test score performance (Achinstein & Ogawa, 2006). Reading First intensified this trend for those schools that received Reading First monies. As a result, schools tended to experience the cumulation and intensification of policy initiatives. Finally, the policy making was serious. The past decade and a half witnessed the use of new and more aggressive policy instruments. Over the course of different policy movements, guidance to schools and teachers became increasingly specified as it moved from the logic of standards (putting forth broad goals and assessing outcomes, but leaving flexibility to local sites in enacting those goals) to mandated curriculum linked with assessments, pacing guides, and close monitoring for fidelity. At the same time, stakes for student performance have increased over time with the advent of test-based accountability linked with sanctions and rewards. These waves of policy have reached into classrooms to change the core activities of reading instruction.

LITERATURE REVIEW

In the rest of this chapter, we review studies that investigate the causes, processes, and consequences of these policy initiatives. In bounding our review, we focused on studies concerned with reading policy that implicated instruction in grades K through 5 and that were published from 1999 until the present. To be included in the review, articles needed to (a) be empirical (rather than essays or opinion or advocacy pieces), (b) have been published in peer-reviewed journals, and (c) have met standards for scholarly articles (for example, we excluded articles that did not have a methodology section). We made one exception to these criteria. Because of the proximity of this review to passage, enactment, and demise of Reading First, we found very few articles published in peer-reviewed journals that investigated Reading First. Given the importance of this policy initiative, we decided to include federally-funded evaluation studies in five states with some of the largest Reading First grants (California, Texas, Florida, Illinois, and Pennsylvania)[6] as well as select cross-state evaluations of Reading First published by research firms that secured contracts to conduct the evaluations. To locate peer-reviewed journal articles, we searched the indexes for all of the major journals of reading instruction, policy, leadership, and general education from 1999 until the present.[7] We also reviewed reference lists in articles we located to point us toward other articles that might have missed. All told, we identified 121 studies of reading policy during this time period and included 87 articles that met our criteria in this review.

In the sections that follow, we review this literature in three parts. First, we review research on the dynamics of policy making in reading instruction. This small body of studies investigates the process of policy making, seeking to uncover how some ideas become embedded in policies and not others and the role of key actors in this process. Given the attention to scientifically-based research in recent legislation, we pay careful attention to studies that investigate the role of research in policy-making activity. Second, we review studies that investigate the process of policy implementation. Here, we review studies that investigate how teachers respond to policy initiatives in their classroom and the individual, organizational, and policy factors that influence when and how teachers respond in particular ways. Finally, we review studies that investigate the impact of policy on student achievement, with a special focus on the impact of Reading First.

READING INSTRUCTION AND THE POLICY-MAKING PROCESS

As reading instruction has become a high profile part of education policy making at both the state and federal level, it has become of increasing interest to reading researchers. In the time since the last *Handbook* edition, reading researchers and others have begun to turn their attention to the dynamics of policy making in reading, perhaps for the first time. Much of the writing about policy making by reading researchers focused on analyzing the degree to which reading legislation is rooted in reading research. This is not surprising given that claims that particular practices supported by legislation are "research-based" and arguments about which research is "scientifically based" have become a central feature of contemporary reading policy debates (Eisenhardt & Towne, 2003; Pearson, 2004). Beyond analysis of the degree to which legislation is research-based, a small group of scholars have also investigated the process by which particular ideas about reading instruction became a part of policy initiatives, asking: What is the process by which some ideas and not others become prominent in the policy arena and become embedded in legislation? Here, we review both of these lines of research.

Most of the literature on policy making in reading has focused on the role of reading research in the policy-making process. Some of this work has analyzed actual pieces of legislation—Reading First, the Reading Excellence Act, or state reading frameworks—to determine the degree to which they are rooted in research (Camilli et al., 2003; Camilli et al., 2006; Pearson, 2004; Pressley & Fingeret, 2007). Other researchers analyze documents that have played prominent roles in the policy-making process, like the National Reading Panel Report (NICHD, 2000) or Bonnie Grossen's "white paper" (1997), which appears to have played an important role in the formation of the California reading policy in the late 1990s (Allington, 1999; Allington & Woodside-Jiron, 1999; Dressman, 1999; Pressley & Fingeret, 2007; Snow, 2000; Taylor, Anderson, Au, & Raphael, 2000). The general strategy of this genre is to examine the claims about best practices in reading put forth in these documents and legislation and analyze the degree to which they are supported by the existing research on reading. Although there is definitely disagreement about the degree to which various documents and legislation are rooted in research (see for example, exchange between Snow, 2000 and Gee, 1999), these studies find a pattern of overstatement of the strength of research findings (Allington & Woodside-Jiron, 1999; Camilli et al., 2003; Camilli et al., 2006; Pressley & Fingeret, 2007; Taylor et al., 2000) and an extrapolation of programmatic solutions from research on student learning, especially in legislation (Allington & Woodside-Jiron, 1999; Pearson, 2004). However, these articles do not analyze the actual policy processes involved. That is, they do not investigate how the particular vision of reading instruction came to be so prominent in state and federal legislation. They do not investigate how particular documents were used in the policy-making process or why these documents and not others came to be influential.

Fortunately, a small body of research has emerged during this time period that sought to address precisely these questions. First, several articles by Cecil Miskel and his colleagues sought to understand the dynamics of federal reading policy during the time leading up to passage of Reading First. Using social network analysis, document analysis, and interviews with key policy informants, this line of work investigates the dynamics of reading policy "issue networks." Issue networks are webs of linkages between people who are involved in and knowledgeable about a particular policy arena. Prior research outside of education has provided evidence that issue networks play a crucial role in policy making because they are the key mechanism through which those inside the policy system (legislatures, congressional staffers, White House staff, etc.) connect with those outside the system (advocacy organizations, researchers, professional organizations, etc.). Through their formal and informal relationships, those in issue networks influence others to support their point of view and mobilize to support particular policy solutions and not others. It is in the context of issue networks that public policies are debated, refined, and negotiated (Heclo, 1978; Kingdon, 1984; McFarland, 1992).

Miskel and his colleagues (McDaniel, Sims, & Miskel, 2001; Miskel & Song, 2004; Song & Miskel, 2005) found that in the late 1990s, the national issues network for reading instruction expanded greatly. They identified 131 organizations that were actively involved in shaping reading policy at the national level. These organizations included traditional reading policy actors such as reading professional organizations and the national teachers unions. But they also found that a host of new actors—including representatives of the business community, the medical community, the special education/disabilities community, and advocacy groups representing the needs of poor children and children of color—had become active players. However, of these 131, Miskel and his colleagues identify a smaller number—18 organizations and 5 individuals—who those in the reading issue network agree are most influential in the policy debates, including the National Institute for Child Heath and Human Development (NICHD), American Federation of Teachers (AFT), International Reading Association (IRA), and the National Education Association (NEA) and such individuals as Reid Lyon from NICHD, Congressman Bill Goodling (who had previously sponsored the Reading Excellence Act), Bob Sweet who was a congressional staffer, Louisa Moats from NICHD, and Marilyn Adams, a prominent reading researcher.[8] Interview data suggests that those who were particularly influential were skilled at disseminating research synthesis that promoted their point of view, including some of the documents that were analyzed in the research reviewed above (e.g., the National Reading Panel Report and the Grossen piece). They also collaborated with one another to bring their message to the fore, had both formal and informal contacts with policy makers in key decision making roles and, perhaps most important, were perceived by policy makers as objective (McDaniel et al., 2001).

But while reading policy activity in the second half of the 1990s was characterized by broad participation, the development of the Reading First legislation in late 2001 was a different story. Miskel and Song (2004) used social network analysis and interviews to map out the issues network for the 18 organizations and 5 influential policy actors identified in the first study. They found that the issue network for Reading First was characterized by a core-periphery structure. At the core were a small number of government actors, especially those in President George W. Bush's domestic policy office who were responsible for drafting the Reading First legislation and moving it through Congress. These core actors were connected to "idea champions" who were non-governmental actors such as Reid Lyon. But, overall, there were remarkably few actors involved in actually drafting and debating the Reading First legislation. This configuration of an issue network is unusual in the literature. However, Miskel and Song (2004) argue that it was made possible because of the consensus that was developed among influentials in the issue network during passage of the Reading Excellence Act in 1998. In the absence of organized opposition or conflict, the insider approach to policy making flourished.

In addition to the work at the federal level, several researchers have also examined the process of policy making at the state level (Allington, 1999; Coburn, 2005a; Cusick & Borman, 2002; Song & Miskel, 2005). Although not all studies use the concept of issue networks, the findings are remarkably consistent with Miskel and his colleagues' analysis at the federal level. These studies paint a portrait of policy making at the state level as occurring in the interaction between government actors and a network of professional organization, advocacy organizations, and university actors. The configuration of these actors and the nature of the positions that they promote influence the focus and content of policy.

State level comparisons suggest that while the size of issue networks and the configuration of key actors varied by state, government actors were generally much more influential (i.e., had greater measures of centrality and prestige) than professional organizations and other interest groups across states (Song & Miskel, 2005). Interview data suggests that limited influence of professional organizations at the state level is due to the fact that many state-level teacher organizations are not focused on the specific content area of reading. Thus, while they are active in state education policy generally, they are less active in subject-matter specific policy making. Furthermore, respondents suggest that many of these organizations tend to focus on implementation issues rather than policy making, limiting their influence in the policy-making process.

There is some disagreement about the degree to which professional reading organizations play an influential role at the state level. While Song and Miskel (2005) provide evidence that teacher organizations had low centrality and prestige in reading issues networks in the eight states in their study including Michigan, Cusick and Borman (2002) paint a different portrait of the role of professional organizations in that state. They use a longitudinal, ethnographic study of policy making in Michigan to provide evidence of the widespread and central role of a network of professional organizations and teacher networks in creating and promoting the state reading framework, although the influence was filtered through bureaucratic authority of the state department of education, which, in turn, mediated political pressure from the state board of education. One explanation for this discrepancy is the fact that the two studies were done at two different historical time periods. Cusick and Borman's study was conducted from 1993 to 1996 and investigated the development of the Michigan English Language Arts Framework. This framework, which promoted constructivist approaches to reading and writing instruction, grew out of what Cusick and Borman characterize as a social movement involving reading profession-als and university researchers that had been developing consensus on this approach to instruc-tion for years. These outside organizations were able to mobilize quickly when the opportunity to write the Frameworks arose. In contrast, Song and Miskel (2005) studied policy making in Michigan during the early 2000s, when a different approach to reading instruction was on the state policy agenda and many states experienced a shift in the configuration of actors who were influential in promoting these policy approaches (Allington, 1999; Coburn, 2005a).

Indeed, Coburn's study of shifts in California reading policy from 1983 to 1999 provides evi-dence that different policy eras have distinctly different configurations of actors. For example, she documents how policy shifts in the late 1980s brought together a grassroots teacher move-ment, professional organizations, and key university researchers with top-down policy initiative led by then State Superintendent Bill Honig to create reading policy promoting literature based instruction. In contrast, in the mid 1990s, efforts to promote greater attention to phonics and phonemic awareness in state policy were initially promoted by a small group of advocates, policy makers, and researchers (many from out of state). Many of the extensive network of actors who were involved in earlier policy initiatives in California were excluded from legislative hearings and task forces in this new period of policy making, and few of the positions they advocated for were considered as part of the policy-making process.[9] Thus, there were different people from different professional and disciplinary backgrounds who were influential in state policy making at different times, accounting for the sharp shifts in California state reading policy in a relatively short period of time.

Taken together, these studies present a first look at the dynamics of policy making in reading during an especially active and fertile time in reading history. But, there is still much to learn. Given the importance of issue networks, we need more studies that help us understand how they are formed and transformed. Existing studies document that they exist, that they are influential, and that they change over time. But we have little information about how and why they exist in the form that they do and what forces cause them to change over time. Similarly, we know that there is often a rather loose relationship between research on reading and the policy-making process, yet some bodies of research do play a role in reading policy. More studies are needed to understand when and under what circumstances research findings move through networks and into the hands of government actors who are crafting policy positions. It is only by understand-ing the processes by which research moves in and through the system and into policy and how its meaning is transformed along the way that reading researchers and others can understand how they can act to form more productive relationships between researchers and policy makers in the service of improving reading instruction for children.

POLICY IMPLEMENTATION

While there is only limited research on the policy-making process in reading instruction, there is an ever-growing body of research that seeks to understand how reading policy, once enacted, moves down and through the policy system and into schools. Most of this scholarship has addressed one of two questions. First, scholars have asked: How are teachers responding to these new reading initiatives? In particular, how are new policy initiatives being implemented in the classroom? And second, some scholars have also asked: What are the factors that influence the implementation process, shaping the degree to which teachers take up new policy ideas in substantive ways? What factors account for teachers' ability and inclination to change their practice in response to policy demands? These questions are critical because they open up the black box between policy enactment and policy outcomes. The answers to these questions provide insight into when and under what conditions some policy initiatives lead to increased student learning and others fail to reach the classroom at all. Thus, studies of the policy implementation process have the potential to provide insight into key points of leverage for supporting and sustaining change in reading instruction over time.

In the sections that follow, we begin by reviewing the findings on how teachers responded to reading policy, with particular attention to the degree and nature of changes in their classroom instruction. We then move on to investigate the factors that shaped how teachers responded, considering individual factors, features of the social context, and features of the policies themselves.

Teachers' Response to Reading Policy

Research during the last decade has investigated teacher responses to a range of policy initiatives as reading policy has shifted rapidly throughout the late 1990s and the early part of the 21st century. In this section, we review the evidence of teachers' response to each kind of policy initiative in turn. We move chronologically, starting where the previous edition of the *Handbook* chapter left off with a review of teacher responses to new state standards, then moving on to review teachers' response to high stakes assessment, and finally to a look at mandated approaches to curriculum implementation that are characteristic of both Reading First and other recent state and district policy initiatives.[10]

Standards.   Only a small number of studies during the period of the review investigated teachers' response to the introduction of new state standards in reading. These studies tended to converge around a single important finding: in implementing state standards, teachers tended to focus on surface features rather than higher level learning outcomes and deeper pedagogical changes promoted by the standards, resulting in superficial implementation (Coburn, 2004, 2005a; McGill-Franzen, Ward, Goatley, Machado, 2002; Ogawa, Sandholtz, & Scribner, 2004; Spillane, 2000). For example, Coburn (2004) studied three California teachers' response to multiple policy messages about reading, including those related to the new state standards. Based on her analysis of teacher responses to 223 policy messages, she developed a typology of teacher responses that ranged from rejection to symbolic response (changing appearances without changing instruction), parallel programs (layering new approaches on top of existing ones), assimilation (transforming new approaches so that they resemble prior practice), and accommodation (restructuring prior practice). She found that the most common response to policy messages by far was assimilation. That is, teachers—even those who were supportive of the reform efforts—came to understand new policy through the lens of their pre-existing practices and beliefs. In so doing, they tended to focus on changing surface aspects of their instruction such as the materials they use or classroom organization while leaving their underlying pedagogical approaches intact. Teachers responded to 49% of all policy messages by assimilating them into their existing instructional approaches compared to 9% of policy messages by restructuring their practice in more fundamental ways characteristic of accommodation. It is also worth noting that teachers also responded to 27% of messages by rejecting them outright.

The degree to which teachers responded to state standards with superficial versus substantive implementation appears to depend, at least in part, on the level of capacity building that was available and that teachers took advantage of (Coburn, 2004; Dutro et al., 2002; McGill-Franzen et al., 2002; Spillane, 2000). For example, in an in-depth longitudinal study of one fifth-grade teacher, Spillane (2000) used the contrast between reading and mathematics instruction to investigate the conditions that support change in practice. He provides evidence that this teacher made substantial changes in her practice in response to new English/Language Arts standards and argues that this was due, in part, to her active participation in the district's rich professional development offerings in reading instruction. Yet, this same teacher participated in only a limited way in professional development related to the new mathematics standards and made only superficial changes in her practice.

Nearly all the studies that investigate teachers' responses to state standards published during this period focus on implementation as learning. These studies emphasize the degree to which standards put forth visions of instruction that often require teachers to learn to teach in new and different ways. Accordingly, most of these studies drew on conceptual frameworks that attended to the dynamics of teacher learning and change. This strategy focused attention on the nature of teachers' opportunities to learn about the instructional foci and approaches presented by standards and frameworks. These studies paid less attention to issues of power and authority, which are often central to studies of policy implementation outside of education. However, a few studies did investigate the way that school districts with authoritarian approaches to leadership created strong parameters within which teachers could learn and make change in their instructional approaches in response to standards (Dutro et al., 2002; McGill-Franzen et al., 2002). Overall, however, the contribution of this set of studies is to identify the learning demands that new reading policy placed on teachers and to investigate the dynamics by which teachers learn and make changes in their practice in response.

High Stakes Assessment.   The greatest number of studies during the review period focused on teachers' response to high stakes assessment. Taken together, these studies document teachers' negative attitudes toward standardized assessment. But they also show that in spite of these negative feelings, teachers did change their practice when tests had high stakes. The nature of teachers' response depended upon the nature of the test.

Nearly all studies that investigate high stakes testing document teachers' widespread negative views. Teachers are especially negative about assessment when it is used for accountability purposes (Hoffman, Assaf, & Paris, 2001; Kauffman, Johnson, Kardos, Liu, & Peske, 2001; McDonnell, 2004; Wright & Choi, 2006). Several survey- and interview-based studies provide evidence that teachers question the degree to which standardized testing accurately measures student learning (Hoffman, Assaf, & Paris, 2001; McDonnell, 2004), especially in cases where the test was in English and students were predominantly English Language Learners (Hoffman et al., 2001; Wright & Choi, 2006). They are also skeptical that the emphasis on testing is beneficial for children (Hoffman et al., 2001).

Yet, at the same time that these studies document teachers' negative attitudes about testing, they also provide evidence that teachers do make changes in their practice in response to high stakes testing. Multiple studies—both survey-based and qualitative case studies—document increased or extensive test preparation activities (Diamond, 2007; Hoffman et al., 2001; McDonnell, 2004; Wright & Choi, 2006), narrowing of the curriculum to tested subjects and tested topics within tested subjects (Diamond, 2007; Hoffman et al., 2001; Sloan, 2006; Ogawa et al., 2004; Wright & Choi, 2006), and redirection of instructional resources to "bubble kids"—those at the margins of proficient whose test scores could influence a school's performance rating—at the expense of both high and low achieving students (Booher-Jennings, 2005; Diamond & Spillane, 2004).

Importantly, the ways in which teachers narrowed curriculum and the nature of test prep activities appears to be related to the nature of the assessment. For example, in his study of 47 teachers in 8 low-income schools in Chicago, Diamond (2007) provides evidence from 105 classroom observations that the city's basic skills test tended to hold in place and reinforce didactic literacy instruction in spite of the presence of standards that emphasized higher order learning outcomes. This was especially true in schools that served large numbers of African American students.

In contrast, in her study of testing policy in North Carolina and Kentucky, McDonnell (2004) found that new state assessments focusing on open-ended prompts, collaborative work, student writing, and higher order outcomes resulted in teacher practice that moved towards these ends. McDonnell analyzed two weeks worth of daily logs of teacher practice and student work assignments for 46 teachers, coding them to assess the degree to which teacher practice and student assignments were consistent with the aims of the new state assessments. She found that teachers in the sample were adding reform practices consistent with state assessments to their instructional routines and that their student assignments reflected classroom activities associated with the assessment reform. However, in a finding that echoes the research on teachers' response to standards reviewed above, McDonnell provides evidence that rather than fundamentally changing their pedagogical approach, teachers added new reform practice on top of existing traditional instruction. Teachers also were more likely to incorporate new activities (more writing assignments, more assignments that explored interdisciplinary connections) than to create instructional assignments that fostered conceptual understanding and critical thinking skills promoted by the testing reform.

Taken together, studies of teachers' response to high stakes accountability provide evidence that teachers shift the nature of their instruction in the direction of the testing content. However, as McDonnell's study illustrates, when the testing content required ambitious or unfamiliar approaches to instruction, teachers tended to change their practice in superficial ways and implement instructional approaches that addressed surface features of the policy rather than their deeper pedagogical implications.

Mandated Curriculum, The final set of studies during the period of review focused on implementation of mandated curriculum. In most of the policy contexts investigated, mandated curricula were part of systems of instructional guidance that included regular interim assessments, pacing schedule, and intensive monitoring with a focus on fidelity of implementation. There are two distinct types of studies investigating this policy strategy: state-level Reading First evaluations (only a subset of which have substantive information on implementation)[11] and small-scale, close-in studies of teachers' responses to mandated curriculum in Reading First and other policy contexts. These studies present a mixed picture about the degree to which teachers used the curriculum as intended and the changes in practice that resulted.

On the one hand, the large-scale evaluations of Reading First that attend to issues of classroom implementation report widespread presence of elements of Reading First, including the core curriculum (DeStefano, Hammer, & Fielder, 2006; Haager, Dhar, Moulton, & McMillian 2006; Zigmond & Bean, 2006). For example, in their evaluation report of the fourth year of Reading First in California, Haager and her colleagues (2006) draw on surveys of teachers, principals, and reading coaches to provide evidence that 98% of Reading First schools across the state had "adequate" implementation of the provisions of Reading First and 4% had "better than adequate" implementation. Schools were considered to have "adequate" implementation if teachers, reading coaches, and principals rated their school as performing adequate on more than 50% of the items on an implementation index that included measures of participation in professional development, school level variables (for example, shared vision for reform), and self-report and coaches' and principals' report of classroom practice.

In contrast, smaller scale observational studies of Reading First and other policy initiatives that stress fidelity to mandated curriculum report that although most teachers were using mandated curricula, there was great variability and limited fidelity in their approach (Achinstein & Ogawa, 2006; Kersten, 2006; Kersten & Pardo, 2007; Sloan, 2006). For example, in his 3-year ethnographic study of three experienced teachers in one urban district in Texas, Sloan (2006) illustrates three entirely different responses to the district's policy of mandated curriculum with explicit scope and sequence, quarterly benchmark assessments, and expanded battery of reading assessments. One teacher entirely ignored the curriculum, continuing with his largely project-based approach to teaching. A second teacher complained bitterly about the new curriculum and pacing schedule, but eventually integrated many key aspects of the curricula into her instruction over time. As her students' performance improved, so did her attitude toward the instructional approaches embodied in the curriculum. A third teacher initially replaced many aspects of her existing reading program with the new curriculum and instructional approaches consistent with the assessments. However, after her students' perennially high test scores went down, she negotiated with the school leadership to allow her the flexibility to return to prior instructional approaches, which included little attention to the adopted curriculum.[12]

These small-scale, observational studies all suggest that when teachers do implement the curriculum, rather than implementing with fidelity, they tend to combine elements of the new curriculum with their prior instructional practice to create hybrid approaches (Achinstein & Ogawa, 2006; Kersten, 2006; Kersten & Pardo, 2007; Sloan, 2006), a finding that is consistent with studies of curriculum implementation that pre-date Reading First (Datnow, Borman, & Stringfield, 2000; Datnow & Castellano, 2000; Hoffman et al., 1998; Remillard, 2000, 2004) and studies of teachers' response to state standards reviewed earlier. Indeed, the only observational study during the current period that provides evidence that teachers actually used highly specified curricula with a high degree of fidelity is a study of new teachers. In their longitudinal study of new teachers' response to the curricula in their districts, Valencia, Place, Martin, and Grossman (2006) investigated 4 teachers, 2 of whom taught in districts with highly specified curriculum linked to pacing schedules and interim assessments. They document how these two teachers taught reading in ways largely guided by the mandated texts in what they characterize as a "procedural" rather than "conceptual" approach to instruction. However, the two teachers were the only ones across the four small-scale studies of mandated curricula that appear to follow the curriculum with a high level of fidelity.

These small-scale studies also document instances where teachers actively resist implementation (Achinstein & Ogawa, 2006; Kersten, 2006; Kersten & Pardo, 2007; Sloan, 2006).[13] For example, in their study of the role of school and district instructional policy on new teachers' socialization, Achinstein and Ogawa (2006) found that 2 of the 9 novice teachers refused to use their school or district's mandated curriculum as intended. In an article that profiles these teachers, the researchers argue that teachers did so because the curricula conflicted with their beliefs about high quality reading instruction and their view of themselves as professionals. Both teachers ultimately left the schools that required fidelity to the curriculum.

It is difficult to reconcile the different portraits of implementation put forth by these two different sets of studies. Large-scale evaluation studies report strong implementation. Small-scale observational studies document high degrees of variability, the widespread presence of hybrid practices, and some degree of resistance. On the one hand, the large-scale evaluation studies have the benefit of drawing data from large numbers of teachers. They have large enough samples to run statistical tests that help them make generalizations and rule out spurious relationships. But, because of the scale of their studies, they are not able to employ very fine-grained measures of classroom practice. For example, Haager et al.'s (2006) study uses a wide range of items for their measure of Reading First implementation at the school level and, in fact, the items that are specific to classroom instruction play only a very small role in their implementation index (they are weighted at only 20% of the overall measure). They also rely on teachers' self-report and principals' and coaches' report of teacher practice rather than direct observation (see Rowan, Correnti, & Miller, 2002 and Hill, 2005 about the limits of surveys in accurately capturing teachers' instructional practice). Other large-scale evaluations of Reading First have measures of classroom implementation that go beyond surveys. However, these studies tend to rely on a very small number of observations—typically 2 a year per teacher—to draw their conclusions. As Rowan and colleagues (2002) suggest, this number of observations is problematic in light of the high level of variability in a given teacher's instruction across time.[14]

At the same time, the in-depth observational approaches favored by case studies provide a more fine-grained rendering of the nature of teachers' reading instruction, especially when the data come from extensive observations and/or are collected over several years. Thus, these studies may be surfacing aspects of instruction that are hidden from view with more general measures of instruction and reveal variation between teachers that is washed out by aggregation to the school or state level, as is the practice in the large-scale evaluations. However, most of the observational studies reviewed in this section provide limited information about their sampling strategy (Kersten, 2006; Kersten & Pardo, 2007) or purposively sampled outlier teachers (for example, Achinstein & Ogawa, 2006). Consequently, it is difficult to ascertain the degree to which the teachers profiled are representative of larger populations of teachers. Thus, while these studies provide evidence that there is variability in teacher practice, the presence of hybrid practices, and teacher resistance to mandated curriculum, we do not know how widespread these phenomena are.

Finally, in highlighting teacher resistance, the small-scale studies of teachers' response to mandated curricula highlight issues of power in the implementation process. Policy makers at multiple levels of the system are using various mechanisms of control—including mandates and monitoring—to ensure that teachers make changes in their classroom practice (in this case, adopt curricula). These articles highlight the fact that teachers do not always respond to this pressure; instead they reject some aspects of policy. However, at the same time that they shine a light on issues of power, studies of mandated curricula tend to neglect issues of learning that were highlighted in studies of standards and, to a lesser extent, standardized testing. That is, they pay little attention to what these policies require teachers to learn and the degree to which teachers have the knowledge and supports to do so. Indeed, most studies of mandated curricula assume that the teachers in the study fully understand the approaches to instruction promoted by the policy and could implement them with ease should they choose to do so.

Summary.   Taken together, studies across all three kinds of reading policy highlight several key findings. First, instructional policy does have the potential to influence teachers' classroom practice. However, when the policy promotes instructional approaches that are ambitious or unfamiliar, teachers are more likely to implement them in superficial ways rather than making fundamental changes in their instructional approach, especially when teachers have limited opportunities to learn about new approaches. Second, because teachers draw on their pre-existing practices to create hybrid approaches, there is likely to be great variability in teachers' implementation of reading policy, even within a single school. Third, studies of high stakes testing suggest that teachers are making changes in practice in response to policy pressures even when the approaches are not in line with their beliefs about high-quality instruction. However, there is also evidence from studies of mandated curricula that under certain conditions, teachers resist policy pressures, although it is hard to discern how widespread this resistance is and when and under what conditions teachers resist policies that promote approaches to instruction that they themselves do not support.

The existing research has a series of methodological limitations. Some of the studies—both large scale and small scale—do not include enough observations of teachers' classrooms to ensure that they are adequately capturing the complexity of teachers' instructional practices or do not discuss changes in classroom instruction with enough precision to get a sense of the predominant or overarching pattern for a given teacher. Additionally, because most studies focus on a single policy at a time and because studies of different kinds of policy focus on different aspects of the policy implementation process, it is very difficult to ascertain the degree to which teachers respond to different policy strategies in different ways. For example, while it perhaps makes intuitive sense that there is greater incidence of resistance to Reading First and other policies centered on mandated curricula because of the aggressive forms of policy intervention they employ (i.e. mandates and extensive monitoring), it is not clear whether the incidence of resistance is in fact higher than in earlier periods. Coburn's study of teachers' response to a range of policy initiatives including state standards reported that teachers rejected 27% of all policy messages (2004). It is not clear if the incidence of resistance to mandated curriculum is higher, lower, or comparable to that figure. Similarly, it is not clear when teachers' limited response to state standards is an issue of learning (as is frequently the inference drawn in those studies) or an instance of resistance (an explanation that is largely absent in studies of standards).

Factors that Influence Teachers' Response to Reading Policy

In addition to documenting how teachers responded to changes in reading policy, some studies published during this time period also investigated the factors that influence when and how teachers respond in particular ways. In so doing, these studies begin to provide insight into the nature of policy implementation processes that produce policy outcomes. In this section, we draw on work by Spillane, Reiser, and Reimer (2002) to organize these findings. In his review of the intersection between policy implementation and cognition, Spillane argued that teachers' response to instructional policy is the result of the interaction between the individual (knowledge, beliefs, and attitudes), the social and organizational situation, and the policy signal (policy design). Taken together, these three categories provide a useful organizational framework for the explanatory factors highlighted in the studies of teacher responses to reading policy. We will address each set of factors in turn.[15]

Individual Factors.   In the last decade, studies of policy implementation have documented the way that individual teachers' prior beliefs, knowledge, and practices influence how they come to understand and enact instructional policy in their classrooms (Guthrie, 1990; Smith, 2000; Spillane, 1999; Spillane & Jennings, 1997; Coburn, 2001b & 2005). As Spillane and his colleagues explain: "Individuals must use their prior knowledge and experience to notice, make sense of, interpret, and react to incoming stimuli—all the while actively constructing meaning from their interactions with the environment, of which policy is part" (2002, pp. 393–394).

Indeed, several studies during this period provide evidence that teachers' *pre-existing knowledge and beliefs about reading instruction* play a major role in how they respond to new reading policies. These studies demonstrate that teachers' pre-existing beliefs and practices influence what they notice about new policy, as they are more likely to focus on aspects of the policy that are familiar and not even notice those that challenge their beliefs and practices (Coburn, 2001b; Spillane et al., 2002). Pre-existing beliefs and practices also shape how teachers come to understand the meaning and implications of reading policy such that teachers with different pre-existing beliefs can understand the same policy in different ways (Coburn, 2001b, 2004; Spillane et al., 2002). Finally, prior beliefs and practice can influence change in classroom practice (Achinstein & Ogawa, 2006; Coburn, 2001b, 2004; Diamond, 2007; Spillane, 2000; Spillane et al., 2002). For example, in her study of three elementary teachers' response to changing reading policy in California from 1983 to 1999, Coburn (2004) provided evidence that teachers' responses to policy was shaped by the degree of congruence between new policy approaches and their pre-existing beliefs and practices. She shows that the greater the congruence of the policy message, the more likely it was that teachers incorporated the approach into their classroom practice in some manner. Thus, teachers responded to 90% of policy messages at high degree of congruence by creating parallel structures (e.g., a teacher adds a block of time for direct instruction of phonics skills and continues to teach phonics in a contextualized manner during small group instruction), assimilating them into their pre-existing practice (e.g., a teacher adopts learning centers but does not permit students to work collaboratively), or restructuring (i.e., accommodating) their practice in fundamental ways (e.g., a teacher learns about comprehension strategy instruction and fundamentally alters how she presents and discuss texts in the classroom). In contrast, the rate of incorporation dropped to 82% at a medium level of congruence and to 38% when congruence was low. However, although teachers were more likely to incorporate new approaches carried by policy with a high degree of congruence, they were also more likely to assimilate new approaches into their existing practice rather than reconstruct their practice in a substantive ways. In fact, teachers were most likely to make substantive changes in their practice in response to policy messages with a medium level of congruence. Just over 16% of the times that teachers incorporated messages at a medium level of congruence and nearly 9% at a low level of congruence, they did so in ways that led to accommodation. Messages with a high level of congruence led to accommodation in only 3% of policy messages.

The foregoing studies emphasize how the content of teachers' knowledge and practices shapes their response to policy. But the depth of teachers' knowledge is also important (Sloan, 2006; Valencia & Wixson, 2000). For example, Sloan's study of three experienced teachers with varied level of content knowledge in reading provides evidence that although mandated curriculum constrained the practice of the teacher with strong content knowledge, making it difficult for her to meet the diverse needs of her students, it improved the quality of instruction for the teachers with weak content knowledge (2006).

In addition to teachers' knowledge, beliefs, and practices, several studies provide evidence that *issues of identity* are also important for how teachers' respond to reading policy (Achinstein & Ogawa, 2006; Kersten, 2006; Kersten & Pardo, 2007; Sloan, 2006; Spillane, 2000). Two aspects of identity are influential: a teacher's identity as a learner and his/her identity as a teacher. In his in-depth, longitudinal study of a single fifth-grade teacher, Spillane (2000) provided evidence that this teacher's identity as a learner influenced how she engaged in professional learning opportunities associated with new content standards and how that, in turn, influenced the changes she made in classroom practice. Recall from our earlier discussion that this teacher had opportunities to change both her literacy and mathematics practice. She engaged in multiple professional opportunities in literacy, but participated in hardly any related to mathematics across the 4 years of the study, even though there were plenty of opportunities available in the district. Spillane argues that the difference in participation was related to the teacher's identity as a learner, which varied substantially between literacy and mathematics. The teacher prioritized literacy in her teaching, saw herself as strong in this regard, and consequently actively sought out learning opportunities in literacy (including, but not limited to those provided by the district). In contrast, she felt insecure about her abilities in mathematics, did not like teaching mathematics, did not see mathematics as central to her teaching mission, and consequently did not engage as actively with available learning opportunities in mathematics. As a result, this teacher made substantial changes in her practice towards the ambitious goals set forth by the literacy standards, she made only superficial changes in her mathematics teaching.

Other scholars focus on how teachers' identity as professionals—their sense of their appropriate role and what it means to be a teacher—influenced their response to reading policy. This body of work, most of which focus on teachers' responses to mandated curricula, suggests that teachers resist following well-specified curricula when this requirement conflicts with their view of themselves as a professional (Achinstein & Ogawa, 2006; Kersten, 2006; Kersten & Pardo, 2007) or when they do not identify strongly with the world of schooling (Sloan, 2006). For example, the two novice teachers who actively resisted the mandated curriculum profiled by Achinstein and Ogawa (2006) had visions of teaching as involving autonomy, creativity, and individuality. Following a highly specified curriculum conflicted with their view of themselves as teachers. Both teachers rejected using the curriculum as intended and ultimately left the schools that required them to do so.

Situation.   Individual characteristics shape teachers' responses to policy but so do the complex social and organizational contexts in which they work. Several facets of these contexts matter for how teachers implement reading policy in their classroom: social interaction with colleagues, school leadership, and features of the district.

Several studies suggest that teachers' *social interaction with their colleagues* influences their decisions about how to implement new approaches to reading instruction. First, patterns of social interaction influence how teachers learn about reading policy in the first place. Reading policy interpenetrates schools to different degrees. There is great variability in the degree to which teachers have access to information about new policy initiatives, especially if it is created at higher levels of the system (Coburn, 2005a; McDonnell, 2004). As suggested by research on social networks (Granovetter, 1973, 1982; Burt, 1992), teachers' connections with each other and those outside the school provide a powerful mechanism for learning about new ideas and approaches promoted by new reading policy, shaping teachers' access to some policy messages and not others (Coburn, 2001b, 2005a; Coburn & Stein, 2006). Second, teachers' interactions with their colleagues influence how they come to understand the meaning and implications of a new policy. Teachers make decisions about how to respond to new policy initiatives in conversation with their colleagues. How they come to understand the nature of instructional change required by a given policy is shaped by who they are interacting with (Coburn, 2001b; Booher-Jennings, 2005). For example, Booher-Jennings (2005) draws on extensive interviews and observations in a single school to provide evidence that teachers responded to high stakes tests by rationing instructional resources—focusing on children at the margins of proficiency (the "bubble kids") rather than high-performing or low-performing students—in part because they felt pressure from colleagues to improve the schools' performance rating. Thus, teachers influenced each other to see rationing as the most appropriate response to the district's high stakes accountability policy.

Beyond social interaction, studies during this period highlight the role of *school leadership* in classroom implementation. Principals influence classroom implementation by emphasizing some aspects of reading policy and not others, shaping teachers' access to some aspects of reading policy and not others (Coburn, 2001b, 2005b; Diamond, 2007; Diamond & Spillane, 2004; Spillane et al., 2002). At a deeper level, school leaders also influence how teachers come to understand the meaning and implication of policy (Anagnostopoulos & Rutledge, 2007; Coburn 2001, 2005b, 2006). Work by Diamond and Spillane (2004) suggested that school leaders' choices about what to emphasize, in turn, are influenced by the performance level of the school. Drawing on interview and observational data from a 4-year study of four low-income schools in Chicago—two high performing and two under threat to probation—Diamond and Spillane provide evidence that many of the practices noted by researchers in earlier studies of high stakes accountability—curriculum narrowing, focus on "bubble kids," extensive test preparation activities, symbolic responses—were more likely to happen in low-performing low-income schools than high- performing low-income schools. School leaders in high-performing schools responded to high-stakes assessment by focusing attention on long-term improvement in all curricular areas (rather than just tested subjects), encouraging teachers to participate in test preparation activities just prior to the tests rather than all year long, and leading teachers to be more reflective and purposeful about instructional change efforts than schools under threat of probation. These studies go beyond the platitude that school leaders are important for instructional reform to begin to unpack the relationship between specific actions by school leaders and teacher learning and instructional change.

Finally, scholars have increasingly identified *features of the school district* as important for teachers' implementation of reading policy. School districts influence implementation by the level and quality of capacity-building activities (coaching and professional development) that they provide to teachers to support instructional change (Dutro et al., 2002; McGill-Franzen et al., 2002; Stein & D'Amico, 2002). Several authors also provide evidence that the degree to which teachers respond to state standards in superficial versus more substantive ways was influenced by the nature of district standards themselves (McGill-Franzen et al., 2002; Ogawa et al., 2004). For example, Ogawa and his colleagues draw on longitudinal data from their study of one California district to investigate the relationship between district standard setting and teachers' classroom practice. They document how the district created three levels of standards, all of which were actually lower than the state standards because district administrators felt that the state standards represented learning outcomes that were too challenging for the children in the districts. Ogawa and his colleagues provide evidence from teacher surveys that teachers in elementary grades tended to pitch their instruction to the lowest level of standards in the district, which focused on basic skills instruction. Interviews with teachers suggest that this focus on basic skills represented a change in practice in response to standards and the accompanying district test rather than a continuation of their existing instructional practice. This suggests that the district's standards and assessment practices mediated state standards, influencing teachers to focus on lower level outcomes rather than higher order outcomes promoted by the state standards.

A study by Booher-Jennings (2005) suggested another way that school districts influence implementation, in this case teachers' response to high-stakes accountability. She argued that teachers consented to engage in rationing of educational resources (e.g., devoting resources disproportionately to the "bubble kids") in part because of their fears of being perceived as a "bad teacher" by their colleagues. The district contributed to this fear by defining good teaching by test score alone and publicizing individual teachers' test scores. Teachers' colleagues enforced this definition of good teaching, creating normative pressure that guided teachers' instructional choices. Taken together, these studies suggest that school districts influence teachers' implementation directly by creating instructional expectations in the form of standards and providing opportunities for teachers to learn new approaches, but also indirectly by creating normative environments and definitions of high quality teaching.

Policy Signal. The final set of factors we will consider are those that relate to the nature of the policy message itself. While implementation researchers outside of education have placed a priority on understanding the role that the design of policy plays in the nature of implementation (Matland, 1995; Mazmanian & Sabatier, 1983; Pressman & Wildavsky, 1984), the nature of the policy itself has received less attention in educational research. Indeed, few of the articles we reviewed on reading policy paid explicit attention to this dimension at all, in spite of the fact that the different policy movements during the last decade used substantively different policy strategies for influencing teacher behavior, resulting in very different policy signals. Nonetheless, there are a few patterns that do emerge from a careful reading of the recent research.

First, several scholars provide evidence that the *degree of ambiguity* of the policy influences how teachers implement reading policy. They provide evidence that when reading policies are ambiguous, teachers struggle to implement in the absence of adequate guidance (McDonnell,

2004; Kauffman, Johnson, Kardos, Liu, & Peske, 2002). For example, in her study of teachers' response to high stakes testing in California, Kentucky, and North Carolina, McDonnell provides evidence that testing policy, while providing a sense of urgency for instructional change, provided little guidance for how teachers should go about improving instruction to produce stronger student outcomes. Drawing on surveys and an analysis of classroom tasks (described earlier), McDonnell provides evidence that teachers had only a "diffuse, shallow understanding of assessment policy goals" (p. 156). Similarly, in their interview-based study of 50 first and second year teachers in Massachusetts, Kauffman and his colleagues (2002) found that in spite of the presence of state standards and assessment, beginning teachers reported that they had very little guidance about what and how to teach. All but a few teachers in their sample reported that they had either no curriculum at all (one-fifth of teachers) or only a list of topics and skills they needed to cover (over one-half) to guide their instruction. In these instances, new teachers struggled to build a curriculum on their own by piecing together materials from multiple sources, often without guidance from their school or district.

Research and theory outside of education suggests that increased ambiguity leads to greater variability in implementation. The basic argument is that the more ambiguous a policy, the greater opportunity for implementers to interpret and enact the policy in a wide range of ways leading to variability in implementation (Mazmanian & Sabatier, 1983). However, our earlier review of teachers' response to reading policies with different degrees of ambiguity (with standards being the most ambiguous and mandated curriculum accompanied by monitoring being the least) found evidence of variability in implementation across all policy strategies. In the absence of studies of that investigate the impact of different policy designs comparatively, and in the absence of common measures of implementation across studies of different policy initiatives, it is difficult to assess whether variation in policy ambiguity leads to greater or lesser variability in teacher implementation.

At the same time, at least one study provides evidence of the downside of too much specification. In their longitudinal study of four new teachers' engagement with reading curricula, Valencia and her colleagues (2006) draw on extensive interviews and repeated observations to provide evidence that the two teachers who worked in schools that had little specification in their curriculum struggled initially but eventually developed much greater understanding of reading instruction, greater flexibility, and more sophisticated instruction over the first three years of their teaching career. In contrast, the two teachers who started their career with highly-specified curricula had a more procedural and less conceptual orientation toward reading instruction and made few changes in their approach to reading instruction during their first three years of teaching. Thus, high specification ensured more support, but also offered fewer opportunities for teacher growth.

Second, several studies provide evidence that the *degree of alignment* among the multiple reading initiatives that teachers experience simultaneously influences implementation. These studies acknowledge the fact that teachers rarely experience a single policy initiative in isolation (Coburn, 2005a; Diamond, 2007; Kersten & Pardo, 2007). In the presence of multiple and at times conflicting reading policies, teachers tend to pick and choose which policy messages to be responsive to and which to ignore. In making these choices, they were more likely to be responsive to policy messages that are more consistent with their beliefs and prior practice. For example, Kersten (2006) painstakingly documented how one experienced third-grade teacher constructed her response to Reading First. Faced with a district curriculum guide that was not aligned with Reading First mandates, the teacher opted to be responsive to district policy when it was consistent with her prior practice. In this way, the presence of multiple and conflicting policies legitimized this teacher's lack of fidelity to some of the tenets of Reading First.

Third, several scholars focus on the degree to which reading initiatives provide *capacity building elements* as part of their policy designs (Coburn, 2005a; Dutro et al., 2002; McDonnell, 2004; Stein & D'Amico, 2002). These studies suggest that opportunities for teachers to learn new instructional approaches are crucial if teachers are to make substantive changes in their classroom practice. For example, in their study of New York City District 2's comprehensive literacy policy, Stein and D'Amico (2002) provide evidence that teachers with higher levels of participation in the district professional development offerings had deeper enactment of the balanced literacy program. More specifically, Stein and D'Amico made 27 observations of 12 teachers, analyzing their instruction along two dimensions: alignment with the balanced literacy program and quality of their instruction. They show that those teachers who had participated in the district's extensive and high quality professional development activities for multiple years tended to have instruction that was both aligned with the policy and of high quality. In contrast, those with more limited experience with professional development tended to have high alignment, but low quality implementation. That is, while the teachers included the various activities associated with the balanced literacy approach in their classroom (high alignment), they implemented them in ways that did not reflect the underlying pedagogical principals that knit the activities together (low quality). The implication is that participation in high quality professional development over an extended period of time enabled teachers to move from more superficial to more substantive enactment of policy.[16]

However, Spillane's study comparing one teachers' response to mathematics versus literacy standards (2000) complicates findings about capacity building. Recall that the teacher in his study worked in a district that had extensive professional development opportunities in both reading and mathematics. Because of differences in this teachers' identity as a learner in literacy versus mathematics, she actively participated in professional development in literacy, but hardly participated at all in professional development in mathematics. This difference was reflected in deep changes in this teachers' literacy instruction compared to only superficial changes in her mathematics instruction. This difference suggests that capacity building efforts may be necessary but not sufficient to support substantive implementation of standards. Rather, there may be an important interaction between elements of the policy, like the nature and quality of mechanisms for capacity building, and features of the individual teacher, such as inclination to reach out and engage with the opportunities that are available.

During the period under review, attention to issues of capacity building as part of policy design was largely confined to investigations of state standards and, to a lesser extent, high stakes assessment. In spite of the fact that Reading First and many other similar policies involve extensive capacity building activities, few studies of mandated curriculum attended to this issue. A few state evaluations of Reading First report data on teachers' and principals' satisfaction with coaching or professional development (Haager et al., 2006; Zigmond & Bean, 2006), but none look at the relationship between the levels and quality of capacity building activities and changes in teachers' classroom practice.

Finally, Coburn (2004, 2005a) provided evidence that the *degree of voluntariness* of policy influences how teachers respond to reading policy. Coburn used a longitudinal design, which provided the opportunity to contrast teachers' responses to multiple reading policies, each of which employed quite different policy strategies. Coburn distinguished between policy that uses normative pressure, putting forth visions of high quality instruction and making arguments for why teachers *should* make changes in practice (for example, standards) versus those that employ regulative pressures, which require teachers to do particular things and enforce this vision of instruction using rules, monitoring, and sanctioning (for example, mandated curricula). Coburn documented how, during the time period of her study, a vast majority of policy messages that teachers encountered were normative rather than regulative. Although teachers were less likely to reject policy messages accompanied by regulative pressure, they were also less likely to incorporate messages accompanied by regulative pressure into their classroom in substantive ways than they were to incorporate those messages offered with normative pressure. Thus, teachers responded to 33.3% of regulative messages symbolically (a kind of mock compliance), 20.8% of regulative messages by assimilating them into their pre-existing instructional approach, but never responded to regulative messages by reconstructing their practice in fundamental ways. In contrast, teachers responded to only 4% of normative messages symbolically, 51.6% by assimilating messages into pre-existing practices, and 10.6% by reconstructing their practice in fundamental ways. It is important to note that data collection for Coburn's study was completed in 1999 before the advent of high stakes testing and mandated curriculum in California. It will be important to see how these findings hold with policy initiatives that make much more extensive use of regulatory pressures than those investigated by Coburn.

Summary.   Taken together, these studies highlight the complex web of factors that influence how and why teachers respond to reading policy in particular ways. They paint a portrait of individual teachers making decisions about their practice in ways that are guided by their history, identity, existing knowledge and practice, but also influenced by the nature and quality of their interaction with their colleagues. The broader school and district context play a role as well, shaping teachers' access to some policy ideas and not others, creating opportunities for teachers to learn, and creating normative expectations for good teaching that shape how teachers see themselves and their colleagues. Finally, these studies provide evidence that the nature of the policy message itself matters, its ambiguity, alignment, instruments for capacity building, and its voluntariness.

However, there is still much to learn. To date, scholars of reading policy have had a tendency to focus greater attention on how teachers respond to new policy initiatives than to dig in and uncover the factors that shape these responses. Those that focus on why teachers respond in particular ways tend to emphasize individual level factors, such as beliefs and identity. As we move from individual to contextual and to features of the policy itself, there are fewer and fewer studies that have taken these factors into account.

Similarly, initial studies have identified a plethora of factors that influence implementation. But few studies have systematically investigated how these factors interact to influence classroom practice. For example, studies suggest that degree of specification and ambiguity influences the nature of implementation. We also know that teachers' depth of content knowledge may matter for how they respond to various kinds of policy. However, there are no studies that investigate how degree of specification and ambiguity interact with teachers' pre-existing content knowledge. Do teachers with different levels of content knowledge respond in different ways to highly specified policies? To more ambiguous policies?

Systematic studies of this sort are hampered because so few researchers compare implementation processes across different kinds of policies or similar policy in different contexts. Because most studies of reading policy are cross-sectional, they investigate teachers' response to a single kind of policy (in this case, standards, high stakes assessment, or mandated curriculum) rather than compare teachers' response across policies with different features (Coburn, 2004, 2005a are exceptions). Similarly, most studies of reading policy investigate teachers in a single district or a single state (Dutro et al., 2002 and McDonnell, 2004 are exceptions). This makes it difficult to make systematic comparisons about how policy context matters for implementation. It also loses the opportunity to investigate the consequences for classroom practice when states or districts implement a single policy—like Reading First—in different ways. In the absence of designs that compare different kinds of policies or similar policies in different contexts, it is very difficult to untangle the role of situation and policy signal in classroom implementation. This, in turn, makes it challenging to investigate how these kinds of factors interact with teacher- or school-level factors to produce patterns in classroom implementation.

As the field matures, it will be important to push our understanding of the factors that influence teachers' implementation further. At a minimum, we need more studies that seek to go beyond documenting how teachers responded to uncover the factors that influence why teachers respond in particular ways. But we also need the development of more precise measures of practice to facilitate comparison of classroom practice across multiple studies. And we need more studies that are designed to facilitate systematic comparisons—between kinds of policy designs, kinds of settings, and teachers with varied beliefs, knowledge, and practices—such that we are able to understand the interactions between the multiple factors that influence classroom implementation of reading policy.

POLICY OUTCOMES: FOCUS ON READING FIRST

In this section we take advantage of a singular opportunity provided by the array of national and state evaluations of federal programs—the Reading First component of No Child Left Behind—over the last decade. Never in the history of reading instruction have we had so many resources focused on early reading achievement, and, as a result, so much evaluation and research evidence gathered in such a concentrated period of time about systematic efforts to reform reading instruction in our schools. The various studies vary in purpose, method, findings, and conclusions, leading observers to conclude that Reading First has been the "Rorschach test" of literacy policy in the United States, or perhaps something more akin to the proverbial elephant described in such contradictory terms by the various blind observers. Even so, there is much to be learned from these evaluations, some of it substantive, but some of it methodological and even ideological.

For this analysis, we took a strategic approach in sampling the overwhelming array of available documents. First, we took careful note of the two large national quasi-experiments on Reading First: the *Reading First Impact Study Final Report* (Gamse et al., 2008) and the *National Evaluation of Early Reading First* (Jackson et al., 2007). Second, we relied on the documents assembled on the website of the Center for Educational Policy (www.cep-dc.org), including their own evaluations of Reading First and their summaries of other work, as well as their links to evaluations conducted by the federal government and other agencies. Of remarkable assistance was the 2007 aptly titled CEP report, *Reading First: Locally Appreciated, Nationally Troubled* (Scott, 2007), which summarized much of the state evaluation data up to that point in time. Third, we made the strategic decision that we could not examine all of the state reports (archived at http://www2.ed.gov/programs/readingfirst/evaluationreports/), so we decided to sample state evaluations of Reading First on a principled basis, looking for both within and between state patterns. We selected 5 states with the largest Reading First Grants (California, Texas, Florida, Pennsylvania, and Illinois) on the grounds that they were the grants that affected the largest number of children and schools in the country. We brought in additional findings and perspectives from the reports from other states when they served to reinforce or extend findings from the 5 large states or provide an alternative perspective.

The National Reports

The two national evaluation studies—the *RF Impact Study* (Gamse et al., 2008) and the *National Evaluation of ERF* (Jackson et al., 2007)—were explicit attempts on behalf of the Institute of Education Sciences (IES) to come as close as possible to meeting the gold standard of a randomized field trial in evaluating the effects of RF and ERF. True random assignment was not possible because of the manner in which funds were allocated. Because the highest rated proposals from eligible districts within each state received the funding, the assignment of treatment (RF or not) to the unit of analysis could not be random. However, in such circumstances, a common alternative to random assignment is the regression discontinuity design (Trochim, 1984). In such a design, under the assumption that the funded units differed from the unfunded units *only on* the variables that underlie the "scores" used to allocate the funding, the scores received on proposals are used to adjust outcome scores in the analysis. The closer the experimental and comparison groups are to the cut score, the better. Thus sampling from units just above and just below to cut score is a common approach to establishing both an experimental and a comparison group. This approach was used in both the *RF Impact Study* and the *Evaluation of ERF*. In what has proven to be a controversial move, the designers of the RF evaluation applied the design tool within districts (selecting schools just above and below the local cut points for school level funding), causing some scholars (e.g., Reading First Advisory Committee, 2008) to worry about between-group contamination of policy and practice initiatives.

The findings in *RF Impact Study* (Gamse et al., 2008) are straightforward. Differences favoring RF schools were found on a number of program implementation variables—total time spent on reading and practicing the "big five" RF components, explicit instruction (grades 1 and 2), high quality instruction (Grade 2 only), time spent on reading (hours per day), focus of professional development on the big five components, and the effective deployment of reading coaches. Implementation differences were not found on student engagement with print, access to differentiated instruction, or the use of diagnostic assessment. On student outcome measures, differences (*ES* of .17) were found favoring the RF schools on a measure of decoding skill in Grade 1 but not on comprehension at any grade. However, these findings are also controversial because they are inconsistent with the state evaluations of RF, most of which demonstrated robust effects favoring RF schools on a range of outcomes (cf. p. 49).

The *Evaluation of ERF* was much less ambitious in scope than the *RF Impact Study*, paralleling the scope of the funding differentiating the two programs. Like the larger study, the ERF study employed a regression discontinuity design with the school site as the unit of analysis, but the unit of selection, as would be expected with pre-school programs, was either a stand-alone pre-school or a "consortium" with several constituent pre-school sites. For both ERF and comparison treatments, classrooms were randomly selected within school sites for participation. The findings also parallel those for the *RF Impact Study*: strong effects on measures of program implementation and weak effects on student outcomes. In particular, ERF demonstrated positive program implementation effects on (a) teachers' professional development opportunities, particularly related to language development and literacy; (b) teachers' sensitivity to children's needs (*ES* = .79); (c) quality of teachers' interactions with students; (d) classroom organization and quality of learning environment; (e) lesson planning; and (f) the relative emphasis during literacy lessons on a range of practices: oral language, book reading, phonological awareness, print and letter knowledge, writing, and screening devices. Of the three classes of outcome measures—print awareness, phonological awareness, and oral language, effects favoring ERF were found only on print awareness. The evaluators also examined the mediating effect of changes in teacher and classroom variables on student achievement, finding a reliable (and predictable) effect only for print and letter knowledge activities on print and letter knowledge achievement.

Looking across the two national studies, a consistent message seems to be that when rigorous quasi-experimental designs are used to evaluate the impact of the complex, multi-faceted programs, it is easier to demonstrate reliable effects on measures of teacher participation and practices than on student outcomes. In this regard, it is worth noting that Dee and Jacob (2009) found, in their broader analysis of the impact of NCLB on student achievement as reflected in a set of broader indicators (scores on fourth- and eighth-grade NAEP), that the evidence for NCLB's influence on mathematics performance is quite strong, while the evidence for impact on reading scores is essentially non-existent.

State Evaluations of Reading First

With some notable exceptions, namely the relatively flat and disappointing results from Texas, the state level evaluations show consistently positive programmatic and student outcomes. The consistent message across the state reports is that Reading First worked, at least as measured by the criteria used to evaluate its impact on school programs, professional development, teacher practices, and student achievement (Carlson, Branum-Martin, Durand, Barr, & Francis, 2008; Foorman, Petscher, Lefsky, & Toste, in press; Haager, Dhar, Moulton, & McMillian, 2008; MGT of America, 2008). By and large, teachers appreciated the various programs (all variations on the "big five" theme—phonemic awareness, phonics, fluency, vocabulary, and comprehension—from the NRP Report), liked and responded well to the staff development provided, and implemented the key components of the enabling legislation.

Even more important, students appeared to benefit from the programmatic changes that were implemented. The general trends, using measures that focused on comprehension reported across these five states, indicate that:

1. Students in Reading First schools outperformed the comparison group, where the comparison group was defined as either as a comparison group of schools (in California),[17] the large sample used to establish the norms for the commercial tests (the SAT in Florida or the ITBS or SAT in Texas) or the achievement level cut scores[18] for the statewide accountability measures in Florida (Grade 3) and Pennsylvania (Grade 3).
2. The Reading First advantage extended to the lowest achieving students. Many states noted substantial reductions in the percentage of students scoring below their "basic" cut scores (or the 25th percentile or 20th percentile for the states using commercial tests). An especially gratifying result is that Florida schools that did not make progress early on were given special assistance in the form of site visits and special coaching and, as a result, were able to accelerate their progress in subsequent years.
3. With a few notable exceptions, traditionally underachieving groups (low-income students, students with disabilities, or ethnic or linguistic minority students) made exceptional progress in comparison to students in the comparison populations. In fact, in some states (California, Florida, and Pennsylvania are the best examples), there was some evidence of actually closing the achievement gap, although it must be recognized that RF seemed to benefit students at all levels of prior achievement and demographic factors.
4. In general, time in the program (the more years students were part of Reading First, the greater the gains), implementation fidelity (the higher the level of implementation, the greater the gains across time), and mobility in both students and teachers (the greater the mobility, the lower the rate of progress) explained variance in school achievement after many other factors, including SES, had been controlled for.

Reconciling the Differences Between State and National Evaluations

So what are we to make of this impressive array of state level findings, all pointing toward the overall efficacy of Reading First, in light of the singularly unimpressive results of the national studies? There are several plausible explanations, all of which should be considered. First, the RF effect emerges in less rigorous designs, such as evaluations that compare RF to population norms or non-comparable comparison groups, but not in more rigorous designs, such as randomized experiments or regression discontinuity designs. It could be, for example, that there are unaccounted for and unintended confounds between RF and non-RF groups in the state evaluations. These confounds could be stem from many potential factors—attention, resources, or intellectual capital that creates a special advantage for an experimental group. If this argument prevails, then we should look beyond the programmatic elements of RF for answers to our questions of what works.

Second, it is logically possible that the RF effect in the evaluation studies is real, and it is the *Reading First Impact Study* and the *Evaluation of Early Reading First* that suffered contamination between treatments. This is exactly the position taken by the National Reading First Advisory Committee (2008) when they saw the draft of the Impact Study. Their concern was that the decision to situate both experimental and control schools within districts and then to allow districts to assign treatment to schools compromised the integrity of the design. They further point out that many districts, in trying to build district capacity for RF, may have unintentionally contaminated the culture(s) of the control schools with ideas and principles emerging from the RF programmatic and professional development efforts. Finally, the National Reading First Advisory Committee expressed a concern about external validity—that the decision to embed the study within districts that used some sort of "rank-ordering" procedure for assigning RF treatment to schools may have inadvertently limited the sample to a restricted subset of schools, thus rendering the sample unrepresentative. If this argument prevails, then we should be asking ourselves questions like: Now that we know that these programmatic elements matter, what else do we need to add to our curricular and professional development portfolios in order to take the next step in reform and innovation?

A third possibility is that the RF effect is real, but not for any of the reasons typically cited by those who support its policy status. This is a variation of the "reading drive" argument put forth long ago by Southgate (1966). The idea is that novelty matters. Once in a while, change is needed to stir things up, offer participants hope and promise, and motivate everyone in the setting to improve. There is a hint of this perspective in the thoughtful set of conclusions offered by the authors of the Pennsylvania report (Bean, Draper, Turner, & Zigmond, in press). Bean and her colleagues conclude that the focus RF provided across Pennsylvania—along with local variation in implementation strategies— was important for the outcomes they observed. Citing McLaughlin's (1976) concept of mutual adaptation between reform and local school culture as an explanatory factor, they argue that strong outcomes in Pennsylvania were due in part to the fact that local districts differentiated their implementation strategy to meet their local needs and capacities, but kept this variation within the framework of RF dictates. In so doing, they were able to achieve implementation that led to strong student outcomes. If this argument prevails, then we should probably look to more open and process-focused approaches to reform— interventions that offer participants prerogative in shaping new initiatives (see Taylor, Pearson, Peterson, & Rodriguez, 2005; or Levin, 1998) within a common framework.

Ultimately, we do not have enough information to know which of these possible interpretations of the conflicting findings is the most accurate. This state of affairs highlights several limitations—methodological and conceptual—in existing research on the outcomes of reading policy in general and Reading First in particular. First, few of these studies use multiple measures of student achievement. As Paris (2005) has argued, it is preferable to have multiple measures of student achievement that range from low-level micro-level enabling skills (e.g., phonemic awareness, phonics, or word identification) to more macro-level outcomes (e.g., comprehension and language development). Doing so allows the researcher to understand the range of phenomena that interventions do or do not influence; a single measure cannot achieve that goal. Second, few of these studies collect measures on pedagogical practice. Absent information about the nature and quality of instruction, it is very difficult to make sense out of achievement results. Without this information, we have little information about the "active ingredients" in these classrooms and interventions.

Third, while all the evaluation studies of Reading First used comparison groups, many of the comparisons were problematic. Comparing the growth of the experimental group with changes in the overall state population or the average performance of the norming group for a commercial assessment, as some state evaluations do, is a poor substitute for a randomly selected control group since we know next to nothing about (a) the natural and unintentional distribution of ingredients of the intervention in a large and diverse norming groups or (b) the demographic similarity of the experimental and norming group. Even more typical control groups can be problematic on two oppositional counts. First, for an intervention like Reading First, contamination is likely to be the norm not the exception. As the California report documented, Reading First was a pervasive reform, extending to fourth and fifth grade in most schools and even to schools that did not receive direct funding; as such there was a natural press for contamination and conceptual seepage in the state's educational reform culture (Haager et al., 2008). Second, business as usual control groups are seldom treated comparably on important and potentially confounding factors such as material resources, professional develop opportunities, and attention—all factors that might motivate teachers to teach in ways that would lead to higher achievement quite independent of the content or focus of the interventions. Finding ways to control for these almost inevitable differences between treatments poses a genuine dilemma for researchers. Developing comparison groups that represent viable alternatives to the intervention under study is one strategy, albeit an expensive one. When random assignment is not possible, as is often the case in school-based evaluations, some scholars advocate for regression discontinuity designs, such as employed in the *Reading First Impact Study* (Gamse et al, 2008) and the *National Evaluation of ERF* (Jackson et al., 2007), but even they introduce vulnerabilities as discussed above (Reading First Advisory Committee, 2009).

We know why most evaluation studies fail to meet these ideals: resources. Evaluation studies rarely have the resources they need to answer the questions they have asked. However, sometimes we need to sacrifice breadth of coverage (testing the entire sample) to achieve greater analytic depth (more measures of more variables, including contextual variables such as instruction). The reallocation of resources in this manner may make it more likely that evaluations can improve our understanding of the impact of ambitious reading policy on student outcomes.

CONCLUSIONS

As policy makers become more and more interested in using policy to influence instruction, it becomes increasingly important to attend to the causes, processes, and outcomes of these efforts. Fortunately, research on reading policy is burgeoning as well. And, we are beginning to learn some crucial lessons about the relationship between reading policy, teachers' classroom practice, and student outcomes. We know that research can influence the development of reading policy, but that influence is dependent upon the structure of the policy issue networks that bring ideas and approaches into the hands of policy makers. We also know that these issue networks can change substantially over time.

We know that various approaches to instructional policy do reach within the classroom door to influence classroom practice. But, if policy is ambitious or unfamiliar, teachers are likely to implement it in superficial or tangential ways in the absence of capacity building efforts. We know, too, that there is likely to be great variability in the ways that teachers implement policy, even within a given school. Teachers will make change in their practice, even when they do not support the instructional approach promoted by the policy. But we also know that teachers can and do actively resist policy, picking and choosing among the plethora of policy messages to implement those that most resemble their pre-existing beliefs and practices. Understanding which of these implementation outcomes happens under what conditions is the next frontier for research. And, indeed, existing research has identified a web of factors—some individual, some social, some contextual, and some features of the policy itself—that influences how teachers respond to policy in their classrooms.

However, even as the research on reading policy begins to develop, there are still notable gaps in our understandings. There is still very little research that investigates the dynamics of policy making. We know little about how issue networks form, how they change over time, and how reading research and researchers become key players in them. This understanding is critical for reading researchers because the more we understand the process by which research moves in and through the system and into policy, the more we can work to form a more productive relationship between research and policy making in the service of improving reading instruction.

Furthermore, in spite of an increase in studies of the process of policy implementation, there is still much to learn about how policy influences teachers' classroom practice. We are beginning to identify the factors that shape implementation of policy, but we know little about when and under what conditions a given factor is important or how they might interact to produce the changes in practice that we see. Existing research has tended to focus on individual factors (i.e., beliefs, knowledge, identity) and paid less attention to organizational context or features of the policy itself. In fact, there are almost no studies that compare different policy approaches to discern how different policy tools (mandates versus capacity building versus accountability mechanisms) influence classroom practice differently. This, in spite of the fact that there is some variability in the same policies across different states (e.g., NCLB and Reading First) and even different districts that would facilitate this sort of comparison. Understanding the implementation process is crucial if we are to open the black box between a policy and its outcomes. Doing so promises to provide insight into strategic levers to support and sustain instructional improvement.

Finally, in spite of increased funding for evaluations of Reading First, there continues to be a paucity of funding for systematic studies of policy outcomes. For many researchers and policy makers, student learning is the bottom line. Yet, there are many significant reading policies with virtually no studies of student outcomes. The Reading Excellence Act, a major piece of federal legislation on reading instruction, received remarkably little research attention. Similarly, there are many state-level policies (e.g., new credentialing requirements for reading teachers in several states) for which we have no systematic analysis of outcomes.

Furthermore, studies of policy implementation and policy outcomes alike are hampered by methodological limitations related to measuring instructional practice. Many studies—especially the large-scale evaluations— have made limited use of classroom observation and other low-inference measures to investigate how teachers are actually responding instructionally. Those studies that do have rich measures of classroom instruction often use unique or idiosyncratic approaches, making comparison across studies difficult. The small-scale studies, which typically have more extensive observational components, often provide little information about sampling choices, so it is difficult to situate the classrooms and schools in the study in the larger sample. All of this makes it difficult to identify just how policy is impacting classroom practice and what features of instruction are associated with increased student learning. If we are truly to understand how policy impacts student outcomes, we need studies that help us understand what is going on instructionally to produce those outcomes. Absent that attention, policy makers have little information to guide the development of policy tools to promote and support efforts to improve reading instruction and student learning.

NOTES

1. While this was the first attention to "scientifically-based" approaches in federal legislation, references to scientifically-based research had appeared in state legislation in California as early as 1996 (Coburn, 2001a; Pearson, 2004) and in Texas by 1997 (Texas State Education Agency, 1997).

2. Student ranking in high school also included scores on a writing, social studies, and science tests.

3. The Texas model later became the blueprint for No Child Left Behind, as key Texas officials took positions in the Department of Education during the Bush administration.

4. It is perhaps interesting to note that the mandate for states to adopt scientifically-based research proved to be fraught with difficulties, as officials at the federal level were found to have pressured states to choose particular materials, some of which were authored by Department of Education officials or advisor. On March 23, 2007, the Government Accountability Office (2007) issued a report corroborating the findings from six reports issued by the U.S. Department of Education's inspector general. In particular, it found that "federal officials failed to safeguard against potential conflicts of interest in administering the program; and they directed some states' and districts' choices of reading texts and assessments, despite legal prohibitions" (Manzo, 2007). In particular, Reading First officials were accused of privileging programs or tests in which they or close associates had a financial interest. They were also accused of steering recipients of Reading First grants away from other programs, including two (Reading Recovery and Success for All) that had been blessed as research-based by the federal What Works Clearinghouse. In most cases, individuals implicated in the scandal resigned from their federal posts to return previous positions or assume new ones before any were publicly asked to step down. A follow up query was initiated by House Education and Labor Committee (Manzo, 2007), but no further actions were taken.

5. The National Reading Panel (NRP) report was mandated directly by Congress and employed the relatively new approach of meta-analysis to distill from existing research what is known about the efficacy of teaching. Yet the selection of topics for review was much less systematic than one might think. The authors of the report were very clear about which topics and studies would be included. It would review only those topics for which there existed a sufficiently large pool of "potentially viable" experimental studies. Hence issues of grouping, the relationship of reading to writing, the role of texts in reading acquisition—just to name a few of the more obvious issues that schools and teachers must address in crafting local reading programs—are not addressed at all. Regarding specific studies, they would include only those that met minimal criteria: employ an experimental or quasi-experimental design with an identifiable comparison group, measure reading as an outcome, describe participants, interventions, study methods, and outcome measures in sufficient detail to "contribute to the validity of any conclusions drawn." Natural experiments of the sort found in large-scale evaluation efforts or epidemiological investigations of relationships between methods and outcomes were excluded. At a meeting of the International Reading Association in 2006, S. Jay Samuels, one of the members of the NRP, announced that another criterion was at work in determining topics—the research interests of the panel members. This revelation suggests the strong possibility that some things did not get studied because no one on the panel found them compelling.

6. At the time we conducted this review, New York state's Reading First evaluation, which would otherwise have been included in the review by these criteria, was not available. However, just prior to the time we submitted the chapter, a Powerpoint presentation of outcome data was posted on the New York Department of Education website. An examination of the data (without benefit of an interpretive narrative) convinced us that the inclusion of the New York data would not have altered our conclusions in this section.

7. The following peer-reviewed journals were reviewed: *American Educational Research Journal, American Journal of Education, Educational Administration Quarterly, Educational Evaluation and Policy Analysis, Educational Policy Analysis Archives, Educational Policy, Elementary School Journal, Journal of Educational Administration, Journal of Educational Change, Journal of Education Policy, Journal of Literacy Research, Leadership and Policy in Schools, Peabody Journal of Education, Reading Research Quarterly, Reading Teacher,* and *Teachers College Record.*

8. That so many researchers and research organizations were found to be highly influential is actually unusual. For example, in his now classic analysis of the dynamics of policy making in health care and

transportation, Kingdon (1984) found that while 66% of his respondents mentioned researchers or academics as players in these policy communities, only 15% of them rated them as very important.

9. See, also, Carnine 1999 for an insider account of policy making in California during the mid to late 1990s.

10. It is important to acknowledge that these are not always distinct policy initiatives. In fact, in many states, these policy approaches tended to be layered on top of one another. Thus, teachers tended to experience the cumulation of these policy strategies over time, rather than discrete policy initiatives.

11. Only 3 of the 5 state-level evaluation reports we reviewed actually reported on levels of implementation of Reading First.

12. Recent large-scale studies of in reading and other subject areas echo this finding about within school variability. For example, in their study of implementation of three Comprehensive School Reform models, Rowan and Correnti (2008) analyzed instructional logs of nearly 2000 teachers in 112 schools and found that 23% of the variance in use of instructional time was among teachers in a single school, while only 5% of the variance was among schools. Similarly, in their study of teachers' response to standards-based accountability in mathematics in three states, Hamilton and her colleagues (2002) found that by far the greatest variability was between teachers within schools rather than between schools or between districts. The proportion of variance on most measures of classroom practice was 0.70 or higher within schools, compared to .20 or lower at the school or district level.

13. There is also some evidence of resistance in at least one large-scale evaluation of Reading First. DeStefano and colleagues (2006) report that respondents from 4 out of 18 Reading First sites that they interviewed over the phone mentioned teacher resistance as one of the challenges they face. However, no further details are available.

14. Rowan et al. (2002) argues that researchers need a minimum of 15-20 classroom observations, spaced out across a school year, in order to draw valid conclusions about classroom instruction given the variability over time and the multi-faceted nature of classroom instruction.

15. In order to be included in this section, studies needed to make an explicit link to classroom practice. For example, a study on the role of principal in implementation of reading policy had to include data that linked principal actions to classroom instruction. Studies that focused on principal leadership—or other factors—absent that link were not included in this review.

16. This finding should be viewed with caution, however, because, as Stein and D'Amico (2002) note, they did not have longitudinal data for their study. Thus, they cannot say with certainty that teachers with implementation that is aligned and high quality moved on a developmental trajectory from superficial implementation to more substantive over time.

17. In California, the evaluators also created a "statistical control group" using statistical methods to illustrate how a school that is similar to Reading First schools would have performed without access to the program.

18. In Pennsylvania (which focused on third grade exclusively), Florida for the third grade FCAT, and California, the norming group for the state test was the entire state sample.

REFERENCES

Achinstein, B., & Ogawa, R. T. (2006). (In)fidelity: What the resistance of new teachers reveals about professional principles and prescriptive educational policies. *Harvard Educational Review, 76*(1), 30–63.

Anagnostopoulos, D., & Rutledge, S. A. (2007). Making sense of school sanctioning policies in urban high schools. *Teachers College Record*, 109(5), 1261–1302.

Allington, R. (1999). Critical issues: Crafting state educational policy: The slippery role of research and researchers. *Journal of Literacy Research, 31*(4), 457–482.

Allington, R. L., & Woodside-Jiron, H. (1999). The politics of literacy teaching: How "research" shaped educational policy. *Educational Researcher, 28*(8), 4–12.

Bean, R., Draper, J., Turner, G., & Zigmond, N. (in press). Reading first in Pennsylvania: Achievement findings after five years. *Journal of Literacy Research*.

Birdyshaw, D., Pesko, E., Wixson, K., & Yochum, N. (2002). From policy to practice: Using literacy standards in early reading instruction. In M. L. Kamil, J. B. Manning, & H. J. Walberg (Eds.), *Successful reading instruction* (pp. 75–99). Greenwich, CT: Information Age Publication/Laboratory for Student Success.

Booher-Jennings, J. (2005). Below the bubble: "Educational triage" and the Texas accountability system. *American Educational Research Journal, 42*(2), 231–268.

Burt, R.S. (1992). *Structural holes: The social structure of competition.* Cambridge, MA: Harvard University Press.

California State Board of Education. (1999). *Guide to the California reading initiative 1996–1999.* Sacramento: California Reading Initiative Center.

Camilli, G., Vargas, S., & Yurecko, M. (2003). Teaching children to read: The fragile link between science and federal education policy [electronic version]. *Education Policy Analysis Archives, 11*(15).

Camilli, G., Wolfe, P., & Smith, M. L. (2006). Meta-analysis and reading policy: Perspectives on teaching children to read. *The Elementary School Journal, 107*(1), 27–37.

Carlson, C. D., Branum-Martin, L., Durand, A., Barr, C., & Francis, D. (2008). *Texas Reading First Initiative: Summary year 4 evaluation report.* University of Houston: Texas Institute for Measurement, Evaluation, and Statistics.

Carnine, D. (1999). Campaigns for moving research into practice. *Remedial and Special Education, 20*(1), 2–6, 35.

Coburn, C. E. (2001a). *Making sense of reading: Logics of reading in the institutional environment and the classroom.* Unpublished doctoral dissertation. Stanford University, Stanford, California.

Coburn, C. E. (2001b). Collective sensemaking about reading: How teachers mediate reading policy in their professional communities. *Educational Evaluation and Policy Analysis, 23*(2), 145–170.

Coburn, C. E. (2004). Beyond decoupling: Rethinking the relationship between the institutional environment and the classroom. *Sociology of Education, 77*(3), 211–244.

Coburn, C. E. (2005a). The role of nonsystem actors in the relationship between policy and practice: The case of reading instruction in California. *Educational Evaluation and Policy Analysis, 27*(1), 23–52.

Coburn, C. E. (2005b). Shaping teacher sensemaking: School leaders and the enactment of reading policy. *Educational Policy, 19*(3), 476–509.

Coburn, C. E. (2006). Framing the problem of reading instruction: Using frame analysis to uncover the microprocesses of policy implementation. *American Educational Research Journal, 43*(3), 343–379.

Coburn, C. E., & Stein, M. K. (2006). Communities of practice theory and the role of teacher professional community in policy implementation. In M. I. Honig (Ed.), *Confronting complexity: Defining the field of education policy implementation* (pp. 25–45). Albany: State University of New York Press.

Colvin, R. L. (1995, September 13). State report urges return to basics in teaching reading. *Los Angeles Times,* p. A1.

Cross, C. T., Riley, R., Sanders, T. (2004). *Political education: National policy comes of age.* New York: Teachers College Press.

Cusick, P. A., & Borman, J. (2002). Reform of and by the system: A case study of a state's effort at curricular and systemic reform. *Teachers College Record, 104*(4), 765–786.

Datnow, A., Borman, G., & Stringfield, S. (2000). School reform through a highly specified curriculum: Implementation and effects of the Core Knowledge Sequence. *The Elementary School Journal, 101*(2), 167–191.

Datnow, A., & Castellano, M. (2000). Teachers' responses to Success for All: How beliefs, experiences, and adaptations shape implementation. *American Educational Research Journal, 37*(3), 775–799.

Dee, T., & Jacob, B. (2009). *The impact of No Child Left Behind on student achievement.* Cambridge, MA: National Bureau of Economic Research.

DeStefano, L., Hammer, V., & Fielder, E. (2006). *Reading First external evaluation (No. 3).* Urbana Campaign: University of Illinois at Urbana Champaign, College of Education.

Diamond, J. B. (2007). Where the rubber meets the road: Rethinking the connection between high-stakes testing policy and classroom instruction. *Sociology of Education, 80*(4), 285–313.

Diamond, J. B., & Spillane, J. P. (2004). High-stakes accountability in urban elementary schools: Challenging or reproducing inequality? *Teachers College Record, 106*(6), 1145–1176.

Dressman, M. (1999). On the use of misuse of research evidence: Decoding two states' reading initiatives. *Reading Research Quarterly, 34*(3), 258–285.

Dutro, E., Fisk, M. C., Koch, R., Roop, L. J., & Wixson, K. K. (2002). When state policies meet local district contexts: Standards-based professional development as a means to individual agency and collective ownership. *Teachers College Record, 104*(4), 787–811.

Edmondson, J. (2005, February 3). Policymaking in education: Understanding influences on the Reading Excellence Act. *Education Policy Analysis Archives, 13*(11). Retrieved December 28, 2006, from http://epaa.asu.edu/epaa/v13n11/

Eisenhardt, M., & Towne, L. (2003). Contestation and change in national policy on "scientifically based" education research. *Educational Researcher, 32*(7), 31–38.

Foorman, B. R., Petscher, Y., Lefsky, E., & Toste, J. R. (in press). Reading First in Florida: Five years of improvement. *Journal of Literacy Research.*

Fuhrman, S. (2004). Introduction. In S. Furhman & R. Elmore (Eds.), *Redesigning accountability systems for education* (pp. 3–14). New York: Teachers College Press.

Gandal, M. (1996). *Making standards matter 1996: An annual 50 state progress report on efforts to raise academic standards.* Washington, DC: American Federation of Teachers.

Gamse, B. C., Jacob, R. ., Horst, M., Boulay, B., & Unlu, F. (2008). *Reading First impact study final report.* National Center for Education Evaluation and Regional Assistance, Institute of Education Sciences. Washington, DC: U.S. Department of Education. (RFISFR) (NCEE 2009-4038).

Gee, J. P. (1999). Reading and the new literacy studies: Reframing the National Academy of Sciences report on reading. *Journal of Literacy Research, 31*(3), 355–374. Retrieved February 9, 2008, from http://findarticles.com/p/articles/mi_qa3785/is_199909/ai_ n8857323/pg_7

Government Accounting Office. (2007). *States report improvements in reading instruction, but additional procedures would clarify education's role in ensuring proper implementation.* Washington, DC: Government Accounting Office.

Granovetter, M. S. (1973). The strength of weak ties. *American Journal of Sociology, 78,* 1360–1380.

Granovetter, M. S. (1982). The strength of weak ties: A network theory revisited. In P. V. Marsden & N. Lin (Eds.), *Social structure and network analysis* (pp. 105–130). Beverly Hills, CA: Sage.

Grossen, B (1997). *Reading recovery: An evaluation of benefits and costs (executive summary).* Eugene: University of Oregon.

Guthrie, J. (1990). *Educational Evaluation and Policy Analysis, 12*(3), 233–353.

Haager, D., Dhar, R., Moulton, M., & McMillian, S. (2006). *The California Reading First Year 4 evaluation report.* Morgan Hill, CA: Educational Data Systems.

Haager, D., Dhar, R., Moulton, M., & McMillan, S. (2008). *The California Reading First Year 7 evaluation report.* Morgan Hill, CA: Educational Data Systems.

Hamilton, L., Stecher, B., & Klein, S. (Eds.). (2002). *Making sense of test-based accountability in education.* Santa Monica, CA: RAND.

Haney, W. (2000). The myth of the Texas Miracle in education [electronic version]. *Education Policy Analysis Archives, 8*(41). Retrieved from at http://olam.ed.asu.edu/apaa

Heclo, H. (1978). Issue networks, and the executive establishment. In A. King (Ed.), *The New American political system* (pp. 87–124). Washington, DC: American Enterprise Institute.

Hill, H.C. (2005). Content across communities: Validating measures of elementary mathematics instruction. *Educational Policy, 19*(3), 447–475.

Hoffman, J. V., Assaf, L. C., & Paris, S. G. (2001). High-stakes testing in reading: Today in Texas, tomorrow? *The Reading Teacher, 54*(5), 482–492.

Hoffman, J. V., McCarthey, S. J., Elliot, B., Bayles, D. L., Price, D. P., Ferree, A., et al. (1998). The literature-based basals in first-grade classrooms: Savior, Satan, or same-old, same-old? *Reading Research Quarterly, 33*(2), 168–197.

Jackson, R., McCoy, A., Pistorino, C., Wilkinson, A., Burghardt, J., Clark, M., et al. (2007). *National evaluation of early Reading First: Final report.* U.S. Department of Education, Institute of Education Sciences, Washington, DC: U.S. Government Printing Office.

Jennings, N. E. (1996). *Interpreting policy in real classrooms: Case studies of state reform and teacher practice.* New York: Teachers College Press.

Kauffman, D., Johnson, S. M., Kardos, S. M., Liu, E., & Peske, H. G. (2002). "Lost at sea": New teachers' experiences with curriculum and assessment. *Teachers College Record, 104*(2), 273–300.

Kersten, J. (2006). Hybridization, resistance, and compliance: Negotiating policies to support literacy achievement. *The New Educator, 2*(2), 103–121.

Kersten, J., & Pardo, L. (2007). Finessing and hybridizing: Innovative literacy practices in Reading First classrooms. *The Reading Teacher, 61*(2), 146–154.

Kingdon, J. W. (1984). *Agendas, alternatives, and public policies.* Boston: Little, Brown.

Levin, H. M. (1998). Accelerated schools: A decade of evolution. In A. Hargreaves, A. Lieberman, M. Fullan, & D. Hopkins (Eds.), *International handbook of educational change, part two* (pp. 807–830). Boston: Kluwer.

Manzo, K. K. (2007, April 3). Reading probe will continue. *Education Week.* Retrieved from http://www.edweek.org/ew/articles/2007/04/04/31read.h26.html

Massachusetts Department of Education. (2004). *The Massachusetts Reading First newsletter: August 2004.* Retrieved August 13, 2006, from http://www.doe.mass.edu/read/newsletter/0905.doc

Massachusetts Department of Education. (2005a). *Overview of the Massachusetts Reading First plan assessment framework.* Retrieved July 24, 2006, from http://www.doe.mass.edu/read/presentations/bsr_assessframework.pps

Massachusetts Department of Education. (2005b). *Second visit monitoring tool for the Massachusetts Reading First Plan.* Retrieved July 21, 2006, from http://www.doe.mass.edu/read/mrfp/visit2.doc

Matland, R. E. (1995). Synthesizing the implementation literature: The ambiguity-conflict model of policy implementation. *Journal of Public Administration and Theory, 5*(2), 145–174.

Mazmanian, D., & Sabatier, P. A. (1983). *Implementation and public policy.* Glenview, IL: Scott, Foresman.

McDaniel, J. E., Sims, C. H., & Miskel, C. G. (2001). The National Reading Policy arena: Policy actors and perceived influence. *Educational Policy, 15*(1), 92–114.

McDonnell, L. M. (2004). *Politics, persuasion, and educational testing.* Cambridge, MA: Harvard University Press.

McFarland, A.S. (1992). Interest groups and the policymaking process. In M. P. Petracca (Ed.), *The Politics of interests: Interest groups transformed* (pp. 58–79). Boulder, CO: Westview Press.

McGill-Franzen, A., Zmach, C., Solic, K., Zeig, J. (2002). The confluence of two policy mandates: Core reading programs and third-grade retention in Florida. *The Elementary School Journal, 107*(1), 67–93.

McGill-Franzen, A., Ward, N., Goatley, V., & Machado, V. (2002). Teachers' use of new standards, frameworks, and assessments: Local cases of NYS elementary grade teachers. *Reading Research and Instruction, 41*(2), 127–148.

Mesmer, H.A. & Karchmer, R.A. (2003). REAlity: How the Reading Excellence Act took form in two schools. *Reading Teacher, 56*(7), 636–645.

MGT of America. (2008). *Illinois Reading First evaluation report: Final, 2007–08.* Washington, DC: author.

Mintrop, H., & Trujillo, T. M. (2005). Corrective action in low performing schools: Lessons for NCLB implementation from first-generation accountability systems. *Education Policy Analysis Archives, 13*(48). Retrieved from http://epaa.asu.edu/epaa/v13n48/

Miskel, C., & Song, M. (2004). Passing Reading First: Prominence and processes in an elite policy network. *Educational Evaluation and Policy Analysis, 26*(2), 89–109.

Moss, M., Fountain, A., Boulay, B., Horst, M., Rodger, C., & Brown-Lyons, M. (2008). *Reading First implementation evaluation: Final report.* Washington, DC: United States Department of Education.

National Reading Panel Report. (2000). *Report of the National Reading Panel: Teaching children to read.* Washington, DC: National Institute for Literacy

Ogawa, R. T., Sandholtz, J. H., & Scribner, S. P. (2004). Standards gap: Unintended consequences of local standards-based reform. *Teachers College Record, 106*(6), 1177–1202.

Paris, S. G. (2005). Reinterpreting the development of reading skills. *Reading Research Quarterly, 40*(2), 184–202.

Pearson, P. D. (2004). The reading wars. *Educational Policy, 18*(1), 216–252.

Pressley, M., & Fingeret, L. (2007). *What we have learned since the National Reading Panel.* New York: Guilford Press.

Pressman, J. L., & Wildavsky, A. (1984). *Implementation.* Berkeley: University of California Press.

Reading First Advisory Committee. (2008). *Response to the Reading First impact study.* Retrieved January 5, 2010, from http://www.ed.gov/programs/readingfirst/statement.pdf

Remillard, J. T. (2000). Can curriculum materials support teachers' learning? Two fourth-grade teachers' use of a new mathematics text. *The Elementary School Journal, 100*(4), 331–350.

Remillard, J. T. (2004). Teachers' orientations toward mathematics curriculum materials: Implications for teacher learning. *Journal for Research in Mathematics, 35*(5), 352–388.

Rowan, B., Correnti, R., & Miller, R. (2002). What large-scale, survey research tells us about teacher effects on student achievement: Insights from the Prospects Study of elementary schools. *Teachers College Record, 104*(8), 1525–1567.

Rowan, B., & Correnti, R. (2008). *Studying reading instruction with teacher logs: Lessons from a study of instructional improvement.* Unpublished manuscript. Ann Arbor: University of Michigan.

Scott, C. (2007). *Reading First: Locally appreciated, nationally troubled.* Washington DC: Center on Educational Policy. Retrieved from http://www.cep-dc.org/

Sloan, K. (2006). Teacher identity and agency in school worlds: Beyond and all-good/all-bad discourse on accountability-explicit curriculum policies. *Curriculum Inquiry, 36*(2), 119–152.

Smith, M. S., & O'Day, J. (1990). Systemic school reform. *Journal of Education Policy, 5*(5), 233–267.

Smith, M. S. (2000). Balancing old and new: An experienced middle school teacher's learning in the context of mathematics instructional reform. *The Elementary School Journal, 100*(4), 351–375.

Snipes, J., Doolittle, F., & Herlihy, C. (2002). *Foundations for success: Case studies of how urban school systems improve student achievement.* DC: Council of Great City Schools.

Snow, C. (2000). On the limits of reframing: Rereading the National Academy of Sciences report on reading. *Journal of Literacy Research, 32*(1), 113–120.

Song, M., & Miskel, C. G. (2005). Who are the influentials? A cross-state social network analysis of the reading policy domain. *Educational Administration Quarterly, 41*(1), 7–48.

Southgate, V. (1966). Approaching I. T. A. results with caution. *Reading Research Quarterly, 1*(3), 35–56.

Spillane, J. P. (1999). External reform initiatives and teachers' efforts to reconstruct their practice: The mediating role of teachers' zones of enactment. *Journal of Curriculum Studies, 31*(2), 143–175.

Spillane, J. P. (2000). Constructing ambitious pedagogy in the fifth grade: The mathematics and literacy divide. *The Elementary School Journal, 100*(4), 307–330.

Spillane, J. P., & Jennings, N. E. (1997). Aligned instructional policy and ambitious pedagogy: Exploring instructional reform from the classroom perspective. *Teachers College Record, 98*(3), 449–481.

Spillane, J. P., Reiser, B. J., & Reimer, T. (2002). Policy implementation and cognition: Reframing and refocusing implementation research. *Review of Educational Research, 72*(3), 387–431.

Stecher, B., Hamilton, L., & Gonzalez, G. (2003). *Working smarter to leave no child behind: Practical insights for school leaders.* Santa Monica, CA: RAND Education.

Stein, M. K., & D'Amico, L. (2002). Inquiry at the crossroads of policy and learning: A study of a district-wide literacy initiative. *Teachers College Record, 104*(7), 1313–1344.

Taylor, B. M., Anderson, R. C., Au, K. H., & Raphael, T. E. (2000). Discretion in the translation of research to policy: A case from beginning reading. *Educational Researcher, 29*(6), 16–26.

Taylor, B. M., Pearson, P. D., Peterson, D. S., & Rodriguez, M. C. (2005). The CIERA school change framework: An evidence-based approach to professional development and school reading improvement. *Reading Research Quarterly, 40*(1), 2–32.

Texas Education Agency. (2002). *Student Success Initiative.* Retrieved February 1, 2010, from http://ritter.tea.state.tx.us/curriculum/ssi.html

Trochim, W. (1984). *Research design for program evaluation: The regression-discontinuity design.* Beverly Hills, CA: Sage

United States Department of Education. (2002). *Guidance for the Reading First Program.* Retrieved November 10, 2007, from http://www.ed.gov/programs/readingfirst/guidance.pdf#search=%22reading%20first%20guidance%22

United States Department of Education. (2004). *Introduction and overview: Reading First.* Retrieved July 16, 2007. from http://www.ed.gov/programs/readingfirst/index.html

Valencia, S. W., Place, N. A., Martin, S., D., & Grossman, P. L. (2006). Curriculum materials for elementary reading: Shackles and scaffolds for four beginning teachers. *The Elementary School Journal, 107*(1), 93–120.

Valencia, S. W., & Wixson, K. K. (2000). Policy-oriented research on literacy standards and assessment. In M. L. Kamil, P. B. Mosenthal, P. D. Pearson, & R. Barr (Eds.), *Handbook of reading research* (Vol. 3, pp. 909–935). Mahwah, NJ: Erlbaum.

Valencia, S.W., & Wixson, K. K. (2001). Inside English/Language Arts standards: What's in a grade? *Reading Research Quarterly, 36*(2), 202–211.

Vasquez Heilig, J. & Darling-Hammond, L. (2008). Accountability Texas-style: The progress and learning of urban minority students in a high-stakes testing context. *Educational Evaluation and Policy Analysis, 30*(2), 75–110.

Wright, W. E., & Choi, D. (2006). The impact of language and high-stakes testing policies on elementary school English language learners in Arizona. *Education Policy Analysis Archives, 14*(13). Retrieved July 30, 2010, from http://epaa.asu.edu/epaa/v14n13/

Zigmond, N., & Bean, R. (2006). *External evaluation of Reading First in Pennsylvania: Annual report, project year 3: 2005–2006.* Unpublished manuscript.

25 Reading and School Reform

Barbara M. Taylor
University of Minnesota

Taffy E. Raphael
University of Illinois at Chicago

Kathryn H. Au
SchoolRise LLC

READING AND SCHOOL REFORM

In constructing this interpretative review—the first on school reform to be included in a *Handbook of Reading Research*—we acknowledge both the rich history on which we are building and establish parameters that must, by their very nature, limit the scope of the research on which we will draw. The review focuses primarily on elementary (K–8) school-level reform initiatives to improve students' reading abilities (i.e., achievement, engagement, dispositions). We believe reading abilities are fundamental to creating an educated citizenry able to compete in a global society as well as fulfill personal goals in life. And we believe that school reform is essential to the overall goal of improving literacy achievement. That schools need reform is not a concept many would debate, but the nature of the reform—particularly reform in reading—has long been open to interpretation.

For example, Berliner (2006, p. 950) argued that "despite the claims of many school critics, only some of America's schools are *not* now succeeding" (italics added). But, he continued by building a compelling argument that schools serving children living in poverty are the ones most in need of reform. Further, he noted that "although the power of schools and educators to influence individual students is never to be underestimated, out-of-school factors associated with poverty play both a powerful and limiting role in what can actually be achieved" (Berliner, 2006, p. 950; see also Darling-Hammond, 2007). In short, the process of school reform is a nested one. Just as teachers and students are nested within schools that influence what they can and cannot achieve, schools are nested within neighborhoods, communities, school districts, states, and nations. And school reform will always be influenced—both positively and negatively—by factors beyond the schools walls. With this caveat, we firmly believe that there is much that reading researchers and educators *can* influence within school boundaries and it is in this spirit that our review describes what we have learned, what we suspect, and what future research is needed for schools to become or remain successful sites for reading development in the 21st century.

This review provides a window into what constitutes school reform in reading as well as illustrative initiatives that demonstrate promise or success in closing the achievement gap for diverse students, within the context created by the federal No Child Left Behind (NCLB, 2002) Act and its demand for increased accountability. We begin with a history of school reform *in general*, on which school reform efforts in reading stand. Next, we turn to *curriculum-based* school reform efforts in reading within the Comprehensive School Reform movement. Third, we examine school reform efforts in reading based in *teacher development*. We conclude by summarizing where we have been and consider what issues should be address in future research on whole-school reform efforts, if this research is to be useful in preparing students to meet this century's new demands.

SETTING THE STAGE: A CONTEXT FOR UNDERSTANDING SCHOOL REFORM IN READING

School reform in reading builds on a substantial body of research and practice dating back to the turn of the last century (Cuban, 1998). The topic remains as important today as it was when initially introduced, and for many of the same reasons cited in research across the decades. In the early part of the 20th century, progressive educators argued that "dramatic social and economic change demands equally dramatic educational change" and that changes must include a focus on the subject matter and how teachers and students handle it (Mirel, 2003, p. 478). Similarly, scholars in the last quarter of the 20th century argued that schools are our nation's hope for insuring equity in access to high quality educational experiences for all learners (Edmonds, 1979). Researchers identified features distinguishing successful or effective schools from less successful ones (e.g., Brookover & Lezotte, 1979, cited in Purkey & Smith, 1983). By the end of the 20th century and early 21st, researchers focused on how to initiate, enact, sustain, and scale successful school reform efforts that move schools designated as ineffective to becoming effective, particularly schools serving students diverse in language, race, ethnicity, and economic situations (e.g., Datnow, Lasky, Stringfield, & Teddlie, 2005).

Throughout the decades of research, scholars uncovered challenges schools face as they engaged in reform efforts, leading to the current recognition that change happens through the work of teachers, principals, parents, and students (Borko, Wolf, Simone, & Uchiyama, 2004) situated within systemic reform at multiple levels (Anyon, 1994; Datnow et al., 2005). Characteristic of current research are studies examining the processes underlying successful school change (e.g., Au, 2005; Borman & Associates, 2005; Raphael, Au, & Goldman, 2009; Mosenthal, Lipson, Mekkelsen, & Thompson, 2003: Taylor, Pearson, Peterson, & Rodriguez, 2005; Timperley & Parr, 2007) and challenges to such change efforts (e.g., Cambone, 1995; Grossman, Wineburg, & Woolworth, 2001; Popkewitz, Tabachnick, & Wehlage, 1982; Uline, Tschannen-Moran, & Perez, 2003).

While school reform researchers share a common goal of improving the quality of education for all students, researchers vary considerably in how they approach the study of this problem. Passow (1984) suggested that the serious study of the processes of educational change and reform emerged in the late 1950s, leading to research in the late 1970s and 1980s that focused on defining features of more and less successful schools (e.g., Austin, 1979; Brookover & Lezotte, 1979; Edmonds, 1979; Purkey & Smith, 1983). The findings from this research led to various lists of distinguishing features, including: (a) strong principal leadership—both administrative and instructional, (b) high expectations for both teacher and student performance, (c) teaching that emphasizes cognitive development as well as warmth toward students, (d) teacher choice in approaches that respond to individual students' needs, (e) reliance on teacher-developed tests and teacher judgments of student achievement, and (f) students' self-efficacy (see, for example, Austin, 1979).

Over the decades, the research evolved from identifying these distinguishing features to studying the impact of the context in which schools are nested and the processes that school faculty and staff engage in within those contexts to improve the quality of their instruction. Researchers examined vehicles with the potential to improve school practices. One key area explored grew out of policy research – examining the impact of new policies at national, state, or district levels (e.g., Dutrow, Fisk, Koch, Roop, & Wixson, 2002; Datnow & Stringfield, 2000; Datnow et al., 2005; Furman, Clune, & Elmore, 1988) on classroom instruction. A second area included studies of changes in teachers' knowledge and practices (e.g., Ahrens, 2005 Duffy, 1993; Griffin & Barnes, 1984; Newmann, King, & Youngs, 2000; Rogers et al., 2006; Santa, 2006), including creating teacher networks (e.g., Stein & D'Amico, 2002) and developing professional communities (e.g., Grossman et al., 2001), as well as adopting and implementing particular curriculum initiatives (see Rowan, Camburn, & Barnes, 2004). A third area examined changes to leadership, their practices, and school organization (e.g., Fink & Brayman, 2006; Spillane, Halverson, & Diamond, 2001; Heckman & Montera, 2009).

Most recently, researchers tackled questions related to sustainability and scaling up of successful reform efforts (e.g., Coburn, 2003; Giles & Hargreaves, 2006; Goldman, 2005; Hatch, 2000; McDonald, Keesler, Nils, & Schneider, 2006; McLaughlin & Mitra, 2001) since "it is one thing to demand that all schools be effective; it is an entirely different matter to assume, without further research, that what has positive effects in one setting will invariably have the same effects in another" (Purkey & Smith, 1983, p. 439). Some researchers examined particular challenges in the school context that potentially derail school reform. For example, Cambone (1995) drew on theory, research, and personal communication with leaders of large-scale reform projects to document the role of time in facilitating or impeding school reform. He documented how critical time is for successful school reform – including time for teachers to learn the new initiative and time for making it their own.

Other researchers provided a window into what constitutes the productive use of time, distinguishing between time spent simply participating in meetings together and time spent on the work of a professional learning community—teachers deepening their disciplinary knowledge as well as learning new pedagogical practices (Grossman et al., 2001). Strike (2004) noted that teachers used time to work together as a professional community with a shared vision that was "expressed in activities through which people cooperate in realizing aims that are rooted in the shared vision" (Strike, 2004, p. 223). Both Grossman and her colleagues and Strike emphasized that such a community was not simply a group of people who were mutually fond of one another, but rather, that it was made up of people who "share a common core of purpose and shared commitment" (Strike, 2004, p. 228). Such a professional community used "time to know colleagues well and to plan for critical action" (Gallego, Hollingsworth, & Whitenack, 2001, p. 261). Community members learned to engage in constructive conflict (Grossman et al., 2001; Uline et al., 2003) so that the work was not derailed by conflicting beliefs and goals that remained beneath the surface. The shared pursuit of their vision, the care that teachers took in initiating students into the work, and the structural features of the school that supported the work (Goddard, Goddard, & Tschannen-Moran, 2007; Irwin & Farr, 2004; Strike, 2004) all contributed to sustainability of the reform effort.

However, studies also reveal a "weak record of sustainability of innovative schools over time" (Giles & Hargreaves, 2006, p. 125) attributed by Giles and Hargreaves to three causes. First, some efforts are not sustainable due to perceptions related to resources, such as imagined or actual need for additional resources, or the beliefs that participants were handpicked or volunteers. Second, some are not sustainable due to factors outside the school's control, such as changing leadership, faculty, or student populations; shifts in policies or district priorities; such pressures outside or internal to the school may draw the school back toward more conventional approaches. Third, some are not sustainable because of changes to the external contexts such as large-scale reform efforts that supercede effective school-level reforms. Other researchers point to the possibility that successful reform efforts are context-specific (Purkey & Smith, 1983), difficult to scale if "large-scale reforms succeed or fail based on issues of local implementation" (Borko et al., 2004, p. 172).

Determining success of an intervention for subsequent scaling has its own set of challenges that stem from the criteria to be adopted for defining success. For example, Cuban (1998) suggested there are tensions that arise from the differences in criteria for policy-makers and practitioners. The former tend to stress effectiveness (how well did the initiative increase test scores?), popularity (how is the initiative perceived by the general public?), and fidelity (is the initiative's implementation faithful to the original conception and the policies that guide it?). In contrast, while practitioners acknowledge the importance of effectiveness, they tend to emphasize adaptability (how easily can the initiative be modified to fit our circumstances?) over fidelity, and longevity (how durable is this initiative in the face of competing agendas?). There are tensions that also reflect differing definitions of scale—is it about increasing the depth of understanding and level of participation (e.g., Coburn, 2003) or about increasing the size of the project, the numbers of participants (McDonald et al., 2006)?

In summary, whole-school reform in reading follows a long tradition of scholarship dedicated to improving the lives of teachers and students, with the goal of insuring that all students' reach the highest levels of success. There are ongoing debates about what such reform must entail, but the history of school reform suggests that success will be determined by attention to the multiple layers in which a reform is embedded, the key participants responsible for the innovation and the community in which they interact, understanding what differentiates more and less successful learning environments, and attention to how to move all students toward success. In the next two sections we examine two different perspectives and related approaches to whole-school reform in reading: (a) curriculum based reform efforts that emphasize effectiveness and fidelity as underlying criteria for success and (b) professional development based reform efforts that emphasize effectiveness, adaptability, and sustainability.

CURRICULUM BASED REFORM EFFORTS: COMPREHENSIVE SCHOOL REFORM

The collection of research studies that constitutes Comprehensive School Reform (CSR) reflects one of the broadest attempts to apply principles of whole-school reform specifically to improvement of the reading curriculum. The hallmark of CSR studies is their focus on the school as a system in which various components of reform must be coordinated to work together. CSR was stimulated by legislation passed by the U.S. Congress in 1997 in response to concerns by policy makers that costly, large-scale federal programs, such as Title I of the Elementary and Secondary Education Act, had led to only modest improvements in student achievement (e.g., Borman & D'Agostino, 1996). The idea was that individual schools should not have to find their own solutions for school improvement but should instead rely on already tested, externally developed models (Borman, Hewes, Overman, & Brown, 2002). At the time, few researchers and educators questioned the reliance on externally developed models; such critiques would come later.

This emphasis on CSR in the 2000s signaled a shift in school reform initiatives, away from the management emphasis prominent in the 1990s to an emphasis on curriculum as a basis for whole-school reform (Skindrud & Gersten, 2006). The criteria for CSR models are: (a) a comprehensive design aligned with the school's curriculum, professional development, and technology, (b) effective, research-based teaching strategies; (c) high quality, ongoing professional development; (d) benchmarks and measurable goals for student achievement, (5) support of administrators and teachers; (e) provisions for the meaningful involvement of parents and community members; (f) assistance from an external partner with expertise in school-wide reform; (g) a plan for evaluating both reform implementation and student results; and (h) coordination of resources available through federal, state, local, and private sources (McCombs & Quiat, 2002). These criteria reflected findings of the school reform research of the day and were consistent with the assumption that a comprehensive, externally developed reform model could readily be used to improve achievement across a wide variety of schools. Because of policy makers' desire to see improvement on a large scale, potential challenges—such as differences among schools and educators' ownership of reform efforts—were not topics that received serious consideration.

Although many CSR models exist, three models have been used in numerous schools and studied in detail and thus serve as the focus for this review. The models are: (a) Accelerated Schools, (b) America's Choice, and (c) Success for All. However, although these programs all fall under the broad umbrella of CSR, they differ in their histories of development, their assumptions about the levers that should be pulled to bring about change, and their potential to improve student achievement.

Accelerated Schools

In 1986 Stanford University professor Henry Levin conducted a project with two elementary schools following a philosophy and process he labeled Accelerated Schools. Levin sought to accelerate the learning, particularly of disadvantaged students, through constructivist teaching and challenging activities, rather than skills-based remediation (Levin, 1987). The guiding principles of Accelerated Schools reflect many of the characteristics scholars have argued are necessary for successful school reform. These include unity of purpose and a common vision of the school shared by educators, students, parents, and the community (Goddard et al., 2007; Strike, 2004); empowerment through shared decision-making and responsibility for changes in curriculum, instruction, and school organization (Grossman et al., 2001); and building on participants' strengths to capture the knowledge and creativity of everyone in the school community. Accelerated Schools relies on what Correnti and Rowan (2007) characterize as "cultural" controls, or an emphasis on philosophical constructs and collaboration, to promote improvement in instruction. The research on Accelerated Schools suggests, however, that while these characteristics are necessary, they may not be sufficient for success in raising students' literacy achievement levels.

Because the program does not prescribe targets for student achievement, curriculum, and instructional practices, Correnti and Rowan (2007) hypothesized that Accelerated Schools would result in fewer observable changes in classroom instruction than more prescriptive programs with clear targets which everyone strives to reach. They found that schools following the Accelerated Schools program did not show teaching practices that differed significantly from those in comparison schools. In an evaluation study of Accelerated Schools, Bloom, Ham, Melton, and O'Brien (2001) found that the program took time to implement and, likely as a result, showed no achievement gains during the first few years. By the fifth year, modest but statistically significant gains on test scores became evident, although these gains were seen primarily in students in the middle range in terms of academic standing, not among those in the low range.

A question raised by the research on Accelerated Schools is what might happen in a CSR model with a stronger and more direct emphasis on changing instruction, although still from a constructivist as opposed to basic skills orientation. We consider models with a constructivist orientation to be those that emphasize literature, comprehension, and meaning making with text, with some attention to word identification. Conversely, those with a basic skills orientation emphasize contrived texts, word identification and phonics, with some attention to comprehension. America's Choice provides such a constructivist model.

America's Choice

The America's Choice program began in 1998 with a launch in 40 schools. This program evolved out of work by the National Center on Education and the Economy (NCEE, http://www.ncee. org/) a not-for-profit organization active in the U.S. standards movement. Like Accelerated Schools, America's Choice seeks to raise student achievement by focusing on elements suggested by research or current policy as central to successful reform. America's Choice emphasizes (a) a standards-based system of assessments with (b) instruction aligned to those standards. America's Choice also emphasizes (c) strong instructional leadership, (d) the building of professional learning communities, and (e) parental and community engagement (Consortium for Policy Research in Education, 2002).

In contrast to Accelerated Schools, in addition to coaching and professional development, America's Choice provides schools with instructional materials and strategies. Instruction is based on readers and writers workshops and genre and author studies at each grade level. The model seeks to promote students' independent reading through classroom libraries, a book of the month, and a campaign in which students are encouraged to read 25 books, as described on the program's website (www.AmericasChoice.org).

In contrast to the "cultural control" characteristic of Accelerated Schools, this program has been described by Correnti and Rowan (2007) as using "professional controls" to foster instructional improvement. For example, schools were typically required to start by improving the teaching of writing, with reading and mathematics to follow, and to create positions for a design coach and a literacy coordinator.

Correnti and Rowan (2007) found the America's Choice strategies of "professional control" to be effective in influencing the teaching of writing, as significant differences were seen in both the quantity and quality of writing instruction, when judged against comparison schools. The Rochester, New York schools studied by May and Supovitz (2006) followed a 3-year implementation plan, with less involvement with NCEE after that. A district official reported that the original program design "started to erode in many places" (p. 245), indicating a problem with sustainability. In a quasi-experimental interrupted time-series analysis, May and Supovitz found that students in America's Choice schools showed significantly higher annual gains in reading performance, when compared to similar students in other schools. However, although lower performing students benefited more than higher performing ones, and minority (African American and Hispanic) students more than students of other ethnicities, America's Choice students' overall level of performance remained below national norms for the standardized achievement test used.

Typical challenges in school reform, highlighted in research on America's Choice, are variability in the implementation of the program and, even in cases of successful implementation, the sustainability of innovative practices as time goes on. Success for All, the final CSR model to be discussed, was designed to promote consistency of implementation.

Success for All

Success for All is by far the most widely used and extensively evaluated of the three major CSR programs. Developed by Robert Slavin of Johns Hopkins University, along with his wife and colleague, Nancy Madden, it was first implemented in 1987 as a pilot program for an inner-city school. The program emphasizes phonics as well as literal comprehension and requires that all students participate in a 90-minute reading period every day taught by teachers who use scripted lessons (Slavin & Madden, 2001). Success for All teachers meet with their students in groups that are typically smaller than regular classes, with students grouped for reading by achievement level rather than by age or grade (i.e., students change classrooms for reading, with students across grade levels mixed to maintain groupings of similar reading ability). Student progress is assessed about every 8–9 weeks. Depending on their assessment results, students may receive tutoring or be moved to another group.

In contrast to the "cultural" control used by Accelerated Schools or "professional" control used by America's Choice, Correnti and Rowan (2007) described Success for All's approach as involving "procedural control." This control stems from the scripting of lessons, strict rules about grouping, and Success for All program monitoring of local activities to promote fidelity of implementation.

Borman et al. (2007) conducted a randomized field trial implementing Success for All in 18 schools with 10,000 students. They found that Success for All showed strong implementation over the 3 years of the study because of its well-specified and prescriptive nature, and its ability to address both organizational and instructional issues. Sterbinsky, Ross, and Redfield (2006) found that teachers in 5 Success for All schools perceived school climate to be somewhat more positive than did teachers in control schools.

Correnti and Rowan (2007) concluded that, of the three major CSR programs, Success for All gave teachers the most detailed plans for instruction, including routines for teaching reading and sequenced, scripted lessons. As a result, teachers did tend to adhere to the program. Similarly, Ross et al. (2004) found the Success for All teachers reported they had gained a thorough understanding of the program, were receiving continuing professional development, valued the professional development provided by SFA, and had made substantial changes to classroom instruction. Comparison teachers working with another model, also highly scripted in design, reported only that they had gained a thorough understanding of the program.

Klingner, Cramer, and Harry (2006) studied the implementation challenges faced by 4 high-need urban schools working with Success for All. Some teachers expressed dissatisfaction with the program and preferred instead to rely on their own teaching and assessment practices. However, because teachers were supposed to adhere strictly to the program, even changes that proved effective were not recognized. The program's lack of flexibility thus became a drawback. In addition, teachers felt that regrouping made it difficult for them to get to know all of their homeroom students' needs as readers. A question raised by Success for All is whether accomplished teachers in schools with prescriptive programs may actually be making adaptations to meet the needs of their students. By downplaying or concealing these adaptations, they may be able to continue to promote student achievement without causing conflict within their schools.

Klingner et al. (2006) found weak support for the lowest performing students, with the kinds of supports recommended by Success for All (e.g., tutoring and parental involvement) proving difficult for schools to implement. Students who did not progress were recycled through the same materials, resulting in a loss of interest in reading. In these situations, boredom was found to be a problem for both teachers and students. A group supposedly consisting of students at similar reading levels in one school included students ranging from first through fifth grade. The younger students—high performers compared to their same-age peers—were motivated to learn while the older students—low performers relative to their same-age peers, were disaffected.

The effects of Success for All on student achievement have been examined in a considerable number of studies. Borman and Hewes (2002) reported positive findings in their study that tracked students at the original Success for All schools through Grade 8 (1986–99). They found the effects of Success for All to compare favorably with those of programs such as the Perry Preschool (Schweinhart, Weikart, & Larner, 1986) that demonstrated lasting achievement effects. When compared to control students, Success for All students showed significantly higher reading scores and were less likely to be placed in special education or retained in the same grade. Borman and Hewes found that Grade 8 students as a group showed reading achievement at the 20th percentile on a nationally normed test, with control students at the 14th percentile; despite the advantage to Success for All students, both groups remained far below national norms. Thus, while Success for All students did benefit from the program, its effects were not powerful enough to overcome other sources of disadvantage, such as family poverty, unsafe neighborhoods, and poorly maintained school facilities, as described by Kozol (1991).

Ross et al. (2004) examined the achievement results of students in Success for All schools at grades 2, 4, and 6 and found no differences with students in the same grades in the district as a whole. In their study of 5 schools, Sterbinsky, Ross, and Redfield (2006) described achievement effects as inconclusive but slightly positive overall for Success for All students in grades 1–3. Skindrud and Gersten (2006) found that the reading achievement of primary grade students in a large urban district was stronger with the Success for All and Open Court programs. In addition, teachers rated Success for All as superior in social outcomes because of its use of cooperative learning, teamwork, and social reinforcement. Borman et al. (2007) reported that

Success for All schools were able to produce broad effects in literacy for children exposed to the program for their first 3 years of their academic careers, as well as for all children, regardless of their number of years of exposure to the reform. In short, although some studies have failed to show positive results for Success for All, there is more evidence for the effectiveness of this CSR model than for any other.

In summary, research on the three major CSR programs reveals both their strengths and weaknesses as models for school reform to improve reading achievement. A continuing challenge with these three programs has been to obtain sizeable gains in reading achievement, particularly for disadvantaged students or students who had previously achieved at low levels. Even when positive results were shown, the reading achievement of disadvantaged students tended to remain far below national norms. The challenge of improving achievement may well be related to the nature of these programs. The more prescriptive the program (i.e., Success for All compared to Accelerated Schools), the easier it is for administrators and teachers to implement. However, a highly prescriptive program may lack the flexibility required to encourage appropriate adaptations by teachers, required to meet the needs of all students. Teachers' orientation toward following a prescription, rather than toward reflective practice and evidence-based teaching, may be related to the programs' emphasis on curriculum enactment and associated professional development that did not tend to build teachers' overall strengths as teachers of reading beyond the boundaries of the particular program. Clearly, a balance is required between specificity of program features and flexibility to address the situations of particular schools, teachers, and students.

A second problem identified across projects was that of sustainability, with evidence in some studies that even initially strong implementations deteriorated over time. Over two decades ago, Bullough, Robert, and Gitlin (1985, p. 224) suggested that prepackaged curriculum "disconnects students from teachers, reduces teaching to technical management of persons and materials, and imposes a furious work pace that limits opportunities for reflection." More recently, Darling-Hammond (2007) noted that such programs have not shown sustainable success for creating successful schools, arguing that instead, successful schools balance professional autonomy with accountability in terms of goals for student learning. Sustainability may well be affected by educators' ownership of a literacy reform effort and whether they believe or learn through experience that it has positive benefits for their school, for their own professional growth, and for their students' learning. The studies described in the next section represent projects that have taken an alternative approach to curriculum-based reform, emphasizing teachers' professional development—including evidence-based teaching and processes for sustainable reform—that support great teacher autonomy balanced with public accountability for increasing students' reading achievement levels.

PROFESSIONAL DEVELOPMENT BASED REFORM EFFORTS

Alternatives to the Comprehensive School Reform models for whole-school reform in reading emphasize investing resources in teacher development more than in program materials. Such approaches share six elements derived from reviews of successful school change efforts. First, participating teachers and administrators must have a good understanding of the key principles of the reform framework they are following (McLaughlin & Mitra, 2001). Second, participants must have an internal commitment to the process of change (Datnow & Stringfield, 2000). Simply buying-in to a reform process through a vote (e.g., 75% agreeing to the reform) is not sufficient (Borman et al., 2003). Third, participants must understand that the reform effort will change over time and that local adaptations are needed (McLaughlin & Mitra, 2002). Fourth, strong building leadership and district support are needed to sustain and scale a successful reform effort (Fink & Brayman, 2006; May & Supovitz, 2006). Fifth, a successful reform effort requires high quality professional development in which participants work together as a professional learning community (Giles & Hargreaves, 2006). And sixth, a successful reform effort requires that teachers develop deeper content knowledge and more effective pedagogy (Cohen & Moffit, 2002; Guiney, 2002; Jennings, 2002).

We draw on seven illustrative research studies conducted in this tradition between 2000 and 2008 as we moved into the 21st century (see Table 25.1). The studies were chosen to reflect adherence to three key features but representing different geo-political contexts. First, all studies supported teachers in schools serving students diverse in languages, race and ethnicity, and economic situations. Second, all demonstrated positive impact on students' reading achievement. Third, all had published results in at least one article that appeared in a recognized archival research source.

In preparation for this review, we searched for articles in archival journals related to literacy instruction, reading achievement, and school improvement (reform, change) that had been published since 2000. Many articles were eliminated from this interpretive review because they did not focus on school-wide reading improvement efforts across multiple grades or they did not report on the efficacy of the reform model as evidenced by positive results related to students' reading achievement. Also, because CSR models were reviewed in the previous section, reports on CSR models were not included in this review of recent reading reform models focusing on teacher professional learning.

Collectively, these studies report on successful approaches to school reform in reading that provide a depth of understanding about essential elements of effective school-wide reading improvement efforts. The studies illustrate the importance of staff support for organizational and individual teacher change and attention to improving classroom practices that address students' individual and collective learning needs and reading abilities.

We discuss the findings from each study in terms of both organizational change and individual teacher change. In the following sections, we begin by describing each study's contributions to our understanding of organizational changes, then summarize the themes that emerge across the studies. We then turn to each study's contributions to our understanding of individual teacher changes and the emerging themes across studies.

Focus on Organizational Change

Consistent among the seven representative studies is the presence of an explicit framework and process for change. Research on school reform in general has demonstrated convincingly that such work is challenging at the collective level. Thus, successful school-wide reading improvement efforts pay close attention to the organizational issues that researchers have demonstrated affect the success and sustainability of any reform effort, beginning with the collaborative understandings amongst staff that must evolve for the effort to be successful (Goddard et al., 2007; Irwin & Farr, 2004; Strike, 2004). We discuss organizational change across projects in terms of: (a) vision, commitment, and ownership of the change process, (b) leadership, (c) deliberate use of data, and (d) collaborative school community.

Vision, Commitment, and Ownership of Change Process.   Vision of, commitment to, and ownership of a school reading improvement effort must be in place for a school staff to sustain an effective effort successfully over time (Strike, 2004). In the Standards Based Change Process (Au, 2005; Au, Raphael, & Mooney, 2008a), external facilitators guided schools as they established a vision for student learning and embarked on a process for change. They also helped teachers and administrators understand the importance of staying the course for 5 years or more to make the improvements necessary to achieve substantial gains in student learning

Table 25.1

Approach		Citation(s)	Description
Standards-Based Change Process	SBC	Au, 2005 Au, Raphael, Mooney (2008) Raphael, Au, Goldman (2009)	Studied in 33 high-poverty schools in Hawaii and 10 schools in Chicago. Schools in Hawaii more effective in implementing the reform saw greater growth in students reading scores than less effective schools. Students in a Chicago school improved in proficiency on the state reading test from 26 to 79%.
School Change in Reading Framework	SCR	Taylor, Pearson, Peterson, & Rodriguez (2005) Taylor, Peterson, Marx, & Chein (2007) Taylor & Peterson (2007) Taylor et al. (2005) Taylor et al. (2007b) Taylor & Peterson (2007b)	Studied in 13 high poverty schools across the U.S. and 46 moderate to high poverty schools in Minnesota. Children on average made significant gains in comprehension from grades 1 through 3. Students demonstrated greater reading growth in schools more successful in implementing the reform than less successful. By the second year in the third study, students in grades 1, 2, and 3 had mean comprehension scores at the 55th, 46th, and 47th percentiles (up from 42nd, 42nd, and 39th, respectively) on a standardized reading test
Literacy Professional Development Model	LPD	Timperly & Parr (2007)	A 2-year school-wide literacy improvement project funded by the New Zealand Ministry of Education and implemented in 91 elementary schools. For all students, the gain in reading achievement was twice the expected gain over the two years of the project (effective size gain = .87). For the lowest 20% of the students, the reading gain was approximately four times the expected gain (ES gain = 1.97).
Acceleration of Achievement in Diverse Schools Project	AADS	McNaughton, Macdonald, Amituanai-Toloa, Lai, & Farry (2006)	Studied 7 high-poverty, culturally and linguistically diverse urban schools in New Zealand over 3 years. After 2 and 3 years, students in years 4–9 of schooling had higher reading achievement than baseline comparison students at these schools (effect sizes from .31 to .59) and higher reading achievement than students at comparison schools (effect sizes from .33 to .61). By the end of the year, the average stanine for the 7 schools for students present during the entire intervention improved from 3.1 to 4.2.
Middle and High Schools Beating the Odds	MHSBO	Langer (2000)	Studied 14 schools with successful middle & high school English programs (e.g., students performing better on state tests than students in demographically similar schools) in New York, Texas, California, and Florida over a 5-year period; and 11 typical middle and high schools in the same states over the same time frame.
Successful Elementary Schools in Vermont	SES-V	Mosenthal, Lipson, Torncello, Russ, & Mekkelsen (2004) Lipson, Mosenthal, Mekkelsen, & Russ (2004)	Studied 6 successful Vermont elementary schools (in which at least 80% of the students at grades 2 and 4 were performing above the state standards in reading). They also studied 3 less successful schools (in which 60% or more of the students in grades 2 and 4 scores below the state standards.)

(continued)

Table 25.1   Continued

Approach		Citation(s)	Description
Successful Elementary School in California	SES-CA	Fisher & Frey (2007)	Studied a large (e.g., 1,500 students), diverse, very high poverty elementary school (e.g., 100% of students on subsidized lunch) in California which made strong progress in students' reading achievement. The mean percent of students in grades 2 through 5 at the proficient or advanced level on the state reading test increased from 12 to 31% over a 6-year period.

and create the organizational structures within the school that are critical to the work (e.g., SBC Process Leadership Team or Lead Literacy Team, grade level meetings). Teachers working within grade level teams developed belief statements about teaching, learning, and literacy; the external facilitator helped teachers identify themes running across grade levels. Next, each grade level team collaborated to generate their vision of what their school's excellent graduating reader would know and be able to do. The facilitator then assisted their SBC leadership team in generating a composite vision of the excellent graduating reader. This composite vision statement was presented to the entire faculty for revision and eventual approval. Teachers, by grade level, continued to develop ownership over their reading curriculum by developing grade level benchmarks and aligning them with those of adjacent grade levels, constructing an evidence system for monitoring students' progress and adjusting instruction in response to students' needs, and ultimately constructing their individual school's literacy curriculum.

Schools using the School Change in Reading process (e.g., Taylor & Peterson, 2007b) had facilitators who focused on helping teachers develop a deep understanding of effective reading instruction and engaged them in collaborative learning experiences to become increasingly effective teachers of reading. Schools embarking on the School Change in Reading process were encouraged to have at least 75%–80% buy-in across teachers and administrators at the beginning of a 2- or 3-year reading improvement effort. Although the reform effort began with an externally provided process for change, the external partner stressed at the onset that teachers and administrators would need to spend more than the initial 2 to 3 years and develop internal motivation and ownership for a continual process of change in order for the effort to be successful and sustainable. Internal leadership was developed through workshops at the onset of the project and throughout the initial 3 years, during which teachers and administrators learned about and discussed essential elements of successful and sustainable school-wide reform efforts: leadership, collaboration, ownership, quality professional development, and effective content knowledge and pedagogy.

The Literacy Professional Development model (Timperley & Parr, 2007) focused on two major components. First, there was a focus on establishing project coherence in which national project leaders, external facilitators, school leadership, and teachers worked toward the three common goals established by the Ministry of Education of (a) increasing student reading achievement, (b) implementing effective literacy instruction, and (c) providing effectively-led professional learning communities. Second, there was a focus on using evidence-informed inquiry and making adaptations in practice at each level of the project. External facilitators and school professionals worked together to construct each school's professional development program. Over time, the expectations developed that everyone involved in the process—the teachers, principals, facilitators, and project leaders—needed to learn, including how to use data to solve problems and modify practices. Project coherence was established through a deeper collective understanding of the school-wide improvement approach being used by all participants. The Ministry of Education established general project goals designed to create project coherence while state leaders provided an external framework for change. However, project leaders, external facilitators, school administrators, and teachers jointly developed the school-wide improvement process and professional learning activities to meet the needs of individual schools.

Collaboration among researchers, schools, and the Ministry of Education, as they worked together to positively impact reading achievement, was a focus in the Acceleration of Achievement in Diverse Schools Project (McNaughton et al., 2006). Researchers established the framework for change over a 3-year period. Like the School Change in Reading project, over time school personnel assumed increasing responsibility for the reform effort. In year 1, researchers and school leaders focused on the analysis of data on students' literacy achievement and on classroom instruction through observations of teaching within classrooms, followed by critical discussions and problem solving related to more effective instructional practices designed to meet students' needs. In year 2, the first year's activities continued and, to begin building internal leadership and ownership, researchers provided ten professional development sessions focused on effective reading instruction to school teams of literacy leaders and teachers. In year 3, school leaders and researchers jointly planned for sustainability by supporting teachers as they engaged in action research projects within school-based, professional learning circles. They studied aspects of effective instruction that met students' and teachers' needs.

In a study of successful middle and high school English programs, Langer (2000) found they all had developed highly coordinated efforts to increase student performance. Effective schools were characterized by teachers and administrators who shared and debated ideas for identifying students' needs, selecting and developing techniques for instructional improvement, and implementing professional learning strategies to help teachers gain new knowledge and apply this knowledge to their daily teaching. Their debates led to targeted, local plans for instructional improvement, coordinated across grades, that were based on the notion of continual modification. Each year teachers expected changes, sometimes minor and sometimes major, in curricular goals and instructional approaches as new research-based ideas surfaced or as test results pointed to student abilities that needed to be strengthened. As students' scores increased, teachers set higher goals. In contrast to other studies (e.g., Au, 2005; Taylor et al., 2005), the schools that Langer studied did not start with an external framework for change; rather the schools developed coordinated efforts over time through which teachers developed a sense of ownership to improve students' abilities.

Mosenthal and colleagues (Mosenthal, Lipson, Torncello, Russ, & Mekkelsen, 2004) studied successful elementary schools that had an 8- to 10-year history of commitment to literacy improvement. Within these successful schools, administrators and teachers worked toward a shared vision for students' literacy achievement that included a collective sense of responsibility for students' learning. This shared vision helped to develop a sense of community among school personnel. As with the schools studied in the Langer (2000) project, these schools did not start with an external framework; rather a framework that was school-specific developed over time.

The process of change in the Fisher and Frey (2007) study began with an elected literacy task force comprised of teachers, parents, and administrators. The site-based management, elected governance committee charged the literacy task force with "developing a plan that could be implemented across grades, program types, and philosophical ideologies" (Fisher & Frey, 2007, p. 33). Over a 3-year period, the task force developed and led a literacy improvement plan and change process for their school. Elected grade level task force members regularly sought feedback from their colleagues about different aspects of literacy instruction. Additional teacher buy-in developed as the plan was formed through this extensive teacher input over time.

Across these studies, five themes emerged that underscore the importance of the members of a school community developing a shared vision for and establishing a long-term commitment

Table 25.2   Vision, Commitment, and Ownership over Reform Process

Theme by Project	Standards-Based Change Process	School Change in Reading Framework	Literacy Professional Development Model	Acceleration of Achievement in Diverse School Project	Middle and High School Beating the Odds	Successful Elementary School in Vermont	Successful Elementary School in California
Initial external framework for change	X	X	X	X			
Internal framework for change					X	X	X
Shared internal vision/ownership for success	X	X	X		X	X	X
Long-term (>2-year) commitment to improvement process	X	X		X	X	X	X
Modifications of improvement process over time	X	X	X	X	X	X	X

to literacy improvement (see Table 25.2). The vision incorporates a framework for change that may come from either an external partner or within the school. Consistent with the findings of Cambone (1995), staff members understand that the process for change that will help them achieve this vision takes time—3 or more years—and that the process itself evolves over time as schools develop increased knowledge, expertise, and experience. It is important to point out that the absence of a check mark in the tables in this section does not indicate that a characteristic was not present in a particular project. It just was not apparent from the published sources that were the basis of this review.

Further, the vision for improvement undergoes modifications and becomes clearer to all participants over time, which—as Cuban (1998) noted—is something that has high value to teachers and administrators and has the potential to contribute to their ownership over the process. The commitment by teachers and administrators tends to become stronger and more universal as students' reading scores increase and as teachers develop increased perceptions of collective efficacy related to their abilities to effect change as well as increased ownership over the school's reading program.

Leadership.   Once a school has an initial level of commitment, strong and shared leadership (Spillane et al., 2001) is critical for the reform effort to move forward with success. In the Standards-Based Change Process, Au (2005) and her colleagues (Au et al., 2008b) worked with schools that had an on-site curriculum leader with deep knowledge of the school and faculty, as well as of literacy instruction. While the principal's visible commitment was important to success, she or he rarely provided leadership for the day-to-day work. Instead, a teacher leader (e.g., Literacy Coordinator, Curriculum Leader, Lead Literacy Teacher) served in that role. The teacher leader was supported by a leadership team that represented each interest group in the school (e.g., grade level teams, school subject groups, special needs teachers) and the school's principal created a school organization that insured teachers ample time to work within and share within and across grade levels as they developed the components of their literacy curriculum. The leadership team kept the reform effort moving forward over multiple years (Au et al., 2008a). Ongoing professional learning for principals, curriculum leaders, and facilitators was an important aspect of each school's work with the Standards-Based Change Process.

Similarly, the most successful schools using the School Change in Reading Framework—those whose students were achieving accelerated growth in reading—had a leadership team that met once a month. The team consisted of an effective teacher leader who served as a literacy coordinator and coach, enthusiastic teacher leaders representing different grade levels and specialists, and a supportive principal (Taylor et al., 2005; Taylor et al., 2007). The leadership team used their time together to consider how to best guide their school. This was seen in the agendas they created for whole school meetings to discuss aspects of the school-wide reading program. Their agendas focused on such aspects as sharing their reform-related successes, collaboration between classroom teachers and special teachers in the delivery of reading instruction, establishment of cross-grade coordinated learning goals related to state and district standards, constructing a school-wide assessment plan, and discussing interventions to meet the needs of struggling readers. Leadership team members took the lead in trying new techniques for reflecting on their practice, such as video sharing or peer coaching. The literacy coordinator orchestrated the multiple aspects of the work. She visited classrooms regularly to model effective teaching practices and to engage in peer coaching conversations with teachers. Each school also received support from an external facilitator experienced with the School Change Framework who worked closely with the literacy coordinator. Ongoing professional learning to develop the leadership abilities of principals, leadership team members, literacy coordinators, and external facilitators was an important part of the reform process.

Each school in the Literacy Professional Development Project (Timperley & Parr, 2007) had a literacy leader, nominated for the position by the external facilitator and appointed by the school, who worked closely with the external facilitator to establish a sustainable professional learning community within their school. Enhancement of leadership knowledge and skills became an increasing focus within the project as leaders gradually realized that simply updating teachers about effective literacy practices would be insufficient to achieve the project's goals. Thus, external facilitators, lead literacy teachers, and principals received ongoing professional development on how to be effective school leaders for their school-wide literacy improvement effort.

In the Accelerated Achievement in Diverse Schools Project (McNaughton et al., 2006), school leaders had prominent roles in each year of the reform. In the first year, senior managers and senior teachers within schools analyzed student achievement data and classroom observation data with project researchers and engaged in problem-solving discussions about how to improve practice. In the second and third years, literacy leaders participated in and provided support and oversight to the professional learning experiences for the teachers at their schools.

Langer (2000) reported on shared leadership that had developed at the effective schools she studied. All of the schools had some components of school-based management and shared decision-making in place. Teachers were given responsibilities such as developing curriculum; setting directions in curriculum and instruction in their school or district; and helping to select new teachers. This, in turn, helped to provide teachers with a sense of ownership related to their teaching and to students' literacy achievement.

All of the successful schools Mosenthal et al. (2004) studied (see also Lipson, Mosenthal, Mekkelsen, & Russ, 2004) were characterized by their stable administrative and curricular leadership, with strong influence on teachers' practice from at least one individual (e.g., principal, teacher) during the 8- to 10-year period that they had been focused on literacy improvement. Moreover, each of the successful schools had strong support in the form of research-based information and suggestions from external partners (e.g., university faculty members, members of a Reading Recovery consortium) that promoted on-site ongoing development and improvement.

Fisher and Frey (2007) reported that the literacy task force led by committed teachers had good principal support for this effort. Also, an elected professional development committee planned for and provided professional development that aligned with the literacy improvement framework.

Collectively, these studies report on shared leadership among a principal, teacher coordinator/coach, and teacher leaders who work together to initiate and refine a process of continuous reading improvement within their school (see Table 25.3).

Typically, there is at least one key teacher leader who is instrumental in initiating and sustaining the reform effort. Also, leadership team members collectively inspire their colleagues to become increasingly engaged in and committed to the school literacy improvement effort over time. External partners also bring ideas and support to the process. Ongoing professional development for effective school leadership was an important component in many of the projects.

Principled Use of Data. The importance of teaching to students' specific needs (Darling-Hammond, 1997) has led to reform efforts that emphasize data-driven instruction or evidence-based teaching. In contrast to the tendency of school systems within the United States to emphasize accountability measures using high stakes standardized testing or assessments

Table 25.3   Leadership

Theme by Project	Standards-Based Change Process	School Change in Reading Framework	Literacy Professional Development Model	Acceleration of Achievement in Diverse School Project	Middle and High School Beating the Odds	Successful Elementary School in Vermont	Successful Elementary School in California
Onsite, designated teacher leader(s)	X	X	X	X		X	X
Principal support and involvement	X	X	X	X	X	X	X
Shared leadership/ Leadership team	X	X	X		X	X	X
External support	X	X	X	X		X	
Ongoing professional development for leadership	X	X	X				

created by publishing companies, the successful reform efforts described in the seven research studies emphasized the use of a broad array of data—included teacher constructed tools—to promote changes in instruction. All projects recognized that the use of data is essential to promote change in a school-wide reading improvement effort (Rogers et al., 2006).

In the Standards-Based Change Process (Au, 2005; Au et al., 2008a), each grade level or subject area team within a school coordinated targets for student performance to insure that students could move steadily toward achieving the school's vision of the excellent graduating reader. To monitor students' progress toward the end-of-year targets, teachers created an evidence system that consisted of benchmarks, evidence sources, procedures for gathering the evidence, and scoring tools. The evidence system was used at the beginning of the year to plan instruction for that year's students, at the middle of the year to evaluate their progress toward the benchmarks and adjust instruction as needed, and at the end of the year to assess overall progress and implications for changes to the evidence system itself and classroom practices—instruction, curricula, and assessment. Teachers maintained assessment handbooks to guide them in the procedures to follow to collect and score work samples consistently. As student scores rose, teachers developed benchmarks and rubrics that were more challenging.

Schools using the School Change in Reading Framework (Taylor et al., 2005; Taylor et al., 2007; Taylor, 2007) received an annual formative report with data that included students' progress in reading and teachers' changes in teaching based on observation data, and teachers' perceptions of school-level collaboration and leadership. Leadership teams attended a data retreat every August to identify strengths and weaknesses as evidenced in their school reports and to propose goals to the whole staff for improving practice during the upcoming year. Schools received support from their external partners on how to develop a school-wide plan for looking at, sharing, and using student reading assessment data on an ongoing basis to impact instruction, to identify students who needed reading interventions, and to help teachers make decisions about supplemental learning activities that would challenge all students at their reading levels. Teachers also received observation data on their teaching three times a year and were encouraged to self-evaluate their lessons by themselves or with support from the literacy coordinator.

Similarly, using data at the student, classroom, school, and project level to impact change was a major component of the Literacy Professional Development Project (Timperley & Parr, 2007). Twice a year external facilitators, school leaders, and teachers looked at data on students' reading abilities; data from teachers' interviews, observations, and written responses to hypothetical lesson scenarios; and data from principal and facilitator interviews. Project personnel used initial data for a needs analysis from which they developed action plans. The plans included criterion statements related to the three major project goals: (a) increased student reading achievement, (b) increased teaching effectiveness, and (c) effectively-led professional learning communities. Semi-annual milestone data reports were created and used to guide discussion focused on progress towards project goals, including discussion of the school participants' progress and the effectiveness of the external facilitators' effectiveness.

Critical analysis of data at the student and classroom level was a cornerstone of the Accelerated Achievement in Diverse Schools Project (McNaughton et al., 2006). Each school participated in a two step process that focused on analysis, feedback, and discussion. In the first step, student data were analyzed to identify students' strengths and weaknesses in literacy, and classroom observation data were analyzed to understand current instruction and teaching needs. In the second step, in discussions among senior teachers, administrators, and researchers, participants raised competing theories of the "problem" and evaluated evidence for competing theories. Teachers and school leaders worked together to answer two key questions, "What are we doing which could have influenced the pattern of student achievement?" and "How can we improve what we are doing to raise student achievement?" (Lai & McNaughton, 2008). School teams of teachers also conducted action research projects and often used pre-test and post-test data to determine if newly implemented aspects of their literacy programs, such as techniques to increase reading vocabulary or to teach critical thinking, were effective (McNaughton et al., 2006).

Teachers in successful schools studied by Langer (2001) deliberately integrated the knowledge and skills to be tested into their ongoing English curriculum. In the less effective schools, teachers tended to teach tested knowledge and skills as a separate activity unrelated to their English curriculum. Mosenthal and colleagues (2004) reported similar findings. Five the six schools in the Vermont study had gone through a period of low student performance in reading and came together as a staff to improve their school-wide approach to reading instruction. Teachers in most of the successful schools regularly used data from student portfolios and running records to inform their instruction.

Fisher and Frey (2007) reported that grade level literacy standards served as the curriculum in the school they studied, and teachers held the belief that students could meet grade level expectations. Like the school teams described by Au and her colleagues (Au 2005; Au, Raphael, & Mooney, 2008a; Au, Raphael, & Mooney, 2008b), common assessment measures were developed by grade level teams to assess students' abilities on grade level standards.

Though there was no single way in which data were used across these studies, in all cases we see that use of data at the student, teacher, and school level serves as a potential change agent (see Table 25.4).

Table 25.4   Principled Use of Data

Theme by Project	Standards-Based Change Process	School Change in Reading Framework	Literacy Professional Development Model	Acceleration of Achievement in Diverse School Project	Middle and High School Beating the Odds	Successful Elementary School in Vermont	Successful Elementary School in California
Deliberate, regular use of student data	X	X	X	X	X	X	X
Common assessments developed by grade levels	X						X
Focus on grade level standards	X				X	X	X
Student gains lead to higher expectations	X	X			X		X
Deliberate use of data on classrooms and schools		X	X	X			

While all projects made deliberate, regular use of student data, some also included data on teachers and the school, some emphasized standards as the driving force, and some used changes in student performance levels as the basis for raising expectations for students in subsequent years. Monitoring student changes and seeing improvements following changes in their instructional practices as part of a school reading improvement effort may help motivate participants to sustain the effort over time.

Collaborative School Community.   Research on successful school-wide improvement efforts has underscored the importance of teachers and administrators becoming a collaborative school community (e.g., Gallego et al., 2001) that ignites the imagination of the participants (Heckman & Montera, 2009) who work together across time (Cambone, 1995), and the findings across these seven studies suggest that such is the case for literacy school reform. In the Standards-Based Change Process, collaboration among teachers within and across grade levels and school subject areas developed through generating a common vision of excellent readers upon graduation from their school, crafting grade level benchmarks, and building a staircase curriculum (Au et al., 2008a). By teaching to this well-articulated, coherent curriculum in which students' learning builds on what was taught the previous year, all grade level teams understood that they played an important role in achieving the goal of students graduating from their school as excellent readers. Furthermore, the collaborative process of developing a common vision, benchmarks, assessments, and curriculum guides, helped teachers develop a sense of ownership over their reading program (Au et al., 2008a).

Teachers in a study of elementary schools that were beating the odds (Taylor, Pearson, Clark, and Walpole, 2000) reported that collaboration in teaching was a major reason for their success. The three areas of peer coaching, teaming, and program consistency were mentioned as aspects of collaboration that teachers valued. Taylor (2007) reported that a sense of collective efficacy was found to be positively related to students' growth in reading and increased over time as teachers were involved in their school-wide School Change in Reading process. This process focused on increased collaboration in teaching, grade level data sharing meetings, and collaborative school-based professional learning experiences.

In the Literacy Professional Development Project (Timperley & Parr, 2007), school collaboration developed through the emphasis on co-constructed analysis of project data and planning for next steps related to the project goals. Also, collaboration developed through the co-construction of learning opportunities and new instructional practices to be implemented in classrooms.

Collaboration in the Accelerated Achievement in Diverse Schools Project (McNaughton et al., 2006) was fostered through the professional learning communities in which teachers and school leaders critically analyzed data on students' literacy achievement and on teaching and then engaged in and reported to others on classroom-based action research projects. However, McNaughton et al. (2006) pointed out that external support from the researchers and funding from the government were key factors contributing to the successes of school learning communities, arguing for the importance of school-research-policy partnerships to foster and sustain change in schools.

In effective middle and high schools (Langer, 2000), teachers developed a sense of collective efficacy—the notion that together they could effect positive change. This sense of agency developed through opportunities for teacher leadership and collaboration related to curriculum development, direction setting for instruction, and problem solving related to their English programs.

Teachers in successful schools in Vermont (Lipson et al., 2004) built a collaborative community with high expectations and a climate of commitment. Open communication among administrators and teachers and a sense of teacher autonomy in making instructional decisions helped to develop a sense of community among school personnel. This positive school culture, however, was missing in the less successful schools Lipson et al. studied.

Fisher and Frey (2007) reported many ways teachers collaborated at the California school they studied. All teachers understood and taught to the core beliefs about literacy and the instructional framework developed at the school. Teachers learned to speak the same language about this instruction. They collaborated on assessments, they selected learning communities to participate in, they observed in each other's classrooms, and through these collaborative activities, they developed a sense of ownership over their learning and their literacy program.

Across these studies, teams of teachers and administrators collaborated in numerous ways (see Table 25.5), both to create a culture that sustained the school improvement activities and in the specific work targeted within each of the frameworks for reform. They collaborated in the development of local literacy improvement projects based on a shared vision and shared in the decision making for their school-wide reading program. Shared decision-making and teachers' participation in a number of collaborative teaching and learning communities helped teachers and administrators develop a sense of ownership and collective efficacy that in turned helped them sustain their continual literacy improvement efforts.

Together, these studies suggest that successful, sustainable reform in literacy involves at least four features of organizational change, from a shared vision of the process to the shared leadership and collaborative workplace required for enacting the change activities, to making decisions based on analysis of data deliberately collected on both student progress and the organization itself. We turn now from the organizational aspects of successful school reform in literacy to factors at the individual level.

Focus on Individual Change

Consistent with research that describes the relationship among teacher development and school reform more generally (e.g., Ancess, 2000; Anyon, 1994), these seven studies of whole school reform in reading demonstrate the importance of individual teacher development of both disci-

Table 25.5 Collaborative School Community

	Standards-Based Change Process	School Change in Reading Framework	Literacy Professional Development Model	Acceleration of Achievement in Diverse School Project	Middle and High School Beating the Odds	Successful Elementary School in Vermont	Successful Elementary School in California
Development of positive culture/collective efficacy	X	X	X	X	X	X	X
Development of collaborative work through reform effort—teaching, PD, vision for students	X	X	X	X	X	X	X

plinary and pedagogical knowledge. The studies reveal the importance of these aspects in their impact on classroom practices related to the integration of assessment, instruction, and curriculum to meet students' individual and collective needs. In this section, we discuss individual change across projects in terms of three features: (a) professional learning and changes in teaching, (b) curriculum coherence and balanced instruction, and (c) providing for complex thinking and motivating learning activities.

Professional Learning and Changes in Teaching. In schools involved in school-wide reading improvement efforts, it is essential that teachers have the opportunity to engage in ongoing, focused, challenging, job-embedded professional learning (e.g., Rogers et al., 2006). The overall goal of this learning is to translate it into increasingly effective reading instruction within the classroom.

Leaders in schools successful with the Standards-Based Change Process (Au et al., 2008b) developed a multiyear plan for school-based professional development that was tied to specific goals for curriculum development designed to improve students' achievement. Through university partners, teachers were provided with approximately eight full days of professional learning spread across 3 years on four sequential "courses" (Au et al., 2008b). First, teachers within schools focused on developing professional learning communities and systems needed to improve students' reading achievement: vision, benchmarks, assessments. Second, teachers focused on students' learning through 3 times a year reporting of results on students' progress towards benchmarks and focused on instruction in high level thinking. Third, teachers learned how to develop curriculum guides that included goals, instructional strategies, instructional materials, and assessments. Fourth, teachers learned how to help students develop portfolios that documented their learning and that could be shared with parents.

Most schools in the Chicago Standards-Based Change Process project had literacy coordinators and/or teacher leaders who participated in a leadership academy in which they completed 12 credits of advanced graduate study in literacy education. Participants learned together in cohorts across a year, completing a course in advanced methods of literacy instruction, a seminar on literacy teacher leadership, and an elective in literacy education. Through this program, literacy leaders enhanced their knowledge of effective literacy instruction as well as their leadership abilities. Similarly, participants from Hawaii participated in quarterly network meetings designed to provide ongoing professional development related to supporting the SBC Process in their schools for both school leaders and classroom teachers.

Teachers in schools that were successful with the School Change in Reading Process engaged in three-times-a month study groups that focused on substantive research-based reading topics focusing on instruction to develop students' decoding abilities, vocabulary, use of comprehension strategies, and higher level thinking abilities (Taylor et al., 2005). Reflection on and change in teaching was at the heart of the professional development model. Teachers met in hour-long study groups three times a month. Study group focused on research-based instruction related to emergent literacy, word recognition, vocabulary, and comprehension, with the topics within these categories determined by teachers based on their needs. In study groups teachers focused on how to make research-based changes in reading instruction, and they engaged in video sharing and looking at student work to improve practice. The video sharing, in particular, provided teachers with concrete examples of teaching around which they could reflect and have conversations about teaching practices. In addition, school-based literacy coordinators and external facilitators visited classrooms to model and coach, and teachers reflected on their teaching through personal analysis of observation data. Protocols tied to elements of effective reading instruction were used in all professional learning experiences to help teachers, in collaborative study groups, with a partner, or on their own, reflect on their practice. In the Minnesota project (Taylor & Peterson, 2007b), all teachers met with other teachers in the state-wide project at three different times each year to learn from one other (e.g., teachers presenting at sessions and round tables), from external partners, and from national literacy experts. Leadership team members across schools met quarterly to learn about effective leadership and sustainability and to share successes and concerns across schools. Literacy coordinators and external facilitators met every six weeks to hone their leadership and coaching abilities.

Timperley and Parr (2007) reported that principles of research-based effective literacy practice drove the professional development in their project. National literacy experts identified principles and practices pertaining to effective literacy instruction. Project leaders with expertise provided professional development to external facilitators who in turn provided professional development to individual schools. Facilitators worked most closely with the nominated literacy lead teacher, helping this literacy leader become a resource and leader in providing ongoing professional learning in literacy within their school. The external facilitator also worked at times with individual teachers. The external facilitator, principal, and literacy leader looked at interview and observation data to construct a school professional development program in which teachers in these schools developed content knowledge related to effective reading instruction that they then put into practice within the contexts of their schools. Schools evaluated their progress towards specific outcomes at sixth-month intervals. Implementing principles and practices with fidelity was not the focus of the professional learning; rather, inquiry and reflection on the impact of their practice was a central part of the learning process.

The need for ongoing professional development for the external facilitators became apparent during the first year of the Timperley and Parr (2007) project. Most facilitators had extensive knowledge about effective reading instruction but little training in how to be an effective collaborative leader. Thus, in the second year, ongoing learning for facilitators focused on how to engage school personnel in conversations about what needed to change within their schools and in how to co-construct plans to achieve needed improvements.

In the second year of the Accelerated Achievement in Diverse Schools Project (McNaughton et al. 2006), specific areas for professional development on reading comprehension and effective instruction were a major undertaking. Ten research-based sessions were led by one of the researchers in which 10–15 teachers and literacy leaders from project schools learned about research-based ideas and completed relevant, classroom-based tasks between sessions. Sessions focused on theoretical concepts of reading comprehension, reading comprehension strategies, the role of vocabulary in comprehension, efforts to increase students' access to rich text, and efforts to include cultural and linguistic resources in learning activities. Tasks included creating instruction focused on comprehension monitoring, implementing an action research project to increase students' vocabulary learning, analysis of the range and types of books in classrooms, and analysis of transcripts from videos of classroom lessons to identify patterns of effective teaching. Teachers also created learning circles in which they observed in each other's classrooms and engaged in follow-up conversations. In year 3, teachers continued with learning circles, and they developed action research projects with pre- and post-tests to assess the effectiveness of various aspects of their literacy programs. These projects were shared at a conference for all participating schools at the end of the year.

Langer (2000) reported that in schools with successful English programs teachers were members of several learning communities. Administrative and teaching colleagues invited each other to participate in professional communities across school, district, and state levels. Teachers elected to join particular groups that provided opportunities for exposure to new ideas and issues in the field, learning that impacted their practice, networking within and across schools, and social interactions that helped to set a positive tone and develop feelings of professionalism and collective efficacy within buildings. Administrators also participated in communities, valuing their importance to professional growth.

Successful schools in Vermont (Lipson et al., 2004) had extensive professional development, and teachers spoke with confidence about their teaching. Also, they were eager to receive feedback and new ideas from their external professional development partners. However, professional learning in these schools was created to meet the context-specific needs of teachers, students, and communities within their unique schools. A one-size-fits all approach to professional development was not followed, and there was not a top-down focus on "training" teachers to acquire knowledge about scientifically based reading research or "training" them to implement best practices in their classrooms. The importance of teachers' voices related to their learning and of differentiated professional learning for teachers was a common theme across the successful schools that were studied.

Fisher and Frey (2007) reported that the instructional framework developed by the literacy task force at their school provided the topics of study for ongoing professional development. The professional development committee, appointed by the literacy task force, developed a professional learning plan a year in advance for the entire school. Members of the professional development committee provided whole group seminars on aspects of the literacy framework (e.g. modeling comprehension, providing small-group phonics lessons, using books clubs). Teachers formed learning communities around topics within the literacy framework. The learning communities met to set agendas, identify professional readings, discuss readings and their instructional practices, and share student work relevant to their topic. Beyond the meetings, teachers within a learning community invited one another into their classrooms to observe instruction related to the topic under study. Because the school was large (e.g., 1,500 students), it had 5 full-time literacy resource teachers who facilitated the activities of professional learning communities as well as engaging in other duties such as peer coaching, working with new teachers, and organizing literacy volunteers.

The six themes that emerged across these studies are listed in Table 25.6. In most studies, professional development in literacy was long-term and well planned. Teachers learned about research-based literacy curriculum and instruction from external partners or literacy leaders within their schools.

However, the importance of teachers going beyond learning about new instructional materials or techniques to focusing on reflection and change in thinking and in teaching was also stressed. Peer modeling and coaching, self-reflection, and dialogue related to pedagogy, curriculum and assessment were techniques that fostered reflection on practice. Most studied reported that teachers learned together as a school-based professional learning community or as a member of multiple communities. In some projects, processes for learning from one another were specifically established. In all studies, authors reported on ways in which professional learning within schools was tailored to meet the needs of teachers and students within schools. Teachers were active participants with choices and responsibilities related to their learning; they were not primarily attendees at traditional top-down, one-size fits all professional development sessions. Further, ongoing professional learning for literacy leaders also occurred. The updating of leaders' knowledge about effective reading instruction was a component of this learning, but the focus on how to become effective leaders was also stressed.

Curriculum Coherence and Balanced Instruction.   Research suggests that to help all students achieve at high levels in reading and writing, teachers in schools engaged in successful school-wide reading improvement efforts focus on developing coherence (Newmann, Smith, Allenworth, & Bryk, 2001) in their reading curricula and providing sound, balanced instruction (Pearson, Raphael, Benson, & Madda, 2007). Further, effective teachers provide challenging, motivating learning activities for all students (e.g., Guthrie et al., 2004). These features were characteristic of the seven illustrative projects.

Table 25.6 Professional Learning and Changes in Teaching

	Standards-Based Change Process	School Change in Reading Framework	Literacy Professional Development Model	Acceleration of Achievement in Diverse School Project	Middle and High School Beating the Odds	Successful Elementary School in Vermont	Successful Elementary School in California
External partners or external learning communities provided some of the professional development on effective literacy curriculum and instruction	X	X	X	X	X	X	X
Schools developed school-based learning communities	X	X	X	X	X	X	X
Professional learning was ongoing, deliberate, and well-planned	X	X	X	X	X	X	X
Reflection on practice tied to instructional change was stressed		X	X	X			X
Professional learning was tailored to schools' unique needs	X	X	X	X	X	X	X
Ongoing learning for literacy leaders was stressed	X	X	X		X		

Teachers in successful schools in the Standards-Based Change Process (Au et al., 2008a) developed a coherent, balanced curriculum across grade levels with a shared understanding of goals for student learning, instruction, and assessment. Beginning with the vision for excellent readers developed by schools followed by clearly defined end-of-year grade level goals to help students reach this vision, teachers in the SBC Process worked together to develop a staircase curriculum. This curriculum was coherent and well coordinated because teachers consciously aligned goals and instruction with adjacent grade levels to insure progression toward the school-wide vision of graduates' literacy knowledge and abilities. Teachers developed grade level curriculum guides that included grade level goals, classroom assessments, instructional materials, and instructional strategies that all teachers had agreed to address. This process, in turn, developed teacher ownership over the reading program. Au (2005) observed that it was the coherent curriculum developed by teachers within a school, not the materials a school had purchased, that led to increasingly effective literacy instruction.

In the School Change in Reading process (Taylor et al., 2005; Taylor et al., 2007) teachers focused on the content and pedagogy of effective, research-based reading instruction as well as differentiated instruction based on students' needs and abilities. Using district-adopted materials, teachers provided balanced instruction by constantly reflecting on the cognitive engagement teaching model (Taylor et al., 2003) in which teachers engage students in high level talk and writing about text in addition to lower level comprehension activities, provide balance in teaching word recognition and comprehension as basic skills and as strategies applied to texts, use a teacher-directed (e.g., telling) or student-support (e.g., coaching) stance towards instruction based on students' needs and abilities, and provide balance in learning activities in which students are actively involved (e.g. students all reading) as well as those in which they are more passively involved (e.g., students involved in turn-taking reading or listening to someone read.) Through study groups, teachers learned to use a common language and similar teaching strategies related to their reading instruction that developed a sense of coherence in their reading program.

Evidence-based curricular and instructional coherence were the foci within the Literacy Professional Development Project (Timperley & Parr, 2007). National experts in literacy identified effective literacy principles and practices related to balanced literacy instruction, and a trainer-of-trainers model was used to help teachers learn how to incorporate these principles and practices in their classrooms. The project had four contracted outcomes which also provided coherence to the work: evidence of improved student achievement, evidence of improved teacher content knowledge, evidence of improved transfer of literacy pedagogy to practice, and evidence of effectively led professional learning communities. Reflections on practice, as opposed to prescriptions for teaching, were stressed in teachers' professional learning.

In the Accelerated Achievement in Diverse Schools Project (McNaughton et al., 2006), schools focused on providing coherent instruction that was linked to various aspects of comprehension such as strategies reader use to understand their reading, vocabulary, engaging texts, and cultural and linguistic links to learning. In the tasks between professional development sessions, teachers engaged in reflection on current and new teaching practices related to the reading comprehension needs and abilities of their students. The framework for effective comprehension instruction began with their external partner, but by the third year, teachers were using literacy circles and action research projects to continue to reflect on and refine their instructional practices.

In secondary schools that were beating the odds (Langer, 2001), teachers moved students from initial skill acquisition or basic understandings to deeper understandings and generation of ideas. English teachers in high performing schools taught students procedural or meta-cognitive strategies in addition to content or skills whereas teachers in more typical schools focused on content or skills alone. Teachers in successful schools worked together on curriculum development, an activity that helped to provide curriculum coherence and high-level instruction.

Teachers in successful elementary schools in Vermont (Lipson et al., 2004) provided balanced literacy instruction involving competent word-level and text-level instruction regardless of the type of reading program the school had adopted. Teachers provided scaffolding to students as needed. Classroom observations revealed that teachers were excellent at classroom management and skillfully provided a complex set of literacy activities in their classroom, including teacher-directed work, independent reading and writing, and work at learning centers.

Fisher and Frey (2007) reported that the literacy task force began by generating core beliefs about literacy learning: learning is social, conversations are critical for learning, reading, writing, and oral language instruction must be integrated, and learners require a gradual increase in responsibility. The literacy instructional framework was developed around these core beliefs and brought coherence to the school's literacy instruction. It focused on balanced instruction including: (a) content driven by state standards (e.g., instruction in emergent literacy, word recognition, fluency, vocabulary, comprehension) and (b) teaching modes (e.g., whole group explicit instruction and modeling, guided small group instruction, collaborative learning, independent practice with conferring, and assessments). Professional development was designed to help all teachers understand the core beliefs and instructional framework. As teachers learned together as a school, they modified their literacy framework with the goal of effective, precision teaching rather than prescriptive curriculum and instruction.

Collectively, these studies focused on school-wide reading improvement demonstrate the importance of ongoing, school-based professional learning related to evidence-based, effective reading instruction where teachers teach from a coherent perspective. In some projects, teachers focused on coherent curriculum development. In others, teachers engaged in ongoing reflection on teaching effectiveness. In all cases, effective instruction, as opposed to adherence to prescriptions for teaching or use of particular purchased materials, was the goal. Teachers focused on providing balanced reading instruction, including the teaching of basic reading skills and more advanced reading strategies related to word recognition and comprehension processes. In the three studies in which external school improvement models were implemented, external partners provided the initial research-based instructional building blocks that evolved into locally owned reading programs within schools. In the other studies, locally developed, site-specific, research-based frameworks for effective reading programs within schools evolved over time (see Table 25.7).

Providing for Complex Thinking and Motivating Learning Activities.   To help all students achieve at high levels in reading and writing, teachers need to teach with an instructional emphasis on complex thinking as well as basic skills (Darling-Hammond, 2003, 2007; Pearson et al., 2007). Across studies, teachers emphasized reading comprehension and students' interactions with texts.

An emphasis on high-level thinking, manifested through an emphasis on reading comprehension and the writing process, is one of four guiding principles of the Standards-Based Change Process (Au & Raphael, 2007). From the onset, teachers in the SBC Process set high expectations for their students' literacy learning through their vision of the excellent reader graduating from their school. Additionally, all teachers in the Chicago project engaged in professional learning that focused on higher level thinking (Au et al., 2008b). This learning focused on effective comprehension strategies instruction as well as instruction that engaged students in higher level thinking about texts.

With the School Change in Reading process, Taylor et al. (2000, 2003, 2005) found that students who showed greater reading growth were in classrooms of teachers who engaged them in more high-level talk and writing about text. These teachers, as compared to teachers who engaged in relatively little high level talk and writing about texts, helped students have conversations about theme and character interpretation and taught students to engage in student-led discussions. Through study groups, teachers learned about high level talk and writing about texts, comprehension strategies instruction, and challenging vocabulary instruction. Through self-reflection supported by protocols and conversations about practice that focused on a model of teaching encouraging students' cognitive engagement in their literacy learning (Taylor et al.,

Table 25.7 Effective Literacy Instruction: Curriculum Coherence and Balanced Instruction

	Standards-Based Change Process	School Change in Reading Framework	Literacy Professional Development Model	Acceleration of Achievement in Diverse School Project	Middle and High School Beating the Odds	Successful Elementary School in Vermont	Successful Elementary School in California
Teach from a coherent perspective	X	X	X	X	X	X	X
Particular focus on curriculum development	X				X		
Particular focus on dimensions of effective instruction		X	X	X		X	X
Provide balanced reading instruction	X	X			X	X	X
Framework for effective instruction began with expertise provided by external partners	X	X	X	X			

2003), teachers, in general, pushed themselves and increased students' opportunities to engage in high level thinking about texts during whole group and small group lessons (Taylor et al., 2005; Taylor & Peterson, 2007a). Also teachers worked to increase the challenge of independent learning activities. Across multiple years in the project, they increased students' reading, discussing, and writing about books at high levels of thinking while working on their own or while working collaboratively with a partner or small group (Taylor & Peterson, 2006).

A key focus for teachers in the Accelerated Achievement in diverse Schools Project (McNaughton et al., 2006) was developing students' self-efficacy and independence as readers and learners. Professional development for teachers centered around comprehension instruction generally, and one dimension focused on teaching students how to monitor and execute control over their reading comprehension. Teachers who saw the highest gains in their students' reading comprehension were particularly skilled in adjusting guidance to their students as they were reading and comprehending texts. In other words, as opposed to providing too little or too much feedback or being limited by a scripted curriculum, they knew what amounts of feedback to provide at what times for different students on varying texts.

Langer (2001) reported that teachers in successful schools also taught students to be strategic learners. They taught students strategies for planning, organizing, completing, and reflecting on the content of their lessons. Effective teachers moved beyond basic concepts to teach and explore deeper understandings of ideas covered in lessons. Also, students were engaged in extensive collaborative work and inquiry learning to develop depth and complexity of understanding in interactions with others. In less successful schools and classrooms, relatively little strategy instruction, deeper level talk about texts, or collaborative work were observed.

Teachers in successful schools in Vermont (Lipson et al., 2004) provided multiple opportunities for students to read, to be read to, and to discuss books. Classrooms also had ample collections of books. Primary grade students read for about 20 minutes a day (beyond teacher-guided reading) and intermediate grade students read for about 50 minutes a day.

In the Fisher and Frey (2007) study, teachers focused on responding to texts and on comprehension strategies instruction within their guided reading groups. In collaborative learning groups, students engaged in literature circles, reciprocal teaching, and word study activities.

Collectively, these studies stress a common theme, instantiated in different ways, that teachers not only taught basic skills, but also made a concerted effort to go far above and beyond the basics (see Table 25.8). They focused on teaching students to be strategic in their comprehension and learning. They gave students ample opportunities to engage in high-level discussions about text. Students engaged in collaborative learning experiences, inquiry learning, and wide reading.

Summary of Professional Development-Based Reading Reform Efforts. The seven projects discussed build on the foundation established by the Comprehensive School Reform (CSR) programs—such as Accelerated Schools, America's Choice, and Success for All. One critique of the CSR programs is the potential lack a good balance between specificity of program features and flexibility. Specificity of features is required to guide teachers in working together within a common framework and to promote continuity of teaching and learning across the grades. Flexibility is required to permit teachers to tailor the approach to fit their own school, classroom, and students. A second critique relates to whether these programs could be sustained over periods of time long enough to see substantial growth in student achievement. The likelihood

Table 25.8   Complex Thinking and Motivating Learning Activities

Theme by Project	Standards-Based Change Process	School Change in Reading Framework	Literacy Professional Development Model	Acceleration of Achievement in Diverse School Project	Middle and High School Beating the Odds	Successful Elementary School in Vermont	Successful Elementary School in California
Focus on strategic readers	X	X		X	X		X
Focus on high level thinking	X	X			X	X	X
Focus on collaborative learning		X			X		X
Focus on motivating, student-led independent learning activities		X			X	X	X

of sustainability is decreased if teachers do not shape and take ownership of the change effort. To build on the foundation established by CSR programs, reading reform efforts would need to achieve a proper balance between specificity of program features and flexibility, while encouraging teachers to take ownership of the change effort, thus fostering sustainability.

We believe the studies of professional development based reading reform approaches suggest that the concerns about balance and sustainability are addressed. First, there was a shared vision of literacy and literacy education, but without highly prescriptive teaching approaches. We see that teachers worked to develop their own and, with peers, their collective knowledge base to insure that students were working toward the highest standards of achievement. Students were not taught simply to achieve at higher levels on a test, but rather—as Pearson (2007) argues to be critical for successful learning—to be able to transfer what they had learned across contexts to further their own learning. Second, the flexibility for teachers to tailor the change effort to their own setting existed because teachers were not participating in "training" but were engaged in professional learning to help them improve their instruction and serve as contributing members to the professional learning community within the school. Third, these change efforts have proven to be sustainable, at least in part because of teachers' ownership. With a consistent emphasis and sufficient time, the projects demonstrated the shift from an externally to internally motivated change effort. The approaches based in professional development reflected both monitoring of and attention to teachers' concerns about their own professional growth, in parallel to their emphasis on students' literacy achievement. Teachers were motivated to improve their own practice as they worked to improve students' motivation and ability to read. Attention was given to the process by which the school-wide professional learning community evolved and teachers came to take ownership of the change effort, with the recognition that this process might well be recursive rather than linear. These seven efforts indicate that whole school reform in reading is no less complex than the decades of research on school reform would indicate. Yet, despite the complexities, these seven studies serve as existence proofs of what is possible when school reform in reading reflects the nested nature of success.

DIRECTIONS FOR FUTURE RESEARCH

With ongoing pressures facing schools to increase reading achievement and close the achievement gap, the need for effective school-based models of reading reform will only increase in the future. Yet, as Heckman and Montera (2009, p. 1) note,

> Our world has drastically changed from the world of the past. Yet, there is one organization in today's world that has changed little from when it was created over 150 years ago. While the knowledge about the organization has fundamentally shifted, this organization's form and procedures have shifted very little...it remains essentially the same in the 21st century as it was in the early to mid-19th century when it began. ...(The) nature of the organization and operation of schooling is at odds with current knowledge of learning, cognition, society human development, and organizational change.

Thus, future research will need to address two broad concerns: (a) increasing the collective data base for sustainable school reform efforts within the boundaries of today's schools, while at the same time research is conducted and (b) pushing the current boundaries of schools such that reform efforts help schools become relevant sites for teaching students to live and work in a rapidly changing, global economy.

Research designed to increase our collective knowledge base within current traditions of schools requires focusing efforts to build the database in areas of impact. Such studies would include replicating and extending research on reform efforts based in professional development rather than fidelity to particular programs. These studies would provide a broader database on which to examine impact on student learning and the factors central to improvements in achievement. Studies are needed to provide information about time and resource allocation at the school level; policies at the district, state, and national levels that drive school-based activities; and professional development at both teacher and administrative levels. They must address issues of long-term sustainability (e.g., beyond 3 to 5 years) in the face of changing initiatives, as well as scaling from relatively small projects of one to a dozen schools to large-scale efforts that reach across large districts and across diverse demographic contexts.

But, while necessary, such studies will not be sufficient for preparing students for today's world. Future research on school reform in literacy must consider the very fundamental nature of schools today, schools that were created on an industrial model that "reflected these ideas of segmented, linear, and time-bound production. The teachers were the workers adding specific knowledge segments to students' minds as students moved from one grade level to the next" (Heckman & Montera, 2009, p. 2). Standards provide a way to make explicit what students are to know at particular points in time and help determine pacing for the linear curriculum. However, research that helps to design schools for the future—where reform isn't about simply doing current practices more successfully, but where it takes into account three critical factors. First, learning today does not happen in the time-bound ways reflected in traditional schooling. The Internet and other innovative technologies have changed both the physical boundaries of school (e.g., the availability of online courses, podcasts) and the very nature of text (e.g., hypertext, web page presentations that are far from traditional linear forms of presentation, gaming). What are the new organizational structures that will shape schools and learning for the future? Second, as described in this review and characteristic of new forms of learning today, few would argue for continuing traditional transmission models of teaching. But much research is needed to understand what a constructivist school reform effort must entail. While we have an extensive research base on which to build, reflected in the earlier and the current volumes of the *Handbook of Reading Research*, taking this research base to the level of whole school reform will require extensive research in the future. Third, in addition to changing the boundaries of time and the form of instruction, future school reform research needs to consider the changing nature of knowledge and skills. The age of "new literacies" is upon us, and this includes interacting with hypermedia, as well as finding, reading, evaluating, and sharing information on the Internet. The majority of schools have much to learn about how to help our students be prepared for reading in the world of today and tomorrow—and research is needed that focuses on how such change can be initiated and sustained.

CONCLUDING COMMENTS

We began this chapter with a look at the history of school reform efforts, noting the lengthy and honorable tradition of research aimed at improving students' learning as well as the work lives of teachers. These earlier studies highlighted the complexity of reform, for example, by identifying multiple factors differentiating more successful from less successful schools. In the next two sections of this chapter, we examined research on two different approaches to whole-school reform in reading. While both of these approaches emphasized results for students, we characterized the first as curriculum based efforts centered on fidelity of implementation, and the second as professional development based efforts centered on effective instruction, adaptability, and sustainability. Both of these research-validated approaches provide models that can be used by schools in their own reform efforts to improve students' literacy abilities. External partners, like the university faculty and researchers who were part of most of the studies included in this review, can assist schools in this important work by providing initial knowledge and support. However, the drive and hard work necessary for long-term change must come from within individual schools.

Curriculum based reform efforts, many of which fall under the aegis of the Comprehensive School Reform movement, start from a premise that has proved extremely appealing to policy makers. This premise is that schools should not have to discover their own solutions for effective reform, and should instead simply be able to adopt existing models, already proven to be successful in other settings. In contrast, professional development based reform efforts have often held little appeal for policy makers. This is in large measure because they begin with the assumption that educators in the schools cannot just copy an existing model and do need to make the reform their own, through the principled adaptation of the reform to their own particular setting, circumstances, and students. Professional development based reform efforts rely more on teaching educators about the principles of effective reform and supporting educators in internalizing and taking ownership of these principles, giving educators some latitude to determine how they can best be instantiated in their own school settings.

We have learned a great deal from studies of curriculum based reform models, yet our own research and experiences have led us to favor professional development based models. We agree with the conclusion of Mosenthal et al. (2004), who found that teachers within successful schools made choices and worked together to enact change tailored to their school communities. These researchers note, "The key to success is not the instructional approach alone but the fit of the approach to the teachers and the school context and the rigor and integrity of its implementation (p. 365)." If teachers have a deep understanding of the principles underlying a reform effort, and take ownership of it, they will know how it should be adapted to address the needs of their school and their students. In our view, integrity in the implementation of a professional development based model has less to do with the exact replication of an existing example and more to do with constructing the adaptation that will work in one's own school.

Langer (2000) concluded that successful schools did not develop from mandates for change or superficial change actions, but rather from an enhanced work environment that invited change, one in which "teachers could feed their professional identities, ideas, and commitments, and also develop and continue to build upon effective strategies for improving student achievement" (p. 436). Successful reading reform efforts need to focus on developing collaborative learning communities, such as those described in this review, that will foster teachers' professional excitement for and commitment to substantive, ongoing improvement in the delivery of effective reading instruction for all students.

Successful reform in reading must address in systematic ways the development of teachers' professional knowledge and practice and not be limited by the false hopes and unrealistic expectations that often accompany a school's adoption of a packaged program. There is a world of difference between the naïve belief that a packaged program is the answer to a school's need for curriculum coherence, and the more sophisticated understanding that a packaged program may provide a good starting point for professional conversations about curriculum coherence.

Teachers need to be thoughtful and adaptable in their teaching to meet the needs of all children, to provide them with excellent learning opportunities, and to help them meet the highest of standards. As Pearson (2007) writes, "Taking responsibility for one's professional knowledge and ensuring that it is used wisely in making difficult decisions in the face of uncertain evidence about how to respond to the widely varying needs, interests, and circumstances of individuals—or what to do next for the common good—have always been the hallmarks of any profession, including teaching" (p. 150).

As we look to the future, we cannot be satisfied with simply "doing school better." We must acknowledge that school reform not only invites but requires educational leaders, as well as teachers in the classroom, to have a solid understanding of principles of effective school reform. We must respect the differences among schools and not perpetuate the misconception that successful schools are cookie cutter images of one another. We must encourage policy makers to give educators the support and time needed to apply research-based principles of school reform to shape the effort that will be effective in improving their students' reading achievement. More and better of the same content and organization is not likely to be the answer for preparing all students to live, work, and enjoy richly fulfilling lives in today's rapidly changing, globalized society. We must, as educational researchers and practitioners, re-imagine the very nature of school reform and look at reform efforts as leading the way to 21st-century education.

REFERENCES

Ahrens, B. C. (2005). Finding a new way: Reinventing a sixth-grade reading program. *Journal of Adolescent and Adult Literacy, 48*(8), 642–654.

Ancess, J. (2000). The reciprocal influence of teacher learning, teaching practice, school restructuring, and student learning outcomes. *Teachers College Record, 102*(3), 590–619.

Anyon, J. (1994). Teacher development and reform in an inner-city school. *Teachers College Record, 96*(1), 14–31.

Au, K. A. (2005). Negotiating the slippery slope: School change and literacy achievement. *Journal of Literacy Research, 37*(3), 267–288.

Au, K. H., & Raphael, T. E. (2007). Classroom assessment and standards-based change. In J. Paratore & R. Mccormick (Eds.), *Classroom literacy assessment* (pp. 306–322). New York: Guilford.

Au, K. H., Raphael, T. E., & Mooney, K. (2008a). Improving reading achievement in elementary schools: Guiding change in a time of standards. In S. B. Wepner & D. S. Strickland (Eds.), *Supervision of reading programs* (4th ed., pp. 71–89). New York: Teachers College Press.

Au, K. H., Raphael, T. E., & Mooney, K. S. (2008b). What we have learned about teacher education to improve literacy achievement in urban schools. In L. Wilkinson, L. Morrow, & V. Chou (Eds.), *Improving the preparation of teachers of reading in urban settings: Policy, practice, pedagogy.* Newark DE: International Reading Association.

Austin, G. R. (1979). Exemplary schools and the search for effectiveness. *Educational Leadership, 37*(1), 10–12, 14.

Berliner, D. C. (2006). Our impoverished view of educational research. *Teachers College Record, 108*(6), 949–995.

Bloom, H. S., Ham, S., Melton, L., & O'Brien, J. (2001). *Evaluating the Accelerated Schools approach: A look at early implementation and impacts on student achievement in eight elementary schools.* New York: Manpower Demonstration Research Corporation.

Borko, H., Wolf, S. A., Simone, G., & Uchiyama, K. P. (2004). Schools in transition: Reform efforts and school capacity in Washington State. *Educational Evaluation and Policy Analysis, 25*(2), 171–201.

Borman, L. M., & Associates. (2005). *Meaningful urban educational reform: Confronting the learning crisis in mathematics and science.* Albany: State University of New York.

Borman, G., Slavin, R., Cheung, A., Chamberlain, A., Madden, N., & Chambers, B. (2007). Final reading outcomes of the national randomized field trial of Success for All. *American Educational Research Journal, 44*(3), 701–731.

Borman, G. D., & D'Agostino, J. V. (1996). Title I and student achievement: A meta-analysis of federal evaluation results. *Education Evaluation and Policy Analysis, 18*, 309–326.

Borman, G. D., & Hewes, G. M. (2002). The long-term effects and cost-effectiveness of Success for All. *Educational Evaluation and Policy Analysis, 24*(4), 243–266.

Borman, G. D., Hewes, G. M., Overman, L. T., & Brown, S. (2002). *Comprehensive school reform and student achievement: A meta-analysis.* Baltimore, MD: Center for Research on the Education of Students Placed At Risk, Johns Hopkins University.

Brookover, W. B., & Lezotte, L. W. (1979). *Changes in school characteristics coincident with changes in student achievement* (No. ERIC Document Reproduction Service No. ED 181005). East Lansing: Institute for Research on Teaching, Michigan State University.

Bullough, R., Robert, V., & Gitlin, A. D. (1985). Schooling and change: A view from the lower rung. *Teachers College Record, 87*(2), 291–237.

Cambone, J. (1995). Time for teachers in school restructuring. *Teachers College Record, 96*(3), 1–32.

Coburn, C. E. (2003). Rethinking scale: Moving beyond numbers to deep and lasting change. *Educational Researcher, 32*(6), 3–12.

Cohen, D. K., & Moffit, S. L. (2002). Standards-based reform and the capacity problem. In *Miles to go…: Reflections on mid-course corrections for standards-based reform* (pp. 53–56). Bethesda, MD: Education Week Press.

Consortium for Policy Research in Education. (2002). *America's Choice school design: A research-based model*. Washington DC: National Center on Education and the Economy.

Correnti, R., & Rowan, B. (2007). Opening up the black box: Literacy instruction in schools participating in three comprehensive school reform programs. *American Educational Research Journal, 44*(2), 298–338.

Cuban, L. (1998). How schools change reforms: Redefining reform success and failure. *Teachers College Record, 99*(3), 453–477.

Darling-Hammond, L. (1997). *The right to learn: A blueprint for creating schools that work*. San Francisco: Jossey-Bass.

Darling-Hammond, L. (2003, February 16). Standards and assessments: Where we are and what we need. Retrieved November 27, 2003, from http://www.tcrecord.org ID 11109

Darling-Hammond, L. (2007). The flat earth and education: How America's commitment to equity will determine our future. *Educational Researcher, 36*(6), 318–334.

Datnow, A., Lasky, S. G., Stringfield, S. C., & Teddlie, C. (2005). Systemic integration for educational reform in racially and linguistically diverse contexts: A summary of the evidence. *Journal of Education for Students Placed at Risk, 10*(4), 445–453.

Datnow, A., & Stringfield, S. C. (2000). Working together for reliable school reform. *Journal of Education for Students Placed at Risk, 5*(1 & 2), 183–204.

Duffy, G. G. (1993). Teachers' progress toward becoming expert strategy teachers. *Elementary School Journal, 94*(2), 109–120.

Dutrow, E., Fisk, M. C., Koch, R., Roop, L. J., & Wixson, K. (2002). When state policies meet local district contexts: Standards-based professional development as a means to individual agency and collective ownership. *Teachers College Record, 104*(4), 787–811.

Edmonds, R. (1979). Effective schools for the urban poor. *Educational Leadership, 37*(1), 15–24.

Fink, D., & Brayman, C. (2006). School leadership succession and the challenges of change. *Educational Administration Quarterly, 42*(1), 62–89.

Fisher, D., & Frey, N. (2007). Implementing a schoolwide literacy framework: Improving achievement in an urban elementary school. *The Reading Teacher, 61*(1), 32–43.

Furman, S., Clune, W. H., & Elmore, R. F. (1988). Research on education reform: Lessons on the implementation of policy. *Teachers College Record, 90*(2), 237–257.

Gallego, M. A., Hollingsworth, S., & Whitenack, D. A. (2001). Relational knowing in the reform of educational cultures. *Teachers College Record, 103*(2), 240–266.

Giles, C., & Hargreaves, A. (2006). The sustainability of innovative schools as learning organizations and professional learning communities during standardized reform. *Education Administration Quarterly, 42*(1), 124–156.

Guiney, E. (2002). A modest proposal: Work on the right problem in the right way. In Pew Forum on Standards-Based Reform. In *Miles to go…:Reflections on mid-course corrections for standards-based reform*. Bethesda, MD: Education Week Press.

Goddard, Y. L., Goddard, R. D., & Tschannen-Moran, M. (2007). A theoretical and empirical investigation of teacher collaboration for school improvement and student achievement in public elementary schools. *Teachers College Record, 109*(4), 877–896.

Goldman, S. R. (2005). Designing for scalable educational improvement. In C. Dede, J. P. Honan, & L. C. Peters (Eds.), *Scaling up success* (pp. 67–96). San Francisco: Jossey-Bass.

Griffin, G. A., & Barnes, S. (1984). School change: A craft-derived and research-based strategy. *Teachers College Record, 86*(1), 103–123.

Grossman, P., Wineburg, S., & Woolworth, S. (2001). Toward a theory of teacher community. *Teachers College Record, 193*(6), 942–1012.

Guthrie, J. T., Wigfield, A., Barbosa, P., Perencevich, K. C., Taboada, A., Davis, M. H., et al. (2004). Increasing reading comprehension and engagement through concept-oriented reading instruction. *Journal of Educational Psychology, 96,* 403–423.

Hatch, T. (2000). What does it take to break the mold? Rhetoric and reality in New American schools. *Teachers College Record, 102*(3), 561–589.

Heckman, P. E., & Montera, V. L. (2009). School reform: The flatworm in a flat world: From entropy to renewal through indigenous invention. *Teachers College Record, 111*(1). Retrieved January 13, 2008, from http://www.tcrecord.org ID Number: 14689

Irwin, J. W., & Farr, W. (2004). Collaborative school communities that support teaching and learning. *Reading & Writing Quarterly, 20,* 343–363.

Jennings, J. (2002). Early victories, serious challenges. In Pew Forum on Standards-Based Reform. In *Miles to go...: Reflections on mid-course corrections for standards-based reform* (pp. 47–52). Bethesda, MD: Education Week Press.

Klingner, J., Cramer, E., & Harry, B. (2006). Challenges in the implementation of Success for All in four high-need urban schools. *Elementary School Journal, 106*(4), 333–349.

Kozol, J. (1991). *Savage inequalities: Children in America's schools.* New York: HarperCollins.

Langer, J. A. (2000). Excellence in English in middle and high school: How teachers' professional lives support student achievement. *American Educational Research Journal, 37*(2), 397–439.

Langer, J. A. (2001). Beating the odds: Teaching middle and high school students to read and write well. *American Educational Research Journal, 38*(4), 837–880.

Lai, M.K., & McNaughton, S. (2008). Raising student achievement in poor, urban communities through evidence-based conversation. In L. Earl & H. Timperley (Eds.), *Professional learning conversation: Challenges in using evidence* (pp. 13–27). Dorddrecht, The Netherlands: Kluwer/Springer.

Levin, H. M. (1987). Accelerated schools for disadvantaged students. *Educational Leadership, 44*(6), 19–21.

Lipson, M.L., Mosenthal, J. H., Mekkelsen, J., & Russ, B. (2004). Building knowledege and fashining success one school at a time. *The Reading Teacher, 57*(6) 534–542.

May, H., & Supovitz, J. A. (2006). Capturing the cumulative effects of school reform: An 11-year study of the impacts of America's Choice on student achievement. *Educational Evaluation and Policy Analysis, 28*(3), 231–257.

McCombs, B. L., & Quiat, M. (2002). What makes a comprehensive school reform model learner centered? *Urban Education, 37*(4), 476–496.

McDonald, S. K., Keesler, V. A., Nils, J. K., & Schneider, B. (2006). Scaling-up exemplary interventions. *Educational Researcher, 35*(3), 15–24.

McLaughlin, M. W., & Mitra, D. (2001). Theory-based change and change-based theory: Going deeper, going broader. *Journal of Educational Change, 2,* 301–323.

McNaughton, S., MacDonald, S., Amituanai-Toloa, M., Lai, M., MacDonald, S., & Farry, S. (2006). *Enhanced teaching and learning of comprehension in year 4–9: Mangere Schools.* Auckland, New Zealand: Uniservices Ltd.

Mirel, J. (2003). Old educational ideas, New American Schools: Progressivism and the rhetoric of educational revolution. *Paedagogica Historica, 39*(4), 477–497.

Mosenthal, J., Lipson, M., Mekkelsen, J., & Thompson, E. (2003). The dynamic environment of success: Representing school improvement in literacy learning and instruction. *Yearbook of the National Reading Conference, 52,* 308–320.

Mosenthal, J., Lipson, M., Torncello, S., Russ, B., & Mekkelsen, J. (2004). Contexts and practices of six schools successful in obtaining reading achievement. *The Elementary School Journal, 41*(5), 343–367.

No Child Left Behind Act of 2001, Pub. L. No. 107–110, 115 Stat. 1425. (2002). Retrieved April 10, 2003, from http://www.ed.gov/offices/OESE/esea

Newmann, F. M., King, M. B., & Youngs, P. (2000). Professional development that addresses schools capacity: Lessons from urban elementary schools. *American Journal of Education, 108,* 259–299.

Newmann, F. M., Smith, B. S., Allenworth, E., & Bryk, A. S. (2001). Instructional program coherence:

What it is and why it should guide school improvement policy? *Education, Evaluation, and Policy Analysis, 23*(4), 297–321.

Passow, A. H. (1984). Educational change and school improvement: Three perspectives. *Teachers College Record, 86*(1), 238–247.

Pearson, D. P. (2007). An endangered species act for literacy education. *Journal of Literacy Research, 39*(2), 145–162.

Pearson, P. D., Raphael, T. E., Benson, V. L., & Madda, C. L. (2007). Balance in the literacy curriculum: Then and now. In L. B. Gambrell & L. M. Morrow (Eds.), *Best practices in literacy instruction* (3rd ed., pp. 30–54). New York: Guilford Press.

Popkewitz, T. S., Tabachnick, B. R., & Wehlage, G. (1982). *The myth of educational reform: A study of school repsonses to a program of change.* Madison: The University of Wisconsin Press.

Purkey, S. C., & Smith, M. S. (1983). Effective schools: A review. *The Elementary School Journal, 83*(4), 427–452.

Raphael, T., Au, K., & Goldman, S. (2009). Whole school instructional improvement through the Standards-based Change Process. In J. Hoffman & Y. Goodman (Eds.), *Changing literacies for changing times: An historical perspective on the future of reading research, public policy, and classroom practices* (pp. 198–229). New York: Routledge.

Rogers, T., Winters, K. L., Bryan, G., Price, J., McCormick, F., House, L., et al. (2006). Developing the IRIS: Toward situated and valid assessment measures in collaborative professional development and school reform in literacy. *The Reading Teacher, 59*(6), 544–553.

Ross, S. M., Nunnery, J. A., Goldfeder, E., McDonald, A., Rachor, R., Hornbeck, M., et al. (2004). Using school reform models to improve reading achievement: A longitudinal study of direct instruction and Success for All in an urban district. *Journal of Education for Students Placed At Risk, 9*(4), 357–388.

Rowan, B., Camburn, E., & Barnes, C. (2004). Benefiting from comprehensive school reform: A review of research on CSR implementation. In C. Cross (Ed.), *Putting the pieces together: Lessons from comprehensive school reform research* (pp. 1–52). Washington, DC: National Clearinghouse for Comprehensive School Reform.

Santa, C. (2006). A vision for adolescent literacy: Ours or theirs? *Journal of Adolescent & Adult Literacy, 49*(6), 466–476.

Schweinhart, L. J., Weikart, D. P., & Larner, M. B. (1986). Consequences of three preschool curriculum models through age 15. *Early Childhood Research Quarterly, 1*, 15–45.

Skindrud, K., & Gersten, R. (2006). An evaluation of two contrasting approaches for improving reding achievement in a large urban district. *Elementary School Journal, 106*(5), 389–407.

Slavin, R., & Madden, N. (Eds.). (2001). *Success for All: Research and reform in elementary education.* New York: Routledge.

Spillane, J. P., Halverson, R., & Diamond, J. B. (2001). Investigating school leadership practice: A distributive perspective. *Educational Researcher, 30*(3), 23–28.

Stein, M. K., & D'Amico, L. (2002). Inquiry at the crossroads of policy and learning: A study of a district-wide literacy initiative. *Teachers College Record, 104*(7), 1313–1344.

Sterbinsky, A., Ross, S. M., & Redfield, D. (2006). Effects of comprehensive school reform on student achievement and school change: A longitudinal multi-site study. *School Effectiveness and School Improvement, 17*(3), 367–397.

Strike, K. A. (2004). Community, the missing element of school reform: Why schools should be more like congregations than banks. *American Journal of Education, 110*, 215–232.

Taylor, B. M. (2007). Tier 1: Effective classroom reading instruction in the elementary grades. In D. Fuchs, L. S. Fuchs, & S. Vaughn (Eds.), *Response to intervention: A framework for reading educators* (pp. 5–25). Newark, DE: International Reading Association.

Taylor, B. M., Pearson, P. D., Peterson, D. S., & Rodriguez, M. C. (2003). Reading growth in high-poverty classrooms: The influence of teacher practices that encourage cognitive engagement in literacy learning. *Elementary School Journal, 104*, 3–28.

Taylor, B. M., Pearson, P. D., Peterson, D. P., & Rodriguez, M. C. (2005). The CIERA school change framework: An evidenced-based approach to professional development and school reading Improvement. . *Reading Research Quarterly, 40*(1), 40–69.

Taylor, B. M., & Peterson, D. S. (2006). *The impact of the school change framework in twenty-three Minnesota REA schools.* St. Paul: University of Minnesota, Center for Reading Research.

Taylor, B. M., & Peterson, D. S. (2007a). Steps for school-wide reading improvement. In B. M. Taylor & J. E. Ysseldyke (Eds.), *Effective instruction for struggling readers, K-6* (pp. 235–249). New York: TC Press.

Taylor, B. M., & Peterson, D. S. (2007b). *Year 2 report of the Minnesota Reading First Cohort 2 School Change project.* St. Paul: University of Minnesota: Minnesota Center for Reading Research.

Taylor, B. M., Peterson, D. S., Marx, M., & Chein, M. (2007). Scaling up a reading reform in high-poverty elementary schools. In B. M. Taylor & J. E. Ysseldyke (Eds.), *Effective instruction for struggling readers, K-6* (pp. 216–234). New York: TC Press.

Taylor, B. M., Pearson, P. D., Clark, K., & Walpole, S. (2000). Effective schools and accomplished teachers: Lessons about primary grade reading instruction in low-income schools. *Elementary School Journal, 101*(2), 121–166.

Timperley, H. S., & Parr, J. M. (2007). Closing the achievement gap through evidence-based inquiry at multilpe levels of the education system. *Journal of Advanced Academics, 19*(1), 90–115.

Uline, C. L., Tschannen-Moran, M., & Perez, L. (2003). Constructive conflict: How controversy can contribute to school improvement. *Teachers College Record, 105*(5), 782–816.

26 Professional Development and Teacher Education for Reading Instruction

Deborah R. Dillon, David G. O'Brien, Mistilina Sato
University of Minnesota, Twin Cities

Catherine M. Kelly
St. Catherine University

INTRODUCTION

Research in reading teacher education and ongoing professional development for practicing teachers has continued to grow in quantity and sophistication since the turn of the 21st century when the last *Handbook of Reading Research* was published. The previous handbook chapter on this topic, "Teaching Teachers to Teach Reading: Paradigm Shifts, Persistent Problems, and Challenges" (Anders, Hoffman, & Duffy, 2000), presented a review of the literature organized around both historical and current perspectives on what we know about preparing teachers of reading and helping them to continue their learning. To accomplish the historical task the authors provided a "Review of Reviews," that revealed "reading researchers have overwhelmingly devoted attention to the process of reading and to the learning of reading (p.723)." By contrast, Anders et al. suggested that attention should be focused on "*how* teachers learn and how that learning is enacted in their professional responsibilities" (p. 723). Duffy (2004) also argued that reading researchers need to think differently about *what* we teach teachers and *how* we prepare them; he also noted that we need to think differently about *when* they are prepared—particularly the time they need to learn to be effective teachers. The need for high quality research on reading teacher preparation and development has been heightened in today's policy context, where the question of what constitutes teacher quality is hotly contested (Cochran-Smith, 2004; Levine, 2006; National Council on Teacher Quality or NCTQ, 2006) and public concerns about whether teachers are well-prepared sometimes leads to policies and legislative initiatives that ignore research findings.

Because comprehensive research reviews and syntheses have been completed recently (e.g., Cochran-Smith & Zeichner, 2005; Darling-Hammond & Bransford, 2005: Snow, Burns, & Griffin, 1998; Snow, Griffin, & Burns, 2005; Risko et al., 2008), we will not replicate those efforts. Rather, the purpose of this chapter is to examine the literature on preservice teacher education (at the elementary and secondary levels), and ongoing professional development in reading teacher education by critically evaluating how research, practice, and policy inform or are informed by research in teacher education. We examine how the relationships among these three elements may in turn impact future research and our practices in teacher development. We also discuss how the links can be strengthened between research and practice to increase the likelihood that policies are based on research. To accomplish these goals, we examined the following:

1. Articles in peer reviewed journals in the field of literacy, teacher education, and professional development, and peer-reviewed syntheses of research.
2. Relevant national syntheses—often conducted by expert panels (e.g., NRP, 2001; Snow et al., 2005).
3. Policy briefs (NCTQ Report, 2006; Smartt & Reschly, 2007).

The following questions guided our review of the national syntheses: Who commissioned each? Who wrote each? What national organizations created research reviews and studies in reading teacher education research? We sought to highlight patterns, understand distinctions, and determine whether each research study, synthesis, or policy brief made an impact and/or moved the field forward. This chapter also provides links between past and recent reviews of published research in reading teacher education to support researchers as they identify questions to study and seek comprehensive answers to their questions. This approach is a direct response to critiques that reading researchers do not always ground their teacher education research historically (Risko et al., 2008).

The remainder of the chapter is organized as follows: We review research on reading teacher education, conducted after 2000, in three sections: elementary preservice preparation, secondary preservice preparation, and continuing professional development. (In the remainder of this review we refer to preservice teachers as PTs.) At the end of each of the three sections, we provide a close analysis to illustrate how important questions and research designs can be used to stimulate thought about the components needed in new research studies that can move the field forward. We conclude the entire chapter with a discussion about the connections or disconnections between research, practice, and policy, offering some recommendations and directions for future research.

Preservice Reading Teacher Education: An Overview

Most research and policy reports we reviewed in the late 1990s through 2000 were focused on preparing teachers to work with elementary age students. For example, in 1999, the American Federation of Teachers (AFT) produced a report, authored by Louisa Moats, titled "Teaching reading IS rocket science: What expert teachers of reading should know and be able to do." This widely circulated document stated that scientists have data to support the notion that 95% of children can be taught to read but that many will never learn to do so without organized, systematic ways enacted by knowledgeable teachers. Moats related that teacher preparation programs have failed to adequately prepare teacher candidates and laid out a core curriculum including understanding the structure of the English language and using validated, reliable, and efficient assessments. The focus of the report was on the rigorous, research-based knowledge and skills and opportunities for practice that should be part of preparation programs; the report also called for licensing authorities to test this knowledge and textbook authors to improve their college methods texts. The National Education Association (NEA) Task Force on Reading (2000) also produced a report that outlines what a complete (versus balanced) reading approach to teaching reading should include, advocating that programs need multiple reading components in ratios determined by the needs of students at various points in their development. The focus was on what complete reading programs should include, with less attention to the specific knowledge and skills required by teachers to enact these programs. These two reports heightened the need for the reading research community to respond by identifying research-based ideas about how (PTs) should be prepared to teach reading. Reading researchers (Fillmore & Snow, 2002; Harmon et al., 2001; Hoffman & Pearson, 2000; National Reading Panel Report, 2000; Strickland, Snow, Griffin, Burns, & McNamara, 2002) also expressed concerns about the need to organize and review the research in reading teacher preparation and determine research-based ways to prepare reading teachers.

One response to this call for action came from Anders and her colleagues (2000) who provided a "review of reviews" section that outlined the focus of research on reading teacher education from about 1900 through the 1980s. This synthesis was followed by an analysis of research studies conducted between 1965 and 1996. Findings from the analysis indicated what teacher educators should do to help PTs learn. They found that there was an increase in teacher preparation research that used diverse methodologies. Anders and colleagues also found that researchers in our field struggle with defining and studying concepts such as teacher knowledge, beliefs, and attitudes and how they impact teacher development and programs.

Anders et al. (2000) concluded that we lack a solid research base upon which to make claims about how teachers should be prepared in the area of reading and that lacking such a base, our field is in danger of individuals outside of the field, such as policy makers, determining what preparation programs should look like and include. Anders and her colleagues called for several types of action: (a) case reports of excellent programs in reading teacher preparation to serve as models; (b) a national database on teacher education programs (e.g., program features, descriptions of participants), (c) self studies by reading researchers of their own programs and practices, (d) increased dialogue between reading teacher educators to share ideas and promote change, and (e) longitudinal studies that document program effectiveness, both in terms of K–12 student learning and cost-effectiveness standards.

THE STATE OF READING TEACHER EDUCATION

We begin at the beginning—by addressing a concern raised in previous reviews about the need for an understanding of where the field stands in how we currently prepare teachers. In 2001 the International Reading Association (IRA) published a book titled *Learning to Teach: Setting the Research Agenda* and outlined the current "state of the state" in research and practices related to reading teacher education (Roller, 2001). The book included a survey of current practices in undergraduate reading teacher education in the U. S., preliminary findings from studies of PT preparation programs focused on providing descriptions of excellent reading teacher preparation (Flint et al., 2001), studies of specific teacher preparation programs (Lalik & Potts, 2001; Au & Maaka, 2001), findings from studies of teachers in their first years or their transition into teaching (Grossman et al., 2001), and research on continuing teacher education and the characteristics of effective teachers (Allington & Johnston, 2001) and schools (Taylor & Pearson, 2001). Roller provided a baseline of research on the state of reading teacher preparation and research directions needed to move the field forward—both necessary steps for reading educators. In this same text, Strickland (2001) and Pearson (2001) discussed the role teaching standards play in reading teacher education. In addition, Pearson (2001) pointed to the need to address increasing levels of knowledge and expertise needed by teachers as they develop their abilities. His recommendations to carefully specify and plot teacher expertise over time are similar to those of Feiman-Nemser (2001) who proposed a professional learning continuum for teacher preparation.

Another IRA initiative was the development of a set of Standards for Reading Professionals (2003), with a revised version due for release in 2010. The IRA Standards moved beyond merely outlining the knowledge that teachers should possess to including statements that indicate what teachers should know *and be able to do* at increasing levels of sophistication. These statements include standards for PTs and individuals moving beyond initial licensure through more advanced levels of preparation, such as the expertise needed by reading specialists (more detail is provided in the professional development section of this chapter). The IRA Standards work and the research efforts outlined in *Learning to Teach Reading* (2001) required that IRA partner with reading researchers to focus on improving reading teacher education. IRA dedicated targeted resources and sustained leadership to complete this project and subsequent research initiatives. This effort was beneficial: Teacher educators were provided with a common, research-based set of concepts to inform their future practices, as well as a research agenda for studying the effectiveness of teacher education programs—primarily at the elementary PT level.

Building a Comprehensive View of the Research in Reading Teacher Preparation

Several large-scale, funded research efforts have been undertaken to address the vacuum in the current research base. These efforts point to effective practices in preparing reading teachers at the preservice level. We present three of these efforts.

National Academy of Education's (NAE) Reading Subcommittee Report.   In contrast to the AFT report and other documents of this nature, Snow and colleagues (2005) make an evidence-based case for a core knowledge base about reading that K–12 teachers need to develop, with the understanding that this knowledge develops over a career-long pathway or framework for thinking about teacher education. Within this framework—called progressive differentiation—teachers learn, enact, assess, and reflect on knowledge gleaned at various points in a career trajectory including preservice, apprentice, novice, experienced, and master teachers. Snow and colleagues argue that teachers engage in these processes at different levels or weights, depending on their experience. For example, PTs primarily engage in developing declarative knowledge about a solid foundation of disciplinary knowledge, but they also need situated, "can-do" procedural knowledge. In comparison, master teachers have considerable knowledge and experience, are reflective, provide stable quality reading instruction, can analyze situations and reflect on these, and lead others in professional development activities. The goal is for first year teachers to exit their preparation programs with a particular level of declarative and procedural knowledge that is stable and allows them to assess, plan, enact, and adapt instruction for the majority of children in the class. Snow and colleagues also lay out what PTs at the K–12 level need to know, supported by considerable research citations, including "useable" knowledge about language structures, reading development, reading in various content areas, texts, word reading, comprehension, assessment, motivation, and how to assist struggling readers. The NAE report benefits reading teacher educators because it compiles the research on what initial and continuing teachers need to know and be able to do, and lays out an argument for a developmental trajectory of how and when teachers learn the knowledge and practices needed to effectively teach reading.

IRA's National Commission on Reading Teacher Preparation.   Simultaneous with the work resulting in the NAE report, IRA's National Commission on Excellence in Elementary Teacher Preparation for Reading Instruction conducted extensive studies of selected teacher education programs. The commission designed three phases of research. For the first phase, Harmon et al. (2001) reported on the critical features of excellent reading teacher preparation programs through the identification of eight Sites of Excellence in Reading Teacher Preparation (SERTE). The eight features of excellence identified through the examination of the SERTE programs are:

1. programs are based on clearly articulated institutional missions (mission),
2. faculty have a clear vision of how the mission is instantiated in the teacher education program (vision),
3. programs deliver broad-based content to meet the needs of diverse students based on current research and professional standards (content),
4. faculty and school personnel model student-centered learning (personalized teaching),
5. carefully supervised apprenticeship experiences are provided (apprenticeship),
6. programs foster the professional identity of preservice teachers and teacher educators within a variety of communities (community),
7. programs are grounded on a discriminating admissions/entry/exit continuum (standards), and

8. faculties strive to maintain the integrity and quality of the literacy program while working within the limited resources and constraints imposed by schools, the university, and the state (autonomy).

The SERTE studies were extended to focus on the transition to teaching literacy years. The commission's next study, as reported in Maloch et al. (2003), used a quasi-experimental design in a longitudinal study of 101teachers, gathering data from a survey and three phone interviews throughout the year. Participants were from one of three groups: beginning teachers who completed an undergraduate reading specialization program at one of three SERTE sites offering multiple programs to students, a second group of beginning teachers who graduated from a general education program at the same three sites (the comparison group), and a third group of beginning teachers graduating from the five additional sites of excellence in reading embedded programs.

The Maloch et al. (2003) study sought to examine the ways in which the graduates from the three aforementioned program types talk about their reading instruction and teaching experiences, and convey their perceptions of the influence of their teacher education programs. The authors found that graduates of the commission-recognized SERTE reading specialization and reading embedded programs were more likely than the general education comparison group to talk about their instruction in ways consistent with effective teaching. For example, these graduates reported providing meaningful and relevant instruction, making an effort to learn more about their students, maintaining enthusiasm for teaching, and seeking ongoing support for their own continued learning. Reading specialization and reading embedded graduates were also specific in the values these graduates assign to their teacher preparation programs. The authors posit that contrary to studies suggesting that teacher education coursework does not transfer to classroom teaching, the results of this study show that quality teacher preparation affects novice teachers' perceptions and understandings of what it means to teach reading.

Hoffman et al. (2005) discuss the third commission study, one designed to investigate the effects of preparation on the transition into teaching and on teaching practices. This quasi-experimental, longitudinal study examined the effects of the completion of an excellent reading teacher education program on experiences as participants enter classrooms, and how teachers' preparation relates to their teaching practice. Three different groups of teachers were observed in the second year of the study: 46 commission program graduates, 28 second-year comparison teachers, and 17 experienced teachers who taught at the same schools as the commission graduates. Of these 92 participants, 61 continued into the third year of the research study. The authors found that commission teachers were more effective than the comparison teachers in creating rich classroom text environments, high engagement with text, and high levels of student understanding and valuing of these texts. The authors posit that participation in a high-quality teacher education program positively influences the experiences of novice teachers.

Sailors, Keehn, Martinez, and Harmon (2005) also examined the perspectives and practices of graduates from SERTE programs. In their article, two distinct but related studies were reported. The first study described what first-year teachers valued about their preservice teacher preparation programs, and the second study examined and described the features of early field experiences related to reading that were offered to students enrolled in SERTE programs. Seventy-three teacher participants were interviewed by telephone during the middle and end of their first year of teaching. While no questions in the first study specifically asked about field experiences, 90% of the beginning teachers identified field experiences as something they valued from their preparation programs. Participants offered global statements of value, as well as specific statements about what they learned: classroom management skills, adapting materials and instruction to meet individual needs, working with students in various contexts, learning from knowledgeable others, and developing professional relationships during field experiences.

In the second study, Sailors et al. (2005) examined course syllabi from the SERTE sites and had a representative faculty member from each site complete a questionnaire addressing information about field experiences not apparent in an examination of syllabi. Through this investigation, the authors identified five common features of the early field experiences of the participating beginning teachers' preparation programs. These features included developing reflective teachers, scaffolding of structured experiences and coursework, scaffolding by a knowledgeable other including classroom teachers and university supervisors, offering placements in a variety of contexts, and one-on-one tutoring experiences. The authors found that there was significant overlap between the features valued by program completers and the common features offered by the SERTE programs.

Maloch and Kinzer (2006) examined a particular program feature, the use of multimedia cases in methods coursework, on 33 graduates as they entered their first year of teaching. Three themes emerged from the survey and interview data. First, 31 of 33 respondents stated that methods courses positively influenced their teaching. Second, respondents reported several factors as influential in their recall of course content, including active involvement, enthusiasm of instructor, and a close connection between field experiences and coursework. And third, respondents reported that the use of multimedia cases influenced their learning in teacher education programs and in their teaching, with 19 respondents identifying the cases as either the first or second most helpful instructional technique used by methods course instructors when presented with a list of techniques.

The IRA SERTE studies indicate that teacher education programs positively influence beginning teachers. This influence can be seen through teachers' descriptions of the features and components of the eight programs, the new teachers' comments about what they learned during their programs and how they are teaching as a result of their preparation, and researchers' observations of PTs as they taught literacy lessons (e.g., these observations revealed aspects of SERTE program goals). This work is also described in "Teaching Reading Well: A Synthesis of IRA's Research on Teacher Preparation for Reading Instruction" (IRA, 2007) and in an extensive review of literature (cf. Risko et al., 2008, detailed later in this paper).

The Snow et al. (2005) and the IRA Commission on Excellence (2007) studies were substantive and high quality efforts to address Anders et al.'s (2000) call for the field to build a credible research base upon which to make claims about how teachers should be prepared in the area of reading.

IRA's Teacher Education Task Force (TETF) Research Review.   The International Reading Association recognized the need and commissioned a critical review of the empirical literature in reading teacher preparation that spanned from 1990 to 2006. This work was undertaken by TETF and recently published in Reading Research Quarterly (Risko et al., 2008). This review of research provides a link between the Anders et al. (2000) Handbook chapter, the six features for reading programs identified by the IRA Commission's Teaching Reading Well (2007) report, and research that has been undertaken recently in the field. The TEFT work also addressed concerns voiced about the small number of reading teacher education studies (11) selected for review in the National Reading Panel Report (2000), noting that the NRP limited number was likely due to a decision within the NRP to include only experimental and quasi-experimental studies.

In the TETF review, the authors identified what research findings say about the best ways to prepare future teachers in the area of reading. First, 298 reading teacher preparation research studies were examined using a carefully designed set of criteria to "assess the quality of the studies" that was open to a variety of methodologies and sensitive to the theoretical frameworks used by researchers. The original pool of studies identified for review was reduced to 82 empirical, peer-reviewed, investigations—all conducted in the United States.

The TETF review analyzed the questions and methodologies used by researchers, included descriptions of participants, data sources and analysis strategies, and summarized patterns and trends across sets of studies. The TEFT authors found that most of the studies were conducted by teacher educators (instructors) at their own institutions, were limited to the time frame of a one-semester PT education course, and used a constructivist perspective (over 50%) when crafting their research questions and designing the studies. Four patterns emerged from the review of literature and macroanalysis: "(a) changes in beliefs and pedagogical knowledge, (b) conditions associated with these changes, (c) use of explicit teaching conditions, and (d) instructional tools commonly used by the teacher educator researchers" (p. 276). Many of the studies focused on studying PTs' beliefs about reading and reading instruction (28%), and teachers' topical knowledge and reflective reasoning (21%). Most of the 82 studies in the final pool used qualitative methodologies and focused on preparing elementary PTs to teach reading; only 11 studies focused on preparing secondary teachers in content area reading coursework. Because so few studies were identified in the area of preparing secondary PTs, most of the TETF review focused on elementary reading teacher preparation. We highlight the elementary teacher preparation findings in the next section and later in this review we focus on the secondary PT findings.

A Focus on Elementary Reading Teacher Preparation Studies.   In their analysis of the beliefs research, the TETF authors drew upon the work by Kane, Sandretto, and Heath (2002), which identified the need for reading researchers to expand the way they think about influencing beliefs and studying changes. In particular, Kane and colleagues suggest that scholars address both stated and enacted (as evidenced by practice) beliefs and the methods used to document beliefs. TETF authors indicated that for the most part, the research on PTs' topical knowledge (and growth as a result of coursework) is disappointing because it fails to advance our understanding of what PTs should know when they leave teacher education programs. Risko and her colleagues (2008) also noted that studies on PT reflection often duplicated previous research findings in the general research on teacher education; namely the finding that reflection deepens when instructors explicitly nurture both the teaching skills and reflective and self-critical dispositions of PTs.

Risko and her colleagues (2008) found that 44% of the studies focused on instructors teaching PTs how to teach reading using explicit instruction, modeling, and demonstration. These instructors also taught PTs how to collect and analyze student data and use it to inform instruction. By experiencing the type of learning that occurred as a result of instructor modeling and through carefully designed practica, PTs often shifted their beliefs about students' abilities to learn (e.g., struggling readers) and embraced effective teaching strategies. In addition, PTs' knowledge of various assessments, how to teach culturally diverse students, and pedagogical skills grew. Prolonged work with students in practica helped this learning process. But generally speaking, PTs were challenged by the expectation that they should use the knowledge gleaned in coursework to reshaping their beliefs and build a portfolio of teaching practices. To give an example, writing personal biographies designed to help PTs reshape beliefs did not appear to help PTs translate their learning into culturally relevant pedagogy when they taught lessons. However, the design of university assignments where PTs were required to gather student data, tutor students by applying what they were learning (knowledge) and then teach the students in culturally relevant ways, led to changes in knowledge and teaching practices. Guided practice in using assessment tools or particular teaching strategies and explicit feedback from instructors and peers, based on the tutoring sessions, also appeared to be important for enhancing learning.

The TETF authors concluded that longitudinal studies are needed to examine teaching across a variety of settings and situations. These longitudinal studies could examine whether the knowledge learned in the limited time PTs are in preservice courses (often procedural knowledge) is developed well enough for PTs to apply it in a flexible, yet effective manner in various situations and with a variety of students over time. Further, as the authors pointed out, literacy research that examines individual differences in PTs' knowledge and pedagogical skill development is important, requiring the use of multiple instruments over time.

Programmatic Research.   A final body of research examined by Risko and her colleagues (2008) focused on programmatic research; unfortunately, it included only six studies. In the study designs researchers either documented the features of programs, how changes in programs were initiated and fostered, or program graduates' perceptions and practices in their first years of teaching. Two studies outlined how university faculty worked to identify and implement research and standards-based program features (Keehn et al., 2003), including designing agreed-upon assignments, clinical experiences, and assessments to strengthen reading teacher preparation (Vagle, Dillon, Davison-Jenkins, LaDuca, & Olson, 2006). One of these programmatic studies focused on reading instructors from four institutions in one state who met together for 3 years to reconceptualize reading teacher preparation and create a Literacy Conceptual Framework or LCF (Dillon et al., 2004; Dillon & Vagle, 2006; Vagle et al., 2006). The LCF offers a vision and a substantive orientation about literacy teaching and learning and identifies 10 key areas of knowledge for PT learning including Reading, Writing, Motivation, and Assessment and Evaluation. Content in each of these areas is organized around several key structures: Foundational Knowledge, Pedagogical Content Knowledge, Instructional Practices and Materials, and Beginning Repertoire. The content is based on a spiraling model of learning—knowledge and pedagogical content knowledge as well as instructional strategies and materials would be introduced, studied, revisited, and studied in more depth as PTs learn to teach, develop as teachers, and become expert in their craft. The LCF and accompanying materials provide opportunities for PTs to critically examine their beliefs as well as develop (a) subject knowledge and pedagogical content knowledge, (b) an understanding of learners—particularly those from diverse backgrounds, (c) tools and skills to teach literacy through "Agreed Upon Assignments," and (d) a "Beginning Repertoire" (BR)—the demonstrated abilities that PTs need to work with children and youth in a variety of ways to enhance literacy learning. The accompanying materials include the Agreed Upon Assignments and pre-and post-assessments tools (surveys and concept maps), used with PTs to determine growth in beliefs and knowledge over the course of their reading preparation programs (Vagle & Dillon, 2006).

Four other studies followed graduates from their preparation programs into their first years of teaching. Findings from these studies point to the importance of providing cohesive content foci and documenting growth in PTs' beliefs and practices during coursework and practica (Grisham, 2000), including structured and carefully supervised early fieldwork (Sailors et al., 2005). Maloch and her colleagues (2003) and Hoffman and his colleagues (2005) followed PTs from their initial programs into their transition to teaching. Based on interviews and surveys, Maloch et al. found that SERTE PTs valued their preparation programs and talked about teaching in ways that indicated that they had taken up effective, student-centered reading instruction. Hoffman et al.'s (2005) observations of SERTE teachers indicated that these individuals were more effective in engaging and teaching students to understand and value texts (a complete description of these SERTE studies was provided earlier in this review).

These studies of programmatic research help us think about the complicated and necessary research we need to address in reading teacher preparation, including: (a) how to develop research-based programs and experiences to best prepare teachers of reading, (b) the impact of preparation programs on teachers as they exit our programs and move into their first years of teaching, and (c) the continued development required for these teachers as they grow in their knowledge and fine-tune their skills in their respective teaching sites, based on the needs of their students.

In the concluding section of their review, Risko et al. (2008) recommend that reading teacher education researchers familiarize themselves with, and build on previous research findings; pursue questions in-depth; use multiple theoretical frameworks; and collaborate across sites to enable more robust designs and findings that can inform policy about teacher preparation.

Additional studies on reading teacher preparation, not included in the Risko et al. (2008) review time frame (2000–2006), focus on the critical need to prepare teachers to work in urban settings. For example, Lazar's (2007) research focused on providing PTs with teaching experiences in urban settings with the goal of shifting PTs' attitudes toward urban students' literacy potential, and bolstering the PTs' confidence in teaching in culturally diverse, urban settings. Significant shifts in dispositions were indicated from ANOVA results of questionnaires coupled with cultural autobiographies. This area of research has also been addressed by researchers in the edited volume "Improving Literacy Achievement in Urban Schools" (Wilkinson, Morrow, & Chou, 2008) where authors note that we do not know the best ways to prepare teachers to work in these settings. However, findings from work where reading teacher education programs have been designed to help urban schools improve students' literacy achievement (Au, Raphael, & Mooney, 2008) can lead us in the right direction, including the type of practica that is key to preparing PTs to work in urban settings (Shanahan, 2008). The ideas in this text challenge reading researchers to understand that preparing teachers for urban settings requires more than what we currently do in teacher education programs. The authors also state that reading educators must address the variation in preparation and experiences provided by the approximately 1,150 U.S. teacher preparation programs (Broemmel, Meller, & Allington, 2008).

Improving urban reading teacher preparation will require carefully designed longitudinal studies, across multiple sites, using multiple theoretical frameworks and mixed methods research designs. This approach will allow reading researchers to document the best ways to prepare new teachers with the knowledge and skills needed to teach effectively in these settings, the practica experiences required, and the impact of these programs as played out in the effectiveness of teachers who graduate and then work in urban settings.

A Closer Look at Transitions to Teaching.   In addition to the work of the IRA's National Commission on Excellence in Elementary Teacher Preparation for Reading Instruction, several other studies focused on the effects of teacher preparation on early career teaching in literacy. Findings from four CELA (Center on English Learning and Achievement) studies (Bickmore, Smagorinsky, Ladd, & O'Donnell-Allen, 2005; Cook, Smagorinsky, Fry, Konopak, & Moore, 2002; Grossman et al., 2000; Smagorinsky, Wright, Murphy, O'Donnell-Allen, & Konopak, 2007) indicated varying degrees to which teachers are able to enact their conceptual understandings introduced in teacher education that were sometimes supported, sometimes seen in conflict with, and sometimes limited by the contexts within which these early-career teachers found themselves teaching. While in each case teachers were able to discuss important concepts from teacher education, the ability to follow through with these visions, ideas, tools, and philosophies were greatly influenced by the inconsistent nature of the instruction regarding these concepts in their teacher education programs.

Several studies made claims about the importance of the initial teaching context for beginning teachers throughout the transition to teaching (Bickmore et al., 2005; Cook et al., 2002; Harste, Leland, Schmidt, Vasquez, & Ociepka, 2004). Similar to the findings regarding conceptual understandings, the authors of these studies concluded that contextual factors (including school motives, curricular materials, mentor teacher beliefs, and support available) were influential on the transition to teaching, particularly when aspects of the initial teaching context of the novice teachers came into conflict (or were perceived to be in conflict) with the philosophies of their preparation.

The need for continued support for novice teachers as they transition from their preparation program into their beginning teaching career was identified in several studies (Massey, 2006; Pomerantz & Pierce, 2004; Pierce & Pomerantz, 2006). Similar to Anders and colleagues (2000), the authors of these transition to teaching studies posit that continued support for novice teachers from mentor teachers, school district personnel, and university educators—specifically guiding them through their early years of teaching in the context of their own classrooms—can help to reinforce learning from preservice programs as well as support new learning regarding the complexities of their particular classroom and instructional contexts.

However, Grossman et al. (2000), warns researchers against drawing definitive conclusions based on studies designed to examine only a teacher's first year of teaching. The limited scope of work following teachers through only their first year of teaching may be insufficient to determine what has or has not been learned and internalized from novice teachers' preparation programs. Further longitudinal work (2–3 years beyond the first year) will be required before claims can be made definitively concerning what teachers are able or unable to enact from their teacher education program.

SECONDARY READING TEACHER PREPARATION

Compared to elementary teacher preparation, there is little empirical work at the secondary level. The low volume of secondary studies is due to the predominant focus on teaching teachers to teach children *how* to read rather than on supporting readers' engagement with a range of genres across disciplines as they continue to learn to read. Hence, there are fewer teacher educators whose primary responsibility is to prepare middle and secondary teachers of reading and fewer courses and field experiences dedicated to the preparation of middle and secondary reading teachers compared to elementary level preparation (Risko et al., 2008).

Middle and secondary teacher education in reading has a dual purpose: One purpose is to prepare teachers who teach reading as a continuation of the elementary focus into middle grades and, to a much lesser extent, into high schools. For example, teachers are prepared to teach "developmental" reading or to teach reading as part of English language arts instruction. The second purpose is to prepare teachers who will teach single subjects—history, science, mathematics, physical education, and English. This second preparation area is particularly challenging because it involves much more than an understanding of reading processes and pedagogy applied to content disciplines; rather, it involves an even deeper understanding of the roles of oral and written language in knowledge production and representation in the disciplines and thus in teaching and learning in these subject areas. This understanding of the intersection of language, literacy, and learning is articulated in a range of ways in teacher education programs. The most common approach for preparing secondary English teachers is to include a range of courses in reading, writing, and literature pedagogy, whereas in such disciplines as math, sciences, social sciences, health, physical education, and the arts, the usual practice is to require a course on literacy in content area instruction. This single course may be developed to complement subject area content or methods courses and field experiences or it may exist as more of a generic course, the content of which PTs are expected to adapt to their respective disciplines.

Risko et al. (2008) discuss briefly much of the foundational work at the secondary level in terms of teachers' beliefs about reading and how those beliefs are mediated by coursework and other experiences in teacher education (e.g., Konopak, Readence, & Wilson, 1994; Linek, Sampson, Raine, Klakamp, & Smith, 2006; Stevens, 2002) with the ultimate goal of connecting PTs' beliefs to practices. At the secondary level, the research on beliefs predominated because literacy educators, at least in the earliest stages of this work, indirectly positioned content teachers as being resistant to the idea that learning about reading and other literacy practices may improve their teaching and their students' engagement and learning (O'Brien & Stewart, 1990; Ratekin, Simpson, Alvermann, Dishner, 1985). Specifically, due to beliefs about the organization of curricula around subject areas, teaching as covering content, beliefs aligned with content expertise, membership in subject subcultures, and preconceived notions about students and texts, literacy teacher educators wanted a better understanding of PTs' resistance beliefs as an important route to improving their practice (Bean & Zulich, 1990, 1992; O'Brien, 1988; O'Brien & Stewart, 1990).

However, positioning secondary content teachers as resistant to incorporating literacy practices is problematic. It assumes that literacy teacher educators' pedagogical knowledge can complement pedagogical knowledge constructed by faculty within the disciplines. And, since instructional strategies adopted by literacy educators are often recommended without benefit of conceptual understanding and socio-historical contexts of disciplinary knowledge and practices generated within disciplines, the idea that generic literacy strategies can be as important or more important than pedagogies that originate in disciplines is questionable (cf. Conley, 2008; Moje, 2007). This assumption of relative importance of literacy frameworks is embodied in the phrase "every teacher a teacher of reading" which, from a pragmatic view, is embraced as a call for all teachers to collectively contribute to help all students with reading. But from the view of teachers in various disciplines, the call is often seen as an unfair demand on their time given their lack of expertise in reading; moreover, it is counter to the institutionalized practices within disciplines (Bean, 2000; O'Brien et al., 1995).

Holt-Reynolds and her colleagues (Anderson & Holt-Reynolds, 1995; Holt-Reynolds, 1992) took a different angle on teacher beliefs about literacy by examining these within the broader field of the scholarship of teaching. They studied the complexities of PTs' beliefs about literacy based on the primacy and importance of personal histories like experiences at "studenting" in various disciplines and how those beliefs mediate, focus their critiques of, or trump, the ideas they encounter in education courses. The researchers noted that the personal histories that inform PTs' beliefs and give them resilience must be taken up as serious points of discussion, ideally by designing experiences so these histories can be brought to the fore.

The recent focus on disciplinary literacy (Alvermann et al., 2011; Moje, 2007, 2008; Shanahan & Shanahan, 2008) also addresses the limitations of teacher education programs that focus on beliefs-modification of "resistant" teachers. Disciplinary literacy pedagogy also debunks the notion that generic reading strategies can simply be adapted to various disciplines. Later, we discuss the specific advantages of disciplinary literacy frameworks in advancing PT teacher education.

Critical Analysis of the Secondary Teacher Education Research

In PT education at the secondary level, research on teacher education practices, however sparse compared to studies of elementary teacher preparation, evidences cumulative progress in what educators know about adolescents (including the shifting nuances of the term *adolescence*), as well as the complexities of supporting their reading skills and strategies development and integrating literacy instruction with the subject disciplines in which adolescents enroll and need support (Jacobs, 2008; Moje, 2007; Heller & Greenleaf, 2007).

Two recent developments have influenced the scholarship on teaching and teacher education at the secondary level. First, adolescent literacy has been presented in policy circles as the "new" literacy crisis (e.g., Biancarosa & Snow, 2004, 2006). Second, adolescent literacy has been targeted, similar to beginning and early reading, with a range of interventions designed to fix the crisis (e.g., Houge, Geier, & Peyton, 2008; Kamil et al., 2008; Lenz, Ehren, & Deshler, 2005). This emphasis on struggling or "striving" readers, and the interventionist direction, positions adolescents as simply older readers who need more skills and strategies instruction to achieve in school and to catch up to more capable peers.

One result of the crisis representation is that more states have or will soon mandate literacy coursework or other experiences for PTs at the PT secondary level. This policy response is at least partly catalyzed by a series of reports published over the last 6 years (e.g., Biancarosa & Snow, 2004; Kamil, 2003; National Governors' Association, 2005; Heller & Greenleaf, 2007). These reports are thoughtful in contextualizing important aspects of adolescent literacy (literacy means *reading* in the reports) and make practical recommendations for how to address the crisis. They also focus needed attention to supporting adolescents in reading. However, the reports begin by highlighting the crisis in terms of a relatively large number of adolescents who "struggle" in reading, using various alarming interpretations of NAEP data and noting an increasing failure of adolescents graduating from high school. The reports also cite students' inability to read the increasingly complex texts they encounter in high school and beyond. The crisis, which has some validity depending on how achievement data are reported and interpreted, amplifies national and state discourses around deficits and intervention. Unfortunately, these discourses ignore the complexities of the broader field of adolescent literacy and the decades of research that have informed secondary preservice reading education and secondary content literacy.

Ironically, just as the research on PT education is leaning toward disciplinary knowledge and discipline-based teaching practices, and promoting collaboration between scholars in literacy and the various disciplines, policy makers are calling for initiatives that ignore these possibilities for collaboration. For example, among policy slogans are the all too familiar exhortations of the past: (a) all teachers are teachers of reading, (b) reading should be taught *in* the content areas (importing reading into disciplines rather than supporting learning in disciplines with literacy practices compatible with disciplines), (c) all teachers can and should help raise adolescents' reading scores (a responsibility that is unreasonable and misplaced). In short, policy is driving an agenda that is reminiscent of the 1960s and 1970s—one that ignores research conducted in the 1980s and 1990s in which literacy was more broadly defined, while also ignoring the most current work that suggests literacy at the secondary level is embedded in and productive of disciplinary practices and knowledge and thus cannot be taught apart from those practices and knowledge.

The policy *response*, at the national, state, and local levels, is that this crisis must be resolved with immediate interventions designed to bring adolescents up to grade level based on performance on state tests. At best, the policy response has required, or will require, more attention to the preparation of teachers who understand how to support readers at the secondary level. At worst, states have formulated, or will formulate, licensure standards or mandated coursework at the secondary level that will revert back to the notion of every teacher being a teacher of reading.

Research Leading to Improved Practices in PT Education at the Secondary Level

Recently the Carnegie Corporation has sponsored a substantial research agenda targeting PT preparation related to adolescent literacy. We will review several of these projects that directly focus on disciplinary literacy and PT preparation. This disciplinary literacy work acknowledges that literacy educators, in order to understand learning within disciplines, need a much deeper understanding of the conceptual domains of each discipline, how the conceptual domains are pedagogically framed to support learning, and how PTs construct their understanding of literacy practices within disciplines. Conceptual and instructional frameworks that originate from within the field of literacy no longer enjoy an elevated status. Rather, frameworks are developed as literacy educators and educators from various disciplines collaboratively construct PT curricula, including literacy courses, methods courses, and field experiences (Douglas, Moje, & Bain, 2008; Moje, Douglas, & Bain, 2007).

Moje and her colleagues at the University of Michigan are studying multiple facets of a PT project including such components as PTs' perceptions of disciplines and disciplinary literacy (Birdyshaw, Moje, Jeppsen, & Bain, 2007), PTs' models of students as readers (Johnson, Stull, Bain, & Moje, 2008) and PTs' models of texts in various disciplines (Birdyshaw & Rackley, 2008). The value of the work conducted at the University of Michigan is partly attributable to the flexibility they have in organizing the PTs into cohorts by disciplines rather than requiring one generic content literacy course and the researchers have found that PTs value the disciplinary cohorting of the literacy course. The post-assessments and interviews across time used in the project show that the PTs take up the literacy strategies more than the students in non-cohorted sections. Perhaps most significant is that even though PTs enrolled in the cohort program are more aware of their responsibility to teach literacy, they encounter a corresponding lack of literacy instruction in their field placement classrooms. And although the project documents a strong sense of responsibility among PTs to engage in disciplinary literacy instruction (e.g., among history/social studies PTs), these PTs have a low sense of agency to effect actual change in students' literacy skills. The work points to the importance of supporting PTs continuing professional development in implementing disciplinary literacy practices.

Another example of a progressive disciplinary approach is work conducted by Shanahan and Shanahan (2008). After studying for 2 years how content experts and secondary teachers read disciplinary texts and make use of strategies, these researchers are constructing recommendations for a revised curriculum in PT education and suggesting revisions on how literacy educators and colleagues in the sciences and liberal arts should more closely collaborate on both coursework and field experiences aligned with disciplines. The researchers point to the benefits of both the careful study of reading by experts in disciplines and the value of collaboration among literacy experts, disciplinary experts, high school teachers, and teacher educators in addressing the unique reading demands in the disciplines.

A third approach proposed by Conley (2008) is to distinguish ineffective generic or "one-size-fits-all" strategies published in the multitude of content literacy texts from more carefully considered cognitive strategies. Conley provides PTs with an approach to cognitive strategies instruction that helps future teachers understand how adolescents learn and how to foster students capacity for lifelong learning. Like the other Carnegie projects, Conley problematizes traditional notions of content literacy strategies instruction and he also explores the complexities of cognitive strategy instruction at the root of many of the instructional recommendations literacy educators have offered to the disciplines.

A fourth example is a project in which Alvermann and her colleagues (Alvermann, Rezak, Mallozzi, Boatright, & Jackson, 2011) constructed an online course for middle school PTs. In the embedded clinical practice component of the class 22 PTs partnered with mentor teachers to create domain-specific lessons for adolescents who struggle to comprehend subject matter. The approach integrated domain knowledge with skills-based instruction in graphic organizers, self-questioning, and summarizing—generic reading strategies shown to be most effective in improving comprehension of written text. The online course also featured a built-in mechanism for mentoring prospective teachers by university instructors with different subject matter expertise. The researchers posited that little is known about how middle school PTs (in this case science PTs) integrate their subject matter knowledge with generic reading strategies they are typically taught in content literacy courses. The researchers also documented a case involving how one science PT worked to make sense of the online class via frameworks for experiencing approximations of preactive and reflective teaching (Grossman & McDonald, 2008), specifically geared toward strengthening understanding of how the strategies-based instruction in reading could be integrated with the concept-based instruction in science. The work points to the importance of understanding and using contradictory discourses across disciplines and questions the traditional notion of importing reading into subject areas with a focus on strategies and text selection, and reinforces the importance of the collaboration between literacy educators and colleagues from the disciplines in constructing courses for PTs.

These research projects critique traditional notions of content literacy and elucidate the design features and logistics of working across literacy and content boundaries to set up PT education programs. These approaches problematize the traditional infusion model—that is, the idea that generic cognitively based strategies PTs encounter in a generic content literacy course can be imported into subject areas.

READING TEACHER PROFESSIONAL DEVELOPMENT

We now turn to research related to the ongoing professional learning and development related to teaching reading. We begin by discussing general principles of professional development. Research-based and professional-consensus recommendations about dimensions of high quality professional development have been synthesized in many sources (e.g., Darling-Hammond, Wei, Andree, Richardson, & Orphanos, 2009; Hawley & Valli, 1999; National Staff Development Council, 2001; Snow et al., 2005). These general principles depict professional development that focuses on specific learning outcomes for students, embeds teacher learning in the teachers' practice, is sustained over time, and provides time for teachers to work together on issues important to them and their schools. This vision of school-embedded professional learning opportunities stands in contrast to traditions of seeking professional development through short-term workshops by experts outside of the school, adopting instructional innovations that are not sustained, and individual teachers seeking ad hoc learning opportunities.

The empirical basis for linking practice-based outcomes to teacher professional development activities is growing. Supovitz (2001) concludes that professional development built on the principles described above has produced outcomes in teaching practices across a variety of research and evaluation studies (e.g., Supovitz & Turner, 2000). Using regression analyses on a national probability sample of mathematics and science teachers, Garet, Porter, Desimone, Birman, & Yoon (2001) identified three features of professional development activities that result in teachers' reports of increased knowledge and skills or changes in classroom practice: (a) focus on content knowledge; (b) opportunities for active learning; and (c) coherence with other learning activities.

Sato, Darling-Hammond, and Wei (2008) reported measurable changes by outside observers in teachers' classroom assessment practices after the teachers engaged in collaborative analysis of their own teaching guided by a set of professional teaching standards. These findings further support the professional consensus around a vision of effective professional development.

Professional Development within Reading Education

Within the field of reading education, Strickland (2002) argues for improving reading achievement through professional development that uses school-based designs (models that use faculty study groups and coaching structures); long term engagement and focus (the recommendation is for no less than a year); collaborative planning among teachers; and building a shared vision for improved instruction. The 2010 IRA Standards for Reading Professionals, currently being drafted, includes six standards that describe the knowledge, skills, and dispositions of reading professionals who can successfully teach diverse student populations: Foundational Knowledge; Curriculum and Instruction; Assessment and Evaluation; Diversity; Literate Environment; and Professional Learning and Leadership. Looking specifically at the standard for professional learning and leadership for reading professionals, the underlying assumptions of effective professional learning are stated as:

1. Effective professional learning is evidence-based in ways that reflect both competent and critical use of relevant research and is thoughtfully planned, ongoing, differentiated and embedded in the work of all faculty members.
2. Effective professional learning is inclusive and collaborative across parents, community, and all school staff, including education support personnel, classroom teachers, specialized personnel, supervisors, and administrators.
3. Effective professional learning is focused on content determined by careful consideration and assessment of the needs of students, teachers, parents, and the larger community of stakeholders.
4. Effective professional learning is supportive of the need for instruction that is responsive to the range of diversity.
5. Effective professional learning is grounded in research related to adult learning and organizational change as well as the research on the learning and teaching of reading.
6. Effective professional learning is based on the use of interpersonal, leadership, and communication skills that build trust and empower teachers.

This view of effective teacher professional learning aligns with the research-based principles described in the previous section. The assumptions emphasize connections between what reading professionals learn and their everyday work in supporting students' literacy development, models collaborative structures, and is built on an expectation that professional learning is not solely dependent on what happens in individual classrooms but reliant on the broader context of the school. These assumptions also go beyond current empirical evidence on effective professional learning design by recommending practices that are inclusive of the broader school and family community, the intentional use of adult learning theory and organizational change theory, and the use of particular skills-sets. These elaborations may underlie some of the effective designs for professional learning, but have not been empirically shown to be necessary to effective designs.

Recent Research on Professional Development for Reading Professionals

Many studies of professional development of practicing reading professionals are concerned with questions related to what processes and structures of professional learning opportunities benefit teachers and their practice. For example, in a case study of four elementary teachers who had engaged in the Literacy Educators Assessing and Developing Early Reading Success (LEADERS) project, Swan (2003) found that the features teachers believed to be most useful in facilitating the implementation of newly learned classroom practices were: (a) support from university, (b) support and collaboration with peers, (c) ability to make decisions about what to implement in classrooms, and (d) the yearlong duration. Similarly, a study of a mentoring program in literacy instruction examined the extent to which teachers learned and implemented the target practices. Six pairs of elementary mentors and classroom teachers participated in the study. Mentor teachers provided training in strategies, met with their teacher partners on an as-needed basis, and kept logs of times the teachers implemented the strategies. Mentors and most of the partners implemented target strategies effectively and all teachers reported satisfaction with the mentoring approach to their professional development. They reported valuing working with a partner, preferred partnering to traditional in-service designs, and both groups perceived themselves as successful in their roles (Vaughn & Coleman, 2004).

The features of professional learning opportunities described in these studies and supported by the teachers as beneficial to their practice align with the principles and assumptions described previously. Both of these studies rely on self-reports by participants about the value of the professional learning design, resulting in a limitation to understanding the impact of the professional development on practice. From these studies, however, we learn from the teachers' perspective about a dimension of professional learning that speaks to the stakes that the teacher has in making changes to his or her classroom practice. For example, Potts et al. (2000) suggested that successful professional development relies not only on collaborative and sustained designs, but also on teacher characteristics such as a willingness to take risks, commitment, and ownership.

Two studies elaborated on how collaboration with other teachers added to teachers' professional learning by describing how their understandings of literacy changed through collaborative conversations (Janisch & Akroft, 2001; Potts et al., 2000). For example, one teacher deepened her understanding of starting from the children's understandings of topics; another teacher developed more focused lesson planning of specific reading strategies; and another teacher saw the benefits of working across disciplines in order to help students see a topic from more than one perspective (Potts et al., 2000).

Ross and McDaniel (2004) addressed a slightly different issue in professional development by looking for transfer of learning from professional development into classroom practice. They explored the impact of an intensive clinical experience in the teaching of reading to struggling readers on the comprehension instructional strategies that teachers incorporate into their practices. Thirty teachers in a graduate reading/language arts program in a large, urban university in California were enrolled in a practicum-based course. Teachers taught a struggling reader one-on-one behind one-way glass while a supervisor and instructor observed. Feedback was given on lesson plans, conferences, and email communication. Teachers kept reflections of lessons, tracking their use of strategies. Self-evaluations based on pre- and post-instructional strategies, strategies tracking sheets, lesson logs, and focus group interviews were also conducted. Of the 26 instructional strategies on the pretest, only 6 were familiar to the majority of the teachers, including KWL, story maps, readers' theater, cloze, story frames, and think-alongs. By the end of the course, the majority of teachers showed familiarity with all but 4 of the 26 strategies. Factors influencing selection of strategies for clinical and classroom settings included individual personalities, experiences, and attitudes; student needs; school environment; and preparation time needed for some strategies (teachers preferred strategies with minimum preparation needed).

We are reminded here that even with the best intentions of increasing teachers' instructional repertoires, teachers in real schools have context-based concerns about what new instructional approaches might mean for them. One study described how a group of teachers (the majority of whom were Latina/o) teaching in high-poverty, urban schools were asked to change their reading instruction from dominantly whole-class, teacher-directed, basals to small group and individualized instruction. When initially interviewed, they raised several challenges that they anticipated in making the instructional changes: concerns about small groups; concerns that students could not work independently; worry about giving up control; difficulty finding texts in Spanish; use of ESL techniques/native language support (Garcia et al., 2006).

Noticeably absent from this brief description of recent research is any study that examined direct observation of changes in teacher practice or the impact of professional learning experiences on student learning outcomes. In the next section, we turn to a discussion about the use of literacy coaches due to the widespread use of this particular professional development model for reading professionals and some recent attention to questions of student outcomes based on this model.

Literacy Coaches

School-based literacy coaches are one of the most common school-based professional development models used today for reading professionals. Literacy coaches serve as instructional coaches for classroom teachers, often providing explicit instruction and guidance on reading and writing processes and instructional strategies. Manifestations of this model of professional development often rest on assumptions that teachers can develop their instructional practices through observations of children's performance, seeing others model instructional practices with students in their own classroom, through talking about their practice with someone viewed as more expert, and through reflection on their own practice.

Currently, most of the education literature on literacy coaching provides useful guidelines and suggestions for developing literacy coaching skills and enacting the role of literacy coach in schools (see, e.g., Allen, 2006; Bean & Caroll, 2006; Casey, 2006; Lyons & Pinnell, 2001; Neufeld & Roper, 2003; Toll, 2005; Walpole & McKenna, 2004). The coaching model is so widely used that The International Reading Association has developed recommendations for the qualifications of reading coaches in the United States (2004) and standards for middle and high school literacy coaches (2006).

The research literature on coaching traces back to Joyce and Showers (1982) and their description of a "peer coaching" model in which pairs of teachers coach each other through a reciprocal analysis and feedback process. These same researchers later found that teachers engaged in a coaching relationship practiced new instructional skills and strategies more frequently and applied them more appropriately in practice than did teachers who worked in isolation (Joyce & Showers, 1996). Other studies have shown that coaching can foster collegial relationships among teachers and deepen teachers' reflections on practice (Gamston, Linder, & Whitaker, 1993) and deepen teachers' understanding of their classroom practices (Edwards & Newton, 1995). Particular instructional practices that have been improved through coaching include use of questioning strategies and facilitating students' interaction with their peers (Kohler, Crilley, & Shearer 1997). Finally, Gibson (2006) described the process of coaching based on a case of expertise and illustrates the variety of knowledge and skills required during lesson observation and feedback sessions.

Several program evaluations that include literacy coaching have been conducted in individual states (see, e.g., Barton & Lavrakas, 2006; Marsh et al., 2008; Reed & Rettig, 2006). Poglinco et al. (2003) conducted an external evaluation of the America's Choice comprehensive school reform model that has schools across the United States. This model of school design uses a school-embedded professional development model led by a full-time literacy coach. The report cited here focused on understanding this literacy coaching model using data from 27 schools. The authors provide a detailed description of the role of the coach, the roll out and implementation of the literacy workshops, and reports on observations of the teaching practices. The evaluation did not assess effects of coaching on teaching practices over time. Several coaching modalities are described, including: instructional modeling, joint planning, co-teaching, formal observation and feedback, informal one-on-one coaching, and mentoring. Teachers generally reacted positively to the in-class coaching, especially when coaches engaged in joint planning or co-teaching. They also appreciated the availability of frequent one-on-one contact with the coach. Classroom observations of teachers showed that "teachers' ability to faithfully reproduce the structures of the literacy workshops closely tracks that of their coaches" (p. 35). This finding raised the question of the extent to which teacher knowledge and practice is dependent on the coach's own mastery of the instructional approaches.

Empirical evidence of the effects of literacy coaches on changing classroom practices of teachers or on student achievement outcomes remains limited. Current studies on the Literacy Collaborative, a coaching model used in over 700 elementary schools in 200 districts across 26 states, are examining changes in teachers' practice (Hough et al., 2008) and the value added effects on student's learning (Biancarosa, Bryk, & Dexter, 2008) using hierarchical linear models on longitudinal data from teachers nested within schools. Preliminary results in measuring change in practice show that after controlling for teacher characteristics, exposure to coaching is positively related to growth in frequency of implementation and expertise-in-enactment as measured on Developing Language and Literacy Teaching rubrics. Further, the level of individual exposure is strongly associated with individual teacher growth in expertise (Hough et al., 2008). The literacy coaching has also shown an association with improvement in student literacy learning as measured by a test of reading comprehension. The degree of student learning gains varies by school and by teacher within schools leaving open-ended questions about the predictive value of variables such as school size, amount of coaching, expertise of coaches, and school staff stability and teacher-level factors including experience teaching, amount of coaching, length of participation in professional development, and frequency and expertise of implementation of instructional practices (Biancarosa, et al., 2008).

A third paper from this larger longitudinal study examined the variations in the amount of coaching teachers received across schools (Atteberry, Bryk, Walker, & Biancarosa, 2008). The researchers report that the average teacher working in a high-implementation school for the full five semesters of their data collection received about 45 hours of one-on-one coaching. However, even within a well-developed coaching model such as the Literacy Collaborative, large variability existed in the amount of coaching a teacher received. "Teachers with less prior training in early literacy, who proactively engage with their colleagues, and who report strong commitment to their school tend to receive a disproportionate amount of the coach's time" (p. 42). Variation among schools was mostly accounted for by school size, with less coaching time per teacher in larger schools. This suggests the need for careful monitoring of coach-to-teacher ratios. Coaches are also more likely to provide more coaching time in schools where teachers and administrators support the coaching activities.

Research repeatedly shows that school-wide results from professional development initiatives are complex problems for researchers to document, but are even more complex to implement and sustain from the practitioner's perspective (see e.g., Taylor, Pearson, Peterson, & Rodriguez, 2004).

An Analysis of One Successful Professional Development Initiative

In this section we use a case of a successful school-based professional development initiative to illustrate the principles of professional development design in action. The study was conducted by Gehsmann and Woodside-Jiron (2005) and describes the school improvement process of a K–5 elementary school in an urban center of New England. South Street School (pseudonym) faced the challenge of supporting its 250 students toward meeting the instructional goals of "reading grade-appropriate text with accuracy, fluency, and comprehension" (p. 184). The challenge seemed most acute for the 20% of the students who were English language learners, many of them recently relocated refugees. All of the students in South Street School received free and reduced lunch and 20% of the students were eligible for special education services. Within the school, there was an overall sense of frustration with student behavior and disciplinary action was unusually high. Teacher turn-over was common with frequent mid-year transfers and resignations. The overall instructional culture of the school was described as fragmented and idio-syncratic with many sporadic efforts to make a change.

South Street School is a success story by both the standards of the state testing system designed to comply with the Federal No Child Left Behind legislation and the experiences of the teachers in the school who worked and lived through the four-year instructional change effort. From 2000 to 2004, the school's reading assessment scores improved dramatically, moving them off of the state's underperforming list. The faculty, although still working to improve the instructional challenges they faced daily, was stable and identified a sense of common vision with other teachers with regard to reading instruction.

Strategies Used to Enact Professional Development Principles.   Strategically, South Street School's approach represented the principles of professional development described earlier. A school-based design was enacted through a steering committee and a school-wide change plan, and required that all teachers participate in the professional development plan. Obstacles to school change were identified and addressed. For example, the high teacher-turnover was resolved by requiring a commitment of 4 years of service in the school by all new teachers. Long-term engagement and focus was created through a 4-year plan with a focus on improving reading instruction and student reading achievement. The vision of improved instruction was enacted through a common instructional model which was introduced to the whole faculty. Both teachers and administrators learned the new instructional model, and the principal was active in observing instruction, offering feedback, and developing her own repertoire in teaching reading. The professional development design relied on teacher collaboration. For example, the steering committee comprised of teachers met regularly, special education was shifted from a pull-out program to a full inclusion model, and a literacy coaching model was adopted.

Elaboration of the Professional Development Principles in Action.   The strategies instituted by South Street School to bring about school change through teacher professional development and improved instruction tell only part of the story of enacting the principle of effective professional development. Further analysis of the case illustrates how complex a school based model for professional learning and instructional change can really be for those who are invested in the instructional improvement through professional development process.

Gehsmann and Woodside-Jiron (2005) identified four themes that were integral to the instructional improvement process: (a) Context: close attention to matching the improvement plan to the school context; (b) Coherence: close alignment between the standards, assessments, teaching practices, and professional development; (c) Coaching: using a coaching model that draws on assessment data to inform instruction; and (d) Compassion: attention to the human aspects of the improvement process both in terms of compassion *for* and compassion *of* those engaged in the change process.

Context: Job-Embedded Professional Development in Complex Contexts.   The approach South Street took was specifically and artfully designed for its context. The notion of school-based designs of professional development and building a shared vision of instruction require much negotiation, deliberation, and strategic planning. Gehsmann and Woodside-Jiron (2005) hint at the struggle and conflict that the school faced to create and enact its school-based plan. They refer to the "considerable pressure" (p. 187) that was exerted on the superintendent to eliminate short-term contracts in South Street and this required "working with" the teachers' union. They also refer to "much turmoil" in getting the South Street staff to agree to the 4-year commitment and mandatory professional development. The authors do not elaborate on these tensions and negotiations, possibly due to their post-analysis of the change process or the limited space for reporting the case. But even these hints reveal that bringing about change is not only a matter of creating a good plan or policy. The district as an organization and the union as a collective had to be willing to bend and flex their policies to accommodate the needs of a particular school in need of improvement.

Coherence: Moving Back and Forth to Move Forward.   Teachers reported that "being on the same page" was a critical component of the school's success. But aligning instruction across multiple classrooms in a school requires that teachers fundamentally change their underlying beliefs about learning, about instruction, and who they envision themselves to be as a teacher. Rather than a strong-arm mandate, an approach that respected and included teachers in the decision-making and change planning process was used. In doing this, the teachers were treated as real people with professional insights, personal passions, and invested interests as opposed to a group of technicians who would adopt and perform discrete teaching tasks without thinking and questioning. Gehsmann and Woodside-Jiron (2005) pointed out that "coaching requires a balance of pressure and support" (p. 186). Instructional innovation requires that teachers move out of their comfort zones and simultaneously requires that systems be in place to support them while they engage in the risk-taking associated with change. Gehsmann and Woodside-Jiron summarized this process as "a feeling of disequilibrium reported by participants ... reminding us that coherence-making is always happening at the edge of chaos (Fullan, 2003)" (p. 190).

Collaboration Among Teachers: Closing the Feedback Loops.   The collaboration among teachers extended beyond the planning phases. The teachers engaged in regular meetings not only to plan instruction, but also to report back on how their efforts were working—what they were learning from their work with the students. They then used their observations and classroom assessments to set new achievement targets and interventions. These ongoing collaborative monitoring sessions provided multiple opportunities for feedback loops in planning, instruction, and assessment. Assessment and observation information was not only collected, but strategically used to improve instruction. The critical steps of closing the feedback loops by reporting what is happening related to student learning and teacher development allowed educators to act on the feedback from classrooms, ultimately propelling the school forward in its improvement plan.

Compassion: Emotional Investment in Professional Development.   The general literature emphasizes that professional development should be focused on specific subject matter expectations and be embedded in the teachers' instructional context. The South Street School case illustrates these principles. But the professional development principles do not always convey how working with children in classrooms can be a very personal process for most teachers. Consistent with the research on the personal dimension of professional development (e.g., Potts et al., 2000), the South Street School case reminds us of the emotional dimensions of teacher development: "We worked hard to replace frustration and low expectations with compassion and action" (p. 194). This final theme was critical to the success of the South Street School professional development initiative.

The findings generated by Gehsmann and Woodside-Jiron (2005) mirror the analysis conducted by Wilson and Berne (1999). This review of research on professional development found that when teachers formed communities of learners, worked with colleagues to build trusting environments where professional discourse and critique could exist, and reconceptualized their teaching and perspectives about the purposes of professional development, change occurred in curriculum and practices. This review also reminds us that it is challenging to document teachers' specific learning during, and as a result of these professional development experiences—primarily due to the need to report the content and the processes involved in these events.

RECOMMENDATIONS FOR FUTURE RESEARCH

Since the last *Handbook of Reading Research* chapter on teacher development (Anders, 2000) the amount of research on the topic has increased and many researchers have followed the recommendations of Anders and her colleagues, resulting in reviews of literature on reading teacher preparation and case studies of effective courses or experiences conducted by individual researchers. In addition, large-scale research projects have been commissioned to study several excellent programs in elementary reading teacher preparation (Harmon et al., 2001). Findings from these investigations and several longitudinal studies of PTs from identified programs (e.g., the SERTE investigations) document literacy program effectiveness beyond preservice preparation, indicating that carefully constructed programs, grounded on the eight elements identified as important for literacy preparation programs and fieldwork, do impact PTs' and K–12 students' learning (Hoffman et al., 2005; Maloch et al., 2003; Sailors et al., 2005). These studies used quasi-experimental designs comparing SERTE PTs and comparison group PTs. The multiple sites, long-term focus, and the methodologies employed make these studies exemplars in the field.

The SERTE studies did not set out to document exactly what content knowledge or pedagogical skills new teachers should know and be able to enact at the end of their preparation programs or how this development plays out over a teacher's career; however this issue was addressed in a report compiled by a panel of researchers sponsored by the National Academy of Education (NAE). Snow et al. (2005) presented a core knowledge base about reading and readers that is important for teachers to develop and discussed how this knowledge base might develop over a teacher's career. Their report, supported by substantial evidence, does not attempt to map the knowledge base onto literacy teacher preparation coursework and experiences, but it does call for "the development of the kinds of powerful experimental long-term studies that definitively link specific aspects of teacher education and teacher learning to teachers' use of specific practices and then to improvements in students' learning" (p. 65). Risko and her colleagues (2008) also indicated that, for the most part, the research on PTs' topical knowledge and growth as a result of coursework is disappointing because it fails to advance our understanding of what PTs should know when they leave teacher education programs. The findings summarized above accentuate the need for research efforts leading to optimal designs for reading teacher preparation programs, including curricula and experiences that address each level of a literacy teacher's development or the "weighting" of knowledge that PTs need versus the knowledge needed by first year, experienced, and master teachers. Although some research efforts document the specific knowledge and practices needed by PTs, including what new teachers need in the form of a "beginning repertoire" (e.g., Dillon et al., 2004), we need more research in this area.

Anders and her colleagues (2000) also noted the importance of building a national database on teacher education programs (e.g., program features, descriptions of participants) in advancing the research agenda in literacy teacher preparation. One answer to this call came from IRA's large-scale review of the literature on PT preparation in reading that identified the research questions and methodologies employed by literacy experts in recent years and patterns in findings from these studies (Risko et al., 2008). Results from this review and other research syntheses indicated that literacy researchers heeded the call for self studies wherein they targeted "local" issues by studying specific courses and practica within their respective programs; and, in some cases, reading teacher educators increased collaborative dialogues among themselves leading to change at particular institutions (Many et al., 2006). Findings indicated that initial and continued teacher development occurs in programs that are: (a) research-based, (b) taught by knowledgeable individuals, (c) grounded in a shared, strong vision of teachers as leaders who support the development of all students, (d) focused on providing teachers with specific knowledge and practices required to teach reading to students at various developmental levels and from diverse backgrounds and settings, (e) committed to using student data to inform instruction, (f) built around systematic, guided opportunities to try out new learning with substantive coaching and feedback provided by knowledgeable others and peers, and (g) informed by teacher and program assessment, including the use of multiple forms of data to document teachers' growth in learning and linking growth in teacher knowledge with the growth of students taught by these teachers. A few "best practices" emerge to guide us in answering the question of how PTs learn best: (a) explicit teaching and modeling of teaching practices; (b) opportunities to discuss and collaborate with others as new information is learned, and (c) long term, focused work on new concepts to enable deep learning to occur.

Although the findings from the studies described above are helpful, we need to ask the critical question of why only 82 studies out of 298 empirical, peer-reviewed, reading teacher preparation research studies met Risko et al.'s quality criteria to be included in the IRA (2008) research review. Perhaps it is because research efforts undertaken in good faith by teacher educators to reform and update reading teacher education at specific universities are highly personal endeavors aimed at improving components of coursework rather than systematic, large-scale, longitudinal efforts aimed at studying comprehensive program revisions within and across university sites. For example, most research reviewed by Risko and her colleagues was conducted by individual course instructors, spanning a single semester, involving small numbers of participants, and yielding data resting on one or two rather than multiple methods of data collection, methodologies, and interpretation. The instruments used to measure PT learning or growth, often lack validation. Hence, the findings may not be persuasive enough to move the field forward in terms of how teachers should be prepared and what their ongoing development should entail. These studies have also tended to focus on *how* to prepare new teachers or have provided a rationale for *why* they should be prepared with certain underlying principles or elements, instead of addressing an integrated approach to studying the *how*, *why*, and *what* involved in reading teacher preparation, transitions into teaching, and teachers' ongoing development.

If research is to inform policy at the national level or offer directions for future research that might inform policy, literacy researchers must target compelling universal problems and generate solutions with implications for teacher education programs as a whole, rather than designing research that responds only to local problems about literacy coursework at particular institutions. Examples of research with this broader focus includes recent studies focused on improving literacy teacher preparation and continued development in urban settings (Wilkinson, Morrow, & Chou, 2008). Future research also needs to address common core knowledges and practices in literacy teacher preparation that are necessary across institutions. In addition, the research agenda must be historically situated and cumulative, guided by a careful synthesis of what we know and still need to know, and informed by a collaborative dialogue among sites within states and beyond. The IRA studies have laid the groundwork for this national research agenda, and we believe that lessons can also be gleaned from the findings of multi-site *program revision studies* that have been conducted in particular states (e.g., Vagle et al., 2006).

Large-scale national studies focused on program revitalization require multi-year funding, careful planning, leadership, and oversight if this complex, labor intensive, longitudinal work is to be completed with integrity and with useable findings. It is logistically challenging to work across institutional requirements and cultures to forge systematic, sustainable changes. But we know these efforts are promising and they address Zeichner's (2005) recommendations that future research studies demonstrate the impact of long-term *multi-institutional* collaborations among teacher education programs. Solutions to programmatic literacy teacher education reform should involve the cooperative efforts of literacy researchers, their disciplinary colleagues within and outside colleges of education, school-based colleagues, and university administrators. Literacy teacher educators are uniquely positioned to work collaboratively with colleagues across and outside of the university. This is particularly true for secondary reading faculty who collaborate with colleagues across disciplines in preparing middle and secondary teachers to better engage students with literacy practices that support learning in their respective teaching disciplines. Funding from within and outside institutions of higher education can provide the time and resources needed for the professional development of literacy faculty and their colleagues both within and across universities and K–12 settings, and this is a critical step towards success.

Second, these studies need to attend to how teachers' knowledge and practices are influenced by their experiences in teacher education programs and into their transition years. Systematic analyses of preservice teachers' formative learning using structured tools such as concept maps, surveys, knowledge assessments, and structured interviews can be effective in documenting the development of PTs' knowledge and beliefs. Understanding PT knowledge and practices and knowing what a beginning repertoire of knowledge and practices entails will require the development of additional reliable and valid formative assessments, the skills researchers need to use these tools to collect and analyze data in credible ways, and the flexibility required to adjust practices and experiences for PTs within an often tightly bound set of courses constrained by state-level standards guiding teacher preparation. Another key strategy for program reform is the examination of a core set of PTs' work (assignments and assessments) within literacy courses and in other teacher preparation experiences. Close examination of new teachers' learning and development—used to inform literacy course and practica planning, revision, and overall program decisions—can press programmatic changes (c.f., Dillon & Vagle, 2006; Vagle & Dillon, 2006).

In addition, we need to conduct formative experimental research that enables literacy educators to document PTs' learning and their impact on K–12 students' learning as these teachers' careers develop and as these individuals move across sites. This research process can be facilitated with the creative design and use of new digital technologies that allow the systematic collection of surveys and assessments of knowledge development at multiple points in time, permit virtual observations of practices, enable remote conversations and interviews, and provide for other ongoing contact with preservice and transition teachers who are geographically mobile. These data can then be fed back into teacher education program redesign, and documented using formative research designs.

Finally, teacher preparation programs can be strengthened by arranging field placements for PTs in sites where high quality, ongoing professional development in literacy is occurring—often designed collaboratively between the same teacher educators preparing the novice teachers and the mentors recruited to work with PTs. As Au and colleagues (2008) noted, the principles and procedures used in high quality professional development can be embedded into preservice coursework and experiences, and Au (2002) found this approach to be even more effective when PTs were placed in schools where teachers were engaged in ongoing professional development with literacy teacher educators.

CONCLUSIONS

Developing research initiatives and launching a new set of longitudinal studies of literacy teacher preparation will require leadership, time, and resources. Policy makers want improvements in teacher preparation now and most will not wait patiently for the results of 4- to 5-year studies. While long-term studies are in process, reading researchers can proactively develop streams of research and development efforts that can be linked up with the larger-scale studies proposed above.

For example, reading professors from 28 institutions in Minnesota are using newly created state-wide reading teacher standards to drive program revisions that are aimed at providing high quality preparation with the goal of consistency and coherence in core elements, knowledge base, and practica experiences for teacher preparation in reading. These professors are meeting together regularly with a group of experienced classroom/mentor teachers to discuss how to draw upon the standards, the IRA components of excellent reading teacher preparation and fieldwork, and the current research on preparing reading teachers, including and the core knowledge base identified by the NAE report and other researchers (Dillon & Boehm, 2010).

In the Minnesota initiative, literacy professors are working at their respective institutions to consider how the reform of literacy courses and experiences fit within larger teacher preparation reform efforts. Many instructors are expanding reading course credit hours or reshaping coursework to provide some foundational knowledge prior to later pedagogical knowledge and experiences. Some educators, particularly at the secondary level, are finding new ways to partner with disciplinary colleagues to co-design coursework and practica experiences, sharing in the creation of assignments and in providing feedback to students. Discipline-based instructors are engaging in substantive conversations with literacy colleagues, literacy colleagues are sharing information, and reading educators are completing syllabi revision, the creation of new assignments and assessments (many that may be used across institutions), and practica experiences that include components identified as effective in the literature. By partnering with K–12 educators—who view this collaboration as a form of professional development—new field sites and practica experiences are being designed with mentors who have co-created the preservice literacy coursework. Research designs are also in place to study the students who graduate from these programs during their transition years to understand what they learned, how that learning impacts their practice, how a new teaching context shapes their actions, and how preparation programs and transition programs can improve using this feedback (Kelly, 2010). Researching and documenting these efforts to enhance practice, and using the results to inform policy, holds promise for effective change in how teachers are prepared in reading. All of this work is occurring under increased pressure from legislators who threaten prescribed content in coursework and narrow tests of foundational reading knowledge for preservice teachers.

The effort in Minnesota is only one of many efforts that literacy leaders are undertaking at various locations worldwide. In this review we highlighted the intersection between research, practice, and policy. We pointed out that promising practices in reading teacher preparation and continued professional development occur when effective practices—gleaned from specific school and classroom contexts, grounded in actions that best support the students in those settings, and documented in well-designed research studies—influence future practices (how teachers are prepared, or how educators who facilitate transition to teaching are supported or how school-wide PD sessions are designed). We also argued that policy should be driven by this interplay between research in reading teacher preparation and development and practice, rather than policy driving teacher preparation practices and research, particularly research that responds to the urgency of select concerns raised by policy makers.

When policy reports or mandates ignore, preempt, or overshadow research, they can move the field in unproductive directions that are difficult to reverse. These reports, which are constructed to further a particular agenda, are often grounded in a "crisis" platform (America's schools are performing abysmally and it's the teachers who are the problem); moreover they vary in the quality of their propositions which, in turn, yield recommendations that are often weakly or narrowly grounded in research. Policy briefs currently pressing teacher preparation are not grounded in the research on how to best prepare teachers of reading (e.g., Moats, 1999, 2000; NCTQ, 2006; Smartt & Reschly, 2007). Instead, they are often grounded on poorly designed studies of course syllabi (NCTQ, 2006) and espouse a narrow view of the knowledge teachers need to teach reading (e.g., Moats, 1999). For example, the policy reports present recommendations based on claims that reading professors are not teaching "scientifically based reading research" (meaning the five components of reading highlighted by the NRP—phonemic awareness, phonics, vocabulary, fluency, and comprehension) in university teacher preparation coursework and attribute waning student achievement on state tests to this inadequate teacher preparation. These policy briefs go so far as to list specific topics that should be included in syllabi and specify how the five components should play out in the selection of course readings and the design of assignments and assessments. Policy makers in several states have also recommended that teachers be required to pass stand-alone tests focused on foundational knowledge, with little regard for the developmental trajectories discussed in reading teacher preparation or the pedagogical knowledge we seek to develop.

Policy grounded on narrow perspectives is often funded with considerable resources. Perhaps the future will levy more caution about how policy is used to change reading teacher practices in light of the recent findings from the Reading First (RF) Impact Study: Final Report (Institute of Education Sciences, 2008). Findings from this report indicated that RF teachers spend more time teaching the five components of reading in grades 1 and 2 and in using the instructional practices they were taught (including professional development in scientifically based reading instruction, support from full-time reading coaches, amount of reading instruction, and supports available for struggling readers). However, results indicated that "Reading First produced a positive and statistically significant impact on decoding among first grade students tested in one school year (spring 2007) … [but] did not produce a statistically significant impact on student reading comprehension test scores in grades one, two or three" (p. xvi and xv). Results varied from school to school because of implementation and contextual factors. Clearly, we need research, grounded on best practices that is funded and can impact policy.

In conclusion, we are reminded of Hoffman and Pearson's (2000) finding that we are making advancements in preparing teachers, moving from technical training-oriented programs to programs based on a view of teaching as a complex domain. Our worry is that current policies and the intense focus of accountability in PT preparation in higher education and K–12 schools will shift teacher preparation backward to a more technical mode, grounded on lists of what needs to be covered in coursework. As reading researchers, we must continue to advance research in reading teacher preparation and development using complex research designs that account for the multiple dimensions of learning and the conditions of learning required to meet students' needs. Improving the quality of our research designs is crucial to credibly answering questions central to our work. We also need to design, and validate better tools and instruments to document teachers' knowledge development and sophisticated changes in reading teaching practices over time. Simultaneously, we must find ways to address concerns raised by the public and policy makers by sharing what we are learning and cogently explaining why these complex designs are required. Forging partnerships with university and school-based educators, policy makers, and business leaders to find financial and intellectual support for these long-term efforts is the key to moving forward in reading teacher education and ongoing professional development in reading.

REFERENCES

Allen, J. (2006). *Becoming a literacy leader: Supporting learning and change*. Portland, ME: Stenhouse.

Allington, R. L., & Johnston, P. H. (2001). What do we know about effective fourth-grade teachers and their classrooms? In C. M. Roller (Ed.), *Learning to teach reading: Setting the research agenda* (pp. 150–165). Newark, DE: International Reading Association.

Alvermann, D. E., Rezak, A. T., Mallozzi, C. A., Boatright, M. D., & Jackson, D. F. (2011). Reflective practice in an online literacy course: Lessons learned from attempts to fuse reading and science instruction. *Teachers College Record, 113.*

Anders, P. L., Hoffman, J. V., & Duffy, G. G. (2000). Teaching teachers to teach reading: Paradigm shifts, persistent problems, and challenges. In M. L. Kamil, P. B. Mosenthal, P. D. Pearson, & R. Barr (Eds.), *Handbook of reading research: Volume* III (pp. 719–742). Mahwah, NJ: Erlbaum.

Anderson, L. M., & Holt-Reynolds, D. (1995). *Prospective teachers' beliefs and teacher education pedagogy: Research based on a teacher educator's practical theory.* East Lansing, MI: National Center for Research on Teacher Learning, Michigan State University.

Atteberry, A., Bryk, A., Walker, L., & Biancarosa, G. (2008). Variations in the amount of coaching in Literacy Collaborative schools. Paper presented at the annual meeting of the American Educational Research Association, New York, NY.

Au, K. H. (2002). Communities of practice: Engagement, imagination, and alignment in research on teacher education. *Journal of Teacher Education, 53,* 222–227.

Au, K. H., & Maaka, M. J. (2001). Teacher education, diversity, and literacy. In C. M. Roller (Ed.), *Learning to teach reading: Setting the research agenda* (pp. 136–149). Newark, DE: International Reading Association.

Au, K. H., Raphael, T. E., & Mooney, K. C. (2008). What we have learned about teacher education to improve literacy achievement in urban schools. In L. C. Wilkinson, L. M. Morrow, & V. Chou (Eds.), *Improving literacy achievement in urban schools: Critical elements in teacher preparation* (pp. 159–184). Newark, DE: International Reading Association.

Barton, R., & Lavrakas, J. (2006). Finding gold at the end of the rainbow: Anchorage's investment in literacy coaching pays big dividends. *Northwest Regional Education Laboratory, 12*(1), 6–11.

Bean, T. W. (1997). Preservice teachers' selection and use of content area literacy strategies. *Journal of Educational Research, 90*(3), 154–163.

Bean, T. W. (2000). Reading in the content areas: Social constructivist dimensions. In M. L. Kamil, P. B. Mosenthal, P. D. Pearson, & R. Barr (Eds.), *Handbook of reading research: Volume III* (pp. 629–644). Mahwah, NJ: Erlbaum.

Bean, R. M. & Carroll, K. E. (2006). The literacy coach as a catalyst for change. In C. Cummins (Ed.), *Understanding and implementing Reading First initiatives: The changing role of administrators* (pp. 139–152). Newark, DE: International Reading Association.

Bean, T. W., & Zulich, J. (1990). Teaching students to learn from text: Preservice content teachers' changing view of their role through the window of student-professor dialogue journals. In J. Zutell & S. McCormick (Eds.), *Literacy theory and research: Analysis from multiple paradigms: Thirty-ninth Yearbook of the National Reading Conference* (pp. 171–178). Chicago: National Reading Conference.

Bean, T. W., & Zulich, J. (1992). A case study of three preservice teachers' beliefs about content area reading through the window of student professor dialogue journals. In C. K. Kinzer & D. J. Leu (Eds.), *Literacy research, theory, and practice: Views from many perspectives: Forty-first yearbook of the National Reading Conference* (pp. 463–474). Chicago: National Reading Conference.

Biancarosa, G., Bryk, A., & Dexter, E. (2008). *Assessing the value-added effects of literacy collaborative professional development on student learning.* Paper presented at the annual meeting of the American Educational Research Association, New York, NY.

Biancarosa, G., & Snow, C. E. (2004). *Reading next—A vision for action and research in middle and high school literacy: A report to the Carnegie Corporation of New York.* Washington, DC: Alliance for Excellent Education.

Bickmore, S., Smagorinsky, P., & O'Donnell-Allen, C. (2005). Tensions between traditions: The role of contexts in learning to teach. *English Education, 38*(1), 23–52.

Birdyshaw, D., Moje, E. B., Jeppsen, A., & Bain, R. (2007). *Preservice teachers' conceptions of disciplines and disciplinary literacy.* Paper presented at the annual meeting of the National Reading Conference, Austin, TX.

Birdyshaw, D., & Rackley, E. (2008). *Preservice teachers' models of text.* Paper presented at the annual meeting of the National Reading Conference, Orlando, FL.

Broemmel, A. D., Meller, W. B., & Allington, R. L. (2008). Preparing expert teachers of reading for urban schools: Models and Variations in the literature. In L. C. Wilkinson, L. M. Morrow, & V. Chou (Eds.),

Improving literacy achievement in urban schools: Critical elements in teacher preparation (pp. 83–104). Newark, DE: International Reading Association.

Cantrell, S. C., & Callaway, P. (2008). High and low implementers of content literacy instruction: Portraits of teacher efficacy. *Teaching and Teacher Education, 24*, 1739–1750.

Casey, K. (2006). *Literacy coaching: The essentials.* Portsmouth, NH: Heinemann.

Cochran-Smith, M. (2004). Promises and politics: Images of research in the discourse of teaching and teacher education. In J. Worthy, B. Maloch, J. V. Hoffman, D. L. Schallert, & C. M. Fairbanks (Eds.), *Fifty-third Yearbook of the National Reading Conference* (pp. 28–44). Oak Creek, WI: National Reading Conference.

Cochran-Smith, M., & Zeichner, K. (Eds.). (2005). *Studying teacher education: The report of the AERA panel on research and teacher education.* Mahwah, NJ: Erlbaum.

Conley, M. W. (2008). Cognitive strategy instruction for adolescents: What we know about the promise, what we don't know about the potential. *Harvard Educational Review, 78*(1), 84–106.

Cook, L. Smagorinsky, P., Fry, P., Konopak, B., & Moore, C. (2002). Problems in developing a constructivist approach to teaching: One' teacher's transition from teacher preparation to teaching. *The Elementary School Journal, 102*(5), 389–413.

Darling-Hammond, L., & Bransford, J. (Eds.). (2005). *Preparing teachers for a changing world: What teachers should learn and be able to do.* San Francisco: Jossey-Bass.

Darling-Hammond, L., Wei, R., Andree, A., Richardson, N., & Orphanos, S. (2009). *Professional learning in the learning profession: A status report on teacher development in the United States and abroad.* Dallas, TX: National Staff Development Council and The School Redesign Network at Stanford University.

Dillon, D. R., & Boehm, E. (2010). *Minnesota Literacy Teacher Educator's Symposia Series: Using state reading teacher standards and research to redesign programs at 28 institutions.* (Unpublished manuscript). University of Minnesota, Twin Cities, MN.

Dillon, D. R., DeLapp, P., Vagle, M., Galda, L., Bigelow, M., Hughes, J., et al. (2004). *A higher education partnership to better prepare K-12 literacy preservice teachers.* Paper presented as part of a symposium at the annual meeting of the National Reading Conference, San Antonio, TX.

Dillon, D. R., & Vagle, M. D. (2006, January). *Collaborating through the complexity: Four teacher education programs' commitment to redesign preservice literacy teacher preparation.* Paper presented at the annual meeting of the American Association of Colleges for Teacher Education, San Diego, CA.

Douglas, E., Moje, E. B., & Bain, R. B. (2008). *Preservice teachers' models of disciplinary subject areas.* Paper presented at the annual meeting of the National Reading Conference, Orlando, FL.

Duffy, G. G. (2004). Teachers who improve reading achievement: What research says about what they do and how to develop them. In D. Strickland & M. L. Kamil (Eds.), *Improving reading instruction through professional development* (pp. 3–22*)*. Norwood, MA: Christopher-Gordon.

Edwards, J. L., & Newton, R. R. (1995). *The effects of cognitive coaching on teacher efficacy and empowerment.* Paper presented at the annual meeting of the American Educational Research Association, San Francisco, CA.

Feiman-Nemser, S. (2001). From preparation to practice: Designing a continuum to strengthen and sustain teaching. *Teachers College Record, 103*(6), 1013–1055.

Fillmore, L. W., & Snow, C. E. (2002). What teachers need to know about language. In C. T. Adger, C. E. Snow, & D. Christian (Eds.), *What teachers need to know about language* (pp. 7–54). McHenry, IL: Delta Systems.

Flint, A. S., Leland, C. H., Patterson, B., Hoffman, J. V., Sailors, M. W., Mast, M. A., et al. (2001). "I'm still figuring out how to do this teaching thing": A cross-site analysis of reading teacher preparation programs on beginning teachers' instructional practices and decisions. In C. M. Roller (Ed.), *Learning to teach reading: Setting the research agenda* (pp. 100–118). Newark, DE: International Reading Association.

Gamston, R., Linder, C., & Whitaker, J. (1993). Reflections on cognitive coaching. *Educational Leadership, 51*(2), 57–61.

García, G. E., Bray, T. M., Mora, R. A., Ricklefs, M. A., Primeaux, J., Engel, L. C., et al. (2006). Working with teachers to change the literacy instruction of Latino students in urban schools. In J. V. Hoffman, D. L., Schallert, C. M. Fairbanks, J. Worthy, & B. Maloch (Eds.), *Fifty-fifth Yearbook of the National Reading Conference* (pp. 155–170). Oak Creek, WI: National Reading Conference.

Garet, M., Porter, A., Desimone, L., Birman, B., & Yoon, K. (2001). What makes professional development effective? Analysis of a national sample of teachers. *American Educational Research Journal, 38*(4), 915–945.

Gehsmann, K. M., & Woodside-Jiron, H. W. (2005). Becoming more effective in the age of accountability: A high-poverty school narrows the literacy achievement gap. In B. Maloch, J. V. Hoffman, D. L., Schallert, C. M. Fairbanks, & J. Worthy (Eds.), *Fifty-fourth Yearbook of the National Reading Conference* (pp. 182–197). Oak Creek, WI: National Reading Conference.

Gibson, S. (2006). Lesson observation and feedback: The practice of an expert reading coach. *Reading Research and Instruction, 45*(4), 295–318.

Grisham, D. L. (2000). Connecting theoretical conceptions of reading to practice: A longitudinal study of elementary school teachers. *Reading Psychology, 21*(2), 145–170.

Grossman, P., & McDonald, M. (2008). Back to the future: Directions for research in teaching and teacher education. *American Educational Research Journal, 45*(1), 184–205.

Grossman, P. L., Valencia, S. W., Evans, K., Thompson, C., Martin, S., & Place, N. (2000). Transitions into teaching: Learning to teach writing in teacher education and beyond. *Journal of Literacy Research, 32*(4), 631–662.

Grossman, P. L., Valencia, S. W., Thompson, C., Martin, S. D., Place, N., & Evans, K. (2001). Transitions into teaching: Learning to teach writing in teacher education and beyond. In C. M. Roller (Ed.), *Learning to teach reading: Setting the research agenda* (pp. 80–99). Newark, DE: International Reading Association.

Harmon, J., Hedrick, W., Martinez, M., Fine, J. C., Eldridge, D., Flint, A. S., et al. (2001). Features of excellence of reading teacher preparation programs. In J. V. Hoffman, D. L. Shallert, C. M. Fairbanks, J. Worthy, & B. Maloch (Eds.), *Fiftieth Yearbook of the National Reading Conference* (pp. 262–274). Oak Creek, WI: National Reading Conference.

Harste, J. C., Leland, C., Schmidt, K., Vasquez, V., & Ociepka, A. (2004, January/February). Practice makes practice, or does it? The relationship between theory and practice in teacher education. *Reading Online, 7*(4). Retrieved from http://readingonline.org/articles/art_index.asp?HREF=harste/index.html

Hawley, W. D., & Valli, L. (1999). The essentials of effective professional development: A new consensus. In L. Darling-Hammond & G. Sykes (Eds.), *Teaching as the learning profession: Handbook for policy and practice* (pp. 127–150). San Francisco: Jossey-Bass.

Heller, R., & Greenleaf, C. (2007). *Literacy instruction in the content areas: Getting to the core of middle and high school improvement.* Washington, DC: Alliance for Excellent Education.

Hoffman, J. V., & Pearson, P. D. (2000). Reading teacher education in the next millennium: What your grandmother's teacher didn't know that your granddaughter's teacher should. *Reading Research Quarterly, 35*(1), 28–44.

Hoffman, J. V., Roller, C., Maloch, B., Sailors, M., Duffy, G., & Beretvas, S. N., (2005). Teachers' preparation to teach reading and their expectations and practices in the first three years of teaching. *Elementary School Journal, 105*(3), 267–287.

Hoffman, J. V., Sailors, M., Duffy, G., & Beretvas, S. N. (2004). The effective elementary classroom literacy environment: Examining the validity of the TEX-IN3 observation system. *Journal of Literacy Research, 36*(3), 303–334.

Houge, T. T., Geier, C., & Peyton, D. (2008). Targeting adolescents' literacy skills using one to-one instruction with research-based practices. *Journal of Adolescent & Adult Literacy, 51*(8), 640–650.

Hough, H. J., Bryk, A., Pinnell, G. S., Kerbow, D., Fountas, I., & Scharer, P. (2008*). Measuring change in the practice of teachers engaged in literacy collaborative professional development: Preliminary results from a four-year study.* Paper presented at the annual meeting of the American Educational Research Association, New York, NY.

Institute of Education Sciences. (2008, November). *Reading First impact study: Final report.* U.S. Department of Education, Office of Planning, Evaluation, and Policy Development, Policy and Program Studies Services. Retrieved June 1, 2009, from http://ies.ed.gov/ncee/pdf/20094038.pdf

International Reading Association. (2003). *Standards for reading professionals—revised 2003.* Newark, DE: Author.

International Reading Association. (2004). *The role and qualifications of the reading coach in the United States.* Newark, DE: Author.

International Reading Association. (2006). *Standards for middle and high school literacy coaches*. Newark, DE: Author.

International Reading Association. (2007). *Teaching reading well: A synthesis of the International Reading Association's research on teacher preparation for reading instruction*. Newark, DE: Author.

Jacobs, V. A. (2008). Adolescent literacy: Putting the crisis in context. *Harvard Educational Review, 78*(1), 7–39.

Janisch, C., & Akroft, A. (2001). Young readers' academy: Opportunities for conversations about literacy teaching and learning. In J. V. Hoffman, D. L., Schallert, C. M. Fairbanks, J. Worthy, & B. Maloch (Eds.), *Fiftieth Yearbook of the National Reading Conference* (pp. 287–299). Oak Creek, WI: National Reading Conference.

Johnson, C., Stull, M., Bain, R., & Moje, E. B. (2008). *Preservice teachers' models of the student as reader*. Paper presented at the annual meeting of the National Reading Conference, Orlando, FL.

Joyce, B., & Showers, B. (1982). The coaching of teaching. *Educational Leadership, 40*(1), 4–10.

Kamil, M. L. (2003, November). *Adolescents and literacy: Reading for the 21st century*. Washington, DC: Alliance for Excellent Education.

Kamil, M. L., Borman, G. D., Dole, J., Kral, C. C., Salinger, T., & Joseph, T. (2008). *Improving adolescent literacy: Effective classroom and intervention practices: A practice guide (NCEE #2008-4027)*. Washington, DC: U.S. Department of Education. Retrieved from http://ies.e: National Center for Education Evaluation and Regional Assistance, Institute of Education Sciences, US Department of Education.

Kane, R., Sandretto, S., & Heath, C. (2002). Telling half the story: A critical review of research on the teaching beliefs and practices of university academics. *Review of Educational Research, 72*(2), 177–228.

Keehn, S., Martinez, M., Harmon, J., Hedrick, W., Steinmetz, L., & Perez, B. (2003). Teacher preparation in reading: A case study of change in one university-based undergraduate program. In *Fifty-second Yearbook of the National Reading Conference* (pp. 230–244). Oak Creek, WI: National Reading Conference.

Kelly, C. (2009). *The transition to teaching reading: Knowledge, beliefs, and identities of novice teachers of reading*. (Unpublished manuscript). University of Minnesota, Twin Cities, MN.

Kohler, F., & Crilley, K., & Shearer, D. D. (1997). Effects of peer coaching on teacher and student outcomes. *Journal of Educational Research, 90*(4), 240–251.

Konopak, B. C., Readence, J. E., & Wilson, E. K. (1994). Preservice and inservice secondary teachers orientations toward content area reading. *Journal of Educational Research, 87*(4), 220–227.

Lalik, R., & Potts, A. (2001). Social reconstructionism as a framework for literacy teacher education. In C. M. Roller (Ed.), *Learning to teach reading: Setting the research agenda* (pp. 119–135). Newark, DE: International Reading Association.

Lazar, A. M. (2007). It's not just about teaching kids to read: Helping preservice teachers acquire a mindset for teaching children in urban communities. *Journal of Literacy Research, 39*(4), 411–443.

Levine, A. (2006). Will universities maintain control of teacher education? *The Magazine of Higher Learning, 38*(4), 36–43.

Lenz, B. K., Ehren, B. J., & Deshler, D. D. (2005). The content literacy continuum: A school reform framework for improving adolescent literacy for all students. *Teaching Exceptional Children, 37*(6), 60–63.

Linek, W. M., Sampson, M. B., Raine, I. L., Klakamp, K., & Smith, B. (2006). Development of literacy beliefs and practices: Preservice teachers with reading specializations in a field-based program. *Reading Horizons, 46*(3), 183–213.

Lyons, C. A., & Pinnell, G. S. (2001). *Systems for change in literacy education: A guide to professional development*. Portsmouth, NH: Heinemann.

Maloch, B., Flint, A. S., Eldridge, D., Harmon, J., Loven, R., Fine, J. C., Bryant-Shanklin, M., & Martinez, M. (2003). Understandings, beliefs, and reported decision making of first-year teachers from different reading teacher preparation programs. *The Elementary School Journal, 103*(5), 431–459.

Many, J., Green, J., Wallace, F. H., Graham, M., Dixey, B., Miller, S., et al. (2006). Understanding the impact of a state-wide reading consortium on literacy teacher educators. *Reading Research and Instruction, 45*(4), 319–352.

Marsh, J. A., McCombs, J. S., Lockwood, J. R., Martorell F., Gerswin, D., Naftel, S., et al. (2008). Supporting literacy across the Sunshine State: A study of Florida middle school reading coaches (MG-762-CC). Santa Monica, CA: RAND Corporation.

Massey, D. D. (2006). "You teach for me; I've had it!" A first-year teacher's cry for help. *Action in Teacher Education, 28*(3), 73–85.

Moats, L. C. (1999). *Teaching reading IS rocket science: What expert teachers of reading should know and be able to do.* Washington, DC: American Federation of Teachers. (Item No. 372).

Moats, L. C. (2000). Whole language lives on: The illusion of "balanced" reading instruction. Washington, DC: Thomas B. Fordham Institute. Retrieved June 4, 2009, from http://www.edexcellence.net/template/index.cfm

Moje, E. B. (2007). Developing socially just subject-matter instruction: A review of the literature on disciplinary literacy teaching. In G. J. Kelly, A. Luke, & J. Green (Eds.), *Review of research in education* (Vol. 31, pp. 1–44). Washington, DC: American Educational Research Association.

Moje, E. B., Douglas, E., & Bain, R. (2007). *How do we study preservice teacher learning? The challenges and possibilities of tools for assessing and studying teacher learning.* Paper presented at the annual meeting of the National Reading Conference. Austin, TX.

National Council on Teacher Quality (NCTQ). (2006). What education schools aren't teaching about reading and what elementary teachers aren't learning. Retrieved June 4, 2009, from http://www.nctq.org/nctq/

National Education Association (NEA). (2000). Report of the National Education Association's Task Force on Reading. Washington, DC: Author.

National Reading Panel. (2000). *Teaching children to read: An evidence-based assessment of the scientific research literature on reading and its implications for reading instruction: Reports of the subgroups.* National Institute of Child Health and Development. Retrieved February 5, 2009, from http://www/nationalreadingpanel.org/Publications/publications.htm

National Staff Development Council. (2001). *NSDC's Standards for Staff Development.* Oxford, Ohio, 2001. Retrieved February 5, 2009, from http://www.nsdc.org/standards/

Neufeld, B., & Roper, D. (2003). *Coaching: A strategy for developing instructional capacity—promises & practicalities.* Washington DC: Aspen Institute Program on Education and Providence, RI: The Annenberg Institute for School Reform. Retrieved February 5, 2009, from http://www.annenberginstitute.org/pdf/Coaching.pdf

O'Brien, D. (1988). Secondary preservice teachers resistance to content reading instruction: A proposal for a broader rationale. In J. E. Readence & R. S. Baldwin (Eds.), *Dialogues in literacy research: Thirty-seventh Yearbook of the National Reading Conference* (pp. 237–243). Chicago: National Reading Conference.

O'Brien, D. G., & Stewart, R. A. (1990). Preservice teachers' perspectives on why every teacher is not a teacher of reading: A qualitative analysis. *Journal of Reading Behavior, 22,* 101–129.

O'Brien , D. G., Stewart, R. A., & Moje, E. B. (1995). Why content literacy is difficult to infuse into the secondary school: Complexities of curriculum, pedagogy, and school culture. *Reading Research Quarterly, 30,* 442–463.

Paglinco, S., Bach, A., Hovde, K., Rosenblum, S., Saunders, M., & Supovitz, J. (2003). *The heart of the matter: The coaching model in America's Choice Schools.* Philadelphia: Consortium for Policy Research in Education, University of Pennsylvania Graduate School of Education. Retrieved February 5, 2009, from http://eric.ed.gov/ERICDocs/data/ericdocs2sql/content_storage_01/0000019b/80/33/b9/78.pdf

Pearson, P. D. (2001). Learning to teach reading: The status of the knowledge base. In C. M. Roller (Ed.), *Learning to teach reading: Setting the research agenda* (pp. 4–19). Newark, DE: International Reading Association.

Pierce, M., & Pomerantz, F. (2006). From preservice to inservice: The evolution of literacy teaching practices and beliefs in novice teachers. In J. V. Hoffman, D. L. Shallert, C. M. Fairbanks, J. Worthy, & B. Maloch (Eds.), *55th yearbook of the National reading Conference* (pp. 235–248). Oak Creek, WI: National Reading Conference.

Pomerantz, F., & Pierce, M. (2004). From literacy methods classes to the real world: Experiences of preservice teachers. *The NERA Journal, 40*(2), 55–62.

Potts, A., Moore, S., Frye, S., Kile, M., Wojtera, C., Criswell, D. (2000). Evolving partnerships: A framework for creating cultures of teacher learning. In T. Shanahan & F. V. Rodriguez-Brown (Eds.), *Forty-ninth Yearbook of the National Reading Conference* (pp. 165–177). Oak Creek, WI: National Reading Conference.

Ratekin, N., Simpson, M. L., Alvermann, D. E., & Dishner, E. K. (1985). Why content teachers resist reading instruction. *Journal of Reading, 28*, 432–437.

Reed, B., & Rettig, R. (2006). Side by side: The Idaho Reading First program finds success by offering targeted professional development to its literacy coaches. *Northwest Regional Education Laboratory, 12*(1), 18–21.

Risko, V. J., Roller, C. M., Cummins, C., Bean, R. M., Block, C. C., Anders, P. L., et al. (2008). A critical analysis of research on reading teacher education. *Reading Research Quarterly, 43*(3), 252–288.

Roller, C. M. (Ed.). (2001). *Learning to teach reading: Setting the research agenda.* Newark, DE: International Reading Association.

Sailors, M., Keehn, S., Martinez, M., & Harmon, J. (2005). Early field experiences offered to and valued by preservice teachers at sites of excellence in reading teacher education programs. *Teacher Education and Practice, 18*(4), 458–470.

Santa, C. M., & Hayes, R. (2009). What we do: Support materials: CRISS Cornerstones. Retrieved June 1, 2009, from http://www.projectcriss.com/criss_cornerstones.php

Sato, M., Wei, R. C., & Darling-Hammond, L. (2008). Improving teachers' assessment practices through professional development: The case of National Board Certification. *American Educational Research Journal, 45*(3), 669–700.

Shanahan, T., & Shanahan, C. (2008). Teaching disciplinary literacy to adolescents: Rethinking content area literacy. *Harvard Educational Review, 78*(1), 40–59.

Showers, B., & Joyce, B. (1982). The coaching of teaching. *Educational Leadership, 40*(1), 4–10.

Showers, B., & Joyce, B. (1996). The evolution of peer coaching. *Educational Leadership, 53*(6), 12–16.

Smagorinsky, P., Cook, L. S., Moore, C., Jackson, A. Y., & Fry, P. G. (2004). Tensions in learning to teach: Accommodation and the development of a teaching identity. *Journal of Teacher Education, 55*(1) 8–24.

Smagorinsky, P., Wright, L., Murphy, A., S., O'Donnell-Allen, C., & Konopak, B. (2007). Student engagement in the teaching and learning of grammar: A case study of an early-career secondary school English teacher. *Journal of Teacher Education, 58*(1), 76–90.

Smartt, S. M., Reschly, D. L. (2007). *Barriers to the preparation of highly qualified teachers in reading* (TQ Research & Policy Brief). Washington, DC: National Comprehensive Center for Teacher Quality. Retrieved June 4, 2009, from http://www.tqsource.org/publications/June2007Brief.pdf

Snow, C. E., Burns, M. S., & Griffin, P. (Eds.). (1998). *Preventing reading difficulties in young children.* Washington, DC: National Academy Press.

Snow, C. E., Griffin, P., & Burns, M. S. (Eds.). (2005). *Knowledge to support the teaching of reading: Preparing teachers for a changing world.* San Francisco: Jossey-Bass.

Stevens, L. P. (2002). Making the road by walking: The transition from content area literacy to adolescent literacy. *Reading Research and Instruction, 41*(3), 267–278.

Strickland, D. S. (2001). The interface of standards, teacher preparation, and research: Improving the quality of teachers. In C. M. Roller (Ed.), *Learning to teach reading: Setting the research agenda* (pp. 20–31). Newark, DE: International Reading Association.

Strickland, D. S., & Kamil, M. S. (Eds.). (2004). Improving reading achievement through professional development. Norwood, MA: Christopher-Gordon.

Strickland, D. S., Snow, C. E., Griffin, P., Burns, M. S., & McNamara, P. (2002). *Preparing our teachers: Opportunities for better reading instruction.* Washington, DC: National Academy Press.

Supovitz, J. A. (2001). Translating teaching practice into improved student achievement. In S. H. Fuhrman (Ed.), *From the capitol to the classroom: Standards-based reform in the states* (pp. 81–98). Chicago: University of Chicago Press.

Supovitz, J. A., & Turner, H. M. (2000). The effects of professional development on science teaching practices and classroom culture. *Journal of Research in Science Teaching, 37*(9), 963–980.

Swan, A. L. (2003). Effective professional development: Tell me and I will hear, show me and I will see, support me and I will evolve. In *Celebrating the freedom of literacy: The Twenty-fifth Yearbook of the College Reading Association* (pp. 239–250). Commerce: Texas A&M.

Taylor, B. M., & Pearson, P. D. (2001). The CIERA School Change Project: Translating research on effective reading instruction and school reform into practice in high-poverty elementary schools. In C. M.

Roller (Ed.), *Learning to teach reading: Setting the research agenda* (pp. 180–189). Newark, DE: International Reading Association.

Taylor, B. M., Pearson, P. D., Peterson, D. S., & Rodriguez, M. C. (2004). The CIERA school change framework: An evidence-based approach to professional development and school reading improvement. *Reading Research Quarterly, 40*(1), 40–69.

The Teaching Commission. (2006). *Teaching at risk: Progress and potholes.* New York City: Author.

Toll, C. A. (2005). *The literacy coach's survival guide: Essential questions and practical answers.* Newark, DE: International Reading Association.

Vagle, M. D., & Dillon, D. R. (2006). *Influencing preservice literacy teacher learning through a multi-institutional collaboration among four teacher education programs.* Paper presented at the annual meeting of the American Educational Research Association, San Francisco, CA.

Vagle, M. D., Dillon, D. R., Davison-Jenkins, J. LaDuca, B., & Olson, V. (2006). Redesigning literacy preservice education at four institutions: A three-year collaborative project. In *Fifty-fifth Yearbook of the National Reading Conference* (pp. 324–340). Oak Creek, WI: The National Reading Conference.

Vaughn, S., & Coleman, M. (2004). The role of mentoring in promoting use of research-based practices in reading. *Remedial and Special Education, 25*(1), 25–38.

Walpole, S., & McKenna, M.C. (2004). *The literacy coach's handbook: A guide to research-based practice.* New York: Guilford.

Wilkinson, L. C., Morrow, L. M., & Chou, V. (Eds.). (2008). *Improving literacy achievement in urban schools: Critical elements in teacher preparation.* Newark, DE: International Reading Association.

Wilson, S. B., & Berne, J. (1999). Teacher learning and the acquisition of professional knowledge: An examination of research on contemporary professional development. In A. Iran-Nejad & P. D. Pearson (Eds.), *Review of research in education* (Vol. 24, pp. 173–209). Washington, DC: American Educational Research Association.

Zeichner, K. (2005). A research agenda for teacher education. In M. Cochran-Smith & K. M. Zeichner (Eds.), *Studying teacher education: The report of the AERA panel on research and teacher education* (pp. 737–759). Washington, DC: American Educational Research Association.

27 Second Language Reading Acquisition

Ludo Verhoeven
Radboud University Nijmegen

Literacy is a lifelong, context-bound set of practices that can vary with time, place, and an individual's needs. One can thus speak of multiple literacies and the importance of language policies that foster cultural diversity. Research has also shown the functional literacy practices via which individuals are socialized into various institutions to vary widely. Functional literacy involves not only the ability to read and write but also the ability to cope with everyday life literacy situations. Functional literacy thus encompasses both literacy conventions and cultural knowledge, which are interrelated. Literacy conventions refer to—among other things—the types of documents that are used in societal institutions such as forms, letters, legal texts, political tracts, religious texts, novels, and poems. The reading of a particular type of document often requires specialized knowledge of that type of document format. Different types of documents, moreover, may call upon different types of cultural background knowledge as well as different values and beliefs.

When it comes to modeling literacy, the sociolinguistic position of minority groups must obviously also be recognized (cf. Fishman, 1980; Hornberger, 2002; Durgunoglu, 1997; Oller & Eilers, 2002; Verhoeven, 1987, 1990). In light of ongoing processes of migration and increased internationalization, minorities are no longer an exception. According to recent census data, minorities currently constitute about a third of the U.S. population (U.S. Census Bureau, 2008). By the year 2042, minorities are projected to become the majority and, for children, this milestone is expected to be reached by 2023. In order to cope in daily life, minority groups often confront the task of communicating in the language of the majority. This language is often acquired as a second language by minority groups. Literacy may be taught in either the children's home language or the mainstream language spoken in the wider community. Whether one or more languages are used for purposes of school instruction and which language and literacy abilities are adopted as educational objectives in the teaching of minority children depends upon the language education policies of the area. It is obviously crucial that minority children acquire literacy in the mainstream language in order to become a citizen of the host society. However, recent statistics show less than 20% of children learning English in U.S. schools to attain state norms for reading comprehension (Kindler, 2002). Such data make it clear that becoming literate in a second language is a challenging task, to say the least.

The focus of this chapter is on second language reading acquisition. To start with, a theoretical framework for bilingualism and learning to read will be presented. Special attention will be devoted to the possibilities for cross-language transfer, which may be beneficial for the development of early literacy and reading skills. From there, the foundations for early language and literacy skills will be considered. Just how the development of language and emergent literacy skills up to the level of preschool can be optimally fostered within an institutional setting will be explored in particular. Special attention will be devoted to the topic of bilingualism and metalinguistic awareness in children. A review of current research will show a sustained level of bilingual development to help children become phonologically aware and quickly grasp the alphabetic code. In addition, the development of the abilities of word decoding and reading comprehension, which are essential for learning to read in general and in a second language as well, will be examined. For each of these abilities, just how linguistic diversity may influence the course of development will be explored. Finally, linguistic diversity in relation to reading acquisition will be considered from an educational perspective.

BILINGUALISM AND LEARNING TO READ

For minority children living in a multilingual environment, a mismatch can occur between the home language and the language of the school. Most minority children thus learn two languages in a successive manner: They typically acquire the ethnic group language within the context of the home and the surrounding community while the second language gradually enters their early lives via the television, contact with peers, and—sometimes—daycare. When these same children enter school, the language input they receive is almost exclusively second-language input. Such minority children thus take part in lessons in the second language but also in more natural second-language interactions with peers and teachers. An essential difference between the language acquisition situations for monolingual versus bilingual children is that bilingual children are exposed to different linguistic systems and must distinguish between the two types of input at some point.

For monolingual children, the task of language acquisition involves only the mastery of a hierarchical set of linguistic abilities that are all connected to an underlying system of background cultural knowledge:

- phonological abilities related to the discrimination and production of speech sounds;
- lexical abilities related to receptive and productive vocabulary;
- syntactic abilities related to sentence processing; and
- text abilities related to the cohesion and coherence of different types of text.

For bilingual children, these abilities must be mastered for two languages as depicted in Figure 27.1.

As can be seen in Figure 27.1, linguistic input can lead to the activation of two language systems, which may be linked to a greater or lesser extent to a system of background knowledge. In working memory, a number of different systems are used to build a conceptual structure from successive input and to draw inferences on the basis of all this information. The model outlined in Figure 27.1 is assumed to be interactive in that it allows for both bottom-up and top-down processing.

The central vertical arrow shows that transfer can take place from one language to the other during language processing. Understanding the nature of cross-language transfer is of great importance for education as such information provides insight into how language learning can be facilitated. The Competition Model bilingualism (MacWhinney, 2004; Hernandez & MacWhinney, 2005) predicts that the level of interaction will depend upon the levels of proficiency in the two languages. Transfer may occur, for example, when new constructions are called for in the one language and have already been grounded in the other language. From previous research, moreover, we know that second-language learners need not relearn the basic categories of language. Taking the analyzed system of the first language as a starting point, that is, second-language learners only need to learn the language-specific devices of the new language. Via self-regulation, children can similarly transfer a variety of the strategies used to acquire the home language to master a second language. In other words, the effective transfer of such strategies can improve the child's capacity to "learn to learn" and thereby facilitate the analysis of knowledge and control of various forms of processing during second language learning.

Having mastered the basic features of two languages, bilingual children are confronted with the task of becoming literate. For many minority children, the first language (L1) initially occu-

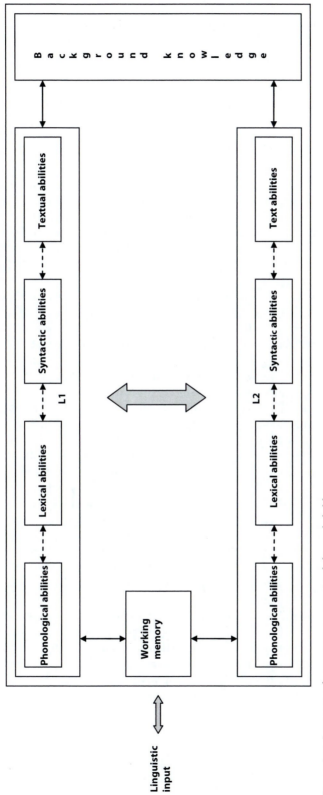

Figure 27.1 Interactive language processing in bilingual children.

pies a favorable position. The development of the L1 has been facilitated by a rich amount of input from the family and the neighborhood, but later exposure conditions may be less favorable and often poor. At school, use of the home language is often prohibited. At best, the home language may be a minimal part of the school curriculum. In both cases, thus, a mismatch exists between the linguistic abilities that the minority child brings to the classroom and the language and literacy curriculum of the school. L2 literacy instruction thus confronts minority children with a complex task. The minority children must master the structure and functions of literacy in a largely unfamiliar language. And while a considerable body of research exists on how children learn to read in a first language, learning to read in a second language has received scant attention. In comparative studies, it has been found that many children indeed experience serious difficulties with learning to read in a second language and that the individual variation in the levels of reading achievement and rates of mastery tends to be much larger among linguistically and culturally diverse learners than among typical learners (e.g., Durgunoglu & Verhoeven, 1998; August & Shanahan, 2006). The pressing question is therefore how linguistic and cultural diversity can affect the process of learning to read in a second language. Three possibilities arise when the model in Figure 27.1 is considered: acquisition on the basis of limited proficiency in L2, acquisition on the basis of limited background knowledge, and acquisition on the basis of transfer from L1.

Limited proficiency in L2 may slow reading development in various ways. Limited L2 phonological abilities may hinder word identification. Limited L2 lexical, syntactic, and text abilities may lead to reading comprehension problems. As a result of inefficient lexical processing, for example, the creation of new lexical entries may be compromised and the size of the L2 reading vocabulary remain limited.

Restricted background knowledge can obviously hinder reading comprehension. Children can have difficulties grasping the meaning of a text when the relevant cultural schemata are not familiar to them. The availability of the cultural schemata associated with curricular materials can therefore be seen as important for culturally and linguistically diverse learners.

Finally, transfer from the home language can also affect the second-language reading process. When literacy skills have been acquired for one language, they can be transferred to another language. In fact, the development of literacy within a bilingual context may show a great deal of interdependencies. With respect to the acquisition of academic language skills, for example, Cummins (1984, 1989, 1991) has hypothesized the role of interdependence to be as follows: *To the extent that instruction in a certain language is effective in promoting proficiency in that language, transfer of this proficiency to another language will occur, provided there is adequate exposure to that other language (either in the school or environment) and adequate motivation to learn that language.* In other words, language transfer can occur from not only L1 to L2 but also from L2 to L1. The so-called interdependence hypothesis further predicts that optimal input in one language can lead to not only better skills in that language but also to a deeper conceptual and linguistic proficiency, which can then facilitate the transfer of various cognitive and language skills across languages. Although the surface aspects of linguistic proficiency, such as vocabulary and specific narrative skills, may thus develop separately within a bilingual context, an underlying proficiency that may be shared across languages can also be assumed to develop. And this brings us to the foundations for early language and literacy development within a bilingual context.

FOUNDATIONS FOR EARLY LITERACY DEVELOPMENT WITHIN A BILINGUAL CONTEXT

To minimize the risk of literacy problems, it is of utmost importance that the foundations for early language and literacy be optimized in minority children. The period of early childhood provides children with important opportunities to develop emergent literacy skills. Longitudinal research has shown language input and literacy support within the home and also in institutional settings to predict kindergarten literacy skills and these skills to predict fourth-grade reading comprehension in turn (Snow, Tabors, & Dickinson, 2001). A critical question is thus how early bilingual development can be promoted and thereby early literacy facilitated.

Early Bilingual Development and Early Literacy

Research on the relations between various family characteristics and children's bilingual language proficiency has focused upon the extent to which and how the family creates an effective home learning environment. In the case of migration, the length of residence for the child and his or her parents host country appears to be critical. Parental attitudes towards L1 maintenance and L2 learning also appear to be of critical importance. Parental attitudes clearly shape the attitudes and motivation of their children. Parents with a positive attitude towards bilingualism tend to foster a positive attitude in their children, and such a positive attitude has been found to lead to more successful second-language learning than a negative or neutral attitude (cf. Delgado-Gaitan, 1990). Another critical family characteristic is language exposure in the home. Fantini (1985) showed various channels of L1 or L2 exposure within the home environment, including communication between family members and communication with people outside the family, to influence both children's first and second-language development.

Depending upon cultural values and the channels of language exposure within the home environment, thus, considerable variation can be detected in the patterns of early first and second-language development. Children with a strong first language foundation within the home and continuous support for this language within the home and wider community will develop language skills that can later be transferred to the second language. Research among very young Spanish-speaking children in Miami indeed shows their first language exposure to greatly facilitate their bilingual development and their second-language English vocabulary in particular (Pearson, Fernández, Lewedag, & Oller, 1997). In the case of parents with limited second-language proficiency, conversely, too much of a focus on the second language may be detrimental for the early language and literacy skills of their children and thereby lead to poor literacy levels at the moment when the children start school (Tabors, 1997; Dickinson & Tabors, 2002).

With respect to the development of children's early literacy, four home factors appear to be crucial (Wasik, 2004): the range of printed materials available within the home (i.e., written language input), the availability of writing materials, the frequency of shared reading, and the responsivity of the children's parents. For purposes of family intervention, the media can also play a significant role. Educational television programs such as Sesame Street, periodicals, and public libraries can provide additional oral written input within the family context. Specific intervention programs such as Head Start may help parents gather L1/L2 resources, including good quality children's books and instruments for drawing and writing (Tabors & Snow, 2001).

Given that the language development of children in modern industrialized societies increasingly occurs within an institutional context, the duration and quality of day care and kindergarten can be viewed as extremely important factors. Institutional care presents immigrant children with a new set of interpersonal relationships and clearly provides them with an opportunity to use language in a meaningful manner and receive feedback from professionals who are usually native speakers of the child's second language. The languages to be used in the curriculum and the educational objectives identified with regard to such are typically determined by the educational model being employed. Four different educational models can be distinguished as described below and summarized in Figure 27.2.

The first model is the so-called home language educational model. Following this model, only L1 is used in the curriculum with L1 maintenance as educational objective. Such a model may be used for the education of children who are likely to return to their country of origin within a brief period of time. The second model is the so-called transitional educational model which starts out

Educational model	Language use in curriculum	Educational objective
Home language	L1 only	L1 maintenance
Transitional	L1 replaced by L2	L1 support + L2 learning
Bilingual	Simultaneous L1-L2	L1 maintenance + L2 learning
Mainstream	L2 only	L2 learning

Figure 27.2 Educational models for early language and literacy instruction.

with language and literacy instruction in the first language but also provides instruction in the second language and switches entirely to this once the child has become proficient in the second language. The first language is thus gradually replaced by the second and just used in this model as a means to attain an optimum literacy learning in the second language. The third model is the so-called bilingual educational model which uses multiple languages in the curriculum and is aimed at fostering biliteracy. Finally, the mainstream educational model uses only the second language in order to attain optimal learning in general and mastery of that language in particular.

In many studies, it has been found that the quality of the interaction patterns within the school classroom is extremely important for immigrant children's first language maintenance and second-language progress (cf. Geva & Genesee, 2006; Martin-Jones & Saxena, 2003). Research on beginning literacy within the context of multilingual classrooms has shown such interactive activities as storybook reading and language games to promote a book orientation on the part of the children and greatly facilitate their vocabulary and language awareness (see Yaden, Rowe, & MacGillivray, 2000). A large body of research has addressed the relations between children's phonological awareness and early literacy. A capacity to distinguish and identify the different phonemes within a word is part of phonological awareness, and strong evidence shows children's phonological awareness helps them discover the correspondences between speech and writing (Bialystok, 2001). Children's vocabulary development has also been found to be highly dependent upon adequate teaching and the provision of extensive possibilities for cross-language transfer (Stahl & Shiel, 1999; Vermeer, 2001). Such preliteracy skills as rhyming, syntactic knowledge, and discourse abilities have also been shown to be quite transferable from one language to the other (Nagy, McClure, & Mir, 1997; Bialystok & Herman, 1999). Finally, many studies conducted in the USA and Canada show children who have participated in a bilingual education program to develop a healthy self-identity and clear appreciation of their own linguistic and cultural backgrounds and current membership (cf. August & Hakuta, 1997; Genesee & Gándara, 1999).

Early Bilingualism and Metalinguistic Awareness

The language situation of most minority children can be characterized as emergent bilingualism with the first language being built up during the early preschool years as the result of linguistic input in L1-speaking homes and the second language later coming into play via L2 playmates and the school. The fact that bilingual children deal with two channels of linguistic input has led to the suggestion that bilingual children may tend to have higher levels of metalinguistic awareness when compared to their monolingual peers (cf. Bialystok, Luk, & Kwan, 2005). In light of this proposal, exploration of the exact conditions under which language transfer typically occurs (cf. Verhoeven, 1990, 2007) and just how particular patterns of bilingual development relate to children's metalinguistic awareness (cf. Genesee & Geva, 2006) becomes paramount.

Metalinguistic awareness is the ability to explicitate one's—often implicit—knowledge of the structure and functions of language (cf. Karmiloff-Smith, 1997). Bialystok and Ryan (1985) suggested earlier that metalinguistic awareness can be characterized in terms of two components, namely the analysis of knowledge and the control of cognitive processing. The analysis component of metalinguistic awareness entails the reorganization of linguistic knowledge into abstract categories. The control component entails the intentional selection and application of knowledge to solve metalinguistic problems (also see Bialystok, 1993, 1994). For the acquisition of literacy, the development of phonological awareness has been shown to be of particular importance (cf. Snow, Burns, & Griffin, 1998; Troia, 1999; Bialystok, 2002). Phonological awareness requires children to consciously reflect upon the phonological segments of spoken words and manipulate these segments in a systematic manner. Phonological awareness thus involves a capacity to focus on speech perception, and this capacity underlies—among other things—the division of words into phonemes or syllables; the recognition of rhymes and alliteration; the use of phonemes and syllables to form words; and the omission, addition, or replacement of phonemes within words. Research shows the development of phonological awareness to progress from the level of syllables and onset-rimes to the more detailed phoneme level (cf. Goswami, 2000). Children find it particularly difficult to make phonemic judgments (i.e., become phonemically aware) because the speech sounds referred to by letters in most alphabetic writing systems are very abstract and virtually imperceptible in spoken language (cf. Nagy & Scott, 2000).

Bilingual children with exposure and access to two sets of languages can be expected to attain relatively high levels of phonological awareness at preschool and kindergarten level precisely because their experience with the two linguistic systems, which includes linguistic transfer, can direct attention to the phonological aspects of language and ultimately result in phonemic awareness. In Figure 27.3, the relations between L1 and L2 development and the emergence of phonemic awareness are visualized. It is shown that L1 and L2 at moment 1 not only predict the same competences at moment 2 but there is also positive transfer from L1 to L2. Moreover, the children's bilingual competence at moment 1 predicts the children's level of general phonological awareness while later in time (moment 2) it predicts their level of phonemic awareness.

The claim that experience with two languages will trigger phonological awareness can be tested in two manners. An indirect test is to show bilingual kindergarten children to have a higher level of phonological awareness than monolingual kindergarten children. In a number studies, an advantage for the learning of spoken language has indeed been reported for bilingual children (cf. Rubin & Turner, 1989; Bruck & Genesee, 1995; Campbell & Sais, 1995). However, as Bialystok (2002) has pointed out, the advantage appears to be mitigated by the age of the children, the nature of the task, and the language pairs involved in the bilingual contrast. A more

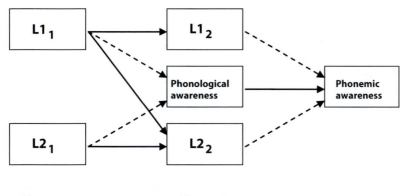

Figure 27.3 Model of bilingual development, language transfer, and the emergence of phonological awareness in children at preschool and kindergarten level.

direct test of the hypothesis that bilingual development stimulates phonological awareness is to examine how specific patterns of first and second-language development relate to the phonological awareness of bilingual children. In two of the few studies along these lines, Bialystok (1988) and Cromdal (1999) showed a high level of bilingualism on the part of already literate school-aged children to be positively associated with a high level of phonological awareness, but neither of the authors considered the relative contributions of the children's first and second-language skills to their phonological awareness. In a different study, Carlisle et al. (1999) showed the levels of first and second-language vocabulary and degree of bilingualism to significantly relate to the phonological awareness of bilingual children who had below-average reading skills. The fact that all of the aforementioned studies involved children who were already literate nevertheless makes it hard to unravel the causal connections between bilingual development and phonological awareness.

In a recent study by Verhoeven (2007), the associations between early bilingualism and phonological awareness were examined for a sample of 75 bilingual Turkish-Dutch children living in the Netherlands. In a longitudinal design, the kindergarten children's Turkish (L1) and Dutch (L2) language abilities were assessed at the both the beginning and end of kindergarten. At the end of kindergarten, the children's phonological awareness was also assessed. Turkish was found to be the dominant language on both occasions. In addition to the expected longitudinal relations, evidence of transfer from L1 to L2 was also found. In addition, the children's L1 and L2 levels of proficiency predicted the onset of both their general phonological and phonemic awareness.

The preceding findings with regard to language interdependence, emergent bilingualism, and children's phonological awareness have important implications for the education of minority children. Given the close links between phonological awareness and emerging literacy, moreover, policy makers should take the findings showing linguistic interdependence to stimulate the development of phonological awareness quite seriously and consider support for bilingual educational programs at the preschool and kindergarten levels. Bilingual education can also stimulate children's more general development in at least two manners. First, attention to the native language of minority children can enhance their self-respect by showing them that that the school respects their native language. Second, sufficient support for the first languages of minority children can enhance their cognitive/academic skills in not only the particular first language but also in the second language.

WORD DECODING IN A SECOND LANGUAGE

In many places throughout the world, children from ethnic minorities are totally immersed in a second-language reading curriculum and minimal attention is paid to their native language reading ability. These children are confronted with the task of learning to read in a language that they have yet to master. Given that most reading instruction strongly draws upon oral language proficiency, minority children may experience a considerable gap between their second-language oral versus reading skills. Reading involves the decoding of spoken language forms from written language forms. That is, the spoken form of a language provides the relevant linguistic units for the decoding of the written form of a language: phonological strings, morphemes, and words. Native speakers of the language to be read thus bring substantial oral language skills to the task (i.e., the necessary phonological, morphosyntactic, and lexical skills). In numerous comparative studies, moreover, the individual variation in the levels of achievement and rates of learning to read and write has been found to be much greater among non-native learners than among native learners (e.g., Durgunoglu & Verhoeven, 1998; Verhoeven & Vermeer, 2006). It is nevertheless by no means clear just how the characteristics of L2 learners affect the course of their reading development.

The automatization of word decoding or the fast and accurate retrieval of the phonological code for written word forms is commonly assumed to play a central role in children's reading development. Word decoding can be defined as the outcome of the interactions between phonological, visual, and meaning information. Phonological connections are further assumed to play a critical role in the consistency of word decoding and learning to read. Children start out with the acquisition of elementary decoding skills, increasingly apply these skills with greater speed and accuracy, and word recognition gradually becomes more automated with the direct recognition of such multi-letter units as consonant clusters, morphemes, syllables, and whole words as a result (Ziegler & Goswami, 2005; Schiff & Calif, 2007). Word decoding can be viewed as a self-teaching device that provides children with feedback regarding attempts to phonologically decode words and allows them to build the orthographic representations for specific words (cf. Share, 1995).

With respect to monolingual children's word decoding skills, researchers agree that children can draw upon three representational systems during the process of learning to identify written words: phonemic mapping, recognition of orthographic patterns, and direct recognition of familiar words. During the process of reading acquisition, children gradually shift from the access of word representations via phonic representations to the access of word representations directly (Perfetti, 1998). Cognitive research on first language reading development has clearly shown lexical representations to be an important source of individual differences on reading tasks (e.g., Plaut, McClelland, Seidenberg, & Patterson, 1996). According to the lexical quality hypothesis (Perfetti & Hart, 2001), the reading skills of children and adults are supported by their word knowledge, which includes the precision of their orthographic, phonological, morphological, and conceptual-semantic representations as in addition the sheer number of words known. Children learning to read in a second language may thus experience greater difficulties with the different representational systems and word recognition than children learning to read in a first language.

Potential Problems in L2 Word Decoding

L2 learners may encounter greater difficulties with the phonemic recoding of letter strings because they lack sufficient knowledge of the oral language (Koda, 1996, 2007). For example, less than full auditory discrimination of phonemes may hamper the assignment of correct pronunciations to individual letters, and L2 readers will thus have greater difficulties pronouncing unfamiliar but otherwise orthographically regular words than L1 readers. When Chiappe and Siegel (1999) compared the reading capacities of English- versus Punjabi-speaking Canadian children, phonological abilities were found to discriminate between the poor versus average readers in both groups. In a different study, Cormier and Kelson (2000) found the phonological abilities of English-speaking children to relate to their word decoding abilities in French immersion classes.

In other research, differences in the abilities of L1 versus L2 learners to make use of orthographic constraints for purposes of word recognition have been documented. L2 learners appear to be less aware of the phonemic distribution rules in the target language than L1 learners and, if L2 learners experience problems with orthographic constraints, they are likely to encounter problems with the reading of more orthographically complex words. Indeed it has been found that French learners of English as a L2 are less efficient than L1 learners in the use of orthographic redundancies to aid word recognition (Frenck-Mestre, 2005) and that a certain level of L2 proficiency is needed for bilinguals to become efficient at the extraction of orthographic cues from L2 words (Vaid & Frenck-Mestre, 2002).

In addition to L1 versus L2 differences in the phonemic recoding of letter strings and the use of orthographic constraints for purposes of word recognition, L1 and L2 differences exist in the efficiency of direct lexical access. Given that L2 learners typically have a smaller vocabulary in the target language than L1 learners, L2 learners may have trouble building visual word representations. L2 readers will therefore lag behind monolingual readers due to the fact that the L2 readers are confronted with the task of learning to read in a language that they have yet to yet to build a sufficient L2 vocabulary (see Jean & Geva, 2009). Similarly, the network of neural connections between the various graphemic, phonological, and semantic nodes needed to read is presumably weaker for L2 readers than for L1 readers. Limited exposure to the second language results in qualitatively weaker word representations and can thereby lead to both slower and less accurate reading. A visual word representation may, for example, only be constructed when a word's meaning is known, which is generally less likely for the L2 reader than the L1 reader. For L1 learners, moreover, word frequency is the best predictor of lexical access; L2 learners benefit less, in contrast, from word frequency for purposes of lexical access. As a result, L2 learners are less efficient at the decoding of low-frequency words using phonic or other cues and, in empirical studies, it has indeed been shown that a later age of acquisition and smaller size of L2 vocabulary and less elaborate L2 lexical entries appears to impede children's L2 reading development (Bernhardt, 2000).

Finally, L2 readers have been found to have difficulties with the reading of more complex, polysyllabic words. This is presumably a consequence of the limited morphological knowledge that minority children bring to the reading situation (Droop & Verhoeven, 2003).

Linguistic Transfer in Word Decoding

Although L2 reading processes may be impeded for various reasons, the results of recent surveys by Verhoeven (2000) and Siegel (2003) show the development of the word decoding skills of LI and L2 learners in the long run to be about equal (see also Lesaux, Koda, Siegel, & Shanahan, 2006). L2 readers may acquire the essentials of the target language during the process of learning to read. It is also possible, however, that the improved word decoding of L2 learners is a result of cross-language transfer. That is, when word reading is construed as the outcome of the interactions between systems referring to the meanings of words (i.e., semantics), the sounds of words (i.e., phonology), and the spelling of words (i.e., orthography) (cf. Seidenberg & McClelland, 1989), bilingual readers can be assumed to have a single shared semantic system at their disposal and two separate phonological and orthographic systems for the first and second languages, respectively (see Figure 27.4).

As depicted in Figure 27.4, the reading of a word in L2 can urge the child to make a connection between the L2 orthographic pattern and its L2 phonology, which is—in turn—associated with the child's semantic system. However, cross-language transfer may take place and make the L1 orthography and L1 phonology systems available at the same time. Orthography and phonology in L1 may thus enhance orthography and phonology in L2, and more so as the two orthographic systems show greater similarities. Simulation studies have indeed provided evidence for the simultaneous access of words in two languages (Dijkstra & van Heuven, 2002; French & Jacquet, 2004). Such processes allow the child to make linguistic and conceptual representations more explicit and carefully structured and also make predictions about L2 on the basis of stored L1 representations (Durgunoglu, 2002; Koda & Reddy, 2008). L2 overlap with L1 and thus transfer at the levels of phonology (Ellis & Schmidt, 1997; Lopez & Greenfield, 2004; Lindsey, Manis, & Bailey, 2003) and orthography (Geva & Siegel, 2000; Deacon, Wade-Woolley, & Kirby, 2009) have indeed been found to help L2 learners build their L2 word decoding skills.

Bilingual approaches to learning to read have been followed to profit from the benefits of cross-language transfer. Slavin and Cheung (2005) reviewed 17 experimental studies compar-

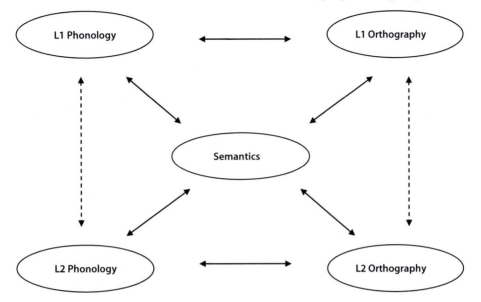

Figure 27.4 Possible roles of phonological, orthographic, and semantic systems in bilingual word recognition.

ing bilingual and English-only reading programs. Of the 13 studies with a focus on elementary reading among Spanish-dominant students, the results of 9 favored a bilingual approach and 4 found no significant differences. Slavin and Cheung thus conclude that although the number of high-quality studies is small, existing evidence favors bilingual approaches to reading instruction particularly when the bilingual approach entails the teaching of reading in the native language and reading in English at different times during the day. Nevertheless, the authors claim that further research using clearly randomized, longitudinal designs is needed to determine how reading success can best be ensured for all English language learners.

SECOND-LANGUAGE READING COMPREHENSION

Having considered word decoding in a second language and its development, we will now turn to reading comprehension in a second language and its development. As will be seen, various linguistic factors, the reader's background knowledge, and the degree of reading engagement all influence the development of second-language reading comprehension.

Role of Linguistic Factors

In the "simple view of reading" proposed by Hoover and Gough (1990), reading comprehension is conceived as the product of word decoding and listening comprehension. It is claimed that listening comprehension or the linguistic processes involved in the comprehension of oral language strongly constrain the process of reading comprehension. In other words, the identification of word meanings, the representations of sentences, the drawing of inferences within and across sentences, and the integration of information are all part of reading comprehension; the identification of underlying text structure (i.e., the text model) is involved as well as getting the global gist of a text (i.e., the situation model) (see Perfetti, Landi & Oakhill, 2005; Verhoeven & Perfetti, 2008). In several studies, evidence for this theoretical framework has been provided.

Word decoding or the fast and accurate retrieval of the phonological code for written word forms, has been found to be essential for the development of reading comprehension. Automated word recognition frees mental resources for closer consideration of the meaning of a text and thereby allows readers to employ reading as a tool for the acquisition of new information and knowledge (NRP, 2000; Perfetti, 1998). Knowledge of word meanings or, in other words, vocabulary skill has also been found to be critical for reading comprehension. Skilled readers are better able to take advantage of word training by remembering a new association between an orthographic form and a meaning than less skilled readers. According to the so-called lexical quality hypothesis (Perfetti & Hart, 2001), moreover, not only the quality of the reader's lexical representations but also the sheer number of available words may directly affect reading comprehension (Verhoeven & van Leeuwe, 2008).

For L2 learners, the limited size of their L2 vocabularies may place their text reading at risk. Vocabulary estimates show major differences between L2 and L1 learners, and the smaller vocabularies of L2 learners may seriously impede their L2 reading. Considerable individual variation can nevertheless be seen to exist in the vocabularies of L2 learners. Grabe (1991) estimated that the vocabulary knowledge of beginning L2 learners can vary from 2000 to 7000 words. When Verhoeven (2000) compared the role of vocabulary in the reading of L1 and L2 learners in the early elementary grades, vocabulary knowledge was found to have more of an impact on the reading of the L2 learners than on the reading of the L1 learners. This finding suggests that children learning to read in a second language should be helped to build their lexical knowledge and that their reading instruction should be matched to this level of knowledge. In addition to quantitative differences in the vocabulary knowledge of L2 versus L1 learners, qualitative differences have also been reported (Verhallen & Schoonen, 1993). The semantic networks of L2 learners appear to be looser than those of L1 learners, for instance. L2 learners thus have not only less extensive vocabularies than L1 learners but also fewer associative links between the words in their vocabularies.

With respect to the role of children's syntactic knowledge in the development of their reading comprehension, a significant relation can be expected (cf. Bernhardt, 2005). The limited syntactic sensitivities of young and/or less experienced readers make the discovery of the structures underlying written sentences a particularly difficult task and may thus create reading comprehension problems at times (cf. Goldman, 2003). Along these lines, Verhoeven (1990) has found the morphosyntactic knowledge of L2 learners to significantly predict their L2 reading comprehension by the end of second grade. Similar findings for young Spanish-English students have been reported by Gottardo (2002). In studies with more advanced learners, moreover, limited syntactic knowledge and a limited awareness of syntactic boundaries have been found to hamper the L2 reading process (Kitajima, 1997).

A full account of the simple view of reading in relation to both first- and second-language learners was evidenced in some recent studies. Droop and Verhoeven (2003) studied the reading comprehension, word decoding, and oral language skills of high and low SES Dutch and low SES minority children with a Turkish and Moroccan background. Several tests to measure reading comprehension, word decoding, oral text comprehension, morphosyntactic knowledge, and vocabulary knowledge were administered at the beginning of third grade, the end of third grade, and the end of fourth grade in the Netherlands. The development of the reading comprehension of both the L1 and L2 learners tended to be influenced more by top-down comprehension processes than by bottom-up word-decoding processes. Relative to the Dutch children, however, the role of oral Dutch turned out to be more prominent in the explanation of the variation in the minority children's reading comprehension than in the Dutch children's reading comprehension. In a similar vein, Proctor, Carlo, August, and Snow (2005) examined the associations between the word decoding and oral proficiency, on the one hand, and reading comprehension, on the other hand, of fourth grade Spanish-speaking learners of English. The English decoding measures included alphabetic knowledge and fluency. The English oral language measures included vocabulary and listening comprehension. The results showed the children's L2 decoding ability to be less predictive than their oral L2 proficiency. Their L2 listening comprehension made an independent, proximal contribution to their L2 reading comprehension while their L2 vocabulary made both proximal and distant contributions. Just like in the study by Droop and Verhoeven, the data from Proctor et al. show L2 oral language proficiency and L2 vocabulary knowledge, in particular, to constitute a crucial predictor of L2 reading comprehension. Finally, Gottardo and Mueller (2009) used L1 and L2 language skills and L2 word decoding to predict the L2 reading comprehension of second grade Spanish-speaking learners of English. L2 oral proficiency and L2 word decoding were found to be the strongest predictors of L2 reading comprehension, which is in line with the simple view of reading.

All of these studies make it clear that the simple view of reading adequately explains the reading comprehension of both first and second-language learners. However, the role of oral proficiency in the target language tends to be more prominent for L2 learners than for L1 learners. In Figure 27.5, just how the simple view of reading can lead to slightly different courses for the development of reading comprehension is depicted.

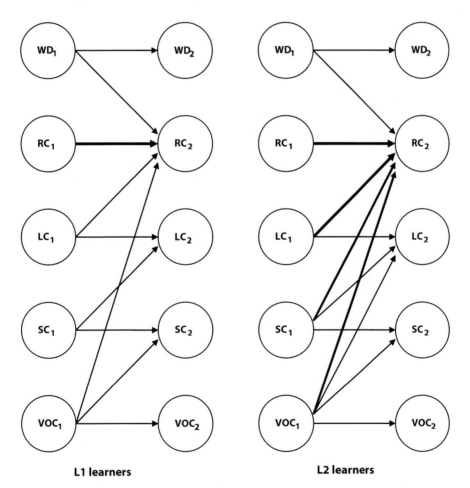

L1 learners   **L2 learners**

Figure 27.5 The simple view of reading in first (L1) and second language (L2) learners: Development of Reading Comprehension (RC) is predicted by Word Decoding (WD) and Listening Comprehension (LC); Listening Comprehension is predicted by Syntax Comprehension (SC), which is predicted—in turn—by Vocabulary (VOC).

For L1 learners, it can be seen that—to start with—reading comprehension is explained by the prior level of reading comprehension. The development of reading comprehension is also explained equally by the children's word decoding abilities and listening comprehension with vocabulary as an additional predictor. In the case of L2 learners, the roles of the children's oral language proficiency and vocabulary are even stronger, and syntax comprehension is also found to play a role.

Role of Background Knowledge

In addition to various linguistic factors, children's background knowledge can influence their reading comprehension. The associations between background knowledge and L1 reading comprehension have been investigated extensively and shown a facilitating effect of having background knowledge of the topic of a text on reading comprehension in both adults and children (see Kucer, 2009). Pritchard (1990) examined the role of cultural schemata on the comprehension processes of proficient 11th-grade readers with an American or Palauan background. Both groups were asked to read two texts in their own native language; the texts described the funeral ceremonies in the two countries. The students were asked to provide a verbal report of their reading strategies while reading the texts and to retell the texts after reading each. On the basis of the verbal descriptions of their reading strategies and subsequent retellings, Pritchard concluded that cultural schemata influenced both the processing strategies used by the readers and their levels of comprehension.

Research has also provided evidence that background knowledge can play a substantial role in second-language reading comprehension. Steffensen, Joag-Dev, and Anderson (1984) found familiarity with the topic of a text to help second-language readers construct meaning. When Malik (1995) studied the oral reading behavior of proficient second-language readers using culturally familiar and unfamiliar texts, cultural schemata significantly affected the reading process in that unfamiliar texts showed less comprehension than familiar texts. Johnson (1981) examined the effects of both linguistic text complexity and cultural origin among Iranian ESL students and American monolingual students. Half of the participants read two unadapted English versions of two stories from different cultural backgrounds: one from Iranian folklore and one from American folklore. The other half read the same two stories but now with simplified English. Multiple-choice questions were asked with regard to both explicit and implicit information from the texts. The results showed the cultural origin of the story to influence the comprehension of the ESL students more than the level of semantic and syntactic complexity (i.e., reading of an adapted versus unadapted form). For the native English readers, however, both the level of syntactic and semantic complexity and the cultural origin of the story affected comprehension: They were better able to understand the unadapted English version and the text based on American folklore.

Droop and Verhoeven (1998) examined the roles of cultural schemata and linguistic complexity in the reading fluency and comprehension of two groups of third-grade children in the Netherlands: monolingual Dutch children and Turkish or Moroccan immigrant children learning Dutch as a second language. The children were given three types of texts that were drawn from standard reading curricula: texts referring to Dutch culture, texts referring to the cultures of immigrants from near Eastern countries from Turkey and Morocco, and neutral texts. For each type of text, two levels of linguistic complexity were distinguished. Using read-aloud protocols, retelling, and questioning, the children's reading performance for the different types of texts was analyzed. A facilitative effect of cultural familiarity was found for both reading comprehension and reading efficiency. For the minority children, this effect was restricted to the linguistically simple texts due to their limited knowledge of the target language, Dutch. These findings demonstrate the role of cultural bias in curricular materials and call for an increased use of culturally authentic materials in both reading curricula and school texts.

Role of Reading Engagement

Reading engagement can be seen as a crucial factor in reading acquisition. If students have to struggle too much with the reading process or what is being read has little or no personal meaning for them, students can disengage. Without motivation and engagement, moreover, even the most advantaged students may not learn much at school. Research has indeed shown that reading engagement can be greatly enhanced when readers are intrinsically motivated and can find personal meaning in what they read (Baker, Afflerbach, & Reinking, 1996). The engagement perspective therefore emphasizes that motivation, cognition, and social interaction are equally important for the development of reading. That is, reading engagement can initiate a positive spiral of reading, knowing, and sharing. Engaged readers want to understand, apply complex cognitive skills for this purpose, and often feel a desire to share the knowledge acquired with others. Texts are read and comprehended not only because the readers are capable of doing this but because they are motivated to do it as well (Guthrie, 2004).

In a series of studies, Guthrie, Wigfield, and Perencevich (2004) demonstrated the positive effects of a concept-oriented reading engagement program for children from varying achievement levels and linguistic-cultural backgrounds. Strengthening a child's reading comprehension and motivation can thus help overcome disadvantages associated with a low socio-economic status and/or minority status. Schools obviously cannot influence the socioeconomic backgrounds of families, but they can adapt their literacy practices to the needs of their students (cf. Campbell, Voelkl, & Donahue, 1997; Cummins, 2000). Given that minority students also tend to live under poor socio-economic conditions, many will experience a mismatch between home and school circumstances. And if the aim of schools is to maintain the status quo, they run the risk of simply perpetuating the structural inequality that already characterizes mainstream versus minority student groups (cf. Au, 1993). Schools should strive to engage their learners as this obviously motivates students; it can also compensate for many inequalities and limited second-language skills. From a recent international comparative study, for example, it was concluded that the level of student reading engagement is a better predictor of reading performance than socioeconomic background (OECD, 2006).

EDUCATIONAL PERSPECTIVE ON SECOND-LANGUAGE READING ACQUISITION

The studies reviewed in this chapter make it clear that the development of children's second-language reading skill is often at-risk. In order to prevent second-language readers from falling behind native language readers, it is essential that continuous learning and genuine input be provided and abrupt changes in reading development thus be avoided. In Figure 27.6, the course of reading development for minority children when viewed from such a perspective is outlined.

In Figure 27.6, it can be seen that the development of children's phonological awareness (PA), L2 word decoding (WD2), and L2 reading comprehension (RC2) are directly influenced by their L2 proficiency and indirectly influenced by their L1 proficiency. It should be emphasized that substantial coverage of the key components of reading as defined by the National Reading Panel is also clearly helpful for minority students (see August & Shanahan, 2006). That is, a focus on phonological awareness, word decoding for purposes of reading fluency, and reading comprehension is of utmost importance for children's second-language reading development in addition to an appreciation of the children's language capacities.

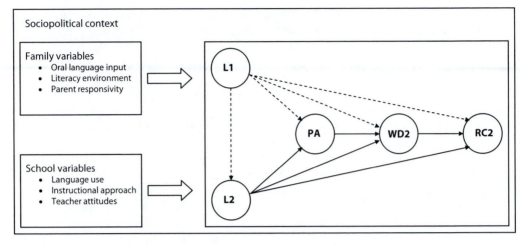

Figure 27.6 Minority children's reading development shows phonological awareness (PA), L2 word decoding (WD2), and L2 reading comprehension (RC2) to be directly influenced by the children's second language proficiency (L2) and indirectly influenced by their first language proficiency (L1) with family and school variables mediating the learning process within a given socio-political context.

In the long run, minority children appear to attain native-like levels of word decoding (see Lesaux et al., 2006). However, the length of residence in the second-language context and exposure to the second language are important mediating factors. If the mismatch between the child's home language and the language of instruction is too large, learning to read in a second language—even at the level of the word—may be problematic. Initial reading instruction should therefore focus—under such circumstances—on the structure of words; special attention should be paid to the fast and accurate retrieval of letter-sound relationships; and the integration of children's phonemic awareness of structural word patterns should be stimulated. Children should also be given abundant opportunities to read graded text materials in order to achieve fluency. A wide variety of well-written and engaging texts that no not exceed the child's frustration level should be provided as well. The better the child's word-decoding skills develop, the more successful his or her reading comprehension will be.

Inspection of Figure 27.6 shows minority children to bring two languages to the classroom situation. It has become evident that early minority language instruction can help bridge the mismatch between the language used in the home and the language used at school while still promoting majority language proficiency (see Cummins, 2000; Genesee, Lindholm-Leary, Saunders, & Christian, 2006; Genesee & Geva, 2006). In this light, it is also important to realize that minority students have developed certain attitudes towards not only their native language and culture but also the majority language and culture and that these attitudes can give rise to specific language and literacy needs. The discovery of the alphabetical principle, moreover, is a very abstract task. A second-language-only approach to literacy interventions in either the home or the school therefore does not seem to fit the linguistic and socio-cultural backgrounds of minority children. Bilingual input during preschool can not only help minority children catch up; it can also help them become phonologically aware. And in subsequent schooling, bilingual instruction can help all children understand the basic principles of word decoding and reading. Given the claim that it is easier for children to build elementary literacy skills in a language for which they have already acquired basic phonological, lexical, and syntactic skills, it is important that both the L1 and L2 oral proficiency of minority children be assessed at the outset of a literacy intervention. Any mismatch between the child's linguistic abilities and the language of instruction can thus be detected and minimized. Research shows both simultaneous and successive literacy interventions in two languages to be feasible. In fact, such programs have been shown to improve students' academic proficiency in general and not delay their second-language literacy skills at all. It should nevertheless be kept in mind that the possibilities for linguistic transfer depend upon not only the structure of the languages and orthographies involved but also the children's level of language and literacy proficiency in both the first and second languages (see Bialystok et al., 2005).

Oral proficiency in the target language (L2) appears to be of critical importance for the acquisition of second-language reading comprehension (cf. Geva & Genesee, 2006). Given the strong relations between vocabulary skills, listening comprehension, and reading comprehension, all of these abilities should be emphasized during children's reading instruction. Children's vocabulary knowledge appears to be an extremely important factor for effective reading comprehension. Intense L2 vocabulary training should therefore be provided throughout the elementary school years. Children should be encouraged to build a large sight vocabulary in order to automatically access word meanings. And, in order to encourage children to not avoid difficult words, lessons should be specifically devoted to the issue of how to read less frequent or tricky words in addition to high frequency but otherwise unfamiliar words. Reading instruction should also be explicitly devoted to the stimulation of deeper levels of processing. Guthrie (2008), for example, stresses the importance of having students reading words from different subject areas and in different contexts. The greater the depth of word meaning aimed at, the more important the use of multiple contexts. With the provision of frequent and varied opportunities to think about the use and meanings of words and the promotion of book reading activities, moreover, teachers can help bridge any gaps in children's reading comprehension (Beck, McKeown, & Kucan, 2002).

Special attention should also be devoted to the structure and content of texts to facilitate the further development of children's reading comprehension skills in general and in their second language in particular. The use of familiar, well-organized, and carefully presented texts can help children learn to identify, summarize, and outline the main ideas in a text (Seidenberg, 1989). At the same time, teachers and educational specialists should consider both the children's L1 and L2 language proficiency and their background knowledge in order to sequence instruction according to the children's abilities. Teachers and educational specialists must recognize that the content of textbooks may not be equally familiar to all children. For the planning of the reading curriculum, it is important to again stress the importance of such prereading activities as the provision of background information, discussion of the content of a story, the building of common ground (i.e., shared experiences), and the explanation of difficult lexical items in order to help children activate and develop their background knowledge. It can be assumed that students often acquire new knowledge from moderately unfamiliar texts that simultaneously offer substantive and structural cues to relevant background information. An engagement perspective can be further recommended to promote reading on the part of children. In addition to a focus on the integration of reading with other subject areas, opportunities for peer discussion and cooperative learning should be provided and the availability of culturally diverse books both inside and outside the classroom should be emphasized (Guthrie, McRae, & Klauda, 2007; Guthrie, Coddington, & Wigfield, 2009).

Figure 27.6 also makes it clear that children's language and literacy development is mediated by family and school variables. With regard to the family, oral language input, literacy resources within the home, and the responsivity of parents greatly influence children's language development and literacy. Home literacy experiences in both L1 and L2 along with responsive parents are positively related to the literacy of children. With regard to the school, at least three factors tend to be crucial for the optimal development of literacy. The first factor is the languages used in the curriculum. As we have seen before a bilingual perspective can highly be recommended. The second school factor is the instructional approach being followed and methods based upon a broad definition of functional literacy in particular. Third, teacher atitudes should be attuned to the attainment of optimal literacy for children from culturally and lingusitically diverse backgrounds. That is, language and literacy objectives should be high but adjusted to the specific educational needs of the children involved.

At least some continuity between the home and school experiences of children is by definition critical within a context of cultural and linguistc diversity (Dickinson & Tabors, 2002). School teams should thus create room for parental involvement and thereby help create some continuity of literacy experiences. Bridging the gap between literacy socialization in the home and literacy education at school can enhance the motivation, engagement, and participation of students at school. Close cooperation between preschool institutions in the area of family activation and school education may be required to harmonize the socialization of children (Snow & Tabors, 2001). The pursuit of continuity in basic education also calls for special attention to the transitions from preschool to early elementary school, early elementary school to later elementary school, and so forth. Starting in the preschool years, moreover, language and literacy education should be organized around powerful learning environments that thus stimulate the meaningful, social, and strategic learning of a language; encourage children to learn independently; and can easily be adapted to the varying learning needs of children. This is particularly important for children who cannot monitor their own learning very well, have difficulties applying what they have learned, and language-delayed children. Remedial teaching may nevertheless be required to prevent language development problems and facilitate mainstreaming (Snow et al., 1998; Garcia & McKoon, 2006).

To conclude this chapter on second-language reading acquisition, the role of minority languages in education should once more be highlighted. The support of minority languages in literacy education may not only help bridge the frequent gap between the language used in the home and the language used at school but also help overcome feelings of ambivalence on the part of minority group members towards the majority group and majority language. Contributions to the first language learning of minority children should thus be defined as an autonomous goal and the first language proficiency of such children viewed as a school subject and evaluated accordingly. In a multi-ethnic society, minority groups may use various written codes that serve—at least partially—distinct functions. The written code of the majority language will presumably be used in societal institutions while the written code of the minority language will be used for primarily intragroup communication and the expression of one's ethnicity. With respect to language and literacy in general, two worldwide trends can be observed. On the one hand, the processes of globalization and internationalization can be seen to occur as a result of mass media, trade, labor migration, and tourism. On the other hand, there is a growing awareness of the significance of cultural and linguistic diversity. A basic policy question within the area of institutional support for literacy is, therefore, how to reconcile these opposing trends—namely, unification and diversification—in multilingual societies. The same question dominates the current debate regarding the unification or diversification of language as language is a prominent feature of both trends and languages are relatively easy to neglect or promote within sociopolitical contexts (see also Cummins, 2009).

REFERENCES

Au, K. H. (1993). *Literacy instruction in multicultural settings.* Orlando, FL: Harcourt Brace.

August, D., & Hakuta, K. (1997). *Improving schooling for language-minority children.* Washington, DC: National Academy Press.

August, D., & Shanahan, T. (Eds.). (2006). *Developing literacy in second-language learners: Report of the National Literacy Panel on language-minority children and youth.* Mahwah, NJ: Erlbaum.

Baker, L., Afflerbach, P., & Reinking, D. (1996). *Developing engaged readers in school and home communities.* Mahwah, NJ: Erlbaum.

Beck, I. L., McKeown, M. G., & Kucan, L. (2002). *Bringing words to life: Robust vocabulary instruction.* New York: Guilford Press.

Bernhardt, E. B. (2000). Second-language reading as a case study of reading scholarship in the 20th century. In M. L. Kamil, P. B. Mosenthal, P. D. Pearson, & R. Barr (Eds.), *Handbook of reading research* (Vol. 3, pp. 791–812). Mahwah, NJ: Erlbaum.

Bernhardt, E. B. (2005). Progress and procrastination in second-language reading. In Mary McGroarty (Ed.), *Annual review of applied linguistics* (pp. 133–150). Cambridge, UK: Cambridge University Press.

Bialystok, E., & Ryan, E.B. (1985). Metacognitive framework for the development of first and second language skills. In D. L. Forrest-Pressley, G. E. MacKinnon, & T. G. Waller (Eds.), *Metacognition, cognition and human performance* (pp. 207–252). New York: Academic Press.

Bialystok, E. (1988). Levels of bilingualism and levels of linguistic awareness. *Developmental Psychology, 24,* 560–567.

Bialystok, E. (1993). Metalinguistic awareness: The development of children's representations of language. In C. Pratt & A. F. Garton (Eds.), *Systems of representation in children* (pp. 211–233). New York: Wiley.

Bialystok, E. (1994). Analysis and control in the development of second language proficiency. *Studies in Second Language Acquisition, 16,* 157–168.

Bialystok, E. (2001). *Bilingualism in development: Language, literacy and cognition.* Cambridge, MA: Cambridge University Press.

Bialystok, E. (2002). Acquisition of literacy in bilingual children: A framework for research. *Language Learning, 52,* 159–199.

Bialystok, E., & Herman, J. (1999). Does bilingualism matter for early literacy? *Bilingualism: Language and Cognition, 2,* 35–44.

Bialystok, E., Luk, G., & Kwan, E. (2005). Bilingualism, biliteracy, and learning to read: Interactions among languages and writing systems. *Scientific Studies of Reading, 9,* 43–61.

Bruck, M., & Genesee, F. (1995). Phonological awareness in young second language learners. *Journal of Child Language, 22,* 307–324.

Campbell, J. R., Voelkl, K. E., & Donahue, P. L. (1997). *Report in brief: NAEP 1996 trends in academic progress.* Washington, DC: U.S. Department of Education, National Center for Education Statistics.

Campbell, R., & Sais, E. (1995). Accelerated metalinguistic (phonological) awareness in bilingual children. *British Journal of Developmental Psychology, 13,* 61–68.

Carlisle, J. F., Beeman, M. M., Davis, L. H., & Spharim, G. (1999). Relationship of metalinguistic capabilities and reading achievement for children who are becoming bilingual. *Applied Psycholinguistics, 20,* 459–478.

Chiappe, P., & Siegel, L. S. (1999). Phonological Awareness and Reading Acquisition in English- and Punjabi-Speaking Canadian Children. *Journal of Educational Psychology, 91,* 1, 20–28.

Cormier, P., & Kelson, S. (2000). The development of sensitivity of plural morphology in children in French immersion and in French-speaking children. *Scientific Studies of Reading, 4,* 267–293.

Cromdal, J. (1999). Childhood bilingualism and metalinguistic skills: Analysis and control in young Swedish-English bilinguals. *Applied Psycholinguistics, 20,* 1–20.

Cummins, J. (1984). Wanted: A theoretical framework for relating language proficiency to academic achievement among bilingual students. In C. Rivera (Ed.), *Language proficiency and academic achievement* (pp. 2–19). Clevedon, UK: Multilingual Matters.

Cummins, J. (1989). Language and literacy acquisition in bilingual contexts. *Journal of Multilingual and Multicultural Development, 10*(1), 17–31.

Cummins, J. (1991). Conversational and academic language proficiency in bilingual contexts. *AILA Review, 8,* 75–89.

Cummins, J. (2000). *Language, power and pedagogy: Bilingual children at the cross-fire.* Clevedon, UK: Multilingual Matters.

Cummins, J. (2009). Literacy and English language learners: A shifting landscape for students, teachers, researchers and policy makers. *Educational Researcher, 38,* 382–384.

Deacon, S. H., Wade-Woolley, L., & Kirby, J. R. (2009). Flexibility in young second-language learners: examining the language specificity of orthographic processing. *Journal of Research in Reading, 32,* 215–229.

Delgado-Gaitan, C. (1990). *Literacy for empowerment: The role of parents in their children's education.* New York: Falmer.

Dickinson, D., & Tabors, P. (2002). Fostering language and literacy in classrooms and homes. *Young Children, 57*(2), 10–18.

Dijkstra, T., & Van Heuven, W. J. B. (2002). The architecture of the bilingual word recognition system: From identification to decision. *Bilingualism, Language and Cognition, 5,* 175–197.

Droop, M., & Verhoeven, L. (1998). Background knowledge, linguistic complexity, and second-language reading comprehension. *Journal of Literacy Research, 30,* 253–271.

Droop, M., & Verhoeven, L. (2003). Language proficiency and reading ability in first- and second-language learners. *Reading Research Quarterly, 38,* 78–103.

Durgunoglu, A.Y., & Verhoeven, L. (Eds.). (1998). *Literacy development in a multilingual context: Cross-cultural perspectives.* Mahwah, NJ: Erlbaum.

Durgunoglu, A.Y. (1997). Bilingual reading: Its components, development and other issues. In A. M. B. de Groot & J. F. Kroll (Eds.), *Tutorials in bilingualism: Psycholinguistic perspectives* (pp. 255–276). Hillsdale, NJ: Erlbaum.

Durgunoglu, A. Y. (2002). Cross-linguistic transfer in literacy development and implications for language learners. *Annals of Dyslexia, 52,* 189–204.

Ellis, N. C., & Schmidt, R. (1997). Morphology and longer distance dependencies: Laboratory research illuminating the A in SLA. *Studies in Second Language Acquisition, 19,* 145–171.

Fantini, A. (1985). *Language acquisition of a bilingual child.* Clevedon, UK: Multilingual Matters.

Fishman, J. A. (1980). Ethnocultural dimensions in the acquisition and retention of biliteracy. *Journal of Basic Writing, 3,* 48–61.

French, R. M., & Jacquet, M. (2004). Understanding bilingual memory : models and data. *Trends in Cognitive Science, 8,* 87–93.

Frenck-Mestre, C. (2005). Eye-movement recording as a tool for studying syntactic processing in a second language. *Second Language Research, 21,* 175–198.

Garcia, G. E., & McKoon, G. (2006). Language and literacy assessment of language-minority students. In D. August & T. Shanahan (Eds.), *Report of the National Literacy Panel on K-12 youth and adolescents* (pp. 597–624). Mahwah, NJ: Erlbaum.

Genesee, F., & Gándara, P. (1999). Bilingual education programs: A cross-national perspective. *Journal of Social Issues, 55,* 665–685.

Genesee, F., & Geva, E. (2006). Cross-linguistic relationships in working memory, phonological processes, and oral language. In D. August & T. Shanahan (Eds.), *Report of the National Literacy Panel on K-12 youth and adolescents* (pp. 175–184). Mahwah, NJ: Erlbaum.

Genesee, F., Lindholm-Leary, K., Saunders, W. & Christian, D. (2006). *Educating English language learners: A synthesis of research evidence.* New York: Cambridge University Press.

Geva, E., & Genesee, F. (2006). First-language oral proficiency and second-language literacy. In D. August & T. Shanahan (Eds.), *Report of the National Literacy Panel on K-12 youth and adolescents* (pp. 147–158). Mahwah, NJ: Erlbaum.

Geva, E., & Siegel, L. S. (2000). Orthographic and cognitive factors in the concurrent development of basic reading skills in two languages. *Reading and Writing: An Interdisciplinary Journal, 12,* 1–30.

Goldman, S. R. (2003). Learning in complex domains: When and why do multiple representations help? *Learning and Instruction, 13,* 239–244.

Goswami U. (2000). Phonological and lexical processes. In M. L. Kamil, P. B. Rosenthal, P. D. Pearson, & R. Barr (Eds.), *Handbook of reading research* (Vol. 3, pp. 251–268). Mahwah, NJ: Erlbaum.

Gottardo, A. (2002). The relationship between language and reading skills in bilingual Spanish-English speakers. *Topics on Language Disorders, 22,* 46–70.

Gottardo, A., & Mueller, J. (2009). Are first- and second-language factors related in predicting second-language reading comprehension? *Journal of Educational Psychology, 101,* 330–344.

Grabe, W. (1991). Current developments in second language reading research. *TESOL Quarterly, 25*(3), 375–406.

Guthrie, J. T. (2004). Teaching for literacy engagement. *Journal of Literacy Research, 36*(1), 1–30.

Guthrie, J. T., Coddington, C. S., & Wigfield, A. (2009). Profiles of motivation for reading among African American and Caucasian students. *Journal of Literacy Research, 41,* 344–363.

Guthrie, J. T., McRae, A., & Klauda, S. L. (2007). Contributions of concept-oriented reading instruction to knowledge about interventions for motivations in reading. *Educational Psychologist, 42,* 237–250.

Guthrie, J. T., Wigfield, A., & Perencevich, K. (Eds.), (2004). *Motivating reading comprehension: Concept-oriented reading instruction.* Mahwah, NJ: Erlbaum.

Hoover, W. A., & Gough, P. B. (1990). The simple view of reading. *Reading and Writing: An Interdisciplinary Journal, 2,* 127–160.

Hornberger, N. H. (2002). *Multilingual language policies and the continua of biliteracy: An ecological approach. Language Policy, 1,* 27–51.

Jean, M., & Geva, E. (2009). The development of vocabulary in English as a second language children and its role in predicting word recognition ability. *Applied Psycholinguistics, 30,* 153–185.

Johnson, P. (1981). Effects on reading comprehension of language complexity and cultural background of a text. *TESOL Quarterly, 15*(2), 169–181.

Karmiloff-Smith, A. (1997). *Beyond modularity.* Cambridge, MA: MIT Press.

Kindler, A. L. (2002). *Survey of the states' limited English proficiency students and available educational programs and services.* Washington, DC: National Clearinghouse for English Language Acquisition.

Kitajima, R. (1997). Referential strategy training for reading comprehension of Japanese texts. *Foreign Language Annals, 30,* 84–97.

Koda, K. (1996). L2 word recognition research: a critical review. *Modern Language Journal, 80,* 450–460.

Koda, K. (2007). Reading and language learning: Cross-linguistic constraints of second language reading development. *Language Learning, 57,* 1–44.

Koda, K., & Reddy, P. (2008). Cross-linguistic transfer in second language reading. *Language Teaching, 41,* 497–508.

Kucer, S. (2009). *Dimensions of literacy.* London: Taylor & Francis

Lesaux, N., Koda, K., Siegel, L., & Shanahan, T. (2006). Development of literacy. In D. August & T. Shanahan (Eds.), *Report of the National Literacy Panel on K-12 youth and adolescents* (pp. 53–74). Mahwah, NJ: Erlbaum.

Lindsey, K. A., Manis, F. R., & Bailey, C. E. (2003). Prediction of first-grade reading in Spanish-speaking English-learners. *Journal of Educational Psychology, 95,* 482–494.

Lopez, L. M., & Greenfield, D. B. (2004). The cross-language transfer of phonological skills of Hispanic Head Start children. *Bilingual Research Journal, 28,* 1–18.

MacWhinney, B. (2004). A unified model of language acquisition. In J. F. Kroll & A. M. B. de Groot (Eds.), *Handbook of bilingualism: Psycholinguistic approaches* (pp. 49–67). Oxford, UK: Oxford University Press.

Malik, A. A. (1995). A psycholinguistic analysis of the reading behavior of EFL-proficient readers using culturally familiar and culturally nonfamiliar expository texts. *American Educational Research Journal, 27,* 205–223.

Martin-Jones, M., & Saxena, M. (2003). Bilingual resources and 'Funds of knowledge' for teaching and learning in multi-ethnic classrooms in Britain. *International Journal of Bilingual Education and Bilingualism, 6,* 267–282.

Nagy, W. E., & Scott, J. A. (2000). Vocabulary processes. In M. L. Kamil, P. B. Rosenthal, P. D. Pearson, & R. Barr (Eds.), *Handbook of reading research* (Vol. 3, pp. 269–284). Mahwah, NJ: Erlbaum.

Nagy, W., McClure, E., & Mir, M. (1997). Linguistic transfer and the use of context by Spanish-English bilinguals. *Applied Psycholinguistics, 18,* 431–452.

National Reading Panel. (2000). *Teaching children to read: An evidence-based assessment of the scientific research literature on reading and its implications for reading instruction.* Washington, DC: The National Institute of Child Health and Human Development.

Organisation for Economic Co-Operation and Development. (OECD). (2006). *Where immigrant students succeed: A comparative review of performance and engagement in PISA 2003.* Paris: OECD.

Oller, K., & Eilers, R. (Eds.). (2002). *Language and literacy in bilingual children.* Clevedon, UK: Multilingual Matters.

Pearson, B. Z., Fernández, S., Lewedag, V., & Oller, D. K. (1997). Input factors in lexical learning of bilingual infants (ages 10 to 30 months). *Applied Psycholinguistics, 18,* 41–58.

Perfetti, C. A. (1998). Learning to read. In P. Reitsma & L. Verhoeven (Eds.), *Literacy problems and interventions* (pp. 15–48). Dordrecht, The Netherlands: Kluwer.

Perfetti, C. A., & Hart, L. (2001). The lexical quality hypothesis. In L. Verhoeven, C. Elbro, & P. Reitsma (Eds.), *Precursors of functional literacy* (pp. 189–214). Amsterdam: John Benjamins.

Perfetti, C. A., Landi, N., & Oakhill, J (2005). The acquisition of reading comprehension skill. In M. J. Snowling & C. Hulme (Eds.), *The science of reading: A handbook* (pp. 227–247). Oxford, UK: Basil Blackwell.

Plaut, D. C., McClelland, J.L., Seidenberg, M. S., & Patterson, K. (1996). Understanding normal and impaired word reading: Computational principles in quasi-regular domains. *Psychological Review, 103,* 56–115.

Pritchard, R. H. (1990). The effects of cultural schemata on reading processing strategies. *Reading Research Quarterly, 25,* 273–295.

Proctor, C. P., Carlo, M., August, D., & Snow, C. E. (2005). Native Spanish-speaking children reading in English: Toward a model of comprehension. *Journal of Educational Psychology, 97*(1), 246–256.

Rubin, H., & Turner, A. (1989). Phonological awareness in young second language learner. *Journal of Child Language, 22,* 307–324.

Schiff, R., & Calif, S. (2007). Role of phonological and morphological awareness in L2 oral word reading. *Language Learning, 57,* 271–298.

Seidenberg, M. S., & McClelland, J. L. (1989). A distributed, developmental model of word recognition and naming. *Psychological Review, 96,* 523–568.

Seidenberg, P. L. (1989). Relating text-processing research to reading and writing instruction for learning disabled students. *Learning Disabilities Focus, 5,* 4–12.

Share, D. L. (1995). Phonological recoding and self-teaching: sine qua non of reading acquisition. *Cognition, 55,* 151–218.

Siegel, L. (2003). Bilingualism and reading. In L. Verhoeven, C. Elbro, & P. Reitsma (Eds.), *Precursors of functional literacy* (pp. 287–302). Amsterdam: John Benjamins.

Slavin, R. E., & Cheung, A. (2005). A synthesis of research on language and reading instruction for English language learners. *Review of Educational Research, 75,* 247–284.

Snow, C. E., Tabors, P. O., Dickinson, D. K. (2001). Language development in the preschool years. In D. K. Dickinson & P. O. Tabors (Eds.), *Beginning literacy with language* (pp. 1–25). Baltimore, MD: Paul H. Brookes.

Snow, C. E., Burns, M. S., & Griffin, P. (1998). *Preventing reading difficulties in young children.* Washington, DC: National Academy Press.

Stahl, S. A., & Shiel, T. G. (1999). Teaching meaning vocabulary: Productive approaches for poor readers. In *Read all about it! Readings to inform the profession* (pp. 291–321). Sacramento: California State Board of Education.

Steffensen M. S., & Joag-Dev, C. (1984). Cultural knowledge and reading. In J. C. Alderson & A. H. Urquhart (Eds.), *Reading in a foreign language* (pp. 48–61). New York: Longman.

Tabors, P. (1997). *One child, two languages: A guide for early childhood educators of children learning English as a second language.* Baltimore, MD: Paul H. Brookes.

Tabors, P., & Snow, C. (2001). Young bilingual children and early literacy development. In S. Neuman & D. Dickinson (Eds.), *Handbook of early literacy research* (pp. 159–178). New York: Guilford Press.

Troia, G. A. (1999). Phonological awareness intervention research: A critical review of the experimental methodology. *Reading Research Quarterly, 34,* 28–52.

U.S. Census Bureau. (2008). *National population projections.* Washington, DC: U.S. Census Bureau.

Vaid, J., & Frenck-Mestre, C. (2002). Do orthographic cues aid language identification? A laterality study with French-English bilinguals. *Brain and Language, 82,* 47–53.

Verhallen, M., & Schoonen, R. (1993). Vocabulary knowledge of monolingual and bilingual children. *Applied Linguistics, 14,* 344–363.

Verhoeven, L. (1987). *Ethnic minority children acquiring literacy.* Berlin: Mouton/DeGruyter.

Verhoeven, L. (1990). Acquisition of reading in a second language. *Reading Research Quarterly, 25*(2), 90–114.

Verhoeven, L. (2000). Components in early second language reading and spelling. *Scientific Studies of Reading, 4,* 313–330.

Verhoeven, L. (2007). Early bilingualism, language transfer, and phonological awareness. *Applied Psycholinguistics, 28,* 425–439.

Verhoeven, L., & Perfetti, C. (2008). Advances in text comprehension: Model, process and development. *Applied Cognitive Psychology, 22,* 293–301.

Verhoeven, L., & van Leeuwe, J. (2008). Predictors of text comprehension development. *Applied Cognitive Psychology, 22,* 407–423.

Verhoeven, L., & Vermeer, A. (2006). Sociocultural variation in literacy achievement. *British Journal of Educational Studies, 54,* 189–211.

Vermeer, A. (2001). Breadth and depth of vocabulary in relation to L1/L2 acquisition and frequency of input. *Applied Psycholinguistics, 22,* 217–234.

Wasik, B. (2004). *Handbook of family literacy.* Mahwah, NJ: Erlbaum.

Yaden, D., Rowe, D. W., & MacGillivray, L. (2000). Emergent literacy: A matter (polyphony) of perspectives. In M. L. Kamil, P. B. Mosenthal, P. D. Pearson, & R. Barr (Eds.), *Handbook of reading research* (Vol. 3, pp. 425–454). Mahwah, NJ: Erlbaum.

Ziegler, J. C., & Goswami, U. (2005). Reading acquisition, developmental dyslexia and skilled reading across languages: A psycholinguistic grain size theory. *Psychological Bulletin, 131,* 3–29.

Zulich, J., Bean, T. W., & Herrick, J. (1992). Charting stages of pre-service teacher development and reflection in a multicultural community through dialogue journal analysis. *Teaching and Teacher Education, 8*(4), 345–360.

28 Reading Instruction for English Language Learners

Claude Goldenberg

Stanford University

The number of students arriving at school not fully proficient in English has grown enormously over the past half century. Forty years ago, the achievement of children from non-English-speaking homes was hardly a national issue. Today it is. The number of students limited in their English abilities has multiplied by 150% nationwide just in the past 15 years; the growth has been even more dramatic in some regions of the country. This demographic change has had a profound impact on schools. Teachers must adjust to the different needs of students from highly diverse backgrounds and with varying degrees of English proficiency. Federal and state accountability requirements since No Child Left Behind was signed into law in 2002 have raised the stakes ever higher, since schools cannot make "adequately yearly progress" unless all student subgroups meet targeted progress benchmarks. But no matter the pressures created by high-stakes testing (which in any case might change under the Obama administration), the moral imperative to improve achievement and opportunities for this group of students grows as their numbers increase. The need for valid research-based knowledge of how to improve these students' literacy attainment has never been greater.

In this chapter I will first provide an overview of this population of students, currently referred to as English language learners (ELLs). Over the years, they have been designated—with varying degrees of accuracy—as bilingual students, English as a second language (ESL) students, limited- or non-English speaking (LES/NES) students, and limited-English proficient (LEP) students. I will then provide a brief historical view of research on ELLs in the United States. Most of the chapter will comprise an analysis of key findings and current trends that should be of greatest salience for educators and policy makers concerned with putting into practice the best research-based knowledge available. The chapter will conclude with implications for practice, policy, and future research.

ELLS IN THE UNITED STATES

In 1990, approximately 2 million public school students—1 of every 20 in grades K–12—were ELLs, that is, spoke English either not at all or with enough limitations that they could not fully participate in mainstream English instruction. Today, there are over 5 million ELLs—1 in 9 public school students in K–12. This 150% increase has occurred during a period when the overall school population has increased by only about 20% (National Clearinghouse for English Language Acquisition, n.d.). Even states not typically associated with ELLs, e.g., South Carolina, North Carolina, Tennessee, Georgia, and Indiana, each saw an increase in the ELL population of 400% or more between 1993–94 and 2003–04 (National Clearinghouse for English Language Acquisition, n.d).

ELLs in the United States come from over 400 different language backgrounds. Contrary to most people's assumptions, most ELLs were born in the United States; fewer than one-quarter of elementary-age ELLs and less than half of secondary-age ELLs are foreign-born (Capps, Fix, Murray, Passel, & Herwantoro, 2005). By far the majority of ELLs—80%—are Spanish-speaking, and most of these are from Mexico and Central America. Although the Latino population in the United States is quite diverse—as is the U.S. immigrant population overall (see Tseng & Lesaux, 2009)—economic and educational levels tend to be lower than either the general population or other immigrants and language minority populations (Larsen, 2004). For example, only 38% of adult immigrants from Mexico and Central America have a high school education, compared to 88% of U.S.-born adults, 85% of immigrants from Europe, and 87% of Asian immigrants. Consequently, most ELLs in the United States are at risk for poor school outcomes not only because of language, but also because of socioeconomic factors.

Speakers of Asian languages (e.g., Vietnamese, Hmong, Chinese, Korean, Khmer, Hindi) comprise about 8% of the ELL population. In general, these populations tend to come from higher educational and economic backgrounds than the Latino population. However, Asians also comprise a highly diverse group with widely varying experiences and characteristics that differ by country and region of origin. For example, more than 50% of the Taiwanese, Indian, and Pakistani populations have college degrees; fewer than 10% of Japanese, Filipino, and Indians live below the poverty line; the median per capita income (in 1999 dollars) of the Taiwanese, Indian, and Japanese populations is greater than $25,000. In contrast, half or fewer U.S. residents of Laotian, Cambodian, or Hmong descent have high school degrees; among Cambodians and Hmong, the poverty rate is 30% or higher and per capita income (in 1999 dollars) $10,000 or lower. Table 28.1 illustrates the diversity in demographic and socioeconomic characteristics among Latino and Asian subgroups in the United States. Note the table includes both foreign- and U.S.-born individuals.

Large Achievement Gaps Between ELLs and English Speakers

Reading and language arts achievement among ELLs in the United States tends to be low, although, again, there is considerable variability. As a group, students who are learning English as a second language consistently underperform compared to their English-speaking peers. In California, for example, approximately 50% of students fluent in English score proficient or advanced on the California Standards Test in English language arts. In contrast, among ELLs *who have been enrolled in school in the U.S. for at least a year,* the percent proficient or advanced in English language arts ranges from a high of 28% in second grade to a dreadfully low 4% in 10th and 11th grades (California Department of Education California STAR Program (n.d.). The national picture shows the same discrepancies. On the 2005 National Assessment of Educational Progress (NAEP), fourth-grade ELLs scored 35 points below non-ELLs in reading, a huge gap since 10 points is approximately equivalent to a grade level. Differences were somewhat smaller but still sizable in math and science. In 2007, the differences between ELLs and non-ELLs were nearly identical to what they were in 2005. Gaps between English-proficient students and ELLs are even larger, and have increased across all subject areas, among eighth and twelfth graders (National Center for Education Statistics, n.d.).

By definition, ELLs are limited in their English proficiency, so it is not surprising that they do more poorly than their English-speaking peers on tests written in English. Their poor test performance is undoubtedly at least partly due to lack of English proficiency. But low test scores might also be due to lagging content knowledge and skills and/or to other factors that interfere with test performance. Whatever the explanation, these achievement gaps should concern us all.

Table 28.1   Demographic Characteristics of Select Hispanic and Asian Subgroups (1, 2)

	Total population	Percent > 25 yrs old	Percent HS graduates	Percent BA+	Percent foreign born (3)	Per capita income (4)	Percent < poverty
White non Hispanic	194,552,774	69%	85%	27%	4%	$24,819	8%
Total Hispanic/ Latino	35,305,818	52%	52%	10%	40%	$12,111	22%
Mexican	20,640,711	49%	46%	7%	42%	$10,918	23%
Cuban	1,241,685	75%	63%	21%	69%	$20,451	14%
Costa Rican	68,588	66%	73%	21%	74%	$16,197	17%
Guatemalan	372,487	63%	39%	7%	85%	$12,083	24%
Honduran	217,569	65%	45%	9%	86%	$11,629	26%
Nicaraguan	177,684	68%	63%	16%	85%	$14,194	18%
Salvadoran	655,165	64%	36%	6%	82%	$12,349	21%
all S. America	1,353,562	69%	76%	25%	80%	$17,645	16%
Puerto Rican	3,406,178	54%	63%	12%	1%	$13,518	25%
Range		36–76%	7–25%	42–86% (5)		$10,918– $20,451	16–26%
Total Asian	10,242,998	65%	80%	44%	68%	$21,823	12%
Cambodian	171,937	50%	47%	9%	68%	$10,366	30%
Chinese mainland	2,314,537	68%	76%	47%	70%	$23,642	13%
Taiwanese	118,048	68%	93%	67%	80%	$25,890	15%
Japanese	796,700	80%	91%	42%	39%	$30,075	9%
Korean	1,076,872	64%	86%	44%	77%	$18,805	14%
Hmong	169,428	32%	40%	7%	56%	$6,600	38%
Laotian	168,707	52%	50%	8%	68%	$11,830	18%
Vietnamese	1,122,528	62%	62%	19%	75%	$15,655	16%
Filipino	1,850,314	68%	87%	44%	68%	$21,267	6%
Pakistani	153,533	57%	82%	54%	77%	$18,096	17%
Indian	1,678,765	62%	87%	64%	74%	$27,514	9%
Range		40–93%	7–67%	39–80%		$6,600– $30,075	6–38%

(1) source: U.S. Census Bureau American FactFinder "Fact Sheet for a Race, Ethnic, or Ancestry Group" available at http:// factfinder.census.gov/servlet/SAFFFactsCharIteration?_submenuId=factsheet_2&_sse=on. Retrieved 4/15/08.
(2) From 2000 Census.
(3) individuals born in Puerto Rico are considered U.S.-born
(4) 1999 dollars
(5) excluding Puerto Ricans

Achievement Differences among ELL Groups

There are also achievement differences among the different ELL groups, although they are very difficult to disentangle from socioeconomic factors known to influence academic outcomes. Kennedy and Park (1994) reported that among students who indicated they spoke a language other than English at home, Asian Americans from East (e.g., China, Japan) and Southeast (e.g., Vietnam, Cambodia) Asia had higher reading scores than Mexican Americans in a nationally representative sample of eighth graders. Kao and Tienda (1995) found similar achievement differences between Asian and Latino youth, although they did not report results by home language use or students' language proficiency. Ima and Rumbaut (1989) found differences in reading achievement among different subgroups of ELL Asian students.

Explanations for such differences among language-minority groups are complex and largely elusive. As Schmid (2001) observed, "the relationship between socioeconomic class, cultural characteristics, social reception, and language proficiency has not been resolved" (p. 82). Schmid further noted research "has revealed that social class heavily influences the academic success" of this population of students (p. 82). Indeed, achievement differences are confounded with socioeconomic status and other dimensions of family life. For example, Kennedy and Park (1994) found that the Asian-origin students spent twice as much time on homework as the Mexican-origin students, which suggests one type of explanation for the achievement difference; but the two groups also differed in family socioeconomic status, which suggests another. Kennedy and Park could not distinguish between the two in their analysis.

Similarly, the relatively high scores among East Asians in Ima and Rumbaut (1989) are at least partly attributable to family socioeconomic status, in particular, parent education. The East Asian group "frequently includes children from 'brain drain' immigrant families (such as those headed by a Taiwanese engineer)" (p. 64). The high grade point averages of East Asian children and the "other immigrant" children in their study might reflect the selective migration pattern of families with highly educated parents. Even within the Southeast Asian group, there were differences: Vietnamese were the highest-achieving, followed by Khmer, Laotian, Chinese-Vietnamese, and finally Hmong. Once parent education, time in the United States, and age of student were taken into account, however, differences in reading achievement across the Southeast Asian subgroups disappeared. These findings reflect the population data reported in Table 28.1.

PAST AND PRESENT RESEARCH ON ELL READING

The history of the *Handbook on Reading Research* mirrors the increased reality and awareness of linguistic diversity in U.S. schools and its significance for literacy education. The first *Handbook*, published in 1984, contained no chapters dealing explicitly with reading in relation to diverse languages and cultures. The second (1991) had two, Heath's analysis of historical and cross-cultural aspects of feeling "literate" and Weber's essay on linguistic diversity and reading in the United States. The third edition of the *Handbook of Reading Research* (2000) had three—Bernhardt's assessment of scholarship on second-language reading, Au's multicultural perspective on policies to improve literacy achievement for cultural/linguistic groups traditionally underserved by U.S. schools, and García's chapter on bilingual children's reading.

In the larger arena of reading research, ELLs were essentially invisible until late in the 20th century, since *the* issue that attracted virtually all attention and enormous controversy was language of instruction, the so-called "bilingual education" debate. As García (2000) observed,

> A problem in locating research on bilingual reading is that the topic historically has been ignored in the second-language field and only recently addressed in the reading field.... researchers in the field of second-language acquisition historically had focused on oral language development, neglecting the study of [literacy] development. (p. 813)

García's observation is ironic, since our strongest findings regarding the achievement of ELLs are precisely about second language *reading* and not about second *language* development. (I discuss these in the next section.) But her larger point, that the study of literacy development among ELLs has been, until recently, relatively neglected, is valid. Research in this field has been traditionally dominated by the debate over bilingual education, that is, whether students who are not proficient in English should be instructed in only English or in their home language as well as in English. This complex and politically and ideologically charged debate, born of the 1960s Civil Rights movement and enmeshed in issues of identity, ethnicity, cultural self-determination, and more recently immigration, dominated the discourse in this area for many years, leaving little room for other issues (see, e.g., Carter, 1970; Carter & Segura, 1979; Crawford, 2004; Goldenberg, 1996).

This field has been evolving since the 1990s, with the pace greatly accelerated since 2000. We also now see much more research dealing with issues of improving literacy outcomes *regardless of language of instruction* (e.g., Calderón, Hertz-Lazarowitz, & Slavin, 1998; Carlo et al., 2004; De La Colina, Parker, Hasbrouck, & Lara-Alecio, 2001; Echevarría, 1995; Escamilla, 1994; Gersten & Jiménez, 1998; Goldenberg & Gallimore, 1991; Gunn, Smolkowski, Biglan, Black, & Blair, 2005; Swanson, Hodson, & Schommer-Aikins, 2005; Vaughn, Mathes, et al., 2006; Vaughn, Linan-Thompson, et al., 2006).

Concurrent with this upsurge of research, three major national reviews conducted by teams of researchers have appeared over the past decade: August and Hakuta (1997), August and Shanahan (2006), known as the "National Literacy Panel," and Genesee, Lindholm-Leary, Saunders, and Christian (2006). All three addressed language of instruction, but went well beyond it to include other factors likely to be at least as important for the school achievement of this population of students, especially curriculum and instruction. As an indication of the increased attention literacy instruction and achievement among ELLs are receiving, practical and helpful articles for teachers now appear regularly in *The Reading Teacher* (e.g., Helman, 2005; Helman & Burns, 2008; Kieffer & Lesaux, 2007), including an ELLs "Department" that appeared in the October, 2007 issue.

Educators concerned with the school success of these students thus have some cause for optimism. The research activity we are seeing could lead to important insights, if not outright breakthroughs, and produce widespread improvements in the literacy achievement of ELLs.

Oral Language and Reading

García's (2000) observation pointed out a tension that has long existed between concern for oral language development (how well ELLs can speak and understand English) and achievement in academic content (reading, writing, and other areas of the curriculum). This tension is understandable, since language skills are so important for success in most areas of the curriculum, particularly reading and anything that involves reading. The fundamental challenge faced by teachers of ELLs, particularly if students are learning to read in an all-English context, is promoting development in two distinct, but related and complex domains—oral language and reading. Discussion of oral language instruction and development per se is beyond the scope of this chapter (interested readers should consult Saunders & O'Brien, 2006, and Saunders & Goldenberg, in press). However, the relationship between oral language and learning to read raises several important questions that cannot be answered with confidence.

One is whether there is some threshold of oral language proficiency ELLs must attain before reading instruction is productive. On the one hand, it stands to reason that until students know some level of English, teaching even rudimentary reading skills in English does not make sense. Not surprisingly, there is a positive association between oral English proficiency and reading achievement in English (Geva, 2006; Saunders & O'Brien, 2006), suggesting that very low levels of oral English proficiency are associated with very low levels of English reading achievement.

On the other hand, however, the fact that oral language proficiency and reading achievement are correlated says nothing about whether students must know English at some level before starting to learn skills and concepts related to English reading. Even a student who speaks no English might be able to learn the sounds of the language, how to segment words into smaller units (e.g., phonemes), how to associate sounds with letters, and how letters/sounds combine to form words. If so, and if instruction is done well and combined with vocabulary teaching and other types of second language instruction, instruction in the "alphabetic principle"—the idea that letters stand for sounds and that sounds can be encoded in letters—could make a positive contribution both to literacy and to oral language development before learners reach any particular oral language threshold. Indeed, a number of studies reviewed below suggest that students who are not proficient in English can still learn critical reading skills and concepts in English *as they learn English*. I know of no direct evidence to corroborate this hypothesis; however, there is a growing consensus, based on studies such as those reviewed here, that ELLs can be taught early literacy skills such as phonological awareness and decoding—and perhaps even more advanced skills—before reaching some specified oral English proficiency level (e.g., Genesee et al., 2006; Gunn et al., 2005).

A second question has to do with expectations for the literacy development (particularly in the earliest stages of learning to read) of students who are limited in their English. Are these students capable of learning at levels and rates comparable to English speakers, assuming they are provided with effective teaching? At first look, the question is puzzling, since it might appear obvious that being limited in English proficiency will, at a minimum, make learning to read more challenging and slower in comparison to the rate of learning for English-proficient students. However, if we consider (a) the evidence described below that instruction in fundamental aspects of reading—phonological awareness, phonics, and decoding—can be just as effective with ELLs as with English speakers, coupled with (b) the growing consensus that reading instruction can proceed regardless of oral English proficiency, perhaps the suggestion that we can expect ELLs in the very early primary grades to make progress comparable to that of English speakers is not so unreasonable. A longitudinal study of Spanish-speaking ELLs by Manis, Lindsey, and Bailey (2004) found early English reading achievement (phonological skills, letter-word identification, passage comprehension) in grades K–2 to be around the 50th national percentile, far higher than might be predicted from the children's very low—3rd to 12th percentile—English oral language scores (memory for sentences and picture vocabulary).

In fact, a recent "Practice Guide" published by the U.S. Department of Education (Gersten et al., 2007) came to just such a conclusion: Assuming good instruction, we should expect early reading progress among ELLs to be comparable to that of non-ELLs. Based on studies of ELLs "who receive their instruction exclusively in the general education classroom alongside their native-English-speaking peers," Gersten et al. wrote,

> ... it is reasonable to expect that English learners can learn to read [in English] at rates similar to those of native speakers if they are provided with high-quality reading instruction. (p. 23)

There are, however, two issues readers should be aware of. The first is that we must distinguish between "rate of acquisition" of skills (phonological awareness, letter-sound mapping, and decoding) and "rate of reading," which requires integration of these skills to produce efficient, or fluent, reading. (My thanks to Sharon Vaughn for helping clarify this distinction.) Even if ELLs acquire discrete skills at the same rate as non-ELLs (the first meaning of "rate"), we do not know whether they can process the information as efficiently (the "rate of reading"). In fact, although teaching children who already speak English to become more fluent readers produces positive effects on reading development (National Reading Panel, 2000), to date the same has not been found among ELLs learning to read in English (Shanahan & Beck, 2006). One very informative study that compared ELLs and non-ELLs on reading rate was reported by Lesaux and Siegel (2003). They found that ELLs were actually more efficient word readers (had higher reading rates) than their non-ELL peers, as indicated by how many words and nonwords per minute they read from lists.

As informative as the Lesaux and Siegel (2003) study is, the problem is that it was conducted in Canada, where the ELL population is far different from that of the United States. This is a more general problem with the conclusion reached by Gersten et al. (2007). With one exception, the studies Gersten et al. cite to support their conclusion that we can expect ELLs to "learn to read at rates similar to those of native speakers" are with ELLs in Canada. (The exception is a study comparing native Dutch and immigrant Turkish children in the Netherlands who had been matched for socioeconomic status.) We must be cautious about how we interpret these studies for the U.S. context. Canada has highly restrictive immigration policies and a very different immigrant population overall. As a result, Canadian ELLs come from families with much higher income and education levels than the U.S. ELL population. The economic and educational chasms between the ELL and English-proficient populations in the United States do not exist in Canada. A recent Canadian newspaper article reported that higher achievement levels among Canadian immigrant children, as compared to immigrant children in other countries, are at least partly due to Canada's attracting "largely ... educated newcomers" (Mahoney, 2007; for more about Canadian immigration requirements see http://www.cic.gc.ca/english/immigrate/index.asp).

In the Lesaux and Siegel (2003) study cited above, for example, the ELL population comprised children from a wide range of language backgrounds—Mandarin, Cantonese, Korean, Spanish, Persian, Polish, and Farsi. There was a range of socioeconomic backgrounds, with no correlation between socioeconomic and ELL status. The ELL population was quite stable as well. Study attrition over 3 years due to changing schools was less than 5% total. Contrast this with typical ELL samples in the United States, where children move or change schools at rates of 5%, 10%, or more *per year* (e.g., Goldenberg, Gallimore, Reese, & Garnier, 2001; Lindsey, Manis, & Bailey, 2000; Manis et al., 2004). (Curiously, the non-ELL sample in Lesaux & Siegel had a very high attrition rate of nearly 25%.) Finally, the ELL sample in Lesaux & Siegel was probably not racially or linguistically isolated. The study included the entire kindergarten cohort in one Canadian district's 30 schools. Approximately 15% of these children were ELLs. Assuming they were roughly evenly distributed across the 30 schools, this represents far less concentration of language-minority students than is typical in the United States., where more than half of ELLs attend schools that have an ELL population greater than 30% and tend to be lower in socioeconomic status than schools with fewer ELLs (August & Shanahan, 2006). In short, the Canadian ELL population has a very different socio-demographic profile than the U.S. ELL population, so we should be very cautious when drawing conclusions from Canadian ELL studies and applying them to ELLs in the United States.

Comparing the Canadian and U.S. ELL experience does suggest an important insight that future research should pursue: Language limitations per se are not what explain achievement differentials between ELLs and English speakers; rather, the explanation resides in aspects of the social context, such as family economic and educational characteristics and the characteristics of the schools children attend. For the moment, however, we do not know with confidence whether and under what conditions typical ELLs in the United States can make progress in their reading development comparable to that of English speakers (Leafstedt, Richards, & Gerber, 2004).

KEY FINDINGS AND CURRENT TRENDS

The current state of our knowledge about how to improve the literacy attainment of ELLs is growing but remains fairly modest. Some findings have been consolidated, and promising lines of inquiry have opened up. What can we conclude that is most likely to be useful to educators and policy makers concerned about the futures of these students? I would draw three principal conclusions:[1] (a) Teaching students reading skills in their first language promotes higher levels of reading achievement *in English*; (b) what we know about good reading instruction for English speakers generally holds true for ELLs learning to read in English—to a point; and (c) when instructed in English, ELLs require additional instructional supports, primarily due to their limited English proficiency.

These three conclusions will frame this section of the chapter, which draws mostly on interventions and experimental studies testing the effects of various strategies, approaches, or programs on the literacy achievement of ELLs.

Teaching Students to Read in the First Language Promotes Higher Levels of Reading in English

We begin with the issue that has driven research—and a great deal of rhetoric and polemics—for most of the second half of the 20th century: Should ELLs be educated in English only or in some mix of English and the student's home language? Nearly three dozen experiments have been reported since the 1960s. These studies have compared the effects of reading instruction that uses students' home language (L1) and second language (L2) to reading instruction that immerses students in the L2 exclusively (which in the U.S. would, of course, be English). Five meta-analyses have been conducted on this topic (Francis, Lesaux, & August, 2006; Greene, 1997; Rolstad, Mahoney, & Glass, 2005; Slavin & Cheung, 2005; Willig, 1985). All reached the same conclusion: *Teaching students to read in the L1 promotes reading achievement in the L2 in comparison to teaching students to read in the L2 exclusively.* The meta-analyses also concluded, not surprisingly, that primary language instruction promotes higher levels of literacy in the primary language.

An important insight provided by Slavin and Cheung (2005) was that many of the studies that demonstrated positive effects of primary language reading instruction used an approach in which students learned to read in their primary language and in English simultaneously--that is, concurrently but at different times of the day. The typical bilingual model has traditionally been sequential, where students learn to read in their L1 then transition to English reading.

Five meta-analyses on the same issue, conducted by independent researchers with diverse perspectives, is highly unusual. That they all reached essentially the same conclusion on a highly controversial issue is extraordinary; in fact, it is unique. The finding that primary language instruction confers benefits for both L1 and L2 reading achievement might in fact be one of the strongest in the entire field of educational research. We should be deeply troubled by the fact that in some states, e.g., California and Arizona, primary language instruction is, with few exceptions, proscribed as a matter of public policy. We are in an era when "scientifically-based practice" has been the preferred slogan of policy makers and many educators, yet policies such as Arizona's and California's are anything but scientifically based.

What Explains the Effects of L1 Reading on L2 Reading?   Different explanations for these consistent findings are available. One is "transfer," that is, if a student learns something (e.g., how to decode or use text comprehension strategies) in one language, he or she will either already know it or can more easily learn it in a second. Another possible, subtly different, explanation is that learning to read in one language contributes to what Riches and Genesee (2006) called "a common underlying reservoir of literacy abilities," which then enables more proficient reading in the L2. Our knowledge of what exactly transfers to L2 when students learn to read in L1 (or vice versa) is imprecise. The basic research here is largely correlational, so it is nearly impossible to determine causal relations or distinguish "transfer" explanations from "underlying reservoir" explanations. (Interested readers are urged to consult Riches and Genesee (2006) and Part II, "Cross-linguistic relationships in Second-language Learners," in August and Shanahan, 2006.) While these and other fine points remain to be resolved, the experimental evidence shows quite clearly that at least at a global level, teaching reading in L1 promotes literacy development in L2.

However, teachers cannot assume that students will automatically use what they know in their L1 when learning to read in a new language. Students sometimes do not realize that knowledge or skills available in their L1 can be applied in their second (e.g., cognates such as *ejemplo* and *example*, decoding skills, reading comprehension strategies). Jiménez (1997) put it this way: "Less successful bilingual readers view their two languages as separate and unrelated, and they often see their non-English language backgrounds as detrimental" (p. 227). Mathes, Pollard-Durodola, Cárdenas-Hagan, Linan-Thompson, and Vaughn (2007) reported similar findings in their summary of four interventions with young struggling ELLs: "… at least with native Spanish speakers who are also struggling readers, transfer does not occur readily, and when it does, it is not sustained over time" (p. 269).

Another possible explanation for lack of transfer, in addition to Jiménez's suggestion that some students see no connection between reading their L1 and L2, is low language proficiency in the L2. That is, in order for knowledge about reading in L1 to transfer and be applied to reading in English, the reader must have sufficient language skills in English to support the transfer (Durgunoglu, 2002). In any case, an implication from these findings is that teachers should be aware of what students know and can do in their primary language so they can help them apply this knowledge and these skills to tasks in English. Knowledge and skills that students possess in L1 should be seen as resources students (and teachers) can draw on to promote knowledge and skills in L2. But students must also receive instruction and opportunities to learn English and academic skills in English. Without these opportunities, English skills will be insufficient to support transfer into English.

Magnitude of Effects on L2 Reading of Teaching Students to Read in L1.   The effects of L1 reading instruction on L2 reading achievement are modest, according to the five meta-analyses cited above. The average effect size of primary language reading instruction is around .35–.40, with estimates ranging from about .20 to about .60. What this means is that teaching students to read in their L1 can boost achievement in the L2 by a total of about 12-15 percentile points (in comparison to students instructed only in English) over 2 to 3 years, the typical length of time for children in the studies. These effects apply to elementary as well as secondary students (although there are far fewer secondary studies). To provide some perspective, the National Reading Panel (2000), which reviewed experimental research on English speakers only, found that the average effect size of phonics instruction is .44, a bit larger than the likely average effect size of primary language reading instruction (studies of phonics instruction are also over a shorter period of time). Primary language reading instruction is clearly no panacea, just as phonics instruction is no panacea. But relatively speaking, it makes a meaningful contribution to ELLs' reading achievement in English.

The meta-analyses also found, not surprisingly, that bilingual education helps ELLs become bilingual and biliterate, which many would consider a desirable outcome. Bilingualism and biliteracy confer numerous advantages—cultural, intellectual, cognitive (e.g., Bialystok, 2001), vocational, and economic (e.g., Saiz & Zoido, 2005). Readers should note, however, that the populations studied by Bialystok, Saiz and Zoido, and other scholars who documented the various advantages of bilingualism are different from the language minority populations that are the subject of this chapter. Their findings did not necessarily draw from individuals who are bilingual by virtue of being language minorities and who receive bilingual schooling as discussed here.

Unresolved Issues in Primary Language Instruction.   Many questions nonetheless remain about primary language reading instruction. For example: Is primary language instruction more beneficial for some learners than for others (e.g., those with weaker or stronger primary language skills; or weaker or stronger English skills)? Is primary language instruction more effective in some settings (e.g., schools in communities where more English is spoken) and with certain ELL populations (e.g., Spanish-speakers, Chinese-speakers, Khmer-speakers)? What should be the relative emphasis between promoting knowledge and skills in the primary language and developing English language proficiency? What level of skill in the students' primary language does the teacher need to possess in order to be effective? We presently cannot answer these questions with confidence, since we lack a body of studies that permit going beyond the general finding about the positive effects of primary language instruction on reading achievement in English.

We also cannot say with confidence whether there is an optimal period of time for students to receive instruction in their primary language. A key difference between two recent syntheses of the research on ELLs, Francis et al. (2006) and Lindholm-Leary (2006), was their conclusion regarding the relationship between length of time students receive primary language instruction and achievement. Lindholm-Leary concluded that more primary language instruction over more years leads to higher levels of ELL achievement in English. This conclusion was based largely on studies and evaluations of "two-way bilingual education," in which children from two language groups (e.g., Spanish and English) participate in a program designed to develop bilingualism and biliteracy in *both* groups. There are different two-way models, but they all involve some combination of L1 and L2 instruction throughout elementary school; some go through middle and high school.

Francis et al. (2006), in contrast, did not include these longer-term studies because they did not have adequate experimental controls. The studies Lindholm-Leary (2006) included did not assure that the achievement of children in contrasting programs (e.g., two-way bilingual and English immersion) was equivalent at the start of the study or that children in different programs had the same demographic characteristics (e.g., parental education and level of English use in the home). Francis et al. only included true experiments or very well-controlled quasi-experiments. All of these were relatively short term; consequently Francis et al. reached no conclusions about the impact of length of time in primary language instruction. Three of the other four meta-analyses—Greene (1997), Slavin and Cheung (2005), and Willig (1985)—were also unable to come to any conclusion about the impact of length of time in primary language instruction on English reading achievement because they also only included studies with the tightest experimental designs.

This already complex issue is complicated further by the question of what our goal is for these students. For promoting achievement only in English, 1 year in primary language instruction might (or might not) be any better than 3 years or 6 years. However, 6 years of primary language instruction might be much more effective than 1 year if the goal is primary language development in addition to English academic competence—that is, full bilingualism. Perhaps this should be our educational goal for ELLs and, for that matter, for all students (see Gándara & Rumberger, 2006).

What We Know About Good Reading Instruction in General Probably also Holds True for ELLs Learning to Read in English—to a Point.   Primary language instruction is not an option for most ELLs in the United States. This might be because of state policy (as in California, Massachusetts, and Arizona), district policy, lack of personnel qualified to provide instruction in students' L1, parental choice, or too many non-English languages to form a large enough primary language class. Whatever the reason, English instruction is what most U.S. students receive (Zehler et al., 2003). The research on instructing ELLs in English is not as solid as the research showing the benefits of primary language reading instruction. But the research we do have points to two important complementary conclusions (or hypotheses). The first one (discussed in this section) is that what we know about effective reading curriculum and instruction for students in general tends to be true for ELLs as well. The second (discussed in the following section) is that when instructed in English, ELLs require instructional modifications, or supports, primarily due to their limited proficiency in English.

In a comprehensive review of the instructional research, Shanahan and Beck (2006) concluded that ELLs learning to read in English, just as English speakers learning to read in English, benefit from explicit teaching of components of literacy. The National Literacy Panel (NLP) began with the components identified by the National Reading Panel (2000) as important for literacy development among English speakers—phonemic awareness, phonics, reading fluency, vocabulary, and reading comprehension—then used these as a framework to synthesize the research with ELLs. (The NLP also reviewed the research on writing instruction for ELLs, but I do not address this topic here.) Although there are undoubtedly other important components, such as background knowledge and motivation, the NLP concluded that what has been identified as important for English speakers' reading development is probably also important for ELLs. This conclusion represents a confirmation of what Fitzgerald (1995a, b) had concluded a decade before: Reading and learning to read in a L1 and L2 "are *substantively* the same... more alike than different" (Fitzgerald (1995a, p. 180). Fitzgerald found "a relatively good fit" between data on L2 readers and "the pre-existing native-language reading theories, models, and views" of reading among English-proficient students (pp. 180–181).

However, the NLP also found that the instructional benefits to ELLs were not the same for all components and not consistently comparable to the instructional benefits for English speakers. This too is consistent with Fitzgerald, who also found "evidence for the specialness of ESL readers' processes" (p. 181), suggesting that views of reading based on English-proficient students are inadequate by themselves to guide reading instruction and policy for ELLs. I will return to this topic in the subsection on "instructional supports" that follows.

I must add one caution before reviewing studies of instruction on reading components. There is a danger in analyzing reading and reading instruction in terms of discreet components such as decoding, vocabulary, fluency, comprehension, and so forth. Although considerable evidence suggests that instruction on these components makes a contribution to reading overall, educators must always remember that competent reading is an integrative and functional act, that is, it requires successfully combining (integrating) a number of skills for the purpose of accomplishing concrete goals (functions). It is certainly useful to think about specific reading components when planning and carrying out instruction; but educators should always be mindful that the payoff comes, ultimately, when they all come together to constitute skilled, informed, and motivated reading. (My thanks to Fred Genesee for reminding me of this crucial fact.)

Phonemic Awareness and Phonics.   The role phonological aspects of reading should play in reading instruction has of course been contentious for a very long time. But the evidence is clear that knowledge or awareness of the sounds of language, how they map to letters, and how letters and sounds combine to form words are essential for successful reading (Adams, 1990; National Reading Panel, 2000). These are by no means the only things teachers need to address as students learn to read; but they are extremely important. They are probably especially critical for children who, for cognitive or experiential reasons, do not grasp the "alphabetic principle" readily.

A number of studies have shown the benefits of instruction for the development of these key early literacy skills and understandings among ELLs. In fact, the effects of instruction on these foundational skills appear to be comparable for ELLs and English speakers (Shanahan & Beck, 2006). A study in England, for example, found that Jolly Phonics had a stronger effect (effect size .46) on ELLs' phonological awareness, alphabet knowledge, and their application to reading and writing than did a Big Books approach; effects were still significant a year later (Stuart, 1999). A study of Puerto Rican first graders found that oral phonemic segmentation training (either in English only or in Spanish then English), followed by instruction for transfer to letters, improved children's segmentation, decoding, and spelling skills; effect size was 2.82 (Larson, 1996, cited in Shanahan & Beck, 2006). An original and follow-up study by Gunn and colleagues (Gunn, Biglan, & Smolkowski, 2000; Gunn, Smolkowski, Biglan, & Black, 2002) showed that supplemental instruction with a phonological and decoding emphasis (including development of reading fluency; see below) produced significant positive effects (effect sizes .29–.38) on the letter- and word-level skills, oral reading fluency, vocabulary, and comprehension of ELLs either with poor achievement or aggressive behavior.

More recent studies continue to provide evidence of the benefits of directly teaching phonological and decoding skills to ELLs, particularly as part of comprehensive approaches to boost early literacy among children at risk for reading problems (e.g., Mathes et al., 2007; Vaughn, Mathes, et al., 2006). We also have evidence that phonological awareness training can help middle school poor ELL readers improve literacy skills (Swanson et al., 2005), although these findings should be interpreted cautiously due to possible non-equivalence between treatment and comparison students.

Oral Reading Fluency.   Reading fluently is not merely reading fast or turning the pages quickly. Reading fluently involves reading accurately, efficiently, and with comprehension, in other words, reading with appropriate speed so that what is being read actually makes sense. If readers cannot read fluently, comprehension is severely compromised. (See Samuels, 2007, for a recent statement on fluency.) While dozens of fluency studies have been conducted with English speakers, the NLP uncovered only two with ELLs. The results of these studies are generally consistent with the results of fluency research in general but are not as conclusive with respect to the role of fluency instruction in developing L2 reading proficiency. Denton (2000, cited in August & Shanahan, 2006), for example, found that fluency instruction for Spanish-speaking ELLs in grades 2–5 led to more rapid gains in oral reading fluency (including reading accuracy) but did not translate into improvement in comprehension. In another study, De La Colina et al. (2001) found that fluency instruction in Spanish for Spanish-English bilinguals led to improvements in oral reading fluency and in reading comprehension. The results were measured in Spanish reading, however; there was no test of impact on English reading.

Other studies have included fluency training as part of comprehensive early intervention programs for ELLs either at risk for reading difficulties or already demonstrating poor reading achievement (Gunn et al., 2005; Mathes et al., 2007). These studies have found effects for reading fluency and reading comprehension, as well as for a range of other outcomes. Because these are multi-component interventions, however, it is very difficult to identify the effects of any one instructional component on any specific reading outcome.

Vocabulary.   Vocabulary is, of course, very important for literacy development, since it is impossible to understand a text fully without understanding virtually all of the words. There is a long history of vocabulary research among English speakers, and the results are well established (Biemiller, 2004): Good vocabulary instruction has a strong effect on students' learning words, and it has a more modest, although still significant and meaningful, effect on reading comprehension. Studies of vocabulary instruction for ELLs, although far fewer, show the same thing: Students are more likely to learn words when they are directly taught, and in the case of students old enough to read, vocabulary instruction helps improve reading comprehension modestly. For English speakers and ELLs alike, word learning is enhanced when the words are taught explicitly, embedded in meaningful contexts, and students are provided with ample opportunities for their repetition and use.

A fifth-grade study (Carlo et al., 2004) showed the relative effectiveness of vocabulary instruction that provided explicit instruction of word meanings, used words from texts likely to interest the students, and provided exposure to and use of the words in numerous contexts, e.g., reading and hearing stories, discussions, posting target words, and writing words and definitions for homework. The experimental program showed an impact on both word learning and, more modestly, reading comprehension, although the article provided insufficient information to compute effects sizes (Shanahan & Beck, 2006). The elements of this program were comparable in many respects to vocabulary instruction that has been found to be effective for English speakers (e.g., Beck, McKeown, & Kucan, 2002). Spycher (2009) reported a small pilot kindergarten study involving two classrooms that also used an instructional model derived from Beck et al. (2002). Spycher found that explicit teaching of science vocabulary helped both ELLs and English speakers learn more words (receptive vocabulary) over the course of a 5-week intervention, in comparison to the control condition where there was only implicit teaching and exposure to the words. The instructional model included saying and repeating words chorally; providing "student-friendly definitions," followed by students' echoing the definition; further explanations and examples; and short-answer questions to promote understanding and use. It was unclear whether the intervention produced an effect on productive vocabulary; moreover, there was no measure of comprehension.

Positive effects of vocabulary instruction on broader reading measures were reported in a third-grade study with Mexican American students. Pérez (1981) found that daily oral instruction in word meanings (emphasizing compound words, synonyms, antonyms, and multiple meanings) led to improvement in oral reading and comprehension. Working with Spanish-speaking first graders, Vaughn-Shavuo (1990; cited in Shanahan & Beck, 2006) found that if students worked on words presented in meaningful narratives, dictated their own sentences using the words, and examined pictures that illustrated the words, they learned more than twice as many words as a group of children who were expected to learn words each presented in the context of a single sentence. Both the Pérez and the Vaughn-Shavuo studies produced very large effect sizes, greater than 1.0.

Based on these few studies, the key seems to be explicit teaching of vocabulary words using instruction that goes beyond the traditional practice of giving a definition and using it in a sentence. Students certainly need definitions and illustrative sentences, but they also need multiple exposures to words in different contexts and opportunities to use them in different ways, what might be characterized as "rich" or "thick" instruction. But even "thin" instruction might help. Collins (2005) showed that Portuguese-speaking kindergartners acquired more vocabulary from storybook reading when the teacher explained new vocabulary. Children with higher initial English scores learned more words, but explaining new words was helpful for all children, regardless of how much English they knew.

Reading Comprehension.   Comprehension is of course what reading is about. We read to comprehend; everything else is a means to this end. But even if everything else is in place—decoding skills, reading fluency, vocabulary—comprehension is not assured. There are at least two additional factors to consider: reading strategies and background knowledge (Pressley, 2000).

First, readers can improve their comprehension by using comprehension strategies. Research on comprehension among English speakers shows reading strategies such as asking questions while reading, making predictions, summarizing, and monitoring comprehension improve reading comprehension. The effect sizes of some of these are as high as 1.0 (National Reading Panel, 2000). In contrast, the National Literacy Panel found the effects of comprehension strategy instruction on ELLs were very weak, perhaps non-existent. The research base is also very limited. In contrast to over 200 studies identified by the National Reading Panel for English speakers, the NLP located only three published studies on reading comprehension strategies that explicitly included ELLs.

For example, Swicegood (1990; cited in Shanahan & Beck, 2006) trained third-grade ELLs to ask themselves questions as they read during their Spanish reading period. There were no effects on either Spanish or English reading. In a study by Shames (1998; cited in Shanahan & Beck, 2006), students receiving reading strategy instruction such as KWL (What I Know; Want to Know; What I Learned) outperformed other groups on a comprehension measure, but the differences were not significant statistically.

Saunders and Goldenberg (2007) reported the effects of "instructional conversations"—not strategy instruction, but rather an interactive discussion between teacher and a small group of students designed to promote comprehension. Students who participated in the instructional conversations demonstrated more sophisticated understanding of a key theme and story concept, compared to students who had received a "basal-type" lesson. On literal comprehension, Saunders and Goldenberg reported an interesting interaction: Among students rated by their teacher as high and medium in English reading and speaking, those in the instructional conversation condition showed higher literal comprehension (over 90% correct responses vs. over 70% for the control condition). Among students rated by the teacher as low in English reading and speaking, there was no difference in literal comprehension between the two conditions. The instructional conversation students actually scored lower than control students on literal comprehension, although the differences were not statistically reliable. If replicated, these results suggest that for lower achieving ELLs, the instructional conversation format might not provide as much support for literal comprehension as a traditional basal-type lesson that involves more recitation and questioning students about story contents.

In general, we lack a robust evidence base about the impact of strategy instruction on ELLs' comprehension. It seems highly likely that we can help ELLs improve their comprehension by teaching comprehension skills directly, although if done in English, the impact will probably depend on English proficiency level. There is no research with ELLs to corroborate this. A meta-analysis reported in Taylor, Stevens, and Asher (2006), however, shows that reading strategy training for L2 learners of all sorts—individuals learning any language, including English as a foreign or second language—is not effective with students in their first year of second-language learning and students in elementary grades, whereas reading strategy training is effective with older students and students with greater second-language experience.

The second factor related to comprehension is background knowledge. As with reading strategies, there is a great deal of research demonstrating the role of background knowledge in reading comprehension (American Educator, 2006; Hirsch, 2006; Pressley, 2000). But in contrast to the research on reading strategies, we have a more robust research base on the role of background knowledge in ELLs' reading comprehension specifically. This research is discussed below in "Instructional Supports in English."

"Complex" and Other Approaches.   In addition to studies that addressed specific literacy components, such as phonics and comprehension, there are studies that address several components simultaneously. The NLP (2000) called these "complex approaches to literacy." They include a wide range of programs and approaches and are such a diverse group it is nearly impossible to come to any general conclusion about "what works," other than the conclusion suggested by the NLP "that we can enhance the literacy development of English-language learners with better instruction" (p. 447). This might appear to be a fairly banal point, but it reinforces one of the principal themes of this chapter: What we know about effective instruction in general is also applicable when thinking about what constitutes effective instruction for ELLs.

The following is a sampling of these types of studies:

1. Success for All (Dianda & Flaherty, 1995), the most thoroughly researched whole-school reform model in the country, has demonstrated positive effects on various outcomes for ELLs, including Spanish reading and English word attack skills, although the effects have not been consistent from one study to the next.
2. A whole-school reform approach reported by Goldenberg (2004) showed a positive effect (compared to students in the rest of the district) on student writing and reading comprehension, in English and Spanish, in a heavily Latino ELL elementary school. This study's findings have been replicated, with stronger effects on ELL students' achievement, in a quasi-experimental study involving nine treatment and six comparison schools (Saunders, Goldenberg, & Gallimore, 2009).
3. In another comprehensive elementary-level study, Tharp (1982) reported positive effects of a year-long program to enhance the reading achievement of first-grade native Hawaiian Creole speakers. The program consisted of increased time on comprehension instruction and instruction accommodated to the children's interactional styles. The study used a strong random-assignment design and found modest effects on reading comprehension.
4. Encouraging students to read has produced different results depending on age and the language in which students are encouraged to read. On the one hand, encouraging reading in the L1 has not been found to affect English literacy skills with older students (Schon, Hopkins, & Davis, 1982); one study in fact found negative effects (Schon, Hopkins, & Vojir, 1985). However, with younger children (kindergarten and first grade) reading in the L1 with parents has produced positive effects on early literacy outcomes *in English* (Hancock, 2002; Roberts, 2008).
5. Encouraging reading in English after school hours has been found to produce positive effect on English reading achievement. Three studies, each with different ELL groups in different countries—Tudor and Hafiz (1989) with Pakistani ELLs in the U.K., Elley (1991) with Fijian speakers learning English (the school language), and Tsang (1996) with Cantonese students learning English in Hong Kong—found comparable results.
6. Tutoring and remediation studies reviewed by the NLP either did not report or did not find effects of remediation on English literacy skills. However, as described previously, more recent studies conducted by Gunn, Vaughn, Mathes, and others have found fairly strong effects, on both English and Spanish reading, of intensive small-group interventions for ELLs at risk for reading problems.

7. A cooperative learning study found positive effects on Spanish writing and English reading for early primary children (Calderón et al., 1998).
8. Saunders (1999) found that an enriched literacy curriculum (e.g., instructional conversations, assigned independent reading, literature logs, comprehension instruction) was associated with better English literacy achievement for ELLs who were transitioning from Spanish to English literacy instruction. However, pre-existing differences among students in the different groups make the results somewhat tenuous.
9. A study of middle school ELLs (Neuman & Koskinen, 1992) found that captioned TV helped students learn academic content more effectively than either (a) reading textbooks or (b) TV without captions. The effects were not general for all units, however, and pre-test differences noted might render the results questionable.

When Instructed in English, ELLs Require Additional Instructional Supports, Primarily Due to Their Limited Proficiency in English

As already discussed, a very important finding that emerged from the National Literacy Panel review was that for some of the components of literacy (most important, perhaps, reading comprehension) instructional impact seems to be weaker for ELLs than for English speakers. This is consistent with Fitzgerald's (1995a, b) conclusion that there are some differences between learning to read in a L1 and L2, even though they are "more alike than different" (see also Bernhardt, 2000, on L2 reading research). The differences Fitzgerald identified included: ELLs did reading tasks more slowly, used fewer metacognitive strategies, monitored comprehension more slowly, and preferred different text structures. The areas of difference Fitzgerald identified might help explain the NLP's findings that instruction targeted at reading comprehension had little or no impact on ELLs' reading (effects of fluency instruction on English reading development are unclear)—speed of processing information and completing tasks and subtasks are slower for students who lack proficiency in the language. Similarly, comprehension processes are more difficult since they rely on more advanced levels of language knowledge and language processing, particularly with respect to vocabulary, syntax, and text structures. Whatever the explanations, however, what seems evident is that ELLs learning to read in English probably need additional supports to make instruction more productive for them.

This is now a very active area, with many researchers and educators offering a wide range of recommendations (e.g., Echevarría, Vogt, & Short, 2008; Gersten & Baker, 2000; Hill & Flynn, 2006). The research basis for most of these, however, is thin. This section reviews briefly some of these recommended supports, broken out into two categories: instructional supports in the primary language and instructional supports in English. Additional information about these strategies can be found in Goldenberg (2008b).

Instructional Supports in the Primary Language.   Although most of the research on primary language use in the classroom has focused on primary language instruction—that is, teaching children academic skills and knowledge in their primary language—another way to use the primary language is for support. In this case, instruction is essentially in English; however, the teacher can use students' primary language strategically to help students gain additional benefit from otherwise all-English instruction. Examples of primary language support include:

1. Clarifications and explanations provided by the teacher, classroom aide, a peer, or a volunteer in the classroom.
2. "Preview-review" (Ovando, Collier, & Combs, 2003), where the teacher introduces new concepts in the primary language, teaches the lesson in English, then afterward reviews the

new content, again in the primary language. A study by Ulanoff and Pucci (1999) provided modest support for the effectiveness of this approach.

3. Pointing out similarities and differences between L1 and English. Examples include teaching symbol-sound similarities and differences between English and other languages that use the Roman alphabet; and pointing out true cognates (e.g., geography and *geografía*) and false cognates (embarrassed and *embarasada*). We do not know the effect of cognate instruction per se (Carlo, August, Fajet, Alfano, Massey, 2006).

4. Teaching reading strategies in the primary language, then having students apply them in English. Fung, Wilkinson, and Moore (2003) found that introducing reciprocal teaching strategies (Palincsar & Brown, 1984) in students' primary language improved reading comprehension in the L2. In contrast, Klingner and Vaughn (1996) did not provide any primary language instruction support and did not find an effect from training special education ELL students on reciprocal teaching. Populations in the Fung et al. (2003) and Klinger and Vaugh (1996) studies were considerably different, so we must be cautious of inferences based on comparisons between the two.

Instructional Supports in English.   A number of supports have been suggested that make use only of English. All have as their goal making lesson content more understandable to ELLs. These include: (a) graphic organizers (tables, charts, semantic maps), (b) redundant key information presented visually, (c) identifying, highlighting, and clarifying difficult words and passages, (d) the teacher, other students, and ELLs themselves summarize and paraphrase, (e) providing extra practice to build automaticity and fluency, (f) highly engaging extended interactions with teacher and peers, (g) adjusting instruction and speech (vocabulary, rate, sentence complexity, (h) targeting both content and English language objectives in every lesson, (i) use of familiar content and linking new learning to student background and experience, and (j) predictable and consistent classroom management routines.

The most common term for this group of strategies is "sheltered instruction." By far the most popular model of this type is the Sheltered Instruction Observation Protocol, or SIOP (Echevarría et al., 2008). The SIOP model has made clear and explicit a large number of instructional adjustments, such as those listed above, and integrated them into a coherent design for planning, delivering, and assessing instruction. To date, only one published study has examined the effects of the SIOP on student learning. These were very modest. Echevarría, Short, and Powers (2006) found a slight improvement in the quality of writing produced by middle-school ELLs whose teachers had received the SIOP training, compared with students of similar backgrounds (students were mostly low-SES; more than 50% Spanish-speaking but from numerous other language and ethnic backgrounds). There have been no reported effects of SIOP training on student reading outcomes.

None of the instructional supports listed above appear to be specific to ELLs (except for possibly including an English language objective in each lesson, although even here many learners might benefit from this). That is, the list above comprises "generic" scaffolds and supports, generally regarded as effective strategies for many students, particularly those who need more learning support than is typically provided in school. Although we have little direct evidence that these supports promote the literacy development of ELLs per se—as opposed to being part of good instruction in general—there are several suggestive studies.

Roberts and Neal (2004) found that pictures helped Spanish-speaking preschoolers with low levels of oral English learn story vocabulary (e.g., dentist, mouse, cap). This finding will surprise no one, but it gains in importance when considered alongside the Collins (2005) study, reported earlier. Collins found that preschool ELLs benefit from informative explanations, just as English speakers do. But Collins also found that children who began with lower English scores learned less than children with higher English scores. That is, knowing less English made it harder to learn additional English words. The Roberts and Neal findings with children who had low language levels suggest that *visual representation* of concepts, not just language-based *explanations*, provided these children with additional support in learning the vocabulary words.

In Carlo et al.'s (2004) fifth-grade vocabulary and reading comprehension study, researchers began with an approach based on principles of vocabulary instruction found to be effective for children who speak English (as discussed above). Carlo et al. included additional elements: activities such as charades that got learners actively involved in manipulating and analyzing word meanings; writing and spelling the words numerous times; and selection of texts and topics on immigration that were expected to resonate with the Mexican and Dominican immigrant students. (The program also included primary language supports such as previewing lessons using Spanish texts, providing teachers with translation equivalents of the target words, and using English-Spanish cognates, such as supermarket and *supermercado*.) Overall, the experimental program produced relatively strong effects on students' learning target vocabulary and smaller, but still significant, effects on reading comprehension. Particularly noteworthy is that the effects of the program were equivalent for ELLs and English-speaking students. Thus, although we cannot determine which (if any) of the extra ELL supports explain the program's impact on these students, Carlo et al.'s demonstration—that with additional supports English instruction can have a similar impact on both ELLs and English speakers—is very important.

The Vaughn, Mathes, et al.'s (2006) interventions discussed previously also suggest that additional instructional supports help ELLs. The foundation for the interventions derived from research with English speakers—phonological training, phonics, decoding, fluency in word recognition and reading connected text, vocabulary, and text comprehension. The researchers then added an oral language component (to promote English oral language development) and a set of what they called "ESL techniques"—clear and repetitive language, repetitive routines, gestures, and high levels of student-teacher interaction. They also included "language support activities" to make sure students understood key vocabulary used in instructions and in connected texts students read. Since the entire intervention was offered as a package, it is impossible to separate out the effects of any component or group of components. The only way to do this would be to compare the results of intervention models with and without the "ESL techniques." It seems entirely reasonable that the ELL supports helped make the intervention successful. However, studies by Gunn and colleagues (Gunn et al., 2000, 2002, 2005) apparently did not include any ELL-specific supports (the interventions were *Reading Mastery* and *Corrective Reading*; no ELL supports were reported), and these studies also showed that supplemental instruction with an emphasis on phonological knowledge, decoding, and fluency improved the reading skills of at-risk ELLs in early elementary school.

Another type of support was suggested by the National Literacy Panel review (Goldenberg, Rueda, & August, 2006)—literacy materials that are meaningful for students and connect with their backgrounds and experiences. Several ethnographic and experimental studies showed the benefits of building on students' knowledge and backgrounds. For example, in two participant observation studies, Kenner (1999, 2000) examined the biliteracy development of an ELL Gujarati (from northwest India) child who attended a London multilingual/multicultural preschool. Parents and children in the preschool were invited to bring literacy materials from home in the L1. These materials were placed in a "home corner" and a "writing area." Parents and children were invited to write in the classroom in different languages and genres—cards, letters to relatives, posters, and travel brochures. Kenner (1999) illustrated connections children made between their home experiences and classroom literacy activities in both English and the L1. In a successor study, Kenner (2000) showed the likely adverse impact on the focal child's bilingual/ biliterate development when she entered an all-English primary school where these types of connections were no longer encouraged by the teacher.

Several studies have also shown that familiar content in reading materials promotes comprehension. This is an important area since, as previously discussed, ELLs are likely to need additional supports in reading comprehension. For example, Abu-Rabia (1996) found that reading comprehension was higher when 15- to 16-year-old Druze (Arab) students (for whom Hebrew was a L2) read a story with Arabic content versus Jewish content; the Druze students also rated stories with Arab content higher in interest value. Both stories were presented in Hebrew and were equal in length and academic difficulty.

There are two important qualifications to these findings relating content familiarity and comprehension. First, ELLs' proficiency in the language of the text influences comprehension much more than their familiarity with passage content (Abu-Rabia, 1996; Lasisi, Falodun, & Onyehalu, 1988); in other words, language proficiency is a more potent factor than content familiarity in influencing reading comprehension. Second, "familiar" does not necessarily mean "culturally familiar." It simply means that students have learned about or have had direct experiences with the content or materials being used. Garcia (1991), for example, found that Hispanic children did as well as or better than non-Hispanic children on a reading comprehension test when the Hispanic children had at least as much background knowledge about the passage content as did the non-Hispanic children. Garcia found two such passages: one about *piñatas* and one about polar bears. The important point is that reading about unfamiliar content (regardless of why it is unfamiliar) in a language that is also unfamiliar will interfere with comprehension. Providing instructional supports by accommodating to ELLs' different experiential bases is likely to be helpful to these students.

This relationship between content familiarity and text comprehension is not unique to any one group, of course. It has long been known that we all are more comfortable with and comprehend familiar material more readily. But given the formidable language challenges ELLs face, teachers should be aware of how they can help students experience additional success by providing familiar reading matter and building on students' backgrounds and experiences.

IMPLICATIONS FOR PRACTICE, POLICY, THEORY, AND RESEARCH

There are many issues in the education of ELLs where there is insufficient research to guide policy and practice. We can, however, lay claim to some things that matter. Chief among these is that (a) teaching children to read in their primary language promotes reading achievement in English; (b) in many important respects what works generally for teaching children to read also works for ELLs; and (c) when ELLs are instructed in English they will probably need additional instructional supports, primarily because of their language limitations.

Framework for Policy and Practice

Our current state of knowledge points to the following instructional framework for promoting high levels of literacy among ELLs:

1. Education policy should be aimed at making primary language instruction feasible for all ELLs. This is admittedly a tall order, since significantly expanding the pool of teachers who can provide instruction in childrens' L1s is not trivial. Moreover, there are some situations, e.g., schools where many languages are spoken among the students, where primary lan-

guage instruction is probably not feasible. But this is nonetheless a worthwhile goal, given that primary language reading instruction develops L1 skills, thereby promoting bilingualism and biliteracy, and promotes reading in English. Primary language instruction can be carried out as children are also learning to read (and learning other academic content) in English, so it need not delay instruction in English academic language skills.

2. Although it is not clear whether more years of primary language instruction promotes greater achievement in English, longer term instruction in the primary language will probably help maintain and develop the primary language, without sacrificing academic development in English.

3. Students should be taught to transfer what they know in their L1 to learning to read in English; teachers should not assume that transfer is automatic.

4. ELLs can learn literacy skills in English even before reaching some threshold of English oral language proficiency. Instruction must be well structured, explicit, and systematic.

5. In general, ELLs probably benefit from instruction in the same components of English literacy as do English speakers. However, because ELLs who are learning to read in English must simultaneously learn literacy skills in English and English oral language skills, instructional supports will almost certainly be necessary. There are many possible supports that teachers can provide, although we lack a robust research base that identifies which, or which types are most productive.

6. These supports will probably be necessary for several years until students are sufficiently proficient in English to permit successful participation in mainstream instruction; more complex learning might require more accommodations or for a longer period.

7. ELLs who exhibit signs of early reading difficulties (e.g., poor phonological awareness, lack of automaticity in letter-sound associations) should receive intensive interventions. The interventions should ideally be in a small-group setting and focus on phonological awareness, phonics, and fluent letter- and word-recognition. An oral English development component would probably also be helpful.

8. It is unclear to what extent limited English proficiency limits or slows down progress in learning to read. It is probably less of an issue in the beginning stages of reading, when the language demands are relatively modest ("learning to read") and much more of an issue as reading begins to require more advanced language skills and is increasingly used to learn new content ("reading to learn"). In any case, educators should strive to help ELLs achieve at levels that are as comparable as possible to the achievement of English speakers.

Although beyond the scope of this chapter, readers should realize that ELLs need intensive and comprehensive oral English language development (ELD), particularly in "academic English." This refers to vocabulary, syntax, genres, and discourse that are essential for academic success, that is, more formal, abstract, and demanding forms of the language (Scarcella, 2003). A growing body of studies has been finding effective ways to teach language skills such as vocabulary (e.g., Carlo et al., 2004; Spycher, 2009) and discrete language functions (Norris & Ortega, 2006). However, we have very little data on what type of English language development instruction accelerates ELLs' progress, or even whether progress can be accelerated (Saunders & O'Brien, 2006; Saunders & Goldenberg, in press).

In addition, ELLs also need academic content Although ELD is crucial, it should not completely supplant instruction designed to promote content knowledge.[2] Content knowledge is essential for reading comprehension (and general academic success) beyond the beginning stages of reading development. Poor vocabulary and inadequate background knowledge create significant obstacles for all students (see, e.g., *American Educator*, 2006; Hirsch, 2006).

Theoretical and Research Considerations

A key set of issues researchers must address has to do with the similarities and differences among students learning to read in their (a) L1 when it is the dominant language of the society (i.e., English speakers learning to read in English); (b) L1 when it is a minority language of the society (i.e., ELLs learning to read in their L1); and (c) L2 when it is the dominant language of the society (i.e., ELLs learning to read in English).

By far the majority of the research we have addresses the first scenario—speakers of the majority language learning to read in that language. Are models of reading derived from this research adequate to understand the second and third scenarios, which is the situation for ELLs? Perhaps not entirely, but they are a very good starting point. We must then take into consideration: (a) knowledge and skills in students' L1 that can contribute to reading in the L1 and L2s, and (b) limitations in L2 knowledge and skills that can interfere with reading in the L2.

A fully elaborated model of reading development among ELLs would also take into account: (a) relationships among language and literacy development in the L1 and L2; (b) how (and whether) L1 and L2 factors play different roles at different points in literacy development and for different components of literacy; and (c) school, family, and community influences on language and literacy at different points in their development.

From a practical standpoint, the most important questions are what teachers can do to help ELLs take advantage of knowledge and skills in the L1 while helping them overcome challenges introduced by limitations in English. In other words, we need research on what can be done instructionally to (a) facilitate transfer from the L1 to English and (b) provide instructional supports for ELLs learning to read in English. At the moment, we have a number of worthwhile and potentially productive ideas, but relatively little research to support explicit guidance on these two crucial instructional issues. Some of the best research that has appeared over the past 5 years has developed and validated intensive early reading interventions for young ELLs at risk for reading difficulty. We must also turn our attention to what the regular classroom teacher can do to promote higher levels of literacy attainment among these children throughout the developmental span. As with reading research in general, by far the greatest attention has been paid to the elementary grades, with attention (and research) dropping off sharply at the secondary level.

Additional research is obviously needed. But we also need to put into practice the results of research we have, such as findings about the contribution of primary language reading instruction to L2 reading achievement and the likely need for instructional supports when ELLs are learning to read in English. Policies that block use of the primary language and limit instructional accommodations for ELLs—such as those in California, Arizona, and Massachusetts—are simply not based on the best evidence available. These policies can create additional obstacles for students and teachers, which is unconscionable under any circumstance, but especially egregious in light of the intense accountability pressures these students and teachers face. There are useful starting points for renewed efforts to improve the achievement of ELLs. We must base policy and practice on the best evidence we have while pushing forward on what we have yet to understand.

ACKNOWLEDGMENTS FOR AUTHOR NOTE

My thanks to Nonie Lesaux for a thorough and critical reading of an earlier draft of this chapter. Thanks as well to Jana Echevarría, Fred Genesee, Sharon Vaughn, Tim Shanahan, Diane August, and Elizabeth Moje for their helpful comments. All errors of fact and interpretation are of course my own.

NOTES

1. See Goldenberg (2008a, b) for additional discussion, including more on practical applications.
2. ELLs in Arizona are to spend 4 hours per day learning exclusively English (Kossan, 2007). This virtually guarantees they will not receive instruction to promote academic content knowledge, which is no less necessary than English proficiency for school success.

REFERENCES

Abu-Rabia, S. (1996). Druze minority students learning Hebrew in Israel: The relationship of attitudes, cultural background, and interest of material to reading comprehension in a second language. *Journal of Multilingual and Multicultural Development, 17*, 415–426.

Adams, M. (1990). *Beginning to read: Thinking and learning about print.* Cambridge, MA: MIT Press.

American Educator (2006, Spring). *Background knowledge* [Entire issue]. Retrieved from http://www.aft. org/pubs-reports/american_educator/issues/spring06/index.htm

August, D., & Hakuta, K. (Eds.). (1997). *Improving schooling for language-minority children: A research agenda.* Washington, DC: National Academy Press.

August, D., & Shanahan, T. (Eds.). (2006). *Developing literacy in second-language learners: Report of the National Literacy Panel on Language-Minority Children and Youth.* Mahwah, NJ: Erlbaum.

Beck, I., McKeown, M., & Kucan, L. (2002). *Bringing words to life: Robust vocabulary instruction.* New York: Guilford.

Bernhardt, E. (2000). Second-language reading as a case study of reading scholarship in the 20th century. In M. Kamil, P. Mosenthal, D. Pearson, & R. Barr (Eds.), *Handbook of reading research* (Vol. 3, pp. 791–811). Mahwah, NJ: Erlbaum.

Bialystok, E. (2001). *Bilingualism in development: Language, literacy, & cognition.* New York: Cambridge University Press.

Biemiller, A. (2004). Teaching vocabulary in the primary grades. In J. F. Baumann & E. J. Kame'enui (Eds.), *Vocabulary instruction: Research to practice* (pp. 28–40). New York: Guilford.

Calderón, M., Hertz-Lazarowitz, R., & Slavin, R. (1998). Effects of bilingual cooperative integrated reading and composition on students making the transition from Spanish to English reading. *Elementary School Journal, 99*, 153–165.

California Department of Education California STAR Program. (n.d.). Retrieved from http://star.cde. ca.gov/star2006

Capps, R., Fix, M., Murray, J., Passel, J. S., & Herwantoro, S. (2005). *The new demography of America's schools: Immigration and the No Child Left Behind act.* Washington, DC: The Urban Institute.

Carlo, M., August, D., Fajet, W., Alfano, A., Massey, S. (2006, April 10). *Is cognate awareness instruction effective in promoting English vocabulary development among third- and fifth-grade Spanish-speaking ELLs?* Paper presented at the annual meeting of the American Educational Research Association, San Francisco, CA.

Carlo, M. S., August, D., McLaughlin, B., Snow, C. E., Dressler, C., Lippman, et al. (2004). Closing the gap: Addressing the vocabulary needs of English language learners in bilingual and mainstream classrooms. *Reading Research Quarterly, 39*, 188–215.

Carter, T. (1970). *Mexican Americans in school: A history of educational neglect.* New York: College Entrance Examination Board.

Carter, T., & Segura, R. (1979). *Mexican Americans in school: A decade of change.* New York: College Entrance Examination Board.

Collins, M. (2005). ESL preschoolers' English vocabulary acquisition from storybook reading. *Reading Research Quarterly, 40*, 406–408.

Crawford, J. (2004). *Educating English Learners: Language diversity in the classroom* (5th ed.). Los Angeles: Bilingual Education Services.

De La Colina, M., Parker, R., Hasbrouck, J., & Lara-Alecio, R. (2001). Intensive intervention in reading fluency for at-risk beginning Spanish readers. *Bilingual Research Journal, 25*, 503–538.

Denton, C.A. (2000). The efficacy of two English reading interventions in a bilingual education program. Unpublished doctoral dissertation, Texas A&M University.

Dianda, M. R., & Flaherty, J. F. (1995). *Report on workstation uses: Effects of Success for All on the reading achievement of first graders in California bilingual programs.* (No. 91002006). Los Alamitos, CA: Southwest Regional Laboratory. (ERIC Document Reproduction Service No. ED394327).

Durgunoglu, A. (2002). Cross-linguistic transfer in literacy development and implications for language learners. *Annals of Dyslexia, 52,* 189–204.

Echevarria, J. (1995). Interactive reading instruction: A comparison of proximal and distal effects of instructional conversations. *Exceptional Children, 61,* 536–552.

Echevarría, J., Short, D., & Powers, K. (2006). School reform and standards-based education: A model for English-language learners. *The Journal of Educational Research, 99,* 195–210.

Echevarría, J., Vogt, M., & Short, D. (2008). *Making content comprehensible for English learners: The SIOP model* (3rd ed.). Boston: Pearson.

Elley, W. B. (1991). Acquiring literacy in a second language: The effect of book-based programs. *Language Learning, 41,* 375–411.

Escamilla, K. (1994). Descubriendo la lectura: An early intervention literacy program in Spanish. *Literacy, Teaching and Learning, 1,* 57–70.

Fitzgerald, J. (1995a). English-as-a-second-language learners' cognitive reading processes: A review of research in the United States. *Review of Educational Research, 65,* 145–190.

Fitzgerald, J. (1995b). English-as-a-second-language reading instruction in the United States: A research review. *Journal of Reading Behavior, 27,* 115–152.

Francis, D., Lesaux, N., & August, D. (2006). Language of instruction. In D. August & T. Shanahan (Eds.), *Developing literacy in second-language learners: Report of the National Literacy Panel on Language-minority Children and Youth* (pp. 365–413). Mahwah, NJ: Erlbaum.

Fung, I., Wilkinson, I., & Moore, D. (2003). L1-assisted reciprocal teaching to improve ESL students' comprehension of English expository text. *Learning and Instruction, 13,* 1–31.

Gándara, P., & Rumberger, R. (2006). *Resource needs for California's English Learners.* Santa Barbara, CA: UC Linguistic Minority Research Institute. Retrieved from http://www.lmri.ucsb.edu/publications/jointpubs.php

Garcia, G. (1991). Factors influencing the English reading test performance of Spanish-speaking Hispanic children. *Reading Research Quarterly, 26,* 371–392.

García, G. (2000). Bilingual children's reading. In M. Kamil, P. Mosenthal, D. Pearson, & R. Barr (Eds.). *Handbook of reading research* (Vol. 3, pp. 813–834). Mahwah, NJ: Erlbaum.

Genesee, F., Lindholm-Leary, K., Saunders, W., & Christian, D. (2006). *Educating English Language Learners.* New York: Cambridge University Press.

Gersten, R., & Baker, S. (2000). What we know about effective instructional practices for English-language learners. *Exceptional Children, 66,* 454–470.

Gersten, R., Baker, S. K., Shanahan, T., Linan-Thompson, S., Collins, P., & Scarcella, R. (2007). *Effective literacy and English language instruction for English Learners in the elementary grades: A practice guide* (NCEE 2007-4011). Washington, DC: National Center for Education Evaluation and Regional Assistance, Institute of Education Sciences, U.S. Department of Education. Retrieved from http://ies.ed.gov/ncee

Gersten, R., & Jiménez, R. (Eds.). (1998). *Promoting learning for culturally and linguistically diverse students: Classroom applications from contemporary research.* Belmont, CA: Wadsworth.

Geva, E. (2006). Second-language oral proficiency and second-language literacy. In D. August & T. Shanahan (Eds.), *Developing literacy in second-language learners: Report of the National Literacy Panel on Language-minority Children and Youth* (pp. 123–139). Mahwah, NJ: Erlbaum.

Goldenberg, C. (1996). Latin American immigration and U.S. schools [Entire issue]. *Social Policy Reports* (Society for Research in Child Development), *10*(1).

Goldenberg, C. (2004). *Successful school change: Creating settings to improve teaching and learning.* New York: Teachers College.

Goldenberg, C. (2008a). Improving achievement for English Language Learners. In S. Neuman (Ed.), *Educating the other America: Top experts tackle poverty, literacy, and achievement in our schools* (pp. 139–162). Baltimore, MD: Brookes.

Goldenberg, C. (2008b). Teaching English Language Learners: What the research does—and does not—say. *American Educator, 32*(2), 8–23, 42–44.

Goldenberg, C., & Gallimore, R. (1991). Local knowledge, research knowledge, and educational change: A case study of first-grade Spanish reading improvement. *Educational Researcher, 20*(8), 2–14.

Goldenberg, C., Gallimore, R., Reese, L., & Garnier, H. (2001). Cause or effect? A longitudinal study of immigrant Latino parents' aspirations and expectations and their children's school performance. *American Educational Research Association Journal, 38*, 547–582.

Goldenberg, C., Rueda, R., & August, D. (2006). In D. August & T. Shanahan (Eds.), *Developing literacy in second-language learners: Report of the National Literacy Panel on language-minority children and youth* (pp. 269–318). Mahwah, NJ: Erlbaum.

Greene, J. (1997). A meta-analysis of the Rossell and Baker review of bilingual education research. *Bilingual Research Journal, 21*, 103–122.

Gunn, B., Biglan, A., & Smolkowski, K. (2000). The efficacy of supplemental instruction in decoding skills for Hispanic and non-Hispanic students in early elementary school. *The Journal of Special Education, 34*, 90–103.

Gunn, B., Smolkowski, K., Biglan, A., & Black, C. (2002). Supplemental instruction in decoding skills for Hispanic and non-Hispanic students in early elementary school: A follow-up. *The Journal of Special Education, 36*, 69–79.

Gunn, B., Smolkowski, K., Biglan, A., Black, C., & Blair, J. (2005). Fostering the development of reading skill through supplemental instruction: Results for Hispanic and non-Hispanic students. *The Journal of Special Education, 39*, 66–85.

Hancock, D. R. (2002). The effects of native language books on the pre-literacy skill development of language minority kindergartners. *Journal of Research in Childhood Education, 17*, 62–68.

Helman, L. (2005). Using literacy assessment results to improve teaching for English-language learners. *The Reading Teacher, 58*, 668–677.

Helman, L., & Burns, M. (2008). What does oral language have to do with it? Helping young English-language learners acquire a sight word vocabulary. *The Reading Teacher, 62*, 14–19.

Hill, J., & Flynn, K. (2006). *Classroom instruction that works with English language learners*. Alexandria, VA: ASCD.

Hirsch, E. (2006). *The knowledge deficit*. Boston: Houghton Mifflin.

Ima, K., & Rumbaut, R. G. (1989). Southeast Asian refugees in American schools: A comparison of fluent-English-proficient and limited-English-proficient students. *Topics in Language Disorders, 9*, 54–75.

Jiménez, R. (1997). The strategic reading abilities and potential of five low-literacy Latina/o readers in middle school. *Reading Research Quarterly, 32*, 224–243.

Kao, G., & Tienda, M. (1995). Optimism and achievement: The educational performance of immigrant youth. *Social Science Quarterly, 76*, 1–19.

Kennedy, E., & Park, H.-S. (1994). Home language as a predictor of academic achievement: A comparative study of Mexican- and Asian-American youth. *Journal of Research and Development in Education, 27*, 188–194.

Kenner, C. (1999). Children's understandings of text in a multilingual nursery. *Language and Education, 13*, 1–16.

Kenner, C. (2000). Biliteracy in a monolingual school system? English and Gujarati in South London. *Language Culture and Curriculum, 13*(1), 13–30.

Kieffer, M., & Lesaux, N. (2007). Breaking down words to build meaning: Morphology, vocabulary, and reading comprehension in the urban classroom. *The Reading Teacher, 61*, 134–144.

Klingner, J., & Vaughn, S. (1996). Reciprocal teaching of reading comprehension strategies for students with learning disabilities who use English as a second language. *Elementary School Journal, 96*, 275–293.

Kossan, P. (2007, July 14). New learners must spend 4 hours a day on English. *The Arizona Republic*. Retrieved from http://www.azcentral.com/arizonarepublic/news/articles/0714english0714.html

Larsen, L. (2004). *The foreign-born population in the United States: 2003*. Current Population Reports, P20-551, U.S. Census Bureau, Washington, D.C.

Lasisi, M. J., Falodun, S., & Onyehalu, A. S. (1988). The comprehension of first- and second-language prose. *Journal of Research in Reading, 11*, 26–35.

Leafstedt, J., Richards, C., & Gerber, M. (2004). Effectiveness of explicit phonological-awareness instruction for at-risk English learners. *Learning Disabilities Research & Practice, 19*, 252–261.

Lesaux, N., & Siegel, L. (2003). The development of reading in children who speak English as a second language. *Developmental Psychology, 39*, 1005–1019.

Lindholm-Leary, K. (2006). Academic achievement. In F. Genesee, K. Lindholm-Leary, W. Saunders, & D. Christian (Eds), *Educating English language learners* (pp. 176–222). New York: Cambridge University Press.

Lindsey, K., Manis, F., & Bailey, C. (2000). Prediction of first-grade reading in Spanish-speaking English-language learners. *Journal of Educational Psychology, 95*, 482–494.

Mahoney, J. (2007, Sept. 18). Canadian immigrant students outpace counterparts elsewhere. *The Globe and Mail.* Retrieved September 21, 2007, from http://www.globeandmail.com

Manis, F., Lindsey, K., & Bailey, C. (2004). Development of reading in grades K–2 in Spanish-speaking English-Language Learners. *Learning Disabilities Research & Practice, 19*, 214–224.

Mathes, P., Pollard-Durodola, S., Cárdenas-Hagan, E., Linan-Thompson, S., & Vaughn, S. (2007). Teaching struggling readers who are native Spanish speakers: What do we know? *Language, Speech, & Hearing Services in Schools, 38*, 260–271.

National Center for Education Statistics. (n.d.). The nation's report card.   Retrieved from http://www. nces.ed.gov/nationsreportcard

National Clearinghouse for English Language Acquisition frequently asked questions. (n.d.). Retrieved from http://www.ncela.gwu.edu/faqs

National Reading Panel. (2000). *Report of the National Reading Panel—Teaching children to read: An evidence-based assessment of the scientific research literature on reading and its implications for reading instruction* (Report of the subgroups). Washington, DC: National Institute of Child Health and Human Development. Retrieved from http://www.nichd.nih.gov/research/supported/nrp.cfm

Neuman, S. B., & Koskinen, P. (1992). Captioned television as comprehensible input: Effects of incidental word learning from context for language minority students. *Reading Research Quarterly, 27*, 94–106.

Norris, J., & Ortega, L. (Eds.) (2006). *Synthesizing research on language learning and teaching.* Philadelphia: John Benjamins.

Ovando, C., Collier, V., & Combs, M.C. (2003). *Bilingual and ESL classrooms: Teaching in multicultural contexts* (3rd ed.). Boston: McGraw Hill.

Palincsar, A., & Brown, A. (1984). Reciprocal teaching of comprehension-fostering and comprehension monitoring activities. *Cognition and Instruction, 1*, 117–175.

Pérez, E. (1981). Oral language competence improves reading skills of Mexican American third graders. *The Reading Teacher, 35*, 24–27.

Pressley, M. (2000). What should comprehension instruction be the instruction of? In M. Kamil, P. Mosenthal, D. Pearson, R. Barr. (Eds.), *Handbook of reading research* (Vol. 3, pp. 545–561). Mahwah, NJ: Erlbaum.

Riches, C., & Genesee, F. (2006). Literacy: Crosslinguistic and crossmodal issues. In F. Genesee, K. Lindholm-Leary, W. Saunders, & D. Christian (Eds.), *Educating English language learners* (pp. 64–108). New York: Cambridge University Press.

Roberts, T. (2008). Home storybook reading in primary or second language with preschool chldren: Evidence of equal effectiveness for second-language vocabulary acquisition. *Reading Research Quarterly, 43*, 103–130.

Roberts, T., & Neal, H. (2004). Relationships among preschool English language learners' oral proficiency in English, instructional experience and literacy development. *Contemporary Educational Psychology, 29*, 283–311.

Rolstad, K. Mahoney, K., & Glass, G. (2005). The big picture: A meta-analysis of program effectiveness research on English Language Learners. *Educational Policy, 19*, 572–594.

Saiz, A., & Zoido, E. (2005). Listening to what the world says: Bilingualism and earnings in the United States. *Review of Economics and Statistics, 87*, 523–538.

Samuels, J. (2007). The DIBELS test: Is speed of barking at print what we mean by reading fluency? *Reading Research Quarterly, 42*, 563–566.

Saunders, W. (1999). Improving literacy achievement for English learners in transitional bilingual programs. *Educational Research and Evaluation, 5*, 345–381.

Saunders, W., & Goldenberg, C. (2007). The effects of an instructional conversation on English Language Learners' concepts of friendship and story comprehension. In R. Horowitz (Ed.), *Talking texts: How speech and writing interact in school learning* (pp. 221–252). Mahwah, NJ: Erlbaum.

Saunders, W., & Goldenberg, C. (in press). Research to guide English Language Development instruction. In D. Dolson & L. Burnham-Massey (Eds.), *Improving education for English learners: Research-based approaches.* Sacramento, CA: CDE Press.

Saunders, W., Goldenberg, C., & Gallimore, R. (2009). Increasing achievement by focusing grade level teams on improving classroom learning: A prospective, quasi-experimental study of Title I schools. *American Educational Research Journal, 46,* 1033–1066

Saunders, W., & O'Brien, G. (2006). Oral language. In F. Genesee, K. Lindholm-Leary, W. Saunders, & D. Christian (Eds), *Educating English language learners* (pp. 14–63). New York: Cambridge University Press.

Scarcella, R. (2003). *Academic English: A conceptual framework* (Technical report 2003-1). Santa Barbara, CA: Linguistic Minority Research Institute. Retrieved from http://lmri.ucsb.edu

Schmid, C. (2001). *Sociology of Education, 74,* 71–87 [Extra Issue: Current of Thought: Sociology of Education at the Dawn of the 21st Century].

Schon, I., Hopkins, K. D., & Davis, W. A. (1982). The effects of books in Spanish and free reading time on Hispanic students' reading abilities and attitudes. *NABE: The Journal for the National Association for Bilingual Education, 7,* 13–20.

Schon, I., Hopkins, K. D., & Vojir, C. (1985). The effects of special reading time in Spanish on the reading abilities and attitudes of Hispanic junior high school students. *Journal of Psycholinguistic Research, 14,* 57–65.

Shanahan, T., & Beck, I. (2006). Effective literacy teaching for English-language learners. In D. August & T. Shanahan (Eds.), *Developing literacy in second-language learners: Report of the National Literacy Panel on language-minority children and youth* (pp. 415–488). Mahwah, NJ: Erlbaum.

Slavin, R., & Cheung, A. (2005). A synthesis of research on language of reading instruction for English Language Learners. *Review of Educational Research, 75,* 247–281.

Spycher, P. (2009). Learning academic language through science in two linguistically diverse kindergarten classes. *The Elementary School Journal, 109,* 360–379.

Stuart, M. (1999). Getting ready for reading: Early phoneme awareness and phonics teaching improves reading and spelling in inner-city second language learners. *British Journal of Educational Psychology, 69,* 587–605.

Swanson, T., Hodson, B., & Schommer-Aikins, M. (2005). An examination of phonological awarenes treatment outcomes for seventh-grade poor readers from a bilingual community. *Language, Speech, and Hearing Service in Schools, 36,* 336–345.

Taylor, A., Stevens, J., & Asher, J. (2006). The effects of Explicit Reading Strategy Training on L2 reading comprehension. In J. Norris & L. Ortega (Eds.). *Synthesizing research on language learning and teaching* (pp. 213–244). Philadelphia: John Benjamins.

Tharp, R. (1982). The effective instruction of comprehension: Results and description of the Kamehameha Early Education Program. *Reading Research Quarterly, 17,* 503–527.

Tsang, W. (1996). Comparing the effects of reading and writing on writing performance. *Applied Linguistics, 17,* 210–233.

Tseng, V., & Lesaux, N. (2009). Immigrant students. In T. Good (Ed.), *21st century education: A reference handbook* (Vol. 2, 105–113), Thousand Oaks, CA: Sage.

Tudor, I., & Hafiz, F. (1989). Extensive reading as a means of input to L2 learning. *Journal of Research in Reading, 12,* 164–178.

Ulanoff, S., & Pucci, S. (1999). Learning words from books: The effects of read-aloud on second language vocabulary acquistion. *Bilingual Research Journal, 23,* 409–422.

Vaughn, S., Linan-Thompson, S., Mathes, P., Cirino, P., Carlson, C., Pollard-Durdola, S., et al. (2006). Effectiveness of Spanish intervention for first-grade English language learners at risk for reading difficulties. *Journal of Learning Disabilities, 39,* 56–73.

Vaughn, S., Mathes, P., Linan-Thompson, S., Cirino, P., Carlson, C., Pollard-Durdola, S., et al. (2006). Effectiveness of an English intervention for first-grade English language learners at risk for reading problems. *The Elementary School Journal, 107,* 154–180.

Willig, A. (1985). A meta-analysis of selected studies on the effectiveness of bilingual education. *Review of Educational Research, 55,* 269–317.

Zehler, A. M., Fleischman, H. L., Hopstock, P. J., Stephenson, T. G., Pendzick, M. L., & Sapru, S. (2003). *Descriptive study of services to LEP students and LEP students with disabilities. Volume I: Research Report.* Arlington VA: Development Associates, Inc.

29 Literacy Out of School

A Review of Research on Programs and Practices

David E. Kirkland and Glynda A. Hull
New York University

INTRODUCTION: THE VALUE OF RESEARCH ON THE MARGINS

Formal schooling has long been considered the primary institution for educating youth, fostering their economic mobility, and inculcating societal values. The teaching of reading and writing—and the skills, knowledge, technologies, dispositions, and identities associated with these and other language arts—are likewise usually assumed to belong to the conventional school day and its arrangement and division of subject matters, timings, and architectures.

Our goal in this review is to explore research on educational institutions, programs, and practices that by most accounts occupy the margins of school-based space and time (cf. Hull & Greeno, 2006). That is, we traverse the historical and contemporary landscape of afterschool and non-school-based organizations and clubs and more loosely collected groupings, gatherings, and affiliations. Our review reveals that such out-of-school spaces can contribute substantively to learning, literacy practices, and the accumulation of literacy experience and expertise, including reading. Out-of-school programs and organizations, we will illustrate, sometimes complement, sometimes extend, and sometimes diverge from understandings of and ways of participating around texts typically promoted through formal educational systems and curricula during the traditional school day. Further, and even more important, this review suggests that for some youth, families, and communities, an eclectic collection of afterschool and out-of-school organizational spaces—a book club, a vacation bible school, a spoken word workshop, a digital storytelling center, a library, a social networking site—can become primary places for literate participation and action (Flower, 2008), agency, and identity-work (e.g., Hull & Katz, 2006; Pleasants, 2008), both long- and short-term. We argue as well that such sites comprise an increasingly important locus for research.

In some ways, such claims should not come as a surprise. After all, in a variety of fields and disciplines, and for several decades running, researchers have observed that children and adults regularly and successfully engage out of school with tasks comparable to the in-school requirements against which they sometimes resist and with which they sometimes struggle or to meet (Hull & Schultz, 2001; Lave, 1988; Saxe, 1990). In a recent study within this tradition, Goldman (2006) followed families ethnographically to document their mathematical understandings and practices out of school. These families were highly skeptical that the researchers would find any mathematical activity of note in their daily lives, but find it the researchers did, and in abundance: figuring percentages, calculating sums, making categories, rounding estimations. The researchers also noted, and with much concern, the disconnect between mathematics in life and mathematics in school.

So it has been for literacy research. Over approximately the last 15 years, there has been an outpouring of research on literacy in out-of-school settings (e.g., Hull & Schultz, 2002), and especially of late, around young people's creation and consumption of new media and popular cultural texts (e.g., Kirkland, 2007). The rub for the field has been, and remains, in understanding how, and sometimes whether, to attempt to connect these practices to school. Our review of out-of-school literacy programs stems from such interests and concerns. Specifically, we have sought to understand:

1. How is literacy learning structured out of school?
2. What programs and practices are in place to help maintain these structures?
3. How might these structures, programs, and practices provide opportunities for literacy researchers to better understand the relationship between literacy in and out of school and improve the literacy development of diverse groups of children, youth, and adults?

This review builds from a growing body of scholarship that has examined out-of-school literacy as a way to understand literate processes such as reading and writing more holistically and thereby, perhaps, more comprehensively and accurately. A concern for representing the landscape of literacy programmatics—that is, the official and unofficial arrangements in which literacy events are learned and practiced—has been key to this research. We have sought here also to illustrate how such programmatics, particularly of out-of-school literacy programs, reveal motivating and sometimes hidden purposes for literacy. Thus, we theorize as to how such purposes might get reshaped out of school depending on whose interests they are designed to serve. There is a potential freshness, then, in looking closely at literacy out of school, which derives from understanding the purposes for which out-of-school literacy programs operate (Luke, 1997).

To get a sense of such purposes, we searched library and web-based archives, scanning historical documents, foundational and recent research studies, which described literacy outside of school contexts. Through our review, we found over 230 studies, predominantly qualitative, that offered detailed accounts of out-of-school literacy worlds. We also examined approximately 30 selected programs in some depth to explore how out-of-school in contexts throughout the United States might look. Lastly, we did not confine our search to the U.S. and ventured where the research led, including several other countries.

LITERACY ACTIVITIES IN THE EVERYDAY LIVES OF YOUTH AND ADULTS IN NON-FORMAL LEARNING ENVIRONMENTS

Even early in the research, some 30 and 40 years ago, we found path-clearing studies that deliberately took as their centerpiece the literacy and language activities that youth and adults engage in as part of their everyday lives and non-formal learning environments. Street's (1984) pivotal examination of Qur'anic-influenced or "maktab" literacy in the commercial venues of small farmers in post-revolution Iran, and his resulting durable formulation of "ideological" versus "autonomous" literacy, remind us forevermore that the schooled versions of literacy are not the only kind, and that literacy depends for its implications on social institutions and conditions. Notable as well is Scribner and Cole's (1981) magnum opus exploring the triliterate, trilingual, triscripted West African Vai, who acquired certain literacies only out of school. Scribner and Cole's careful definition of literacy as multiple practices consisting of differing and distinctive configurations of skills, knowledge, and technology has proved especially significant to the field.

Heath (1983), in one of the most field-altering studies of literacy, demonstrated how language patterns, including ways of writing and reading and the textual ecologies of communities, varied with social class and had serious implications for many children whose "reading habitus" (Sterponi, 2007) differed from the valuations and uses of texts found in the mostly middle-class and white institution of school. And Cook-Gumperz (1986) novelly argued that in 18th-century England, not only did reading instruction take place primarily out of school in religious settings, but also literacy instruction, when taken to school, had as its impetus the control of reading practices rather than their promotion and expansion. Each of these landmark studies, often cited in previous editions of this handbook, offered importantly divergent commentaries on the commonplace assumption that schooling is the predominant sponsor of literacy.

If the extent of literacy out of school, in all of its variety of meaning-making practices, symbol systems, participant structures, and sponsorships, should not come as a surprise to most students of literacy theory, the current emphasis in the United States upon afterschool and extra-school programs and systems is likely to startle most. As documented by the National Center for Educational Statistics (Parsad, Lewis, & Tice, 2009), approximately half of all U.S. public elementary schools now have afterschool programs located on site—some 25,000 of them. Many programs in U.S. elementary, middle, and high schools are now supported by federal pass-through funds via 21st Century Community Learning Centers, authorized under Title X, Part I, of the Elementary and Secondary Education Act. President Obama has pledged to double this funding to serve a million more children (The Promise Audit, n.d.).

Even as many literacy theorists and out-of-school researchers centered their interest on non-formal settings, the trend in publicly funded afterschool programs has increasingly been to extend the formal school day. Suddenly, it seems, the landscape of education has shifted, as participation in some kind of post-school-day program, especially for academic assistance but also for "enrichment," becomes the norm. This trend, we should note, appears transnational. Smith (2006) has documented the rise of corporatization of formal and informal schooling in England, for example, paralleling to a large extent developments in the United States. In Hertz-Lazarowitz's (1999) study of cooperative learning in Israel's Jewish and Arab schools, out-of-school programs simultaneously served the functions of maintaining common community cultures and helping individuals keep pace or catch up in a changing world. Out-of-school literacy programs such as the "faith-based" efforts that Hertz-Lazarowitz described are situated locally but also serve global interests. There are increasing references as well to extra-school programs in so-called "developing" and "transforming" societies, where they sometimes serve as alternatives to rather than extensions of the school day (cf. Sahni, in press). In such cases, national governments and international organizations such as UNESCO often endorse particular local literacy programs to promote national identity and extend opportunities to individuals lacking access to reading and writing skills, particularly when these skills are thought to coincide with civic development (Tagoe, 2008).

In the United States, the public funding of afterschool programs has been accompanied by a sudden growth in a range of ancillary services and organizations. There are clearinghouses that supply resources for programs, centers that promote, encourage, and disseminate research on non-school time, and non-profits that provide services and advocate for funding and recognition of the role that organized afterschool programs play. These include the National Institute on Out-of-School Time (http://www.niost.org/), the After School Corporation (http://www.tascorp.org/), the Center for After-School Excellence (http://www.afterschoolexcellence.org/), and the Afterschool Alliance (http://www.afterschoolalliance.org/). Federally sponsored programs tend to serve schools in poor neighborhoods and the youth who attend them, whereas wealthier parents favor privately operated tutorial programs and exam preparation centers, for which there is now a huge market, even as they supply elaborate technological resources and opportunities to learn inside the home.

There are important questions to consider in the variety of scenarios where literacy is occasioned or sponsored out of school. How can researchers further understand and explore the anatomy of literacy out of school, particularly when the purposes of out-of-school literacy programs have often shifted away from or, alternately, mapped squarely onto larger school-based aims? How might literacy activities in the everyday lives of youth and adults in non-formal learning environments find utility in formal venues, such as schools? To address these questions, we describe a wide range of research on out-of-school literacy. For analytical purposes, we have organized the research using three categories—community-based literacy, afterschool literacy programs, and extra-school literacy programs—indicative of the alternative spacings, timings, and structures of out-of-school literacy activities and efforts.

Community-Based Literacy Programs

As the literature on community-based, afterschool, and extra-school programs continuously suggests, shifts from the goals of schooling sometimes carry important consequences for the communities and cultures of youth and their families. Peck, Flower, and Higgins's (1995) research on "community literacy" demonstrated this point. They described how communities offer opportunities for intercultural communication, social action, and activism for their members. Tensions between community literacy and school literacy, Peck et al. found, thus get catalyzed in various programs that occupy the "liminal" space between centers and margins (cf. Bakhtin, 1981; Kirkland & Jackson, 2009; Lave & Wenger, 1991).

When accommodating centralizing pressures—such as the force behind standardized reading assessments—some communities have created their own sorts of programs to enhance access to successful reading performance as measured by standardized reading assessments (Cushman, 2002; Heath, 1983; Lave & Wenger, 1991). By contrast, when resisting centralizing pressures, some communities have created programs to protect and sustain community culture or simply to provide educational opportunities that schools have not been designed to promote (Au & Jordon, 1981; Auerbach, 1992; Carter, 2007; Jocson, 2006; Morrell, 2003).

Still, many community-based literacy programs have lived with the kinds of tension that Grabill (2001), for instance, grappled with in his research, where the goals of out-of-school literacy programs face threats of co-optation by more dominant interests. Similar kinds of co-optation may have been at play also in Kelly's (1992) study of a group of Hmong elementary school students who performed better in word recognition after receiving primary language instruction. As the students grew older and greater emphasis was placed on English readiness and reading comprehension, and as community scaffolds diminished, Kelly found no differences between the performance of second and fourth graders. There could be many explanations for this other than a co-opting of literate practices. For example, the comprehension instruction could have been insufficient. A fair bit of literature on early reading programs shows gains to about third grade, with scores hitting a plateau beyond third. Most research suggests that this is probably due to the nature of instruction being inadequate to the task of reading comprehension at more "advanced" levels and in content-area domains. Whatever the case, Kelly's study highlighted an important link and perhaps tension between literacy learning in school and cultural identity outside it.

Kendrick and Hissani's research (2007) provided what we see as another example of such links and tensions between literacy learning and cultural identity. They examined the decisions of 15 women in rural Uganda who participated in an adult literacy program in order to become independent letter readers and found that the community's desire to produce readers and writers among its members provided the raison d'etre for this particular community literacy program. Three overlapping issues constituted this desire: problems associated with the loss of privacy that comes with not being able to read private letters; dependence on others to read personal letters; and potential marital strife arising from being unable to understand letter content. Kendrick and Hissani thus illustrated a common tension in community-based literacy programs: Many serve multiple and sometimes competing needs—here, the need to promote reading readiness coupled with the need to maintain cultural identity. In the community that Kendrick and Hissani observed, reading readiness for women sometimes conflicted with women's traditional gender roles. However, ironically, Kendrick and Hissani suggest that being able to read had also become an important aspect in the changing identities of rural Ugandan women.

The research on out-of-school literacy programs also illuminates themes of connecting and belonging, where reading is essential but not always the central goal. In less formal ways, some families have sponsored their own literacy events to promote family cohesion. In such cases, families play a key role in structuring, sanctioning, and supporting community literacy practice. For example, in her study of Al-Anon family groups, Bharij (2001) described Alcoholics Anonymous meetings as literacy events in which community literacy practices, such as reading role-play scenarios and writing commitment forms, are used in therapy and for mutual support.

Lee and Hawkins (2008) detailed how community-based afterschool programs served low-income Hmong immigrant youth who draw on knowledge of Hmong culture, history, and family structure and mainstream American culture to connect to children and adolescents in ways that schools do not. Although these centers—where family and ethic communities act as epicenters—appear less successful in providing youth with literacy-rich activities that promote school success, collaborative school- and community-based afterschool literacy programs may have been able to bridge the academic and cultural barriers that marginalize some youth, particularly low-income immigrant youth (Lee & Hawkins, 2008).

This should come as no surprise. In ethnic communities there has long been a tradition of community sponsorship of literacy. African American communities are a case in point. McHenry (2002) showed how literary societies formed during the last century in middle-class African American communities to encourage literacy through the collective discussion of texts. These societies allowed African Americans to develop a public voice; their literary activities were fundamentally political, connected to questions of citizenship, participation in American democracy, and resistance to oppression. Regardless of their intent, the societies encouraged African Americans to become readers and producers of texts, training "individuals to claim the authority of language and effectively use it to participate in reasoned and civil public debate" (McHenry, 2002, p. 102). Carter (2007), who studied the African American Read-In program sponsored by the National Council of Teachers of English, described groups of African Americans coming together to read excerpts from literary works by African American authors. Her description of the African American Read-in program is reminiscent of McHenry's work; both descriptions acknowledge the countless contributions of African American authors, and both programs provide communities a deeper sense of their literate legacies and the means by which cultural literacies are preserved.

In recent years, researchers have also shown how communities' literacy programs have extended cultural literacies. Fisher (2004), for example, examined the significance of the inextricable connection between past and present cultural literacy activities in African American communities. Building on the work of Heath and McHenry (Heath, 1983; McHenry, 2002; McHenry & Heath, 1994), Fisher found that community literacy activities such as spoken word poetry events and writing collectives contribute to an historical continuum. Carter (2007) and Fisher (2004), examining the preservation and extension of cultural literacies, illustrated how culturally- and community-based literacy programs have goals not associated with the typical school day. Much of this research has begun to highlight themes of change and social transformation, where out-of-school literacy programs can be seen to privilege literacies crucial for participating in community and cultural life.

Grabill's (2001) research also illustrated themes of change and social transformation. Examining the policies and practices of the district community literacy program, Grabill focused on the following issues: (a) identifying disciplinary gaps and institutional power; (b) locating the meaning and value of literacy; (c) designing community literacy programs as vehicles for helping people gain access to resources, knowledge, literacies, and institutions; (d) exploring the concepts of community and community literacy; and (e) discovering tactics for making educational institutions more relevant and responsive to learners. He concluded that institutions affecting community literacy programs can be redesigned in a participatory fashion that both empowers the programs' users and improves the institutions attempting to meet the users' needs.

In this instance, it might be helpful to consider the critical complexities of community-based youth literacy practice. Mahiri and Sablo's (1996) examination of the out-of-school literacy practices of urban youth suggested that youth bring their communities to their literacy events. That is, aspects of the motivations, functions, genres, and themes of the students' voluntary writing illustrated the knowledge they brought to this writing. In particular, the voluntary, outside-school writings of a 15-year-old high school female and a 17-year-old high school male revealed that the students' voluntary prose and verse helped them to make sense of their lives and social environments, provided them with a partial sanctuary from the grim realities of everyday life, and gave them a sense of personal status and satisfaction.

In both the Grabill and the Mahiri and Sablo studies, geographic features of communities-based literacy were viewed as at least as important as cultural features. That is, both rural and urban contexts carried their own weight in shaping and supporting the literacy needs of their members. In his most recent work, Mahiri (2004) extended this understanding by showing how many community-based literacy programs serve as in-between sites that link home and school. Their ability to close distances, to bring together home and school, Mahiri found, is valued by community members. Still, a growing body of studies documents the vast distances that continue to exist between home and school for many youth. To be successful in life, these young people must navigate distances and perform culture crossings rarely explained in or supported by schools (Pastor, 2008; Rosenthal & Feldman, 1996; Yi, 2007). The procession from home to school requires them to find their own way through channels of difference and sometimes treacherous social and cultural climates.

At times, however, these cultural distances take a backseat to larger social ones. In this vein, Noll and Watkins (2003) discussed the literacy experiences of homeless students who took part in a project designed to stabilize and enrich their educational environment. These homeless children exploited the realities of their daily lives outside school to develop understandings of what they read. Similarly, in a case study of American Indian adolescents' literacy attitudes, performance, and construction of meaning in home, community, and school, Noll (1998) found that community literacy provided participants with an outlet to explore their senses of identity and examine critical issues related to prejudice, discrimination, and racism.

Afterschool Literacy Programs

In the wake of the vast swell of publicly sponsored afterschool programs in the United States, debates and tensions have likewise arisen. These often center on whether such programs should serve the purpose of extending schooling, thereby offering more of what has been offered in the normal school day, or their aims and activities should be broader, more eclectic, and/or more youth-centered, not more of the same, but something different and perhaps better (Noam, Biancarosa, & Dechausay, 2003).

There is the related worry that afterschool is fast becoming "tracked," with poorer kids the recipients of test preparation and remediation after school, while their more economically advantaged counterparts enjoy debate, music, and the arts. Sometimes there are attempts at a rapprochement, as in Hill's (2007) descriptions of enrichment-type, youth-development-oriented afterschool programs. Hill studied these programs with support from the Bowne Foundation, which has led the afterschool field with grants to teachers and researchers to support scholarship and also provides publication opportunities through its After School Matters series. Although most of the programs described in Hill's collection drew importantly on a "youth development" approach (cf. Eidman-Aadahl, 2002; Eccles & Gootman, 2002) and represented a range of enrichment opportunities—from comic book writing and fashion modeling to forensics contests and science experiments out-of-doors—they calibrated their curricula to academic standards as well.

Walking such a middle ground, or representing one's program in ways that capture this balance, is no doubt seen as more and more attractive and necessary, as funding for afterschool efforts is increasingly tied to demonstrating a positive effect on academic achievement as determined by evaluation research, itself linked to comparisons of standardized test score data as specified by No Child Left Behind regulations. In fact, the vast majority of research done on afterschool programming consists of evaluation studies. There has been controversy over the impact of afterschool programs, with a few studies claiming no effect or negative ones, as well as debate over the validity of the research itself (cf. U.S. Department of Education, 2003; Mahoney, Larson, Eccles, & Lord, 2005). One large-scale analysis called into question achievement effects (James-Burdumy et al., 2005) and another (Lauer et al., 2006) documented achievement gains only in homework help programs. In the main, however, studies have repeatedly shown academic and social gains for youth who regularly attend afterschool compared to those who do not, in some cases including improvement in measures of reading. (cf. Durlak & Weissberg, 2007; Shernoff & Vandell, 2008).

As one might imagine, much of the research on these programs, including evaluation studies as noted earlier, tends to affirm a shared finding—that afterschool literacy programs of almost any kind retread notions of literacy. For example, the Los Angeles BEST After School Enrichment Program was designed to "provide a safe haven for children, ages 5 to 12" (LA's BEST After School Enrichment Program, n.d.). It operates out of 180 elementary school sites each day during the critical hours after school reportedly at no cost to parents. Programs such as LA's BEST extend the goal of teaching reading into a larger goal of providing a safe place for students after school. It was established in 1988 in partnership among the City of Los Angeles, the Los Angeles Unified School District, and the private sector. At the end of each school day, LA's BEST provides students with homework assistance, a cognitively based enrichment activity (i.e., science club, math club, literacy activity), a fun recreational activity of their choosing (i.e., dance, sports, art, cooking), and a nutritious snack.

It also uses the commercial curriculum "KidzLit," a "research-based" literacy program developed by the Developmental Studies Center[1] specifically for use in afterschool programs. Unlike many afterschool literacy programs, the curriculum is aligned with NCTE standards. A sample K–3 package on LA's BEST's Web site is made up of eight 10-book sets on a variety of themes. A sample lesson plan on "Amos and Boris" by William Steig emphasizes word recognition and how to be a good friend—a peculiar goal for reading. Research conducted by the Developmental Studies Center, the company that developed the LA's BEST curriculum, to demonstrate the program's effectiveness, reported "significant progress" in various measures of reading proficiency.

Hartry, Fitzgerald, and Porter (2008) explained that schools and districts often view an extended school day as a promising way to address the literacy needs of their lowest-performing students by devoting more time to reading instruction. Harris (2008) suggests that such "afterschool" programs serve the necessity of youth "information literacy" development. Yet, implementing a structured reading program in an afterschool setting is not always easy and does not always lead to improved reading proficiency. Although structured reading programs may help teachers use afterschool instructional time more effectively, the research of Hartry et al. and Harris suggests that the degree to which the programs improve student outcomes depends on the effectiveness of their implementation. For example, Hartry et al. focused on program implementation in one district as part of a randomized controlled trial. The researchers found that successful implementation of a structured reading program in an afterschool setting depended on thoughtful preparation, suitable resources, and ongoing attention. However, youth engagement, attendance, and performance remained perennial and key issues—more so even than implementation—for afterschool literacy program success (Foley & Eddins, 2001).

Like LA's BEST, the 100 Book Challenge is an afterschool program to stimulate independent reading among students. Its entire system is organized and delivered to schools directly from the American Reading Company and includes all books, materials, software tools, and professional development. 100 Book Challenge is currently used in more than 600 schools in 95 districts of 24 states and the District of Columbia. More than 100,000 students nationwide participate in the program. At all times, students can self-select books they want to read. The book leveling system uses a phonics, vocabulary, and comprehension infrastructure, catalogued on "skills cards" to support student, teacher and parent learning. For afterschool programs, 100 Book Challenge recommends its Research Labs, six-week, hour-a-day programs that combine reading, writing, discussion, and research, culminating in a final project: a student-authored-and-illustrated book. Although programs such as Research Labs have gained national attention, these programs seem to target proficient or at least interested readers, whereas students who are not motivated by traditional pathways into literacy go unserved.

In recent years, new afterschool literacy programs have been created with underserved populations in mind. Zierk (2000) described a program, Sports PLUS After School, which combined sports and literature to help improve students' reading, writing, and comprehension skills. The program sought to promote links between children's personal development and self-esteem, and to forge links between sports, literature, and daily life. Other programs have used socially relevant material such as comic books (Bitz, 2004; Cowan, 1999; Jacobs, 2007) or digital media and popular cultural materials (e.g., Hull & Katz, 2006) to engage youth.

Cole and colleagues (Cole, 1996; Gutiérrez, 2008; Vasquez, 2003) have for a number of years created networks of afterschool programs that link community organizations with universities and offer alternative learning spaces informed by cultural historical activity theory. These programs emphasize play as well as learning. Still other programs respond to factors such as boredom caused by the intense formalizing of literacy learning in school (Alvermann, Young, Green, & Wisenbaker, 1999; Schwarz & Stolow, 2006; Warren & Yost, 2001). The goal of such afterschool literacy sites is pleasure and engagement in literacy practices, which for Capalongo-Bernadowski (2007) was vital to literacy learning.

Despite the centrality of pleasure and play in new afterschool literacy programs, Hull (2007) described the afterschool literacy universe as marginal to the school world. Its marginality to school, however, downplays its importance. The literature on afterschool programs confirms that schools alone are widely viewed as insufficient for promoting the literacy activities needed to develop citizens in the 21st century and the social and cultural values that stem from citizenship. Although afterschool programs like KidzLit and 100 Books Challenge offer individuals extended opportunities to gain or improve their literacy proficiency, they also offer a space away from school—fueled by alternative theories of literacy learning that see pleasure, play, and relevance as essential to the developmental experience.

Extra-School Literacy Programs

Out-of-school-literacy researchers also seem interested in the extra-school sites that house out-of-school literacy programs. Dressman (1997), for example, wrote about the role of libraries in establishing literacy rituals within communities, where new technologies complicate the picture of out-of-school literacies (Del-Castillo, Garcia-Varela, & Lacasa, 2003). In their ethnographic study of family and community literacy practices in a neighborhood public library, Ward and Wason-Ellam (2005) found that the public library was a hub of what they call "contiguous communities of practice" (p. 92). They described libraries as situated within contexts, such as neighborhoods and other settings, that feature shifting boundaries between formal and informal literacies and between traditional print media and multimodal literacies. Their study revealed the dynamic nature of literacy practices in extra-school settings, which programmatically have supported both the formal and informal literacies of families and communities.

Neuman, Khan, and Dondolo (2008) looked specifically at the Rural Education and Development (READ) program, run through newly created community libraries in Nepal. "READ set out to address the high rates of illiteracy and poverty in Nepal through the development of these libraries" (p. 513). Based on their examination of READ program evaluations, Neuman et al. concluded that such programs offer strong supports for community members. Programs like READ, therefore, hinge on the benefits of community libraries to provide access to literacy for members and improve economic and social development for a nation's citizens. READ libraries, in particular, promoted a "book culture" in Nepal by helping communities—in place of schools—encourage the development of multimodal literacies. Such a view of libraries, Neuman et al. suggested, may effectively inform literacy efforts and spur the development of extra-school spaces throughout the world (cf. Biancarosa & Snow, 2006).

While libraries have operated as one of the main localities for literacy learning beyond school, they are far from being the only extra-school location that encourages literacy learning. Increasingly, correctional institutions have become sites, tightly woven within the prison-industrial complex, to encourage the development of literacies. Through her work on literacy in prison populations, Dawe (2007) offered evidence that adult prisoners and offenders who participate in vocational education and training (VET) during their sentence are less likely to re-offend. She argued that a reduction in recidivism represents significant cost savings to communities. Hence, the goal of such programs angle beyond the individual pursuit of literacy to providing savings for communities and their members.

Muth and Kiser (2008) were less celebratory of prison literacy programs. Based on their research findings, Muth and Kiser suggested that, in many U.S. prisons, an overuse of individualized instruction silences literacy learners and reinforces oppressive notions about what knowledge is and whose knowledge counts. In these classrooms, methods that invite learners to tap their background knowledge, reflect on their worlds, and dialogue with others to construct meaning—commonplace in K–12 education and even corporate HRD practices—seem radically at odds with top-down prison cultures and output-based programs.

Despite cross-purposes and competing ideas, different locations in the extra-school world have intersected—in the name of literacy—in interesting ways. Take, for example, the case of the Book Em! Program, whereby police and librarians work together to foster greater community investment in literacy (Burnette, 1998). Programs like Book Em!, which extend the notion of school, demonstrate how schools alone cannot fully support youth literacy development. As a result, institutions as distinctly different as churches and prisons have served as literacy locations in addition to and sometimes in place of schools (Cornelius, 1991; Henriques, 1982). All together, a diverse and sometimes contentious set of locations—from government facilities to corporately run businesses, from libraries to churches—frames the out-of-school literacy world.

Concerns must be voiced, however, when the out-of-school world, once the domain of community-based organizations, faith-based institutions, and social service agencies, which may operate through different epistemological and pedagogical traditions, seems to become more homogenous in aims and approach via the advent of prepackaged curricula and funding streams with strings attached. One interesting example of these concerns is Smith's (2006) account of the growth in the numbers of what he termed "informal" educators (cf. Knowles, 1950), who are increasingly called upon to work within schools and formal education in Great Britain.

Smith explained that informal education has traditionally been grounded in distinctive practices that value democracy, local institutions (churches, community organizations), and the benefits of dialogue, reciprocity, and cooperation, as opposed to individualism and commodification, hallmarks of the neoliberal enterprise (cf. Hursh, 2007). He worried that traditions associated with informal education are being overwhelmed by the push to regulate and standardize, and that there are fewer spaces for the values of informal education to flourish within schools. Yet Smith also observed that informal and formal education and learning do not depend merely on physical context or setting, and he thereby helpfully moved the field beyond the in-school and out-of-school divide that sometimes characterizes the discourse of literacy studies today (Schultz & Hull, 2008; cf. Hull & Greeno, 2006).

Notwithstanding, out-of-school literacy programs have had some critics over time, such as the charge that early on, at the end of the 19th and the beginning of the 20th centuries in the United States, they actually interfered with immigrant children's free play on the streets (Halpern, 2003). However, the literature on these institutions and programs and their activities and practices is on the whole hopeful (cf. Halpin, 2003). Greene (1990) wrote about the leap of imagination and belief that characterizes successful participants in "second chance" educational efforts, such as adult literacy programs or alternative schools. It could be said that, as institutions, extra-school efforts have successfully managed that leap.

As Heath (1998) noted about community-based youth organizations focused on the arts, the best of such programs are characterized by their teachers' faith in youthful abilities and their commitment to the creation of spaces where youth are viewed, not as deficient—as "struggling readers," for example—but as promising and full of ability and potential (cf. Hull, Kenney, Marple, & Forsman-Schneider, 2006). And at least at some historical moments, extra-school educational programs have provided the means, unavailable elsewhere, for the construction and transmission of critical and crucial knowledge and points of view. The Freedom Schools, conducted in churches during the summertime as part of the Civil Rights movement of the 1960s, come to mind (Perlstein, 1990). It is not surprising, then, that out-of-school venues have also been viewed as potential hospitable locales for the design and implementation of educational innovations that don't flourish in school (Cole, 1996; Vasquez, 2003; Hull & Nelson, in press).

CONCLUSION

In our walk through the landscape of current out-of-school literacy programs and activities, we have maintained that the usual ways of differentiating the nature, aims, and practices of out-of-school from school-day institutions and practices do not do justice to the complexity of their histories, purposes, and practices. A hard-and-fast distinction between school and out-of-school literacy rarely holds, as purposes, methods, and conceptions morph, deviate from one another, and become localized. There are significant points of irony, too, in the commonality of sites such as prisons, libraries, backyards, and soup kitchens, whose institutional walls metaphorically collapse through their complementary attempts to encourage literacy (Brandt, 1998; Hull & Schultz, 2001, 2002).

Through our review of literacy out of school—in communities and in afterschool and extra-school programs—we have attempted to make clear that non-school hours are increasingly viewed and used as educational time, though that time and its associated spaces are filled and shaped by a range of sponsors, ideologies, purposes, and practices, sometimes in surprising and sometimes in predictable ways. While federal pass-through funding and particular conceptions of achievement and reading currently dominate afterschool programming, other configurations, purposes, and sponsors "poach," to use de Certeau's (1984) terminology, taking and making opportunities for the exercise of a variety of literacy practices and purposes, especially in extra-school and community settings.

A utopian spirit infuses most current representations of literacy practices in out-of-school settings, and we conclude our review with some like-minded hopefulness about the role of afterschool programs, community literacy efforts, and extra-school institutions in research and practice, but we offer several concerns as well. Reading researchers can find abundant work to do after school, especially in evaluating programs designed to improve reading achievement and required by conditions of funding to demonstrate particular kinds of academic improvement. We expect such research to continue apace. Researchers would also do well, however, to attend to the enrichment activities in which opportunities to read and write are embedded—e.g., art, music, debate, and drama. Such activities are often expected to justify their worth by accounting for their contribution to the more utilitarian aims of schooling. More usefully, researchers could helpfully document the development of literate habits of mind and hand in a host of activities, from play-based to explicitly instructional. Another concern that should be rigorously investigated in evaluation research is the extent to which school-based pressures to improve achievement test scores creates a tracking system after school, whereby poor children tend to receive remediation and test preparation, whereas their more advantaged peers have access to enrichment activities.

Reading researchers who are interested in studying literate aims that satisfy personal and civic and community goals may wish to locate their research in certain out-of-school worlds, using such worlds to investigate potentially different conceptions of and perspectives on learning, texts, and identity formation. For example, youth can sometimes achieve during afterschool hours a measure of freedom from school-based identities that position them as uncooperative or non-academically inclined (Hull, Kenney, Marple, & Forsman-Schneider, 2006), reinventing themselves as engaged participants in learning and their communities.

To be sure, current educational policy related to out-of-school worlds illustrates the power of schooling as an institution to assimilate and transform innovation (cf. Tyack, 1979; Hull, 2007). If schooling can be expected to encroach upon and incorporate afterschool worlds, however, those worlds can also be expected to push back and innovate by bringing to the fore goals, interests, dispositions, and practices that sometimes complement, sometimes depart from, and sometimes oppose those that dominate the school day. Thus, reading researchers and reading educators who are interested in conflicts and rapprochements between the center and the margins of teaching and learning; who desire an educational arena somewhat less calcified and more nimble than bureaucracy has made the institution of formal schooling; and who want to entertain and explore conceptions and practices of literacy that reflect a diversity of individual, community, organizational, and civic desires and motivations, would do well to consider out-of-school learning as a locus for inquiry and for program development.

The question that remains is the place of reading in the landscape of community-based programs and the afterschool world. This chapter is, in fact, the first in the handbook series to treat afterschool as a domain for reading research and practice. On the one hand, it does not take long to discover that reading is an extremely popular focus, and that many of the same kinds of reading instruction—on phonemic awareness, vocabulary development, strategy instruction, and reading comprehension—that occur during school also occur in a similar fashion beyond the schoolhouse door. Out-of-school has arrived as an important locus for reading instruction via prepackaged curricula, as scores of commercial reading programs advertise materials targeted toward afterschool and summer. Their approaches are buttressed by results from a range of research studies—for example, that individual tutoring helps to prevent reading difficulties, and that some youth enrolled in reading programs afterschool outperform others who don't attend (U.S. Dept. of Education and Dept. of Justice, 2000).

On the other hand, a great deal of reading, as well as other literacy-related engagement with texts, symbol systems, and information and communication technologies, occurs as part of a wider range of activities, diverse purposes, and institutional affiliations in afterschool and out-of-school programs. At their most innovative, such patterns of engagement may offer fresh takes on meaning-making in the 21st century and expansive insights for reading researchers and educators to apply both in and out of school.

NOTES

1. Developmental Studies Center, a non-profit organization, is headed by Eric Schaps and receives funding from a large number of sources, primarily private foundations.

REFERENCES

Alvermann, D. E., Young, J. P., Green, C., & Wisenbaker, J. M. (1999). Adolescents' perceptions and negotiations of literacy practices in after-school read and talk clubs. *American Educational Research Journal, 36,* 221–224.

Au, K. H., & Jordon, C. (1981). Teaching reading to Hawaiian children: Finding a culturally appropriate solution. In H. H. Trueba, G. P. Guthrie, & K. H. Au (Eds.), *Culture in the bilingual classroom: Studies in classroom ethnography* (pp. 139–152). Rowley, MA: Newberry House.

Auerbach, E. (1992). Literacy and Ideology. *Annual Review of Applied Linguistics, 12,* 71–85.

Bakhtin, M. M. (1981). *The dialogic imagination: Four essays* (M. Holquist & C. Emerson, Trans.). Austin: University of Texas Press.

Bharij, S. (2001). Literacy in Al-Anon family groups. *RaPAL Bulletin* (43), 18–20.

Biancarosa, G., & Snow, C.E. (2006). *Reading next—a vision for action and research in middle and high school literacy: A report from Carnegie Corporation of New York.* Washington, DC: Alliance for Excellent Education.

Bitz, M. (2004). The comic book project: Forging alternative pathways to literacy. *Journal of Adolescent & Adult Literacy, 47*(7), 574–586.

Brandt, D. (1998). Sponsors of literacy. *College Composition and Communication, 49*(2), 165–185.

Burnette, S. (1998). Book 'Em! Cops and Librarians Working Together. *American Libraries, 29*(2), 48–50.

Capalongo-Bernadowski, C. (2007). Book clubs at work. *Library Media Connection, 26*(3), 32.

Carter, S. P. (2007). The African American read-in: Celebrating black writers and supporting youth. *English Journal, 96*(4), 22–23.

de Certeau, M. (1984). *The practice of everyday life.* Berkeley: University of California Press.

Cole, M. (1996). *Cultural psychology: A once and future discipline.* Cambridge, MA: Harvard University Press.

Cook-Gumperz, J. (1986). Literacy and schooling: An unchanging equation? In J. Cook-Gumperz (Ed.), *The social construction of literacy* (pp. 16–44). Cambridge,UK: Cambridge University Press.

Cornelius, J. D. (1991). *"When I can read my title clear": Literacy, slavery, and religion in the antebellum South.* Columbia: University of South Carolina Press.

Cowan, P. (1999). "Drawn" into the community: Re-considering the artwork of Latino adolescents. *Visual Studies, 14*(1), 91–101.

Cushman, E. (2002). Sustainable service learning programs. *College Composition and Communication, 54*(1), 45–65.

Dawe, S. (2007). *Vocational education and training for adult prisoners and offenders in Australia: Research readings.* Adelaide, Australia: National Center for Vocational Education and Training.

Del-Castillo, H., Garcia-Varela, A. B., & Lacasa, P. (2003). Literacies through media: Identity and discourse in the process of constructing a web site. *International Journal of Educational Research, 39,* 885–891.

Dressman, M. (1997). Congruence, resistance, liminality: Reading and ideology in three school libraries. *Curriculum Inquiry, 27,* 267–315.

Durlak, J. A., & Weissberg, R. P. (2007). *The impact of after-school programs that promote personal and social skills.* Chicago: Collaborative for Academic, Social, and Emotional Learning.

Eccles, J., & Gootman, J.A. (Eds.). (2002). *Community programs to promote youth development.* Washington, DC: National Academy Press.

Eidman-Aadahl, E. (2002). Got some time, got a place, got the word: Collaborating for literacy learning and youth development. In G. Hull & K. Schultz (Eds.), *School's out! Bridging out-of-school literacies with classroom practice* (pp. 241–60). New York: Teachers College Press.

Fisher, M. T. (2004). "The song is unfinished": The new literate and literary and their institutions. *Written Communication, 21*(3), 290–313.

Flower, L. (2008). *Community literacy and the rhetoric of public engagement.* Carbondale: Southern Illiniois University Press.

Foley, E. M., & Eddins, G. (2001). *Preliminary analysis of Virtual Y after-school program participants' patterns of school attendance and academic performance: Final evaluation report, program year 1999–2000.* New York: Fordham University, National Center for Schools and Communities. Retrieved from http://www.ncscatfordham.org/pages/page33.cfm

Goldman, S. (2006). A new angle on families: Connecting the mathematics of life with school mathematics. In Z. Bekerman, N. C. Burbules, & D. Silberman-Keller (Eds.), *Learning in places: The informal education reader* (pp. 53–76). New York: Peter Lang.

Grabill, J. T. (2001). *Community literacy programs and the politics of change.* Albany: State University of New York Press.

Greene, M. (1990). Revision and interpretation: Opening spaces for the second chance. In D. Inbar (Ed.), *Second chance in education* (pp. 37–48). London: Falmer.

Gutiérrez, K. D. (2008). Developing a sociocritical literacy in the third space. *Reading Research Quarterly, 43*(2), 148–164.

Halpern (2003). *Making play work: The promise of afterschool programs for low-income children.* New York: Teachers College Press.

Halpin, D. (2003). *Hope and education: The role of the utopian imagination.* London: Routledge.

Harris, B. R. (2008). Communities as Necessity in Information Literacy Development: Challenging the Standards. *Journal of Academic Librarianship, 34*(3), 248.

Hartry, A., Fitzgerald, R., & Porter, K. (2008). Implementing a structured reading program in an afterschool setting: Problems and ootential solutions. *Harvard Educational Review, 78*(1), 181–210.

Heath, S. B. (1983). *Ways with words: Language, life and work in communities and classrooms.* Cambridge, MA: Cambridge University Press.

Heath, S. B. (1998). Living the arts through language plus learning: A report on community-based youth organizations. *Americans for the Arts Monographs, 2*(7), 1–19.

Henriques, Z. W. (1982). *Imprisoned mothers and their children.* New York: University Press of America.

Hertz-Lazarowitz, R. (1999). Cooperative learning in Israel's Jewish and Arab schools: A community approach. *Theory Into Practice, 38*(2), 105–113.

Hill, S. (Ed.). (2007). *Afterschool matters: Creative programs that connect youth development and student achievement.* Thousand Oaks, CA: Corwin.

Hull, G., & Greeno, J. (2006). Identity and agency in non-school and school worlds. In Z. Bekerman, N. C. Burbules, & D. Silberman-Keller (Eds.), *Learning in places: The informal education reader* (pp. 77–97). New York: Peter Lang.

Hull, G. (2007). Foreword: After-school talks back. In S. Hill (Ed.), *Afterschool matters: Creative programs that connect youth development and student achievement* (pp. ix–xx). Thousand Oaks, CA: Corwin.

Hull, G., & Katz, M. (2006). Crafting an agentive self: Case studies on digital storytelling. *Research in the Teaching of English, 41*(1), 43–81.

Hull, G., Kenney, N., Marple, S., & Forsman-Schneider, A. (2006). *Many versions of masculine: Explorations of boys' identity formation through multimodal composing in an after-school program.* The Robert F. Bowne Foundation's Occasional Papers Series. New York: Robert F. Bowne Foundation.

Hull, G., & Nelson, M. (in press). Literacy, media, and morality: Making the case for an aesthetic turn. In M. Prinsloo & M. Baynham (Eds.), *The future of literacy studies.* Houndmills, UK: Palgrave Macmillan.

Hull, G., & Schultz, K. (2001). Literacy and learning out of school: A review of theory and research. *Review of Educational Research, 71*(4), 575–611.

Hull, G., & Schultz, K. (Eds.). (2002). *School's out! Bridging out-of-school literacies with classroom practice.* New York: Teachers College Press.

Hursh, D. (2007). Assessing No Child Left Behind and the rise of neoliberal educational policies. *American Educational Research Journal, 44*(3), 493–518.

Jacobs, D. (2007). Marveling at "The man called Nova": Comics as sponsors of multimodal literacy. *College Composition and Communication, 59*(2), 180–205.

James-Burdumy, S., Dynarski, M., Moore, M., Deke, J., Mansfield, W., Pistorino, C., et al. (2005). *When schools stay open late: The national evaluation of the 21st century community learning centers program.* Washington, DC: U.S. Department of Education Institute of Education Sciences National Center for Education Evaluation and Regional Assistance.

Jocson, K. M. (2006). "Bob Dylan and Hip Hop": Intersecting literacy practices in youth poetry communities. *Written Communication, 23*(3), 231–259.

Kelly, C. (1992). *Teaching Hmong literacy skills to Hmong elementary students: Its effect on English reading competencies.* (ERIC Document Reproduction Service No. ED393067)

Kendrick, M. E., & Hissani, H. (2007). Letters, imagined communities, and literate identities: Perspectives from rural Ugandan women. *Journal of Literacy Research, 39*(2), 195.

Kirkland, D. (2007). The power of their text: Teaching hip hop in the secondary English classroom. In K. Keaton & P. R. Schmidt (Eds.), *Closing the gap: English educators address the tensions between teacher preparation and teaching writing in secondary schools* (pp. 129–145). Charlotte, NC: Information Age.

Kirkland, D., & Jackson, A. (2009). "We Real Cool": Toward a theory of black masculine Literacy. *Reading Research Quarterly, 44*(3), 278–297.

Knowles, M. S. (1950). *Informal adult education.* New York: Association Press.

LA's BEST After School Enrichment Program. (n.d.). *Welcome to LA's BEST.* Retrieved May 27, 2009, from http://www.lasbest.org

Lauer, P. A., Akiba, M., Wilkerson, S. B., Apthorp, H. S., Snow, D., & Martin-Glenn, M. L. (2006). Out-of-school time programs: A meta-analysis of effects for at-risk students. *Review of Educational Research, 76,* 275–313.

Lave, J. (1988). *Cognition in practice: Mind, mathematics, and culture in everyday life.* Cambridge, UK: Cambridge University Press.

Lave, J., & Wenger, E. (1991). *Situated learning: Legitimate peripheral participation.* New York: Cambridge University Press.

Lee, S. J., & Hawkins, M. R. (2008). "Family Is here": Learning in community-based after-school programs. *Theory Into Practice, 47*(1), 51–58.

Luke, A. (1997). *Critical literacy: An introduction.* St. Leonards, Australia: Allen & Unwin.

Mahiri, J. (2004). *What they don't learn in school: Literacy in the lives of urban youth.* New York: Peter Lang.

Mahiri, J., & Sablo, S. (1996). Writing for their lives: The non-School literacy of California. *Journal of Negro Education, 65*(2), 164–180.

Mahoney, J. L., Larson, R. W., Eccles, J. S., & Lord, H. (2005). Organized activities as development contexts for children and adolescents. In J. L. Mahoney R. W. Larson, & J. S. Eccles (Eds.), *Organized activities as contexts of development: Extracurricular activities, after-school, and community programs* (pp. 3–22). Mahwah, NJ: Erlbaum.

McHenry, E. (2002). *Forgotten readers: Recovering the lost history of African-American literary societies.* Durham, NC: Duke University Press.

McHenry, E., & Heath, S. B. (1994). The literate and the literary: African Americans as writers and readers-1830–1940. *Written Communication, 11*(4), 419–444.

Morrell, E. (2003). *Writing the word and the world: Critical literacy as critical textual production.* Paper presented at the 54th Annual Meeting of the Conference on College Composition and Communication, New York, NY. Retrieved from http://eric.edu.gov (ERIC Document Reproduction Service No. ED475208)

Muth, B., & Kiser, M. (2008). Radical conversations: Part two—Cultivating social-constructivist learning methods in ABE classrooms. *Journal of Correctional Education, 59*(4), 349–366.

Neuman, S. B., Khan, N., & Dondolo, T. (2008). When I give, I own: Building literacy through READ community libraries in Nepal. *Reading Teacher, 61*(7), 513–522.

Noam, G. G., Biancarosa, G., & Dechausay, N. (2003). *Afterschool education: Approaches to an emerging field.* Cambridge, MA: Harvard University Press.

Noll, E. (1998). Experiencing literacy in and out of school: Case studies of two American Indian youths [Sioux Indians]. *Journal of Literacy Research, 30*(2), 205–232.

Noll, E., & Watkins, R. (2003). The impact of homelessness on children's literacy experiences. *The Reading Teacher, 57*(4), 362–371.

Parsad, B., Lewis, L., & Tice, P. (2009). After-school program in public elementary schools. Washington, DC: U.S. Department of Education, National Center for Education Statistics. Retrieved from http://nces.ed.gov/pubs2009/2009043.pdf

Pastor, A. M. R. (2008). Competing language ideologies in a bilingual/bicultural after-school program in southern California. *Journal of Latinos and Education, 7*(1), 4–24.

Peck, W. C., Flower, L., & Higgins, L. (1995). Community literacy. *CCC, 46*(2), 199–222.

Perlstein, D. (1990). Teaching freedom: SNCC and the creation of the Mississippi Freedom Schools. *History of Education Quarterly, 30*(3), 297–324.

Pleasants, H. (2008). Negotiating identity projects: Exploring the digital storytelling experiences of three African American girls. In M. L. Hill & L. Vasudevan (Eds.), *Media, learning, and sites of possibility* (pp. 205–234). New York: Peter Lang.

The Promise Audit: Tracking President Obama's progress on campaign promises. (n.d.). Retrieved May 10, 2009, from http://promises.nationaljournal.com/education/double-funding-for-after-school-programs/

Rosenthal, D. A., & Feldman, S. S. (1996). Crossing the border: Chinese adolescents in the West. In S. Lau (Ed.), *Growing up the Chinese way: Chinese child and adolescent development* (pp. 287–320). Hong Kong: Chinese University Press.

Sahni, U. (in press). Finding "self," finding "home": Drama in education. *Canadian Theatre Review.*

Saxe, G. (1990). *Culture and cognitive development: Studies in mathematical understanding.* Hillsdale, NJ: Erlbaum.

Schultz, K., & Hull, G. (2008). Literacy in and out of US schools. In B. Street (Ed.), *The encyclopedia of language and education* (Vol. 2, pp. 239–250). Heidelberg, Germany: Kluwer.

Schwarz, E., & Stolow, D. (2006). Twenty-first century learning in afterschool. *New Directions for Youth Development: Theory, Practice, and Research, 110*, 81–99.

Scribner, S., & Cole, M. (1981). *The psychology of literacy.* Cambridge, MA: Harvard University Press.

Shernoff, D. J., & Vandell, D. L. (2008, Fall). Youth engagement and quality of experience in afterschool program. *Afterschool Matters Occasional Paper Series, 9*, 1–14.

Smith, M. K. (2006). Beyond the curriculum: Fostering associational life in schools. In Z. Bekerman, N. C. Burbules, & D. Silberman-Keller (Eds.), *Learning in places: The informal education reader* (pp. 9–33). New York: Peter Lang.

Sterponi, L. (2007). Clandestine interactional reading: Intertextuality and double-voicing under the desk. *Linguistics and Education, 18*(1), 1–23.

Street, B. (1984). *Literacy in theory and practice.* Cambridge, UK: Cambridge University Press.

Tagoe, M. (2008). Challenging the orthodoxy of literacy: Realities of moving from personal to community empowerment through "Reflect" in Ghana. *International Journal of Lifelong Education, 27*, 707–728.

Tyack, D. B. (1979). The high school as a social service agency: Historical perspectives on current policy issues. *Educational Evaluation and Policy Analysis, 1*(5), 45–57.

U.S. Department of Education, Office of the Under Secretary. (2003). *When schools stay open late: The national evaluation of the 21st century learning centers program, first year findings.* Washington, DC: U.S. Government Printing Office.

U.S. Department of Education and U.S. Department of Justice. (April, 2000). *Working for children and families: Safe and smart after-school programs.* Washington, DC: U.S. Government Printing Office.

Vasquez, O. A. (2003). *La Clase Magica: Imagining optimal possibilities in a bilingual community of learners.* Mahwah, NJ: Erlbaum.

Ward, A., & Wason-Ellam, L. (2005). Reading beyond school: Literacies in a neighbourhood library. *Canadian Journal of Education, 28*(1/2), 98–109.

Warren, A., & Yost, A. (2001). Making afterschool count: Communities & schools working together. *Making Afterschool Count, 4*(1), 34.

Yi, Y. (2007). Engaging literacy: A biliterate student's composing practices beyond school. *Journal of Second Language Writing, 16*(1), 23–39.

Zierk, T. (2000). The Power of play: A literature-based after school sports program for urban youth. *Afterschool Matters, 1*(1), 12–17.

30 Family Literacy
A Current View of Research on Parents and Children Learning Together

Flora V. Rodríguez-Brown
University of Illinois at Chicago

INTRODUCTION

The influence of family literacy practices has been widely researched for many years. Heath (1983) described how children acquire basic cognitive and linguistic skills, as well as an understanding of language and its uses within the context of the family. Others have examined and described the effects of parents' efforts to support early literacy learning in low socioeconomic status (SES) settings where parents had low levels of formal education as well as cultural and linguistic differences (Morrow, 1995; Reese, Gallimore, & Goldenberg, 1999; Taylor, 1983). However, it has been during the last 20 years that family literacy as an "educational construct" (Purcell-Gates, 2000) has become relevant to policymakers, teachers, and communities, as research on the effect of learning at home informs the field.

In spite of the existent research into practices of family literacy, there is still disagreement on a definition of the construct. As stated by Purcell-Gates (2000):

> There is a real lack of agreement as to what family literacy is, what it means for schooling, what it means for literacy development, and how, or if, we should go about researching it, instituting it, promoting it, or even "doing it," whatever "it" may be! (p. 853)

In this chapter, I describe the family literacy construct as currently conceptualized by researchers, policymakers, families, and practitioners. In order to do so, I first describe the historical trajectory of the concept, including issues related to its definition. Then, I discuss current research on family literacy from different paradigms and program perspectives, namely the home literacy environment, and sociocultural aspects of home literacy learning. Finally, I describe and illustrate how the construct has been contextualized through interventions which follow different ideologies in working with families as they support their children's literacy learning.

REVIEW PROCEDURES

The field of research in family literacy is still "evolving" (Purcell-Gates, 2000, p. 853). Although the focus of this chapter is on research in family literacy and home literacy practices published from 2000 to 2007, some major studies prior to 2000 were included because of their importance to the topic and the fact that they were not included in previous reviews. Both qualitative and quantitative studies were reviewed as well as theoretical contributions that have enhanced the concept of family literacy both as an educational construct and as a field of research.

Identifiers used to locate research publications in family literacy included family literacy, learning at home, and family literacy models, among others. Content searches were conducted in journals, books, and Google Scholar to identify possibly candidates for inclusion in the review.

Once studies were identified, they were grouped by three major topics: the home learning environment (HLE) and literacy learning, sociocultural studies related to learning at home, and family literacy programs or models. Subsequently, the sociocultural studies related to learning at home were categorized according to different perspectives. Research on family literacy models and interventions in the chapter included programs or models which were not covered in prior reviews, and those included come from publications and reports which described research designs, data analysis, and findings explaining the effectiveness of the interventions.

In terms of methodology, the studies were characterized as qualitative when they included naturalistic observations and provided in depth descriptions of the ways in which children and their parents or caretakers interact with written text. These studies might discuss a variety of literacy activities but usually involved small sample sizes. For example, Purcell-Gates' study (2007) included 24 children; Delgado-Gaitan (1993) studied 8 families.

Quantitative studies included in the chapter attempted to predict outcomes in relation to different indicators and involved larger samples. Some of the studies desegregated the data by race, ethnicity, or SES. The focus of many of these studies was shared reading. Also, in some of the quantitative studies the home literacy environment was defined as complex and multifaceted. These studies included more variables in order to allow for more variability in outcomes. For example, Burgess, Hetch, and Lonigan (2002) utilized several conceptualizations including parents' ability and disposition to engage in literacy activities (as determined by parents' occupation and education) and shared reading activities which included measures of a child's active participation in literacy activity, a child's observation of literacy activity, and an overall mix of both.

DEFINING FAMILY LITERACY

The term "family literacy" has different meanings when viewed from different perspectives. When it is considered an "educational construct" (Purcell-Gates, 2000), there is disagreement as to whether it is a field of study or an intervention. The term family literacy originated with Taylor's (1983) descriptive ethnography. This was followed by other descriptive studies (Purcell-Gates, 1995, 1996; Taylor & Dorsey-Gaines, 1988; Teale, 1986) that examined home literacy practices in various settings and found different levels of congruency between the home literacy practices of the families studied and those of the schools the children attended.

As recently as 2005, Paratore describes the problem of defining family literacy as follows:

> To some, family literacy is an explanatory concept—a way to describe how parents and children read and write together and alone during everyday activities. To others, family literacy is a program or a curriculum—a construct for teaching parents how to prepare for success in school. (p. 394)

Some in the field define family literacy as programs that support families from low educational and economic backgrounds to help parents become self-sufficient, get jobs, and also support their children's learning. For example, McCoy and Watts (1992) describe family literacy as a "community-based initiative designed to break the cycle of illiteracy" (p. 1) among parents, children, and families. The National Center for Family Literacy (NCFL, 1995) labels their program as family literacy, saying it is an intergenerational program which integrates adult literacy instruction and early childhood education for undereducated families. It includes:

1. Interactive literacy activities between parents and their children;
2. Training for parents regarding how to be the primary teacher for their children and full partners in the education of their children;
3. Parent literacy training that leads to economic self-sufficiency; and
4. Age appropriate education to prepare children for success in school and life experiences.

Thus, as described above, family literacy is defined in a broad sense which is more related to community literacy in that it includes not only children and parents involved in literacy learning, but also intervention programs that serve adults and children within families and communities in order to empower them toward self-sufficiency. Similar views of family literacy are shared by several others (e.g., Moneyhun, 1997; Peck, Flowers, & Higgins, 1995), who use the term "family literacy" to refer to community-based adult literacy programs.

Another perspective, however, describes family literacy as home literacy practices that involve oral and written texts in support of children's literacy learning. This view recognizes the literacy knowledge that families already possess and addresses the need to expand the home repertoire of literacy practices (Reese et al., 1999; Rodríguez-Brown, 2004, 2009). Definitions from this perspective are based on the families' contributions to literacy learning and recognize that new literacy strategies might be needed to create some congruency between what is learned at home and what is expected at school. In support of this view, Morrow, Paratore, and Tracey (as cited in Morrow, 1995) define family literacy as follows:

> Family literacy encompasses the ways parents, children and extended family members use literacy at home and in their community. Sometimes, family literacy occurs naturally during the routines of daily living and helps adults and children "get things done." These events might include using drawings or writings to share ideas; composing notes or letters to communicate messages; making lists; reading and following directions; or sharing stories and ideas through conversations, reading, and writing. Family literacy may be initiated purposefully by a parent or may occur spontaneously as parents and children go about the business of their daily lives. Family literacy activities may also reflect the ethnic, racial, or cultural heritage of the families involved. (pp. 7–8)

The International Reading Association's Family Literacy Commission takes a similar stance on family literacy and has adapted this definition for use on their Web site (www.reading.org/downloads/parents/p6_1045_family.pdf) and in publications.

However, not everyone agrees with this definition. One critique to this definition is that it is "a general and vague description of family literacy without theoretical foundations or means of implementation" (De Bruin-Parecki, Paris, & Seidenberg, 1996, p. 1). Others believe that the concept of family literacy should be open, allowing researchers or program developers to create an operational definition that matches their own purposes.

For the purpose of this chapter, family literacy is defined as parent/family/child interactions at home and in the community that support the early literacy learning of all children. In a diverse society parents might define their role as their children's first teachers differently, and they teach their children using a variety of discourse patterns and cultural models—defined as different ways to interact with words, and the environment, in general, and with books, as children are exposed to reading and writing.

The family literacy definition currently used in government programs, and also supported by the National Center for Family Literacy, includes only one true component of family literacy: Interactive literacy activities between parents and their children. The other three components are related to adult education and compensatory pre-school experiences, using middle-class values and ways of learning, for children who are culturally and/or linguistically different. There is no consideration of what parents already contribute to their children's learning situation or the ways they support their children's learning at home.

The definition by Morrow (1995), which has been embraced by the International Reading Association (IRA), is closer to the way family literacy is defined here. An explicit statement needs to be made to explain that, in a diverse society, parents might share literacy with their children in different manners, which should be respected and celebrated. These differences could be used as steppingstones to learning different ways to become literate, and would facilitate all children's transition between home and school.

OVERVIEW OF PREVIOUS RESEARCH

Since Taylor used the term "family literacy" in 1983 to describe literacy learning at home, the area of family literacy has developed both as an educational construct (Purcell-Gates, 2000) and as a field of research. Foundational research examined literacy learning at home and the role of parents in this development. It described how children acquire basic cognitive and linguistic skills within the context of the family (Heath, 1983), and that a rich home literacy environment has an impact on children's success in school and in life (Heath, 1983; Morrow, 1995; Taylor & Dorsey-Gaines, 1988). Studies during this time also examined topics such as the effects of parents' efforts in support of early literacy learning even when their educational levels were low (Taylor & Dorsey-Gaines); and the role of parent-child interactions with books and how these interactions affect children's emergent literate behaviors, literacy learning, and future school success (Teale & Sulzby, 1986). Some early research on family literacy focused on how children learned different things about literacy from their home environment. Studies by Clay (1979) showed how children learned about concepts of print at home, while Burgess (1982) studied the acquisition of letters, and Purcell-Gates (1988) described how children learned about characteristics of written registers through interactions with parents in activities such as shared book readings.

Research of this period also discovered critical differences in family literacy practices. For example, some found that parents with low educational levels engaged in literacy activities at home for different purposes than those of mainstream parents (Taylor, 1983; Taylor & Dorsey-Gaines, 1988). Taylor and Dorsey-Gaines stated that "families use literacy for a wide variety of purposes (social, technical, and aesthetic purposes), for a wide variety of audiences, and in a wide variety of situations" (p. 202). However, this view of family literacy is often overlooked because of the belief that these home-situated family literacy practices do not lead to early literacy learning from a mainstream perspective (Purcell-Gates, 1995). Because culturally diverse children do not always exhibit the same literacy behaviors that are expected in mainstream classrooms, teachers and other school personnel often do not recognize, or see a "deficit" with, the literacy knowledge that low SES, culturally different children bring from home.

Later studies shifted the research focus to these cultural differences in family literacy, exemplified by Snow and Tabors' statement (1996) that literacy is more than print skills acquired in a print-rich environment. They felt that the scope of family literacy practices needed to be expanded and diversified, especially for emergent readers and writers, whereby the contributions of different cultural ways and discourses were recognized and their effects on literacy development studied.

For those who view literacy as a cultural practice (defined as literacy in practice as it occurs in the lives of people and as a mediator of social life), whether parents transmit knowledge, model literacy behaviors, or engage children in meaningful literacy activities, children are learning through literacy practices that are specific to the culture of the home (Beals, De Temple, & Dickinson, 1994; Dyson, 2003). Dyson described how first-grade children from diverse backgrounds used authentic home literacy practices as they learned to read and write. This study illustrated how children in diverse settings follow different paths to literacy than mainstream populations. The paths were determined not only by what children learned in school but also by the multiple ways in which they practiced literacy at home.

More recently, studies in the field have focused on the effectiveness of family literacy programs and the theoretical basis for their development (Paratore, 2001; Rodríguez-Brown, 2004). Other areas of current research include the role of discourse (Gee, 1999; Rogers, 2003) and cultural models of the literacy practices of minority homes and their congruence or incongruence with literacies validated in school settings (Gutiérrez, 2002; Reese & Gallimore, 2000; Reese & Goldenberg, 2006).

FOUNDATIONAL RESEARCH IN FAMILY LITERACY

Research findings serve to inform the field of family literacy on existing practices across different types of families. Research also describes the effects of different home literacy practices on children's learning, school preparedness, and possible interventions that could facilitate the transition from home to school for children from culturally and linguistically different families. This section presents basic research studies, both empirical and descriptive, that are related to home literacy practices. The varying definitions of family literacy result in different perspectives for research in this area.

Research on Home Literacy Environments and Language/Literacy Learning

Conceptualizations of Home Literacy Environments.   All children benefit from home literacy environments that foster language and literacy development. One of the main areas of research in family literacy is the influence of home literacy environments on the development of emergent literacy skills or specific literacy-related skills (e.g., vocabulary) of young children. Some researchers (e.g., Griffin & Morrison, 1997) have found that the home literacy environment is multifaceted and that various components of the environment might affect literacy development and educational outcomes in different ways. Griffin and Morrison examined the role of magazine and newspaper subscriptions, library use, television viewing, and shared book readings on learning at home. They found that these activities supported the development of receptive vocabulary skills, word recognition skills, and math skills in young children. Similar results were reported by Leseman and de Jong (1998). Other enrichment activities such as singing songs, chanting nursery rhymes, telling stories, and playing rhyming games have also been found to improve literacy and language learning outcomes (Baker, Scher, & Mackler, 1997).

Data for this study were collected through parents' self-reports of their children's preferences during shared reading (the book, the interaction, or the routine), their interests (making requests, listening), and actions (using words, pretending to read). The outcomes were reported by desegregating the sample by income. The findings show that low-income and under educated parents tended to favor drill and practice of reading skills over more informal playful opportunities for literacy learning.

Some foundational research is based on complex conceptualizations of the home literacy environment that include not only literacy activities and beliefs, but also family functioning variables, routines and resources, and the quality of relationships between family members and the children's teachers. Burgess et al. (2002) compared the predictive value of six different conceptualizations of home literacy environment (parents' ability to engage in literacy activities, parents' education and occupation, shared readings, child participation in literacy activities, child as observant of literacy activities, child participant and observer of literacy activities, and an aggregate of all of the above) and the literacy outcomes of preschoolers. Using regression analysis, they found that conceptualizations that included an active home literacy environment explained the most variance in literacy scores.

Another conceptualization of the home literacy environment is taken by Bennett, Weigel, and Martin (2002) who studied the relationship between family environment and children's language and literacy skills with middle-class families and their children. They used three theoretical models (Family as Educator, Resilient Family, and Parent-Child Care Partnership) as described in Snow, Barnes, Chandler, Goodman, and Hemphill (1991) in order to explain the contributions of families to their children's literacy learning. In the Family as Educator model, the family is defined as an educating agent, positively affecting children's language and literacy development. The Resilient Family model sees resilience as more than an issue of income. The model considers how the family functions, how it is organized, how well it manages its resources, and how it copes with the internal and external stresses that all families face. Finally, the Parent-Child-Care Partnership model is based on the belief that parents who support school efforts to teach their children are more successful in enhancing their children's language and literacy achievements. Results from the Bennett et al. (2002) study showed that only the Family as Educator model was related to oral language and literacy acquisition outcomes. As defined by Snow et al. (1991) under this model parents support children's literacy learning by providing books at home, helping their children with homework, exposing children to other people and activities, and having high expectations for their children's education. The results of this study could be explained by the differences in literacy interactions between parents and preschoolers as opposed to parent interactions with elementary school children.

Shared Book Readings and the Home Literacy Environment.   Most of the research on the home literacy environment conceptualizes it in relation to parent-child joint book reading and its influence on children's acquisition of oral language and literacy (Burgess, 1997; Sénéchal, LeFevre, Thomas, & Daley, 1998), as well as the children's motivation to read (Baker et al., 1997).

There is limited research that examines the effects of joint book reading at home on preschool children's interest and motivation to read (Lyon, 1999). In a recent study, Baker and Scher (2002) compared parental attitudes toward early reading and children's interest in reading. They found that mothers who identified the reason for reading as pleasure predicted a higher motivation for their children's enjoyment and value of literacy. Those who associated book reading interactions with learning produced a negative impact on their children's interest in literacy. Kaderavek and Justice (2005) hypothesized that a negative orientation to literacy sometimes occurred due to the directive adult language style used during book reading.

Research studies that investigate joint book readings in the home also assess the effects on children's oral language skills, literacy skills, or a combination of both. For example, Roberts, Jurgens, and Buchinal (2005) investigated the role of home literacy practices on low-income, African American preschool children's emergent literacy skills. The study examined four specific factors (shared book reading frequency, maternal book reading strategies, child's enjoyment of reading, and maternal sensitivity) and a global measure of the quality and responsiveness of the home environment during the preschool years. They found that the best predictor of children's oral language and literacy skills was the global measure of responsiveness and support of the home environment.

Van Steensel (2006) investigated shared book reading effects on young children's academic achievement in a study with diverse populations in Holland. Controlling for background characteristics, van Steensel found that the home literacy environment had an effect on children's vocabulary in Grade 1 and on general reading comprehension in grades 1 and 2. Considerable variability was found in home literacy environments among and within ethnic and low SES groups. Van Steensel interpreted the variability within groups as a by-product of acculturation. He felt that some ethnic and low SES parents engaged in activities such as shared reading, singing songs, and library visits once they learned that those were practices of the mainstream Dutch society.

Working with a different cultural group, Gallimore and Reese (1999) found similar acculturation effects. Their study was based on a longitudinal database, which includes observations of Mexican families before and after their children started school. The parents in the study had been in the United States between 10 and 40 years, and they were first generation immigrants whose identity was tied to their home countries. The study showed that the Mexican parents in the study who were from low economic backgrounds started reading to their children at home once their children started school, and the parents learned about U.S. schools' expectations about their role as the children's first teachers. The researchers believed that parents adjusted to new environmental expectations because of the value that schools attach to sharing literacy. Based on the results of this study and other similar research, Goldenberg (2004) stated that home literacy environment measures were better predictors of children's literacy scores than such static factors as ethnicity and SES. The Gallimore and Reese (1999) study supported the findings in Roberts et al. (2005) described above, which found that in the measurement of home literacy environments global measures are more predictive than discrete measures.

Studies with bilingual populations have also assessed the development of language and literacy skills as a result of shared book readings. Using bilingual (Spanish/English) families, Quiroz (2004) studied the influence of narratives on knowledge, memory, and language acquisition. She examined specifically the relationship between the interaction styles of bilingual parents during book reading and homework and their children's language skills. She defined a narrative style of reading as one of just reading the book, while the descriptive style allowed for interaction (use of questions, clarifications, extensions) between the mother and child while book sharing. The sample for the study included 50 low SES Spanish-speaking families. The data included a phone interview, a home visit interview, a book-sharing activity, a homework activity and the children's oral language achievement scores. Results showed that bilingual mothers tended to use slightly more narrative than descriptive styles while interacting with their children. Narrative style was positively associated with typical indicators of home literacy environment (number of books at home, income). Descriptive language styles were positively associated with discourse markers, such as questions and answers observed in parent-child interactions. Both styles of reading were effective but resulted in different outcomes for the children. The most significant finding was that narrative style in Spanish (as a language acquisition and early childhood intervention) was a significant and strong predictor of children's language development in English (as measured by word frequency during narrative production and memory for sentences scores).

Focusing specifically on oral language skills, Snow and Páez (2004) discussed research by Dickinson and Tabors (2001) and Snow and Tabors (1993) that identified the relevance that language experiences and early exposure to literacy have in children's language development and later literacy acquisition. Based on the research, Snow and Páez concluded that knowledge such as vocabulary, understanding concepts of print and phonological awareness were very important for later literacy development.

Owing to the large data base (3,001 children and their caregivers), data from the National Head Start Research and Evaluation Project, have generated a number of studies over the years that relate home literacy environments of the populations studied to the language, literacy, and cognitive development of low-income infants and toddlers. In general, findings show variation in children's oral language and pre-literacy experiences, and a consistent predictive relationship between the home literacy environment and the children's language development.

Other studies using Head Start data investigate the use of shared book experiences across different types of families. One of these studies by Bradley, Corwyn, McAdoo, and Coll (2001) found that low-income families were likely to read less frequently (at least several times a week) with their young children than other economic groups.

Raikes et al. (2004), using a subset of the Head Start data, tried to determine which maternal and children's characteristics affected the frequency of reading and book availability, and what the reciprocal effects of book reading and children's language skills were over time. The analysis showed a wide variability in self-reports of shared book reading. Mothers reported that they read more to girls than to boys. Those who were high school graduates read more to their toddlers than those who were not. White, African American, or English-speaking Hispanic mothers reported reading more to their children than Spanish-speaking mothers. The availability of books paralleled the frequency of book reading at home. At each age level for which data was collected, shared reading was significantly related to child language skills at that age, and also predicted reading achievement at subsequent ages.

Summary of Home Literacy Environment Research

In summary, research on home literacy environments and early literacy learning as described above shows that the concept of "home literacy environment" is multifaceted. Different components, activities, and interaction styles used during shared readings at home support the development of different literacy skills in young children. Conceptualizations of the home literacy environment include activities such as shared book reading, and also more complicated conceptualizations which include not only literacy activities but beliefs, routines, resources, and the quality of the interactions between parents and children.

Some of the studies discussed used large data sets, particularly from the National Head Start Program. Other studies involved small samples. Several studies included diverse populations and some of them desegregated the data to report effects across different types of families (mostly by ethnicity and SES). Data collection for these studies included structured observations, self-reports, and interviews as well as outcome measures mostly related to receptive vocabulary and concepts of print. The findings from the studies showed a positive relationship between a rich literacy environment defined in terms of opportunities to share readings, the quality of the interactions between parent and child while reading, as well as the existence of resources that support literacy learning. Research on conceptualizations, which included an active home literacy environment, explained most of the variance in studies that measured literacy outcomes, mostly through receptive vocabulary measures.

Although the studies of home literacy environment with diverse populations discussed here showed a positive relationship between home literacy environments, literacy practices, interaction styles, and language and literacy acquisition, it is critical to note that the designs of the studies were based on what is expected from mainstream populations. The measures used and the observations made were related to a norm which might not reflect the cultural and linguistic differences of the subjects involved in the study. For example, minority, low SES, and culturally different parents were expected to show the same styles of interaction, cultural ways, and/or strategies used by White, middle-class families or they were considered to be "disadvantaged" or in "deficit." There was no recognition of the families' culturally specific literacy practices and how they might contribute to the language and literacy learning situation or what their children know. In order to illustrate a framework that challenges these limitations, in the following section a sociocultural perspective on family literacy research is discussed.

A SOCIOCULTURAL RESEARCH PERSPECTIVE ON FAMILY LITERACY

Researchers who take a sociocultural perspective in the study of family literacy observe and describe ways in which families share literacy with their children at home and in the community in order to learn what children know about language and literacy, rather than report on what the children do not know in relation to the expectations of school systems, which are based on White, middle-class values and experiences. The studies are qualitative in nature and samples are small. This research perspective contrasts with the home literacy environment studies in which the purpose of the research is to describe globally what families do in support of their children's literacy learning rather than to explain the outcomes in relation to acquired literacy skills which is prevalent in the research described in the previous section. Kersten (2007) argues that it is important for research related to the construct of family literacy to focus on the description of the rich literacy lives of low SES families exemplified by the work of Taylor and Dorsey-Gaines (1988). She quotes Barton and Hamilton's (1998) claim that today, "the term family literacy is part of a deficit model because it focuses on what low socioeconomic (SES) families and children lack as compared to middle-class ones rather than on their strengths" (p. 152) and argues for the importance of providing accounts of local literacies that are often at "odds with other public images of literacy" (p. 4).

A sociocultural perspective of family literacy argues that literacy learning cannot be abstracted from the cultural practices and the context of its development (Gutíerrez, 2002). From this, it follows that the acquisition of literacy is a socially mediated process supported by the forms of mediation that are available as well as individual participation across different cultural practices. This perspective is based on the viewpoint that culture is central to learning in general and helps mediate human activity. Moll (2000) states that culture per se cannot be isolated, but can be studied by examining how people live. Culture is not equated with race, ethnicity, or a set of traits assumed to exist among members of a community (Gutíerrez & Rogoff, 2003).

Studies of literacy practices from this perspective do not question whether or how well children can read and write but rather ask what children know about literacy and how it is intrinsically informed by their social and cultural upbringing (Gutíerrez, Baquedano-Lopez, Alvarez & Chiu, 1999; Moll, Saez, & Dworin, 2001; Rueda & McIntyre, 2002). Some studies conducted from a sociocultural perspective are descriptive of a specific cultural group. Others investigate differences in literacy practices not only among cultures but also between the home culture and school literacy expectations. In order to examine different studies in family literacy from a sociocultural perspective, I have separated them by central topics.

Research on Discontinuities Between Home and School

A number of studies with different populations (Latinos, Hmong, African Americans, working-class youth, and Native Americans) have investigated discontinuities between learning at home and school from a sociocultural perspective (e.g., Foster, 1995; Gallimore, Boggs, & Jordan, 1974; Laureau, 1989; Moll, 1994; Purcell-Gates, 1995; Reese & Gallimore, 2000; Trueba, Jacobs, & Kirton, 1990; Valdes, 1996). The large number of studies reflects the interest of qualitative researchers in issues of incongruence between ways of learning at home and school and how these differences might affect minority children's learning. In general, these studies examine discontinuities related to differences in cultural ways of learning, the linguistic and literacy knowledge that children bring from home, discourse, and the school expectations for both children and families.

Foster (1995) analyzed and discussed discontinuities between home and school for African Americans; Gallimore, Boggs, and Jordan (1974) examined conflicts between Hawaiian children and their teachers, which were a byproduct of differences between socialization patterns used at home and literacy learning at school. A sociological study by Laureau (1989) examined and explained the cultural ways that parents from different social classes used to shape their young children's literacy learning experiences at home and their impact in schools designed to serve the needs of mainstream middle-class populations. Moll (1994) discussed knowledge and cultural ways related to early literacy learning existing in Hispanic homes, which were seldom recognized or valued by schools. Purcell-Gates (1995) explored the functions and effects of home literacy practices and cultural ways on the lives of children and schools. She explained that

> social class differences have predicted literacy skill achievement. If you are a child born into a family that is not middle class and educated, your chances of achieving a literacy level equal to that of another child born into such a family is low. (pp. 179–180)

Reese and Gallimore (2000) and Valdes (1996) described cultural ways existing in Mexican families that support literacy learning which were not validated by schools, and Trueba, Jacobs, and Kirton (1990) described discontinuities between home and school that led to school problems and misunderstandings of Hmong refugees in a small town school in the United States. In addition, Cazden (1986) and Tharp (1989) documented existing discontinuities for some cultural groups between home and school in such areas as linguistic codes, narrative patterns, motivation, participant structures, teaching strategies, and learning styles.

Not everyone agrees that discontinuity between ways of learning at home and school is an explanation for literacy learning problems that culturally different children have once they get to school. Weisner, Gallimore, and Jordan (1988) criticize this discontinuity perspective because of within group variability. They believe that there are within group differences in SES, parents' education, language used at home, and other variables among individuals from specific ethnic and/or racial groups. There is also a danger in stereotyping individuals when characteristics are generalized to an entire group of people, especially in studies that are descriptive in nature. Chandler, Argyris, Barnes, Goodman, and Snow (1985) also have pointed out that variability within different cultural groups and the ways that people adapt to change and new circumstances might affect the literacy acquisition of their children.

Explaining the failure of culturally different children as a consequence of discontinuities between home and school might further support a deficit perspective, which sees the cultural ways of non-mainstream groups as inadequate rather than different. However, the fact that schools tend to favor middle-class cultural ways and values seems to hurt the opportunity for success of children whose language and culture are different from what is expected in school settings.

Researchers such as Weisner (1997) and Gutíerrez and Rogoff (2003) perceive problems with studying issues of discontinuity between home and school under the assumptions that culture is static and categorical, and that differences also can be defined as traits. Therefore, they call for an approach to the study of home-school discontinuities that takes into account the histories and valued practices of cultural groups—a cultural-historical approach to the study of learning at home versus learning at school. Within this approach, learning is studied as "a process occurring within activity" (p. 20), where the characteristics of the individual (histories and valued practices) are imbedded in the context in which the activity takes place.

Issues of discontinuity, individual variability, group traits, and cultural ways of learning have been studied from a variety of perspectives and with various approaches or models. Each perspective colors the analysis of the data and thus the results and interpretations of the researchers. Research from several perspectives is examined next.

Cultural Practices Perspective and Literacy Learning

Cultural practices are defined as authentic literacy practices existing in the every day life of children, which informally support their literacy learning, and contrast with the ways literacy is learned in institutional settings such as schools. In discussions of family literacy practices, one of the recurring topics is the cultural mismatches among the discourse and literacy learning experiences of homes, schools, and communities (Heath, 1983; Moll, Amanti, Neff, & Gonzalez, 1992; Rogers, 2001). Mismatches have educational implications as pointed out by Purcell-Gates (1996), Taylor (1983), Teale (1986) and Gee (1996), among others, who have stated that children who share the most with the culture of schools are those who find more congruency with schools' practices, and therefore they are better able to succeed in school. In addition, the attitudes of educators toward minority students with different literacy backgrounds can result in differential treatment in the classroom and lowered expectations and opportunities. Luke (1996) has used the construct of "capital" to reveal and examine ways in which groups of people or individuals are favored within particular social and economic contexts. Bourdieu (1974) explained how schools use "objective processes which continually exclude children from the less privileged classes" (p. 32). Examples include the school and the teachers overlooking ways in which culturally different children interact with texts, or the discourse patterns which those children bring from home, which are different from what is expected in school and which may differ from mainstream children.

Although non-mainstream families often hold different or contrasting views about literacy and schooling, research conducted with these families shows that they value and respect the literacy learned in school (Carger, 1996; McCarthey, 2000). According to Purcell-Gates (2007), "the impact, or influence, of school-based or privileged literacy practices on individuals' out-of-school socioculturally situated literacy practices" (p. 15) is an area that needs to be researched and theorized. For this reason, Purcell-Gates has developed the Cultural Practices of Literacy Study (CPLS) with the goal "to explore and begin to theorize the relationships between situated literacy practices and literacy as it is learned within formal school contexts" (pp. 198–199). For the purpose of her study, sociocultural groups are defined as:

> groups of individuals who share common, and often unrecognized or nonconscious, values, beliefs, social structures, norms, conventions, activities and discursive practices. Sociocultural groups may be marked by race, ethnicity, language, gender, class, age…Individuals may participate as members in multiple sociocultural groups as they engage in different aspects of their life. (p. 17)

Recent results of the Purcell-Gates' study group have the potential to inform other researchers and educators about the differences in literacy practices at home and school, and how these differences might be mediated to insure all students' success in school. One of the main differences is related to the different types of authentic materials that support diverse children's early literacy learning at home, in comparison with materials used at school.

Discourse Perspective and Literacy Learning

Another perspective for exploring discontinuities between home and school is through the study of discourse. Gee's framework (1996) on discourse has been influential in the area of family literacy research, and it is important to examine further its meaning. Discourse is a theoretical construct that provides a way to examine discourse practices across settings (home vs. school) and explain mismatches and discontinuities that often separate home and community discourse from that of the schools and other social institutions (Gee, 1996). It has been used to explain the discontinuity for culturally and linguistically different children (Moll et al., 1992; Purcell-Gates, 1995).

Gee (1999) makes a distinction between d (discourse), which refers to "language-in-use or stretches of language (like conversations or stories)" (p. 17), and D (Discourse), which includes linguistic aspects of language and also beliefs, sociocultural issues, and political issues related to language. Gee calls D "language plus 'other stuff'" (p. 17). The "other stuff" includes beliefs, symbols, objects, tools, and places connected to a particular identity. Gee believes that discourses do not have discrete borders, so school discourse can influence home discourse, as described by Purcell-Gates (2007).

According to Gee (1996), children acquire their primary discourse at home and in the community by exposure, immersion, and practice. As children learn their primary discourse, they also learn ways of believing, practicing, and performing literacy. Children who have the least trouble in the transition between home and school are those from homes and communities where the discourse and cultural ways of learning are similar to those used in school settings. The primary discourse of children from White, middle-class families is very similar to the school discourse. Children from culturally and linguistically diverse families, however, bring to the school setting primary discourses that can be quite different from the school discourse. In addition, school personnel often do not recognize the literacy knowledge that minority children possess (Rogers, 2003). As a result, learning the secondary discourse of school is tenuous for these children.

Working from the discourse perspective, Rogers (2003) studied the out-of-school literacy practices of an African American family. Her studies of discourse intersect ideology and subjectivity, which inform the literacy practices of the family in her study. Building on the work of others (Delpit, 1995; Erickson, 1993; Gee, 1996; Heath, 1983; Mercado & Moll, 1997), Rogers situated her research on family literacy practices "within the cultural discursive mismatch social debate" (p. 4). She described the discourse mismatch as a "lack of alignment between the culture, language and knowledge of working-class students and dominant institutions such as schools" (p. 5). Rogers used the discourse construct (d/D and primary vs. secondary discourse) because she felt it provided a better explanation of the differences between home and school.

Beyond the differences in discourse practices in the family that she studied, Rogers (2003) found that there are issues of ideology, subjectivity, and power among discursive contexts. She saw problems with setting up boundaries between primary and secondary discourses and also addressed the issue of ideology acquisition as students learn secondary discourses.

This discourse framework also has been used to demonstrate that children who do well in school often have access to "schooled" literacy (Purcell-Gates, 1996; Taylor, 1983; Teale, 1986). These include stories the children hear or read, question-and-answer interaction patterns, multiple experiences with a variety of genres of books and texts within the context of their home, and primary discourses which are more congruent with the one used at school. The cultural practices perspective and the discourse perspective are approaches to the study of family literacy practices and the differences between those practices and what is expected of students in a mainstream classroom. The discourse construct is effective for studying the use of language as a specific aspect of literacy in the home. Both perspectives also examine the knowledge and skills that children learn in their specific cultural setting, regardless of their congruency with school expectations.

This particular type of study has the potential to inform educators and change the ways in which literacy is taught in schools. We need more research that describes what happens to culturally different children when they attend schools where teachers value and understand how different cultural ways and literacy models support early literacy learning, and try to create congruence between learning at home and at school. These studies could be complemented by quantitative studies which could measure literacy learning outcomes for children in those settings.

The studies discussed here illustrate how differences in cultural practices and discourse could create incongruence between home and school that can affect literacy learning. Their findings suggest a need to accept and connect with the knowledge and cultural ways that children from diverse families bring from home, in order to facilitate their transition into schooling. This suggests a need for schools to adapt their teaching approaches to include and accept multiple cultural ways of learning. Rather than expecting non-mainstream families to change and learn White middle-class values and cultural ways of learning, educators need to redesign schooling and learning in ways that are appropriate to diverse settings where multiple paths toward literacy learning are accepted and celebrated.

Specific Home Literacy Practices and Mismatches Between Home and School

The studies discussed in this section employ a sociocultural perspective toward specific features of home literacy practices that contribute to a mismatch between home and school. Rather than a simple measure of children's language and literacy skills, these studies describe how language skills are related to academic success as well as variables such as reading practices, learning styles, resources in the home, and literacy practices that differ from mainstream practices.

According to Vernon-Feagans, Hammer, Miccio, and Manlove (2001), superior narrative skills in poor African American children correlated negatively with literacy, while the narrative skills of Caucasian students in the same classrooms were positively related to achievement and school literacy. The authors believe that a deficit explanation of early literacy acquisition and experiences of minority children exists because of a narrow view about literacy and culture. When the participants in a study are minorities, a problem occurs if literacy is seen as a neutral practice because a view of literacy as neutral tends to privilege literacy practices and values of White, middle-class communities.

In relation to social class, studies have found that some literacy practices are not valued in school, regardless of the family's ethnicity. Believing that school-based literacy practices help marginalize the literacy activity that exists in the homes of poor children, Knobel and Lankshear (2003) analyzed three research studies involving children who were culturally different and/or from low-income homes (Hicks, 2002; Pahl, 2002; Volk & De Acosta, 2001). They found that the knowledge the children in these studies brought to school was not recognized or acknowledged by the teachers. For example, the subject in Hicks' study was White, from a low SES family, and used literacy practices that were not valued in school, although his family thought he was a gifted learner. Hicks explained this discontinuity as a case of "dissonance between school practices and working class values" (p. 99).

Using case studies, Compton-Lilly (2007) examined home literacy practices that were valued and others that were devalued in mainstream classrooms. She looked specifically at the reading practices of nine mothers and their children. Similar to the subjects in Hicks' (2002) study, the mothers demonstrated reading abilities that were recognized and valued in the home setting but not at school. For example, some non-mainstream mothers read newspapers, novels, and on one case American history texts despite the negative assumptions teachers at her school routinely made about parents in the community. In addition, the mothers in this study shared books and other texts with their children and helped them with their homework. Many of these shared reading practices reflected sophisticated understandings about reading such as making sure that children understood what they read rather than focusing on decoding. Other reading practices reflected parental school experiences rather than current reading pedagogy (i.e., having children copy words in order to learn them, practicing with flashcards). In both cases, these practices demonstrate the commitment that parents exhibited in helping children to become readers. Compton-Lilly (2004) reported that her case studies "demonstrate that parents and children often display reading abilities and fulfill roles related to reading and schooling that are highly valued within the local communities and families but generally remain unnoticed and unappreciated by official institutions" (p. 78). If schools expect that parents support their children in their transition to schooling, the parents' cultural ways should be recognized, even when their literacy practices may be different at home from the ones used at school. Schools could use some of the cultural ways from their children's homes to connect with parents and then, introduce them to alternative ways to read books or share literacy with their children. Success in school, according to Compton-Lilly, "is contingent on a complex set of practices and ways of being that often fail to reflect the rich strengths and abilities that are valued in the home communities" (p. 75). For example, Compton-Lilly reported how she used children's jump rope rhymes and clapping rhymes as early literacy texts in her first-grade classroom when it became evident that her students were not familiar with the traditional nursery rhymes that were part of the first-grade curriculum.

Rather than ignoring the differing literacy skills and strengths of non-mainstream students, such as the role of storytelling in the early literacy lives of children; or the different conceptions about writing that children bring from home; or the nature of parent-child interactions during shared readings, Compton-Lilly (2004) argues that educators ought to capitalize on the knowledge that diverse families contribute to today's schools. She asserts that:

> the abilities that diverse families bring to school are not only tools to engage students with academic tasks but also valuable skills and abilities that can translate into ways of being that have significant value within school contexts. (p. 97)

In doing research with culturally and linguistically different families, it is important to understand that incongruence may exist between the ways that children learn literacy at home and the expected literacy practices at school. The study of cultural ways and literacy practices in diverse settings needs to take into consideration that there are multiple ways to become literate as described in Dyson (2003), instead of perceiving anything that is not grounded in White, middle-class ways as deficient.

Some studies from a sociocultural perspective describe and report on the availability of literacy materials and resources in the home environment as well as how those materials and resources are used in literacy activities. Makin (2003) discussed research that highlighted the influence of the home environment on literacy learning (Cairney, 2003; Purcell-Gates, 1996; Saracho, 2002) as she explained the lack of congruency between what and how children learn at home and at school. She found that in many situations the home environment was rich in available resources, but the use of resources was restricted to a narrow range of books, paper, and writing implements for some children. In addition, if materials in bilingual homes are in the native language, children might have more difficulty making the transition to English materials at school. She stated:

> When a print rich environment is restricted to the dominant language, children whose home language or dialect is a language or a dialect other than the standard language or dialect of power within a society face many difficulties in literacy learning…Research studies confirm that cultural as well as linguistic differences are often overlooked in such cases and that the children often learn the new language at the expense of their communities' languages or dialects. (p. 332)

Another topic for research within this perspective is the family's attitudes toward literacy and learning. It is believed that bilingual families might have more disparity in this area than low SES, English-speaking families. In a sociocultural ethnography of family literacy practices in a Chinese community, Li (2002) explored the intersection between home literacy, culture, and schooling through case studies of four Chinese immigrant children. Her book described the challenges faced by the children and their families as they tried to understand an educational system very different from their own. She found that Chinese parents' views about being literate were embedded in Confucian principles, which influenced the way literacy was learned and taught, with an emphasis on rote memory, copying, and imitating as one became literate. Chinese families saw learning as a formal and individual activity. Learning for these families was gaining knowledge and, therefore there was no room for creative or social activities. Chinese "parents regard schools as a place for knowledge and discipline and their own role as one of moral supporters" (p. 176). Differences in practices found across the families in the study were attributed to differences in educational attainment of the parents, which also was an important factor in parents' understanding and adapting to new ways of becoming literate. Li concluded that "because literacy is a 'cultural practice,' parents from different cultures have different beliefs about what it means to be literate, how to acquire literacy and the role of schooling in achieving literacy" (p. 170).

Li, like Valdes (1996) and Auerbach (1995), found problematic the use of interventions that are created to fix differences or deficits as perceived by schools and teachers. Li supports partnerships between home and school that investigate, celebrate, and validate students' and their families' multiple literacies and cultural resources.

An enrichment alternative to deficit based interventions are programs that accept and celebrate the cultural ways used in diverse homes in support of the children literacy learning, and use that knowledge as stepping-stones to new ways to share literacy. These interventions help create congruency among different ways to become literate and create bridges that facilitate the children's transition between learning at home and school.

Looking at similar issues with another cultural group, Valdes (1996) found that the Latino parents in her study believed that everyone had different talents and there were different ways to show intelligence. Furthermore they did not give schooling high significance. Instead, it was more important for children to learn to discipline themselves, respect others, and take responsibility for younger siblings. These values determined how the families viewed their children's schooling and learning at home. This study showed another role of culture and the home in the development of children's literacy practices, and it also raised awareness of discontinuity between home and school, especially in cases where the values and beliefs at home and school were different.

Cultural Models and Literacy Learning

Gallimore and Goldenberg (2001) define cultural models as

> shared schema or normative understandings of how the world works, or ought to work.... Cultural models encode shared environmental and event interpretations, what is valued, and ideal, what settings should be enacted and avoided, who should participate, the rules of the interaction, and the purpose of the interaction. (p. 47)

Although diverse families often have values and beliefs about learning and literacy that differ significantly from mainstream families, these beliefs might change after exposure to and experience with classroom expectations and practices. To study changes in beliefs and literacy practices at home with new immigrant Mexican families, Reese and Gallimore (2000) used a cultural model approach to studying learning at home, specifically early literacy development in children. The cultural models approach had been used previously in other studies of socialization and child development across different cultures (D'Andrade, 1995; LeVine, 1977; Weisner,

1997). In this approach, researchers view culture as a flexible and dynamic construct rather than an unchanging and external force.

Reese and Gallimore (2000) described the effect that parents' views and beliefs about literacy have on the way they structured activities to support literacy learning at home. One belief found among many new immigrants was that children learned to read through repeated practice when they started school. Reese and Gallimore feel that this belief, or cultural model, is derived from the experiences of previous generations who lived in rural ranchos where there was little formal schooling. This belief, along with others in the Latino cultural model, guides what most immigrant families do with their children.

However, Gallimore and Reese (1999) had previously reported that Mexican immigrant parents did not feel that their cultural models were static; rather, they considered their beliefs to be flexible and adaptable to new circumstances. For example, once parents learned that reading to children at home supported literacy learning at school, they complied with the teachers' assignments and suggestions. Reese and Gallimore (2000) stated that:

> …while parents did not initially share the teacher's view that reading aloud to young children was helpful in terms of their subsequent literacy development, they did follow through on teacher suggestions and requirements to read at home and appreciated the effects that this newly appropriated activity had produced. (pp. 130–131)

In this particular situation, continuity between home and school was created in response to teachers' requests and not just from parents' observations in the new environment. Perhaps the viewpoint that cultural models are flexible helps to explain why new immigrant parents were willing to modify and adapt their cultural ways in a new context.

According to Reese and Gallimore (2000), changes in the Mexican parents' cultural models for literacy development were not seen as threats to their traditional values. Rather, the researchers viewed parents as "powerful agents of adaptation."

Because of the flexible nature of the cultural model, Reese and Gallimore (2000) found that continuities and discontinuities co-exist in home-school literacy interactions. This finding contrasts with discontinuity explanations from previous research, (e.g., Goldenberg & Gallimore, 1995), which describes discontinuities and no commonalities between learning at home and school as immigrant parents adapt to their new context.

From the previously discussed studies, we have found that research studies conducted from a sociocultural perspective describe, explain, and sometimes justify the values, beliefs, and practices of diverse families on literacy and learning. This body of research also has the potential to mediate the effects of deficit perspectives and to highlight the skills, knowledge, and strengths that students bring to the classroom.

RESEARCH RELATED TO FAMILY LITERACY PROGRAMS AS INTERVENTIONS

Research discussed above has shown how the contributions of low SES and minority parents to early literacy learning are different from those of middle-class parents. Other research shows that discourses and cultural ways that low SES and minority children bring to the learning situation are generally not recognized in schools, which are based on values of a White, middle-class population. Examples of differences in discourse and cultural ways which might be incongruent with school expectations include interaction patterns between adults and children. Who starts an interaction? Can a child talk at any time? Who chooses the book to read? What types of questions does parent or child ask? They also include the use and purpose of storytelling in support of children's language development. In relation to shared-readings, the narrative styles can vary from what is expected by teachers. Some parents might believe their role is to read the story from beginning to end, with no interactions, while other parents may extend the story while reading. In keeping with their belief about their role as teachers, some parents may teach values and morals as they read a story.

Because of the lack of congruency between the ways that non-mainstream children learn at home and those used at school, family literacy programs have been created as interventions to help mostly low SES and culturally different parents prepare their children for school and in order to facilitate the transition between home and school for these children. These programs have different purposes and designs, and are based on different definitions of family literacy. Some programs teach parents how to support their children's literacy learning in a school-like manner; other programs emphasize the use of authentic, culturally relevant experiences where parents create literacy experiences with their children at home and in the community.

Deficit Model

Auerbach (1995) has found that many programs are developed from a deficit perspective (e.g., Even Start, Early Access to Success in Education [EASE]). These programs or interventions are based on the premise that low SES and minority parents do not provide young children with preschool literacy experiences that prepare them for future school success. The programs then, try to teach parents how to support their children's literacy learning in ways that are expected by schools, without acknowledging minority parents' contributions to their children's learning, which might be informed by different cultural ways, discourse, and languages than the mainstream.

Enrichment Model

In contrast, enrichment programs (e.g., FLAME, ILP models) recognize the knowledge, cultural ways, and discourses of the home. They use what parents already do with their children at home as a starting point and add new literacy practices in order to create some congruency between what children learn at home and at school (Gutíerrez & Rogoff, 2003; Paratore, 2001; Rodríguez-Brown, 2004).

A number of researchers support an enrichment perspective in the development of family literacy programs. Auerbach (1995) believed that such programs recognize parents' strengths. Goldenberg, Reese and Gallimore (1992) agreed with this view, stating that "intervention plans must be informed by parents' understandings no less than by our own, presumably more scientific ones" (p. 530). Because of the culturally different ways in which families share literacy, Heath (1983) suggested that school programs should also make accommodations to the types of literacy children practice at home rather than focus on the practices of middle-class mainstream families. Delgado-Gaitan, in her 1993 ethnography of a community-based literacy program in Carpinteria, California, called COPLA (Comite de Padres Latinos/Committee of Latin Parents), has provided evidence that programs that are directed toward culturally and linguistically diverse families empower parents to learn more about schools and school literacy and gain confidence in their relationships with teachers and the schools. Their children can benefit from new and additional literacy interactions at home.

For most enrichment programs, family literacy is defined as learning at home in ways that are culturally relevant to the families. The programs raise awareness of and respect for cultural and linguistic differences that the participants might bring into the program as well as differences in discourse and cultural ways of learning between home and school (Gee, 1999; Rogers, 2001,

2002). They design activities that use "funds of knowledge" (Moll & Greenberg, 1990) from the community as resources to new learning.

Enrichment programs allow parents to share literacy with their children in the language they know better and to continue to share literacy activities that are culturally specific even though they do not resemble school activities. Features such as storytelling keep the program relevant to the populations involved in the program, regardless of language or culture (Auerbach, 1989). At the same time, families are introduced to new activities and practices that support literacy learning at school but which are still culturally and linguistically appropriate for the family. Parents also learn to appreciate their role as their children's first teachers and to value their participation and volunteering in school activities that support their children's learning.

Research on Specific Program Models

Research and evaluation studies with family literacy programs examine the effects of interventions on the home literacy environment or provide descriptions of how program participation changes the home learning environment and parent-child literacy interactions (Paratore, 2001; Rodríguez-Brown, 2004). Evidence of changes can be found in artifacts such as parents' self-reports, samples of parents' writing, or portfolios that parents prepare to share with teachers (Paratore, 2001). Some programs, such as Project FLAME (Rodríguez-Brown, 2004, 2009) collect data through observations, standardized tests for both adults and children, and parent self-reporting of home literacy practices. Project FLAME and the Intergenerational Literacy program (ILP) models have already been discussed in previous reviews of research on family literacy (Purcell-Gates, 2000). In the following pages, descriptions, as well as research and evaluation findings, from several family literacy models are included. The program models discussed in this chapter were chosen because of the availability of research publications and evaluation findings that explain their effectiveness and their effects on low SES, culturally, and/or linguistically different families and their children.

Project Early Access to Success in Education (EASE) (Jordan, Snow, & Porche, 2000) is described as a family literacy "...intervention designed to provide parents...with a theoretical understanding of how to help their children with scaffolded-interactive-practices to facilitate their children's early literacy development..." (p. 524). The program provides parents with ideas to support their children's oral development with a focus on vocabulary, the use of narratives, and exposition.

The program design is supported by previous research, which shows that certain characteristics of family literacy make school literacy easier for children. According to Snow (2001), opportunities in high quality language interactions prepare children for the task of text comprehension after basic skills are in place. Also, preschoolers' engagement in oral extended discourse increases kindergarten and first-grade reading outcomes (Dickinson & Tabors, 1991). Children's talk that includes narratives, explanations, and extensions over several turns that occur during shared readings and during toy play also supports learning (Beals & De Temple, 1993). In addition, storybook reading promotes literacy development and the benefits of print-related, parent-child activities (Sénéchal et al., 1998).

The program presents models of effective language interactions through systematic parent coaching and an increase in the number of interactions through structured parent activities over time. The program recognizes literacy attainment as a set of abilities that include both language and literacy, and believes that parent training's efficacy has an effect on children's language and literacy abilities.

The evaluation of Project EASE (Jordan et al., 2000) included a sample of 240 children attending kindergarten—177 children who participated in the intervention and 71 children in a control group. These children attended four Title I schools in high poverty areas that were considered low scoring schools according to standardized tests scores.

The intervention used through Project EASE included four training or coaching sessions for parents over a five-month period. Each training session was followed by opportunities for structured parent-child activities that supported practice and interaction. Also, teachers sent home scripted activities (interactions, demonstrations) using pre-selected books.

The data used in the study included a parent survey (self-report of parent literacy practices at home), a measure of verbal receptive vocabulary, and subtests from an instrument called CAPS, which measured vocabulary, story comprehension, sequencing in story production, letter recognition, sound awareness (onset-rime), and concepts of print (environmental print, forming words, and invented spelling).

For analysis purposes, the data were organized into three composite variables (language, print, and sounds). Control variables included home literacy environment (a composite score), home literacy activities, and program participation. Data analysis included descriptive statistics, Pearson correlations, and regression. The results showed that the program (intervention) had the most effect on the language skills of children. Parents' attendance to sessions determined the size of the effect. The results from the PPVT show no effect on vocabulary development. This finding was explained by the authors as related to the fact that the PPVT measures incidental vocabulary acquisition and may not be related to the curriculum used in the program. The authors claimed that the size of the effects of the program was better than expected. They believe that a more serious investment is needed to find program effects. They cited a limitation with the fact that the study was not longitudinal and with the use of self-reports, rather than observations to account for home literacy practices and environments.

From a sociocultural perspective, it is important to consider the relevance of the program or intervention activities for all participant families, whether the families see themselves as part of the program, and whether what they know is valued by the program. The program is scripted and it seems as if no consideration is given to characteristics of the population to be served. Were the participants' cultural ways, discourses, and knowledge acknowledged in the development of the intervention? In other words, in planning the intervention, were any of the families' practices seen as resources, which could facilitate a home-school connection, and/or create some congruency between the ways the participants' children learn at home and at school?

Another well-known family literacy model is the Even Start program, which as a family service intervention includes four components: (a) early childhood education, (b) parenting education, (c) adult education, and (d) parent-child joint literacy activities. Only the last component relates to parent-child interactions that support literacy learning. The program is considered a national family literacy model, and it is funded by the United States Department of Education.

The third and most recent evaluation of Even Start was made public in 2003 (St. Pierre et al., 2003). The evaluation included an empirical study (EDS) with a randomized sample of program participants and a control group of non-participants. The sample for the study included an overrepresentation of Hispanics; most of the sample came from urban areas.

According to the researchers, all the instruments (surveys, tests) were developed or existed in English and Spanish since about 33% of Even Start participants were Hispanic. No measure of language proficiency (English) was used with the parents or the children to determine the language to be used for data collection. Parents' self-reports of language proficiency for themselves and their children determined the language used in all data collection procedures.

The findings from the study showed that Even Start children and their parents made gains in literacy assessments and other measures. However, children in the program did not gain more than children in the control group. In general, Even Start parents and their children showed small gains on the literacy measures and scored low in relation to national norms when they left the program. In interpreting the data, the authors explained that Even Start serves a very disadvantaged population.

From the evaluation report, it appears that time spent in program activities is central to program effectiveness. Since the program participants appear to be diverse, one wonders whether the purpose of the program is clear to the families, and whether the relevance of program activities to a diverse population (SES, race, ethnicity, culture, and language) could explain the reported lack of interest in these activities. Perhaps services offered to these families do not take into account their strengths and their contributions to their children's learning within their own cultural and economical milieus. Also, there is no recognition that many of the subjects have a native language other than English, and many of them have knowledge that they could demonstrate or explain better in their native language.

Another program model that has been studied is the Learning Together: Read and Write with your Child (Phillips, Hayden, & Norris, 2007). This family literacy program was developed in Alberta, Canada and directed toward preschool children and their families. The program includes a series of activities designed to improve children's literacy, the parents' literacy, and the ability of parents to support their children's literacy learning.

A longitudinal study (Phillips et al., 2007) of the effectiveness of the program was conducted between 2001 and 2006. Participants in the study were low-income, low-educational background parents and their children. The study was grounded on the premise that parental interactive strategies, and the quantity and variety of print materials available in the home were factors that could affect children's preparation for meaningful formal literacy instruction.

Results of the study showed an effect between parents' education and reading ability and their children's reading ability at preschool age. Controlling for the children's literacy level at the beginning of the intervention, the data showed that the intervention worked for all participant children. The results also showed that ethnicity and native language were predictors of parents' literacy level. As in many other programs, the results showed that parents acquired and implemented more home literacy activities as a result of the program. They also showed appreciation and a sense of efficacy in learning new strategies to engage and respond to their children's emergent literacy learning. Parents were able to help their children learn reading and writing at home and also showed an interest in improving their own literacy.

Finally, Words-to-Go! A Family Literacy Program (Reutzel, Fawson, & Smith, 2006) was program designed for settings in which the Words-to-Go curriculum materials were used in classrooms. The program involves parents in their children's early literacy with a focus on vocabulary development. The intervention for parents includes training through a set of three workshops directly related to the content of the Words-to-Go program used in their children's classrooms. Also, during the school year, teachers send home weekly lessons for parents to share with their children. A pretest, posttest comparison of first graders' word reading, word writing ability, and criterion-referenced test performance in reading showed significant effects in favor of the group that participated in the Words-to-Go program. Positive perceptions toward the program were reported by parents, teachers, and children.

The research studies with a variety of family literacy models described above are just a sample of current programs whose effectiveness has been evaluated or researched. Other studies of family literacy interventions for which there is research data and that show positive results for parental involvement in children's learning are described in Saint-Laurent and Giasson (2005), Mandel-Morrow, Kuhn, and Schwanenflugel (2006) and Dworin (2006).

METHODOLOGY ISSUES IN THE STUDY OF FAMILY LITERACY

Validity of Self-Reported Data

One of the problems that arises when joint book reading is a major variable in a study of the home literacy environment is the validity of the data collected since most data collected is self-reported. Parents are asked to record the frequency of joint readings and other literacy practices during activities with their children. It is believed that they might report information that reflects what they think the researchers expect, rather than what they actually do with their child. This is especially true in studies with large databases, such as the National Head Start and Evaluation Project.

In order to increase the validity of self-reported data, particularly in studies that involve shared readings, researchers have designed alternative ways to collect data on the quality and quantity of shared readings at home. One of the alternatives, used by Sénéchal, LeFevre, Hudson, and Lawson (1996), includes the development of a list of book titles and authors that are popular for young children. Then they ask participants in a study to mark the book titles and authors that they recognize. This procedure may not, however, be valid for low SES, culturally diverse, and linguistically families since the lists are usually based on what middle-class parents read to their children. The use of mixed methods whereby observational data and survey data are collected in order to explain the home literacy environments could facilitate the validation of survey reported data, especially when observations are carried out in a randomized manner.

Studies with Bilingual Families and Their Children

One of the main concerns with the existing research on home literacy environment in bilingual homes, mostly Spanish/English, is that the language proficiency of the participants is not assessed. This has implications for the choice of instruments used, and the validity for data collected, including data collected through surveys. Researchers should question the validity of data collected in English when the subjects are not proficient in English.

Instruments designed to account for the home literacy environment should also take into considerations the variation in discourse patterns and cultural models used in diverse families. This becomes relevant in the interpretation of findings in general, and particularly when explaining the language and literacy development of children in bilingual or multilingual settings. These issues and their effect on the home literacy environment of culturally different children should not be overlooked in future research in family literacy from different perspectives.

Snow (2004) has raised questions and concerns about research conducted in homes where English is the second language, specifically the use of data from the Head Start Project. Her concerns are related to the equivalence in the vocabulary outcomes for children tested in Spanish and in English. For research with Spanish/English bilingual children where the measured outcome is vocabulary knowledge, it is necessary to account for children's vocabulary knowledge in both English and Spanish, in order to determine the full extent of their vocabulary development. Since both languages are used at home and in the community, the children might know words in either Spanish or English, according to the domains in which the words are used.

Another concern is with the use of vocabulary assessments in the native language of the children, which are most often translations from tests in English. Many of the vocabulary tests in English include vocabulary chosen according to the frequency of use in English. The frequency of word use in other languages, such as Spanish, might be different than in English and, as such, the tests might not be equivalent in difficulty. The issue of norms and the type of populations used in the norming of tests that exist in two languages also needs consideration in the selection of instruments that exist in two languages (e.g., Spanish/English).

Like Snow (2004), I question how research studies account for the effects of differences in the literacy environment in bilingual homes. For example, how do researchers account for differences in literacy interactions between bilingual children and their parents when they use books or other materials in Spanish rather than English? If parents have access to materials, such as children's books, written in their native language, there could be a difference in the type of shared reading activities and interactions between them and their children. Parents who are not fully proficient in English may be able to read more fluently, ask more questions, and extend the stories when they do shared-readings in Spanish. The reading fluency of the parents, the questions they ask, and how they interact in relation to the story with their children affect the way parents see their role as language brokers and literacy models, and might have an effect on the outcomes of research with bilingual children and their families. Access to reading materials in the language that parents know best and the type of interaction between parent and child during shared readings is critical in supporting the richness of the home literacy environment.

Use of Variables in Family Literacy Research

A major problem with current research in the home literacy environment is that most studies use only variables such as ethnicity or race and SES for analysis purposes. Differences in cultural ways and discourse patterns in situated practices that have been observed in different types of homes could be contextualized as new variables in a quantifiable manner. Variables that account for cultural differences in the way parents perceive their role as teachers and the role of parents' beliefs about literacy learning and schooling could enrich the findings of these studies and facilitate the understanding of diversity in home literacy environments. Findings from observational studies could facilitate the design and validation of new quantifiable variables which are socioculturally complex and which could be used in large quantitative studies from which generalizations can be made.

SUMMARY

Research on family literacy that is currently available comes from a variety of disciplines (literacy, early childhood education, educational psychology) and programs (Head Start, Even Start). Current family literacy research addresses populations with disabilities, culturally and/or linguistic minority populations, and mainstream groups.

Many of the studies discussed in this review explored the effects of specific interventions; the home literacy environment and/or parent-child interactions during shared reading and/or writing at home, and included a control group with matched characteristics. The preferred methodology used in home literacy environment studies was parents' self-reports of home literacy practices and their frequency (although a few studies also included some home observation to validate the results from the self-reported data). Most of the studies found that SES and parents' education made a difference in the frequency with which parents read or did literacy activities with their children at home. Parents who were poor and did not have much education did not share literacy with their children as often as parents who were financially better off and more educated. Some studies desegregated the data according to race, ethnicity, and immigration status. The data from these studies showed that parents who were English Language Learners (ELL) carried out fewer educational activities at home than parents in any of the other groups studied.

A limitation with current research on home literacy environment is the set of variables being used for analysis purposes. As explained before, there is a need for complex socioculturally derived variables, other than ethnicity, race, and socioeconomic status that should be included in the design of future family literacy research. Observational studies designed to complement quantitative research designs would contribute to the validation of these variables, facilitate the creation of more complex quantifiable variables, and assist in the interpretation of findings.

Also, as discussed earlier, since shared or joint reading accounts for much of the information collected and reported in home literacy environment studies, the nature of the data collected has to include more than parents' self-reports on frequency of joint reading activities. The use of mixed methods whereby observational data and survey data are collected in order to explain the home literacy environments could facilitate the validation of survey reported data, especially when observations are carried out in a randomized manner.

This review includes a body of qualitative research based on a sociocultural perspective that describes the nature and quality of parent-child interactions during shared reading with diverse families, and research that deals with congruency and continuity between the cultural ways and discourses of diverse families and school environments. Issues of what is valued as literacy knowledge in early literacy learning are supported by strong theoretical frameworks: Purcell-Gates (2007) on cultural practices of literacy, and Moll (2005) on the influence and value of community knowledge on literacy learning. Also, Gutiérrez and Rogoff (2003), Gallimore and Goldenberg (2001), Reese et al. (1999), and Reese and Goldenberg (2006) provide theoretical frameworks that take into account a definition of culture not as traits of cultural groups, but as situated learning in which diverse populations are seen as willing to change behaviors and accommodate the multiple spaces and understandings of literacy learning in their lives. More research in family literacy is needed; especially involving the above described theoretical frameworks and paradigms.

There is also a need for more studies that focus on possible barriers for diverse populations to understand, participate in, and benefit from current interventions that are grounded in middle-class mainstream values. Studies of the effectiveness of interventions which recognize differences in values, beliefs, discourses, and cultural ways in diverse populations and add new strategies to parents' repertoire in support of minority children's transition between home and school are also greatly needed. These studies, mostly qualitative in nature, should provide a strong basis for the development of hypotheses, which could also be studied under quantitative paradigms. Across all paradigms, researchers studying diverse populations should be aware of within-group differences in the interpretation of findings.

In spite of the amount of research on the influence of home literacy environments and parent-child interactions, there is a great need for longitudinal studies that could explain the effects of these activities across several years of schooling. We know that the different research paradigms discussed in the chapter complement each other and, as such, should contribute further to what we currently know about families' contributions to their children's literacy learning. Also, more long-term descriptive research is needed on cultural literacy practices among diverse populations, and the role and characteristics of their authentic literacy that supports children's literacy learning in those communities. In support of an easier transition between home and school for children from low SES, diverse families, there is also a need to study the nature, availability, and use of authentic materials in these families' homes and communities and also how these materials support their children's literacy learning. Longitudinal studies of the long-term impact of both deficit and enrichment family literacy program models would make a powerful contribution to the existing literature. It is also important to note that research of parent-child home literacy interactions with older children is almost non-existent.

Finally, since some of the research with families shows that current school expectations are incongruent with cultural ways of learning and discourses of diverse families (low SES, culturally and linguistically different), there is a need for qualitative research that examines what and how children learn literacy at home so that schools learn how to make connections with home learning practices in diverse communities as steppingstones to school learning. The home/school connection is a two-way street (Rodríguez-Brown, 2009). That is, it is necessary to support culturally diverse families in learning about different ways to support their children's learning at home, but is also important for schools to learn, understand, and recognize the contributions of culturally and linguistically different families to their children's learning in order to find functions and applications of this knowledge in their curricula and methodologies. In a diverse society and in the era of globalization, the application of this knowledge in educational settings will make schooling more relevant to the needs of all children.

REFERENCES

Auerbach, E. R. (1989). Toward a social-contextual approach to family literacy. *Harvard Educational Review, 59*, 165–181.

Auerbach, E. R. (1995). Deconstructing the discourse of strengths in family literacy. *Journal of Reading Behavior, 27*, 643–661.

Baker, L., & Scher, D. (2002). Beginning readers' motivation for reading in relation to parental beliefs and home reading experiences. *Reading Psychology, 23*, 239–269.

Baker, L., Scher, D., & Mackler, K. (1997). Home and family influences on motivation for reading. *Educational Psychology, 32*, 69–82.

Barton, D., & Hamilton, M. (1998). *Local literacies: Reading and writing in one community.* New York: Routledge.

Beals, D. E., & De Temple, J. M. (1993). Home contributions to early language and literacy development. In D. Leu & C. Kinzer (Eds.), *Examining central issues in literacy research, theory, and practice. Forty-second yearbook of the National Reading Conference* (pp. 207–215). Chicago: National Reading Conference.

Beals, D., De Temple, J., & Dickinson, D. (1994). Talking and listening that support early literacy development of children from low-income families. In D. Dickinson (Ed.), *Bridges to literacy: Children, families and schools* (pp. 19–42). Cambridge, MA: Blackwell.

Bennett, K. K., Weigel, D. J., & Martin, S. S. (2002). Children's acquisition of early literacy skills: Examining families contributions. *Early Childhood Research Quarterly, 17*, 295–317.

Bourdieu, P. (1974). The school as a conservative force: Scholastic and cultural inequalities. In J. Eggleston (Ed.), *Contemporary research in the sociology of education* (pp. 32–46). London: Methuen.

Bradley, R., Corwyn, R., McAdoo, H. P., & Coll, C. G. (2001). The home environments of children in the United States part I: Variations by age, ethnicity and poverty status. *Child Development, 72*, 1844–1867.

Burgess, J. (1982). The effects of a training program for parents of preschoolers on the children's school readiness. *Reading Improvement, 19*, 313–318.

Burgess, S. (1997). The role of shared reading in the development of phonological awareness: A longitudinal study of middle to upper middle-class children. *Early Child Development and Care, 70*, 37–43.

Burgess, S. R., Hetch, S. A., & Lonigan, C. J. (2002). Relations of the home literacy environment (HLE) to the development of reading-related abilities: A one year longitudinal study. *Reading Research Quarterly, 37*, 408–426.

Cairney, T. H. (2003). Literacy within family life. In N. Hall, J. Larson, & J. Marsch (Eds.), *Handbook of early childhood literacy* (pp. 85–98). London: Sage.

Carger, C. (1996). *Of borders and dreams.* New York: Teachers College Press.

Cazden, C. (1986). Classroom discourse. In M. C. Wittrock (Ed.), *Handbook of research on teaching* (3rd ed., pp. 432–463). New York: MacMillan.

Chandler J., Argyris, D., Barnes, W., Goodman, I., & Snow, C. (1985). Parents as teachers: Observations of low-income parents and children in a homework-like task. In B. Schieffelin, & P. Gilmore (Eds.), *The acquisition of literacy: Ethnographic perspectives* (pp. 171–187). Norwood, NJ: Ablex.

Clay, M. M. (1979). *Stones—The concepts about print test.* Auckland, New Zealand: Heinemann.

Compton-Lilly, C. (2004). *Confronting racism, poverty and power.* Portsmouth, NH: Heinemann.

Compton-Lilly, C. (2007). The complexities of reading capital in two Puerto Rican families. *Reading Research Quarterly, 42*, 72–98.

D'Andrade, R. (1995). *The development of cognitive anthropology.* Cambridge, MA: Cambridge University Press.

De Bruin-Parecki, A., Paris, S. G., & Seidenberg, J. L. (1996). *Characteristics of effective family literacy programs in Michigan.* (NCAL Technical Report TR96-07). Ann Arbor: University of Michigan, National Center on Adult Literacy.

Delgado-Gaitan, C. (1993). Research and policy in reconceptualizing family-schools relationships. In P. Phelan & A. Locke-Davidson (Eds.), *Renegotiating cultural diversity in American schools* (pp. 139–158). New York: Teachers College Press.

Delpit, L. (1995). *Other people's children: Cultural conflict in the classroom*. New York: New Press.

Dickinson, D., & Tabors, P. O. (1991). Early literacy: Linkages between home, school and literacy achievement at age five. *Journal of Research in Childhood Education, 6*(1), 30–46.

Dickinson, D. K., & Tabors, P. O. (Eds.). (2001). *Beginning literacy with language*. Baltimore: Brookes.

Dworin, J. E. (2006). The family stories project: Using funds of knowledge for writing. *The Reading Teacher, 59*, 510–520

Dyson, A. H. (2003). *The brothers and sisters learn to write: Popular literacies in childhood and school cultures*. New York: Teachers College Press.

Erickson, F. (1993). Transformation and school success: The politics and culture of educational achievement. In E. Jacob, & C. Jordan (Eds.), *Minority education: Anthropological perspectives* (pp. 27–52). Westport, CT: Greenwood.

Foster, M. (1995). African American teachers and culturally relevant pedagogy. In J. A. Banks & C. A. M. Banks (Eds.), *Handbook of research in multicultural education* (pp. 570–581). New York: Macmillan.

Gallimore, R., Boggs, J. W., & Jordan, C. (1974). *Culture, behavior and education: A study of Hawaiian-Americans*. Beverly Hills, CA: Sage.

Gallimore, R., & Goldenberg, C. (2001). Analyzing cultural models and settings to connect minority achievement and school improvement research. *Educational Psychologist, 36*(1), 45–56.

Gallimore, R., & Reese, L. J. (1999). Mexican immigrants in urban California: Forging adaptations from familiar and new cultural resources. In M. C. Foblets, & C. I. Pang (Eds.), *Culture, ethnicity and immigration* (pp. 245–263). Leuven, Belgium: ACCO.

Gee, J. P. (1996). *Social linguistics and literacies: Ideologies in discourses*. London: Farmer Press.

Gee, J. P. (1999). *An introduction to discourse analysis: Theory and method*. New York: Routledge.

Goldenberg, C. N. (2004). Literacy for low-income children in the 21st century. In N. Unrau & R. Rudell (Eds.), *Theoretical models and processes of reading* (pp. 1636–1666). Newark, DE: Internaional Reading Association.

Goldenberg, C. N., & Gallimore, R. (1995). Immigrant Latino parents' values and beliefs about their children's education: Continuities and discontinuities across cultures and generations. In P. Pintrich, & M. Maehr (Eds.), *Advances in motivation and achievement* (Vol. 9, pp. 183–228). Greenwich, CT: Ablex.

Goldenberg, C. N., Reese, L., & Gallimore, R. (1992). Effects of literacy materials from school on Latino children's home experiences and early reading achievement. *American Journal of Education, 100*, 497–536.

Griffin, E. A., & Morrison, F. J. (1997). The unique contributions of home literacy environment to differences in early literacy learning. *Early Child Development and Care, 127/128*, 233–243.

Gutiérrez, K. (2002). Studying cultural practices in urban learning communities. *Human Development, 45*, 312–321.

Gutiérrez, K. D., Baquedano-Lopez, P., Alvarez, H., & Chiu, M. M. (1999). Building a culture of collaboration through hybrid language practices. *Theory Into Practice, 38*(2), 87–93.

Gutiérrez, K. D., & Rogoff, B. (2003). Cultural ways of learning: Individual traits or repertoires of practice. *Educational Researcher, 32*(5), 15–25.

Heath, S. B. (1983). *Ways with words: Language, life and work in community and classrooms*. Cambridge, England: Cambridge University Press.

Hicks, D. (2002). *Reading lives: Working-class children and literacy learning*. New York: Teachers College Press.

Jordan, C. E., Snow, C. E., & Porche, M. V. (2000). Project EASE: The effects of a family literacy project on kindergarten students' early literacy skills. *Reading Research Quarterly, 34*, 524–546.

Kaderavek, J. N., & Justice, L. A. (2005). Mother-child storybook interactions: Literacy orientation of preschoolers with hearing impairment. *Journal of Early Childhood Literacy, 7*(1), 49–72.

Kersten, J. (2007). Literacy and choice: Urban students' perceptions of links between home, school and community literacy practices. In V. Purcell-Gates (Ed.), *Cultural practices of literacy: Case studies of language, literacy, social practice, and power* (pp. 133–154). Mahwah, NJ: Erlbaum.

Knobel, M., & Lankshear, C. (2003). Researching young children's out-of-school literacy practices. In N. Hall, J. Larson, & J. Marsch (Eds.), *Handbook of early childhood literacy* (pp. 51–65). London: Sage.

Laureau, A. (1989). *Home advantage: Social class and parental intervention.* New York: Farmer Press.

Leseman, P. P., & de Jong, P. F. (1998). Home literacy: Opportunity, instruction, cooperation and socio-emotional quality predicting early literacy development. *Reading Research Quarterly, 33,* 294–319.

LeVine, R. (1977). Child rearing as cultural adaptation. In P. Leiderman, S. Tulkin, & A. Rosenfeld (Eds.), *Culture and infancy* (pp. 15–27). New York: Academic.

Li, G. (2002). *East is east, West is west?: Home literacy, culture and schooling.* New York: Peter Lang.

Luke, A. (1996). Genres of power? Literacy education and the production of capital. In R. Hasan, & G. Williams (Eds.), *Literacy in society* (pp. 308–338). New York: Longman.

Lyon, G. R. (1999). The NICHD research program in reading development, reading disorders and reading instruction: A summary of research findings. *Keys to successful learning: A national summit on research in learning disabilities.* Washington, DC: National Center for Learning Disabilities.

Makin, L. (2003). Creating positive literacy learning environments in early childhood. In N. Hall, J. Larson, & J. Marsch (Eds.), *Handbook of early childhood literacy* (pp. 327–337). London: Sage.

Mandel-Morrow, L., Kuhn, M. R., & Schwanenflugel, P. J. (2006). The family fluency program. *The Reading Teacher, 60,* 322–333.

McCarthey, S. J. (2000). Home-school connections: A review of literature. *The Journal of Educational Research, 93,* 145–182.

McCoy, L., & Watts, T. (1992). *Learning together: Family literacy in Ontario.* Kingston, Ontario, Canada: Family Literacy Interest Group of the Ontario Reading Association.

Mercado, C. I., & Moll, L. C. (1997). The study of funds of knowledge: Collaborative research in Latino homes. *CENTRO, The Journal of the Center for Puerto Rican Studies, IX* (9), 26–42.

Moll, L. C. (1994). Literacy research in community and classrooms: A sociocultural approach. In R. B. Rudell & H. Singer (Eds.), *Theoretical models and processes of reading* (pp. 179–207). Newark, DE: International Reading Association.

Moll, L. C. (2000). Inspired by Vygotsky: Ethnographic experiments in education. In C. Lee & P. Smagorinsky (Eds.), *Vygotskian perspectives on literacy research: Constructing meaning through collaborative inquiry* (pp. 256–268). New York: Cambridge University Press.

Moll, L. C. (2005). Reflections and possibilities. In N. Gonzalez, L. Moll, & C. Amanti (Eds.), *Funds of knowledge: Theorizing practice in households, communities and classrooms* (pp. 275–288). Mahwah, NJ: Erlbaum.

Moll, L. C., Amanti, C., Neff, D., & Gonzalez, N. (1992). Funds of knowledge for teaching: Using a qualitative approach to connect homes and classrooms. *Theory Into Practice, 31,* 132–141.

Moll, L. C., & Greenberg, J. B. (1990). Creating zones of possibilities: Combining social contexts for instruction. In L. C. Moll (Ed.), *Vygotsky and education* (pp. 319–348). New York: Cambridge University Press.

Moll, L., Saez, R., & Dworin, J. (2001). Exploring biliteracy: Two student case studies of writing as a social practice. *Elementary School Journal, 101,* 435–449.

Moneyhun, C. A. (1997, March). *"Work to be done": Community literacy as a new model of social action for literacy educators.* Paper presented at the annual meeting of the Conference on College Composition and Communication. Phoenix, AZ. (ERIC Document Reproduction Service No. 407-677)

Morrow, L. M. (Ed.). (1995). *Family literacy: Connections in schools and communities.* Newark, DE: International Reading Association.

National Center for Family Literacy (NCFL). (1995). *Family literacy: An overview.* Louisville, KY: Author.

Pahl, K. (2002). Ephemera, mess and miscellaneous piles: Text and practices in families. *Journal of Early Childhood Literacy, 2,* 145–166.

Paratore, J. R. (2001). *Opening doors, opening opportunities: Family literacy in an urban community.* Needham Heights, MA: Allyn & Bacon.

Paratore, J. R. (2005). Approaches to family literacy: Exploring the possibilities. *The Reading Teacher, 59,* 394–396.

Peck, W. C., Flowers, L., & Higgins, L. (1995). Community literacy. *College Composition and Communication, 46,* 199–222.

Phillips, L. M., Hayden, R., & Norris, S. (2007). *Family literacy matters: A longitudinal parent-child literacy intervention.* Calgary, Alberta, Canada: Detselig Enterprises.

Purcell-Gates, V. (1988). Lexical and syntactic knowledge of written narrative held by well-read-to kindergartners and second graders. *Research on the Teaching of English, 22,* 128–160.

Purcell-Gates, V. (1995). *Other people's words: The cycle of illiteracy.* Cambridge, MA: Harvard University Press.

Purcell-Gates, V. (1996). Stories, coupons, and the TV Guide: Relationships between home literacy experiences and emergent literacy knowledge. *Reading Research Quarterly, 31,* 406–428.

Purcell-Gates, V. (2000). Family literacy. In M. L. Kamil, P. B. Mosenthal, P. D. Pearson, & R. Barr (Eds.), *Handbook of reading research* (Volume 3, pp. 853–870). Mahwah, NJ: Erlbaum.

Purcell-Gates, V. (2007). *Cultural practices of literacy: Case studies of language, literacy, social practice, and power.* Mahwah, NJ: Erlbaum.

Quiroz, B. (2004, June). *Mothers' narratives and children's literacy skills in Spanish-speaking families.* Paper presented at the Head Start's 7th National Research Conference, Washington, DC.

Raikes, H. H., Pan, B. A., Luze, G., Tamis-LeMonda, C. S., Brooks-Gunn, J., Constantine, J., et al. (2004, June). *Predictors of mother-toddler book reading in low-income families and child language and cognitive outcomes at 14, 24 and 36 months.* Paper presented at the Head Start's 7th National Research Conference in Washington, DC.

Reese, L., & Gallimore, R. (2000). Immigrant Latinos' cultural models of literacy development: An alternative perspective on home-school discontinuities. *American Journal of Education, 108,* 103–134.

Reese, L., Gallimore, R., & Goldenberg, C. N. (1999). Job-required literacy, home literacy environments, and school reading: Early literacy experiences of immigrant Latino Children. In J. G. Lipson & L. A. McSpadden (Eds.), *Negotiating power and place at the margins: Selected papers on refugees and immigrant* (Vol. 7, pp. 232–269). Washington, DC: American Anthropological Association.

Reese, L., & Goldenberg, C. (2006). Community contexts for literacy development of Latina/o children: Contrasting case studies. *Anthropology of Education Quarterly, 37*(1), 42–61.

Reutzel, D. R., Fawson, P. C., & Smith, J. A. (2006). Words to go: Evaluating a first-grade parent involvement program for "making" words at home. *Reading Research and Instruction, 45,* 119–160.

Roberts, J., Jurgens, J., & Buchinal, M. (2005). The role of literacy practices in preschool children's language and emergent literacy skills. *Journal of Speech, Language and Hearing Research, 48,* 345–359.

Rodríguez-Brown, F. V. (2004). Project FLAME: A parent support family literacy model. In B. Wasik (Ed.), *Handbook of family literacy* (pp. 213–229). Mahwah, NJ: Erlbaum.

Rodríguez-Brown, F. V. (2009). *The home-school connection: Lessons learned in a culturally and linguistically diverse community.* New York: Routledge.

Rogers, R. (2001). Family literacy and cultural models. *National Reading Conference Yearbook, 50,* 96–114.

Rogers, R. (2002). Between contexts: A critical analysis of family literacy, discursive practices, and literacy subjectivities. *Reading Research Quarterly, 37,* 248–277.

Rogers, R. (2003). *A critical discourse analysis of family literacy practices: Power in and out of print.* Mahwah, NJ: Erlbaum.

Rueda, R., & McIntyre, E. (2002). Toward universal literacy. In S. Stringfield, & D. Land (Eds.), *Education at risk students: One hundred-first yearbook of the National Society for the Study of Education* (pp. 189–209). Chicago: University of Chicago Press.

Saint-Laurent, L., & Giasson, J. (2005). Effects of family literacy program adapting intervention to first-graders' evolution of reading and writing. *Journal of Early Childhood Literacy, 5,* 253–278.

St. Pierre, R., Ricciuti, A., Tao, F., Creps, C., Rimzius, T., Swartz, J., et al. (2003). *Third national Even Start evaluation: Program impacts and implications for improvement.* Jessup, MD: ED Pubs.

Saracho, O. (2002). Family literacy: Exploring family practices. *Early Child Development and Care, 172,* 113–122.

Sénéchal, M., LeFevre, J., Hudson, E., & Lawson, P. (1996). Knowledge of storybooks as a predictor of young children's vocabulary. *Journal of Educational Psychology, 88,* 520–536.

Sénéchal, M., LeFevre, J., Thomas, E., & Daley, K. (1998). Differential effects of home literacy experiences on the development of oral and written language. *Reading Research Quarterly, 33,* 96–116.

Snow, C. E. (2001). Literacy and language: Relationships during the preschool years. In S. W. Beck & P. O. Nabors (Eds.), *Language and literacy: Beyond the here and now* (pp. 161–186). Cambridge, MA: Harvard Educational Review.

Snow, C. E. (2004, June). *Language and literacy environments of toddlers in low-income families: Relations to cognitive and language development.* Discussant at Head Start 7th National Research Conference, Washington, DC.

Snow, C. E., Barnes, W., Chandler, J., Goodman, I., & Hemphill L. (1991). *Unfulfilled expectations: Home and school influences in literacy.* Cambridge, MA: Harvard University.

Snow, C. E., & Páez, M. M. (2004). The Head Start classroom as an oral language environment: What should the performance standards be? In E. Ziegler, & S. Styfco (Eds.), *The Head Start debates* (pp. 113–128). Baltimore: Brookes.

Snow, C. E., & Tabors, P. O. (1993). Language skills that relate to literacy development. In B. Spodek & O. Saracho (Eds.), *Yearbook in early childhood education, Vol. 4* (pp. 116–138). New York: Teachers College Press.

Snow, C., & Tabors, P. O. (1996). Intergenerational transfer of literacy. In L. A. Benjamin, & J. Lord (Eds.), *Family literacy: Directions in research and implications for practice* (pp. 73–80). Washington, DC: U. S. Department of Education, Office of Educational Research and Improvement.

Taylor, D. (1983). *Family literacy: Young children learning to read and write.* Exeter, NH: Heinemann.

Taylor, D., & Dorsey-Gaines, C. (1988). *Growing up literate: Learning from inner-city families.* Portsmouth, NH: Heinemann.

Teale, W. H. (1986). Home background and young children's literacy development. In W. H. Teale & E. Sulsby (Eds.), *Emergent literacy: Writing and reading* (pp. 173–206). Norwood, NJ: Ablex.

Teale, W. H., & Sulzby, E. (Eds.). (1986). *Emergent literacy: Writing and reading.* Norwood, NJ: Ablex.

Tharp, R. G. (1989). Culturally compatible education: A formula for designing effective classrooms. In H. T. Trueba, G. Spindler, & L. Spindler (Eds.), *What do anthropologists have to say about dropouts?* (pp. 51–66). New York: Farmer Press.

Trueba, H., Jacobs, L., & Kirton, E. (1990). *Cultural conflict and adaptation: The case of Hmong children in American society.* New York: Farmer Press.

Valdes, G. (1996). *Con respeto: Bridging the differences between culturally diverse families and schools.* New York: Teachers College Press.

Van Steensel, R. (2006). Relations between socio-cultural factors, the home literacy environment and children's literacy development. *Journal of Research in Reading, 29,* 367–382.

Vernon-Feagans, L., Hammer, C. S., Miccio, A., & Manlove, E. (2001). Early language and literacy skills in low-income African American and Hispanic children. In S. Neuman & D. K. Dickinson (Eds.), *Handbook for research on early literacy* (pp. 192–210). New York: Guilford.

Volk, D., & de Acosta, M. (2001). "Many different ladders, many ways to climb…": literacy events in the bilingual, classrooms, home and community of three Puerto Rican kindergartners. *Journal of Early Childhood Literacy, 1,* 193–223.

Weisner, T. (1997). The ecocultural project of human development: Why ethnography and its findings matter. *Ethos, 25,* 1977–1990.

Weisner, T., Gallimore, R., & Jordan, C. (1988). Unpackaging cultural effects on classroom learning: Native Hawaiian peer assistance and child-generated activity. *Anthropology and Education Quarterly, 19,* 327–353.

Index

eBooks

eBooks – at www.eBookstore.tandf.co.uk

A library at your fingertips!

eBooks are electronic versions of printed books. You can store them on your PC/laptop or browse them online.

They have advantages for anyone needing rapid access to a wide variety of published, copyright information.

eBooks can help your research by enabling you to bookmark chapters, annotate text and use instant searches to find specific words or phrases. Several eBook files would fit on even a small laptop or PDA.

NEW: Save money by eSubscribing: cheap, online access to any eBook for as long as you need it.

Annual subscription packages

We now offer special low-cost bulk subscriptions to packages of eBooks in certain subject areas. These are available to libraries or to individuals.

For more information please contact webmaster.ebooks@tandf.co.uk

We're continually developing the eBook concept, so keep up to date by visiting the website.

www.eBookstore.tandf.co.uk